ACCOUNTING

27e

Chapters 14–26

Carl S. Warren
Professor Emeritus of Accounting
University of Georgia, Athens

James M. Reeve
Professor Emeritus of Accounting
University of Tennessee, Knoxville

Jonathan E. Duchac
Professor of Accounting
Wake Forest University

CENGAGE Learning™

Australia • Brazil • Japan • Korea • Mexico • Singapore • Spain • United Kingdom • United States

CENGAGE Learning

Accounting, 27e
Chapters 14–26

Carl S. Warren
James M. Reeve
Jonathan E. Duchac

Senior Vice President, General Manager, Social Sciences, Humanities, and Business: Erin Joyner

Executive Product Director: Mike Schenk

Product Director: Jason Fremder

Senior Product Manager: Matthew Filimonov

Content Development Manager: Daniel Celenza

Senior Content Developer: Diane Bowdler

Product Assistant: Aiyana Moore

Executive Marketing Manager: Robin LeFevre

Marketing Coordinator: Hillary Johns

Senior Digital Production Project Manager: Jessica Robbe

Senior Digital Content Specialist: Tim Ross

Senior Content Project Manager: Tim Bailey

Manufacturing Planner: Doug Wilke

Production Service: Cenveo Publisher Services, Inc.

Senior Art Director: Michelle Kunkler

Cover Designer: cmillerdesign

Internal Designer: Ke Design

Intellectual Property
  Analyst: Brittani Morgan
  Project Manager: Betsy Hathaway

For product information and technology assistance, contact us at **Cengage Learning Customer & Sales Support, 1-800-354-9706**

For permission to use material from this text or product, submit all requests online at **www.cengage.com/permissions**

Further permissions questions can be emailed to **permissionrequest@cengage.com**

Library of Congress Control Number: 2016961921

ISBN: 978-1-337-27211-7

Cengage Learning
20 Channel Center Street
Boston, MA 02210
USA

Cengage Learning is a leading provider of customized learning solutions with employees residing in nearly 40 different countries and sales in more than 125 countries around the world. Find your local representative at **www.cengage.com**.

Cengage Learning products are represented in Canada by Nelson Education, Ltd.

To learn more about Cengage Learning Solutions, visit **www.cengage.com**

Purchase any of our products at your local college store or at our preferred online store **www.cengagebrain.com**

Printed in Canada
Print Number: 01 Print Year: 2016

The Warren/Reeve/Duchac Family

The Warren/Reeve/Duchac Family of solutions provides a host of options to fit your exact teaching style—all with an integrated technology solution.

Sole Proprietorship Approach

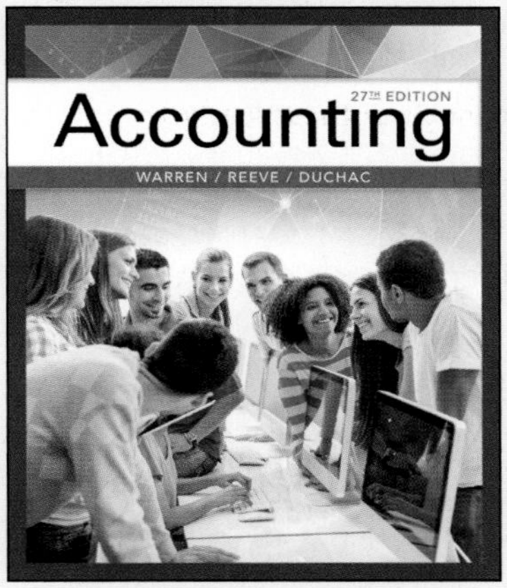

- 26 Chapters
- 65% Financial Accounting/
  35% Managerial Accounting

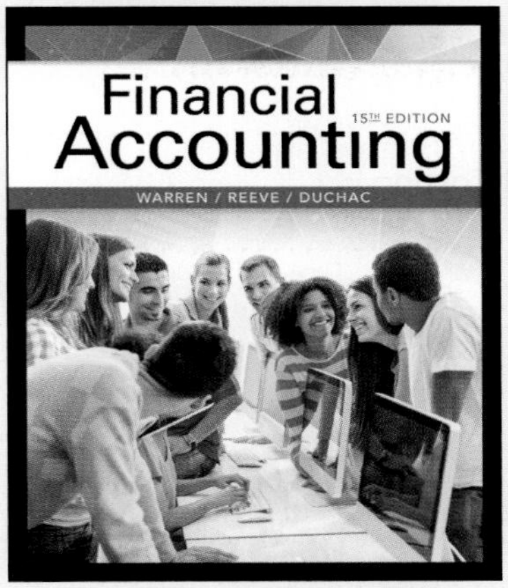

- Financial Chapters 1–17 from *Accounting, 27e*

Corporate Approach

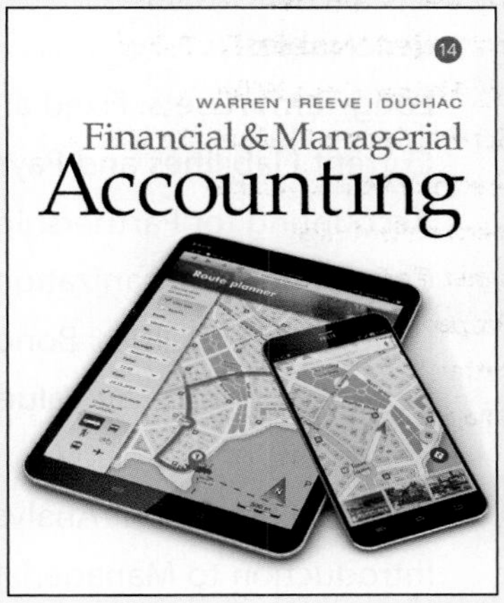

- 26 Chapters
- 50% Financial Accounting/
  50% Managerial Accounting

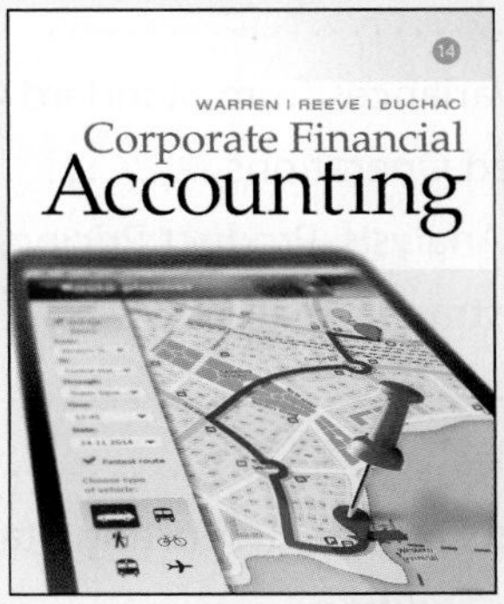

- Chapters 1–14 from *Financial & Managerial Accounting, 14e*

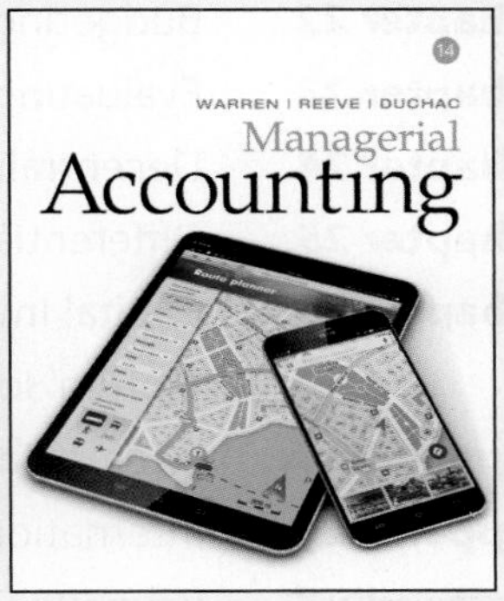

- Chapters 13–26 from *Financial & Managerial Accounting, 14e*

Brief Contents

The Warren Vision

Warren/Reeve/Duchac's *Accounting 27e* gives students a solid foundation in accounting to prepare them for future business courses and the real world.

1. Helps students connect concepts to the bigger picture with features such as the new **Chapter-Opening Schema**.

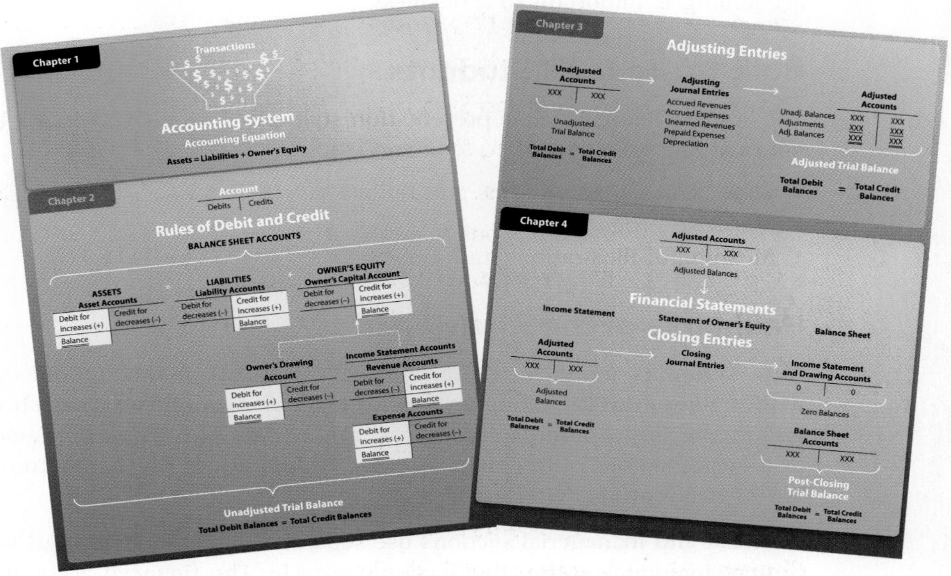

2. **Accounting Cycle Coverage** provides an unmatched foundation so students are prepared to succeed in later chapters.

3. Helps learners appreciate why accounting is important to business and a prosperous society with new tools such as the **Why It Matters Concept Clips**.

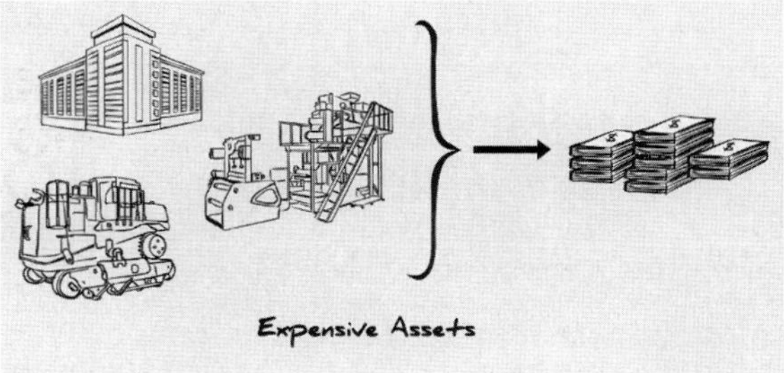

Expensive Assets

4. A **presentation style** built for the way this generation reads and assimilates information.

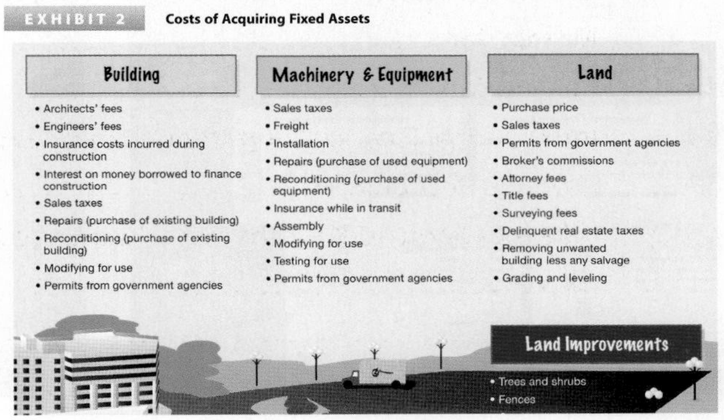

EXHIBIT 2
Costs of Acquiring Fixed Assets
Building
• Architects' fees
• Engineers' fees
• Insurance costs incurred during construction
• Interest on money borrowed to finance construction
• Sales taxes
• Repairs (purchase of existing building)
• Reconditioning (purchase of existing building)
• Modifying for use
• Permits from government agencies
Machinery & Equipment
• Sales taxes
• Freight
• Installation
• Repairs (purchase of used equipment)
• Reconditioning (purchase of used equipment)
• Insurance while in transit
• Assembly
• Modifying for use
• Testing for use
• Permits from government agencies
Land
• Purchase price
• Sales taxes
• Permits from government agencies
• Broker's commissions
• Attorney fees
• Title fees
• Surveying fees
• Delinquent real estate taxes
• Removing unwanted building less any salvage
• Grading and leveling
Land Improvements
• Trees and shrubs
• Fences

Features

Roadmap for Success

Warren/Reeve/Duchac's *Accounting 27e* makes it easy for you to give students a solid foundation in accounting without overwhelming students. Warren covers the fundamentals AND motivates students to learn by showing how accounting is important to a business.

Built for Today's Students

The Warren/Reeve/Duchac presentation style provides content in a way that this generation reads and assimilates information.

- Short, concise paragraphs and bullets
- Stepwise progression
- Meaningful illustrations and graphs

Hallmarks of the Revision

New schemas provide a roadmap of accounting that emphasizes the big picture. Each chapter begins with a new graphic Schema, or Roadmap of Accounting, that shows readers how the chapter material fits within the larger context of the overall book. With this approach, students view chapter concepts as part of a larger whole rather than as mere independent pieces of knowledge, for a truly functional understanding of accounting.

Financial and managerial sections use separate schemas. A four-part schema (Chs. 1–4) demonstrates how chapter content integrates within the accounting cycle. The financial accounting chapters' schema (Chs. 5–17) highlights chapter content within a set of integrated financial statements. A separate managerial accounting schema (Chs. 18–26) shows how chapter content integrates within the managerial accounting functions.

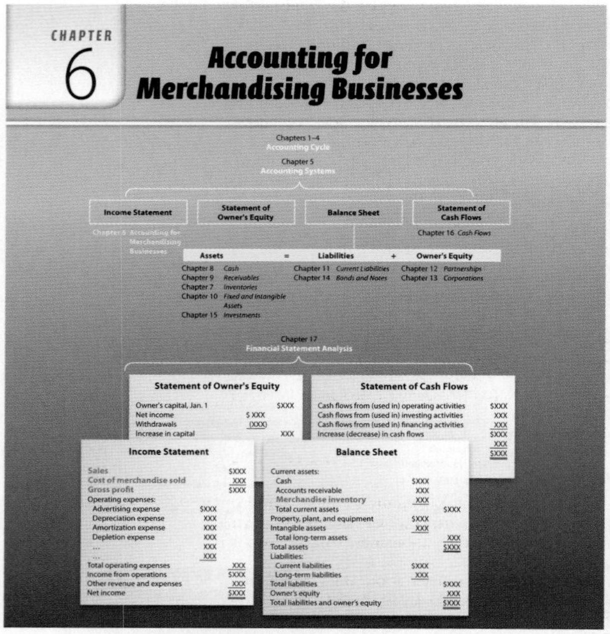

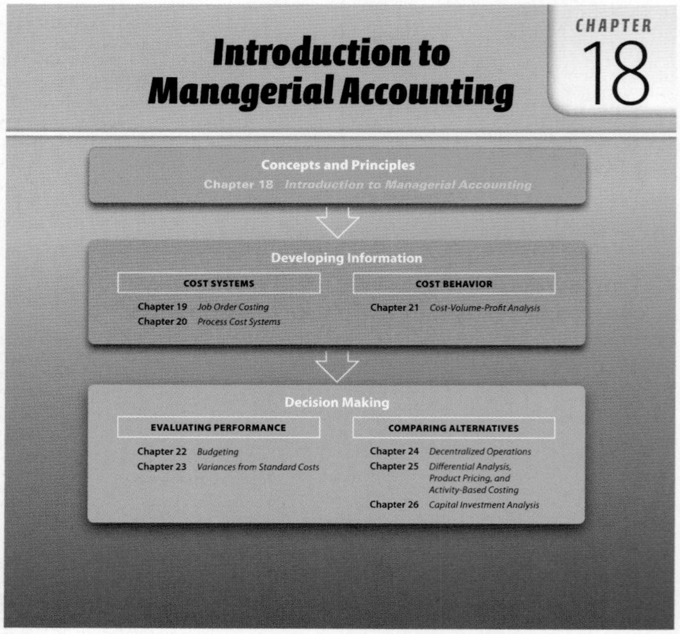

Revised and refreshed real company chapter openers engage readers from the start. New and fresh chapter openers introduce and briefly describe a real company and how its challenges relate to the chapter content. Links to this opening company appear throughout the chapter to reinforce the importance of what readers are learning.

CHAPTER 7

Best Buy

Assume that in September, you purchased a Sony HDTV from Best Buy. At the same time, you purchased a Denon surround sound system for $599.99. You liked your surround sound so well that in November, you purchased an identical Denon system on sale for $549.99 for your bedroom TV. Over the holidays, you moved to a new apartment and in the process of unpacking discovered that one of the Denon surround sound systems was missing. Luckily, your renters or homeowners insurance policy will cover the theft, but the insurance company needs to know the cost of the system that was stolen.

The Denon systems were identical. However, to respond to the insurance company, you will need to identify which system was stolen. Was it the first system, which cost $599.99, or was it the second system, which cost $549.99? Whichever system you choose will determine the amount that you receive from the insurance company.

Merchandising businesses such as Best Buy make similar assumptions when identical merchandise is purchased at different costs. For example, Best Buy may have purchased thousands of Denon surround sound systems over the past year at different costs. At the end of a period, some of the Denon systems will still be in inventory, and some will have been sold. But which costs relate to the sold systems, and which costs relate to the systems still in inventory? Best Buy's assumption about inventory costs can involve large dollar amounts and, thus, can have a significant impact on the financial statements. For example, Best Buy reported $5,731 million of inventory and net loss of $1,231 million for a recent year.

This chapter discusses such issues as how to determine the cost of merchandise in inventory and the cost of merchandise sold. However, it begins by discussing the importance of control over inventory.

Link to Best Buy
Best Buy values its inventory at lower of cost or market based upon cost and the amount it expects to realize from the sale.

Thus, the merchandise would be valued at $650, which is the lower of its cost of $1,000 and its market value of $650.

The lower-of-cost-or-market method can be applied in one of three ways. The cost, market price, and any declines could be determined for:

- Each item in the inventory
- Each major class or category of inventory
- Inventory as a whole

The amount of any price decline is included in the cost of merchandise sold. This, in turn, reduces gross profit and net income in the period in which the price declines occur. This matching of price declines to the period in which they occur is the primary advantage of using the lower-of-cost-or-market method.

Revised end-of-chapter assignments (homework) provide important hands-on practice. Refined, meaningful review and applications at the end of each chapter include Discussion Questions, Practice Exercises (A and B versions), Exercises, Problems (Series A and B), and Cases & Projects that emphasize ethics, teamwork, and communication skills.

Cases & Projects

Ethics

CP 5-1 Ethics in Action

Netbooks Inc. provides accounting applications for business customers on the Internet for a monthly subscription. Netbooks customers run their accounting system on the Internet; thus, the business data and accounting software reside on the servers of Netbooks Inc. The senior management of Netbooks believes that once a customer begins to use Netbooks, it is very difficult to cancel the service. That is, customers are "locked in" because it is difficult to move the business data from Netbooks to another accounting application even though the customers own their own data. Therefore, Netbooks has decided to entice customers with an initial low monthly price that is half the normal monthly rate for the first year of services. After a year, the price will be increased to the regular monthly rate. Netbooks management believes that customers will have to accept the full price because customers will be "locked in" after one year of use.

a. Discuss whether the half-price offer is an ethical business practice.

b. Discuss whether customer "lock-in" is an ethical business practice.

Team Activity

Real World

CP 5-2 Team Activity

The two leading software application providers for supply chain management (SCM) and customer relationship management (CRM) software are JDA and Salesforce.com, respectively. In groups of two or three, go to the website of each company (www.jda.com and www.salesforce.com, respectively) and list the services provided by each company's software.

Communication

Real World

CP 5-3 Communication

Internet-based accounting software is a recent trend in business computing. Major software firms such as Oracle, SAP, and NetSuite are running their core products on the Internet using cloud computing. NetSuite is one of the most popular small-business Internet-based accounting systems.

Go to NetSuite Inc.'s website at www.netsuite.com. Read about the product and prepare a memo to management defining cloud-based accounting. Also outline the advantages and disadvantages of using cloud-based accounting compared to running software on a company's internal computer network.

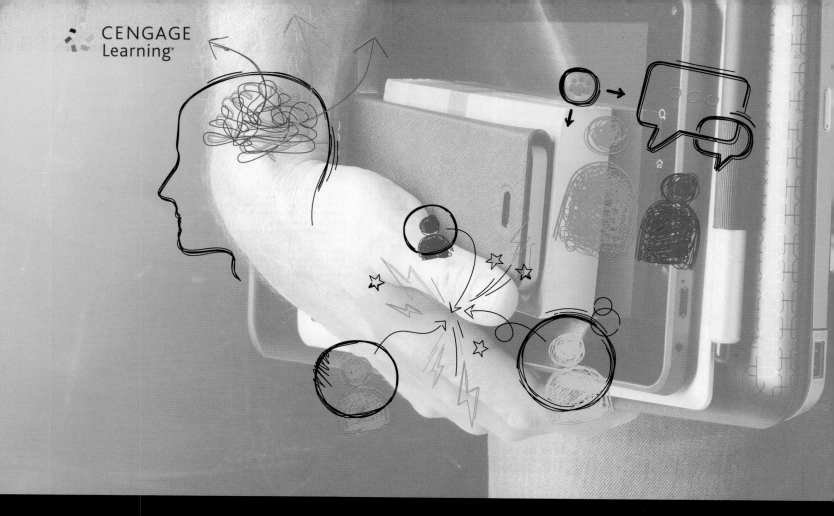

Closing the gap, one step at a time.

CENGAGE**NOW**v2

Multi-Panel View

One of the biggest complaints students have about online homework is the scrolling, which prevents students from seeing the big picture and understanding the accounting system. This new Multi-Panel View in CengageNOWv2 enables students to see all the elements of a problem on one screen.

- Students make connections and see the tasks as connected components in the accounting process.
- Dramatically reduced scrolling eliminates student frustration.

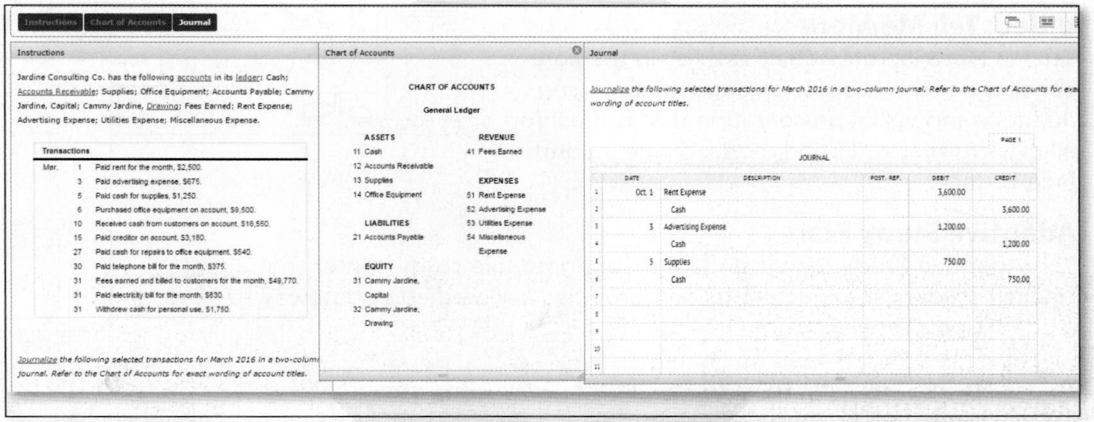

Blank Sheet of Paper Experience

Many students perform well on homework but struggle when it comes to exams. Now, with the new Blank Sheet of Paper Experience, students must problem-solve on their own, just as they would if taking a test on a blank sheet of paper. This discourages overreliance on the system.

- Students must refer to the Chart of Accounts and decide for themselves which account is impacted.
- The number of accounts in each transaction is not given away.
- Whether the account should be debited or credited is not given away.
- Transactions may be entered in any order (as long as the entries are correct).

Adaptive Feedback

Adaptive Feedback responds to students based upon their unique answers and alerts them to the type of error they have made without giving away the answer.

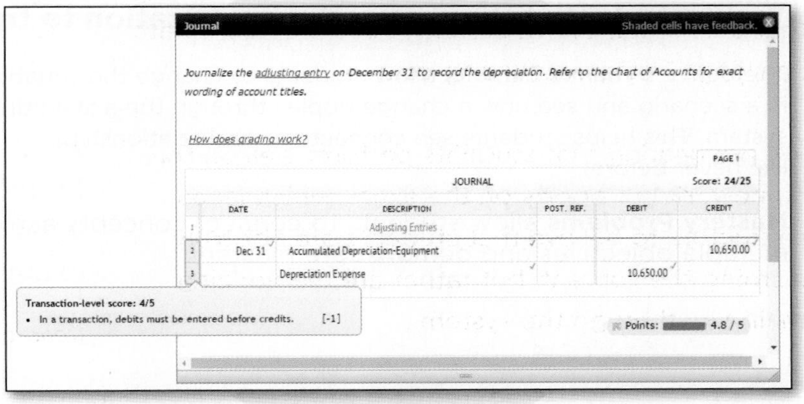

From Motivation to Mastery

MASTERY
APPLICATION
MOTIVATION

MOTIVATION:
Engage students and better prepare them for class.

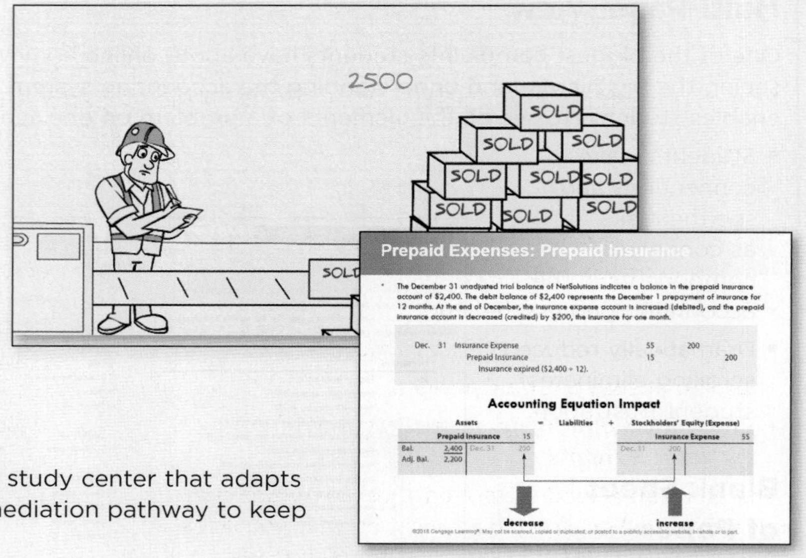

NEW **Video: Animated Concept Clips**
Animated Concept Clips are brief captivating video clips that expose students to why a concept is important and how the concept is used in the real world.

Video: Tell Me More
Tell Me More lecture activities explain the core concepts of the chapter through an engaging auditory and visual presentation that is ideal for all class formats—flipped mode, online, hybrid, face-to-face.

Adaptive Study Plan
The Adaptive Study Plan is an assignable/gradable study center that adapts to each student's unique needs and provides a remediation pathway to keep students progressing.

APPLICATION:
Help students apply accounting concepts.

Video: Show Me How
Linked to end-of-chapter problems in CengageNOWv2, Show Me How problem demonstration videos provide a step-by-step model of a similar problem.

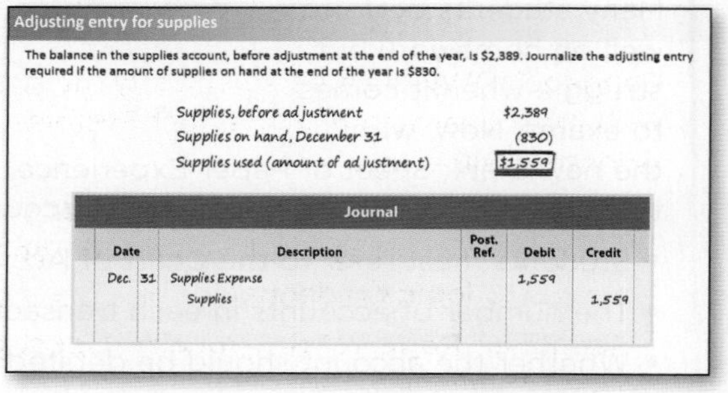

MASTERY:
Teach students to go beyond memorization to true understanding.

Interactive **Dynamic Exhibits** allow students to change the variables in a scenario and see how a change ripples through the accounting system. This helps students see connections and relationships like never before!

Mastery Problems allow students to connect concepts across multiple objectives and demonstrate mastery.

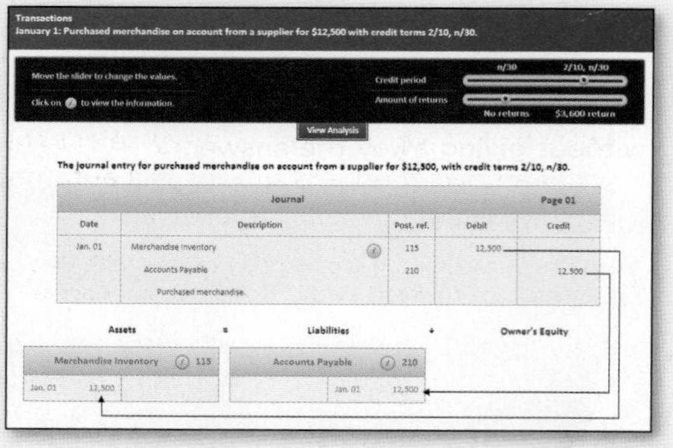

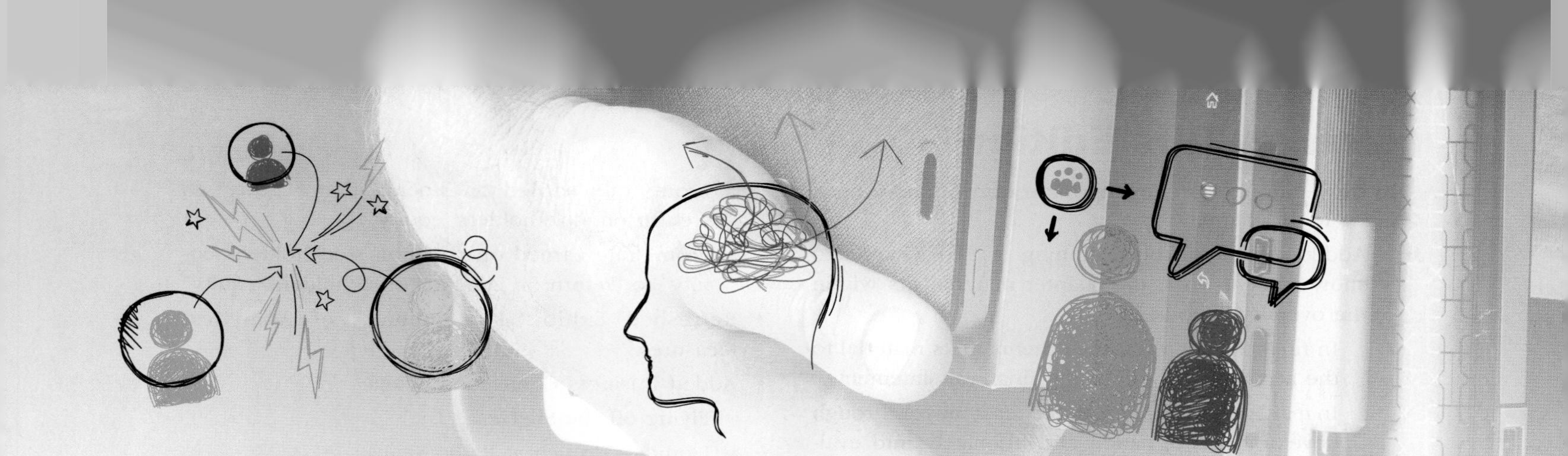

And that's not all...

You might also want to learn about the MindTap eReader, our LMS integration options, and more.

MindTap eReader

The MindTap eReader is the most robust digital reading experience available.

- Fully optimized for the iPad.
- Note-taking, highlighting, and more.
- Offline access to smartphones.
- Embedded digital media such as the Dynamic Exhibits.

The MindTap eReader also features ReadSpeaker®, an online text-to-speech application that vocalizes, or "speechenables," online educational content.

LMS Integration

CengageNOWv2 can be seamlessly integrated with most Learning Management Systems. Adopters will enjoy:

- **A Seamless User Experience**—Access your Cengage resources seamlessly using only your LMS login credentials.
- **Simplified Registration Process**—Get students up and running faster!
- **Content Customization and Deep Linking**—Use our Content Selector to create a unique learning path for students that blends your content with Cengage Learning activities, eText, and more within your LMS course.
- **Automatic Grade Synchronization***—Need to have your course grades recorded in your LMS gradebook? No problem. Simply select the activities you want synched and grades will automatically be recorded in your LMS gradebook.

* Grade synchronization is currently available with Blackboard, Brightspace (powered by D2L), Angel 8, and Canvas.

ADA Accessibility

Cengage Learning is committed to making its educational materials accessible to users of all abilities. We are steadily working to increase accessibility and create a full spectrum of usable tools, features, and choices that are accessible for users of all abilities. All new Cengage Learning products and services are designed with accessibility in mind.

- With the latest release of CengageNOWv2:
  - Images and graphics have been converted to HTML tables so that they can be read by screen readers.
  - The assignment experience now offers proper heading structure to support easy navigation with assistive technology.
- CengageNOWv2 solutions offer high contrast and well-structured HTML, which helps support screen reader interactivity.
- All videos are created with closed captioning and transcripts available for download.
- The MindTap eReader is HTML-based and compatible with most screen reading assistive software. The eReader supports browser settings for high-contrast narrative text, variable font sizes, and multiple foreground and background color options.

For more information on accessibility, please visit www.cengage.com/accessibility.

iPad Tablet Compatibility

CengageNOWv2 is fully compatible with the iPad and other tablet devices, with the exception of General Ledger (CLGL) and Excel Tutorials, which are flash based.

New to This Edition

In this edition, the following improvements have been made to all chapters:

- Added schema at the beginning of each chapter to show students how the chapter material fits within the overall textbook.
  - In financial chapters, the schema links material to the accounting cycle or the financial statements.
  - In managerial chapters, the schema moves through developing information and ultimately into evaluating and analyzing information to make decisions.
- Updated dates and real company information for currency.
- Added "Link to" for the opening company to interweave real-world references through each chapter.
- Refreshed end-of-chapter assignments with different numerical values and updated information.
- Revised Cases & Projects to include Ethics in Action, Team Activity, and Communication in every chapter.

Chapter 14

- Added Business Connection box on Investor Bond Price Risk.
- Refreshed Financial Analysis and Interpretation discussion of times interest earned, focusing on intra-industry comparisons.

Chapter 15

- Refreshed Interest Timeline exhibits to clearly illustrate the timing of interest accruals.

Chapter 16

- Added Business Connection boxes:
  - Cash Crunch!
  - Growing Pains at Twitter
- Updated and expanded Financial Analysis and Interpretation discussion of free cash flow.

Chapter 17

- Revised learning objectives on liquidity analysis and solvency analysis.
- Added learning objective on Analyzing and Interpreting Financial Statements.
- Name changes to several ratios:
  - From "number of times interest charges are earned" to "times interest earned"
  - From "ratio of assets to sales" to "asset turnover"
  - From "rate earned on total assets" to "return on total assets"
  - From "rate earned on stockholders' equity" to "return on stockholders' equity"
  - From "rate earned on common stockholders' equity" to "return on common stockholders' equity"
- Refreshed Exhibit 13, Summary of Analytical Measures.
- Added Business Connection boxes:
  - Flying off the Shelves
  - Liquidity Crunch at Radio Shack
  - Gearing for Profit
- Updated Comprehensive Problem for Nike's recent financial statements.

Chapter 18

- Revised chapter title.
- Added new learning objective on Sustainability and Accounting.
- Added Business Connection box on Line and Staff for Service Companies.

Chapter 19

- Added Business Connection boxes:
  - 3D Printing
  - Advanced Robotics

Chapter 20

- References to "just-in-time processing" are changed to "lean manufacturing" to reflect use of more contemporary terms.
- Added new Business Connection box on Sustainable Papermaking.

Chapter 21

- Added Business Connection boxes:
  - Booking Fees
  - Airline Industry Break-Even

Chapter 22

- Added new Business Connection box on Mad Men; it shows the U.S. companies with the largest advertising budgets.

Chapter 23

- Revised chapter title.

Chapter 24

- Revised chapter title.
- Refreshed Exhibit 3, Responsibility Accounting Reports for Cost Centers.
- Added Business Connection box on Coca-Cola Company: Go West Young Man.

Chapter 25

- Eliminated the step structure at the beginning of the chapter to provide a less complex analysis framework.
- Improved the explanation of the differential analysis table illustration at the beginning of the chapter.
- The differential make vs. buy analysis table has an added revenue line that is set at "zero." Thus, income and loss can now be arithmetically determined.
- Added new Business Connection box on The ABC's of Schwab; it shows how Charles Schwab Corporation uses activity-based costing.

Chapter 26

- Added new section on capital investment analysis for sustainability.
- Added new exercises for capital investment analysis for sustainability.

Instructor Resources

Solutions Manual

Author-written and carefully verified multiple times to ensure accuracy and consistency with the text, the Solutions Manual contains answers to the Discussion Questions, Practice Exercises, Exercises, Problems (Series A and Series B), Continuing Problems, Comprehensive Problems, and Cases & Projects that appear in the text. These solutions help you easily plan, assign, and efficiently grade assignments.

Test Bank

Test Bank content is delivered via Cengage Learning Testing, powered by Cognero®, a flexible, online system that allows you to:

- Author, edit, and manage test bank content
- Create multiple test versions in an instant
- Deliver tests from your LMS, from your classroom, or through CengageNOWv2
- Export tests in Word format

Companion Website

This robust companion website provides immediate access to a rich array of teaching and learning resources—including the Instructor's Manual, PowerPoint slides, and Excel Template Solutions. Easily download the instructor resources you need from the password-protected, instructor-only section of the site.

Instructor's Manual Discover new ways to engage your students by using the Instructor's Manual ideas for class discussion, group learning activities, writing exercises, and Internet activities. Moreover, simplify class preparation by reviewing a brief summary of each chapter, a detailed chapter synopsis, teaching tips regarding a suggested approach to the material, questions students frequently ask in the classroom, lecture aids, and demonstration problems in the Instructor's Manual. Quickly identify the assignments that best align your course with the assignment preparation grid that includes information about learning objective coverage, difficulty level and Bloom's taxonomy categorization, time estimates, and accrediting standard alignment for business programs, AICPA, ACBSP, and IMA.

PowerPoint Slides Bring your lectures to life with slides designed to clarify difficult concepts for your students. The lecture PowerPoints include key terms and definitions, equations, examples, and exhibits from the textbook. Descriptions for all graphics in the PowerPoints are included to enhance PowerPoint usability for students with disabilities.

Excel Template Solutions Excel Templates are provided for selected long or complicated end-of-chapter exercises and problems to assist students as they set up and work the problems. Certain cells are coded to display a red asterisk when an incorrect answer is entered, which helps students stay on track. Selected problems that can be solved using these templates are designated by an icon in the textbook and are listed in the assignment preparation grid in the Instructor's Manual. The Excel Template Solutions provide answers to these templates.

Practice Set Solutions Establish a fundamental understanding of the accounting cycle for your students with Practice Sets, which require students to complete one month of transactions for a fictional company. Brief descriptions of each Practice Set are provided in the Table of Contents. The Practice Set Solutions provide answers to these practice sets.

Student Resources

Study Guide

Now available free in CengageNOWv2, the Study Guide allows students to easily assess what they know with a "Do You Know" checklist covering the key points in each chapter. To further test their comprehension, students can work through Practice Exercises, which include a "strategy" hint and solution so they can continue to practice applying key accounting concepts.

Working Papers

Students will find the tools they need to help work through end-of-chapter assignments with the Working Papers. The preformatted templates provide a starting point by giving students a basic structure for problems and journal entries. Working Papers are available in a printed format as a bundle option.

Practice Sets

For more in-depth application of accounting practices, instructors may choose from among six different Practice Sets for long-term assignments. Each Practice Set requires students to complete one month of transactions for a fictional company. Practice Sets can be solved manually or with the Cengage Learning General Ledger software.

General Ledger

Website

Designed specifically for your students' accounting needs, this website features student PowerPoint slides and Excel Templates, as well as the Study Guides.

- **PowerPoint Slides:** Students can easily take notes or review difficult concepts with the student version of this edition's PowerPoint slides.
- **Excel Templates:** These Excel Templates help students stay on track. If students enter an incorrect answer in certain cells, a red asterisk will appear to let them know something is wrong. Problems that can be solved using these templates are designated by an icon.

EXCEL

Acknowledgments

The many enhancements to this edition of *Accounting* are the direct result of one-on-one interviews, surveys, reviews, and focus groups with instructors at institutions across the country. We would like to take this opportunity to thank those who helped us better understand the challenges of the principles of accounting course and provided valuable feedback on our content and digital assets.

Debbie Adkins, Remington College Online
Sharon Agee, Rollins College
Sol. Ahiarah, SUNY Buffalo State
John G. Ahmad, Northern Virginia Community College
Janice Akeo, Butler Community College
Dave Alldredge, Salt Lake Community College
Robert Almon, South Texas College
Lynn Almond, Virginia Tech
Elizabeth Ammann, Lindenwood University
Sheila Ammons, Austin Community College
Anne Marie Anderson, Raritan Valley Community College
Rick Andrews, Sinclair Community College
Leah Arrington, Northwest Mississippi Community College
Christopher Ashley, Everest College
John Babich, Kankakee Community College
Felicia R. Baldwin, Richard J. Daley College
Sara Barritt, Northeast Community College
Geoffrey D. Bartlett, Drake University
Jan Barton, Emory University
Robert E. (Reb) Beatty, Anne Arundel Community College
Eric Blazer, Millersville University
Cindy Bleasdal, Hilbert College
Cynthia Bolt, The Citadel
Anna Boulware, St. Charles Community College
Gary Bower, Community College of Rhode Island
Thomas Branton, Alvin Community College
Gregory Brookins, Santa Monica College
Esther S. Bunn, Stephen F. Austin State University
Jacqueline Burke, Hofstra University
Lisa Busto, William Rainey Harper College
Thane Butt, Champlain College
Marci Butterfield, University of Utah
Magan Calhoun, Austin Peay State University
Julia M. Camp, Providence College
Kirk Canzano, Long Beach City College
Roy Carson, Anne Arundel Community College
Cassandra H. Catlett, Carson Newman University
David Centers, Grand Valley State University
Machiavelli W. Chao, University of California, Irvine
Bea Chiang, The College of New Jersey
Linda Christiansen, Indiana University Southeast
Lawrence Chui, University of St. Thomas
Colleen Chung, Miami Dade College
Tony Cioffi, Lorain County Community College
Sandra Cohen, Columbia College Chicago
Debora Constable, Georgia Perimeter College
Susan Cordes, Johnson County Community College
Leonard Cronin, University Center Rochester
Louann Hofheins Cummings, The University of Findlay
Sue Cunningham, Rowan Cabarrus Community College
Don Curfman, McHenry County College
Robin D'Agati, Palm Beach State College
Dori Danko, Grand Valley State University
Emmanuel Danso, Palm Beach State College
Bruce L. Darling, University of Oregon
Dorothy Davis, University of Louisiana Monroe
Rebecca Grava Davis, East Mississippi Community College
Julie Dawson, Carthage College
Christopher Demaline, Central Arizona College
Carol Dickerson, Chaffey College
Patricia Doherty, Boston University School of Management
Michael P. Dole, Marquette University
Karen C. Elsom, Fayetteville Technical Community College
Nancy Emerson, North Dakota State University
James M. Emig, Villanova University
Bruce England, Massasoit Community College
Lucile Faurel, University of California, Irvine
Robert Foster, Los Angeles Pierce College
Kimberly Franklin, St. Louis Community College
Michael J. Gallagher, DeSales University
Ann Gervais, Springfield Technical Community College
Alex Gialanella, Manhattanville College
Michael Goeken, Northwest Vista College
Nino Gonzalez, El Paso Community College
Saturnino (Nino) Gonzalez, El Paso Community College

Lori A. Grady, Bucks County Community College
Carol Graham, The University of San Francisco
Marina Grau, Houston Community College
Gloria Grayless, Sam Houston State University
Tim Green, North Georgia Technical College
Ann Gregory, South Plains College
Timothy Griffin, Hillsborough Community College
Sheila Guillot, Lamar State College-Port Arthur
Michael Gurevitz, Montgomery College
Keith Hallmark, Calhoun Community College
Rebecca Hancock, El Paso Community College
Martin Hart, Manchester Community College
Len Heritage, Tacoma Community College
Katherine Sue Hewitt, Klamath Community College
Merrily Hoffman, San Jacinto College
Jose Hortensi, Miami Dade College
Jana Hosmer, Blue Ridge Community College
Aileen Huang, Santa Monica College
Marianne James, California State University, Los Angeles
Cynthia Johnson, University of Arkansas at Little Rock
Lori Johnson, Minnesota State University Moorhead
Odessa Jordan, Calhoun Community College
Stani Kantcheva, Cincinnati State Technical and Community College
Chris Kinney, Mount Wachusett Community College
Taylor Klett, Sam Houston State University
Stacy Kline, Drexel University
Pamela Knight, Columbus Technical College
W. Jeff Knight, Flagler College
Lynn Krausse, Bakersfield College
Barbara Kren, Marquette University
Jeffrey T. Kunz, Carroll University
Steven J. LaFave, Augsburg College
Tara Laken, Joliet Junior College
Meg Costello Lambert, Oakland Community College
Richard Lau, California State University, Los Angeles
Suzanne Laudadio, Durham Technical Community College
Greg Lauer, North Iowa Area Community College
David E. Laurel, South Texas College
Michael Lawrence, Mt. Hood Community College
Charles J. F. Leflar, University of Arkansas
Jennifer LeSure, Ivy Tech Community College
Bruce Leung, City College of San Francisco
Charles Lewis, Houston Community College
Erik Lindquist, Lansing Community College
Harold Little, Western Kentucky University
James Lock, Northern Virginia Community College
Katy Long, Hill College
Dawn Lopez, Johnson & Wales University
Ming Lu, Santa Monica College
Angelo Luciano, Columbia College Chicago
Debbie Luna, El Paso Community College
Jennifer Mack, Lindenwood University
Suneel Maheshwari, Marshall University
Ajay Maindiratta, New York University
Richard Mandau, Piedmont Technical College
Michele Martinez, Hillsborough Community College
Michelle A. McFeaters, Grove City College
Noel McKeon, Florida State College at Jacksonville
Chris McNamara, Finger Lakes Community College
Kevin McNelis, New Mexico State University
Glenn (Mel) McQueary, Houston Community College
Brenda McVey, Green River Community College
Pam Meyer, University of Louisiana at Lafayette
Jeanette Milius, Iowa Western Community College
Cynthia J. Miller, University of Kentucky
Linda Miller, Northeast Community College
Julie Miller Millmann, Chippewa Valley Technical College
Rita Mintz, Calhoun Community College
Jill Mitchell, Northern Virginia Community College
Timothy J. Moran, Aurora University
Michelle Moshier, University at Albany
Linda Muren, Cuyahoga Community College
Andrea Murowski, Brookdale Community College
Johnna Murray, University of Missouri-St. Louis
Adam Myers, Texas A&M University
John Nader, Davenport University
Joseph M. Nicassio, Westmoreland County Community College
Lisa Novak, Mott Community College
Jamie O'Brien, South Dakota State University
Ron O'Brien, Fayetteville Technical Community College
Robert A. Pacheco, Masssasoit Community College
Edwin Pagan, Passaic County Community College
Judy Patrick, Minnesota State Community and Technical College
Sy Pearlman, California State University, Long Beach
Aaron Pennington, York College of Pennsylvania
Rachel Pernia, Essex County College
Dawn Peters, Southwestern Illinois College
April Poe, University of the Incarnate Word
Michael P. Prockton, Finger Lakes Community College
Kristen Quinn, Northern Essex Community College
La Vonda Ramey, Schoolcraft College
Marcela Raphael, Chippewa Valley Technical College
Jenny Resnick, Santa Monica College
Rick Rinetti, Los Angeles City College
Cecile Roberti, Community College of Rhode Island
Shani N. Robinson, Sam Houston State University
Patrick Rogan, Cosumnes River College
Lawrence A. Roman, Cuyahoga Community College
Debbie Rose, Northeast Wisconsin Technical College
Leah Russell, Holyoke Community College

John H. Sabbagh, Northern Essex Community College
Lynn K. Saubert, Radford University
Marie Saunders, Dakota County Technical College
Michael G. Schaefer, Blinn College
Jennifer Schneider, University of North Georgia
Darlene Schnuck, Waukesha County Technical College
John Seilo, Irvine Valley College
Mon Sellers, Lone Star College-North Harris
Perry Sellers, Lone Star College System
Jim Shelton, Harding University
Ercan Sinmaz, Houston Community College
Lee Smart, Southwest Tennessee Community College
Gerald Smith, University of Northern Iowa
Judy Smith, Parkland College
Ryan Smith, Columbia College
Jennifer Spring Sneed, Arkansas State University-Newport
Nancy L. Snow, University of Toledo
Sharif Soussi, Charter Oak State College
Marilyn Stansbury, Calvin College
Larry G. Stephens, Austin Community College
Dawn W. Stevens, Northwest Mississippi Community College
Joel Strong, St. Cloud State University
Timothy Swenson, Sullivan University
Linda H. Tarrago, Hillsborough Community College
Denise Teixeira, Chemeketa Community College
Teresa Thompson, Chaffey Community College
Judith A. Toland, Bucks County Community College
Lana Tuss, Chemeketa Community College
Robert Urell, Irvine Valley College
Jeff Varblow, College of Lake County
John Verani, White Mountains Community College
Patricia Walczak, Lansing Community College
Terri Walsh, Seminole State College
James Webb, University of the Pacific
Wanda Wong, Chabot College
Patricia Worsham, Norco College
Judith Zander, Grossmont College
Mary Zenner, College of Lake County

About the Authors

Carl S. Warren

Terry R. Spray InHisImage Studios

Dr. Carl S. Warren is Professor Emeritus of Accounting at the University of Georgia, Athens. Dr. Warren has taught classes at the University of Georgia, University of Iowa, Michigan State University, and University of Chicago. He focused his teaching efforts on principles of accounting and auditing. Dr. Warren received his PhD from Michigan State University and his BBA and MA from the University of Iowa. During his career, Dr. Warren published numerous articles in professional journals, including *The Accounting Review*, *Journal of Accounting Research*, *Journal of Accountancy*, *The CPA Journal*, and *Auditing: A Journal of Practice & Theory*. Dr. Warren has served on numerous committees of the American Accounting Association, the American Institute of Certified Public Accountants, and the Institute of Internal Auditors. He also has consulted with numerous companies and public accounting firms. His outside interests include handball, golf, skiing, backpacking, and fly-fishing.

James M. Reeve

Charles J. Garvey III / Garvey Photography

Dr. James M. Reeve is Professor Emeritus of Accounting and Information Management at the University of Tennessee. Professor Reeve taught full time as part of the accounting faculty for 25 years after graduating with his PhD from Oklahoma State University. He presently teaches part time at UT. His teaching efforts focused on Senior Executive MBA programs. His research interests are varied and include work in managerial accounting, supply chain management, lean manufacturing, and information management. He has published over 40 articles in academic and professional journals, including *Journal of Cost Management*, *Journal of Management Accounting Research*, *Accounting Review*, *Management Accounting Quarterly*, *Supply Chain Management Review*, and *Accounting Horizons*. He has consulted or provided training around the world for a variety of organizations, including Boeing, Procter & Gamble, Norfolk Southern, Hershey Foods, Coca-Cola, and Sony. When not writing books, Dr. Reeve plays golf and is involved in faith-based activities.

Jonathan Duchac

© Ken Bennett

Dr. Jonathan Duchac is the Wayne Calloway Professor of Accounting and Acting Associate Dean of Accounting Programs at Wake Forest University. He earned his PhD in accounting from the University of Georgia and currently teaches introductory and advanced courses in financial accounting. Dr. Duchac has received a number of awards during his career, including the Wake Forest University Outstanding Graduate Professor Award, the T.B. Rose Award for Instructional Innovation, and the University of Georgia Outstanding Teaching Assistant Award. In addition to his teaching responsibilities, Dr. Duchac has served as Accounting Advisor to Merrill Lynch Equity Research, where he worked with research analysts in reviewing and evaluating the financial reporting practices of public companies. He has testified before the U.S. House of Representatives, the Financial Accounting Standards Board, and the Securities and Exchange Commission and has worked with a number of major public companies on financial reporting and accounting policy issues. In addition to his professional interests, Dr. Duchac is an avid mountain biker and snow skier.

Contents

Chapter 13 Corporations: Organization, Stock Transactions, and Dividends 628

Chapter 14 Long-Term Liabilities: Bonds and Notes 675

Chapter 15 Investments and Fair Value Accounting 719

Chapter 21 Cost-Volume-Profit Analysis 1020

Chapter 22 Budgeting 1074

Chapter 23 Evaluating Variances from Standard Costs 1124

ACCOUNTING

27e

Chapters 14–26

CHAPTER 14

Long-Term Liabilities: Bonds and Notes

Chapters 1–4
Accounting Cycle

Chapter 5
Accounting Systems

Income Statement

Chapter 6 *Accounting for Merchandising Businesses*

Statement of Owner's Equity

Balance Sheet

Statement of Cash Flows

Chapter 16 *Cash Flows*

Assets = Liabilities + Owner's Equity

Assets

Chapter 8 *Cash*
Chapter 9 *Receivables*
Chapter 7 *Inventories*
Chapter 10 *Fixed and Intangible Assets*
Chapter 15 *Investments*

Liabilities

Chapter 11 *Current Liabilities*
Chapter 14 Long-Term Liabilities: Bonds and Notes

Owner's Equity

Chapter 12 *Accounting for Partnerships and Limited Liability Companies*
Chapter 13 *Corporations*

Chapter 17
Financial Statement Analysis

Statement of Retained Earnings

Retained earnings, Jan. 1		$XXX
Net income	$ XXX	
Dividends	(XXX)	
Increase in retained earnings		XXX

Statement of Cash Flows

Cash flows from (used in) operating activities	$XXX
Cash flows from (used in) investing activities	XXX
Cash flows from (used in) financing activities	XXX
Increase (decrease) in cash flows	$XXX
	XXX
	$XXX

Income Statement

Sales		$XXX
Cost of merchandise sold		XXX
Gross profit		$XXX
Operating expenses:		
Advertising expense	$XXX	
Depreciation expense	XXX	
Amortization expense	XXX	
Depletion expense	XXX	
...	XXX	
...	XXX	
Total operating expenses		XXX
Income from operations		$XXX
Other revenue and expenses		
Interest expense		XXX
Net income		$XXX

Balance Sheet

Current assets:		
Cash	$XXX	
Accounts receivable	XXX	
Inventory	XXX	
Total current assets		$XXX
Property, plant, and equipment	$XXX	
Intangible assets	XXX	
Total long-term assets		XXX
Total assets		$XXX
Liabilities:		
Current liabilities	$XXX	
Long-term liabilities:	XXX	
Bonds payable	XXX	
Notes payable	XXX	
Total liabilities		$XXX
Stockholders' equity		XXX
Total liabilities and stockholders' equity		$XXX

CHAPTER

14

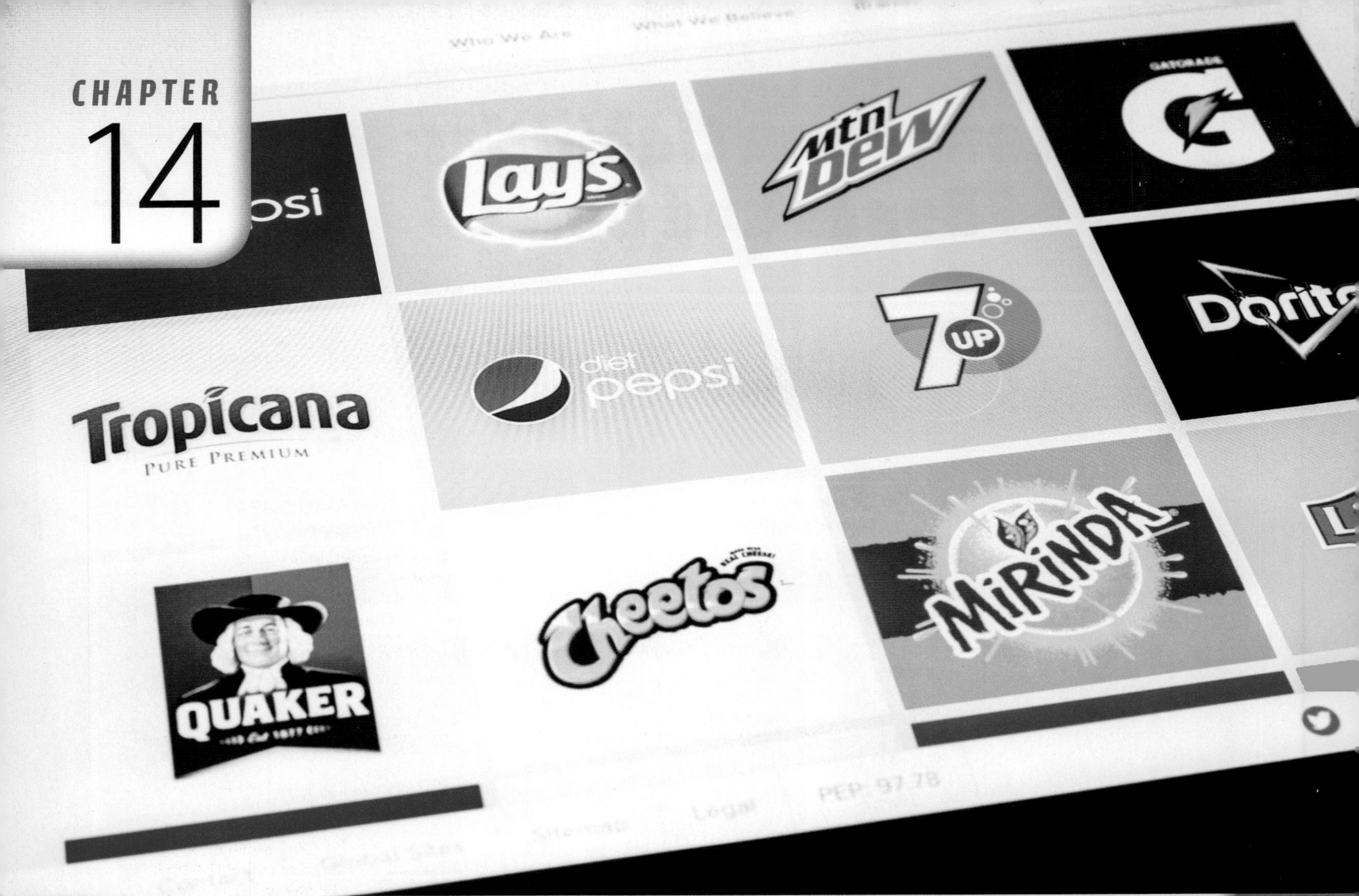

RADU BERCAN/SHUTTERSTOCK.COM

PepsiCo, Inc.

PepsiCo, Inc. is best known for its beverages, which include Pepsi, Diet Pepsi, Gatorade, Mountain Dew, Diet Mountain Dew, Tropicana fruit juices, and Aquafina water.* However, PepsiCo also produces a variety of foods, which include Lay's potato chips, Fritos corn chips, Doritos, Cheetos, Quaker oatmeal, Aunt Jemima mixes and syrups, and Cap'n Crunch cereal. PepsiCo produces, distributes, and sells its products in over 200 countries.

PepsiCo uses a variety of methods to finance its operations, including long-term debt and stock. A recent balance sheet revealed that over 75% of its total assets are financed with liabilities, and 66% of these liabilities are long-term. Included in PepsiCo's long-term liabilities are a variety of notes and bonds. For example, PepsiCo has $13,640 million of bonds maturing throughout 2020–2044 with interest rates of 3.9% and 4.0%. In this chapter, we will discuss the accounting and reporting of bonds payable and installment notes payable.

*The brands listed here are trademarked by PepsiCo.

Learning Objectives

After studying this chapter, you should be able to:

Example Exercises (EE) are shown in **green.**

Obj. 1 **Compute the potential impact of long-term borrowing on earnings per share.**

Financing Corporations

Determining earnings per share under alternative financing plans — EE **14-1**

Obj. 2 **Describe the characteristics and terminology of bonds payable.**

Nature of Bonds Payable

Bond Characteristics and Terminology

Proceeds from Issuing Bonds

Obj. 3 **Describe and illustrate the accounting for bonds payable.**

Accounting for Bonds Payable

Bonds Issued at Face Amount	EE **14-2**
Bonds Issued at a Discount	EE **14-3**
Amortizing a Bond Discount	EE **14-4**
Bonds Issued at a Premium	EE **14-5**
Amortizing a Bond Premium	EE **14-6**
Bond Redemption	EE **14-7**

Obj. 4 **Describe and illustrate the accounting for installment notes.**

Installment Notes

Issuing an Installment Note

Annual Payments — EE **14-8**

Obj. 5 **Describe and illustrate the reporting of long-term liabilities, including bonds and installment notes payable.**

Reporting Long-Term Liabilities

Obj. 6 **Describe and illustrate how the times interest earned ratio is used to evaluate a company's financial condition.**

Financial Analysis and Interpretation: Times Interest Earned Ratio

Compute Times Interest Earned — EE **14-9**

At a Glance 14 Page 700

Financing Corporations

Obj. 1 Compute the potential impact of long-term borrowing on earnings per share.

Corporations finance their operations using the following sources:

- Short-term debt, such as purchasing goods or services on account
- Long-term debt, such as issuing bonds or notes payable
- Equity, such as issuing common or preferred stock

Short-term debt, including the purchase of goods and services on account and the issuance of short-term notes payable, was discussed in Chapter 11. Issuing equity in the form of common or preferred stock was discussed in Chapter 13. This chapter focuses on the use of long-term debt such as bonds and notes payable to finance a company's operations.

A **bond** is an interest-bearing note that requires periodic interest payments, with the face amount to be repaid at the maturity date. For example, a 12% bond requires the company issuing the bond to pay 12% interest on the face amount of the bonds every year. As creditors of the corporation, bondholder claims on the corporation's assets rank ahead of stockholders.

One of the main factors that influences the decision to issue debt or equity is the effect that various financing alternatives will have on earnings per share. **Earnings per share (EPS)** measures the income earned by each share of common stock. It is computed as follows:[1]

$$\text{Earnings per Share} = \frac{\text{Net Income} - \text{Preferred Dividends}}{\text{Number of Common Shares Outstanding}}$$

1 Earnings per share is also discussed in the *Financial Analysis and Interpretation* section of Chapter 13 and in Chapter 17.

To illustrate the effects that issuing debt can have on earnings per share, consider the following alternative plans for financing Boz Corporation, a $4,000,000 company:

	Plan 1		Plan 2		Plan 3	
	Amount	**Percent**	**Amount**	**Percent**	**Amount**	**Percent**
Issue 12% bonds	—	0%	—	0%	$2,000,000	50%
Issue preferred 9% stock, $50 par value	—	0	$2,000,000	50	1,000,000	25
Issue common stock, $10 par value	$4,000,000	100	2,000,000	50	1,000,000	25
Total amount of financing	$4,000,000	100%	$4,000,000	100%	$4,000,000	100%

The company must choose one of these plans. Each plan finances some of the corporation's operations by issuing common stock. However, the percentage financed by common stock varies from 100% (Plan 1) to 25% (Plan 3).

Assume the following data for Boz Corporation:

- Earnings before interest and income taxes are $800,000.
- The tax rate is 40%.
- All bonds or stocks are issued at their par or face amount.

The effect of the preceding financing plans on Boz's net income and earnings per share is shown in Exhibit 1.

EXHIBIT 1

Effect of Alternative Financing Plans—$800,000 Earnings

Dynamic Exhibit

	Plan 1	Plan 2	Plan 3
12% bonds	—	—	$2,000,000
Preferred 9% stock, $50 par	—	$2,000,000	1,000,000
Common stock, $10 par	$4,000,000	2,000,000	1,000,000
Total	$4,000,000	$4,000,000	$4,000,000
Earnings before interest and income tax	$ 800,000	$ 800,000	$ 800,000
Interest on bonds	—	—	(240,000)[a]
Income before income tax	$ 800,000	$ 800,000	$ 560,000
Income tax	(320,000)[b]	(320,000)[b]	(224,000)[b]
Net income	$ 480,000	$ 480,000	$ 336,000
Dividends on preferred stock	—	(180,000)[c]	(90,000)[c]
Available for dividends on common stock	$ 480,000	$ 300,000	$ 246,000
Shares of common stock outstanding	÷ 400,000[d]	÷ 200,000[d]	÷ 100,000[d]
Earnings per share on common stock	$ 1.20	$ 1.50	$ 2.46

[a] $2,000,000 bonds × 12%
[b] Income before income tax × 40%
[c] Preferred stock × 9%
[d] Common stock ÷ $10 par value per share

Exhibit 1 indicates that when earnings are strong, Plan 3 has the highest earnings per share, making it most attractive for common shareholders. This is because the company is generating more than enough net income to cover the bond interest. If the estimated earnings are more than $800,000, the difference between the earnings per share to common stockholders under Plans 1 and 3 is even greater.[2]

Lower earnings, however, have the opposite effect. If earnings are reduced to $440,000, as illustrated in Exhibit 2, Plans 1 and 2 become more attractive to common stockholders. This is because more of the company's earnings are being used to pay bond interest, leaving less net income attributable to common stockholders.

2 The higher earnings per share under Plan 3 is due to a finance concept known as *leverage*. This concept is discussed further in Chapter 18.

EXHIBIT 2

Effect of Alternative Financing Plans—$440,000 Earnings

Dynamic Exhibit

	Plan 1	Plan 2	Plan 3
12% bonds	—	—	$2,000,000
Preferred 9% stock, $50 par	—	$2,000,000	1,000,000
Common stock, $10 par	$4,000,000	2,000,000	1,000,000
Total	$4,000,000	$4,000,000	$4,000,000
Earnings before interest and income tax	$ 440,000	$ 440,000	$ 440,000
Interest on bonds	—	—	(240,000)
Income before income tax	$ 440,000	$ 440,000	$ 200,000
Income tax	(176,000)	(176,000)	(80,000)
Net income	$ 264,000	$ 264,000	$ 120,000
Dividends on preferred stock	—	(180,000)	(90,000)
Available for dividends on common stock	$ 264,000	$ 84,000	$ 30,000
Shares of common stock outstanding	÷ 400,000	÷ 200,000	÷ 100,000
Earnings per share on common stock	$ 0.66	$ 0.42	$ 0.30

In addition to earnings per share, the corporation should consider other factors in deciding among the financing plans. For example, if bonds are issued, the interest and the face value of the bonds at maturity must be paid. If these payments are not made, the bondholders could seek court action and force the company into bankruptcy. In contrast, a corporation is not legally obligated to pay dividends on preferred or common stock.

Example Exercise 14-1 Alternative Financing Plans

Obj. 1

Gonzales Co. is considering the following alternative plans for financing its company:

	Plan 1	Plan 2
Issue 10% bonds (at face value)	—	$2,000,000
Issue common stock, $10 par	$3,000,000	1,000,000

Income tax is estimated at 40% of income.

Determine the earnings per share of common stock under the two alternative financing plans, assuming that income before bond interest and income tax is $750,000.

Follow My Example 14-1

	Plan 1	Plan 2
Earnings before bond interest and income tax	$ 750,000	$ 750,000
Interest on bonds	—	(200,000)[2]
Income before income tax	$ 750,000	$ 550,000
Income tax	(300,000)[1]	(220,000)[3]
Net income	$ 450,000	$ 330,000
Dividends on preferred stock	—	—
Available for dividends on common stock	$ 450,000	$ 330,000
Shares of common stock outstanding	÷300,000	÷100,000
Earnings per share on common stock	$ 1.50	$ 3.30

[1]$750,000 × 40% [2]$2,000,000 × 10% [3]$550,000 × 40%

Practice Exercises: PE 14-1A, PE 14-1B

Nature of Bonds Payable

Obj. 2 Describe the characteristics and terminology of bonds payable.

Corporate bonds normally differ in face amount, interest rates, interest payment dates, and maturity dates. Bonds also differ in other ways such as whether corporate assets are pledged in support of the bonds.

Bond Characteristics and Terminology

The face amount of each bond is called the *principal*. This is the amount that must be repaid on the dates the bonds mature. The principal is usually $1,000, or a multiple of $1,000. The interest on bonds may be payable annually, semiannually, or quarterly. Most bonds pay interest semiannually.

The underlying contract between the company issuing bonds and the bondholders is called a **bond indenture**. This contract can be written in different ways, depending on the financing needs of the company. The two most common types of bonds are term bonds and serial bonds. When all bonds of an issue mature at the same time, they are called *term bonds*. If the bonds mature over several dates, they are called *serial bonds*. For example, one-tenth of an issue of $1,000,000 bonds, or $100,000, may mature 16 years from the issue date, another $100,000 in the 17th year, and so on.

There are also a variety of more complicated bond structures. For example, *convertible bonds* may be exchanged for shares of common stock, and *callable bonds* may be redeemed by the corporation prior to maturity. These bonds are discussed in intermediate and advanced accounting texts.

Proceeds from Issuing Bonds

When a corporation issues bonds, the proceeds received for the bonds depend on the following:

- The face amount of the bonds, which is the amount due at the maturity date
- The interest rate on the bonds
- The market rate of interest for similar bonds

The face amount and the interest rate on the bonds are identified in the bond indenture. The interest rate to be paid on the face amount of the bond is called the **contract rate** or *coupon rate*.

Link to PepsiCo

PepsiCo's 2.75% bonds maturing in 2023 were recently selling for less than their face value.

The **market rate of interest**, sometimes called the **effective rate of interest**, is the rate determined from sales and purchases of similar bonds. The market rate of interest is affected by a variety of factors, including investors' expectations of current and future economic conditions.

By comparing the market and contract rates of interest, it can be determined whether the bonds will sell for more than, for less than, or at their face amount, as shown in Exhibit 3.

EXHIBIT 3 **Issuing Bonds at a Discount, at Face Amount, and at a Premium**

If: Market Rate > Contract Rate	**If:** Market Rate = Contract Rate	**If:** Market Rate < Contract Rate

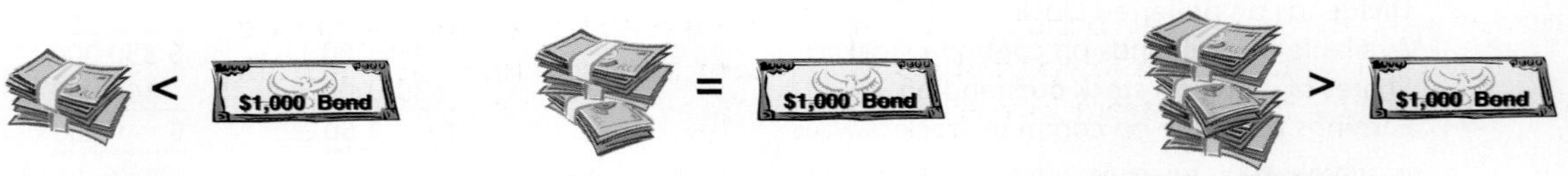

Less than $1,000	**$1,000**	**More than $1,000**
Then: Selling Price < Face Amount	**Then:** Selling Price = Face Amount	**Then:** Selling Price > Face Amount
Sold at a DISCOUNT	Sold at FACE AMOUNT	Sold at a PREMIUM

If the market rate equals the contract rate, bonds will sell at the **face amount**.

If the market rate is greater than the contract rate, the bonds will sell for less than their face value. The face amount of the bonds less the selling price is called a **discount**. A bond sells at a discount because buyers are not willing to pay the full face amount for bonds with a contract rate that is lower than the market rate.

If the market rate is less than the contract rate, the bonds will sell for more than their face value. The selling price of the bonds less the face amount is called a **premium**. A bond sells at a premium because buyers are willing to pay more than the face amount for bonds with a contract rate that is higher than the market rate.

The price of a bond is quoted as a percentage of the bond's face value. For example, a $1,000 bond quoted at 98 could be purchased or sold for $980 ($1,000 × 0.98). Likewise, bonds quoted at 109 could be purchased or sold for $1,090 ($1,000 × 1.09).

Link to PepsiCo

PepsiCo's 4.5% bonds maturing in 2023 were recently selling for over 110% of their face value.

Business Connection

INVESTOR BOND PRICE RISK

Corporate bonds are purchased as investments by both individuals and institutions. Bonds issued by financially strong issuers provide a compelling balance of risk and reward, as they provide the investor with both a steady stream of interest payments and the repayment of the principal at maturity. Thus, high-quality bond investments are considered less risky than equity investments. However, this does not mean that bond investors have no price risk. Bond prices move in the opposite direction as changes in market interest rates, as shown below.

Market Rate of Interest	Market Price of Bonds
Increase	Decrease
Decrease	Increase

The magnitude of a bond's price change depends on its maturity. When market interest rates change, the price of short-term bonds fluctuates less than the price of long-term bonds with a comparable interest rate. This is illustrated in the following table:

Bond Term	Contract Rate	Estimated Price of $1,000 Par Value Bond if Market Interest Rate Doubles	Estimated Price of $1,000 Par Value Bond if Market Interest Rate Halves
1 year	0.5%	$995	$1,002
5 years	1.5%	931	1,037
10 years	2.0%	838	1,095
30 years	3.0%	587	1,360

The greater price variability of long-term bonds makes them a riskier investment than short-term bonds. This is one of the reasons longer-term bonds typically have higher coupon rates than shorter-term bonds. As a result, the bond's term must be considered in evaluating both the risk and return of a bond investment.

Accounting for Bonds Payable

Obj. 3 Describe and illustrate the accounting for bonds payable.

Bonds may be issued at their face amount, a discount, or a premium. When bonds are issued at less or more than their face amount, the discount or premium must be amortized over the life of the bonds. At the maturity date, the face amount must be repaid. In some situations, a corporation may redeem bonds before their maturity date by repurchasing them from investors.

Bonds Issued at Face Amount

If the market rate of interest is equal to the contract rate of interest, the bonds will sell for their face amount or at a price of 100. To illustrate, assume that on January 1, 20Y5, Eastern Montana Communications Inc. issued the following bonds:

Face amount	$100,000
Contract rate of interest	12%
Interest paid semiannually on June 30 and December 31.	
Term of bonds	5 years
Market rate of interest	12%

Since the contract rate of interest and the market rate of interest are the same, the bonds will sell at their face amount. The entry to record the issuance of the bonds is as follows:

20Y5					
Jan.	1	Cash		100,000	
		Bonds Payable			100,000
		Issued $100,000 bonds payable at face amount.			

Every six months (on June 30 and December 31) after the bonds are issued, interest of $6,000 ($100,000 × 12% × ½ year) is paid. The first interest payment on June 30, 20Y5, is recorded as follows:

20Y5					
June	30	Interest Expense		6,000	
		Cash			6,000
		Paid six months' interest on bonds.			

At the maturity date, the payment of the principal of $100,000 is recorded as follows:

20Y9					
Dec.	31	Bonds Payable		100,000	
		Cash			100,000
		Paid bond principal at maturity date.			

Example Exercise 14-2 Issuing Bonds at Face Amount — Obj. 3

On January 1, the first day of the fiscal year, a company issues a $1,000,000, 6%, five-year bond that pays semiannual interest of $30,000 ($1,000,000 × 6% × ½ year), receiving cash of $1,000,000. Journalize the entries to record (a) the issuance of the bonds at their face amount, (b) the first interest payment on June 30, and (c) the payment of the principal on the maturity date.

Follow My Example 14-2

a.	Cash	1,000,000	
	Bonds Payable		1,000,000
b.	Interest Expense	30,000	
	Cash		30,000
c.	Bonds Payable	1,000,000	
	Cash		1,000,000

Practice Exercises: PE 14-2A, PE 14-2B

Bonds Issued at a Discount

Note

Bonds will sell at a discount when the market rate of interest is higher than the contract rate.

If the market rate of interest is greater than the contract rate of interest, the bonds will sell for less than their face amount. This is because investors are not willing to pay the full face amount for bonds that pay a lower contract rate of interest than the rate they could earn on similar bonds (market rate). The difference between the face amount and the selling price of the bonds is the bond discount.[3]

3 The price that investors are willing to pay for the bonds depends on present value concepts. Present value concepts, including the computation of bond prices, are described and illustrated in Appendix 1 at the end of this chapter.

To illustrate, assume that on January 1, 20Y5, Western Wyoming Distribution Inc. issued the following bonds:

Face amount	$100,000
Contract rate of interest	12%
Interest paid semiannually on June 30 and December 31.	
Term of bonds	5 years
Market rate of interest	13%

Because the contract rate of interest is less than the market rate of interest, the bonds will sell at less than their face amount. Assuming that the bonds sell for $96,406, the entry to record the issuance of the bonds is as follows:

20Y5					
Jan.	1	Cash		96,406	
		Discount on Bonds Payable		3,594	
		Bonds Payable			100,000
		Issued $100,000 bonds at discount.			

The $96,406 is the amount investors are willing to pay for bonds that have a lower contract rate of interest (12%) than the market rate (13%). The discount is the market's way of adjusting the contract rate of interest to the higher market rate of interest.

The account, Discount on Bonds Payable, is a contra account to Bonds Payable and has a normal debit balance. It is subtracted from Bonds Payable to determine the carrying amount (or book value) of the bonds payable. The **carrying amount** of bonds payable is the face amount of the bonds less any unamortized discount or plus any unamortized premium. Thus, after the preceding entry, the carrying amount of the bonds payable is $96,406 ($100,000 − $3,594).

Link to PepsiCo

PepsiCo's 3.6% bonds maturing in 2042 were selling for less than 94% of their face value, which implies that the market rate of interest for equivalent bonds is more than the 3.6% contract rate.

Example Exercise 14-3 Issuing Bonds at a Discount **Obj. 3**

On the first day of the fiscal year, a company issues a $1,000,000, 6%, five-year bond that pays semiannual interest of $30,000 ($1,000,000 × 6% × ½), receiving cash of $936,420. Journalize the entry to record the issuance of the bonds.

Follow My Example 14-3

Cash	936,420	
Discount on Bonds Payable	63,580	
Bonds Payable		1,000,000

Practice Exercises: PE 14-3A, PE 14-3B

Amortizing a Bond Discount

Every period, a portion of the bond discount must be reduced and added to interest expense to reflect the passage of time. This process, called **amortization**, increases the contract rate of interest on a bond to the market rate of interest that existed on the date the bonds were issued. The entry to amortize a bond discount is as follows:

		Interest Expense		XXX	
		Discount on Bonds Payable			XXX

Business Connection

U.S. GOVERNMENT DEBT

Like many corporations, the U.S. government issues debt to finance its operations. Currently, debt provides approximately 15% of the total annual funding needs of the U.S. government. The remainder comes from taxes. The debt is issued by the U.S. Treasury Department in the form of U.S. Treasury bills, notes, and bonds. An individual investor can purchase these as an investment through the TreasuryDirect® website or through a broker. Treasury securities have the following characteristics:

	Issued at	Interest Paid	Term
U.S. Treasury bills	Discount	None	1 year or less
U.S. Treasury notes	Face value	Semiannual	1 to 10 years
U.S. Treasury bonds	Face value	Semiannual	30 years

Recently, 10-year notes had a contract rate of 2.26%. The contract interest rate for government securities will normally be lowest for Treasury bills and largest for Treasury bonds.

The preceding entry may be made annually as an adjusting entry, or it may be combined with the semiannual interest payment. In the latter case, the entry would be as follows:

		Interest Expense		XXX	
		Discount on Bonds Payable			XXX
		Cash (amount of semiannual interest)			XXX

The straight-line method is used to compute the amortization of a bond discount. This method provides equal amounts of amortization each period[4]. To illustrate, amortization of the Western Wyoming Distribution bond discount of $3,594 is computed as follows:

Discount on bonds payable	$3,594
Term of bonds	5 years
Semiannual amortization.....................	$359.40 ($3,594 ÷ 10 periods)

The combined entry to record the first interest payment and the amortization of the discount is as follows:

20Y5					
June	30	Interest Expense		6,359.40	
		Discount on Bonds Payable			359.40
		Cash			6,000.00
		Paid semiannual interest and amortized 1/10 of bond discount.			

The preceding entry is made on each interest payment date. Thus, the amount of the semiannual interest expense on the bonds ($6,359.40) remains the same over the life of the bonds.

The effect of the discount amortization is to increase the interest expense from $6,000.00 to $6,359.40 on every semiannual interest payment date. In effect, this increases the contract rate of interest from 12% to a rate of interest that approximates the market rate of 13%. In addition, as the discount is amortized, the carrying amount of the bonds increases until it equals the face amount of the bonds on the maturity date.

4 The effective interest rate method is required by generally accepted accounting principles. However, the straight-line method may be used if the results do not differ significantly from the interest method. The straight-line method is used in this chapter. The effective interest rate method is described and illustrated in Appendix 2 at the end of this chapter.

Example Exercise 14-4 Discount Amortization

Obj. 3

Using the bond from Example Exercise 14-3, journalize the first interest payment and the amortization of the related bond discount.

Follow My Example 14-4

Interest Expense	36,358	
Discount on Bonds Payable		6,358
Cash		30,000
Paid interest and amortized the bond discount ($63,580 ÷ 10).		

Practice Exercises: PE 14-4A, PE 14-4B

Bonds Issued at a Premium

If the market rate of interest is less than the contract rate of interest, the bonds will sell for more than their face amount. This is because investors are willing to pay more for bonds that pay a higher contract rate of interest than the rate they could earn on similar bonds (market rate).

Note

Bonds will sell at a premium when the market rate of interest is less than the contract rate.

To illustrate, assume that on January 1, 20Y5, Northern Idaho Transportation Inc. issued the following bonds:

Face amount	$100,000
Contract rate of interest	12%
Interest paid semiannually on June 30 and December 31.	
Term of bonds	5 years
Market rate of interest	11%

Because the contract rate of interest is more than the market rate of interest, the bonds will sell for more than their face amount. Assuming that the bonds sell for $103,769, the entry to record the issuance of the bonds is as follows:

20Y5					
Jan.	1	Cash		103,769	
		Bonds Payable			100,000
		Premium on Bonds Payable			3,769
		Issued $100,000 bonds at a premium.			

The $3,769 premium is the extra amount investors are willing to pay for bonds that have a higher contract rate of interest (12%) than the market rate (11%). The premium is the market's way of adjusting the contract rate of interest to the lower market rate of interest.

The account Premium on Bonds Payable has a normal credit balance. It is added to Bonds Payable to determine the carrying amount (or book value) of the bonds payable. Thus, after the preceding entry, the carrying amount of the bonds payable is $103,769 ($100,000 + $3,769).

Example Exercise 14-5 Issuing Bonds at a Premium

Obj. 3

On the first day of the fiscal year, a company issues a $2,000,000, 12%, five-year bond that pays semiannual interest of $120,000 ($2,000,000 × 12% × ½), receiving cash of $2,154,440. Journalize the bond issuance.

(Continued)

Follow My Example 14-5

Cash	2,154,440	
Premium on Bonds Payable		154,440
Bonds Payable		2,000,000

Practice Exercises: PE 14-5A, PE 14-5B

Amortizing a Bond Premium

Like bond discounts, a bond premium must be amortized over the life of the bond. The amortization of a bond premium decreases the contract rate of interest on a bond to the market rate of interest that existed on the date the bonds were issued. The amortization can be computed using either the straight-line or the effective interest rate method. The entry to amortize a bond premium is as follows:

	Premium on Bonds Payable	XXX	
	Interest Expense		XXX

The preceding entry may be made annually as an adjusting entry, or it may be combined with the semiannual interest payment. In the latter case, it would be:

	Interest Expense	XXX	
	Premium on Bonds Payable	XXX	
	Cash (amount of semiannual interest)		XXX

To illustrate, amortization of the preceding premium of $3,769 is computed as follows using the straight-line method:

Premium on bonds payable	$3,769
Term of bonds	5 years
Semiannual amortization	$376.90 ($3,769 ÷ 10 periods)

The combined entry to record the first interest payment and the amortization of the premium is as follows:

20Y5				
June	30	Interest Expense	5,623.10	
		Premium on Bonds Payable	376.90	
		Cash		6,000.00
		Paid semiannual interest and amortized 1/10 of bond premium.		

The preceding entry is made on each interest payment date. Thus, the amount of the semiannual interest expense ($5,623.10) on the bonds remains the same over the life of the bonds.

The effect of the premium amortization is to decrease the interest expense from $6,000.00 to $5,623.10. In effect, this decreases the rate of interest from 12% to a rate of interest that approximates the market rate of 11%. In addition, as the premium is amortized, the carrying amount of the bonds decreases until it equals the face amount of bonds on the maturity date.

Example Exercise 14-6 Premium Amortization Obj. 3

Using the bond from Example Exercise 14-5, journalize the first interest payment and the amortization of the related bond premium.

Follow My Example 14-6

Interest Expense	104,556	
Premium on Bonds Payable	15,444	
Cash		120,000
Paid interest and amortized the bond premium ($154,440 ÷ 10).		

Practice Exercises: PE 14-6A, PE 14-6B

Business Connection

BOND RATINGS

When purchasing bonds, investors are very interested in understanding how likely it is that the bond issuer will be able to repay the bond principal and associated interest. To help them assess this likelihood, independent rating agencies review and grade the financial condition of companies that issue bonds. For example, the Standard & Poor's rating agency rates bonds on a scale from D (lowest) to AAA (highest). Bonds with a rating of BBB- or higher are called *investment grade* because they are issued by companies in sound financial condition and are considered to be reasonably safe investments. Bonds issued by companies in relatively weak financial condition receive ratings below BBB-, reflecting the higher potential for default or nonpayment. These lesser quality bonds are referred to as *non-investment grade* or *junk* bonds. The market rate of interest on junk bonds is much higher than the market rate on investment grade bonds, which compensates bond investors for junk bonds' higher risk of default.

Bond Redemption

A corporation may redeem or call bonds before they mature. This is often done when the market rate of interest declines below the contract rate of interest. In such cases, the corporation may issue new bonds at a lower interest rate and use the proceeds to redeem the original bond issue.

Callable bonds can be redeemed by the issuing corporation within the period of time and at the price stated in the bond indenture. Normally, the call price is above the face value. A corporation may also redeem its bonds by purchasing them on the open market.[5]

A corporation usually redeems its bonds at a price different from the carrying amount (or book value) of the bonds. A gain or loss may be realized on a bond redemption as follows:

- A *gain* is recorded if the price paid for redemption is below the bond carrying amount.
- A *loss* is recorded if the price paid for the redemption is above the carrying amount.

Gains and losses on the redemption of bonds are reported in the *Other revenue (loss)* section of the income statement.

To illustrate, assume that on June 30, 20Y5, a corporation has the following bond issue:

Face amount of bonds	$100,000
Premium on bonds payable	4,000*

*After the semiannual interest payment and premium amortization have been recorded.

5 Some bond indentures require the corporation issuing the bonds to transfer cash to a special cash fund, called a *sinking fund,* over the life of the bond. Such funds help assure investors that there will be adequate cash to pay the bonds at their maturity date.

On June 30, 20Y5, the corporation redeemed one-fourth ($25,000) of these bonds in the market for $24,000. The entry to record the redemption is as follows:

20Y5				
June	30	Bonds Payable	25,000	
		Premium on Bonds Payable	1,000	
		Cash		24,000
		Gain on Redemption of Bonds		2,000
		Redeemed $25,000 bonds for $24,000.		

In the preceding entry, only the portion of the premium related to the redeemed bonds ($4,000 × 25% = $1,000) is removed. The difference between the carrying amount of the bonds redeemed, $26,000 ($25,000 + $1,000), and the redemption price, $24,000, is recorded as a gain.

Assume that the corporation calls the remaining $75,000 of outstanding bonds, which are held by a private investor, for $79,500 on July 1, 20Y5. The entry to record the redemption is as follows:

20Y5				
July	1	Bonds Payable	75,000	
		Premium on Bonds Payable	3,000	
		Loss on Redemption of Bonds	1,500	
		Cash		79,500
		Redeemed $75,000 bonds for $79,500.		

Example Exercise 14-7 Redemption of Bonds Payable — Obj. 3

A $500,000 bond issue on which there is an unamortized discount of $40,000 is redeemed for $475,000. Journalize the redemption of the bonds.

Follow My Example 14-7

Bonds Payable	500,000	
Loss on Redemption of Bonds	15,000	
Discount on Bonds Payable		40,000
Cash		475,000

Practice Exercises: PE 14-7A, PE 14-7B

Obj. 4 Describe and illustrate the accounting for installment notes.

Installment Notes

Corporations often finance their operations by issuing bonds payable. As an alternative, corporations may issue a different kind of notes payable called installment notes. An **installment note** is a debt that requires the borrower to make equal periodic payments to the lender for the term of the note. Unlike bonds, each note payment includes the following:

- Payment of a portion of the amount initially borrowed, called the *principal*
- Payment of interest on the outstanding balance

At the end of the note's term, the principal will have been repaid in full.

Installment notes are often used to purchase specific assets such as equipment and are often secured by the purchased asset. When a note is secured by an asset, it is called a **mortgage note**. If the borrower fails to pay a mortgage note, the lender has the right to take possession of the pledged asset and sell it to pay off the debt. Mortgage notes are typically issued by an individual bank.

Real World

Individuals typically use mortgage notes when buying a house or car.

Issuing an Installment Note

When an installment note is issued, an entry is recorded debiting Cash and crediting Notes Payable. To illustrate, assume that Lewis Company issues the following installment note to City National Bank on January 1, 20Y4:

Principal amount of note	$24,000
Interest rate	6%
Term of note	5 years
Annual payments	$5,698[6]

The entry to record the issuance of the note is as follows:

20Y4				
Jan.	1	Cash	24,000	
		Notes Payable		24,000
		Issued installment note for cash.		

Annual Payments

The preceding note payable requires Lewis Company to repay the principal and interest in equal payments of $5,698 beginning December 31, 20Y4, for each of the next five years. Unlike bonds, however, each installment note payment includes an interest and principal component.

The interest portion of an installment note payment is computed by multiplying the interest rate by the carrying amount (book value) of the note at the beginning of the period. The principal portion of the payment is then computed as the difference between the total installment note payment (cash paid) and the interest component. These computations are illustrated in Exhibit 4 (rounded to the nearest dollar).

Amortization of Installment Notes EXHIBIT 4

Year Ending December 31	A January 1 Carrying Amount	B Note Payment (Cash Paid)	C Interest Expense (6% of January 1 Note Carrying Amount)		D Decrease in Notes Payable (B – C)	E December 31 Carrying Amount (A – D)
20Y4	$24,000	$ 5,698	$ 1,440	(6% of $24,000)	$ 4,258	$19,742
20Y5	19,742	5,698	1,185	(6% of $19,742)	4,513	15,229
20Y6	15,229	5,698	914	(6% of $15,229)	4,784	10,445
20Y7	10,445	5,698	627	(6% of $10,445)	5,071	5,374
20Y8	5,374	5,698	324*	(6% of $5,374)	5,374	—
		$28,490	$4,490		$24,000	

*Rounded ($5,374 – $5,698).

1. The January 1, 20Y4, carrying value (Column A) equals the amount borrowed from the bank. The January 1 balance in the following years equals the December 31 balance from the prior year.
2. The note payment (Column B) remains constant at $5,698, the annual cash payment required by the bank.
3. The interest expense (Column C) is computed at 6% times the installment note carrying amount at the beginning of each year. Since the carrying amount decreases each year, the interest expense decreases each year.
4. Notes payable decreases each year by the amount of the principal repayment (Column D). The principal repayment is computed by subtracting the interest expense (Column C) from the total payment (Column B). The principal repayment (Column D) increases each year as the interest expense decreases (Column C).

6 The amount of the annual payment is calculated by using the present value concepts discussed in Appendix 1 at the end of this chapter. The annual payment of $5,698 is computed by dividing the $24,000 loan amount by the present value of an annuity of $1 for five periods at 6% (4.21236) from Exhibit 10 (rounded to the nearest dollar).

5. The carrying amount on December 31 (Column E) of the note decreases from $24,000, the initial amount borrowed, to $0 at the end of the five years.

The entry to record the first payment on December 31, 20Y4, is as follows:

20Y4				
Dec.	31	Interest Expense	1,440	
		Notes Payable	4,258	
		Cash		5,698
		Paid principal and interest on installment note.		

The entry to record the second payment on December 31, 20Y5, is as follows:

20Y5				
Dec.	31	Interest Expense	1,185	
		Notes Payable	4,513	
		Cash		5,698
		Paid principal and interest on installment note.		

As the prior entries show, the cash payment is the same in each year. The interest and principal payments, however, changes each year. This is because the carrying amount (book value) of the note decreases each year as principal is paid, which decreases the interest component the next period.

The entry to record the final payment on December 31, 20Y8, is as follows:

20Y8				
Dec.	31	Interest Expense	324	
		Notes Payable	5,374	
		Cash		5,698
		Paid principal and interest on installment note.		

After the final payment, the carrying amount on the note is zero, indicating that the note has been paid in full. Any assets that secure the note would then be released by the bank.

Example Exercise 14-8 Journalizing Installment Notes — Obj. 4

On the first day of the fiscal year, a company issues a $30,000, 10%, five-year installment note that has annual payments of $7,914. The first note payment consists of $3,000 of interest and $4,914 of principal repayment.

a. Journalize the entry to record the issuance of the installment note.

b. Journalize the first annual note payment.

Follow My Example 14-8

a.	Cash	30,000	
	Notes Payable		30,000
b.	Interest Expense	3,000	
	Notes Payable	4,914	
	Cash		7,914

Practice Exercises: PE 14-8A, PE 14-8B

INTEGRITY, OBJECTIVITY, AND ETHICS IN BUSINESS

THE RATINGS GAME

In February 2013, the United States Justice Department filed a lawsuit against the three main credit rating agencies (**Moody's**, **Standard & Poor's**, and **Fitch**) for inflating their ratings on high risk bond issuances between 2004 and 2007. During this time period, the three ratings agencies gave their highest rating (AAA) to debt securities that were, in fact, highly risky. During the financial crisis of 2008, most of these bonds experienced significant drops in value, leaving investors with huge losses. The Justice Department lawsuit alleges that the ratings agencies were aware of the high risks associated with these bonds but inflated their ratings because of the large fee they received for providing a rating on these bonds. In 2015, Standard & Poor's settled this and related lawsuits for $1.5 billion.

Sources: "U.S. vs. S&P: The Rating Game," *Chicago Tribune*, February 6, 2013; "S&P Reaches $1.5 Billion Deal with U.S., States over Crisis-Era Ratings," Reuters, *Business News*, February 3, 2015.

Reporting Long-Term Liabilities

Obj. 5 Describe and illustrate the reporting of long-term liabilities, including bonds and notes payable.

Bonds payable and notes payable are reported as liabilities on the balance sheet. Any portion of the bonds or notes that is due within one year is reported as a current liability. Any remaining bonds or notes are reported as a long-term liability.

Any unamortized premium is reported as an addition to the face amount of the bonds. Any unamortized discount is reported as a deduction from the face amount of the bonds. A description of the bonds and notes should also be reported either on the face of the financial statements or in the accompanying notes.

The reporting of bonds and notes payable for **Mornin' Joe** follows:

Mornin' Joe
Balance Sheet
December 31, 20Y6

Current liabilities:		
Accounts payable	$133,000	
Notes payable (current portion)	200,000	
Salaries and wages payable	42,000	
Payroll taxes payable	16,400	
Interest payable	40,000	
Total current liabilities		$ 431,400
Long-term liabilities:		
Bonds payable, 8%, due December 31, 2030	$500,000	
Unamortized discount	(16,000)	$ 484,000
Notes payable		1,400,000
Total long-term liabilities		$1,884,000
Total liabilities		$2,315,400

Financial Analysis and Interpretation: Times Interest Earned Ratio

Obj. 6 Describe and illustrate how the times interest earned ratio is used to evaluate a company's financial condition.

FAI

As we have discussed, the assets of a company are subject to (1) the claims of creditors and (2) the rights of owners. As creditors, bondholders are concerned primarily with the company's ability to make its periodic interest payments and repay the face amount of the bonds at maturity.

Analysts assess the risk that bondholders will not receive their interest payments by computing the **times interest earned** ratio during the year as follows:

$$\text{Times Interest Earned} = \frac{\text{Income Before Income Tax} + \text{Interest Expense}}{\text{Interest Expense}}$$

This ratio computes the number of times interest payments could be paid out of current period earnings. Because interest payments reduce income tax expense, the ratio is computed using income before tax. High values of this ratio are considered favorable. In contrast, low values are considered unfavorable. Values of this ratio less than 1.0 suggest that the firm is unable to cover interest payments from current period income before tax. Such a situation could eventually lead to loan defaults.

To illustrate, the following data were taken from recent annual reports of four companies in the soft drink beverage industry—PepsiCo, Inc., The Coca-Cola Company, Dr Pepper Snapple Group, Inc., and Monster Beverage Corporation (in thousands):

	PepsiCo	Coca-Cola	Dr Pepper Snapple	Monster
Interest expense	$ 909,000	$ 483,000	$ 109,000	$ 1,676
Income before income tax expense	8,757,000	9,325,000	1,073,000	745,788

The times interest earned is computed as follows for all four companies:

	PepsiCo	Coca-Cola	Dr Pepper Snapple	Monster
Interest expense	$ 909,000	$ 483,000	$ 109,000	$ 1,676
Income before income tax expense	8,757,000	9,325,000	1,073,000	745,788
Income before income tax expense + Interest expense	$9,666,000	$9,808,000	$1,182,000	$747,464
Times interest earned	10.6*	20.3**	10.8***	446.0****

*($9,666,000 ÷ $909,000)
**($9,808,000 ÷ $483,000)
***($1,182,000 ÷ $109,000)
****($747,464 ÷ $1,676)

Monster is much smaller than the other three beverage companies. However, it has a times interest earned ratio of 446.0, which is much greater than the other three companies. This is because Monster has no long-term debt and only a small amount of short-term bank loans. Among the other three beverage companies, Coca-Cola has twice the interest coverage of PepsiCo and Dr Pepper Snapple. Since all of the ratios are in excess of 10, all of the companies generate enough income before tax to pay (cover) their interest payments. As a result, bondholders of these companies have extremely good protection in the event of an earnings decline.

Example Exercise 14-9 Times Interest Earned — Obj. 6

Harris Industries reported the following on the company's income statement in 20Y7 and 20Y6:

	20Y7	20Y6
Interest expense	$ 200,000	$180,000
Income before income tax expense	1,000,000	720,000

a. Determine the times interest earned ratio for 20Y7 and 20Y6.
b. Is times interest earned ratio improving or declining?

Follow My Example 14-9

a. 20Y7:

$$\text{Times interest earned: } \frac{\$1{,}000{,}000 + \$200{,}000}{\$200{,}000} = 6.0$$

20Y6:

$$\text{Times interest earned: } \frac{\$720{,}000 + \$180{,}000}{\$180{,}000} = 5.0$$

b. The times interest earned has increased from 5.0 in 20Y6 to 6.0 in 20Y7. Thus, the debtholders have improved confidence in the company's ability to make its interest payments.

Practice Exercises: PE 14-9A, PE 14-9B

APPENDIX 1

Present Value Concepts and Pricing Bonds Payable

When a corporation issues bonds, the price that investors are willing to pay for the bonds depends on the following:

- The face amount of the bonds, which is the amount due at the maturity date
- The periodic interest to be paid on the bonds
- The market rate of interest

An investor determines how much to pay for the bonds by computing the present value of the bond's future cash receipts, using the market rate of interest. A bond's future cash receipts include its face value at maturity and the periodic interest payments.

Present Value Concepts

The concept of present value is based on the time value of money. The *time value of money concept* recognizes that cash received today is worth more than the same amount of cash to be received in the future.

To illustrate, what would you rather have: $1,000 today or $1,000 one year from now? You would rather have the $1,000 today because it could be invested to earn interest. For example, if the $1,000 could be invested to earn 10% interest per year, the $1,000 will accumulate to $1,100 ($1,000 plus $100 interest) in one year. In this sense, you can think of the $1,000 in hand today as the **present value** of $1,100 to be received a year from today. This present value is illustrated in Exhibit 5.

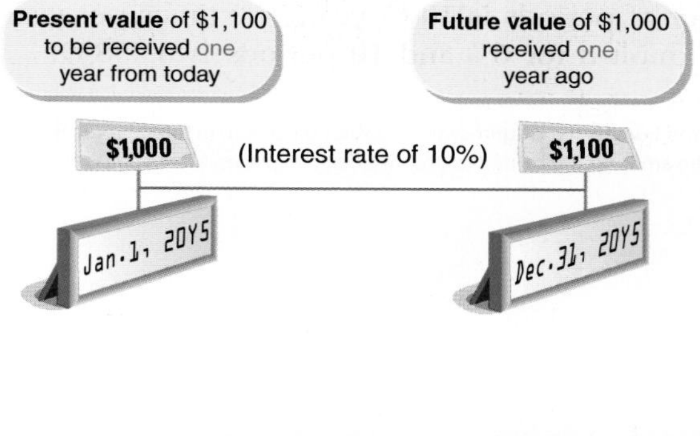

EXHIBIT 5

Present Value and Future Value

A related concept to present value is **future value**. To illustrate, using the preceding example illustrated in Exhibit 5, the $1,100 to be received on December 31, 20Y5, is the *future value* of $1,000 on January 1, 20Y5, assuming an interest rate of 10%.

Present Value of an Amount To illustrate the present value of an amount, assume that $1,000 is to be received in one year. If the market of interest is 10%, the present value of the $1,000 is $909.09 ($1,000 ÷ 1.10). This present value is illustrated in Exhibit 6.

EXHIBIT 6

Present Value of an Amount to Be Received in One Year

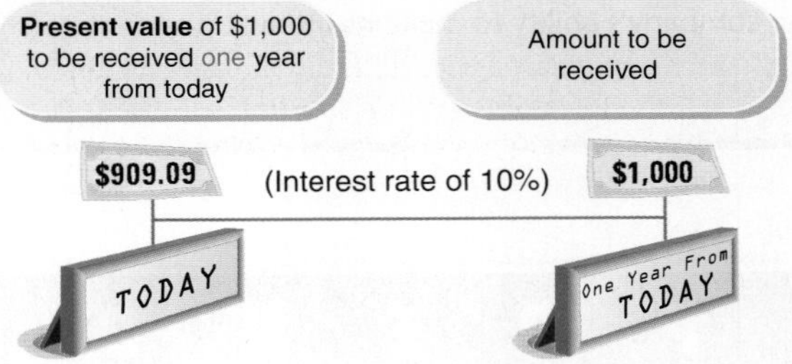

If the $1,000 is to be received in two years, with interest of 10% compounded at the end of the first year, the present value is $826.45 ($909.09 ÷ 1.10). This present value is illustrated in Exhibit 7.

EXHIBIT 7

Present Value of an Amount to Be Received in Two Years

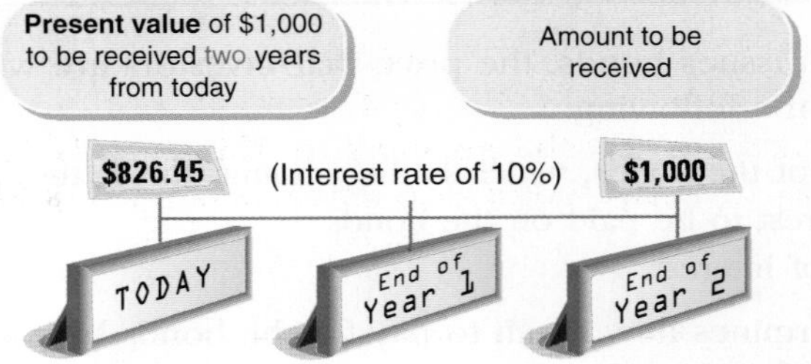

Real World

Spreadsheet software and business calculators have built-in present value functions that can also be used to calculate present values.

The present value of an amount to be received in the future can be determined by a series of divisions as illustrated in Exhibits 5, 6, and 7. In practice, however, it is easier to use a table of present values.

The *present value of $1* table is used to find the present value factor for $1 to be received after a number of periods in the future. The amount to be received is then multiplied by this factor to determine its present value.

To illustrate, Exhibit 8 is a partial table of the present value of $1.[7] Exhibit 8 indicates that the present value of $1 to be received in two years with a market rate of interest of 10% a year is 0.82645. Multiplying $1,000 to be received in two years by 0.82645 yields $826.45 ($1,000 × 0.82645). This amount is the same as the amount computed earlier. In Exhibit 8, the Periods column represents the number of compounding periods, and the percentage columns represent the compound interest rate per period. Thus, the present value factor from Exhibit 8 for 12% for five years is 0.56743. If the interest is compounded semiannually, the interest rate is 6% (12% ÷ 2), and the number of periods is 10 (5 years × 2 times per year). Thus, the present value factor from Exhibit 8 for 6% and 10 periods is 0.55839.

7 To simplify the illustrations and homework assignments, the tables presented in this chapter are limited to 10 periods for a small number of interest rates and the amounts are carried to only five decimal places. More complete interest tables are presented in Appendix A of the text.

Present Value of $1 at Compound Interest EXHIBIT 8

Periods	4%	4½%	5%	5½%	6%	6½%	7%	10%	11%	12%	13%
1	0.96154	0.95694	0.95238	0.94787	0.94340	0.93897	0.93458	0.90909	0.90090	0.89286	0.88496
2	0.92456	0.91573	0.90703	0.89845	0.89000	0.88166	0.87344	0.82645	0.81162	0.79719	0.78315
3	0.88900	0.87630	0.86384	0.85161	0.83962	0.82785	0.81630	0.75131	0.73119	0.71178	0.69305
4	0.85480	0.83856	0.82270	0.80722	0.79209	0.77732	0.76290	0.68301	0.65873	0.63552	0.61332
5	0.82193	0.80245	0.78353	0.76513	0.74726	0.72988	0.71299	0.62092	0.59345	0.56743	0.54276
6	0.79031	0.76790	0.74622	0.72525	0.70496	0.68533	0.66634	0.56447	0.53464	0.50663	0.48032
7	0.75992	0.73483	0.71068	0.68744	0.66506	0.64351	0.62275	0.51316	0.48166	0.45235	0.42506
8	0.73069	0.70319	0.67684	0.65160	0.62741	0.60423	0.58201	0.46651	0.43393	0.40388	0.37616
9	0.70259	0.67290	0.64461	0.61763	0.59190	0.56735	0.54393	0.42410	0.39092	0.36061	0.33288
10	0.67556	0.64393	0.61391	0.58543	0.55839	0.53273	0.50835	0.38554	0.35218	0.32197	0.29459

Some additional examples using Exhibit 8 follow:

	Number of Periods	Interest Rate	Present Value of $1 Factor from Exhibit 8
10% for *two* years compounded *annually*	2	10%	0.82645
10% for *two* years compounded *semiannually*	4	5%	0.82270
10% for *three* years compounded *semiannually*	6	5%	0.74622
12% for *five* years compounded *semiannually*	10	6%	0.55839

Present Value of the Periodic Receipts A series of equal cash receipts spaced equally in time is called an **annuity**. The **present value of an annuity** is the sum of the present values of each cash receipt. To illustrate, assume that $100 is to be received annually for two years and that the market rate of interest is 10%. Using Exhibit 8, the present value of the receipt of the two amounts of $100 is $173.55, as shown in Exhibit 9.

EXHIBIT 9

Present Value of an Annuity

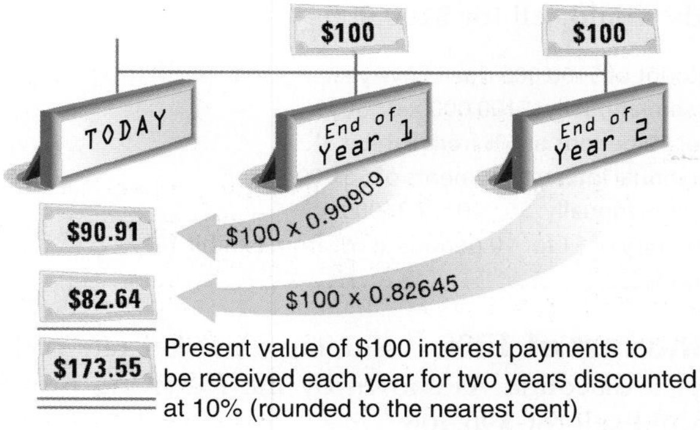

Instead of using present value of $1 tables to determine the present value of each cash flow separately, such as in Exhibit 8, the present value of an annuity can be computed in a single step. Using a value from the *present value of an annuity of $1* table in Exhibit 10, the present value of the entire annuity can be calculated by multiplying the equal cash payment times the appropriate present value of an annuity of $1.

To illustrate, the present value of $100 to be received at the end of each of the next two years at 10% compound interest per period is $173.55 ($100 × 1.73554). This amount is the same amount computed previously using the present value of $1.

EXHIBIT 10 **Present Value of an Annuity of $1 at Compound Interest**

Periods	4%	4½%	5%	5½%	6%	6½%	7%	10%	11%	12%	13%
1	0.96154	0.95694	0.95238	0.94787	0.94340	0.93897	0.93458	0.90909	0.90090	0.89286	0.88496
2	1.88609	1.87267	1.85941	1.84632	1.83339	1.82063	1.80802	1.73554	1.71252	1.69005	1.66810
3	2.77509	2.74896	2.72325	2.69793	2.67301	2.64848	2.62432	2.48685	2.44371	2.40183	2.36115
4	3.62990	3.58753	3.54595	3.50515	3.46511	3.42580	3.38721	3.16987	3.10245	3.03735	2.97447
5	4.45182	4.38998	4.32948	4.27028	4.21236	4.15568	4.10020	3.79079	3.69590	3.60478	3.51723
6	5.24214	5.15787	5.07569	4.99553	4.91732	4.84101	4.76654	4.35526	4.23054	4.11141	3.99755
7	6.00205	5.89270	5.78637	5.68297	5.58238	5.48452	5.38929	4.86842	4.71220	4.56376	4.42261
8	6.73274	6.59589	6.46321	6.33457	6.20979	6.08875	5.97130	5.33493	5.14612	4.96764	4.79677
9	7.43533	7.26879	7.10782	6.95220	6.80169	6.65610	6.51523	5.75902	5.53705	5.32825	5.13166
10	8.11090	7.91272	7.72173	7.53763	7.36009	7.18883	7.02358	6.14457	5.88923	5.65022	5.42624

Pricing Bonds

The selling price of a bond is the sum of the present values of:

- The face amount of the bonds due at the maturity date
- The periodic interest to be paid on the bonds

The market rate of interest is used to compute the present value of both the face amount and the periodic interest.

To illustrate the pricing of bonds, assume that Southern Utah Communications Inc. issued the following bond on January 1:

Face amount	$100,000
Contract rate of interest	12%
Interest paid semiannually on June 30 and December 31.	
Term of bonds	5 years

Market Rate of Interest of 12% Assuming a market rate of interest of 12%, the bonds would sell for their face amount. As shown by the following present value computations, the bonds would sell for $100,000:

Present value of face amount of $100,000 due in five years, at 12% compounded semiannually: $100,000 × 0.55839 (present value of $1 for 10 periods at 6% from Exhibit 8)	$ 55,839
Present value of 10 semiannual interest payments of $6,000, at 12% compounded semiannually: $6,000 × 7.36009 (present value of an annuity of $1 for 10 periods at 6% from Exhibit 10)	44,161
Total present value of bonds	$100,000

Market Rate of Interest of 13% Assuming a market rate of interest of 13%, the bonds would sell at a discount. As shown by the following present value computations, the bonds would sell for $96,406:[8]

Present value of face amount of $100,000 due in five years, at 13% compounded semiannually: $100,000 × 0.53273 (present value of $1 for 10 periods at 6½% from Exhibit 8)	$53,273
Present value of 10 semiannual interest payments of $6,000, at 13% compounded semiannually: $6,000 × 7.18883 (present value of an annuity of $1 for 10 periods at 6½% from Exhibit 10)	43,133
Total present value of bonds	$96,406

8 Some corporations issue bonds called *zero-coupon bonds* that provide for only the payment of the face amount at maturity. Such bonds sell for large discounts. In this example, such a bond would sell for $53,273, which is the present value of the face amount.

Market Rate of Interest of 11% Assuming a market rate of interest of 11%, the bonds would sell at a premium. As shown by the following present value computations, the bonds would sell for $103,769:

Present value of face amount of $100,000 due in five years, at 11% compounded semiannually: $100,000 × 0.58543 (present value of $1 for 10 periods at 5½% from Exhibit 8)	$ 58,543
Present value of 10 semiannual interest payments of $6,000, at 11% compounded semiannually: $6,000 × 7.53763 (present value of an annuity of $1 for 10 periods at 5½% from Exhibit 10)	45,226
Total present value of bonds	$103,769

As shown, the selling price of the bond varies with the present value of the bond's face amount at maturity, interest payments, and the market rate of interest.

APPENDIX 2

Interest Rate Method of Amortization

The effective interest rate method of amortization is an alternative method for amortizing the discount or premium on a bond, which provides for a constant *rate* of interest over the life of the bonds. As the discount or premium is amortized, the carrying amount of the bonds changes. As a result, interest expense also changes each period. This is in contrast to the straight-line method, which provides for a constant *amount* of interest expense each period.

The interest rate used in the effective interest rate method of amortization, sometimes called the *interest method*, is the market rate on the date the bonds are issued. The carrying amount of the bonds is multiplied by this interest rate to determine the interest expense for the period. The difference between the interest expense and the interest payment is the amount of discount or premium to be amortized for the period.

Amortization of Discount by the Interest Method

To illustrate, the following data taken from the chapter illustration of issuing bonds at a discount are used:

Face value of 12%, five-year bonds, interest compounded semiannually	$100,000
Present value of bonds at effective (market) rate of interest of 13%	(96,406)
Discount on bonds payable	$ 3,594

Exhibit 11 illustrates the interest method for the preceding bonds. Exhibit 11 begins with six columns. The first column is not lettered. The remaining columns are lettered A through E. The exhibit was then prepared as follows:

Step 1. List the interest payment dates in the first column, which for the preceding bond are 10 interest payment dates (semiannual interest over five years). Also list on the first line (above the first interest payment) the initial amount of discount in Column D and the initial carrying amount (selling price) of the bonds in Column E.

Step 2. List in Column A the semiannual interest payments, which for the preceding bond are $6,000 ($100,000 × 6%).

Step 3. Compute the interest expense in Column B by multiplying the bond carrying amount at the beginning of each period times 6½%, which is the semiannual effective interest (market) rate (13% ÷ 2).

Step 4. In Column C, compute the discount to be amortized each period by subtracting the interest payment in Column A ($6,000) from the interest expense for the period shown in Column B.

EXHIBIT 11 **Amortization of Discount on Bonds Payable**

Interest Payment Date	A Interest Paid (6% of Face Amount)	B Interest Expense (6½% of Bond Carrying Amount)	C Discount Amortization (B – A)	D Unamortized Discount (D – C)	E Bond Carrying Amount ($100,000 – D)
				$3,594	$ 96,406
June 30, 20Y5	$6,000	$6,266 (6½% of $96,406)	$266	3,328	96,672
Dec. 31, 20Y5	6,000	6,284 (6½% of $96,672)	284	3,044	96,956
June 30, 20Y6	6,000	6,302 (6½% of $96,956)	302	2,742	97,258
Dec. 31, 20Y6	6,000	6,322 (6½% of $97,258)	322	2,420	97,580
June 30, 20Y7	6,000	6,343 (6½% of $97,580)	343	2,077	97,923
Dec. 31, 20Y7	6,000	6,365 (6½% of $97,923)	365	1,712	98,288
June 30, 20Y8	6,000	6,389 (6½% of $98,288)	389	1,323	98,677
Dec. 31, 20Y8	6,000	6,414 (6½% of $98,677)	414	909	99,091
June 30, 20Y9	6,000	6,441 (6½% of $99,091)	441	468	99,532
Dec. 31, 20Y9	6,000	6,470 (6½% of $99,532)	468*	—	100,000

*Cannot exceed unamortized discount.

Step 5. Compute the remaining unamortized discount by subtracting the amortized discount in Column C for the period from the unamortized discount at the beginning of the period in Column D.

Step 6. Compute the bond carrying amount at the end of the period by subtracting the unamortized discount at the end of the period in Column D from the face amount of the bonds ($100,000).

Steps 3–6 are repeated for each interest payment.

As shown in Exhibit 11, the interest expense increases each period as the carrying amount of the bond increases. Also, the unamortized discount decreases each period to zero at the maturity date. Finally, the carrying amount of the bonds increases from $96,406 to $100,000 (the face amount) at maturity.

The entry to record the first interest payment on June 30, 20Y5, and the related discount amortization is as follows:

20Y5					
June	30	Interest Expense		6,266	
		Discount on Bonds Payable			266
		Cash			6,000
		Paid semiannual interest and amortized bond discount for ½ year.			

If the amortization is recorded only at the end of the year, the amount of the discount amortized on December 31, Year 1, would be $550. This is the sum of the first two semiannual amortization amounts ($266 and $284) from Exhibit 11.

Amortization of Premium by the Interest Method

To illustrate, the following data taken from the chapter illustration of issuing bonds at a premium are used:

Present value of bonds at effective (market) rate of interest of 11%..........	$103,769
Face value of 12%, five-year bonds, interest compounded semiannually..........	(100,000)
Premium on bonds payable..........	$ 3,769

Exhibit 12 illustrates the interest method for the preceding bonds. Exhibit 12 begins with six columns. The first column is not lettered. The remaining columns are lettered A through E. The exhibit was then prepared as follows:

Amortization of Premium on Bonds Payable EXHIBIT 12

Interest Payment Date	A Interest Paid (6% of Face Amount)	B Interest Expense (5½% of Bond Carrying Amount)	C Premium Amortization (A – B)	D Unamortized Premium (D – C)	E Bond Carrying Amount ($100,000 + D)
				$3,769	$103,769
June 30, 20Y5	$6,000	$5,707 (5½% of $103,769)	$293	3,476	103,476
Dec. 31, 20Y5	6,000	5,691 (5½% of $103,476)	309	3,167	103,167
June 30, 20Y6	6,000	5,674 (5½% of $103,167)	326	2,841	102,841
Dec. 31, 20Y6	6,000	5,656 (5½% of $102,841)	344	2,497	102,497
June 30, 20Y7	6,000	5,637 (5½% of $102,497)	363	2,134	102,134
Dec. 31, 20Y7	6,000	5,617 (5½% of $102,134)	383	1,751	101,751
June 30, 20Y8	6,000	5,596 (5½% of $101,751)	404	1,347	101,347
Dec. 31, 20Y8	6,000	5,574 (5½% of $101,347)	426	921	100,921
June 30, 20Y9	6,000	5,551 (5½% of $100,921)	449	472	100,472
Dec. 31, 20Y9	6,000	5,526 (5½% of $100,472)	472*	—	100,000

*Cannot exceed unamortized premium.

Step 1. List the number of interest payments in the first column, which for the preceding bond are 10 interest payments (semiannual interest over five years). Also list on the first line the initial amount of premium in Column D and the initial carrying amount of the bonds in Column E.

Step 2. List in Column A the semiannual interest payments, which for the preceding bond are $6,000 ($100,000 × 6%).

Step 3. Compute the interest expense in Column B by multiplying the bond carrying amount at the beginning of each period times 5½%, which is the semiannual effective interest (market) rate (11% ÷ 2).

Step 4. In Column C, compute the premium to be amortized each period by subtracting the interest expense for the period shown in Column B from the interest payment in Column A ($6,000).

Step 5. Compute the remaining unamortized premium by subtracting the amortized premium in Column C for the period from the unamortized premium at the beginning of the period in Column D.

Step 6. Compute the bond carrying amount at the end of the period by adding the unamortized premium at the end of the period in Column D to the face amount of the bonds ($100,000).

Steps 3–6 are repeated for each interest payment.

As shown in Exhibit 12, the interest expense decreases each period as the carrying amount of the bond decreases. Also, the unamortized premium decreases each period to zero at the maturity date. Finally, the carrying amount of the bonds decreases from $103,769 to $100,000 (the face amount) at maturity.

The entry to record the first interest payment on June 30, 20Y5, and the related premium amortization is as follows:

20Y5				
June	30	Interest Expense	5,707	
		Premium on Bonds Payable	293	
		Cash		6,000
		Paid semiannual interest and amortized bond premium for 1/2 year.		

If the amortization is recorded only at the end of the year, the amount of the premium amortized on December 31, Year 1, would be $602. This is the sum of the first two semiannual amortization amounts ($293 and $309) from Exhibit 12.

At a Glance 14

Obj. 1 Compute the potential impact of long-term borrowing on earnings per share.

Key Points Corporations can finance their operations by issuing short-term debt, long-term debt, or equity. One of the many factors that influence a corporation's decision on whether it should issue long-term debt or equity is the effect each alternative has on earnings per share.

Learning Outcomes	Example Exercises	Practice Exercises
• Define the concept of a bond.		
• Calculate and compare the effect of alternative long-term financing plans on earnings per share.	**EE14-1**	**PE14-1A, 14-1B**

Obj. 2 Describe the characteristics and terminology of bonds payable.

Key Points A corporation that issues bonds enters into a contract, or bond indenture.

When a corporation issues bonds, the price that buyers are willing to pay for the bonds depends on (1) the face amount of the bonds, (2) the periodic interest to be paid on the bonds, and (3) the market rate of interest.

Learning Outcomes	Example Exercises	Practice Exercises
• Define the characteristics of a bond.		
• Describe the various types of bonds.		
• Describe the factors that determine the price of a bond.		

Obj. 3 Describe and illustrate the accounting for bonds payable.

Key Points The journal entry for issuing bonds payable debits Cash and credits Bonds Payable. Any difference between the face amount of the bonds and the selling price is debited to Discount on Bonds Payable or credited to Premium on Bonds Payable when the bonds are issued. The discount or premium on bonds payable is amortized to interest expense over the life of the bonds.

At the maturity date, the entry to record the repayment of the face value of a bond is a debit to Bonds Payable and a credit to Cash.

When a corporation redeems bonds before they mature, Bonds Payable is debited for the face amount of the bonds, the premium (discount) on bonds payable account is debited (credited) for its unamortized balance, Cash is credited, and any gain or loss on the redemption is recorded.

Learning Outcomes	Example Exercises	Practice Exercises
• Journalize the issuance of bonds at face value and the payment of periodic interest.	**EE14-2**	**PE14-2A, 14-2B**
• Journalize the issuance of bonds at a discount.	**EE14-3**	**PE14-3A, 14-3B**
• Journalize the amortization of a bond discount.	**EE14-4**	**PE14-4A, 14-4B**
• Journalize the issuance of bonds at a premium.	**EE14-5**	**PE14-5A, 14-5B**
• Journalize the amortization of a bond premium.	**EE14-6**	**PE14-6A, 14-6B**
• Describe bond redemptions.		
• Journalize the redemption of bonds payable.	**EE14-7**	**PE14-7A, 14-7B**

Obj. 4 **Describe and illustrate the accounting for installment notes.**

Key Points An installment note requires the borrower to make equal periodic payments to the lender for the term of the note. Unlike bonds, the annual payment in an installment note consists of both principal and interest. The journal entry for the annual payment debits Interest Expense and Notes Payable and credits Cash for the amount of the payment. After the final payment, the carrying amount on the note is zero.

Learning Outcomes	Example Exercises	Practice Exercises
• Define the characteristics of an installment note.		
• Journalize the issuance of installment notes.	EE14-8	PE14-8A, 14-8B
• Journalize the annual payment for an installment note.		

Obj. 5 **Describe and illustrate the reporting of long-term liabilities, including bonds and installment notes payable.**

Key Points Bonds payable and notes payable are usually reported as long-term liabilities. If the balance sheet date is within one year, they are reported as current liabilities. A discount on bonds should be reported as a deduction from the related bonds payable. A premium on bonds should be reported as an addition to related bonds payable.

Learning Outcomes	Example Exercises	Practice Exercises
• Illustrate the balance sheet presentation of bonds payable and notes payable.		

Obj. 6 **Describe and illustrate how the times interest earned ratio is used to evaluate a company's financial condition.**

Key Points The times interest earned ratio measures the risk to bondholders that a company will not be able to make its interest payments. It is computed by dividing income before income tax plus interest expense by interest expense. This ratio computes the number of times interest payments could be paid out of current period earnings.

Learning Outcomes	Example Exercises	Practice Exercises
• Describe and compute the times interest earned ratio.	EE14-9	PE14-9A, 14-9B
• Interpret the times interest earned ratio.		

Illustrative Problem

The fiscal year of Russell Inc., a manufacturer of acoustical supplies, ends December 31. Selected transactions for the period 20Y1 through 20Y8, involving bonds payable issued by Russell Inc., are as follows:

20Y1

June 30. Issued $2,000,000 of 25-year, 7% callable bonds dated June 30, 20Y1, for cash of $1,920,000. Interest is payable semiannually on June 30 and December 31.

Dec. 31. Paid the semiannual interest on the bonds. The bond discount is amortized annually in a separate journal entry.

(Continued)

Dec. 31. Recorded straight-line amortization of $1,600 of discount on the bonds.

20Y2

June 30. Paid the semiannual interest on the bonds. The bond discount is amortized annually in a separate journal entry.

Dec. 31. Paid the semiannual interest on the bonds. The bond discount is amortized annually in a separate journal entry.

31. Recorded straight-line amortization of $3,200 of discount on the bonds.

20Y8

June 30. Recorded the redemption of the bonds, which were called at 101.5. The balance in the bond discount account is $57,600 after the payment of interest and amortization of discount have been recorded. Record the redemption only.

Instructions

1. Journalize entries to record the preceding transactions.
2. Determine the amount of interest expense for 20Y1 and 20Y2.
3. Determine the carrying amount of the bonds as of December 31, 20Y2.

Solution

1.

20Y1					
June	30	Cash		1,920,000	
		Discount on Bonds Payable		80,000	
		Bonds Payable			2,000,000
Dec.	31	Interest Expense*		70,000	
		Cash			70,000
	31	Interest Expense		1,600	
		Discount on Bonds Payable			1,600
		Amortization of discount from July 1 to December 31.			
20Y2					
June	30	Interest Expense		70,000	
		Cash			70,000
Dec.	31	Interest Expense		70,000	
		Cash			70,000
	31	Interest Expense		3,200	
		Discount on Bonds Payable			3,200
		Amortization of discount from January 1 to December 31.			
20Y8					
June	30	Bonds Payable		2,000,000	
		Loss on Redemption of Bonds Payable		87,600	
		Discount on Bonds Payable			57,600
		Cash			2,030,000

*$2,000,000 × 7% × 1/2

2. a. 20Y1: $71,600 = $70,000 + $1,600

b. 20Y2: $143,200 = $70,000 + $70,000 + $3,200

3. Initial carrying amount of bonds

Initial carrying amount of bonds	$1,920,000
Discount amortized on December 31, 20Y1	1,600
Discount amortized on December 31, 20Y2	3,200
Carrying amount of bonds, December 31, 20Y2	$1,924,800

Key Terms

amortization (683)
annuity (695)
bond (677)
bond indenture (680)
carrying amount (683)
contract rate (680)
discount (680)
earnings per share (EPS) (677)
effective interest rate method (684)
effective rate of interest (680)
face amount (680)
future value (694)
installment note (688)
market rate of interest (680)
mortgage notes (688)
premium (681)
present value (693)
present value of annuity (695)
times interest earned (692)

Discussion Questions

1. Describe the two distinct obligations incurred by a corporation when issuing bonds.
2. Explain the meaning of each of the following terms as they relate to a bond issue: (a) convertible and (b) callable.
3. If you asked your broker to buy you a 12% bond when the market interest rate for such bonds was 11%, would you expect to pay more or less than the face amount for the bond? Explain.
4. A corporation issues $26,000,000 of 9% bonds to yield interest at the rate of 7%. (a) Was the amount of cash received from the sale of the bonds greater or less than $26,000,000? (b) Identify the following amounts as they relate to the bond issue: (1) face amount, (2) market or effective rate of interest, (3) contract rate of interest, and (4) maturity amount.
5. If bonds issued by a corporation are sold at a discount, is the market rate of interest greater or less than the contract rate?
6. The following data relate to a $2,000,000, 8% bond issued for a selected semiannual interest period:

Bond carrying amount at beginning of period	$2,125,000
Interest paid during period	160,000
Interest expense allocable to the period	148,750

(a) Were the bonds issued at a discount or at a premium? (b) What is the unamortized amount of the discount or premium account at the beginning of the period? (c) What account was debited to amortize the discount or premium?

7. Bonds Payable has a balance of $5,000,000, and Discount on Bonds Payable has a balance of $150,000. If the issuing corporation redeems the bonds at 98, is there a gain or loss on the bond redemption?
8. What is a mortgage note?
9. Fleeson Company needs additional funds to purchase equipment for a new production facility and is considering either issuing bonds payable or borrowing the money from a local bank in the form of an installment note. How does an installment note differ from a bond payable?
10. In what section of the balance sheet would a bond payable be reported if (a) it is payable within one year and (b) it is payable beyond one year?

Practice Exercises

Example Exercises

EE 14-1 p. 679 **Show Me How**

PE 14-1A Alternative financing plans OBJ. 1

Frey Co. is considering the following alternative financing plans:

	Plan 1	Plan 2
Issue 5% bonds (at face value)	$6,000,000	$2,000,000
Issue preferred $1 stock, $20 par	—	6,000,000
Issue common stock, $25 par	6,000,000	4,000,000

Income tax is estimated at 40% of income.

Determine the earnings per share of common stock, assuming that income before bond interest and income tax is $800,000.

EE 14-1 p. 679 **Show Me How**

PE 14-1B Alternative financing plans OBJ. 1

Brower Co. is considering the following alternative financing plans:

	Plan 1	Plan 2
Issue 10% bonds (at face value)	$4,000,000	$2,500,000
Issue preferred $2.50 stock, $25 par	—	3,000,000
Issue common stock, $10 par	4,000,000	2,500,000

Income tax is estimated at 40% of income.

Determine the earnings per share of common stock, assuming that income before bond interest and income tax is $2,000,000.

EE 14-2 p. 682 **Show Me How**

PE 14-2A Issuing bonds at face amount OBJ. 3

On January 1, the first day of the fiscal year, a company issues a $5,000,000, 6%, 10-year bond that pays semiannual interest of $150,000 ($5,000,000 × 6% × ½ year), receiving cash of $5,000,000. Journalize the entries to record (a) the issuance of the bonds, (b) the first interest payment on June 30, and (c) the payment of the principal on the maturity date.

EE 14-2 p. 682 **Show Me How**

PE 14-2B Issuing bonds at face amount OBJ. 3

On January 1, the first day of the fiscal year, a company issues an $800,000, 4%, 10-year bond that pays semiannual interest of $16,000 ($800,000 × 4% × ½ year), receiving cash of $800,000. Journalize the entries to record (a) the issuance of the bonds, (b) the first interest payment on June 30, and (c) the payment of the principal on the maturity date.

EE 14-3 p. 683 **Show Me How**

PE 14-3A Issuing bonds at a discount OBJ. 3

On the first day of the fiscal year, a company issues a $2,500,000, 4%, five-year bond that pays semiannual interest of $50,000 ($2,500,000 × 4% × ½), receiving cash of $2,390,599. Journalize the bond issuance.

EE 14-3 p. 683 **Show Me How**

PE 14-3B Issuing bonds at a discount OBJ. 3

On the first day of the fiscal year, a company issues a $3,000,000, 11%, five-year bond that pays semiannual interest of $165,000 ($3,000,000 × 11% × ½), receiving cash of $2,889,599. Journalize the bond issuance.

EE 14-4 p. 685 **Show Me How**

PE 14-4A Discount amortization OBJ. 3

Using the bond from Practice Exercise 14-3A, journalize the first interest payment and the amortization of the related bond discount. Round to the nearest dollar.

Show Me How — EE 14-4 *p. 685*

PE 14-4B Discount amortization **OBJ. 3**

Using the bond from Practice Exercise 14-3B, journalize the first interest payment and the amortization of the related bond discount. Round to the nearest dollar.

Show Me How — EE 14-5 *p. 685*

PE 14-5A Issuing bonds at a premium **OBJ. 3**

On the first day of the fiscal year, a company issues a $7,500,000, 8%, five-year bond that pays semiannual interest of $300,000 ($7,500,000 × 8% × ½), receiving cash of $7,811,873. Journalize the bond issuance.

Show Me How — EE 14-5 *p. 685*

PE 14-5B Issuing bonds at a premium **OBJ. 3**

On the first day of the fiscal year, a company issues an $8,000,000, 11%, five-year bond that pays semiannual interest of $440,000 ($8,000,000 × 11% × ½), receiving cash of $8,308,869. Journalize the bond issuance.

Show Me How — EE 14-6 *p. 687*

PE 14-6A Premium amortization **OBJ. 3**

Using the bond from Practice Exercise 14-5A, journalize the first interest payment and the amortization of the related bond premium. Round to the nearest dollar.

Show Me How — EE 14-6 *p. 687*

PE 14-6B Premium amortization **OBJ. 3**

Using the bond from Practice Exercise 14-5B, journalize the first interest payment and the amortization of the related bond premium. Round to the nearest dollar.

Show Me How — EE 14-7 *p. 688*

PE 14-7A Redemption of bonds payable **OBJ. 3**

A $1,500,000 bond issue on which there is an unamortized discount of $70,100 is redeemed for $1,455,000. Journalize the redemption of the bonds.

Show Me How — EE 14-7 *p. 688*

PE 14-7B Redemption of bonds payable **OBJ. 3**

A $1,200,000 bond issue on which there is an unamortized premium of $63,956 is redeemed for $1,250,000. Journalize the redemption of the bonds.

Show Me How — EE 14-8 *p. 690*

PE 14-8A Journalizing installment notes **OBJ. 4**

On the first day of the fiscal year, a company issues $65,000, 6%, five-year installment notes that have annual payments of $15,431. The first note payment consists of $3,900 of interest and $11,531 of principal repayment.

a. Journalize the entry to record the issuance of the installment notes.

b. Journalize the first annual note payment.

Show Me How — EE 14-8 *p. 690*

PE 14-8B Journalizing installment notes **OBJ. 4**

On the first day of the fiscal year, a company issues $45,000, 8%, six-year installment notes that have annual payments of $9,734. The first note payment consists of $3,600 of interest and $6,134 of principal repayment.

a. Journalize the entry to record the issuance of the installment notes.

b. Journalize the first annual note payment.

Show Me How — EE 14-9 *p. 692*

FAI

PE 14-9A Times interest earned **OBJ. 6**

Berry Company reported the following on the company's income statement in two recent years:

	Current Year	Prior Year
Interest expense	$ 320,000	$ 300,000
Income before income tax expense	3,200,000	3,600,000

(Continued)

a. Determine the times interest earned ratio for the current year and the prior year. Round to one decimal place.

b. Is the number of times interest charges are earned improving or declining?

EE 14-9 p. 692 Show Me How

FAI

PE 14-9B Times interest earned **OBJ. 6**

Averill Products Inc. reported the following on the company's income statement in two recent years:

	Current Year	Prior Year
Interest expense	$ 440,000	$ 400,000
Income before income tax expense	5,544,000	4,400,000

a. Determine the times interest earned ratio for the current year and the prior year. Round to one decimal place.

b. Is the number of times interest charges are earned improving or declining?

Exercises

EX 14-1 Effect of financing on earnings per share **OBJ. 1**

✔ b. $1.00

Excel

Show Me How

Domanico Co., which produces and sells biking equipment, is financed as follows:

Bonds payable, 6% (issued at face amount)	$5,000,000
Preferred $2.00 stock, $100 par	5,000,000
Common stock, $25 par	5,000,000

Income tax is estimated at 40% of income.

Determine the earnings per share of common stock, assuming that the income before bond interest and income tax is (a) $600,000, (b) $800,000, and (c) $1,200,000.

EX 14-2 Evaluate alternative financing plans **OBJ. 1**

Based on the data in Exercise 14-1, what factors other than earnings per share should be considered in evaluating these alternative financing plans?

EX 14-3 Corporate financing **OBJ. 1**

Real World

The financial statements for Nike, Inc., are presented in Appendix D at the end of the text. What is the major source of financing for Nike?

EX 14-4 Bond price **OBJ. 3**

Real World

Stone Energy Corporation's 7.5% bonds due in 2022 were reported as selling for 82.95.

Were the bonds selling at a premium or at a discount? Why is Stone Energy Corporation able to sell its bonds at this price?

EX 14-5 Entries for issuing bonds **OBJ. 3**

Show Me How

Thomson Co. produces and distributes semiconductors for use by computer manufacturers. Thomson Co. issued $900,000 of 10-year, 7% bonds on May 1 of the current year at face value, with interest payable on May 1 and November 1. The fiscal year of the company is the calendar year. Journalize the entries to record the following selected transactions for the current year:

May 1. Issued the bonds for cash at their face amount.

Nov. 1. Paid the interest on the bonds.

Dec. 31. Recorded accrued interest for two months.

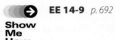

✔ b. $781,118

Show Me How

EX 14-6 Entries for issuing bonds and amortizing discount by straight-line method OBJ. 2, 3

On the first day of its fiscal year, Chin Company issued $10,000,000 of five-year, 7% bonds to finance its operations of producing and selling home improvement products. Interest is payable semiannually. The bonds were issued at a market (effective) interest rate of 8%, resulting in Chin Company receiving cash of $9,594,415.

a. Journalize the entries to record the following:
   1. Issuance of the bonds.
   2. First semiannual interest payment. The bond discount amortization is combined with the semiannual interest payment. Round your answer to the nearest dollar.
   3. Second semiannual interest payment. The bond discount amortization is combined with the semiannual interest payment. Round your answer to the nearest dollar.

b. Determine the amount of the bond interest expense for the first year.

c. Explain why the company was able to issue the bonds for only $9,594,415 rather than for the face amount of $10,000,000.

Show Me How

EX 14-7 Entries for issuing bonds and amortizing premium by straight-line method OBJ. 2, 3

Smiley Corporation wholesales repair products to equipment manufacturers. On April 1, Year 1, Smiley Corporation issued $20,000,000 of five-year, 9% bonds at a market (effective) interest rate of 8%, receiving cash of $20,811,010. Interest is payable semiannually on April 1 and October 1. Journalize the entries to record the following:

a. Issuance of bonds on April 1.

b. First interest payment on October 1 and amortization of bond premium for six months, using the straight-line method. The bond premium amortization is combined with the semiannual interest payment. Round to the nearest dollar.

c. Explain why the company was able to issue the bonds for $20,811,010 rather than for the face amount of $20,000,000.

Show Me How

EX 14-8 Entries for issuing and calling bonds; loss OBJ. 3

Adele Corp., a wholesaler of music equipment, issued $22,000,000 of 20-year, 7% callable bonds on March 1, 20Y1, at their face amount, with interest payable on March 1 and September 1. The fiscal year of the company is the calendar year. Journalize the entries to record the following selected transactions:

20Y1

Mar. 1. Issued the bonds for cash at their face amount.

Sept. 1. Paid the interest on the bonds.

20Y5

Sept. 1. Called the bond issue at 102, the rate provided in the bond indenture. (Omit entry for payment of interest.)

Show Me How

EX 14-9 Entries for issuing and calling bonds; gain OBJ. 3

Emil Corp. produces and sells wind-energy-driven engines. To finance its operations, Emil Corp. issued $15,000,000 of 20-year, 9% callable bonds on May 1, 20Y1, at their face amount, with interest payable on May 1 and November 1. The fiscal year of the company is the calendar year. Journalize the entries to record the following selected transactions:

20Y1

May 1. Issued the bonds for cash at their face amount.

Nov. 1. Paid the interest on the bonds.

20Y5

Nov. 1. Called the bond issue at 96, the rate provided in the bond indenture. (Omit entry for payment of interest.)

Show Me How

EX 14-10 Entries for installment note transactions **OBJ. 4**

On the first day of the fiscal year, Shiller Company borrowed $85,000 by giving a seven-year, 7% installment note to Soros Bank. The note requires annual payments of $15,772, with the first payment occurring on the last day of the fiscal year. The first payment consists of interest of $5,950 and principal repayment of $9,822.

a. Journalize the entries to record the following:
   1. Issued the installment note for cash on the first day of the fiscal year.
   2. Paid the first annual payment on the note.

b. Explain how the notes payable would be reported on the balance sheet at the end of the first year.

Show Me How

EX 14-11 Entries for installment note transactions **OBJ. 4**

On January 1, Year 1, Luzak Company issued a $120,000, five-year, 6% installment note to McGee Bank. The note requires annual payments of $28,488, beginning on December 31, Year 1. Journalize the entries to record the following:

Year 1

Jan. 1. Issued the note for cash at its face amount.

Dec. 31. Paid the annual payment on the note, which consisted of interest of $7,200 and principal of $21,288.

Year 4

Dec. 31. Paid the annual payment on the note, including $3,134 of interest. The remainder of the payment reduced the principal balance on the note.

Excel

Show Me How

EX 14-12 Entries for installment note transactions **OBJ. 4**

On January 1, Year 1, Bryson Company obtained a $147,750, four-year, 7% installment note from Campbell Bank. The note requires annual payments of $43,620, beginning on December 31, Year 1.

a. Prepare an amortization table for this installment note, similar to the one presented in Exhibit 4.

b. Journalize the entries for the issuance of the note and the four annual note payments.

c. Describe how the annual note payment would be reported in the Year 1 income statement.

EX 14-13 Reporting bonds **OBJ. 5**

At the beginning of the current year, two bond issues (Simmons Industries 7%, 20-year bonds and Hunter Corporation 8%, 10-year bonds) were outstanding. During the year, the Simmons Industries bonds were redeemed and a significant loss on the redemption of bonds was reported as cost of merchandise sold on the income statement. At the end of the year, the Hunter Corporation bonds were reported as a noncurrent liability. The maturity date on the Hunter Corporation bonds was early in the following year.

Identify the flaws in the reporting practices related to the two bond issues.

Real World

FAI

EX 14-14 Times interest earned **OBJ. 6**

The following data were taken from recent annual reports of Southwest Airlines, which operates a low-fare airline service to more than 50 cities in the United States:

	Current Year	Prior Year
Interest expense	$147,000,000	$194,000,000
Income before income tax	685,000,000	323,000,000

a. Determine the times interest earned ratio for the current and preceding years. Round to one decimal place.

b. What conclusions can you draw?

FAI

EX 14-15 Times interest earned **OBJ. 6**

Loomis, Inc. reported the following on the company's income statement in two recent years:

	Current Year	Prior Year
Interest expense	$ 13,500,000	$ 16,000,000
Income before income tax expense	310,500,000	432,000,000

a. Determine the times interest earned ratio for the current year and the prior year. Round to one decimal place.

b. Is this ratio improving or declining?

FAI

EX 14-16 Times interest earned **OBJ. 6**

Iacouva Company reported the following on the company's income statement for two recent years:

	Current Year	Prior Year
Interest expense	$5,000,000	$5,000,000
Income before income tax	3,500,000	6,000,000

a. Determine the times interest earned ratio for the current year and the prior year. Round to one decimal place.

b. What conclusions can you draw?

Appendix 1

EX 14-17 Present value of amounts due

Tommy John is going to receive $1,000,000 in three years. The current market rate of interest is 10%.

a. Using the present value of $1 table in Exhibit 8, determine the present value of this amount compounded annually.

b. Why is the present value less than the $1,000,000 to be received in the future?

Appendix 1

EX 14-18 Present value of an annuity

Determine the present value of $200,000 to be received at the end of each of four years, using an interest rate of 7%, compounded annually, as follows:

a. By successive computations, using the present value table in Exhibit 8.

b. By using the present value table in Exhibit 10.

c. Why is the present value of the four $200,000 cash receipts less than the $800,000 to be received in the future?

Appendix 1

EX 14-19 Present value of an annuity

✔ $44,160,540

On January 1, you win $60,000,000 in the state lottery. The $60,000,000 prize will be paid in equal installments of $6,000,000 over 10 years. The payments will be made on December 31 of each year, beginning on December 31 of the current year. If the current interest rate is 6%, determine the present value of your winnings. Use the present value tables in Appendix A.

Appendix 1

EX 14-20 Present value of an annuity

Assume the same data as in Exercise 14-19, except that the current interest rate is 10%. Will the present value of your winnings using an interest rate of 10% be more than the present value of your winnings using an interest rate of 6%? Why or why not?

Appendix 1
EX 14-21 Present value of bonds payable; discount

Pinder Co. produces and sells high-quality video equipment. To finance its operations, Pinder Co. issued $25,000,000 of five-year, 7% bonds, with interest payable semiannually, at a market (effective) interest rate of 9%. Determine the present value of the bonds payable, using the present value tables in Exhibits 8 and 10. Round to the nearest dollar.

Appendix 1
EX 14-22 Present value of bonds payable; premium

✔ $45,323,443

Moss Co. issued $42,000,000 of five-year, 11% bonds, with interest payable semiannually, at a market (effective) interest rate of 9%. Determine the present value of the bonds payable using the present value tables in Exhibits 8 and 10. Round to the nearest dollar.

Appendix 2
EX 14-23 Amortize discount by interest method

✔ b. $3,923,959

On the first day of its fiscal year, Ebert Company issued $50,000,000 of 10-year, 7% bonds to finance its operations. Interest is payable semiannually. The bonds were issued at a market (effective) interest rate of 9%, resulting in Ebert Company receiving cash of $43,495,895. The company uses the interest method.

a. Journalize the entries to record the following:
   1. Sale of the bonds.
   2. First semiannual interest payment, including amortization of discount. Round to the nearest dollar.
   3. Second semiannual interest payment, including amortization of discount. Round to the nearest dollar.
b. Compute the amount of the bond interest expense for the first year.
c. Explain why the company was able to issue the bonds for only $43,495,895 rather than for the face amount of $50,000,000.

Appendix 2
EX 14-24 Amortize premium by interest method

✔ b. $1,662,619

Shunda Corporation wholesales parts to appliance manufacturers. On January 1, Year 1, Shunda Corporation issued $22,000,000 of five-year, 9% bonds at a market (effective) interest rate of 7%, receiving cash of $23,829,684. Interest is payable semiannually. Shunda Corporation's fiscal year begins on January 1. The company uses the interest method.

a. Journalize the entries to record the following:
   1. Sale of the bonds.
   2. First semiannual interest payment, including amortization of premium. Round to the nearest dollar.
   3. Second semiannual interest payment, including amortization of premium. Round to the nearest dollar.
b. Determine the bond interest expense for the first year.
c. Explain why the company was able to issue the bonds for $23,829,684 rather than for the face amount of $22,000,000.

Appendix 1 and Appendix 2
EX 14-25 Compute bond proceeds, amortizing premium by interest method, and interest expense

✔ a. $37,702,483
✔ c. $225,620

Ware Co. produces and sells motorcycle parts. On the first day of its fiscal year, Ware Co. issued $35,000,000 of five-year, 12% bonds at a market (effective) interest rate of 10%, with interest payable semiannually. Compute the following, presenting figures used in your computations:

a. The amount of cash proceeds from the sale of the bonds. Use the tables of present values in Exhibits 8 and 10. Round to the nearest dollar.

b. The amount of premium to be amortized for the first semiannual interest payment period, using the interest method. Round to the nearest dollar.

c. The amount of premium to be amortized for the second semiannual interest payment period, using the interest method. Round to the nearest dollar.

d. The amount of the bond interest expense for the first year.

Appendix 1 and Appendix 2

EX 14-26 Compute bond proceeds, amortizing discount by interest method, and interest expense

✔ a. $71,167,524
✔ b. $670,051

Boyd Co. produces and sells aviation equipment. On the first day of its fiscal year, Boyd Co. issued $80,000,000 of five-year, 9% bonds at a market (effective) interest rate of 12%, with interest payable semiannually. Compute the following, presenting figures used in your computations:

a. The amount of cash proceeds from the sale of the bonds. Use the tables of present values in Exhibits 8 and 10. Round to the nearest dollar.

b. The amount of discount to be amortized for the first semiannual interest payment period, using the interest method. Round to the nearest dollar.

c. The amount of discount to be amortized for the second semiannual interest payment period, using the interest method. Round to the nearest dollar.

d. The amount of the bond interest expense for the first year.

Problems: Series A

PR 14-1A Effect of financing on earnings per share OBJ. 1

✔ 1. Plan 3: $1.44

Excel

Three different plans for financing an $18,000,000 corporation are under consideration by its organizers. Under each of the following plans, the securities will be issued at their par or face amount, and the income tax rate is estimated at 40% of income:

	Plan 1	Plan 2	Plan 3
8% Bonds	—	—	$ 9,000,000
Preferred 4% stock, $20 par	—	$ 9,000,000	4,500,000
Common stock, $10 par	$18,000,000	9,000,000	4,500,000
Total	$18,000,000	$18,000,000	$18,000,000

Instructions

1. Determine the earnings per share of common stock for each plan, assuming that the income before bond interest and income tax is $2,100,000.
2. Determine the earnings per share of common stock for each plan, assuming that the income before bond interest and income tax is $1,050,000.
3. Discuss the advantages and disadvantages of each plan.

PR 14-2A Bond discount, entries for bonds payable transactions OBJ. 2, 3

✔ 3. $1,535,897

General Ledger

Show Me How

On July 1, Year 1, Danzer Industries Inc. issued $40,000,000 of 10-year, 7% bonds at a market (effective) interest rate of 8%, receiving cash of $37,282,062. Interest on the bonds is payable semiannually on December 31 and June 30. The fiscal year of the company is the calendar year.

Instructions

1. Journalize the entry to record the amount of cash proceeds from the issuance of the bonds on July 1, Year 1.
2. Journalize the entries to record the following:

   a. The first semiannual interest payment on December 31, Year 1, and the amortization of the bond discount, using the straight-line method. Round to the nearest dollar.

(Continued)

b. The interest payment on June 30, Year 2, and the amortization of the bond discount, using the straight-line method. Round to the nearest dollar.

3. Determine the total interest expense for Year 1.
4. Will the bond proceeds always be less than the face amount of the bonds when the contract rate is less than the market rate of interest?
5. (Appendix 1) Compute the price of $37,282,062 received for the bonds by using the present value tables in Appendix A at the end of the text. Round to the nearest dollar.

PR 14-3A Bond premium, entries for bonds payable transactions — OBJ. 2, 3

✓ 3. $1,168,704

General Ledger

Campbell Inc. produces and sells outdoor equipment. On July 1, Year 1, Campbell Inc. issued $25,000,000 of 10-year, 10% bonds at a market (effective) interest rate of 9%, receiving cash of $26,625,925. Interest on the bonds is payable semiannually on December 31 and June 30. The fiscal year of the company is the calendar year.

Instructions

1. Journalize the entry to record the amount of cash proceeds from the issuance of the bonds on July 1, Year 1.
2. Journalize the entries to record the following:
   a. The first semiannual interest payment on December 31, Year 1, and the amortization of the bond premium, using the straight-line method. Round to the nearest dollar.
   b. The interest payment on June 30, Year 2, and the amortization of the bond premium, using the straight-line method. Round to the nearest dollar.
3. Determine the total interest expense for Year 1.
4. Will the bond proceeds always be greater than the face amount of the bonds when the contract rate is greater than the market rate of interest?
5. (Appendix 1) Compute the price of $26,625,925 received for the bonds by using the present value tables in Appendix A at the end of the text. Round to the nearest dollar.

PR 14-4A Entries for bonds payable and installment note transactions — OBJ. 3, 4

✓ 3. $64,317,346

Excel

General Ledger

Show Me How

The following transactions were completed by Winklevoss Inc., whose fiscal year is the calendar year:

Year 1

July 1. Issued $74,000,000 of 20-year, 11% callable bonds dated July 1, Year 1, at a market (effective) rate of 13%, receiving cash of $63,532,267. Interest is payable semiannually on December 31 and June 30.

Oct. 1. Borrowed $200,000 by issuing a six-year, 6% installment note to Nicks Bank. The note requires annual payments of $40,673, with the first payment occurring on September 30, Year 2.

Dec. 31. Accrued $3,000 of interest on the installment note. The interest is payable on the date of the next installment note payment.

31. Paid the semiannual interest on the bonds. The bond discount amortization of $261,693 is combined with the semiannual interest payment.

Year 2

June 30. Paid the semiannual interest on the bonds. The bond discount amortization of $261,693 is combined with the semiannual interest payment.

Sept. 30. Paid the annual payment on the note, which consisted of interest of $12,000 and principal of $28,673.

Dec. 31. Accrued $2,570 of interest on the installment note. The interest is payable on the date of the next installment note payment.

31. Paid the semiannual interest on the bonds. The bond discount amortization of $261,693 is combined with the semiannual interest payment.

Year 3

June 30. Recorded the redemption of the bonds, which were called at 98. The balance in the bond discount account is $9,420,961 after payment of interest and amortization of discount have been recorded. Record the redemption only.

Sept. 30. Paid the second annual payment on the note, which consisted of interest of $10,280 and principal of $30,393.

Instructions

1. Journalize the entries to record the foregoing transactions. Round all amounts to the nearest dollar.
2. Indicate the amount of the interest expense in (a) Year 1 and (b) Year 2.
3. Determine the carrying amount of the bonds as of December 31, Year 2.

Appendix 1 and Appendix 2

PR 14-5A Bond discount, entries for bonds payable transactions, interest method of amortizing bond discount

✔ 3. $1,491,282

On July 1, Year 1, Danzer Industries Inc. issued $40,000,000 of 10-year, 7% bonds at a market (effective) interest rate of 8%, receiving cash of $37,282,062. Interest on the bonds is payable semiannually on December 31 and June 30. The fiscal year of the company is the calendar year.

Instructions

1. Journalize the entry to record the amount of cash proceeds from the issuance of the bonds.
2. Journalize the entries to record the following:
   a. The first semiannual interest payment on December 31, Year 1, and the amortization of the bond discount, using the interest method. Round to the nearest dollar.
   b. The interest payment on June 30, Year 2, and the amortization of the bond discount, using the interest method. Round to the nearest dollar.
3. Determine the total interest expense for Year 1.

Appendix 1 and Appendix 2

PR 14-6A Bond premium, entries for bonds payable transactions, interest method of amortizing bond premium

✔ 3. $1,198,167

Campbell, Inc. produces and sells outdoor equipment. On July 1, Year 1, Campbell, Inc. issued $25,000,000 of 10-year, 10% bonds at a market (effective) interest rate of 9%, receiving cash of $26,625,925. Interest on the bonds is payable semiannually on December 31 and June 30. The fiscal year of the company is the calendar year.

Instructions

1. Journalize the entry to record the amount of cash proceeds from the issuance of the bonds.
2. Journalize the entries to record the following:
   a. The first semiannual interest payment on December 31, Year 1, and the amortization of the bond premium, using the interest method. Round to the nearest dollar.
   b. The interest payment on June 30, Year 2, and the amortization of the bond premium, using the interest method. Round to the nearest dollar.
3. Determine the total interest expense for Year 1.

Problems: Series B

PR 14-1B Effect of financing on earnings per share **OBJ. 1**

✔ 1. Plan 3: $2.84

Excel

Three different plans for financing an $80,000,000 corporation are under consideration by its organizers. Under each of the following plans, the securities will be issued at their par or face amount, and the income tax rate is estimated at 40% of income:

(Continued)

	Plan 1	Plan 2	Plan 3
9% Bonds	—	—	$40,000,000
Preferred 5% stock, $25 par	—	$40,000,000	20,000,000
Common stock, $20 par	$80,000,000	40,000,000	20,000,000
Total	$80,000,000	$80,000,000	$80,000,000

Instructions

1. Determine for each plan the earnings per share of common stock, assuming that the income before bond interest and income tax is $10,000,000.
2. Determine for each plan the earnings per share of common stock, assuming that the income before bond interest and income tax is $6,000,000.
3. Discuss the advantages and disadvantages of each plan.

PR 14-2B Bond discount, entries for bonds payable transactions

OBJ. 2, 3

✔ 3. $2,392,269

General Ledger

Show Me How

On July 1, Year 1, Livingston Corporation, a wholesaler of manufacturing equipment, issued $46,000,000 of 20-year, 10% bonds at a market (effective) interest rate of 11%, receiving cash of $42,309,236. Interest on the bonds is payable semiannually on December 31 and June 30. The fiscal year of the company is the calendar year.

Instructions

1. Journalize the entry to record the amount of cash proceeds from the issuance of the bonds on July 1, Year 1.
2. Journalize the entries to record the following:
   a. The first semiannual interest payment on December 31, Year 1, and the amortization of the bond discount, using the straight-line method. Round to the nearest dollar.
   b. The interest payment on June 30, Year 2, and the amortization of the bond discount, using the straight-line method. Round to the nearest dollar.
3. Determine the total interest expense for Year 1.
4. Will the bond proceeds always be less than the face amount of the bonds when the contract rate is less than the market rate of interest?
5. (Appendix 1) Compute the price of $42,309,236 received for the bonds by using the present value tables in Appendix A at the end of the text. Round to the nearest dollar.

PR 14-3B Bond premium, entries for bonds payable transactions

OBJ. 2, 3

✔ 3. $3,494,977

General Ledger

Rodgers Corporation produces and sells football equipment. On July 1, Year 1, Rodgers Corporation issued $65,000,000 of 10-year, 12% bonds at a market (effective) interest rate of 10%, receiving cash of $73,100,469. Interest on the bonds is payable semiannually on December 31 and June 30. The fiscal year of the company is the calendar year.

Instructions

1. Journalize the entry to record the amount of cash proceeds from the issuance of the bonds on July 1, Year 1.
2. Journalize the entries to record the following:
   a. The first semiannual interest payment on December 31, Year 1, and the amortization of the bond premium, using the straight-line method. Round to the nearest dollar.
   b. The interest payment on June 30, Year 2, and the amortization of the bond premium, using the straight-line method. Round to the nearest dollar.
3. Determine the total interest expense for Year 1.
4. Will the bond proceeds always be greater than the face amount of the bonds when the contract rate is greater than the market rate of interest?
5. (Appendix 1) Compute the price of $73,100,469 received for the bonds by using the present value tables in Appendix A at the end of the text. Round to the nearest dollar.

✔ 3. $61,644,484

Excel

General Ledger

Show Me How

PR 14-4B Entries for bonds payable and installment note transactions **OBJ. 3, 4**

The following transactions were completed by Montague Inc., whose fiscal year is the calendar year:

Year 1

July 1. Issued $55,000,000 of 10-year, 9% callable bonds dated July 1, Year 1, at a market (effective) rate of 7%, receiving cash of $62,817,040. Interest is payable semiannually on December 31 and June 30.

Oct. 1. Borrowed $450,000 by issuing a six-year, 8% installment note to Intexicon Bank. The note requires annual payments of $97,342, with the first payment occurring on September 30, Year 2.

Dec. 31. Accrued $9,000 of interest on the installment note. The interest is payable on the date of the next installment note payment.

31. Paid the semiannual interest on the bonds. The bond premium amortization of $390,852 is combined with the semiannual interest payment.

Year 2

June 30. Paid the semiannual interest on the bonds. The bond premium amortization of $390,852 is combined with the semiannual interest payment.

Sept. 30. Paid the annual payment on the note, which consisted of interest of $36,000 and principal of $61,342.

Dec. 31. Accrued $7,773 of interest on the installment note. The interest is payable on the date of the next installment note payment.

31. Paid the semiannual interest on the bonds. The bond premium amortization of $390,852 is combined with the semiannual interest payment.

Year 3

June 30. Recorded the redemption of the bonds, which were called at 103. The balance in the bond premium account is $6,253,632 after payment of interest and amortization of premium have been recorded. Record the redemption only.

Sept. 30. Paid the second annual payment on the note, which consisted of interest of $31,093 and principal of $66,249.

Instructions

1. Journalize the entries to record the foregoing transactions.
2. Indicate the amount of the interest expense in (a) Year 1 and (b) Year 2.
3. Determine the carrying amount of the bonds as of December 31, Year 2.

Appendix 1 and Appendix 2

PR 14-5B Bond discount, entries for bonds payable transactions, interest method of amortizing bond discount

✔ 3. $2,327,008

On July 1, Year 1, Livingston Corporation, a wholesaler of manufacturing equipment, issued $46,000,000 of 20-year, 10% bonds at a market (effective) interest rate of 11%, receiving cash of $42,309,236. Interest on the bonds is payable semiannually on December 31 and June 30. The fiscal year of the company is the calendar year.

Instructions

1. Journalize the entry to record the amount of cash proceeds from the issuance of the bonds.
2. Journalize the entries to record the following:
   a. The first semiannual interest payment on December 31, Year 1, and the amortization of the bond discount, using the interest method. Round to the nearest dollar.
   b. The interest payment on June 30, Year 2, and the amortization of the bond discount, using the interest method. Round to the nearest dollar.
3. Determine the total interest expense for Year 1.

Appendix 1 and Appendix 2
PR 14-6B Bond premium, entries for bonds payable transactions, interest method of amortizing bond premium

✓ 3. $3,655,023

Rodgers Corporation produces and sells football equipment. On July 1, Year 1, Rodgers Corporation issued $65,000,000 of 10-year, 12% bonds at a market (effective) interest rate of 10%, receiving cash of $73,100,469. Interest on the bonds is payable semiannually on December 31 and June 30. The fiscal year of the company is the calendar year.

Instructions

1. Journalize the entry to record the amount of cash proceeds from the issuance of the bonds.
2. Journalize the entries to record the following:
   a. The first semiannual interest payment on December 31, Year 1, and the amortization of the bond premium, using the interest method. Round to the nearest dollar.
   b. The interest payment on June 30, Year 2, and the amortization of the bond premium, using the interest method. Round to the nearest dollar.
3. Determine the total interest expense for Year 1.

Cases & Projects

CP 14-1 Ethics in Action

Ethics

CEG Capital Inc. is a large holding company that uses long-term debt extensively to fund its operations. At December 31, the company reported total assets of $100 million, total debt of $55 million, and total equity of $45 million. In January, the company issued $11 billion in long-term bonds to investors at par value. This was the largest debt issuance in the company's history, and it significantly increased the company's ratio of total debt to total equity. Five days after the debt issuance, CEG filed legal documents to prepare for an additional $50 billion long-term bond issue. As a result of this filing, the price of the $11 billion in bonds that the company issued earlier in the week dropped to 94 because of the increased risk associated with the company's debt. The investors in the original $11 billion bond issuance were not informed of the company's plans to issue additional debt so quickly after the initial bond issue.

Did CEG Capital act unethically by not disclosing to initial bond investors its immediate plans to issue an additional $50 billion debt offering?

CP 14-2 Team Activity

Team Activity

Real World

In teams, select a public company that interests you. Obtain the company's most recent annual report on Form 10-K. The Form 10-K is a company's annually required filing with the Securities and Exchange Commission (SEC). It includes the company's financial statements and accompanying notes. The Form 10-K can be obtained either (a) by referring to the investor relations section of the company's website or (b) by using the company search feature of the SEC's EDGAR database service found at www.sec.gov/edgar/searchedgar/companysearch.html.

1. Based on the information in the company's most recent annual report, answer the following questions:
   a. How much long-term debt does the company report at the end of the most recent year presented?
   b. Does the company have any bonds outstanding at the end of the most recent year? If so, read the supporting notes to the financial statements and determine the following:
      (1) The contract rate of interest on the bond issue(s)
      (2) The discount or premium on the bond issue(s)
      (3) The due date of the bond issue(s)
      (4) The total amount of any bonds that will mature within one year of the balance sheet date
2. Based on your answers to the questions in requirement 1, evaluate the company's debt position.

CP 14-3 Communication

Communication

Nordbock Inc. reports the following outstanding bond issue on its December 31, 20Y1, balance sheet:

$1,000,000, 7%, 10-year bonds that pay interest semiannually.

The bonds have been outstanding for five years and were originally issued at face amount. The company is considering redeeming these bonds on January 1, 20Y2, at 103 and issuing new $1,000,000, 5%, five-year bonds at their face amount. These bonds would pay interest semiannually on June 30 and December 31.

Write a brief memo to Liz Nolan, the chief financial officer, discussing the costs of redeeming the existing bonds, the proceeds from issuing the new bonds, and whether this is a good financial decision.

CP 14-4 Present values

Alex Kelton recently won the jackpot in the Colorado lottery while he was visiting his parents. When he arrived at the lottery office to collect his winnings, he was offered the following three payout options:

a. Receive $100,000,000 in cash today.

b. Receive $25,000,000 today and $9,000,000 per year for eight years, with the first payment being received one year from today.

c. Receive $15,000,000 per year for 10 years, with the first payment being received one year from today.

Assuming that the effective rate of interest is 7%, which payout option should Alex select? Use the present value tables in Appendix A. Explain your answer and provide any necessary supporting calculations.

CP 14-5 Preferred stock vs. bonds

Xentec Inc. has decided to expand its operations to owning and operating golf courses. The following is an excerpt from a conversation between the chief executive officer, Peter Kilgallon, and the vice president of finance, Dan Baron:

Peter: Dan, have you given any thought to how we're going to manage the acquisition of Sweeping Bluff Golf Course?

Dan: Well, the two basic options, as I see it, are to issue either preferred stock or bonds. The equity market is a little depressed right now. The rumor is that the Federal Reserve Bank's going to increase the interest rates either this month or next.

Peter: Yes. I've heard the rumor. The problem is that we can't wait around to see what's going to happen. We'll have to move on this next week if we want any chance to complete the acquisition of Sweeping Bluff Golf Course.

Dan: Well, the bond market is strong right now. Maybe we should issue debt this time around.

Peter: That's what I would have guessed as well. Sweeping Bluff Golf Course's financial statements look pretty good, except for the volatility of its income and cash flows. But that's characteristic of the industry.

Discuss the advantages and disadvantages of issuing preferred stock versus bonds.

CP 14-6 Financing business expansion

You hold a 25% common stock interest in YouOwnIt, a family-owned construction equipment company. Your sister, who is the manager, has proposed an expansion of plant facilities at an expected cost of $26,000,000. Two alternative plans have been suggested as methods of financing the expansion. Each plan is briefly described as follows:

Plan 1. Issue $26,000,000 of 20-year, 8% notes at face amount

Plan 2. Issue an additional 550,000 shares of $10 par common stock at $20 per share, and $15,000,000 of 20-year, 8% notes at face amount

(Continued)

The balance sheet as of the end of the previous fiscal year is as follows:

YouOwnIt, Inc.
Balance Sheet
December 31, 20Y7

Assets	
Current assets	$15,000,000
Property, plant, and equipment	22,500,000
Total assets	$37,500,000
Liabilities and Stockholders' Equity	
Liabilities	$ 11,250,000
Common stock, $10	4,000,000
Paid-in capital in excess of par	500,000
Retained earnings	21,750,000
Total liabilities and stockholders' equity	$ 37,500,000

Net income has remained relatively constant over the past several years. The expansion program is expected to increase yearly income before bond interest and income tax from $2,667,000 in the previous year to $5,000,000 for this year. Your sister has asked you, as the company treasurer, to prepare an analysis of each financing plan.

1. Prepare a table indicating the expected earnings per share on the common stock under each plan. Assume an income tax rate of 40%. Round to the nearest cent.
2. a. Discuss the factors that should be considered in evaluating the two plans.
   b. Which plan offers greater benefit to the present stockholders? Give reasons for your opinion.

CP 14-7 Times interest earned

Real World

FAI

The following financial data (in thousands) were taken from recent financial statements of Staples, Inc.:

	Year 3	Year 2	Year 1
Interest expense	$ 173,751	$ 214,824	$ 237,025
Earnings before taxes	1,459,141	1,356,595	1,155,894

1. Determine the times interest earned ratio for Staples in Year 3, Year 2, and Year 1? Round your answers to one decimal place.
2. Evaluate this ratio for Staples.

Investments and Fair Value Accounting

Chapters 1–4
Accounting Cycle

Chapter 5
Accounting Systems

Income Statement	**Statement of Owner's Equity**	**Balance Sheet**	**Statement of Cash Flows**

Chapter 6 *Accounting for Merchandising Businesses*

Chapter 16 *Cash Flows*

Assets	=	**Liabilities**	+	**Owner's Equity**

Chapter 8 *Cash*
Chapter 9 *Receivables*
Chapter 7 *Inventories*
Chapter 10 *Fixed and Intangible Assets*
Chapter 15 Investments and Fair Value Accounting

Chapter 11 *Current Liabilities*
Chapter 14 *Long-Term Liabilities: Bonds and Notes*

Chapter 12 *Accounting for Partnerships and Limited Liability Companies*
Chapter 13 *Corporations*

Chapter 17
Financial Statement Analysis

Statement of Owner's Equity

Owner's capital, Jan. 1	$XXX
Net income	$XXX
	XXX

Statement of Cash Flows

Cash flows from (used in) operating activities	$XXX
Cash flows from (used in) investing activities	XXX
	XXX
	$XXX
	XXX
	$XXX

Income Statement

Sales	$XXX
Cost of merchandise sold	XXX
Gross profit	$XXX
Total operating expenses	XXX
Income from operations	$XXX
Other revenue and expenses:	
Interest revenue	XXX
Unrealized gain (loss) on available -for-sale investments	XXX
Unrealized gain (loss) on trading investments	XXX
Equity income in investment	XXX
Net income	$XXX

Balance Sheet

Current assets:		
Cash	$XXX	
Accounts receivable	XXX	
Merchandise inventory	XXX	
Available-for-sale investments	XXX	
Trading investments	XXX	
Total current assets		$XXX
Equity investments	$XXX	
Property, plant, and equipment	XXX	
Intangible assets	XXX	
Total long-term assets		XXX
Total assets		$XXX
Liabilities:		
Current liabilities		$XXX
Long-term liabilities		XXX
Total liabilities		$XXX
Stockholders' equity		XXX
Total liabilities and stockholders' equity		$XXX

CHAPTER 15

MARDIS COERS/GETTY IMAGES

Deere & Company

You invest cash to earn more cash. For example, you could deposit cash in a bank account to earn interest. You could also invest in preferred or common stocks; or in corporate or U.S. government notes and bonds.

Preferred and common stock can be purchased through a stock exchange such as the **New York Stock Exchange (NYSE)**. Preferred stock is purchased primarily with the expectation of earning dividends. Common stock is purchased with the expectation of earning dividends and realizing gains from an increase in the price of the stock.

Corporate and U.S. government bonds can also be purchased through a bond exchange. Bonds are purchased with the primary expectation of earning interest revenue.

Companies make investments for many of the same reasons you would as an individual. For example, **Deere & Company**, a manufacturer of agricultural and construction machinery, has invested approximately $437 million of available cash in stocks and bonds. These investments are held by Deere & Company for interest, dividends, and expected price increases.

Unlike most individuals, however, companies also purchase significant amounts of the outstanding common stock of other companies for strategic reasons. For example, Deere & Company has more than $303 million invested in companies where it owns between 20% and 50% of the outstanding shares. The vast majority of these investments are international manufacturing partners.

Investments in debt and equity securities give rise to a number of accounting issues. These issues are described and illustrated in this chapter.

Learning Objectives

After studying this chapter, you should be able to:

Example Exercises (EE) are shown in **green.**

Obj. 1 **Describe why companies invest in debt and equity securities.**

Why Companies Invest
Investing Cash in Current Operations
Investing Cash in Temporary Investments
Investing Cash in Long-Term Investments

Obj. 2 **Describe and illustrate the accounting for debt investments.**

Accounting for Debt Investments
Purchase of Bonds
Interest Revenue
Sale of Bonds — EE 15-1

Obj. 3 **Describe and illustrate the accounting for equity investments.**

Accounting for Equity Investments
Cost Method: Less Than 20% Ownership — EE 15-2
Equity Method: Between 20%–50% Ownership — EE 15-3
Consolidation: More Than 50% Ownership

Obj. 4 **Describe and illustrate valuing and reporting investments in the financial statements.**

Valuing and Reporting Investments
Trading Securities — EE 15-4
Available-for-Sale Securities — EE 15-5
Held-to-Maturity Securities
Summary

Obj. 5 **Describe fair value accounting and its effects on the financial statements.**

Fair Value Accounting
Effect of Fair Value Accounting on the Financial Statements

Obj. 6 **Describe and illustrate the computation of dividend yield.**

Financial Analysis and Interpretation:
Dividend Yield — EE 15-6

At a Glance 15 Page 740

Why Companies Invest

Obj. 1 Describe why companies invest in debt and equity securities.

Most companies generate cash from their operations. This cash can be used for the following investment purposes:

- Investing in current operations
- Investing in temporary investments to earn additional revenue
- Investing in long-term investments in stock of other companies for strategic reasons

Investing Cash in Current Operations

Cash is often used to support the current operating activities of a company. For example, cash may be used to replace worn-out equipment or to purchase new, more efficient and productive equipment. In addition, cash may be reinvested in the company to expand its current operations. For example, a retailer based in the northwest United States might decide to expand by opening stores in the Midwest.

The accounting for the use of cash in current operations has been described and illustrated in earlier chapters. For example, Chapter 10 illustrated the use of cash for purchasing property, plant, and equipment. In this chapter, we describe and illustrate the use of cash for investing in temporary investments and the stock of other companies.

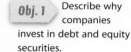

Investing Cash in Temporary Investments

A company may temporarily have excess cash that is not needed for use in its current operations. This is often the case when a company has a seasonal operating cycle. For example, a significant portion of the annual merchandise sales of a retailer occurs during the fall holiday season. As a result, retailers often experience a large increase in cash during this period, which is not needed until the spring buying season.

Instead of letting excess cash remain idle in a checking account, most companies invest their excess cash in temporary investments. In doing so, companies invest in securities such as:

- **Debt securities**, which are notes and bonds that pay interest and have a fixed maturity date.
- **Equity securities**, which are preferred and common stock that represent ownership in a company and do not have a fixed maturity date.

Investments in debt and equity securities, termed **investments** or *temporary investments*, are reported in the Current Assets section of the balance sheet.

The primary objective of investing in temporary investments is as follows:

- Earn interest revenue
- Receive dividends
- Realize gains from increases in the market price of the securities

Investments in certificates of deposit and other securities that do not normally change in value are disclosed on the balance sheet as *cash and cash equivalents*. Such investments are held primarily for their interest revenue.

Investing Cash in Long-Term Investments

A company may invest cash in the debt or equity of another company as a long-term investment. Long-term investments may be held for the same investment objectives as temporary investments. However, long-term investments often involve the purchase of a significant portion of the stock of another company. Such investments usually have a strategic purpose, such as:

- *Reduction of costs:* When one company buys another company, the combined company may be able to reduce administrative expenses. For example, a combined company does not need two chief executive officers (CEOs) or chief financial officers (CFOs).
- *Replacement of management:* If the purchased company has been mismanaged, the acquiring company may replace the company's management and, thus, improve operations and profits.
- *Expansion:* The acquiring company may purchase a company because it has a complementary product line, territory, or customer base. The new combined company may be able to serve customers better than the two companies could separately.
- *Integration:* A company may integrate operations by acquiring a supplier or customer. Acquiring a supplier may provide a more stable or uninterrupted supply of resources. Acquiring a customer may also provide a market for the company's products or services.

Obj. 2 Describe and illustrate the accounting for debt investments.

Accounting for Debt Investments

Debt securities include notes and bonds issued by corporations and governmental organizations. Most companies invest excess cash in bonds as investments to earn interest revenue.

The accounting for bond investments[1] includes recording the following:

- Purchase of bonds
- Interest revenue
- Sale of bonds

1 Debt investments may also include installment notes and short-term notes. The accounting for these debt investments is covered in intermediate and advanced accounting courses.

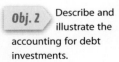

Purchase of Bonds

The purchase of bonds is recorded by debiting an investments account for the purchase price of the bonds, including any brokerage commissions. (A *brokerage commission* is the fee charged by the agent who arranges the transaction between the buyer and seller.) If the bonds are purchased between interest dates, the purchase price includes accrued interest since the last interest payment. This is because the seller has earned the accrued interest, but the buyer will receive the accrued interest when it is paid.

To illustrate, assume that Homer Company purchases $18,000 of U.S. Treasury bonds at their face amount on March 17, 20Y6, plus accrued interest for 45 days. The bonds have an interest rate of 6%, payable on July 31 and January 31.

The entry to record the purchase of the U.S. Treasury bonds is as follows:

20Y6					
Mar.	17	Investments—U.S. Treasury Bonds		18,000	
		Interest Receivable		135	
		Cash			18,135
		Purchased $18,000, 6% U.S. Treasury bonds.			

Because Homer Company purchased the bonds on March 17, it is also purchasing the accrued interest for 45 days (January 31 to March 17), as shown in Exhibit 1. The accrued interest of $135 is computed as follows:[2]

$$\text{Accrued Interest} = \$18{,}000 \times 6\% \times (45 \div 360) = \$135$$

The accrued interest is recorded by debiting Interest Receivable for $135. Investments is debited for the purchase price of the bonds of $18,000.

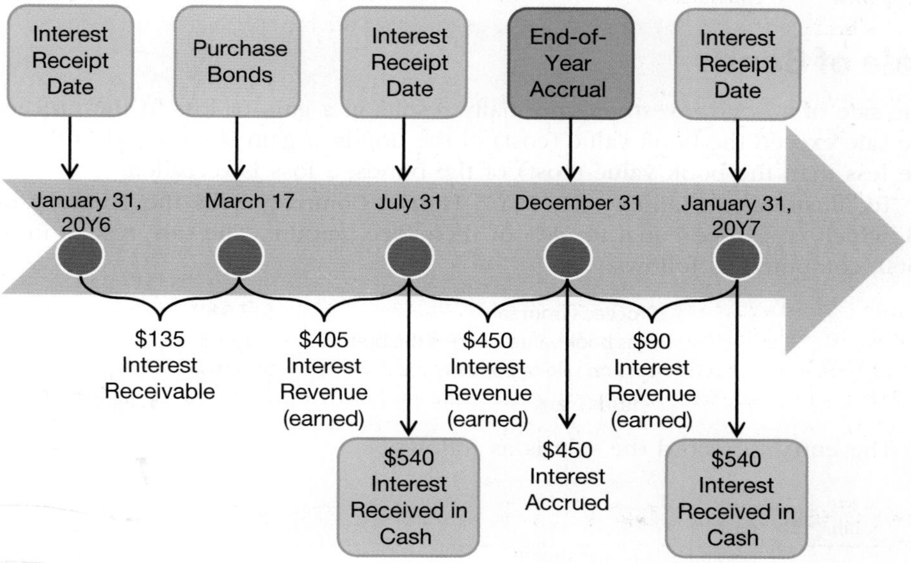

EXHIBIT 1

Interest Timeline

Interest Revenue

On July 31, Homer Company receives a semiannual interest payment of $540 ($18,000 × 6% × ½). The $540 interest includes the $135 accrued interest that Homer Company purchased with the bonds on March 17. Thus, Homer has earned $405 ($540 − $135) of interest revenue since purchasing the bonds, as shown in Exhibit 1.

2 To simplify, a 360-day year is used to compute interest.

The receipt of the interest on July 31 is recorded as follows:

20Y6				
July	31	Cash	540	
		Interest Receivable		135
		Interest Revenue		405
		Received semiannual interest.		

Homer Company's accounting period ends on December 31. Thus, an adjusting entry must be made to accrue interest for five months (August 1 to December 31) of $450 ($18,000 × 6% × 5/12), as shown in Exhibit 1. The adjusting entry to record the accrued interest is as follows:

20Y6				
Dec.	31	Interest Receivable	450	
		Interest Revenue		450
		Accrued five months of interest.		

For the year ended December 31, 20Y6, Homer Company would report Interest Revenue of $855 ($405 + $450) as part of Other Income on its income statement.

The receipt of the semiannual interest of $540 on January 31, 20Y7, is recorded as follows:

20Y7				
Jan.	31	Cash	540	
		Interest Revenue		90
		Interest Receivable		450
		Received semiannual interest		

Sale of Bonds

The sale of a bond investment normally results in a gain or loss. If the proceeds from the sale exceed the book value (cost) of the bonds, a gain is recorded. If the proceeds are less than the book value (cost) of the bonds, a loss is recorded.

To illustrate, on January 31, 20Y7, Homer Company sells the Treasury bonds at 98, which is a price equal to 98% of their face amount. The sale results in a loss of $360, computed as follows:

Proceeds from sale	$17,640*
Less book value (cost) of the bonds	18,000
Loss on sale of bonds	$ (360)

*$18,000 × 98%

The entry to record the sale is as follows:

20Y7				
Jan.	31	Cash	17,640	
		Loss on Sale of Investment	360	
		Investments—U.S. Treasury Bonds		18,000
		Sold U.S. Treasury bonds.		

Link to Deere & Company

Deere & Company recently reported $385 million of investments in government and corporate bonds.

There is no accrued interest upon the sale because the interest payment date is also January 31. If the sale were between interest dates, interest accrued since the last interest payment date would be added to the sale proceeds and credited to Interest Revenue. The loss on the sale of bond investments is reported as part of Other Income (Loss) on Homer Company's income statement.

Example Exercise 15-1 Bond Investment Transactions Obj. 2

Journalize the entries to record the following selected bond investment transactions for Fly Company:

1. Purchased for cash $40,000 of Tyler Company 10% bonds at 100 plus accrued interest of $500.
2. Received the first semiannual interest.
3. Sold $30,000 of the bonds at 102 plus accrued interest of $110.

Follow My Example 15-1

1. Investments—Tyler Company Bonds	40,000	
Interest Receivable	500	
Cash		40,500
2. Cash	2,000*	
Interest Receivable		500
Interest Revenue		1,500
*$40,000 × 10% × ½		
3. Cash	30,710*	
Interest Revenue		110
Gain on Sale of Investments		600
Investments—Tyler Company Bonds		30,000

*Sale proceeds ($30,000 × 102%)	$30,600
Accrued interest	110
Total proceeds from sale	$30,710

Practice Exercises: PE 15-1A, PE 15-1B

Accounting for Equity Investments

Obj. 3 Describe and illustrate the accounting for equity investments.

A company may invest in the preferred or common stock of another company. The company investing in another company's stock is the **investor**. The company whose stock is purchased is the **investee**.

The percent of the investee's outstanding stock purchased by the investor determines the degree of control that the investor has over the investee. This, in turn, determines the accounting method used to record the stock investment, as shown in Exhibit 2.

EXHIBIT 2 Stock Investments

Percent of Outstanding Stock Owned by Investor	Degree of Control of Investor over Investee	Accounting Method
Less than 20%	No control	Cost method
Between 20% and 50%	Significant influence	Equity method
Greater than 50%	Control	Consolidation

Cost Method: Less Than 20% Ownership

If the investor purchases less than 20% of the outstanding stock of the investee, the investor is considered to have no control over the investee. In this case, it is assumed that the investor purchased the stock primarily to earn dividends or to realize gains on price increases of the stock.

Investments of less than 20% of the investee's outstanding stock are accounted for using the **cost method**. Under the cost method, entries are recorded for the following transactions:

- Purchase of stock
- Receipt of dividends
- Sale of stock

Purchase of Stock The purchase of stock is recorded at its cost. Any brokerage commissions are included as part of the cost.

To illustrate, assume that on May 1, Bart Company purchases 2,000 shares of Lisa Company common stock at $49.90 per share plus a brokerage commission of $200. The entry to record the purchase of the stock is as follows:

May	1	Investments—Lisa Company Stock		100,000	
		Cash			100,000
		Purchased 2,000 shares of Lisa Company common stock [($49.90 × 2,000 shares) + $200].			

Receipt of Dividends On July 31, Bart Company receives a dividend of $0.40 per share from Lisa Company. The entry to record the receipt of the dividend is as follows:

July	31	Cash		800	
		Dividend Revenue			800
		Received dividend on Lisa Company common stock (2,000 shares × $0.40).			

Dividend Revenue is reported as part of Other Income on Bart Company's income statement.

Sale of Stock The sale of a stock investment normally results in a gain or loss. A gain is recorded if the proceeds from the sale exceed the book value (cost) of the stock. A loss is recorded if the proceeds from the sale are less than the book value (cost).

To illustrate, on September 1, Bart Company sells 1,500 shares of Lisa Company stock for $54.50 per share less a $160 commission. The sale results in a gain of $6,590, computed as follows:

Proceeds from sale	$81,590*
Book value (cost) of the stock	75,000**
Gain on sale	$ 6,590

*($54.50 × 1,500 shares) − $160
**($100,000 ÷ 2,000 shares) × 1,500 shares

The entry to record the sale is as follows:

Sept.	1	Cash		81,590	
		Gain on Sale of Investments			6,590
		Investments—Lisa Company Stock			75,000
		Sold 1,500 shares of Lisa Company common stock.			

The gain on the sale of investments is reported as part of Other Income on Bart Company's income statement.

Example Exercise 15-2 Stock Investment Transactions

Obj. 3

On September 1, 1,500 shares of Monroe Company are acquired at a price of $24 per share plus a $40 brokerage commission. On October 14, a $0.60-per-share dividend was received on the Monroe Company stock. On November 11, 750 shares (half) of Monroe Company stock were sold for $20 per share less a $45 brokerage commission. Prepare the journal entries for the original purchase, dividend, and sale.

Follow My Example 15-2

Sept. 1	Investments—Monroe Company Stock	36,040*	
	Cash		36,040
	*(1,500 shares × $24 per share) + $40		
Oct. 14	Cash	900*	
	Dividend Revenue		900
	*$0.60 per share × 1,500 shares		
Nov. 11	Cash	14,955*	
	Loss on Sale of Investments	3,065	
	Investments—Monroe Company Stock		18,020**
	*(750 shares × $20) − $45		
	**$36,040 × ½		

Practice Exercises: PE 15-2A, PE 15-2B

Equity Method: Between 20%–50% Ownership

If the investor purchases between 20% and 50% of the outstanding stock of the investee, the investor is considered to have a ***significant influence*** over the investee. In this case, it is assumed that the investor purchased the stock primarily for strategic reasons, such as developing a supplier relationship.

Investments of between 20% and 50% of the investee's outstanding stock are accounted for using the **equity method**. Under the equity method, the stock is recorded initially at its cost, including any brokerage commissions. This is the same as under the cost method.

Under the equity method, the investment account is adjusted for the investor's share of the net income and dividends of the investee. These adjustments are as follows:

- *Net Income:* The investor records its share of the net income of the investee as an increase in the investment account. Its share of any net loss is recorded as a decrease in the investment account.
- *Dividends:* The investor's share of cash dividends received from the investee decreases the investment account.

Purchase of Stock To illustrate, assume that Simpson Inc. purchased a 40% interest in Flanders Corporation's common stock on January 2, 20Y6, for $350,000. The entry to record the purchase is as follows:

20Y6				
Jan.	2	Investment in Flanders Corporation Stock	350,000	
		Cash		350,000
		Purchased 40% of Flanders Corporation stock.		

Recording Investee Net Income For the year ended December 31, 20Y6, Flanders Corporation reported net income of $105,000. Under the equity method, Simpson Inc. (the investor) records its share of Flanders net income, as follows:

20Y6				
Dec.	31	Investment in Flanders Corporation Stock	42,000	
		Income of Flanders Corporation		42,000
		Recorded 40% share of Flanders Corporation net income, $105,000 × 40%.		

Income of Flanders Corporation is reported on Simpson Inc.'s income statement. Depending on its significance, it may be reported separately or as part of *Other Income*. If Flanders had a loss during the period, then the journal entry would be a debit to Loss of Flanders Corporation and a credit to the investment account.

Recording Investee Dividends During the year, Flanders Corporation declared and paid cash dividends of $45,000. Under the equity method, Simpson Inc. (the investor) records its share of Flanders dividends as follows:

20Y6				
Dec.	31	Cash	18,000	
		Investment in Flanders Corporation Stock		18,000
		Recorded 40% share of Flanders Corporation dividends, $45,000 × 40%.		

The effect of recording 40% of Flanders Corporation's net income and dividends is to increase the investment account by $24,000 ($42,000 − $18,000). Thus, Investment in Flanders Corporation Stock increases from $350,000 to $374,000, as shown in Exhibit 3.

EXHIBIT 3

Investment and Dividends

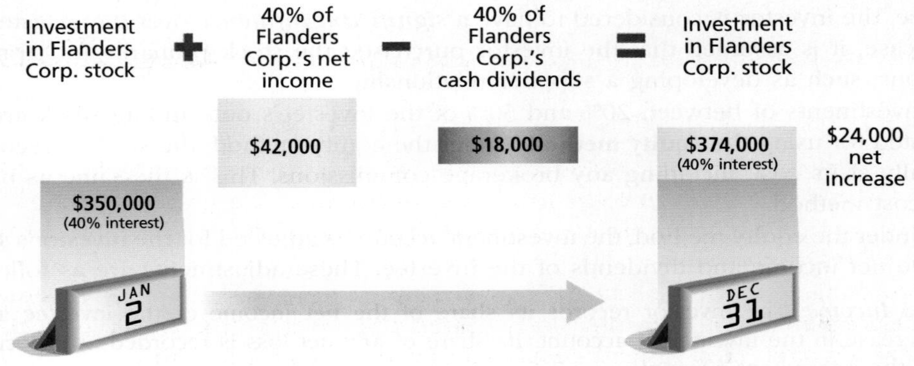

Under the equity method, the investment account reflects the investor's proportional changes in the net book value of the investee. For example, Flanders Corporation's net book value increased by $60,000 (net income of $105,000 less dividends of $45,000) during the year. As a result, Simpson Inc.'s share of Flanders' net book value increased by $24,000 ($60,000 × 40%). Investments accounted for under the equity method are classified on the balance sheet as noncurrent assets.

Sale of Stock Under the equity method, a gain or loss is normally recorded from the sale of an investment. A gain is recorded if the proceeds exceed the *book value* of the investment. A loss is recorded if the proceeds are less than the *book value* of the investment.

To illustrate, if Simpson Inc. sold Flanders Corporation's stock on January 1, 20Y7, for $400,000, a gain of $26,000 would be reported, computed as follows:

Proceeds from sale	$400,000
Book value of stock investment	374,000
Gain on sale	$ 26,000

The entry to record the sale is as follows:

20Y7				
Jan.	1	Cash	400,000	
		Investment in Flanders Corporation Stock		374,000
		Gain on Sale of Flanders Corporation Stock		26,000
		Sold Flanders Corporation stock.		

Link to Deere & Company

In a recent year, Deere & Company reported equity method investments of $303.4 million.

Example Exercise 15-3 Equity Method

Obj. 3

On January 2, Olson Company acquired 35% of the outstanding stock of Bryant Company for $140,000. For the year ended December 31, Bryant Company earned income of $44,000 and paid dividends of $20,000. Prepare the entries for Olson Company for the purchase of the stock, the share of Bryant income, and the dividends received from Bryant Company.

Follow My Example 15-3

Jan. 2	Investment in Bryant Company Stock	140,000	
	Cash		140,000
Dec. 31	Investment in Bryant Company Stock	15,400*	
	Income of Bryant Company		15,400
	*Recorded 35% of Bryant income, 35% × $44,000		
31	Cash	7,000*	
	Investment in Bryant Company Stock		7,000
	*Recorded 35% of Bryant's $20,000 dividend, 35% × $20,000		

Practice Exercises: PE 15-3A, PE 15-3B

Consolidation: More Than 50% Ownership

If the investor purchases more than 50% of the outstanding stock of the investee, the investor is considered to have *control* over the investee. In this case, it is assumed that the investor purchased the stock of the investee primarily for strategic reasons.

The purchase of more than 50% ownership of the investee's stock is termed a **business combination**. Companies may combine in order to produce more efficiently, diversify product lines, expand geographically, or acquire know-how.

A corporation owning all or a majority of the voting stock of another corporation is called a **parent company**. The corporation that is controlled is called the **subsidiary company**.

Parent and subsidiary corporations often continue to maintain separate accounting records and prepare their own financial statements. In such cases, at the end of the year, the financial statements of the parent and subsidiary are combined and reported as a single company. These combined financial statements are called **consolidated financial statements**. Such statements are normally identified by adding *and Subsidiary(ies)* to the name of the parent corporation or by adding *Consolidated* to the statement title.

To the external stakeholders of the parent company, consolidated financial statements are more meaningful than separate statements for each corporation. This is because the parent company, in substance, controls the subsidiaries. The accounting for business combinations, including preparing consolidated financial statements, is described and illustrated in advanced accounting courses and textbooks.

Link to Deere & Company

The financial statements of Deere & Company represent the consolidation of all the companies in which Deere & Company owns more than 50%.

Business Connection

MORE CASH MEANS MORE INVESTMENTS FOR DRUG COMPANIES

Patented drugs are the life blood of the pharmaceutical industry. Drug companies with extensive portfolios of patented drugs generate significant cash flows from operating activities. As a result, these companies often have extensive amounts of cash on hand to invest in other companies. Near the end of 2015, the five biggest drug makers had in excess of $45 billion in cash and investments. Many analysts anticipated that these companies would use this excess cash to acquire smaller biotechnology and drug companies for their patented drugs and their ongoing research activities.

Source: "Mergers and Acquisitions on the Rise in 2013 as Big Pharma Companies Hold Record Amounts of Cash on Hand," *Five Star Equities Market Research Report*. February 7, 2013.

Obj. 4 Describe and illustrate valuing and reporting investments in the financial statements.

Valuing and Reporting Investments

Debt and equity securities are *financial assets* that are often traded on public exchanges such as the New York Stock Exchange. As a result, their market value can be observed and, thus, objectively determined. For this reason, generally accepted accounting principles (GAAP) allow some debt securities and require equity securities where there is less than a 20% ownership interest to be valued in the accounting records and financial statements at their fair market values.

These securities are classified as follows:

- Trading securities
- Available-for-sale securities
- Held-to-maturity securities

Trading Securities

Trading securities are debt and equity securities that are purchased to earn short-term profits from changes in their market prices. Trading securities are often held by banks, mutual funds, insurance companies, and other financial institutions.

Because trading securities are held as a short-term investment, they are reported as a current asset on the balance sheet. Trading securities are valued as a portfolio (group) of securities using the securities' fair values. **Fair value** is the market price that the company would receive for a security if it were sold. A change in the fair value of the portfolio (group) of trading securities is recognized as an **unrealized gain or loss** for the period.

To illustrate, assume that Maggie Company purchased a portfolio of trading securities during 20Y6. On December 31, 20Y6, the cost and fair values of the securities were as follows:

Name	Number of Shares	Total Cost	Total Fair Value
Armour Company	400	$ 5,000	$ 7,200
Maven, Inc.	500	11,000	7,500
Polaris Co.	200	8,000	10,600
Total		$24,000	$25,300

The portfolio of trading securities is reported at its fair value of $25,300. An adjusting entry is made to record the increase in the fair value of $1,300 ($25,300 – $24,000). In order to maintain a record of the original cost of the securities, a valuation account, called *Valuation Allowance for Trading Investments*, is debited for $1,300 and Unrealized Gain on Trading Investments is credited for $1,300.[3]

3 We assume that the valuation allowance account has a beginning balance of zero to simplify our illustrations.

The adjusting entry on December 31, 20Y6, to record the fair value of the portfolio of trading securities is as follows:

20Y6				
Dec.	31	Valuation Allowance for Trading Investments	1,300	
		Unrealized Gain on Trading Investments		1,300
		To record increase in fair value of trading securities.		

Unrealized Gain on Trading Investments is reported on the income statement. Depending on its significance, it may be reported separately or as Other Income on the income statement. The valuation allowance is reported on the December 31, 20Y6, balance sheet as follows:

Maggie Company
Balance Sheet (selected items)
December 31, 20Y6

Current assets:		
Cash		$120,000
Trading investments (at cost)	$24,000	
Plus valuation allowance for trading investments	1,300	
Trading investments (at fair value)		25,300

If the fair value of the portfolio of trading securities was less than the cost, then the adjustment would debit Unrealized Loss on Trading Investments and credit Valuation Allowance for Trading Investments for the difference. Unrealized Loss on Trading Investments would be reported on the income statement as Other Expenses. Valuation Allowance for Trading Investments would be shown on the balance sheet as a *deduction* from Trading Investments (at cost).

Over time, the valuation allowance account is adjusted to reflect the difference between the cost and the fair value of the portfolio. Thus, increases in the valuation allowance account from the beginning of the period will result in an adjustment to record an unrealized gain, similar to the preceding journal entry. Likewise, decreases in the valuation allowance account from the beginning of the period will result in an adjustment to record an unrealized loss.

Example Exercise 15-4 Valuing Trading Securities at Fair Value

Obj. 4

On January 1, 20Y6, Valuation Allowance for Trading Investments had a zero balance. On December 31, 20Y6, the cost of the trading securities portfolio was $79,200, and the fair value was $76,800. Prepare the December 31, 20Y6, adjusting journal entry to record the unrealized gain or loss on trading investments.

Follow My Example 15-4

20Y6			
Dec. 31	Unrealized Loss on Trading Investments	2,400	
	Valuation Allowance for Trading Investments		2,400*
	To record decrease in fair value of trading investments.		

*Trading investments at fair value, December 31, 20Y6	$ 76,800
Less trading investments at cost, December 31, 20Y6	79,200
Unrealized loss on trading investments	$ (2,400)

Practice Exercises: PE 15-4A, PE 15-4B

INTEGRITY, OBJECTIVITY, AND ETHICS IN BUSINESS

SOCIALLY RESPONSIBLE INVESTING

Socially responsible investing is a growing trend in the United States and Europe that focuses on making investments to improve society. Socially responsible investors attempt to balance investment return with social good by seeking out investments in companies that (1) are environmentally friendly, (2) do not infringe on human rights in the production of a product or provision of a service, and (3) are anti-discriminatory. In some situations, socially responsible investors target emerging markets to both generate a return and help overcome social challenges. In addition, some socially responsible investors refuse to invest in companies that produce alcohol, tobacco, or weapons.

Available-for-Sale Securities

Available-for-sale securities are debt and equity securities that are not held for trading, not held to maturity, and not held for strategic reasons. The accounting for available-for-sale securities is similar to the accounting for trading securities, except for the reporting of changes in fair values. Specifically, changes in the fair values of *trading securities* are reported as an unrealized gain or loss on the income statement. In contrast, changes in the fair values of *available-for-sale securities* are reported as part of stockholders' equity and, thus, excluded from the income statement.

To illustrate, assume that the three securities Maggie Company purchased during 20Y6 are classified as available-for-sale securities instead of as trading securities. On December 31, 20Y6, the cost and fair values of the securities were as follows:

Link to Deere & Company

Deere & Company has a $14 million valuation allowance for available-for-sale securities.

Name	Number of Shares	Total Cost	Total Fair Value
Armour Company	400	$ 5,000	$ 7,200
Maven, Inc.	500	11,000	7,500
Polaris Co.	200	8,000	10,600
Total		$24,000	$25,300

The portfolio of available-for-sale securities is reported at its fair value of $25,300. An adjusting entry is made to record the increase in fair value of $1,300 ($25,300 – $24,000). In order to maintain a record of the original cost of the securities, a valuation account, called *Valuation Allowance for Available-for-Sale Investments*, is debited for $1,300. This account is similar to the valuation account used for trading securities.

Unlike trading securities, the December 31, 20Y6, adjusting entry credits a stockholders' equity account instead of an income statement account.[4] The $1,300 increase in fair value is credited to Unrealized Gain (Loss) on Available-for-Sale Investments.

The adjusting entry on December 31, 20Y6, to record the fair value of the portfolio of available-for-sale securities is as follows:

20Y6					
Dec.	31	Valuation Allowance for Available-for-Sale Investments		1,300	
		Unrealized Gain (Loss) on Available-for-Sale Investments			1,300
		To record increase in fair value of available-for-sale investments.			

4 This is a rare exception to the rule that every adjusting entry must affect an income statement and a balance sheet account.

A credit balance in Unrealized Gain (Loss) on Available-for-Sale Investments is added to stockholders' equity, while a debit balance is subtracted from stockholders' equity.

The valuation allowance and the unrealized gain are reported on the December 31, 20Y6, balance sheet as follows:

Maggie Company
Balance Sheet
December 31, 20Y6

Current assets:			
Cash		$120,000	
Available-for-sale investments (at cost)	$24,000		
Plus valuation allowance for available-for-sale investments	1,300		←
Available-for-sale investments (at fair value)		25,300	
			Equal
Stockholders' equity:			
Common stock		$ 10,000	
Paid-in capital in excess of par		150,000	
Retained earnings		250,000	
Unrealized gain (loss) on available-for-sale investments		1,300	←
Total stockholders' equity		$411,300	

As shown, Unrealized Gain (Loss) on Available-for-Sale Investments is reported as an addition to stockholders' equity. In future years, the cumulative effects of unrealized gains and losses are reported in this account. Because 20Y6 was the first year that Maggie Company purchased available-for-sale securities, the unrealized gain is reported as the balance of Unrealized Gain (Loss) on Available-for-Sale Investments. This treatment is supported under the theory that available-for-sale securities will be held longer than trading securities, so changes in fair value over time have a greater opportunity to cancel out. Thus, these changes are not reported on the income statement, as is the case with trading securities.

If the fair value was less than the cost, then the adjustment would debit Unrealized Gain (Loss) on Available-for-Sale Investments and credit Valuation Allowance for Available-for-Sale Investments for the difference. Unrealized Gain (Loss) on Trading Investments would be reported in the Stockholders' Equity section as a negative item. Valuation Allowance for Available-for-Sale Investments would be shown on the balance sheet as a deduction from Available-for-Sale Investments (at cost).

Over time, the valuation allowance account is adjusted to reflect the difference between the cost and the fair value of the portfolio. Thus, increases in the valuation allowance from the beginning of the period will result in an adjustment to record an increase in the valuation and unrealized gain (loss) accounts, similar to the journal entry illustrated earlier. Likewise, decreases in the valuation allowance from the beginning of the period will result in an adjustment to record decreases in the valuation and unrealized gain (loss) accounts.

Link to Deere & Company

Deere & Company classifies all of its investments in debt securities and qualifying equity securities as available-for-sale securities.

Example Exercise 15-5 Valuing Available-for-Sale Securities at Fair Value — Obj. 4

On January 1, 20Y6, Valuation Allowance for Available-for-Sale Investments had a zero balance. On December 31, 20Y6, the cost of the available-for-sale securities was $45,700 and the fair value was $50,000.

Prepare the adjusting entry to record the unrealized gain or loss for available-for-sale investments on December 31, 20Y6.

Follow My Example 15-5

20Y6			
Dec. 31	Valuation Allowance for Available-for-Sale Investments	4,300*	
	Unrealized Gain (Loss) on Available-for-Sale Investments		4,300
	To record increase in fair value of available-for-sale securities.		

*Available-for-sale investments at fair value, December 31, 20Y6	$50,000
Less available-for-sale investments at cost, December 31, 20Y6	45,700
Unrealized gain (loss) on available-for-sale investments	$ 4,300

Practice Exercises: PE 15-5A, PE 15-5B

Held-to-Maturity Securities

Held-to-maturity securities are debt investments, such as notes or bonds, that a company intends to hold until their maturity date. Held-to-maturity securities are purchased primarily to earn interest revenue.

If a held-to-maturity security will mature within a year, it is reported as a current asset on the balance sheet. Held-to-maturity securities maturing beyond a year are reported as noncurrent assets.

Only securities with maturity dates, such as corporate notes and bonds, are classified as held-to-maturity securities. Equity securities are not held-to-maturity securities because they have no maturity date.

Held-to-maturity bond investments are recorded at their cost, including any brokerage commissions, as illustrated earlier in this chapter. If the interest rate on the bonds differs from the market rate of interest, the bonds may be purchased at a premium or discount. In such cases, the premium or discount is amortized over the life of the bonds.

Held-to-maturity bond investments are reported on the balance sheet at their amortized cost. The accounting for held-to-maturity investments, including premium and discount amortization, is described in advanced accounting texts.

Summary

Exhibit 4 summarizes the valuation and balance sheet reporting of trading, available-for-sale, and held-to-maturity securities.

EXHIBIT 4

Summary of Valuing and Reporting of Investments

	Trading Securities	**Available-for-Sale Securities**	**Held-to-Maturity Securities**
Valued at:	**Fair Value**	**Fair Value**	**Amortized Cost**
Changes in valuation are reported as:	Unrealized gain or loss in the income statement as Other Income (loss).	Accumulated unrealized gain or loss is reported in stockholders' equity on the balance sheet.	Not applicable. Held-to-maturity securities are reported at cost.*
Reported on the balance sheet as:	Cost of investments plus or minus valuation allowance.	Cost of investments plus or minus valuation allowance.	Amortized cost of investment.
Classified on balance sheet as:	A current asset.	Either a current or non-current asset, depending on management's intent.	Either a current or noncurrent asset, depending on remaining term to maturity.

*Premium or discount amortization is reported as part of interest revenue on the income statement.

Common stock investments in trading and available-for-sale securities are typically less than 20% of the outstanding common stock of the investee. The portfolios are reported at fair value using the valuation allowance account, while the individual securities are accounted for using the cost method. Investments between 20% and 50% of the outstanding common stock of the investee are accounted for using the equity method illustrated earlier in this chapter. Equity method investments are classified as noncurrent assets on the balance sheet.

The balance sheet reporting for the investments of **Mornin' Joe** follows:

Mornin' Joe
Balance Sheet
December 31, 20Y6

Assets			
Current assets:			
Cash and cash equivalents		$235,000	
Trading investments (at cost)	$420,000		
Plus valuation allowance for trading investments	45,000	465,000	
Accounts receivable	$305,000		
Less allowance for doubtful accounts	12,300	292,700	
Merchandise inventory—at lower of cost (first-in, first-out method) or market		120,000	
Prepaid insurance		24,000	
Total current assets			$1,136,700
Investments:			
Investment in AM Coffee (equity method)			565,000
Property, plant, and equipment:			

Mornin' Joe invests in trading securities and does not have investments in held-to-maturity or available-for-sale securities. Mornin' Joe also owns 40% of AM Coffee Corporation, which is accounted for using the equity method. Mornin' Joe intends to keep its investment in AM Coffee indefinitely for strategic reasons; thus, its investment in AM Coffee is classified as a noncurrent asset. Such investments are normally reported before property, plant, and equipment.

Mornin' Joe reported an Unrealized Gain on Trading Investments of $5,000 and Equity Income in AM Coffee of $57,000 in the Other Income and Expense section of its income statement, as follows:

Mornin' Joe
Income Statement
For the Year Ended December 31, 20Y6

Sales		$5,402,100
Cost of merchandise sold		2,160,000
Gross profit		$3,242,100
Total operating expenses		2,608,700
Income from operations		$ 633,400
Other revenue and expense:		
Interest revenue	$ 18,000	
Interest expense	(136,000)	
Loss on disposal of fixed asset	(23,000)	
Unrealized gain on trading investments	5,000	
Equity income in AM Coffee	57,000	(79,000)
Income before income taxes		$ 554,400
Income tax expense		132,800
Net income		$ 421,600

Business Connection

WARREN BUFFETT: THE SAGE OF OMAHA

Beginning in 1962, Warren Buffett, one of the world's wealthiest and most successful investors, began buying shares of **Berkshire Hathaway**. He eventually took control of the company and transformed it from a textile manufacturing company into an investment holding company. Today, Berkshire Hathaway holds more than $125 billion in cash and cash equivalents, equity securities, and debt securities. Berkshire's largest holdings include **The Coca-Cola Company**, **American Express**, **Wells Fargo**, and **Procter & Gamble**. Berkshire Class A common stock trades near $212,000 per share, the highest priced share on the **New York Stock Exchange**.

Buffett compares his investment style to hitting a baseball: "Ted Williams, one of the greatest hitters in the game, stated, 'my argument is, to be a good hitter, you've got to get a good ball to hit. It's the first rule of the book. If I have to bite at stuff that is out of my happy zone, I'm not a .344 hitter. I might only be a .250 hitter.'" Buffett states, "Charlie (Buffett's partner) and I agree and will try to wait for (investment) opportunities that are well within our 'happy zone.'" One of Buffet's recent "happy zone" investments was the acquisition of **Burlington Northern Santa Fe Railroad** for $34 billion.

Warren Buffett as the CEO of Berkshire Hathaway earns a salary of only $100,000 per year, which is the lowest CEO salary for a company of its size in the United States. However, he personally owns approximately 38% of the company, making him worth more than $70 billion. What will Buffett do with this wealth? He has decided to give nearly all of it to philanthropic causes through the **Bill and Melinda Gates Foundation**.

Source: Warren E. Buffett, *The Essays of Warren Buffett: Lessons for Corporate America*, edited by Lawrence A. Cunningham, p. 234.

Fair Value Accounting

Obj. 5 Describe fair value accounting and its effects on the financial statements.

Fair value is the price that would be received from selling an asset. Fair value assumes that this transaction occurs under *normal* business conditions.

As illustrated earlier, generally accepted accounting principles require trading and available-for-sale investments to be recorded at their fair value. This differs from the traditional historical cost measurement basis, which records assets such as inventory and property, plant, and equipment at their purchase price. As a result, financial statements include some assets that are reported at their historical cost (inventory, property, plant, and equipment), and other assets that are reported at their fair value (trading and available-for-sale securities).

Over the past several decades, the financial statements of companies in most industries have included more fair value measures. This is partially due to the Financial Accounting Standards Board's increased willingness to apply fair value to certain assets and transactions. As the ability to measure fair value becomes more reliable, a greater number of assets and transactions are likely to be reported at fair value. A more detailed discussion of fair value is provided in intermediate and advanced financial accounting courses.

Effect of Fair Value Accounting on the Financial Statements

The use of fair values for valuing assets and liabilities affects the financial statements. Specifically, the balance sheet and income statement could be affected.

Balance Sheet When an asset is reported at its fair value, any difference between the asset's original cost or prior period's fair value must be recorded. As we illustrated for trading and available-for-sale securities, this difference is reported in a valuation allowance. The account, Valuation Allowance for Trading Investments, was used earlier in this chapter to adjust trading securities to their fair values.

Available-for-sale securities are reported at fair value in the balance sheet. Changes in their fair values are not recognized on the income statement, but are included as part of stockholders' equity through the comprehensive income and accumulated other comprehensive income accounts. These accounts are described in the appendix to this chapter.

Income Statement Trading securities are also reported at fair value in the balance sheet. However, instead of recording the changes in the fair values of trading securities as part of stockholders' equity, the unrealized gains or losses are reported on the income statement.

Financial Analysis and Interpretation: Dividend Yield

Obj. 6 Describe and illustrate the computation of dividend yield.

The **dividend yield** measures the rate of return to stockholders based on cash dividends. Dividend yield is most often computed for common stock because preferred stock has a stated dividend rate. In contrast, the cash dividends paid on common stock normally vary with the profitability of the corporation.

The dividend yield is computed as follows:

$$\text{Dividend Yield} = \frac{\text{Dividends per Share of Common Stock}}{\text{Market Price per Share of Common Stock}}$$

To illustrate, the market price of Deere & Company was $76.26 at the end of a recent fiscal year. During the preceding year, Deere & Company had paid dividends of $2.40 per share. Thus, the dividend yield of Deere & Company's common stock is computed as follows:

$$\text{Dividend Yield} = \frac{\text{Dividends per Share of Common Stock}}{\text{Market Price per Share of Common Stock}} = \frac{\$2.40}{\$76.26} = 3.1\%$$

Deere & Company pays a dividend yield of slightly more than 3.1%. The dividend yield is first a function of a company's profitability, or ability to pay a dividend. Deere & Company has sufficient profitability to pay a dividend. Second, a company's dividend yield is a function of management's alternative use of funds. If a company has sufficient growth opportunities, funds may be directed toward internal investment rather than toward paying dividends.

The dividend yield will vary from day to day because the market price of a corporation's stock varies day to day. Current dividend yields are provided with news service quotations of market prices, such as The Wall Street Journal or Yahoo! Finance.

Recent dividend yields for some selected companies are as follows:

Company	Dividend Yield (%)
Alphabet (Google)	None
Best Buy	3.6
Coca-Cola Company	3.1
Deere & Company	3.1
Duke Energy	4.1
Facebook	None
Microsoft	2.8
Verizon Communications	4.4

As can be seen, the dividend yield varies widely across firms. Growth firms tend to retain their earnings to fund future growth. Thus, Facebook and Alphabet (Google) pay no dividends. Common stockholders of these companies expect to earn most of their return from stock price appreciation. In contrast, Duke Energy and Verizon Communications are regulated utilities that provide a return to common stockholders mostly through dividends. Best Buy, Coca-Cola, Deere & Company, and Microsoft provide a mix of dividends and expected stock price appreciation to their common stockholders.

Example Exercise 15-6 Dividend Yield

Obj. 6

On March 11, 20Y6, Sheldon Corporation had a market price of $58 per share of common stock. For the previous year, Sheldon paid an annual dividend of $2.90 per share. Compute the dividend yield for Sheldon Corporation.

Follow My Example 15-6

$$\text{Dividend Yield} = \frac{\text{Dividends per Share of Common Stock}}{\text{Market Price per Share of Common Stock}}$$

$$= \frac{\$2.90}{\$58} = 0.05, \text{ or } 5\%$$

Practice Exercises: PE 15-6A, PE 15-6B

APPENDIX

Comprehensive Income

Comprehensive income is defined as all changes in stockholders' equity during a period, except those resulting from dividends and stockholders' investments. Comprehensive income is computed by adding or subtracting *other comprehensive income* to (from) net income, as follows:

Net income	$XXX
Other comprehensive income	XXX
Comprehensive income	$XXX

Other comprehensive income items include unrealized gains and losses on available-for-sale securities as well as other items such as foreign currency and pension liability adjustments. The *cumulative* effect of other comprehensive income is reported on the balance sheet as **accumulated other comprehensive income**.

Companies are required to report comprehensive income in the financial statements in one of the following two ways:

- On the income statement, or
- In a separate statement of comprehensive income that immediately follows the income statement.

In the earlier illustration, Maggie Company had reported an unrealized gain of $1,300 on available-for-sale investments. This unrealized gain would be reported in the Stockholders' Equity section of Maggie's 20Y6 balance sheet, as follows:

Maggie Company
Balance Sheet
December 31, 20Y6

Stockholders' equity:	
Common stock	$ 10,000
Excess of issue price over par	150,000
Retained earnings	250,000
Unrealized gain (loss) on available-for-sale investments	1,300
Total stockholders' equity	$411,300

Alternatively, Maggie Company could have reported the unrealized gain as part of accumulated other comprehensive income as follows:

Maggie Company
Balance Sheet
December 31, 20Y6

Stockholders' equity:	
Common stock	$ 10,000
Excess of issue price over par	150,000
Retained earnings	250,000
Accumulated other comprehensive income:	
Unrealized gain on available-for-sale investments	1,300
Total stockholders' equity	$411,300

The accounting for comprehensive income is an advanced accounting topic that will be covered in greater detail in advanced accounting courses.

At a Glance 15

Obj. 1 Describe why companies invest in debt and equity securities.

Key Points Cash can be used to (1) invest in current operations, (2) invest to earn additional revenue in marketable securities, or (3) invest in marketable securities for strategic reasons.

Learning Outcomes	*Example Exercises*	*Practice Exercises*
• Describe the ways excess cash is used by a business.		
• Describe the purpose of temporary investments.		
• Describe the strategic purpose of long-term investments.		

Obj. 2 Describe and illustrate the accounting for debt investments.

Key Points The accounting for debt investments includes recording the purchase, interest revenue, and sale of the debt. Both the purchase and sale date may include accrued interest.

Learning Outcomes	*Example Exercises*	*Practice Exercises*
• Prepare journal entries to record the purchase of a debt investment, including accrued interest.	**EE15-1**	**PE15-1A, 15-1B**
• Prepare journal entries for interest revenue from debt investments.	**EE15-1**	**PE15-1A, 15-1B**
• Prepare journal entries to record the sale of a debt investment at a gain or loss.	**EE15-1**	**PE15-1A, 15-1B**

Obj. 3 Describe and illustrate the accounting for equity investments.

Key Points The accounting for equity investments differs, depending on the degree of control. Accounting for investments of less than 20% of the outstanding stock (no control) of the investee includes recording the purchase of stock, the receipt of dividends, and the sale of stock at a gain or loss. Investments of 20%–50% of the outstanding stock of an investee are considered to have significant influence and are accounted for under the *equity method*. An investment for more than 50% of the outstanding stock of an investee is treated as a *business combination* and is accounted for using *consolidated financial statements*.

Learning Outcomes	Example Exercises	Practice Exercises
• Describe the accounting for less than 20%, 20%–50%, and greater than 50% investments.		
• Prepare journal entries to record the purchase of a stock investment.	EE15-2	PE15-2A, 15-2B
• Prepare journal entries for the receipt of dividends.	EE15-2	PE15-2A, 15-2B
• Prepare journal entries for the sale of a stock investment at a gain or loss.	EE15-2	PE15-2A, 15-2B
• Prepare journal entries for the equity earnings of an equity method investee under the equity method.	EE15-3	PE15-3A, 15-3B
• Prepare journal entries for the dividends received from an equity method investee under the equity method.	EE15-3	PE15-3A, 15-3B
• Describe a business combination, parent company, and subsidiary company.		
• Describe consolidated financial statements.		

Obj. 4 Describe and illustrate valuing and reporting investments in the financial statements.

Key Points Equity security investments of 20%–50% of the outstanding stock (not control) may be classified as either (1) trading securities, or (2) available-for-sale securities Investments in debt securities can be classified as either (1) trading securities, (2) available-for-sale securities, or (3) held-to-maturity securities. *Trading securities* are valued at *fair value*, with unrealized gains and losses reported on the income statement. *Available-for-sale securities* are reported at fair value with unrealized gains or losses reported in the Stockholders' Equity section of the balance sheet. *Held-to-maturity* investments are valued at amortized cost.

Learning Outcomes	Example Exercises	Practice Exercises
• Describe trading securities, held-to-maturity securities, and available-for-sale securities.		
• Prepare journal entries to record the change in the fair value of a trading security portfolio.	EE15-4	PE15-4A, 15-4B
• Describe and illustrate the reporting of trading securities on the balance sheet.		
• Prepare journal entries to record the change in fair value of an available-for-sale security portfolio.	EE15-5	PE15-5A, 15-5B
• Describe and illustrate the reporting of available-for-sale securities on the balance sheet.		
• Describe the accounting for held-to-maturity debt securities.		

Obj. 5 Describe fair value accounting and its effects on the financial statements.

Key Points There is a trend toward fair value accounting in generally accepted accounting principles. Fair value is the price that would be received to sell an asset.

Learning Outcomes	Example Exercises	Practice Exercises
• Describe fair value accounting.		
• Describe how fair value accounting impacts the balance sheet and income statement.		

Obj. 6 Describe and illustrate the computation of dividend yield.

Key Points The dividend yield measures the cash return from common dividends as a percent of the market price of the common stock. The ratio is computed as dividends per share of common stock divided by the market price per share of common stock.

Learning Outcomes	Example Exercises	Practice Exercises
• Compute dividend yield.	EE15-6	PE15-6A, 15-6B
• Describe how dividend yield measures the return to stockholders from dividends.		

Illustrative Problem

The following selected investment transactions were completed by Rosewell Company during Year 1, its first year of operations:

Year 1

Jan. 11. Purchased 800 shares of Bryan Company stock as an available-for-sale security at $23 per share plus an $80 brokerage commission.

Feb. 6. Purchased $40,000 of 8% U.S. Treasury bonds at their face amount plus accrued interest for 36 days. The bonds pay interest on January 1 and July 1. The bonds were classified as held-to-maturity securities.

Mar. 3. Purchased 1,900 shares of Cohen Company stock as a trading security at $48 per share plus a $152 brokerage commission.

Apr. 5. Purchased 2,400 shares of Lyons Inc. stock as an available-for-sale security at $68 per share plus a $120 brokerage commission.

May 12. Purchased 200,000 shares of Myers Company at $37 per share plus an $8,000 brokerage commission. Myers Company has 800,000 common shares issued and outstanding. The equity method was used for this investment.

July 1. Received semiannual interest on bonds purchased on February 6.

Aug. 29. Sold 1,200 shares of Cohen Company stock at $61 per share less a $90 brokerage commission.

Oct. 5. Received an $0.80-per-share dividend on Bryan Company stock.

Nov. 11. Received a $1.10-per-share dividend on Myers Company stock.

16. Purchased 3,000 shares of Morningside Company stock as a trading security for $52 per share plus a $150 brokerage commission.

Year 1

Dec. 31. Accrued interest on U.S. Treasury bonds.

31. Myers Company earned $1,200,000 during the year. Rosewell recorded its share of Myers Company earnings, using the equity method.

31. Prepared adjusting entries for the portfolios of trading and available-for-sale securities based on the following fair values (stock prices):

Bryan Company	$21
Cohen Company	43
Lyons Inc.	88
Myers Company	40
Morningside Company	45

Instructions

1. Journalize the preceding transactions.
2. Prepare the balance sheet disclosure for Rosewell Company's investments on December 31, Year 1. Assume that held-to-maturity investments are classified as noncurrent assets.

Solution

1.

Year 1				
Jan.	11	Investments—Bryan Company	18,480*	
		Cash		18,480
		*(800 shares × $23 per share) + $80		
Feb.	6	Investments—U.S. Treasury Bonds	40,000	
		Interest Receivable	320*	
		Cash		40,320
		*$40,000 × 8% × (36 days ÷ 360 days)		
Mar.	3	Investments—Cohen Company	91,352*	
		Cash		91,352
		*(1,900 shares × $48 per share) + $152		
Apr.	5	Investments—Lyons Inc.	163,320*	
		Cash		163,320
		*(2,400 shares × $68 per share) + $120		
May	12	Investment in Myers Company	7,408,000*	
		Cash		7,408,000
		*(200,000 shares × $37 per share) + $8,000		
July	1	Cash	1,600*	
		Interest Receivable		320
		Interest Revenue		1,280
		*$40,000 × 8% × ½		

(Continued)

Year 1				
Aug.	29	Cash	73,110*	
		Investments—Cohen Company		57,696**
		Gain on Sale of Investments		15,414
		*(1,200 shares × $61 per share) – $90		
		**1,200 shares × ($91,352 ÷ 1,900 shares)		

Oct.	5	Cash	640	
		Dividend Revenue		640
		*800 shares × $0.80 per share		

Nov.	11	Cash	220,000	
		Investment in Myers Company Stock		220,000
		*200,000 shares × $1.10 per share		

Nov.	16	Investments—Morningside Company	156,150*	
		Cash		156,150
		*(3,000 shares × $52 per share) + $150		

Dec.	31	Interest Receivable	1,600	
		Interest Revenue		1,600
		Accrued interest, $40,000 × 8% × ½.		

Dec.	31	Investment in Myers Company Stock	300,000	
		Income of Myers Company		300,000
		Recorded equity income, $1,200,000 × (200,000 shares ÷ 800,000 shares).		

Dec.	31	Unrealized Loss on Trading Investments	24,706	
		Valuation Allowance for Trading Investments		24,706
		Recorded decease in fair value of trading investments, $165,100 – $189,806.		

Name	**Number of Shares**	**Total Cost**	**Total Fair Value**
Cohen Company	700	$ 33,656	$ 30,100*
Morningside Company	3,000	156,150	135,000**
Total		$189,806	$165,100

*700 shares × $43 per share
**3,000 shares × $45 per share

Note: Myers Company is valued using the equity method; thus, the fair value is not used.

Year 1				
Dec.	31	Valuation Allowance for Available-for-Sale Investments	46,200	
		Unrealized Gain (Loss) on Available-for-Sale Investments		46,200
		Recorded increase in fair value of available-for-sale investments, $228,000 – $181,800.		

Name	Number of Shares	Total Cost	Total Fair Value
Bryan Company	800	$ 18,480	$ 16,800*
Lyons Inc.	2,400	163,320	211,200**
Total		$181,800	$228,000

*800 shares × $21 per share
**2,400 shares × $88 per share

2.

Rosewell Company
Balance Sheet (Selected)
December 31, Year 1

Assets

Current assets:		
Cash		$ XXX,XXX
Trading investments (at cost)	$189,806	
Less valuation allowance for trading investments	24,706	
Trading investments at fair value		165,100
Available-for-sale investments (at cost)	$181,800	
Plus valuation allowance for available-for-sale investments	46,200	
Available-for-sale investments at fair value		228,000
Investments:		
Held-to-maturity investments		40,000
Investment in Myers Company (equity method)		7,488,000

Stockholders' equity:	
Common stock	$ XX,XXX
Paid-in capital in excess of par	XXX,XXX
Retained earnings	XXX,XXX
Unrealized gain on available-for-sale investments	46,200
Total stockholders' equity	$ XXX,XXX

Key Terms

accumulated other comprehensive income (739)
available-for-sale securities (732)
business combination (729)
comprehensive income (739)
consolidated financial statements (729)
cost method (726)
debt securities (722)
dividend yield (737)
equity method (727)
equity securities (722)
fair value (730)
held-to-maturity securities (734)
investee (725)
investments (722)
investor (725)
other comprehensive income (739)
parent company (729)
subsidiary company (729)
trading securities (730)
unrealized gain or loss (730)

Discussion Questions

1. Why might a business invest cash in temporary investments?
2. What causes a gain or loss on the sale of a bond investment?
3. When is the equity method the appropriate accounting for equity investments?
4. How does the accounting for a dividend received differ between the cost method and the equity method?
5. If an investor owns more than 50% of an investee, how is the investment treated on the investor's financial statements?
6. What is the major difference in the accounting for a portfolio of trading securities and a portfolio of available-for-sale securities?
7. If Valuation Allowance for Available-for-Sale Investments has a credit balance, how is it treated on the balance sheet?
8. How would a debit balance in Unrealized Gain (Loss) on Available-for-Sale Investments be reported in the financial statements?
9. What are the factors contributing to the trend toward fair value accounting?
10. How are the balance sheet and income statement affected by fair value accounting?

Practice Exercises

Example Exercises

Show Me How EE 15-1 p. 725

PE 15-1A Bond investment transactions **OBJ. 2**

Journalize the entries to record the following selected bond investment transactions for Hall Trust:

a. Purchased for cash $240,000 of Medina City 6% bonds at 100 plus accrued interest of $3,600.
b. Received first semiannual interest payment.
c. Sold $120,000 of the bonds at 98 plus accrued interest of $600.

Show Me How EE 15-1 p. 725

PE 15-1B Bond investment transactions **OBJ. 2**

Journalize the entries to record the following selected bond investment transactions for Starks Products:

a. Purchased for cash $120,000 of Iceline, Inc. 5% bonds at 100 plus accrued interest of $1,000.
b. Received first semiannual interest payment.
c. Sold $60,000 of the bonds at 101 plus accrued interest of $500.

Show Me How EE 15-2 p. 727

PE 15-2A Stock investment transactions **OBJ. 3**

On January 23, 10,000 shares of Tolle Company are acquired at a price of $30 per share plus a $100 brokerage commission. On April 12, a $0.50-per-share dividend was received on the Tolle Company stock. On June 10, 4,000 shares of the Tolle Company stock were sold for $34 per share less a $100 brokerage commission. Prepare the journal entries for the original purchase, the dividend, and the sale under the cost method.

Show Me How EE 15-2 p. 727

PE 15-2B Stock investment transactions **OBJ. 3**

On September 12, 2,000 shares of Aspen Company are acquired at a price of $50 per share plus a $200 brokerage commission. On October 15, a $0.50-per-share dividend was received on the Aspen Company stock. On November 10, 1,200 shares of the Aspen Company stock were sold for $42 per share less a $150 brokerage commission. Prepare the journal entries for the original purchase, the dividend, and the sale under the cost method.

Show Me How EE 15-3 *p. 729*

PE 15-3A Equity method **OBJ. 3**

On January 2, Cohan Company acquired 40% of the outstanding stock of Sanger Company for $500,000. For the year ended December 31, Sanger Company earned income of $80,000 and paid dividends of $30,000. Prepare the entries for Cohan Company for the purchase of the stock, the share of Sanger income, and the dividends received from Sanger Company.

Show Me How EE 15-3 *p. 729*

PE 15-3B Equity method **OBJ. 3**

On January 2, Yorkshire Company acquired 40% of the outstanding stock of Fain Company for $600,000. For the year ended December 31, Fain Company earned income of $140,000 and paid dividends of $50,000. Prepare the entries for Yorkshire Company for the purchase of the stock, the share of Fain income, and the dividends received from Fain Company.

Show Me How EE 15-4 *p. 731*

PE 15-4A Valuing trading securities at fair value **OBJ. 4**

On January 1, Valuation Allowance for Trading Investments had a zero balance. On December 31, the cost of the trading securities portfolio was $260,000, and the fair value was $214,000. Prepare the December 31 adjusting journal entry to record the unrealized gain or loss on trading investments.

Show Me How EE 15-4 *p. 731*

PE 15-4B Valuing trading securities at fair value **OBJ. 4**

On January 1, Valuation Allowance for Trading Investments had a zero balance. On December 31, the cost of the trading securities portfolio was $41,500, and the fair value was $46,300. Prepare the December 31 adjusting journal entry to record the unrealized gain or loss on trading investments.

Show Me How EE 15-5 *p. 734*

PE 15-5A Valuing available-for-sale securities at fair value **OBJ. 4**

On January 1, Valuation Allowance for Available-for-Sale Investments had a zero balance. On December 31, the cost of the available-for-sale securities was $60,250, and the fair value was $57,500. Prepare the adjusting entry to record the unrealized gain or loss on available-for-sale investments on December 31.

Show Me How EE 15-5 *p. 734*

PE 15-5B Valuing available-for-sale securities at fair value **OBJ. 4**

On January 1, Valuation Allowance for Available-for-Sale Investments had a zero balance. On December 31, the cost of the available-for-sale securities was $24,260, and the fair value was $26,350. Prepare the adjusting entry to record the unrealized gain or loss on available-for-sale investments on December 31.

Show Me How EE 15-6 *p. 738*

FAI

PE 15-6A Dividend yield **OBJ. 6**

On June 30, Setzer Corporation had a market price of $100 per share of common stock. For the previous year, Setzer paid an annual dividend of $4.00. Compute the dividend yield for Setzer Corporation.

Show Me How EE 15-6 *p. 738*

FAI

PE 15-6B Dividend yield **OBJ. 6**

On October 23, Wilkerson Company had a market price of $40 per share of common stock. For the previous year, Wilkerson paid an annual dividend of $1.20. Compute the dividend yield for Wilkerson Company.

Exercises

EX 15-1 Entries for investment in bonds, interest, and sale of bonds — OBJ. 2

Show Me How

Gonzalez Company acquired $200,000 of Walker Co., 6% bonds on May 1 at their face amount. Interest is paid semiannually on May 1 and November 1. On November 1, Gonzalez Company sold $70,000 of the bonds for 97.

Journalize entries to record the following in Year 1:

a. The initial acquisition of the bonds on May 1.

b. The semiannual interest received on November 1.

c. The sale of the bonds on November 1.

d. The accrual of $1,300 interest on December 31.

EX 15-2 Entries for investments in bonds, interest, and sale of bonds — OBJ. 2

Show Me How

Torres Investments acquired $160,000 of Murphy Corp., 5% bonds at their face amount on October 1, Year 1. The bonds pay interest on October 1 and April 1. On April 1, Year 2, Torres sold $60,000 of Murphy Corp. bonds at 102.

Journalize the entries to record the following:

a. The initial acquisition of the Murphy Corp. bonds on October 1, Year 1.

b. The adjusting entry for three months of accrued interest earned on the Murphy Corp. bonds on December 31, Year 1.

c. The receipt of semiannual interest on April 1, Year 2.

d. The sale of $60,000 of Murphy Corp. bonds on April 1, Year 2, at 102.

EX 15-3 Entries for investment in bonds, interest, and sale of bonds — OBJ. 2

✔ Oct. 31, Loss on sale of investments, $400

Show Me How

Bocelli Co. purchased $120,000 of 6%, 20-year Sanz County bonds on May 11, Year 1, directly from the county, at their face amount plus accrued interest. The bonds pay semiannual interest on April 1 and October 1. On October 31, Year 1, Bocelli Co. sold $30,000 of the Sanz County bonds at 99 plus $150 accrued interest less a $100 brokerage commission.

Provide journal entries for the following:

a. The purchase of the bonds on May 11 plus 40 days of accrued interest.

b. Semiannual interest on October 1.

c. Sale of the bonds on October 31.

d. Adjusting entry for accrued interest of $1,365 on December 31, Year 1.

EX 15-4 Entries for investment in bonds, interest, and sale of bonds — OBJ. 2

✔ Aug. 30, Loss on sale of investments, $700

Show Me How

The following bond investment transactions were completed during a recent year by Starks Company:

Year 1

Jan. 31. Purchased 75, $1,000 government bonds at 100 plus accrued interest of $375 (one month). The bonds pay 6% annual interest on July 1 and January 1.

July 1. Received semiannual interest on bond investment.

Aug. 30. Sold 35, $1,000 bonds at 98 plus $350 accrued interest (two months).

a. Journalize the entries for these transactions.

b. Provide the December 31, Year 1, adjusting journal entry for semiannual interest earned on the bonds.

EX 15-5 Interest on bond investments — OBJ. 2

On February 1, Hansen Company purchased $120,000 of 5%, 20-year Knight Company bonds at their face amount plus one month's accrued interest. The bonds pay interest on January 1 and July 1. On October 1, Hansen Company sold $40,000 of the Knight Company bonds acquired on February 1, plus three months' accrued interest. On December 31, three months' interest was accrued for the remaining bonds.

Determine the interest earned by Hansen Company on Knight Company bonds for the year.

EX 15-6 Entries for investment in stock, receipt of dividends, and sale of shares OBJ. 3

✔ c. Gain on sale of investments, $47,860

Show Me How

On February 22, Stewart Corporation acquired 12,000 shares of the 400,000 outstanding shares of Edwards Co. common stock at $50 plus commission charges of $120. On June 1, a cash dividend of $1.40 per share was received. On November 12, 4,000 shares were sold at $62 less commission charges of $100.

Using the cost method, journalize the entries for (a) the purchase of stock, (b) the receipt of dividends, and (c) the sale of 4,000 shares.

EX 15-7 Entries for investment in stock, receipt of dividends, and sale of shares OBJ. 3

✔ Sept. 10, Loss on sale of investments, $6,150

Show Me How

The following equity investment transactions were completed by Romero Company during a recent year:

Apr. 10. Purchased 5,000 shares of Dixon Company for a price of $25 per share plus a brokerage commission of $75.

July 8. Received a quarterly dividend of $0.60 per share on the Dixon Company investment.

Sept. 10. Sold 2,000 shares for a price of $22 per share less a brokerage commission of $120.

Journalize the entries for these transactions.

EX 15-8 Entries for stock investments, dividends, and sale of stock OBJ. 3

✔ Sept. 25, Dividend revenue, $520

Show Me How

Yerbury Corp. manufactures construction equipment. Journalize the entries to record the following selected equity investment transactions completed by Yerbury during a recent year:

Feb. 2. Purchased for cash 5,300 shares of Wong Inc. stock for $20 per share plus a $110 brokerage commission.

Mar. 6. Received dividends of $0.30 per share on Wong Inc. stock.

June 7. Purchased 2,000 shares of Wong Inc. stock for $26 per share plus a $120 brokerage commission.

July 26. Sold 6,000 shares of Wong Inc. stock for $35 per share less a $100 brokerage commission. Yerbury assumes that the first investments purchased are the first investments sold.

Sept. 25. Received dividends of $0.40 per share on Wong Inc. stock.

EX 15-9 Entries for stock investments, dividends, and sale of stock OBJ. 3

Show Me How

Seamus Industries Inc. buys and sells investments as part of its ongoing cash management. The following investment transactions were completed during the year:

Feb. 24. Acquired 1,000 shares of Tett Co. stock for $85 per share plus a $150 brokerage commission.

May 16. Acquired 2,500 shares of Issacson Co. stock for $36 per share plus a $100 commission.

July 14. Sold 400 shares of Tett Co. stock for $100 per share less a $75 brokerage commission.

Aug. 12. Sold 750 shares of Issacson Co. stock for $32.50 per share less an $80 brokerage commission.

Oct. 31. Received dividends of $0.40 per share on Tett Co. stock.

Journalize the entries for these transactions.

EX 15-10 Equity method for stock investment OBJ. 3

Show Me How

At a total cost of $5,600,000, Herrera Corporation acquired 280,000 shares of Tran Corp. common stock as a long-term investment. Herrera Corporation uses the equity method of accounting for this investment. Tran Corp. has 800,000 shares of common stock outstanding, including the shares acquired by Herrera Corporation.

(Continued)

a. Journalize the entries by Herrera Corporation to record the following information:
   1. Tran Corp. reports net income of $600,000 for the current period.
   2. A cash dividend of $0.50 per common share is paid by Tran Corp. during the current period.

b. Why is the equity method appropriate for the Tran Corp. investment?

EX 15-11 Equity method for stock investment **OBJ. 3**

✔ b. $14,900,000

Excel

Show Me How

On January 4, Year 1, Ferguson Company purchased 480,000 shares of Silva Company directly from one of the founders for a price of $30 per share. Silva has 1,200,000 shares outstanding, including the Daniels shares. On July 2, Year 1, Silva paid $750,000 in total dividends to its shareholders. On December 31, Year 1, Silva reported a net income of $2,000,000 for the year. Ferguson uses the equity method in accounting for its investment in Silva.

a. Provide the Ferguson Company journal entries for the transactions involving its investment in Silva Company during Year 1.

b. Determine the December 31, Year 1, balance of the investment in Silva Company stock account.

EX 15-12 Equity method for stock investment with loss **OBJ. 3**

On January 6, Year 1, Bulldog Co. purchased 34% of the outstanding stock of Gator Co. for $212,000. Gator Co. paid total dividends of $24,000 to all shareholders on June 30. Gator had a net loss of $56,000 for Year 1.

a. Journalize Bulldog's purchase of the stock, receipt of the dividends, and the adjusting entry for the equity loss in Gator Co. stock.

b. Compute the balance of Investment in Gator Co. Stock on December 31, Year 1.

c. How does valuing an investment under the equity method differ from valuing an investment at fair value?

EX 15-13 Equity method for stock investment **OBJ. 3**

Hawkeye Company's balance sheet reported, under the equity method, its long-term investment in Raven Company for comparative years as follows:

	Dec. 31, Year 2	Dec. 31, Year 1
Investment in Raven Company stock (in millions)	$281	$264

In addition, the Year 2 Hawkeye Company income statement disclosed equity earnings in the Raven Company investment as $25 million. Hawkeye Company neither purchased nor sold Raven Company stock during Year 2. The fair value of the Raven Company stock investment on December 31, Year 2, was $310 million.

Explain the change in Investment in Raven Company Stock from December 31, Year 1, to December 31, Year 2.

EX 15-14 Missing statement items, trading investments **OBJ. 4**

✔ g. $6,000

JED Capital Inc. makes investments in trading securities. Selected income statement items for the years ended December 31, Year 2 and Year 3, plus selected items from comparative balance sheets, are as follows:

JED Capital Inc.
Selected Income Statement Items
For the Years Ended December 31, Year 2 and Year 3

	Year 2	Year 3
Operating income	a.	e.
Unrealized gain (loss)	b.	$(11,000)
Net income	c.	28,000

JED Capital Inc.
Selected Balance Sheet Items
December 31, Year 1, Year 2, and Year 3

	Dec. 31, Year 1	Dec. 31, Year 2	Dec. 31, Year 3
Trading investments, at cost	$144,000	$168,000	$205,000
Valuation allowance for trading investments	(12,000)	17,000	g.
Trading investments, at fair value	d.	f.	h.
Retained earnings	$210,000	$245,000	i.

There were no dividends.

Determine the missing lettered items.

Show Me How

EX 15-15 Fair value journal entries, trading investments **OBJ. 3, 4**

The investments of Charger Inc. include a single investment: 14,500 shares of Raiders Inc. common stock purchased on February 24, Year 1, for $38 per share including brokerage commission. These shares were classified as trading securities. As of the December 31, Year 1, balance sheet date, the share price had increased to $42 per share.

a. Journalize the entries to acquire the investment on February 24 and record the adjustment to fair value on December 31, Year 1.

b. How is the unrealized gain or loss for trading investments reported on the financial statements?

Show Me How

EX 15-16 Fair value journal entries, trading investments **OBJ. 3, 4**

Gruden Bancorp Inc. purchased a portfolio of trading securities during Year 1. The cost and fair value of this portfolio on December 31, Year 1, was as follows:

Name	Number of Shares	Total Cost	Total Fair Value
Griffin Inc.	1,600	$ 40,000	$ 44,800
Luck Company	1,250	37,500	33,750
Wilson Company	1,000	40,000	37,000
Total		$117,500	$115,550

On May 10, Year 2, Gruden Bancorp Inc. purchased 1,200 shares of Carroll Inc. at $29 per share plus a $100 brokerage commission.

Provide the journal entries to record the following:

a. The adjustment of the trading security portfolio to fair value on December 31, Year 1.

b. The May 10, Year 2, purchase of Carroll Inc. stock.

✔ a. Dec. 31, Year 1, Unrealized gain on trading investments, $17,500

Excel

EX 15-17 Fair value journal entries, trading investments **OBJ. 3, 4**

Last Unguaranteed Financial Inc. purchased the following trading securities during Year 1, its first year of operations:

Name	Number of Shares	Cost
Arden Enterprises Inc.	5,000	$150,000
French Broad Industries Inc.	2,750	66,000
Pisgah Construction Inc.	1,600	104,000
Total		$320,000

The market price per share for the trading security portfolio on December 31, Year 1, was as follows:

	Market Price per Share, Dec. 31, Year 1
Arden Enterprises Inc.	$34
French Broad Industries Inc.	26
Pisgah Construction Inc.	60

a. Provide the journal entry to adjust the trading security portfolio to fair value on December 31, Year 1.

b. Assume that the market prices of the portfolio were the same on December 31, Year 2, as they were on December 31, Year 1. What would be the journal entry to adjust the portfolio to fair value?

EX 15-18 Balance sheet presentation, trading investments **OBJ. 4**

The income statement for Delta-tec Inc. for the year ended December 31, Year 2, was as follows:

Delta-tec Inc.
Income Statement (selected items)
For the Year Ended December 31, Year 2

Income from operations	$299,700
Gain on sale of investments	17,800
Unrealized loss on trading investments	(72,500)
Net income	$245,000

The balance sheet dated December 31, Year 1, showed a Retained Earnings balance of $825,000. During Year 2, the company purchased trading investments for the first time at a cost of $346,000. In addition, trading investments with a cost of $66,000 were sold at a gain during Year 2. The company paid $65,000 in dividends during Year 2.

a. Determine the December 31, Year 2, Retained Earnings balance.

b. Provide the December 31, Year 2, balance sheet presentation for Trading Investments.

EX 15-19 Missing statement items, available-for-sale securities **OBJ. 4**

✔ f. $(11,000)

Highland Industries Inc. makes investments in available-for-sale securities. Selected income statement items for the years ended December 31, Year 2 and Year 3, plus selected items from comparative balance sheets, are as follows:

Highland Industries Inc.
Selected Income Statement Items
For the Years Ended December 31, Year 2 and Year 3

	Year 2	Year 3
Operating income	a.	g.
Gain (loss) from sale of investments	$7,500	$(12,000)
Net income (loss)	b.	(21,000)

Highland Industries Inc.
Selected Balance Sheet Items
December 31, Year 1, Year 2, and Year 3

	Dec. 31, Year 1	Dec. 31, Year 2	Dec. 31, Year 3
Assets			
Available-for-sale investments, at cost	$ 90,000	$ 86,000	$102,000
Valuation allowance for available-for-sale investments	12,000	(11,000)	h.
Available-for-sale investments, at fair value	c.	e.	i.
Stockholders' Equity			
Unrealized gain (loss) on available-for-sale investments	d.	f.	(16,400)
Retained earnings	$175,400	$220,000	j.

There were no dividends.

Determine the missing lettered items.

EX 15-20 Fair value journal entries, available-for-sale investments **OBJ. 3, 4**

The investments of Steelers Inc. include a single investment: 33,100 shares of Bengals Inc. common stock purchased on September 12, Year 1, for $13 per share including brokerage commission. These shares were classified as available-for-sale securities. As of the December 31, Year 1, balance sheet date, the share price declined to $11 per share.

a. Journalize the entries to acquire the investment on September 12 and record the adjustment to fair value on December 31, Year 1.

b. How is the unrealized gain or loss for available-for-sale investments disclosed on the financial statements?

EX 15-21 Fair value journal entries, available-for-sale investments **OBJ. 3, 4**

Hurricane Inc. purchased a portfolio of available-for-sale securities in Year 1, its first year of operations. The cost and fair value of this portfolio on December 31, Year 1, was as follows:

Name	Number of Shares	Total Cost	Total Fair Value
Tornado Inc.	800	$14,000	$15,600
Tsunami Corp.	1,250	31,250	35,000
Typhoon Corp.	2,140	43,870	42,800
Total		$89,120	$93,400

On June 12, Year 2, Hurricane purchased 1,450 shares of Rogue Wave Inc. at $45 per share plus a $100 brokerage commission.

a. Provide the journal entries to record the following:

1. The adjustment of the available-for-sale security portfolio to fair value on December 31, Year 1.
2. The June 12, Year 2, purchase of Rogue Wave Inc. stock.

b. How are unrealized gains and losses treated differently for available-for-sale securities than for trading securities?

Excel

EX 15-22 Fair value journal entries, available-for-sale investments **OBJ. 3, 4**

Storm, Inc. purchased the following available-for-sale securities during Year 1, its first year of operations:

Name	Number of Shares	Cost
Dust Devil, Inc.	1,900	$ 81,700
Gale Co.	850	68,000
Whirlwind Co.	2,850	114,000
Total		$263,700

The market price per share for the available-for-sale security portfolio on December 31, Year 1, was as follows:

	Market Price per Share, Dec. 31, Year 1
Dust Devil, Inc.	$40
Gale Co.	75
Whirlwind Co.	42

a. Provide the journal entry to adjust the available-for-sale security portfolio to fair value on December 31, Year 1.

b. Describe the income statement impact from the December 31, Year 1, journal entry.

EX 15-23 Balance sheet presentation of available-for-sale investments **OBJ. 4**

During Year 1, its first year of operations, Galileo Company purchased two available-for-sale investments as follows:

Security	Shares Purchased	Cost
Hawking Inc.	900	$44,000
Pavlov Co.	1,780	38,000

Assume that as of December 31, Year 1, the Hawking Inc. stock had a market value of $50 per share and the Pavlov Co. stock had a market value of $24 per share. Galileo Company had net income of $300,000 and paid no dividends for the year ended December 31, Year 1. All of the available-for-sale investments are classified as current assets.

(Continued)

a. Prepare the Current Assets section of the balance sheet presentation for the available-for-sale investments.

b. Prepare the Stockholders' Equity section of the balance sheet to reflect the earnings and unrealized gain (loss) for the available-for-sale investments.

EX 15-24 Balance sheet presentation of available-for-sale investments **OBJ. 4**

During Year 2, Copernicus Corporation held a portfolio of available-for-sale securities having a cost of $185,000. There were no purchases or sales of investments during the year. The market values at the beginning and end of the year were $225,000 and $160,000, respectively. The net income for Year 2 was $180,000, and no dividends were paid during the year. The Stockholders' Equity section of the balance sheet was as follows on December 31, Year 1:

Copernicus Corporation
Stockholders' Equity
December 31, Year 1

Common stock	$ 50,000
Paid-in capital in excess of par	250,000
Retained earnings	340,000
Unrealized gain on available-for-sale investments	40,000
Total	$680,000

Prepare the Stockholders' Equity section of the balance sheet for December 31, Year 2.

EX 15-25 Dividend yield **OBJ. 6**

Real World
FAI

At the market close on May 12 of a recent year, McDonald's Corporation had a closing stock price of $129.51. In addition, McDonald's Corporation had a dividend per share of $3.56 during the previous year.

Determine McDonald's Corporation's dividend yield. Round to one decimal place.

EX 15-26 Dividend yield **OBJ. 6**

✔ a. Dec. 31, current year, 2.24%

Real World
FAI

The market price for Microsoft Corporation closed at $55.48 and $46.45 on December 31, current year, and previous year, respectively. The dividends per share were $1.24 for current year and $1.12 for previous year.

a. Determine the dividend yield for Microsoft on December 31, current year, and previous year. Round percentages to two decimal places.

b. Interpret these measures.

EX 15-27 Dividend yield **OBJ. 6**

Real World
FAI

eBay Inc. developed a web-based marketplace at www.ebay.com, in which individuals can buy and sell a variety of items. eBay also acquired PayPal, an online payments system that allows businesses and individuals to send and receive online payments securely. In a recent annual report, eBay published the following dividend policy:

We have never paid cash dividends on our stock and currently anticipate that we will continue to retain any future earnings for the foreseeable future.

Given eBay's dividend policy, why would investors be attracted to its stock?

Appendix
EX 15-28 Comprehensive income

On May 12, Year 1, Chewco Co. purchased 2,000 shares of Jedi Inc. for $112 per share, including the brokerage commission. The Jedi investment was classified as an available-for-sale security. On December 31, Year 1, the fair value of Jedi Inc. was $124 per share. The net income of Chewco Co. was $50,000 for Year 1.

Compute the comprehensive income for Chewco Co. for the year ended December 31, Year 1.

Appendix
EX 15-29 Comprehensive income

On December 31, Year 1, Valur Co. had the following available-for-sale investment disclosure within the Current Assets section of the balance sheet:

Available-for-sale investments (at cost)	$145,000
Plus valuation allowance for available-for-sale investments	40,000
Available-for-sale investments (at fair value)	$185,000

There were no purchases or sales of available-for-sale investments during Year 2. On December 31, Year 2, the fair value of the available-for-sale investment portfolio was $200,000. The net income of Valur Co. was $210,000 for Year 2.

Compute the comprehensive income for Valur Co. for the year ended December 31, Year 2.

Problems: Series A

General Ledger

Show Me How

PR 15-1A Debt investment transactions, available-for-sale valuation **OBJ. 2, 4**

Soto Industries Inc. is an athletic footware company that began operations on January 1, Year 1. The following transactions relate to debt investments acquired by Soto Industries Inc., which has a fiscal year ending on December 31:

Year 1

Apr. 1. Purchased $100,000 of Welch Co. 6%, 15-year bonds at their face amount plus accrued interest of $500. The bonds pay interest semiannually on March 1 and September 1.

June 1. Purchased $210,000 of Bailey 4%, 10-year bonds at their face amount plus accrued interest of $700. The bonds pay interest semiannually on May 1 and November 1.

Sept. 1. Received semiannual interest on the Welch Co. bonds.

30. Sold $40,000 of Welch Co. bonds at 97 plus accrued interest of $200.

Nov. 1. Received semiannual interest on the Bailey bonds.

Dec. 31. Accrued $1,200 interest on the Welch Co. bonds.

31. Accrued $1,400 interest on the Bailey bonds.

Year 2

Mar. 1. Received semiannual interest on the Welch Co. bonds.

May 1. Received semiannual interest on the Bailey bonds.

Instructions

1. Journalize the entries to record these transactions.
2. If the bond portfolio is classified as available for sale, what impact would this have on financial statement disclosure?

Excel

PR 15-2A Stock investment transactions, trading securities **OBJ. 3, 4**

Rios Financial Co. is a regional insurance company that began operations on January 1, Year 1. The following transactions relate to trading securities acquired by Rios Financial Co., which has a fiscal year ending on December 31:

Year 1

Feb. 1. Purchased 7,500 shares of Caldwell Inc. as a trading security at $50 per share plus a brokerage commission of $75.

May 1. Purchased 3,000 shares of Holland Inc. as a trading security at $42 plus a brokerage commission of $90.

(Continued)

July 1. Sold 4,500 shares of Caldwell Inc. for $46 per share less a $110 brokerage commission.

31. Received an annual dividend of $0.50 per share on Caldwell Inc. stock.

Dec. 31. The portfolio of trading securities was adjusted to fair values of $47 and $40 per share for Caldwell Inc. and Holland Inc., respectively.

Year 2

Apr. 1. Purchased 5,000 shares of Fuller Inc. as a trading security at $25 per share plus a $100 brokerage commission.

July 31. Received an annual dividend of $0.52 per share on Caldwell Inc. stock.

Oct. 14. Sold 1,000 shares of Fuller Inc. for $28 per share less a $110 brokerage commission.

Dec. 31. The portfolio of trading securities had a cost of $376,200 and a fair value of $420,000, requiring a debit balance in Valuation Allowance for Trading Investments of $43,800 ($420,000 − $376,200). Thus, the credit balance from December 31, Year 1, is to be adjusted to the new balance.

Instructions

1. Journalize the entries to record these transactions.
2. Prepare the investment-related current asset balance sheet presentation for Rios Financial Co. on December 31, Year 2.
3. How are unrealized gains or losses on trading investments presented in the financial statements of Rios Financial Co.?

PR 15-3A Stock investment transactions, equity method and available-for-sale securities OBJ. 3, 4

Excel

Forte Inc. produces and sells theater set designs and costumes. The company began operations on January 1, Year 1. The following transactions relate to securities acquired by Forte Inc., which has a fiscal year ending on December 31:

Year 1

Jan. 22. Purchased 22,000 shares of Sankal Inc. as an available-for-sale security at $18 per share, including the brokerage commission.

Mar. 8. Received a cash dividend of $0.22 per share on Sankal Inc. stock.

Sept. 8. A cash dividend of $0.25 per share was received on the Sankal stock.

Oct. 17. Sold 3,000 shares of Sankal Inc. stock at $16 per share less a brokerage commission of $75.

Dec. 31. Sankal Inc. is classified as an available-for-sale investment and is adjusted to a fair value of $25 per share. Use the valuation allowance for available-for-sale investments account in making the adjustment.

Year 2

Jan. 10. Purchased an influential interest in Imboden Inc. for $720,000 by purchasing 96,000 shares directly from the estate of the founder of Imboden Inc. There are 300,000 shares of Imboden Inc. stock outstanding.

Mar. 10. Received a cash dividend of $0.30 per share on Sankal Inc. stock.

Sept. 12. Received a cash dividend of $0.25 per share plus an extra dividend of $0.05 per share on Sankal Inc. stock.

Dec. 31. Received $57,600 of cash dividends on Imboden Inc. stock. Imboden Inc. reported net income of $450,000 in Year 2. Forte Inc. uses the equity method of accounting for its investment in Imboden Inc.

31. Sankal Inc. is classified as an available-for-sale investment and is adjusted to a fair value of $22 per share. Use the valuation allowance for available-for-sale investments account in making the adjustment for the decrease in fair value from $25 to $22 per share.

Instructions

1. Journalize the entries to record these transactions.
2. Prepare the investment-related asset and stockholders' equity balance sheet presentation for Forte Inc. on December 31, Year 2, assuming that the Retained Earnings balance on December 31, Year 2, is $389,000.

PR 15-4A Investment reporting

OBJ. 2, 3, 4

✔ h. $(5,800)

Excel

O'Brien Industries Inc. is a book publisher. The comparative unclassified balance sheets for December 31, Year 2 and Year 1 follow. Selected missing balances are shown by letters.

O'Brien Industries Inc.
Balance Sheet
December 31, Year 2 and Year 1

	Dec. 31, Year 2	Dec. 31, Year 1
Cash	$233,000	$220,000
Accounts receivable (net)	136,530	138,000
Available-for-sale investments (at cost)—Note 1	$ a.	$103,770
Less valuation allowance for available-for-sale investments	b.	2,500
Available-for-sale investments (fair value)	$ c.	$101,270
Interest receivable	$ d.	—
Investment in Jolly Roger Co. stock—Note 2	e.	$ 77,000
Office equipment (net)	115,000	130,000
Total assets	$ f.	$666,270
Accounts payable	$ 69,400	$ 65,000
Common stock	70,000	70,000
Excess of issue price over par	225,000	225,000
Retained earnings	g.	308,770
Unrealized gain (loss) on available-for-sale investments	h.	(2,500)
Total liabilities and stockholders' equity	$ i.	$666,270

Note 1. Investments are classified as available for sale. The investments at cost and fair value on December 31, Year 1, are as follows:

	No. of Shares	Cost per Share	Total Cost	Total Fair Value
Bernard Co. stock	2,250	$17	$ 38,250	$ 37,500
Chadwick Co. stock	1,260	52	65,520	63,770
			$103,770	$101,270

Note 2. The investment in Jolly Roger Co. stock is an equity method investment representing 30% of the outstanding shares of Jolly Roger Co.

The following selected investment transactions occurred during Year 2:

May 5. Purchased 3,080 shares of Gozar Inc. at $30 per share including brokerage commission. Gozar Inc. is classified as an available-for-sale security.

Oct. 1. Purchased $40,000 of Nightline Co. 6%, 10-year bonds at 100. The bonds are classified as available for sale. The bonds pay interest on October 1 and April 1.

9. Dividends of $12,500 are received on the Jolly Roger Co. investment.

Dec. 31. Jolly Roger Co. reported a total net income of $112,000 for Year 2. O'Brien Industries Inc. recorded equity earnings for its share of Jolly Roger Co. net income.

31. Accrued three months of interest on the Nightline bonds.

31. Adjusted the available-for-sale investment portfolio to fair value, using the following fair value per-share amounts:

Available-for-Sale Investments	Fair Value
Bernard Co. stock	$15.40 per share
Chadwick Co. stock	$46.00 per share
Gozar Inc. stock	$32.00 per share
Nightline Co. bonds	$98 per $100 of face amount

(Continued)

Dec. 31. Closed the O'Brien Industries Inc. net income of $146,230. O'Brien Industries Inc. paid no dividends during the year.

Instructions

Determine the missing letters in the unclassified balance sheet. Provide appropriate supporting calculations.

Problems: Series B

PR 15-1B Debt investment transactions, available-for-sale valuation — OBJ. 2, 4

General Ledger

Show Me How

Rekya Mart Inc. is a general merchandise retail company that began operations on January 1, Year 1. The following transactions relate to debt investments acquired by Rekya Mart Inc., which has a fiscal year ending on December 31:

Year 1

Apr. 1. Purchased $90,000 of Smoke Bay 6%, 10-year bonds at their face amount plus accrued interest of $900. The bonds pay interest semiannually on February 1 and August 1.

May 16. Purchased $42,000 of Geotherma Co. 4%, 12-year bonds at their face amount plus accrued interest of $70. The bonds pay interest semiannually on May 1 and November 1.

Aug. 1. Received semiannual interest on the Smoke Bay bonds.

Sept. 1. Sold $12,000 of Smoke Bay bonds at 101 plus accrued interest of $60.

Nov. 1. Received semiannual interest on the Geotherma Co. bonds.

Dec. 31. Accrued $1,950 interest on the Smoke Bay bonds.

31. Accrued $280 interest on the Geotherma Co. bonds.

Year 2

Feb. 1. Received semiannual interest on the Smoke Bay bonds.

May 1. Received semiannual interest on the Geotherma Co. bonds.

Instructions

1. Journalize the entries to record these transactions.
2. If the bond portfolio is classified as available for sale, what impact would this have on financial statement disclosure?

PR 15-2B Stock investment transactions, trading securities — OBJ. 3, 4

Excel

Zeus Investments Inc. is a regional investment company that began operations on January 1, Year 1. The following transactions relate to trading securities acquired by Zeus Investments Inc., which has a fiscal year ending on December 31:

Year 1

Feb. 14. Purchased 4,800 shares of Apollo Inc. as a trading security at $26 per share plus a brokerage commission of $192.

Apr. 1. Purchased 2,300 shares of Ares Inc. as a trading security at $19 per share plus a brokerage commission of $92.

June 1. Sold 600 shares of Apollo Inc. for $32 per share less a $100 brokerage commission.

27. Received an annual dividend of $0.20 per share on Apollo Inc. stock.

Dec. 31. The portfolio of trading securities was adjusted to fair values of $33 and $18.50 per share for Apollo Inc. and Ares Inc., respectively.

Year 2

Mar. 14. Purchased 1,200 shares of Athena Inc. as a trading security at $65 per share plus a $120 brokerage commission.

June 26. Received an annual dividend of $0.21 per share on Apollo Inc. stock.

July 30. Sold 480 shares of Athena Inc. for $60 per share less a $50 brokerage commission.

Dec. 31. The portfolio of trading securities had a cost of $200,032 and a fair value of $188,000, requiring a credit balance in Valuation Allowance for Trading Investments of $12,032 ($188,000 – $200,032). Thus, the debit balance from December 31, Year 1, is to be adjusted to the new balance.

Instructions

1. Journalize the entries to record these transactions.
2. Prepare the investment-related current asset balance sheet presentation for Zeus Investments Inc. on December 31, Year 2.
3. How are unrealized gains or losses on trading investments presented in the financial statements of Zeus Investments Inc.?

PR 15-3B Stock investment transactions, equity method and available-for-sale securities

OBJ. 3, 4

Excel

Glacier Products Inc. is a wholesaler of rock climbing gear. The company began operations on January 1, Year 1. The following transactions relate to securities acquired by Glacier Products Inc., which has a fiscal year ending on December 31:

Year 1

Jan. 18. Purchased 9,000 shares of Malmo Inc. as an available-for-sale investment at $40 per share, including the brokerage commission.

July 22. A cash dividend of $3 per share was received on the Malmo stock.

Oct. 5. Sold 500 shares of Malmo Inc. stock at $58 per share less a brokerage commission of $100.

Dec. 18. Received a regular cash dividend of $30 per share on Malmo Inc. stock.

31. Malmo Inc. is classified as an available-for-sale investment and is adjusted to a fair value of $36 per share. Use the valuation allowance for available-for-sale investments account in making the adjustment.

Year 2

Jan. 25. Purchased an influential interest in Helsi Co. for $800,000 by purchasing 75,000 shares directly from the estate of the founder of Helsi. There are 250,000 shares of Helsi Co. stock outstanding.

July 16. Received a cash dividend of $3 per share on Malmo Inc. stock.

Dec. 16. Received a cash dividend of $3 per share plus an extra dividend of $0.20 per share on Malmo Inc. stock.

31. Received $38,000 of cash dividends on Helsi Co. stock. Helsi Co. reported net income of $170,000 in Year 2. Glacier Products Inc. uses the equity method of accounting for its investment in Helsi Co.

31. Malmo Inc. is classified as an available-for-sale investment and is adjusted to a fair value of $44 per share. Use the valuation allowance for available-for-sale investments account in making the adjustment for the increase in fair value from $36 to $44 per share.

Instructions

1. Journalize the entries to record the preceding transactions.
2. Prepare the investment-related asset and stockholders' equity balance sheet presentation for Glacier Products Inc. on December 31, Year 2, assuming that the Retained Earnings balance on December 31, Year 2, is $700,000.

PR 15-4B Investment reporting

OBJ. 2, 3, 4

✔ b. $4,680

Excel

Teasdale Inc. manufactures and sells commercial and residential security equipment. The comparative unclassified balance sheets for December 31, Year 2 and Year 1 are provided below. Selected missing balances are shown by letters.

Teasdale Inc.
Balance Sheet
December 31, Year 2 and Year 1

	Dec. 31, Year 2	Dec. 31, Year 1
Cash	$160,000	$156,000
Accounts receivable (net)	115,000	108,000
Available-for-sale investments (at cost)—Note 1	$ a.	$ 91,200
Plus valuation allowance for available-for-sale investments	b.	8,776
Available-for-sale investments (fair value)	$ c.	$ 99,976
Interest receivable	$ d.	—
Investment in Wright Co. stock—Note 2	e.	$ 69,200
Office equipment (net)	96,000	105,000
Total assets	$ f.	$538,176
Accounts payable	$ 91,000	$ 72,000
Common stock	80,000	80,000
Excess of issue price over par	250,000	250,000
Retained earnings	g.	127,400
Unrealized gain (loss) on available-for-sale investments	h.	8,776
Total liabilities and stockholders' equity	$ i.	$538,176

Note 1. Investments are classified as available for sale. The investments at cost and fair value on December 31, Year 1, are as follows:

	No. of Shares	Cost per Share	Total Cost	Total Fair Value
Alvarez Inc. stock	960	$38.00	$36,480	$39,936
Hirsch Inc. stock	1,900	28.80	54,720	60,040
			$91,200	$99,976

Note 2. The Investment in Wright Co. stock is an equity method investment representing 30% of the outstanding shares of Wright Co.

The following selected investment transactions occurred during Year 2:

Mar. 18. Purchased 800 shares of Richter Inc. at $40, including brokerage commission. Richter is classified as an available-for-sale security.

July 12. Dividends of $12,000 are received on the Wright Co. investment.

Oct. 1. Purchased $24,000 of Toon Co. 4%, 10-year bonds at 100. The bonds are classified as available for sale. The bonds pay interest on October 1 and April 1.

Dec. 31. Wright Co. reported a total net income of $80,000 for Year 2. Teasdale recorded equity earnings for its share of Wright Co. net income.

31. Accrued interest for three months on the Toon Co. bonds purchased on October 1.

31. Adjusted the available-for-sale investment portfolio to fair value, using the following fair value per-share amounts:

Available-for-Sale Investments	Fair Value
Alvarez Inc. stock	$41.50 per share
Hirsch Inc. stock	$26.00 per share
Richter Inc. stock	$48.00 per share
Toon Co. bonds	101 per $100 of face amount

31. Closed the Teasdale Inc. net income of $51,240. Teasdale Inc. paid no dividends during the year.

Instructions

Determine the missing letters in the unclassified balance sheet. Provide appropriate supporting calculations.

Comprehensive Problem 4

General Ledger

Selected transactions completed by Equinox Products Inc. during the fiscal year ended December 31, Year 1, were as follows:

a. Issued 15,000 shares of $20 par common stock at $30, receiving cash.

b. Issued 4,000 shares of $80 par preferred 5% stock at $100, receiving cash.

c. Issued $500,000 of 10-year, 5% bonds at 104, with interest payable semiannually.

d. Declared a quarterly dividend of $0.50 per share on common stock and $1.00 per share on preferred stock. On the date of record, 100,000 shares of common stock were outstanding, no treasury shares were held and 20,000 shares of preferred stock were outstanding.

e. Paid the cash dividends declared in (d).

f. Purchased 7,500 shares of Solstice Corp. at $40 per share plus a $150 brokerage commission. The investment is classified as an available-for-sale investment.

g. Purchased 8,000 shares of treasury common stock at $33 per share.

h. Purchased 40,000 shares of Pinkberry Co. stock directly from the founders for $24 per share. Pinkberry has 125,000 shares issued and outstanding. Equinox Products Inc. treated the investment as an equity method investment.

i. Declared a $1.00 quarterly cash dividend per share on preferred stock. On the date of record, 20,000 shares of preferred stock had been issued.

j. Paid the cash dividends to the preferred stockholders.

k. Received $27,500 dividend from Pinkberry Co. investment in (h).

l. Purchased $90,000 of Dream Inc. 10-year, 5% bonds, directly from the issuing company, at their face amount plus accrued interest of $375. The bonds are classified as a held-to-maturity long-term investment.

m. Sold, at $38 per share, 2,600 shares of treasury common stock purchased in (g).

n. Received a dividend of $0.60 per share from the Solstice Corp. investment in (f).

o. Sold 1,000 shares of Solstice Corp. at $45, including commission.

p. Recorded the payment of semiannual interest on the bonds issued in (c) and the amortization of the premium for six months. The amortization is determined using the straight-line method.

q. Accrued interest for three months on the Dream Inc. bonds purchased in (l).

r. Pinkberry Co. recorded total earnings of $240,000. Equinox Products recorded equity earnings for its share of Pinkberry Co. net income.

s. The fair value for Solstice Corp. stock was $39.02 per share on December 31, Year 1. The investment is adjusted to fair value, using a valuation allowance account. Assume that Valuation Allowance for Available-for-Sale Investments had a beginning balance of zero.

Instructions

1. Journalize the selected transactions.
2. After all of the transactions for the year ended December 31, Year 1, had been posted [including the transactions recorded in part (1) and all adjusting entries], the data that follows were taken from the records of Equinox Products Inc.
   a. Prepare a multiple-step income statement for the year ended December 31, Year 1, concluding with earnings per share. In computing earnings per share, assume that the average number of common shares outstanding was 100,000 and preferred dividends were $100,000. Round earnings per share to the nearest cent.
   b. Prepare a retained earnings statement for the year ended December 31, Year 1.
   c. Prepare a balance sheet in report form as of December 31, Year 1.

(Continued)

Income statement data:	
Advertising expense	$ 150,000
Cost of merchandise sold	3,700,000
Delivery expense	30,000
Depreciation expense—office buildings and equipment	30,000
Depreciation expense—store buildings and equipment	100,000
Dividend revenue	4,500
Gain on sale of investment	4,980
Income from Pinkberry Co. investment	76,800
Income tax expense	140,500
Interest expense	21,000
Interest revenue	2,720
Miscellaneous administrative expense	7,500
Miscellaneous selling expense	14,000
Office rent expense	50,000
Office salaries expense	170,000
Office supplies expense	10,000
Sales	5,254,000
Sales commissions	185,000
Sales salaries expense	385,000
Store supplies expense	21,000

Retained earnings and balance sheet data:	
Accounts payable	$ 194,300
Accounts receivable	545,000
Accumulated depreciation—office buildings and equipment	1,580,000
Accumulated depreciation—store buildings and equipment	4,126,000
Allowance for doubtful accounts	8,450
Available-for-sale investments (at cost)	260,130
Bonds payable, 5%, due 20Y2	500,000
Cash	246,000
Common stock, $20 par (400,000 shares authorized; 100,000 shares issued, 94,600 outstanding)	2,000,000
Dividends:	
Cash dividends for common stock	155,120
Cash dividends for preferred stock	100,000
Goodwill	500,000
Income tax payable	44,000
Interest receivable	1,125
Investment in Pinkberry Co. stock (equity method)	1,009,300
Investment in Dream Inc. bonds (long term)	90,000
Merchandise inventory (December 31, Year 1), at lower of cost (FIFO) or market	778,000
Office buildings and equipment	4,320,000
Paid-in capital from sale of treasury stock	13,000
Excess of issue price over par—common stock	886,800
Excess of issue price over par—preferred stock	150,000
Preferred 5% stock, $80 par (30,000 shares authorized; 20,000 shares issued)	1,600,000
Premium on bonds payable	19,000
Prepaid expenses	27,400
Retained earnings, January 1, Year 1	9,319,725
Store buildings and equipment	12,560,000
Treasury stock (5,400 shares of common stock at cost of $33 per share)	178,200
Unrealized gain (loss) on available-for-sale investments	(6,500)
Valuation allowance for available-for-sale investments	(6,500)

Cases & Projects

Ethics

CP 15-1 Ethics in Action

Financial assets include stocks and bonds. These are fairly simple securities that can often be valued using quoted market prices. However, there are more complex financial instruments that do not have quoted market prices. These complex securities must still be valued on the balance sheet at fair value. Generally accepted accounting principles require that the reporting entity use assumptions in valuing investments when market prices or critical valuation inputs are unobservable.

What are the ethical considerations in making subjective valuations of these complex financial instruments?

Real World

CP 15-2 Reporting investments

Group Project

In groups of three or four, find the latest annual report for Microsoft Corporation. The annual report can be found on the company's website at www.microsoft.com/msft/default.mspx.

The notes to the financial statements include details of Microsoft's investments. Find the notes that provide details of its investments (Note 4) and the income from its investments (Note 3).

From these disclosures, answer the following questions:

1. What is the total cost of investments?
2. What is the fair value (recorded value) of investments?
3. What is the total unrealized gain from investments?
4. What is the total unrealized loss from investments?
5. What percent of total investments (at fair value) are:
   a. Cash and equivalents?
   b. Short-term investments?
   c. Equity and other investments (long term)?
6. What was the total combined dividend and interest revenue?
7. What was the recognized net gain or loss from sale of investments?

Real World

CP 15-3 Warren Buffett and "look-through" earnings

Berkshire Hathaway, the investment holding company of Warren Buffett, reports its "less than 20% ownership" investments according to generally accepted accounting principles. However, it also provides additional disclosures that it terms "look-through" earnings.

Warren Buffett states,

Many of these companies (in the less than 20%-owned category) pay out relatively small proportions of their earnings in dividends. This means that only a small proportion of their earning power is recorded in our own current operating earnings. But, while our reported operating earnings reflect only the dividends received from such companies, our economic well-being is determined by their earnings, not their dividends.

The value to Berkshire Hathaway of retained earnings (of our investees) is not determined by whether we own 100%, 50%, 20%, or 1% of the businesses in which they reside. . . . Our perspective on such "forgotten-but-not-gone" earnings is simple: the way they are accounted for is of no importance, but their ownership and subsequent utilization is all-important. We care not whether the auditors hear a tree fall in the forest; we do care who owns the tree and what's next done with it.

I believe the best way to think about our earnings is in terms of "look-through" results, calculated as follows: Take $250 million, which is roughly our share of the operating earnings retained by our investees (<20% ownership holdings); subtract . . . incremental taxes we would have owed had that $250 million been paid to us in dividends; then add the remainder, $220 million, to our reported earnings of $371 million. Thus, our "look-through" earnings were about $590 million.

Source: Warren Buffett, *The Essays of Warren Buffett: Lessons for Corporate America*, edited by Lawrence A. Cunningham, pp. 180–183 (excerpted).

Write a brief memo to your instructor, explaining look through-earnings and why Mr. Buffet favors look-through earnings.

CP 15-4 Benefits of fair value

On July 16, 20Y1, Wyatt Corp. purchased 40 acres of land for $350,000. The land has been held for a future plant site until the current date, December 31, 20Y9. On December 18, 20Y9, TexoPete Inc. purchased 40 acres of land for $2,000,000 to be used for a distribution center. The TexoPete land is located next to the Wyatt Corp. land. Thus, both Wyatt Corp. and TexoPete Inc. own nearly identical pieces of land.

1. What are the valuations of land on the balance sheets of Wyatt Corp. and TexoPete Inc. using generally accepted accounting principles?
2. How might fair value accounting aid comparability when evaluating these two companies?

CP 15-5 International fair value accounting

IFRS

International Financial Reporting Standard No. 16 provides companies the option of valuing property, plant, and equipment at either historical cost or fair value. If fair value is selected, then the property, plant, and equipment must be revalued periodically to fair value. Under fair value, if there is an increase in the value of the property, plant, and equipment during the reporting period, then the increase is credited to stockholders' equity. However, if there is a decrease in fair value, then the decrease is reported as an expense for the period.

How is the international accounting treatment for changes in fair value for property, plant, and equipment similar to investments?

CHAPTER 16

Statement of Cash Flows

Chapters 1–4
Accounting Cycle

Chapter 5
Accounting Systems

Income Statement	**Retained Earnings Statement**	**Balance Sheet**	**Statement of Cash Flows**
Chapter 6 *Accounting for Merchandising Businesses*			**Chapter 16 Statement of Cash Flows**

Assets	=	**Liabilities**	+	**Stockholders' Equity**
Chapter 8 *Cash* Chapter 9 *Receivables* Chapter 7 *Inventories* Chapter 10 *Fixed and Intangible Assets* Chapter 15 *Investments*		Chapter 11 *Current Liabilities and Payroll* Chapter 14 *Bonds and Notes*		Chapter 12 *Partnerships* Chapter 13 *Corporations*

Chapter 17
Financial Statement Analysis

Retained Earnings Statement

Retained earnings, Jan. 1		$XXX
Net income	$ XXX	
Dividends	(XXX)	
…		…XX
…		…X

Income Statement

Sales		$XXX
Cost of merchandise sold		XXX
Gross profit		$XXX
Operating expenses:		
Advertising expense	$XXX	
Depreciation expense	XXX	
Wages expense	XXX	
Utilities expense	XXX	
…	XXX	
…	XXX	
Total operating expenses		XXX
Income from operations		$XXX
Other revenue and expenses		XXX
Net income		$XXX

Statement of Cash Flows

Cash flows from operating activities	$XXX
Cash flows from (used for) investing activities	XXX
Cash flows from (used for) financing activities	XXX
Increase (decrease) in cash	$XXX
Cash, January 1	XXX
Cash, December 31	$XXX

Cur…		
Ca…		
Ac…		
In…		
Property, plant, and equipment	$XXX	
Intangible assets	XXX	
Total long-term assets		XXX
Total assets		$XXX
Liabilities:		
Current liabilities	$XXX	
Long-term liabilities	XXX	
Total liabilities		$XXX
Stockholders' equity:		
Retained earnings	$XXX	
Common stock	XXX	
Total stockholders' equity		XXX
Total liabilities and stockholders' equity		$XXX

CHAPTER

16

National Beverage Co.

Suppose you receive $100 from an event. Does it make a difference what the event was? Yes, it does! If you receive $100 for your birthday, then it's a gift. If you receive $100 as a result of working part-time for a week, then it's from earnings. If you receive $100 as a loan, then it's money that you will have to pay back in the future. If you sell your iPod for $100, then it's the result of selling an asset. These examples illustrate that not all cash flows are the same, and the source of the cash has different meanings and implications for your future. You would much rather receive a $100 gift than take out a $100 loan. Likewise, company stakeholders view inflows and outflows of cash differently, depending on their source.

Companies are required to report information about the events causing a change in cash over a period of time. This information is reported in the statement of cash flows. One such company is **National Beverage**, which is known for its innovative soft drinks and alternative beverages. You have probably seen the company's **Shasta** and **Faygo** soft drinks or **LaCroix**, **Everfresh**, and **Crystal Bay** drinks at your local grocery or convenience store. As with any company, cash is important to National Beverage. Without cash, National Beverage would be unable to expand its brands, distribute its product, support extreme sports, or provide a return for its owners. Thus, its managers are concerned about the sources and uses of cash.

In previous chapters, we used the income statement, balance sheet, statement of retained earnings, and other information to analyze the effects of management decisions on a business's financial position and operating performance. In this chapter, we focus on the events causing a change in cash by presenting the preparation and use of the statement of cash flows.

Learning Objectives

After studying this chapter, you should be able to:

Example Exercises (EE) are shown in **green.**

Obj. 1 **Describe the cash flow activities reported in the statement of cash flows.**

Reporting Cash Flows

Cash Flows from Operating Activities	EE **16-1**
Cash Flows from (used for) Investing Activities	EE **16-1**
Cash Flows from (used for) Financing Activities	EE **16-1**
Noncash Investing and Financing Activities	
Format of the Statement of Cash Flows	
No Cash Flow per Share	

Obj. 2 **Prepare a statement of cash flows, using the indirect method.**

Preparing the Statement of Cash Flows—The Indirect Method

Net Income	
Adjustments to Net Income	EE **16-2, 3, 4**
Dividends and Dividends Payable	
Common Stock	
Bonds Payable	
Building and Accumulated Depreciation—Building	
Land	EE **16-5**
Preparing the Statement of Cash Flows	

Obj. 3 **Prepare a statement of cash flows, using the direct method.**

Preparing the Statement of Cash Flows—The Direct Method

Cash Received from Customers	EE **16-6**
Cash Payments for Merchandise	EE **16-7**
Cash Payments for Operating Expenses	
Gain on Sale of Land	
Interest Expense	
Cash Payments for Income Taxes	
Reporting Cash Flows from Operating Activities—Direct Method	

Obj. 4 **Describe and illustrate the use of free cash flow in evaluating a company's cash flow.**

Financial Analysis and Interpretation: Free Cash Flow

Compute Free Cash Flow	EE **16-8**

At a Glance 16 Page 792

Reporting Cash Flows

Obj. 1 Describe the cash flow activities reported in the statement of cash flows.

The **statement of cash flows** reports a company's cash inflows and outflows for a period.[1] The statement of cash flows provides useful information about a company's ability to do the following:

- Generate cash from operations
- Maintain and expand its operating capacity
- Meet its financial obligations
- Pay dividends

The statement of cash flows is used by managers in evaluating past operations and in planning future investing and financing activities. It is also used by external users such as investors and creditors to assess a company's profit potential and ability to pay its debt and to pay dividends.

The statement of cash flows reports three types of cash flow activities, as follows:

1. **Cash flows from operating activities** are the cash flows from transactions that affect the net income of the company.

   Example: Purchase and sale of merchandise by a retailer.
2. **Cash flows from (used for) investing activities** are the cash flows received from or used for transactions that affect investments in the noncurrent assets of the company.

   Example: Purchase and sale of fixed assets, such as equipment and buildings.

Note

The statement of cash flows reports cash flows from operating, investing, and financing activities.

1 As used in this chapter, *cash* refers to cash and cash equivalents. Examples of cash equivalents include short-term, highly liquid investments such as money market accounts, bank certificates of deposit, and U.S. Treasury bills.

3. **Cash flows from (used for) financing activities** are the cash flows received from or used for transactions that affect the debt and equity of the company.

   Example: Issuing or retiring equity and debt securities.

The cash flows are reported in the statement of cash flows as follows:

Cash flows from operating activities	$XXX
Cash flows from (used for) investing activities	XXX
Cash flows from (used for) financing activities	XXX
Increase (decrease) in cash	$XXX
Cash at the beginning of the period	XXX
Cash at the end of the period	$XXX

The ending cash on the statement of cash flows equals the cash reported on the company's balance sheet at the end of the year.

Exhibit 1 illustrates the sources (increases) and uses (decreases) of cash by each of the three cash flow activities. A *source* of cash causes the cash flow to increase and is called a *cash inflow*. A *use* of cash causes cash flow to decrease and is called *cash outflow*.

EXHIBIT 1 **Sources and Uses of Cash**

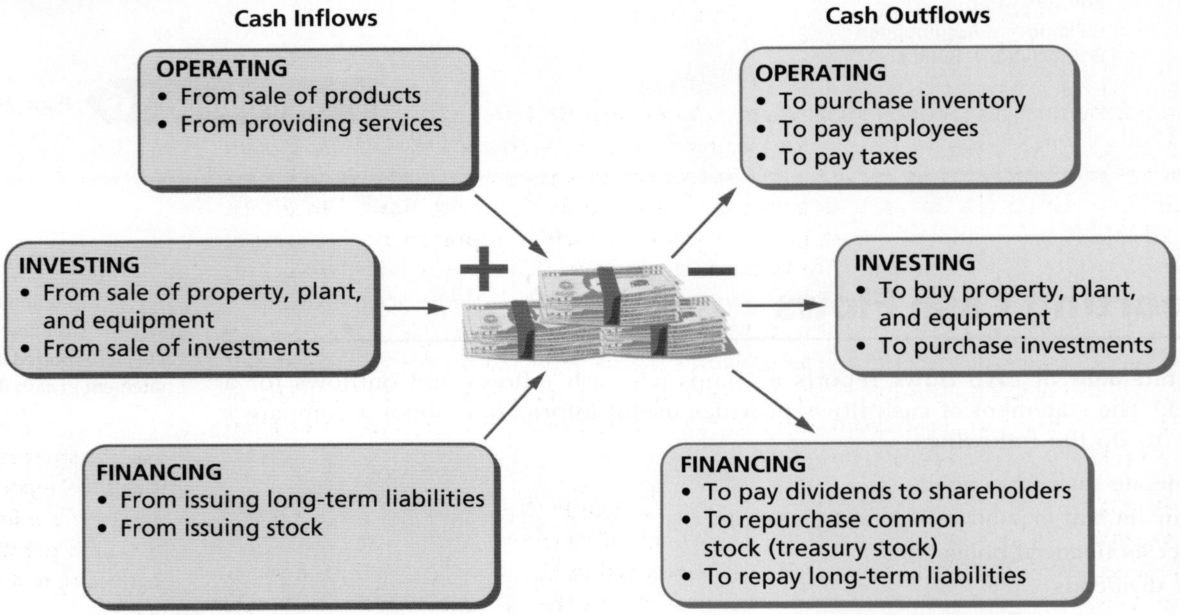

Cash Flows from Operating Activities

Cash flows from operating activities reports the cash inflows and outflows from a company's day-to-day operations. Companies may select one of two alternative methods for reporting cash flows from operating activities in the statement of cash flows:

- The direct method
- The indirect method

Both methods result in the same amount of cash flows from operating activities. They differ in the way they report cash flows from operating activities.

The Direct Method The **direct method** reports operating cash inflows (receipts) and cash outflows (payments) as follows:

Cash flows from operating activities:		
Cash received from customers	$ XXX	
Cash payments for merchandise	(XXX)	
Cash payments for operating expenses	(XXX)	
Cash payments for interest	(XXX)	
Cash payments for income taxes	(XXX)	
Net cash flow from operating activities		$XXX

The primary operating cash inflow is cash received from customers. The primary operating cash outflows are cash payments for merchandise, operating expenses, interest, and income tax payments. The cash received from operating activities less the cash payments for operating activities is the net cash flow from operating activities.

The primary advantage of the direct method is that it *directly* reports cash receipts and cash payments in the statement of cash flows. Its primary disadvantage is that these data may not be readily available in the accounting records. Thus, the direct method is normally more costly to prepare and, as a result, is used infrequently in practice.

The Indirect Method The **indirect method** reports cash flows from operating activities by beginning with net income and adjusting it for revenues and expenses that do not involve the receipt or payment of cash, as follows:

Cash flows from operating activities:		
Net income	$XXX	
Adjustments to reconcile net income to net cash flow from operating activities	XXX	
Net cash flow from operating activities		$XXX

The adjustments to reconcile net income to net cash flow from operating activities include such items as depreciation and gains or losses on fixed assets. Changes in current operating assets and liabilities such as accounts receivable or accounts payable are also added or deducted, depending on their effect on cash flows.[2] In effect, these additions and deductions adjust net income, which is reported on an accrual accounting basis, to cash flows from operating activities, which is a cash basis.

A primary advantage of the indirect method is that it reconciles the differences between net income and net cash flows from operations. In doing so, it shows how net income is related to the ending cash balance that is reported on the balance sheet.

Because the data are readily available, the indirect method is less costly to prepare than the direct method. As a result, the indirect method of reporting cash flows from operations is most commonly used in practice.

Link to National Beverage

National Beverage uses the indirect method of reporting the cash flows from operating activities in its statement of cash flows.

Comparing the Direct and Indirect Methods Exhibit 2 illustrates the Cash flows from operating activities section of the statement of cash flows for **NetSolutions**. Exhibit 2 shows the direct and indirect methods using the NetSolutions data from Chapter 1. As Exhibit 2 illustrates, both methods report the same amount of net cash flow from operating activities, $2,900.

Cash Flow from Operations: Direct and Indirect Methods—NetSolutions EXHIBIT 2

Direct Method

Cash flows from operating activities:	
Cash received from customers	$ 7,500
Cash payments for expenses and payments to creditors	(4,600)
Net cash flow from operating activities	$ 2,900

Indirect Method

Cash flows from operating activities:	
Net income	$3,050
Increase in accounts payable	400
Increase in supplies	(550)
Net cash flow from operating activities	$2,900

the same

2 Current operating assets include all current assets other than cash, and all current liabilities other than dividends payable.

Business Connection

CASH CRUNCH!

The Wet Seal, Inc., a young women's clothing retailer, filed for bankruptcy protection. The cash flows from operating activities for the three years prior to bankruptcy (in thousands) follow:

	Year 3	Year 2	Year 1
Cash provided (used in) operating activities	$(17,589)	$(26,191)	$61,900

As can be seen, cash flows from operating activities trended into negative territory during the two years prior to the firm's bankruptcy. Thus, when cash flows from operating activities are negative, it can lead to financial distress.

Cash Flows from (Used for) Investing Activities

Link to National Beverage

For a recent year, **National Beverage** reported net cash used in investing activities of $9,725,000.

Cash flows from (used for) investing activities show the cash inflows and outflows related to changes in a company's long-term assets. Cash flows from (used for) investing activities are reported on the statement of cash flows as follows:

Cash flows from (used for) investing activities:		
Cash from investing activities	$ XXX	
Cash used for investing activities	(XXX)	
Net cash flows from (used for) investing activities		$XXX

Cash inflows from investing activities normally arise when cash is received from selling fixed assets, investments, and intangible assets. Cash outflows normally include payments to purchase fixed assets, investments, and intangible assets.

Cash Flows from (Used for) Financing Activities

Link to National Beverage

For a recent year, **National Beverage** reported net cash used in financing activities of $25,771,000.

Cash flows from (used for) financing activities show the cash inflows and outflows related to changes in a company's long-term liabilities and stockholders' equity. Cash flows from (used for) financing activities are reported on the statement of cash flows as follows:

Cash flows from (used for) financing activities:		
Cash from financing activities	$ XXX	
Cash used for financing activities	(XXX)	
Net cash flow from (used for) financing activities		$XXX

Cash inflows from financing activities normally arise when cash is received from issuing long-term debt or equity securities. For example, issuing bonds, notes payable, preferred stock, and common stock creates cash inflows from financing activities. Cash outflows from financing activities include paying cash dividends, repaying long-term debt, and acquiring treasury stock.

Noncash Investing and Financing Activities

A company may enter into transactions involving investing and financing activities that do not *directly* affect cash. For example, a company may issue common stock to retire long-term debt. Although this transaction does not directly affect cash, it does eliminate future cash payments for interest and for paying the bonds when they mature. Because such transactions *indirectly* affect cash flows, they are reported in a separate section of the statement of cash flows. This section usually appears at the bottom of the statement of cash flows.

Format of the Statement of Cash Flows

The statement of cash flows presents the cash flows generated by, or used for, the three activities previously discussed: operating, investing, and financing. These three activities are always reported in the same order, following the format illustrated in Exhibit 3.

EXHIBIT 3

Format of the Statement of Cash Flows

COMPANY NAME
Statement of Cash Flows
For the Year Ended XXXX

Cash flows from operating activities:		
(List of individual items, as illustrated in Exhibit 1)	$XXX	
Net cash flows from operating activities		$XXX
Cash flows from (used for) investing activities:		
(List of individual items, as illustrated in Exhibit 1)	$XXX	
Net cash flows from (used for) investing activities		XXX
Cash flows from (used for) financing activities:		
(List of individual items, as illustrated in Exhibit 1)	$XXX	
Net cash flows from (used for) financing activities		XXX
Increase (decrease) in cash		$XXX
Cash at the beginning of the period		XXX
Cash at the end of the period		$XXX
Noncash investing and financing activites		$XXX

No Cash Flow per Share

Cash flow per share is sometimes reported in the financial press. As reported, cash flow per share is normally computed as *cash flow from operations divided by the number of common shares outstanding*. However, such reporting may be misleading because of the following:

- Users may misinterpret cash flow per share as the per-share amount available for dividends. This would not be the case if the cash generated by operations is required for repaying loans or for reinvesting in the business.
- Users may misinterpret cash flow per share as equivalent to (or better than) earnings per share.

For these reasons, the financial statements, including the statement of cash flows, should not report cash flow per share.

Example Exercise 16-1 Classifying Cash Flows — Obj. 1

Identify whether each of the following would be reported as an operating, investing, or financing activity in the statement of cash flows:

a. Purchase of patent
b. Payment of cash dividend
c. Disposal of equipment
d. Cash sales
e. Purchase of treasury stock
f. Payment of wages expense

Follow My Example 16-1

a. Investing
b. Financing
c. Investing
d. Operating
e. Financing
f. Operating

Practice Exercises: PE 16-1A, PE 16-1B

Obj. 2 Prepare a statement of cash flows, using the indirect method.

Preparing the Statement of Cash Flows—The Indirect Method

The indirect method of reporting cash flows from operating activities uses the logic that a change in any balance sheet account (including cash) can be analyzed in terms of changes in the other balance sheet accounts. Thus, by analyzing changes in noncash balance sheet accounts, any change in the cash account can be *indirectly* determined.

To illustrate, the accounting equation can be solved for cash as follows:

$$\text{Assets} = \text{Liabilities} + \text{Stockholders' Equity}$$
$$\text{Cash} + \text{Noncash Assets} = \text{Liabilities} + \text{Stockholders' Equity}$$
$$\text{Cash} = \text{Liabilities} + \text{Stockholders' Equity} - \text{Noncash Assets}$$

Therefore, any change in the cash account can be determined by analyzing changes in the liability, stockholders' equity, and noncash asset accounts as follows:

$$\textit{Change}\text{ in Cash} = \textit{Change}\text{ in Liabilities} + \textit{Change}\text{ in Stockholders' Equity} - \textit{Change}\text{ in Noncash Assets}$$

Under the indirect method, there is no order in which the balance sheet accounts must be analyzed. However, net income (or net loss) is the first amount reported on the statement of cash flows. Because net income (or net loss) is a component of any change in Retained Earnings, the first account normally analyzed is Retained Earnings.

To illustrate the indirect method, the income statement and comparative balance sheets for **Rundell Inc.**, shown in Exhibit 4, are used. Ledger accounts and other data supporting the income statement and balance sheet are presented as needed.[3]

EXHIBIT 4

Income Statement and Comparative Balance Sheet

Rundell Inc.
Income Statement
For the Year Ended December 31, 20Y8

Sales		$1,180,000
Cost of merchandise sold		790,000
Gross profit		$ 390,000
Operating expenses:		
Depreciation expense	$ 7,000	
Other operating expenses	196,000	
Total operating expenses		203,000
Income from operations		$ 187,000
Other revenue and expense:		
Gain on sale of land	$ 12,000	
Interest expense	(8,000)	4,000
Income before income tax		$ 191,000
Income tax expense		83,000
Net income		$ 108,000

3 An appendix that discusses using a spreadsheet (work sheet) as an aid in assembling data for the statement of cash flows is presented at the end of this chapter. This appendix illustrates the use of this spreadsheet in reporting cash flows from operating activities using the indirect method.

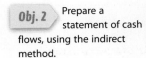

EXHIBIT 4

Income Statement and Comparative Balance Sheet (*Continued*)

Rundell Inc.
Comparative Balance Sheet
December 31, 20Y8 and 20Y7

	20Y8	20Y7	Increase (Decrease)
Assets			
Cash	$ 97,500	$ 26,000	$ 71,500
Accounts receivable (net)	74,000	65,000	9,000
Inventories	172,000	180,000	(8,000)
Land	80,000	125,000	(45,000)
Building	260,000	200,000	60,000
Accumulated depreciation—building	(65,300)	(58,300)	(7,000)*
Total assets	$618,200	$537,700	$ 80,500
Liabilities			
Accounts payable (merchandise creditors)	$ 43,500	$ 46,700	$ (3,200)
Accrued expenses payable (operating expenses)	26,500	24,300	2,200
Income taxes payable	7,900	8,400	(500)
Dividends payable	14,000	10,000	4,000
Bonds payable	100,000	150,000	(50,000)
Total liabilities	$191,900	$239,400	$ (47,500)
Stockholders' Equity			
Common stock ($2 par)	$ 24,000	$ 16,000	$ 8,000
Paid-in capital in excess of par	120,000	80,000	40,000
Retained earnings	282,300	202,300	80,000
Total stockholders' equity	$426,300	$298,300	$128,000
Total liabilities and stockholders' equity	$618,200	$537,700	$ 80,500

*There is a $7,000 increase to Accumulated Depreciation—Building, which is a contra asset account. As a result, the $7,000 increase in this account must be subtracted in summing to the increase in Total assets of $80,500.

Net Income

Rundell Inc.'s net income for 20Y8 is $108,000, as shown on the income statement in Exhibit 4. Since net income is closed to Retained Earnings, net income also helps explain the change in retained earnings during the year. The retained earnings account for Rundell is as follows:

Account *Retained Earnings* — Account No.

Date		Item	Debit	Credit	Balance Debit	Balance Credit
20Y8 Jan.	1	Balance				202,300
June	30	Dividends declared	14,000			188,300
Dec.	31	Net income		108,000		296,300
	31	Dividends declared	14,000			282,300

The retained earnings account indicates that the $80,000 ($108,000 – $28,000) change resulted from net income of $108,000 and cash dividends of $28,000. The net income of $108,000 is the first amount reported in the Cash flows from operating activities section. The impact of the dividends of $28,000 on cash flows will be included as part of financing activities.

Adjustments to Net Income

The net income of $108,000 reported by **Rundell Inc.** does not equal the cash flows from operating activities for the period. This is because net income is determined using the accrual method of accounting.

Under the accrual method of accounting, revenues and expenses are recorded at different times from when cash is received or paid. For example, merchandise may be sold on account and the cash received at a later date. Likewise, insurance premiums may be paid in the current period but expensed in a following period.

Thus, under the indirect method, adjustments to net income must be made to determine cash flows from operating activities. The typical adjustments to net income are shown in Exhibit 5.[4]

EXHIBIT 5 **Adjustments to Net Income (Loss) Using the Indirect Method**

		Increase (Decrease)
	Net income (loss)	$ XXX
	Adjustments to reconcile net income to net cash flow from operating activities:	
Step 1	Depreciation of fixed assets	XXX
Step 1	Amortization of intangible assets	XXX
Step 2	Losses on disposal of assets	XXX
Step 2	Gains on disposal of assets	(XXX)
Step 3	Changes in current operating assets and liabilities:	
	Increases in noncash current operating assets	(XXX)
	Decreases in noncash current operating assets	XXX
	Increases in current operating liabilities	XXX
	Decreases in current operating liabilities	(XXX)
	Net cash flow from operating activities	$ XXX or $(XXX)

Subtract	Add
Increases in accounts receivable	Decreases in accounts receivable
Increases in inventory	Decreases in inventory
Increases in prepaid expenses	Decreases in prepaid expenses
Decreases in accounts payable	Increases in accounts payable
Decreases in accrued expenses payable	Increases in accrued expenses payable
Decreases in income taxes payable	Increases in income taxes payable

Net income is normally adjusted to cash flows from operating activities, using the following steps:

Step 1. Expenses that do not affect cash are added. Such expenses decrease net income but do not involve cash payments and, thus, are added to net income.

Example: Depreciation of fixed assets and amortization of intangible assets are non-cash expenses that are added to net income.

Step 2. Losses on the disposal of assets are added and gains on the disposal of assets are deducted. The disposal (sale) of assets is an investing activity rather than an operating activity. However, the losses and gains are reported as part of net income. As a result, any *losses* on disposal of assets are *added* back to net income. Likewise, any *gains* on disposal of assets are *deducted* from net income.

Example: Land costing $100,000 is sold for $90,000. The loss of $10,000 is added back to net income.

4 Other items that also require adjustments to net income to obtain cash flows from operating activities include amortization of bonds payable discounts (add), losses on debt retirement (add), amortization of bonds payable premiums (deduct), and gains on retirement of debt (deduct). These topics are covered in advanced accounting courses.

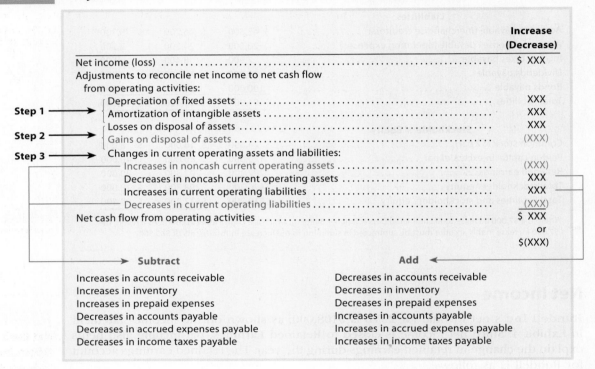

Step 3. Changes in current operating assets and liabilities are added or deducted as follows:

- Increases in noncash current operating assets are deducted.
- Decreases in noncash current operating assets are added.
- Increases in current operating liabilities are added.
- Decreases in current operating liabilities are deducted.

Example: A sale of $10,000 on account increases sales, accounts receivable, and net income by $10,000. However, no cash is received or paid. Thus, the $10,000 increase in accounts receivable is deducted from net income. Similar adjustments are required for the changes in the other current asset and liability accounts, such as inventory, prepaid expenses, accounts payable, accrued expenses payable, and income taxes payable, as shown in Exhibit 5.

Link to National Beverage

For a recent year, **National Beverage** reported changes in current asset and liability accounts for accounts receivable, inventory, prepaid assets, accounts payable, and accrued liabilities.

Example Exercise 16-2 Adjustments to Net Income—Indirect Method

Obj. 2

Omni Corporation's accumulated depreciation increased by $12,000, while $3,400 of patent amortization was recognized between balance sheet dates. There were no purchases or sales of depreciable or intangible assets during the year. In addition, the income statement showed a gain of $4,100 from the sale of land. Reconcile Omni's net income of $50,000 to net cash flow from operating activities.

Follow My Example 16-2

Net income	$50,000
Adjustments to reconcile net income to net cash flow from operating activities:	
Depreciation	12,000
Amortization of patents	3,400
Gain from sale of land	(4,100)
Net cash flow from operating activities	$61,300

Practice Exercises: PE 16-2A, PE 16-2B

The Cash flows from operating activities section of **Rundell Inc.**'s statement of cash flows is shown in Exhibit 6.

EXHIBIT 6

Net Cash Flow from Operating Activities—Indirect Method

Cash flows from operating activities:			
Net income		$108,000	
Adjustments to reconcile net income to net cash flow from operating activities:			
Depreciation	7,000		Step 1
Gain on sale of land	(12,000)		Step 2
Changes in current operating assets and liabilities:			
Increase in accounts receivable	(9,000)		Step 3
Decrease in inventories	8,000		Step 3
Decrease in accounts payable	(3,200)		Step 3
Increase in accrued expenses payable	2,200		Step 3
Decrease in income taxes payable	(500)		Step 3
Net cash flow from operating activities		$100,500	

Rundell's net income of $108,000 is converted to cash flows from operating activities of $100,500 as follows:

Step 1. Add depreciation of $7,000.

Analysis: The comparative balance sheet in Exhibit 4 indicates that Accumulated Depreciation—Building increased by $7,000. Given that there was no other activity in this account, as shown on the following page, depreciation expense for the year was $7,000 on the building:

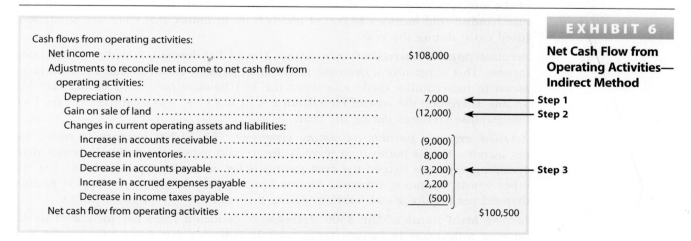

Account *Accumulated Depreciation—Building*					Account No.	
					Balance	
Date		**Item**	**Debit**	**Credit**	**Debit**	**Credit**
20Y8 Jan.	1	Balance				58,300
Dec.	31	Depreciation for year		7,000		65,300

Step 2. Deduct the gain on the sale of land of $12,000.
Analysis: The income statement in Exhibit 4 reports a gain of $12,000 from the sale of land. The proceeds, which include the gain, are reported in the Investing section of the statement of cash flows.[5] Thus, the gain of $12,000 is deducted from net income in determining cash flows from operating activities.

Step 3. Add and deduct changes in current operating assets and liabilities excluding cash.
Analysis: The increases and decreases in the current operating asset and current liability accounts excluding cash are as follows:

	December 31		Increase
Accounts	**20Y8**	**20Y7**	**(Decrease)**
Accounts Receivable (net)	$ 74,000	$ 65,000	$ 9,000
Inventories	172,000	180,000	(8,000)
Accounts Payable (merchandise creditors)	43,500	46,700	(3,200)
Accrued Expenses Payable (operating expenses)	26,500	24,300	2,200
Income Taxes Payable	7,900	8,400	(500)

Accounts receivable (net): The $9,000 increase is deducted from net income. This is because the $9,000 increase in accounts receivable indicates that sales on account were $9,000 more than the cash received from customers. Thus, sales (and net income) includes $9,000 that was not received in cash during the year.

Inventories: The $8,000 decrease is added to net income. This is because the $8,000 decrease in inventories indicates that the cost of merchandise *sold* exceeds the cost of the merchandise *purchased* during the year by $8,000. In other words, the cost of merchandise sold includes $8,000 of goods from inventory that were not purchased (used cash) during the year.

Accounts payable (merchandise creditors): The $3,200 decrease is deducted from net income. This is because a decrease in accounts payable indicates that the cash *payments* to merchandise creditors exceed the merchandise *purchased on account* by $3,200. Therefore, the cost of merchandise sold is $3,200 less than the cash paid to merchandise creditors during the year.

Accrued expenses payable (operating expenses): The $2,200 increase is added to net income. This is because an increase in accrued expenses payable indicates that operating expenses exceed the cash payments for operating expenses by $2,200. In other words, operating expenses reported on the income statement include $2,200 that did not require a cash outflow during the year.

Income taxes payable: The $500 decrease is deducted from net income. This is because a decrease in income taxes payable indicates that taxes paid exceed the amount of taxes incurred during the year by $500. In other words, the amount reported on the income statement for income tax expense is less than the amount paid by $500.

Using the preceding analyses, Rundell's net income of $108,000 is converted to cash flows from operating activities of $100,500 as shown in Exhibit 6.

5 The reporting of the proceeds (cash flows) from the sale of land as part of investing activities is discussed later in this chapter.

Example Exercise 16-3 Changes in Current Operating Assets and Liabilities—Indirect Method

Obj. 2

Victor Corporation's current operating assets and liabilities from the company's comparative balance sheet were as follows:

	Dec. 31, 20Y8	Dec. 31, 20Y7
Accounts receivable	$ 6,500	$ 4,900
Inventory	12,300	15,000
Accounts payable	4,800	5,200

Adjust Victor's net income of $70,000 for changes in current operating assets and liabilities to arrive at net cash flow from operating activities.

Follow My Example 16-3

Net income	$70,000
Adjustments to reconcile net income to net cash flow from operating activities:	
Changes in current operating assets and liabilities:	
Increase in accounts receivable	(1,600)
Decrease in inventory	2,700
Decrease in accounts payable	(400)
Net cash flow from operating activities	$70,700

Practice Exercises: PE 16-3A, PE 16-3B

INTEGRITY, OBJECTIVITY, AND ETHICS IN BUSINESS

CREDIT POLICY AND CASH FLOW

Investors frequently use net cash flow from operating activities to assess a company's financial health. If a company is financially healthy, net cash flow from operating activities should be roughly consistent with accrual basis net income. Questions arise, however, when a company's net cash flow from operating activities significantly lags net income. Two scenarios can cause this to happen:

- Sales on account are never collected in cash.
- Large cash purchases for inventory are never sold or sell at a very slow pace.

Both of these scenarios increase net income, without a corresponding increase in net cash flow from operating activities. Prudent investors are often skeptical when they observe these scenarios and tend to avoid these types of investments until the cash flows become clear.

Source: M. Argersinger, "How Companies Fake It (With Cash Flow)," *Daily Finance Investor Center*, July 17, 2011.

Example Exercise 16-4 Cash Flows from Operating Activities—Indirect Method

Obj. 2

Omicron Inc. reported the following data:

Net income	$120,000
Depreciation expense	12,000
Loss on disposal of equipment	15,000
Increase in accounts receivable	5,000
Decrease in accounts payable	2,000

Prepare the Cash flows from operating activities section of the statement of cash flows, using the indirect method.

(Continued)

Follow My Example 16-4

Cash flows from operating activities:		
Net income	$120,000	
Adjustments to reconcile net income to net cash flow from operating activities:		
Depreciation expense	12,000	
Loss on disposal of equipment	15,000	
Changes in current operating assets and liabilities:		
Increase in accounts receivable	(5,000)	
Decrease in accounts payable	(2,000)	
Net cash flow from operating activities		$140,000

Practice Exercises: PE 16-4A, PE 16-4B

Dividends and Dividends Payable

The retained earnings account of **Rundell Inc.** indicates that cash dividends of $28,000 were declared during the year. However, the following dividends payable account indicates that only $24,000 of dividends were paid during the year:

Account *Dividends Payable* Account No.

Date		Item	Debit	Credit	Balance Debit	Balance Credit
20Y8 Jan.	1	Balance				10,000
	10	Cash paid	10,000		—	—
June	30	Dividends declared		14,000		14,000
July	10	Cash paid	14,000		—	—
Dec.	31	Dividends declared		14,000		14,000

Cash dividends paid during the year can also be computed by adjusting the dividends declared during the year for the change in the dividends payable account as follows:

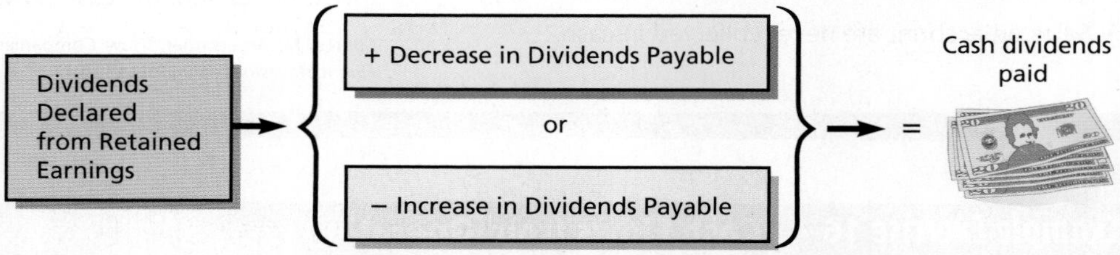

The cash dividends paid by Rundell Inc. during 20Y8 are $24,000, computed as follows:

Dividends declared ($14,000 + $14,000)	$28,000
Increase in Dividends Payable	(4,000)
Cash dividends paid	$24,000

Because dividend payments are a financing activity, the dividend payment of $24,000 is reported in the financing activities section of the statement of cash flows, as follows:

Cash flows from (used for) financing activities:	
Cash used for dividends....................................	$(24,000)

Common Stock

The common stock account of **Rundell Inc.** increased by $8,000, and the paid-in capital in excess of par—common stock account increased by $40,000, as follows:

Account *Common Stock* — Account No.

Date		Item	Debit	Credit	Balance Debit	Balance Credit
20Y8 Jan.	1	Balance				16,000
Nov.	1	4,000 shares issued for cash		8,000		24,000

Account *Paid-In Capital in Excess of Par—Common Stock* — Account No.

Date		Item	Debit	Credit	Balance Debit	Balance Credit
20Y8 Jan.	1	Balance				80,000
Nov.	1	4,000 shares issued for cash		40,000		120,000

These increases were from issuing 4,000 shares of common stock for $12 per share. This cash inflow is reported in the financing activities section as follows:

Cash flows from (used for) financing activities:	
Cash from sale of common stock...........................	$48,000

Bonds Payable

The bonds payable account of **Rundell Inc.** decreased by $50,000, as follows:

Account *Bonds Payable* — Account No.

Date		Item	Debit	Credit	Balance Debit	Balance Credit
20Y8 Jan.	1	Balance				150,000
June	1	Retired by payment of cash at face amount	50,000			100,000

This decrease is from retiring the bonds by a cash payment for their face amount. This cash outflow is reported in the financing activities section as follows:

Cash flows from (used for) financing activities:	
Cash used to retire bonds payable..........................	$(50,000)

Building and Accumulated Depreciation—Building

The building account of **Rundell Inc.** increased by $60,000, and the accumulated depreciation—building account increased by $7,000, as follows:

Account *Building*						Account No.
					Balance	
Date		**Item**	**Debit**	**Credit**	**Debit**	**Credit**
20Y8 Jan.	1	Balance			200,000	
Dec.	27	Purchased for cash	60,000		260,000	

Account *Accumulated Depreciation—Building*						Account No.
					Balance	
Date		**Item**	**Debit**	**Credit**	**Debit**	**Credit**
20Y8 Jan.	1	Balance				58,300
Dec.	31	Depreciation for the year		7,000		65,300

The purchase of a building for cash of $60,000 is reported as an outflow of cash in the investing activities section as follows:

Cash flows from (used for) investing activities:	
Cash used for purchase of building..........................	$(60,000)

The credit in the accumulated depreciation—building account represents depreciation expense for the year. This depreciation expense of $7,000 on the building was added to net income in determining cash flows from operating activities, as reported in Exhibit 6.

Land

The $45,000 decline in the land account of **Rundell Inc.** was from two transactions, as follows:

Account *Land*						Account No.
					Balance	
Date		**Item**	**Debit**	**Credit**	**Debit**	**Credit**
20Y8 Jan.	1	Balance			125,000	
June	8	Sold for $72,000 cash		60,000	65,000	
Oct.	12	Purchased for $15,000 cash	15,000		80,000	

The June 8 transaction is the sale of land with a cost of $60,000 for $72,000 in cash. The $72,000 proceeds from the sale are reported in the investing activities section as follows:

Cash flows from (used for) investing activities:	
Cash from sale of land	$72,000

The proceeds of $72,000 include the $12,000 gain on the sale of land and the $60,000 cost (book value) of the land. As shown in Exhibit 6, the $12,000 gain is deducted from net income in the Cash flows from operating activities section. This is so that the $12,000 cash inflow related to the gain is not included twice as a cash inflow.

The October 12 transaction is the purchase of land for cash of $15,000. This transaction is reported as an outflow of cash in the investing activities section as follows:

Cash flows from (used for) investing activities:	
Cash used for purchase of land	$(15,000)

Example Exercise 16-5 Land Transactions on the Statement of Cash Flows — Obj. 2

Alpha Corporation purchased land for $125,000. Later in the year, the company sold a different piece of land with a book value of $165,000 for $200,000. How are the effects of these transactions reported on the statement of cash flows?

Follow My Example 16-5

The gain on the sale of the land is deducted from net income, as follows:

Gain on sale of land	$ (35,000)

The purchase and sale of land are reported as part of cash flows from investing activities, as follows:

Cash received from sale of land	$ 200,000
Cash used for purchase of land	(125,000)

Practice Exercises: PE 16-5A, PE 16-5B

Preparing the Statement of Cash Flows

The statement of cash flows for **Rundell Inc.**, using the indirect method, is shown in Exhibit 7. The statement of cash flows indicates that cash increased by $71,500 during the year. The most significant increase in net cash flows ($100,500) was from operating activities. The most significant use of cash ($26,000) was for financing activities. The ending balance of cash on December 31, 20Y8, is $97,500. This ending cash balance is also reported on the December 31, 20Y8, balance sheet shown in Exhibit 4.

Rundell Inc.
Statement of Cash Flows
For the Year Ended December 31, 20Y8

Cash flows from operating activities:		
Net income	$108,000	
Adjustments to reconcile net income to net cash flow from operating activities:		
Depreciation	7,000	
Gain on sale of land	(12,000)	
Changes in current operating assets and liabilities:		
Increase in accounts receivable	(9,000)	
Decrease in inventories	8,000	
Decrease in accounts payable	(3,200)	
Increase in accrued expenses payable	2,200	
Decrease in income taxes payable	(500)	
Net cash flow from operating activities		$100,500
Cash flows from (used for) investing activities:		
Cash from sale of land	$ 72,000	
Cash used for purchase of land	(15,000)	
Cash used for purchase of building	(60,000)	
Net cash flow used for investing activities		(3,000)
Cash flows from (used for) financing activities:		
Cash from sale of common stock	$ 48,000	
Cash used to retire bonds payable	(50,000)	
Cash used for dividends	(24,000)	
Net cash flow used for financing activities		(26,000)
Increase (decrease) in cash		$ 71,500
Cash at the beginning of the year		26,000
Cash at the end of the year		$ 97,500

EXHIBIT 7

Statement of Cash Flows—Indirect Method

Link to National Beverage

In a recent statement of cash flows, **National Beverage** reported net cash provided by operating activities of $58,020,000, net cash used for investing activities of $9,725,000, and net cash used for financing activities of $25,771,000 for a net increase in cash of $22,524,000 for the year.

Business Connection

GROWING PAINS

Twitter, Inc. is a global social media platform used for real-time self-expression and conversation within the limits of 140-character tweets. Twitter is a new, fast-growing company. The cash flows from operating, investing, and financing activities are summarized for its first three years as a public company (in thousands):

	Cash provided from (used in)			
	Operating activities	**Investing activities**	**Financing activities**	**Net change for year**
Year 1	$(27,935)	$ 49,443	$ (37,124)	$ (15,616)
Year 2	1,398	(1,306,066)	1,942,176	637,508
Year 3	81,796	(1,097,272)	1,691,722	676,246

One can see the significant improvement in Twitter's cash flows from operations from Year 1 to Year 3. This indicates that Twitter is succeeding as a new company and is able to provide cash from operations after only three years of operating as a public company. However, as a new company, Twitter must make significant investments in order to expand. This is clear in the trend in cash flows used in investing activities. Since the cash flows from operations are insufficient to fund this growth, the company must obtain cash from financing activities. We see significant sources of cash from stockholders in Year 2 and Year 3, which was used to expand and provide future flexibility.

Obj. 3 Prepare a statement of cash flows, using the direct method.

Preparing the Statement of Cash Flows—The Direct Method

The direct method reports cash flows from operating activities as follows:

Cash flows from operating activities:		
Cash received from customers	$ XXX	
Cash payments for merchandise	(XXX)	
Cash payments for operating expenses	(XXX)	
Cash payments for interest	(XXX)	
Cash payments for income taxes	(XXX)	
Net cash flow from operating activities		$XXX

The investing and financing activities sections of the statement of cash flows are exactly the same under both the direct and indirect methods. The amount of net cash flow from operating activities is also the same, but the manner in which it is reported is different.

Under the direct method, the income statement is adjusted to cash flows from operating activities as shown in Exhibit 8.

EXHIBIT 8

Converting Income Statement to Cash Flows from Operating Activities Using the Direct Method

Income Statement	Adjusted to	Cash Flows from Operating Activities
Sales	→	Cash received from customers
Cost of merchandise sold	→	Cash payments for merchandise
Operating expenses:		
Depreciation expense	N/A	N/A
Other operating expenses	→	Cash payments for operating expenses
Gain on sale of land	N/A	N/A
Interest expense	→	Cash payments for interest
Income tax expense	→	Cash payments for income taxes
Net income	→	Net cash flow from operating activities

N/A—Not applicable

As shown in Exhibit 8, depreciation expense is not adjusted or reported as part of cash flows from operating activities. This is because deprecation expense does not involve a cash outflow. The gain on the sale of the land is also not adjusted and is not reported as part of cash flows from operating activities. This is because the cash flow from operating activities is determined directly, rather than by reconciling net income. The cash proceeds from the sale of the land are reported as an investing activity.

To illustrate the direct method, the income statement and comparative balance sheet for Rundell Inc., shown in Exhibit 4, are used.

Cash Received from Customers

The income statement (shown in Exhibit 4) of **Rundell Inc.** reports sales of $1,180,000. To determine the *cash received from customers*, the $1,180,000 is adjusted for any increase or decrease in accounts receivable. The adjustment is summarized in Exhibit 9.

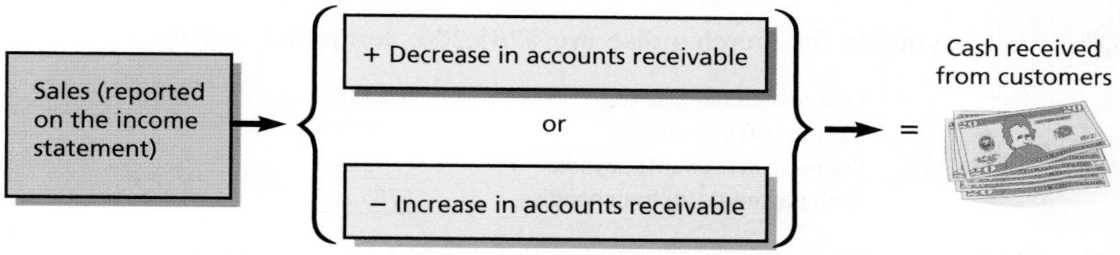

EXHIBIT 9

Determining the Cash Received from Customers

The cash received from customers is $1,171,000, computed as follows:

Sales	$1,180,000
Increase in accounts receivable	(9,000)
Cash received from customers	$1,171,000

The increase of $9,000 in accounts receivable (shown in Exhibit 4) during 20Y8 indicates that sales on account exceeded cash received from customers by $9,000. In other words, sales include $9,000 that did not result in a cash inflow during the year. Thus, $9,000 is deducted from sales to determine the cash received from customers.

Example Exercise 16-6 Cash Received from Customers—Direct Method — *Obj. 3*

Sales reported on the income statement were $350,000. The accounts receivable balance declined $8,000 over the year. Determine the amount of cash received from customers.

Follow My Example 16-6

Sales	$350,000
Decrease in accounts receivable	8,000
Cash received from customers	$ 358,000

Practice Exercises: PE 16-6A, PE 16-6B

Cash Payments for Merchandise

The income statement (shown in Exhibit 4) for **Rundell Inc.** reports cost of merchandise sold of $790,000. To determine the cash payments for merchandise, the $790,000 is adjusted for any increases or decreases in inventories and accounts payable. Assuming that the accounts payable are owed to merchandise suppliers, the adjustment is summarized in Exhibit 10.

EXHIBIT 10

Determining the Cash Payments for Merchandise

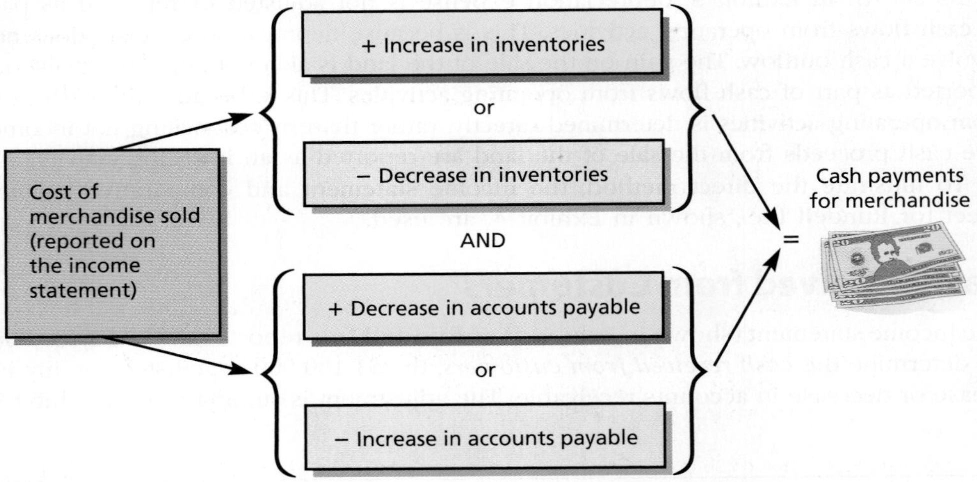

The cash payments for merchandise are $785,200, computed as follows:

Cost of merchandise sold	$790,000
Decrease in inventories	(8,000)
Decrease in accounts payable	3,200
Cash payments for merchandise	$785,200

The $8,000 decrease in inventories (from Exhibit 4) indicates that the merchandise sold exceeded the cost of the merchandise purchased by $8,000. In other words, the cost of merchandise sold includes $8,000 of goods sold from inventory that did not require a cash outflow during the year. Thus, $8,000 is deducted from the cost of merchandise sold in determining the cash payments for merchandise.

The $3,200 decrease in accounts payable (from Exhibit 4) indicates that cash payments for merchandise were $3,200 more than the purchases on account during 20Y8. Therefore, $3,200 is added to the cost of merchandise sold in determining the cash payments for merchandise.

Example Exercise 16-7 Cash Payments for Merchandise—Direct Method **Obj. 3**

The cost of merchandise sold reported on the income statement was $145,000. The accounts payable balance increased by $4,000, and the inventory balance increased by $9,000 over the year. Determine the amount of cash paid for merchandise.

Follow My Example 16-7

Cost of merchandise sold	$145,000
Increase in inventories	9,000
Increase in accounts payable	(4,000)
Cash paid for merchandise	$150,000

Practice Exercises: PE 16-7A, PE 16-7B

Cash Payments for Operating Expenses

The income statement for **Rundell Inc.** (from Exhibit 4) reports total operating expenses of $203,000, which includes depreciation expense of $7,000. Because depreciation expense does not require a cash outflow, it is omitted from cash payments for operating expenses.

To determine the cash payments for operating expenses, the other operating expenses (excluding depreciation) of $196,000 ($203,000 – $7,000) are adjusted for any increase or decrease in prepaid and accrued expenses. Assuming that Rundell Inc.'s accrued expenses payable are all operating expenses, this adjustment is summarized in Exhibit 11.

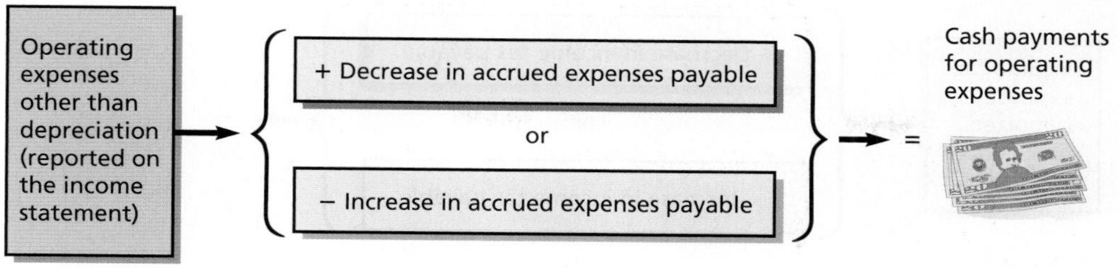

EXHIBIT 11

Determining the Cash Payments for Operating Expenses

The cash payments for operating expenses are $193,800, computed as follows:

Operating expenses other than depreciation	$196,000
Increase in accrued expenses payable	(2,200)
Cash payments for operating expenses	$193,800

The increase in accrued expenses payable (from Exhibit 4) indicates that the cash payments for operating expenses were $2,200 less than the amount reported for operating expenses during the year. Thus, $2,200 is deducted from the operating expenses in determining the cash payments for operating expenses.

Rundell Inc. had no prepaid expenses and thus, there was no operating expense adjustment for prepaid expense. When prepaid expenses exist, operating expenses are also adjusted for any increase or decrease in prepaid expenses. Increases (decreases) in prepaid expenses are added to (subtracted from) other operating expenses to determine the cash payments for operating expenses.

Gain on Sale of Land

The income statement for **Rundell Inc.** (from Exhibit 4) reports a gain of $12,000 on the sale of land. The sale of land is an investing activity. Thus, the proceeds from the sale, which include the gain, are reported as part of the investing activities section.

Interest Expense

The income statement for **Rundell Inc.** (from Exhibit 4) reports interest expense of $8,000. To determine the cash payments for interest, the $8,000 is adjusted for any increases or decreases in interest payable. The adjustment is summarized in Exhibit 12.

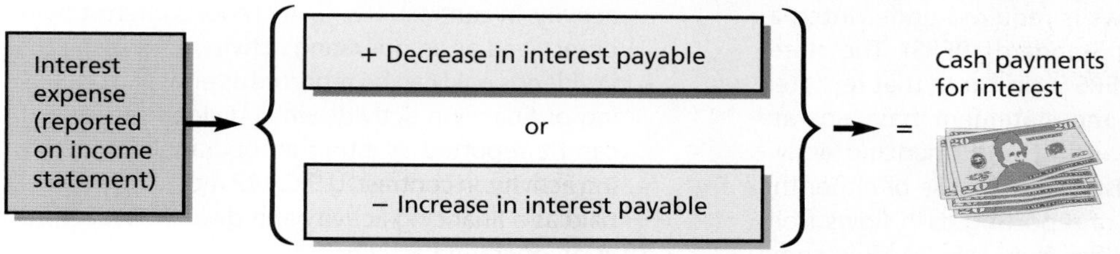

EXHIBIT 12

Determining the Cash Payments for Interest

The comparative balance sheet of Rundell in Exhibit 4 indicates no interest payable. This is because the interest expense on the bonds payable is paid on June 1 and December 31. Because there is no interest payable, no adjustment of the interest expense of $8,000 is necessary.

Cash Payments for Income Taxes

The income statement for **Rundell Inc.** (from Exhibit 4) reports income tax expense of $83,000. To determine the cash payments for income taxes, the $83,000 is adjusted for any increases or decreases in income taxes payable. The adjustment is summarized in Exhibit 13.

EXHIBIT 13

Determining the Cash Payments for Income Taxes

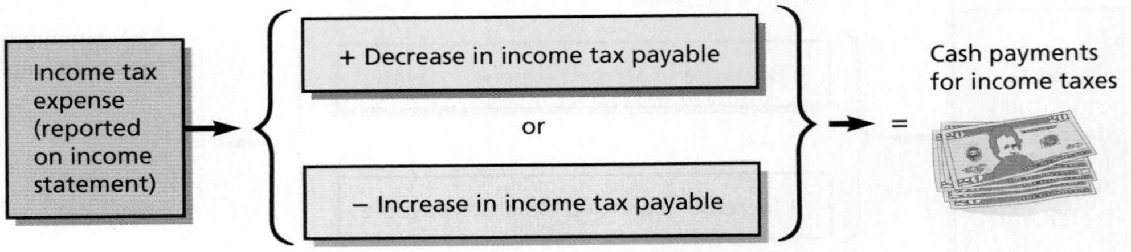

The cash payments for income taxes are $83,500, computed as follows:

Income tax expense	$83,000
Decrease in income taxes payable	500
Cash payments for income taxes	$83,500

The $500 decrease in income taxes payable (from Exhibit 4) indicates that the cash payments for income taxes were $500 more than the amount reported for income tax expense during 20Y8. Thus, $500 is added to the income tax expense in determining the cash payments for income taxes.

Reporting Cash Flows from Operating Activities—Direct Method

The statement of cash flows for **Rundell Inc.**, using the direct method for reporting cash flows from operating activities, is shown in Exhibit 14. The portions of the statement that differ from those prepared under the indirect method are highlighted.

Exhibit 14 also includes the separate schedule reconciling net income and net cash flow from operating activities. This schedule is included in the statement of cash flows when the direct method is used. This schedule is similar to the Cash flows from operating activities section prepared under the indirect method.

International Connection

IFRS IFRS FOR STATEMENT OF CASH FLOWS

The statement of cash flows is required under International Financial Reporting Standards (IFRS). The statement of cash flows under IFRS is similar to that reported under U.S. GAAP in that the statement has separate sections for operating, investing, and financing activities. Like U.S. GAAP, IFRS also allow the use of either the indirect or direct method of reporting cash flows from operating activities. IFRS differ from U.S. GAAP in some minor areas, including:

- Interest paid can be reported as either an operating or financing activity, while interest received can be reported as either an operating or investing activity. In contrast, U.S. GAAP reports interest paid or received as an operating activity.
- Dividends paid can be reported as either an operating or financing activity, while dividends received can be reported as either an operating or investing activity. In contrast, U.S. GAAP reports dividends paid as a financing activity and dividends received as an operating activity.
- Cash flows to pay taxes are reported as a separate line in the operating activities, in contrast to U.S. GAAP, which does not require a separate line disclosure.

EXHIBIT 14

Statement of Cash Flows—Direct Method

Rundell Inc.
Statement of Cash Flows
For the Year Ended December 31, 20Y8

Cash flows from operating activities:		
Cash received from customers	$1,171,000	
Cash payments for merchandise	(785,200)	
Cash payments for operating expenses	(193,800)	
Cash payments for interest	(8,000)	
Cash payments for income taxes	(83,500)	
Net cash flow from operating activities		$100,500
Cash flows from (used for) investing activities:		
Cash from sale of land	$ 72,000	
Cash used for purchase of land	(15,000)	
Cash used for purchase of building	(60,000)	
Net cash flow used for investing activities		(3,000)
Cash flows from (used for) financing activities:		
Cash from sale of common stock	$ 48,000	
Cash used to retire bonds payable	(50,000)	
Cash used for dividends	(24,000)	
Net cash flow used for financing activities		(26,000)
Increase (decrease) in cash		$ 71,500
Cash at the beginning of the year		26,000
Cash at the end of the year		$ 97,500
Schedule Reconciling Net Income with Cash Flows from Operating Activities:		
Cash flows from operating activities:		
Net income		$108,000
Adjustments to reconcile net income to net cash flow from operating activities:		
Depreciation		7,000
Gain on sale of land		(12,000)
Changes in current operating assets and liabilities:		
Increase in accounts receivable		(9,000)
Decrease in inventory		8,000
Decrease in accounts payable		(3,200)
Increase in accrued expenses payable		2,200
Decrease in income taxes payable		(500)
Net cash flow from operating activities		$100,500

Financial Analysis and Interpretation: Free Cash Flow

Obj. 4 Describe and illustrate the use of free cash flow in evaluating a company's cash flow.

FAI

A valuable tool for evaluating the profitability of a business is free cash flow. **Free cash flow** measures the operating cash flow available to a company after it purchases the property, plant, and equipment (PP&E) necessary to maintain its current operations. Since the investments in PP&E necessary to maintain current operations cannot often be determined from financial statements, analysts estimate this amount using the cash used to purchase PP&E, as shown in the statement of cash flows. Thus, free cash flow is computed as follows:

Cash flows from operating activities	$ XXX
Cash used to purchase property, plant, and equipment	(XXX)
Free cash flow	$ XXX

The free cash flow can be expressed as a percentage of sales in order to provide a relative measure that can be compared over time or to other companies. This ratio is computed as follows:

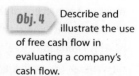

$$\text{Ratio of Free Cash Flow to Sales} = \frac{\text{Free Cash Flow}}{\text{Sales}}$$

Positive free cash flow is considered favorable. A company that has free cash flow is able to fund growth and acquisitions, retire debt, purchase treasury stock, and pay dividends. A company with no free cash flow may have limited financial flexibility, potentially leading to liquidity problems.

To illustrate, information from the annual reports of National Beverage for three recent years is as follows (in thousands):

	Year 3	Year 2	Year 1
Cash flows from operating activities	$ 58,020	$ 52,383	$ 40,264
Cash used to purchase property, plant, and equipment	11,630	12,124	9,693
Sales	645,825	641,135	662,007

The free cash flow is computed for the three years as follows:

	Year 3	Year 2	Year 1
Cash flows from operating activities	$ 58,020	$ 52,383	$40,264
Cash used to purchase property, plant, and equipment	(11,630)	(12,124)	(9,693)
Free cash flow	$ 46,390	$ 40,259	$30,571

As can be seen, free cash flow has increased across the three years. In Year 3, it is nearly 52% higher than in Year 1 [($46,390 – $30,571) ÷ $30,571]. The ratio of free cash flow to sales is as follows (rounded to one decimal place):

	Year 3	Year 2	Year 1
Ratio of free cash flow to sales	7.2%	6.3%	4.6%
	($46,390 ÷ $645,825)	($40,259 ÷ $641,135)	($30,571 ÷ $662,007)

The ratio of free cash flow to sales has also increased across these three years, from 4.6% in Year 1 to 7.2% in Year 3, which is a 57% increase [(7.2% – 4.6%) ÷ 4.6%].

Example Exercise 16-8 Free Cash Flow

Obj. 4

Omnicron Inc. reported the following on the company's cash flow statement in 20Y8 and 20Y7:

	20Y8	20Y7
Net cash flow from operating activities	$ 140,000	$120,000
Net cash flow used for investing activities	(120,000)	(80,000)
Net cash flow used for financing activities	(20,000)	(32,000)

Seventy-five percent of the net cash flow used for investing activities was used to replace existing capacity.

a. Determine Omnicron's free cash flow.

b. Has Omnicron's free cash flow improved or declined from 20Y7 to 20Y8?

Follow My Example 16-8

a.

	20Y8	20Y7
Net cash flow from operating activities	$140,000	$120,000
Investments in fixed assets to maintain current production	(90,000)[1]	(60,000)[2]
Free cash flow	$ 50,000	$ 60,000

[1] $120,000 × 75%
[2] $80,000 × 75%

b. The change from $60,000 to $50,000 indicates an unfavorable trend.

Practice Exercises: PE 16-8A, PE 16-8B

APPENDIX

Spreadsheet (Work Sheet) for Statement of Cash Flows—The Indirect Method

A spreadsheet (work sheet) may be used in preparing the statement of cash flows. However, whether or not a spreadsheet (work sheet) is used, the concepts presented in this chapter are not affected.

The data for Rundell Inc., presented in Exhibit 4, are used as a basis for illustrating the spreadsheet (work sheet) for the indirect method. The steps in preparing this spreadsheet (work sheet), shown in Exhibit 15, are as follows:

Step 1. List the title of each balance sheet account in the Accounts column.

Step 2. For each balance sheet account, enter its balance as of December 31, 20Y7, in the first column and its balance as of December 31, 20Y8, in the last column. Place the credit balances in parentheses.

Step 3. Add the December 31, 20Y7 and 20Y8 column totals, which should total to zero.

Step 4. Analyze the change during the year in each noncash account to determine its net increase (decrease) and classify the change as affecting cash flows from operating activities, investing activities, financing activities, or noncash investing and financing activities.

Step 5. Indicate the effect of the change on cash flows by making entries in the Transactions columns.

Step 6. After all noncash accounts have been analyzed, enter the net increase (decrease) in cash during the period.

Step 7. Add the Debit and Credit Transactions columns. The totals should be equal.

Analyzing Accounts

In analyzing the noncash accounts (Step 4), try to determine the type of cash flow activity (operating, investing, or financing) that led to the change in the account. As each noncash account is analyzed, an entry (Step 5) is made on the spreadsheet (work sheet) for the type of cash flow activity that caused the change. After all noncash accounts have been analyzed, an entry (Step 6) is made for the increase (decrease) in cash during the period.

The entries made on the spreadsheet are not posted to the ledger. They are only used in preparing and summarizing the data on the spreadsheet.

The order in which the accounts are analyzed is not important. However, it is more efficient to begin with Retained Earnings and proceed upward in the account listing.

Retained Earnings

The spreadsheet (work sheet) shows a Retained Earnings balance of $202,300 at December 31, 20Y7, and $282,300 at December 31, 20Y8. Thus, Retained Earnings increased $80,000 during the year. This increase is from the following:

- Net income of $108,000
- Declaring cash dividends of $28,000

To identify the cash flows from these activities, two entries are made on the spreadsheet.

EXHIBIT 15 **End-of-Period Spreadsheet (Work Sheet) for Statement of Cash Flows—Indirect Method**

Step 2

	A	B	C	D	E	F	G
1	**Rundell Inc.**						
2	**End-of-Period Spreadsheet (Work Sheet) for Statement of Cash Flows**						
3	**For the Year Ended December 31, 20Y8**						
4		**Balance,**		**Transactions**			**Balance,**
5	**Accounts**	**Dec. 31, 20Y7**		**Debit**		**Credit**	**Dec. 31, 20Y8**
6	Cash	26,000	(o)	71,500			97,500
7	Accounts receivable (net)	65,000	(n)	9,000			74,000
8	Inventories	180,000			(m)	8,000	172,000
9	Land	125,000	(k)	15,000	(l)	60,000	80,000
10	Building	200,000	(j)	60,000			260,000
11	Accumulated depreciation—building	(58,300)			(i)	7,000	(65,300)
12	Accounts payable (merchandise creditors)	(46,700)	(h)	3,200			(43,500)
13	Accrued expenses payable (operating expenses)	(24,300)			(g)	2,200	(26,500)
14	Income taxes payable	(8,400)	(f)	500			(7,900)
15	Dividends payable	(10,000)			(e)	4,000	(14,000)
16	Bonds payable	(150,000)	(d)	50,000			(100,000)
17	Common stock	(16,000)			(c)	8,000	(24,000)
18	Paid-in capital in excess of par	(80,000)			(c)	40,000	(120,000)
19	Retained earnings	(202,300)	(b)	28,000	(a)	108,000	(282,300)
20	Totals	0		237,200		237,200	0
21	Operating activities:						
22	Net income		(a)	108,000			
23	Depreciation of building		(i)	7,000			
24	Gain on sale of land				(l)	12,000	
25	Increase in accounts receivable				(n)	9,000	
26	Decrease in inventories		(m)	8,000			
27	Decrease in accounts payable				(h)	3,200	
28	Increase in accrued expenses payable		(g)	2,200			
29	Decrease in income taxes payable				(f)	500	
30	Investing activities:						
31	Sale of land		(l)	72,000			
32	Purchase of land				(k)	15,000	
33	Purchase of building				(j)	60,000	
34	Financing activities:						
35	Issued common stock		(c)	48,000			
36	Retired bonds payable				(d)	50,000	
37	Declared cash dividends				(b)	28,000	
38	Increase in dividends payable		(e)	4,000			
39	Increase (decrease) in cash				(o)	71,500	
40	Totals			249,200		249,200	
41							

Step 1 (rows 6–20) — Step 3 (row 20 totals, columns B and G)

Steps 4–7

The $108,000 is reported on the statement of cash flows as part of cash flows from operating activities. Thus, an entry is made in the Transactions columns on the spreadsheet, as follows:

(a) Operating Activities—Net Income................................	108,000	
Retained Earnings..		108,000

The preceding entry accounts for the net income portion of the change to Retained Earnings. It also identifies the cash flow in the bottom portion of the spreadsheet as related to operating activities.

The $28,000 of dividends is reported as a financing activity on the statement of cash flows. Thus, an entry is made in the Transactions columns on the spreadsheet, as follows:

(b)	Retained Earnings	28,000	
	Financing Activities—Declared Cash Dividends		28,000

The preceding entry accounts for the dividends portion of the change to Retained Earnings. It also identifies the cash flow in the bottom portion of the spreadsheet as related to financing activities. The $28,000 of declared dividends will be adjusted later for the actual amount of cash dividends paid during the year.

Other Accounts

The entries for the other noncash accounts are made in the spreadsheet in a manner similar to entries (a) and (b). A summary of these entries follows:

(c)	Financing Activities—Issued Common Stock	48,000	
	Common Stock		8,000
	Paid-In Capital in Excess of Par—Common Stock		40,000
(d)	Bonds Payable	50,000	
	Financing Activities—Retired Bonds Payable		50,000
(e)	Financing Activities—Increase in Dividends Payable	4,000	
	Dividends Payable		4,000
(f)	Income Taxes Payable	500	
	Operating Activities—Decrease in Income Taxes Payable		500
(g)	Operating Activities—Increase in Accrued Expenses Payable	2,200	
	Accrued Expenses Payable		2,200
(h)	Accounts Payable	3,200	
	Operating Activities—Decrease in Accounts Payable		3,200
(i)	Operating Activities—Depreciation of Building	7,000	
	Accumulated Depreciation—Building		7,000
(j)	Building	60,000	
	Investing Activities—Purchase of Building		60,000
(k)	Land	15,000	
	Investing Activities—Purchase of Land		15,000
(l)	Investing Activities—Sale of Land	72,000	
	Operating Activities—Gain on Sale of Land		12,000
	Land		60,000
(m)	Operating Activities—Decrease in Inventories	8,000	
	Inventories		8,000
(n)	Accounts Receivable	9,000	
	Operating Activities—Increase in Accounts Receivable		9,000
(o)	Cash	71,500	
	Net Increase in Cash		71,500

After all the balance sheet accounts are analyzed and the entries made on the spreadsheet (work sheet), all the operating, investing, and financing activities are identified in the bottom portion of the spreadsheet. The accuracy of the entries is verified by totaling the Debit and Credit Transactions columns. The totals of the columns should be equal.

Preparing the Statement of Cash Flows

The statement of cash flows prepared from the spreadsheet is identical to the statement in Exhibit 7. The data for the three sections of the statement are obtained from the bottom portion of the spreadsheet.

At a Glance 16

Obj. 1 Describe the cash flow activities reported in the statement of cash flows.

Key Points The statement of cash flows reports cash receipts and cash payments by three types of activities: operating activities, investing activities, and financing activities. Cash flows from operating activities reports the cash inflows and outflows from a company's day-to-day operations. Cash flows from (used for) investing activities reports the cash inflows and outflows related to changes in a company's long-term assets. Cash flows from (used for) financing activities reports the cash inflows and outflows related to changes in a company's long-term liabilities and stockholders' equity. Investing and financing for a business may be affected by transactions that do not involve cash. The effect of such transactions should be reported in a separate schedule accompanying the statement of cash flows.

Learning Outcome	Example Exercises	Practice Exercises
• Classify transactions that either provide or use cash into operating, investing, or financing activities.	EE16-1	PE16-1A, 16-1B

Obj. 2 Prepare a statement of cash flows, using the indirect method.

Key Points The indirect method reports cash flows from operating activities by adjusting net income for revenues and expenses that do not involve the receipt or payment of cash. Noncash expenses such as depreciation are added back to net income. Gains and losses on the disposal of assets are added to or deducted from net income. Changes in current operating assets and liabilities are added to or subtracted from net income, depending on their effect on cash. Cash flows from (used for) investing activities and cash flows from (used for) financing activities are reported below cash flows from operating activities in the statement of cash flows.

Learning Outcomes	Example Exercises	Practice Exercises
• Determine cash flows from operating activities under the indirect method by adjusting net income for noncash expenses and gains and losses from asset disposals.	EE16-2	PE16-2A, 16-2B
• Determine cash flows from operating activities under the indirect method by adjusting net income for changes in current operating assets and liabilities.	EE16-3	PE16-3A, 16-3B
• Prepare the Cash flows from operating activities section of the statement of cash flows, using the indirect method.	EE16-4	PE16-4A, 16-4B
• Prepare the Cash flows from (used for) investing activities and Cash flows from (used for) financing activities sections of the statement of cash flows.	EE16-5	PE16-5A, 16-5B

Obj. 3 Prepare a statement of cash flows, using the direct method.

Key Points The amount of cash flows from operating activities is the same under both the direct and indirect methods, but the manner in which cash flows operating activities is reported is different. The direct method reports cash flows from operating activities by major classes of operating cash receipts and cash payments. The difference between the major classes of total operating cash receipts and total operating cash payments is the net cash flow from operating activities. The Cash flows from (used for) investing and financing activities sections of the statement are the same under both the direct and indirect methods.

Learning Outcome	Example Exercises	Practice Exercises
• Prepare the Cash flows from operating activities section of the statement of cash flows under the direct method.	EE16-6 EE16-7	PE16-6A, 16-6B PE16-7A, 16-7B

Obj. 4 **Describe and illustrate the use of free cash flow in evaluating a company's cash flow.**

Key Points Free cash flow measures the operating cash flow available for company use after purchasing the fixed assets that are necessary to maintain current productive capacity. It is calculated by subtracting these fixed asset purchases from net cash flow from operating activities. A company with strong free cash flow is able to fund internal growth, retire debt, pay dividends, and enjoy financial flexibility. A company with weak free cash flow has much less financial flexibility.

Learning Outcomes	*Example Exercises*	*Practice Exercises*
• Describe free cash flow.		
• Calculate and evaluate free cash flow.	**EE16-8**	**PE16-8A, 16-8B**

Illustrative Problem

The comparative balance sheet of Dowling Company for December 31, 20Y6 and 20Y5, is as follows:

Dowling Company
Comparative Balance Sheet
December 31, 20Y6 and 20Y5

	20Y6	**20Y5**
Assets		
Cash	$ 140,350	$ 95,900
Accounts receivable (net)	95,300	102,300
Inventories	165,200	157,900
Prepaid expenses	6,240	5,860
Investments (long-term)	35,700	84,700
Land	75,000	90,000
Buildings	375,000	260,000
Accumulated depreciation—buildings	(71,300)	(58,300)
Machinery and equipment	428,300	428,300
Accumulated depreciation—machinery and equipment	(148,500)	(138,000)
Patents	58,000	65,000
Total assets	$1,159,290	$1,093,660
Liabilities and Stockholders' Equity		
Accounts payable (merchandise creditors)	$ 43,500	$ 46,700
Accrued expenses payable (operating expenses)	14,000	12,500
Income taxes payable	7,900	8,400
Dividends payable	14,000	10,000
Mortgage note payable, due in 10 years	40,000	0
Bonds payable	150,000	250,000
Common stock, $30 par	450,000	375,000
Excess of issue price over par—common stock	66,250	41,250
Retained earnings	373,640	349,810
Total liabilities and stockholders' equity	$1,159,290	$1,093,660

(Continued)

The income statement for Dowling Company follows:

Dowling Company Income Statement For the Year Ended December 31, 20Y6		
Sales		$1,100,000
Cost of merchandise sold		710,000
Gross profit		$ 390,000
Operating expenses:		
Depreciation expense	$ 23,500	
Patent amortization	7,000	
Other operating expenses	196,000	
Total operating expenses		226,500
Income from operations		$ 163,500
Other revenue and expense:		
Gain on sale of investments	$ 11,000	
Interest expense	(26,000)	(15,000)
Income before income tax		$ 148,500
Income tax expense		50,000
Net income		$ 98,500

An examination of the accounting records revealed the following additional information applicable to 20Y6:

a. Land costing $15,000 was sold for $15,000.

b. A mortgage note was issued for $40,000.

c. A building costing $115,000 was constructed.

d. 2,500 shares of common stock were issued at $40 in exchange for the bonds payable.

e. Cash dividends declared were $74,670.

Instructions

1. Prepare a statement of cash flows, using the indirect method of reporting cash flows from operating activities.
2. Prepare a statement of cash flows, using the direct method of reporting cash flows from operating activities. For purposes of the direct method, the adjustment to arrive at cash payments for operating expenses includes changes in prepaid expenses.

Solution

1.

Dowling Company
Statement of Cash Flows—Indirect Method
For the Year Ended December 31, 20Y6

Cash flows from operating activities:		
Net income	$ 98,500	
Adjustments to reconcile net income to net cash flow from operating activities:		
Depreciation	23,500	
Amortization of patents	7,000	
Gain on sale of investments	(11,000)	
Changes in current operating assets and liabilities:		
Decrease in accounts receivable	7,000	
Increase in inventories	(7,300)	
Increase in prepaid expenses	(380)	
Decrease in accounts payable	(3,200)	
Increase in accrued expenses payable	1,500	
Decrease in income taxes payable	(500)	
Net cash flow from operating activities		$115,120
Cash flows from (used for) investing activities:		
Cash from sale of investments	$ 60,000[1]	
Cash from sale of land	15,000	
Cash used for construction of building	(115,000)	
Net cash flow used for investing activities		(40,000)
Cash flows from (used for) financing activities:		
Cash from issuing mortgage note payable	$ 40,000	
Cash used for dividends	(70,670)[2]	
Net cash flow used for financing activities		(30,670)
Increase (decrease) in cash		$ 44,450
Cash at the beginning of the year		95,900
Cash at the end of the year		$140,350

Schedule of Noncash Investing and Financing Activities:

Issued common stock to retire bonds payable	$100,000

[1] $60,000 = $11,000 gain + $49,000 (decrease in investments)

[2] $70,670 = $74,670 – $4,000 (increase in dividends)

(Continued)

2.

Dowling Company
Statement of Cash Flows—Direct Method
For the Year Ended December 31, 20Y6

Cash flows from operating activities:		
Cash received from customers[1]	$1,107,000	
Cash paid for merchandise[2]	(720,500)	
Cash paid for operating expenses[3]	(194,880)	
Cash paid for interest expense	(26,000)	
Cash paid for income tax[4]	(50,500)	
Net cash flow from operating activities		$115,120
Cash flows from (used for) investing activities:		
Cash from sale of investments	$ 60,000[5]	
Cash from sale of land	15,000	
Cash used for construction of building	(115,000)	
Net cash flow used for investing activities		(40,000)
Cash flows from (used for) financing activities:		
Cash from issuing mortgage note payable	$ 40,000	
Cash used for dividends[6]	(70,670)	
Net cash flow used for financing activities		(30,670)
Increase (decrease) in cash		$ 44,450
Cash at the beginning of the year		95,900
Cash at the end of the year		$140,350

Schedule of Noncash Investing and Financing Activities:

Issued common stock to retire bonds payable $100,000

Schedule Reconciling Net Income with Cash Flows from Operating Activities[7]

Computations:

[1]$1,100,000 + $7,000 = $1,107,000
[2]$710,000 + $3,200 + $7,300 = $720,500
[3]$196,000 + $380 – $1,500 = $194,880
[4]$50,000 + $500 = $50,500
[5]$60,000 = $11,000 gain + $49,000 (decrease in investments)
[6]$74,670 + $10,000 – $14,000 = $70,670
[7]The content of this schedule is the same as the operating activities section of part (1) of this solution and is not reproduced here for the sake of brevity.

Key Terms

cash flow per share (771)
cash flows from (used for) financing activities (768)
cash flows from (used for) investing activities (767)
cash flows from operating activities (767)
direct method (768)
free cash flow (787)
indirect method (769)
statement of cash flows (767)

Discussion Questions

1. What is the principal advantage and the principal disadvantage of the direct method of reporting cash flows from operating activities?
2. What are the major advantages of the indirect method of reporting cash flows from operating activities?
3. A corporation issued $2,000,000 of common stock in exchange for $2,000,000 of fixed assets. Where would this transaction be reported on the statement of cash flows?
4. A retail business, using the accrual method of accounting, owed merchandise creditors (accounts payable) $320,000 at the beginning of the year and $350,000 at the end of the year. How would the $30,000 increase be used to adjust net income in determining the amount of cash flows from operating activities by the indirect method?
5. If salaries payable was $100,000 at the beginning of the year and $75,000 at the end of the year, should the $25,000 decrease be added to or deducted from income to determine the amount of cash flows from operating activities by the indirect method? Explain.
6. A long-term investment in bonds with a cost of $500,000 was sold for $600,000 cash. (a) What was the gain or loss on the sale? (b) What was the effect of the transaction on cash flows? (c) How would the transaction be reported on the statement of cash flows if cash flows from operating activities are reported by the indirect method?
7. A corporation issued $2,000,000 of 20-year bonds for cash at 98. How would the transaction be reported on the statement of cash flows?
8. Fully depreciated equipment costing $50,000 is discarded. What is the effect of the transaction on cash flows if (a) $15,000 cash is received for the equipment, (b) no cash is received for the equipment?
9. For the current year, Packers Company decided to switch from the indirect method to the direct method for reporting cash flows from operating activities on the statement of cash flows. Will the change cause the amount of net cash flow from operating activities to be larger, smaller, or the same compared to the indirect method being used? Explain.
10. Name five common major classes of operating cash receipts or operating cash payments presented on the statement of cash flows when the cash flows from operating activities are reported by the direct method.

Practice Exercises

Example Exercises

Show Me How EE 16-1 *p. 771*

PE 16-1A Classifying cash flows

OBJ. 1

Identify whether each of the following would be reported as an operating, investing, or financing activity on the statement of cash flows:

a. Retirement of bonds payable
b. Purchase of inventory for cash
c. Cash sales
d. Repurchase of common stock
e. Payment of accounts payable
f. Disposal of equipment

Show Me How EE 16-1 *p. 771*

PE 16-1B Classifying cash flows

OBJ. 1

Identify whether each of the following would be reported as an operating, investing, or financing activity on the statement of cash flows:

a. Purchase of investments
b. Purchase of equipment
c. Payment for selling expenses
d. Collection of accounts receivable
e. Cash received from customers
f. Issuance of bonds payable

EE 16-2 p. 775 Show Me How

PE 16-2A Adjustments to net income—indirect method

OBJ. 2

Ripley Corporation's accumulated depreciation—furniture account increased by $11,575, while $2,500 of patent amortization was recognized between balance sheet dates. There were no purchases or sales of depreciable or intangible assets during the year. In addition, the income statement showed a loss of $3,400 from the sale of land. Reconcile a net income of $224,500 to net cash flow from operating activities.

EE 16-2 p. 775 Show Me How

PE 16-2B Adjustments to net income—indirect method

OBJ. 2

Ya Wen Corporation's accumulated depreciation—equipment account increased by $8,750, while $3,250 of patent amortization was recognized between balance sheet dates. There were no purchases or sales of depreciable or intangible assets during the year. In addition, the income statement showed a gain of $18,750 from the sale of investments. Reconcile a net income of $175,000 to net cash flow from operating activities.

EE 16-3 p. 777 Show Me How

PE 16-3A Changes in current operating assets and liabilities—indirect method

OBJ. 2

Zwilling Corporation's comparative balance sheet for current assets and liabilities was as follows:

	Dec. 31, Year 2	Dec. 31, Year 1
Accounts receivable	$35,000	$39,500
Inventory	22,500	18,450
Accounts payable	18,500	16,300
Dividends payable	43,200	53,100

Adjust net income of $320,000 for changes in operating assets and liabilities to arrive at net cash flow from operating activities.

EE 16-3 p. 777 Show Me How

PE 16-3B Changes in current operating assets and liabilities—indirect method

OBJ. 2

Huluduey Corporation's comparative balance sheet for current assets and liabilities was as follows:

	Dec. 31, Year 2	Dec. 31, Year 1
Accounts receivable	$18,000	$14,400
Inventory	34,800	29,700
Accounts payable	27,600	20,700
Dividends payable	8,400	10,800

Adjust net income of $160,000 for changes in operating assets and liabilities to arrive at net cash flow from operating activities.

EE 16-4 p. 777 Show Me How

PE 16-4A Cash flows from operating activities—indirect method

OBJ. 2

Demers Inc. reported the following data:

Net income	$490,000
Depreciation expense	52,000
Gain on disposal of equipment	26,500
Decrease in accounts receivable	32,400
Decrease in accounts payable	12,350

Prepare the Cash flows from operating activities section of the statement of cash flows, using the indirect method.

Show Me How EE 16-4 *p. 777*

PE 16-4B Cash flows from operating activities—indirect method **OBJ. 2**

Staley Inc. reported the following data:

Net income	$280,000
Depreciation expense	48,000
Loss on disposal of equipment	19,520
Increase in accounts receivable	17,280
Increase in accounts payable	8,960

Prepare the Cash flows from operating activities section of the statement of cash flows, using the indirect method.

Show Me How EE 16-5 *p. 781*

PE 16-5A Land transactions on the statement of cash flows **OBJ. 2**

Simkin Corporation purchased land for $420,000. Later in the year, the company sold a different piece of land with a book value of $155,000 for $110,000. How are the effects of these transactions reported on the statement of cash flows?

Show Me How EE 16-5 *p. 781*

PE 16-5B Land transactions on the statement of cash flows **OBJ. 2**

IZ Corporation purchased land for $400,000. Later in the year, the company sold a different piece of land with a book value of $200,000 for $240,000. How are the effects of these transactions reported on the statement of cash flows?

Show Me How EE 16-6 *p. 783*

PE 16-6A Cash received from customers—direct method **OBJ. 3**

Sales reported on the income statement were $480,000. The accounts receivable balance increased $54,000 over the year. Determine the amount of cash received from customers.

Show Me How EE 16-6 *p. 783*

PE 16-6B Cash received from customers—direct method **OBJ. 3**

Sales reported on the income statement were $112,000. The accounts receivable balance decreased $10,500 over the year. Determine the amount of cash received from customers.

Show Me How EE 16-7 *p. 784*

PE 16-7A Cash payments for merchandise—direct method **OBJ. 3**

The cost of merchandise sold reported on the income statement was $770,000. The accounts payable balance decreased $44,000, and the inventory balance decreased by $66,000 over the year. Determine the amount of cash paid for merchandise.

Show Me How EE 16-7 *p. 784*

PE 16-7B Cash payments for merchandise—direct method **OBJ. 3**

The cost of merchandise sold reported on the income statement was $240,000. The accounts payable balance increased $12,000, and the inventory balance increased by $19,200 over the year. Determine the amount of cash paid for merchandise.

Show Me How EE 16-8 *p. 788* FAI

PE 16-8A Free cash flow **OBJ. 4**

McMahon Inc. reported the following on the company's statement of cash flows in Year 2 and Year 1:

	Year 2	Year 1
Net cash flow from operating activities	$ 294,000	$ 280,000
Net cash flow used for investing activities	(224,000)	(252,000)
Net cash flow used for financing activities	(63,000)	(42,000)

Seventy percent of the net cash flow used for investing activities was used to replace existing capacity.

(Continued)

a. Determine McMahon's free cash flow for both years.
b. Has McMahon's free cash flow improved or declined from Year 1 to Year 2?

EE 16-8 *p. 788* **Show Me How**

FAI

PE 16-8B Free cash flow **OBJ. 4**

Dillin Inc. reported the following on the company's statement of cash flows in Year 2 and Year 1:

	Year 2	Year 1
Net cash flow from operating activities	$476,000	$455,000
Net cash flow used for investing activities	(427,000)	(378,000)
Net cash flow used for financing activities	(42,000)	(58,800)

Eighty percent of the net cash flow used for investing activities was used to replace existing capacity.

a. Determine Dillin's free cash flow for both years.
b. Has Dillin's free cash flow improved or declined from Year 1 to Year 2?

Exercises

EX 16-1 Cash flows from operating activities—net loss **OBJ. 1**

Real World

On its income statement for a recent year, American Airlines Group, Inc., the parent company of American Airlines, reported a net *loss* of $1,834 million from operations. On its statement of cash flows, it reported $675 million of cash flows from operating activities.

Explain this apparent contradiction between the loss and the positive cash flows.

EX 16-2 Effect of transactions on cash flows **OBJ. 1**

✔ a. Cash payment, $411,000

State the effect (cash receipt or payment and amount) of each of the following transactions, considered individually, on cash flows:

a. Retired $400,000 of bonds, on which there was $3,000 of unamortized discount, for $411,000.
b. Sold 20,000 shares of $5 par common stock for $22 per share.
c. Sold equipment with a book value of $55,800 for $60,000.
d. Purchased land for $650,000 cash.
e. Purchased a building by paying $50,000 cash and issuing a $450,000 mortgage note payable.
f. Sold a new issue of $500,000 of bonds at 98.
g. Purchased 10,000 shares of $40 par common stock as treasury stock at $50 per share.
h. Paid dividends of $1.50 per share. There were 1,000,000 shares issued and 120,000 shares of treasury stock.

EX 16-3 Classifying cash flows **OBJ. 1**

Identify the type of cash flow activity for each of the following events (operating, investing, or financing):

a. Redeemed bonds
b. Issued preferred stock
c. Paid cash dividends
d. Net income
e. Sold equipment
f. Purchased treasury stock
g. Purchased patents
h. Purchased buildings
i. Sold long-term investments
j. Issued bonds
k. Issued common stock

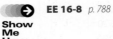

EX 16-4 Cash flows from operating activities—indirect method

OBJ. 2

Indicate whether each of the following would be added to or deducted from net income in determining net cash flow from operating activities by the indirect method:

a. Increase in merchandise inventory
b. Increase in prepaid expenses
c. Depreciation of fixed assets
d. Gain on disposal of fixed assets
e. Amortization of patent
f. Increase in notes payable due in 120 days to vendors
g. Increase in accounts payable
h. Decrease in wages payable
i. Decrease in notes receivable due in 60 days from customers
j. Decrease in accounts receivable
k. Loss on retirement of long-term debt

EX 16-5 Cash flows from operating activities—indirect method

OBJ. 1, 2

✔ Net cash flow from operating activities, $103,850

Show Me How

The net income reported on the income statement for the current year was $73,600. Depreciation recorded on store equipment for the year amounted to $27,400. Balances of the current asset and current liability accounts at the beginning and end of the year are as follows:

	End of Year	Beginning of Year
Cash	$23,500	$18,700
Accounts receivable (net)	56,000	48,000
Merchandise inventory	35,500	40,000
Prepaid expenses	4,750	7,000
Accounts payable (merchandise creditors)	21,800	16,800
Wages payable	4,900	5,800

a. Prepare the Cash flows from operating activities section of the statement of cash flows, using the indirect method.

b. Briefly explain why net cash flow from operating activities is different from net income.

EX 16-6 Cash flows from operating activities—indirect method

OBJ. 1, 2

✔ Net cash flow from operating activities, $260,850

Show Me How

The net income reported on the income statement for the current year was $185,000. Depreciation recorded on equipment and a building amounted to $96,000 for the year. Balances of the current asset and current liability accounts at the beginning and end of the year are as follows:

	End of Year	Beginning of Year
Cash	$ 75,000	$ 86,150
Accounts receivable (net)	84,550	90,000
Inventories	186,200	175,000
Prepaid expenses	3,600	4,500
Accounts payable (merchandise creditors)	91,500	110,000
Salaries payable	7,200	4,000

a. Prepare the Cash flows from operating activities section of the statement of cash flows, using the indirect method.

b. If the direct method had been used, would the net cash flow from operating activities have been the same? Explain.

EX 16-7 Cash flows from operating activities—indirect method

OBJ. 1, 2

✔ Net cash flow from operating activities, $651,300

Show Me How

The income statement disclosed the following items for the year:

Depreciation expense	$ 65,000
Gain on disposal of equipment	27,500
Net income	620,000

(Continued)

The changes in the current asset and liability accounts for the year are as follows:

	Increase (Decrease)
Accounts receivable	$11,200
Inventory	(6,350)
Prepaid insurance	(1,200)
Accounts payable	(4,200)
Income taxes payable	1,650
Dividends payable	2,500

a. Prepare the Cash flows from operating activities section of the statement of cash flows, using the indirect method.

b. Briefly explain why net cash flows from operating activities is different from net income.

Show Me How

EX 16-8 Determining cash payments to stockholders **OBJ. 2**

The board of directors declared cash dividends totaling $585,000 during the current year. The comparative balance sheet indicates dividends payable of $167,625 at the beginning of the year and $146,250 at the end of the year. What was the amount of cash payments to stockholders during the year?

EX 16-9 Reporting changes in equipment on statement of cash flows **OBJ. 2**

An analysis of the general ledger accounts indicates that office equipment, which cost $202,500 and on which accumulated depreciation totaled $84,375 on the date of sale, was sold for $101,250 during the year. Using this information, indicate the items to be reported on the statement of cash flows.

EX 16-10 Reporting changes in equipment on statement of cash flows **OBJ. 2**

An analysis of the general ledger accounts indicates that delivery equipment, which cost $200,000 and on which accumulated depreciation totaled $60,000 on the date of sale, was sold for $132,500 during the year. Using this information, indicate the items to be reported on the statement of cash flows.

EX 16-11 Reporting land transactions on statement of cash flows **OBJ. 2**

On the basis of the details of the following fixed asset account, indicate the items to be reported on the statement of cash flows:

ACCOUNT *Land* ACCOUNT NO.

Date		Item	Debit	Credit	Balance Debit	Balance Credit
Jan.	1	Balance			868,000	
Mar.	12	Purchased for cash	104,300		972,300	
Oct.	4	Sold for $95,550		63,840	908,460	

EX 16-12 Reporting stockholders' equity items on statement of cash flows **OBJ. 2**

On the basis of the following stockholders' equity accounts, indicate the items, exclusive of net income, to be reported on the statement of cash flows. There were no unpaid dividends at either the beginning or the end of the year.

ACCOUNT *Common Stock, $40 par* ACCOUNT NO.

Date		Item	Debit	Credit	Balance Debit	Balance Credit
Jan.	1	Balance, 120,000 shares				4,800,000
Apr.	2	30,000 shares issued for cash		1,200,000		6,000,000
June	30	4,400-share stock dividend		176,000		6,176,000

ACCOUNT ***Paid-In Capital in Excess of Par—Common Stock*** **ACCOUNT NO.**

Date		Item	Debit	Credit	Balance Debit	Balance Credit
Jan.	1	Balance				360,000
Apr.	2	30,000 shares issued for cash		720,000		1,080,000
June	30	Stock dividend		114,400		1,194,400

ACCOUNT ***Retained Earnings*** **ACCOUNT NO.**

Date		Item	Debit	Credit	Balance Debit	Balance Credit
Jan.	1	Balance				2,000,000
June	30	Stock dividend	290,440			1,709,560
Dec.	30	Cash dividend	463,200			1,246,360
	31	Net income		1,440,000		2,686,360

EX 16-13 Reporting land acquisition for cash and mortgage note on statement of cash flows **OBJ. 2**

On the basis of the details of the following fixed asset account, indicate the items to be reported on the statement of cash flows:

ACCOUNT ***Land*** **ACCOUNT NO.**

Date		Item	Debit	Credit	Balance Debit	Balance Credit
Jan.	1	Balance			156,000	
Feb.	10	Purchased for cash	246,000		402,000	
Nov.	20	Purchased with long-term mortgage note	324,000		726,000	

EX 16-14 Reporting issuance and retirement of long-term debt **OBJ. 2**

On the basis of the details of the following bonds payable and related discount accounts, indicate the items to be reported in the financing activities section of the statement of cash flows, assuming no gain or loss on retiring the bonds:

ACCOUNT ***Bonds Payable*** **ACCOUNT NO.**

Date		Item	Debit	Credit	Balance Debit	Balance Credit
Jan.	1	Balance				750,000
	2	Retire bonds	150,000			600,000
June	30	Issue bonds		450,000		1,050,000

ACCOUNT ***Discount on Bonds Payable*** **ACCOUNT NO.**

Date		Item	Debit	Credit	Balance Debit	Balance Credit
Jan.	1	Balance			33,750	
	2	Retire bonds		12,000	21,750	
June	30	Issue bonds	30,000		51,750	
Dec.	31	Amortize discount		2,625	49,125	

EX 16-15 Determining net income from net cash flow from operating activities OBJ. 2

✔ Net income, $341,770

Show Me How

Curwen Inc. reported net cash flow from operating activities of $357,500 on its statement of cash flows for a recent year ended December 31. The following information was reported in the Cash flows from operating activities section of the statement of cash flows, using the indirect method:

Decrease in income taxes payable	$ 7,700
Decrease in inventories	19,140
Depreciation	29,480
Gain on sale of investments	13,200
Increase in accounts payable	5,280
Increase in prepaid expenses	2,970
Increase in accounts receivable	14,300

a. Determine the net income reported by Curwen Inc. for the year ended December 31.

b. Briefly explain why Curwen's net income is different from net cash flow from operating activities.

EX 16-16 Cash flows from operating activities—indirect method OBJ. 2

✔ Net cash flow from operating activities, $58,020

Excel

Real World

Selected data derived from the income statement and balance sheet of National Beverage Co. for a recent year are as follows:

Income statement data (in thousands):	
Net income	$49,311
Gain on disposal of property	1,188
Depreciation expense	11,580
Other items involving noncash expense	1,383
Balance sheet data (in thousands):	
Increase in accounts receivable	1,746
Decrease in inventory	990
Increase in prepaid expenses	605
Decrease in accounts payable and other current liabilities	1,705

a. Prepare the Cash flows from operating activities section of the statement of cash flows, using the indirect method for National Beverage Co.

b. Interpret your results in part (a).

EX 16-17 Statement of cash flows—indirect method OBJ. 2

✔ Net cash flow from operating activities, $38

Excel

Show Me How

The comparative balance sheet of Olson-Jones Industries Inc. for December 31, 20Y2 and 20Y1, is as follows:

	Dec. 31, 20Y2	Dec. 31, 20Y1
Assets		
Cash	$183	$ 14
Accounts receivable (net)	55	49
Inventories	117	99
Land	250	330
Equipment	205	175
Accumulated depreciation—equipment	(68)	(42)
Total assets	$742	$625
Liabilities and Stockholders' Equity		
Accounts payable (merchandise creditors)	$ 51	$ 37
Dividends payable	5	—
Common stock, $1 par	125	80
Paid-in capital: Excess of issue price over par—common stock	85	70
Retained earnings	476	438
Total liabilities and stockholders' equity	$742	$625

The following additional information is taken from the records:

1. Land was sold for $120.
2. Equipment was acquired for cash.
3. There were no disposals of equipment during the year.
4. The common stock was issued for cash.
5. There was a $62 credit to Retained Earnings for net income.
6. There was a $24 debit to Retained Earnings for cash dividends declared.

a. Prepare a statement of cash flows, using the indirect method of presenting cash flows from operating activities.

b. Was Olson-Jones Industries Inc.'s net cash flow from operations more or less than net income? What is the source of this difference?

EX 16-18 Statement of cash flows—indirect method **OBJ. 2**

The following statement of cash flows for Shasta Inc. was not correctly prepared:

Shasta Inc.
Statement of Cash Flows
For the Year Ended December 31, 20Y9

Cash flows from operating activities:		
Net income	$ 360,000	
Adjustments to reconcile net income to net cash flow from operating activities:		
Depreciation	100,800	
Gain on sale of investments	17,280	
Changes in current operating assets and liabilities:		
Increase in accounts receivable	27,360	
Increase in inventories	(36,000)	
Increase in accounts payable	(3,600)	
Decrease in accrued expenses payable	(2,400)	
Net cash flow from operating activities		$ 463,440
Cash flows from (used for) investing activities:		
Cash from sale of investments	$ 240,000	
Cash used for purchase of land	(259,200)	
Cash used for purchase of equipment	(432,000)	
Net cash flow used for investing activities		(415,200)
Cash flows from (used for) financing activities:		
Cash from sale of common stock	$ 312,000	
Cash used for dividends	(132,000)	
Net cash flow from financing activities		180,000
Increase (decrease) in cash		$ 47,760
Cash at the end of the year		192,240
Cash at the beginning of the year		$ 240,000

a. List the errors you find in the statement of cash flows. The cash balance at the beginning of the year was $240,000. All other amounts are correct, except the cash balance at the end of the year.

b. Prepare a corrected statement of cash flows.

✔ a. $801,900

EX 16-19 Cash flows from operating activities—direct method **OBJ. 3**

The cash flows from operating activities are reported by the direct method on the statement of cash flows. Determine the following:

a. If sales for the current year were $753,500 and accounts receivable decreased by $48,400 during the year, what was the amount of cash received from customers?

b. If income tax expense for the current year was $50,600 and income tax payable decreased by $5,500 during the year, what was the amount of cash payments for income taxes?

c. Briefly explain why the cash received from customers in (a) is different from sales.

EX 16-20 Cash paid for merchandise purchases OBJ. 3

Real World

The cost of merchandise sold for Kohl's Corporation for a recent year was $12,265 million. The balance sheet showed the following current account balances (in millions):

	Balance, End of Year	Balance, Beginning of Year
Merchandise inventories	$4,038	$3,814
Accounts payable	1,251	1,511

Determine the amount of cash payments for merchandise.

EX 16-21 Determining selected amounts for cash flows from operating activities—direct method OBJ. 3

✔ a. $1,025,800

Selected data taken from the accounting records of Ginis Inc. for the current year ended December 31 are as follows:

	Balance, December 31	Balance, January 1
Accrued expenses payable (operating expenses)	$ 12,650	$ 14,030
Accounts payable (merchandise creditors)	96,140	105,800
Inventories	178,020	193,430

During the current year, the cost of merchandise sold was $1,031,550 and the operating expenses other than depreciation were $179,400. The direct method is used for presenting the cash flows from operating activities on the statement of cash flows.

Determine the amount reported on the statement of cash flows for (a) cash payments for merchandise and (b) cash payments for operating expenses.

EX 16-22 Cash flows from operating activities—direct method OBJ. 3

✔ Net cash flow from operating activities, $96,040

The income statement of Booker T Industries Inc. for the current year ended June 30 is as follows:

Sales		$511,000
Cost of merchandise sold		290,500
Gross profit		$220,500
Operating expenses:		
Depreciation expense	$ 39,200	
Other operating expenses	105,000	
Total operating expenses		144,200
Income before income tax		$ 76,300
Income tax expense		21,700
Net income		$ 54,600

Changes in the balances of selected accounts from the beginning to the end of the current year are as follows:

	Increase (Decrease)
Accounts receivable (net)	$(11,760)
Inventories	3,920
Prepaid expenses	(3,780)
Accounts payable (merchandise creditors)	(7,980)
Accrued expenses payable (operating expenses)	1,260
Income tax payable	(2,660)

a. Prepare the Cash flows from operating activities section of the statement of cash flows, using the direct method.

b. What does the direct method show about a company's cash flows from operating activities that is not shown using the indirect method?

✔ Net cash flow from operating activities, $123,860

EX 16-23 Cash flows from operating activities—direct method **OBJ. 3**

The income statement for Rhino Company for the current year ended June 30 and balances of selected accounts at the beginning and the end of the year are as follows:

Sales		$445,500
Cost of merchandise sold		154,000
Gross profit		$291,500
Operating expenses:		
Depreciation expense	$ 38,500	
Other operating expenses	115,280	
Total operating expenses		153,780
Income before income tax		$137,720
Income tax expense		39,600
Net income		$ 98,120

	End of Year	Beginning of Year
Accounts receivable (net)	$36,300	$31,240
Inventories	92,400	80,300
Prepaid expenses	14,520	15,840
Accounts payable (merchandise creditors)	67,540	62,700
Accrued expenses payable (operating expenses)	19,140	20,900
Income tax payable	4,400	4,400

Prepare the Cash flows from operating activities section of the statement of cash flows, using the direct method.

Show Me How

FAI

EX 16-24 Free cash flow **OBJ. 4**

Sweeter Enterprises Inc. has cash flows from operating activities of $539,000. Cash flows used for investments in property, plant, and equipment totaled $210,000, of which 75% of this investment was used to replace existing capacity.

a. Determine the free cash flow for Sweeter Enterprises Inc.

b. How might a lender use free cash flow to determine whether or not to give Sweeter Enterprises Inc. a loan?

Real World

FAI

EX 16-25 Free cash flow **OBJ. 4**

The financial statements for Nike, Inc., are provided in Appendix C at the end of the text.

a. Determine the free cash flow for the most recent fiscal year. Assume that 90% of the additions to property, plant, and equipment were used to maintain productive capacity. Round to the nearest thousand dollars.

b. How might a lender use free cash flow to determine whether or not to give Nike, Inc., a loan?

c. Would you feel comfortable giving Nike a loan, based on the free cash flow calculated in (a)?

FAI

EX 16-26 Free cash flow **OBJ. 4**

Lovato Motors Inc. has cash flows from operating activities of $720,000. Cash flows used for investments in property, plant, and equipment totaled $440,000, of which 85% of this investment was used to replace existing capacity.

Determine the free cash flow for Lovato Motors Inc.

Problems: Series A

PR 16-1A Statement of cash flows—indirect method

OBJ. 2

✔ Net cash flow from operating activities, $490,000

Excel

Show Me How

The comparative balance sheet of Navaria Inc. for December 31, 20Y3 and 20Y2, is shown as follows:

	Dec. 31, 20Y3	Dec. 31, 20Y2
Assets		
Cash	$ 155,000	$ 150,000
Accounts receivable (net)	450,000	400,000
Inventories	770,000	750,000
Investments	0	100,000
Land	500,000	0
Equipment	1,400,000	1,200,000
Accumulated depreciation—equipment	(600,000)	(500,000)
Total assets	$2,675,000	$2,100,000
Liabilities and Stockholders' Equity		
Accounts payable	$ 340,000	$ 300,000
Accrued expenses payable	45,000	50,000
Dividends payable	30,000	25,000
Common stock, $4 par	700,000	600,000
Paid-in capital: Excess of issue price over par—common stock	200,000	175,000
Retained earnings	1,360,000	950,000
Total liabilities and stockholders' equity	$2,675,000	$2,100,000

Additional data obtained from an examination of the accounts in the ledger for 20Y3 are as follows:

a. The investments were sold for $175,000 cash.
b. Equipment and land were acquired for cash.
c. There were no disposals of equipment during the year.
d. The common stock was issued for cash.
e. There was a $500,000 credit to Retained Earnings for net income.
f. There was a $90,000 debit to Retained Earnings for cash dividends declared.

Instructions

Prepare a statement of cash flows, using the indirect method of presenting cash flows from operating activities.

PR 16-2A Statement of cash flows—indirect method

OBJ. 2

✔ Net cash flow from operating activities, $225,000

Excel

Show Me How

The comparative balance sheet of Yellow Dog Enterprises Inc. at December 31, 20Y8 and 20Y7, is as follows:

	Dec. 31, 20Y8	Dec. 31, 20Y7
Assets		
Cash	$ 80,000	$ 100,000
Accounts receivable (net)	275,000	300,000
Merchandise inventory	510,000	400,000
Prepaid expenses	15,000	10,000
Equipment	1,070,000	750,000
Accumulated depreciation—equipment	(200,000)	(160,000)
Total assets	$1,750,000	$1,400,000

	Dec. 31, 20Y8	Dec. 31, 20Y7
Liabilities and Stockholders' Equity		
Accounts payable (merchandise creditors)	$ 100,000	$ 90,000
Mortgage note payable	0	400,000
Common stock, $10 par	600,000	200,000
Paid-in capital: Excess of issue price over par—common stock	300,000	100,000
Retained earnings	750,000	610,000
Total liabilities and stockholders' equity	$1,750,000	$1,400,000

Additional data obtained from the income statement and from an examination of the accounts in the ledger for 20Y8 are as follows:

a. Net income, $190,000.

b. Depreciation reported on the income statement, $115,000.

c. Equipment was purchased at a cost of $395,000, and fully depreciated equipment costing $75,000 was discarded, with no salvage realized.

d. The mortgage note payable was not due for six years, but the terms permitted earlier payment without penalty.

e. 40,000 shares of common stock were issued at $15 for cash.

f. Cash dividends declared and paid, $50,000.

Instructions

Prepare a statement of cash flows, using the indirect method.

PR 16-3A Statement of cash flows—indirect method

OBJ. 2

✔ Net cash flow from operating activities, $(169,600)

Excel

The comparative balance sheet of Whitman Co. at December 31, 20Y2 and 20Y1, is as follows:

	Dec. 31, 20Y2	Dec. 31, 20Y1
Assets		
Cash	$ 918,000	$ 964,800
Accounts receivable (net)	828,900	761,940
Inventories	1,268,460	1,162,980
Prepaid expenses	29,340	35,100
Land	315,900	479,700
Buildings	1,462,500	900,900
Accumulated depreciation—buildings	(408,600)	(382,320)
Equipment	512,280	454,680
Accumulated depreciation—equipment	(141,300)	(158,760)
Total assets	$4,785,480	$4,219,020
Liabilities and Stockholders' Equity		
Accounts payable (merchandise creditors)	$ 922,500	$ 958,320
Bonds payable	270,000	0
Common stock, $25 par	317,000	117,000
Paid-in capital: Excess of issue price over par—common stock	758,000	558,000
Retained earnings	2,517,980	2,585,700
Total liabilities and stockholders' equity	$4,785,480	$4,219,020

The noncurrent asset, noncurrent liability, and stockholders' equity accounts for 20Y2 are as follows:

ACCOUNT ***Land*** **ACCOUNT NO.**

Date		Item	Debit	Credit	Balance Debit	Balance Credit
20Y2						
Jan.	1	Balance			479,700	
Apr.	20	Realized $151,200 cash from sale		163,800	315,900	

(Continued)

ACCOUNT ***Buildings*** **ACCOUNT NO.**

Date		Item	Debit	Credit	Balance Debit	Balance Credit
20Y2						
Jan.	1	Balance			900,900	
Apr.	20	Acquired for cash	561,600		1,462,500	

ACCOUNT ***Accumulated Depreciation—Buildings*** **ACCOUNT NO.**

Date		Item	Debit	Credit	Balance Debit	Balance Credit
20Y2						
Jan.	1	Balance				382,320
Dec.	31	Depreciation for year		26,280		408,600

ACCOUNT ***Equipment*** **ACCOUNT NO.**

Date		Item	Debit	Credit	Balance Debit	Balance Credit
20Y2						
Jan.	1	Balance			454,680	
	26	Discarded, no salvage		46,800	407,880	
Aug.	11	Purchased for cash	104,400		512,280	

ACCOUNT ***Accumulated Depreciation—Equipment*** **ACCOUNT NO.**

Date		Item	Debit	Credit	Balance Debit	Balance Credit
20Y2						
Jan.	1	Balance				158,760
	26	Equipment discarded	46,800			111,960
Dec.	31	Depreciation for year		29,340		141,300

ACCOUNT ***Bonds Payable*** **ACCOUNT NO.**

Date		Item	Debit	Credit	Balance Debit	Balance Credit
20Y2						
May	1	Issued 20-year bonds		270,000		270,000

ACCOUNT ***Common Stock, $25 par*** **ACCOUNT NO.**

Date		Item	Debit	Credit	Balance Debit	Balance Credit
20Y2						
Jan.	1	Balance				117,000
Dec.	7	Issued 8,000 shares of common stock for $50 per share		200,000		317,000

ACCOUNT ***Paid-In Capital in Excess of Par—Common Stock*** **ACCOUNT NO.**

Date		Item	Debit	Credit	Balance Debit	Balance Credit
20Y2						
Jan.	1	Balance				558,000
Dec.	7	Issued 8,000 shares of common stock for $50 per share		200,000		758,000

ACCOUNT ***Retained Earnings*** **ACCOUNT NO.**

Date		Item	Debit	Credit	Balance Debit	Balance Credit
20Y2						
Jan.	1	Balance				2,585,700
Dec.	31	Net loss	35,320			2,550,380
	31	Cash dividends	32,400			2,517,980

Instructions

Prepare a statement of cash flows, using the indirect method of presenting cash flows from operating activities.

✔ Net cash flow from operating activities, $293,600

Excel

General Ledger

Show Me How

PR 16-4A Statement of cash flows—direct method **OBJ. 3**

The comparative balance sheet of Canace Products Inc. for December 31, 20Y6 and 20Y5, is as follows:

	Dec. 31, 20Y6	Dec. 31, 20Y5
Assets		
Cash	$ 643,400	$ 679,400
Accounts receivable (net)	566,800	547,400
Inventories	1,011,000	982,800
Investments	0	240,000
Land	520,000	0
Equipment	880,000	680,000
Accumulated depreciation	(244,400)	(200,400)
Total assets	$3,376,800	$2,929,200
Liabilities and Stockholders' Equity		
Accounts payable	$ 771,800	$ 748,400
Accrued expenses payable	63,400	70,800
Dividends payable	8,800	6,400
Common stock, $2 par	56,000	32,000
Paid-in capital: Excess of issue price over par—common stock	408,000	192,000
Retained earnings	2,068,800	1,879,600
Total liabilities and stockholders' equity	$3,376,800	$2,929,200

The income statement for the year ended December 31, 20Y6, is as follows:

Sales		$5,980,000
Cost of merchandise sold		2,452,000
Gross profit		$3,528,000
Operating expenses:		
Depreciation expense	$ 44,000	
Other operating expenses	3,100,000	
Total operating expenses		3,144,000

(Continued)

Operating income	$ 384,000
Other expense:	
Loss on sale of investments	(64,000)
Income before income tax	$ 320,000
Income tax expense	102,800
Net income	$ 217,200

Additional data obtained from an examination of the accounts in the ledger for 20Y6 are as follows:

a. Equipment and land were acquired for cash.
b. There were no disposals of equipment during the year.
c. The investments were sold for $176,000 cash.
d. The common stock was issued for cash.
e. There was a $28,000 debit to Retained Earnings for cash dividends declared.

Instructions

Prepare a statement of cash flows, using the direct method of presenting cash flows from operating activities.

PR 16-5A Statement of cash flows—direct method applied to PR 16-1A **OBJ. 3**

✔ Net cash flow from operating activities, $490,000

Excel

The comparative balance sheet of Navaria Inc. for December 31, 20Y3 and 20Y2, is as follows:

	Dec. 31, 20Y3	Dec. 31, 20Y2
Assets		
Cash	$ 155,000	$ 150,000
Accounts receivable (net)	450,000	400,000
Inventories	770,000	750,000
Investments	0	100,000
Land	500,000	0
Equipment	1,400,000	1,200,000
Accumulated depreciation—equipment	(600,000)	(500,000)
Total assets	$2,675,000	$2,100,000
Liabilities and Stockholders' Equity		
Accounts payable	$ 340,000	$ 300,000
Accrued expenses payable	45,000	50,000
Dividends payable	30,000	25,000
Common stock, $4 par	700,000	600,000
Paid-in capital: Excess of issue price over par—common stock	200,000	175,000
Retained earnings	1,360,000	950,000
Total liabilities and stockholders' equity	$2,675,000	$2,100,000

The income statement for the year ended December 31, 20Y3, is as follows:

Sales		$3,000,000
Cost of merchandise sold		1,400,000
Gross profit		$1,600,000
Operating expenses:		
Depreciation expense	$ 100,000	
Other operating expenses	950,000	
Total operating expenses		1,050,000
Operating income		$ 550,000
Other income:		
Gain on sale of investments		75,000
Income before income tax		$ 625,000
Income tax expense		125,000
Net income		$ 500,000

Additional data obtained from an examination of the accounts in the ledger for 20Y3 are as follows:

a. The investments were sold for $175,000 cash.
b. Equipment and land were acquired for cash.
c. There were no disposals of equipment during the year.
d. The common stock was issued for cash.
e. There was a $90,000 debit to Retained Earnings for cash dividends declared.

Instructions

Prepare a statement of cash flows, using the direct method of presenting cash flows from operating activities.

Problems: Series B

PR 16-1B Statement of cash flows—indirect method

OBJ. 2

✔ Net cash flow from operating activities, $154,260

Excel

Show Me How

The comparative balance sheet of Merrick Equipment Co. for December 31, 20Y9 and 20Y8, is as follows:

	Dec. 31, 20Y9	Dec. 31, 20Y8
Assets		
Cash	$ 70,720	$ 47,940
Accounts receivable (net)	207,230	188,190
Inventories	298,520	289,850
Investments	0	102,000
Land	295,800	0
Equipment	438,600	358,020
Accumulated depreciation—equipment	(99,110)	(84,320)
Total assets	$1,211,760	$901,680
Liabilities and Stockholders' Equity		
Accounts payable	$ 205,700	$194,140
Accrued expenses payable	30,600	26,860
Dividends payable	25,500	20,400
Common stock, $1 par	202,000	102,000
Paid-in capital: Excess of issue price over par—common stock	354,000	204,000
Retained earnings	393,960	354,280
Total liabilities and stockholders' equity	$1,211,760	$901,680

Additional data obtained from an examination of the accounts in the ledger for 20Y9 are as follows:

a. Equipment and land were acquired for cash.
b. There were no disposals of equipment during the year.
c. The investments were sold for $91,800 cash.
d. The common stock was issued for cash.
e. There was a $141,680 credit to Retained Earnings for net income.
f. There was a $102,000 debit to Retained Earnings for cash dividends declared.

Instructions

Prepare a statement of cash flows, using the indirect method of presenting cash flows from operating activities.

PR 16-2B Statement of cash flows—indirect method

OBJ. 2

✔ Net cash flow from operating activities, $561,400

Excel

Show Me How

The comparative balance sheet of Harris Industries Inc. at December 31, 20Y4 and 20Y3, is as follows:

	Dec. 31, 20Y4	Dec. 31, 20Y3
Assets		
Cash	$ 443,240	$ 360,920
Accounts receivable (net)	665,280	592,200
Inventories	887,880	1,022,560
Prepaid expenses	31,640	25,200
Land	302,400	302,400
Buildings	1,713,600	1,134,000
Accumulated depreciation—buildings	(466,200)	(414,540)
Machinery and equipment	781,200	781,200
Accumulated depreciation—machinery and equipment	(214,200)	(191,520)
Patents	106,960	112,000
Total assets	$4,251,800	$3,724,420
Liabilities and Stockholders' Equity		
Accounts payable	$ 837,480	$ 927,080
Dividends payable	32,760	25,200
Salaries payable	78,960	87,080
Mortgage note payable, due in 10 years	224,000	0
Bonds payable	0	390,000
Common stock, $5 par	200,400	50,400
Paid-in capital: Excess of issue price over par—common stock	366,000	126,000
Retained earnings	2,512,200	2,118,660
Total liabilities and stockholders' equity	$4,251,800	$3,724,420

An examination of the income statement and the accounting records revealed the following additional information applicable to 20Y4:

a. Net income, $524,580.
b. Depreciation expense reported on the income statement: buildings, $51,660; machinery and equipment, $22,680.
c. Patent amortization reported on the income statement, $5,040.
d. A building was constructed for $579,600.
e. A mortgage note for $224,000 was issued for cash.
f. 30,000 shares of common stock were issued at $13 in exchange for the bonds payable.
g. Cash dividends declared, $131,040.

Instructions

Prepare a statement of cash flows, using the indirect method.

PR 16-3B Statement of cash flows—indirect method

OBJ. 2

✔ Net cash flow from operating activities, $162,800

Excel

The comparative balance sheet of Coulson, Inc. at December 31, 20Y2 and 20Y1, is as follows:

	Dec. 31, 20Y2	Dec. 31, 20Y1
Assets		
Cash	$ 300,600	$ 337,800
Accounts receivable (net)	704,400	609,600
Inventories	918,600	865,800
Prepaid expenses	18,600	26,400
Land	990,000	1,386,000

Buildings	$1,980,000	$ 990,000
Accumulated depreciation—buildings	(397,200)	(366,000)
Equipment	660,600	529,800
Accumulated depreciation—equipment	(133,200)	(162,000)
Total assets	$5,042,400	$4,217,400
Liabilities and Stockholders' Equity		
Accounts payable	$ 594,000	$ 631,200
Income taxes payable	26,400	21,600
Bonds payable	330,000	0
Common stock, $20 par	320,000	180,000
Paid-in capital: Excess of issue price over par—common stock	950,000	810,000
Retained earnings	2,822,000	2,574,600
Total liabilities and stockholders' equity	$5,042,400	$4,217,400

The noncurrent asset, noncurrent liability, and stockholders' equity accounts for 20Y2 are as follows:

ACCOUNT ***Land*** **ACCOUNT NO.**

Date		Item	Debit	Credit	Balance Debit	Balance Credit
20Y2						
Jan.	1	Balance			1,386,000	
Apr.	20	Realized $456,000 cash from sale		396,000	990,000	

ACCOUNT ***Buildings*** **ACCOUNT NO.**

Date		Item	Debit	Credit	Balance Debit	Balance Credit
20Y2						
Jan.	1	Balance			990,000	
Apr.	20	Acquired for cash	990,000		1,980,000	

ACCOUNT ***Accumulated Depreciation—Buildings*** **ACCOUNT NO.**

Date		Item	Debit	Credit	Balance Debit	Balance Credit
20Y2						
Jan.	1	Balance				366,000
Dec.	31	Depreciation for year		31,200		397,200

ACCOUNT ***Equipment*** **ACCOUNT NO.**

Date		Item	Debit	Credit	Balance Debit	Balance Credit
20Y2						
Jan.	1	Balance			529,800	
	26	Discarded, no salvage		66,000	463,800	
Aug.	11	Purchased for cash	196,800		660,600	

(Continued)

ACCOUNT ***Accumulated Depreciation—Equipment*** **ACCOUNT NO.**

Date		Item	Debit	Credit	Balance Debit	Balance Credit
20Y2						
Jan.	1	Balance				162,000
	26	Equipment discarded	66,000			96,000
Dec.	31	Depreciation for year		37,200		133,200

ACCOUNT ***Bonds Payable*** **ACCOUNT NO.**

Date		Item	Debit	Credit	Balance Debit	Balance Credit
20Y2						
May	1	Issued 20-year bonds		330,000		330,000

ACCOUNT ***Common Stock, $20 par*** **ACCOUNT NO.**

Date		Item	Debit	Credit	Balance Debit	Balance Credit
20Y2						
Jan.	1	Balance				180,000
Dec.	7	Issued 7,000 shares of common stock for $40 per share		140,000		320,000

ACCOUNT ***Paid-In Capital in Excess of Par—Common Stock*** **ACCOUNT NO.**

Date		Item	Debit	Credit	Balance Debit	Balance Credit
20Y2						
Jan.	1	Balance				810,000
Dec.	7	Issued 7,000 shares of common stock for $40 per share		140,000		950,000

ACCOUNT ***Retained Earnings*** **ACCOUNT NO.**

Date		Item	Debit	Credit	Balance Debit	Balance Credit
20Y2						
Jan.	1	Balance				2,574,600
Dec.	31	Net income		326,600		2,901,200
	31	Cash dividends	79,200			2,822,000

Instructions

Prepare a statement of cash flows, using the indirect method of presenting cash flows from operating activities.

✔ Net cash flow from operating activities, $509,220

Excel

General Ledger

Show Me How

PR 16-4B Statement of cash flows—direct method

OBJ. 3

The comparative balance sheet of Martinez Inc. for December 31, 20Y4 and 20Y3, is as follows:

	Dec. 31, 20Y4	Dec. 31, 20Y3
Assets		
Cash	$ 661,920	$ 683,100
Accounts receivable (net)	992,640	914,400
Inventories	1,394,400	1,363,800
Investments	0	432,000
Land	960,000	0
Equipment	1,224,000	984,000
Accumulated depreciation—equipment	(481,500)	(368,400)
Total assets	$4,751,460	$4,008,900
Liabilities and Stockholders' Equity		
Accounts payable	$1,080,000	$ 966,600
Accrued expenses payable	67,800	79,200
Dividends payable	100,800	91,200
Common stock, $5 par	130,000	30,000
Paid-in capital: Excess of issue price over par—common stock	950,000	450,000
Retained earnings	2,422,860	2,391,900
Total liabilities and stockholders' equity	$4,751,460	$4,008,900

The income statement for the year ended December 31, 20Y4, is as follows:

Sales		$4,512,000
Cost of merchandise sold		2,352,000
Gross profit		$2,160,000
Operating expenses:		
Depreciation expense	$ 113,100	
Other operating expenses	1,344,840	
Total operating expenses		1,457,940
Operating income		$ 702,060
Other income:		
Gain on sale of investments		156,000
Income before income tax		$ 858,060
Income tax expense		299,100
Net income		$ 558,960

Additional data obtained from an examination of the accounts in the ledger for 20Y4 are as follows:

a. Equipment and land were acquired for cash.
b. There were no disposals of equipment during the year.
c. The investments were sold for $588,000 cash.
d. The common stock was issued for cash.
e. There was a $528,000 debit to Retained Earnings for cash dividends declared.

Instructions

Prepare a statement of cash flows, using the direct method of presenting cash flows from operating activities.

PR 16-5B Statement of cash flows—direct method applied to PR 16-1B

OBJ. 3

✔ Net cash flow from operating activities, $154,260

Excel

The comparative balance sheet of Merrick Equipment Co. for Dec. 31, 20Y9 and 20Y8, is as follows:

	Dec. 31, 20Y9	Dec. 31, 20Y8
Assets		
Cash	$ 70,720	$ 47,940
Accounts receivable (net)	207,230	188,190
Inventories	298,520	289,850
Investments	0	102,000
Land	295,800	0
Equipment	438,600	358,020
Accumulated depreciation—equipment	(99,110)	(84,320)
Total assets	$1,211,760	$901,680
Liabilities and Stockholders' Equity		
Accounts payable	$ 205,700	$194,140
Accrued expenses payable	30,600	26,860
Dividends payable	25,500	20,400
Common stock, $1 par	202,000	102,000
Paid-in capital: Excess of issue price over par—common stock	354,000	204,000
Retained earnings	393,960	354,280
Total liabilities and stockholders' equity	$1,211,760	$901,680

The income statement for the year ended December 31, 20Y9, is as follows:

Sales		$2,023,898
Cost of merchandise sold		1,245,476
Gross profit		$ 778,422
Operating expenses:		
Depreciation expense	$ 14,790	
Other operating expenses	517,299	
Total operating expenses		532,089
Operating income		$ 246,333
Other expenses:		
Loss on sale of investments		(10,200)
Income before income tax		$ 236,133
Income tax expense		94,453
Net income		$ 141,680

Additional data obtained from an examination of the accounts in the ledger for 20Y9 are as follows:

a. Equipment and land were acquired for cash.
b. There were no disposals of equipment during the year.
c. The investments were sold for $91,800 cash.
d. The common stock was issued for cash.
e. There was a $102,000 debit to Retained Earnings for cash dividends declared.

Instructions

Prepare a statement of cash flows, using the direct method of presenting cash flows from operating activities.

Cases & Projects

Ethics

CP 16-1 Ethics in Action

Lucas Hunter, president of Simmons Industries Inc., believes that reporting operating cash flow per share on the income statement would be a useful addition to the company's just completed financial statements. The following discussion took place between Lucas Hunter and Simmons' controller, John Jameson, in January, after the close of the fiscal year:

Lucas: I've been reviewing our financial statements for the last year. I am disappointed that our net income per share has dropped by 10% from last year. This won't look good to our shareholders. Is there anything we can do about this?

John: What do you mean? The past is the past, and the numbers are in. There isn't much that can be done about it. Our financial statements were prepared according to generally accepted accounting principles, and I don't see much leeway for significant change at this point.

Lucas: No, no. I'm not suggesting that we "cook the books." But look at the cash flow from operating activities on the statement of cash flows. The cash flow from operating activities has increased by 20%. This is very good news—and, I might add, useful information. The higher cash flow from operating activities will give our creditors comfort.

John: Well, the cash flow from operating activities is on the statement of cash flows, so I guess users will be able to see the improved cash flow figures there.

Lucas: This is true, but somehow I think this information should be given a much higher profile. I don't like this information being "buried" in the statement of cash flows. You know as well as I do that many users will focus on the income statement. Therefore, I think we ought to include an operating cash flow per share number on the face of the income statement—someplace under the earnings per share number. In this way, users will get the complete picture of our operating performance. Yes, our earnings per share dropped this year, but our cash flow from operating activities improved! And all the information is in one place where users can see and compare the figures. What do you think?

John: I've never really thought about it like that before. I guess we could put the operating cash flow per share on the income statement, underneath the earnings per share amount. Users would really benefit from this disclosure. Thanks for the idea—I'll start working on it.

Lucas: Glad to be of service.

How would you interpret this situation? Is John behaving in an ethical and professional manner?

Team Activity

Real World

CP 16-2 Team Activity

In teams, select a public company that interests you. Obtain the company's most recent annual report on Form 10-K. The Form 10-K is a company's annually required filing with the Securities and Exchange Commission (SEC). It includes the company's financial statements and accompanying notes. The Form 10-K can be obtained either (a) by referring to the investor relations section of the company's website or (b) by using the company search feature of the SEC's EDGAR database service found at www.sec.gov/edgar/searchedgar/companysearch.html.

1. Based on the information in the company's most recent annual report, answer the following questions:
   a. What is the net cash flows from operating activities reported by the company at the end of the most recent year?
   b. What is the net cash flows from (used for) investing activities reported by the company at the end of the most recent year?
   c. What is the net cash flows from (used for) financing activities reported by the company at the end of the most recent year?
   d. What was the net increase (or decrease) in cash during the year?
2. Evaluate the company's cash inflows and outflows.

CP 16-3 Communication

Communication

Tidewater Inc., a retailer, provided the following financial information for its most recent fiscal year:

Net income	$945,000
Return on invested capital	8%
Cash flows from operating activities	$(1,428,000)
Cash flows from investing activities	$600,000
Cash flows from financing activities	$900,000

The company's Cash flows from operating activities section is as follows:

Net income	$ 945,000
Depreciation	210,000
Increase in accounts receivable	(1,134,000)
Increase in inventory	(1,260,000)
Decrease in accounts payable	(189,000)
Net cash flow from operating activities	$(1,428,000)

An examination of the financial statements revealed the following additional information:

- Revenues increased during the year as a result of an aggressive marketing campaign aimed at increasing the number of new "Tidewater Card" credit card customers. This is the company's branded credit card, which can only be used at Tidewater stores. The credit card balances are accounts receivable on Tidewater's balance sheet.
- Some suppliers have made their merchandise available at a deep discount. As a result, the company purchased large quantities of these goods in an attempt to improve the company's profitability.
- In recent years, the company has struggled to pay its accounts payable on time. The company has improved on this during the past year and is nearly caught up on overdue payables balances.
- The company reported net losses in each of the two prior years.

Write a brief memo to your instructor evaluating the financial condition of Tidewater Inc.

CP 16-4 Using the statement of cash flows

You are considering an investment in a new start-up company, Giraffe Inc., an Internet service provider. A review of the company's financial statements reveals a negative retained earnings. In addition, it appears as though the company has been running a negative cash flow from operating activities since the company's inception.

How is the company staying in business under these circumstances? Could this be a good investment?

CP 16-5 Analysis of statement of cash flows

Dillip Lachgar is the president and majority shareholder of Argon Inc., a small retail chain store. Recently, Dillip submitted a loan application for Argon Inc. to Compound Bank. It called for a $600,000, 9%, 10-year loan to help finance the construction of a building and the purchase of store equipment, costing a total of $750,000. This will enable Argon Inc. to open a store in the town of Compound. Land for this purpose was acquired last year. The bank's loan officer requested a statement of cash flows in addition to the most recent income statement, balance sheet, and retained earnings statement that Dillip had submitted with the loan application.

As a close family friend, Dillip asked you to prepare a statement of cash flows. From the records provided, you prepared the following statement:

Argon Inc.
Statement of Cash Flows
For the Year Ended December 31, 20Y7

Cash flows from operating activities:		
Net income	$ 300,000	
Adjustments to reconcile net income to net cash flow from operating activities:		
Depreciation	84,000	
Gain on sale of investments	(30,000)	
Changes in current operating assets and liabilities:		
Decrease in accounts receivable	21,000	
Increase in inventories	(42,000)	
Increase in accounts payable	30,000	
Decrease in accrued expenses payable	(6,000)	
Net cash flow from operating activities		$ 357,000
Cash flows from (used for) investing activities:		
Cash from investments sold	$ 180,000	
Cash used for purchase of store equipment	(120,000)	
Net cash flow from investing activities		60,000
Cash flows from (used for) financing activities:		
Cash used for dividends	$ (126,000)	
Net cash flow used for financing activities		(126,000)
Increase (decrease) in cash		$ 291,000
Cash at the beginning of the year		108,000
Cash at the end of the year		$ 399,000
Schedule of Noncash Financing and Investing Activities:		
Issued common stock for land		$ 240,000

After reviewing the statement, Dillip telephoned you and commented, "Are you sure this statement is right?" Dillip then raised the following questions:

1. "How can depreciation be a cash flow?"
2. "Issuing common stock for the land is listed in a separate schedule. This transaction has nothing to do with cash! Shouldn't this transaction be eliminated from the statement?"
3. "How can the gain on the sale of investments be a deduction from net income in determining the cash flow from operating activities?"
4. "Why does the bank need this statement anyway? They can compute the increase in cash from the balance sheets for the last two years."

After jotting down Dillip's questions, you assured him that this statement was "right." But to alleviate Dillip's concern, you arranged a meeting for the following day.

a. How would you respond to each of Dillip's questions?

b. Do you think that the statement of cash flows enhances the chances of Argon Inc. receiving the loan? Discuss.

Team Activity

Real World

FAI

CP 16-6 Team Activity

This activity will require two teams to retrieve cash flow statement information from the Internet. One team is to obtain the most recent year's statement of cash flows for Johnson & Johnson; the other team, the most recent year's statement of cash flows for JetBlue Airways Corp.

The statement of cash flows is included as part of the annual report information that is a required disclosure to the Securities and Exchange Commission (SEC). SEC documents can be retrieved using the EdgarScan™ service at www.sec.gov/edgar/searchedgar/companysearch.html.

(Continued)

To obtain annual report information, key a company name in the appropriate space. EdgarScan will list the reports available to you for the company you've selected. Select the most recent annual report filing, identified as a 10-K or 10-K405. EdgarScan provides an outline of the report, including the separate financial statements.

As a group, compare the two statements of cash flows.

a. How are Johnson & Johnson and JetBlue Airways Corp. similar or different regarding cash flows?

b. Compute and compare the free cash flow for each company, assuming that additions to property, plant, and equipment replace current capacity.

CHAPTER 17

Financial Statement Analysis

Chapters 1–4
Accounting Cycle

Chapter 5
Accounting Systems

Income Statement	**Retained Earnings Statement**	**Balance Sheet**	**Statement of Cash Flows**
Chapter 6 *Accounting for Merchandising Businesses*			Chapter 16 *Statement of Cash Flows*

Assets	=	**Liabilities**	+	**Stockholders' Equity**
Chapter 8 *Cash*		Chapter 11 *Current Liabilities and Payroll*		Chapter 12 *Partnerships*
Chapter 9 *Receivables*		Chapter 14 *Bonds and Notes*		Chapter 13 *Corporations*
Chapter 7 *Inventories*				
Chapter 10 *Fixed and Intangible Assets*				
Chapter 15 *Investments*				

Chapter 17
Financial Statement Analysis

Retained Earnings Statement

Retained earnings, Jan. 1		$XXX
Net income	$ XXX	
Dividends	(XXX)	

Statement of Cash Flows

Cash flows from operating activities	$XXX
Cash flows from investing activities	XXX
Cash flows from financing activities	XXX
	$XXX
	XXX
	$XXX

Income Statement

Sales		$XXX
Cost of goods sold		XXX
Gross profit		$XXX
Operating expenses:		
Advertising expense	$XXX	
Depreciation expense	XXX	
Amortization expense	XXX	
Depletion expense	XXX	
…	XXX	
…	XXX	
Total operating expenses		XXX
Income from operations		$XXX
Other revenue and expenses		XXX
Net income		$XXX

Balance Sheet

Current assets:		
Cash	$XXX	
Accounts receivable	XXX	
Inventory	XXX	
Total current assets		$XXX
Long-term assets:		
Fixed assets	$XXX	
Intangible assets	XXX	
Total long-term assets		XXX
Total assets		$XXX
Liabilities:		
Current liabilities	$XXX	
Long-term liabilities	XXX	
Total liabilities		$XXX
Stockholders' equity		XXX
Total liabilities and stockholders' equity		$XXX

CHAPTER 17

©JOSHUA RAINEY PHOTOGRAPHY/SHUTTERSTOCK.COM

Nike, Inc.

"Just do it." These three words identify one of the most recognizable brands in the world, **Nike**. While this phrase inspires athletes to "compete and achieve their potential," it also defines the company.

Nike began in 1964 as a partnership between University of Oregon track coach Bill Bowerman and one of his former student-athletes, Phil Knight. The two began by selling shoes imported from Japan out of the back of Knight's car to athletes at track-and-field events. As sales grew, the company opened retail outlets, calling itself **Blue Ribbon Sports**. The company also began to develop its own shoes. In 1971, the company commissioned a graphic design student at Portland State University to develop the swoosh logo for a fee of $35. In 1978, the company changed its name to Nike, and in 1980, it sold its first shares of stock to the public.

Nike would have been a great company to invest in at the time. If you had invested in Nike's common stock back in 1990, you would have paid $5 per share. As of September 2016, Nike's stock was worth over $55 per share. Unfortunately, you can't invest using hindsight.

How can you select companies in which to invest? Like any significant purchase, you should do some research to guide your investment decision. If you were buying a car, for example, you might go to **Edmunds.com** to obtain reviews, ratings, prices, specifications, options, and fuel economies to evaluate different vehicles. In selecting companies in which to invest, you can use financial analysis to gain insight into a company's past performance and future prospects. This chapter describes and illustrates common financial data that can be analyzed to assist you in making investment decisions such as whether or not to invest in Nike's stock.

Source: http://news.nike.com

Learning Objectives

After studying this chapter, you should be able to:

Example Exercises (EE) are shown in **green.**

Obj. 1 **Describe the techniques and tools used to analyze financial statement information.**

Analyzing and Interpreting Financial Statements
The Value of Financial Statement Information
Techniques for Analyzing Financial Statements

Obj. 2 **Describe and illustrate basic financial statement analytical methods.**

Basic Analytical Methods
Horizontal Analysis — EE 17-1
Vertical Analysis — EE 17-2
Common-Sized Statements

Obj. 3 **Describe and illustrate how to use financial statement analysis to assess liquidity.**

Analyzing Liquidity
Current Position Analysis — EE 17-3
Accounts Receivable Analysis — EE 17-4
Inventory Analysis — EE 17-5

Obj. 4 **Describe and illustrate how to use financial statement analysis to assess solvency.**

Analyzing Solvency
Ratio of Fixed Assets to Long-Term Liabilities
Ratio of Liabilities to Stockholders' Equity — EE 17-6
Times Interest Earned — EE 17-7

Obj. 5 **Describe and illustrate how to use financial statement analysis to assess profitability.**

Analyzing Profitability
Asset Turnover — EE 17-8
Return on Total Assets — EE 17-9
Return on Stockholders' Equity
Return on Common Stockholders' Equity — EE 17-10
Earnings per Share on Common Stock
Price-Earnings Ratio — EE 17-11
Dividends per Share
Dividend Yield
Summary of Analytical Measures

Obj. 6 **Describe the contents of corporate annual reports.**

Corporate Annual Reports
Management Discussion and Analysis
Report on Internal Control
Report on Fairness of the Financial Statements

At a Glance 17 Page 852

Analyzing and Interpreting Financial Statements

Obj. 1 Describe the techniques and tools used to analyze financial statement information.

The objective of accounting is to provide relevant and timely information to support the decision-making needs of financial statement users. Bankers, creditors, and investors all rely on financial statements to provide insight into a company's financial condition and performance. This chapter discusses the value of financial statement information, techniques used to evaluate financial statements, and how this information can be used in decision making.

The Value of Financial Statement Information

General-purpose financial statements are distributed to a wide range of potential users, providing each group with valuable information about a company's economic performance and financial condition. Users typically evaluate this information along three dimensions: liquidity, solvency, and profitability.

Liquidity Short-term creditors such as banks and financial institutions are concerned primarily with whether a company will be able to repay short-term borrowings such as loans and notes. As such, they are most interested in evaluating a company's ability to convert assets into cash, which is called **liquidity**.

Solvency Long-term creditors such as bondholders loan money for long periods of time. Thus, they are interested in evaluating a company's ability to make its periodic interest payments and repay the face amount of debt at maturity, which is called **solvency**.

Profitability Investors such as stockholders are the owners of the company. They benefit from increases in the price of a company's shares and are interested in evaluating the potential for the price of the company's stock to increase. The price of a company's stock depends on a variety of factors, including the company's current and potential future earnings. As such, investors focus on evaluating a company's ability to generate earnings, which is called **profitability**.

Techniques for Analyzing Financial Statements

Financial statement users rely on the following techniques to analyze and interpret a company's financial performance and condition:

- **Analytical methods** examine changes in the amount and percentage of financial statement items within and across periods.
- **Ratios** express a financial statement item or set of financial statement items as a percentage of another financial statement item in order to measure an important economic relationship as a single number.

Both analytical methods and ratios can be used to compare a company's financial performance over time or to another company.

- *Comparisons over Time:* The comparison of a financial statement item or ratio with the same item or ratio from a prior period often helps the user identify trends in a company's economic performance, financial condition, liquidity, solvency, and profitability.
- *Comparisons Between Companies:* The comparison of a financial statement item or ratio to another company in the same industry can provide insight into a company's economic performance and financial condition relative to its competitors.

Obj. 2 Describe and illustrate basic financial statement analytical methods.

Basic Analytical Methods

Users analyze a company's financial statements using a variety of analytical methods. Three such methods are:

- Horizontal analysis
- Vertical analysis
- Common-sized statements

Horizontal Analysis

The analysis of increases and decreases in the amount and percentage of comparative financial statement items is called **horizontal analysis**. Each item on the most recent statement is compared with the same item on one or more earlier statements in terms of the following:

- *Amount* of increase or decrease
- *Percent* of increase or decrease

When comparing statements, the earlier statement is normally used as the base year for computing increases and decreases.

Exhibit 1 illustrates horizontal analysis for the December 31, 20Y6 and 20Y5 balance sheets of Lincoln Company. In Exhibit 1, the December 31, 20Y5, balance sheet (the earliest year presented) is used as the base year.

EXHIBIT 1

Comparative Balance Sheet—Horizontal Analysis

Lincoln Company
Comparative Balance Sheet
December 31, 20Y6 and 20Y5

	Dec. 31, 20Y6	Dec. 31, 20Y5	Increase (Decrease) Amount	Increase (Decrease) Percent
Assets				
Current assets	$ 550,000	$ 533,000	$ 17,000	3.2%
Long-term investments	95,000	177,500	(82,500)	(46.5%)
Property, plant, and equipment (net)	444,500	470,000	(25,500)	(5.4%)
Intangible assets	50,000	50,000	—	—
Total assets	$1,139,500	$1,230,500	$ (91,000)	(7.4%)
Liabilities				
Current liabilities	$ 210,000	$ 243,000	$ (33,000)	(13.6%)
Long-term liabilities	100,000	200,000	(100,000)	(50.0%)
Total liabilities	$ 310,000	$ 443,000	$(133,000)	(30.0%)
Stockholders' Equity				
Preferred 6% stock, $100 par	$ 150,000	$ 150,000	$ —	—
Common stock, $10 par	500,000	500,000	—	—
Retained earnings	179,500	137,500	42,000	30.5%
Total stockholders' equity	$ 829,500	$ 787,500	$ 42,000	5.3%
Total liabilities and stockholders' equity	$1,139,500	$1,230,500	$ (91,000)	(7.4%)

Exhibit 1 indicates that total assets decreased by $91,000 (7.4%), liabilities decreased by $133,000 (30.0%), and stockholders' equity increased by $42,000 (5.3%). Since the long-term investments account decreased by $82,500, it appears that most of the decrease in long-term liabilities of $100,000 was achieved through the sale of long-term investments.

The balance sheets in Exhibit 1 may be expanded or supported by a separate schedule that includes the individual asset and liability accounts. For example, Exhibit 2 is a supporting schedule of Lincoln Company's current asset accounts.

EXHIBIT 2

Comparative Schedule of Current Assets—Horizontal Analysis

Lincoln Company
Comparative Schedule of Current Assets
December 31, 20Y6 and 20Y5

	Dec. 31, 20Y6	Dec. 31, 20Y5	Increase (Decrease) Amount	Increase (Decrease) Percent
Cash	$ 90,500	$ 64,700	$ 25,800	39.9%
Temporary investments	75,000	60,000	15,000	25.0%
Accounts receivable, net	115,000	120,000	(5,000)	(4.2%)
Inventories	264,000	283,000	(19,000)	(6.7%)
Prepaid expenses	5,500	5,300	200	3.8%
Total current assets	$550,000	$533,000	$ 17,000	3.2%

Exhibit 2 indicates that while cash and temporary investments increased, accounts receivable and inventories decreased. The decrease in accounts receivable could be caused by improved collection policies, which would increase cash. The decrease in inventories could be caused by increased sales.

Exhibit 3 illustrates horizontal analysis for the 20Y6 and 20Y5 income statements of Lincoln Company. Exhibit 3 indicates an increase in sales of $298,000, or 24.8%.

EXHIBIT 3

Comparative Income Statement—Horizontal Analysis

Lincoln Company
Comparative Income Statement
For the Years Ended December 31, 20Y6 and 20Y5

			Increase (Decrease)	
	20Y6	**20Y5**	**Amount**	**Percent**
Sales	$1,498,000	$1,200,000	$298,000	24.8%
Cost of goods sold	1,043,000	820,000	223,000	27.2%
Gross profit	$ 455,000	$ 380,000	$ 75,000	19.7%
Selling expenses	$ 191,000	$ 147,000	$ 44,000	29.9%
Administrative expenses	104,000	97,400	6,600	6.8%
Total operating expenses	$ 295,000	$ 244,400	$ 50,600	20.7%
Income from operations	$ 160,000	$ 135,600	$ 24,400	18.0%
Other revenue	8,500	11,000	(2,500)	(22.7%)
	$ 168,500	$ 146,600	$ 21,900	14.9%
Other expense (interest)	6,000	12,000	(6,000)	(50.0%)
Income before income tax	$ 162,500	$ 134,600	$ 27,900	20.7%
Income tax expense	71,500	58,100	13,400	23.1%
Net income	$ 91,000	$ 76,500	$ 14,500	19.0%

However, the percentage increase in sales of 24.8% was accompanied by an even greater percentage increase in the cost of goods sold of 27.2%. Thus, gross profit increased by only 19.7% compared to the 24.8% increase in sales.

Exhibit 3 also indicates that selling expenses increased by 29.9%. Thus, the 24.8% increases in sales could have been caused by an advertising campaign, which increased selling expenses. Administrative expenses increased by only 6.8%, total operating expenses increased by 20.7%, and income from operations increased by 18.0%. Interest expense decreased by 50.0%. This decrease was probably caused by the 50.0% decrease in long-term liabilities (Exhibit 1). Overall, net income increased by 19.0%, a favorable result.

Link to Nike

For a recent year, Nike's net income increased by 21.5%.

Exhibit 4 illustrates horizontal analysis for the 20Y6 and 20Y5 retained earnings statements of **Lincoln Company**. Exhibit 4 indicates that retained earnings increased by 30.5% for the year. The increase is due to net income of $91,000 for the year, less dividends of $49,000.

EXHIBIT 4

Comparative Retained Earnings Statement—Horizontal Analysis

Lincoln Company
Comparative Retained Earnings Statement
For the Years Ended December 31, 20Y6 and 20Y5

			Increase (Decrease)	
	20Y6	**20Y5**	**Amount**	**Percent**
Retained earnings, January 1	$137,500	$100,000	$37,500	37.5%
Net income	91,000	76,500	14,500	19.0%
Total	$228,500	$176,500	$52,000	29.5%
Dividends:				
Preferred stock dividends	$ 9,000	$ 9,000	—	—
Common stock dividends	40,000	30,000	$10,000	33.3%
Total dividends	$ 49,000	$ 39,000	$10,000	25.6%
Retained earnings, December 31	$179,500	$137,500	$42,000	30.5%

Example Exercise 17-1 Horizontal Analysis

Obj. 2

The comparative cash and accounts receivable balances for a company follow:

	Dec. 31, Current Year	Dec. 31, Previous Year
Cash	$62,500	$50,000
Accounts receivable (net)	74,400	80,000

Based on this information, what is the amount and percentage of increase or decrease that would be shown on a balance sheet with horizontal analysis?

Follow My Example 17-1

Cash	$12,500 increase ($62,500 – $50,000), or 25%
Accounts receivable	$5,600 decrease ($74,400 – $80,000), or (7%)

Practice Exercises: PE 17-1A, PE 17-1B

Vertical Analysis

The percentage analysis of the relationship of each component in a financial statement to a total within the statement is called **vertical analysis.** Although vertical analysis is applied to a single statement, it may be applied on the same statement over time. This enhances the analysis by showing how the percentages of each item have changed over time.

In vertical analysis of the balance sheet, the percentages are computed as follows:

- Each asset item is stated as a percent of the total assets.
- Each liability and stockholders' equity item is stated as a percent of the total liabilities and stockholders' equity.

Exhibit 5 illustrates the vertical analysis of the December 31, 20Y6 and 20Y5 balance sheets of **Lincoln Company**. Exhibit 5 indicates that current assets have increased from 43.3% to 48.3% of total assets. Long-term investments decreased from 14.4% to 8.3% of total assets. Stockholders' equity increased from 64.0% to 72.8%, with a comparable decrease in liabilities.

Link to Nike

For a recent year, Nike's current assets were 73.6% of total assets.

EXHIBIT 5

Comparative Balance Sheet—Vertical Analysis

Lincoln Company
Comparative Balance Sheet
December 31, 20Y6 and 20Y5

	Dec. 31, 20Y6		Dec. 31, 20Y5	
	Amount	**Percent**	**Amount**	**Percent**
Assets				
Current assets	$ 550,000	48.3%	$ 533,000	43.3%
Long-term investments	95,000	8.3	177,500	14.4
Property, plant, and equipment (net)	444,500	39.0	470,000	38.2
Intangible assets	50,000	4.4	50,000	4.1
Total assets	$1,139,500	100.0%	$1,230,500	100.0%
Liabilities				
Current liabilities	$ 210,000	18.4%	$ 243,000	19.7%
Long-term liabilities	100,000	8.8	200,000	16.3
Total liabilities	$ 310,000	27.2%	$ 443,000	36.0%
Stockholders' Equity				
Preferred 6% stock, $100 par	$ 150,000	13.2%	$ 150,000	12.2%
Common stock, $10 par	500,000	43.9	500,000	40.6
Retained earnings	179,500	15.7	137,500	11.2
Total stockholders' equity	$ 829,500	72.8%	$ 787,500	64.0%
Total liabilities and stockholders' equity	$1,139,500	100.0%	$1,230,500	100.0%

In a vertical analysis of the income statement, each item is stated as a percent of sales. Exhibit 6 illustrates the vertical analysis of the 20Y6 and 20Y5 income statements of Lincoln Company.

EXHIBIT 6

Comparative Income Statement—Vertical Analysis

Lincoln Company
Comparative Income Statement
For the Years Ended December 31, 20Y6 and 20Y5

	20Y6		20Y5	
	Amount	Percent	Amount	Percent
Sales	$1,498,000	100.0%	$1,200,000	100.0%
Cost of goods sold	1,043,000	69.6	820,000	68.3
Gross profit	$ 455,000	30.4%	$ 380,000	31.7%
Selling expenses	$ 191,000	12.8%	$ 147,000	12.3%
Administrative expenses	104,000	6.9	97,400	8.1
Total operating expenses	$ 295,000	19.7%	$ 244,400	20.4%
Income from operations	$ 160,000	10.7%	$ 135,600	11.3%
Other revenue	8,500	0.6	11,000	0.9
	$ 168,500	11.3%	$ 146,600	12.2%
Other expense (interest)	6,000	0.4	12,000	1.0
Income before income tax	$ 162,500	10.9%	$ 134,600	11.2%
Income tax expense	71,500	4.8	58,100	4.8
Net income	$ 91,000	6.1%	$ 76,500	6.4%

Exhibit 6 indicates a decrease in the gross profit rate from 31.7% in 20Y5 to 30.4% in 20Y6. Although this is only a 1.3 percentage point (31.7% – 30.4%) decrease, in dollars of potential gross profit, it represents a decrease of $19,474 (1.3% × $1,498,000) based on 20Y6 sales. Thus, a small percentage decrease can have a large dollar effect.

Example Exercise 17-2 Vertical Analysis — Obj. 2

Income statement information for Lee Corporation follows:

Sales	$100,000
Cost of goods sold	65,000
Gross profit	$ 35,000

Prepare a vertical analysis of the income statement for Lee Corporation.

Follow My Example 17-2

	Amount	Percentage	
Sales	$100,000	100%	($100,000 ÷ $100,000)
Cost of goods sold	65,000	65	($65,000 ÷ $100,000)
Gross profit	$ 35,000	35%	($35,000 ÷ $100,000)

Practice Exercises: PE 17-2A, PE 17-2B

Common-Sized Statements

In a **common-sized statement**, all items are expressed as percentages, with no dollar amounts shown. Common-sized statements are often useful for comparing one company with another or for comparing a company with industry averages.

Exhibit 7 illustrates common-sized income statements for **Lincoln Company** and Madison Corporation. Exhibit 7 indicates that Lincoln has a slightly higher gross profit percentage (30.4%) than Madison (30.0%). However, Lincoln has a higher percentage of selling expenses (12.8%) and administrative expenses (6.9%) than does Madison (11.5% and 4.1%). As a result, the income from operations as a percentage of sales of Lincoln (10.7%) is less than that of Madison (14.4%).

EXHIBIT 7

Common-Sized Income Statements

	Lincoln Company	Madison Corporation
Sales	100.0%	100.0%
Cost of goods sold	69.6	70.0
Gross profit	30.4%	30.0%
Selling expenses	12.8%	11.5%
Administrative expenses	6.9	4.1
Total operating expenses	19.7%	15.6%
Income from operations	10.7%	14.4%
Other revenue	0.6	0.6
	11.3%	15.0%
Other expense (interest)	0.4	0.5
Income before income tax	10.9%	14.5%
Income tax expense	4.8	5.5
Net income	6.1%	9.0%

The unfavorable difference of 3.7 (14.4% – 10.7%) percentage points in income from operations would concern the managers and other stakeholders of Lincoln. The underlying causes of the difference should be investigated and possibly corrected. For example, Lincoln may decide to outsource some of its administrative duties so that its administrative expenses are more comparative to that of Madison.

Link to Nike

For a recent year, Nike's net income was 9.7% of sales.

Analyzing Liquidity

Obj. 3 Describe and illustrate how to use financial statement analysis to assess liquidity.

Liquidity analysis evaluates the ability of a company to convert current assets into cash. Banks and other short-term creditors rely heavily on liquidity analysis, because they are interested in evaluating a company's ability to repay loans and short-term notes. Exhibit 8 shows three categories of measures used to evaluate a company's liquidity. These ratios and measures focus upon a company's current position (current assets and liabilities), accounts receivable, and inventory.

EXHIBIT 8

Liquidity Ratios and Measures

Current Position Analysis	Accounts Receivable Analysis	Inventory Analysis
Working Capital	Accounts Receivable Turnover	Inventory Turnover
Current Ratio	Number of Days' Sales in Receivables	Number of Days' Sales in Inventory
Quick Ratio		

Current Position Analysis

Current position analysis evaluates a company's ability to pay its current liabilities. This information helps short-term creditors determine how quickly they will be repaid. This analysis includes:

- Working capital
- Current ratio
- Quick ratio

Working Capital A company's **working capital** is computed as follows:

Working Capital = Current Assets − Current Liabilities

To illustrate, the working capital for **Lincoln Company** for 20Y6 and 20Y5 is computed as follows:

	20Y6	20Y5
Current assets	$ 550,000	$ 533,000
Current liabilities	(210,000)	(243,000)
Working capital	$ 340,000	$ 290,000

The working capital is used to evaluate a company's ability to pay current liabilities. A company's working capital is often monitored monthly, quarterly, or yearly by creditors and other debtors. However, it is difficult to use working capital to compare companies of different sizes. For example, working capital of $250,000 may be adequate for a local sporting goods store, but it would be inadequate for **Nike**.

Current Ratio The **current ratio**, sometimes called the *working capital ratio*, is computed as follows:

$$\text{Current Ratio} = \frac{\text{Current Assets}}{\text{Current Liabilities}}$$

To illustrate, the current ratio for **Lincoln Company** is computed as follows:

	20Y6	20Y5
Current assets	$550,000	$533,000
Current liabilities	$210,000	$243,000
Current ratio	2.6 ($550,000 ÷ $210,000)	2.2 ($533,000 ÷ $243,000)

Link to Nike

For a recent five-year period, **Nike**'s average current ratio was 2.9.

The current ratio is a more reliable indicator of a company's ability to pay its current liabilities than is working capital, and it is much easier to compare across companies. To illustrate, assume that as of December 31, 20Y6, the working capital of a competitor is much greater than Lincoln's $340,000, but its current ratio is only 1.3. Considering these facts alone, Lincoln is in a more favorable position to obtain short-term credit than the competitor because it has a higher current ratio.

Quick Ratio One limitation of working capital and the current ratio is that they do not consider the types of current assets a company has and how easily they can be turned into cash. Because of this, two companies may have the same working capital and current ratios but differ significantly in their ability to pay their current liabilities.

To illustrate, the current assets and liabilities for Lincoln Company and Jefferson Company as of December 31, 20Y6, are as follows:

	Lincoln Company	Jefferson Company
Current assets:		
Cash	$ 90,500	$ 45,500
Temporary investments	75,000	25,000
Accounts receivable (net)	115,000	90,000
Inventories	264,000	380,000
Prepaid expenses	5,500	9,500
Total current assets	$ 550,000	$ 550,000
Current assets	$ 550,000	$ 550,000
Current liabilities	(210,000)	(210,000)
Working capital	$ 340,000	$ 340,000
Current ratio (Current assets ÷ Current liabilities)	2.6	2.6

Lincoln and Jefferson both have a working capital of $340,000 and current ratios of 2.6. Jefferson, however, has more of its current assets in inventories. These inventories must be sold and the receivables collected before all the current liabilities can be paid. This takes time. In addition, if the market for its product declines, Jefferson may have difficulty selling its inventory. This, in turn, could impair its ability to pay its current liabilities.

In contrast, Lincoln's current assets contain more cash, temporary investments, and accounts receivable, which can easily be converted to cash. Thus, Lincoln is in a stronger current position than Jefferson to pay its current liabilities.

A ratio that captures this difference and measures the "instant" debt-paying ability of a company is the **quick ratio**, sometimes called the *acid-test ratio*. The quick ratio is computed as follows:

$$\text{Quick Ratio} = \frac{\text{Quick Assets}}{\text{Current Liabilities}}$$

Quick assets are cash and other current assets that can be easily converted to cash. Quick assets normally include cash, temporary investments, and receivables but exclude inventories and prepaid assets.

To illustrate, the quick ratios for Lincoln Company and Jefferson Company are computed as follows:

	Lincoln Company	Jefferson Company
Quick assets:		
Cash	$ 90,500	$ 45,500
Temporary investments	75,000	25,000
Accounts receivable (net)	115,000	90,000
Total quick assets	$280,500	$160,500
Current liabilities	$210,000	$210,000
Quick ratio	1.3 ($280,500 ÷ $210,000)	0.8 ($160,500 ÷ $210,000)

Example Exercise 17-3 Current Position Analysis

Obj. 3

The following items are reported on a company's balance sheet:

Cash	$300,000
Temporary investments	100,000
Accounts receivable (net)	200,000
Inventory	200,000
Accounts payable	400,000

Determine (a) the current ratio and (b) the quick ratio. Round to one decimal place.

(Continued)

Follow My Example 17-3

a. Current Ratio = Current Assets ÷ Current Liabilities
= ($300,000 + $100,000 + $200,000 + $200,000) ÷ $400,000
= 2.0

b. Quick Ratio = Quick Assets ÷ Current Liabilities
= ($300,000 + $100,000 + $200,000) ÷ $400,000
= 1.5

Practice Exercises: PE 17-3A, PE 17-3B

Accounts Receivable Analysis

A company's ability to collect its accounts receivable is called **accounts receivable analysis**. It includes the computation and analysis of the following:

- Accounts receivable turnover
- Number of days' sales in receivables

Collecting accounts receivable as quickly as possible improves a company's liquidity. In addition, the cash collected from receivables may be used to improve or expand operations. Quick collection of receivables also reduces the risk of uncollectible accounts.

Accounts Receivable Turnover The **accounts receivable turnover** is computed as follows:

$$\text{Accounts Receivable Turnover} = \frac{\text{Sales}^1}{\text{Average Accounts Receivable}}$$

To illustrate, the accounts receivable turnover for Lincoln Company for 20Y6 and 20Y5 is computed as follows. Lincoln's accounts receivable balance at the beginning of 20Y5 is $140,000.

	20Y6	20Y5
Sales	$1,498,000	$1,200,000
Accounts receivable (net):		
Beginning of year	$ 120,000	$ 140,000
End of year	115,000	120,000
Total	$ 235,000	$ 260,000
Average accounts receivable	$117,500 ($235,000 ÷ 2)	$130,000 ($260,000 ÷ 2)
Accounts receivable turnover	12.7 ($1,498,000 ÷ $117,500)	9.2 ($1,200,000 ÷ $130,000)

The increase in Lincoln's accounts receivable turnover from 9.2 to 12.7 indicates that the collection of receivables has improved during 20Y6. This may be due to a change in how credit is granted, collection practices, or both.

For Lincoln, the average accounts receivable was computed using the accounts receivable balance at the beginning and the end of the year. When sales are seasonal and, thus, vary throughout the year, monthly balances of receivables are often used. Also, if sales on account include notes receivable as well as accounts receivable, notes and accounts receivable are normally combined for analysis.

1 If known, *credit* sales should be used in the numerator. Because credit sales are not normally known by external users, we use sales in the numerator.

Number of Days' Sales in Receivables The **number of days' sales in receivables** is computed as follows:

$$\text{Number of Days' Sales in Receivables} = \frac{\text{Average Accounts Receivable}}{\text{Average Daily Sales}}$$

where

$$\text{Average Daily Sales} = \frac{\text{Sales}}{\text{365 days}}$$

To illustrate, the number of days' sales in receivables for **Lincoln Company** is computed as follows:

	20Y6	20Y5
Average accounts receivable	$117,500 ($235,000 ÷ 2)	$130,000 ($260,000 ÷ 2)
Average daily sales	$4,104 ($1,498,000 ÷ 365)	$3,288 ($1,200,000 ÷ 365)
Number of days' sales in receivables	28.6 ($117,500 ÷ $4,104)	39.5 ($130,000 ÷ $3,288)

The number of days' sales in receivables is an estimate of the time (in days) that the accounts receivable have been outstanding. The number of days' sales in receivables is often compared with a company's credit terms to evaluate the efficiency of the collection of receivables.

To illustrate, if Lincoln's credit terms are 2/10, n/30, then Lincoln was very *inefficient* in collecting receivables in 20Y5. In other words, receivables should have been collected in 30 days or less but were being collected in 39.5 days. Although collections improved during 20Y6 to 28.6 days, there is probably still room for improvement. On the other hand, if Lincoln's credit terms are n/45, then there is probably little room for improving collections.

Example Exercise 17-4 Accounts Receivable Analysis **Obj. 3**

A company reports the following:

Sales	$960,000
Average accounts receivable (net)	48,000

Determine (a) the accounts receivable turnover and (b) the number of days' sales in receivables. Round to one decimal place.

Follow My Example 17-4

a. Accounts Receivable Turnover = Sales ÷ Average Accounts Receivable
= $960,000 ÷ $48,000
= 20.0

b. Number of Days' Sales in Receivables = Average Accounts Receivable ÷ Average Daily Sales
= $48,000 ÷ ($960,000 ÷ 365) = $48,000 ÷ $2,630
= 18.3 days

Practice Exercises: PE 17-4A, PE 17-4B

Inventory Analysis

A company's ability to manage its inventory effectively is evaluated using **inventory analysis**. It includes the computation and analysis of the following:

- Inventory turnover
- Number of days' sales in inventory

Excess inventory decreases liquidity by tying up funds (cash) in inventory. In addition, excess inventory increases insurance expense, property taxes, storage costs, and other related expenses. These expenses further reduce funds that could be used elsewhere to improve or expand operations.

Excess inventory also increases the risk of losses because of price declines or obsolescence of the inventory. On the other hand, a company should keep enough inventory in stock so that it doesn't lose sales because of lack of inventory.

Inventory Turnover The **inventory turnover** is computed as follows:

$$\text{Inventory Turnover} = \frac{\text{Cost of Goods Sold}}{\text{Average Inventory}}$$

To illustrate, the inventory turnover for **Lincoln Company** for 20Y6 and 20Y5 is computed as follows. Lincoln's inventory balance at the beginning of 20Y5 is $311,000.

	20Y6	20Y5
Cost of goods sold	$1,043,000	$820,000
Inventories:		
Beginning of year	$ 283,000	$311,000
End of year	264,000	283,000
Total	$ 547,000	$594,000
Average inventory	$273,500 ($547,000 ÷ 2)	$297,000 ($594,000 ÷ 2)
Inventory turnover	3.8 ($1,043,000 ÷ $273,500)	2.8 ($820,000 ÷ $297,000)

The increase in Lincoln's inventory turnover from 2.8 to 3.8 indicates that the management of inventory has improved in 20Y6. The inventory turnover improved because of an increase in the cost of goods sold, which indicates more sales and a decrease in the average inventories.

Link to Nike

For a recent five-year period, Nike's average inventory turnover was 4.3.

What is considered a good inventory turnover varies by type of inventory, company, and industry. For example, grocery stores have a higher inventory turnover than jewelers or furniture stores. Likewise, within a grocery store, perishable foods have a higher turnover than the soaps and cleansers.

Number of Days' Sales in Inventory The **number of days' sales in inventory** is computed as follows:

$$\text{Number of Days' Sales in Inventory} = \frac{\text{Average Inventory}}{\text{Average Daily Cost of Goods Sold}}$$

where

$$\text{Average Daily Cost of Goods Sold} = \frac{\text{Cost of Goods Sold}}{\text{365 days}}$$

To illustrate, the number of days' sales in inventory for **Lincoln Company** is computed as follows:

	20Y6	20Y5
Average inventory	$273,500 ($547,000 ÷ 2)	$297,000 ($594,000 ÷ 2)
Average daily cost of goods sold	$2,858 ($1,043,000 ÷ 365)	$2,247 ($820,000 ÷ 365)
Number of days' sales in inventory	95.7 ($273,500 ÷ $2,858)	132.2 ($297,000 ÷ $2,247)

The number of days' sales in inventory is a rough measure of the length of time it takes to purchase, sell, and replace the inventory. Lincoln's number of days' sales in inventory improved from 132.2 days to 95.7 days during 20Y6. This is a major improvement in managing inventory.

Example Exercise 17-5 Inventory Analysis

Obj. 3

A company reports the following:

Cost of goods sold	$560,000
Average inventory	112,000

Determine (a) the inventory turnover and (b) the number of days' sales in inventory. Round to one decimal place.

Follow My Example 17-5

a. Inventory Turnover = Cost of Goods Sold ÷ Average Inventory
= $560,000 ÷ $112,000
= 5.0

b. Number of Days' Sales in Inventory = Average Inventory ÷ Average Daily Cost of Goods Sold
= $112,000 ÷ ($560,000 ÷ 365) = $112,000 ÷ $1,534
= 73.0 days

Practice Exercises: PE 17-5A, PE 17-5B

Business Connection

FLYING OFF THE SHELVES

Two companies with a fast inventory turnover relative to their industries are Apple Inc. and Costco Wholesale Corporation:

	Inventory Turnover	Industry	Industry Average
Apple	53.2	Technology	15.6
Costco	11.5	Retail	7.7

Apple turns over its inventory approximately every week. There are two primary reasons for this performance. First, Apple does not manufacture its products, but contracts their manufacture by others. Thus, Apple has no inventory related to manufacturing. Second, the Apple Store inventory moves very quickly due to the popularity of its products. Costco is ranked number one in the retail industry for inventory turns. This is because Costco employs a club warehouse model that stocks a minimum variety of highly popular products. Products that don't sell quickly are removed from its offerings.

Analyzing Solvency

Obj. 4 Describe and illustrate how to use financial statement analysis to assess solvency.

Solvency analysis evaluates a company's ability to pay its long-term debts. Bondholders and other long-term creditors use solvency analysis to evaluate a company's ability to (1) repay the face amount of debt at maturity and (2) make periodic interest payments. Three common solvency ratios are shown in Exhibit 9.

EXHIBIT 9

Solvency Ratios

Solvency Ratios		
Ratio of Fixed Assets to Long-Term Liabilities	Ratio of Liabilities to Stockholders' Equity	Times Interest Earned

Ratio of Fixed Assets to Long-Term Liabilities

Fixed assets are often pledged as security for long-term notes and bonds. The **ratio of fixed assets to long-term liabilities** provides a measure of how much fixed assets a company has to support its long-term debt. This measures a company's ability to repay the face amount of debt at maturity and is computed as follows:

$$\text{Ratio of Fixed Assets to Long-Term Liabilities} = \frac{\text{Fixed Assets (net)}}{\text{Long-Term Liabilities}}$$

To illustrate, the ratio of fixed assets to long-term liabilities for **Lincoln Company** is computed as follows:

	20Y6	20Y5
Fixed assets (net)	$444,500	$470,000
Long-term liabilities	$100,000	$200,000
Ratio of fixed assets to long-term liabilities	4.4 ($444,500 ÷ $100,000)	2.4 ($470,000 ÷ $200,000)

Link to Nike

For a recent year, **Nike**'s ratio of fixed assets to long-term liabilities was 1.0.

During 20Y6, Lincoln's ratio of fixed assets to long-term liabilities increased from 2.4 to 4.4. This increase was due primarily to Lincoln paying off one-half of its long-term liabilities in 20Y6.

Ratio of Liabilities to Stockholders' Equity

The **ratio of liabilities to stockholders' equity** measures how much of the company is financed by debt and equity. It is computed as follows:

$$\text{Ratio of Liabilities to Stockholders' Equity} = \frac{\text{Total Liabilities}}{\text{Total Stockholders' Equity}}$$

To illustrate, the ratio of liabilities to stockholders' equity for **Lincoln Company** is computed as follows:

	20Y6	20Y5
Total liabilities	$310,000	$443,000
Total stockholders' equity	$829,500	$787,500
Ratio of liabilities to stockholders' equity	0.4 ($310,000 ÷ $829,500)	0.6 ($443,000 ÷ $787,500)

Link to Nike

For a recent five-year period, **Nike**'s average ratio of liabilities to stockholders' equity was 0.6.

Lincoln's ratio of liabilities to stockholders' equity decreased from 0.6 to 0.4 during 20Y6. The lower ratio indicates that Lincoln's liabilities as a proportion of equity is decreasing. This is an improvement and indicates that the margin of safety for Lincoln's creditors is improving.

Example Exercise 17-6 Solvency Analysis

Obj. 4

The following information was taken from Acme Company's balance sheet:

Fixed assets (net)	$1,400,000
Long-term liabilities	400,000
Total liabilities	560,000
Total stockholders' equity	1,400,000

Determine the company's (a) ratio of fixed assets to long-term liabilities and (b) ratio of liabilities to total stockholders' equity. Round to one decimal place.

Follow My Example 17-6

a. Ratio of Fixed Assets to Long-Term Liabilities = Fixed Assets ÷ Long-Term Liabilities
= $1,400,000 ÷ $400,000
= 3.5

b. Ratio of Liabilities to Total Stockholders' Equity = Total Liabilities ÷ Total Stockholders' Equity
= $560,000 ÷ $1,400,000
= 0.4

Practice Exercises: PE 17-6A, PE 17-6B

Times Interest Earned

The **times interest earned**, sometimes called the *coverage ratio*, measures the risk that interest payments will not be made if earnings decrease. It is computed as follows:

$$\text{Times Interest Earned} = \frac{\text{Income Before Income Tax} + \text{Interest Expense}}{\text{Interest Expense}}$$

Interest expense is paid before income taxes. In other words, interest expense is deducted in determining taxable income and, thus, income tax. For this reason, income *before taxes* is used in computing the times interest earned.

The *higher* the ratio, the more likely interest payments will be paid if earnings decrease. To illustrate, the times interest earned for **Lincoln Company** is computed as follows:

	20Y6	20Y5
Income before income tax	$162,500	$134,600
Interest expense	6,000	12,000
Amount available to pay interest	$168,500	$146,600
Times interest earned	28.1 ($168,500 ÷ $6,000)	12.2 ($146,600 ÷ $12,000)

The times interest earned improved from 12.2 to 28.1 during 20Y6. The higher ratio indicates that the relationship between the amount of income available to pay interest and the amount of interest expense has improved. Lincoln has more than enough earnings (28 times) to make its interest payments.

Link to Nike

For a recent year, **Nike**'s times interest earned ratio was nine times higher than the industry average.

Example Exercise 17-7 Times Interest Earned **Obj. 4**

Acme Company reports the following:

Income before income tax	$250,000
Interest expense	100,000

Determine the times interest earned ratio. Round to one decimal place.

Follow My Example 17-7

Times Interest Earned = (Income Before Income Tax + Interest Expense) ÷ Interest Expense
= ($250,000 + $100,000) ÷ $100,000
= 3.5

Practice Exercises: PE 17-7A, PE 17-7B

Business Connection

LIQUIDITY CRUNCH

RadioShack Corporation, an electronics retailer, filed for bankruptcy protection. Information on the company's liquidity and solvency for the three years prior to bankruptcy follow:

	20Y3	20Y2	20Y1
Liquidity measures:			
Working capital (in thousands)	$748,400	$1,003,700	$1,176,700
Current ratio	2.3	2.0	2.9
Quick ratio	0.7	1.0	1.5
Solvency measures:			
Ratio of liabilities to stockholders' equity	6.7	2.8	1.9
Ratio of fixed assets to long-term liabilities	0.2	0.3	0.3

The data show that the company's liquidity and solvency measures deteriorated in the years prior to the firm's bankruptcy. All three of the company's liquidity measures declined significantly during the three-year period, indicating a growing risk that the company would not be able to repay its current liabilities. The ratio of liabilities to stockholder's equity also increased significantly during this period, indicating that the company might not be able to repay its long-term debts. Finally, the ratio of fixed assets to long-term liabilities began to deteriorate in 20Y3, indicating that fewer assets would be available to secure the company's long-term liabilities.

Obj. 5 Describe and illustrate how to use financial statement analysis to assess profitability.

Analyzing Profitability

Profitability analysis evaluates the ability of a company to generate future earnings. This ability depends on the relationship between the company's operating results and the assets the company has available for use in its operations. Thus, the relationship between income statement and balance sheet items are used to evaluate profitability.

Common profitability ratios are shown in Exhibit 10.

EXHIBIT 10

Profitability Ratios

Profitability Ratios		
Asset Turnover	Return on Stockholders' Equity	Price-Earnings Ratio
Return on Total Assets	Return on Common Stockholders' Equity	Dividends per Share
	Earnings per Share on Common Stock	Dividend Yield

Asset Turnover

The **asset turnover** ratio measures how effectively a company uses its assets. It is computed as follows:

$$\text{Asset Turnover} = \frac{\text{Sales}}{\text{Average Total Assets}}$$

To illustrate, the asset turnover for **Lincoln Company** is computed as follows. Total assets are $1,187,500 at the beginning of 20Y5.

	20Y6	20Y5
Sales	$1,498,000	$1,200,000
Total assets:		
Beginning of year	$1,230,500	$1,187,500
End of year	1,139,500	1,230,500
Total	$2,370,000	$2,418,000
Average total assets	$1,185,000 ($2,370,000 ÷ 2)	$1,209,000 ($2,418,000 ÷ 2)
Asset turnover	1.3 ($1,498,000 ÷ $1,185,000)	1.0 ($1,200,000 ÷ $1,209,000)

For Lincoln, the average total assets was computed using total assets at the beginning and end of the year. The average total assets could also be based on monthly or quarterly averages.

The asset turnover ratio indicates that Lincoln's use of its assets has improved in 20Y6. This was due primarily to the increase in sales in 20Y6.

Example Exercise 17-8 Asset Turnover Obj. 5

A company reports the following:

Sales	$2,250,000
Average total assets	1,500,000

Determine the asset turnover ratio. Round to one decimal place.

Follow My Example 17-8

Asset Turnover Ratio = Sales ÷ Average Total Assets
= $2,250,000 ÷ $1,500,000
= 1.5

Practice Exercises: PE 17-8A, PE 17-8B

Return on Total Assets

The **return on total assets** measures the profitability of total assets, without considering how the assets are financed. In other words, this rate is not affected by the portion of assets financed by creditors or stockholders. It is computed as follows:

$$\text{Return on Total Assets} = \frac{\text{Income + Interest Expense}}{\text{Average Total Assets}}$$

The return on total assets is computed by adding interest expense to net income. By adding interest expense to net income, the effect of whether the assets are financed by creditors (debt) or stockholders (equity) is eliminated. Because net income includes any income earned from long-term investments, the average total assets includes long-term investments as well as the net operating assets.

To illustrate, the return on total assets by **Lincoln Company** is computed as follows. Total assets are $1,187,500 at the beginning of 20Y5.

	20Y6	20Y5
Net income	$ 91,000	$ 76,500
Interest expense	6,000	12,000
	$ 97,000	$ 88,500
Total assets:		
Beginning of year	$1,230,500	$1,187,500
End of year	1,139,500	1,230,500
Total	$2,370,000	$2,418,000
Average total assets	$1,185,000 ($2,370,000 ÷ 2)	$1,209,000 ($2,418,000 ÷ 2)
Return on total assets	8.2% ($97,000 ÷ $1,185,000)	7.3% ($88,500 ÷ $1,209,000)

The return on total assets improved from 7.3% to 8.2% during 20Y6.

The *return on operating assets* is sometimes computed when there are large amounts of nonoperating income and expense. It is computed as follows:

$$\text{Return on Operating Assets} = \frac{\text{Income from Operations}}{\text{Average Operating Assets}}$$

Because Lincoln does not have a significant amount of nonoperating income and expense, the return on operating assets is not illustrated.

Example Exercise 17-9 Return on Total Assets — Obj. 5

A company reports the following income statement and balance sheet information for the current year:

Net income	$ 125,000
Interest expense	25,000
Average total assets	2,000,000

Determine the return on total assets. Round percentage to one decimal place.

Follow My Example 17-9

Return on Total Assets = (Net Income + Interest Expense) ÷ Average Total Assets
= ($125,000 + $25,000) ÷ $2,000,000
= $150,000 ÷ $2,000,000
= 7.5%

Practice Exercises: PE 17-9A, PE 17-9B

Return on Stockholders' Equity

The **return on stockholders' equity** measures the rate of income earned on the amount invested by the stockholders. It is computed as follows:

$$\text{Return on Stockholders' Equity} = \frac{\text{Net Income}}{\text{Average Total Stockholders' Equity}}$$

To illustrate, the return on stockholders' equity for **Lincoln Company** is computed as follows. Total stockholders' equity is $750,000 at the beginning of 20Y5.

	20Y6	20Y5
Net income	$ 91,000	$ 76,500
Total stockholders' equity:		
Beginning of year	$ 787,500	$ 750,000
End of year	829,500	787,500
Total	$1,617,000	$1,537,500
Average total stockholders' equity	$808,500 ($1,617,000 ÷ 2)	$768,750 ($1,537,500 ÷ 2)
Return on stockholders' equity	11.3% ($91,000 ÷ $808,500)	10.0% ($76,500 ÷ $768,750)

The return on stockholders' equity improved from 10.0% to 11.3% during 20Y6.

Leverage involves using debt to increase the return on an investment. The return on stockholders' equity is normally higher than the return on total assets. This is because of the effect of leverage.

For **Lincoln Company**, the effect of leverage for 20Y6 is 3.1% and for 20Y5 is 2.7% computed as follows:

	20Y6	20Y5
Return on stockholders' equity	11.3%	10.0%
Return on total assets	(8.2)	(7.3)
Effect of leverage	3.1%	2.7%

Link to Nike

For a recent five-year period, **Nike's** average return on stockholders' equity was 23.9%.

Exhibit 11 shows the 20Y6 and 20Y5 effects of leverage for Lincoln.

EXHIBIT 11

Effect of Leverage

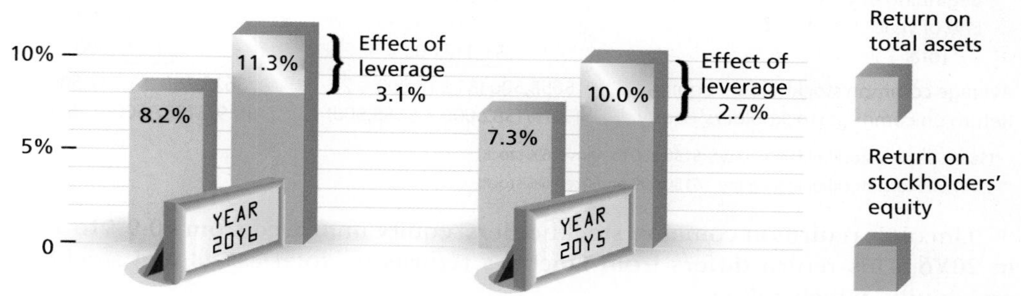

Business Connection

GEARING FOR PROFIT

Another term for leverage is "financial gearing." **Exxon Mobil Corporation**, a worldwide-integrated energy company, is an example of a company that uses leverage for financial advantage. Exxon had a return on total assets of 9.35% for a recent year, while its return on stockholders' equity was 18.7%. Thus, Exxon is "geared" 2:1 by using debt on its balance sheet. Exxon is very profitable; thus, leverage is beneficial. In contrast, **Chesapeake Energy**, an oil and gas exploration company, had return on assets of –7.5% for a recent 12-month period and return on stockholders' equity of –25%. In this case, the over 3:1 leverage (25% ÷ 7.5%) creates a financial disadvantage because the company is experiencing losses.

Return on Common Stockholders' Equity

The **return on common stockholders' equity** measures the rate of profits earned on the amount invested by the common stockholders. It is computed as follows:

$$\text{Return on Common Stockholders' Equity} = \frac{\text{Net Income} - \text{Preferred Dividends}}{\text{Average Common Stockholders' Equity}}$$

Because preferred stockholders rank ahead of the common stockholders in their claim on earnings, any preferred dividends are subtracted from net income in computing the return on common stockholders' equity.

Lincoln Company had $150,000 par value of 6% preferred stock outstanding on December 31, 20Y6 and 20Y5. Thus, preferred dividends of $9,000 ($150,000 × 6%) are deducted from net income. Lincoln's common stockholders' equity is determined as follows:

	December 31		
	20Y6	20Y5	20Y4
Common stock, $10 par	$500,000	$500,000	$500,000
Retained earnings	179,500	137,500	100,000
Common stockholders' equity	$679,500	$637,500	$600,000

The retained earnings on December 31, 20Y4, of $100,000 is the same as the retained earnings on January 1, 20Y5, as shown in Lincoln's retained earnings statement in Exhibit 4.

Using this information, the return on common stockholders' equity for Lincoln is computed as follows:

	20Y6	20Y5
Net income	$ 91,000	$ 76,500
Preferred dividends	(9,000)	(9,000)
Total	$ 82,000	$ 67,500
Common stockholders' equity:		
Beginning of year	$ 637,500	$ 600,000
End of year	679,500*	637,500**
Total	$1,317,000	$1,237,500
Average common stockholders' equity	$658,500 ($1,317,000 ÷ 2)	$618,750 ($1,237,500 ÷ 2)
Return on common stockholders' equity	12.5% ($82,000 ÷ $658,500)	10.9% ($67,500 ÷ $618,750)

*($829,500 total stockholders' equity – $150,000 preferred 6% stock)
**($787,500 total stockholders' equity – $150,000 preferred 6% stock)

Lincoln's return on common stockholders' equity improved from 10.9% to 12.5% in 20Y6. This return differs from Lincoln's returns on total assets and stockholders' equity, which follow:

	20Y6	20Y5
Return on total assets	8.2%	7.3%
Return on stockholders' equity	11.3%	10.0%
Return on common stockholders' equity	12.5%	10.9%

These returns differ because of leverage, as discussed in the preceding section.

Example Exercise 17-10 Return on Stockholders' Equity Obj. 5

A company reports the following:

Net income	$ 125,000
Preferred dividends	5,000
Average stockholders' equity	1,000,000
Average common stockholders' equity	800,000

Determine (a) the return on stockholders' equity and (b) the return on common stockholders' equity. Round percentages to one decimal place.

Follow My Example 17-10

a. Return on Stockholders' Equity = Net Income ÷ Average Stockholders' Equity
= $125,000 ÷ $1,000,000
= 12.5%

b. Return on Common Stockholders' Equity = (Net Income – Preferred Dividends) ÷ Average Common Stockholders' Equity
= ($125,000 – $5,000) ÷ $800,000
= 15.0%

Practice Exercises: PE 17-10A, PE 17-10B

Earnings per Share on Common Stock

Earnings per share (EPS) on common stock measures the share of profits that are earned by a share of common stock. Earnings per share must be reported on the income statement. As a result, earnings per share (EPS) is often reported in the financial press. It is computed as follows:

$$\text{Earnings per Share (EPS) on Common Stock} = \frac{\text{Net Income} - \text{Preferred Dividends}}{\text{Shares of Common Stock Outstanding}}$$

When preferred and common stock are outstanding, preferred dividends are subtracted from net income to determine the income related to the common shares.

To illustrate, the earnings per share (EPS) of common stock for **Lincoln Company** is computed as follows:

	20Y6	20Y5
Net income	$91,000	$76,500
Preferred dividends	(9,000)	(9,000)
Total	$82,000	$67,500
Shares of common stock outstanding	50,000	50,000
Earnings per share on common stock	$1.64 ($82,000 ÷ 50,000)	$1.35 ($67,500 ÷ 50,000)

Lincoln had $500,000 par value of $10 common stock, and $150,000 par value of 6% preferred stock outstanding on December 31, 20Y6 and 20Y5. The preferred dividends of $9,000 ($150,000 × 6%) are deducted from net income in computing earnings per share on common stock. This amount is divided by the 50,000 common shares outstanding, which is computed by dividing the $500,000 par value of the common stock by the $10 par value per share.

Lincoln did not issue any additional shares of common stock in 20Y6. If Lincoln had issued additional shares in 20Y6, a weighted average of common shares outstanding during the year would have been used.

Lincoln's earnings per share (EPS) on common stock improved from $1.35 to $1.64 during 20Y6.

Lincoln has a simple capital structure with only common stock and preferred stock outstanding. Many corporations, however, have complex capital structures with various types of equity securities outstanding, such as convertible preferred stock, stock options, and stock warrants. In such cases, the possible effects of such securities on the shares of common stock outstanding are considered in reporting earnings per share. These possible effects are reported separately as *earnings per common share assuming dilution* or *diluted earnings per share*. This topic is described and illustrated in advanced accounting courses and textbooks.

Link to Nike

On a recent income statement, **Nike** reported net income of $2,693 million.

Price-Earnings Ratio

The **price-earnings (P/E) ratio** on common stock measures a company's future earnings prospects. It is often quoted in the financial press and is computed as follows:

$$\text{Price-Earnings (P/E) Ratio} = \frac{\text{Market Price per Share of Common Stock}}{\text{Earnings per Share on Common Stock}}$$

To illustrate, the price-earnings (P/E) ratio for **Lincoln Company** is computed as follows:

	20Y6	20Y5
Market price per share of common stock	$41.00	$27.00
Earnings per share on common stock	$1.64	$1.35
Price-earnings ratio on common stock	25 ($41 ÷ $1.64)	20 ($27 ÷ $1.35)

The price-earnings ratio improved from 20 to 25 during 20Y6. In other words, a share of common stock of Lincoln was selling for 20 times earnings per share at the end of 20Y5. At the end of 20Y6, the common stock was selling for 25 times earnings per share. This indicates that the market expects Lincoln to experience favorable earnings in the future.

Example Exercise 17-11 Earnings per Share and Price-Earnings Ratio — Obj. 5

A company reports the following:

Net income	$250,000
Preferred dividends	$15,000
Shares of common stock outstanding	20,000
Market price per share of common stock	$35.25

a. Determine the company's earnings per share on common stock.
b. Determine the company's price-earnings ratio. Round to one decimal place.

Follow My Example 17-11

a. Earnings per Share on Common Stock = (Net Income – Preferred Dividends) ÷ Shares of Common Stock Outstanding
= ($250,000 – $15,000) ÷ 20,000
= $11.75

b. Price-Earnings Ratio = Market Price per Share of Common Stock ÷ Earnings per Share on Common Stock
= $35.25 ÷ $11.75
= 3.0

Practice Exercises: PE 17-11A, PE 17-11B

Dividends per Share

Dividends per share measures the extent to which earnings are being distributed to common shareholders. It is computed as follows:

$$\text{Dividends per Share} = \frac{\text{Dividends on Common Stock}}{\text{Shares of Common Stock Outstanding}}$$

To illustrate, the dividends per share for **Lincoln Company** are computed as follows:

	20Y6	20Y5
Dividends on common stock	$40,000	$30,000
Shares of common stock outstanding	50,000	50,000
Dividends per share of common stock	$0.80 ($40,000 ÷ 50,000)	$0.60 ($30,000 ÷ 50,000)

The dividends per share of common stock increased from $0.60 to $0.80 during 20Y6.

Dividends per share are often reported with earnings per share. Comparing the two per-share amounts indicates the extent to which earnings are being retained for use in operations. To illustrate, the dividends and earnings per share for **Lincoln Company** are shown in Exhibit 12.

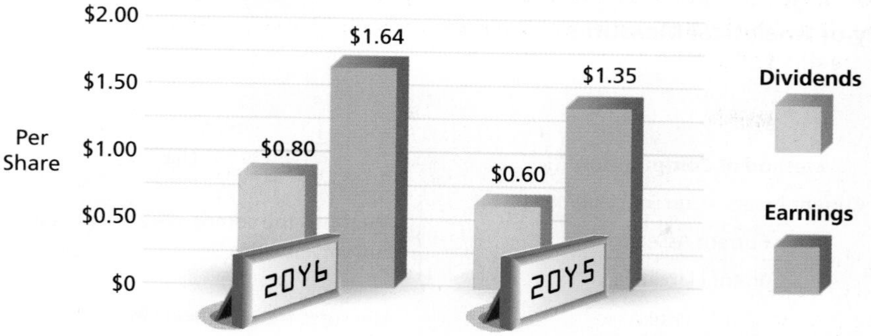

EXHIBIT 12

Dividends and Earnings per Share of Common Stock

Dividend Yield

The **dividend yield** on common stock measures the rate of return to common stockholders from cash dividends. It is of special interest to investors whose objective is to earn revenue (dividends) from their investment. It is computed as follows:

$$\text{Dividend Yield} = \frac{\text{Dividends per Share of Common Stock}}{\text{Market Price per Share of Common Stock}}$$

To illustrate, the dividend yield for **Lincoln Company** is computed as follows:

	20Y6	20Y5
Dividends per share of common stock	$0.80	$0.60
Market price per share of common stock	$41.00	$27.00
Dividend yield on common stock	2.0% ($0.80 ÷ $41)	2.2% ($0.60 ÷ $27)

The dividend yield declined slightly from 2.2% to 2.0% in 20Y6. This decline was due primarily to the increase in the market price of Lincoln's common stock.

Link to Nike

For a recent five-year period, Nike's average dividend yield was 1.24%.

Business Connection

INVESTING FOR YIELD

Companies that provide attractive dividend yields are often mature companies found in stable industries. Examples of such industries are public utilities and food. Coca-Cola, Procter & Gamble, Kellogg's, Consolidated Edison, Southern Company, and General Mills all have attractive dividend yields in excess of 3%. Procter & Gamble has had 58 consecutive years of dividend payouts, and Kellogg's has not reduced its dividend for 56 years. The stability of the food industry has allowed these companies to maintain dividends for many years. Growth companies such as Google and Facebook do not pay dividends, because they use their cash to grow the business. Investors in such growth companies expect to make their return from stock price appreciation rather than dividends. Mark Cuban, billionaire, Shark Tank® investor, and owner of the Dallas Mavericks, stated, "I believe non-dividend stocks aren't much more than baseball cards. They are worth what you can convince someone to pay for it."

Quote source: Tim Parker, "The Top Ten Dividend Quotes," *Dividend.com*, August 29, 2012.

Summary of Analytical Measures

Exhibit 13 shows a summary of the liquidity, solvency and profitability measures discussed in this chapter. The type of industry and the company's operations usually affect which measures are used. In many cases, additional measures are used for a specific industry. For example, airlines use *revenue per passenger mile* and *cost per available seat* as profitability measures. Likewise, hotels use *occupancy rates* as a profitability measure.

EXHIBIT 13 **Summary of Analytical Measures**

Liquidity Measures

	Method of Computation	Use
Working Capital	Current Assets – Current Liabilities	Measures the company's ability to pay current liabilities.
Current Ratio	$\frac{\text{Current Assets}}{\text{Current Liabilities}}$	
Quick Ratio	$\frac{\text{Quick Assets}}{\text{Current Liabilities}}$	Measures the company's instant debt-paying ability.
Accounts Receivable Turnover	$\frac{\text{Sales}}{\text{Average Accounts Receivable}}$	Measures the company's efficiency in collecting receivables and in the management of credit.
Numbers of Days' Sales in Receivables	$\frac{\text{Average Accounts Receivable}}{\text{Average Daily Sales}}$	
Inventory Turnover	$\frac{\text{Cost of Goods Sold}}{\text{Average Inventory}}$	Measures the company's efficiency in managing inventory.
Number of Days' Sales in Inventory	$\frac{\text{Average Inventory}}{\text{Average Daily Cost of Goods Sold}}$	

Solvency Measures

Ratio of Fixed Assets to Long-Term Liabilities	$\frac{\text{Fixed Assets (net)}}{\text{Long-Term Liabilities}}$	Measures the margin of safety available to long-term creditors.
Ratio of Liabilities to Stockholders' Equity	$\frac{\text{Total Liabilities}}{\text{Total Stockholders' Equity}}$	Measures how much of the company is financed by debt and equity.
Times Interest Earned	$\frac{\text{Income Before Income Tax + Interest Expense}}{\text{Interest Expense}}$	Measures the risk that interest payments will not be made if earnings decrease.

Profitability Measures

Asset Turnover	$\frac{\text{Sales}}{\text{Average Total Assets}}$	Measures how effectively a company uses its assets.
Return on Total Assets	$\frac{\text{Net Income + Interest Expense}}{\text{Average Total Assets}}$	Measures the profitability of a company's assets.
Return on Stockholders' Equity	$\frac{\text{Net Income}}{\text{Average Total Stockholders' Equity}}$	Measures the profitability of the investment by stockholders.
Return on Common Stockholders' Equity	$\frac{\text{Net Income – Preferred Dividends}}{\text{Average Common Stockholders' Equity}}$	Measures the profitability of the investment by common stockholders.
Earnings per Share (EPS) on Common Stock	$\frac{\text{Net Income – Preferred Dividends}}{\text{Shares of Common Stock Outstanding}}$	
Price-Earnings (P/E) Ratio	$\frac{\text{Market Price per Share of Common Stock}}{\text{Earnings per Share on Common Stock}}$	Measures future earnings prospects, based on the relationship between market value of common stock and earnings.
Dividends per Share	$\frac{\text{Dividends on Common Stock}}{\text{Shares of Common Stock Outstanding}}$	Measures the extent to which earnings are being distributed to common stockholders.
Dividend Yield	$\frac{\text{Dividends per Share of Common Stock}}{\text{Market Price per Share of Common Stock}}$	Measures the rate of return to common stockholders in terms of dividends.

The analytical measures shown in Exhibit 13 are a useful starting point for analyzing a company's liquidity, solvency, and profitability. However, they are not a substitute for sound judgment. The general economic and business environment should always be considered in analyzing a company's future prospects. In addition, any trends and interrelationships among the measures should be studied carefully.

Corporate Annual Reports

Obj. 6 Describe the contents of corporate annual reports.

IFRS See Appendix B for more information.

Public corporations issue annual reports summarizing their operating activities for the past year and plans for the future. Such annual reports include the financial statements and the accompanying notes. In addition, annual reports normally include the following sections:

- Management discussion and analysis
- Report on internal control
- Report on fairness of the financial statements

Management Discussion and Analysis

Management's Discussion and Analysis (MD&A) is required in annual reports filed with the Securities and Exchange Commission. It includes management's analysis of current operations and its plans for the future. Typical items included in the MD&A are as follows:

- Management's analysis and explanations of any significant changes between the current and prior years' financial statements.
- Important accounting principles or policies that could affect interpretation of the financial statements, including the effect of changes in accounting principles or the adoption of new accounting principles.
- Management's assessment of the company's liquidity and the availability of capital to the company.
- Significant risk exposures that might affect the company.
- Any "off-balance-sheet" arrangements such as leases not included in the financial statements. Such arrangements are discussed in advanced accounting courses and textbooks.

Report on Internal Control

The Sarbanes-Oxley Act of 2002 requires a report on internal control by management. The report states management's responsibility for establishing and maintaining internal control. In addition, management's assessment of the effectiveness of internal controls over financial reporting is included in the report.

INTEGRITY, OBJECTIVITY, AND ETHICS IN BUSINESS

CHARACTERISTICS OF FINANCIAL STATEMENT FRAUD

Each year, the Association of Certified Fraud Examiners conducts a worldwide survey examining the characteristics of corporate fraud. The most recent study found the following:

- 43.3% of frauds were detected by a tip from an employee or someone close to the company.
- Frauds committed by owners and executives tended to be much larger than those caused by employees.
- Most people who are caught committing fraud are first-time offenders with clean employment histories.
- In 81% of the cases, the person committing the fraud displayed one or more behavioral red flags, such as living beyond his or her means, having financial difficulties, and having excessive control issues.

Fraud examiners can use these trends to help them narrow their focus when searching for fraud.

Source: *2012 Report to the Nations*, Association of Certified Fraud Examiners, 2012.

Sarbanes-Oxley also requires a public accounting firm to verify management's conclusions on internal control. Thus, two reports on internal control, one by management and one by a public accounting firm, are included in the annual report. In some situations, these may be combined into a single report on internal control.

Report on Fairness of the Financial Statements

All publicly held corporations are required to have an independent audit (examination) of their financial statements. The Certified Public Accounting (CPA) firm that conducts the audit renders an opinion, called the *Report of Independent Registered Public Accounting Firm*, on the fairness of the statements.

An opinion stating that the financial statements present fairly the financial position, results of operations, and cash flows of the company is said to be an *unmodified opinion*, sometimes called a *clean opinion*. Any report other than an unmodified opinion raises a red flag for financial statement users and requires further investigation as to its cause. The types and nature of audit opinions are covered in more detail in advanced courses on auditing.

The annual report of Nike Inc. is shown in Appendix D. The Nike report includes the financial statements as well as Management's Discussion and Analysis, Report on Internal Control, and the Report on Fairness of the Financial Statements.

APPENDIX

Unusual Items on the Income Statement

Generally accepted accounting principles require that unusual items be reported separately on the income statement. This is because such items do not occur frequently and are typically unrelated to current operations. Without separate reporting of these items, users of the financial statements might be misled about current and future operations.

Unusual items on the income statement are classified as one of the following:

- Affecting the *current period* income statement
- Affecting a *prior period* income statement

Unusual Items Affecting the Current Period's Income Statement

Discontinued operations are an unusual item that affects the current period's:

- Income statement presentation
- Earnings per share presentation

Discontinued operations are reported separately on the income statement for any period in which they occur.

Income Statement Presentation A company may discontinue a component of its operations by selling or abandoning the component's operations. For example, a retailer might decide to sell its product only online and, thus, discontinue selling its merchandise at its retail outlets (stores).

If the discontinued component is (1) the result of a strategic shift and (2) has a major effect on the entity's operations and financial results, any gain or loss on discontinued operations is reported on the income statement as a *Gain (or loss) from discontinued operations*. It is reported immediately following *Income from continuing operations*.

To illustrate, assume that Jones Corporation produces and sells electrical products, hardware supplies, and lawn equipment. Because of a lack of profits, Jones discontinues its electrical products operation and sells the remaining inventory and other assets at a loss of $100,000. Exhibit 14 illustrates the reporting of the loss on discontinued operations.[2]

EXHIBIT 14

Unusual Items in the Income Statement

Jones Corporation
Income Statement
For the Year Ended December 31, 20Y2

Sales	$12,350,000
Cost of goods sold	5,800,000
Gross profit	$ 6,550,000
Selling and administrative expenses	5,240,000
Income from continuing operations before income tax	$ 1,310,000
Income tax expense	620,000
Income from continuing operations	$ 690,000
Loss on discontinued operations	(100,000)
Net income	$ 590,000

In addition, a note to the financial statements should describe the operations sold, including the date operations were discontinued, and details about the assets, liabilities, income, and expenses of the discontinued component.

Earnings per Share Earnings per common share should be reported separately for discontinued operations. To illustrate, a partial income statement for Jones Corporation is shown in Exhibit 15. The company has 200,000 shares of common stock outstanding.

EXHIBIT 15

Income Statement with Earnings per Share

Jones Corporation
Income Statement
For the Year Ended December 31, 20Y2

Earnings per common share:	
Income from continuing operations	$ 3.45
Loss on discontinued operations	(0.50)
Net income	$ 2.95

Exhibit 15 reports earnings per common share for income from continuing operations, discontinued operations. However, only earnings per share for income from continuing operations and net income are required by generally accepted accounting principles. The other per-share amounts may be presented in the notes to the financial statements.

2 The gain or loss on discontinued operations is reported net of any tax effects. To simplify, the tax effects are not specifically identified in Exhibit 14.

Unusual Items Affecting the Prior Period's Income Statement

An unusual item may occur that affects a prior period's income statement. Two such items are as follows:

- Errors in applying generally accepted accounting principles
- Changes from one generally accepted accounting principle to another

If an error is discovered in a prior period's financial statement, the prior-period statement and all following statements are restated and thus corrected.

A company may change from one generally accepted accounting principle to another. In this case, the prior-period financial statements are restated as if the new accounting principle had always been used as discussed in Chapter 11.

For both of the preceding items, the current period earnings are not affected. That is, only the earnings reported in prior periods are restated. However, because the prior earnings are restated, the beginning balance of Retained Earnings may also have to be restated. This, in turn, may cause the restatement of other balance sheet accounts. Illustrations of these types of adjustments and restatements are provided in advanced accounting courses.

At a Glance 17

Obj. 1 Describe the techniques and tools used to analyze financial statement information.

Key Points Financial statements provide important information that users rely on to make economic decisions. This information is evaluated along three dimensions: liquidity, solvency, and profitability. Two common techniques are used to analyze a company's financial performance and condition: analytical methods and ratios. Both analytical methods and ratios can be used to compare a company's financial performance over time or to another company.

Learning Outcome	Example Exercises	Practice Exercises
• Describe the techniques used to analyze a company's financial performance.		

Obj. 2 Describe and illustrate basic financial statement analytical methods.

Key Points Financial statements provide much of the information users need to make economic decisions. Analytical procedures are used to compare items on a current financial statement with related items on earlier financial statements or to examine relationships within a financial statement.

Learning Outcomes	Example Exercises	Practice Exercises
• Prepare a horizontal analysis from a company's financial statements.	EE17-1	PE17-1A, 17-1B
• Prepare a vertical analysis from a company's financial statements.	EE17-2	PE17-2A, 17-2B
• Prepare a common-sized financial statement.		

Obj. 3 Describe and illustrate how to use financial statement analysis to assess liquidity.

Key Points Liquidity analysis evaluates a company's ability to convert current assets into cash. Short-term creditors use liquidity analysis to evaluate a company's ability to repay short-term debts by focusing on a company's current position, accounts receivable, and inventory. The measures and ratios used to evaluate a company's liquidity include (1) working capital, (2) current ratio, (3) quick ratio, (4) accounts receivable turnover, (5) number of days' sales in receivables, (6) inventory turnover, and (7) number of days' sales in inventory.

Learning Outcomes	Example Exercises	Practice Exercises
• Determine working capital.		
• Compute and interpret the current ratio.		
• Compute and interpret the quick ratio.	EE17-3	PE17-3A, 17-3B
• Compute and interpret accounts receivable turnover.	EE17-4	PE17-4A, 17-4B
• Compute and interpret the number of days' sales in receivables.		
• Compute and interpret inventory turnover.		
• Compute and interpret the number of days' sales in inventory.	EE17-5	PE17-5A, 17-5B

Obj. 4 Describe and illustrate how to use financial statement analysis to assess solvency.

Key Points Solvency analysis evaluates the ability of a company to pay its long-term debts. Long-term creditors use solvency analysis to evaluate a company's ability to make its periodic interest payments and repay the face amount of bonds at maturity. Solvency is normally assessed by examining (1) the ratio of fixed assets to long-term liabilities, (2) the ratio of liabilities to stockholders' equity, and (3) the times interest earned ratio.

Learning Outcomes	Example Exercises	Practice Exercises
• Compute and interpret the ratio of fixed assets to long-term liabilities.		
• Compute and interpret the ratio of liabilities to stockholders' equity.	EE17-6	PE17-6A, 17-6B
• Compute and interpret the times interest earned ratio.	EE17-7	PE17-7A, 17-7B

Obj. 5 Describe and illustrate to to use financial statement analysis to assess profitability.

Key Points Profitability analysis focuses on the relationship between operating results (income statement) and assets (balance sheet). Profitability analyses include (1) the asset turnover ratio, (2) the return on total assets, (3) the return on stockholders' equity, (4) the return on common stockholders' equity, (5) earnings per share on common stock, (6) the price-earnings ratio, (7) dividends per share, and (8) dividend yield.

Learning Outcomes	Example Exercises	Practice Exercises
• Compute and interpret the asset turnover ratio.	EE17-8	PE17-8A, 17-8B
• Compute and interpret the return on total assets.	EE17-9	PE17-9A, 17-9B
• Compute and interpret the return on stockholders' equity.		
• Compute and interpret the return on common stockholders' equity.	EE17-10	PE17-10A, 17-10B
• Compute and interpret the price-earnings ratio.	EE17-11	PE17-11A, 17-11B
• Compute and interpret dividends per share and dividend yield.		
• Describe the uses and limitations of analytical measures.		

Obj. 6 Describe the contents of corporate annual reports.

Key Points Public corporations issue annual reports summarizing their operating activities for the past year and plans for the future. In addition to the financial statements and accompanying notes, annual reports include Management's Discussion and Analysis (MD&A), a report on internal control, and a report on fairness of the financial statements.

Learning Outcome	Example Exercises	Practice Exercises
• Describe the elements of a corporate annual report.		

Illustrative Problem

Rainbow Paint Co.'s comparative financial statements for the years ending December 31, 20Y9 and 20Y8, are as follows. The market price of Rainbow Paint's common stock was $25 on December 31, 20Y9, and $30 on December 31, 20Y8.

Rainbow Paint Co.
Comparative Income Statement
For the Years Ended December 31, 20Y9 and 20Y8

	20Y9	20Y8
Sales	$5,000,000	$3,200,000
Cost of goods sold	3,400,000	2,080,000
Gross profit	$1,600,000	$1,120,000
Selling expenses	$ 650,000	$ 464,000
Administrative expenses	325,000	224,000
Total operating expenses	$ 975,000	$ 688,000
Income from operations	$ 625,000	$ 432,000
Other revenue	25,000	19,200
	$ 650,000	$ 451,200
Other expense (interest)	105,000	64,000
Income before income tax	$ 545,000	$ 387,200
Income tax expense	300,000	176,000
Net income	$ 245,000	$ 211,200

Rainbow Paint Co.
Comparative Retained Earnings Statement
For the Years Ended December 31, 20Y9 and 20Y8

	20Y9	20Y8
Retained earnings, January 1	$723,000	$581,800
Net income	245,000	211,200
Total	$968,000	$793,000
Dividends:		
Preferred stock dividends	$ 40,000	$ 40,000
Common stock dividends	45,000	30,000
Total dividends	$ 85,000	$ 70,000
Retained earnings, December 31	$883,000	$723,000

(Continued)

Rainbow Paint Co.
Comparative Balance Sheet
December 31, 20Y9 and 20Y8

	20Y9	20Y8
Assets		
Current assets:		
Cash	$ 175,000	$ 125,000
Temporary investments	150,000	50,000
Accounts receivable (net)	425,000	325,000
Inventories	720,000	480,000
Prepaid expenses	30,000	20,000
Total current assets	$1,500,000	$1,000,000
Long-term investments	250,000	225,000
Property, plant, and equipment (net)	2,093,000	1,948,000
Total assets	$3,843,000	$3,173,000
Liabilities		
Current liabilities	$ 750,000	$ 650,000
Long-term liabilities:		
Mortgage note payable, 10%, due in five years	$ 410,000	$ —
Bonds payable, 8%, due in 15 years	800,000	800,000
Total long-term liabilities	$1,210,000	$ 800,000
Total liabilities	$1,960,000	$1,450,000
Stockholders' Equity		
Preferred 8% stock, $100 par	$ 500,000	$ 500,000
Common stock, $10 par	500,000	500,000
Retained earnings	883,000	723,000
Total stockholders' equity	$1,883,000	$1,723,000
Total liabilities and stockholders' equity	$3,843,000	$3,173,000

Instructions

Determine the following measures for 20Y9, rounding percentages and ratios other than per-share amounts to one decimal place:

1. Working capital
2. Current ratio
3. Quick ratio
4. Accounts receivable turnover
5. Number of days' sales in receivables
6. Inventory turnover
7. Number of days' sales in inventory
8. Ratio of fixed assets to long-term liabilities
9. Ratio of liabilities to stockholders' equity
10. Times interest earned
11. Asset turnover
12. Return on total assets
13. Return on stockholders' equity
14. Return on common stockholders' equity
15. Earnings per share on common stock
16. Price-earnings ratio
17. Dividends per share
18. Dividend yield

Solution

(Ratios are rounded to one decimal place.)

1. Working capital: $750,000

   $1,500,000 – $750,000

2. Current ratio: 2.0

   $1,500,000 ÷ $750,000

3. Quick ratio: 1.0

   $750,000 ÷ $750,000

4. Accounts receivable turnover: 13.3

   $5,000,000 ÷ [($425,000 + $325,000) ÷ 2]

5. Number of days' sales in receivables: 27.4 days

   $5,000,000 ÷ 365 days = $13,699 average daily sales

   $375,000 ÷ $13,699

6. Inventory turnover: 5.7

   $3,400,000 ÷ [($720,000 + $480,000) ÷ 2]

7. Number of days' sales in inventory: 64.4 days

   $3,400,000 ÷ 365 days = $9,315 average daily cost of goods sold

   $600,000 ÷ $9,315

8. Ratio of fixed assets to long-term liabilities: 1.7

   $2,093,000 ÷ $1,210,000

9. Ratio of liabilities to stockholders' equity: 1.0

   $1,960,000 ÷ $1,883,000

10. Times interest earned: 6.2

    ($545,000 + $105,000) ÷ $105,000

11. Asset turnover: 1.4

    $5,000,000 ÷ [($3,843,000 + $3,173,000) ÷ 2]

12. Return on total assets: 10.0%

    ($245,000 + $105,000) ÷ [($3,843,000 + $3,173,000) ÷ 2]

13. Return on stockholders' equity: 13.6%

    $245,000 ÷ [($1,883,000 + $1,723,000) ÷ 2]

14. Return on common stockholders' equity: 15.7%

    ($245,000 – $40,000) ÷ [($1,383,000 + $1,223,000) ÷ 2]

15. Earnings per share on common stock: $4.10

    ($245,000 – $40,000) ÷ 50,000 shares

16. Price-earnings ratio: 6.1

    $25 ÷ $4.10

17. Dividends per share: $0.90

    $45,000 ÷ 50,000 shares

18. Dividend yield: 3.6%

    $0.90 ÷ $25

Key Terms

accounts receivable analysis (834)
accounts receivable turnover (834)
analytical methods (826)
asset turnover (840)
common-sized statement (830)
current position analysis (832)
current ratio (832)
dividend yield (847)
dividends per share (846)
earnings per share (EPS) on common stock (844)
horizontal analysis (826)
inventory analysis (835)
inventory turnover (836)
leverage (842)
liquidity (825)
Management's Discussion and Analysis (MD&A) (849)
number of days' sales in inventory (836)
number of days' sales in receivables (835)
price-earnings (P/E) ratio (845)
profitability (826)
quick assets (833)
quick ratio (833)
ratio of fixed assets to long-term liabilities (838)
ratio of liabilities to stockholders' equity (838)
ratios (826)
return on common stockholders' equity (843)
return on stockholders' equity (842)
return on total assets (841)
solvency (826)
times interest earned (839)
vertical analysis (829)
working capital (832)

Discussion Questions

1. Briefly explain the difference between liquidity, solvency, and profitability analysis.
2. What is the advantage of using comparative statements for financial analysis rather than statements for a single date or period?
3. A company's current year net income (after income tax) is 25% larger than that of the preceding year. Does this indicate improved operating performance? Why or why not?
4. How would the current and quick ratios of a service business compare?
5. a. Why is a high inventory turnover considered to be a positive indicator?
   b. Is it possible to have a high inventory turnover and a high number of days' sales in inventory? Why?
6. What do the following data, taken from a comparative balance sheet, indicate about the company's ability to borrow additional long-term debt in the current year as compared to the preceding year?

	Current Year	Preceding Year
Fixed assets (net)	$1,260,000	$1,360,000
Total long-term liabilities	300,000	400,000

7. a. How does the return on total assets differ from the return on stockholders' equity?
   b. Which ratio is normally higher? Why?
8. Real World Kroger, a grocery store, recently had a price-earnings ratio of 17.5, while the average price-earnings ratio in the grocery store industry was 21.4. What might explain this difference?
9. Real World The dividend yield of Suburban Propane was 10.2% in a recent year, and the dividend yield of Google was 0% in the same year. What might explain the difference between these ratios?
10. Describe two reports provided by independent auditors in the annual report to shareholders.

Practice Exercises

Example Exercises

Show Me How **EE 17-1** *p. 829*

PE 17-1A Horizontal analysis **OBJ. 2**

The comparative temporary investments and inventory balances of a company follow.

	Current Year	Previous Year
Temporary investments	$44,000	$40,000
Inventory	57,000	60,000

Based on this information, what is the amount and percentage of increase or decrease that would be shown on a balance sheet with horizontal analysis?

Show Me How **EE 17-1** *p. 829*

PE 17-1B Horizontal analysis **OBJ. 2**

The comparative accounts payable and long-term debt balances for a company follow.

	Current Year	Previous Year
Accounts payable	$111,000	$100,000
Long-term debt	132,680	124,000

Based on this information, what is the amount and percentage of increase or decrease that would be shown on a balance sheet with horizontal analysis?

Show Me How **EE 17-2** *p. 830*

PE 17-2A Vertical analysis **OBJ. 2**

Income statement information for Omega Corporation follows:

Sales	$500,000
Cost of goods sold	300,000
Gross profit	200,000

Prepare a vertical analysis of the income statement for Omega Corporation.

Show Me How **EE 17-2** *p. 830*

PE 17-2B Vertical analysis **OBJ. 2**

Income statement information for Einsworth Corporation follows:

Sales	$1,200,000
Cost of goods sold	780,000
Gross profit	420,000

Prepare a vertical analysis of the income statement for Einsworth Corporation.

Show Me How **EE 17-3** *p. 833*

PE 17-3A Current position analysis **OBJ. 3**

The following items are reported on a company's balance sheet:

Cash	$100,000
Marketable securities	50,000
Accounts receivable (net)	60,000
Inventory	70,000
Accounts payable	140,000

Determine (a) the current ratio and (b) the quick ratio. Round to one decimal place.

EE 17-3 p. 833 **Show Me How**

PE 17-3B Current position analysis

OBJ. 3

The following items are reported on a company's balance sheet:

Cash	$210,000
Marketable securities	120,000
Accounts receivable (net)	110,000
Inventory	160,000
Accounts payable	200,000

Determine (a) the current ratio and (b) the quick ratio. Round to one decimal place.

EE 17-4 p. 835 **Show Me How**

PE 17-4A Accounts receivable analysis

OBJ. 3

A company reports the following:

Sales	$1,500,000
Average accounts receivable (net)	100,000

Determine (a) the accounts receivable turnover and (b) the number of days' sales in receivables. Round to one decimal place.

EE 17-4 p. 835 **Show Me How**

PE 17-4B Accounts receivable analysis

OBJ. 3

A company reports the following:

Sales	$4,000,000
Average accounts receivable (net)	200,000

Determine (a) the accounts receivable turnover and (b) the number of days' sales in receivables. Round to one decimal place.

EE 17-5 p. 837 **Show Me How**

PE 17-5A Inventory analysis

OBJ. 3

A company reports the following:

Cost of goods sold	$660,000
Average inventory	60,000

Determine (a) the inventory turnover and (b) the number of days' sales in inventory. Round to one decimal place.

EE 17-5 p. 837 **Show Me How**

PE 17-5B Inventory analysis

OBJ. 3

A company reports the following:

Cost of goods sold	$435,000
Average inventory	72,500

Determine (a) the inventory turnover and (b) the number of days' sales in inventory. Round to one decimal place.

EE 17-6 p. 838 **Show Me How**

PE 17-6A Long-term solvency analysis

OBJ. 4

The following information was taken from Sigmund Company's balance sheet:

Fixed assets (net)	$1,050,000
Long-term liabilities	750,000
Total liabilities	850,000
Total stockholders' equity	500,000

Determine the company's (a) ratio of fixed assets to long-term liabilities and (b) ratio of liabilities to stockholders' equity. Round to one decimal place.

Show Me How EE 17-6 *p. 838*

PE 17-6B Long-term solvency analysis **OBJ. 4**

The following information was taken from Charu Company's balance sheet:

Fixed assets (net)	$860,000
Long-term liabilities	200,000
Total liabilities	600,000
Total stockholders' equity	250,000

Determine the company's (a) ratio of fixed assets to long-term liabilities and (b) ratio of liabilities to stockholders' equity. Round to one decimal place.

Show Me How EE 17-7 *p. 839*

PE 17-7A Times interest earned **OBJ. 4**

A company reports the following:

Income before income tax	$4,000,000
Interest expense	400,000

Determine the times interest earned ratio. Round to one decimal place.

Show Me How EE 17-7 *p. 839*

PE 17-7B Times interest earned **OBJ. 4**

A company reports the following:

Income before income tax	$8,000,000
Interest expense	500,000

Determine the times interest earned ratio. Round to one decimal place.

Show Me How EE 17-8 *p. 841*

PE 17-8A Asset turnover **OBJ. 5**

A company reports the following:

Sales	$1,800,000
Average total assets	1,125,000

Determine the asset turnover ratio. Round to one decimal place.

Show Me How EE 17-8 *p. 841*

PE 17-8B Asset turnover **OBJ. 5**

A company reports the following:

Sales	$4,400,000
Average total assets	2,000,000

Determine the asset turnover ratio. Round to one decimal place.

Show Me How EE 17-9 *p. 842*

PE 17-9A Return on total assets **OBJ. 5**

A company reports the following income statement and balance sheet information for the current year:

Net income	$ 250,000
Interest expense	100,000
Average total assets	2,500,000

Determine the return on total assets. Round percentage to one decimal place.

EE 17-9 p. 842
Show Me How

PE 17-9B Return on total assets OBJ. 5

A company reports the following income statement and balance sheet information for the current year:

Net income	$ 410,000
Interest expense	90,000
Average total assets	5,000,000

Determine the return on total assets. Round percentage to one decimal place.

EE 17-10 p. 844
Show Me How

PE 17-10A Common stockholders' profitability analysis OBJ. 5

A company reports the following:

Net income	$ 375,000
Preferred dividends	75,000
Average stockholders' equity	2,500,000
Average common stockholders' equity	1,875,000

Determine (a) the return on stockholders' equity and (b) the return on common stockholders' equity. Round percentages to one decimal place.

EE 17-10 p. 844
Show Me How

PE 17-10B Common stockholders' profitability analysis OBJ. 5

A company reports the following:

Net income	$1,000,000
Preferred dividends	50,000
Average stockholders' equity	6,250,000
Average common stockholders' equity	3,800,000

Determine (a) the return on stockholders' equity and (b) the return on common stockholders' equity. Round percentages to one decimal place.

EE 17-11 p. 846
Show Me How

PE 17-11A Earnings per share and price-earnings ratio OBJ. 5

A company reports the following:

Net income	$185,000
Preferred dividends	$25,000
Shares of common stock outstanding	100,000
Market price per share of common stock	$20

a. Determine the company's earnings per share on common stock.

b. Determine the company's price-earnings ratio. Round to one decimal place.

EE 17-11 p. 846
Show Me How

PE 17-11B Earnings per share and price-earnings ratio OBJ. 5

A company reports the following:

Net income	$410,000
Preferred dividends	$60,000
Shares of common stock outstanding	50,000
Market price per share of common stock	$84

a. Determine the company's earnings per share on common stock.

b. Determine the company's price-earnings ratio. Round to one decimal place.

Exercises

EX 17-1 Vertical analysis of income statement

OBJ. 2

✔ a. Current year net income: $360,000; 9% of sales

Show Me How

Revenue and expense data for Innovation Quarter Inc. for two recent years are as follows:

	Current Year	Previous Year
Sales	$4,000,000	$3,600,000
Cost of goods sold	2,280,000	1,872,000
Selling expenses	600,000	648,000
Administrative expenses	520,000	360,000
Income tax expense	240,000	216,000

a. Prepare an income statement in comparative form, stating each item for both years as a percent of sales. Round to the nearest whole percentage.

b. Comment on the significant changes disclosed by the comparative income statement.

EX 17-2 Vertical analysis of income statement

OBJ. 2

✔ a. Current fiscal year income from continuing operations, 12.3% of revenues

Excel

Real World

The following comparative income statement (in thousands of dollars) for two recent fiscal years was adapted from the annual report of Speedway Motorsports, Inc., owner and operator of several major motor speedways, such as the Atlanta, Texas, and Las Vegas Motor Speedways.

	Current Year	Previous Year
Revenues:		
Admissions	$100,694	$100,798
Event-related revenue	146,980	146,849
NASCAR broadcasting revenue	217,469	207,369
Other operating revenue	31,320	29,293
Total revenues	$496,463	$484,309
Expenses and other:		
Direct expense of events	$104,303	$102,196
NASCAR event management fees	133,682	128,254
Other direct operating expenses	19,541	18,513
General and administrative	177,926	194,120
Total expenses and other	$435,452	$443,083
Income from continuing operations	$ 61,011	$ 41,226

a. Prepare a comparative income statement for these two years in vertical form, stating each item as a percent of revenues. Round percentages to one decimal place.

b. Comment on the significant changes.

EX 17-3 Common-sized income statement

OBJ. 2

✔ A. Tannenhill net income: $120,000; 3.0% of sales

Show Me How

Revenue and expense data for the current calendar year for Tannenhill Company and for the electronics industry are as follows. Tannenhill's data are expressed in dollars. The electronics industry averages are expressed in percentages.

(Continued)

	Tannenhill Company	Electronics Industry Average
Sales	$4,000,000	100%
Cost of goods sold	2,120,000	60
Gross profit	$1,880,000	40%
Selling expenses	$1,080,000	24%
Administrative expenses	640,000	14
Total operating expenses	$1,720,000	38%
Operating income	$ 160,000	2%
Other revenue	120,000	3
	$ 280,000	5%
Other expense	80,000	2
Income before income tax	$ 200,000	3%
Income tax expense	80,000	2
Net income	$ 120,000	1%

a. Prepare a common-sized income statement comparing the results of operations for Tannenhill Company with the industry average. Round to the nearest whole percentage.

b. As far as the data permit, comment on significant relationships revealed by the comparisons.

EX 17-4 Vertical analysis of balance sheet

OBJ. 2

✔ Retained earnings, Current year, 36.8%

Excel

Show Me How

Balance sheet data for Alvarez Company on December 31, the end of two recent fiscal years, follow:

	Current Year	Previous Year
Current assets	$2,500,000	$1,840,000
Property, plant, and equipment	5,600,000	6,072,000
Intangible assets	1,900,000	1,288,000
Current liabilities	2,000,000	1,380,000
Long-term liabilities	3,400,000	3,680,000
Common stock	920,000	920,000
Retained earnings	3,680,000	3,220,000

Prepare a comparative balance sheet for both years, stating each asset as a percent of total assets and each liability and stockholders' equity item as a percent of the total liabilities and stockholders' equity. Round percentages to one decimal place.

EX 17-5 Horizontal analysis of the income statement

OBJ. 2

✔ a. Net income increase, 66.0%

Excel

Show Me How

Income statement data for Winthrop Company for two recent years ended December 31 are as follows:

	Current Year	Previous Year
Sales	$2,280,000	$2,000,000
Cost of goods sold	1,960,000	1,750,000
Gross profit	$ 320,000	$ 250,000
Selling expenses	$ 156,500	$ 125,000
Administrative expenses	122,000	100,000
Total operating expenses	$ 278,500	$ 225,000
Income before income tax	$ 41,500	$ 25,000
Income tax expense	16,600	10,000
Net income	$ 24,900	$ 15,000

a. Prepare a comparative income statement with horizontal analysis, indicating the increase (decrease) for the current year when compared with the previous year. Round percentages to one decimal place.

b. What conclusions can be drawn from the horizontal analysis?

✔ a. Current year working capital, $1,170,000

Show Me How

EX 17-6 Current position analysis

OBJ. 3

The following data were taken from the balance sheet of Nilo Company at the end of two recent fiscal years:

	Current Year	Previous Year
Current assets:		
Cash	$ 414,000	$ 320,000
Marketable securities	496,800	336,000
Accounts and notes receivable (net)	619,200	464,000
Inventories	351,900	272,000
Prepaid expenses	188,100	208,000
Total current assets	$2,070,000	$1,600,000
Current liabilities:		
Accounts and notes payable (short-term)	$ 675,000	$ 600,000
Accrued liabilities	225,000	200,000
Total current liabilities	$ 900,000	$ 800,000

a. Determine for each year (1) the working capital, (2) the current ratio, and (3) the quick ratio. Round ratios to one decimal place.

b. What conclusions can be drawn from these data as to the company's ability to meet its currently maturing debts?

✔ a. (1) Current year's current ratio, 1.1

Real World

EX 17-7 Current position analysis

OBJ. 3

PepsiCo, Inc., the parent company of Frito-Lay snack foods and Pepsi beverages, had the following current assets and current liabilities at the end of two recent years:

	Current Year (in millions)	Previous Year (in millions)
Cash and cash equivalents	$ 6,297	$ 4,067
Short-term investments, at cost	322	358
Accounts and notes receivable, net	7,041	6,912
Inventories	3,581	3,827
Prepaid expenses and other current assets	1,479	2,277
Short-term obligations	4,815	6,205
Accounts payable	12,274	11,949

a. Determine the (1) current ratio and (2) quick ratio for both years. Round to one decimal place.

b. What conclusions can you draw from these data about PepsiCo's liquidity?

EX 17-8 Current position analysis

OBJ. 3

The bond indenture for the 10-year, 9% debenture bonds issued January 2, 20Y5, required working capital of $100,000, a current ratio of 1.5, and a quick ratio of 1.0 at the end of each calendar year until the bonds mature. At December 31, 20Y6, the three measures were computed as follows:

1. Current assets:

Cash	$102,000	
Temporary investments	48,000	
Accounts and notes receivable (net)	120,000	
Inventories	36,000	
Prepaid expenses	24,000	
Intangible assets	124,800	
Property, plant, and equipment	55,200	
Total current assets (net)		$510,000
Current liabilities:		
Accounts and short-term notes payable	$ 96,000	
Accrued liabilities	204,000	
Total current liabilities		300,000
Working capital		$210,000

(Continued)

2. Current ratio	1.7	$510,000 ÷ $300,000
3. Quick ratio..	1.2	$115,200 ÷ $ 96,000

a. List the errors in the determination of the three measures of current position analysis.

b. Is the company satisfying the terms of the bond indenture? Explain.

EX 17-9 Accounts receivable analysis **OBJ. 3**

✔ a. Accounts receivable turnover, 20Y3, 8.2

Show Me How

The following data are taken from the financial statements of Sigmon Inc. Terms of all sales are 2/10, n/45.

	20Y3	20Y2	20Y1
Accounts receivable, end of year	$ 725,000	$ 650,000	$600,000
Sales on account	5,637,500	4,687,500	

a. For 20Y2 and 20Y3, determine (1) the accounts receivable turnover and (2) the number of days' sales in receivables. Round to the nearest dollar and one decimal place.

b. What conclusions can be drawn from these data concerning accounts receivable and credit policies?

EX 17-10 Accounts receivable analysis **OBJ. 3**

✔ a. 1. Lestrade, 7.0

Xavier Stores Company and Lestrade Stores Inc. are large retail department stores. Both companies offer credit to their customers through their own credit card operations. Information from the financial statements for both companies for two recent years is as follows (in millions):

	Xavier	Lestrade
Sales	$8,500,000	$4,585,000
Credit card receivables—beginning	820,000	600,000
Credit card receviables—ending	880,000	710,000

a. Determine the (1) accounts receivable turnover and (2) the number of days' sales in receivables for both companies. Round to one decimal place.

b. Compare the two companies with regard to their credit card policies.

EX 17-11 Inventory analysis **OBJ. 3**

✔ a. Inventory turnover, current year, 9.0

Show Me How

The following data were extracted from the income statement of Keever Inc.:

	Current Year	Previous Year
Sales	$18,500,000	$20,000,000
Beginning inventories	940,000	860,000
Cost of goods sold	9,270,000	10,800,000
Ending inventories	1,120,000	940,000

a. Determine for each year (1) the inventory turnover and (2) the number of days' sales in inventory. Round to the nearest dollar and one decimal place.

b. What conclusions can be drawn from these data concerning the inventories?

EX 17-12 Inventory analysis **OBJ. 3**

✔ a. QT inventory turnover, 32.1

QT, Inc. and Elppa Computers, Inc. compete with each other in the personal computer market. QT assembles computers to customer orders, building and delivering a computer within four days of a customer entering an order online. Elppa, on the other hand, builds computers for inventory prior to receiving an order. These computers are sold from inventory once an order is received. Selected financial information for both companies from recent financial statements follows (in millions):

	QT	Elppa
Sales	$56,940	$120,357
Cost of goods sold	44,754	92,385
Inventory, beginning of period	1,382	6,317
Inventory, end of period	1,404	7,490

a. Determine for both companies (1) the inventory turnover and (2) the number of days' sales in inventory. Round to one decimal place.

b. Interpret the inventory ratios in the context of both companies' operating strategies.

✔ a. Ratio of liabilities to stockholders' equity, current year, 0.9

EX 17-13 Ratio of liabilities to stockholders' equity and times interest earned **OBJ. 4**

The following data were taken from the financial statements of Hunter Inc. for December 31 of two recent years:

	Current Year	Previous Year
Accounts payable	$ 924,000	$ 800,000
Current maturities of serial bonds payable	200,000	200,000
Serial bonds payable, 10%	1,000,000	1,200,000
Common stock, $10 par value	250,000	250,000
Paid-in capital in excess of par	1,250,000	1,250,000
Retained earnings	860,000	500,000

The income before income tax was $480,000 and $420,000 for the current and previous years, respectively.

a. Determine the ratio of liabilities to stockholders' equity at the end of each year. Round to one decimal place.

b. Determine the times interest earned ratio for both years. Round to one decimal place.

c. What conclusions can be drawn from these data as to the company's ability to meet its currently maturing debts?

✔ a. Hasbro, 1.8

Real World

EX 17-14 Ratio of liabilities to stockholders' equity and times interest earned **OBJ. 4**

Hasbro, Inc. and Mattel, Inc. are the two largest toy companies in North America. Condensed liabilities and stockholders' equity from a recent balance sheet are shown for each company as follows (in thousands):

	Hasbro	Mattel
Liabilities:		
Current liabilities	$ 1,064,647	$ 1,645,572
Long-term debt	1,547,115	1,800,000
Other liabilities	404,883	473,863
Total liabilities	$ 3,016,645	$ 3,919,435
Stockholders' equity:		
Common stock	$ 104,847	$ 441,369
Additional paid in capital	893,630	1,789,870
Retained earnings	3,852,321	3,745,815
Accumulated other comprehensive loss and other equity items	(146,001)	(848,899)
Treasury stock, at cost	(3,040,895)	(2,494,901)
Total stockholders' equity	$ 1,663,902	$ 2,633,254
Total liabilities and stockholders' equity	$ 4,680,547	$ 6,522,689

The income from operations and interest expense from the income statement for each company were as follows (in thousands):

(Continued)

	Hasbro	Mattel
Income from operations (before income tax)	$603,915	$463,915
Interest expense	97,122	85,270

a. Determine the ratio of liabilities to stockholders' equity for both companies. Round to one decimal place.

b. Determine the times interest earned ratio for both companies. Round to one decimal place.

c. Interpret the ratio differences between the two companies.

EX 17-15 Ratio of liabilities to stockholders' equity and ratio of fixed assets to long-term liabilities **OBJ. 4**

✔ a. Mondelez International, Inc., 1.3

Real World

Recent balance sheet information for two companies in the food industry, Mondelez International, Inc. and The Hershey Company, is as follows (in thousands):

	Mondelez	Hershey
Net property, plant, and equipment	$10,010,000	$1,674,071
Current liabilities	14,873,000	1,471,110
Long-term debt	15,574,000	1,530,967
Other long-term liabilities	12,816,000	716,013
Stockholders' equity	32,215,000	1,036,749

a. Determine the ratio of liabilities to stockholders' equity for both companies. Round to one decimal place.

b. Determine the ratio of fixed assets to long-term liabilities for both companies. Round to one decimal place.

c. Interpret the ratio differences between the two companies.

EX 17-16 Asset turnover **OBJ. 5**

✔ a. YRC, 2.5

Real World

Three major segments of the transportation industry are motor carriers such as YRC Worldwide, railroads such as Union Pacific, and transportation logistics services such as C.H. Robinson Worldwide, Inc. Recent financial statement information for these three companies follows (in thousands):

	YRC	Union Pacific	C.H. Robinson
Sales	$4,832,400	$21,813,000	$13,476,084
Average total assets	1,939,800	53,486,000	3,199,348

a. Determine the asset turnover for all three companies. Round to one decimal place.

b. Assume that the asset turnover for each company represents its respective industry segment. Interpret the differences in the asset turnover in terms of the operating characteristics of each of the respective segments.

EX 17-17 Profitability ratios **OBJ. 5**

✔ a. Return on total assets, 20Y7, 11.0%

Show Me How

The following selected data were taken from the financial statements of Vidahill Inc. for December 31, 20Y7, 20Y6, and 20Y5:

	20Y7	20Y6	20Y5
Total assets	$5,200,000	$5,000,000	$4,800,000
Notes payable (6% interest)	2,500,000	2,500,000	2,500,000
Common stock	250,000	250,000	250,000
Preferred 2.5% stock, $100 par (no change during year)	500,000	500,000	500,000
Retained earnings	1,574,000	1,222,000	750,000

The 20Y7 net income was $411,000, and the 20Y6 net income was $462,500. No dividends on common stock were declared between 20Y5 and 20Y7. Preferred dividends were declared and paid in full in 20Y6 and 20Y7.

a. Determine the return on total assets, the return on stockholders' equity, and the return on common stockholders' equity for the years 20Y6 and 20Y7. Round percentages to one decimal place.

b. What conclusions can be drawn from these data as to the company's profitability?

✔a. Year 3 return on total assets, 12.2%

Real World

EX 17-18 Profitability ratios **OBJ. 5**

Ralph Lauren Corporation sells apparel through company-owned retail stores. Recent financial information for Ralph Lauren follows (in thousands):

	Fiscal Year 3	Fiscal Year 2
Net income	$567,600	$479,500
Interest expense	18,300	22,200

	Fiscal Year 3	Fiscal Year 2	Fiscal Year 1
Total assets (at end of fiscal year)	$4,981,100	$4,648,900	$4,356,500
Total stockholders' equity (at end of fiscal year)	3,304,700	3,116,600	2,735,100

Assume that the apparel industry average return on total assets is 8.0% and the average return on stockholders' equity is 10.0% for the year ended April 2, Year 3.

a. Determine the return on total assets for Ralph Lauren for fiscal Years 2 and 3. Round percentages to one decimal place.

b. Determine the return on stockholders' equity for Ralph Lauren for fiscal Years 2 and 3. Round percentages to one decimal place.

c. Evaluate the two-year trend for the profitability ratios determined in (a) and (b).

d. Evaluate Ralph Lauren's profit performance relative to the industry.

✔ c. Asset turnover, 2.5

EX 17-19 Six measures of solvency or profitability **OBJ. 4, 5**

The following data were taken from the financial statements of Gates Inc. for the current fiscal year.

Property, plant, and equipment (net)			$ 3,200,000
Liabilities:			
Current liabilities		$1,000,000	
Note payable, 6%, due in 15 years		2,000,000	
Total liabilities			$ 3,000,000
Stockholders' equity:			
Preferred $10 stock, $100 par (no change during year)			$ 1,000,000
Common stock, $10 par (no change during year)			2,000,000
Retained earnings:			
Balance, beginning of year	$1,570,000		
Net income	930,000	$2,500,000	
Preferred dividends	$ 100,000		
Common dividends	400,000	500,000	
Balance, end of year			2,000,000
Total stockholders' equity			$ 5,000,000
Sales			$18,750,000
Interest expense			$ 120,000

Assuming that total assets were $7,000,000 at the beginning of the current fiscal year, determine the following: (a) ratio of fixed assets to long-term liabilities, (b) ratio of liabilities to stockholders' equity, (c) asset turnover, (d) return on total assets, (e) return on stockholders' equity, and (f) return on common stockholders' equity. Round ratios and percentages to one decimal place as appropriate.

EX 17-20 Five measures of solvency or profitability **OBJ. 4, 5**

✔ c. Price-earnings ratio, 10.0

The balance sheet for Garcon Inc. at the end of the current fiscal year indicated the following:

Bonds payable, 8%	$5,000,000
Preferred $4 stock, $50 par	2,500,000
Common stock, $10 par	5,000,000

Income before income tax was $3,000,000, and income taxes were $1,200,000 for the current year. Cash dividends paid on common stock during the current year totaled $1,200,000. The common stock was selling for $32 per share at the end of the year. Determine each of the following: (a) times interest earned ratio, (b) earnings per share on common stock, (c) price-earnings ratio, (d) dividends per share of common stock, and (e) dividend yield. Round ratios and percentages to one decimal place, except for per-share amounts.

EX 17-21 Earnings per share, price-earnings ratio, dividend yield **OBJ. 5**

✔ b. Price-earnings ratio, 15.0

Show Me How

The following information was taken from the financial statements of Tolbert Inc. for December 31 of the current fiscal year:

Common stock, $20 par (no change during the year)	$10,000,000
Preferred $4 stock, $40 par (no change during the year)	2,500,000

The net income was $1,750,000, and the declared dividends on the common stock were $1,125,000 for the current year. The market price of the common stock is $45 per share.

For the common stock, determine (a) the earnings per share, (b) the price-earnings ratio, (c) the dividends per share, and (d) the dividend yield. Round ratios and percentages to one decimal place, except for per-share amounts.

EX 17-22 Price-earnings ratio; dividend yield **OBJ. 5**

✔ a. Alphabet (Google), 29.9

Real World

The table that follows shows the stock price, earnings per share, and dividends per share for three companies for a recent year:

	Price	Earnings per Share	Dividends per Share
Deere & Company	$ 82.29	$ 4.98	$2.40
Alphabet (Google)	735.72	24.58	0.00
The Coca-Cola Company	44.60	1.66	1.40

a. Determine the price-earnings ratio and dividend yield for the three companies. Round ratios and percentages to one decimal place as appropriate.

b. Explain the differences in these ratios across the three companies.

Appendix

EX 17-23 Earnings per share, discontinued operations

✔ b. Earnings per share on common stock, $7.60

The net income reported on the income statement of Cutler Co. was $4,000,000. There were 500,000 shares of $10 par common stock and 100,000 shares of $2 preferred stock outstanding throughout the current year. The income statement included a gain on discontinued operations of $400,000 after applicable income tax. Determine the per-share figures for common stock for (a) income before discontinued operations and (b) net income.

Appendix

EX 17-24 Income statement and earnings per share for discontinued operations

Apex Inc. reports the following for a recent year:

Income from continuing operations before income tax	$1,000,000
Loss from discontinued operations	$240,000*
Weighted average number of shares outstanding	20,000
Applicable tax rate	40%

*Net of any tax effect.

a. Prepare a partial income statement for Apex Inc., beginning with income from continuing operations before income tax.

b. Determine the earnings per common share for Apex Inc., including per-share amounts for unusual items.

Appendix

EX 17-25 Unusual items

Explain whether Colston Company correctly reported the following items in the financial statements:

a. In a recent year, the company discovered a clerical error in the prior year's accounting records. As a result, the reported net income for the previous year was overstated by $45,000. The company corrected this error by restating the prior-year financial statements.

b. In a recent year, the company voluntarily changed its method of accounting for long-term construction contracts from the percentage of completion method to the completed contract method. Both methods are acceptable under generally acceptable accounting principles. The cumulative effect of this change was reported as a separate component of income in the current period income statement.

Problems: Series A

PR 17-1A Horizontal analysis of income statement — OBJ. 2

✔ 1. Sales, 12.0% increase

Excel | General Ledger | Show Me How

For 20Y2, McDade Company reported a decline in net income. At the end of the year, T. Burrows, the president, is presented with the following condensed comparative income statement:

McDade Company
Comparative Income Statement
For the Years Ended December 31, 20Y2 and 20Y1

	20Y2	20Y1
Sales	$16,800,000	$15,000,000
Cost of goods sold	11,500,000	10,000,000
Gross profit	$ 5,300,000	$ 5,000,000
Selling expenses	$ 1,770,000	$ 1,500,000
Administrative expenses	1,220,000	1,000,000
Total operating expenses	$ 2,990,000	$ 2,500,000
Income from operations	$ 2,310,000	$ 2,500,000
Other revenue	256,950	225,000
Income before income tax	$ 2,566,950	$ 2,725,000
Income tax expense	1,413,000	1,500,000
Net income	$ 1,153,950	$ 1,225,000

Instructions

1. Prepare a comparative income statement with horizontal analysis for the two-year period, using 20Y1 as the base year. Round percentages to one decimal place.
2. To the extent the data permit, comment on the significant relationships revealed by the horizontal analysis prepared in (1).

PR 17-2A Vertical analysis of income statement — OBJ. 2

✔ 1. Net income, 20Y2, 10.0%

Excel | General Ledger

For 20Y2, Tri-Comic Company initiated a sales promotion campaign that included the expenditure of an additional $50,000 for advertising. At the end of the year, Lumi Neer, the president, is presented with the following condensed comparative income statement:

(Continued)

Tri-Comic Company
Comparative Income Statement
For the Years Ended December 31, 20Y2 and 20Y1

	20Y2	20Y1
Sales	$1,500,000	$1,250,000
Cost of goods sold	510,000	475,000
Gross profit	$ 990,000	$ 775,000
Selling expenses	$ 270,000	$ 200,000
Administrative expenses	180,000	156,250
Total operating expenses	$ 450,000	$ 356,250
Income from operations	$ 540,000	$ 418,750
Other revenue	60,000	50,000
Income before income tax	$ 600,000	$ 468,750
Income tax expense	450,000	375,000
Net income	$ 150,000	$ 93,750

Instructions

1. Prepare a comparative income statement for the two-year period, presenting an analysis of each item in relationship to sales for each of the years. Round percentages to one decimal place.
2. To the extent the data permit, comment on the significant relationships revealed by the vertical analysis prepared in (1).

PR 17-3A Effect of transactions on current position analysis

OBJ. 3

✔ 2. c. Current ratio, 2.0

Excel

Data pertaining to the current position of Forte Company follow:

Cash	$412,500
Marketable securities	187,500
Accounts and notes receivable (net)	300,000
Inventories	700,000
Prepaid expenses	50,000
Accounts payable	200,000
Notes payable (short-term)	250,000
Accrued expenses	300,000

Instructions

1. Compute (a) the working capital, (b) the current ratio, and (c) the quick ratio. Round ratios in parts b through j to one decimal place.
2. List the following captions on a sheet of paper:

Transaction	Working Capital	Current Ratio	Quick Ratio

Compute the working capital, the current ratio, and the quick ratio after each of the following transactions and record the results in the appropriate columns. *Consider each transaction separately* and assume that only that transaction affects the data given. Round to one decimal place.

a. Sold marketable securities at no gain or loss, $70,000.
b. Paid accounts payable, $125,000.
c. Purchased goods on account, $110,000.
d. Paid notes payable, $100,000.
e. Declared a cash dividend, $150,000.
f. Declared a common stock dividend on common stock, $50,000.
g. Borrowed cash from bank on a long-term note, $225,000.
h. Received cash on account, $125,000.
i. Issued additional shares of stock for cash, $600,000.
j. Paid cash for prepaid expenses, $10,000.

✔ 5. Number of days' sales in receivables, 18.3

Excel

PR 17-4A Measures of liquidity, solvency, and profitability

OBJ. 3, 4, 5

The comparative financial statements of Marshall Inc. are as follows. The market price of Marshall common stock was $82.60 on December 31, 20Y2.

Marshall Inc.
Comparative Retained Earnings Statement
For the Years Ended December 31, 20Y2 and 20Y1

	20Y2	20Y1
Retained earnings, January 1	$3,704,000	$3,264,000
Net income	600,000	550,000
Total	$4,304,000	$3,814,000
Dividends:		
On preferred stock	$ 10,000	$ 10,000
On common stock	100,000	100,000
Total dividends	$ 110,000	$ 110,000
Retained earnings, December 31	$4,194,000	$3,704,000

Marshall Inc.
Comparative Income Statement
For the Years Ended December 31, 20Y2 and 20Y1

	20Y2	20Y1
Sales	$10,850,000	$10,000,000
Cost of goods sold	6,000,000	5,450,000
Gross profit	$ 4,850,000	$ 4,550,000
Selling expenses	$ 2,170,000	$ 2,000,000
Administrative expenses	1,627,500	1,500,000
Total operating expenses	$ 3,797,500	$ 3,500,000
Income from operations	$ 1,052,500	$ 1,050,000
Other revenue	99,500	20,000
	$ 1,152,000	$ 1,070,000
Other expense (interest)	132,000	120,000
Income before income tax	$ 1,020,000	$ 950,000
Income tax expense	420,000	400,000
Net income	$ 600,000	$ 550,000

Marshall Inc.
Comparative Balance Sheet
December 31, 20Y2 and 20Y1

	20Y2	20Y1
Assets		
Current assets:		
Cash	$1,050,000	$ 950,000
Marketable securities	301,000	420,000
Accounts receivable (net)	585,000	500,000
Inventories	420,000	380,000
Prepaid expenses	108,000	20,000
Total current assets	$ 2,464,000	$2,270,000
Long-term investments	800,000	800,000
Property, plant, and equipment (net)	5,760,000	5,184,000
Total assets	$ 9,024,000	$8,254,000
Liabilities		
Current liabilities	$ 880,000	$ 800,000
Long-term liabilities:		
Mortgage note payable, 6%	$ 200,000	$ 0
Bonds payable, 4%	3,000,000	3,000,000
Total long-term liabilities	$ 3,200,000	$3,000,000
Total liabilities	$ 4,080,000	$3,800,000
Stockholders' Equity		
Preferred 4% stock, $5 par	$ 250,000	$ 250,000
Common stock, $5 par	500,000	500,000
Retained earnings	4,194,000	3,704,000
Total stockholders' equity	$ 4,944,000	$4,454,000
Total liabilities and stockholders' equity	$ 9,024,000	$8,254,000

(Continued)

Instructions

Determine the following measures for 20Y2, rounding to one decimal place, including percentages, except for per-share amounts:

1. Working capital
2. Current ratio
3. Quick ratio
4. Accounts receivable turnover
5. Number of days' sales in receivables
6. Inventory turnover
7. Number of days' sales in inventory
8. Ratio of fixed assets to long-term liabilities
9. Ratio of liabilities to stockholders' equity
10. Times interest earned
11. Asset turnover
12. Return on total assets
13. Return on stockholders' equity
14. Return on common stockholders' equity
15. Earnings per share on common stock
16. Price-earnings ratio
17. Dividends per share of common stock
18. Dividend yield

PR 17-5A Solvency and profitability trend analysis **OBJ. 4, 5**

✔ 1. c. 20Y8, 1.5

Addai Company has provided the following comparative information:

	20Y8	20Y7	20Y6	20Y5	20Y4
Net income	$ 273,406	$ 367,976	$ 631,176	$ 884,000	$ 800,000
Interest expense	616,047	572,003	528,165	495,000	440,000
Income tax expense	31,749	53,560	106,720	160,000	200,000
Total assets (ending balance)	4,417,178	4,124,350	3,732,443	3,338,500	2,750,000
Total stockholders' equity (ending balance)	3,706,557	3,433,152	3,065,176	2,434,000	1,550,000
Average total assets	4,270,764	3,928,396	3,535,472	3,044,250	2,475,000
Average total stockholders' equity	3,569,855	3,249,164	2,749,588	1,992,000	1,150,000

You have been asked to evaluate the historical performance of the company over the last five years.

Selected industry ratios have remained relatively steady at the following levels for the last five years:

	20Y4–20Y8
Return on total assets	28%
Return on stockholders' equity	18%
Times interest earned	2.7
Ratio of liabilities to stockholders' equity	0.4

Instructions

1. Prepare four line graphs with the ratio on the vertical axis and the years on the horizontal axis for the following four ratios, rounding to one decimal place:
   a. Return on total assets
   b. Return on stockholders' equity
   c. Times interest earned
   d. Ratio of liabilities to stockholders' equity

   Display both the company ratio and the industry benchmark on each graph. That is, each graph should have two lines.
2. Prepare an analysis of the graphs in (1).

Problems: Series B

✔ 1. Sales, 30.0% increase

Excel

General Ledger

Show Me How

PR 17-1B Horizontal analysis of income statement

OBJ. 2

For 20Y2, Macklin Inc. reported a significant increase in net income. At the end of the year, John Mayer, the president, is presented with the following condensed comparative income statement:

Macklin Inc.
Comparative Income Statement
For the Years Ended December 31, 20Y2 and 20Y1

	20Y2	20Y1
Sales	$910,000	$700,000
Cost of goods sold	441,000	350,000
Gross profit	$469,000	$350,000
Selling expenses	$ 139,150	$115,000
Administrative expenses	99,450	85,000
Total operating expenses	$238,600	$200,000
Income from operations	$230,400	$150,000
Other revenue	65,000	50,000
Income before income tax	$295,400	$200,000
Income tax expense	65,000	50,000
Net income	$230,400	$150,000

Instructions

1. Prepare a comparative income statement with horizontal analysis for the two-year period, using 20Y1 as the base year. Round percentages to one decimal place.
2. To the extent the data permit, comment on the significant relationships revealed by the horizontal analysis prepared in (1).

✔ 1. Net income, 20Y1, 14.0%

Excel

General Ledger

PR 17-2B Vertical analysis of income statement

OBJ. 2

For 20Y2, Fielder Industries Inc. initiated a sales promotion campaign that included the expenditure of an additional $40,000 for advertising. At the end of the year, Leif Grando, the president, is presented with the following condensed comparative income statement:

Fielder Industries Inc.
Comparative Income Statement
For the Years Ended December 31, 20Y2 and 20Y1

	20Y2	20Y1
Sales	$1,300,000	$1,180,000
Cost of goods sold	682,500	613,600
Gross profit	$ 617,500	$ 566,400
Selling expenses	$ 260,000	$ 188,800
Adminstrative expenses	169,000	177,000
Total operating expenses	$ 429,000	$ 365,800
Income from operations	$ 188,500	$ 200,600
Other revenue	78,000	70,800
Income before income tax	$ 266,500	$ 271,400
Income tax expense	117,000	106,200
Net income	$ 149,500	$ 165,200

Instructions

1. Prepare a comparative income statement for the two-year period, presenting an analysis of each item in relationship to sales for each of the years. Round percentages to one decimal place.
2. To the extent the data permit, comment on the significant relationships revealed by the vertical analysis prepared in (1).

PR 17-3B Effect of transactions on current position analysis

OBJ. 3

✔ 2. g. Quick ratio, 1.6

Excel

Data pertaining to the current position of Lucroy Industries Inc. follow:

Cash	$ 800,000
Marketable securities	550,000
Accounts and notes receivable (net)	850,000
Inventories	700,000
Prepaid expenses	300,000
Accounts payable	1,200,000
Notes payable (short-term)	700,000
Accrued expenses	100,000

Instructions

1. Compute (a) the working capital, (b) the current ratio, and (c) the quick ratio. Round ratios in parts b through j to one decimal place.
2. List the following captions on a sheet of paper:

Transaction	Working Capital	Current Ratio	Quick Ratio

Compute the working capital, the current ratio, and the quick ratio after each of the following transactions and record the results in the appropriate columns. *Consider each transaction separately* and assume that only that transaction affects the data given. Round to one decimal place.

a. Sold marketable securities at no gain or loss, $500,000.
b. Paid accounts payable, $287,500.
c. Purchased goods on account, $400,000.
d. Paid notes payable, $125,000.
e. Declared a cash dividend, $325,000.
f. Declared a common stock dividend on common stock, $150,000.
g. Borrowed cash from bank on a long-term note, $1,000,000.
h. Received cash on account, $75,000.
i. Issued additional shares of stock for cash, $2,000,000.
j. Paid cash for prepaid expenses, $200,000.

PR 17-4B Measures of liquidity, solvency and profitability

OBJ. 3, 4, 5

✔ 9. Ratio of liabilities to stockholders' equity, 0.4

Excel

The comparative financial statements of Stargel Inc. are as follows. The market price of Stargel common stock was $119.70 on December 31, 20Y2.

Stargel Inc.
Comparative Retained Earnings Statement
For the Years Ended December 31, 20Y2 and 20Y1

	20Y2	20Y1
Retained earnings, January 1	$5,375,000	$4,545,000
Net income	900,000	925,000
Total	$6,275,000	$5,470,000
Dividends:		
Preferred stock dividends	$ 45,000	$ 45,000
Common stock dividends	50,000	50,000
Total dividends	$ 95,000	$ 95,000
Retained earnings, December 31	$6,180,000	$5,375,000

Stargel Inc.
Comparative Income Statement
For the Years Ended December 31, 20Y2 and 20Y1

	20Y2	20Y1
Sales	$10,000,000	$9,400,000
Cost of goods sold	5,350,000	4,950,000
Gross profit	$ 4,650,000	$4,450,000
Selling expenses	$ 2,000,000	$1,880,000
Administrative expenses	1,500,000	1,410,000
Total operating expenses	$ 3,500,000	$3,290,000
Income from operations	$ 1,150,000	$1,160,000
Other revenue	150,000	140,000
	$ 1,300,000	$1,300,000
Other expense (interest)	170,000	150,000
Income before income tax	$ 1,130,000	$1,150,000
Income tax expense	230,000	225,000
Net income	$ 900,000	$ 925,000

Stargel Inc.
Comparative Balance Sheet
December 31, 20Y2 and 20Y1

	20Y2	20Y1
Assets		
Current assets:		
Cash	$ 500,000	$ 400,000
Marketable securities	1,010,000	1,000,000
Accounts receivable (net)	740,000	510,000
Inventories	1,190,000	950,000
Prepaid expenses	250,000	229,000
Total current assets	$3,690,000	$3,089,000
Long-term investments	2,350,000	2,300,000
Property, plant, and equipment (net)	3,740,000	3,366,000
Total assets	$9,780,000	$8,755,000
Liabilities		
Current liabilities	$ 900,000	$ 880,000
Long-term liabilities:		
Mortgage note payable, 10%	$ 200,000	$ 0
Bonds payable, 10%	1,500,000	1,500,000
Total long-term liabilities	$1,700,000	$1,500,000
Total liabilities	$2,600,000	$2,380,000
Stockholders' Equity		
Preferred $0.90 stock, $10 par	$ 500,000	$ 500,000
Common stock, $5 par	500,000	500,000
Retained earnings	6,180,000	5,375,000
Total stockholders' equity	$7,180,000	$6,375,000
Total liabilities and stockholders' equity	$9,780,000	$8,755,000

Instructions

Determine the following measures for 20Y2, rounding to one decimal place including percentages, except for per-share amounts:

1. Working capital
2. Current ratio
3. Quick ratio
4. Accounts receivable turnover
5. Number of days' sales in receivables

(Continued)

6. Inventory turnover
7. Number of days' sales in inventory
8. Ratio of fixed assets to long-term liabilities
9. Ratio of liabilities to stockholders' equity
10. Times interest earned
11. Asset turnover
12. Return on total assets
13. Return on stockholders' equity
14. Return on common stockholders' equity
15. Earnings per share on common stock
16. Price-earnings ratio
17. Dividends per share of common stock
18. Dividend yield

PR 17-5B Solvency and profitability trend analysis **OBJ. 4, 5**

✔ 1. b. 20Y7, 32.9%

Crosby Company has provided the following comparative information:

	20Y8	20Y7	20Y6	20Y5	20Y4
Net income	$ 5,571,720	$ 3,714,480	$ 2,772,000	$ 1,848,000	$ 1,400,000
Interest expense	1,052,060	891,576	768,600	610,000	500,000
Income tax expense	1,225,572	845,222	640,320	441,600	320,000
Total assets (ending balance)	29,378,491	22,598,839	17,120,333	12,588,480	10,152,000
Total stockholders' equity (ending balance)	18,706,200	13,134,480	9,420,000	6,648,000	4,800,000
Average total assets	25,988,665	19,859,586	14,854,406	11,370,240	8,676,000
Average total stockholders' equity	15,920,340	11,277,240	8,034,000	5,724,000	4,100,000

You have been asked to evaluate the historical performance of the company over the last five years.

Selected industry ratios have remained relatively steady at the following levels for the last five years:

	20Y4–20Y8
Return on total assets	19%
Return on stockholders' equity	26%
Times interest earned	3.4
Ratio of liabilities to stockholders' equity	1.4

Instructions

1. Prepare four line graphs with the ratio on the vertical axis and the years on the horizontal axis for the following four ratios, rounding ratios and percentages to one decimal place:
   a. Return on total assets
   b. Return on stockholders' equity
   c. Times interest earned
   d. Ratio of liabilities to stockholders' equity

   Display both the company ratio and the industry benchmark on each graph. That is, each graph should have two lines.
2. Prepare an analysis of the graphs in (1).

Nike, Inc., Problem

Financial statement analysis

The financial statements for Nike, Inc., are presented in Appendix D at the end of the text. Use the following additional information (in thousands):

Accounts receivable at May 31, 2014	$ 3,117
Inventories at May 31, 2014	4,142
Total assets at May 31, 2014	18,594
Stockholders' equity at May 31, 2014	12,000

Instructions

1. Determine the following measures for the fiscal years ended May 31, 2016, and May 31, 2015. Round ratios and percentages to one decimal place.
   a. Working capital
   b. Current ratio
   c. Quick ratio
   d. Accounts receivable turnover
   e. Number of days' sales in receivables
   f. Inventory turnover
   g. Number of days' sales in inventory
   h. Ratio of liabilities to stockholders' equity
   i. Asset turnover
   j. Return on total assets.
   k. Return on common stockholders' equity
   l. Price-earnings ratio, assuming that the market price was $54.90 per share on May 29, 2016, and $52.81 per share on May 30, 2015
   m. Percentage relationship of net income to sales
2. What conclusions can be drawn from these analyses?

Cases & Projects

CP 17-1 Ethics in Action

Ethics

Rodgers Industries Inc. completed its fiscal year on December 31. Near the end of the fiscal year, the company's Internal Audit Department determined that an important internal control procedure had not been functioning properly. The head of Internal Audit, Dash Riprock, reported the internal control failure to the company's chief accountant, Todd Barleywine. Todd reported the failure to the company's chief financial officer, Josh McCoy. After discussing the issue, Josh instructed Todd not to inform the external auditors of the internal control failure and to fix the problem quietly after the end of the fiscal year. The external auditors did not discover the internal control failure during their audit. In March, after the audit was complete, the company released its annual report, including associated reports by management. As chief financial officer, Josh authorized the release of Management's Report on Internal Control, which stated that the management team believed that the company's internal controls were effective during the period covered by the annual report.

Did Josh behave ethically in this situation? Explain your answer.

Team Activity

Real World

CP 17-2 Team Activity

In teams, select a public company that interests you. Obtain the company's most recent annual report on Form 10-K. The Form 10-K is a company's annually required filing with the Securities and Exchange Commission (SEC). It includes the company's financial statements and accompanying notes. The Form 10-K can be obtained either (a) by referring to the investor relations section of the company's website or (b) by using the company search feature of the SEC's EDGAR database service found at www.sec.gov/edgar/searchedgar/companysearch.html.

1. Based on the information in the company's annual report, compute the following for the most recent year, rounding ratios and percentages to one decimal place, except for per-share amounts:
   a. Liquidity analysis:
      (1) Working capital
      (2) Current ratio
      (3) Quick ratio
      (4) Accounts receivable turnover
      (5) Number of days' sales in receivables
      (6) Inventory turnover
      (7) Number of days' sales in inventory
   b. Solvency analysis:
      (1) Ratio of liabilities to stockholders' equity
      (2) Times interest earned
   c. Profitability analysis:
      (1) Asset turnover
      (2) Return on total assets
      (3) Return on stockholders' equity
      (4) Earnings per share
      (5) Price-earnings ratio

Communication

CP 17-3 Communication

The president of Freeman Industries Inc. made the following statement in the annual report to shareholders: "The founding family and majority shareholders of the company do not believe in using debt to finance future growth. The founding family learned from hard experience during the Great Depression that debt can cause loss of flexibility and eventual loss of corporate control. The company will not place itself at such risk again. As such, all future growth will be financed either by stock sales to the public or by internally generated resources."

Write a brief memo to the company's president, Boss Freeman, outlining the errors in his logic.

Real World

CP 17-4 Common-sized income statements

The condensed income statements through income from operations for Amazon.com, Inc., Best Buy, Inc., and Wal-Mart Stores, Inc. for a recent fiscal year follow (in millions):

	Amazon	Best Buy	Wal-Mart
Sales	$88,988	$40,339	$485,651
Cost of sales	62,752	31,292	365,086
Gross profit	$26,236	$ 9,047	$120,565
Selling, general, and administrative expenses	26,058	7,592	93,418
Operating expenses	0	5	0
Income from operations	$ 178	$ 1,450	$ 27,147

1. Prepare comparative common-sized income statements for each company. Round percentages to one decimal place.
2. Use the common-sized analysis to compare the financial performance of the three companies.

Real World

CP 17-5 Profitability analysis

Deere & Company manufactures and distributes farm and construction machinery that it sells around the world. In addition to its manufacturing operations, Deere's credit division loans money to customers to finance the purchase of their farm and construction equipment.

The following information is available for three recent years (in millions except per-share amounts):

	Year 3	Year 2	Year 1
Net income (loss)	$3,064.7	$2,799.9	$1,865.0
Preferred dividends	$0.00	$0.00	$0.00
Interest expense	$782.8	$759.4	$811.4
Shares outstanding for computing earnings per share	397	417	424
Cash dividend per share	$1.79	$1.52	$1.16
Average total assets	$52,237	$45,737	$42,200
Average stockholders' equity	$6,821	$6,545	$5,555
Average stock price per share	$79.27	$80.48	$61.18

1. Calculate the following ratios for each year, rounding ratios and percentages to one decimal place, except for per-share amounts:
   a. Return on total assets
   b. Return on stockholders' equity
   c. Earnings per share
   d. Dividend yield
   e. Price-earnings ratio
2. Based on these data, evaluate Deere's profitability.

Real World

CP 17-6 Comprehensive profitability and solvency analysis

Marriott International, Inc., and **Hyatt Hotels Corporation** are two major owners and managers of lodging and resort properties in the United States. Abstracted income statement information for the two companies is as follows for a recent year (in millions):

	Marriott	Hyatt
Operating profit before other expenses and interest	$ 677	$ 39
Other revenue (expenses)	54	118
Interest expense	(180)	(54)
Income before income taxes	$ 551	$103
Income tax expense	93	37
Net income	$ 458	$ 66

Balance sheet information is as follows:

	Marriott	Hyatt
Total liabilities	$7,398	$2,125
Total stockholders' equity	1,585	5,118
Total liabilities and stockholders' equity	$8,983	$7,243

(Continued)

The average liabilities, average stockholders' equity, and average total assets are as follows:

	Marriott	Hyatt
Average total liabilities	$7,095	$2,132
Average total stockholders' equity	1,364	5,067
Average total assets	8,458	7,199

1. Determine the following ratios for both companies, rounding ratios and percentages to one decimal place:
   a. Return on total assets
   b. Return on stockholders' equity
   c. Times interest earned
   d. Ratio of total liabilities to stockholders' equity
2. Based on the information in (1), analyze and compare the two companies' solvency and profitability.

CHAPTER 18

Introduction to Managerial Accounting

Concepts and Principles

Chapter 18 *Introduction to Managerial Accounting*

Developing Information

COST SYSTEMS

Chapter 19 *Job Order Costing*
Chapter 20 *Process Cost Systems*

COST BEHAVIOR

Chapter 21 *Cost-Volume-Profit Analysis*

Decision Making

EVALUATING PERFORMANCE

Chapter 22 *Budgeting*
Chapter 23 *Variances from Standard Costs*

COMPARING ALTERNATIVES

Chapter 24 *Decentralized Operations*
Chapter 25 *Differential Analysis, Product Pricing, and Activity-Based Costing*
Chapter 26 *Capital Investment Analysis*

CHAPTER

18

PAVEL LOSEVSKY/FOTOLIA

Gibson Guitars

Gibson guitars have been used by musical legends over the years, including B.B. King, Chet Atkins, Brian Wilson (Beach Boys), Jimmy Page (Led Zeppelin), Jackson Browne, John Fogerty, Jose Feliciano, Miranda Lambert, and Wynonna Judd. Known for its quality, **Gibson Guitars** celebrated its 120th anniversary in 2014.

Staying in business for 120 years requires a thorough understanding of how to manufacture high-quality guitars. In addition, it requires knowledge of how to account for the costs of making guitars. For example, Gibson needs cost information to answer the following questions:

- What should be the selling price of its guitars?
- How many guitars does it have to sell in a year to cover its costs and earn a profit?
- How many employees should the company have working on each stage of the manufacturing process?
- How would purchasing automated equipment affect the costs of its guitars?

This chapter introduces managerial accounting concepts that are useful in addressing these questions. This chapter begins by describing managerial accounting and its relationship to financial accounting. Following this overview, the management process is described along with the role of managerial accounting. Finally, characteristics of managerial accounting reports, managerial accounting terms, and uses of managerial accounting information are described and illustrated.

Source: www.gibson.com/Gibson/History.aspx

Learning Objectives

After studying this chapter, you should be able to:

Example Exercises (EE) are shown in **green**.

Obj. 1 **Describe managerial accounting and the role of managerial accounting in a business.**

Managerial Accounting
Differences Between Managerial and Financial Accounting
The Management Accountant in the Organization
The Management Process — EE 18-1
Uses of Managerial Accounting Information

Obj. 2 **Describe and illustrate the following costs: direct and indirect costs; direct materials, direct labor, and factory overhead costs; and product and period costs.**

Manufacturing Operations: Costs and Terminology
Direct and Indirect Costs
Manufacturing Costs — EE 18-2, 3, 4

Obj. 3 **Describe sustainable business activities and eco-efficiency measures.**

Sustainability and Accounting
Sustainability
Eco-Efficiency Measures in Managerial Accounting

Obj. 4 **Describe and illustrate the following statements for a manufacturing business: balance sheet, statement of cost of goods manufactured, and income statement.**

Financial Statements for a Manufacturing Business
Balance Sheet for a Manufacturing Business
Income Statement for a Manufacturing Business — EE 18-5

At a Glance 18 Page 904

Managerial Accounting

Obj. 1 Describe managerial accounting and the role of managerial accounting in a business.

Managers make numerous decisions during the day-to-day operations of a business and in planning for the future. Managerial accounting provides much of the information used for these decisions.

Some examples of managerial accounting information along with the chapter in which it is described and illustrated follow:

- Classifying manufacturing and other costs and reporting them in the financial statements (Chapter 18)
- Determining the cost of manufacturing a product or providing a service (Chapters 19 and 20)
- Estimating the behavior of costs for various levels of activity and assessing cost-volume-profit relationships (Chapter 21)
- Planning for the future by preparing budgets (Chapter 22)
- Evaluating manufacturing costs by comparing actual with expected results (Chapter 23)
- Evaluating decentralized operations by comparing actual and budgeted costs as well as computing various measures of profitability (Chapter 24)
- Evaluating special decision-making situations by comparing differential revenues and costs and allocating product costs using activity-based costing (Chapter 25)
- Evaluating alternative proposals for long-term investments in fixed assets (Chapter 26)

Link to Gibson Guitars

Orville Gibson, founder of **Gibson Guitars**, started producing guitars in 1894 in Kalamazoo, Michigan. He produced guitars and mandolins based on the archtop design of violins.

Differences Between Managerial and Financial Accounting

Accounting information is often divided into two types: financial and managerial. Exhibit 1 shows the relationship between financial accounting and managerial accounting.

Financial accounting information is reported at fixed intervals (monthly, quarterly, yearly) in general-purpose financial statements. These financial statements—the income statement, retained earnings statement, balance sheet, and statement of cash flows—present timely information about the results of operations and the financial

EXHIBIT 1 **Financial Accounting and Managerial Accounting**

	Financial Statements	Management Reports
Users of Information	External users and company management	Management
Nature of Information	Objective	Objective and subjective
Guidelines for Preparation	Prepared according to GAAP	Prepared according to management needs
Timeliness of Reporting	Prepared at fixed intervals	Prepared at fixed intervals and on an as-needed basis
Focus of Reporting	Company as a whole	Company as a whole or segment

condition of a business. These statements are based on objective historical data and are prepared according to generally accepted accounting principles (GAAP) in order to meet the decision-making needs of external users such as:

- Investors
- Creditors
- Government agencies
- The general public

Link to Gibson Guitars

Gibson Mandolin-Guitar Mfg. Co., Ltd. was formed in 1902 in Kalamazoo, Michigan, with the support of five investors.

Managers of a company also use general-purpose financial statements. For example, in planning future operations, managers often begin by evaluating the current income statement and statement of cash flows.

Managerial accounting information is designed to meet the specific needs of a company's management. This information includes the following:

- Historical data, which provide *objective measures* of past operations
- Estimated data, which provide *subjective estimates* about future decisions

Management uses both types of information in directing daily operations, planning future operations, and developing business strategies.

Unlike the financial statements prepared in financial accounting, managerial accounting reports are not required to be:

- Prepared according to generally accepted accounting principles (GAAP). This is because *only* the company's management uses the information. Also, in many cases, GAAP is not relevant to the specific decision-making needs of management.
- Prepared at fixed intervals (monthly, quarterly, yearly). Although some management reports are prepared at fixed intervals, most reports are prepared as management needs the information.
- Prepared for the business as a whole. Most management reports are prepared for products, projects, sales territories, or other segments of the company.

Link to Gibson Guitars

Chicago Musical Instrument Company purchased Gibson in 1944.

The Management Accountant in the Organization

In most companies, departments or similar organizational units are assigned responsibilities for specific functions or activities. The operating structure of a company can be shown in an *organization chart*.

Exhibit 2 is a partial organization chart for Callaway Golf Company, the manufacturer and distributor of golf clubs, clothing, and other products.

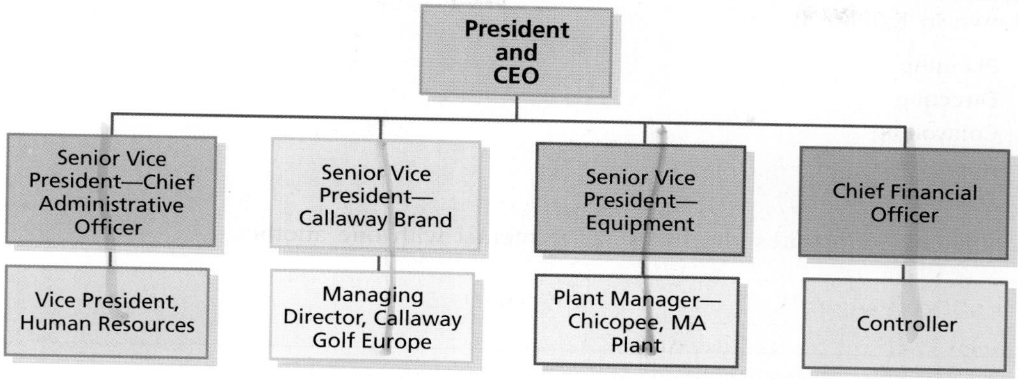

EXHIBIT 2

Partial Organization Chart for Callaway Golf Company

The departments in a company can be viewed as having either of the following:

- Line responsibilities
- Staff responsibilities

A **line department** is directly involved in providing goods or services to the customers of the company. For Callaway Golf (shown in Exhibit 2), the following occupy line positions:

- Senior Vice President—Equipment
- Plant Manager—Chicopee, MA Plant
- Senior Vice President—Callaway Brand
- Managing Director, Callaway Golf Europe

Individuals in these positions are responsible for manufacturing and selling Callaway's products.

A **staff department** provides services, assistance, and advice to the departments with line or other staff responsibilities. A staff department has no direct authority over a line department. For Callaway Golf (Exhibit 2), the following are staff positions:

- Senior Vice President—Chief Administrative Officer
- Vice President, Human Resources
- Chief Financial Officer
- Controller

In most companies, the **controller** is the chief management accountant. The controller's staff consists of a variety of other accountants who are responsible for specialized accounting functions such as the following:

- Systems and procedures
- General accounting
- Budgets and budget analysis
- Special reports and analysis
- Taxes
- Cost accounting

Experience in managerial accounting is often an excellent training ground for senior management positions. This is not surprising because accounting touches all phases of a company's operations.

Link to Gibson Guitars

One of Gibson's most influential managers was Ted McCarty, who was the company president from 1950–1966. During this period, Gibson was known for its innovations. For example, in 1954, McCarty invented the tune-o-matic bridge with adjustable saddles.

The Management Process

As a staff department, managerial accounting supports management and the management process. The **management process** has the following five basic phases, as shown in Exhibit 3:

- Planning
- Directing
- Controlling
- Improving
- Decision making

As Exhibit 3 illustrates, the five phases interact with one another.

EXHIBIT 3

The Management Process

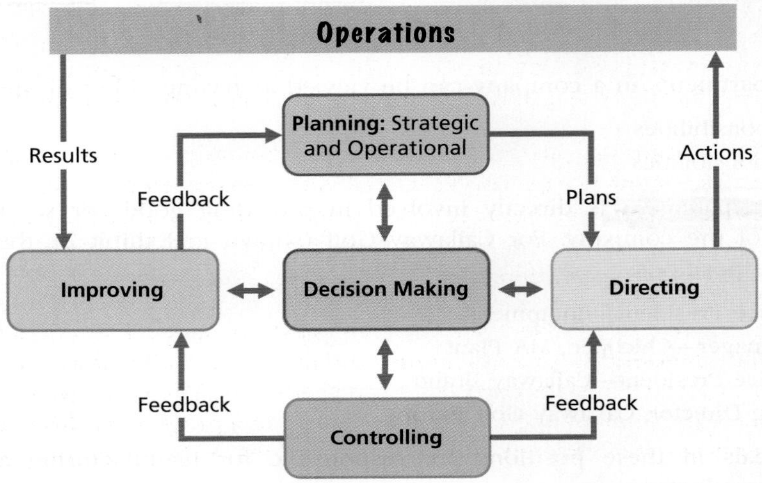

Business Connection

LINE AND STAFF FOR SERVICE COMPANIES

The terms *line* and *staff* may also be applied to service organizations. Some examples follow:

Service Industry	Line	Staff
Airline	Crew, baggage handling, and gate staff	Information systems, accounting, and human resources
Hotel	Housekeeping and reception staff	Maintenance, hotel manager, and grounds
Hospital	Doctors, nurses, and other caregivers	Admissions, records, and billing
Banking	Tellers, loan officers, trust officers, and brokers	Branch manager, information systems
Telecommunications	Sales, customer service, and customer installation staff	Information systems, regional management, and network maintenance

Planning Management uses **planning** in developing the company's **objectives (goals)** and translating these objectives into courses of action. For example, a company may set an objective to increase market share by 15% by introducing three new products. The actions to achieve this objective might be as follows:

- Increase the advertising budget
- Open a new sales territory
- Increase the research and development budget

Planning may be classified as follows:

- **Strategic planning**, which is developing long-term actions to achieve the company's objectives. These long-term actions are called **strategies**, which often involve periods of 5 to 10 years.
- **Operational planning**, which develops short-term actions for managing the day-to-day operations of the company.

Directing The process by which managers run day-to-day operations is called **directing**. An example of directing is a production supervisor's efforts to keep the production line moving without interruption (downtime). A credit manager's development of guidelines for assessing the ability of potential customers to pay their bills is also an example of directing.

Controlling Monitoring operating results and comparing actual results with the expected results is **controlling**. This **feedback** allows management to isolate areas for further investigation and possible remedial action. It may also lead to revising future plans. This philosophy of controlling by comparing actual and expected results is called **management by exception**.

Improving Feedback is also used by managers to support continuous process improvement. **Continuous process improvement** is the philosophy of continually improving employees, business processes, and products. The objective of continuous improvement is to eliminate the *source* of problems in a process. In this way, the right products (services) are delivered in the right quantities at the right time.

Decision Making Inherent in each of the preceding management processes is **decision making**. In managing a company, management must continually decide among alternative actions. For example, in directing operations, managers must decide on an operating structure, training procedures, and staffing of day-to-day operations.

Managerial accounting supports managers in all phases of the management process. For example, accounting reports comparing actual and expected operating results help managers plan and improve current operations. Such a report might compare the actual and expected costs of defective materials. If the cost of defective materials is unusually high, management might decide to change suppliers.

Uses of Managerial Accounting Information

As mentioned earlier, managerial accounting provides information and reports for managers to use in operating a business. Some examples of how managerial accounting could be used by Gibson Guitars include the following:

- The cost of manufacturing each guitar could be used to determine its selling price.
- Comparing the costs of guitars over time can be used to monitor and control the cost of direct materials, direct labor, and factory overhead.
- Performance reports could be used to identify any large amounts of scrap or employee downtime. For example, large amounts of unusable wood (scrap) after the cutting process should be investigated to determine the underlying cause. Such scrap may be caused by saws that have not been properly maintained.
- A report could analyze the potential efficiencies and dollar savings of purchasing a new computerized saw to speed up the production process.

Link to Gibson Guitars

Gibson struggled financially from 1966–1986. The company was purchased and sold several times and experienced declining sales.

- A report could analyze how many guitars need to be sold to cover operating costs and expenses. Such information could be used to set monthly selling targets and bonuses for sales personnel.

As the prior examples illustrate, managerial accounting information can be used for a variety of purposes. In the remaining chapters of this text, we examine these and other areas of managerial accounting.

Example Exercise 18-1 The Management Process — Obj. 1

Three phases of the management process are planning, controlling, and improving. Match the following descriptions to the proper phase:

Phase of management process	Description
Planning	a. Monitoring the operating results of implemented plans and comparing the actual results with expected results.
Controlling	b. Rejects solving individual problems with temporary solutions that fail to address the root cause of the problem.
Improving	c. Used by management to develop the company's objectives.

Follow My Example 18-1

Planning (c), Controlling (a), and Improving (b)

Practice Exercises: PE 18-1A, PE 18-1B

Obj. 2 Describe and illustrate the following costs: direct and indirect costs; direct materials, direct labor, and factory overhead costs; and product and period costs.

Manufacturing Operations: Costs and Terminology

The operations of a business can be classified as service, merchandising, or manufacturing. The accounting for service and merchandising businesses has been described and illustrated in earlier chapters. For this reason, the remaining chapters of this text focus primarily on manufacturing businesses. Most of the managerial accounting concepts discussed, however, also apply to service and merchandising businesses.

As a basis for illustration of manufacturing operations, a guitar manufacturer, **Legend Guitars**, is used. Exhibit 4 is an overview of Legend's guitar manufacturing operations.

EXHIBIT 4 **Guitar-Making Operations of Legend Guitars**

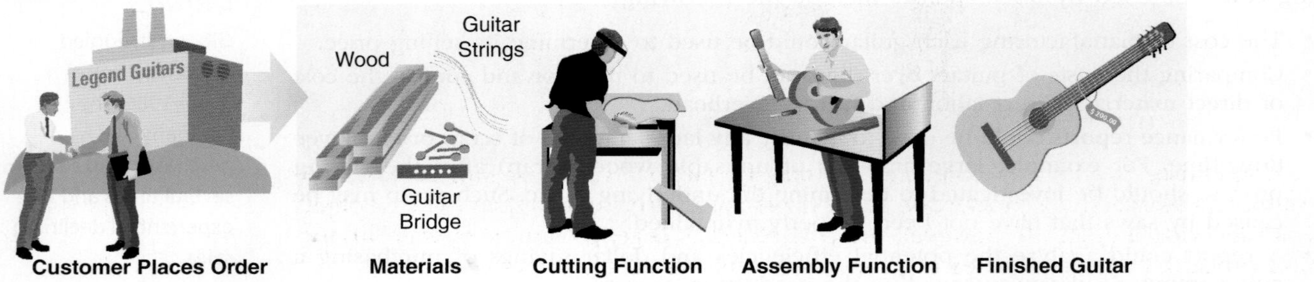

Legend's guitar-making process begins when a customer places an order for a guitar. Once the order is accepted, the manufacturing process begins by obtaining the necessary materials. An employee then cuts the body and neck of the guitar out of raw lumber. Once the wood is cut, the body and neck of the guitar are assembled. When the assembly is complete, the guitar is painted and finished.

Link to Gibson Guitars
Gibson provides tours of its Memphis guitar factory located at 145 Lt. George W. Lee Avenue.

Direct and Indirect Costs

A **cost** is a payment of cash or the commitment to pay cash in the future for the purpose of generating revenues. For example, cash (or credit) used to purchase equipment is the cost of the equipment. If equipment is purchased by exchanging assets other than cash, the current market value of the assets given up is the cost of the equipment purchased.

In managerial accounting, costs are classified according to the decision-making needs of management. For example, costs are often classified by their relationship to a segment of operations, called a **cost object**. A cost object may be a product, a sales territory, a department, or an activity such as research and development. Costs identified with cost objects are either direct costs or indirect costs.

Direct costs are identified with and can be traced to a cost object. For example, as shown in Exhibit 5, the cost of wood (materials) used by **Legend Guitars** in manufacturing a guitar is a direct cost of the guitar.

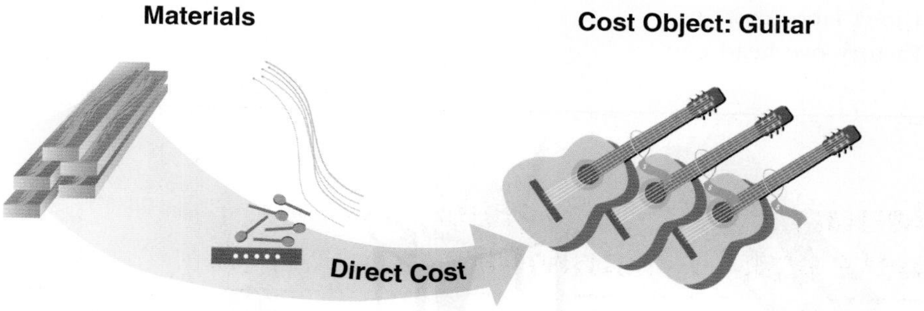

EXHIBIT 5
Direct Costs of Legend Guitars

Indirect costs cannot be identified with or traced to a cost object. For example, as shown in Exhibit 6, the salaries of the **Legend Guitars** production supervisors are indirect costs of producing a guitar. Although the production supervisors contribute to the production of a guitar, their salaries cannot be identified with or traced to any individual guitar.

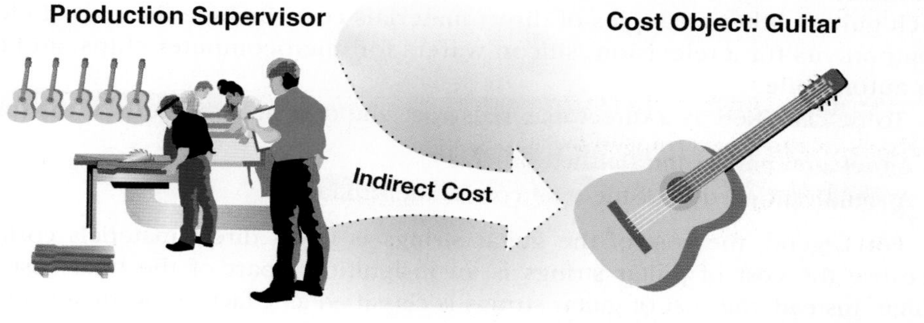

EXHIBIT 6
Indirect Costs of Legend Guitars

Depending on the cost object, a cost may be either a direct or indirect cost. For example, the salaries of production supervisors are indirect costs when the cost object is an individual guitar. If, however, the cost object is Legend Guitars' overall production process, then the salaries of production supervisors are direct costs.

This process of classifying a cost as direct or indirect is illustrated in Exhibit 7.

EXHIBIT 7

Classifying Direct and Indirect Costs

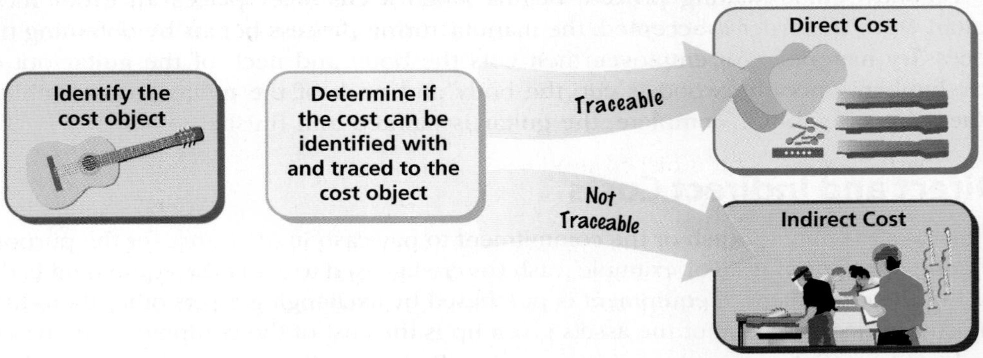

Manufacturing Costs

The cost of a manufactured product includes the cost of materials used in making the product. In addition, the cost of a manufactured product includes the cost of converting the materials into a finished product. For example, **Legend Guitars** uses employees and machines to convert wood (and other supplies) into finished guitars. Thus, as shown in Exhibit 8, the cost of a finished guitar (the cost object) includes the following:

- Direct materials cost
- Direct labor cost
- Factory overhead cost

EXHIBIT 8

Manufacturing Costs of Legend Guitars

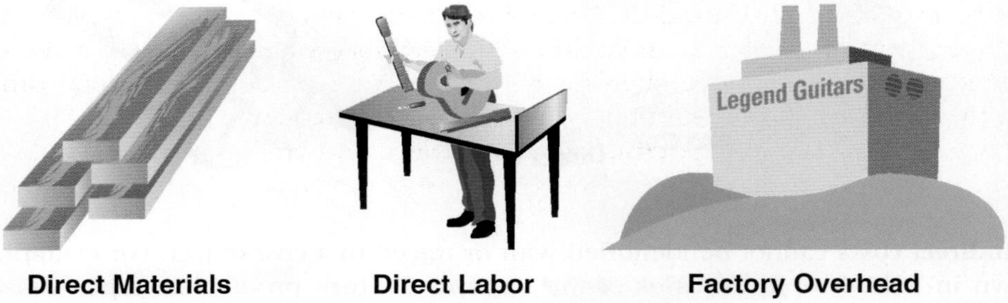

Direct Materials Cost Manufactured products begin with raw materials that are converted into finished products. The cost of any material that is an integral part of the finished product is classified as a **direct materials cost**. For **Legend Guitars**, direct materials cost includes the cost of the wood used in producing each guitar. Other examples of direct materials costs include the cost of electronic components for a television, silicon wafers for microcomputer chips, and tires for an automobile.

To be classified as a direct materials cost, the cost must be *both* of the following:

- An integral part of the finished product
- A significant portion of the total cost of the product

For Legend, the cost of the guitar strings is not a direct materials cost. This is because the cost of guitar strings is an insignificant part of the total cost of each guitar. Instead, the cost of guitar strings is classified as a factory overhead cost, which is discussed later.

Direct Labor Cost Most manufacturing processes use employees to convert materials into finished products. The cost of employee wages that is an integral part of the finished product is classified as **direct labor cost**. For **Legend Guitars**, direct labor cost includes the wages of the employees who cut each guitar out of raw lumber and assemble it. Other examples of direct labor costs include mechanics' wages for repairing an automobile, machine operators' wages for manufacturing tools, and assemblers' wages for assembling a laptop computer.

Like a direct materials cost, a direct labor cost must meet *both* of the following criteria:

- An integral part of the finished product
- A significant portion of the total cost of the product

For Legend, the wages of the janitors who clean the factory are not a direct labor cost. This is because janitorial costs are not an integral part or a significant cost of each guitar. Instead, janitorial costs are classified as a factory overhead cost, which is discussed next.

Factory Overhead Cost Costs other than direct materials and direct labor that are incurred in the manufacturing process are combined and classified as **factory overhead cost**. Factory overhead is sometimes called **manufacturing overhead** or **factory burden**.

All factory overhead costs are indirect costs of the product. Some factory overhead costs include the following:

- Cost of heating and lighting the factory
- Cost of repairing and maintaining factory equipment
- Property taxes on factory buildings and land
- Insurance on factory buildings
- Depreciation on factory plant and equipment

Factory overhead cost also includes materials and labor costs that do not enter directly into the finished product. Examples include the cost of oil used to lubricate machinery and the wages of janitorial and supervisory employees. Also, if the costs of direct materials or direct labor are not a significant portion of the total product cost, these costs may be classified as factory overhead costs.

For Legend Guitars, the costs of guitar strings and janitorial wages are factory overhead costs. Additional factory overhead costs of making guitars are as follows:

- Sandpaper
- Buffing compound
- Glue
- Power (electricity) to run the machines
- Depreciation of the machines and building
- Salaries of production supervisors

Business Connection

OVERHEAD COSTS

Defense contractors such as General Dynamics, Boeing, and Lockheed Martin sell products such as airplanes, ships, and military equipment to the U.S. Department of Defense. Building large products such as these requires a significant investment in facilities and tools, all of which are classified as factory overhead costs. As a result, factory overhead costs are a much larger portion of the cost of goods sold for defense contractors than they are in other industries. For example, a U.S. General Accounting Office study of six defense contractors found that overhead costs were almost one-third the price of the final product. This is more than three times greater than the factory overhead costs for a laptop computer, which are typically about 10% of the price of the final product.

Example Exercise 18-2 Direct Materials, Direct Labor, and Factory Overhead Obj. 2

Identify the following costs as direct materials (DM), direct labor (DL), or factory overhead (FO) for a baseball glove manufacturer:

a. Leather used to make a baseball glove
b. Coolants for machines that sew baseball gloves
c. Wages of assembly line employees
d. Ink used to print a player's autograph on a baseball glove

Follow My Example 18-2

a. DM
b. FO
c. DL
d. FO

Practice Exercises: PE 18-2A, PE 18-2B

Prime Costs and Conversion Costs Direct materials, direct labor, and factory overhead costs may be grouped together for analysis and reporting. Two such common groupings are as follows:

- **Prime costs**, which consist of direct materials and direct labor costs
- **Conversion costs**, which consist of direct labor and factory overhead costs

Conversion costs are the costs of converting the materials into a finished product. Direct labor is both a prime cost and a conversion cost, as shown in Exhibit 9.

EXHIBIT 9

Prime Costs and Conversion Costs

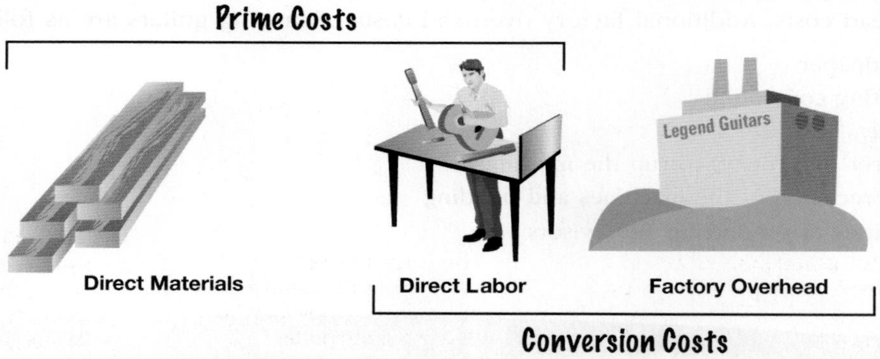

Example Exercise 18-3 Prime and Conversion Costs Obj. 2

Identify the following costs as a prime cost (P), conversion cost (C), or both (B) for a baseball glove manufacturer:

a. Leather used to make a baseball glove
b. Coolants for machines that sew baseball gloves
c. Wages of assembly line employees
d. Ink used to print a player's autograph on a baseball glove

Follow My Example 18-3

a. P
b. C
c. B
d. C

Practice Exercises: PE 18-3A, PE 18-3B

Product Costs and Period Costs For financial reporting purposes, costs are classified as product costs or period costs.

- **Product costs** consist of manufacturing costs: direct materials, direct labor, and factory overhead.
- **Period costs** consist of selling and administrative expenses. *Selling expenses* are incurred in marketing the product and delivering the product to customers. *Administrative expenses* are incurred in managing the company and are not directly related to the manufacturing or selling functions.

Examples of product costs and period costs for **Legend Guitars** are presented in Exhibit 10.

Note

Product costs consist of direct materials, direct labor, and factory overhead costs.

Examples of Product Costs and Period Costs—Legend Guitars **EXHIBIT 10**

Product (Manufacturing) Costs

Direct Materials Cost
- Wood used in neck and body

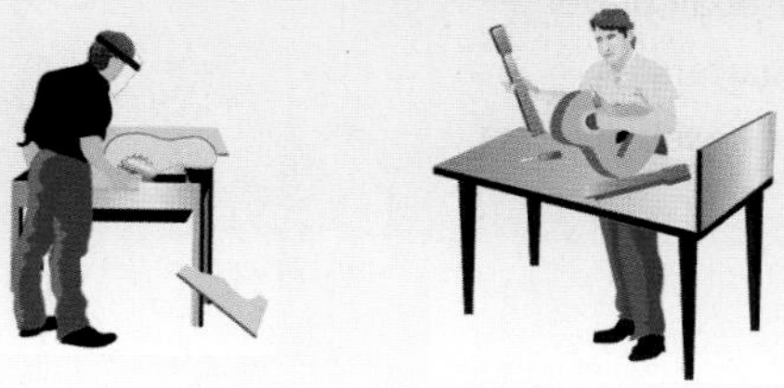

Direct Labor Cost
- Wages of saw operator
- Wages of employees who assemble the guitar

Factory Overhead
- Guitar strings
- Wages of janitor
- Power to run the machines
- Depreciation expense—factory building
- Sandpaper and buffing materials
- Glue used in assembly of the guitar
- Salary of production supervisors

Period (Nonmanufacturing) Costs

Selling Expenses
- Advertising expenses
- Sales salaries expenses
- Commissions expenses

Administrative Expenses
- Office salaries expense
- Office supplies expense
- Depreciation expense—office building and equipment

To facilitate control, selling and administrative expenses may be reported by level of responsibility. For example, selling expenses may be reported by products, salespersons, departments, divisions, or territories. Likewise, administrative expenses may be reported by areas such as human resources, computer services, legal, accounting, or finance.

The impact on the financial statements of product and period costs is summarized in Exhibit 11. As product costs are incurred, they are recorded and reported on the balance sheet as *inventory*. When the inventory is sold, the cost of the manufactured product sold is reported as *cost of goods sold* on the income statement. Period costs are reported as *expenses* on the income statement in the period in which they are incurred and, thus, never appear on the balance sheet.

EXHIBIT 11

Product Costs, Period Costs, and the Financial Statements

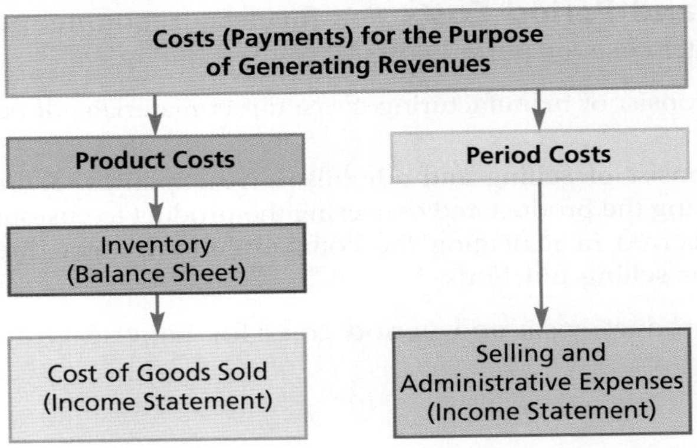

Example Exercise 18-4 Product and Period Costs — Obj. 2

Identify the following costs as a product cost or a period cost for a baseball glove manufacturer:

a. Leather used to make a baseball glove
b. Cost of endorsement from a professional baseball player
c. Office supplies used at the company headquarters
d. Ink used to print a player's autograph on the baseball glove

Follow My Example 18-4

a. Product cost
b. Period cost
c. Period cost
d. Product cost

Practice Exercises: PE 18-4A, PE 18-4B

Obj. 3 Describe sustainable business activities and eco-efficiency measures.

Sustainability and Accounting

Managers must consider the social and environmental settings in which a business operates, in order to make sound strategic and operational decisions. Issues such as population growth, resource scarcity, declining ecosystems, increasing urbanization, and climate change all have a direct impact on a company's potential for success. As a result, managers are using new management techniques and tools that consider these issues.

Sustainability

Sustainability is the practice of operating a business to maximize profits while attempting to preserve the environment, economy, and needs of future generations. Sustainability practices acknowledge that a company's long-term success requires the continued availability of natural resources and a productive social environment. Examples of sustainable business activities are provided in Exhibit 12.

Sustainable Business Activities EXHIBIT 12

Category	Description	Example
Agriculture	Using farming and ranching techniques that do not damage or disrupt the environment	Mixed farming, crop rotation, multiple cropping
Energy	Generating energy with little or no pollution	Wind turbines, solar power
Engineering and Construction	Designing and constructing buildings that are highly efficient in using natural resources, while minimizing pollution	Recycled building materials, high-efficiency heating and cooling systems, renewable energy generation
Transportation	Using transportation methods that result in little pollution and have a minimal impact on the environment	Expanded public transportation systems, green vehicles, biofuel-powered vehicles
Waste Minimization	Using recycling and reuse practices that reduce the amount of waste disposed in landfills	Curbside recycling collection, composting, reusable products (e.g., water bottles)

Eco-Efficiency Measures in Managerial Accounting

Sustainability information can provide important feedback to guide a company's strategic and operational decision making. Managers can use this information to increase revenue, control costs, and allocate resources efficiently. **Eco-efficiency measures** are a form of managerial accounting information that helps managers evaluate the savings generated by using fewer natural resources in a company's operations. Examples of eco-efficiency measures are provided in Exhibit 13.

EXHIBIT 13

Eco-Efficiency Measures

Energy Efficiency	Energy cost savings from replacing lighting fixtures in a production facility with energy-efficient lighting
Material Use Efficiency	Materials cost savings from reducing the amount of product packaging materials
Fuel Efficiency	Fuel cost savings from replacing gas-powered vehicles with hybrid or alternative energy-source vehicles
Waste Efficiency	Waste removal cost savings from recycling and reusing waste and by-product materials

Sustainability information can also benefit external financial statement users in their decision making. The risks and opportunities that a company faces are tied to the environment in which it operates and provide important insights into the potential for success. As such, external financial statement users may require sustainability information to evaluate investment and credit decisions. The **Sustainability Accounting Standards Board (SASB)** was organized in 2011 to develop accounting standards that help companies report decision-useful sustainability information to external financial statement users. While the SASB's standards are not required, they are designed to provide sustainability information that complements required financial statement information.

INTEGRITY, OBJECTIVITY, AND ETHICS IN BUSINESS

ENVIRONMENTAL MANAGERIAL ACCOUNTING

Throughout the last decade, environmental issues have become an increasingly important part of the business environment for most companies. Companies and managers must now consider the environmental impact of their business decisions in the same way they would consider other operational issues. To help managers make sound business decisions, the emerging field of environmental management accounting focuses on calculating the environmental-related costs of business decisions. Environmental managerial accountants evaluate a variety of issues such as the volume and level of emissions, the estimated costs of different levels of emissions, and the impact that environmental costs have on product cost. Managers use these results to assess the environmental effects of their business decisions.

Obj. 4 Describe and illustrate the following statements for a manufacturing business: balance sheet, statement of cost of goods manufactured, and income statement.

Financial Statements for a Manufacturing Business

The retained earnings and cash flow statements for a manufacturing business are similar to those illustrated in earlier chapters for service and merchandising businesses. However, the balance sheet and income statement for a manufacturing business are more complex. This is because a manufacturer makes the products that it sells and, thus, must record and report product costs. The reporting of product costs affects primarily the balance sheet and the income statement.

Balance Sheet for a Manufacturing Business

A manufacturing business reports three types of inventory on its balance sheet as follows:

- **Materials inventory** (sometimes called raw materials inventory). This inventory consists of the costs of the direct and indirect materials that have not entered the manufacturing process.

  Examples for **Legend Guitars**: Wood, guitar strings, glue, sandpaper
- **Work in process inventory.** This inventory consists of the direct materials, direct labor, and factory overhead costs for products that have entered the manufacturing process but are not yet completed (in process).

  Example for Legend: Unfinished (partially assembled) guitars
- **Finished goods inventory.** This inventory consists of completed (or finished) products that have not been sold.

  Example for Legend: Unsold guitars

Link to Gibson Guitars

In January 1986, guitar enthusiasts Henry Juszkiewicz and David Berryman purchased **Gibson**. Together they restored Gibson's reputation for innovation and quality. Under their leadership, Gibson began generating profits.

Exhibit 14 illustrates the reporting of inventory on the balance sheet for a merchandising and a manufacturing business. MusicLand Stores, Inc., a retailer of musical instruments, reports only Merchandise Inventory. In contrast, **Legend Guitars**, a manufacturer of guitars, reports Finished Goods, Work in Process, and Materials inventories. In both balance sheets, inventory is reported in the Current assets section.

Income Statement for a Manufacturing Business

The income statements for merchandising and manufacturing businesses differ primarily in the reporting of the cost of merchandise (goods) *available for sale* and *sold* during the period. These differences are shown in Exhibit 15.

EXHIBIT 14

Balance Sheet Presentation of Inventory in Manufacturing and Merchandising Companies

MusicLand Stores, Inc.
Balance Sheet
December 31, 20Y8

Current assets:	
Cash	$ 25,000
Accounts receivable (net)	85,000
Merchandise inventory	142,000
Supplies	10,000
Total current assets	$262,000

Legend Guitars
Balance Sheet
December 31, 20Y8

Current assets:		
Cash		$ 21,000
Accounts receivable (net)		120,000
Inventories:		
Finished goods	$62,500	
Work in process	24,000	
Materials	35,000	121,500
Supplies		2,000
Total current assets		$264,500

EXHIBIT 15

Income Statements for Merchandising and Manufacturing Businesses

Merchandising Business

Income Statement

Sales		$XXX
Beginning merchandise inventory	$XXX	
Plus net purchases	XXX	
Merchandise available for sale	$XXX	
Less ending merchandise inventory	XXX	
Cost of merchandise sold		XXX
Gross profit		$XXX

Manufacturing Business

Income Statement

Sales		$XXX
Beginning finished goods inventory	$XXX	
Plus cost of goods manufactured	XXX	
Cost of finished goods available for sale	$XXX	
Less ending finished goods inventory	XXX	
Cost of goods sold		XXX
Gross profit		$XXX

A merchandising business purchases merchandise ready for resale to customers. The total cost of the **merchandise available for sale** during the period is determined as follows:

$$\text{Beginning Merchandise Inventory} + \text{Net Purchases} = \text{Merchandise Available for Sale}$$

The **cost of merchandise sold** is determined as follows:

$$\text{Cost of Merchandise Available for Sale} - \text{Ending Merchandise Inventory} = \text{Cost of Merchandise Sold}$$

A manufacturer makes the products it sells, using direct materials, direct labor, and factory overhead. The total cost of making products that are available for sale during the period is called the **cost of goods manufactured**.

The **cost of finished goods available for sale** is determined as follows:

Beginning Finished Goods Inventory + Cost of Goods Manufactured = Cost of Finished Goods Available for Sale

The **cost of goods sold** is determined as follows:

Cost of Finished Goods Available for Sale − Ending Finished Goods Inventory = Cost of Goods Sold

Cost of goods manufactured is required to determine the *cost of goods sold* and, thus, to prepare the income statement. The cost of goods manufactured is often determined by preparing a **statement of cost of goods manufactured.**[1] This statement summarizes the cost of goods manufactured during the period, as follows:

Statement of Cost of Goods Manufactured

Beginning work in process inventory			$XXX
Direct materials:			
Beginning materials inventory	$XXX		
Purchases	XXX		
Cost of materials available for use	$XXX		
Less ending materials inventory	XXX		
Cost of direct materials used		$XXX	
Direct labor		XXX	
Factory overhead		XXX	
Total manufacturing costs incurred			XXX
Total manufacturing costs			$XXX
Less ending work in process inventory			XXX
Cost of goods manufactured			$XXX

To illustrate, the following data for **Legend Guitars** are used:

	Jan. 1, 20Y8	Dec. 31, 20Y8
Inventories:		
Materials	$ 65,000	$ 35,000
Work in process	30,000	24,000
Finished goods	60,000	62,500
Total inventories	$155,000	$121,500
Manufacturing costs incurred during 20Y8:		
Materials purchased		$100,000
Direct labor		110,000
Factory overhead:		
Indirect labor	$ 24,000	
Depreciation on factory equipment	10,000	
Factory supplies and utility costs	10,000	44,000
Total		$254,000
Sales		$366,000
Selling expenses		20,000
Administrative expenses		15,000

The statement of cost of goods manufactured is prepared using the following three steps:

Step 1. Determine the *cost of materials used.*
Step 2. Determine the *total manufacturing costs incurred.*
Step 3. Determine the *cost of goods manufactured.*

1 Chapters 19 and 20 describe and illustrate the use of job order and process cost systems. As will be discussed, these systems do not require a statement of cost of goods manufactured.

Exhibit 16 summarizes how manufacturing costs flow to the income statement and balance sheet of a manufacturing business.

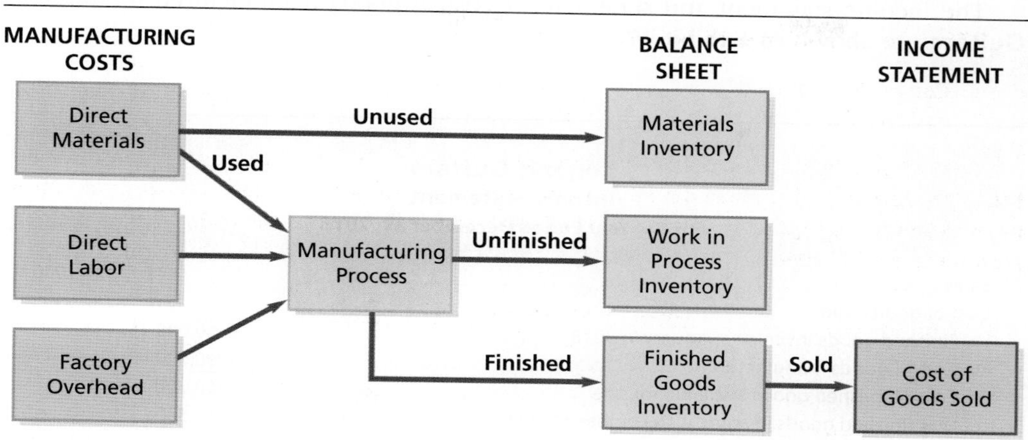

EXHIBIT 16

Flow of Manufacturing Costs

Using the data for **Legend Guitars**, the steps for determining the cost of materials used, total manufacturing costs incurred, and cost of goods manufactured are computed as follows:

Step 1. The *cost of materials used* in production is determined as follows:

Materials inventory, January 1, 20Y8	$ 65,000
Add materials purchased	100,000
Cost of materials available for use	$ 165,000
Less materials inventory, December 31, 20Y8	35,000
Cost of direct materials used	$ 130,000

The January 1, 20Y8 (beginning), materials inventory of $65,000 is added to the cost of materials purchased of $100,000 to yield the $165,000 total cost of materials that are available for use during 20Y8. Deducting the December 31, 20Y8 (ending), materials inventory of $35,000 yields the $130,000 cost of direct materials used in production.

Step 2. The *total manufacturing costs incurred* is determined as follows:

Direct materials used in production (Step 1)	$ 130,000
Direct labor	110,000
Factory overhead	44,000
Total manufacturing costs incurred	$284,000

The total manufacturing costs incurred in 20Y8 of $284,000 are determined by adding the direct materials used in production (Step 1), the direct labor cost, and the factory overhead costs.

Step 3. The *cost of goods manufactured* is determined as follows:

Work in process inventory, January 1, 20Y8	$ 30,000
Total manufacturing costs incurred (Step 2)	284,000
Total manufacturing costs	$ 314,000
Less work in process inventory, December 31, 20Y8	24,000
Cost of goods manufactured	$290,000

The cost of goods manufactured of $290,000 is determined by adding the total manufacturing costs incurred (Step 2) to the January 1, 20Y8 (beginning), work in process inventory of $30,000. This yields total manufacturing costs of $314,000. The December 31, 20Y8 (ending), work in process inventory of $24,000 is then deducted to determine the cost of goods manufactured of $290,000.

The income statement and statement of cost of goods manufactured for **Legend Guitars** are shown in Exhibit 17.

EXHIBIT 17

Manufacturing Company—Income Statement with Statement of Cost of Goods Manufactured

Dynamic Exhibit

Legend Guitars
Income Statement
For the Year Ended December 31, 20Y8

Sales		$366,000
Cost of goods sold:		
Finished goods inventory, January 1, 20Y8	$ 60,000	
Cost of goods manufactured	290,000	
Cost of finished goods available for sale	$350,000	
Less finished goods inventory, December 31, 20Y8	62,500	
Cost of goods sold		287,500
Gross profit		$ 78,500
Operating expenses:		
Selling expenses	$ 20,000	
Administrative expenses	15,000	
Total operating expenses		35,000
Net income		$ 43,500

Legend Guitars
Statement of Cost of Goods Manufactured
For the Year Ended December 31, 20Y8

Work in process inventory, January 1, 20Y8			$ 30,000
Direct materials:			
Materials inventory, January 1, 20Y8	$ 65,000		
Purchases	100,000		
Cost of materials available for use	$165,000		
Less materials inventory, December 31, 20Y8	35,000		
Cost of direct materials used		$130,000	
Direct labor		110,000	
Factory overhead:			
Indirect labor	$ 24,000		
Depreciation on factory equipment	10,000		
Factory supplies and utility costs	10,000		
Total factory overhead		44,000	
Total manufacturing costs incurred			284,000
Total manufacturing costs			$314,000
Less work in process inventory, December 31, 20Y8			24,000
Cost of goods manufactured			$290,000

Example Exercise 18-5 Cost of Goods Sold, Cost of Goods Manufactured

Obj. 4

Gauntlet Company has the following information for January:

Cost of direct materials used in production	$25,000
Direct labor	35,000
Factory overhead	20,000
Work in process inventory, January 1	30,000
Work in process inventory, January 31	25,000
Finished goods inventory, January 1	15,000
Finished goods inventory, January 31	12,000

For January, determine (a) the cost of goods manufactured and (b) the cost of goods sold.

Follow My Example 18-5

a.	Work in process inventory, January 1		$ 30,000
	Cost of direct materials used	$ 25,000	
	Direct labor	35,000	
	Factory overhead	20,000	
	Total manufacturing costs incurred during January		80,000
	Total manufacturing costs		$110,000
	Less work in process inventory, January 31		25,000
	Cost of goods manufactured		$ 85,000
b.	Finished goods inventory, January 1	$ 15,000	
	Cost of goods manufactured	85,000	
	Cost of finished goods available for sale	$100,000	
	Less finished goods inventory, January 31	12,000	
	Cost of goods sold	$ 88,000	

Practice Exercises: PE 18-5A, PE 18-5B

SERVICE FOCUS

MANAGERIAL ACCOUNTING IN THE SERVICE INDUSTRY

All businesses can benefit from managerial accounting whether they manufacture a product or provide a service. Service businesses such as professional service firms, restaurants, maintenance companies, and airlines need managerial accounting information to direct daily operations, plan future operations, and develop business strategies.

For example, **The Walt Disney Company** relies heavily on managerial accounting to manage its operations. Disney uses budgets and financial forecasts to plan costs and allocate resources between its various business units. Based on these budgets and financial forecasts, Disney directs its operations by determining how to staff its theme parks and off-cycle its theme park rides for maintenance. Operations are controlled by a variety of qualitative and quantitative metrics that provide feedback on the efficiency and quality of the customer experience. To ensure the best guest experience, Disney Theme Parks manages operations in small business units to maximize management ownership and responsibility. The results of Disney's deployment and use of managerial accounting have been impressive. The Walt Disney Company is typically ranked number 1 in *Fortune*'s listing of the 10 most admired companies for quality.

At a Glance 18

Obj. 1 **Describe managerial accounting and the role of managerial accounting in a business.**

Key Points Managerial accounting is a staff function that supports the management process by providing reports to aid management in planning, directing, controlling, improving, and decision making. This differs from financial accounting, which provides information to users outside the organization. Managerial accounting reports are designed to meet the specific needs of management and aid management in planning long-term strategies and running the day-to-day operations.

Learning Outcomes	Example Exercises	Practice Exercises
• Describe the differences between financial accounting and managerial accounting.		
• Describe the role of the management accountant in the organization.		
• Describe the role of managerial accounting in the management process.	EE18-1	PE18-1A, 18-1B

Obj. 2 **Describe and illustrate the following costs: direct and indirect costs; direct materials, direct labor, and factory overhead costs; and product and period costs.**

Key Points Manufacturing companies use machinery and labor to convert materials into a finished product. A direct cost can be directly traced to a finished product, while an indirect cost cannot. The cost of a finished product is made up of three components: direct materials, direct labor, and factory overhead.

These three manufacturing costs can be categorized into prime costs (direct materials and direct labor) or conversion costs (direct labor and factory overhead). Product costs consist of the elements of manufacturing cost—direct materials, direct labor, and factory overhead—while period costs consist of selling and administrative expenses.

Learning Outcomes	Example Exercises	Practice Exercises
• Describe a cost object.		
• Classify a cost as a direct or indirect cost for a cost object.		
• Describe direct materials cost.	EE18-2	PE18-2A, 18-2B
• Describe direct labor cost.	EE18-2	PE18-2A, 18-2B
• Describe factory overhead cost.	EE18-2	PE18-2A, 18-2B
• Describe prime costs and conversion costs.	EE18-3	PE18-3A, 18-3B
• Describe product costs and period costs.	EE18-4	PE18-4A, 18-4B

Obj. 3 **Describe sustainable business activities and eco-efficiency measures.**

Key Points To make sound strategic and operational decisions, managers must consider the social and environmental conditions in which their company operates. Sustainability is the practice of operating a business to maximize profits while attempting to preserve the environment, economy, and needs of future generations. Sustainability information provides important internal feedback that helps guide a company's strategic and operational decision making. This information also helps users of external financial statements evaluate the risks and opportunities a company faces that are tied to the environment in which it operates.

Learning Outcomes	*Example Exercises*	*Practice Exercises*
• Describe sustainability.		
• Describe eco-efficiency measures.		

Obj. 4 **Describe and illustrate the following statements for a manufacturing business: balance sheet, statement of cost of goods manufactured, and income statement.**

Key Points The financial statements of manufacturing companies differ from those of merchandising companies. Manufacturing company balance sheets report three types of inventory: materials, work in process, and finished goods. The income statement of manufacturing companies reports the cost of goods sold, which is the total manufacturing cost of the goods sold. The income statement is supported by the statement of cost of goods manufactured, which provides the details of the cost of goods manufactured during the period.

Learning Outcomes	*Example Exercises*	*Practice Exercises*
• Describe materials inventory.		
• Describe work in process inventory.		
• Describe finished goods inventory.		
• Describe the differences between merchandising and manufacturing company balance sheets.		
• Prepare a statement of cost of goods manufactured.	**EE18-5**	**PE18-5A, 18-5B**
• Prepare an income statement for a manufacturing company.	**EE18-5**	**PE18-5A, 18-5B**

Illustrative Problem

The following is a list of costs that were incurred in producing this textbook:

a. Insurance on the factory building and equipment
b. Salary of the vice president of finance
c. Hourly wages of printing press operators during production
d. Straight-line depreciation on the printing presses used to manufacture the text
e. Electricity used to run the presses during the printing of the text
f. Sales commissions paid to textbook representatives for each text sold
g. Paper on which the text is printed
h. Book covers used to bind the pages

(Continued)

i. Straight-line depreciation on an office building
j. Salaries of staff used to develop artwork for the text
k. Glue used to bind pages to cover

Instructions

With respect to the manufacture and sale of this text, classify each cost as either a product cost or a period cost. Indicate whether each product cost is a direct materials cost, a direct labor cost, or a factory overhead cost. Indicate whether each period cost is a selling expense or an administrative expense.

Solution

	Product Cost			Period Cost	
Cost	**Direct Materials Cost**	**Direct Labor Cost**	**Factory Overhead Cost**	**Selling Expense**	**Administrative Expense**
a.			X		
b.					X
c.		X			
d.			X		
e.			X		
f.				X	
g.	X				
h.	X				
i.					X
j.			X		
k.			X		

Key Terms

continuous process improvement (889)
controller (887)
controlling (889)
conversion costs (894)
cost (891)
cost object (891)
cost of finished goods available for sale (900)
cost of goods manufactured (899)
cost of goods sold (900)
cost of merchandise sold (899)
decision making (889)
direct costs (891)
direct labor cost (892)
direct materials cost (892)
directing (889)
eco-efficiency measures (897)
factory burden (893)
factory overhead cost (893)
feedback (889)
financial accounting (885)
finished goods inventory (898)
indirect costs (891)
line department (887)
management by exception (889)
management process (888)
managerial accounting (886)
manufacturing overhead (893)
materials inventory (898)
merchandise available for sale (899)
objectives (goals) (889)
operational planning (889)
period costs (895)
planning (889)
prime costs (894)
product costs (895)
staff department (887)
statement of cost of goods manufactured (900)
strategic planning (889)
strategies (889)
sustainability (897)
Sustainability Accounting Standards Board (SASB) (897)
work in process inventory (898)

Discussion Questions

1. What are the major differences between financial accounting and managerial accounting?
2. a. Differentiate between a department with line responsibility and a department with staff responsibility.
   b. In an organization that has a Sales Department and a Personnel Department, among others, which of the two departments has (1) line responsibility and (2) staff responsibility?
3. What manufacturing cost term is used to describe the cost of materials that are an integral part of the manufactured end product?
4. Distinguish between prime costs and conversion costs.
5. What is the difference between a product cost and a period cost?
6. Name the three inventory accounts for a manufacturing business and describe what each balance represents at the end of an accounting period.
7. In what order should the three inventories of a manufacturing business be presented on the balance sheet?
8. What three categories of manufacturing costs are included in the cost of finished goods and the cost of work in process?
9. Describe sustainability and sustainable business practices.
10. How does the Cost of goods sold section of the income statement differ between merchandising and manufacturing companies?

Practice Exercises

Example Exercises

Show Me How — EE 18-1 *p. 890*

PE 18-1A Management process

OBJ. 1

Three phases of the management process are controlling, planning, and decision making. Match the following descriptions to the proper phase:

Phase of management process	Description
Controlling	a. Monitoring the operating results of implemented plans and comparing the actual results with expected results.
Planning	b. Inherent in planning, directing, controlling, and improving.
Decision making	c. Long-range courses of action.

Show Me How — EE 18-1 *p. 890*

PE 18-1B Management process

OBJ. 1

Three phases of the management process are planning, directing, and controlling. Match the following descriptions to the proper phase:

Phase of management process	Description
Planning	a. Developing long-range courses of action to achieve goals.
Directing	b. Isolating significant departures from plans for further investigation and possible remedial action. It may lead to a revision of future plans.
Controlling	c. Process by which managers, given their assigned levels of responsibilities, run day-to-day operations.

EE 18-2 p. 894
Show Me How

PE 18-2A Direct materials, direct labor, and factory overhead OBJ. 2

Identify the following costs as direct materials (DM), direct labor (DL), or factory overhead (FO) for an automobile manufacturer:

a. Wages of employees that operate painting equipment
b. Wages of the plant supervisor
c. Steel
d. Oil used for assembly line machinery

EE 18-2 p. 894
Show Me How

PE 18-2B Direct materials, direct labor, and factory overhead OBJ. 2

Identify the following costs as direct materials (DM), direct labor (DL), or factory overhead (FO) for a magazine publisher:

a. Staples used to bind magazines
b. Wages of printing machine employees
c. Maintenance on printing machines
d. Paper used in the magazine

EE 18-3 p. 894
Show Me How

PE 18-3A Prime and conversion costs OBJ. 2

Identify the following costs as a prime cost (P), conversion cost (C), or both (B) for an automobile manufacturer:

a. Wages of employees that operate painting equipment
b. Wages of the plant manager
c. Steel
d. Oil used for assembly line machinery

EE 18-3 p. 894
Show Me How

PE 18-3B Prime and conversion costs OBJ. 2

Identify the following costs as a prime cost (P), conversion cost (C), or both (B) for a magazine publisher:

a. Paper used for the magazine
b. Wages of printing machine employees
c. Glue used to bind magazine
d. Maintenance on printing machines

EE 18-4 p. 896
Show Me How

PE 18-4A Product and period costs OBJ. 2

Identify the following costs as a product cost or a period cost for an automobile manufacturer:

a. Steel
b. Wages of employees that operate painting equipment
c. Rent on office building
d. Sales staff salaries

EE 18-4 p. 896
Show Me How

PE 18-4B Product and period costs OBJ. 2

Identify the following costs as a product cost or a period cost for a magazine publisher:

a. Sales salaries
b. Paper used for the magazine
c. Maintenance on printing machines
d. Depreciation expense—corporate headquarters

Show Me How EE 18-5 *p. 903*

PE 18-5A Cost of goods sold, cost of goods manufactured **OBJ. 4**

Timbuk 3 Company has the following information for March:

Cost of direct materials used in production	$21,000
Direct labor	54,250
Factory overhead	35,000
Work in process inventory, March 1	87,500
Work in process inventory, March 31	92,750
Finished goods inventory, March 1	36,750
Finished goods inventory, March 31	42,000

For March, determine (a) the cost of goods manufactured and (b) the cost of goods sold.

Show Me How EE 18-5 *p. 903*

PE 18-5B Cost of goods sold, cost of goods manufactured **OBJ. 4**

Glenville Company has the following information for April:

Cost of direct materials used in production	$280,000
Direct labor	324,000
Factory overhead	188,900
Work in process inventory, April 1	72,300
Work in process inventory, April 30	76,800
Finished goods inventory, April 1	39,600
Finished goods inventory, April 30	41,200

For April, determine (a) the cost of goods manufactured and (b) the cost of goods sold.

Exercises

EX 18-1 Classifying costs as materials, labor, or factory overhead **OBJ. 2**

Indicate whether each of the following costs of an automobile manufacturer would be classified as direct materials cost, direct labor cost, or factory overhead cost:

a. Wheels
b. Glass used in the vehicle's windshield
c. Wages of assembly line worker
d. V8 automobile engine
e. Depreciation of robotic assembly line equipment
f. Steering wheel
g. Painting safety masks for employees working in the paint room
h. Salary of test driver

Real World

EX 18-2 Classifying costs as materials, labor, or factory overhead **OBJ. 2**

Indicate whether the following costs of Procter & Gamble, a maker of consumer products, would be classified as direct materials cost, direct labor cost, or factory overhead cost:

a. Resins for body wash products
b. Scents and fragrances used in making soaps and detergents
c. Plant manager salary for the Iowa City, Iowa, plant
d. Depreciation on the Auburn, Maine, manufacturing plant

(Continued)

e. Depreciation on assembly line in the Mehoopany, Pennsylvania, paper products plant
f. Maintenance supplies
g. Packaging materials, which are a significant portion of the total product cost
h. Wages of production line employees at the Pineville, Louisiana, soap and detergent plant
i. Wages paid to Packaging Department employees in the Bear River City, Utah, paper products plant
j. Salary of process engineers

EX 18-3 Classifying costs as factory overhead **OBJ. 2**

Real World

Which of the following items are properly classified as part of factory overhead for Ford Motor Company, a maker of heavy automobiles and trucks?

a. Plant manager's salary at Buffalo, New York, stamping plant, which manufactures auto and truck subassemblies
b. Depreciation on Flat Rock, Michigan, assembly plant
c. Dividends paid to shareholders
d. Machine lubricant used to maintain the assembly line at the Louisville, Kentucky, assembly plant
e. Leather to be used on vehicles that have leather interiors
f. Depreciation on mechanical robots used on the assembly line
g. Consultant fees for a study of production line efficiency
h. Dealership sales incentives
i. Vice president of human resources' salary
j. Property taxes on the Detriot, Michigan, headquarters building

---

EX 18-4 Classifying costs as product or period costs **OBJ. 2**

Real World

For apparel manufacturer Abercrombie & Fitch, Inc., classify each of the following costs as either a product cost or a period cost:

a. Cost of information technology support for the corporate headquarters
b. Depreciation on sewing machines
c. Fabric used during production
d. Depreciation on office equipment
e. Advertising expenses
f. Repairs and maintenance costs for sewing machines
g. Salary of production quality control supervisor
h. Utility costs for office building
i. Sales commissions
j. Salaries of distribution center personnel
k. Wages of sewing machine operators
l. Factory janitorial supplies
m. Chief financial officer's salary
n. Travel costs of media relations employees
o. Factory supervisors' salaries
p. Oil used to lubricate sewing machines
q. Property taxes on factory building and equipment

EX 18-5 Concepts and terminology **OBJ. 1, 2**

From the choices presented in parentheses, choose the appropriate term for completing each of the following sentences:

a. Advertising costs are usually viewed as (period, product) costs.
b. Feedback is often used to (improve, direct) operations.
c. Payments of cash or the commitment to pay cash in the future for the purpose of generating revenues are (costs, expenses).

d. A product, a sales territory, a department, or an activity to which costs are traced is called a (direct cost, cost object).

e. The balance sheet of a manufacturer would include an account for (cost of goods sold, work in process inventory).

f. Factory overhead costs combined with direct labor costs are called (prime, conversion) costs.

g. The implementation of automatic, robotic factory equipment normally (increases, decreases) the direct labor component of product costs.

EX 18-6 Concepts and terminology

OBJ. 1, 2

From the choices presented in parentheses, choose the appropriate term for completing each of the following sentences:

a. The phase of the management process that uses process information to eliminate the source of problems in a process so that the process delivers the correct product in the correct quantities is called (directing, improving).

b. Direct labor costs combined with factory overhead costs are called (prime, conversion) costs.

c. The salaries of salespeople are normally considered a (period, product) cost.

d. The plant manager's salary would be considered (direct, indirect) to the product.

e. Long-term plans are called (strategic, operational) plans.

f. Materials for use in production are called (supplies, materials inventory).

g. An example of factory overhead is (electricity used to run assembly line, CEO salary).

EX 18-7 Classifying costs in a service company

OBJ. 2

A partial list of the costs for Wisconsin and Minnesota Railroad, a short hauler of freight, follows. Classify each cost as either indirect or direct. For purposes of classifying each cost, use the train as the cost object.

a. Cost to lease (rent) railroad cars

b. Cost of track and bed (ballast) replacement

c. Diesel fuel costs

d. Cost to lease (rent) train locomotives

e. Depreciation of terminal facilities

f. Maintenance costs of right-of-way, bridges, and buildings

g. Salaries of dispatching and communications personnel

h. Headquarters information technology support staff salaries

i. Safety training costs

j. Wages of train engineers

k. Wages of switch and classification yard personnel

l. Costs of accident cleanup

EX 18-8 Sustainability and eco-efficiency measures

OBJ. 3

Four types of eco-efficiency measures are identified below. Match the following descriptions to the proper eco-efficiency measures:

1. Energy efficiency	a. Cost savings from recycling and reusing waste and by-product materials
2. Fuel efficiency	b. Cost savings from reducing the amount of product packaging materials
3. Material use efficiency	c. Cost savings from replacing lighting fixtures in a production facility with energy-efficient lighting
4. Waste efficiency	d. Cost savings from replacing gas-powered vehicles with hybrid or alternative energy-source vehicles

EX 18-9 Classifying costs **OBJ. 2, 4**

The following report was prepared for evaluating the performance of the plant manager of Marching Ants Inc. Evaluate and correct this report.

Marching Ants Inc.
Manufacturing Costs
For the Quarter Ended June 30

Materials used in production (including $56,200 of indirect materials)	$ 607,500
Direct labor (including $84,400 maintenance salaries)	562,500
Factory overhead:	
Supervisor salaries	517,500
Heat, light, and power	140,650
Sales salaries	348,750
Promotional expenses	315,000
Insurance and property taxes—plant	151,900
Insurance and property taxes—corporate offices	219,400
Depreciation—plant and equipment	123,750
Depreciation—corporate offices	90,000
Total	$3,076,950

EX 18-10 Financial statements of a manufacturing firm **OBJ. 4**

✔ a. Net income, $145,000

Show Me How

The following events took place for Digital Vibe Manufacturing Company during January, the first month of its operations as a producer of digital video monitors:

a. Purchased $168,500 of materials.
b. Used $149,250 of direct materials in production.
c. Incurred $360,000 of direct labor wages.
d. Incurred $120,000 of factory overhead.
e. Transferred $600,000 of work in process to finished goods.
f. Sold goods for $875,000.
g. Sold goods with a cost of $525,000.
h. Incurred $125,000 of selling expense.
i. Incurred $80,000 of administrative expense.

Using the information given, complete the following:

a. Prepare the January income statement for Digital Vibe Manufacturing Company.
b. Determine the Materials Inventory, Work in Process Inventory, and Finished Goods Inventory balances at the end of the first month of operations.

EX 18-11 Manufacturing company balance sheet **OBJ. 4**

Show Me How

Partial balance sheet data for Diesel Additives Company at August 31 are as follows:

Finished goods inventory	$ 89,400	Supplies	$ 13,800
Prepaid insurance	9,000	Materials inventory	26,800
Accounts receivable	348,200	Cash	167,500
Work in process inventory	61,100		

Prepare the Current assets section of Diesel Additives Company's balance sheet at August 31.

Show Me How

EX 18-12 Cost of direct materials used in production for a manufacturing company **OBJ. 4**

Okaboji Manufacturing Company reported the following materials data for the month ending November 30:

Materials purchased	$490,900
Materials inventory, November 1	64,900
Materials inventory, November 30	81,300

Determine the cost of direct materials used in production by Okaboji during the month ended November 30.

✔ e. $165,000

Show Me How

EX 18-13 Cost of goods manufactured for a manufacturing company **OBJ. 4**

Two items are omitted from each of the following three lists of cost of goods manufactured statement data. Determine the amounts of the missing items, identifying them by letter.

Work in process inventory, August 1	$ 19,660	$ 41,650	(e)
Total manufacturing costs incurred during August	332,750	(c)	1,075,000
Total manufacturing costs	(a)	$515,770	$1,240,000
Work in process inventory, August 31	23,500	54,000	(f)
Cost of goods manufactured	(b)	(d)	$1,068,000

Show Me How

EX 18-14 Cost of goods manufactured for a manufacturing company **OBJ. 4**

The following information is available for Ethtridge Manufacturing Company for the month ending July 31:

Cost of direct materials used in production	$1,150,000
Direct labor	966,000
Work in process inventory, July 1	316,400
Work in process inventory, July 31	355,500
Total factory overhead	490,500

Determine Ethtridge's cost of goods manufactured for the month ended July 31.

✔ d. $470,000

EX 18-15 Income statement for a manufacturing company **OBJ. 4**

Two items are omitted from each of the following three lists of cost of goods sold data from a manufacturing company income statement. Determine the amounts of the missing items, identifying them by letter.

Finished goods inventory, June 1	$ 116,600	$ 38,880	(e)
Cost of goods manufactured	825,900	(c)	180,000
Cost of finished goods available for sale	(a)	$540,000	$1,100,000
Finished goods inventory, June 30	130,000	70,000	(f)
Cost of goods sold	(b)	(d)	$ 945,000

✔ a. Total manufacturing costs, $4,325,700

Excel

Show Me How

EX 18-16 Statement of cost of goods manufactured for a manufacturing company **OBJ. 4**

Cost data for Disksan Manufacturing Company for the month ended January 31 are as follows:

Inventories	**January 1**	**January 31**
Materials	$180,000	$145,500
Work in process	334,600	290,700
Finished goods	675,000	715,000

(Continued)

Direct labor	$2,260,000
Materials purchased during January	1,375,000
Factory overhead incurred during January:	
Indirect labor	115,000
Machinery depreciation	90,000
Heat, light, and power	55,000
Supplies	18,500
Property taxes	10,000
Miscellaneous costs	33,100

a. Prepare a cost of goods manufactured statement for January.
b. Determine the cost of goods sold for January.

EX 18-17 Cost of goods sold, profit margin, and net income for a manufacturing company OBJ. 4

✔ a. Cost of goods sold, $4,595,000

Show Me How

The following information is available for Bandera Manufacturing Company for the month ending January 31:

Cost of goods manufactured	$4,490,000
Selling expenses	530,000
Administrative expenses	340,000
Sales	6,600,000
Finished goods inventory, January 1	880,000
Finished goods inventory, January 31	775,000

For the month ended January 31, determine Bandera's (a) cost of goods sold, (b) gross profit, and (c) net income.

EX 18-18 Cost flow relationships OBJ. 4

✔ a. $330,000

Excel

Show Me How

The following information is available for the first month of operations of Bahadir Company, a manufacturer of mechanical pencils:

Sales	$792,000
Gross profit	462,000
Cost of goods manufactured	396,000
Indirect labor	171,600
Factory depreciation	26,400
Materials purchased	244,200
Total manufacturing costs for the period	455,400
Materials inventory, ending	33,000

Using the information given, determine the following missing amounts:

a. Cost of goods sold
b. Finished goods inventory at the end of the month
c. Direct materials cost
d. Direct labor cost
e. Work in process inventory at the end of the month

EX 18-19 Uses of managerial accounting in a service company LO 1, 4

Real World

Priceline.com allows customers to bid on hotel rooms by "naming their price." This "name your price" process allows customers to obtain a better rate on a hotel room than they might be able to obtain by reserving their room directly from the hotel. The hotel can also benefit from this transaction by filling empty hotel rooms during periods of low occupancy.

Natalie Mooney bids $85 for a night's stay at the Hotel Monaco in Seattle on Saturday August 10. The Hotel Monaco is not fully booked that evening and would likely accept any reasonable bids. How might the Hotel Monaco use managerial accounting information to decide whether or not to accept Natalie's bid?

Problems: Series A

PR 18-1A Classifying costs

OBJ. 2

The following is a list of costs that were incurred in the production and sale of large commercial airplanes:

a. Cost of electronic guidance system installed in the airplane cockpit
b. Special advertising campaign in *Aviation World* magazine
c. Salary of chief compliance officer of company
d. Salary of chief financial officer
e. Decals for cockpit door, the cost of which is immaterial to the cost of the final product
f. Cost of electrical wiring throughout the airplane
g. Cost of normal scrap from production of airplane body
h. Instrument panel installed in the airplane cockpit
i. Depreciation on factory equipment
j. Masks for use by painters in painting the airplane body
k. Cost of paving the headquarters employee parking lot
l. Turbo-charged airplane engine
m. Prebuilt leather seats installed in the first-class cabin
n. Human Resources Department costs for the year
o. Hourly wages of employees that assemble the airplane
p. Salary of the Marketing Department personnel
q. Oil to lubricate factory equipment
r. Yearly cost of the maintenance contract for robotic equipment
s. Hydraulic pumps used in the airplane's flight control system
t. Cost of miniature replicas of the airplane used to promote and market the airplane
u. Metal used for producing the airplane body
v. Power used by painting equipment
w. Annual bonus paid to the chief operating officer of the company
x. Interior trim material used throughout the airplane cabin
y. Salary of plant manager
z. Annual fee to a celebrity to promote the aircraft

Instructions

Classify each cost as either a product cost or a period cost. Indicate whether each product cost is a direct materials cost, a direct labor cost, or a factory overhead cost. Indicate whether each period cost is a selling expense or an administrative expense. Use the following tabular headings for your answer, placing an "X" in the appropriate column:

	Product Costs			Period Costs	
Cost	Direct Materials Cost	Direct Labor Cost	Factory Overhead Cost	Selling Expense	Administrative Expense

PR 18-2A Classifying costs

OBJ. 2

The following is a list of costs incurred by several businesses:

a. Cost of fabric used by clothing manufacturer
b. Maintenance and repair costs for factory equipment
c. Rent for a warehouse used to store raw materials and work in process
d. Wages of production quality control personnel
e. Oil lubricants for factory plant and equipment

(Continued)

f. Depreciation of robot used to assemble a product
g. Travel costs of marketing executives to annual sales meeting
h. Depreciation of copying machines used by the Marketing Department
i. Fees charged by collection agency on past-due customer accounts
j. Electricity used to operate factory machinery
k. Maintenance costs for factory equipment
l. Pens, paper, and other supplies used by the Accounting Department in preparing various managerial reports
m. Charitable contribution to United Fund
n. Depreciation of microcomputers used in the factory to coordinate and monitor the production schedules
o. Fees paid to lawn service for office grounds upkeep
p. Cost of sewing machine needles used by a shirt manufacturer
q. Cost of plastic for a telephone being manufactured
r. Telephone charges by president's office
s. Cost of 30-second television commercial
t. Surgeon's fee for heart bypass surgery
u. Depreciation of tools used in production
v. Wages of a machine operator on the production line
w. Salary of the vice president of manufacturing operations
x. Factory janitorial supplies

Instructions

Classify each of the preceding costs as a product cost or period cost. Indicate whether each product cost is a direct materials cost, a direct labor cost, or a factory overhead cost. Indicate whether each period cost is a selling expense or an administrative expense. Use the following tabular headings for preparing your answer, placing an "X" in the appropriate column:

	Product Costs			Period Costs	
Cost	Direct Materials Cost	Direct Labor Cost	Factory Overhead Cost	Selling Expense	Administrative Expense

PR 18-3A Cost classifications for a service company **OBJ. 2**

A partial list of Foothills Medical Center's costs follows:

a. Cost of laundry services for operating room personnel
b. Salary of intensive care personnel
c. Depreciation on patient rooms
d. Cost of blood tests
e. Nurses' salaries
f. Cost of patient meals
g. Overtime incurred in the Patient Records Department due to a computer failure
h. Operating room supplies used on patients (catheters, sutures, etc.)
i. Doctor's fee
j. Cost of X-ray test
k. Cost of maintaining the staff and visitors' cafeteria
l. Cost of drugs used for patients
m. Cost of intravenous solutions used for patients
n. Cost of improvements on the employee parking lot
o. Salary of the nutritionist
p. General maintenance of the hospital
q. Cost of advertising hospital services on television
r. Cost of new heart wing
s. Training costs for nurses
t. Depreciation of X-ray equipment
u. Utility costs of the hospital

Instructions

1. What would be Foothills Medical Center's most logical definition for the final cost object? Explain.
2. Identify whether each of the costs is to be classified as direct or indirect. For purposes of classifying each cost as direct or indirect, use the patient as the cost object.

PR 18-4A Manufacturing income statement, statement of cost of goods manufactured **OBJ. 2, 4**

✔ 1. b. Yakima, $1,330,000

Excel

Several items are omitted from the income statement and cost of goods manufactured statement data for two different companies for the month of May.

	Rainier Company	Yakima Company
Materials inventory, May 1	$ 100,000	$ 48,200
Materials inventory, May 31	(a)	50,000
Materials purchased	950,000	710,000
Cost of direct materials used in production	938,500	(a)
Direct labor	2,860,000	(b)
Factory overhead	1,800,000	446,000
Total manufacturing costs incurred during May	(b)	2,484,200
Total manufacturing costs	5,598,500	2,660,600
Work in process inventory, May 1	400,000	176,400
Work in process inventory, May 31	382,000	(c)
Cost of goods manufactured	(c)	2,491,500
Finished goods inventory, May 1	615,000	190,000
Finished goods inventory, May 31	596,500	(d)
Sales	9,220,000	4,550,000
Cost of goods sold	(d)	2,470,000
Gross profit	(e)	(e)
Operating expenses	1,000,000	(f)
Net income	(f)	1,500,000

Instructions

1. Determine the amounts of the missing items, identifying them by letter.
2. Prepare Yakima Company's statement of cost of goods manufactured for May.
3. Prepare Yakima Company's income statement for May.

PR 18-5A Statement of cost of goods manufactured and income statement for a manufacturing company **OBJ. 2, 4**

✔ 1. Cost of goods manufactured, $1,989,250

Excel Show Me How

The following information is available for Robstown Corporation for 20Y8:

Inventories	January 1	December 31
Materials	$ 44,250	$31,700
Work in process	63,900	80,000
Finished goods	101,200	99,800

(*Continued*)

Advertising expense	$ 400,000
Depreciation expense—office equipment	30,000
Depreciation expense—factory equipment	80,000
Direct labor	1,100,000
Heat, light, and power—factory	53,300
Indirect labor	115,000
Materials purchased	556,600
Office salaries expense	$ 318,000
Property taxes—factory	40,000
Property taxes—office building	25,000
Rent expense—factory	27,000
Sales	3,850,000
Sales salaries expense	200,000
Supplies—factory	9,500
Miscellaneous costs—factory	11,400

Instructions

1. Prepare the statement of cost of goods manufactured.
2. Prepare the income statement.

Problems: Series B

PR 18-1B Classifying costs

OBJ. 2

The following is a list of costs that were incurred in the production and sale of lawn mowers:

a. Premiums on insurance policy for factory buildings
b. Tires for lawn mowers
c. Filter for spray gun used to paint the lawn mowers
d. Paint used to coat the lawn mowers, the cost of which is immaterial to the cost of the final product
e. Plastic for outside housing of lawn mowers
f. Salary of factory supervisor
g. Hourly wages of operators of robotic machinery used in production
h. Engine oil used in mower engines prior to shipment
i. Salary of vice president of marketing
j. Property taxes on the factory building and equipment
k. Cost of advertising in a national magazine
l. Gasoline engines installed in the lawn mowers
m. Electricity used to run the robotic machinery
n. Straight-line depreciation on the robotic machinery used to manufacture the lawn mowers
o. Salary of quality control supervisor who inspects each lawn mower before it is shipped
p. Attorney fees for drafting a new lease for headquarters offices
q. Payroll taxes on hourly assembly line employees
r. Telephone charges for company controller's office
s. Steering wheels for lawn mowers
t. Factory cafeteria cashier's wages
u. Cash paid to outside firm for janitorial services for factory
v. Maintenance costs for new robotic factory equipment, based on hours of usage
w. Cost of boxes used in packaging lawn mowers, which are a significant portion of the total product cost

x. License fees for use of patent for lawn mower blade, based on the number of lawn mowers produced
y. Steel used in producing the lawn mowers
z. Commissions paid to sales representatives, based on the number of lawn mowers sold

Instructions

Classify each cost as either a product cost or a period cost. Indicate whether each product cost is a direct materials cost, a direct labor cost, or a factory overhead cost. Indicate whether each period cost is a selling expense or an administrative expense. Use the following tabular headings for your answer, placing an "X" in the appropriate column:

	Product Costs			Period Costs	
Cost	Direct Materials Cost	Direct Labor Cost	Factory Overhead Cost	Selling Expense	Administrative Expense

PR 18-2B Classifying costs

OBJ. 2

The following is a list of costs incurred by several businesses:

a. Salary of quality control supervisor
b. Packing supplies for products sold. These supplies are a very small portion of the total cost of the product.
c. Factory operating supplies
d. Depreciation of factory equipment
e. Hourly wages of warehouse laborers
f. Wages of company controller's secretary
g. Maintenance and repair costs for factory equipment
h. Paper used by commercial printer
i. Entertainment expenses for sales representatives
j. Protective glasses for factory machine operators
k. Sales commissions
l. Cost of hogs for meat processor
m. Cost of telephone operators for a toll-free hotline to help customers operate products
n. Hard drives for a microcomputer manufacturer
o. Lumber used by furniture manufacturer
p. Wages of a machine operator on the production line
q. First-aid supplies for factory workers
r. Tires for an automobile manufacturer
s. Paper used by Computer Department in processing various managerial reports
t. Seed for grain farmer
u. Health insurance premiums paid for factory workers
v. Costs of information technology support for the corporate headquarters
w. Costs for television advertisement
x. Executive bonus for vice president of marketing

Instructions

Classify each of the preceding costs as a product cost or period cost. Indicate whether each product cost is a direct materials cost, a direct labor cost, or a factory overhead cost. Indicate whether each period cost is a selling expense or an administrative expense. Use the following tabular headings for preparing your answer. Place an "X" in the appropriate column.

	Product Costs			Period Costs	
Cost	Direct Materials Cost	Direct Labor Cost	Factory Overhead Cost	Selling Expense	Administrative Expense

PR 18-3B Cost classifications for a service company **OBJ. 2**

A partial list of The Grand Hotel's costs follows:

a. Cost to mail a customer survey
b. Wages of convention setup employees
c. Pay-per-view movie rental costs (in rooms)
d. Cost of food
e. Cost of room mini-bar supplies
f. Training for hotel restaurant servers
g. Cost to paint lobby
h. Cost of laundering towels and bedding
i. Champagne for guests
j. Salary of the hotel manager
k. Depreciation of the hotel
l. Cost of valet parking
m. Wages of bellhops
n. Cost to replace lobby furniture
o. Cost of advertising in local newspaper
p. Wages of desk clerks
q. Wages of maids
r. Cost of new carpeting
s. Guest room telephone costs for long-distance calls
t. Cost of soaps and shampoos for rooms
u. Utility cost
v. Wages of kitchen employees
w. General maintenance supplies

Instructions

1. What would be The Grand Hotel's most logical definition for the final cost object? Explain.
2. Identify whether each of the costs is to be classified as direct or indirect. For purposes of classifying each cost as direct or indirect, use the hotel guest as the cost object.

PR 18-4B Manufacturing income statement, statement of cost of goods manufactured **OBJ. 2, 4**

✔ 1. c. On Company, $800,800

Excel

Several items are omitted from the income statement and cost of goods manufactured statement data for two different companies for the month of December.

	On Company	Off Company
Materials inventory, December 1	$ 65,800	$ 195,300
Materials inventory, December 31	(a)	91,140
Materials purchased	282,800	(a)
Cost of direct materials used in production	317,800	(b)
Direct labor	387,800	577,220
Factory overhead	148,400	256,060
Total manufacturing costs incurred in December	(b)	1,519,000
Total manufacturing costs	973,000	1,727,320
Work in process inventory, December 1	119,000	208,320
Work in process inventory, December 31	172,200	(c)
Cost of goods manufactured	(c)	1,532,020
Finished goods inventory, December 1	$ 224,000	$ 269,080
Finished goods inventory, December 31	197,400	(d)
Sales	1,127,000	1,944,320
Cost of goods sold	(d)	1,545,040
Gross profit	(e)	(e)
Operating expenses	117,600	(f)
Net income	(f)	164,920

Instructions

1. Determine the amounts of the missing items, identifying them by letter.
2. Prepare On Company's statement of cost of goods manufactured for December.
3. Prepare On Company's income statement for December.

✔ 1. Cost of goods manufactured, $367,510

Excel

Show Me How

PR 18-5B Statement of cost of goods manufactured and income statement for a manufacturing company

OBJ. 2, 4

The following information is available for Shanika Company for 20Y6:

Inventories	January 1	December 31
Materials	$ 77,350	$ 95,550
Work in process	109,200	96,200
Finished goods	113,750	100,100

Advertising expense	$ 68,250
Depreciation expense—office equipment	22,750
Depreciation expense—factory equipment	14,560
Direct labor	186,550
Heat, light, and power—factory	5,850
Indirect labor	23,660
Materials purchased	123,500
Office salaries expense	77,350
Property taxes—factory	4,095
Property taxes—headquarters building	13,650
Rent expense—factory	6,825
Sales	864,500
Sales salaries expense	136,500
Supplies—factory	3,250
Miscellaneous costs—factory	4,420

Instructions

1. Prepare the statement of cost of goods manufactured.
2. Prepare the income statement.

Cases & Projects

Ethics

CP 18-1 Ethics in Action

Avett Manufacturing Company allows employees to purchase materials, such as metal and lumber, for personal use at a price equal to the company's cost. To purchase materials, an employee must complete a materials requisition form, which must then be approved by the employee's immediate supervisor. Brian Dadian, an assistant cost accountant, then charges the employee an amount based on Avett's net purchase cost.

Brian is in the process of replacing a deck on his home and has requisitioned lumber for personal use, which has been approved in accordance with company policy. In computing the cost of the lumber, Brian reviewed all the purchase invoices for the past year. He then used the lowest price to compute the amount due the company for the lumber.

The Institute of Management Accountants (IMA) is the professional organization for managerial accountants. The IMA has established four principles of ethical conduct for its members: honesty, fairness, objectivity, and responsibility. These principles are available at the IMA Web site: www.imanet.org.

Using the IMA's four principles of ethical conduct, evaluate Brian's behavior. Has he acted in an ethical manner? Why?

Team Activity

CP 18-2 Team Activity

In teams, visit a local restaurant. As you observe the operation, consider the costs associated with running the business. As a team, identify as many costs as you can and classify them according to the following table headings:

Cost	Direct Materials	Direct Labor	Overhead	Selling Expenses

Communication

CP 18-3 Communication

Todd Johnson is the vice president of Finance for Boz Zeppelin Industries, Inc. At a recent finance meeting, Todd made the following statement: "The managers of a company should use the same information as the shareholders of the firm. When managers use the same information to guide their internal operations as shareholders use in evaluating their investments, the managers will be aligned with the stockholders' profit objectives."

Prepare a one-half page memo to Todd discussing any concerns you might have with his statement.

CP 18-4 Managerial accounting in the management process

For each of the following managers, describe how managerial accounting could be used to satisfy strategic or operational objectives:

1. The vice president of the Information Systems Division of a bank.
2. A hospital administrator.
3. The chief executive officer of a food company. The food company is divided into three divisions: Nonalcoholic Beverages, Snack Foods, and Fast-Food Restaurants.
4. The manager of the local campus copy shop.

CP 18-5 Classifying costs

Geek Chic Company provides computer repair services for the community. Obie Won's computer was not working, and he called Geek Chic for a home repair visit. Geek Chic Company's technician arrived at 2:00 PM to begin work. By 4:00 PM, the problem was diagnosed as a failed circuit board. Unfortunately, the technician did not have a new circuit board in the truck because the technician's previous customer had the same problem and a board was used on that visit. Replacement boards were available back at Geek Chic Company's shop. Therefore, the technician drove back to the shop to retrieve a replacement board. From 4:00 to 5:00 PM, Geek Chic Company's technician drove the round trip to retrieve the replacement board from the shop.

At 5:00 PM, the technician was back on the job at Obie's home. The replacement procedure is somewhat complex because a variety of tests must be performed once the board is installed. The job was completed at 6:00 PM.

Obie's repair bill showed the following:

Circuit board	$100
Labor charges	300
Total	$400

Obie was surprised at the size of the bill and asked for more detail supporting the calculations. Geek Chic Company responded with the following explanations:

Cost of materials:	
Purchase price of circuit board	$ 80
Markup on purchase price to cover storage and handling	20
Total materials charge	$100

The labor charge per hour is detailed as follows:

2:00–3:00 PM	$ 70
3:00–4:00 PM	60
4:00–5:00 PM	80
5:00–6:00 PM	90
Total labor charge	$300

Further explanations in the differences in the hourly rates are as follows:

First hour:	
Base labor rate	$42
Fringe benefits	10
Overhead (other than storage and handling)	8
Total base labor rate	$60
Additional charge for first hour of any job to cover the cost of vehicle depreciation, fuel, and employee time in transit. A 30-minute transit time is assumed.	10
	$70
Third hour:	
Base labor rate	$60
The trip back to the shop includes vehicle depreciation and fuel; therefore, a charge was added to the hourly rate to cover these costs. The round trip took an hour.	20
	$80
Fourth hour:	
Base labor rate	$60
Overtime premium for time worked in excess of an eight-hour day (starting at 5:00 PM) is equal to 1.5 times the base rate.	30
	$90

1. If you were in Obie's position, how would you respond to the bill? Are there parts of the bill that appear incorrect to you? If so, what argument would you employ to convince Geek Chic Company that the bill is too high?
2. Use the headings that follow to construct a table. Fill in the table by listing the costs identified in the activity in the left-hand column. For each cost, place a check mark in the appropriate column identifying the correct cost classification. Assume that each service call is a job.

Cost	Direct Materials	Direct Labor	Overhead

CP 18-6 Using managerial accounting information

The following situations describe decision scenarios that could use managerial accounting information:

1. The manager of High Times Restaurant wants to determine the price to charge for various lunch plates.
2. By evaluating the cost of leftover materials, the plant manager of a precision tool facility wants to determine how effectively the plant is being run.
3. The division controller of West Coast Supplies needs to determine the cost of products left in inventory.
4. The manager of the Maintenance Department of a large manufacturing company wants to plan next year's anticipated expenditures.

For each situation, discuss how managerial accounting information could be used.

CHAPTER 19

Job Order Costing

Concepts and Principles

Chapter 18 *Introduction to Managerial Accounting*

Developing Information

COST SYSTEMS

Chapter 19 ***Job Order Costing***

Chapter 20 *Process Cost Systems*

COST BEHAVIOR

Chapter 21 *Cost-Volume-Profit Analysis*

Decision Making

EVALUATING PERFORMANCE

Chapter 22 *Budgeting*

Chapter 23 *Variances from Standard Costs*

COMPARING ALTERNATIVES

Chapter 24 *Decentralized Operations*

Chapter 25 *Differential Analysis, Product Pricing, and Activity-Based Costing*

Chapter 26 *Capital Investment Analysis*

BOB DAEMMRICH/PHOTOEDIT

Gibson Guitar

The selling price of a Gibson guitar ranges from less than $500 to over $11,000 for a Gibson 2015 Wes Montgomery electric guitar. These differences in selling prices reflect the quality of the materials and the craftsmanship required in making a guitar. In all cases, however, the selling price of a guitar must be greater than the cost of producing it. So how does **Gibson** determine the cost of producing a guitar?

Costs associated with creating a guitar include materials such as wood and strings, the wages of employees who build the guitar, and factory overhead. To determine the purchase price of a guitar, Gibson identifies and records the costs that go into the guitar during each step of the manufacturing process. As the guitar moves through the production process, the costs of direct materials, direct labor, and factory overhead are recorded. When the guitar is complete, the costs that have been recorded are added up to determine the cost of the guitar. The company then prices the guitar to achieve a level of profit.

This chapter describes a job order cost accounting system that illustrates how costs could be recorded and accumulated in manufacturing a guitar. The chapter also describes how a job order cost system could be used by service businesses.

Source: www.gibson.com/Gibson/History.aspx

Learning Objectives

After studying this chapter, you should be able to:

Example Exercises (EE) are shown in **green**.

Obj. 1 **Describe cost accounting systems used by manufacturing businesses.**

Cost Accounting Systems Overview
Job Order Cost Systems
Process Cost Systems

Obj. 2 **Describe and illustrate a job order cost accounting system.**

Job Order Cost Systems for Manufacturing Businesses

Materials	EE 19-1
Factory Labor	EE 19-2
Factory Overhead	EE 19-3, 19-4
Work in Process	EE 19-5
Finished Goods	
Sales and Cost of Goods Sold	
Period Costs	
Summary of Cost Flows for Legend Guitars	

Obj. 3 **Describe the use of job order cost information for decision making.**

Job Order Costing for Decision Making

Obj. 4 **Describe job order cost accounting systems for service businesses.**

Job Order Cost Systems for Service Businesses
Types of Service Businesses
Flow of Costs in a Service Job Order Cost System

At a Glance 19 Page 943

Obj. 1 Describe cost accounting systems used by manufacturing businesses.

Cost Accounting Systems Overview

Cost accounting systems measure, record, and report product costs. Managers use product costs for setting product prices, controlling operations, and developing financial statements.

The two main types of cost accounting systems for manufacturing operations are job order cost and process cost systems. Each system differs in how it accumulates and records costs.

Job Order Cost Systems

A **job order cost system** provides product costs for each quantity of product that is manufactured. Each quantity of product that is manufactured is called a *job*. Job order cost systems are often used by companies that manufacture custom products for customers or batches of similar products. For example, an apparel manufacturer such as Levi Strauss & Co. or a guitar manufacturer such as Gibson Guitars would use a job order cost system.

This chapter illustrates the job order cost system. As a basis for illustration, Legend Guitars, a manufacturer of guitars, is used.[1]

Process Cost Systems

A **process cost system** provides product costs for each manufacturing department or process. Process cost systems are often used by companies that manufacture units of a product that are indistinguishable from each other and are manufactured using a continuous production process. Examples are oil refineries, paper producers, chemical processors, and food processors. The process cost system is illustrated in Chapter 20.

1 Legend Guitars' manufacturing operation is described in more detail in Chapter 18.

Job Order Cost Systems for Manufacturing Businesses

Obj. 2 Describe and illustrate a job order cost accounting system.

A job order cost system records and summarizes manufacturing costs by jobs. The flow of manufacturing costs in a job order system is illustrated in Exhibit 1.

EXHIBIT 1

Flow of Manufacturing Costs

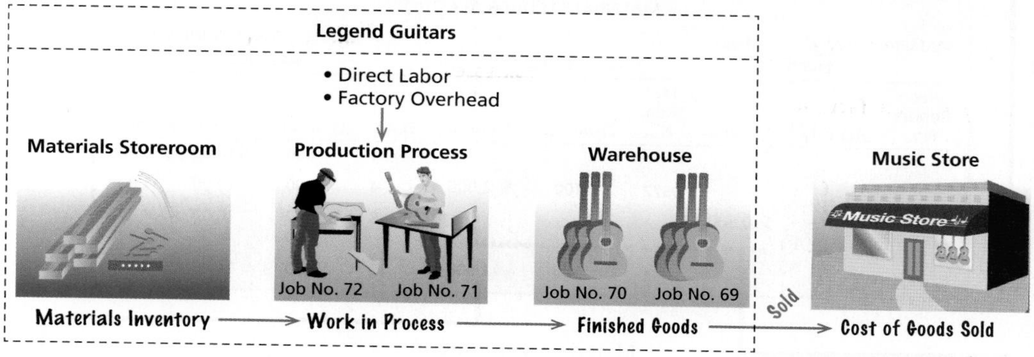

Exhibit 1 indicates that although the materials for Jobs 71 and 72 have been added, both jobs are still in the production process. Thus, Jobs 71 and 72 are part of *Work in Process Inventory*. In contrast, Exhibit 1 indicates that Jobs 69 and 70 have been completed. Thus, Jobs 69 and 70 are part of *Finished Goods Inventory*. Exhibit 1 also indicates that when finished guitars are sold to music stores, their costs become part of *Cost of Goods Sold*.

In a job order cost accounting system, perpetual inventory controlling accounts and subsidiary ledgers are maintained for materials, work in process, and finished goods inventories as shown in Exhibit 2.

Link to Gibson Guitars

At any one point in time, Gibson will have materials, work in process, and finished goods inventories.

EXHIBIT 2

Inventory Ledger Accounts

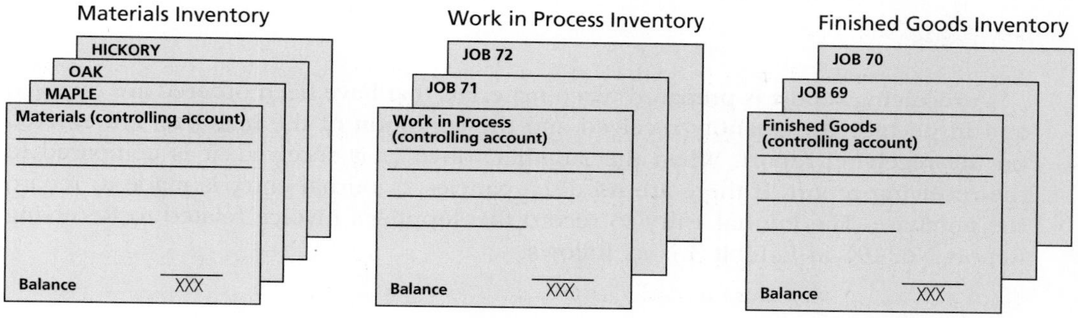

Materials

The materials account in the general ledger is a controlling account. A separate account for each type of material is maintained in a subsidiary **materials ledger**.

Exhibit 3 shows **Legend Guitars**' materials ledger account for maple. Increases (debits) and decreases (credits) to the materials account are as follows:

- Increases (debits) are based on *receiving reports* such as Receiving Report No. 196 for $10,500, which is supported by the supplier's invoice.

- Decreases (credits) are based on *materials requisitions* such as Requisition No. 672 for $2,000 for Job 71 and Requisition No. 704 for $11,000 for Job 72.

EXHIBIT 3

Materials Information and Cost Flows

Receiving Report No. 196 ← **Supplier Invoice $10,500**

MATERIALS LEDGER ACCOUNT

MATERIAL: No. 8 Wood—Maple — ORDER POINT: 500 ft.

RECEIVED			ISSUED			BALANCE			
Rec. Report No.	Quantity	Amount	Mat. Req. No.	Quantity	Amount	Date	Quantity	Unit Price	Amount
						Dec. 1	600	$10.00	$ 6,000
			672	200	$ 2,000	4	400	10.00	4,000
196	750	$10,500				8	400 750	10.00 14.00	4,000 10,500
			704	900	11,000	12	250	14.00	3,500

Materials Requisitions

MATERIALS REQUISITION

REQUISITION NO.: 672
JOB NO.: 71

Description	Quantity Issued	Unit Price	Amount
No. 8 Wood—Maple	200	$10.00	$2,000
Total Issued			$2,000

MATERIALS REQUISITION

REQUISITION NO.: 704
JOB NO.: 72

Description	Quantity Issued	Unit Price	Amount
No. 8 Wood—Maple No. 8 Wood—Maple	400 500	$10.00 14.00	$ 4,000 7,000
Total Issued			$11,000

Job Cost Sheets

Job 71
20 units of Jazz Series guitars

Balance, Dec. 1	$3,000
Direct Materials	2,000
Direct Labor	
Factory Overhead	

Job 72
60 units of American Series guitars

Direct Materials	$11,000
Direct Labor	
Factory Overhead	

Link to Gibson Guitars

Gibson Guitars uses a variety of woods (direct materials) in making guitars, including cedar.

A **receiving report** is prepared when materials that have been ordered are received and inspected. The quantity received and the condition of the materials are entered on the receiving report. When the supplier's invoice is received, it is compared to the receiving report. If there are no discrepancies, a journal entry is made to record the purchase. The journal entry to record the supplier's invoice related to Receiving Report No. 196 in Exhibit 3 is as follows:

a.	Materials		10,500	
	Accounts Payable			10,500
	Materials purchased during December.			

The storeroom releases materials for use in manufacturing when a **materials requisition** is received. Examples of materials requisitions are shown in Exhibit 3.

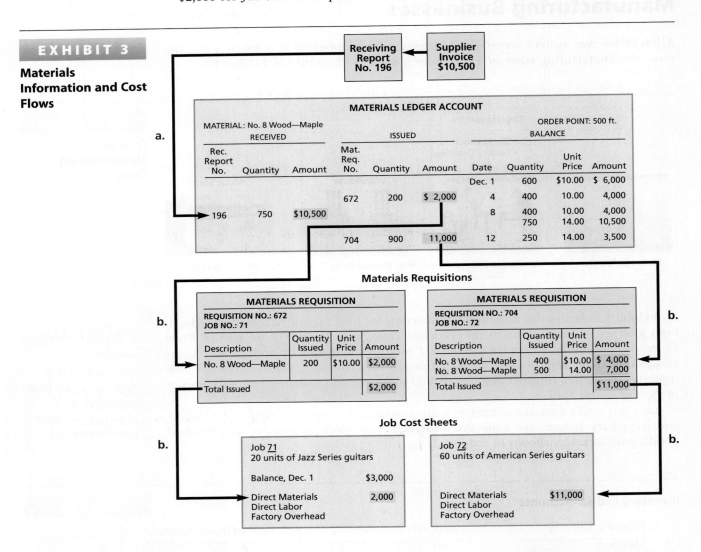

The materials requisitions for each job serve as the basis for recording materials used. For direct materials, the quantities and amounts from the materials requisitions are posted to job cost sheets. **Job cost sheets**, which are also illustrated in Exhibit 3, make up the work in process subsidiary ledger.

Exhibit 3 shows the posting of $2,000 of direct materials to Job 71 and $11,000 of direct materials to Job 72.[2] Job 71 is an order for 20 units of Jazz Series guitars, while Job 72 is an order for 60 units of American Series guitars.

A summary of the materials requisitions is used as a basis for the journal entry recording the materials used for the month. For direct materials, this entry increases (debits) Work in Process and decreases (credits) Materials as follows:

	b.	Work in Process	13,000	
		Materials		13,000
		Materials requisitioned to jobs ($2,000 + $11,000).		

Many companies use computerized information processes to record the use of materials. In such cases, storeroom employees electronically record the release of materials, which automatically updates the materials ledger and job cost sheets.

INTEGRITY, OBJECTIVITY, AND ETHICS IN BUSINESS

PHONY INVOICE SCAMS

A popular method for defrauding a company is to issue a phony invoice. The scam begins by initially contacting the target firm to discover details of key business contacts, business operations, and products. The swindler then uses this information to create a fictitious invoice. The invoice will include names, figures, and other details to give it the appearance of legitimacy. This type of scam can be avoided if invoices are matched with receiving documents prior to issuing a check.

Example Exercise 19-1 Issuance of Materials — Obj. 2

On March 5, Hatch Company purchased 400 units of raw materials at $14 per unit. During March, raw materials were requisitioned for production as follows: 200 units for Job 101 at $12 per unit and 300 units for Job 102 at $14 per unit. Journalize the entry on March 5 to record the purchase and on March 31 to record the requisition from the materials storeroom.

Follow My Example 19-1

Mar. 5	Materials	5,600*	
	Accounts Payable		5,600
31	Work in Process	6,600**	
	Materials		6,600

*$5,600 = 400 × $14

**Job 101	$2,400 = 200 × $12
Job 102	4,200 = 300 × $14
Total	$6,600

Practice Exercises: PE 19-1A, PE 19-1B

2 To simplify, Exhibit 4 and this chapter use the first-in, first-out cost flow method.

Factory Labor

When employees report for work, they may use *electronic badges, clock cards,* or *in-and-out cards* to clock in. When employees work on an individual job, they use **time tickets** to record the amount of time they have worked on a specific job. Exhibit 4 illustrates time tickets for Jobs 71 and 72 at **Legend Guitars**.

EXHIBIT 4

Labor Information and Cost Flows

Dynamic Exhibit

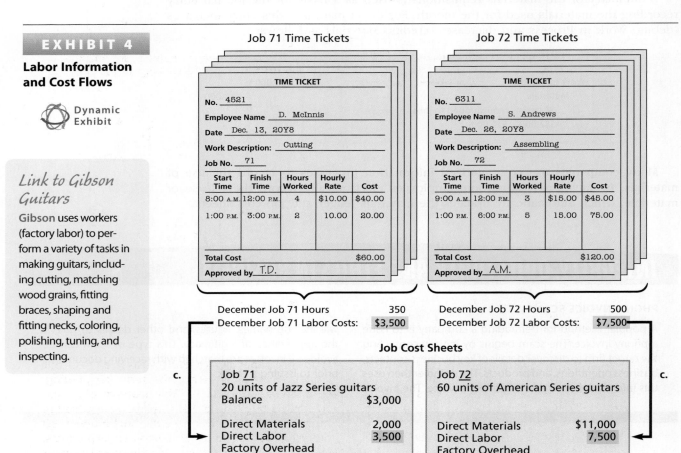

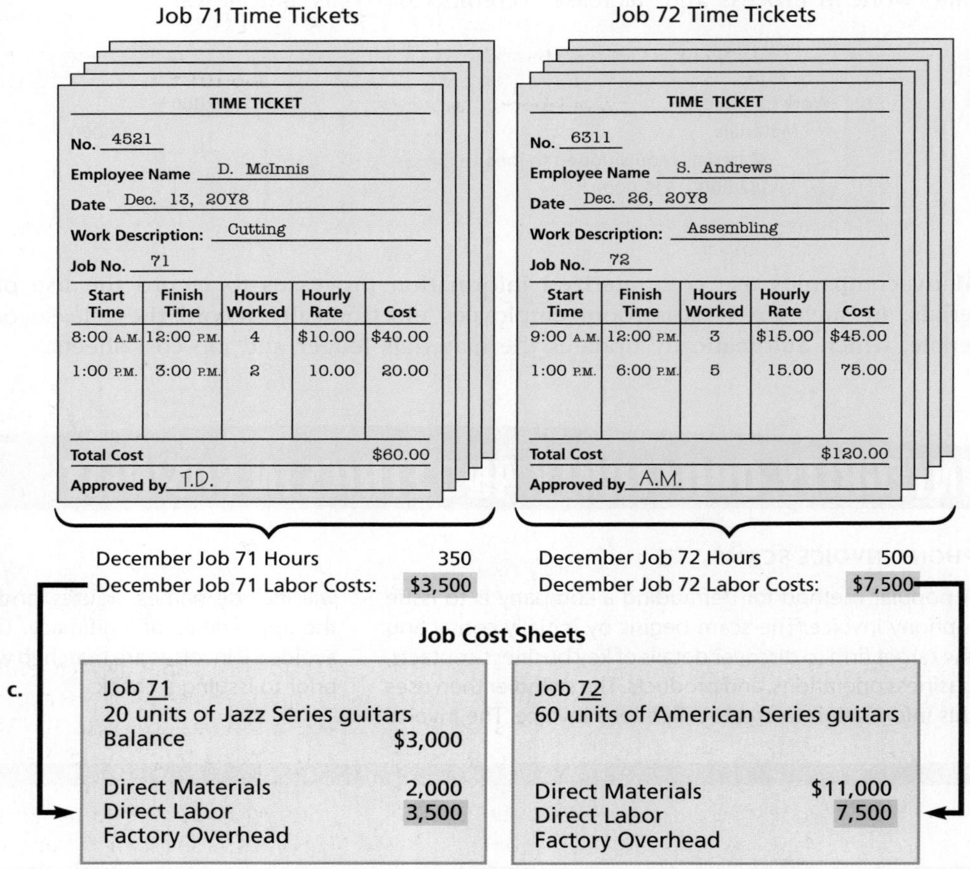

Link to Gibson Guitars

Gibson uses workers (factory labor) to perform a variety of tasks in making guitars, including cutting, matching wood grains, fitting braces, shaping and fitting necks, coloring, polishing, tuning, and inspecting.

Exhibit 4 shows that on December 13, 20Y8, D. McInnis spent six hours working on Job 71 at an hourly rate of $10 for a cost of $60 (6 hrs. × $10). Exhibit 4 also indicates that a total of 350 hours was spent by employees on Job 71 during December for a total cost of $3,500. This total direct labor cost of $3,500 is posted to the job cost sheet for Job 71, as shown in Exhibit 4.

Likewise, Exhibit 4 shows that on December 26, 20Y8, S. Andrews spent eight hours on Job 72 at an hourly rate of $15 for a cost of $120 (8 hrs. × $15). A total of 500 hours was spent by employees on Job 72 during December for a total cost of $7,500. This total direct labor cost of $7,500 is posted to the job cost sheet for Job 72, as shown in Exhibit 4.

A summary of the time tickets is used as the basis for the journal entry recording direct labor for the month. This entry increases (debits) Work in Process and increases (credits) Wages Payable, as follows:

	c.	Work in Process	11,000	
		Wages Payable		11,000
		Factory labor used in production of jobs ($3,500 + $7,500).		

As with direct materials, many businesses use computerized information processing to record direct labor. In such cases, employees may log their time directly into computer terminals at their workstations. In other cases, employees may be issued magnetic cards, much like credit cards, to log in and out of work assignments.

Example Exercise 19-2 Direct Labor Costs **Obj. 2**

During March, Hatch Company accumulated 800 hours of direct labor costs on Job 101 and 600 hours on Job 102. The total direct labor was incurred at a rate of $16 per direct labor hour for Job 101 and $12 per direct labor hour for Job 102. Journalize the entry to record the flow of labor costs into production during March.

Follow My Example 19-2

Work in Process	20,000*	
Wages Payable		20,000

*Job 101	$12,800	= 800 hrs. × $16
Job 102	7,200	= 600 hrs. × $12
Total	$20,000	

Practice Exercises: PE 19-2A, PE 19-2B

Business Connection

3D PRINTING

3D printing is a technology that creates a three-dimensional product from an "additive" process. "Additive" means the product is built from plastic, metal, or other material that is built layer by successive layer until the final object is complete. The layers are very thin, allowing for extremely precise final specifications. The process is like printing on a piece of paper (which adds a layer of ink), but in three dimensions, hence the term 3D printing. The machines that add the thin material layers are computer controlled, so that the layers are added in exactly the right way to create the final product. 3D printers can manufacture very complex final products. 3D printing fits well within a job shop environment because the technology provides an economical way to create custom products.

Factory Overhead

Factory overhead includes all manufacturing costs except direct materials and direct labor. Factory overhead costs come from a variety of sources, including the following:

- *Indirect materials* comes from a summary of materials requisitions.
- *Indirect labor* comes from the salaries of production supervisors and the wages of other employees such as janitors.
- *Factory power* comes from utility bills.
- *Factory depreciation* comes from Accounting Department computations of depreciation.

To illustrate the recording of factory overhead, assume that **Legend Guitars** incurred $4,600 of overhead during December, which included $500 of indirect materials, $2,000 of indirect labor, $900 of utilities, and $1,200 of factory depreciation.

The $500 of indirect materials consisted of $200 of glue and $300 of sandpaper. The entry to record the factory overhead is as follows:

		d.	Factory Overhead		4,600	
			Materials			500
			Wages Payable			2,000
			Utilities Payable			900
			Accumulated Depreciation			1,200
			Factory overhead incurred in production.			

Business Connection

ADVANCED ROBOTICS

Boston Consulting Group (BCG) believes that the use of advanced robotics in manufacturing is about to take off. It estimates that by 2025, 25% of all tasks will be automated through robotics, driving a 10–30% increase in productivity. China, the United States, Japan, Germany, and South Korea will be the primary drivers of this trend. BCG anticipates that significant use of advanced robotics will have a number of important impacts on manufacturing:

- Robotics will reduce the need to move factories to low-labor cost countries to save costs.
- Robotics will reduce the size of manufacturing facilities, allowing for greater flexibility and a more regional focus.
- The economic costs of robotics will decline, opening up their broad use.
- The workforce will require new skills, such as programming and technical maintenance, to support robotic manufacturing. For example, Shenzhen Everwin Precision Technology recently announced plans to replace 90% of its 1,800 employees with advanced robotics in the near future. The remaining employees will be retrained to work with the robots.

Increasing use of robots will cause direct labor to go down while factory overhead will increase. As a result, accurate factory overhead allocation will become increasingly important in these advanced manufacturing environments.

Source: Boston Consulting Group, *The Shifting Economics of Global Manufacturing: How a Takeoff in Advanced Robotics Will Power the Next Productivity Surge*, February 2015.

Example Exercise 19-3 Factory Overhead Costs

Obj. 2

During March, Hatch Company incurred factory overhead costs as follows: indirect materials, $800; indirect labor, $3,400; utilities cost, $1,600; and factory depreciation, $2,500. Journalize the entry to record the factory overhead incurred during March.

Follow My Example 19-3

Factory Overhead	8,300	
Materials		800
Wages Payable		3,400
Utilities Payable		1,600
Accumulated Depreciation—Factory		2,500

Practice Exercises: PE 19-3A, PE 19-3B

Allocating Factory Overhead Unlike direct labor and direct materials, factory overhead is *indirectly* related to the jobs. That is, factory overhead costs cannot be identified with or traced to specific jobs. For this reason, factory overhead costs are allocated to jobs. The process by which factory overhead or other costs are assigned to a cost object, such as a job, is called **cost allocation**.

The factory overhead costs are *allocated* to jobs using a common measure related to each job. This measure is called an **activity base**, *allocation base*, or *activity driver*. The activity base used to allocate overhead should reflect the consumption or use of factory overhead costs. Three common activity bases used to allocate factory overhead costs are direct labor hours, direct labor cost, and machine hours.

Predetermined Factory Overhead Rate Factory overhead costs are normally allocated or *applied* to jobs using a **predetermined factory overhead rate**. The predetermined factory overhead rate is computed as follows:

$$\text{Predetermined Factory Overhead Rate} = \frac{\text{Estimated Total Factory Overhead Costs}}{\text{Estimated Activity Base}}$$

To illustrate, assume that Legend Guitars estimates the total factory overhead cost as $50,000 for the year and the activity base as 10,000 direct labor hours. The predetermined factory overhead rate of $5 per direct labor hour is computed as follows:

$$\text{Predetermined Factory Overhead Rate} = \frac{\$50{,}000}{10{,}000\text{ direct labor hours}} = \$5\text{ per direct labor hour}$$

As illustrated, the predetermined overhead rate is computed using *estimated* amounts at the beginning of the period. This is because managers need timely information on the product costs of each job. If a company waited until all overhead costs were known at the end of the period, the allocated factory overhead would be accurate but not timely. Only through timely reporting can managers adjust manufacturing methods or product pricing.

Many companies use a more precise method for accumulating and allocating factory overhead costs called **activity-based costing**. This method uses a different overhead rate for each type of factory overhead activity, such as inspecting, moving, and machining. Activity-based costing is discussed and illustrated in Chapter 25.

Applying Factory Overhead to Work in Process Legend Guitars applies factory overhead using a rate of $5 per direct labor hour. The factory overhead applied to each job is recorded in the job cost sheets, as shown in Exhibit 5.

Exhibit 5 shows that 850 direct labor hours were used in Legend Guitars' December operations. Based on the time tickets, 350 hours can be traced to Job 71 and 500 hours can be traced to Job 72.

Using a factory overhead rate of $5 per direct labor hour, $4,250 of factory overhead is applied as follows:

	Direct Labor Hours	Factory Overhead Rate	Factory Overhead Applied
Job 71	350	$5	$1,750 (350 hrs. × $5)
Job 72	500	5	2,500 (500 hrs. × $5)
Total	850		$4,250

As shown in Exhibit 5, the applied overhead is posted to each job cost sheet. Factory overhead of $1,750 is posted to Job 71, which results in a total product cost on December 31, 20Y8, of $10,250. Factory overhead of $2,500 is posted to Job 72, which results in a total product cost on December 31, 20Y8, of $21,000.

The journal entry to apply factory overhead increases (debits) Work in Process and credits Factory Overhead. This journal entry to apply overhead to Jobs 71 and 72 is as follows:

e.	Work in Process		4,250	
	Factory Overhead			4,250
	Factory overhead applied to jobs according to the predetermined overhead rate (850 hrs. × $5).			

EXHIBIT 5

Applying Factory Overhead to Jobs

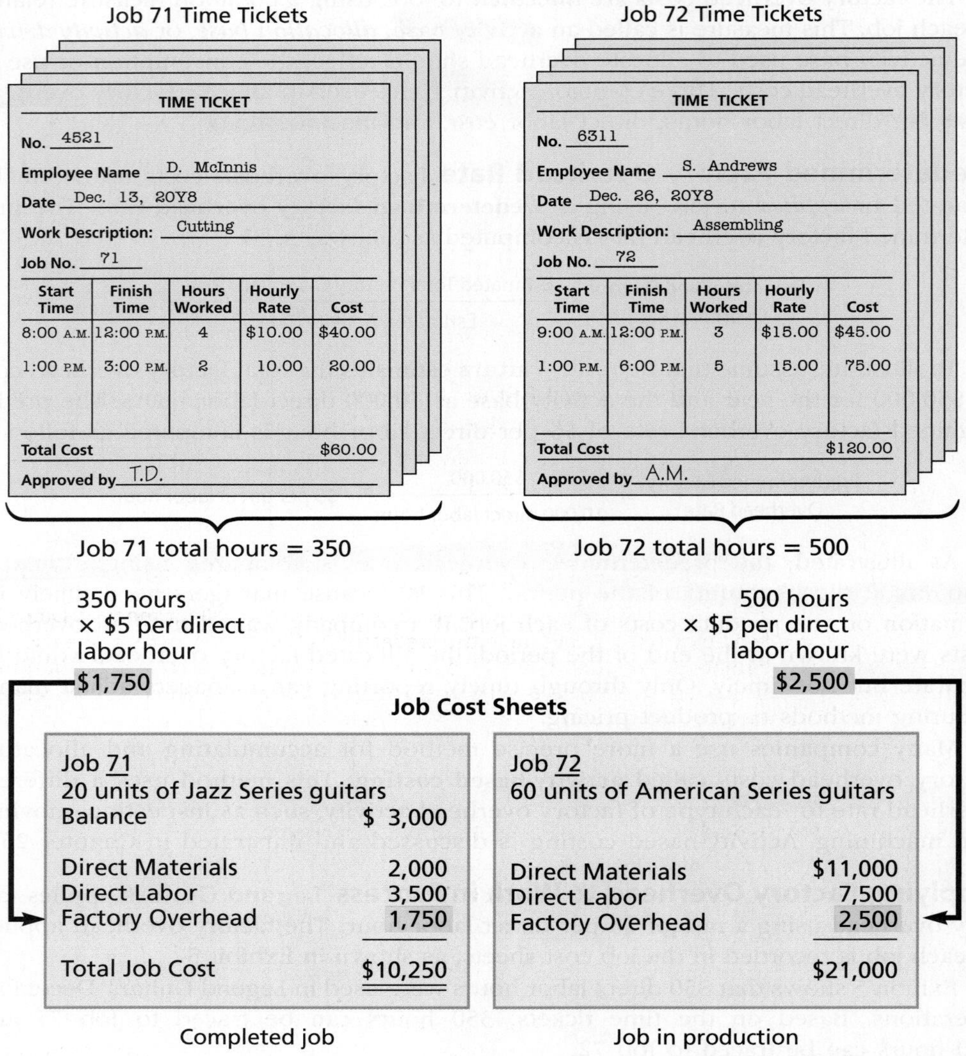

To summarize, the factory overhead account is:

- Increased (debited) for the *actual overhead* costs incurred, as shown for transaction (d).
- Decreased (credited) for the *applied overhead*, as shown for transaction (e).

The actual and applied overhead usually differ because the actual overhead costs are normally different from the estimated overhead costs. Depending on whether actual overhead is greater or less than applied overhead, the factory overhead account will have either a debit or credit ending balance as follows:

- If the applied overhead is *less than* the actual overhead incurred, the factory overhead account will have a debit balance. This debit balance is called **underapplied factory overhead** or *underabsorbed factory overhead*.
- If the applied overhead is *more than* the actual overhead incurred, the factory overhead account will have a credit balance. This credit balance is called **overapplied factory overhead** or *overabsorbed factory overhead*.

The factory overhead account for Legend Guitars, which follows, illustrates both underapplied and overapplied factory overhead. Specifically, the December 1, 20Y8, credit balance of $200 represents overapplied factory overhead. In contrast, the December 31, 20Y8, debit balance of $150 represents underapplied factory overhead.

Account *Factory Overhead* *Account No.*

Date		Item	Post. Ref.	Debit	Credit	Balance Debit	Balance Credit
20Y8 Dec.	1	Balance					200
	31	Factory overhead cost incurred		4,600		4,400	
	31	Factory overhead cost applied			4,250	150	

Underapplied balance (150)
Overapplied balance (200)

If the balance of factory overhead (either underapplied or overapplied) becomes large, the balance and related overhead rate should be investigated. For example, a large balance could be caused by changes in manufacturing methods. In this case, the factory overhead rate should be revised.

Example Exercise 19-4 Applying Factory Overhead — Obj. 2

Hatch Company estimates that total factory overhead costs will be $100,000 for the year. Direct labor hours are estimated to be 25,000. For Hatch Company, (a) determine the predetermined factory overhead rate using direct labor hours as the activity base, (b) determine the amount of factory overhead applied to Jobs 101 and 102 in March using the data on direct labor hours from Example Exercise 19-2, and (c) prepare the journal entry to apply factory overhead to both jobs in March according to the predetermined overhead rate.

Follow My Example 19-4

a. $4.00 per direct labor hour = $100,000 ÷ 25,000 direct labor hours

b.

Job 101	$3,200	= 800 hours × $4.00 per hour
Job 102	2,400	= 600 hours × $4.00 per hour
Total	$5,600	

c.

Work in Process	5,600	
Factory Overhead		5,600

Practice Exercises: PE 19-4A, PE 19-4B

Disposal of Factory Overhead Balance During the year, the balance in the factory overhead account is carried forward and reported as a deferred debit or credit on the monthly (interim) balance sheets. However, any balance in the factory overhead account should not be carried over to the next year. This is because any such balance applies only to operations of the current year.

If the estimates for computing the predetermined overhead rate are reasonably accurate, the ending balance of Factory Overhead should be relatively small. For this reason, the balance of Factory Overhead at the end of the year is disposed of by transferring it to the cost of goods sold account as follows:[3]

- If there is an ending debit balance (underapplied overhead) in the factory overhead account, it is disposed of by the entry that follows:

		Cost of Goods Sold		XXX	
		Factory Overhead			XXX
		Transfer of underapplied overhead to cost of goods sold.			

Link to Gibson Guitars

Gibson incurs a variety of overhead costs in making guitars, including depreciation on buildings and equipment.

3 An ending balance in the factory overhead account may also be allocated among the work in process, finished goods, and cost of goods sold accounts. This brings these accounts into agreement with the actual costs incurred. This approach is rarely used and is only required for large ending balances in the factory overhead account. For this reason, it will not be used in this text.

- If there is an ending credit balance (overapplied overhead) in the factory overhead account, it is disposed of by the entry that follows:

	Factory Overhead		XXX	
	Cost of Goods Sold			XXX
	Transfer of overapplied overhead to cost of goods sold.			

To illustrate, the journal entry to dispose of **Legend Guitars**' December 31, 20Y8, underapplied overhead balance of $150 is as follows:

f.	Cost of Goods Sold		150	
	Factory Overhead			150
	Closed underapplied factory overhead to cost of goods sold.			

Work in Process

During the period, Work in Process is increased (debited) for the following:

- Direct materials cost
- Direct labor cost
- Applied factory overhead cost

To illustrate, the work in process account for **Legend Guitars** is shown in Exhibit 6. The balance of Work in Process on December 1, 20Y8 (beginning balance), was $3,000.

EXHIBIT 6

Job Cost Sheets and the Work in Process Controlling Account

Job Cost Sheets

Job 71	
20 units of Jazz Series guitars	
Balance	$ 3,000
Direct Materials	2,000
Direct Labor	3,500
Factory Overhead	1,750
Total Job Cost	$10,250
Unit Cost	$512.50

Job 72	
60 units of American Series guitars	
Direct Materials	$11,000
Direct Labor	7,500
Factory Overhead	2,500
Total Job Cost	$21,000

g.

Account *Work in Process* — *Account No.*

Date		Item	Post. Ref.	Debit	Credit	Balance Debit	Balance Credit
20Y8 Dec.	1	Balance				3,000	
	31	Direct materials		13,000		16,000	
	31	Direct labor		11,000		27,000	
	31	Factory overhead		4,250		31,250	
	31	Jobs completed—Job 71			10,250	21,000	

As shown in Exhibit 6, this balance relates to Job 71, which was the only job in process on this date. During December, Work in Process was debited for the following:

- Direct materials cost of $13,000 [transaction (b)] based on materials requisitions
- Direct labor cost of $11,000 [transaction (c)] based on time tickets
- Applied factory overhead of $4,250 [transaction (e)] based on the predetermined overhead rate of $5 per direct labor hour

The preceding Work in Process debits are supported by the detail postings to job cost sheets for Jobs 71 and 72, as shown in Exhibit 6.

During December, Job 71 was completed. Upon completion, the product costs (direct materials, direct labor, factory overhead) are totaled. This total is divided by the number of units produced to determine the cost per unit. Thus, the 20 Jazz Series guitars produced as Job 71 cost $512.50 ($10,250 ÷ 20) per guitar.

After completion, Job 71 is transferred from Work in Process to Finished Goods by the following entry:

	g.	Finished Goods	10,250	
		Work in Process		10,250
		Job 71 completed in December.		

Job 72 was started in December but was not completed by December 31, 20Y8. Thus, Job 72 is still part of work in process on December 31, 20Y8. As shown in Exhibit 6, the balance of the job cost sheet for Job 72 ($21,000) is also the December 31, 20Y8, balance of Work in Process.

Example Exercise 19-5 Job Costs

Obj. 2

At the end of March, Hatch Company had completed Jobs 101 and 102. Job 101 is for 500 units, and Job 102 is for 1,000 units. Using the data from Example Exercises 19-1, 19-2, and 19-4, determine (a) the balance on the job cost sheets for Jobs 101 and 102 at the end of March and (b) the cost per unit for Jobs 101 and 102 at the end of March.

Follow My Example 19-5

a.

	Job 101	Job 102
Direct materials	$ 2,400	$ 4,200
Direct labor	12,800	7,200
Factory overhead	3,200	2,400
Total costs	$18,400	$13,800

b. Job 101 $36.80 = $18,400 ÷ 500 units
Job 102 $13.80 = $13,800 ÷ 1,000 units

Practice Exercises: PE 19-5A, PE 19-5B

Finished Goods

The finished goods account is a controlling account for the subsidiary **finished goods ledger** or *stock ledger*. Each account in the finished goods ledger contains cost data for the units manufactured, units sold, and units on hand.

Exhibit 7 illustrates the finished goods ledger account for **Legend Guitars**' Jazz Series guitars.

Exhibit 7 indicates that 40 Jazz Series guitars were on hand on December 1, 20Y8. During the month, 20 additional Jazz guitars were completed and transferred to Finished Goods from the completion of Job 71. In addition, the beginning inventory of 40 Jazz guitars was sold during the month.

EXHIBIT 7

Finished Goods Ledger Account

ITEM: *Jazz Series guitars*

Manufactured			Shipped			Balance			
Job Order No.	Quantity	Amount	Ship Order No.	Quantity	Amount	Date	Quantity	Amount	Unit Cost
						Dec. 1	40	$20,000	$500.00
			643	40	$20,000	9	—	—	—
71	20	$10,250				31	20	10,250	512.50

Sales and Cost of Goods Sold

Link to Gibson Guitars

A virtual tour of **Gibson**'s Bozeman, Montana, manufacturing plant can be found at www2.gibson.com. The Bozeman plant makes acoustical guitars similar to those illustrated in this chapter. Acoustical guitars that do not require power or amps to produce sound are often used for folk and country music. Electric guitars are most often used for heavy metal and rock music.

During December, **Legend Guitars** sold 40 Jazz Series guitars for $850 each, generating total sales of $34,000 ($850 × 40 guitars). Exhibit 7 indicates that the cost of these guitars was $500 per guitar, or a total cost of $20,000 ($500 × 40 guitars). The entries to record the sale and related cost of goods sold are as follows:

	h.	Accounts Receivable		34,000		
		Sales			34,000	
		Revenue received from guitars sold on account.				

	i.	Cost of Goods Sold		20,000		
		Finished Goods			20,000	
		Cost of 40 Jazz Series guitars sold.				

In a job order cost accounting system, the preparation of a statement of cost of goods manufactured, which was discussed in Chapter 18, is not necessary. This is because job order costing uses the perpetual inventory system; thus, the cost of goods sold can be determined directly from the finished goods ledger as illustrated in Exhibit 7.

Period Costs

Period costs are used in generating revenue during the current period but are not involved in the manufacturing process. As discussed in Chapter 18, *period costs* are recorded as expenses of the current period as either selling or administrative expenses.

Selling expenses are incurred in marketing the product and delivering sold products to customers. Administrative expenses are incurred in managing the company but are not related to the manufacturing or selling functions. During December, **Legend Guitars** recorded the following selling and administrative expenses:

	j.	Sales Salaries Expense		2,000		
		Office Salaries Expense		1,500		
		Salaries Payable			3,500	
		Recorded December period costs.				

Summary of Cost Flows for Legend Guitars

Exhibit 8 shows the cost flows through the manufacturing accounts of **Legend Guitars** for December. In addition, summary details of the following subsidiary ledgers are shown:

- *Materials Ledger*—the subsidiary ledger for Materials

EXHIBIT 8 **Flow of Manufacturing Costs for Legend Guitars**

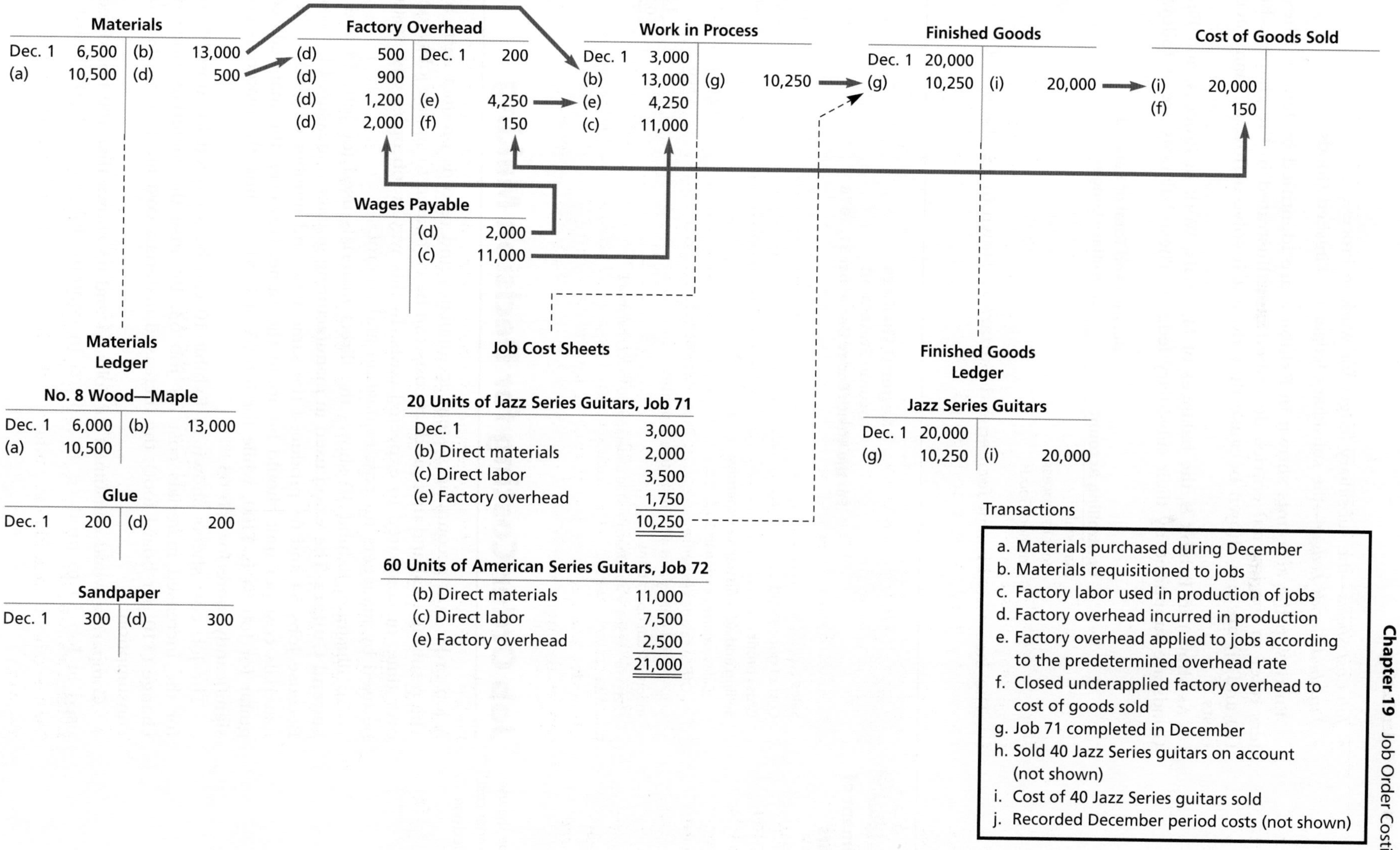

- *Job Cost Sheets*—the subsidiary ledger for Work in Process
- *Finished Goods Ledger*—the subsidiary ledger for Finished Goods

Entries in the accounts shown in Exhibit 8 are identified by letters. These letters refer to the journal entries described and illustrated in the chapter. Entries (h) and (j) are not shown because they do not involve a flow of manufacturing costs.

As shown in Exhibit 8, the balances of Materials, Work in Process, and Finished Goods are supported by their subsidiary ledgers. These balances are as follows:

Controlling Account	Balance and Total of Related Subsidiary Ledger
Materials	$ 3,500
Work in Process	21,000
Finished Goods	10,250

The income statement for Legend Guitars is shown in Exhibit 9.

EXHIBIT 9

Income Statement of Legend Guitars

Legend Guitars
Income Statement
For the Month Ended December 31, 20Y8

Sales		$34,000
Cost of goods sold		20,150*
Gross profit		$13,850
Selling and administrative expenses:		
Sales salaries expense	$2,000	
Office salaries expense	1,500	
Total selling and administrative expenses		3,500
Income from operations		$10,350

*$20,150 = ($500 × 40 guitars) + $150 underapplied factory overhead

Obj. 3 Describe the use of job order cost information for decision making.

Job Order Costing for Decision Making

A job order cost accounting system accumulates and records product costs by jobs. The resulting total and unit product costs can be compared to similar jobs, compared over time, or compared to expected costs. In this way, a job order cost system can be used by managers for cost evaluation and control.

To illustrate, Exhibit 10 shows the direct materials used for Jobs 54 and 63 for Legend Guitars. The wood used in manufacturing guitars is measured in board feet. Because Jobs 54 and 63 produced the same type and number of guitars, the direct materials cost per unit should be about the same. However, the materials cost per guitar for Job 54 is $100, while for Job 63, it is $125. Thus, the materials costs are significantly more for Job 63.

The job cost sheets shown in Exhibit 10 can be analyzed for possible reasons for the increased materials cost for Job 63. Because the materials price did not change ($10 per board foot), the increased materials cost must be related to wood consumption.

Comparing wood consumed for Jobs 54 and 63 shows that 400 board feet were used in Job 54 to produce 40 guitars. In contrast, Job 63 used 500 board feet to

EXHIBIT 10

Comparing Data from Job Cost Sheets

Job 54
Item: 40 Jazz Series guitars

	Materials Quantity (board feet)	Materials Price	Materials Amount
Direct materials:			
No. 8 Wood—Maple	400	$10.00	$4,000
Direct materials per guitar			$ 100*

*$4,000 ÷ 40

Job 63
Item: 40 Jazz Series guitars

	Materials Quantity (board feet)	Materials Price	Materials Amount
Direct materials:			
No. 8 Wood—Maple	500	$10.00	$5,000
Direct materials per guitar			$ 125*

*$5,000 ÷ 40

produce the same number of guitars. Thus, an investigation should be undertaken to determine the cause of the extra 100 board feet used for Job 63. Possible explanations could include the following:

- A new employee who was not properly trained cut the wood for Job 63. As a result, there was excess waste and scrap.
- The wood used for Job 63 was purchased from a new supplier. The wood was of poor quality, which created excessive waste and scrap.
- The cutting tools needed repair and were not properly maintained. As a result, the wood was miscut, which created excessive waste and scrap.
- The instructions attached to the job were incorrect. The wood was cut according to the instructions. The incorrect instructions were discovered later in assembly. As a result, the wood had to be recut and the initial cuttings scrapped.

Job Order Cost Systems for Service Businesses

Obj. 4 Describe job order cost accounting systems for service businesses.

A job order cost accounting system may be used by a service business. However, whether a service business uses a job order cost system depends upon the nature of the service provided to customers.

Types of Service Businesses

Hotels, taxis, newspapers, attorneys, accountants, and hospitals provide services to customers. Some of these businesses, such as law firms, accounting firms, and hospitals, rely on job order costing to manage and control costs. However, not all service businesses are able to practically apply job order costing. These include businesses such as hotels, taxi services, and newspapers.

A service business using job order costing normally renders a service that is unique to each customer with related costs that vary significantly with each customer. For example, while hotels provide a service, the service is the same for each guest on any given night.

In contrast, an attorney or a hospital provides a unique service for each client or patient. In addition, each client or patient incurs costs that are unique to him or her. For this reason, law firms and hospitals normally use job order cost systems.[4] Other examples of service businesses using job order cost systems include advertising agencies, event planners, and car repair shops.

Flow of Costs in a Service Job Order Cost System

A service business using a job order cost system views each customer, client, or patient as a separate job for which costs are accumulated and reported.

Since a service is being provided, the primary product costs are normally direct labor and overhead. Any materials or supplies used in rendering services are usually insignificant. As a result, materials and supply costs may be included as part of the overhead cost.

Like a manufacturing business, the direct labor and overhead costs of rendering services to clients are accumulated in a work in process account. Work in Process is supported by a cost ledger with a job cost sheet for each client.

When a job is completed and the client is billed, the costs are transferred to a cost of services account. Cost of Services is similar to the cost of goods sold account for a merchandising or manufacturing business. A finished goods account and related finished goods ledger are not necessary. This is because services cannot be inventoried and the revenues for the services are recorded upon completion.

In practice, other considerations unique to service businesses may need to be considered. For example, a service business may bill clients on a weekly or monthly basis rather than upon completion of a job. In such cases, a portion of the costs related to each billing is transferred from the work in process account to the cost of services account. A service business may also bill clients for services in advance, which would be accounted for as deferred revenue until the services are completed.

The flow of costs through a service business using a job order cost accounting system is shown in Exhibit 11.

EXHIBIT 11 **Flow of Costs Through a Service Business**

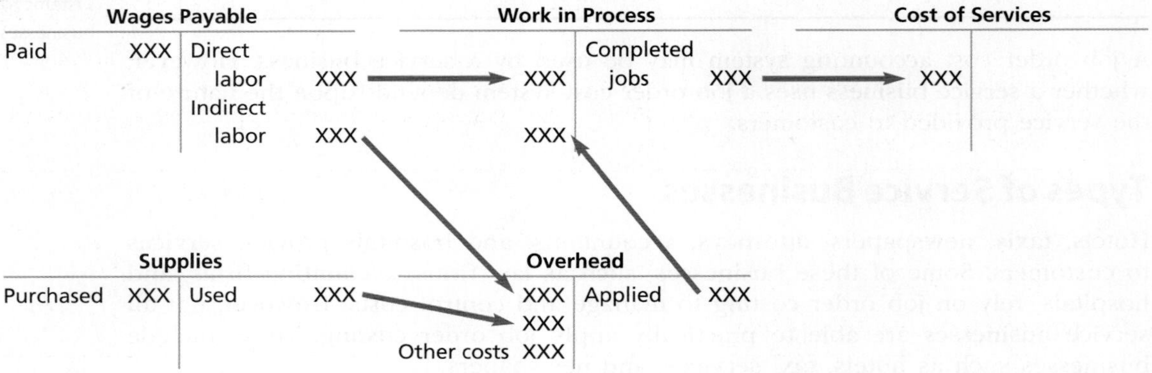

4 Service businesses using job order cost systems normally require each customer, client, or patient to sign a contract that describes the nature of the service being rendered.

SERVICE FOCUS

JOB ORDER COSTING IN A LAW FIRM

Law firms typically use job order costing to track the costs of individual legal cases or client engagements. The costs of each job are accumulated in a job cost sheet, just as in a manufacturing firm. However, because a law firm is a service firm, there are no direct materials costs. The primary cost comes from the direct labor of the professional staff.

Law firms like Constangy, Brooks, Smith & Prophete, a national law firm specializing in employment law and labor relations, uses a job order costing system to track the cost of individual cases. The direct labor costs of the professional staff are determined by multiplying the time that each attorney spends on an individual case by the attorney's hourly billing rate. Billing rates vary depending on the rank of the attorney doing the work. In addition, any costs that can be attributed directly to a specific engagement are added to the engagement's job cost sheet. For example, if a case requires the legal team to travel to another city to interview witnesses, the cost of that travel is added to the job cost sheet for that specific client. Indirect costs such as support staff, office supplies, and office rent are accumulated as overhead costs and allocated to individual jobs using an activity base such as professional service hours.

At a Glance 19

Obj. 1 Describe cost accounting systems used by manufacturing businesses.

Key Points A cost accounting system accumulates product costs. The two primary cost accounting systems are the job order and the process cost systems. Job order cost systems accumulate costs for each quantity of product that passes through the factory. Process cost systems accumulate costs for each department or process within the factory.

Learning Outcomes	Example Exercises	Practice Exercises
• Describe a cost accounting system.		
• Describe a job order cost system.		
• Describe a process cost system.		

Obj. 2 **Describe and illustrate a job order cost accounting system.**

Key Points A job order cost system accumulates costs for each quantity of product, or "job," that passes through the factory. Direct materials, direct labor, and factory overhead are accumulated on the job cost sheet, which is the subsidiary cost ledger for each job. Direct materials and direct labor are assigned to individual jobs based on the quantity used. Factory overhead costs are assigned to each job based on an activity base that reflects the use of factory overhead costs.

Learning Outcomes	Example Exercises	Practice Exercises
• Describe the flow of materials and how materials costs are assigned.		
• Prepare the journal entry to record materials used in production.	EE19-1	PE19-1A, 19-1B
• Describe how factory labor hours are recorded and how labor costs are assigned.		
• Prepare the journal entry to record factory labor used in production.	EE19-2	PE19-2A, 19-2B
• Describe and illustrate how factory overhead costs are accumulated and assigned.	EE19-3 EE19-4	PE19-3A, 19-3B PE19-4A, 19-4B
• Compute the predetermined overhead rate.	EE19-4	PE19-4A, 19-4B
• Describe and illustrate how to dispose of the balance in the factory overhead account.		
• Describe and illustrate how costs are accumulated for work in process and finished goods inventories.	EE19-5	PE19-5A, 19-5B
• Describe how costs are assigned to the cost of goods sold.	EE19-6	PE19-6A, 19-6B
• Describe and illustrate the flow of costs.		

Obj. 3 **Describe the use of job order cost information for decision making.**

Key Points Job order cost systems can be used to evaluate cost performance. Unit costs can be compared over time to determine whether product costs are staying within expected ranges.

Learning Outcome	Example Exercises	Practice Exercises
• Describe and illustrate how job cost sheets can be used to investigate possible reasons for increased product costs.		

Obj. 4 **Describe job order cost accounting systems for service businesses.**

Key Points Job order cost accounting systems can be used by service businesses to plan and control operations. Because the product is a service, the focus is on direct labor and overhead costs. The costs of providing a service are accumulated in a work in process account and transferred to a cost of services account upon completion.

Learning Outcome	Example Exercises	Practice Exercises
• Describe how service businesses use a job order cost system.		

Illustrative Problem

Wildwing Entertainment Inc. is a manufacturer that uses a job order cost system. The following data summarize the operations related to production for March, the first month of operations:

a. Materials purchased on account, $15,500.

b. Materials requisitioned and labor used:

	Materials	Factory Labor
Job No. 100	$2,650	$1,770
Job No. 101	1,240	650
Job No. 102	980	420
Job No. 103	3,420	1,900
Job No. 104	1,000	500
Job No. 105	2,100	1,760
For general factory use	450	650

c. Factory overhead costs incurred on account, $2,700.

d. Depreciation of machinery, $1,750.

e. Factory overhead is applied at a rate of 70% of direct labor cost.

f. Jobs completed: Nos. 100, 101, 102, 104.

g. Jobs 100, 101, and 102 were shipped, and customers were billed for $8,100, $3,800, and $3,500, respectively.

Instructions

1. Journalize the entries to record these transactions.
2. Determine the account balances for Work in Process and Finished Goods.
3. Prepare a schedule of unfinished jobs to support the balance in the work in process account.
4. Prepare a schedule of completed jobs on hand to support the balance in the finished goods account.

Solution

		Debit	Credit
1.	a. Materials	15,500	
	Accounts Payable		15,500
	b. Work in Process	11,390	
	Materials		11,390
	Work in Process	7,000	
	Wages Payable		7,000
	Factory Overhead	1,100	
	Materials		450
	Wages Payable		650
	c. Factory Overhead	2,700	
	Accounts Payable		2,700
	d. Factory Overhead	1,750	
	Accumulated Depreciation—Machinery		1,750
	e. Work in Process	4,900	
	Factory Overhead (70% of $7,000)		4,900
	f. Finished Goods	11,548	
	Work in Process		11,548

(Continued)

Computation of the cost of jobs finished:

Job	Direct Materials	Direct Labor	Factory Overhead	Total
Job No. 100	$2,650	$1,770	$1,239	$ 5,659
Job No. 101	1,240	650	455	2,345
Job No. 102	980	420	294	1,694
Job No. 104	1,000	500	350	1,850
				$11,548

g. Accounts Receivable	15,400	
Sales		15,400
Cost of Goods Sold	9,698	
Finished Goods		9,698

Cost of jobs sold computation:

Job No. 100	$5,659
Job No. 101	2,345
Job No. 102	1,694
	$9,698

2. Work in Process: $11,742 ($11,390 + $7,000 + $4,900 – $11,548)

Finished Goods: $1,850 ($11,548 – $9,698)

3. **Schedule of Unfinished Jobs**

Job	Direct Materials	Direct Labor	Factory Overhead	Total
Job No. 103	$3,420	$1,900	$1,330	$ 6,650
Job No. 105	2,100	1,760	1,232	5,092
Balance of Work in Process, March 31				$11,742

4. **Schedule of Completed Jobs**

Job No. 104:	
Direct materials	$1,000
Direct labor	500
Factory overhead	350
Balance of Finished Goods, March 31	$1,850

Key Terms

activity base (933)
activity-based costing (933)
cost accounting systems (926)
cost allocation (932)
finished goods ledger (937)
job cost sheets (929)
job order cost system (926)
materials ledger (927)
materials requisition (928)
overapplied factory overhead (934)
predetermined factory overhead rate (933)
process cost system (926)
receiving report (928)
time tickets (930)
underapplied factory overhead (934)

Discussion Questions

1. a. Name two principal types of cost accounting systems.
   b. Which system provides for a separate record of each particular quantity of product that passes through the factory?
   c. Which system accumulates the costs for each department or process within the factory?
2. What kind of firm would use a job order cost system?
3. Which account is used in the job order cost system to accumulate direct materials, direct labor, and factory overhead applied to production costs for individual jobs?
4. What document is the source for (a) debiting the accounts in the materials ledger and (b) crediting the accounts in the materials ledger?
5. What is a job cost sheet?
6. What is the difference between a clock card and time ticket?
7. Discuss how the predetermined factory overhead rate can be used in job order cost accounting to assist management in pricing jobs.
8. a. How is a predetermined factory overhead rate calculated?
   b. Name three common bases used in calculating the rate.
9. a. What is (1) overapplied factory overhead and (2) underapplied factory overhead?
   b. If the factory overhead account has a debit balance, was factory overhead underapplied or overapplied?
10. Describe how a job order cost system can be used for professional service businesses.

Practice Exercises

Example Exercises

Show Me How

EE 19-1 *p. 929*

PE 19-1A Issuance of materials **OBJ. 2**

On May 7, Bergan Company purchased on account 10,000 units of raw materials at $8 per unit. During May, raw materials were requisitioned for production as follows: 7,500 units for Job 200 at $8 per unit and 1,480 units for Job 305 at $5 per unit. Journalize the entry on May 7 to record the purchase and on May 31 to record the requisition from the materials storeroom.

Show Me How

EE 19-1 *p. 929*

PE 19-1B Issuance of materials **OBJ. 2**

On August 4, Rothchild Company purchased on account 12,000 units of raw materials at $14 per unit. During August, raw materials were requisitioned for production as follows: 5,000 units for Job 40 at $8 per unit and 6,200 units for Job 42 at $14 per unit. Journalize the entry on August 4 to record the purchase and on August 31 to record the requisition from the materials storeroom.

Show Me How

EE 19-2 *p. 931*

PE 19-2A Direct labor costs **OBJ. 2**

During May, Bergan Company accumulated 2,500 hours of direct labor costs on Job 200 and 3,000 hours on Job 305. The total direct labor was incurred at a rate of $28 per direct labor hour for Job 200 and $24 per direct labor hour for Job 305. Journalize the entry to record the flow of labor costs into production during May.

Show Me How EE 19-2 p. 931

PE 19-2B Direct labor costs OBJ. 2

During August, Rothchild Company accumulated 3,500 hours of direct labor costs on Job 40 and 4,200 hours on Job 42. The total direct labor was incurred at a rate of $25.00 per direct labor hour for Job 40 and $23.50 per direct labor hour for Job 42. Journalize the entry to record the flow of labor costs into production during August.

Show Me How EE 19-3 p. 932

PE 19-3A Factory overhead costs OBJ. 2

During May, Bergan Company incurred factory overhead costs as follows: indirect materials, $8,800; indirect labor, $6,600; utilities cost, $4,800; and factory depreciation, $9,000. Journalize the entry to record the factory overhead incurred during May.

Show Me How EE 19-3 p. 932

PE 19-3B Factory overhead costs OBJ. 2

During August, Rothchild Company incurred factory overhead costs as follows: indirect materials, $17,500; indirect labor, $22,000; utilities cost, $9,600; and factory depreciation, $17,500. Journalize the entry to record the factory overhead incurred during August.

Show Me How EE 19-4 p. 935

PE 19-4A Applying factory overhead OBJ. 2

Bergan Company estimates that total factory overhead costs will be $620,000 for the year. Direct labor hours are estimated to be 80,000. For Bergan Company, (a) determine the predetermined factory overhead rate using direct labor hours as the activity base, (b) determine the amount of factory overhead applied to Jobs 200 and 305 in May using the data on direct labor hours from Practice Exercise 19-2A, and (c) prepare the journal entry to apply factory overhead to both jobs in May according to the predetermined overhead rate.

Show Me How EE 19-4 p. 935

PE 19-4B Applying factory overhead OBJ. 2

Rothchild Company estimates that total factory overhead costs will be $810,000 for the year. Direct labor hours are estimated to be 90,000. For Rothchild Company, (a) determine the predetermined factory overhead rate using direct labor hours as the activity base, (b) determine the amount of factory overhead applied to Jobs 40 and 42 in August using the data on direct labor hours from Practice Exercise 19-2B, and (c) prepare the journal entry to apply factory overhead to both jobs in August according to the predetermined overhead rate.

Show Me How EE 19-5 p. 937

PE 19-5A Job costs OBJ. 2

At the end of May, Bergan Company had completed Jobs 200 and 305. Job 200 is for 2,390 units, and Job 305 is for 2,053 units. Using the data from Practice Exercises 19-1A, 19-2A, and 19-4A, determine (a) the balance on the job cost sheets for Jobs 200 and 305 at the end of May and (b) the cost per unit for Jobs 200 and 305 at the end of May.

Show Me How EE 19-5 p. 937

PE 19-5B Job costs OBJ. 2

At the end of August, Rothchild Company had completed Jobs 40 and 42. Job 40 is for 10,000 units, and Job 42 is for 11,000 units. Using the data from Practice Exercises 19-1B, 19-2B, and 19-4B, determine (a) the balance on the job cost sheets for Jobs 40 and 42 at the end of August and (b) the cost per unit for Jobs 40 and 42 at the end of August.

Exercises

EX 19-1 Transactions in a job order cost system

OBJ. 2

Five selected transactions for the current month are indicated by letters in the following T accounts in a job order cost accounting system:

Materials	
	(a)

Work in Process	
(a)	(d)
(b)	
(c)	

Wages Payable	
	(b)

Finished Goods	
(d)	(e)

Factory Overhead	
(a)	(c)
(b)	

Cost of Goods Sold	
(e)	

Describe each of the five transactions.

EX 19-2 Cost of materials issuances under the FIFO method

✔ b. $2,280

Excel

OBJ. 2

An incomplete subsidiary ledger of materials inventory for May is as follows:

RECEIVED			ISSUED			BALANCE			
Receiving Report Number	Quantity	Unit Price	Materials Requisition Number	Quantity	Amount	Date	Quantity	Unit Price	Amount
						May 1	285	$30.00	$8,550
40	130	$32.00				May 4	____	____	____
			91	365		May 10	____	____	____
44	110	38.00				May 21	____	____	____
			97	100		May 27	____	____	____

a. Complete the materials issuances and balances for the materials subsidiary ledger under FIFO.

b. Determine the materials inventory balance at the end of May.

c. Journalize the summary entry to transfer materials to work in process.

d. Explain how the materials ledger might be used as an aid in maintaining inventory quantities on hand.

EX 19-3 Entry for issuing materials

Show Me How

OBJ. 2

Materials issued for the current month are as follows:

Requisition No.	Material	Job No.	Amount
103	Plastic	400	$ 2,800
104	Steel	402	24,000
105	Glue	Indirect	1,620
106	Rubber	403	3,200
107	Titanium	404	31,600

Journalize the entry to record the issuance of materials.

EX 19-4 Entries for materials

OBJ. 2

✔ c. Fabric, $35,500

GenX Furnishings manufactures designer furniture. GenX Furnishings uses a job order cost system. Balances on June 1 from the materials ledger are as follows:

Fabric	$40,500
Polyester filling	28,600
Lumber	62,400
Glue	6,550

The materials purchased during June are summarized from the receiving reports as follows:

Fabric	$440,000
Polyester filling	180,000
Lumber	360,000
Glue	40,000

Materials were requisitioned to individual jobs as follows:

	Fabric	Polyester Filling	Lumber	Glue	Total
Job 601	$205,000	$ 75,000	$120,000		$400,000
Job 602	110,000	36,000	88,000		234,000
Job 603	130,000	55,000	125,000		310,000
Factory overhead—indirect materials				$34,800	34,800
Total	$445,000	$166,000	$333,000	$34,800	$978,800

The glue is not a significant cost, so it is treated as indirect materials (factory overhead).

a. Journalize the entry to record the purchase of materials in June.

b. Journalize the entry to record the requisition of materials in June.

c. Determine the June 30 balances that would be shown in the materials ledger accounts.

EX 19-5 Entry for factory labor costs

OBJ. 2

Show Me How

A summary of the time tickets for the current month follows:

Job No.	Amount	Job No.	Amount
100	$ 3,500	Indirect	$ 9,100
101	6,650	111	8,620
104	21,900	115	2,760
108	14,440	117	18,550

Journalize the entry to record the factory labor costs.

EX 19-6 Entry for factory labor costs

OBJ. 2

The weekly time tickets indicate the following distribution of labor hours for three direct labor employees:

	Hours			
	Job 301	Job 302	Job 303	Process Improvement
Tom Couro	10	15	13	2
David Clancy	12	12	14	2
Jose Cano	11	13	15	1

The direct labor rate earned per hour by the three employees is as follows:

Tom Couro	$32
David Clancy	36
Jose Cano	28

The process improvement category includes training, quality improvement, and other indirect tasks.

a. Journalize the entry to record the factory labor costs for the week.

b. Assume that Jobs 301 and 302 were completed but not sold during the week and that Job 303 remained incomplete at the end of the week. How would the direct labor costs for all three jobs be reflected on the financial statements at the end of the week?

Show Me How

EX 19-7 Entries for direct labor and factory overhead **OBJ. 2**

Townsend Industries Inc. manufactures recreational vehicles. Townsend uses a job order cost system. The time tickets from November jobs are summarized as follows:

Job 201	$6,240
Job 202	7,000
Job 203	5,210
Job 204	6,750
Factory supervision	4,000

Factory overhead is applied to jobs on the basis of a predetermined overhead rate of $18 per direct labor hour. The direct labor rate is $40 per hour.

a. Journalize the entry to record the factory labor costs.

b. Journalize the entry to apply factory overhead to production for November.

✔ b. $40.80 per direct labor hour

Show Me How

EX 19-8 Factory overhead rates, entries, and account balance **OBJ. 2**

Sundance Solar Company operates two factories. The company applies factory overhead to jobs on the basis of machine hours in Factory 1 and on the basis of direct labor hours in Factory 2. Estimated factory overhead costs, direct labor hours, and machine hours are as follows:

	Factory 1	Factory 2
Estimated factory overhead cost for fiscal year beginning March 1	$12,900,000	$10,200,000
Estimated direct labor hours for year		250,000
Estimated machine hours for year	600,000	
Actual factory overhead costs for March	$12,990,000	$10,090,000
Actual direct labor hours for March		245,000
Actual machine hours for March	610,000	

a. Determine the factory overhead rate for Factory 1.

b. Determine the factory overhead rate for Factory 2.

c. Journalize the entries to apply factory overhead to production in each factory for March.

d. Determine the balances of the factory overhead accounts for each factory as of March 31 and indicate whether the amounts represent over- or underapplied factory overhead.

EX 19-9 Predetermined factory overhead rate

OBJ. 2

Show Me How

Street Runner Engine Shop uses a job order cost system to determine the cost of performing engine repair work. Estimated costs and expenses for the coming period are as follows:

Engine parts	$ 740,000
Shop direct labor	500,000
Shop and repair equipment depreciation	40,000
Shop supervisor salaries	133,000
Shop property taxes	22,000
Shop supplies	10,000
Advertising expense	20,000
Administrative office salaries	71,400
Administrative office depreciation expense	6,000
Total costs and expenses	$1,542,400

The average shop direct labor rate is $20 per hour.

Determine the predetermined shop overhead rate per direct labor hour.

EX 19-10 Predetermined factory overhead rate

OBJ. 2

✔ a. $290 per hour

Show Me How

Poehling Medical Center has a single operating room that is used by local physicians to perform surgical procedures. The cost of using the operating room is accumulated by each patient procedure and includes the direct materials costs (drugs and medical devices), physician surgical time, and operating room overhead. On January 1 of the current year, the annual operating room overhead is estimated to be:

Disposable supplies	$299,600
Depreciation expense	75,000
Utilities	32,000
Nurse salaries	278,500
Technician wages	126,900
Total operating room overhead	$812,000

The overhead costs will be assigned to procedures based on the number of surgical room hours. Poehling Medical Center expects to use the operating room an average of eight hours per day, seven days per week. In addition, the operating room will be shut down two weeks per year for general repairs.

a. Calculate the estimated number of operating room hours for the year.

b. Determine the predetermined operating room overhead rate for the year.

c. Bill Harris had a five-hour procedure on January 22. How much operating room overhead would be charged to his procedure, using the rate determined in part (b)?

d. During January, the operating room was used 240 hours. The actual overhead costs incurred for January were $67,250. Determine the overhead under- or overapplied for the period.

EX 19-11 Entry for jobs completed; cost of unfinished jobs

OBJ. 2

✔ b. $62,200

Show Me How

The following account appears in the ledger prior to recognizing the jobs completed in January:

Work in Process	
Balance, January 1	$ 72,000
Direct materials	390,000
Direct labor	500,000
Factory overhead	250,000

Jobs finished during January are summarized as follows:

Job 210	$200,000	Job 224	$225,000
Job 216	288,000	Job 230	436,800

a. Journalize the entry to record the jobs completed.

b. Determine the cost of the unfinished jobs at January 31.

✔ d. $73,750

EX 19-12 Entries for factory costs and jobs completed **OBJ. 2**

Old School Publishing Inc. began printing operations on January 1. Jobs 301 and 302 were completed during the month, and all costs applicable to them were recorded on the related cost sheets. Jobs 303 and 304 are still in process at the end of the month, and all applicable costs except factory overhead have been recorded on the related cost sheets. In addition to the materials and labor charged directly to the jobs, $8,000 of indirect materials and $12,400 of indirect labor were used during the month. The cost sheets for the four jobs entering production during the month are as follows, in summary form:

Job 301	
Direct materials	$10,000
Direct labor	8,000
Factory overhead	6,000
Total	$24,000

Job 302	
Direct materials	$20,000
Direct labor	17,000
Factory overhead	12,750
Total	$49,750

Job 303	
Direct materials	$24,000
Direct labor	18,000
Factory overhead	—

Job 304	
Direct materials	$14,000
Direct labor	12,000
Factory overhead	—

Journalize the summary entry to record each of the following operations for January (one entry for each operation):

a. Direct and indirect materials used

b. Direct and indirect labor used

c. Factory overhead applied to all four jobs (a single overhead rate is used based on direct labor cost)

d. Completion of Jobs 301 and 302

✔ a. Income from operations, $137,200

Excel

EX 19-13 Financial statements of a manufacturing firm **OBJ. 2**

The following events took place for Focault Inc. during July 20Y2, the first month of operations as a producer of road bikes:

- Purchased $320,000 of materials
- Used $275,000 of direct materials in production
- Incurred $236,000 of direct labor wages
- Applied factory overhead at a rate of 75% of direct labor cost
- Transferred $652,000 of work in process to finished goods
- Sold goods with a cost of $630,000
- Sold goods for $1,120,000
- Incurred $252,800 of selling expenses
- Incurred $100,000 of administrative expenses

a. Prepare the July income statement for Focault. Assume that Focault uses the perpetual inventory method.

b. Determine the inventory balances at the end of the first month of operations.

OBJ. 3

EX 19-14 Decision making with job order costs

Alvarez Manufacturing Inc. is a job shop. The management of Alvarez Manufacturing Inc. uses the cost information from the job sheets to assess cost performance. Information on the total cost, product type, and quantity of items produced is as follows:

Date	Job No.	Product	Quantity	Amount
Jan. 2	1	TT	520	$16,120
Jan. 15	22	SS	1,610	20,125
Feb. 3	30	SS	1,420	25,560
Mar. 7	41	TT	670	15,075
Mar. 24	49	SLK	2,210	22,100
May 19	58	SLK	2,550	31,875
June 12	65	TT	620	10,540
Aug. 18	78	SLK	3,110	48,205
Sept. 2	82	SS	1,210	16,940
Nov. 14	92	TT	750	8,250
Dec. 12	98	SLK	2,700	52,650

a. Develop a graph for *each* product (three graphs) with Job Number (in date order) on the horizontal axis and Unit Cost on the vertical axis. Use this information to determine Alvarez Manufacturing Inc.'s cost performance over time for the three products.

b. What additional information would you require in order to investigate Alvarez Manufacturing Inc.'s cost performance more precisely?

OBJ. 3

EX 19-15 Decision making with job order costs

Raneri Trophies Inc. uses a job order cost system for determining the cost to manufacture award products (plaques and trophies). Among the company's products is an engraved plaque that is awarded to participants who complete a training program at a local business. The company sells the plaques to the local business for $80 each.

Each plaque has a brass plate engraved with the name of the participant. Engraving requires approximately 30 minutes per name. Improperly engraved names must be redone. The plate is screwed to a walnut backboard. This assembly takes approximately 15 minutes per unit. Improper assembly must be redone using a new walnut backboard.

During the first half of the year, Raneri had two separate plaque orders. The job cost sheets for the two separate jobs indicated the following information:

Job 101	**May 4**		
	Cost per Unit	**Units**	**Job Cost**
Direct materials:			
Wood	$20/unit	40 units	$ 800
Brass	15/unit	40 units	600
Engraving labor	20/hr.	20 hrs.	400
Assembly labor	30/hr.	10 hrs.	300
Factory overhead	10/hr.	30 hrs.	300
			$2,400
Plaques shipped			÷ 40
Cost per plaque			$ 60

Job 105	**June 10**		
	Cost per Unit	**Units**	**Job Cost**
Direct materials:			
Wood	$20/unit	34 units	$ 680
Brass	15/unit	34 units	510
Engraving labor	20/hr.	17 hrs.	340
Assembly labor	30/hr.	8.5 hrs.	255
Factory overhead	10/hr.	25.5 hrs.	255
			$2,040
Plaques shipped			÷ 30
Cost per plaque			$ 68

a. Why did the cost per plaque increase from $60 to $68?

b. What improvements would you recommend for Raneri Trophies Inc.?

✔ b. Underapplied, $5,530

EX 19-16 Job order cost accounting for a service company **OBJ. 4**

The law firm of Furlan and Benson accumulates costs associated with individual cases, using a job order cost system. The following transactions occurred during July:

July 3. Charged 175 hours of professional (lawyer) time at a rate of $150 per hour to the Obsidian Co. breech of contract suit to prepare for the trial

10. Reimbursed travel costs to employees for depositions related to the Obsidian case, $12,500

14. Charged 260 hours of professional time for the Obsidian trial at a rate of $185 per hour

18. Received invoice from consultants Wadsley and Harden for $30,000 for expert testimony related to the Obsidian trial

27. Applied office overhead at a rate of $62 per professional hour charged to the Obsidian case

31. Paid administrative and support salaries of $28,500 for the month

31. Used office supplies for the month, $4,000

31. Paid professional salaries of $74,350 for the month

31. Billed Obsidian $172,500 for successful defense of the case

a. Provide the journal entries for each of these transactions.

b. How much office overhead is over- or underapplied?

c. Determine the gross profit on the Obsidian case, assuming that over- or underapplied office overhead is closed monthly to cost of services.

✔ d. Dr. Cost of Services, $2,827,750

EX 19-17 Job order cost accounting for a service company **OBJ. 4**

The Fly Company provides advertising services for clients across the nation. The Fly Company is presently working on four projects, each for a different client. The Fly Company accumulates costs for each account (client) on the basis of both direct costs and allocated indirect costs. The direct costs include the charged time of professional personnel and media purchases (air time and ad space). Overhead is allocated to each project as a percentage of media purchases. The predetermined overhead rate is 65% of media purchases.

On August 1, the four advertising projects had the following accumulated costs:

	August 1 Balances
Vault Bank	$270,000
Take Off Airlines	80,000
Sleepy Tired Hotels	210,000
Tastee Beverages	115,000
Total	$675,000

(Continued)

During August, The Fly Company incurred the following direct labor and media purchase costs related to preparing advertising for each of the four accounts:

	Direct Labor	Media Purchases
Vault Bank	$ 190,000	$ 710,000
Take Off Airlines	85,000	625,000
Sleepy Tired Hotels	372,000	455,000
Tastee Beverages	421,000	340,000
Total	$1,068,000	$2,130,000

At the end of August, both the Vault Bank and Take Off Airlines campaigns were completed. The costs of completed campaigns are debited to the cost of services account.

Journalize the summary entry to record each of the following for the month:

a. Direct labor costs
b. Media purchases
c. Overhead applied
d. Completion of Vault Bank and Take Off Airlines campaigns

Problems: Series A

PR 19-1A Entries for costs in a job order cost system

OBJ. 2

General Ledger

Show Me How

Munson Co. uses a job order cost system. The following data summarize the operations related to production for July:

a. Materials purchased on account, $225,750
b. Materials requisitioned, $217,600, of which $17,600 was for general factory use
c. Factory labor used, $680,000, of which $72,300 was indirect
d. Other costs incurred on account for factory overhead, $330,000; selling expenses, $180,000; and administrative expenses, $126,000
e. Prepaid expenses expired for factory overhead, $27,500; for selling expenses, $8,100; and for administrative expenses, $5,250
f. Depreciation of office building was $44,500; of office equipment, $16,800; and of factory equipment, $55,100
g. Factory overhead costs applied to jobs, $548,000
h. Jobs completed, $1,140,000
i. Cost of goods sold, $1,128,000

Instructions

Journalize the entries to record the summarized operations.

PR 19-2A Entries and schedules for unfinished jobs and completed jobs

OBJ. 2

✔ 3. Work in Process balance, $27,288

Excel

General Ledger

Tybee Industries Inc. uses a job order cost system. The following data summarize the operations related to production for January, the first month of operations:

a. Materials purchased on account, $29,800.

b. Materials requisitioned and factory labor used:

Job	Materials	Factory Labor
301	$2,960	$2,775
302	3,620	3,750
303	2,400	1,875
304	8,100	6,860
305	5,100	5,250
306	3,750	3,340
For general factory use	1,080	4,100

c. Factory overhead costs incurred on account, $5,500.

d. Depreciation of machinery and equipment, $1,980.

e. The factory overhead rate is $54 per machine hour. Machine hours used:

Job	Machine Hours
301	25
302	36
303	30
304	72
305	40
306	25
Total	228

f. Jobs completed: 301, 302, 303, and 305.

g. Jobs were shipped and customers were billed as follows: Job 301, $8,250; Job 302, $11,200; Job 303, $15,000.

Instructions

1. Journalize the entries to record the summarized operations.
2. Post the appropriate entries to T accounts for Work in Process and Finished Goods, using the identifying letters as transaction codes. Insert memo account balances as of the end of the month.
3. Prepare a schedule of unfinished jobs to support the balance in the work in process account.
4. Prepare a schedule of completed jobs on hand to support the balance in the finished goods account.

Excel

PR 19-3A Job order cost sheet

OBJ. 2, 3

Remnant Carpet Company sells and installs commercial carpeting for office buildings. Remnant Carpet Company uses a job order cost system. When a prospective customer asks for a price quote on a job, the estimated cost data are inserted on an unnumbered job cost sheet. If the offer is accepted, a number is assigned to the job and the costs incurred are recorded in the usual manner on the job cost sheet. After the job is completed, reasons for the variances between the estimated and actual costs are noted on the sheet. The data are then available to management in evaluating the efficiency of operations and in preparing quotes on future jobs. On October 1, Remnant Carpet Company gave Jackson

(Continued)

Consulting an estimate of $9,450 to carpet the consulting firm's newly leased office. The estimate was based on the following data:

Estimated direct materials:	
200 sq. ft. at $35 per sq. ft.	$7,000
Estimated direct labor:	
16 hours at $20 per hour	320
Estimated factory overhead (75% of direct labor cost)	240
Total estimated costs	$7,560
Markup (25% of production costs)	1,890
Total estimate	$9,450

On October 3, Jackson Consulting signed a purchase contract, and the delivery and installation was completed on October 10.

The related materials requisitions and time tickets are summarized as follows:

Materials Requisition No.	Description	Amount
112	140 sq. ft. at $35	$4,900
114	68 sq. ft. at $35	2,380

Time Ticket No.	Description	Amount
H10	10 hours at $20	$200
H11	10 hours at $20	200

Instructions

1. Complete that portion of the job order cost sheet that is prepared when the estimate is given to the customer.
2. Record the costs incurred and prepare a job order cost sheet. Comment on the reasons for the variances between actual costs and estimated costs. For this purpose, assume that the additional square feet of material used in the job were spoiled, the factory overhead rate has proven to be satisfactory, and an inexperienced employee performed the work.

PR 19-4A Analyzing manufacturing cost accounts

OBJ. 2

✓ g. $751,870

Excel

Fire Rock Company manufactures designer paddle boards in a wide variety of sizes and styles. The following incomplete ledger accounts refer to transactions that are summarized for June:

Materials

June 1	Balance	82,500	June 30	Requisitions	(a)
30	Purchases	330,000			

Work in Process

June 1	Balance	(b)	June 30	Completed jobs	(f)
30	Materials	(c)			
30	Direct labor	(d)			
30	Factory overhead applied	(e)			

Finished Goods

June 1	Balance	0	June 30	Cost of goods sold	(g)
30	Completed jobs	(f)			

Wages Payable

			June 30	Wages incurred	330,000

Factory Overhead

June 1	Balance	33,000	June 30	Factory overhead applied	(e)
30	Indirect labor	(h)			
30	Indirect materials	44,000			
30	Other overhead	237,500			

In addition, the following information is available:

a. Materials and direct labor were applied to the following jobs in June:

Job No.	Style	Quantity	Direct Materials	Direct Labor
201	T100	550	$ 55,000	$ 41,250
202	T200	1,100	93,500	71,500
203	T400	550	38,500	22,000
204	S200	660	82,500	69,300
205	T300	480	60,000	48,000
206	S100	380	22,000	12,400
	Total	3,720	$351,500	$264,450

b. Factory overhead is applied to each job at a rate of 140% of direct labor cost.

c. The June 1 Work in Process balance consisted of two jobs, as follows:

Job No.	Style	Work in Process, June 1
201	T100	$16,500
202	T200	44,000
Total		$60,500

d. Customer jobs completed and units sold in June were as follows:

Job No.	Style	Completed in June	Units Sold in June
201	T100	X	440
202	T200	X	880
203	T400		0
204	S200	X	570
205	T300	X	420
206	S100		0

Instructions

1. Determine the missing amounts associated with each letter. Provide supporting calculations by completing a table with the following headings:

Job No.	Quantity	June 1 Work in Process	Direct Materials	Direct Labor	Factory Overhead	Total Cost	Unit Cost	Units Sold	Cost of Goods Sold

2. Determine the June 30 balances for each of the inventory accounts and factory overhead.

PR 19-5A Flow of costs and income statement

OBJ. 2

✔ 1. Income from operations, $432,000

Excel

Ginocera Inc. is a designer, manufacturer, and distributor of low-cost, high-quality stainless steel kitchen knives. A new kitchen knife series called the Kitchen Ninja was released for production in early 20Y8. In January, the company spent $600,000 to develop a late-night advertising infomercial for the new product. During 20Y8, the company spent $1,400,000 advertising the product through these infomercials. In addition, the company incurred $800,000 in legal costs. The knives were ready for manufacture on January 1, 20Y8.

Ginocera uses a job order cost system to accumulate costs associated with the kitchen knife. The unit direct materials cost for the knife is as follows:

Hardened steel blanks (used for knife shaft and blade)	$4.00
Wood (for handle)	1.50
Packaging	0.50

(Continued)

The production process is straightforward. First, the hardened steel blanks, which are purchased directly from a raw material supplier, are stamped into a single piece of metal that includes both the blade and the shaft. The stamping machine requires one hour per 250 knives.

After the knife shafts are stamped, they are brought to an assembly area where an employee attaches the handle to the shaft and packs the knife in a decorative box. The direct labor cost is $0.50 per unit.

The knives are sold to stores. Each store is given promotional materials such as posters and aisle displays. Promotional materials cost $60.00 per store. In addition, shipping costs average $0.20 per knife.

Total completed production was 1,200,000 units during the year. Other information is as follows:

Number of customers (stores)	60,000
Number of knives sold	1,120,000
Wholesale price (to store) per knife	$16

Factory overhead cost is applied to jobs at the rate of $800 per stamping machine hour after the knife blanks are stamped. There were an additional 25,000 stamped knives, handles, and cases waiting to be assembled on December 31, 20Y8.

Instructions

1. Prepare an annual income statement for the Kitchen Ninja knife series, including supporting calculations, from the information provided.
2. Determine the balances in the work in process and finished goods inventories for the Kitchen Ninja knife series on December 31, 20Y8.

Problems: Series B

PR 19-1B Entries for costs in a job order cost system

OBJ. 2

General Ledger

Show Me How

Royal Technology Company uses a job order cost system. The following data summarize the operations related to production for March:

a. Materials purchased on account, $770,000
b. Materials requisitioned, $680,000, of which $75,800 was for general factory use
c. Factory labor used, $756,000, of which $182,000 was indirect
d. Other costs incurred on account for factory overhead, $245,000; selling expenses, $171,500; and administrative expenses, $110,600
e. Prepaid expenses expired for factory overhead, $24,500; for selling expenses, $28,420; and for administrative expenses, $16,660
f. Depreciation of factory equipment was $49,500; of office equipment, $61,800; and of office building, $14,900
g. Factory overhead costs applied to jobs, $568,500
h. Jobs completed, $1,500,000
i. Cost of goods sold, $1,375,000

Instruction

Journalize the entries to record the summarized operations.

PR 19-2B Entries and schedules for unfinished jobs and completed jobs

OBJ. 2

✔ 3. Work in Process balance, $127,880

Hildreth Company uses a job order cost system. The following data summarize the operations related to production for April, the first month of operations:

a. Materials purchased on account, $147,000.

Excel General Ledger

b. Materials requisitioned and factory labor used:

Job No.	Materials	Factory Labor
101	$19,320	$19,500
102	23,100	28,140
103	13,440	14,000
104	38,200	36,500
105	18,050	15,540
106	18,000	18,700
For general factory use	9,000	20,160

c. Factory overhead costs incurred on account, $6,000.

d. Depreciation of machinery and equipment, $4,100.

e. The factory overhead rate is $40 per machine hour. Machine hours used:

Job	Machine Hours
101	154
102	160
103	126
104	238
105	160
106	174
Total	1,012

f. Jobs completed: 101, 102, 103, and 105.

g. Jobs were shipped and customers were billed as follows: Job 101, $62,900; Job 102, $80,700; Job 105, $45,500.

Instructions

1. Journalize the entries to record the summarized operations.
2. Post the appropriate entries to T accounts for Work in Process and Finished Goods, using the identifying letters as transaction codes. Insert memo account balances as of the end of the month.
3. Prepare a schedule of unfinished jobs to support the balance in the work in process account.
4. Prepare a schedule of completed jobs on hand to support the balance in the finished goods account.

Excel

PR 19-3B Job order cost sheet

OBJ. 2, 3

Stretch and Trim Carpet Company sells and installs commercial carpeting for office buildings. Stretch and Trim Carpet Company uses a job order cost system. When a prospective customer asks for a price quote on a job, the estimated cost data are inserted on an unnumbered job cost sheet. If the offer is accepted, a number is assigned to the job, and the costs incurred are recorded in the usual manner on the job cost sheet. After the job is completed, reasons for the variances between the estimated and actual costs are noted on the sheet. The data are then available for management to use in evaluating the efficiency of operations and in preparing quotes on future jobs. On May 9, Stretch and Trim gave Lunden Consulting an estimate of $18,044 to carpet the consulting firm's newly leased office. The estimate was based on the following data:

Estimated direct materials:	
400 sq. ft. at $32 per sq. ft.	$12,800
Estimated direct labor:	
30 hours at $20 per hour	600
Estimated factory overhead (80% of direct labor cost)	480
Total estimated costs	$13,880
Markup (30% of production costs)	4,164
Total estimate	$18,044

(Continued)

On May 10, Lunden Consulting signed a purchase contract, and the carpet was delivered and installed on May 15.

The related materials requisitions and time tickets are summarized as follows:

Materials Requisition No.	Description	Amount
132	360 sq. ft. at $32	$11,520
134	50 sq. ft. at $32	1,600

Time Ticket No.	Description	Amount
H9	18 hours at $19	$342
H12	18 hours at $19	342

Instructions

1. Complete that portion of the job order cost sheet that would be prepared when the estimate is given to the customer. Round factory overhead applied to the nearest dollar.
2. Record the costs incurred and prepare a job order cost sheet. Comment on the reasons for the variances between actual costs and estimated costs. For this purpose, assume that the additional square feet of material used in the job were spoiled, the factory overhead rate has proven to be satisfactory, and an inexperienced employee performed the work.

PR 19-4B Analyzing manufacturing cost accounts

OBJ. 2

✔ g. $700,284

Excel

Clapton Company manufactures custom guitars in a wide variety of styles. The following incomplete ledger accounts refer to transactions that are summarized for May:

Materials

May 1	Balance	105,600	May 31	Requisitions	(a)
31	Purchases	500,000			

Work in Process

May 1	Balance	(b)	May 31	Completed jobs	(f)
31	Materials	(c)			
31	Direct labor	(d)			
31	Factory overhead applied	(e)			

Finished Goods

May 1	Balance	0	May 31	Cost of goods sold	(g)
31	Completed jobs	(f)			

Wages Payable

			May 31	Wages incurred	396,000

Factory Overhead

May 1	Balance	26,400	May 31	Factory overhead applied	(e)
31	Indirect labor	(h)			
31	Indirect materials	15,400			
31	Other overhead	122,500			

In addition, the following information is available:

a. Materials and direct labor were applied to the following jobs in May:

Job No.	Style	Quantity	Direct Materials	Direct Labor
101	AF1	330	$ 82,500	$ 59,400
102	AF3	380	105,400	72,600
103	AF2	500	132,000	110,000
104	VY1	400	66,000	39,600
105	VY2	660	118,800	66,000
106	AF4	330	66,000	30,800
	Total	2,600	$570,700	$378,400

b. Factory overhead is applied to each job at a rate of 50% of direct labor cost.
c. The May 1 Work in Process balance consisted of two jobs, as follows:

Job No.	Style	Work in Process, May 1
101	AF1	$26,400
102	AF3	46,000
Total		$72,400

d. Customer jobs completed and units sold in May were as follows:

Job No.	Style	Completed in May	Units Sold in May
101	AF1	X	264
102	AF3	X	360
103	AF2		0
104	VY1	X	384
105	VY2	X	530
106	AF4		0

Instructions
1. Determine the missing amounts associated with each letter. Provide supporting calculations by completing a table with the following headings:

Job No.	Quantity	May 1 Work in Process	Direct Materials	Direct Labor	Factory Overhead	Total Cost	Unit Cost	Units Sold	Cost of Goods Sold

2. Determine the May 31 balances for each of the inventory accounts and factory overhead.

PR 19-5B Flow of costs and income statement

OBJ. 2

✔ 1. Income from operations, $656,000

Excel

Technology Accessories Inc. is a designer, manufacturer, and distributor of accessories for consumer electronic products. Early in 20Y3, the company began production of a leather cover for tablet computers, called the iLeather. The cover is made of stitched leather with a velvet interior and fits around most tablet computers. In January, $750,000 was spent on developing marketing and advertising materials. For the first six months of 20Y2, the company spent $1,400,000 promoting the iLeather. The product was ready for manufacture on January 21, 20Y3.

Technology Accessories Inc. uses a job order cost system to accumulate costs for the iLeather. Direct materials unit costs for the iLeather are as follows:

Leather	$10.00
Velvet	5.00
Packaging	0.40
Total	$15.40

The actual production process for the iLeather is fairly straightforward. First, leather is brought to a cutting and stitching machine. The machine cuts the leather and stitches an exterior edge into the product. The machine requires one hour per 125 iLeathers.

After the iLeather is cut and stitched, it is brought to assembly, where assembly personnel affix the velvet interior and pack the iLeather for shipping. The direct labor cost for this work is $0.50 per unit.

The completed packages are then sold to retail outlets through a sales force. The sales force is compensated by a 20% commission on the wholesale price for all sales.

Total completed production was 500,000 units during the year. Other information is as follows:

Number of iLeather units sold in 20Y3	460,000
Wholesale price per unit	$40

(Continued)

Factory overhead cost is applied to jobs at the rate of $1,250 per machine hour. An additional 22,000 cut and stitched iLeathers were waiting to be assembled on December 31, 20Y3.

Instructions

1. Prepare an annual income statement for the iLeather product, including supporting calculations, from the information provided.
2. Determine the balances in the finished goods and work in process inventories for the iLeather product on December 31, 20Y3.

Cases & Projects

CP 19-1 Communication

Communication

TAC Industries sells heavy equipment to large corporations and to federal, state, and local governments. Corporate sales are the result of a competitive bidding process, where TAC competes against other companies based on selling price. Sales to the government, however, are determined on a cost plus basis, where the selling price is determined by adding a fixed markup percentage to the total job cost.

Tandy Lane is the cost accountant for the Equipment Division of TAC Industries Inc. The division is under pressure from senior management to improve income from operations. As Tandy reviewed the division's job cost sheets, she realized that she could increase the division's income from operations by moving a portion of the direct labor hours that had been assigned to the job order cost sheets of corporate customers onto the job order costs sheets of government customers. She believed that this would create a win–win for the division by (1) reducing the cost of corporate jobs and (2) increasing the cost of government jobs whose profit is based on a percentage of job cost. Tandy submitted this idea to her division manager, who was impressed by her creative solution for improving the division's profitability.

Is Tandy's plan ethical? Explain.

CP 19-2 Predetermined overhead rates

As an assistant cost accountant for Mississippi Industries, you have been assigned to review the activity base for the predetermined factory overhead rate. The president, Tony Favre, has expressed concern that the over- or underapplied overhead has fluctuated excessively over the years.

An analysis of the company's operations and use of the current overhead rate (direct labor cost) has narrowed the possible alternative overhead bases to direct labor cost and machine hours. For the past five years, the following data have been gathered:

	Year 5	Year 4	Year 3	Year 2	Year 1
Actual overhead	$ 790,000	$ 870,000	$ 935,000	$ 845,000	$ 760,000
Applied overhead	777,000	882,000	924,000	840,000	777,000
(Over-) underapplied overhead	$ 13,000	$ (12,000)	$ 11,000	$ 5,000	$ (17,000)
Direct labor cost	$3,885,000	$4,410,000	$4,620,000	$4,200,000	$3,885,000
Machine hours	93,000	104,000	111,000	100,400	91,600

In teams:

1. Calculate a predetermined factory overhead rate for each alternative base, assuming that rates would have been determined by relating the total amount of factory overhead for the past five years to the base.
2. For each of the past five years, determine the over- or underapplied overhead based on the two predetermined overhead rates developed in part (1).
3. Which predetermined overhead rate would you recommend? Discuss the basis for your recommendation.

Communication

CP 19-3 Communication

Carol Creedence, the plant manager of the Clearwater Company's Revival plant, has prepared the following graph of the unit costs from the job cost reports for the plant's highest volume product, Product CCR:

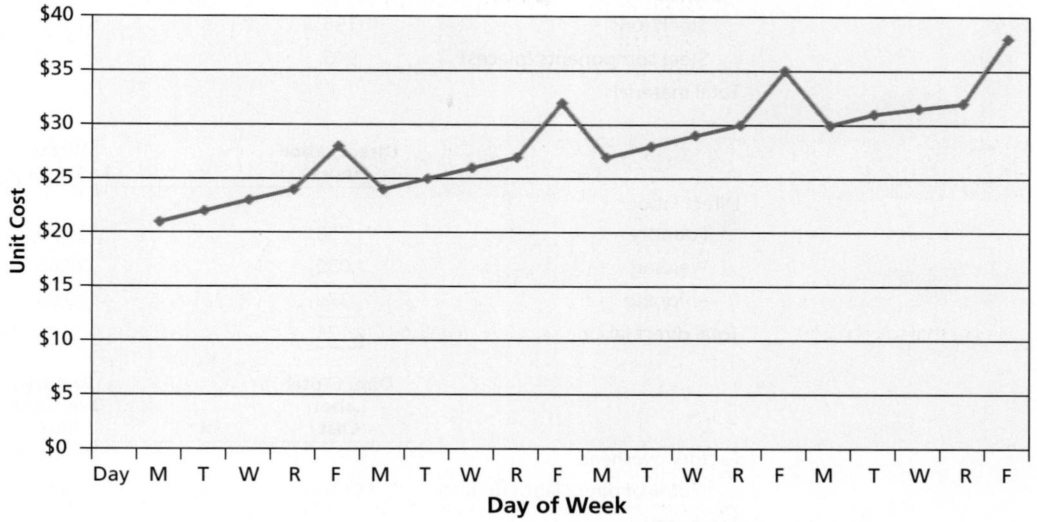

Carol is concerned about the erratic and increasing cost of Product CCR and has asked for your help. Prepare a half-page memo to Carol, interpreting this graph and requesting any additional information that might be needed to explain this situation.

CP 19-4 Job order decision making and rate deficiencies

RIRA Company makes attachments such as backhoes and grader and bulldozer blades for construction equipment. The company uses a job order cost system. Management is concerned about cost performance and evaluates the job cost sheets to learn more about the cost effectiveness of the operations. To facilitate a comparison, the cost sheet for Job 206 (50 backhoe buckets completed in October) was compared with Job 228, which was for 75 backhoe buckets completed in December. The two job cost sheets follow:

Job 206

Item: 50 backhoe buckets

Materials:	**Direct Materials Quantity**	×	**Direct Materials Price**	=	**Amount**
Steel (tons)	105		$1,200		$126,000
Steel components (pieces)	630		7		4,410
Total materials					$130,410
Direct labor:	**Direct Labor Hours**	×	**Direct Labor Rate**	=	**Amount**
Foundry	400		$22.50		$ 9,000
Welding	550		27.00		14,850
Shipping	180		18.00		3,240
Total direct labor	1,130				$ 27,090
	Direct Total Labor Cost	×	**Factory Overhead Rate**	=	**Amount**
Factory overhead					
(200% of direct labor dollars)	$27,090	×	200%		$ 54,180
Total cost					$ 211,680
Total units					÷ 50
Unit cost (rounded)					$4,233.60

(Continued)

Job 228

Item: 75 backhoe buckets

	Direct Materials Quantity	×	Direct Materials Price	=	Amount
Materials:					
Steel (tons)	195		$1,100		$214,500
Steel components (pieces)	945		7		6,615
Total materials					$221,115

	Direct Labor Hours	×	Direct Labor Rate	=	Amount
Direct labor:					
Foundry	750		$22.50		$ 16,875
Welding	1,050		27.00		28,350
Shipping	375		18.00		6,750
Total direct labor	2,175				$ 51,975

	Direct Total Labor Cost	×	Factory Overhead Rate	=	Amount
Factory overhead					
(200% of direct labor dollars)	$51,975	×	200%		$ 103,950
Total cost					$ 377,040
Total units					÷ 75
Unit cost					$5,027.20

Management is concerned with the increase in unit costs over the months from October to December. To understand what has occurred, management interviewed the purchasing manager and quality manager.

Purchasing Manager: Prices have been holding steady for our raw materials during the first half of the year. I found a new supplier for our bulk steel that was willing to offer a better price than we received in the past. I saw these lower steel prices and jumped at them, knowing that a reduction in steel prices would have a very favorable impact on our costs.

Quality Manager: Something happened around mid-year. All of a sudden, we were experiencing problems with respect to the quality of our steel. As a result, we've been having all sorts of problems on the shop floor in our foundry and welding operation.

1. Analyze the two job cost sheets and identify why the unit costs have changed for the backhoe buckets. Complete the following schedule to help in your analysis:

Item	Input Quantity per Unit—Job 206	Input Quantity per Unit—Job 228
Steel		
Foundry labor		
Welding labor		

2. How would you interpret what has happened in light of your analysis and the interviews?

CP 19-5 Recording manufacturing costs

Todd Lay just began working as a cost accountant for Enteron Industries Inc., which manufactures gift items. Todd is preparing to record summary journal entries for the month. Todd begins by recording the factory wages as follows:

Wages Expense	60,000	
Wages Payable		60,000

Then the factory depreciation:

Depreciation Expense—Factory Machinery	20,000	
Accumulated Depreciation—Factory Machinery		20,000

Todd's supervisor, Jeff Fastow, walks by and notices the entries. The following conversation takes place:

Jeff: That's a very unusual way to record our factory wages and depreciation for the month.

Todd: What do you mean? This is the way I was taught in school to record wages and depreciation. You know, debit an expense and credit Cash or payables or, in the case of depreciation, credit Accumulated Depreciation.

Jeff: Well, it's not the credits I'm concerned about. It's the debits—I don't think you've recorded the debits correctly. I wouldn't mind if you were recording the administrative wages or office equipment depreciation this way, but I've got real questions about recording factory wages and factory machinery depreciation this way.

Todd: Now I'm really confused. You mean this is correct for administrative costs but not for factory costs? Well, what am I supposed to do—and why?

1. Play the role of Jeff and answer Todd's questions.
2. Why would Jeff accept the journal entries if they were for administrative costs?

CHAPTER

20

Process Cost Systems

Concepts and Principles

Chapter 18 *Introduction to Managerial Accounting*

Developing Information

COST SYSTEMS

Chapter 19 *Job Order Costing*

Chapter 20 ***Process Cost Systems***

COST BEHAVIOR

Chapter 21 *Cost-Volume-Profit Analysis*

Decision Making

EVALUATING PERFORMANCE

Chapter 22 *Budgeting*

Chapter 23 *Variances from Standard Costs*

COMPARING ALTERNATIVES

Chapter 24 *Decentralized Operations*

Chapter 25 *Differential Analysis, Product Pricing, and Activity-Based Costing*

Chapter 26 *Capital Investment Analysis*

MICHAEL STRAUCH/STREETCARMIKE.COM

Dreyer's Ice Cream

In making ice cream, an electric ice cream maker is used to mix ingredients, which include milk, cream, sugar, and flavoring. After the ingredients are added, the mixer is packed with ice and salt to cool the ingredients and then turned on.

After mixing for half of the required time, would you have ice cream? Of course not, because the ice cream needs to mix longer to freeze. Now assume that you ask the question:

What costs have I incurred so far in making ice cream?

The answer to this question requires knowing the cost of the ingredients and electricity. The ingredients are added at the beginning; thus, all the ingredient costs have been incurred. Because the mixing is only half complete, only 50% of the electricity cost has been incurred. Therefore, the answer to the preceding question is:

All the materials costs and half the electricity costs have been incurred.

These same cost concepts apply to larger ice cream processes like those of **Dreyer's Ice Cream** (a subsidiary of **Nestlé**), manufacturer of Dreyer's® and Edy's® ice cream. Dreyer's mixes ingredients in 3,000-gallon vats in much the same way you would using an electric ice cream maker. Dreyer's also records the costs of the ingredients, labor, and factory overhead used in making ice cream. These costs are used by managers for decisions such as setting prices and improving operations.

This chapter describes and illustrates process cost systems that are used by manufacturers such as Dreyer's. In addition, the use of cost of production reports in decision making is described. Finally, the principles of lean manufacturing are discussed.

Learning Objectives

After studying this chapter, you should be able to:

Example Exercises (EE) are shown in **green.**

Obj. 1 **Describe process cost systems.**

Process Cost Systems
Comparing Job Order and Process Cost Systems — EE 20-1
Cost Flows for a Process Manufacturer

Obj. 2 **Prepare a cost of production report.**

Cost of Production Report
Step 1: Determine the Units to Be Assigned Costs — EE 20-2
Step 2: Compute Equivalent Units of Production — EE 20-3, 20-4
Step 3: Determine the Cost per Equivalent Unit — EE 20-5
Step 4: Allocate Costs to Units Transferred Out and Partially Completed Units — EE 20-6
Preparing the Cost of Production Report

Obj. 3 **Journalize entries for transactions using a process cost system.**

Journal Entries for a Process Cost System — EE 20-7

Obj. 4 **Describe and illustrate the use of cost of production reports for decision making.**

Using the Cost of Production Report for Decision Making
Cost per Equivalent Unit Between Periods
Cost Category Analysis — EE 20-8
Yield

Obj. 5 **Compare lean manufacturing with traditional manufacturing processing.**

Lean Manufacturing
Traditional Production Process
Lean Production Process

At a Glance 20 Page 996

Obj. 1 Describe process cost systems.

Process Cost Systems

A **process manufacturer** produces products that are indistinguishable from each other using a continuous production process. For example, an oil refinery processes crude oil through a series of steps to produce a barrel of gasoline. One barrel of gasoline, the product, cannot be distinguished from another barrel. Other examples of process manufacturers include paper producers, chemical processors, aluminum smelters, and food processors.

INTEGRITY, OBJECTIVITY, AND ETHICS IN BUSINESS

ON BEING GREEN

Process manufacturing often involves significant energy and material resources, which can be harmful to the environment. Thus, many process manufacturing companies, such as chemical, electronic, and metal processors, must address environmental issues. Companies such as DuPont, Intel, Apple, and Alcoa are at the forefront of providing environmental solutions for their products and processes. For example, Apple provides free recycling programs for Macs®, iPhones®, and iPads®. Apple recovers more than 90% by weight of the original product in reusable components, glass, and plastic. You can even receive a free gift card for voluntarily recycling an older Apple product.

Source: Apple website.

The cost accounting system used by process manufacturers is called the **process cost system.** A process cost system records product costs for each manufacturing department or process.

In contrast, a job order manufacturer produces custom products for customers or batches of similar products. For example, a custom printer produces wedding invitations, graduation announcements, or other special print items that are tailored to the specifications of each customer. Each item manufactured is unique to itself. Other examples of job order manufacturers include furniture manufacturers, shipbuilders, and home builders.

As described and illustrated in Chapter 19, the cost accounting system used by job order manufacturers is called the *job order cost system.* A job order cost system records product cost for each job, using job cost sheets.

Some examples of process and job order companies and their products are shown in Exhibit 1.

EXHIBIT 1

Examples of Process Cost and Job Order Companies

Process Manufacturing Companies		Job Order Companies	
Company	**Product**	**Company**	**Product**
Pepsi	soft drinks	Walt Disney	movies
Alcoa	aluminum	Nike, Inc.	athletic shoes
Intel	computer chip	Nicklaus Design	golf courses
ExxonMobil	Gasoline	Tennessee Heritage	log homes
Hershey	chocolate bars	DDB Advertising Agency	advertising

Comparing Job Order and Process Cost Systems

Process and job order cost systems are similar in that each system:

- Records and summarizes product costs.
- Classifies product costs as direct materials, direct labor, and factory overhead.
- Allocates factory overhead costs to products.
- Uses perpetual inventory system for materials, work in process, and finished goods.
- Provides useful product cost information for decision making.

Process and job costing systems are different in several ways. As a basis for illustrating these differences, the cost systems for **Frozen Delight** and **Legend Guitars** are used.

Exhibit 2 illustrates the process cost system for Frozen Delight, an ice cream manufacturer. As a basis for comparison, Exhibit 2 also illustrates the job order cost system for Legend Guitars, a custom guitar manufacturer. Legend Guitars was described and illustrated in Chapters 18 and 19.

Exhibit 2 indicates that Frozen Delight manufactures ice cream, using two departments:

- The Mixing Department mixes the ingredients, using large vats.
- The Packaging Department puts the ice cream into cartons for shipping to customers.

Because each gallon of ice cream is similar, product costs are recorded in each department's work in process account. As shown in Exhibit 2, Frozen Delight accumulates (records) the cost of making ice cream in ***work in process accounts*** for the Mixing and Packaging departments.

The product costs of making a gallon of ice cream include:

- *Direct materials costs,* which include milk, cream, sugar, and packing cartons. All materials costs are added at the beginning of the process for both the Mixing Department and the Packaging Department.

Link to Dreyer's Ice Cream

William Dreyer, an ice cream maker, and Joseph Edy, a candy maker, founded Dreyer's and Edy's Grand Ice Cream in 1928. The ice cream was sold out of their ice cream parlor on Grand Avenue in Oakland, California.

EXHIBIT 2 **Process Cost and Job Order Cost Systems**

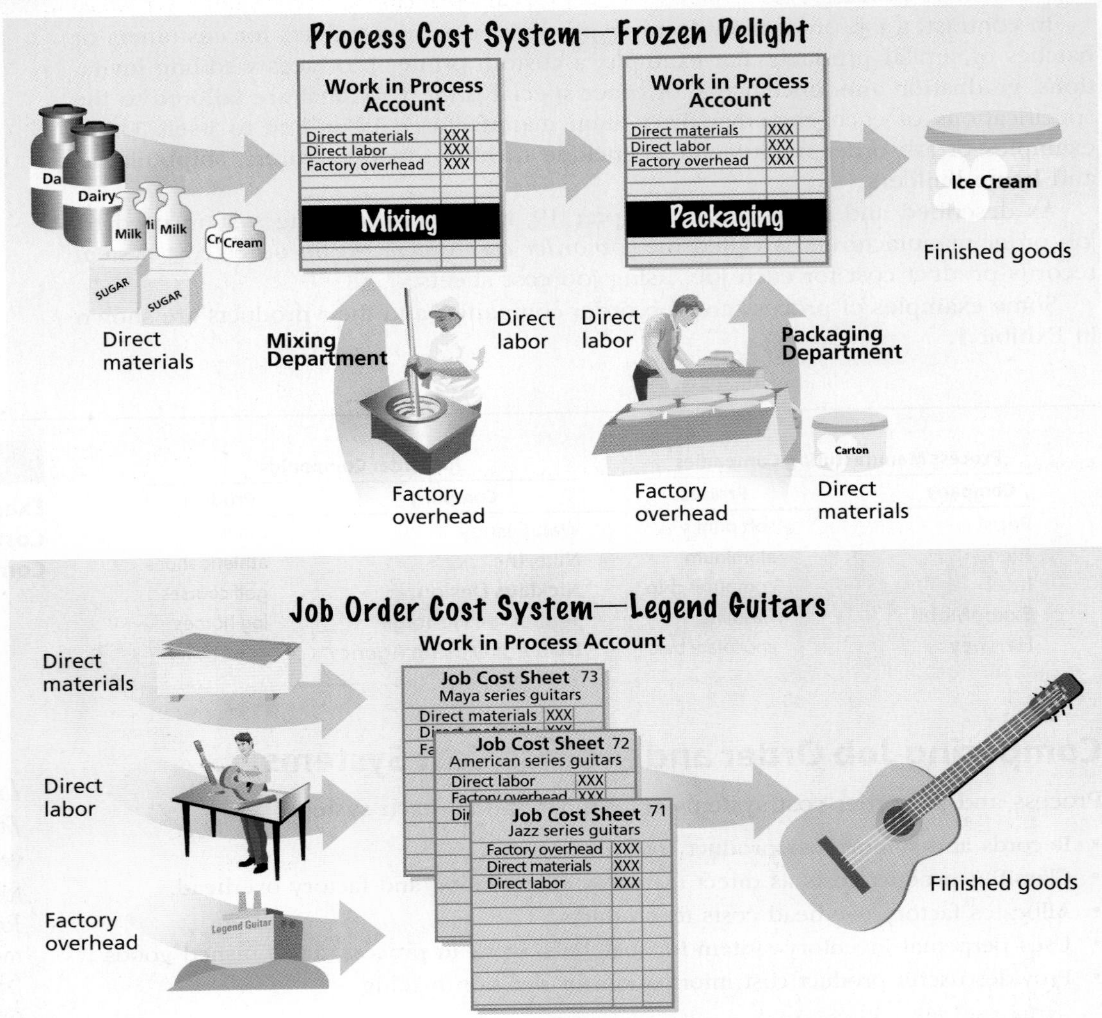

- *Direct labor costs,* which are incurred by employees in each department who run the equipment and load and unload product.
- *Factory overhead costs,* which include the utility costs (power) and depreciation on the equipment.

When the Mixing Department completes the mixing process, its product costs are transferred to the Packaging Department. When the Packaging Department completes its process, the product costs are transferred to Finished Goods. In this way, the cost of the product (a gallon of ice cream) accumulates across the entire production process.

In contrast, Exhibit 2 shows that Legend Guitars accumulates (records) product costs by jobs, using a job cost sheet for each type of guitar. Thus, Legend Guitars uses just one work in process account. As each job is completed, its product costs are transferred to Finished Goods.

In a job order cost system, the work in process at the end of the period is the sum of the job cost sheets for partially completed jobs. In a process cost system, the work in process at the end of the period is the sum of the costs remaining in each department account at the end of the period.

Example Exercise 20-1 Job Order versus Process Costing — Obj. 1

Which of the following industries would normally use job order costing systems, and which would normally use process costing systems?

Home construction	Computer chips
Beverages	Cookies
Military aircraft	Video game design and production

Follow My Example 20-1

Home construction	Job order costing
Beverages	Process costing
Military aircraft	Job order costing
Computer chips	Process costing
Cookies	Process costing
Video game design and production	Job order costing

Practice Exercises: PE 20-1A, PE 20-1B

Cost Flows for a Process Manufacturer

Exhibit 3 illustrates the *physical flow* of materials for **Frozen Delight**. Ice cream is made in a manufacturing plant in much the same way you would make it at home, except on a larger scale.

Physical Flows for a Process Manufacturer — EXHIBIT 3

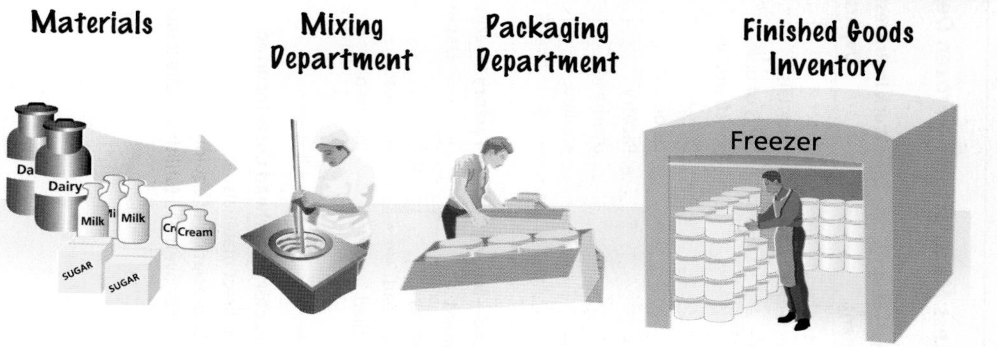

In the Mixing Department, direct materials in the form of milk, cream, and sugar are placed into a vat. An employee fills each vat, sets the cooling temperature, and sets the mix speed. The vat is cooled as the direct materials are being mixed by agitators (paddles). Factory overhead includes equipment depreciation and indirect materials.

In the Packaging Department, the ice cream is received from the Mixing Department in a form ready for packaging. The Packaging Department uses direct labor and factory overhead to package the ice cream into one-gallon containers. The ice cream is then transferred to finished goods, where it is frozen and stored in refrigerators prior to shipment to customers.

The *cost flows* in a process cost accounting system are similar to the *physical flow* of materials illustrated in Exhibit 3. The cost flows for **Frozen Delight** are illustrated in Exhibit 4 as follows:

a. The cost of materials purchased is recorded in the materials account.
b. The cost of direct materials used by the Mixing and Packaging departments is recorded in the work in process accounts for each department.

Link to Dreyer's Ice Cream

Dreyer's slow-churned ice cream uses a proprietary process that mixes nonfat milk slowly. This process, called low-temperature extrusion, allows ice cream to be made with one-third fewer calories and half the fat while tasting like normal ice cream.

Real World

Materials costs can be as high as 70% of the total product costs for many process manufacturers.

EXHIBIT 4 **Cost Flows for a Process Manufacturer—Frozen Delight**

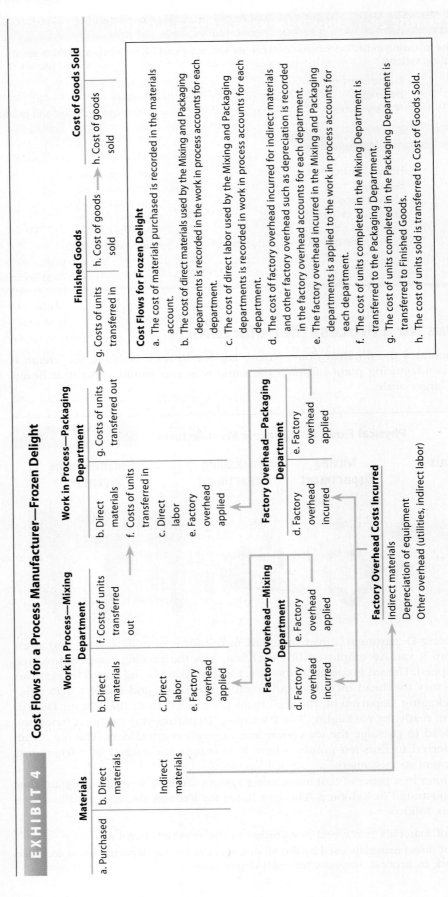

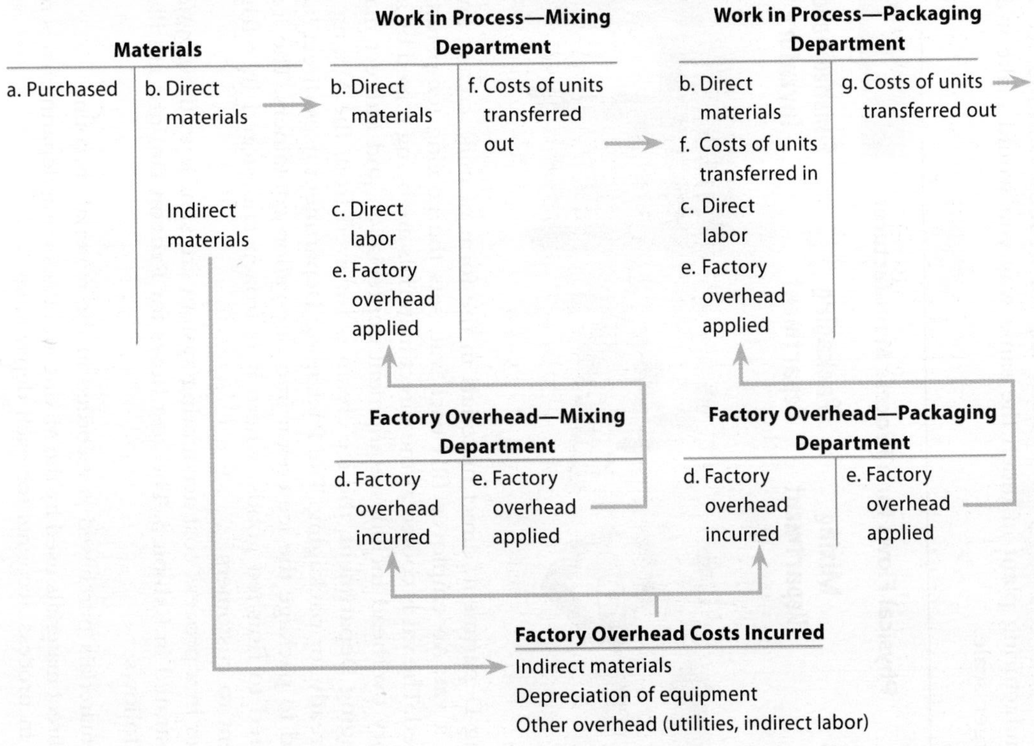

Cost Flows for Frozen Delight

a. The cost of materials purchased is recorded in the materials account.
b. The cost of direct materials used by the Mixing and Packaging departments is recorded in the work in process accounts for each department.
c. The cost of direct labor used by the Mixing and Packaging departments is recorded in work in process accounts for each department.
d. The cost of factory overhead incurred for indirect materials and other factory overhead such as depreciation is recorded in the factory overhead accounts for each department.
e. The factory overhead incurred in the Mixing and Packaging departments is applied to the work in process accounts for each department.
f. The cost of units completed in the Mixing Department is transferred to the Packaging Department.
g. The cost of units completed in the Packaging Department is transferred to Finished Goods.
h. The cost of units sold is transferred to Cost of Goods Sold.

c. The cost of direct labor used by the Mixing and Packaging departments is recorded in work in process accounts for each department.
d. The cost of factory overhead incurred for indirect materials and other factory overhead such as depreciation is recorded in the factory overhead accounts for each department.
e. The factory overhead incurred in the Mixing and Packaging departments is applied to the work in process accounts for each department.
f. The cost of units completed in the Mixing Department is transferred to the Packaging Department.
g. The cost of units completed in the Packaging Department is transferred to Finished Goods.
h. The cost of units sold is transferred to Cost of Goods Sold.

As shown in Exhibit 4, the Mixing and Packaging departments have separate factory overhead accounts. The factory overhead costs incurred for indirect materials, depreciation, and other overhead are debited to each department's factory overhead account. The overhead is applied to work in process by debiting each department's work in process account and crediting the department's factory overhead account.

Exhibit 4 illustrates how the Mixing and Packaging departments have separate work in process accounts. Each work in process account is debited for direct materials, direct labor, and applied factory overhead. In addition, the work in process account for the Packaging Department is debited for the cost of the units transferred in from the Mixing Department. Each work in process account is credited for the cost of the units transferred to the next department.

Finally, Exhibit 4 shows that the finished goods account is debited for the cost of the units transferred from the Packaging Department. The finished goods account is credited for the cost of the units sold, which is debited to the cost of goods sold account.

Link to Dreyer's Ice Cream

Dreyer's is currently a subsidiary of Nestlé, which produces Dreyer's ice cream at its Bakersfield, California, plant.

Business Connection

SUSTAINABLE PAPERMAKING

We discussed social and environmental sustainability in the introductory managerial chapter. Processing companies involved with papermaking, refining, and chemical processing focus on sustainability because of their impact on the environment. For example, papermaking requires the use of large amounts of wood fiber (cellulous), energy, and water. Thus, papermakers are actively involved in sustainability efforts to reduce the negative environmental impacts from the use of these resources. To illustrate, International Paper Company provides an annual report to external stakeholders identifying its progress toward several sustainability objectives. A recent report identified six sustainability areas:

1. **Safety:** Improve worker health and safety, resulting in a 68% reduction in life-impacting injuries.
2. **Water use:** Identify and implement water conservation opportunities at each paper mill.
3. **Greenhouse gas emissions:** Reduce greenhouse gases by using renewable carbon-neutral biomass to meet over 70% of energy needs.
4. **Forest stewardship:** Implement sustainable forest management practices that provide a low-cost wood supply while simultaneously conserving primary forests.
5. **Ethics and compliance:** Train suppliers in the company's Supplier Code of Conduct.
6. **Stakeholder engagement:** Engage with communities, customers, and governments by participating in conferences, providing donations, and volunteering.

Source: *In Our Nature: Sustainability Year in Review 2014*, International Paper Company.

Obj. 2 Prepare a cost of production report.

Cost of Production Report

In a process cost system, the cost of units transferred out of each processing department must be determined along with the cost of any partially completed units remaining in the department. The report that summarizes these costs is a cost of production report.

The **cost of production report** summarizes the production and cost data for a department as follows:

- The units the department is accountable for and the disposition of those units
- The product costs incurred by the department and the allocation of those costs between completed (transferred out) and partially completed units

A cost of production report is prepared using the following four steps:

Step 1. Determine the units to be assigned costs.
Step 2. Compute equivalent units of production.
Step 3. Determine the cost per equivalent unit.
Step 4. Allocate costs to units transferred out and partially completed units.

Preparing a cost of production report requires making a cost flow assumption. Like merchandise inventory, costs can be assumed to flow through the manufacturing process, using the first-in, first-out (FIFO), last in, first-out (LIFO), or average cost methods. Because the **first-in, first-out (FIFO) method** is often the same as the physical flow of units, the FIFO method is used in this chapter.[1]

To illustrate, a cost of production report for the Mixing Department of **Frozen Delight** for July is prepared. The July data for the Mixing Department are as follows:

Inventory in process, July 1, 5,000 gallons:		
Direct materials cost, for 5,000 gallons	$5,000	
Conversion costs, for 5,000 gallons, 70% completed	1,225	
Total inventory in process, July 1		$ 6,225
Direct materials cost for July, 60,000 gallons		66,000
Direct labor cost for July		10,500
Factory overhead applied for July		7,275
Total production costs to account for		$ 90,000
Gallons transferred to Packaging in July (includes units in process on July 1), 62,000 gallons		?
Inventory in process, July 31, 3,000 gallons, 25% completed as to conversion costs		?

By preparing a cost of production report, the cost of the gallons transferred to the Packaging Department in July and the ending work in process inventory in the Mixing Department are determined. These amounts are indicated by question marks (?).

Step 1: Determine the Units to Be Assigned Costs

The first step is to determine the units to be assigned costs. A unit can be any measure of completed production, such as tons, gallons, pounds, barrels, or cases. For **Frozen Delight**, a unit is a gallon of ice cream.

The Mixing Department is accountable for 65,000 gallons of direct materials during July, computed as follows:

1 The average cost method is illustrated in an appendix to this chapter.

Total units (gallons) charged to production:	
In process, July 1	5,000 gallons
Received from materials storage	60,000
Total units (gallons) accounted for	65,000 gallons

For July, the following three groups of units (gallons) are assigned costs:

Group 1. Units (gallons) in beginning work in process inventory on July 1.
Group 2. Units (gallons) started and completed during July.
Group 3. Units (gallons) in ending work in process inventory on July 31.

Exhibit 5 illustrates these groups of units (gallons) in the Mixing Department for July. The 5,000 gallons of beginning inventory were completed and transferred to the Packaging Department. During July, 60,000 gallons of material were started (entered into mixing). Of the 60,000 gallons started in July, 3,000 gallons were incomplete on July 31. Thus, 57,000 gallons (60,000 – 3,000) were started and completed in July.

The total units (gallons) to be assigned costs for July are summarized as follows:

Group 1	Inventory in process, July 1, completed in July	5,000 gallons
Group 2	Started and completed in July	57,000
	Transferred out to the Packaging Department in July	62,000 gallons
Group 3	Inventory in process, July 31	3,000
	Total units (gallons) to be assigned costs	65,000 gallons

The total gallons to be assigned costs (65,000) equal the total gallons accounted for (65,000) by the Mixing Department.

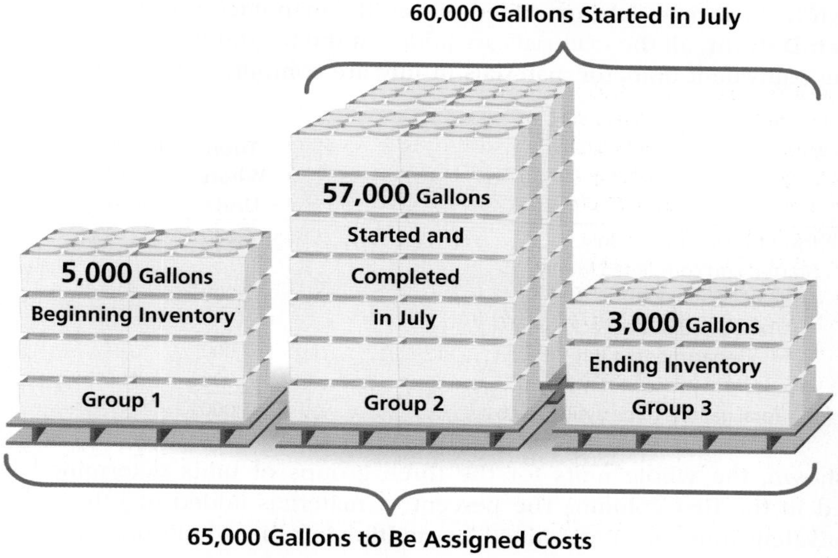

EXHIBIT 5

July Units to Be Costed—Mixing Department

Example Exercise 20-2 Units to Be Assigned Costs **Obj. 2**

Rocky Springs Beverage Company has two departments, Blending and Bottling. The Bottling Department received 57,000 liters from the Blending Department. During the period, the Bottling Department completed 58,000 liters, including 4,000 liters of work in process at the beginning of the period. The ending work in process was 3,000 liters. How many liters were started and completed during the period?

Follow My Example 20-2

54,000 liters started and completed (58,000 completed – 4,000 beginning work in process), or (57,000 started – 3,000 ending work in process)

Practice Exercises: PE 20-2A, PE 20-2B

Step 2: Compute Equivalent Units of Production

Whole units are the number of units in production during a period, whether completed or not. **Equivalent units of production** are the portion of whole units that are complete with respect to materials or conversion (direct labor and factory overhead) costs.

To illustrate, assume that a 1,000-gallon batch (vat) of ice cream at **Frozen Delight** is only 40% complete in the mixing process on May 31. Thus, the batch is only 40% complete as to conversion costs such as power. In this case, the whole units and equivalent units of production are as follows:

	Whole Units	Equivalent Units
Materials costs	1,000 gallons	1,000 gallons
Conversion costs	1,000 gallons	400 gallons (1,000 × 40%)

Because the materials costs are all added at the beginning of the process, the materials costs are 100% complete for the 1,000-gallon batch of ice cream. Thus, the whole units and equivalent units for materials costs are 1,000 gallons. However, because the batch is only 40% complete as to conversion costs, the equivalent units for conversion costs are 400 gallons.

Equivalent units for materials and conversion costs are usually determined separately as shown earlier. This is because materials and conversion costs normally enter production at different times and rates. In contrast, direct labor and factory overhead normally enter production at the same time and rate. For this reason, direct labor and factory overhead are combined as conversion costs in computing equivalent units.

Materials Equivalent Units To compute equivalent units for materials, it is necessary to know how materials are added during the manufacturing process. In the case of **Frozen Delight**, all the materials are added at the beginning of the mixing process. Thus, the equivalent units for materials in July are computed as follows:

		Total Whole Units	Percent Materials Added in July	Equivalent Units for Direct Materials
Group 1	Inventory in process, July 1	5,000	0%	0
Group 2	Started and completed in July (62,000 − 5,000)	57,000	100%	57,000
	Transferred out to Packaging Department in July	62,000	—	57,000
Group 3	Inventory in process, July 31	3,000	100%	3,000
	Total gallons to be assigned cost	65,000		60,000

As shown, the whole units for the three groups of units determined in Step 1 are listed in the first column. The percent of materials added in July is then listed. The equivalent units are determined by multiplying the whole units by the percent of materials added.

To illustrate, the July 1 inventory (Group 1) has 5,000 gallons of whole units, which are complete as to materials. That is, all the direct materials for the 5,000 gallons in process on July 1 were added in June. Thus, the percent of materials added in July is zero, and the equivalent units added in July are zero.

The 57,000 gallons started and completed in July (Group 2) are 100% complete as to materials. Thus, the equivalent units for the gallons started and completed in July are 57,000 (57,000 × 100%) gallons. The 3,000 gallons in process on July 31 (Group 3) are also 100% complete as to materials because all materials are added at the beginning of the process. Therefore, the equivalent units for the inventory in process on July 31 are 3,000 (3,000 × 100%) gallons.

The equivalent units for direct materials for **Frozen Delight** are summarized in Exhibit 6.

Direct Materials Equivalent Units EXHIBIT 6

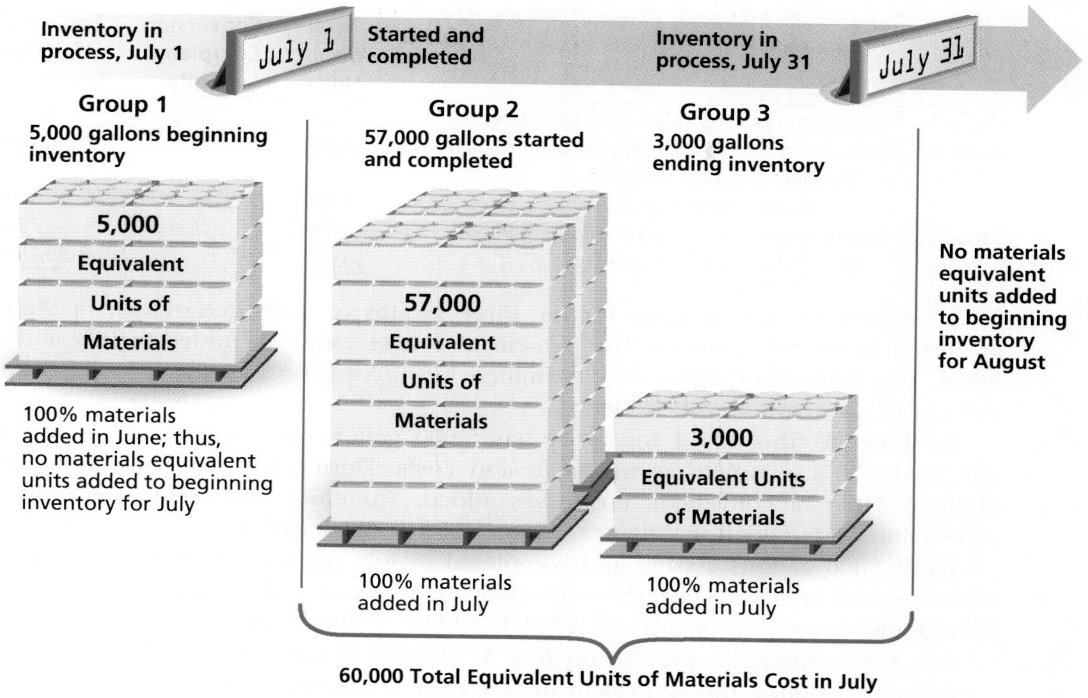

Example Exercise 20-3 Equivalent Units of Materials Cost

Obj. 2

The Bottling Department of Rocky Springs Beverage Company had 4,000 liters in the beginning work in process inventory (30% complete). During the period, 58,000 liters were completed. The ending work in process inventory was 3,000 liters (60% complete). What are the total equivalent units for direct materials if materials are added at the beginning of the process?

Follow My Example 20-3

Total equivalent units for direct materials are 57,000, computed as follows:

	Total Whole Units	Percent Materials Added in Period	Equivalent Units for Direct Materials
Inventory in process, beginning of period	4,000	0%	0
Started and completed during the period	54,000*	100%	54,000
Transferred out of Bottling (completed)	58,000	—	54,000
Inventory in process, end of period	3,000	100%	3,000
Total units to be assigned costs	61,000		57,000

*58,000 – 4,000

Practice Exercises: PE 20-3A, PE 20-3B

Conversion Equivalent Units To compute equivalent units for conversion costs, it is necessary to know how direct labor and factory overhead enter the manufacturing process. Direct labor, utilities, and equipment depreciation are often incurred uniformly during processing. For this reason, it is assumed that **Frozen Delight** incurs conversion costs evenly throughout its manufacturing process. Thus, the equivalent units for conversion costs in July are computed as follows:

		Total Whole Units	Percent Conversion Completed in July	Equivalent Units for Conversion
Group 1	Inventory in process, July 1 (70% completed)	5,000	30%	1,500
Group 2	Started and completed in July (62,000 − 5,000)	57,000	100%	57,000
	Transferred out to Packaging Department in July	62,000	—	58,500
Group 3	Inventory in process, July 31 (25% completed)......	3,000	25%	750
	Total gallons to be assigned cost	65,000		59,250

As shown, the whole units for the three groups of units determined in Step 1 are listed in the first column. The percent of conversion costs added in July is then listed. The equivalent units are determined by multiplying the whole units by the percent of conversion costs added.

To illustrate, the July 1 inventory has 5,000 gallons of whole units (Group 1), which are 70% complete as to conversion costs. During July, the remaining 30% (100% – 70%) of conversion costs was added. Therefore, the equivalent units of conversion costs added in July are 1,500 (5,000 × 30%) gallons.

The 57,000 gallons started and completed in July (Group 2) are 100% complete as to conversion costs. Thus, the equivalent units of conversion costs for the gallons started and completed in July are 57,000 (57,000 × 100%) gallons.

The 3,000 gallons in process on July 31 (Group 3) are 25% complete as to conversion costs. Hence, the equivalent units for the inventory in process on July 31 are 750 (3,000 × 25%) gallons.

The equivalent units for conversion costs for **Frozen Delight** are summarized in Exhibit 7.

EXHIBIT 7 **Conversion Equivalent Units**

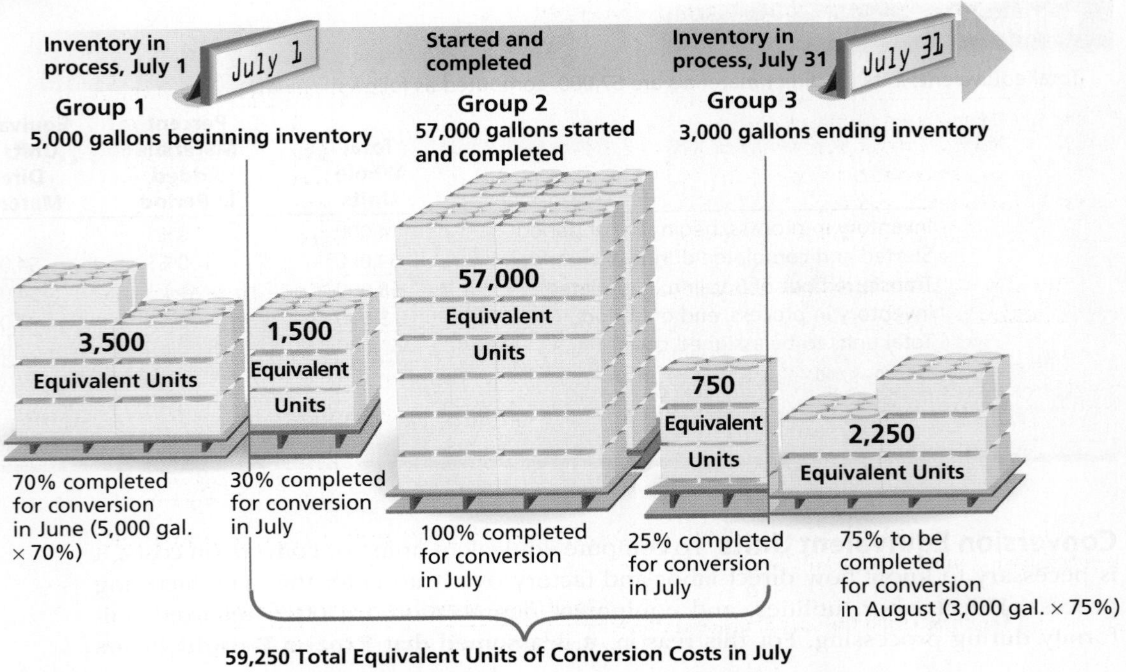

Example Exercise 20-4 Equivalent Units of Conversion Costs

Obj. 2

The Bottling Department of Rocky Springs Beverage Company had 4,000 liters in the beginning work in process inventory (30% complete). During the period, 58,000 liters were completed. The ending work in process inventory was 3,000 liters (60% complete). What are the total equivalent units for conversion costs?

Follow My Example 20-4

	Total Whole Units	Percent Conversion Completed in Period	Equivalent Units for Conversion
Inventory in process, beginning of period	4,000	70%	2,800
Started and completed during the period	54,000*	100%	54,000
Transferred out of Bottling (completed)	58,000	—	56,800
Inventory in process, end of period	3,000	60%	1,800
Total units to be assigned costs	61,000		58,600

*58,000 − 4,000

Practice Exercises: PE 20-4A, PE 20-4B

Step 3: Determine the Cost per Equivalent Unit

The next step in preparing the cost of production report is to compute the cost per equivalent unit for direct materials and conversion costs. The **cost per equivalent unit** for direct materials and conversion costs is computed as follows:

$$\text{Direct Materials Cost per Equivalent Unit} = \frac{\text{Total Direct Materials Cost for the Period}}{\text{Total Equivalent Units of Direct Materials}}$$

$$\text{Conversion Cost per Equivalent Unit} = \frac{\text{Total Conversion Costs for the Period}}{\text{Total Equivalent Units of Conversion Costs}}$$

The July direct materials and conversion cost equivalent units for Frozen Delight's Mixing Department from Step 2 are as follows:

		Equivalent Units	
		Direct Materials	Conversion
Group 1	Inventory in process, July 1	0	1,500
Group 2	Started and completed in July (62,000 – 5,000)	57,000	57,000
	Transferred out to Packaging Department in July	57,000	58,500
Group 3	Inventory in process, July 31	3,000	750
	Total gallons to be assigned cost	60,000	59,250

The direct materials and conversion costs incurred by Frozen Delight in July are repeated as follows:

Direct materials		$66,000
Conversion costs:		
Direct labor	$10,500	
Factory overhead	7,275	17,775
Total product costs		$83,775

The direct materials and conversion costs per equivalent unit are $1.10 and $0.30 per gallon, computed as follows:

$$\text{Direct Materials Cost per Equivalent Unit} = \frac{\text{Total Direct Materials Cost for the Period}}{\text{Total Equivalent Units of Direct Materials}}$$

$$\text{Direct Materials Cost per Equivalent Unit} = \frac{\$66{,}000}{60{,}000 \text{ gallons}} = \$1.10 \text{ per gallon}$$

$$\text{Conversion Cost per Equivalent Unit} = \frac{\text{Total Conversion Costs for the Period}}{\text{Total Equivalent Units of Conversion Costs}}$$

$$\text{Conversion Cost per Equivalent Unit} = \frac{\$17{,}775}{59{,}250 \text{ gallons}} = \$0.30 \text{ per gallon}$$

The preceding costs per equivalent unit are used in Step 4 to allocate the direct materials and conversion costs to the completed and partially completed units.

Example Exercise 20-5 Cost per Equivalent Unit

Obj. 2

The cost of direct materials transferred into the Bottling Department of Rocky Springs Beverage Company is $22,800. The conversion cost for the period in the Bottling Department is $8,790. The total equivalent units for direct materials and conversion are 57,000 liters and 58,600 liters, respectively. Determine the direct materials and conversion costs per equivalent unit.

Follow My Example 20-5

$$\text{Direct Materials Cost per Equivalent Unit} = \frac{\$22{,}800}{57{,}000 \text{ liters}} = \$0.40 \text{ per liter}$$

$$\text{Conversion Cost per Equivalent Unit} = \frac{\$8{,}790}{58{,}600 \text{ liters}} = \$0.15 \text{ per liter}$$

Practice Exercises: PE 20-5A, PE 20-5B

Step 4: Allocate Costs to Units Transferred Out and Partially Completed Units

Product costs must be allocated to the units transferred out and the partially completed units on hand at the end of the period. The product costs are allocated using the costs per equivalent unit for materials and conversion costs that were computed in Step 3.

The total production costs to be assigned for **Frozen Delight** in July are $90,000, computed as follows:

Inventory in process, July 1, 5,000 gallons:	
Direct materials cost, for 5,000 gallons	$ 5,000
Conversion costs, for 5,000 gallons, 70% completed	1,225
Total inventory in process, July 1	$ 6,225
Direct materials cost for July, 60,000 gallons	66,000
Direct labor cost for July	10,500
Factory overhead applied for July	7,275
Total production costs to account for	$90,000

The units to be assigned these costs follow. The costs to be assigned these units are indicated by question marks (?).

		Units	Total Cost
Group 1	Inventory in process, July 1, completed in July	5,000 gallons	?
Group 2	Started and completed in July	57,000	?
	Transferred out to the Packaging Department in July	62,000 gallons	?
Group 3	Inventory in process, July 31	3,000	?
	Total	65,000 gallons	$90,000

Group 1: Inventory in Process on July 1 The 5,000 gallons of inventory in process on July 1 (Group 1) were completed and transferred out to the Packaging Department in July. The cost of these units of $6,675 is determined as follows:

	Direct Materials Costs	Conversion Costs	Total Costs
Inventory in process, July 1 balance			$6,225
Equivalent units for completing the July 1 in-process inventory	0	1,500	
Cost per equivalent unit	× $1.10	× $0.30	
Cost to complete July 1 in-process inventory	0	$450	450
Cost of July 1 in-process inventory transferred to Packaging Department			$6,675

As shown, $6,225 of the cost of the July 1 in-process inventory of 5,000 gallons was carried over from June. This cost plus the cost of completing the 5,000 gallons in July was transferred to the Packaging Department during July. The cost of completing the 5,000 gallons during July is $450. The $450 represents the conversion costs necessary to complete the remaining 30% of the processing. No direct materials costs were added in July because all the materials costs had been added in June. Thus, the cost of the 5,000 gallons in process on July 1 (Group 1) transferred to the Packaging Department is $6,675.

Group 2: Started and Completed The 57,000 units started and completed in July (Group 2) incurred all (100%) of their direct materials and conversion costs in July. Thus, the cost of the 57,000 gallons started and completed is $79,800, computed by multiplying 57,000 gallons by the costs per equivalent unit for materials and conversion costs as follows:

	Direct Materials Costs	Conversion Costs	Total Costs
Units started and completed in July	57,000 gallons	57,000 gallons	
Cost per equivalent unit	× $1.10	× $0.30	
Cost of the units started and completed in July	$62,700	$17,100	$79,800

The total cost of $86,475 transferred to the Packaging Department in July is the sum of the beginning inventory cost and the costs of the units started and completed in July, computed as follows:

Group 1	Cost of July 1 in-process inventory	$ 6,675
Group 2	Cost of the units started and completed in July	79,800
	Total costs transferred to Packaging Department in July	$86,475

Group 3: Inventory in Process on July 31 The 3,000 gallons in process on July 31 (Group 3) incurred all their direct materials costs and 25% of their conversion costs in July. The cost of these partially completed units of $3,525 is computed as follows:

	Direct Materials Costs	Conversion Costs	Total Costs
Equivalent units in ending inventory	3,000 gallons	750 gallons	
Cost per equivalent unit	× $1.10	× $0.30	
Cost of July 31 in-process inventory	$3,300	$225	$3,525

The 3,000 gallons in process on July 31 received all (100%) of their materials in July. Therefore, the direct materials cost incurred in July is $3,300 (3,000 × $1.10). The conversion costs of $225 represent the cost of the 750 (3,000 × 25%) equivalent gallons multiplied by the cost of $0.30 per equivalent unit for conversion costs. The sum of the direct materials cost ($3,300) and the conversion costs ($225) equals the total cost of the July 31 work in process inventory of $3,525 ($3,300 + $225).

To summarize, the total manufacturing costs for Frozen Delight in July were assigned as follows. In doing so, the question marks (?) for the costs to be assigned to units in Groups 1, 2, and 3 have been answered.

		Units	Total Cost
Group 1	Inventory in process, July 1, completed in July	5,000 gallons	$ 6,675
Group 2	Started and completed in July	57,000	79,800
	Transferred out to the Packaging Department in July	62,000 gallons	$86,475
Group 3	Inventory in process, July 31	3,000	3,525
	Total	65,000 gallons	$90,000

Example Exercise 20-6 Cost of Units Transferred Out and Ending Work in Process

Obj. 2

The costs per equivalent unit of direct materials and conversion in the Bottling Department of Rocky Springs Beverage Company are $0.40 and $0.15, respectively. The equivalent units to be assigned costs are as follows:

	Equivalent Units	
	Direct Materials	**Conversion**
Inventory in process, beginning of period	0	2,800
Started and completed during the period	54,000	54,000
Transferred out of Bottling (completed)	54,000	56,800
Inventory in process, end of period	3,000	1,800
Total units to be assigned costs	57,000	58,600

The beginning work in process inventory had a cost of $1,860. Determine the cost of units transferred out and the ending work in process inventory.

Follow My Example 20-6

	Direct Materials Costs		Conversion Costs	Total Costs
Inventory in process, beginning balance				$ 1,860
Inventory in process, to complete	0	+	2,800 × $0.15	420
Started and completed during the period	54,000 × $0.40	+	54,000 × $0.15	29,700
Transferred out of Bottling (completed)				$31,980
Inventory in process, end of period	3,000 × $0.40	+	1,800 × $0.15	1,470
Total costs assigned by the Bottling Department				$33,450
Completed and transferred out of production	$31,980			
Inventory in process, ending	$ 1,470			

Practice Exercises: PE 20-6A, PE 20-6B

Preparing the Cost of Production Report

A cost of production report is prepared for each processing department at periodic intervals. The report summarizes the following production quantity and cost data:

- The units for which the department is accountable and the disposition of those units
- The production costs incurred by the department and the allocation of those costs between completed (transferred out) and partially completed units

Using Steps 1–4, the July cost of production report for **Frozen Delight**'s Mixing Department is shown in Exhibit 8. During July, the Mixing Department was accountable for 65,000 units (gallons). Of these units, 62,000 units were completed and transferred to the Packaging Department. The remaining 3,000 units are partially completed and are part of the in-process inventory as of July 31.

The Mixing Department was responsible for $90,000 of production costs during July. The cost of goods transferred to the Packaging Department in July was $86,475. The remaining cost of $3,525 is part of the in-process inventory as of July 31.

Cost of Production Report for Frozen Delight's Mixing Department—FIFO EXHIBIT 8

	A	B	C	D	E	
1		**Frozen Delight**				
2		**Cost of Production Report—Mixing Department**				
3		**For the Month Ended July 31**				Step 1
4						Step 2
5		Whole Units	Equivalent Units			
6	**UNITS**		Direct Materials	Conversion		
7	Units charged to production:					
8	Inventory in process, July 1	5,000				
9	Received from materials storeroom	60,000				
10	Total units accounted for by the Mixing Department	65,000				
11						
12	Units to be assigned costs:					
13	Inventory in process, July 1 (70% completed)	5,000	0	1,500		
14	Started and completed in July	57,000	57,000	57,000		
15	Transferred to Packaging Department in July	62,000	57,000	58,500		
16	Inventory in process, July 31 (25% completed)	3,000	3,000	750		
17	Total units to be assigned costs	65,000	60,000	59,250		
18						
19				**Costs**		
20	**COSTS**		Direct Materials	Conversion	Total	
21						
22	Cost per equivalent unit:					Step 3
23	Total costs for July in Mixing Department		$ 66,000	$ 17,775		
24	Total equivalent units (from Step 2)		÷60,000	÷59,250		
25	Cost per equivalent unit		$ 1.10	$ 0.30		
26						
27	Costs assigned to production:					
28	Inventory in process, July 1				$ 6,225	
29	Costs incurred in July				83,775[a]	
30	Total costs accounted for by the Mixing Department				$90,000	
31						
32						
33	Cost allocated to completed and partially					Step 4
34	completed units:					
35	Inventory in process, July 1 balance				$ 6,225	
36	To complete inventory in process, July 1		$ 0 +	$ 450[b] =	450	
37	Cost of completed July 1 work in process				$ 6,675	
38	Started and completed in July		62,700[c] +	17,100[d] =	79,800	
39	Transferred to Packaging Department in July				$86,475	
40	Inventory in process, July 31		$ 3,300[e] +	$ 225[f] =	3,525	
41	Total costs assigned by the Mixing Department				$90,000	
42						

[a]$66,000 + $10,500 + $7,275 = $83,775 [b]1,500 units × $0.30 = $450 [c]57,000 units × $1.10 = $62,700 [d]57,000 units × $0.30 = $17,100
[e]3,000 units × $1.10 = $3,300 [f]750 units × $0.30 = $225

Journal Entries for a Process Cost System

Obj. 3 Journalize entries for transactions using a process cost system.

The journal entries to record the cost flows and transactions for a process cost system are illustrated in this section. As a basis for illustration, the July transactions for **Frozen Delight** are used. To simplify, the entries are shown in summary form, even though many of the transactions would be recorded daily.

a. Purchased materials, including milk, cream, sugar, packaging, and indirect materials on account, $88,000.

a.	Materials	88,000	
	Accounts Payable		88,000

b. The Mixing Department requisitioned milk, cream, and sugar, $66,000. This is the total amount from the original July data. Packaging materials of $8,000 were requisitioned by the Packaging Department. Indirect materials for the Mixing and Packaging departments were $4,125 and $3,000, respectively.

b.	Work in Process—Mixing	66,000	
	Work in Process—Packaging	8,000	
	Factory Overhead—Mixing	4,125	
	Factory Overhead—Packaging	3,000	
	Materials		81,125

c. Incurred direct labor in the Mixing and Packaging departments of $10,500 and $12,000, respectively.

c.	Work in Process—Mixing	10,500	
	Work in Process—Packaging	12,000	
	Wages Payable		22,500

d. Recognized equipment depreciation for the Mixing and Packaging departments of $3,350 and $1,000, respectively.

d.	Factory Overhead—Mixing	3,350	
	Factory Overhead—Packaging	1,000	
	Accumulated Depreciation—Equipment		4,350

e. Applied factory overhead to Mixing and Packaging departments of $7,275 and $3,500, respectively.

e.	Work in Process—Mixing	7,275	
	Work in Process—Packaging	3,500	
	Factory Overhead—Mixing		7,275
	Factory Overhead—Packaging		3,500

f. Transferred costs of $86,475 from the Mixing Department to the Packaging Department per the cost of production report in Exhibit 8.

f.	Work in Process—Packaging	86,475	
	Work in Process—Mixing		86,475

g. Transferred goods of $106,000 out of the Packaging Department to Finished Goods according to the Packaging Department cost of production report (not illustrated).

g.	Finished Goods—Ice Cream	106,000	
	Work in Process—Packaging		106,000

h. Recorded the cost of goods sold out of the finished goods inventory of $107,000.

	h.	Cost of Goods Sold		107,000	
		Finished Goods—Ice Cream			107,000

Exhibit 9 shows the flow of costs for each transaction. The highlighted amounts in Exhibit 9 were determined from assigning the costs in the Mixing Department. These amounts were computed and are shown at the bottom of the cost of production report for the Mixing Department in Exhibit 8. Likewise, the amount transferred out of the Packaging Department to Finished Goods would have also been determined from a cost of production report for the Packaging Department.

Frozen Delight's Cost Flows **EXHIBIT 9**

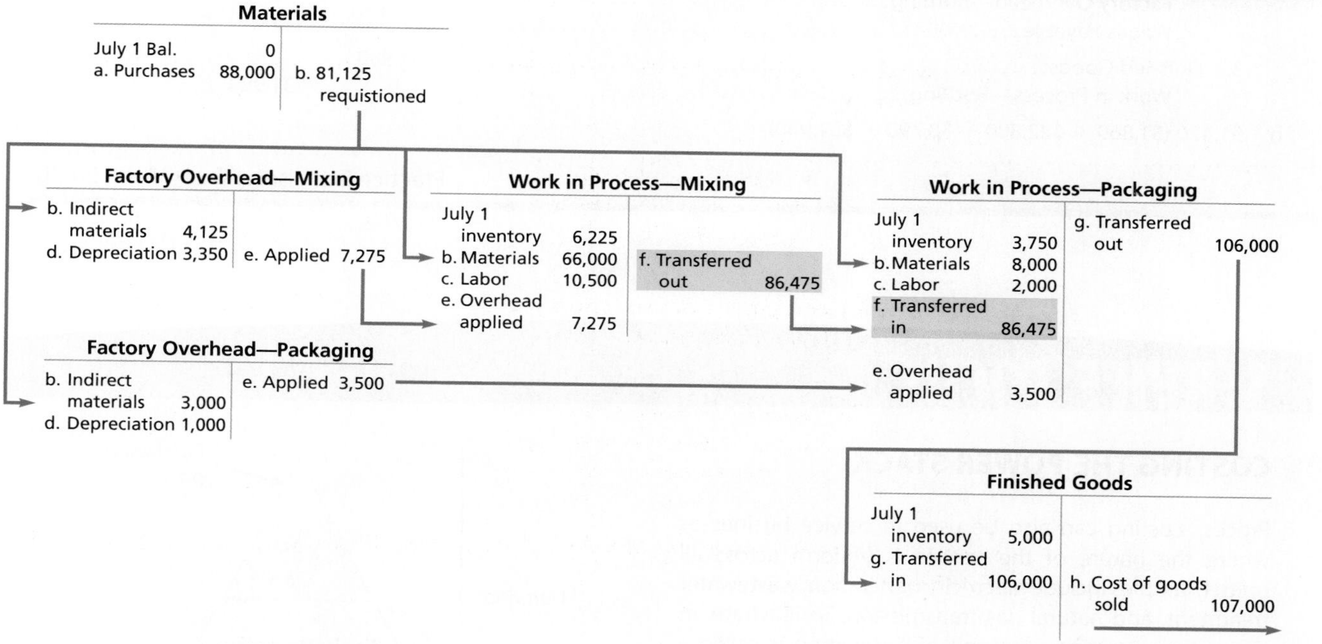

The ending inventories for Frozen Delight are reported on the July 31 balance sheet as follows:

Materials	$ 6,875
Work in Process—Mixing Department	3,525
Work in Process—Packaging Department	7,725
Finished Goods	4,000
Total inventories	$22,125

The $3,525 balance of Work in Process—Mixing Department is the amount determined from the bottom of the cost of production report in Exhibit 8.

Example Exercise 20-7 Process Cost Journal Entries

Obj. 3

The cost of materials transferred into the Bottling Department of Rocky Springs Beverage Company is $22,800, including $20,000 from the Blending Department and $2,800 from the materials storeroom. The conversion cost for the period in the Bottling Department is $8,790 ($3,790 factory overhead applied and $5,000 direct labor). The total cost transferred to Finished Goods for the period was $31,980. The Bottling Department had a beginning inventory of $1,860.

a. Journalize (1) the cost of transferred-in materials, (2) conversion costs, and (3) the costs transferred out to Finished Goods.

b. Determine the balance of Work in Process—Bottling at the end of the period.

Follow My Example 20-7

a.	1. Work in Process—Bottling	22,800	
	Work in Process—Blending		20,000
	Materials		2,800
	2. Work in Process—Bottling	8,790	
	Factory Overhead—Bottling		3,790
	Wages Payable		5,000
	3. Finished Goods	31,980	
	Work in Process—Bottling		31,980

b. $1,470 ($1,860 + $22,800 + $8,790 − $31,980)

Practice Exercises: PE 20-7A, PE 20-7B

SERVICE FOCUS

COSTING THE POWER STACK

Process costing can also be used in service businesses where the nature of the service is uniform across all units. Examples include electricity generation, wastewater treatment, and natural gas transmission. To illustrate, in generating electricity, the unit of production is called a *megawatt hour*, where each megawatt hour is the same across all sources of generation.

Unlike product manufacturing, service companies often do not have inventory. For example, in generating electricity, the electricity cannot be stored. Thus, electric companies such as **Duke Energy Corporation** match the production of electricity to the demand in real time. Electric companies use what is termed the *power stack* to match power supply to demand by arranging generating facilities in order of cost per megawatt hour. The least cost per megawatt hour facilities satisfy initial demand at the bottom of the stack, while the highest cost per megawatt hour power sources are placed at top of the stack to satisfy peak loads, as illustrated in the following graph:

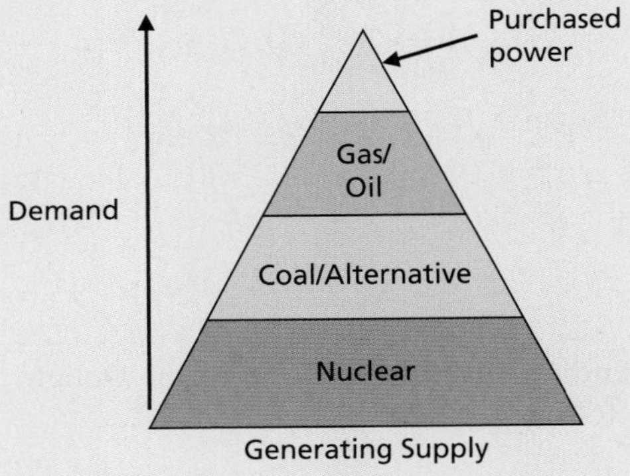

The cost per megawatt hour is determined using process costing by accumulating the conversion costs such as equipment depreciation, labor, and maintenance plus the cost of fuel for each facility. These costs are divided by the megawatt hours generated. Because there are no inventories, the additional complexity of equivalent units is avoided. The resulting cost per megawatt hour by facility is used to develop the power stack.

Using the Cost of Production Report for Decision Making

Obj. 4 Describe and illustrate the use of cost of production reports for decision making.

The cost of production report is often used by managers for decisions involving the control and improvement of operations. To illustrate, cost of production reports for **Frozen Delight** and **Holland Beverage Company** are used. Finally, the computation and use of yield are discussed.

Cost per Equivalent Unit Between Periods

The cost of production report for the Mixing Department is shown in Exhibit 8. The cost per equivalent unit for June can be determined from the beginning inventory. The original Frozen Delight data indicate that the July 1 inventory in process of $6,225 consists of the following costs:

Direct materials cost, 5,000 gallons	$5,000
Conversion costs, 5,000 gallons, 70% completed	1,225
Total inventory in process, July 1	$6,225

Using the preceding data, the June costs per equivalent unit of materials and conversion costs can be determined as follows:

$$\text{Direct Materials Cost per Equivalent Unit} = \frac{\text{Total Direct Materials Cost for the Period}}{\text{Total Equivalent Units of Direct Materials}}$$

$$\text{Direct Materials Cost per Equivalent Unit} = \frac{\$5{,}000}{5{,}000 \text{ gallons}} = \$1.00 \text{ per gallon}$$

$$\text{Conversion Cost per Equivalent Unit} = \frac{\text{Total Conversion Costs for the Period}}{\text{Total Equivalent Units of Conversion Costs}}$$

$$\text{Conversion Cost per Equivalent Unit} = \frac{\$1{,}225}{(5{,}000 \times 70\%) \text{ gallons}} = \$0.35 \text{ per gallon}$$

In July, the cost per equivalent unit of materials increased by $0.10 per gallon, while the cost per equivalent unit for conversion costs decreased by $0.05 per gallon, computed as follows:

	July*	June	Increase (Decrease)
Cost per equivalent unit for direct materials	$1.10	$1.00	$ 0.10
Cost per equivalent unit for conversion costs	0.30	0.35	(0.05)

*From Exhibit 8

Frozen Delight's management could use the preceding analysis as a basis for investigating the increase in the direct materials cost per equivalent unit and the decrease in the conversion cost per equivalent unit.

Cost Category Analysis

A cost of production report may be prepared showing more cost categories beyond just direct materials and conversion costs. This greater detail can help managers isolate problems and seek opportunities for improvement.

To illustrate, the Blending Department of Holland Beverage Company prepared cost of production reports for April and May. To simplify, assume that the Blending Department had no beginning or ending work in process inventory in either month. That is, all units started were completed in each month. The cost of production reports showing multiple cost categories for April and May in the Blending Department are as follows:

	A	B	C
1	Cost of Production Reports		
2	Holland Beverage Company—Blending Department		
3	For the Months Ended April 30 and May 31		
4		April	May
5	Direct materials	$ 20,000	$ 40,600
6	Direct labor	15,000	29,400
7	Energy	8,000	20,000
8	Repairs	4,000	8,000
9	Tank cleaning	3,000	8,000
10	Total	$ 50,000	$106,000
11	Units completed	÷100,000	÷200,000
12	Cost per unit	$ 0.50	$ 0.53
13			

The May results indicate that total unit costs have increased from $0.50 to $0.53, or 6% in May. To determine the possible causes for this increase, the cost of production report is restated in per-unit terms by dividing the costs by the number of units completed, as follows:

	A	B	C	D
1	Blending Department			
2	Per-Unit Expense Comparisons			
3		April	May	% Change
4	Direct materials	$0.200	$0.203	1.50%
5	Direct labor	0.150	0.147	−2.00%
6	Energy	0.080	0.100	25.00%
7	Repairs	0.040	0.040	0.00%
8	Tank cleaning	0.030	0.040	33.33%
9	Total	$0.500	$0.530	6.00%
10				

Both energy and tank cleaning per-unit costs have increased significantly in May. These increases should be further investigated. For example, the increase in energy may be due to the machines losing fuel efficiency. This could lead management to repair the machines. The tank cleaning costs could be investigated in a similar fashion.

Yield

In addition to unit costs, managers of process manufacturers are also concerned about yield. The **yield** is computed as follows:

$$\text{Yield} = \frac{\text{Quantity of Material Output}}{\text{Quantity of Material Input}}$$

To illustrate, assume that 1,000 pounds of sugar enter the Packaging Department and 980 pounds of sugar were packed. The yield is 98%, computed as follows:

$$\text{Yield} = \frac{\text{Quantity of Material Output}}{\text{Quantity of Material Input}} = \frac{\text{980 pounds}}{\text{1,000 pounds}} = 98\%$$

Thus, two percent (100% – 98%) or 20 pounds of sugar were lost or spilled during the packing process. Managers can investigate significant changes in yield over time or significant differences in yield from industry standards.

Example Exercise 20-8 Using Process Costs for Decision Making **Obj. 4**

The cost of energy consumed in producing good units in the Bottling Department of Rocky Springs Beverage Company was $4,200 and $3,700 for March and April, respectively. The number of equivalent units produced in March and April was 70,000 liters and 74,000 liters, respectively. Evaluate the change in the cost of energy between the two months.

Follow My Example 20-8

$$\text{Energy cost per liter, March} = \frac{\$4,200}{70,000 \text{ liters}} = \$0.06$$

$$\text{Energy cost per liter, April} = \frac{\$3,700}{74,000 \text{ liters}} = \$0.05$$

The cost of energy has improved by 1 cent per liter between March and April.

Practice Exercises: PE 20-8A, PE 20-8B

Lean Manufacturing

Obj. 5 Compare lean manufacturing with traditional manufacturing processing.

The objective of most manufacturers is to produce products with high quality, low cost, and instant availability. In attempting to achieve this objective, many manufacturers have implemented lean manufacturing. **Lean manufacturing** is a management approach that produces products with high quality, low cost, fast response, and immediate availability. Lean manufacturing obtains efficiencies and flexibility by reorganizing the traditional production process.

Traditional Production Process

A traditional manufacturing process for a furniture manufacturer is shown in Exhibit 10. The product (chair) moves through seven processes. In each process, workers are assigned a specific job, which is performed repeatedly as unfinished products are received from the preceding department. The product moves from process to process as each function or step is completed.

EXHIBIT 10

Traditional Production Line

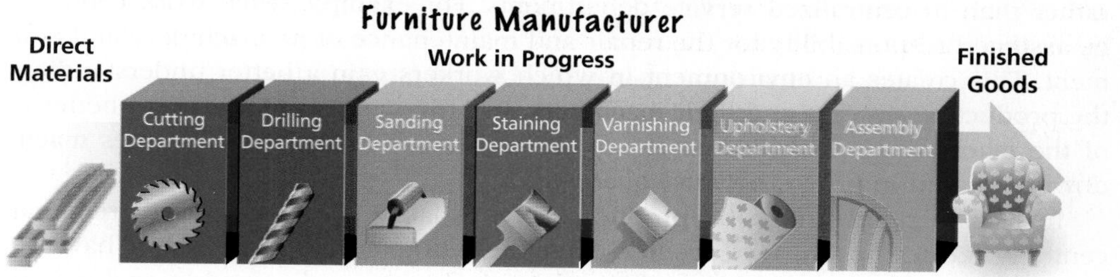

For the furniture maker in Exhibit 10, the product (chair) moves through the following processes:

1. In the Cutting Department, the wood is cut to design specifications.
2. In the Drilling Department, the wood is drilled to design specifications.
3. In the Sanding Department, the wood is sanded.
4. In the Staining Department, the wood is stained.
5. In the Varnishing Department, varnish and other protective coatings are applied.
6. In the Upholstery Department, fabric and other materials are added.
7. In the Assembly Department, the product (chair) is assembled.

In the traditional production process, supervisors enter materials into manufacturing to keep all the manufacturing departments (processes) operating. Some departments, however, may process materials more rapidly than others. In addition, if one department stops because of machine breakdowns, for example, the preceding departments usually continue production in order to avoid idle time. In such cases, a buildup of work in process inventories results in some departments.

Lean Production Process

In lean manufacturing, processing functions are combined into work centers, sometimes called **manufacturing cells**. For example, the seven departments illustrated in Exhibit 10 might be reorganized into the following three work centers:

1. Work Center 1 performs the cutting, drilling, and sanding functions.
2. Work Center 2 performs the staining and varnishing functions.
3. Work Center 3 performs the upholstery and assembly functions.

The preceding lean manufacturing process is illustrated in Exhibit 11.

EXHIBIT 11

Lean Production Line

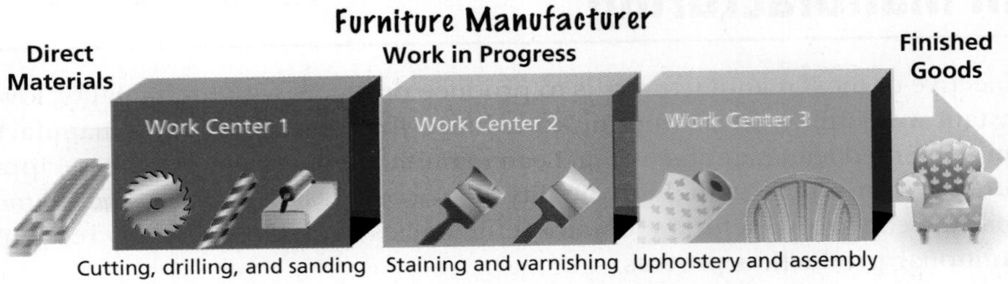

In traditional manufacturing, a worker typically performs only one function. However, in lean manufacturing, work centers complete several functions. Thus, workers are often cross-trained to perform more than one function. Research has indicated that workers who perform several functions identify better with the end product. This creates pride in the product and improves quality and productivity.

The activities supporting the manufacturing process are called *service activities*. For example, repair and maintenance of manufacturing equipment are service activities. In lean manufacturing, service activities may be assigned to individual work centers rather than to centralized service departments. For example, each work center may be assigned responsibility for the repair and maintenance of its machinery and equipment. This creates an environment in which workers gain a better understanding of the production process and their machinery. In turn, workers tend to take better care of the machinery, which decreases repairs and maintenance costs, reduces machine downtime, and improves product quality.

In lean manufacturing, the product is often placed on a movable carrier that is centrally located in the work center. After the workers in a work center have completed their activities with the product, the entire carrier and any additional materials are moved just in time to satisfy the demand or need of the next work center. In this sense, the product is said to be "pulled through." Each work center is connected to other work centers through information contained on a Kanban, which is a Japanese term for cards.

In summary, the primary objective of lean manufacturing is to increase the efficiency of operations. This is achieved by eliminating waste and simplifying the production process. At the same time, lean manufacturing continually improves the manufacturing process and product quality.

Real World

Before Caterpillar implemented JIT, a transmission traveled 10 miles through the factory and required 1,000 pieces of paper to support the manufacturing process. After implementing lean manufacturing, a transmission travels only 200 feet and requires only 10 pieces of paper.

APPENDIX

Average Cost Method

A cost flow assumption must be used as product costs flow through manufacturing processes. In this chapter, the first-in, first-out cost flow method was used for the Mixing Department of Frozen Delight. In this appendix, the average cost flow method is illustrated for S&W Ice Cream Company (S&W).

Determining Costs Using the Average Cost Method

S&W's operations are similar to those of Frozen Delight. Like Frozen Delight, S&W mixes direct materials (milk, cream, sugar) in refrigerated vats and has two manufacturing departments, Mixing and Packaging.

The manufacturing data for the Mixing Department for July are as follows:

Inventory in process, July 1, 5,000 gallons (70% completed)	$ 6,200
Direct materials cost incurred in July, 60,000 gallons	66,000
Direct labor cost incurred in July	10,500
Factory overhead applied in July	6,405
Total production costs to account for	$89,105
Cost of goods transferred to Packaging in July (includes units in process on July 1), 62,000 gallons	?
Cost of work in process inventory, July 31, 3,000 gallons, 25% completed as to conversion costs	?

Using the average cost method, the objective is to allocate the total costs of production of $89,105 to the following:

- The 62,000 gallons completed and transferred to the Packaging Department
- The 3,000 gallons in the July 31 (ending) work in process inventory

The preceding costs show two question marks. These amounts are determined by preparing a cost of production report, using the following four steps:

Step 1. Determine the units to be assigned costs.
Step 2. Compute equivalent units of production.
Step 3. Determine the cost per equivalent unit.
Step 4. Allocate costs to transferred out and partially completed units.

Under the average cost method, all production costs (materials and conversion costs) are combined for determining equivalent units and cost per equivalent unit.

Step 1: Determine the Units to Be Assigned Costs The first step is to determine the units to be assigned costs. A unit can be any measure of completed production, such as tons, gallons, pounds, barrels, or cases. For S&W, a unit is a gallon of ice cream.

S&W's Mixing Department had 65,000 gallons of direct materials to account for during July, as shown here.

Total gallons to account for:	
Inventory in process, July 1	5,000 gallons
Received from materials storeroom	60,000
Total units to account for by the Packaging Department	65,000 gallons

There are two groups of units to be assigned costs for the period.

Group 1	Units completed and transferred out
Group 2	Units in the July 31 (ending) work in process inventory

During July, the Mixing Department completed and transferred 62,000 gallons to the Packaging Department. Of the 60,000 gallons started in July, 57,000 (60,000 − 3,000) gallons were completed and transferred to the Packaging Department. Thus, the ending work in process inventory consists of 3,000 gallons.

The total units (gallons) to be assigned costs for S&W can be summarized as follows:

Group 1	Units transferred out to the Packaging Department in July	62,000 gallons
Group 2	Inventory in process, July 31	3,000
	Total gallons to be assigned costs	65,000 gallons

The total units (gallons) to be assigned costs (65,000 gallons) equal the total units to account for (65,000 gallons).

Step 2: Compute Equivalent Units of Production S&W has 3,000 gallons of whole units in the work in process inventory for the Mixing Department on July 31. Because these units are 25% complete, the number of equivalent units in process in the Mixing Department on July 31 is 750 gallons (3,000 gallons × 25%). Because the units transferred to the Packaging Department have been completed, the whole units (62,000 gallons) transferred are the same as the equivalent units transferred.

The total equivalent units of production for the Mixing Department are determined by adding the equivalent units in the ending work in process inventory to the units transferred and completed during the period, computed as follows:

Equivalent units completed and transferred to the Packaging Department during July	62,000 gallons
Equivalent units in ending work in process, July 31	750
Total equivalent units	62,750 gallons

Step 3: Determine the Cost per Equivalent Unit Because materials and conversion costs are combined under the average cost method, the cost per equivalent unit is determined by dividing the total production costs by the total equivalent units of production as follows:

$$\text{Cost per Equivalent Unit} = \frac{\text{Total Production Costs}}{\text{Total Equivalent Units}}$$

$$\text{Cost per Equivalent Unit} = \frac{\text{Total Production Costs}}{\text{Total Equivalent Units}} = \frac{\$89{,}105}{62{,}750 \text{ gallons}} = \$1.42$$

The cost per equivalent unit is used in Step 4 to allocate the production costs to the completed and partially completed units.

Step 4: Allocate Costs to Transferred Out and Partially Completed Units

The cost of transferred and partially completed units is determined by multiplying the cost per equivalent unit times the equivalent units of production. For S&W's Mixing Department, these costs are determined as follows:

Group 1	Transferred out to the Packaging Department (62,000 gallons × $1.42)	$88,040
Group 2	Inventory in process, July 31 (3,000 gallons × 25% × $1.42)	1,065
	Total production costs assigned	$89,105

The Cost of Production Report

The July cost of production report for S&W's Mixing Department is shown in Exhibit 12.

This cost of production report summarizes the following:

- The units for which the department is accountable and the disposition of those units
- The production costs incurred by the department and the allocation of those costs between completed and partially completed units

Cost of Production Report for S&W's Mixing Department—Average Cost **EXHIBIT 12**

	A	B	C
1	**S&W Ice Cream Company**		
2	**Cost of Production Report—Mixing Department**		
3	**For the Month Ended July 31**		
4	**UNITS**	Step 1	Step 2
5		Whole Units	Equivalent Units
6			of Production
7	Units to account for during production:		
8	Inventory in process, July 1	5,000	
9	Received from materials storeroom	60,000	
10	Total units accounted for by the Mixing Department	65,000	
11			
12	Units to be assigned costs:		
13	Transferred to Packaging Department in July	62,000	62,000
14	Inventory in process, July 31 (25% completed)	3,000	750
15	Total units to be assigned costs	65,000	62,750
16			
17	**COSTS**		**Costs**
18			
19	Cost per equivalent unit: (Step 3)		
20	Total production costs for July in Mixing Department		$89,105
21	Total equivalent units (from Step 2)		÷62,750
22	Cost per equivalent unit		$ 1.42
23			
24	Costs assigned to production:		
25	Inventory in process, July 1		$ 6,200
26	Direct materials, direct labor, and factory overhead incurred in July		82,905
27	Total costs accounted for by the Mixing Department		$89,105
28			
29			
30	Costs allocated to completed and partially completed units: (Step 4)		
31	Transferred to Packaging Department in July (62,000 gallons × $1.42)		$88,040
32	Inventory in process, July 31 (3,000 gallons × 25% × $1.42)		1,065
33	Total costs assigned by the Mixing Department		$89,105
34			

At a Glance 20

Obj. 1 Describe process cost systems.

Key Points The process cost system is best suited for industries that mass produce identical units of a product. Costs are charged to processing departments rather than to jobs as with the job order cost system. These costs are transferred from one department to the next until production is completed.

Learning Outcomes	Example Exercises	Practice Exercises
• Identify the characteristics of a process manufacturer.		
• Compare and contrast the job order cost system with the process cost system.	EE20-1	PE20-1A, 20-1B
• Describe the physical and cost flows of a process manufacturer.		

Obj. 2 Prepare a cost of production report.

Key Points Manufacturing costs must be allocated between the units that have been completed and those that remain within the department. This allocation is accomplished by allocating costs using equivalent units of production.

Learning Outcomes	Example Exercises	Practice Exercises
• Determine the whole units charged to production and to be assigned costs.	EE20-2	PE20-2A, 20-2B
• Compute the equivalent units with respect to materials.	EE20-3	PE20-3A, 20-3B
• Compute the equivalent units with respect to conversion.	EE20-4	PE20-4A, 20-4B
• Compute the costs per equivalent unit.	EE20-5	PE20-5A, 20-5B
• Allocate the costs to beginning inventory, units started and completed, and ending inventory.	EE20-6	PE20-6A, 20-6B
• Prepare a cost of production report.		

Obj. 3 Journalize entries for transactions using a process cost system.

Key Points Prepare the summary journal entries for materials, labor, applied factory overhead, and transferred costs incurred in production.

Learning Outcomes	Example Exercises	Practice Exercises
• Prepare journal entries for process costing transactions.	EE20-7	PE20-7A, 20-7B
• Summarize cost flows in T account form.		
• Compute the ending inventory balances.		

Obj. 4 **Describe and illustrate the use of cost of production reports for decision making.**

Key Points The cost of production report provides information for controlling and improving operations. The report(s) can provide details of a department for a single period or over a period of time.

Yield measures the quantity of output of production relative to the inputs.

Learning Outcomes	*Example Exercises*	*Practice Exercises*
• Evaluate the change in the cost per equivalent unit between two periods.		
• Prepare and evaluate a report showing the change in costs per unit by multiple cost categories for comparative periods.	**EE20-8**	**PE20-8A, 20-8B**
• Compute and interpret yield.		

Obj. 5 **Compare lean manufacturing with traditional manufacturing processing.**

Key Points The lean manufacturing philosophy focuses on reducing time, cost, and poor quality within the process.

Learning Outcome	*Example Exercises*	*Practice Exercises*
• Identify the characteristics of lean manufacturing.		

Illustrative Problem

Southern Aggregate Company manufactures concrete by a series of four processes. All materials are introduced in Crushing. From Crushing, the materials pass through Sifting, Baking, and Mixing, emerging as finished concrete. All inventories are costed by the first-in, first-out method.

The balances in the accounts Work in Process—Mixing and Finished Goods were as follows on May 1:

Inventory in Process—Mixing (2,000 units, 1/4 completed with regard to conversion)	$ 13,700
Finished Goods (1,800 units at $8.00 a unit)	14,400

The following costs were charged to Work in Process—Mixing during May:

Direct materials transferred from Baking: 15,200 units at $6.50 a unit	$ 98,800
Direct labor	17,200
Factory overhead	11,780
Total	$127,780

During May, 16,000 units of concrete were completed and 15,800 units were sold. Inventories on May 31 were as follows:

Inventory in Process—Mixing: 1,200 units, 1/2 completed with regard to conversion
Finished Goods: 2,000 units

(*Continued*)

Instructions

1. Prepare a cost of production report for the Mixing Department.
2. Determine the cost of goods sold (indicate number of units and unit costs).
3. Determine the finished goods inventory, May 31.

Solution

1.

	A	B	C	D	E
1	**Southern Aggregate Company**				
2	**Cost of Production Report—Mixing Department**				
3	**For the Month Ended May 31**				
4			Equivalent Units		
5	**UNITS**	Whole Units	Direct Materials	Conversion	
6	Units charged to production:				
7	Inventory in process, May 1	2,000			
8	Received from Baking	15,200			
9	Total units accounted for by the Mixing Department	17,200			
10					
11	Units to be assigned costs:				
12	Inventory in process, May 1 (25% completed with regards to conversion)	2,000	0	1,500	
13	Started and completed in May	14,000	14,000	14,000	
14	Transferred to finished goods in May	16,000	14,000	15,500	
15	Inventory in process, May 31 (50% completed with regards to conversion)	1,200	1,200	600	
16	Total units to be assigned costs	17,200	15,200	16,100	
17					
18				**Costs**	
19	**COSTS**		Direct Materials	Conversion	Total
20	Cost per equivalent unit:				
21	Total costs for May in Mixing Department		$ 98,800	$ 28,980*	
22	Total equivalent units (row 16)		÷15,200	÷16,100	
23	Cost per equivalent unit		$ 6.50	$ 1.80	
24	* $17,200 + $11,780				
25	Costs assigned to production:				
26	Inventory in process, May 1				$ 13,700
27	Costs incurred in May				127,780
28	Total costs accounted for by the Mixing Department				$141,480
29					
30	Cost allocated to completed and partially				
31	completed units:				
32	Inventory in process, May 1 balance				$ 13,700
33	To complete inventory in process, May 1		$ 0	$ 2,700[a]	2,700
34	Cost of completed May 1 work in process				$ 16,400
35	Started and completed in May		91,000[b]	25,200[c]	116,200
36	Transferred to finished goods in May				$132,600
37	Inventory in process, May 31		7,800[d]	1,080[e]	8,880
38	Total costs assigned by the Mixing Department				$141,480
39					

[a]1,500 × $1.80 = $2,700 [b]14,000 × $6.50 = $91,000 [c]14,000 × $1.80 = $25,200 [d]1,200 × $6.50 = $7,800 [e]600 × $1.80 = $1,080

2. Cost of goods sold:

1,800 units at $8.00	$ 14,400	(from finished goods beginning inventory)
2,000 units at $8.20*	16,400	(from inventory in process beginning inventory)
12,000 units at $8.30**	99,600	(from May production started and completed)
15,800 units	$130,400	

*($13,700 + $2,700) ÷ 2,000
**$116,200 ÷ 14,000

3. Finished goods inventory, May 31:

2,000 units at $8.30 $16,600

Key Terms

cost of production report (976)
cost per equivalent unit (981)
equivalent units of production (978)
first-in, first-out (FIFO) method (976)
lean manufacturing (991)
manufacturing cells (992)
process cost system (971)
process manufacturer (970)
whole units (978)
yield (990)

Discussion Questions

1. Which type of cost system, process or job order, would be best suited for each of the following: (a) TV assembler, (b) building contractor, (c) automobile repair shop, (d) paper manufacturer, and (e) custom jewelry manufacturer? Give reasons for your answers.
2. In job order cost accounting, the three elements of manufacturing cost are charged directly to job orders. Why is it not necessary to charge manufacturing costs in process cost accounting to job orders?
3. In a job order cost system, direct labor and factory overhead applied are debited to individual jobs. How are these items treated in a process cost system and why?
4. Why is the cost per equivalent unit often determined separately for direct materials and conversion costs?
5. What is the purpose for determining the cost per equivalent unit?
6. Rameriz Company is a process manufacturer with two production departments, Blending and Filling. All direct materials are introduced in Blending from the materials store area. What is included in the cost transferred to Filling?
7. What is the most important purpose of the cost of production report?
8. How are cost of production reports used for controlling and improving operations?
9. How is "yield" determined for a process manufacturer?
10. How does lean manufacturing differ from the conventional manufacturing process?

Practice Exercises

Example Exercises

EE 20-1 *p. 973* Show Me How

PE 20-1A Job order versus process costing **OBJ. 1**

Which of the following industries would typically use job order costing, and which would typically use process costing?

Steel manufactuirng	Computer chip manufacturing
Business consulting	Candy making
Web designer	Designer clothes manufacturing

EE 20-1 *p. 973* Show Me How

PE 20-1B Job order versus process costing **OBJ. 1**

Which of the following industries would typically use job order costing, and which would typically use process costing?

Dentist	Movie studio
Gasoline refining	Paper manufacturing
Flour mill	Custom printing

Show Me How EE 20-2 p. 977

PE 20-2A Units to be assigned costs OBJ. 2

Eve Cosmetics Company consists of two departments, Blending and Filling. The Filling Department received 50,000 ounces from the Blending Department. During the period, the Filling Department completed 46,000 ounces, including 4,000 ounces of work in process at the beginning of the period. The ending work in process inventory was 8,000 ounces. How many ounces were started and completed during the period?

Show Me How EE 20-2 p. 977

PE 20-2B Units to be assigned costs OBJ. 2

Keystone Steel Company has two departments, Casting and Rolling. In the Rolling Department, ingots from the Casting Department are rolled into steel sheet. The Rolling Department received 8,500 tons from the Casting Department. During the period, the Rolling Department completed 7,900 tons, including 400 tons of work in process at the beginning of the period. The ending work in process inventory was 1,000 tons. How many tons were started and completed during the period?

Show Me How EE 20-3 p. 979

PE 20-3A Equivalent units of materials cost OBJ. 2

The Filling Department of Eve Cosmetics Company had 4,000 ounces in beginning work in process inventory (60% complete). During the period, 46,000 ounces were completed. The ending work in process inventory was 8,000 ounces (25% complete). What are the total equivalent units for direct materials if materials are added at the beginning of the process?

Show Me How EE 20-3 p. 979

PE 20-3B Equivalent units of materials cost OBJ. 2

The Rolling Department of Keystone Steel Company had 400 tons in beginning work in process inventory (20% complete). During the period, 7,900 tons were completed. The ending work in process inventory was 1,000 tons (30% complete). What are the total equivalent units for direct materials if materials are added at the beginning of the process?

Show Me How EE 20-4 p. 981

PE 20-4A Equivalent units of conversion costs OBJ. 2

The Filling Department of Eve Cosmetics Company had 4,000 ounces in beginning work in process inventory (60% complete). During the period, 46,000 ounces were completed. The ending work in process inventory was 8,000 ounces (25% complete). What are the total equivalent units for conversion costs?

Show Me How EE 20-4 p. 981

PE 20-4B Equivalent units of conversion costs OBJ. 2

The Rolling Department of Keystone Steel Company had 400 tons in beginning work in process inventory (20% complete). During the period, 7,900 tons were completed. The ending work in process inventory was 1,000 tons (30% complete). What are the total equivalent units for conversion costs?

Show Me How EE 20-5 p. 982

PE 20-5A Cost per equivalent unit OBJ. 2

The cost of direct materials transferred into the Filling Department of Eve Cosmetics Company is $20,000. The conversion cost for the period in the Filling Department is $4,560. The total equivalent units for direct materials and conversion are 50,000 ounces and 45,600 ounces, respectively. Determine the direct materials and conversion costs per equivalent unit.

Show Me How EE 20-5 p. 982

PE 20-5B Cost per equivalent unit OBJ. 2

The cost of direct materials transferred into the Rolling Department of Keystone Steel Company is $510,000. The conversion cost for the period in the Rolling Department is $81,200. The total equivalent units for direct materials and conversion are 8,500 tons and 8,120 tons, respectively. Determine the direct materials and conversion costs per equivalent unit.

Show Me How EE 20-6 *p. 984*

PE 20-6A Cost of units transferred out and ending work in process — OBJ. 2

The costs per equivalent unit of direct materials and conversion in the Filling Department of Eve Cosmetics Company are $0.40 and $0.10, respectively. The equivalent units to be assigned costs are as follows:

	Equivalent Units	
	Direct Materials	**Conversion**
Inventory in process, beginning of period	0	1,600
Started and completed during the period	42,000	42,000
Transferred out of Filling (completed)	42,000	43,600
Inventory in process, end of period	8,000	2,000
Total units to be assigned costs	50,000	45,600

The beginning work in process inventory had a cost of $1,800. Determine the cost of completed and transferred-out production and the ending work in process inventory.

Show Me How EE 20-6 *p. 984*

PE 20-6B Cost of units transferred out and ending work in process — OBJ. 2

The costs per equivalent unit of direct materials and conversion in the Rolling Department of Keystone Steel Company are $60 and $10, respectively. The equivalent units to be assigned costs are as follows:

	Equivalent Units	
	Direct Materials	**Conversion**
Inventory in process, beginning of period	0	320
Started and completed during the period	7,500	7,500
Transferred out of Rolling (completed)	7,500	7,820
Inventory in process, end of period	1,000	300
Total units to be assigned costs	8,500	8,120

The beginning work in process inventory had a cost of $25,000. Determine the cost of completed and transferred-out production and the ending work in process inventory.

Show Me How EE 20-7 *p. 988*

PE 20-7A Process cost journal entries — OBJ. 3

The cost of materials transferred into the Filling Department of Eve Cosmetics Company is $20,000, including $14,000 from the Blending Department and $6,000 from the materials storeroom. The conversion cost for the period in the Filling Department is $4,560 ($1,600 factory overhead applied and $2,960 direct labor). The total cost transferred to Finished Goods for the period was $22,960. The Filling Department had a beginning inventory of $1,800.

a. Journalize (1) the cost of transferred-in materials, (2) conversion costs, and (3) the costs transferred out to Finished Goods.

b. Determine the balance of Work in Process—Filling at the end of the period.

Show Me How EE 20-7 *p. 988*

PE 20-7B Process cost journal entries — OBJ. 3

The cost of materials transferred into the Rolling Department of Keystone Steel Company is $510,000 from the Casting Department. The conversion cost for the period in the Rolling Department is $81,200 ($54,700 factory overhead applied and $26,500 direct labor). The total cost transferred to Finished Goods for the period was $553,200. The Rolling Department had a beginning inventory of $25,000.

a. Journalize (1) the cost of transferred-in materials, (2) conversion costs, and (3) the costs transferred out to Finished Goods.

b. Determine the balance of Work in Process—Rolling at the end of the period.

EE 20-8 p. 991

Show Me How

PE 20-8A Using process costs for decision making OBJ. 4

The costs of energy consumed in producing good units in the Baking Department of Pan Company were $14,875 and $14,615 for June and July, respectively. The number of equivalent units produced in June and July was 42,500 pounds and 39,500 pounds, respectively. Evaluate the change in the cost of energy between the two months.

EE 20-8 p. 991

Show Me How

PE 20-8B Using process costs for decision making OBJ. 4

The costs of materials consumed in producing good units in the Forming Department of Thomas Company were $76,000 and $77,350 for September and October, respectively. The number of equivalent units produced in September and October was 800 tons and 850 tons, respectively. Evaluate the change in the cost of materials between the two months.

Exercises

Real World

EX 20-1 Entries for materials cost flows in a process cost system OBJ. 1, 3

The Hershey Company manufactures chocolate confectionery products. The three largest raw materials are cocoa, sugar, and dehydrated milk. These raw materials first go into the Blending Department. The blended product is then sent to the Molding Department, where the bars of candy are formed. The candy is then sent to the Packing Department, where the bars are wrapped and boxed. The boxed candy is then sent to the distribution center, where it is eventually sold to food brokers and retailers.

Show the accounts debited and credited for each of the following business events:

a. Materials used by the Blending Department
b. Transfer of blended product to the Molding Department
c. Transfer of chocolate to the Packing Department
d. Transfer of boxed chocolate to the distribution center
e. Sale of boxed chocolate

Real World

EX 20-2 Flowchart of accounts related to service and processing departments OBJ. 1

Alcoa Inc. is the world's largest producer of aluminum products. One product that Alcoa manufactures is aluminum sheet products for the aerospace industry. The entire output of the Smelting Department is transferred to the Rolling Department. Part of the fully processed goods from the Rolling Department are sold as rolled sheet, and the remainder of the goods are transferred to the Converting Department for further processing into sheared sheet.

Prepare a diagram using T accounts showing the flow of costs from the processing department accounts into the finished goods accounts and then into the cost of goods sold account. The relevant accounts are as follows:

Cost of Goods Sold	Finished Goods—Rolled Sheet
Materials	Finished Goods—Sheared Sheet
Factory Overhead—Smelting Department	Work in Process—Smelting Department
Factory Overhead—Rolling Department	Work in Process—Rolling Department
Factory Overhead—Converting Department	Work in Process—Converting Department

Real World

Show Me How

EX 20-3 Entries for flow of factory costs for process cost system OBJ. 1, 3

Domino Foods, Inc., manufactures a sugar product by a continuous process involving three production departments—Refining, Sifting, and Packing. Assume that records indicate that direct materials, direct labor, and applied factory overhead for the first department, Refining, were $400,000, $150,000, and $100,000, respectively. Also, work in process in the Refining Department at the beginning of the period totaled $40,000, and work in process at the end of the period totaled $35,000.

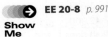

Journalize the entries to record (a) the flow of costs into the Refining Department during the period for (1) direct materials, (2) direct labor, and (3) factory overhead and to record (b) the transfer of production costs to the second department, Sifting.

EX 20-4 Factory overhead rate, entry for applying factory overhead, and factory overhead account balance **OBJ. 1, 3**

✔ a. 125%

Show Me How

The chief cost accountant for Kenner Beverage Co. estimated that total factory overhead cost for the Blending Department for the coming fiscal year beginning May 1 would be $3,000,000 and total direct labor costs would be $2,400,000. During May, the actual direct labor cost totaled $198,400 and factory overhead cost incurred totaled $253,200.

a. What is the predetermined factory overhead rate based on direct labor cost?

b. Journalize the entry to apply factory overhead to production for May.

c. What is the May 31 balance of the account Factory Overhead—Blending Department?

d. Does the balance in part (c) represent over- or underapplied factory overhead?

EX 20-5 Equivalent units of production **OBJ. 2**

✔ Direct materials, 16,800 units

Show Me How

The Converting Department of Soft Touch Towel and Tissue Company had 1,200 units in work in process at the beginning of the period, which were 25% complete. During the period, 16,000 units were completed and transferred to the Packing Department. There were 2,000 units in process at the end of the period, which were 40% complete. Direct materials are placed into the process at the beginning of production. Determine the number of equivalent units of production with respect to direct materials and conversion costs.

EX 20-6 Equivalent units of production **OBJ. 2**

✔ a. Conversion, 96,720 units

Show Me How

Units of production data for the two departments of Pacific Cable and Wire Company for November of the current fiscal year are as follows:

	Drawing Department	Winding Department
Work in process, November 1	5,000 units, 40% completed	3,200 units, 80% completed
Completed and transferred to next processing department during November	95,000 units	95,100 units
Work in process, November 30	6,200 units, 60% completed	3,100 units, 15% completed

If all direct materials are placed in process at the beginning of production, determine the direct materials and conversion equivalent units of production for November for (a) the Drawing Department and (b) the Winding Department.

EX 20-7 Equivalent units of production **OBJ. 2**

✔ b. Conversion, 335,100

Show Me How

The following information concerns production in the Baking Department for March. All direct materials are placed in process at the beginning of production.

ACCOUNT *Work in Process—Baking Department* **ACCOUNT NO.**

Date		Item	Debit	Credit	Balance Debit	Balance Credit
Mar.	1	Bal., 18,000 units, ¼ completed			14,760	
	31	Direct materials, 336,000 units	252,000		266,760	
	31	Direct labor	40,000		306,760	
	31	Factory overhead	60,530		367,290	
	31	Goods finished, 330,000 units		346,410	20,880	
	31	Bal. ? units, ⅖ completed			20,880	

a. Determine the number of units in work in process inventory at March 31.

b. Determine the equivalent units of production for direct materials and conversion costs in March.

EX 20-8 Costs per equivalent unit

OBJ. 2, 4

✔ a. 2. Conversion cost per equivalent unit, $0.30

Show Me How

a. Based on the data in Exercise 20-7, determine the following for March:

1. Direct materials cost per equivalent unit
2. Conversion cost per equivalent unit
3. Cost of the beginning work in process completed during March
4. Cost of units started and completed during March
5. Cost of the ending work in process

b. Assuming that the direct materials cost is the same for February and March, did the conversion cost per equivalent unit increase, decrease, or remain the same in March?

EX 20-9 Equivalent units of production

OBJ. 2

Real World

Kellogg Company manufactures cold cereal products, such as *Frosted Flakes*. Assume that the inventory in process on March 1 for the Packing Department included 1,200 pounds of cereal in the packing machine hopper (enough for 800 24-oz. boxes) and 800 empty 24-oz. boxes held in the package carousel of the packing machine. During March, 65,400 boxes of 24-oz. cereal were packaged. Conversion costs are incurred when a box is filled with cereal. On March 31, the packing machine hopper held 900 pounds of cereal and the package carousel held 600 empty 24-oz. (1½-lb.) boxes. Assume that once a box is filled with cereal, it is immediately transferred to the finished goods warehouse.

Determine the equivalent units of production for cereal, boxes, and conversion costs for March. An equivalent unit is defined as "pounds" for cereal and "24-oz. boxes" for boxes and conversion costs.

EX 20-10 Costs per equivalent unit

OBJ. 2

✔ c. $2.40

Show Me How

Georgia Products Inc. completed and transferred 89,000 particle board units of production from the Pressing Department. There was no beginning inventory in process in the department. The ending in-process inventory was 2,400 units, which were 3/5 complete as to conversion cost. All materials are added at the beginning of the process. Direct materials cost incurred was $219,360, direct labor cost incurred was $28,100, and factory overhead applied was $12,598.

Determine the following for the Pressing Department:

a. Total conversion cost
b. Conversion cost per equivalent unit
c. Direct materials cost per equivalent unit

EX 20-11 Equivalent units of production and related costs

OBJ. 2

✔ a. 1,000 units

Excel

Show Me How

The charges to Work in Process—Assembly Department for a period, together with information concerning production, are as follows. All direct materials are placed in process at the beginning of production.

Work in Process—Assembly Department

Bal., 1,600 units, 35% completed	17,440	To Finished Goods, 29,600 units	?
Direct materials, 29,000 units @ $9.50	275,500		
Direct labor	84,600		
Factory overhead	39,258		
Bal. ? units, 45% completed	?		

Determine the following:

a. The number of units in work in process inventory at the end of the period
b. Equivalent units of production for direct materials and conversion
c. Costs per equivalent unit for direct materials and conversion
d. Cost of the units started and completed during the period

✔ a. 1. $21,808

EX 20-12 Cost of units completed and in process

OBJ. 2, 4

a. Based on the data in Exercise 20-11, determine the following:

1. Cost of beginning work in process inventory completed this period
2. Cost of units transferred to finished goods during the period
3. Cost of ending work in process inventory
4. Cost per unit of the completed beginning work in process inventory, rounded to the nearest cent

b. Did the production costs change from the preceding period? Explain.

c. Assuming that the direct materials cost per unit did not change from the preceding period, did the conversion costs per equivalent unit increase, decrease, or remain the same for the current period?

EX 20-13 Errors in equivalent unit computation

OBJ. 2

Napco Refining Company processes gasoline. On June 1 of the current year, 6,400 units were 3/5 completed in the Blending Department. During June, 55,000 units entered the Blending Department from the Refining Department. During June, the units in process at the beginning of the month were completed. Of the 55,000 units entering the department, all were completed except 5,200 units that were 1/5 completed. The equivalent units for conversion costs for June for the Blending Department were computed as follows:

Equivalent units of production in June:	
To process units in inventory on June 1: 6,400 × 3/5	3,840
To process units started and completed in June: 55,000 – 6,400	48,600
To process units in inventory on June 30: 5,200 × 1/5	1,040
Equivalent units of production	53,480

List the errors in the computation of equivalent units for conversion costs for the Blending Department for June.

✔ a. 12,400 units

Show Me How

EX 20-14 Cost per equivalent unit

OBJ. 2

The following information concerns production in the Forging Department for November. All direct materials are placed into the process at the beginning of production, and conversion costs are incurred evenly throughout the process. The beginning inventory consists of $9,000 of direct materials.

ACCOUNT ***Work in Process—Forging Department*** **ACCOUNT NO.**

Date		Item	Debit	Credit	Balance Debit	Balance Credit
Nov.	1	Bal., 900 units, 60% completed			10,566	
	30	Direct materials, 12,900 units	123,840		134,406	
	30	Direct labor	21,650		156,056	
	30	Factory overhead	16,870		172,926	
	30	Goods transferred, ? units		?	?	
	30	Bal., 1,400 units, 70% completed			?	

a. Determine the number of units transferred to the next department.

b. Determine the costs per equivalent unit of direct materials and conversion.

c. Determine the cost of units started and completed in November.

EX 20-15 Costs per equivalent unit and production costs

OBJ. 2, 4

✔ a. $11,646

Based on the data in Exercise 20-14, determine the following:

a. Cost of beginning work in process inventory completed in November
b. Cost of units transferred to the next department during November
c. Cost of ending work in process inventory on November 30
d. Costs per equivalent unit of direct materials and conversion included in the November 1 beginning work in process
e. The November increase or decrease in costs per equivalent unit for direct materials and conversion from the previous month

EX 20-16 Cost of production report

OBJ. 2, 4

✔ a. 4. $2,092

Excel

The debits to Work in Process—Roasting Department for Morning Brew Coffee Company for August, together with information concerning production, are as follows:

Work in process, August 1, 700 pounds, 20% completed		$ 3,479*
*Direct materials (700 × $4.70)	$3,290	
Conversion (700 × 20% × $1.35)	189	
	$3,479	
Coffee beans added during August, 14,300 pounds		65,780
Conversion costs during August		21,942
Work in process, August 31, 400 pounds, 42% completed		?
Goods finished during August, 14,600 pounds		?

All direct materials are placed in process at the beginning of production.

a. Prepare a cost of production report, presenting the following computations:
   1. Direct materials and conversion equivalent units of production for August
   2. Direct materials and conversion costs per equivalent unit for August
   3. Cost of goods finished during August
   4. Cost of work in process at August 31
b. Compute and evaluate the change in cost per equivalent unit for direct materials and conversion from the previous month (July).

EX 20-17 Cost of production report

OBJ. 2, 4

✔ Conversion cost per equivalent unit, $5.10

The Cutting Department of Karachi Carpet Company provides the following data for January. Assume that all materials are added at the beginning of the process.

Work in process, January 1, 1,400 units, 75% completed		$ 22,960*
*Direct materials (1,400 × $12.65)	$17,710	
Conversion (1,400 × 75% × $5.00)	5,250	
	$22,960	
Materials added during January from Weaving Department, 58,000 units		$742,400
Direct labor for January		134,550
Factory overhead for January		151,611
Goods finished during January (includes goods in process, January 1), 56,200 units		—
Work in process, January 31, 3,200 units, 30% completed		—

a. Prepare a cost of production report for the Cutting Department.
b. Compute and evaluate the change in the costs per equivalent unit for direct materials and conversion from the previous month (December).

✔ b. $29,760

EX 20-18 Cost of production and journal entries **OBJ. 1, 2, 3, 4**

AccuBlade Castings Inc. casts blades for turbine engines. Within the Casting Department, alloy is first melted in a crucible, then poured into molds to produce the castings. On May 1, there were 230 pounds of alloy in process, which were 60% complete as to conversion. The Work in Process balance for these 230 pounds was $32,844, determined as follows:

Direct materials (230 × $132)	$30,360
Conversion (230 × 60% × $18)	2,484
	$32,844

During May, the Casting Department was charged $350,000 for 2,500 pounds of alloy and $19,840 for direct labor. Factory overhead is applied to the department at a rate of 150% of direct labor. The department transferred out 2,530 pounds of finished castings to the Machining Department. The May 31 inventory in process was 44% complete as to conversion.

a. Prepare the following May journal entries for the Casting Department:
   1. The materials charged to production
   2. The conversion costs charged to production
   3. The completed production transferred to the Machining Department
b. Determine the Work in Process—Casting Department May 31 balance.
c. Compute and evaluate the change in the costs per equivalent unit for direct materials and conversion from the previous month (April).

✔ b. $14,319

EX 20-19 Cost of production and journal entries **OBJ. 1, 2, 3**

Lighthouse Paper Company manufactures newsprint. The product is manufactured in two departments, Papermaking and Converting. Pulp is first placed into a vessel at the beginning of papermaking production. The following information concerns production in the Papermaking Department for March:

ACCOUNT ***Work in Process—Papermaking Department*** **ACCOUNT NO.**

Date		Item	Debit	Credit	Balance Debit	Balance Credit
Mar.	1	Bal., 2,600 units, 35% completed			9,139	
	31	Direct materials, 105,000 units	330,750		339,889	
	31	Direct labor	40,560		380,449	
	31	Factory overhead	54,795		435,244	
	31	Goods transferred, 103,900 units		?	?	
	31	Bal., 3,700 units, 80% completed			?	

a. Prepare the following March journal entries for the Papermaking Department:
   1. The materials charged to production
   2. The conversion costs charged to production
   3. The completed production transferred to the Converting Department
b. Determine the Work in Process—Papermaking Department March 31 balance.

EX 20-20 Process costing for a service company **OBJ. 4**

Madison Electric Company uses a fossil fuel (coal) plant for generating electricity. The facility can generate 900 megawatts (million watts) per hour. The plant operates 600 hours during March. Electricity is used as it is generated; thus, there are no inventories at the beginning or end of the period. The March conversion and fuel costs are as follows:

Conversion costs	$40,500,000
Fuel	10,800,000
Total	$51,300,000

(Continued)

Madison also has a wind farm that can generate 100 megawatts per hour. The wind farm receives sufficient wind to run 300 hours for March. The March conversion costs for the wind farm (mostly depreciation) are as follows:

Conversion costs	$2,700,000

a. Determine the cost per megawatt hour (MWh) for the fossil fuel plant and the wind farm to identify the lowest cost facility in March.

b. Why are equivalent units of production not needed in determining the cost per megawatt hour (MWh) for generating electricity?

c. What advantage does the fossil fuel plant have over the wind farm?

EX 20-21 Decision making **OBJ. 4**

Excel

Mystic Bottling Company bottles popular beverages in the Bottling Department. The beverages are produced by blending concentrate with water and sugar. The concentrate is purchased from a concentrate producer. The concentrate producer sets higher prices for the more popular concentrate flavors. A simplified Bottling Department cost of production report separating the cost of bottling the four flavors follows:

	A	B	C	D	E
1		**Orange**	**Cola**	**Lemon-Lime**	**Root Beer**
2	Concentrate	$ 4,625	$129,000	$105,000	$ 7,600
3	Water	1,250	30,000	25,000	2,000
4	Sugar	3,000	72,000	60,000	4,800
5	Bottles	5,500	132,000	110,000	8,800
6	Flavor changeover	3,000	4,800	4,000	10,000
7	Conversion cost	1,750	24,000	20,000	2,800
8	Total cost transferred to finished goods	$19,125	$391,800	$324,000	$36,000
9	Number of cases	2,500	60,000	50,000	4,000
10					

Beginning and ending work in process inventories are negligible, so they are omitted from the cost of production report. The flavor changeover cost represents the cost of cleaning the bottling machines between production runs of different flavors.

Prepare a memo to the production manager, analyzing this comparative cost information. In your memo, provide recommendations for further action, along with supporting schedules showing the total cost per case and cost per case by cost element. Round all supporting calculations to the nearest cent.

EX 20-22 Decision making **OBJ. 4**

Pix Paper Inc. produces photographic paper for printing digital images. One of the processes for this operation is a coating (solvent spreading) operation, where chemicals are coated onto paper stock. There has been some concern about the cost performance of this operation. As a result, you have begun an investigation. You first discover that all materials and conversion prices have been stable for the last six months. Thus, increases in prices for inputs are not an explanation for increasing costs. However, you have discovered three possible problems from some of the operating personnel whose quotes follow:

Operator 1: "I've been keeping an eye on my operating room instruments. I feel as though our energy consumption is becoming less efficient."

Operator 2: "Every time the coating machine goes down, we produce waste on shutdown and subsequent startup. It seems as though during the last half year, we have had more unscheduled machine shutdowns than in the past. Thus, I think our yields must be dropping."

Operator 3: "My sense is that our coating costs are going up. It seems as though we are spreading a thicker coating than we should. Perhaps the coating machine needs to be recalibrated."

The Coating Department had no beginning or ending inventories for any month during the study period. The following data from the cost of production report are made available:

	A	B	C	D	E	F	G
1		January	February	March	April	May	June
2	Paper stock	$67,200	$63,840	$60,480	$64,512	$57,120	$53,760
3	Coating	$11,520	$11,856	$12,960	$15,667	$16,320	$18,432
4	Conversion cost (incl. energy)	$38,400	$36,480	$34,560	$36,864	$32,640	$30,720
5	Pounds input to the process	100,000	95,000	90,000	96,000	85,000	80,000
6	Pounds transferred out	96,000	91,200	86,400	92,160	81,600	76,800
7							

a. Prepare a table showing the paper cost per output pound, coating cost per output pound, conversion cost per output pound, and yield (pounds transferred out/pounds input) for each month. Round costs to the nearest cent and yield to the nearest whole percent.

b. Interpret your table results.

EX 20-23 Lean manufacturing

OBJ. 5

The following are some quotes provided by a number of managers at Hawkeye Machining Company regarding the company's planned move toward a lean manufacturing system:

Director of Sales: I'm afraid we'll miss some sales if we don't keep a large stock of items on hand just in case demand increases. It only makes sense to me to keep large inventories in order to ensure product availability for our customers.

Director of Purchasing: I'm very concerned about moving to a lean system for materials. What would happen if one of our suppliers were unable to make a shipment? A supplier could fall behind in production or have a quality problem. Without some safety stock in our materials, our whole plant would shut down.

Director of Manufacturing: If we go to lean manufacturing, I think our factory output will drop. We need in-process inventory in order to "smooth out" the inevitable problems that occur during manufacturing. For example, if a machine that is used to process a product breaks down, it will starve the next machine if I don't have in-process inventory between the two machines. If I have in-process inventory, then I can keep the next operation busy while I fix the broken machine. Thus, the in-process inventories give me a safety valve that I can use to keep things running when things go wrong.

How would you respond to these managers?

Appendix

EX 20-24 Equivalent units of production: average cost method

✔ a. 17,000

The Converting Department of Tender Soft Tissue Company uses the average cost method and had 1,900 units in work in process that were 60% complete at the beginning of the period. During the period, 15,800 units were completed and transferred to the Packing Department. There were 1,200 units in process that were 30% complete at the end of the period.

a. Determine the number of whole units to be accounted for and to be assigned costs for the period.

b. Determine the number of equivalent units of production for the period.

Appendix

EX 20-25 Equivalent units of production: average cost method

✔ a. 12,100 units to be accounted for

Units of production data for the two departments of Atlantic Cable and Wire Company for July of the current fiscal year are as follows:

	Drawing Department	Winding Department
Work in process, July 1	500 units, 50% completed	350 units, 30% completed
Completed and transferred to next processing department during July	11,400 units	10,950 units
Work in process, July 31	700 units, 55% completed	800 units, 25% completed

Each department uses the average cost method.

a. Determine the number of whole units to be accounted for and to be assigned costs and the equivalent units of production for the Drawing Department.

b. Determine the number of whole units to be accounted for and to be assigned costs and the equivalent units of production for the Winding Department.

Appendix
EX 20-26 Equivalent units of production: average cost method

✔ a. 3,100

The following information concerns production in the Finishing Department for May. The Finishing Department uses the average cost method.

ACCOUNT *Work in Process—Finishing Department* ACCOUNT NO.

Date		Item	Debit	Credit	Balance Debit	Balance Credit
May	1	Bal., 4,200 units, 70% completed			36,500	
	31	Direct materials, 23,600 units	125,800		162,300	
	31	Direct labor	75,400		237,700	
	31	Factory overhead	82,675		320,375	
	31	Goods transferred, 24,700 units		308,750	11,625	
	31	Bal., ? units, 30% completed			11,625	

a. Determine the number of units in work in process inventory at the end of the month.
b. Determine the number of whole units to be accounted for and to be assigned costs and the equivalent units of production for May.

Appendix
EX 20-27 Equivalent units of production and related costs

✔ b. 8,820 units

Excel

The charges to Work in Process—Baking Department for a period as well as information concerning production are as follows. The Baking Department uses the average cost method, and all direct materials are placed in process during production.

Work in Process—Baking Department

Bal., 900 units, 40% completed	2,466	To Finished Goods, 8,100 units	?
Direct materials, 8,400 units	34,500		
Direct labor	16,200		
Factory overhead	8,574		
Bal., 1,200 units, 60% completed	?		

Determine the following:
a. The number of whole units to be accounted for and to be assigned costs
b. The number of equivalent units of production
c. The cost per equivalent unit
d. The cost of units transferred to Finished Goods
e. The cost of units in ending Work in Process

Appendix
EX 20-28 Cost per equivalent unit: average cost method

✔ a. $26.00

The following information concerns production in the Forging Department for June. The Forging Department uses the average cost method.

ACCOUNT *Work in Process—Forging Department* ACCOUNT NO.

Date		Item	Debit	Credit	Balance Debit	Balance Credit
June	1	Bal., 500 units, 40% completed			5,000	
	30	Direct materials, 3,700 units	49,200		54,200	
	30	Direct labor	25,200		79,400	
	30	Factory overhead	25,120		104,520	
	30	Goods transferred, 3,600 units		?	?	
	30	Bal., 600 units, 70% completed			?	

a. Determine the cost per equivalent unit.
b. Determine cost of units transferred to Finished Goods.
c. Determine the cost of units in ending Work in Process.

✔ Cost per equivalent unit, $3.60

Appendix
EX 20-29 Cost of production report: average cost method

The increases to Work in Process—Roasting Department for Highlands Coffee Company for May as well as information concerning production are as follows:

Work in process, May 1, 1,150 pounds, 40% completed	$ 1,700
Coffee beans added during May, 10,900 pounds	28,600
Conversion costs during May	12,504
Work in process, May 31, 800 pounds, 80% completed	—
Goods finished during May, 11,250 pounds	—

Prepare a cost of production report, using the average cost method.

✔ Cost per equivalent unit, $9.00

Excel

Appendix
EX 20-30 Cost of production report: average cost method

Prepare a cost of production report for the Cutting Department of Dalton Carpet Company for January. Use the average cost method with the following data:

Work in process, January 1, 3,400 units, 75% completed	$ 23,000
Materials added during January from Weaving Department, 64,000 units	366,200
Direct labor for January	105,100
Factory overhead for January	80,710
Goods finished during January (includes goods in process, January 1), 63,500 units	—
Work in process, January 31, 3,900 units, 10% completed	—

Problems: Series A

✔ 2. Materials January 31 balance, $46,500

General Ledger

Show Me How

PR 20-1A Entries for process cost system **OBJ. 1, 3**

Port Ormond Carpet Company manufactures carpets. Fiber is placed in process in the Spinning Department, where it is spun into yarn. The output of the Spinning Department is transferred to the Tufting Department, where carpet backing is added at the beginning of the process and the process is completed. On January 1, Port Ormond Carpet Company had the following inventories:

Finished Goods	$62,000
Work in Process—Spinning Department	35,000
Work in Process—Tufting Department	28,500
Materials	17,000

Departmental accounts are maintained for factory overhead, and both have zero balances on January 1.

Manufacturing operations for January are summarized as follows:

a. Materials purchased on account	$500,000
b. Materials requisitioned for use:	
Fiber—Spinning Department	$275,000
Carpet backing—Tufting Department	110,000
Indirect materials—Spinning Department	46,000
Indirect materials—Tufting Department	39,500

(Continued)

c. Labor used:

Direct labor—Spinning Department	$185,000
Direct labor—Tufting Department	98,000
Indirect labor—Spinning Department	18,500
Indirect labor—Tufting Department	9,000

d. Depreciation charged on fixed assets:

Spinning Department	$ 12,500
Tufting Department	8,500

e. Expired prepaid factory insurance:

Spinning Department	$ 2,000
Tufting Department	1,000

f. Applied factory overhead:

Spinning Department	$ 80,000
Tufting Department	55,000

g. Production costs transferred from Spinning Department to Tufting Department	$547,000
h. Production costs transferred from Tufting Department to Finished Goods	$807,200
i. Cost of goods sold during the period	$795,200

Instructions

1. Journalize the entries to record the operations, identifying each entry by letter.
2. Compute the January 31 balances of the inventory accounts.
3. Compute the January 31 balances of the factory overhead accounts.

PR 20-2A Cost of production report

OBJ. 2, 4

✔ 1. Conversion cost per equivalent unit, $0.76

Excel

Arabica Highland Coffee Company roasts and packs coffee beans. The process begins by placing coffee beans into the Roasting Department. From the Roasting Department, coffee beans are then transferred to the Packing Department. The following is a partial work in process account of the Roasting Department at July 31:

ACCOUNT ***Work in Process—Roasting Department*** **ACCOUNT NO.**

Date		Item	Debit	Credit	Balance	
					Debit	**Credit**
July	1	Bal., 30,000 units, 10% completed			121,800	
	31	Direct materials, 155,000 units	620,000		741,800	
	31	Direct labor	90,000		831,800	
	31	Factory overhead	33,272		865,072	
	31	Goods transferred, 149,000 units		?		
	31	Bal., ? units, 45% completed			?	

Instructions

1. Prepare a cost of production report and identify the missing amounts for Work in Process—Roasting Department.
2. Assuming that the July 1 work in process inventory includes $119,400 of direct materials, determine the increase or decrease in the cost per equivalent unit for direct materials and conversion between June and July.

PR 20-3A Equivalent units and related costs; cost of production report; entries

OBJ. 2, 3, 4

✔ 2. Transferred to Packaging Dept., $40,183

Excel

White Diamond Flour Company manufactures flour by a series of three processes, beginning with wheat grain being introduced in the Milling Department. From the Milling Department, the materials pass through the Sifting and Packaging departments, emerging as packaged refined flour.

The balance in the account Work in Process—Sifting Department was as follows on July 1:

Work in Process—Sifting Department (900 units, $\frac{3}{5}$ completed):	
Direct materials (900 × \$2.05)	\$1,845
Conversion (900 × $\frac{3}{5}$ × \$0.40)	216
	\$2,061

The following costs were charged to Work in Process—Sifting Department during July:

Direct materials transferred from Milling Department:	
15,700 units at \$2.15 a unit	\$33,755
Direct labor	4,420
Factory overhead	2,708

During July, 15,500 units of flour were completed. Work in Process—Sifting Department on July 31 was 1,100 units, $\frac{4}{5}$ completed.

Instructions

1. Prepare a cost of production report for the Sifting Department for July.
2. Journalize the entries for costs transferred from Milling to Sifting and the costs transferred from Sifting to Packaging.
3. Determine the increase or decrease in the cost per equivalent unit from June to July for direct materials and conversion costs.
4. Discuss the uses of the cost of production report and the results of part (3).

PR 20-4A Work in process account data for two months; cost of production reports

OBJ. 1, 2, 3, 4

✔ 1. c. Transferred to finished goods in April, \$49,818

Excel

Hearty Soup Co. uses a process cost system to record the costs of processing soup, which requires the cooking and filling processes. Materials are entered from the cooking process at the beginning of the filling process. The inventory of Work in Process—Filling on April 1 and debits to the account during April were as follows:

Bal., 800 units, 30% completed:	
Direct materials (800 × \$4.30)	\$ 3,440
Conversion (800 × 30% × \$1.75)	420
	\$ 3,860
From Cooking Department, 7,800 units	\$34,320
Direct labor	8,562
Factory overhead	6,387

During April, 800 units in process on April 1 were completed, and of the 7,800 units entering the department, all were completed except 550 units that were 90% completed.

Charges to Work in Process—Filling for May were as follows:

From Cooking Department, 9,600 units	\$44,160
Direct labor	12,042
Factory overhead	6,878

During May, the units in process at the beginning of the month were completed, and of the 9,600 units entering the department, all were completed except 300 units that were 35% completed.

Instructions

1. Enter the balance as of April 1 in a four-column account for Work in Process—Filling. Record the debits and credits in the account for April. Construct a cost of production report and present computations for determining (a) equivalent units of production for materials and conversion; (b) cost per equivalent unit; (c) cost of goods finished, differentiating between units started in the prior period and units started and finished in April; and (d) work in process inventory.
2. Provide the same information for May by recording the May transactions in the four-column work in process account. Construct a cost of production report and present the May computations (a through d) listed in part (1).

(Continued)

3. Comment on the change in costs per equivalent unit for March through May for direct materials and conversion costs.

Appendix
PR 20-5A Cost of production report: average cost method

✔ Cost per equivalent unit, $2.70

Excel

Sunrise Coffee Company roasts and packs coffee beans. The process begins in the Roasting Department. From the Roasting Department, the coffee beans are transferred to the Packing Department. The following is a partial work in process account of the Roasting Department at December 31:

ACCOUNT ***Work in Process—Roasting Department*** **ACCOUNT NO.**

Date		Item	Debit	Credit	Balance Debit	Balance Credit
Dec.	1	Bal., 10,500 units, 75% completed			21,000	
	31	Direct materials, 210,400 units	246,800		267,800	
	31	Direct labor	135,700		403,500	
	31	Factory overhead	168,630		572,130	
	31	Goods transferred, 208,900 units		?	?	
	31	Bal., ? units, 25% completed			?	

Instructions

Prepare a cost of production report, using the average cost method, and identify the missing amounts for Work in Process—Roasting Department.

Problems: Series B

PR 20-1B Entries for process cost system

OBJ. 1, 3

✔ 2. Materials July 31 balance, $11,390

General Ledger

Show Me How

Preston & Grover Soap Company manufactures powdered detergent. Phosphate is placed in process in the Making Department, where it is turned into granulars. The output of Making is transferred to the Packing Department, where packaging is added at the beginning of the process. On July 1, Preston & Grover Soap Company had the following inventories:

Finished Goods	$13,500
Work in Process—Making	6,790
Work in Process—Packing	7,350
Materials	5,100

Departmental accounts are maintained for factory overhead, which both have zero balances on July 1.

Manufacturing operations for July are summarized as follows:

a. Materials purchased on account	$149,800
b. Materials requisitioned for use:	
Phosphate—Making Department	$105,700
Packaging—Packing Department	31,300
Indirect materials—Making Department	4,980
Indirect materials—Packing Department	1,530
c. Labor used:	
Direct labor—Making Department	$ 32,400
Direct labor—Packing Department	40,900
Indirect labor—Making Department	15,400
Indirect labor—Packing Department	18,300

d. Depreciation charged on fixed assets:	
Making Department	$ 10,700
Packing Department	7,900
e. Expired prepaid factory insurance:	
Making Department	$ 2,000
Packing Department	1,500
f. Applied factory overhead:	
Making Department	$ 32,570
Packing Department	30,050
g. Production costs transferred from Making Department to Packing Department	$166,790
h. Production costs transferred from Packing Department to Finished Goods	$263,400
i. Cost of goods sold during the period	$265,200

Instructions

1. Journalize the entries to record the operations, identifying each entry by letter.
2. Compute the July 31 balances of the inventory accounts.
3. Compute the July 31 balances of the factory overhead accounts.

✔ 1. Conversion cost per equivalent unit, $6.00

Excel

PR 20-2B Cost of production report

OBJ. 2, 4

Bavarian Chocolate Company processes chocolate into candy bars. The process begins by placing direct materials (raw chocolate, milk, and sugar) into the Blending Department. All materials are placed into production at the beginning of the blending process. After blending, the milk chocolate is then transferred to the Molding Department, where the milk chocolate is formed into candy bars. The following is a partial work in process account of the Blending Department at October 31:

ACCOUNT ***Work in Process—Blending Department*** **ACCOUNT NO.**

Date		Item	Debit	Credit	Balance Debit	Balance Credit
Oct.	1	Bal., 2,300 units, 3/5 completed			46,368	
	31	Direct materials, 26,000 units	429,000		475,368	
	31	Direct labor	100,560		575,928	
	31	Factory overhead	48,480		624,408	
	31	Goods transferred, 25,700 units		?		
	31	Bal., ? units, 1/5 completed			?	

Instructions

1. Prepare a cost of production report and identify the missing amounts for Work in Process—Blending Department.
2. Assuming that the October 1 work in process inventory includes direct materials of $38,295, determine the increase or decrease in the cost per equivalent unit for direct materials and conversion between September and October.

✔ 2. Transferred to finished goods, $705,376

Excel

PR 20-3B Equivalent units and related costs; cost of production report; entries

OBJ. 2, 3, 4

Dover Chemical Company manufactures specialty chemicals by a series of three processes, all materials being introduced in the Distilling Department. From the Distilling Department, the materials pass through the Reaction and Filling departments, emerging as finished chemicals.

The balance in the account Work in Process—Filling was as follows on January 1:

(Continued)

Work in Process—Filling Department	
(3,400 units, 60% completed):	
Direct materials (3,400 × $9.58)	$32,572
Conversion (3,400 × 60% × $3.90)	7,956
	$40,528

The following costs were charged to Work in Process—Filling during January:

Direct materials transferred from Reaction Department: 52,300 units at $9.50 a unit	$496,850
Direct labor	101,560
Factory overhead	95,166

During January, 53,000 units of specialty chemicals were completed. Work in Process—Filling Department on January 31 was 2,700 units, 30% completed.

Instructions

1. Prepare a cost of production report for the Filling Department for January.
2. Journalize the entries for costs transferred from Reaction to Filling and the costs transferred from Filling to Finished Goods.
3. Determine the increase or decrease in the cost per equivalent unit from December to January for direct materials and conversion costs.
4. Discuss the uses of the cost of production report and the results of part (3).

PR 20-4B Work in process account data for two months; cost of production reports **OBJ. 1, 2, 3, 4**

✓ 1. c. Transferred to finished goods in September, $702,195

Excel

Pittsburgh Aluminum Company uses a process cost system to record the costs of manufacturing rolled aluminum, which consists of the smelting and rolling processes. Materials are entered from smelting at the beginning of the rolling process. The inventory of Work in Process—Rolling on September 1 and debits to the account during September were as follows:

Bal., 2,600 units, ¼ completed:	
Direct materials (2,600 × $15.50)	$40,300
Conversion (2,600 × ¼ × $8.50)	5,525
	$45,825
From Smelting Department, 28,900 units	462,400
Direct labor	158,920
Factory overhead	101,402

During September, 2,600 units in process on September 1 were completed, and of the 28,900 units entering the department, all were completed except 2,900 units that were ⅘ completed.

Charges to Work in Process—Rolling for October were as follows:

From Smelting Department, 31,000 units	$511,500
Direct labor	162,850
Factory overhead	104,494

During October, the units in process at the beginning of the month were completed, and of the 31,000 units entering the department, all were completed except 2,000 units that were ⅖ completed.

Instructions

1. Enter the balance as of September 1 in a four-column account for Work in Process—Rolling. Record the debits and credits in the account for September. Construct a cost of production report and present computations for determining (a) equivalent units of production for materials and conversion; (b) cost per equivalent unit; (c) cost of goods finished, differentiating between units started in the prior period and units started and finished in September; and (d) work in process inventory.

2. Provide the same information for October by recording the October transactions in the four-column work in process account. Construct a cost of production report and present the October computations (a through d) listed in part (1).
3. Comment on the change in costs per equivalent unit for August through October for direct materials and conversion cost.

✔ Transferred to Packaging Dept., $54,000

Excel

Appendix
PR 20-5B Cost of production report: average cost method

Blue Ribbon Flour Company manufactures flour by a series of three processes, beginning in the Milling Department. From the Milling Department, the materials pass through the Sifting and Packaging departments, emerging as packaged refined flour.

The balance in the account Work in Process—Sifting Department was as follows on May 1:

Work in Process—Sifting Department (1,500 units, 75% completed)	$3,400

The following costs were charged to Work in Process—Sifting Department during May:

Direct materials transferred from Milling Department: 18,300 units	$32,600
Direct labor	14,560
Factory overhead	7,490

During May, 18,000 units of flour were completed and transferred to finished goods. Work in Process—Sifting Department on May 31 was 1,800 units, 75% completed.

Instructions

Prepare a cost of production report for the Sifting Department for May, using the average cost method.

Cases & Projects

Ethics

CP 20-1 Ethics in Action

Assume that you are the division controller for Auntie M's Cookie Company. Auntie M has introduced a new chocolate chip cookie called Full of Chips, and it is a success. As a result, the product manager responsible for the launch of this new cookie was promoted to division vice president and became your boss. A new product manager, Bishop, has been brought in to replace the promoted manager. Bishop notices that the Full of Chips cookie uses a great deal of chips, which increases the cost of the cookie. As a result, Bishop has ordered that the amount of chips used in the cookies be reduced by 10%. The manager believes that a 10% reduction in chips will not adversely affect sales but will reduce costs and, hence, improve margins. The increased margins would help Bishop meet profit targets for the period.

You are looking over some cost of production reports segmented by cookie line. You notice that there is a drop in the materials costs for Full of Chips. On further investigation, you discover why the chip costs have declined (fewer chips). Both you and Bishop report to the division vice president, who was the original product manager for Full of Chips. You are trying to decide what to do, if anything.

Discuss the options you might consider.

Team Activity

Real World

CP 20-2 Team Activity

The following categories represent typical process manufacturing industries:

Beverages	Metals
Chemicals	Petroleum refining
Food	Pharmaceuticals
Forest and paper products	Soap and cosmetics

In groups of two or three, for each category, identify one company (following your instructor's specific instructions) and determine the following:

(Continued)

1. Typical products manufactured by the selected company, including brand names
2. Typical raw materials used by the selected company
3. Types of processes used by the selected company

Use annual reports, the Internet, or library resources in doing this activity.

CP 20-3 Communication

Communication

Jamarcus Bradshaw, plant manager of Georgia Paper Company's papermaking mill, was looking over the cost of production reports for July and August for the Papermaking Department. The reports revealed the following:

	July	August
Pulp and chemicals	$295,600	$304,100
Conversion cost	146,000	149,600
Total cost	$441,600	$453,700
Number of tons	÷ 1,200	÷ 1,130
Cost per ton	$ 368	$ 401.50

Jamarcus was concerned about the increased cost per ton from the output of the department. As a result, he asked the plant controller to perform a study to help explain these results. The controller, Leann Brunswick, began the analysis by performing some interviews of key plant personnel in order to understand what the problem might be. Excerpts from an interview with Len Tyson, a paper machine operator, follow:

Len: We have two papermaking machines in the department. I have no data, but I think paper machine No. 1 is applying too much pulp and, thus, is wasting both conversion and materials resources. We haven't had repairs on paper machine No. 1 in a while. Maybe this is the problem.

Leann: How does too much pulp result in wasted resources?

Len: Well, you see, if too much pulp is applied, then we will waste pulp material. The customer will not pay for the extra product; we just use more material to make the product. Also, when there is too much pulp, the machine must be slowed down in order to complete the drying process. This results in additional conversion costs.

Leann: Do you have any other suspicions?

Len: Well, as you know, we have two products—green paper and yellow paper. They are identical except for the color. The color is added to the papermaking process in the paper machine. I think that during August these two color papers have been behaving differently. I don't have any data, but it seems as though the amount of waste associated with the green paper has increased.

Leann: Why is this?

Len: I understand that there has been a change in specifications for the green paper, starting near the beginning of August. This change could be causing the machines to run poorly when making green paper. If that is the case, the cost per ton would increase for green paper.

Leann also asked for a database printout providing greater detail on August's operating results.

September 9 Requested by: Leann Brunswick

Papermaking Department—August detail

	A	B	C	D	E	F
1	Production					
2	Run	Paper		Material	Conversion	
3	Number	Machine	Color	Costs	Costs	Tons
4	1	1	Green	40,300	18,300	150
5	2	1	Yellow	41,700	21,200	140
6	3	1	Green	44,600	22,500	150
7	4	1	Yellow	36,100	18,100	120
8	5	2	Green	38,300	18,900	160
9	6	2	Yellow	33,900	15,200	140
10	7	2	Green	35,600	18,400	130
11	8	2	Yellow	33,600	17,000	140
12		Total		304,100	149,600	1,130
13						

Prior to preparing a report, Leann resigned from Georgia Paper Company to start her own business. You have been asked to take the data that Leann collected and write a memo to Jamarcus Bradshaw with a recommendation to management. Your memo should include analysis of the August data to determine whether the paper machine or the paper color explains the increase in the unit cost from July. Include any supporting schedules that are appropriate. Round all calculations to the nearest cent.

Real World

CP 20-4 Accounting for materials costs

In papermaking operations for companies such as International Paper Company, wet pulp is fed into paper machines, which press and dry pulp into a continuous sheet of paper. The paper is formed at very high speeds (60 mph). Once the paper is formed, the paper is rolled onto a reel at the back end of the paper machine. One of the characteristics of papermaking is the creation of "broke" paper. Broke is paper that fails to satisfy quality standards and is therefore rejected for final shipment to customers. Broke is recycled back to the beginning of the process by combining the recycled paper with virgin (new) pulp material. The combination of virgin pulp and recycled broke is sent to the paper machine for papermaking. Broke is fed into this recycle process continuously from all over the facility.

In this industry, it is typical to charge the papermaking operation with the cost of direct materials, which is a mixture of virgin materials and broke. Broke has a much lower cost than does virgin pulp. Therefore, the more broke in the mixture, the lower the average cost of direct materials to the department. Papermaking managers frequently comment on the importance of broke for keeping their direct materials costs down.

a. How do you react to this accounting procedure?

b. What "hidden costs" are not considered when accounting for broke as described?

CP 20-5 Analyzing unit costs

Midstate Containers Inc. manufactures cans for the canned food industry. The operations manager of a can manufacturing operation wants to conduct a cost study investigating the relationship of tin content in the material (can stock) to the energy cost for enameling the cans. The enameling was necessary to prepare the cans for labeling. A higher percentage of tin content in the can stock increases the cost of material. The operations manager believed that a higher tin content in the can stock would reduce the amount of energy used in enameling. During the analysis period, the amount of tin content in the steel can stock was increased every month from April to September. The following operating reports were available from the controller:

	A	B	C	D	E	F	G
1		April	May	June	July	August	September
2	Materials	$ 14,000	$ 34,800	$ 33,000	$ 21,700	$ 28,800	$ 33,000
3	Energy	13,000	28,800	24,200	14,000	17,100	16,000
4	Total cost	$ 27,000	$ 63,600	$ 57,200	$ 35,700	$ 45,900	$ 49,000
5	Units produced	÷50,000	÷120,000	÷110,000	÷ 70,000	÷ 90,000	÷100,000
6	Cost per unit	$ 0.54	$ 0.53	$ 0.52	$ 0.51	$ 0.51	$ 0.49
7							

Differences in materials unit costs were entirely related to the amount of tin content.

Interpret this information and report to the operations manager your recommendations with respect to tin content.

CHAPTER

21

Cost-Volume-Profit Analysis

Concepts and Principles

Chapter 18 *Introduction to Managerial Accounting*

Developing Information

COST SYSTEMS

Chapter 19 *Job Order Costing*
Chapter 20 *Process Costing*

COST BEHAVIOR

Chapter 21 *Cost-Volume-Profit Analysis*

Decision Making

EVALUATING PERFORMANCE

Chapter 22 *Budgeting*
Chapter 23 *Variances from Standard Costs*

COMPARING ALTERNATIVES

Chapter 24 *Decentralized Operations*
Chapter 25 *Differential Analysis, Product Pricing, and Activity-Based Costing*
Chapter 26 *Capital Investment Analysis*

SCOTT OLSON/GETTY IMAGES

CHAPTER 21

Ford Motor Company

Making a profit isn't easy for U.S. auto manufacturers like the **Ford Motor Company**. The cost of materials, labor, equipment, and advertising means it is very expensive to produce cars and trucks.

How many cars does Ford need to produce and sell to break even? The answer depends on the relationship between Ford's sales revenue and costs. Some of Ford's costs, like direct labor and materials, change in direct proportion to the number of vehicles that are built. Other costs, such as the costs of manufacturing equipment, are fixed and do not change with the number of vehicles that are produced. Ford breaks even when it generates enough sales revenue to cover both its fixed and variable costs.

During the depths of the 2009 recession, Ford renegotiated labor contracts with its employees. These renegotiations reduced the direct labor cost incurred to build each car, which lowered the number of cars the company needed to sell to break even by 45%.

As with Ford, understanding how costs behave and the relationship between costs, profits, and volume is important for all businesses. This chapter discusses commonly used methods for classifying costs according to how they change, and illustrates how to determine the number of units that must be sold for a company to break even. Techniques that management can use to evaluate costs in order to make sound business decisions are also discussed.

Source: J. Booton, "Moody's Upgrades Ford's Credit Rating, Returns Blue Oval Trademark," *Fox Business*, May 22, 2012.

Learning Objectives

After studying this chapter, you should be able to:

Example Exercises (EE) are shown in **green**.

Obj. 1 **Classify costs as variable costs, fixed costs, or mixed costs.**

Cost Behavior
Variable Costs
Fixed Costs
Mixed Costs — EE 21-1
Summary of Cost Behavior Concepts

Obj. 2 **Compute the contribution margin, the contribution margin ratio, and the unit contribution margin.**

Cost-Volume-Profit Relationships
Contribution Margin
Contribution Margin Ratio
Unit Contribution Margin — EE 21-2

Obj. 3 **Determine the break-even point and sales necessary to achieve a target profit.**

Mathematical Approach to Cost-Volume-Profit Analysis
Break-Even Point — EE 21-3
Target Profit — EE 21-4

Obj. 4 **Using a cost-volume-profit chart and a profit-volume chart, determine the break-even point and sales necessary to achieve a target profit.**

Graphic Approach to Cost-Volume-Profit Analysis
Cost-Volume-Profit (Break-Even) Chart
Profit-Volume Chart
Use of Computers in Cost-Volume-Profit Analysis
Assumptions of Cost-Volume-Profit Analysis

Obj. 5 **Compute the break-even point for a company selling more than one product, the operating leverage, and the margin of safety.**

Special Cost-Volume-Profit Relationships
Sales Mix Considerations — EE 21-5
Operating Leverage — EE 21-6
Margin of Safety — EE 21-7

At a Glance 21 Page 1050

Obj. 1 Classify costs as variable costs, fixed costs, or mixed costs.

Cost Behavior

Cost behavior is the manner in which a cost changes as a related activity changes. The behavior of costs is useful to managers for a variety of reasons. For example, knowing how costs behave allows managers to predict profits as sales and production volumes change. Knowing how costs behave is also useful for estimating costs, which affects a variety of decisions such as whether to replace a machine.

Understanding the behavior of a cost depends on the following:

- Identifying the activities that cause the cost to change. These activities are called **activity bases** (or *activity drivers*).
- Specifying the range of activity over which the changes in the cost are of interest. This range of activity is called the **relevant range**.

To illustrate, assume that a hospital is concerned about planning and controlling patient food costs. A good activity base is the number of patients who *stay* overnight in the hospital. The number of patients who are *treated* is not as good an activity base because some patients are outpatients and, thus, do not consume food. Once an activity base is identified, food costs can then be analyzed over the range of the number of patients who normally stay in the hospital (the relevant range).

Costs are normally classified as variable costs, fixed costs, or mixed costs.

Link to Ford Motor Company

The first vehicle built by Henry Ford in 1896 was a Quadracycle that consisted of four bicycle wheels powered by a four-horsepower engine. The first Ford Model A was sold by Ford Motor Company in 1903. In 1908, the Ford Model T was introduced, which had sales of 15 million before its production was halted in 1927.

Source: www.corporate.ford.com

Variable Costs

Variable costs are costs that vary in proportion to changes in the activity base. When the activity base is units produced, direct materials and direct labor costs are normally classified as variable costs.

To illustrate, assume that Jason Sound Inc. produces stereo systems. The parts for the stereo systems are purchased from suppliers for $10 per unit and are assembled by Jason Sound. For Model JS-12, the direct materials costs for the relevant range of 5,000 to 30,000 units of production are as follows:

Number of Units of Model JS-12 Produced	Direct Materials Cost per Unit	Total Direct Materials Cost
5,000 units	$10	$ 50,000
10,000	10	100,000
15,000	10	150,000
20,000	10	200,000
25,000	10	250,000
30,000	10	300,000

As shown, variable costs have the following characteristics:

- *Cost per unit* remains the same regardless of changes in the activity base. For Jason Sound, units produced is the activity base. For Model JS-12, the cost per unit is $10.
- *Total cost* changes in proportion to changes in the activity base. For Model JS-12, the direct materials cost for 10,000 units ($100,000) is twice the direct materials cost for 5,000 units ($50,000).

Exhibit 1 illustrates how the variable costs for direct materials for Model JS-12 behave in total and on a per-unit basis as production changes.

Link to Ford Motor Company

Changing emission, fuel economy, and safety standards increase the variable cost of each vehicle manufactured by Ford Motor Company.

Variable Cost Graphs **EXHIBIT 1**

Dynamic Exhibit

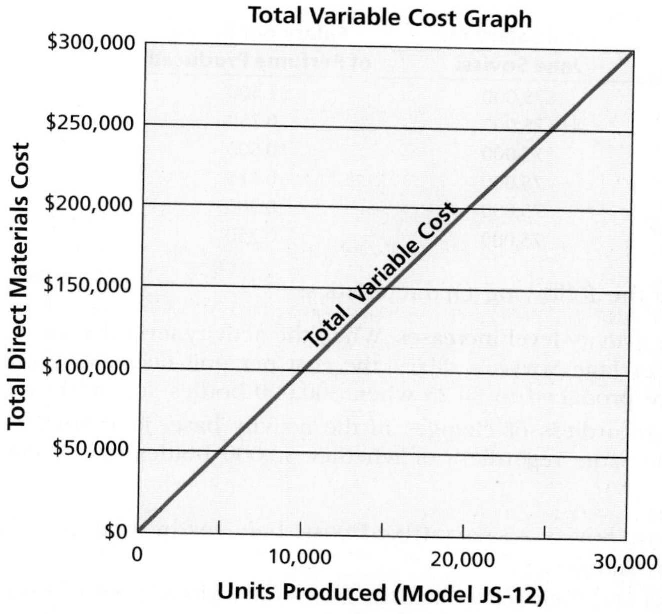

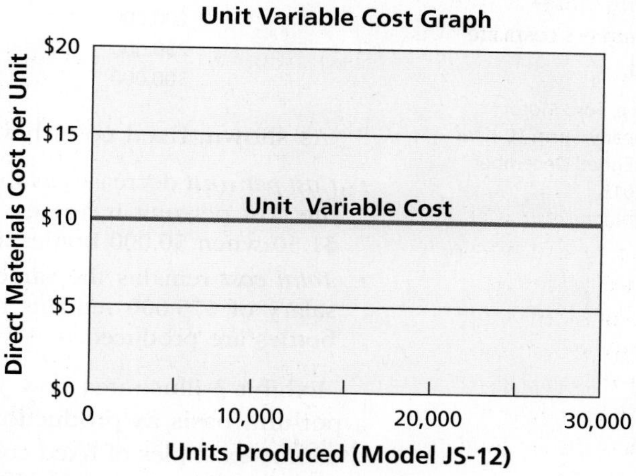

Some examples of variable costs and their related activity bases for various types of businesses are shown in Exhibit 2.

EXHIBIT 2

Variable Costs and Their Activity Bases

Type of Business	Cost	Activity Base
University	Instructor salaries	Number of classes
Passenger airline	Fuel	Number of miles flown
Manufacturing	Direct materials	Number of units produced
Hospital	Nurse wages	Number of patients
Hotel	Maid wages	Number of guests
Bank	Teller wages	Number of banking transactions

Fixed Costs

Fixed costs are costs that remain the same in total dollar amount as the activity base changes. When the activity base is units produced, many factory overhead costs such as straight-line depreciation are classified as fixed costs.

To illustrate, assume that Minton Inc. manufactures, bottles, and distributes perfume. The production supervisor is Jane Sovissi, who is paid a salary of $75,000 per year. For the relevant range of 50,000 to 300,000 bottles of perfume, the total fixed cost of $75,000 does not vary as production increases. As a result, the fixed cost per bottle decreases as the units produced increase. This is because the fixed cost is spread over a larger number of bottles, as follows:

Link to Ford Motor Company

A high proportion of **Ford Motor Company**'s costs are fixed.

Source: Ford Motor Company, Form 10-K for Year Ended December 31, 2015.

Number of Bottles of Perfume Produced	Total Salary for Jane Sovissi	Salary per Bottle of Perfume Produced
50,000 bottles	$75,000	$1.500
100,000	75,000	0.750
150,000	75,000	0.500
200,000	75,000	0.375
250,000	75,000	0.300
300,000	75,000	0.250

As shown, fixed costs have the following characteristics:

- *Cost per unit* decreases as the activity level increases. When the activity level decreases, the cost per unit increases. For Jane Sovissi's salary, the cost per unit decreases from $1.50 when 50,000 bottles are produced to $0.25 when 300,000 bottles are produced.
- *Total cost* remains the same regardless of changes in the activity base. Jane Sovissi's salary of $75,000 remains the same regardless of whether 50,000 bottles or 300,000 bottles are produced.

Exhibit 3 illustrates how Jane Sovissi's salary (fixed cost) behaves in total and on a per-unit basis as production changes.

Some examples of fixed costs and their related activity bases for various types of businesses are shown in Exhibit 4. In each of these cases, the cost is fixed to the level of activity.

Mixed Costs

Mixed costs are costs that have characteristics of both a variable and a fixed cost. Mixed costs are sometimes called *semivariable* or *semifixed costs.*

To illustrate, assume that Simpson Inc. manufactures sails, using rented machinery. The rental charges are as follows:

Rental Charge = $15,000 per year + $1 for each hour used in excess of 10,000 hours

Fixed Cost Graphs EXHIBIT 3

Dynamic Exhibit

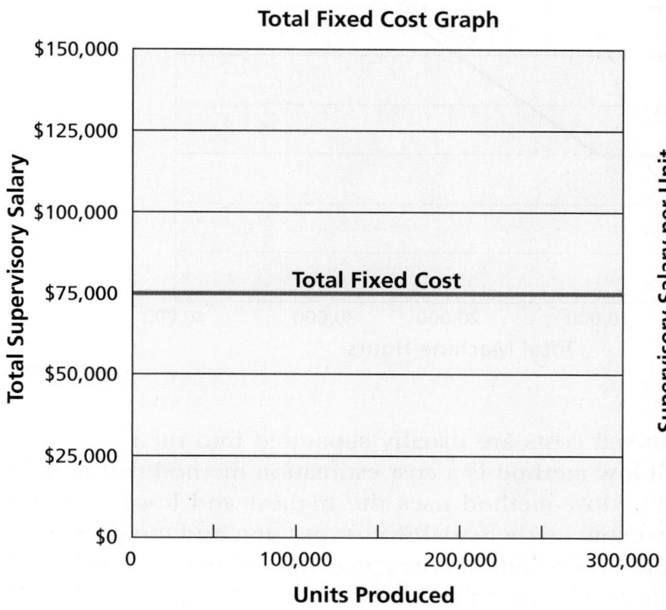

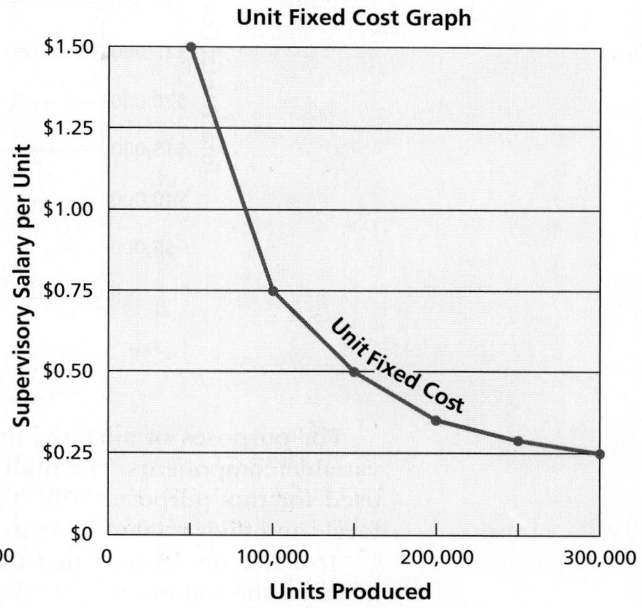

EXHIBIT 4

Fixed Costs and Their Activity Bases

Type of Business	Fixed Cost	Activity Base
University	Building (straight-line) depreciation	Number of students
Passenger airline	Airplane (straight-line) depreciation	Number of miles flown
Manufacturing	Plant manager salary	Number of units produced
Hospital	Property insurance	Number of patients
Hotel	Property taxes	Number of guests
Bank	Branch manager salary	Number of customer accounts

The rental charges for various hours used within the relevant range of 8,000 hours to 40,000 hours are as follows:

Hours Used	Rental Charge
8,000 hours	$15,000
12,000	$17,000 {$15,000 + [(12,000 hrs. – 10,000 hrs.) × $1]}
20,000	$25,000 {$15,000 + [(20,000 hrs. – 10,000 hrs.) × $1]}
40,000	$45,000 {$15,000 + [(40,000 hrs. – 10,000 hrs.) × $1]}

Exhibit 5 illustrates the preceding mixed cost behavior.

EXHIBIT 5

Mixed Costs

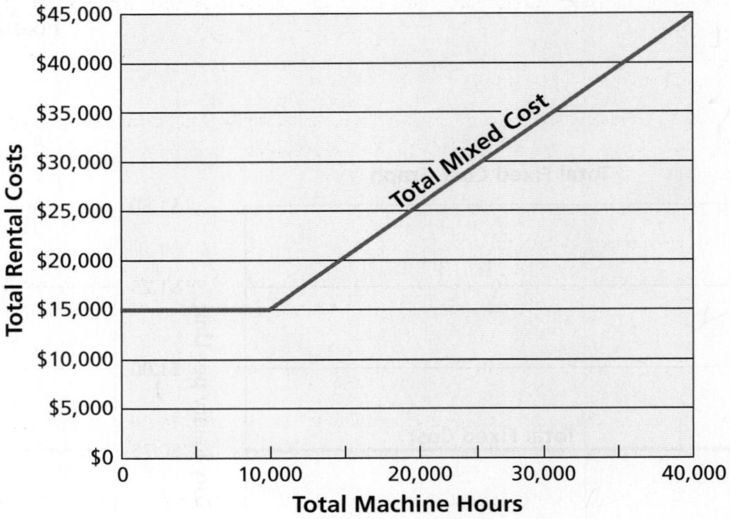

For purposes of analysis, mixed costs are usually separated into their fixed and variable components. The **high-low method** is a cost estimation method that may be used for this purpose.[1] The high-low method uses the highest and lowest activity levels and their related costs to estimate the variable cost per unit and the fixed cost.

To illustrate, assume that the Equipment Maintenance Department of Kason Inc. incurred the following costs during the past five months:

	Units Produced	Total Cost
June	1,000 units	$45,550
July	1,500	52,000
August	2,100	61,500
September	1,800	57,500
October	750	41,250

The number of units produced is the activity base, and the relevant range is the units produced between June and October. For Kason, the difference between the units produced and the total costs at the highest and lowest levels of production are as follows:

	Units Produced	Total Cost
Highest level	2,100 units	$61,500
Lowest level	750	41,250
Difference	1,350 units	$20,250

The total fixed cost does not change with changes in production. Thus, the $20,250 difference in the total cost is the change in the total variable cost. Dividing this difference of $20,250 by the difference in production is an estimate of the variable cost per unit. For Kason, this estimate is $15, computed as follows:

$$\text{Variable Cost per Unit} = \frac{\text{Difference in Total Cost}}{\text{Difference in Units Produced}}$$

$$= \frac{\$20{,}250}{1{,}350 \text{ units}} = \$15 \text{ per unit}$$

The fixed cost is estimated by subtracting the total variable costs from the total costs for the units produced, as follows:

$$\text{Fixed Cost} = \text{Total Costs} - (\text{Variable Cost per Unit} \times \text{Units Produced})$$

1 Other methods of estimating costs, such as the scattergraph method and the least squares method, are discussed in cost accounting textbooks.

The fixed cost is the same at the highest and lowest levels of production, as follows for Kason:

Highest level (2,100 units)

Fixed Cost = Total Costs – (Variable Cost per Unit × Units Produced)
= $61,500 – ($15 × 2,100 units)
= $61,500 – $31,500
= $30,000

Lowest level (750 units)

Fixed Cost = Total Costs – (Variable Cost per Unit × Units Produced)
= $41,250 – ($15 × 750 units)
= $41,250 – $11,250
= $30,000

Using the variable cost per unit and the fixed cost, the total equipment maintenance cost for Kason can be computed for various levels of production as follows:

Total Cost = (Variable Cost per Unit × Units Produced) + Fixed Costs
= ($15 × Units Produced) + $30,000

To illustrate, the estimated total cost of 2,000 units of production is $60,000, computed as follows:

Total Cost = ($15 × Units Produced) + $30,000
= ($15 × 2,000 units) + $30,000 = $30,000 + $30,000
= $60,000

Link to Ford

In 2011, Ford Motor Company entered into a collective bargaining agreement with the United Auto Workers union that provides for lump-sum payments in lieu of general wage increases. This has the effect of making wages more like a mixed cost.

Source: Ford Motor Company, Form 10-K for Year Ended December 31, 2011.

Example Exercise 21-1 High-Low Method

Obj. 1

The manufacturing costs of Alex Industries for the first three months of the year follow:

	Total Cost	Units Produced
January	$ 80,000	1,000 units
February	125,000	2,500
March	100,000	1,800

Using the high-low method, determine (a) the variable cost per unit and (b) the total fixed cost.

Follow My Example 21-1

a. $30 per unit = ($125,000 – $80,000) ÷ (2,500 – 1,000)
b. $50,000 = $125,000 – ($30 × 2,500), or $80,000 – ($30 × 1,000)

Practice Exercises: PE 21-1A, PE 21-1B

Summary of Cost Behavior Concepts

The cost behavior of variable costs and fixed costs is summarized in Exhibit 6.

EXHIBIT 6

Variable and Fixed Cost Behavior

	Effect of Changing Activity Level	
Cost	**Total Amount**	**Per-Unit Amount**
Variable	Increases and decreases proportionately with activity level.	Remains the same regardless of activity level.
Fixed	Remains the same regardless of activity level.	Increases and decreases inversely with activity level.

Mixed costs contain a fixed cost component that is incurred even if nothing is produced. For analysis, the fixed and variable cost components of mixed costs are separated using the high-low method.

Exhibit 7 provides some examples of variable, fixed, and mixed costs for the activity base of *units produced.*

EXHIBIT 7

Variable, Fixed, and Mixed Costs

Variable Costs	Fixed Costs	Mixed Costs
• Direct materials • Direct labor • Electricity expense • Supplies	• Straight-line depreciation • Property taxes • Production supervisor salaries • Insurance expense	• Quality Control Department salaries • Purchasing Department salaries • Maintenance expenses • Warehouse expenses

One method of reporting variable and fixed costs is called **variable costing** or *direct costing*. Under variable costing, only the variable manufacturing costs (direct materials, direct labor, and variable factory overhead) are included in the product cost. The fixed factory overhead is treated as an expense of the period in which it is incurred. Variable costing is described and illustrated in the appendix to this chapter.

Business Connection

BOOKING FEES

A major fixed cost for a concert promoter is the booking fee for the act. The booking fee is the amount to be paid to the act for a single show at a venue. Degy Entertainment, a booking agency, provided a list of asking prices for several popular acts. The following is a sampling from the list.

Taylor Swift	$1,000,000+
Justin Timberlake	$1,000,000+
Rihanna	$500K–$750K
Katy Perry	$500K
Keith Urban	$400K–$600K
Maroon 5	$400K–$600K
Kanye West	$400K–$600K
Carrie Underwood	$400K–$500K
Alicia Keys	$350k–$500K
Bruno Mars	$200K–$400K
Pitbull	$200K–$300K
Ke$ha	$150K–$200K
The Script	$125K–$175K

The promoter must cover these fixed costs with ticket revenues; thus, the size of the booking fee is necessarily related to the popularity of the act represented by the number of potential tickets sold and the ticket price.

Source: Zachery Crockett, "How Much Does It Cost to Book Your Favorite Band?" *Priceconomics.com*, May 16, 2014.

Obj. 2 Compute the contribution margin, the contribution margin ratio, and the unit contribution margin.

Cost-Volume-Profit Relationships

Cost-volume-profit analysis is the examination of the relationships among selling prices, sales and production volume, costs, expenses, and profits. Cost-volume-profit analysis is useful for managerial decision making. Some of the ways cost-volume-profit analysis may be used include the following:

- Analyzing the effects of changes in selling prices on profits
- Analyzing the effects of changes in costs on profits
- Analyzing the effects of changes in volume on profits
- Setting selling prices
- Selecting the mix of products to sell
- Choosing among marketing strategies

Contribution Margin

Contribution margin is especially useful because it provides insight into the profit potential of a company. **Contribution margin** is the excess of sales over variable costs, computed as follows:

Contribution Margin = Sales − Variable Costs

To illustrate, assume the following data for Lambert Inc.:

Sales	50,000 units
Sales price per unit	\$20 per unit
Variable cost per unit	\$12 per unit
Fixed costs	\$300,000

Exhibit 8 illustrates an income statement for Lambert prepared in a contribution margin format.

EXHIBIT 8

Contribution Margin Income Statement Format

Sales (50,000 units × \$20)	\$1,000,000
Variable costs (50,000 units × \$12)	600,000
Contribution margin (50,000 units × \$8)	\$ 400,000
Fixed costs	300,000
Income from operations	\$ 100,000

Lambert's contribution margin of \$400,000 is available to cover the fixed costs of \$300,000. Once the fixed costs are covered, any additional contribution margin increases income from operations.

Contribution Margin Ratio

Contribution margin can also be expressed as a percentage. The **contribution margin ratio**, sometimes called the *profit-volume ratio*, indicates the percentage of each sales dollar available to cover fixed costs and to provide income from operations. The contribution margin ratio is computed as follows:

$$\text{Contribution Margin Ratio} = \frac{\text{Contribution Margin}}{\text{Sales}}$$

The contribution margin ratio is 40% for Lambert Inc., computed as follows:

$$\text{Contribution Margin Ratio} = \frac{\$400{,}000}{\$1{,}000{,}000} = 40\%$$

The contribution margin ratio is most useful when the increase or decrease in sales volume is measured in sales *dollars*. In this case, the change in sales dollars multiplied by the contribution margin ratio equals the change in income from operations, computed as follows:

Change in Income from Operations = Change in Sales Dollars × Contribution Margin Ratio

To illustrate, if Lambert adds \$80,000 in sales from the sale of an additional 4,000 units, its income from operations will increase by \$32,000, computed as follows:

Change in Income from Operations = Change in Sales Dollars × Contribution Margin Ratio
= \$80,000 × 40%
= \$32,000

The preceding analysis is confirmed by the contribution margin income statement of Lambert that follows:

Sales (54,000 units × $20)	$1,080,000
Variable costs (54,000 units × $12)	648,000*
Contribution margin (54,000 units × $8)	$ 432,000**
Fixed costs	300,000
Income from operations	$ 132,000

*$1,080,000 × 60%
**$1,080,000 × 40%

Income from operations increased from $100,000 to $132,000 when sales increased from $1,000,000 to $1,080,000. Variable costs as a percentage of sales are equal to 100% minus the contribution margin ratio. Thus, in the preceding income statement, the variable costs are 60% (100% – 40%) of sales, or $648,000 ($1,080,000 × 60%). The total contribution margin, $432,000, can also be computed directly by multiplying the total sales by the contribution margin ratio ($1,080,000 × 40%).

In the preceding analysis, factors other than sales volume, such as variable cost per unit and sales price, are assumed to remain constant. If such factors change, their effect must also be considered.

The contribution margin ratio is also useful in developing business strategies. For example, assume that a company has a high contribution margin ratio and is producing below 100% of capacity. In this case, a large increase in income from operations can be expected from an increase in sales volume. Therefore, the company might consider implementing a special sales campaign to increase sales. In contrast, a company with a small contribution margin ratio will probably want to give more attention to reducing costs before attempting to promote sales.

Unit Contribution Margin

The unit contribution margin is also useful for analyzing the profit potential of proposed decisions. The **unit contribution margin** is computed as follows:

Unit Contribution Margin = Sales Price per Unit – Variable Cost per Unit

To illustrate, if Lambert Inc.'s unit selling price is $20 and its variable cost per unit is $12, the unit contribution margin is $8, computed as follows:

Unit Contribution Margin = Sales Price per Unit – Variable Cost per Unit
= $20 – $12
= $8

The unit contribution margin is most useful when the increase or decrease in sales volume is measured in sales *units* (quantities). In this case, the change in sales volume (units) multiplied by the unit contribution margin equals the change in income from operations, computed as follows:

Change in Income from Operations = Change in Sales Units × Unit Contribution Margin

To illustrate, assume that Lambert's sales could be increased by 15,000 units, from 50,000 units to 65,000 units. Lambert's income from operations would increase by $120,000 (15,000 units × $8), computed as follows:

Change in Income from Operations = Change in Sales Units × Unit Contribution Margin
= 15,000 units × $8
= $120,000

The preceding analysis is confirmed by the contribution margin income statement of Lambert that follows, which shows that income increased to $220,000 when 65,000 units are sold. The income statement in Exhibit 8 indicates income of $100,000 when 50,000 units are sold. Thus, selling an additional 15,000 units increases income by $120,000 ($220,000 – $100,000).

Sales (65,000 units × $20)	$1,300,000
Variable costs (65,000 units × $12)	780,000
Contribution margin (65,000 units × $8)	$ 520,000
Fixed costs	300,000
Income from operations	$ 220,000

Unit contribution margin analysis is useful information for managers. For example, in the preceding illustration, Lambert could spend up to $120,000 for special advertising or other product promotions to increase sales by 15,000 units and still increase income.

Example Exercise 21-2 Contribution Margin — **Obj. 2**

Molly Company sells 20,000 units at $12 per unit. Variable costs are $9 per unit, and fixed costs are $25,000. Determine the (a) contribution margin ratio, (b) unit contribution margin, and (c) income from operations.

Follow My Example 21-2

a. 25% = ($12 – $9) ÷ $12, or ($240,000 – $180,000) ÷ $240,000

b. $3 per unit = $12 – $9

c.

Sales	$240,000	(20,000 units × $12 per unit)
Variable costs	180,000	(20,000 units × $9 per unit)
Contribution margin	$ 60,000	[20,000 units × ($12 – $9)]
Fixed costs	25,000	
Income from operations	$ 35,000	

Practice Exercises: PE 21-2A, PE 21-2B

Mathematical Approach to Cost-Volume-Profit Analysis

Obj. 3 Determine the break-even point and sales necessary to achieve a target profit.

The mathematical approach to cost-volume-profit analysis uses equations to determine the following:

- Sales necessary to break even
- Sales necessary to make a target or desired profit

Break-Even Point

The **break-even point** is the level of operations at which a company's revenues and expenses are equal, as shown in Exhibit 9. At break-even, a company reports neither income nor a loss from operations.

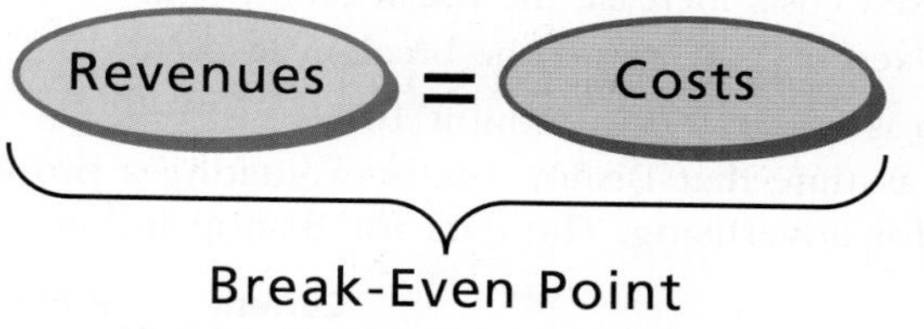

EXHIBIT 9

Break-Even Point

The break-even point in *sales units* is computed as follows:

$$\text{Break-Even Sales (units)} = \frac{\text{Fixed Costs}}{\text{Unit Contribution Margin}}$$

To illustrate, assume the following data for Baker Corporation:

Fixed costs	$90,000
Unit selling price	$25
Unit variable cost	15
Unit contribution margin	$10

The break-even point for Baker is 9,000 units, computed as follows:

$$\text{Break-Even Sales (units)} = \frac{\text{Fixed Costs}}{\text{Unit Contribution Margin}} = \frac{\$90{,}000}{\$10} = 9{,}000 \text{ units}$$

The following income statement for Baker verifies the break-even point of 9,000 units:

Sales (9,000 units × $25)	$225,000
Variable costs (9,000 units × $15)	135,000
Contribution margin	$ 90,000
Fixed costs	90,000
Income from operations	$ 0

As shown in Baker's income statement, the break-even point is $225,000 (9,000 units × $25) of sales. The break-even point in *sales dollars* can be determined directly as follows:

$$\text{Break-Even Sales (dollars)} = \frac{\text{Fixed Costs}}{\text{Contribution Margin Ratio}}$$

The contribution margin ratio can be computed using the unit contribution margin and unit selling price as follows:

$$\text{Contribution Margin Ratio} = \frac{\text{Unit Contribution Margin}}{\text{Unit Selling Price}}$$

The contribution margin ratio for Baker is 40%, computed as follows:

$$\text{Contribution Margin Ratio} = \frac{\text{Unit Contribution Margin}}{\text{Unit Selling Price}} = \frac{\$10}{\$25} = 40\%$$

Thus, the break-even sales dollars for Baker of $225,000 can be computed directly as follows:

$$\text{Break-Even Sales (dollars)} = \frac{\text{Fixed Costs}}{\text{Contribution Margin Ratio}} = \frac{\$90{,}000}{40\%} = \$225{,}000$$

Link to Ford Motor Company

Ford Motor reported that its 2014 operations in the Middle East and Africa were at break-even.

Source: Ford Motor Company, Form 10-K for Year Ended December 31, 2014.

The break-even point is affected by changes in the fixed costs, unit variable costs, and unit selling price.

Effect of Changes in Fixed Costs Fixed costs do not change in total with changes in the level of activity. However, fixed costs may change because of other factors such as advertising campaigns, changes in property tax rates, or changes in factory supervisors' salaries.

Changes in fixed costs affect the break-even point as follows:

- Increases in fixed costs increase the break-even point.
- Decreases in fixed costs decrease the break-even point.

This relationship is illustrated in Exhibit 10.

To illustrate, assume that Bishop Co. is evaluating a proposal to budget an additional $100,000 for advertising. The data for Bishop follow:

	Current	Proposed
Unit selling price	$90	$90
Unit variable cost	70	70
Unit contribution margin	$20	$20
Fixed costs	$600,000	$700,000

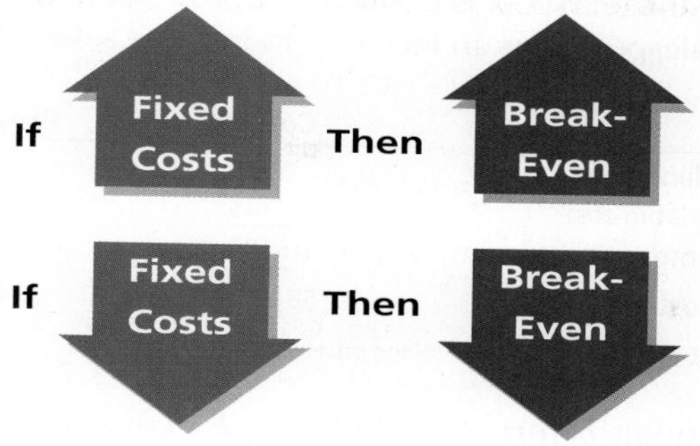

EXHIBIT 10

Effect of Change in Fixed Costs on Break-Even Point

Bishop's break-even point *before* the additional advertising expense of $100,000 is 30,000 units, computed as follows:

$$\text{Break-Even Sales (units)} = \frac{\text{Fixed Costs}}{\text{Unit Contribution Margin}} = \frac{\$600{,}000}{\$20} = 30{,}000 \text{ units}$$

Bishop's break-even point *after* the additional advertising expense of $100,000 is 35,000 units, computed as follows:

$$\text{Break-Even Sales (units)} = \frac{\text{Fixed Costs}}{\text{Unit Contribution Margin}} = \frac{\$700{,}000}{\$20} = 35{,}000 \text{ units}$$

As shown for Bishop, the $100,000 increase in advertising (fixed costs) requires an additional 5,000 units (35,000 – 30,000) of sales to break even.[2] In other words, an increase in sales of 5,000 units is required in order to generate an additional $100,000 of total contribution margin (5,000 units × $20) to cover the increased fixed costs.

Effect of Changes in Unit Variable Costs Unit variable costs do not change with changes in the level of activity. However, unit variable costs may be affected by other factors such as changes in the cost per unit of direct materials, changes in the wage rate for direct labor, or changes in the sales commission paid to salespeople.

Changes in unit variable costs affect the break-even point as follows:

- Increases in unit variable costs increase the break-even point.
- Decreases in unit variable costs decrease the break-even point.

This relationship is illustrated in Exhibit 11.

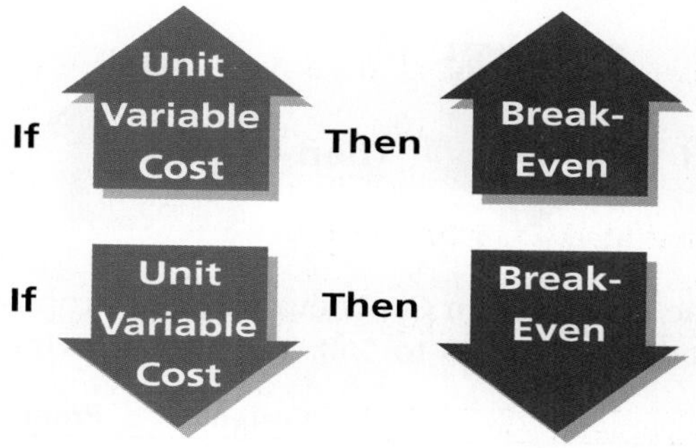

EXHIBIT 11

Effect of Change in Unit Variable Cost on Break-Even Point

2 The increase of 5,000 units can also be computed by dividing the increase in fixed costs of $100,000 by the unit contribution margin, $20, as follows: 5,000 units = $100,000 ÷ $20.

To illustrate, assume that Park Co. is evaluating a proposal to pay an additional 2% commission on sales to its salespeople as an incentive to increase sales. The data for Park follow:

	Current	Proposed
Unit selling price	$250	$250
Unit variable cost	145	150*
Unit contribution margin	$105	$100
Fixed costs	$840,000	$840,000

*$150 = $145 + (2% × $250 unit selling price)

Park's break-even point *before* the additional 2% commission is 8,000 units, computed as follows:

$$\text{Break-Even Sales (units)} = \frac{\text{Fixed Costs}}{\text{Unit Contribution Margin}} = \frac{\$840{,}000}{\$105} = 8{,}000 \text{ units}$$

If the 2% sales commission proposal is adopted, unit variable costs will increase by $5 ($250 × 2%), from $145 to $150 per unit. This increase in unit variable costs will decrease the unit contribution margin from $105 to $100 ($250 – $150). Thus, Park's break-even point *after* the additional 2% commission is 8,400 units, computed as follows:

$$\text{Break-Even Sales (units)} = \frac{\text{Fixed Costs}}{\text{Unit Contribution Margin}} = \frac{\$840{,}000}{\$100} = 8{,}400 \text{ units}$$

As shown for Park, an additional 400 units of sales will be required in order to break even. This is because if 8,000 units are sold, the new unit contribution margin of $100 provides only $800,000 (8,000 units × $100) of contribution margin. Thus, $40,000 more contribution margin is necessary to cover the total fixed costs of $840,000. This additional $40,000 of contribution margin is provided by selling 400 more units (400 units × $100).

Effect of Changes in Unit Selling Price Changes in the unit selling price affect the unit contribution margin and, thus, the break-even point. Specifically, changes in the unit selling price affect the break-even point as follows:

- Increases in the unit selling price decrease the break-even point.
- Decreases in the unit selling price increase the break-even point.

This relationship is illustrated in Exhibit 12.

EXHIBIT 12

Effect of Change in Unit Selling Price on Break-Even Point

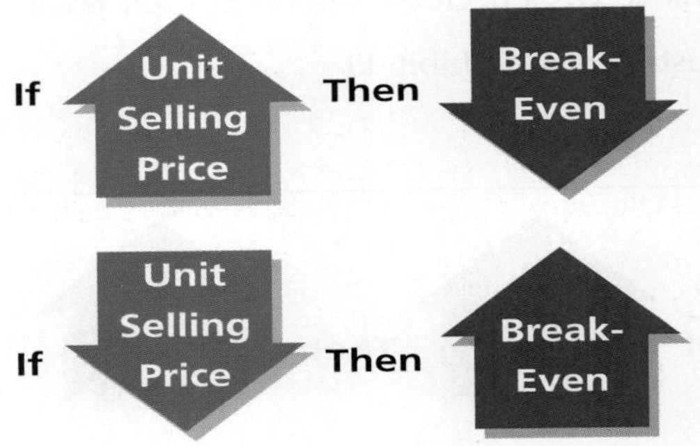

To illustrate, assume that Graham Co. is evaluating a proposal to increase the unit selling price of its product from $50 to $60. The data for Graham follow:

	Current	Proposed
Unit selling price	$50	$60
Unit variable cost	30	30
Unit contribution margin	$20	$30
Fixed costs	$600,000	$600,000

Graham's break-even point *before* the price increase is 30,000 units, computed as follows:

$$\text{Break-Even Sales (units)} = \frac{\text{Fixed Costs}}{\text{Unit Contribution Margin}} = \frac{\$600{,}000}{\$20} = 30{,}000 \text{ units}$$

The increase of $10 per unit in the selling price increases the unit contribution margin by $10. Thus, Graham's break-even point *after* the price increase is 20,000 units, computed as follows:

$$\text{Break-Even Sales (units)} = \frac{\text{Fixed Costs}}{\text{Unit Contribution Margin}} = \frac{\$600{,}000}{\$30} = 20{,}000 \text{ units}$$

As shown for Graham, the price increase of $10 increased the unit contribution margin by $10, which decreased the break-even point by 10,000 units (30,000 units – 20,000 units).

Summary of Effects of Changes on Break-Even Point The break-even point in sales changes in the same direction as changes in the variable cost per unit and fixed costs. In contrast, the break-even point in sales changes in the opposite direction as changes in the unit selling price. These changes on the break-even point in sales are summarized in Exhibit 13.

EXHIBIT 13

Effects of Changes in Selling Price and Costs on Break-Even Point

Type of Change	Direction of Change	Effect of Change on Break-Even Sales
Fixed cost	↑	↑
	↓	↓
Unit variable cost	↑	↑
	↓	↓
Unit selling price	↑	↓
	↓	↑

Example Exercise 21-3 Break-Even Point

Obj. 3

Nicolas Enterprises sells a product for $60 per unit. The variable cost is $35 per unit, while fixed costs are $80,000. Determine the (a) break-even point in sales units and (b) break-even point in sales units assuming that the selling price is increased to $67 per unit.

Follow My Example 21-3

a. 3,200 units = $80,000 ÷ ($60 – $35)

b. 2,500 units = $80,000 ÷ ($67 – $35)

Practice Exercises: PE 21-3A, PE 21-3B

Target Profit

At the break-even point, sales and costs are exactly equal. However, the goal of most companies is to make a profit.

Business Connection

AIRLINE INDUSTRY BREAK-EVEN

Airlines measure revenues and costs by available seat miles. An available seat mile is one seat (empty or filled) flying one mile. Thus, the average revenue earned per available seat mile is termed the RASM, and the average cost per available seat mile is termed the CASM. The operating break-even occurs when the RASM equals the CASM. Since airlines have high aircraft fixed costs, filling passenger seats is an important contributor to exceeding break-even. This is measured by the average proportion of seats filled across all flights, which is termed the load factor. In addition, important variable costs such as labor and fuel impact the break-even performance. Thus, airlines monitor employee productivity and fuel costs to maintain profitability. The RASM, CASM, and load factor for a recent year for major airlines are as follows:

	American Airlines	United Airlines	Delta Air Lines	Southwest Airlines	US Airways
RASM	$0.129	$0.124	$0.132	$0.135	$0.125
CASM	0.082	0.079	0.089	0.075	0.077
RASM – CASM	$0.047	$0.045	$0.043	$0.060	$0.048
Load factor	82%	84%	85%	82%	83%

As can be seen, all the major airlines are operating above their break-even points, with Southwest Airlines demonstrating the best profit performance by these metrics. All the load factors are more than 80%, indicating that the airlines are using their aircraft efficiently.

Source: MIT Airline Data Project.

By modifying the break-even equation, the sales required to earn a target or desired amount of profit may be computed. For this purpose, target profit is added to the break-even equation, as follows:

$$\text{Sales (units)} = \frac{\text{Fixed Costs} + \text{Target Profit}}{\text{Unit Contribution Margin}}$$

To illustrate, assume the following data for Waltham Co.:

Fixed costs	$200,000
Target profit	100,000
Unit selling price	$75
Unit variable cost	45
Unit contribution margin	$30

The sales necessary for Waltham to earn the target profit of $100,000 would be 10,000 units, computed as follows:

$$\text{Sales (units)} = \frac{\text{Fixed Costs} + \text{Target Profit}}{\text{Unit Contribution Margin}} = \frac{\$200{,}000 + \$100{,}000}{\$30} = 10{,}000 \text{ units}$$

The following income statement for Waltham verifies this computation:

Sales (10,000 units × $75)	$750,000	
Variable costs (10,000 units × $45)	450,000	
Contribution margin (10,000 units × $30)	$300,000	
Fixed costs	200,000	
Income from operations	$100,000	← Target profit

As shown in the income statement for Waltham, sales of $750,000 (10,000 units × $75) are necessary to earn the target profit of $100,000. The sales of $750,000 needed to earn the target profit of $100,000 can be computed directly using the contribution margin ratio, computed as follows:

$$\text{Contribution Margin Ratio} = \frac{\text{Unit Contribution Margin}}{\text{Unit Selling Price}} = \frac{\$30}{\$75} = 40\%$$

$$\text{Sales (dollars)} = \frac{\text{Fixed Costs} + \text{Target Profit}}{\text{Contribution Margin Ratio}}$$

$$= \frac{\$200,000 + \$100,000}{40\%} = \frac{\$300,000}{40\%} = \$750,000$$

Example Exercise 21-4 Target Profit **Obj. 3**

Forest Company sells a product for $140 per unit. The variable cost is $60 per unit, and fixed costs are $240,000. Determine the (a) break-even point in sales units and (b) the sales units required to achieve a target profit of $50,000.

Follow My Example 21-4

a. 3,000 units = $240,000 ÷ ($140 – $60)

b. 3,625 units = ($240,000 + $50,000) ÷ ($140 – $60)

Practice Exercises: PE 21-4A, PE 21-4B

INTEGRITY, OBJECTIVITY, AND ETHICS IN BUSINESS

ORPHAN DRUGS

Each year, pharmaceutical companies develop new drugs that cure a variety of physical conditions. In order to be profitable, drug companies must sell enough of a product for a reasonable price to exceed break-even. Break-even points, however, create a problem for drugs, called "orphan drugs," targeted at rare diseases. These drugs are typically expensive to develop and have low sales volumes, making it impossible to achieve break-even. To ensure that orphan drugs are not overlooked, Congress passed the Orphan Drug Act, which provides incentives for pharmaceutical companies to develop drugs for rare diseases that might not generate enough sales to reach break-even. The program has been a great success. Since 1982, more than 200 orphan drugs have come to market, such as Novartis AG's drug for the treatment of Paget's disease.

Graphic Approach to Cost-Volume-Profit Analysis

Obj. 4 Using a cost-volume-profit chart and a profit-volume chart, determine the break-even point and sales necessary to achieve a target profit.

Cost-volume-profit analysis can be presented as a graph as well as an equation. Many managers prefer the graphic form because the operating profit or loss for different levels can be easily seen.

Cost-Volume-Profit (Break-Even) Chart

A **cost-volume-profit chart**, sometimes called a *break-even chart*, graphically shows sales, costs, and the related profit or loss for various levels of units sold. It assists in understanding the relationship among sales, costs, and operating profit or loss.

To illustrate, the cost-volume-profit chart in Exhibit 14 is based on the following data for Munoz Co.:

Total fixed costs	$100,000
Unit selling price	$50
Unit variable cost	30
Unit contribution margin	$20

The cost-volume-profit chart in Exhibit 14 is constructed using the following steps:

Step 1. Volume in units of sales is indicated along the horizontal axis. The range of volume shown is the relevant range in which the company expects to operate. Dollar amounts of total sales and total costs are indicated along the vertical axis.

Step 2. A total sales line is plotted by connecting the point at zero on the left corner of the graph to a second point on the chart. The second point is determined by multiplying the maximum number of units in the relevant range, which is found on the far right of the horizontal axis, by the unit sales price. A line is then drawn through both of these points. This is the total sales line. For Munoz, the maximum number of units in the relevant range is 10,000. The second point on the line is determined by multiplying the 10,000 units by the $50 unit selling price to get the second point for the total sales line of $500,000 (10,000 units × $50). The sales line is drawn upward to the right from zero through the $500,000 point at the end of the relevant range.

Step 3. A total cost line is plotted by beginning with total fixed costs on the vertical axis. A second point is determined by multiplying the maximum number of units in the relevant range, which is found on the far right of the horizontal axis by the unit variable costs, and adding the total fixed costs. A line is then drawn through both of these points. This is the total cost line. For Munoz, the maximum number of units in the relevant range is 10,000. The second point on the line is determined by multiplying the 10,000 units by the $30 unit variable cost and then adding the $100,000 total fixed costs to get the second point for the total estimated costs of $400,000 [(10,000 units × $30) + $100,000]. The cost line is drawn upward to the right from $100,000 on the vertical axis through the $400,000 point at the end of the relevant range.

Step 4. The break-even point is the intersection point of the total sales and total cost lines. A vertical dotted line drawn downward at the intersection point indicates the units of sales at the break-even point. A horizontal dotted line drawn to the left at the intersection point indicates the sales dollars and costs at the break-even point.

EXHIBIT 14

Cost-Volume-Profit Chart

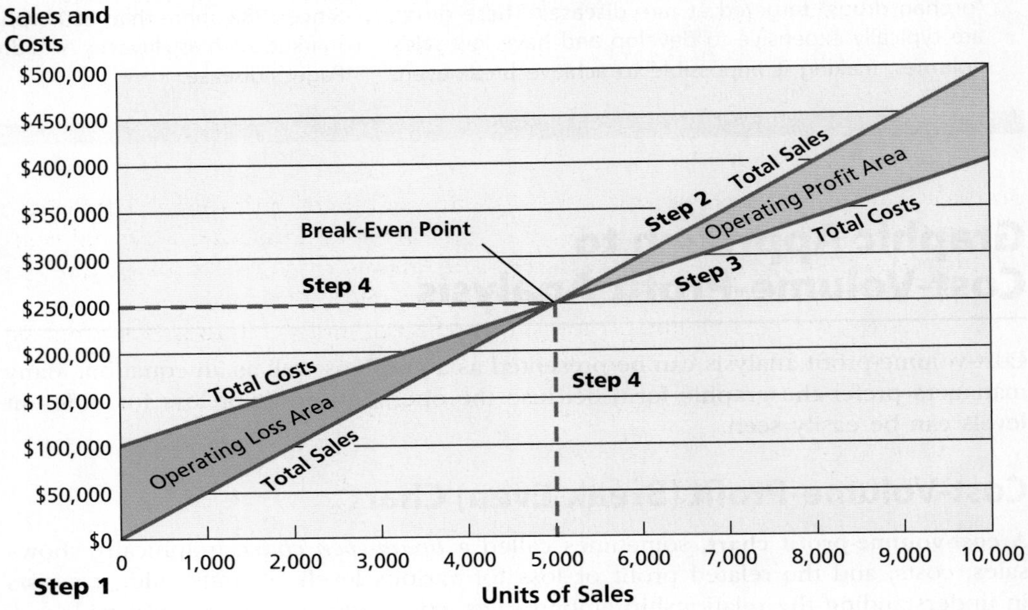

In Exhibit 14, the break-even point for Munoz is $250,000 of sales, which represents sales of 5,000 units. Operating profits will be earned when sales levels are to the right of the break-even point (*operating profit area*). Operating losses will be incurred when sales levels are to the left of the break-even point (*operating loss area*).

Changes in the unit selling price, total fixed costs, and unit variable costs can be analyzed by using a cost-volume-profit chart. Using the data in Exhibit 14, assume that Munoz is evaluating a proposal to reduce fixed costs by $20,000. In this case, the total fixed costs would be $80,000 ($100,000 – $20,000).

Under this scenario, the total sales line is not changed, but the total cost line will change. As shown in Exhibit 15, the total cost line is redrawn, starting at the $80,000 point (total fixed costs) on the vertical axis. The second point is determined by multiplying the maximum number of units in the relevant range, which is found on the far right of the horizontal axis, by the unit variable costs and adding the fixed costs. For Munoz, this is the total estimated cost for 10,000 units, which is $380,000 [(10,000 units × $30) + $80,000]. The cost line is drawn upward to the right from $80,000 on the vertical axis through the $380,000 point. The revised cost-volume-profit chart in Exhibit 15 indicates that the break-even point for Munoz decreases to $200,000 and 4,000 units of sales.

EXHIBIT 15

Revised Cost-Volume-Profit Chart

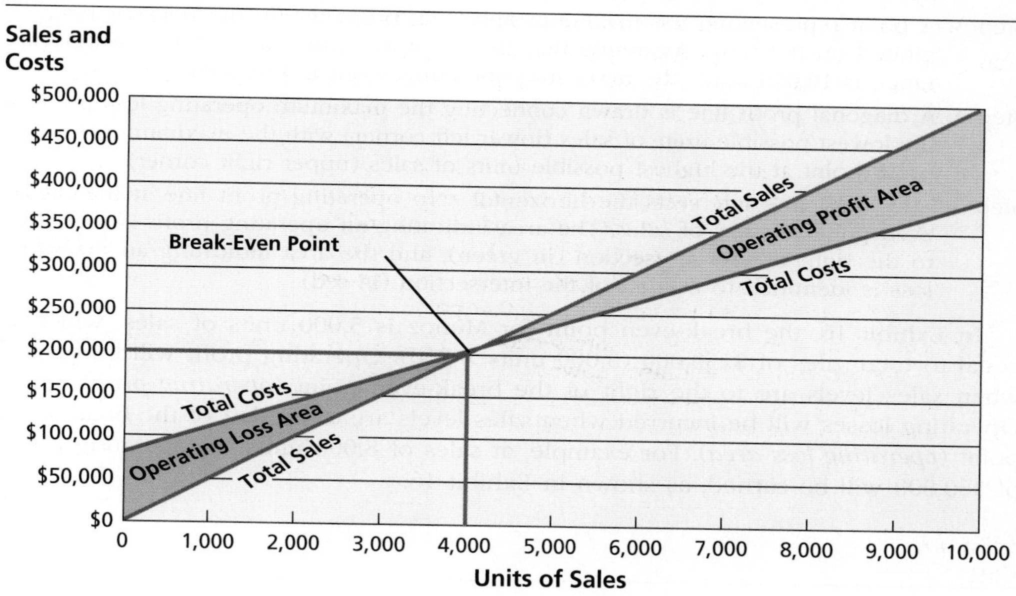

Profit-Volume Chart

Another graphic approach to cost-volume-profit analysis is the profit-volume chart. The **profit-volume chart** plots only the difference between total sales and total costs (or profits). In this way, the profit-volume chart allows managers to determine the operating profit (or loss) for various levels of units sold.

To illustrate, the profit-volume chart for Munoz Co. in Exhibit 16 is based on the same data used in Exhibit 14. These data are as follows:

Total fixed costs	$100,000
Unit selling price	$50
Unit variable cost	30
Unit contribution margin	$20

The maximum operating loss is equal to the fixed costs of $100,000. Assuming that the maximum units that can be sold within the relevant range is 10,000 units, the maximum operating profit is $100,000, computed as follows:

Sales (10,000 units × $50)	$500,000
Variable costs (10,000 units × $30)	300,000
Contribution margin (10,000 units × $20)	$200,000
Fixed costs	100,000
Operating profit	$100,000 ← Maximum profit

The profit-volume chart in Exhibit 16 is constructed using the following steps:

Step 1. Volume in units of sales is indicated along the horizontal axis. The range of volume shown is the relevant range in which the company expects to operate. In Exhibit 16, the maximum units of sales is 10,000 units. Dollar amounts indicating operating profits and losses are shown along the vertical axis.

Step 2. A point representing the maximum operating loss is plotted on the vertical axis at the left. This loss is equal to the total fixed costs at the zero level of sales. Thus, the maximum operating loss is equal to the fixed costs of $100,000.

Step 3. A point representing the maximum operating profit within the relevant range is plotted on the right. Assuming that the maximum unit sales within the relevant range is 10,000 units, the maximum operating profit is $100,000.

Step 4. A diagonal profit line is drawn connecting the maximum operating loss point at the lowest possible units of sales (lower left corner) with the maximum operating profit point at the highest possible units of sales (upper right corner).

Step 5. The profit line intersects the horizontal zero operating profit line at the break-even point in units of sales. The area indicating an operating profit is identified to the right of the intersection (in green), and the area indicating an operating loss is identified to the left of the intersection (in red).

In Exhibit 16, the break-even point for Munoz is 5,000 units of sales, which is equal to total sales of $250,000 (5,000 units × $50). Operating profit will be earned when sales levels are to the right of the break-even point (*operating profit area*). Operating losses will be incurred when sales levels are to the left of the break-even point (*operating loss area*). For example, at sales of 8,000 units, an operating profit of $60,000 will be earned, as shown in Exhibit 16.

EXHIBIT 16

Profit-Volume Chart

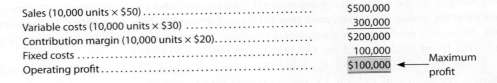

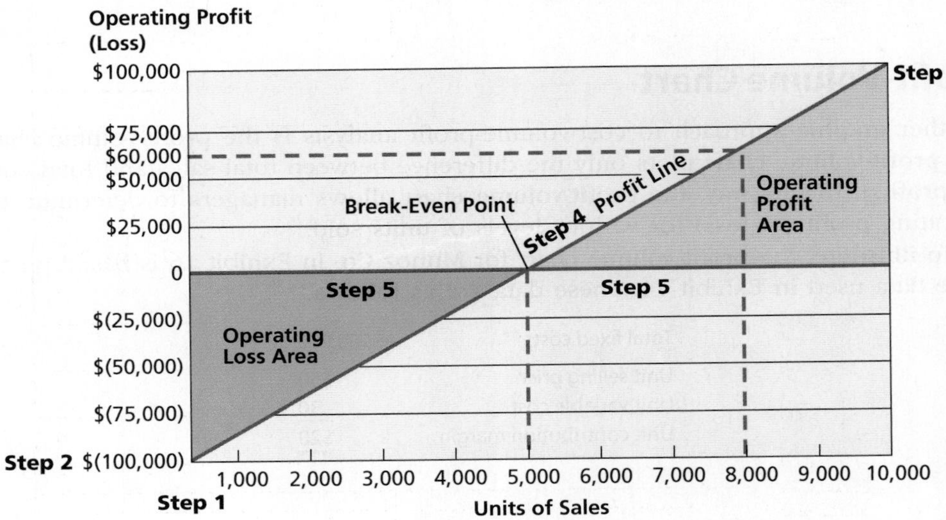

The effect of changes in the unit selling price, total fixed costs, and unit variable costs on profit can be analyzed using a profit-volume chart. Using the data in Exhibit 16, consider the effect that a $20,000 increase in fixed costs will have on profit. In this case, the total fixed costs will increase to $120,000 ($100,000 + $20,000), and the maximum operating loss will also increase to $120,000. At the maximum sales of 10,000 units, the maximum operating profit would be $80,000, computed as follows:

Sales (10,000 units × $50)	$500,000	
Variable costs (10,000 units × $30)	300,000	
Contribution margin (10,000 units × $20)	$200,000	
Fixed costs	120,000	
Operating profit	$ 80,000	← Revised maximum profit

A revised profit-volume chart is constructed by plotting the maximum operating loss and maximum operating profit points and drawing the revised profit line. The original and revised profit-volume charts for Munoz are shown in Exhibit 17.

EXHIBIT 17

Original Profit-Volume Chart and Revised Profit-Volume Chart

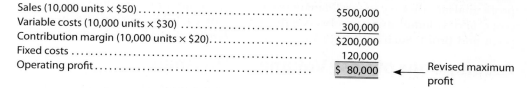

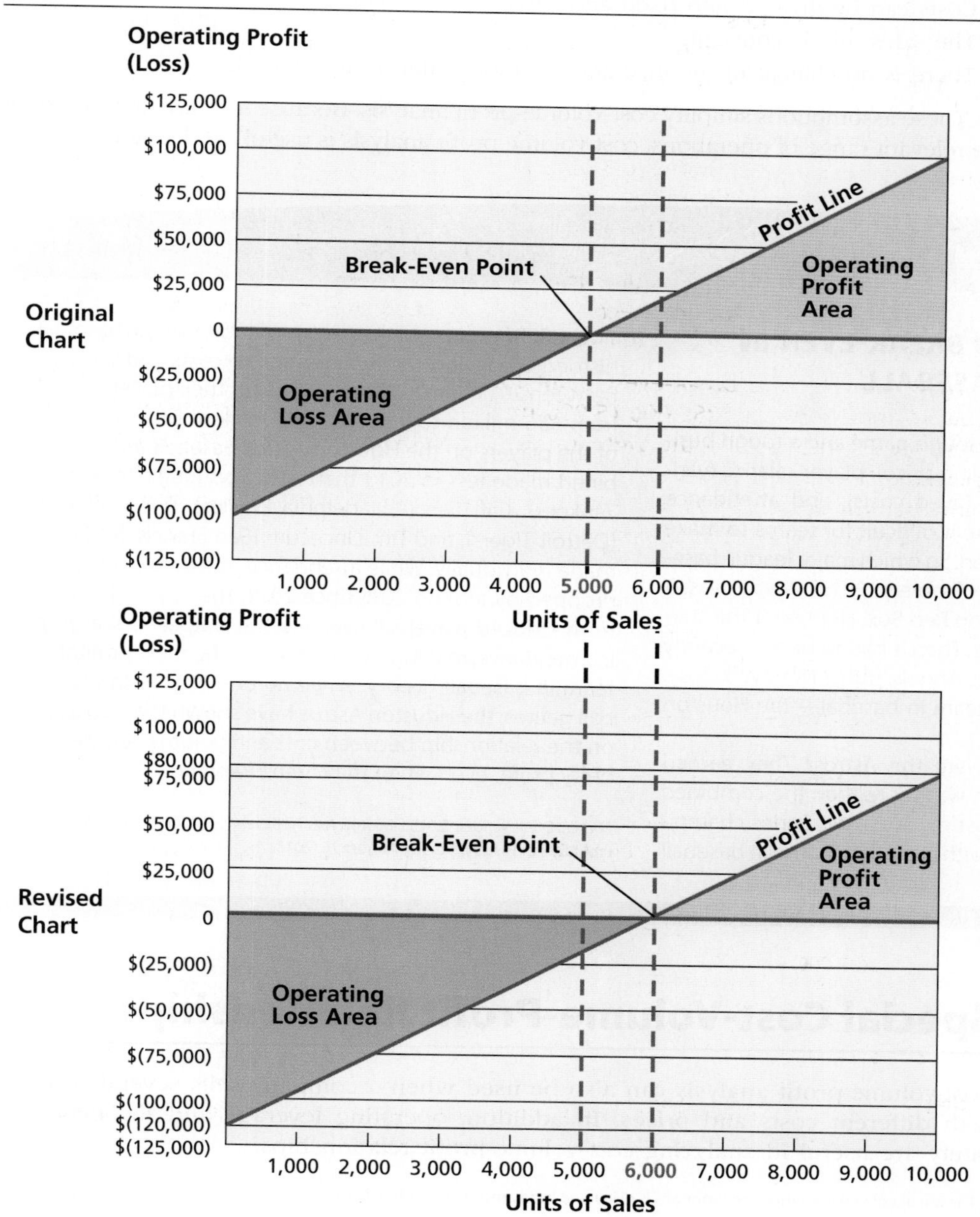

The revised profit-volume chart indicates that the break-even point for Munoz is 6,000 units of sales. This is equal to total sales of $300,000 (6,000 units × $50). The operating loss area of the chart has increased, while the operating profit area has decreased.

Use of Computers in Cost-Volume-Profit Analysis

With computers, the graphic approach and the mathematical approach to cost-volume-profit analysis are easy to use. Managers can vary assumptions regarding selling prices, costs, and volume and can observe the effects of each change on the break-even point and profit. Such an analysis is called a *"what if"* analysis or *sensitivity* analysis.

Assumptions of Cost-Volume-Profit Analysis

Cost-volume-profit analysis depends on several assumptions. The primary assumptions are as follows:

- Total sales and total costs can be represented by straight lines.
- Within the relevant range of operating activity, the efficiency of operations does not change.
- Costs can be divided into fixed and variable components.
- The sales mix is constant.
- There is no change in the inventory quantities during the period.

These assumptions simplify cost-volume-profit analysis. Because they are often valid for the relevant range of operations, cost-volume-profit analysis is useful for decision making.[3]

SERVICE FOCUS

PROFIT, LOSS, AND BREAK-EVEN IN MAJOR LEAGUE BASEBALL

Major League Baseball is a tough game and a tough business. Ticket prices (unit selling price), player salaries (variable costs), stadium fees (fixed costs), and attendance (volume) converge to make it difficult for teams to make a profit or at least break even. So which major league baseball team was the most profitable in 2013? Well, it wasn't the World Champion Boston Red Sox. Nor was it the star-studded New York Yankees. Then it had to be the recently turned around Los Angeles Angels, right? Not even close. It was actually the worst team in baseball—the Houston Astros.

Just how profitable were the Astros? They earned $99 million in 2013, which was more than the combined 2013 profits of the six most recent World Series champions. How could the team with the worst record in baseball since 2005 have one of the most profitable years in baseball history? By paying careful attention to costs and volume. Between 2011 and 2013, the Astros cut their player payroll from $56 million to less than $13 million. That's right; all of the players on the Houston Astros baseball team combined made less in 2013 than Alex Rodriguez (New York Yankees), Cliff Lee (Philadelphia Phillies), Prince Fielder (Detroit Tigers), and Tim Lincecum (San Francisco Giants) made individually. While attendance at Astros games has dropped by around 20% since 2011, the cost reductions from reduced player salaries have far outpaced the drop in attendance, making the 2013 Astros the most profitable team in baseball history. While no one likes losing baseball games, the Houston Astros have shown that focusing on the relationship between cost and volume can yield a hefty profit, even when they aren't winning.

Source: D. Alexander, "2013 Houston Astros: Baseball's Worst Team Is the Most Profitable In History," *Forbes*, August 26, 2013.

Obj. 5 Compute the break-even point for a company selling more than one product, the operating leverage, and the margin of safety.

Special Cost-Volume-Profit Relationships

Cost-volume-profit analysis can also be used when a company sells several products with different costs and prices. In addition, operating leverage and the margin of safety are useful in analyzing cost-volume-profit relationships.

3 The impact of violating these assumptions is discussed in advanced accounting texts.

Sales Mix Considerations

Many companies sell more than one product at different selling prices. In addition, the products normally have different unit variable costs and, thus, different unit contribution margins. In such cases, break-even analysis can still be performed by considering the sales mix. The **sales mix** is the relative distribution of sales among the products sold by a company.

To illustrate, assume that Cascade Company sold Products A and B during the past year, as follows:

Total fixed costs $200,000

	Product A	Product B
Unit selling price	$90	$140
Unit variable cost	70	95
Unit contribution margin	$20	$ 45
Units sold	8,000	2,000
Sales mix	80%	20%

The sales mix for Products A and B is expressed as a percentage of total units sold. For Cascade, a total of 10,000 (8,000 + 2,000) units were sold during the year. Therefore, the sales mix is 80% (8,000 ÷ 10,000) for Product A and 20% for Product B (2,000 ÷ 10,000), as shown in Exhibit 18. The sales mix could also be expressed as the ratio 80:20.

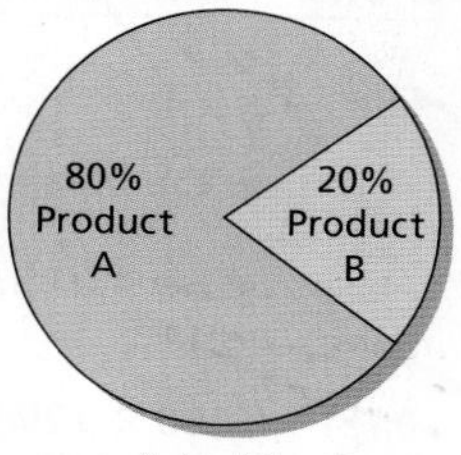

Sales Mix

EXHIBIT 18

Multiple Product Sales Mix

For break-even analysis, it is useful to think of Products A and B as components of one overall enterprise product called E. The unit selling price of E equals the sum of the unit selling prices of each product multiplied by its sales mix percentage. Likewise, the unit variable cost and unit contribution margin of E equal the sum of the unit variable costs and unit contribution margins of each product multiplied by its sales mix percentage.

For Cascade, the unit selling price, unit variable cost, and unit contribution margin for E are computed as follows:

Product E			Product A		Product B
Unit selling price of E	$100	=	($90 × 0.8)	+	($140 × 0.2)
Unit variable cost of E	75	=	($70 × 0.8)	+	($95 × 0.2)
Unit contribution margin of E	$ 25	=	($20 × 0.8)	+	($45 × 0.2)

Cascade has total fixed costs of $200,000. The break-even point of 8,000 units of E can be determined as follows using the unit selling price, unit variable cost, and unit contribution margin of E:

$$\text{Break-Even Sales (units) for E} = \frac{\text{Fixed Costs}}{\text{Unit Contribution Margin}} = \frac{\$200{,}000}{\$25} = 8{,}000 \text{ units}$$

Because the sales mix for Products A and B is 80% and 20%, respectively, the break-even quantity of A is 6,400 units (8,000 units × 80%) and B is 1,600 units (8,000 units × 20%).

The preceding break-even analysis is verified in Exhibit 19.

Link to Ford Motor Company

The sales mix of cars and trucks has a major impact on profitability. Ford Motor Company's overall profitability.

EXHIBIT 19

Break-Even Sales: Multiple Products

	Product A	Product B	Total
Sales:			
6,400 units × $90	$576,000		$576,000
1,600 units × $140		$224,000	224,000
Total sales	$576,000	$224,000	$800,000
Variable costs:			
6,400 units × $70	$448,000		$448,000
1,600 units × $95		$152,000	152,000
Total variable costs	$448,000	$152,000	$600,000
Contribution margin	$128,000	$ 72,000	$200,000
Fixed costs			200,000
Income from operations		Break-even point →	$ 0

The effects of changes in the sales mix on the break-even point can be determined by assuming a different sales mix. The break-even point of E can then be recomputed.

Example Exercise 21-5 Sales Mix and Break-Even Analysis

Obj. 5

Megan Company has fixed costs of $180,000. The unit selling price, variable cost per unit, and contribution margin per unit for the company's two products are as follows:

Product	Selling Price	Variable Cost per Unit	Contribution Margin per Unit
Q	$160	$100	$60
Z	100	80	20

The sales mix for products Q and Z is 75% and 25%, respectively. Determine the break-even point in units of Q and Z.

Follow My Example 21-5

Unit selling price of E:	[($160 × 0.75) + ($100 × 0.25)] =	$145
Unit variable cost of E:	[($100 × 0.75) + ($80 × 0.25)] =	95
Unit contribution margin of E		$ 50

Break-Even Sales (units) for E = $180,000 ÷ $50 = 3,600 units
Break-Even Sales (units) for Q = 3,600 units of E × 75% = 2,700 units of Product Q
Break-Even Sales (units) for Z = 3,600 units of E × 25% = 900 units of Product Z

Practice Exercises: PE 21-5A, PE 21-5B

Operating Leverage

The relationship between a company's contribution margin and income from operations is measured by **operating leverage**. A company's operating leverage is computed as follows:

$$\text{Operating Leverage} = \frac{\text{Contribution Margin}}{\text{Income from Operations}}$$

The difference between contribution margin and income from operations is fixed costs. Thus, companies with high fixed costs will normally have high operating leverage. Examples of such companies include airline and automotive companies, like Ford Motor Company. Low operating leverage is normal for companies that are labor-intensive, such as professional service companies, which have low fixed costs.

To illustrate operating leverage, assume the following data for Jones Inc. and Wilson Inc.:

	Jones Inc.	Wilson Inc.
Sales	$400,000	$400,000
Variable costs	300,000	300,000
Contribution margin	$100,000	$100,000
Fixed costs	80,000	50,000
Income from operations	$ 20,000	$ 50,000

As shown, Jones and Wilson have the same sales, the same variable costs, and the same contribution margin. However, Jones has larger fixed costs than Wilson and, thus, a higher operating leverage. The operating leverage for each company is computed as follows:

Jones Inc.

$$\text{Operating Leverage} = \frac{\text{Contribution Margin}}{\text{Income from Operations}} = \frac{\$100{,}000}{\$20{,}000} = 5$$

Wilson Inc.

$$\text{Operating Leverage} = \frac{\text{Contribution Margin}}{\text{Income from Operations}} = \frac{\$100{,}000}{\$50{,}000} = 2$$

Operating leverage can be used to measure the impact of changes in sales on income from operations. Using operating leverage, the effect of changes in sales on income from operations is computed as follows:

$$\begin{array}{c}\text{Percent Change in}\\\text{Income from Operations}\end{array} = \begin{array}{c}\text{Percent Change in}\\\text{Sales}\end{array} \times \begin{array}{c}\text{Operating}\\\text{Leverage}\end{array}$$

To illustrate, assume that sales increased by 10%, or $40,000 ($400,000 × 10%), for Jones and Wilson. The percent increase in income from operations for Jones and Wilson is computed as follows:

Jones Inc.

$$\begin{array}{c}\text{Percent Change in}\\\text{Income from Operations}\end{array} = \begin{array}{c}\text{Percent Change in}\\\text{Sales}\end{array} \times \begin{array}{c}\text{Operating}\\\text{Leverage}\end{array}$$

$$= 10\% \times 5 = 50\%$$

Wilson Inc.

$$\begin{array}{c}\text{Percent Change in}\\\text{Income from Operations}\end{array} = \begin{array}{c}\text{Percent Change in}\\\text{Sales}\end{array} \times \begin{array}{c}\text{Operating}\\\text{Leverage}\end{array}$$

$$= 10\% \times 2 = 20\%$$

As shown, Jones's income from operations increases by 50%, while Wilson's income from operations increases by only 20%. The validity of this analysis is shown in the following income statements for Jones and Wilson based on the 10% increase in sales:

	Jones Inc.	Wilson Inc.
Sales	$440,000	$440,000
Variable costs	330,000	330,000
Contribution margin	$110,000	$110,000
Fixed costs	80,000	50,000
Income from operations	$ 30,000	$ 60,000

The preceding income statements indicate that Jones's income from operations increased from $20,000 to $30,000, a 50% increase ($10,000 ÷ $20,000). In contrast, Wilson's income from operations increased from $50,000 to $60,000, a 20% increase ($10,000 ÷ $50,000).

Because even a small increase in sales will generate a large percentage increase in income from operations, Jones might consider ways to increase sales. Such actions

Link to Ford Motor Company

Ford Motor Company has a high proportion of fixed costs with the result that small changes in units sold can significantly affect its overall profitability.

Source: Ford Motor Company, Form 10-K for Year Ended December 31, 2014.

could include special advertising or sales promotions. In contrast, Wilson might consider ways to increase operating leverage by reducing variable costs.

The impact of a change in sales on income from operations for companies with high and low operating leverage is summarized in Exhibit 20.

EXHIBIT 20

Effect of Operating Leverage on Income from Operations

Operating Leverage	Percentage Impact on Income from Operations from a Change in Sales
High	Large
Low	Small

Example Exercise 21-6 Operating Leverage

Obj. 5

Tucker Company reports the following data:

Sales	$750,000
Variable costs	500,000
Contribution margin	$250,000
Fixed costs	187,500
Income from operations	$ 62,500

Determine Tucker Company's operating leverage.

Follow My Example 21-6

$$\text{Operating Leverage} = \frac{\text{Contribution Margin}}{\text{Income from Operations}} = \frac{\$250,000}{\$62,500} = 4.0$$

Practice Exercises: PE 21-6A, PE 21-6B

Margin of Safety

The **margin of safety** indicates the possible decrease in sales that may occur before an operating loss results. Thus, if the margin of safety is low, even a small decline in sales revenue may result in an operating loss.

The margin of safety may be expressed in the following ways:

- Dollars of sales
- Units of sales
- Percent of current sales

To illustrate, assume the following data:

Sales	$250,000
Sales at the break-even point	200,000
Unit selling price	25

The margin of safety in dollars of sales is $50,000 ($250,000 – $200,000). The margin of safety in units is 2,000 units ($50,000 ÷ $25). The margin of safety expressed as a percent of current sales is 20%, computed as follows:

$$\text{Margin of Safety} = \frac{\text{Sales} - \text{Sales at Break-Even Point}}{\text{Sales}}$$

$$= \frac{\$250,000 - \$200,000}{\$250,000} = \frac{\$50,000}{\$250,000} = 20\%$$

Therefore, the current sales may decline $50,000, 2,000 units, or 20% before an operating loss occurs.

Example Exercise 21-7 Margin of Safety *Obj. 5*

Rachel Company has sales of $400,000, and the break-even point in sales dollars is $300,000. Determine the company's margin of safety as a percent of current sales.

Follow My Example 21-7

$$\text{Margin of Safety} = \frac{\text{Sales} - \text{Sales at Break-Even Point}}{\text{Sales}} = \frac{\$400{,}000 - \$300{,}000}{\$400{,}000} = \frac{\$100{,}000}{\$400{,}000} = 25\%$$

Practice Exercises: PE 21-7A, PE 21-7B

APPENDIX

Variable Costing

The cost of manufactured products consists of direct materials, direct labor, and factory overhead. The reporting of all these costs in financial statements is called **absorption costing**. Absorption costing is required under generally accepted accounting principles for financial statements distributed to external users. However, alternative reports may be prepared for decision-making purposes by managers and other internal users. One such alternative reporting is *variable costing* or *direct costing*.

In *variable costing*, the cost of goods manufactured is composed only of variable costs. Thus, the cost of goods manufactured consists of direct materials, direct labor, and *variable* factory overhead.

In a variable costing income statement, *fixed* factory overhead costs do not become a part of the cost of goods manufactured. Instead, fixed factory overhead costs are treated as a period expense. The differences between absorption and variable cost of goods manufactured is summarized in Exhibit 21.

EXHIBIT 21

Absorption Versus Variable Cost of Goods Manufactured

Cost of Goods Manufactured	
Absorption Costing	**Variable Costing**
Direct materials	Direct materials
Direct labor	Direct labor
Variable factory overhead	Variable factory overhead
Fixed factory overhead	

The form of a variable costing income statement is as follows:

Sales		$XXX
Variable cost of goods sold		XXX
Manufacturing margin		$XXX
Variable selling and administrative expenses		XXX
Contribution margin		$XXX
Fixed costs:		
Fixed manufacturing costs	$XXX	
Fixed selling and administrative expenses	XXX	XXX
Income from operations		$XXX

Manufacturing margin is the excess of sales over variable cost of goods sold.

Manufacturing Margin = Sales − Variable Cost of Goods Sold

Variable cost of goods sold consists of direct materials, direct labor, and variable factory overhead for the units sold. *Contribution margin* is the excess of manufacturing margin over variable selling and administrative expenses.

Contribution Margin = Manufacturing Margin − Variable Selling and Administrative Expenses

Subtracting fixed costs from contribution margin yields *income from operations.*

Income from Operations = Contribution Margin − Fixed Costs

The variable costing income statement facilitates managerial decision making because manufacturing margin and contribution margin are reported directly. As illustrated in this chapter, contribution margin is used in break-even analysis and other analyses.

To illustrate the variable costing income statement, assume that Martinez Co. manufactures 15,000 units, which are sold at a price of $50. The related costs and expenses for Martinez are as follows:

	Total Cost	Number of Units	Unit Cost
Manufacturing costs:			
Variable	$375,000	15,000	$25
Fixed	150,000	15,000	10
Total	$525,000		$35
Selling and administrative expenses:			
Variable ($5 per unit sold)	$ 75,000		
Fixed	50,000		
Total	$125,000		

Exhibit 22 shows the variable costing income statement prepared for Martinez. The computations are shown in parentheses.

EXHIBIT 22

Variable Costing Income Statement

Sales (15,000 × $50)		$750,000
Variable cost of goods sold (15,000 × $25)		375,000
Manufacturing margin		$375,000
Variable selling and administrative expenses (15,000 × $5)		75,000
Contribution margin		$300,000
Fixed costs:		
Fixed manufacturing costs	$150,000	
Fixed selling and administrative expenses	50,000	200,000
Income from operations		$100,000

Exhibit 23 illustrates the absorption costing income statement prepared for Martinez. The absorption costing income statement does not distinguish between variable and fixed costs. All manufacturing costs are included in the cost of goods sold. Deducting the cost of goods sold from sales yields the *gross profit.* Deducting the selling and administrative expenses from gross profit yields the *income from operations.*

The relationship between variable and absorption costing *income from operations* is summarized in Exhibit 24.

EXHIBIT 23

Absorption Costing Income Statement

Sales (15,000 × $50)	$750,000
Cost of goods sold (15,000 × $35)	525,000
Gross profit	$225,000
Selling and administrative expenses ($75,000 + $50,000)	125,000
Income from operations	$100,000

Relationship Between Variable and Absorption Costing Income

EXHIBIT 24

If	Units Sold < Units Manufactured	
Then	Variable Costing Income < Absorption Costing Income	
If	Units Sold > Units Manufactured	
Then	Variable Costing Income > Absorption Costing Income	

In Exhibits 22 and 23, Martinez manufactured and sold 15,000 units. Thus, the variable and absorption costing income statements reported the same income from operations of $100,000. However, assume that only 12,000 units of the 15,000 units Martinez manufactured were sold. Exhibit 25 shows the related variable and absorption costing income statements.

Exhibit 25 shows a $30,000 ($70,000 – $40,000) difference in income from operations. This difference is due to the fixed manufacturing costs. All of the $150,000 of fixed manufacturing costs is included as a period expense in the variable costing statement. However, the 3,000 units of ending inventory in the absorption costing statement include $30,000 (3,000 units × $10) of fixed manufacturing costs. By being included in inventory, this $30,000 is excluded from the current cost of goods sold. Thus, the absorption costing income from operations is $30,000 higher than the income from operations for variable costing.

A similar analysis could be used to illustrate that income from operations under variable costing is greater than income from operations under absorption costing when the units manufactured are less than the units sold.

Under absorption costing, increases or decreases in income from operations can result from changes in inventory levels. For example, for Martinez, a 3,000 increase in ending inventory created a $30,000 increase in income from operations under absorption costing. Such increases (decreases) could be misinterpreted by managers using absorption costing as operating efficiencies (inefficiencies). This is one of the reasons that variable costing is often used by managers for cost control, product pricing, and production planning. Such uses of variable costing are discussed in advanced accounting texts.

EXHIBIT 25

Units Manufactured Exceed Units Sold

Variable Costing Income Statement		
Sales (12,000 × $50)		$600,000
Variable cost of goods sold:		
Variable cost of goods manufactured (15,000 × $25)	$375,000	
Less ending inventory (3,000 × $25)	75,000	
Variable cost of goods sold		300,000
Manufacturing margin		$300,000
Variable selling and administrative expenses (12,000 × $5)		60,000
Contribution margin		$240,000
Fixed costs:		
Fixed manufacturing costs	$150,000	
Fixed selling and administrative expenses	50,000	200,000
Income from operations		$ 40,000
Absorption Costing Income Statement		
Sales (12,000 × $50)		$600,000
Cost of goods sold:		
Cost of goods manufactured (15,000 × $35)	$525,000	
Less ending inventory (3,000 × $35)	105,000	
Cost of goods sold		420,000
Gross profit		$180,000
Selling and administrative expenses [(12,000 × $5) + $50,000]		110,000
Income from operations		$ 70,000

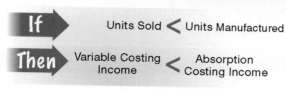

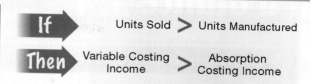

At a Glance 21

Obj. 1 Classify costs as variable costs, fixed costs, or mixed costs.

Key Points Variable costs vary in proportion to changes in the level of activity. Fixed costs remain the same in total dollar amount as the level of activity changes. Mixed costs are comprised of both fixed and variable costs.

Learning Outcomes	*Example Exercises*	*Practice Exercises*
• Describe variable costs.		
• Describe fixed costs.		
• Describe mixed costs.		
• Separate mixed costs, using the high-low method.	**EE21-1**	**PE21-1A, 21-1B**

Obj. 2 Compute the contribution margin, the contribution margin ratio, and the unit contribution margin.

Key Points Contribution margin is the excess of sales revenue over variable costs and can be expressed as a ratio (contribution margin ratio) or a dollar amount (unit contribution margin).

Learning Outcomes	*Example Exercises*	*Practice Exercises*
• Describe the contribution margin.		
• Compute the contribution margin ratio.	**EE21-2**	**PE21-2A, 21-2B**
• Compute the unit contribution margin.	**EE21-2**	**PE21-2A, 21-2B**

Obj. 3 Determine the break-even point and sales necessary to achieve a target profit.

Key Points The break-even point is the point at which a business's revenues exactly equal costs. The mathematical approach to cost-volume-profit analysis uses the unit contribution margin concept and mathematical equations to determine the break-even point and the volume necessary to achieve a target profit.

Learning Outcomes	*Example Exercises*	*Practice Exercises*
• Compute the break-even point in units.	**EE21-3**	**PE21-3A, 21-3B**
• Describe how changes in fixed costs affect the break-even point.		
• Describe how changes in variable costs affect the break-even point.		
• Describe how a change in the unit selling price affects the break-even point.	**EE21-3**	**PE21-3A, 21-3B**
• Modify the break-even equation to compute the unit sales required to earn a target profit.	**EE21-4**	**PE21-4A, 21-4B**

Obj. 4 **Using a cost-volume-profit chart and a profit-volume chart, determine the break-even point and sales necessary to achieve a target profit.**

Key Points Graphical methods can be used to determine the break-even point and the volume necessary to achieve a target profit. A cost-volume-profit chart focuses on the relationship among costs, sales, and operating profit or loss. The profit-volume chart focuses on profits rather than revenues and costs.

Learning Outcomes	Example Exercises	Practice Exercises
• Describe how to construct a cost-volume-profit chart.		
• Determine the break-even point, using a cost-volume-profit chart.		
• Describe how to construct a profit-volume chart.		
• Determine the break-even point, using a profit-volume chart.		
• Describe factors affecting the reliability of cost-volume-profit analysis.		

Obj. 5 **Compute the break-even point for a company selling more than one product, the operating leverage, and the margin of safety.**

Key Points Cost-volume-profit relationships can be used for analyzing (1) sales mix, (2) operating leverage, and (3) margin of safety.

Learning Outcomes	Example Exercises	Practice Exercises
• Compute the break-even point for a mix of products.	EE21-5	PE21-5A, 21-5B
• Compute operating leverage.	EE21-6	PE21-6A, 21-6B
• Compute the margin of safety.	EE21-7	PE21-7A, 21-7B

Illustrative Problem

Wyatt Inc. expects to maintain the same inventories at the end of the year as at the beginning of the year. The estimated fixed costs for the year are $288,000, and the estimated variable costs per unit are $14. It is expected that 60,000 units will be sold at a price of $20 per unit. Maximum sales within the relevant range are 70,000 units.

Instructions

1. What is (a) the contribution margin ratio and (b) the unit contribution margin?
2. Determine the break-even point in units.
3. Construct a cost-volume-profit chart, indicating the break-even point.
4. Construct a profit-volume chart, indicating the break-even point.
5. What is the margin of safety?

(*Continued*)

Solution

1. a. Contribution Margin Ratio $= \dfrac{\text{Sales} - \text{Variable Costs}}{\text{Sales}}$

$$= \frac{(60{,}000 \text{ units} \times \$20) - (60{,}000 \text{ units} \times \$14)}{(60{,}000 \text{ units} \times \$20)}$$

$$= \frac{\$1{,}200{,}000 - \$840{,}000}{\$1{,}200{,}000} = \frac{\$360{,}000}{\$1{,}200{,}000}$$

$$= 30\%$$

b. Unit Contribution Margin = Unit Selling Price − Unit Variable Costs
= \$20 − \$14 = \$6

2. Break-Even Sales (units) $= \dfrac{\text{Fixed Costs}}{\text{Unit Contribution Margin}}$

$$= \frac{\$288{,}000}{\$6} = 48{,}000 \text{ units}$$

3.

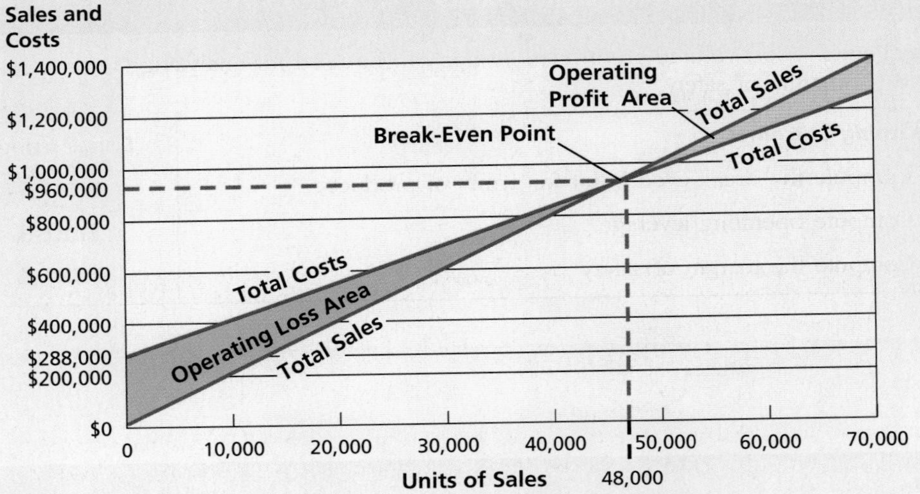

4.

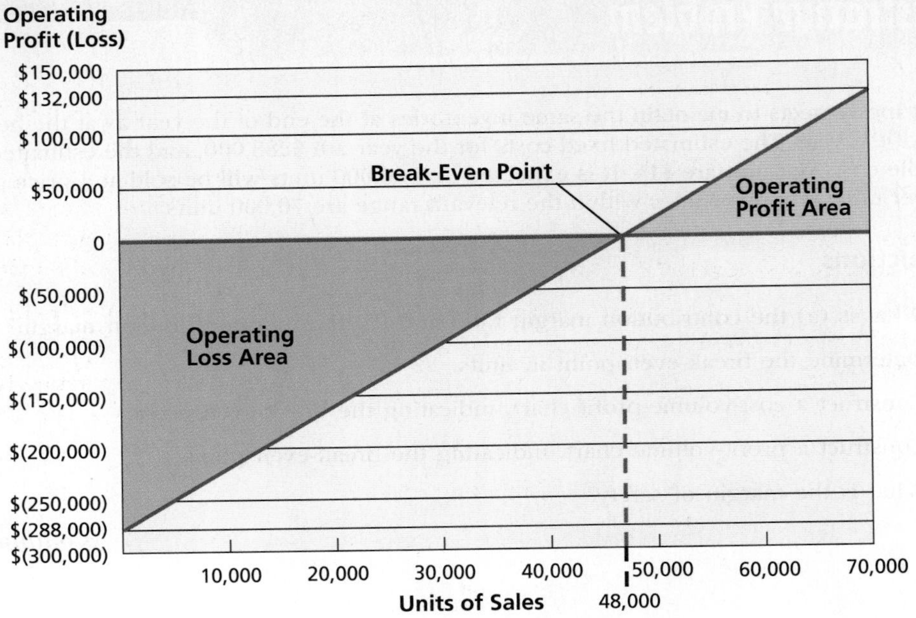

5. Margin of safety:

Expected sales (60,000 units × $20)	$1,200,000
Break-even point (48,000 units × $20)	960,000
Margin of safety	$ 240,000

or

$$\text{Margin of Safety} = \frac{\text{Sales} - \text{Sales at Break-Even Point}}{\text{Sales}}$$

$$= \frac{\$240{,}000}{\$1{,}200{,}000} = 20\%$$

Key Terms

absorption costing (1047)
activity bases (drivers) (1022)
break-even point (1031)
contribution margin (1029)
contribution margin ratio (1029)
cost behavior (1022)
cost-volume-profit analysis (1028)
cost-volume-profit chart (1037)
fixed costs (1024)
high-low method (1026)
margin of safety (1046)
mixed costs (1024)
operating leverage (1044)
profit-volume chart (1039)
relevant range (1022)
sales mix (1043)
unit contribution margin (1030)
variable costing (1028)
variable costs (1022)

Discussion Questions

1. Describe how total variable costs and unit variable costs behave with changes in the level of activity.
2. How would the following costs be classified (variable or fixed) if units produced was the activity base?
   a. Direct materials costs
   b. Electricity costs of $0.35 per kilowatt-hour
3. Describe how total fixed costs and unit fixed costs behave with changes in the level of activity.
4. In applying the high-low method of cost estimation to mixed costs, how is the total fixed cost estimated?
5. If fixed costs increase, what would be the impact on the (a) contribution margin? (b) income from operations?
6. An examination of the accounting records of Clowney Company disclosed a high contribution margin ratio and production at a level below maximum capacity. Based on this information, suggest a likely means of improving income from operations. Explain.
7. If the unit cost of direct materials is decreased, what effect will this change have on the break-even point?
8. Both Austin Company and Hill Company had the same unit sales, total costs, and income from operations for the current fiscal year; yet, Austin Company had a lower break-even point than Hill Company. Explain the reason for this difference in break-even points.
9. How does the sales mix affect the calculation of the break-even point?
10. What does operating leverage measure, and how is it computed?

Practice Exercises

Example Exercises

EE 21-1 p. 1027
Show Me How

OBJ. 1

PE 21-1A High-low method

The manufacturing costs of Ackerman Industries for the first three months of the year follow:

	Total Cost	Units Produced
January	$1,900,000	20,000 units
February	2,250,000	27,000
March	2,400,000	30,000

Using the high-low method, determine (a) the variable cost per unit and (b) the total fixed cost.

EE 21-1 p. 1027
Show Me How

OBJ. 1

PE 21-1B High-low method

The manufacturing costs of Carrefour Enterprises for three months of the year follow:

	Total Cost	Units Produced
July	$300,000	2,700 units
August	440,000	5,500
September	325,000	3,500

Using the high-low method, determine (a) the variable cost per unit and (b) the total fixed cost.

EE 21-2 p. 1031
Show Me How

OBJ. 2

PE 21-2A Contribution margin

Lanning Company sells 160,000 units at $45 per unit. Variable costs are $27 per unit, and fixed costs are $975,000. Determine (a) the contribution margin ratio, (b) the unit contribution margin, and (c) income from operations.

EE 21-2 p. 1031
Show Me How

OBJ. 2

PE 21-2B Contribution margin

Weidner Company sells 22,000 units at $30 per unit. Variable costs are $24 per unit, and fixed costs are $40,000. Determine (a) the contribution margin ratio, (b) the unit contribution margin, and (c) income from operations.

EE 21-3 p. 1035
Show Me How

OBJ. 3

PE 21-3A Break-even point

Bigelow Inc. sells a product for $800 per unit. The variable cost is $600 per unit, while fixed costs are $1,200,000. Determine (a) the break-even point in sales units and (b) the break-even point if the selling price were increased to $850 per unit.

EE 21-3 p. 1035
Show Me How

OBJ. 3

PE 21-3B Break-even point

Elrod Inc. sells a product for $75 per unit. The variable cost is $45 per unit, while fixed costs are $48,000. Determine (a) the break-even point in sales units and (b) the break-even point if the selling price were increased to $95 per unit.

EE 21-4 p. 1037
Show Me How

OBJ. 3

PE 21-4A Target profit

Ramirez Inc. sells a product for $80 per unit. The variable cost is $60 per unit, and fixed costs are $2,000,000. Determine (a) the break-even point in sales units and (b) the break-even point in sales units if the company desires a target profit of $250,000.

EE 21-4 *p. 1037*
Show Me How

PE 21-4B Target profit

OBJ. 3

Scrushy Company sells a product for $150 per unit. The variable cost is $110 per unit, and fixed costs are $200,000. Determine (a) the break-even point in sales units and (b) the break-even point in sales units if the company desires a target profit of $50,000.

EE 21-5 *p. 1044*
Show Me How

PE 21-5A Sales mix and break-even analysis

OBJ. 5

Wide Open Industries Inc. has fixed costs of $475,000. The unit selling price, variable cost per unit, and contribution margin per unit for the company's two products follow:

Product	Selling Price	Variable Cost per Unit	Contribution Margin per Unit
AA	$145	$105	$40
BB	110	75	35

The sales mix for Products AA and BB is 60% and 40%, respectively. Determine the break-even point in units of AA and BB.

EE 21-5 *p. 1044*
Show Me How

PE 21-5B Sales mix and break-even analysis

OBJ. 5

Einhorn Company has fixed costs of $105,000. The unit selling price, variable cost per unit, and contribution margin per unit for the company's two products follow:

Product	Selling Price	Variable Cost per Unit	Contribution Margin per Unit
QQ	$50	$35	$15
ZZ	60	30	30

The sales mix for Products QQ and ZZ is 40% and 60%, respectively. Determine the break-even point in units of QQ and ZZ.

EE 21-6 *p. 1046*
Show Me How

PE 21-6A Operating leverage

OBJ. 5

SungSam Enterprises reports the following data:

Sales	$340,000
Variable costs	180,000
Contribution margin	$160,000
Fixed costs	80,000
Income from operations	$ 80,000

Determine SungSam Enterprises's operating leverage.

EE 21-6 *p. 1046*
Show Me How

PE 21-6B Operating leverage

OBJ. 5

Westminster Co. reports the following data:

Sales	$875,000
Variable costs	425,000
Contribution margin	$450,000
Fixed costs	150,000
Income from operations	$300,000

Determine Westminster Co.'s operating leverage.

EE 21-7 *p. 1047*
Show Me How

PE 21-7A Margin of safety

OBJ. 5

Liu Inc. has sales of $48,500,000, and the break-even point in sales dollars is $31,040,000. Determine the company's margin of safety as a percent of current sales.

EE 21-7 *p. 1047*
Show Me How

PE 21-7B Margin of safety

OBJ. 5

Junck Company has sales of $550,000, and the break-even point in sales dollars is $385,000. Determine the company's margin of safety as a percent of current sales.

Exercises

OBJ. 1

EX 21-1 Classify costs

Following is a list of various costs incurred in producing replacement automobile parts. With respect to the production and sale of these auto parts, classify each cost as variable, fixed, or mixed.

1. Cost of labor for hourly workers
2. Factory cleaning costs, $6,000 per month
3. Hourly wages of machine operators
4. Computer chip (purchased from a vendor)
5. Electricity costs, $0.20 per kilowatt-hour
6. Metal
7. Salary of plant manager
8. Property taxes, $165,000 per year on factory building and equipment
9. Plastic
10. Oil used in manufacturing equipment
11. Rent on warehouse, $10,000 per month plus $25 per square foot of storage used
12. Property insurance premiums, $3,600 per month plus $0.01 for each dollar of property over $1,200,000
13. Straight-line depreciation on the production equipment
14. Pension cost, $1.00 per employee hour on the job
15. Packaging

OBJ. 1

EX 21-2 Identify cost graphs

The following cost graphs illustrate various types of cost behavior:

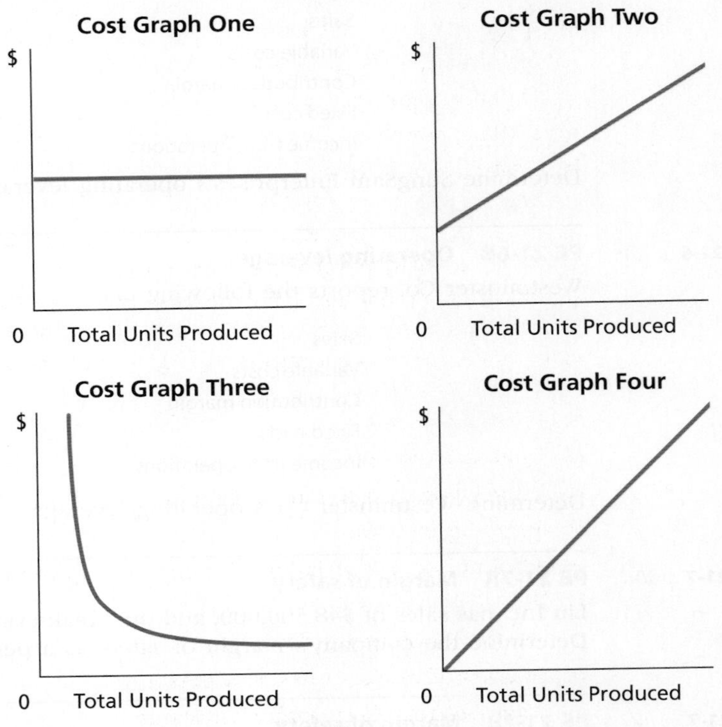

For each of the following costs, identify the cost graph that best illustrates its cost behavior as the number of units produced increases:

a. Total direct materials cost
b. Electricity costs of $1,000 per month plus $0.10 per kilowatt-hour
c. Per-unit cost of straight-line depreciation on factory equipment
d. Salary of quality control supervisor, $20,000 per month
e. Per-unit direct labor cost

EX 21-3 Identify activity bases

OBJ. 1

For a major university, match each cost in the following table with the activity base most appropriate to it. An activity base may be used more than once or not used at all.

Cost:

1. Instructor salaries
2. Admissions office salaries
3. Student records office salaries
4. Financial aid office salaries
5. Housing personnel wages
6. Office supplies

Activity Base:

a. Student credit hours
b. Number of students living on campus
c. Number of enrollment applications
d. Number of students
e. Number of enrolled students and alumni
f. Number of financial aid applications

EX 21-4 Identify activity bases

OBJ. 1

From the following list of activity bases for an automobile dealership, select the base that would be most appropriate for each of these costs: (1) preparation costs (cleaning, oil, and gasoline costs) for each car received, (2) salespersons' commission of 5% of the sales price for each car sold, and (3) administrative costs for ordering cars.

a. Number of cars sold
b. Dollar amount of cars ordered
c. Number of cars ordered
d. Number of cars on hand
e. Number of cars received
f. Dollar amount of cars sold
g. Dollar amount of cars received
h. Dollar amount of cars on hand

Real World

EX 21-5 Identify fixed and variable costs

OBJ. 1

Intuit Inc. develops and sells software products for the personal finance market, including popular titles such as Quickbooks® and TurboTax®. Classify each of the following costs and expenses for this company as either variable or fixed to the number of units produced and sold:

a. Packaging costs
b. Sales commissions
c. Property taxes on general offices
d. Shipping expenses
e. Straight-line depreciation of computer equipment
f. President's salary
g. Salaries of software developers
h. Salaries of human resources personnel
i. Wages of telephone order assistants
j. Users' guides

EX 21-6 Relevant range and fixed and variable costs

OBJ. 1

✔ a. $30.00

Show Me How

Vogel Inc. manufactures memory chips for electronic toys within a relevant range of 45,000 to 75,000 memory chips per year. Within this range, the following partially completed manufacturing cost schedule has been prepared:

Components produced	45,000	60,000	75,000
Total costs:			
Total variable costs	$ 1,350,000	(d)	(j)
Total fixed costs	810,000	(e)	(k)
Total costs	$2,160,000	(f)	(l)
Cost per unit:			
Variable cost per unit	(a)	(g)	(m)
Fixed cost per unit	(b)	(h)	(n)
Total cost per unit	(c)	(i)	(o)

Complete the cost schedule, identifying each cost by the appropriate letter (a) through (o).

EX 21-7 High-low method

OBJ. 1

✔ a. $175.50 per unit

Excel

Show Me How

Ziegler Inc. has decided to use the high-low method to estimate the total cost and the fixed and variable cost components of the total cost. The data for various levels of production are as follows:

Units Produced	Total Costs
80,000	$25,100,000
92,000	27,206,000
120,000	32,120,000

a. Determine the variable cost per unit and the total fixed cost.

b. Based on part (a), estimate the total cost for 115,000 units of production.

EX 21-8 High-low method for a service company

OBJ. 1

✔ Fixed cost, $600,000

Show Me How

Boston Railroad decided to use the high-low method and operating data from the past six months to estimate the fixed and variable components of transportation costs. The activity base used by Boston Railroad is a measure of railroad operating activity, termed "gross-ton miles," which is the total number of tons multiplied by the miles moved.

	Transportation Costs	Gross-Ton Miles
January	$1,776,000	560,000
February	2,700,000	1,000,000
March	1,650,000	500,000
April	1,860,000	600,000
May	1,440,000	400,000
June	1,566,000	460,000

Determine the variable cost per gross-ton mile and the total fixed cost.

EX 21-9 Contribution margin ratio

OBJ. 2

✔ a. 35%

Show Me How

a. Yountz Company budgets sales of $2,400,000, fixed costs of $525,000, and variable costs of $1,560,000. What is the contribution margin ratio for Yountz Company?

b. If the contribution margin ratio for Vera Company is 40%, sales were $3,400,000, and fixed costs were $800,000, what was the income from operations?

EX 21-10 Contribution margin and contribution margin ratio — OBJ. 2

✔ b. 34.6%

Real World

Show Me How

For a recent year, McDonald's company-owned restaurants had the following sales and expenses (in millions):

Sales	$18,169.3
Food and packaging	$ 6,129.7
Payroll	4,756.0
Occupancy (rent, depreciation, etc.)	4,402.6
General, selling, and administrative expenses	2,487.9
	$17,776.2
Income from operations	$ 393.1

Assume that the variable costs consist of food and packaging; payroll; and 40% of the general, selling, and administrative expenses.

a. What is McDonald's contribution margin? Round to the nearest tenth of a million (one decimal place).

b. What is McDonald's contribution margin ratio? Round to one decimal place.

c. How much would income from operations increase if same-store sales increased by $500 million for the coming year, with no change in the contribution margin ratio or fixed costs? Round your answer to the nearest tenth of a million (one decimal place).

EX 21-11 Break-even sales and sales to realize income from operations — OBJ. 3

✔ b. 154,000 units

Show Me How

For the current year ended October 31, Yentling Company expects fixed costs of $14,000,000, a unit variable cost of $200, and a unit selling price of $300.

a. Compute the anticipated break-even sales (units).

b. Compute the sales (units) required to realize income from operations of $1,400,000.

EX 21-12 Break-even sales — OBJ. 3

✔ a. 168.9 million barrels

Real World

Anheuser-Busch InBev Companies, Inc., reported the following operating information for a recent year (in millions):

Net sales	$47,063
Cost of goods sold	$18,756
Selling, general and administration	12,999
	$31,755
Income from operations	$15,308*

*Before special items

In addition, assume that Anheuser-Busch InBev sold 400 million barrels of beer during the year. Assume that variable costs were 75% of the cost of goods sold and 50% of selling, general and administration expenses. Assume that the remaining costs are fixed. For the following year, assume that Anheuser-Busch InBev expects pricing, variable costs per barrel, and fixed costs to remain constant, except that new distribution and general office facilities are expected to increase fixed costs by $300 million.

a. Compute the break-even number of barrels for the current year. *Note:* For the selling price per barrel and variable costs per barrel, round to the nearest cent. Also present the break-even units in millions of barrels.

b. Compute the anticipated break-even number of barrels for the following year.

EX 21-13 Break-even sales — OBJ. 3

✔ a. 15,000 units

Show Me How

Currently, the unit selling price of a product is $1,500, the unit variable cost is $1,200, and the total fixed costs are $4,500,000. A proposal is being evaluated to increase the unit selling price to $1,600.

a. Compute the current break-even sales (units).

b. Compute the anticipated break-even sales (units), assuming that the unit selling price is increased to the proposed $1,600, and all costs remain constant.

EX 21-14 Break-even analysis **OBJ. 3**

The Junior League of Yadkinville, California, collected recipes from members and published a cookbook entitled *Food for Everyone*. The book will sell for $18 per copy. The chairwoman of the cookbook development committee estimated that the club needed to sell 2,000 books to break even on its $4,000 investment. What is the variable cost per unit assumed in the Junior League's analysis?

EX 21-15 Break-even analysis **OBJ. 3**

Real World

Media outlets such as ESPN and Fox Sports often have websites that provide in-depth coverage of news and events. Portions of these websites are restricted to members who pay a monthly subscription to gain access to exclusive news and commentary. These websites typically offer a free trial period to introduce viewers to the site. Assume that during a recent fiscal year, ESPN.com spent $4,200,000 on a promotional campaign for the ESPN .com website that offered two free months of service for new subscribers. In addition, assume the following information:

Number of months an average new customer stays with the service (including the two free months)	14 months
Revenue per month per customer subscription	$10.00
Variable cost per month per customer subscription	$5.00

Determine the number of new customer accounts needed to break even on the cost of the promotional campaign. In forming your answer, (1) treat the cost of the promotional campaign as a fixed cost and (2) treat the revenue less variable cost per account for the subscription period as the unit contribution margin.

EX 21-16 Break-even analysis for a service company **OBJ. 3**

Excel

Real World

Sprint Nextel is one of the largest digital wireless service providers in the United States. In a recent year, it had approximately 32.5 million direct subscribers (accounts) that generated revenue of $35,345 million. Costs and expenses for the year were as follows (in millions):

Cost of revenue	$20,841
Selling, general, and administrative expenses	9,765
Depreciation	2,239

Assume that 70% of the cost of revenue and 30% of the selling, general, and administrative expenses are variable to the number of direct subscribers (accounts).

a. What is Sprint Nextel's break-even number of accounts, using the data and assumptions given? Round units (accounts) and per-account amounts to one decimal place.

b. How much revenue per account would be sufficient for Sprint Nextel to break even if the number of accounts remained constant?

EX 21-17 Cost-volume-profit chart **OBJ. 4**

✔ b. $1,500,000

For the coming year, Loudermilk Inc. anticipates fixed costs of $600,000, a unit variable cost of $75, and a unit selling price of $125. The maximum sales within the relevant range are $2,500,000.

a. Construct a cost-volume-profit chart.

b. Estimate the break-even sales (dollars) by using the cost-volume-profit chart constructed in part (a).

c. What is the main advantage of presenting the cost-volume-profit analysis in graphic form rather than equation form?

✔ b. $400,000

EX 21-18 Profit-volume chart **OBJ. 4**

Using the data for Loudermilk Inc. in Exercise 21-17, (a) determine the maximum possible operating loss, (b) compute the maximum possible operating profit, (c) construct a profit-volume chart, and (d) estimate the break-even sales (units) by using the profit-volume chart constructed in part (c).

EX 21-19 Break-even chart **OBJ. 4**

Name the following chart and identify the items represented by the letters (a) through (f):

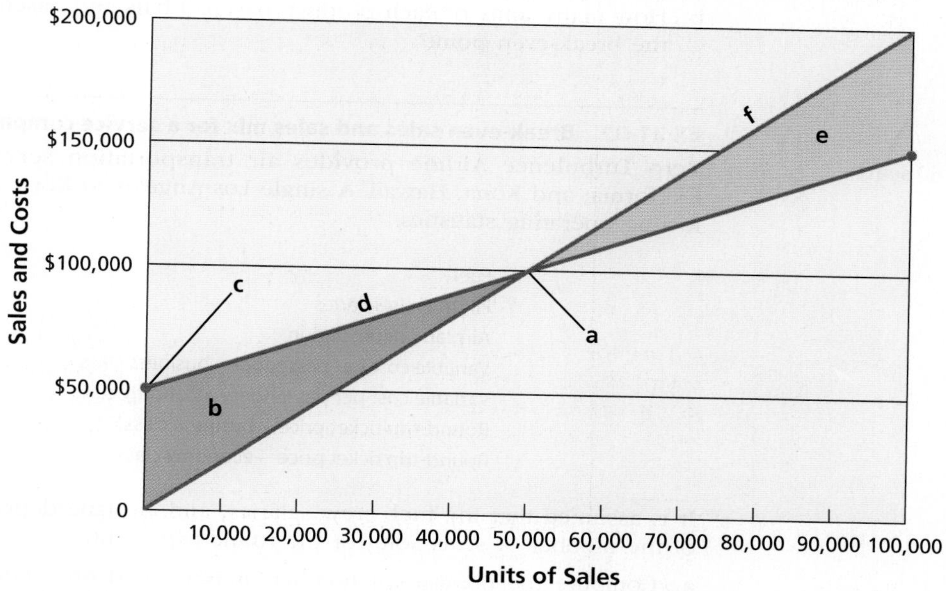

EX 21-20 Break-even chart **OBJ. 4**

Name the following chart and identify the items represented by the letters (a) through (f):

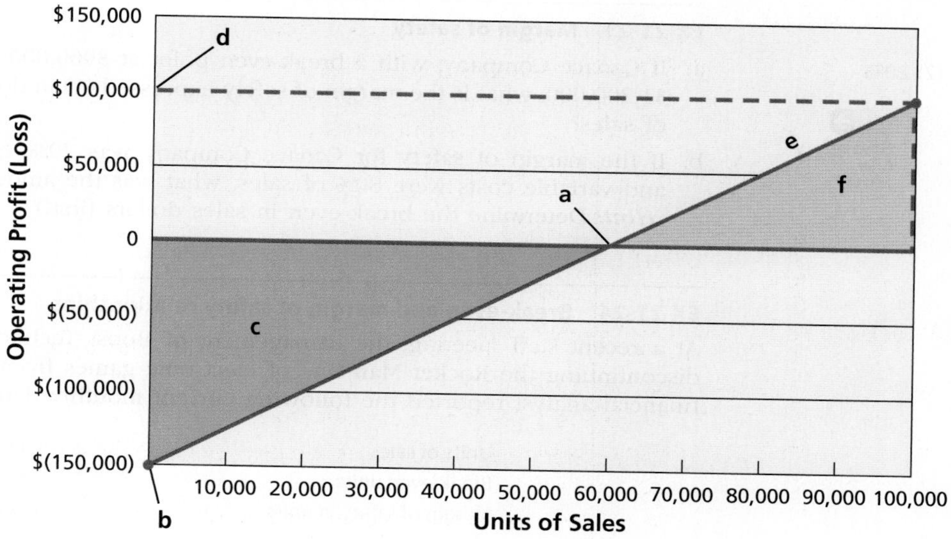

✔ a. 15,500 units

Show Me How

EX 21-21 Sales mix and break-even sales **OBJ. 5**

Dragon Sports Inc. manufactures and sells two products, baseball bats and baseball gloves. The fixed costs are $620,000, and the sales mix is 40% bats and 60% gloves. The unit selling price and the unit variable cost for each product are as follows:

Products	Unit Selling Price	Unit Variable Cost
Bats	$ 90	$50
Gloves	105	65

a. Compute the break-even sales (units) for the overall product, E.

b. How many units of each product, baseball bats and baseball gloves, would be sold at the break-even point?

✔ a. 60 seats

EX 21-22 Break-even sales and sales mix for a service company **OBJ. 5**

Zero Turbulence Airline provides air transportation services between Los Angeles, California; and Kona, Hawaii. A single Los Angeles to Kona round-trip flight has the following operating statistics:

Fuel	$7,000
Flight crew salaries	3,200
Airplane depreciation	3,480
Variable cost per passenger—business class	140
Variable cost per passenger—economy class	120
Round-trip ticket price—business class	800
Round-trip ticket price—economy class	300

It is assumed that the fuel, crew salaries, and airplane depreciation are fixed, regardless of the number of seats sold for the round-trip flight.

a. Compute the break-even number of seats sold on a single round-trip flight for the overall product, E. Assume that the overall product mix is 10% business class and 90% economy class tickets.

b. How many business class and economy class seats would be sold at the break-even point?

✔ a. (2) 20%

Show Me How

EX 21-23 Margin of safety **OBJ. 5**

a. If Canace Company, with a break-even point at $960,000 of sales, has actual sales of $1,200,000, what is the margin of safety expressed (1) in dollars and (2) as a percentage of sales?

b. If the margin of safety for Canace Company was 20%, fixed costs were $1,875,000, and variable costs were 80% of sales, what was the amount of actual sales (dollars)? (*Hint:* Determine the break-even in sales dollars first.)

EX 21-24 Break-even and margin of safety relationships **OBJ. 5**

At a recent staff meeting, the management of Boost Technologies Inc. was considering discontinuing the Rocket Man line of electronic games from the product line. The chief financial analyst reported the following current monthly data for the Rocket Man:

Units of sales	420,000
Break-even units	472,500
Margin of safety in units	29,400

For what reason would you question the validity of these data?

EX 21-25 Operating leverage

OBJ. 5

✔ a. Beck, 5.0

Beck Inc. and Bryant Inc. have the following operating data:

	Beck Inc.	Bryant Inc.
Sales	$1,250,000	$2,000,000
Variable costs	750,000	1,250,000
Contribution margin	$ 500,000	$ 750,000
Fixed costs	400,000	450,000
Income from operations	$ 100,000	$ 300,000

a. Compute the operating leverage for Beck Inc. and Bryant Inc.

b. How much would income from operations increase for each company if the sales of each increased by 20%?

c. Why is there a difference in the increase in income from operations for the two companies? Explain.

Appendix

EX 21-26 Items on variable costing income statement

In the following equations, based on the variable costing income statement, identify the items designated by X:

a. Net Sales – X = Manufacturing Margin

b. Manufacturing Margin – X = Contribution Margin

c. Contribution Margin – X = Income from Operations

Appendix

EX 21-27 Variable costing income statement

✔ a. Contribution margin, $1,934,400

Excel

On July 31, the end of the first month of operations, Rhys Company prepared the following income statement, based on the absorption costing concept:

Sales (96,000 units)		$4,440,000
Cost of goods sold:		
Cost of goods manufactured	$3,120,000	
Less ending inventory (24,000 units)	624,000	
Cost of goods sold		2,496,000
Gross profit		$1,944,000
Selling and administrative expenses		288,000
Income from operations		$1,656,000

a. Prepare a variable costing income statement, assuming that the fixed manufacturing costs were $132,000 and the variable selling and administrative expenses were $115,200.

b. Reconcile the absorption costing income from operations of $1,656,000 with the variable costing income from operations determined in (a).

Appendix

EX 21-28 Absorption costing income statement

✔ a. Gross profit, $1,435,600

On June 30, the end of the first month of operations, Tudor Manufacturing Co. prepared the following income statement, based on the variable costing concept:

(Continued)

Excel

Sales (420,000 units)		$7,450,000
Variable cost of goods sold:		
Variable cost of goods manufactured (500,000 units × $14 per unit)	$7,000,000	
Less ending inventory (80,000 units × $14 per unit)	1,120,000	
Variable cost of goods sold		5,880,000
Manufacturing margin		$1,570,000
Variable selling and administrative expenses		80,000
Contribution margin		$1,490,000
Fixed costs:		
Fixed manufacturing costs	$ 160,000	
Fixed selling and administrative expenses	75,000	235,000
Income from operations		$1,255,000

a. Prepare an absorption costing income statement.
b. Reconcile the variable costing income from operations of $1,255,000 with the absorption costing income from operations determined in (a).

Problems: Series A

PR 21-1A Classify costs

OBJ. 1

Seymour Clothing Co. manufactures a variety of clothing types for distribution to several major retail chains. The following costs are incurred in the production and sale of blue jeans:

a. Shipping boxes used to ship orders
b. Consulting fee of $200,000 paid to industry specialist for marketing advice
c. Straight-line depreciation on sewing machines
d. Salesperson's salary, $10,000 plus 2% of the total sales
e. Fabric
f. Dye
g. Thread
h. Salary of designers
i. Brass buttons
j. Legal fees paid to attorneys in defense of the company in a patent infringement suit, $50,000 plus $87 per hour
k. Insurance premiums on property, plant, and equipment, $70,000 per year plus $5 per $30,000 of insured value over $8,000,000
l. Rental costs of warehouse, $5,000 per month plus $4 per square foot of storage used
m. Supplies
n. Leather for patches identifying the brand on individual pieces of apparel
o. Rent on plant equipment, $50,000 per year
p. Salary of production vice president
q. Janitorial services, $2,200 per month
r. Wages of machine operators
s. Electricity costs of $0.10 per kilowatt-hour
t. Property taxes on property, plant, and equipment

Instructions

Classify the preceding costs as fixed, variable, or mixed. Use the following tabular headings and place an X in the appropriate column. Identify each cost by letter in the cost column.

Cost	Fixed Cost	Variable Cost	Mixed Cost

✔ 2. (b) $50

Show Me How

PR 21-2A Break-even sales under present and proposed conditions **OBJ. 2, 3**

Darby Company, operating at full capacity, sold 500,000 units at a price of $94 per unit during the current year. Its income statement is as follows:

Sales		$ 47,000,000
Cost of goods sold		25,000,000
Gross profit		$ 22,000,000
Expenses:		
Selling expenses	$4,000,000	
Administrative expenses	3,000,000	
Total expenses		7,000,000
Income from operations		$15,000,000

The division of costs between variable and fixed is as follows:

	Variable	Fixed
Cost of goods sold	70%	30%
Selling expenses	75%	25%
Administrative expenses	50%	50%

Management is considering a plant expansion program for the following year that will permit an increase of $3,760,000 in yearly sales. The expansion will increase fixed costs by $1,800,000 but will not affect the relationship between sales and variable costs.

Instructions

1. Determine the total variable costs and the total fixed costs for the current year.
2. Determine (a) the unit variable cost and (b) the unit contribution margin for the current year.
3. Compute the break-even sales (units) for the current year.
4. Compute the break-even sales (units) under the proposed program for the following year.
5. Determine the amount of sales (units) that would be necessary under the proposed program to realize the $15,000,000 of income from operations that was earned in the current year.
6. Determine the maximum income from operations possible with the expanded plant.
7. If the proposal is accepted and sales remain at the current level, what will the income or loss from operations be for the following year?
8. Based on the data given, would you recommend accepting the proposal? Explain.

✔ 1. 12,000 units

PR 21-3A Break-even sales and cost-volume-profit chart **OBJ. 3, 4**

For the coming year, Cleves Company anticipates a unit selling price of $100, a unit variable cost of $60, and fixed costs of $480,000.

Instructions

1. Compute the anticipated break-even sales (units).
2. Compute the sales (units) required to realize a target profit of $240,000.
3. Construct a cost-volume-profit chart, assuming maximum sales of 20,000 units within the relevant range.
4. Determine the probable income (loss) from operations if sales total 16,000 units.

✔ 1. 1,000 units

PR 21-4A Break-even sales and cost-volume-profit chart **OBJ. 3, 4**

Last year Hever Inc. had sales of $500,000, based on a unit selling price of $250. The variable cost per unit was $175, and fixed costs were $75,000. The maximum sales within Hever Inc.'s relevant range are 2,500 units. Hever Inc. is considering a proposal to spend an additional $33,750 on billboard advertising during the current year in an attempt to increase sales and utilize unused capacity.

(Continued)

Instructions

1. Construct a cost-volume-profit chart indicating the break-even sales for last year. Verify your answer, using the break-even equation.
2. Using the cost-volume-profit chart prepared in part (1), determine (a) the income from operations for last year and (b) the maximum income from operations that could have been realized during the year. Verify your answers using the mathematical approach to cost-volume-profit analysis.
3. Construct a cost-volume-profit chart indicating the break-even sales for the current year, assuming that a noncancellable contract is signed for the additional billboard advertising. No changes are expected in the unit selling price or other costs. Verify your answer, using the break-even equation.
4. Using the cost-volume-profit chart prepared in part (3), determine (a) the income from operations if sales total 2,000 units and (b) the maximum income from operations that could be realized during the year. Verify your answers using the mathematical approach to cost-volume-profit analysis.

PR 21-5A Sales mix and break-even sales

OBJ. 5

✔ 1. 4,030 units

Data related to the expected sales of laptops and tablets for Tech Products Inc. for the current year, which is typical of recent years, are as follows:

Products	Unit Selling Price	Unit Variable Cost	Sales Mix
Laptops	$1,600	$800	40%
Tablets	850	350	60%

The estimated fixed costs for the current year are $2,498,600.

Instructions

1. Determine the estimated units of sales of the overall (total) product, E, necessary to reach the break-even point for the current year.
2. Based on the break-even sales (units) in part (1), determine the unit sales of both laptops and tablets for the current year.
3. Assume that the sales mix was 50% laptops and 50% tablets. Compare the break-even point with that in part (1). Why is it so different?

PR 21-6A Contribution margin, break-even sales, cost-volume-profit chart, margin of safety, and operating leverage

OBJ. 2, 3, 4, 5

✔ 2. 25%

Excel

Wolsey Industries Inc. expects to maintain the same inventories at the end of 20Y8 as at the beginning of the year. The total of all production costs for the year is therefore assumed to be equal to the cost of goods sold. With this in mind, the various department heads were asked to submit estimates of the costs for their departments during the year. A summary report of these estimates is as follows:

	Estimated Fixed Cost	Estimated Variable Cost (per unit sold)
Production costs:		
Direct materials	—	$ 46
Direct labor	—	40
Factory overhead	$200,000	20
Selling expenses:		
Sales salaries and commissions	110,000	8
Advertising	40,000	—
Travel	12,000	—
Miscellaneous selling expense	7,600	1
Administrative expenses:		
Office and officers' salaries	132,000	—
Supplies	10,000	4
Miscellaneous administrative expense	13,400	1
Total	$525,000	$120

It is expected that 21,875 units will be sold at a price of $160 a unit. Maximum sales within the relevant range are 27,000 units.

Instructions

1. Prepare an estimated income statement for 20Y8.
2. What is the expected contribution margin ratio?
3. Determine the break-even sales in units and dollars.
4. Construct a cost-volume-profit chart indicating the break-even sales.
5. What is the expected margin of safety in dollars and as a percentage of sales?
6. Determine the operating leverage.

Problems: Series B

PR 21-1B Classify costs

OBJ. 1

Cromwell Furniture Company manufactures sofas for distribution to several major retail chains. The following costs are incurred in the production and sale of sofas:

a. Fabric for sofa coverings
b. Wood for framing the sofas
c. Legal fees paid to attorneys in defense of the company in a patent infringement suit, $25,000 plus $160 per hour
d. Salary of production supervisor
e. Cartons used to ship sofas
f. Rent on experimental equipment, $50 for every sofa produced
g. Straight-line depreciation on factory equipment
h. Rental costs of warehouse, $30,000 per month
i. Property taxes on property, plant, and equipment
j. Insurance premiums on property, plant, and equipment, $25,000 per year plus $25 per $25,000 of insured value over $16,000,000
k. Springs
l. Consulting fee of $120,000 paid to efficiency specialists
m. Electricity costs of $0.13 per kilowatt-hour
n. Salesperson's salary, $80,000 plus 4% of the selling price of each sofa sold
o. Foam rubber for cushion fillings
p. Janitorial supplies, $2,500 per month
q. Employer's FICA taxes on controller's salary of $180,000
r. Salary of designers
s. Wages of sewing machine operators
t. Sewing supplies

Instructions

Classify the preceding costs as fixed, variable, or mixed. Use the following tabular headings and place an X in the appropriate column. Identify each cost by letter in the cost column.

Cost	Fixed Cost	Variable Cost	Mixed Cost

PR 21-2B Break-even sales under present and proposed conditions

OBJ. 2, 3

✓ 3. 29,375 units

Show Me How

Howard Industries Inc., operating at full capacity, sold 64,000 units at a price of $45 per unit during the current year. Its income statement is as follows:

Sales		$2,880,000
Cost of goods sold		1,400,000
Gross profit		$1,480,000
Expenses:		
Selling expenses	$400,000	
Administrative expenses	387,500	
Total expenses		787,500
Income from operations		$ 692,500

The division of costs between variable and fixed is as follows:

	Variable	Fixed
Cost of goods sold	75%	25%
Selling expenses	60%	40%
Administrative expenses	80%	20%

Management is considering a plant expansion program for the following year that will permit an increase of $900,000 in yearly sales. The expansion will increase fixed costs by $212,500 but will not affect the relationship between sales and variable costs.

Instructions

1. Determine the total fixed costs and the total variable costs for the current year.
2. Determine (a) the unit variable cost and (b) the unit contribution margin for the current year.
3. Compute the break-even sales (units) for the current year.
4. Compute the break-even sales (units) under the proposed program for the following year.
5. Determine the amount of sales (units) that would be necessary under the proposed program to realize the $692,500 of income from operations that was earned in the current year.
6. Determine the maximum income from operations possible with the expanded plant.
7. If the proposal is accepted and sales remain at the current level, what will the income or loss from operations be for the following year?
8. Based on the data given, would you recommend accepting the proposal? Explain.

PR 21-3B Break-even sales and cost-volume-profit chart

OBJ. 3, 4

✓ 1. 20,000 units

For the coming year, Culpeper Products Inc. anticipates a unit selling price of $150, a unit variable cost of $110, and fixed costs of $800,000.

Instructions

1. Compute the anticipated break-even sales (units).
2. Compute the sales (units) required to realize income from operations of $300,000.
3. Construct a cost-volume-profit chart, assuming maximum sales of 40,000 units within the relevant range.
4. Determine the probable income (loss) from operations if sales total 32,000 units.

PR 21-4B Break-even sales and cost-volume-profit chart

OBJ. 3, 4

✓ 1. 3,000 units

Last year Parr Co. had sales of $900,000, based on a unit selling price of $200. The variable cost per unit was $125, and fixed costs were $225,000. The maximum sales within Parr Co.'s relevant range are 7,500 units. Parr Co. is considering a proposal to spend an additional $112,500 on billboard advertising during the current year in an attempt to increase sales and utilize unused capacity.

Instructions

1. Construct a cost-volume-profit chart indicating the break-even sales for last year. Verify your answer, using the break-even equation.
2. Using the cost-volume-profit chart prepared in part (1), determine (a) the income from operations for last year and (b) the maximum income from operations that could have been realized during the year. Verify your answers.
3. Construct a cost-volume-profit chart indicating the break-even sales for the current year, assuming that a noncancellable contract is signed for the additional billboard advertising. No changes are expected in the selling price or other costs. Verify your answer, using the break-even equation.
4. Using the cost-volume-profit chart prepared in part (3), determine (a) the income from operations if sales total 6,000 units and (b) the maximum income from operations that could be realized during the year. Verify your answers.

PR 21-5B Sales mix and break-even sales

OBJ. 5

✔ 1. 4,500 units

Data related to the expected sales of two types of frozen pizzas for Norfolk Frozen Foods Inc. for the current year, which is typical of recent years, are as follows:

Products	Unit Selling Price	Unit Variable Cost	Sales Mix
12″ Pizza	$12	$3	30%
16″ Pizza	15	4	70%

The estimated fixed costs for the current year are $46,800.

Instructions

1. Determine the estimated units of sales of the overall (total) product, E, necessary to reach the break-even point for the current year.
2. Based on the break-even sales (units) in part (1), determine the unit sales of both the 12″ pizza and 16″ pizza for the current year.
3. Assume that the sales mix was 50% 12″ pizza and 50% 16″ pizza. Compare the break-even point with that in part (1). Why is it so different?

PR 21-6B Contribution margin, break-even sales, cost-volume-profit chart, margin of safety, and operating leverage

OBJ. 2, 3, 4, 5

✔ 3. 8,000 units

Excel

Belmain Co. expects to maintain the same inventories at the end of 20Y7 as at the beginning of the year. The total of all production costs for the year is therefore assumed to be equal to the cost of goods sold. With this in mind, the various department heads were asked to submit estimates of the costs for their departments during the year. A summary report of these estimates is as follows:

	Estimated Fixed Cost	Estimated Variable Cost (per unit sold)
Production costs:		
Direct materials	—	$50.00
Direct labor	—	30.00
Factory overhead	$ 350,000	6.00
Selling expenses:		
Sales salaries and commissions	340,000	4.00
Advertising	116,000	—
Travel	4,000	—
Miscellaneous selling expense	2,300	1.00
Administrative expenses:		
Office and officers' salaries	325,000	—
Supplies	6,000	4.00
Miscellaneous administrative expense	8,700	1.00
Total	$1,152,000	$96.00

(Continued)

It is expected that 12,000 units will be sold at a price of $240 a unit. Maximum sales within the relevant range are 18,000 units.

Instructions

1. Prepare an estimated income statement for 20Y7.
2. What is the expected contribution margin ratio?
3. Determine the break-even sales in units and dollars.
4. Construct a cost-volume-profit chart indicating the break-even sales.
5. What is the expected margin of safety in dollars and as a percentage of sales?
6. Determine the operating leverage.

Cases & Projects

CP 21-1 Ethics in Action

Ethics

Edward Seymour is a financial consultant to Cornish Inc., a real estate syndicate. Cornish finances and develops commercial real estate (office buildings) projects. The completed projects are then sold as limited partnership interests to individual investors. The syndicate makes a profit on the sale of these partnership interests. Edward provides financial information for prospective investors in a document called the offering "prospectus." This document discusses the financial and legal details of the limited partnership investment.

One of the company's current projects, called JEDI 2, has the partnership borrowing money from a local bank to build a commercial office building. The interest rate on the loan is 6.5% for the first four years. After four years, the interest rate jumps to 15% for the remaining 20 years of the loan. The interest expense is one of the major costs of this project and significantly affects the number of renters needed for the project to break even. In the prospectus, Edward has prominently reported that the break-even occupancy for the first four years is 65%. This is the amount of office space that must be leased to cover the interest and general upkeep costs during the first four years. The 65% break-even point is very low compared to similar projects and thus communicates a low risk to potential investors. Edward uses the 65% break-even rate as a major marketing tool in selling the limited partnership interests. Buried in the fine print of the prospectus is additional information that would allow an astute investor to determine that the break-even occupancy jumps to 95% after the fourth year when the interest rate on the loan increases to 15%. Edward believes prospective investors are adequately informed of the investment's risk.

Is Edward behaving ethically? Explain your answer.

CP 21-2 Team Activity

Team Activity

Real World

Break-even analysis is an important tool for managing any business, including colleges and universities. In a group, identify three areas where break-even analysis might be used at your college or university. For each area, identify the revenues, fixed costs, and variable costs.

CP 21-3 Communication

Communication

Sun Airlines is a commercial airline that targets business and nonbusiness travelers. In recent months, the airline has been unprofitable. The company has break-even sales volume of 75% of capacity, which is significantly higher than the industry average of 65%. Sun's CEO, Neil Armstrong, is concerned about the recent string of losses and is considering a strategic plan that could reduce the break-even sales volume by increasing ticket prices. He has asked for your help in evaluating this plan.

Write a brief memo to Neil Armstrong evaluating this strategy.

CP 21-4 Break-even analysis

Somerset Inc. has finished a new video game, *Snowboard Challenge*. Management is now considering its marketing strategies. The following information is available:

Anticipated sales price per unit	$80
Variable cost per unit*	$35
Anticipated volume	1,000,000 units
Production costs	$20,000,000
Anticipated advertising	$15,000,000

*The cost of the video game, packaging, and copying costs.

Two managers, James Hamilton and Thomas Seymour, had the following discussion of ways to increase the profitability of this new offering:

James: I think we need to think of some way to increase our profitability. Do you have any ideas?

Thomas: Well, I think the best strategy would be to become aggressive on price.

James: How aggressive?

Thomas: If we drop the price to $60 per unit and maintain our advertising budget at $15,000,000, I think we will generate total sales of 2,000,000 units.

James: I think that's the wrong way to go. You're giving up too much on price. Instead, I think we need to follow an aggressive advertising strategy.

Thomas: How aggressive?

James: If we increase our advertising to a total of $25,000,000, we should be able to increase sales volume to 1,400,000 units without any change in price.

Thomas: I don't think that's reasonable. We'll never cover the increased advertising costs.

Which strategy is best: Do nothing, follow the advice of Thomas Seymour, or follow James Hamilton's strategy?

CP 21-5 Variable costs and activity bases in decision making

The owner of Warwick Printing, a printing company, is planning direct labor needs for the upcoming year. The owner has provided you with the following information for next year's plans:

	One Color	Two Color	Three Color	Four Color	Total
Number of banners	212	274	616	698	1,800

Each color on the banner must be printed one at a time. Thus, for example, a four-color banner will need to be run through the printing operation four separate times. The total production volume last year was 800 banners, as follows:

	One Color	Two Color	Three Color	Total
Number of banners	180	240	380	800

As you can see, the four-color banner is a new product offering for the upcoming year. The owner believes that the expected 1,000-unit increase in volume from last year means that direct labor expenses should increase by 125% (1,000 ÷ 800). What do you think?

CP 21-6 Variable costs and activity bases in decision making

Sales volume has been dropping at Mumford Industries. During this time, however, the Shipping Department manager has been under severe financial constraints. The manager knows that most of the Shipping Department's effort is related to pulling inventory from the warehouse for each order and performing the paperwork. The paperwork involves preparing shipping documents for each order. Thus, the pulling and paperwork effort associated with each sales order is essentially the same, regardless of the size of the

(Continued)

order. The Shipping Department manager has discussed the financial situation with senior management. Senior management has responded by pointing out that because sales volume has been dropping, the amount of work in the Shipping Department also should be dropping. Thus, senior management told the Shipping Department manager that costs should be decreasing in the department.

The Shipping Department manager prepared the following information:

Month	Sales Volume	Number of Customer Orders	Sales Volume per Order
January	$472,000	1,180	400
February	475,800	1,220	390
March	456,950	1,235	370
April	425,000	1,250	340
May	464,750	1,430	325
June	421,200	1,350	312
July	414,000	1,380	300
August	430,700	1,475	292

Given this information, how would you respond to senior management?

CHAPTER 22

Budgeting

Concepts and Principles

Chapter 18 *Introduction to Managerial Accounting*

Developing Information

COST SYSTEMS

Chapter 19 *Job Order Costing*

Chapter 20 *Process Costing*

COST BEHAVIOR

Chapter 21 *Cost-Volume-Profit Analysis*

Decision Making

EVALUATING PERFORMANCE

Chapter 22 ***Budgeting***

Chapter 23 *Variances from Standard Costs*

COMPARING ALTERNATIVES

Chapter 24 *Decentralized Operations*

Chapter 25 *Differential Analysis, Product Pricing, and Activity-Based Costing*

Chapter 26 *Capital Investment Analysis*

CHAPTER
22

JONATHAN FERREY/GETTY IMAGES

Hendrick Motorsports

You may have financial goals for your life. To achieve these goals, it is necessary to plan for future expenses. For example, you may consider taking a part-time job to save money for school expenses for the coming school year. How much money would you need to earn and save in order to pay these expenses? One way to find an answer to this question would be to prepare a budget. A budget would show an estimate of your expenses associated with school, such as tuition, fees, and books. In addition, you would have expenses for day-to-day living, such as rent, food, and clothing. You might also have expenses for travel and entertainment. Once the school year begins, you can use the budget as a tool for guiding your spending priorities during the year.

The budget is used in businesses in much the same way it can be used in personal life. For example, **Hendrick Motorsports**, featuring drivers Dale Earnhardt, Jr., Jeff Gordon, and Jimmie Johnson, uses budget information to remain one of the most valuable racing teams in NASCAR. Hendrick uses budgets to keep revenues greater than expenses. For example, Hendrick plans revenues from car sponsorships and winnings. Primary and secondary sponsorships (car decals) can provide as much as 70% of the revenues for a typical race team. Costs include salaries, engines, tires, cars, travel, and research and development. In addition, star drivers such as Dale Earnhardt, Jr. can earn as much as $28 million in salary, winnings, and endorsements. Overall, Hendrick is estimated to earn $179 million in revenues and $16.6 million in operating income from its four race teams. The budget provides the company with a "game plan" for the year. In this chapter, you will see how budgets can be used for financial planning and control.

Sources: Kurt Badenhausen, "Hendrick Motorsports Tops List of Nascar's Most Valuable Teams," *Forbes*, March 13, 2013; Bob Pockrass, "NASCAR's Highest Paid Drivers Make Their Money from a Variety of Sources," *Sporting News*, December 4, 2012; and Ed Hilton, "Under the Hood at Hendrick Motorsports", *Chicago Tribune*, July 13, 2007.

Learning Objectives

After studying this chapter, you should be able to:

Example Exercises (EE) are shown in **green.**

Obj. 1 **Describe budgeting, its objectives, and its impact on human behavior.**

Nature and Objectives of Budgeting
Objectives of Budgeting
Human Behavior and Budgeting

Obj. 2 **Describe the basic elements of the budget process, the two major types of budgeting, and the use of computers in budgeting.**

Budgeting Systems
Static Budget
Flexible Budget — EE 22-1
Computerized Budgeting Systems

Obj. 3 **Describe the master budget for a manufacturing company.**

Master Budget

Obj. 4 **Prepare the basic operating budgets for a manufacturing company.**

Operating Budgets
Sales Budget
Production Budget — EE 22-2
Direct Materials Purchases Budget — EE 22-3
Direct Labor Cost Budget — EE 22-4
Factory Overhead Cost Budget
Cost of Goods Sold Budget — EE 22-5
Selling and Administrative Expenses Budget
Budgeted Income Statement

Obj. 5 **Prepare financial budgets for a manufacturing company.**

Financial Budgets
Cash Budget — EE 22-6
Capital Expenditures Budget
Budgeted Balance Sheet

At a Glance 22 Page 1096

Obj. 1 Describe budgeting, its objectives, and its impact on human behavior.

Nature and Objectives of Budgeting

Budgets play an important role for organizations of all sizes and forms. For example, budgets are used in managing the operations of government agencies, churches, hospitals, and other nonprofit organizations. Individuals and families also use budgeting in managing their financial affairs. This chapter describes and illustrates budgeting for a manufacturing company.

Link to Hendrick Motorsports

Hendrick Motorsports holds a record of 11 NASCAR Sprint Cup Series Championships won by the following drivers: 6 by Jimmie Johnson, 4 by Jeff Gordon, and 1 by Terry Labonte.

Objectives of Budgeting

Budgeting involves (1) establishing specific goals, (2) executing plans to achieve the goals, and (3) periodically comparing actual results with the goals. In doing so, budgeting affects the following managerial functions:

- Planning
- Directing
- Controlling

The relationships of these activities are illustrated in Exhibit 1.

EXHIBIT 1 **Planning, Directing, and Controlling**

Planning involves setting goals to guide decisions and help motivate employees. The planning process often identifies where operations can be improved.

Directing involves decisions and actions to achieve budgeted goals. A budgetary unit of a company is called a **responsibility center**. Each responsibility center is led by a manager who has the authority and responsibility for achieving the center's budgeted goals.

Controlling involves comparing actual performance against the budgeted goals. Such comparisons provide feedback to managers and employees about their performance. If necessary, responsibility centers can use such feedback to adjust their activities in the future.

Human Behavior and Budgeting

Human behavior problems can arise in the budgeting process in the following situations:

- Budgeted goals are set too tight, which are very hard or impossible to achieve.
- Budgeted goals are set too loose, which are very easy to achieve.
- Budgeted goals conflict with the objectives of the company and employees.

These behavior problems are illustrated in Exhibit 2.

EXHIBIT 2

Human Behavior Problems in Budgeting

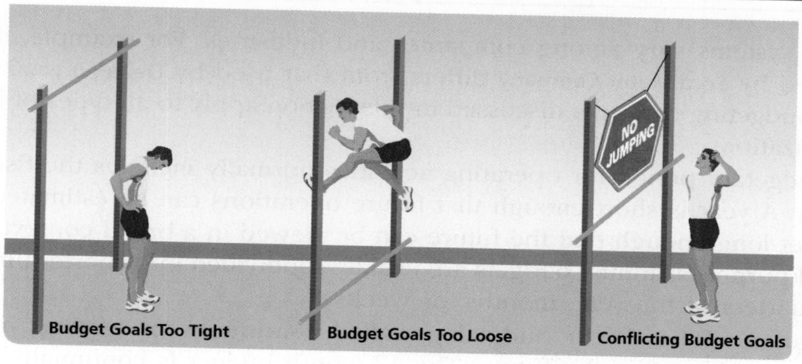

Setting Budget Goals Too Tightly Employees and managers may become discouraged if budgeted goals are set too high. That is, if budgeted goals are viewed as unrealistic or unachievable, the budget may have a negative effect on the ability of the company to achieve its goals.

Reasonable, attainable goals are more likely to motivate employees and managers. For this reason, it is important for employees and managers to be involved in the budgeting process. Involving employees in the budgeting process provides them with a sense of control and, thus, more of a commitment in meeting budgeted goals.

Setting Budget Goals Too Loosely Although it is desirable to establish attainable goals, it is undesirable to plan budget goals that are too easy. Such budget "padding" is termed **budgetary slack**. Managers may plan slack in their budgets to provide a "cushion" for unexpected events. However, slack budgets may create inefficiency by reducing the budgetary incentive to trim spending.

Setting Conflicting Budget Goals **Goal conflict** occurs when the employees' or managers' self-interest differs from the company's objectives or goals. To illustrate, assume that the sales department manager is given an increased sales goal and as a result accepts customers who are poor credit risks. Thus, while the sales department might meet sales goals, the overall firm may suffer reduced profitability from bad debts.

INTEGRITY, OBJECTIVITY, AND ETHICS IN BUSINESS

BUDGET GAMES

The budgeting system is designed to plan and control a business. However, it is common for the budget to be "gamed" by its participants. For example, managers may pad their budgets with excess resources. In this way, the managers have additional resources for unexpected events during the period. If the budget is being used to establish the incentive plan, then sales managers have incentives to understate the sales potential of a territory to ensure hitting their quotas. Other times, managers engage in "land grabbing," which occurs when they overstate the sales potential of a territory to guarantee access to resources. If managers believe that unspent resources will not roll over to future periods, then they may be encouraged to "spend it or lose it," causing wasteful expenditures. These types of problems can be partially overcome by separating the budget into planning and incentive components. This is why many organizations have two budget processes, one for planning resources and another more challenging budget for motivating managers.

Obj. 2 Describe the basic elements of the budget process, the two major types of budgeting, and the use of computers in budgeting.

Budgeting Systems

Budgeting systems vary among companies and industries. For example, the budget system used by Ford Motor Company differs from that used by Delta Air Lines. However, the basic budgeting concepts discussed in this section apply to all types of businesses and organizations.

The budgetary period for operating activities normally includes the fiscal year of a company. A year is short enough that future operations can be estimated fairly accurately, yet long enough that the future can be viewed in a broad context. However, for control purposes, annual budgets are usually subdivided into shorter time periods, such as quarters of the year, months, or weeks.

A variation of fiscal-year budgeting, called **continuous budgeting**, maintains a 12-month projection into the future. The 12-month budget is continually revised by replacing the data for the month just ended with the budget data for the same month in the next year. A continuous budget is illustrated in Exhibit 3.

EXHIBIT 3 **Continuous Budgeting**

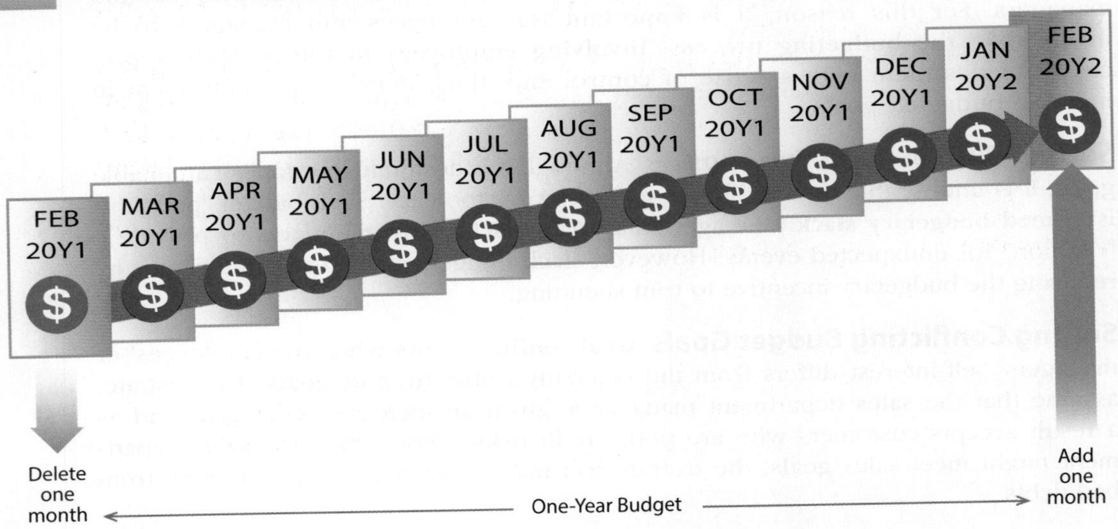

Developing an annual budget usually begins several months prior to the end of the current year. This responsibility is normally assigned to a budget committee. Such a committee often consists of the budget director, the controller, the treasurer, the production manager, and the sales manager. The budget process is monitored and summarized by the Accounting Department, which reports to the committee.

There are several methods of developing budget estimates. One method, called **zero-based budgeting**, requires managers to estimate sales, production, and other operating data as though operations are being started for the first time. This approach has the benefit of taking a fresh view of operations each year. A more common approach is to start with last year's budget and revise it for actual results and expected changes for the coming year. Two major budgets using this approach are the static budget and the flexible budget.

Link to Hendrick Motorsports

Rick Hendrick uses budgeting in **Hendrick Motorsports** as well as the **Hendrick Automotive Group.** The Hendrick Automotive Group is the largest privately held dealership group in the United States with 120 retail franchises.

Static Budget

A **static budget** shows the expected results of a responsibility center for only one activity level. Once the budget has been determined, it is not changed, even if the activity changes. Static budgeting is used by many service companies; by governmental entities; and for some functions of manufacturing companies, such as purchasing, engineering, and accounting.

To illustrate, the static budget for the Assembly Department of Colter Manufacturing Company is shown in Exhibit 4.

EXHIBIT 4

Static Budget

	A	B
1	**Colter Manufacturing Company**	
2	**Assembly Department Budget**	
3	**For the Year Ending July 31, 20Y8**	
4	Direct labor	$40,000
5	Electric power	5,000
6	Supervisor salaries	15,000
7	Total department costs	$60,000
8		

A disadvantage of static budgets is that they do not adjust for changes in activity levels. For example, assume that the Assembly Department of Colter Manufacturing spent $70,800 for the year ended July 31, 20Y8. Thus, the Assembly Department spent $10,800 ($70,800 – $60,000), or 18% ($10,800 ÷ $60,000) more than budgeted. Is this good news or bad news?

The first reaction is that this is bad news and the Assembly Department was inefficient in spending more than budgeted. However, assume that the Assembly Department's budget was based on plans to assemble 8,000 units during the year. If 10,000 units were actually assembled, the additional $10,800 spent in excess of budget might be good news. That is, the Assembly Department assembled 25% (2,000 units ÷ 8,000 units) more than planned for only 18% more cost. In this case, a static budget may not be useful for controlling costs.

SERVICE FOCUS

FILM BUDGETING

Service businesses, like film and entertainment, use budgets as a road map to control expenses. In film production, the budget is a valuable tool to manage the tension between creative expression and cost.

The film budget is a static budget that can be divided into three major categories:

- above the line
- below the line
- post-production costs

The *above the line* costs include costs attributed to creative talent, such as the lead cast's and director's salaries and script fees. The *below the line* costs include the remaining costs to create the film, including location, costume, and prop rentals; permits; and other production costs. The *post-production costs* include the costs to complete the film, including editing, sound, and special effects. Marketing has a separate budget.

The total cost of the film is influenced by many decisions, including the cost of story rights, location, star quality of creative talent, union representation in the production crew, music, and special effects. Even a low-budget indie (independent) documentary could easily have a budget of more than $1 million. In contrast, a special effect-laden Hollywood film could have a budget in excess of $200 million.

Flexible Budget

Note

Flexible budgets show expected results for several activity levels.

Unlike static budgets, **flexible budgets** show the expected results of a responsibility center for several activity levels. A flexible budget is, in effect, a series of static budgets for different levels of activity.

To illustrate, a flexible budget for the Assembly Department of Colter Manufacturing Company is shown in Exhibit 5.

EXHIBIT 5

Flexible Budget

	A	B	C	D
1	**Colter Manufacturing Company**			
2	**Assembly Department Budget**			
3	**For the Year Ending July 31, 20Y8**			
4		**Level 1**	**Level 2**	**Level 3**
5	Units of production	8,000	9,000	10,000 ← Step 1
6	Variable cost:			
7	Direct labor ($5 per unit)	$40,000	$45,000	$50,000
8	Electric power ($0.50 per unit)	4,000	4,500	5,000
9	Total variable cost	$44,000	$49,500	$55,000
10	Fixed cost:			
11	Electric power	$ 1,000	$ 1,000	$ 1,000
12	Supervisor salaries	15,000	15,000	15,000
13	Total fixed cost	$16,000	$16,000	$16,000
14	Total department costs	$60,000	$65,500	$71,000
15				

Step 2 (rows 6–12)

Step 3 (columns B–D)

Link to Hendrick Motorsports

Rick Hendrick started by selling used cars. At age 26, he invested all of his assets in a struggling Chevrolet dealership, becoming the youngest Chevrolet dealer in the United States. This dealership was the predecessor of the Hendrick Automotive Group.

A flexible budget is constructed as follows:

Step 1. Identify the relevant activity levels. The relevant levels of activity could be expressed in units, machine hours, direct labor hours, or some other activity base. In Exhibit 5, the levels of activity are 8,000, 9,000, and 10,000 units of production.

Step 2. Identify the fixed and variable cost components of the costs being budgeted. In Exhibit 5, the electric power cost is separated into its fixed cost ($1,000 per year) and variable cost ($0.50 per unit). The direct labor is a variable cost, and the supervisor salaries are all fixed costs.

Step 3. Prepare the budget for each activity level by multiplying the variable cost per unit by the activity level and then adding the monthly fixed cost.

With a flexible budget, actual costs can be compared to the budgeted costs for actual activity. To illustrate, assume that the Assembly Department spent $70,800 to produce 10,000 units. Exhibit 5 indicates that the Assembly Department was *under* budget by $200 ($71,000 – $70,800).

Under the static budget in Exhibit 4, the Assembly Department was $10,800 *over* budget. This comparison is illustrated in Exhibit 6.

The flexible budget for the Assembly Department is more accurate and useful than the static budget. This is because the flexible budget adjusts for changes in the level of activity. Flexible budgets can be used in service businesses when the variable costs can be associated to an activity. For example, hospital room expenses are related to number of patients, or transportation fuel costs are related to number of miles.

EXHIBIT 6

Static and Flexible Budgets

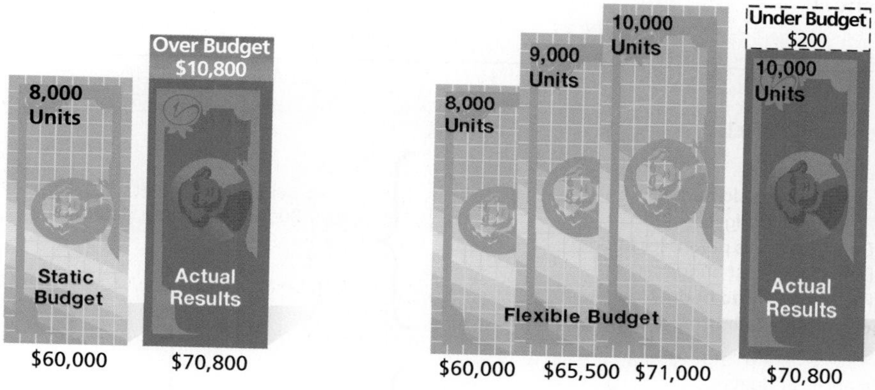

Example Exercise 22-1 Flexible Budgeting **Obj. 2**

At the beginning of the period, the Assembly Department budgeted direct labor of $45,000 and supervisor salaries of $30,000 for 5,000 hours of production. The department actually completed 6,000 hours of production. Determine the budget for the department, assuming that it uses flexible budgeting.

Follow My Example 22-1

Variable cost:	
Direct labor (6,000 hours × $9* per hour)	$54,000
Fixed cost:	
Supervisor salaries	30,000
Total department costs	$84,000

*$45,000 ÷ 5,000 hours

Practice Exercises: PE 22-1A, PE 22-1B

Computerized Budgeting Systems

In developing budgets, companies use a variety of computerized approaches. Two of the most popular computerized approaches use:

- Spreadsheet software such as Microsoft® Excel®
- Integrated budget and planning (B&P) software systems

Spreadsheets ease budget preparation by summarizing budget information in linked spreadsheets across the organization. In addition, the impact of proposed changes in various assumptions or operating alternatives can be analyzed on a spreadsheet.

B&P software systems use the web (intranet) to link thousands of employees during the budget process. Employees can input budget data onto web pages that are integrated and summarized throughout the company. In this way, a company can quickly and consistently integrate top-level strategies and goals to lower-level operational goals.

Obj. 3 Describe the master budget for a manufacturing company.

Master Budget

The **master budget** is an integrated set of operating and financial budgets for a period of time. Most companies prepare a master budget on a yearly basis. Exhibit 7 shows that the operating budgets can be used to prepare a budgeted income statement, while the financial budgets provide information for a budgeted balance sheet.

EXHIBIT 7

Master Budget for a Manufacturing Company

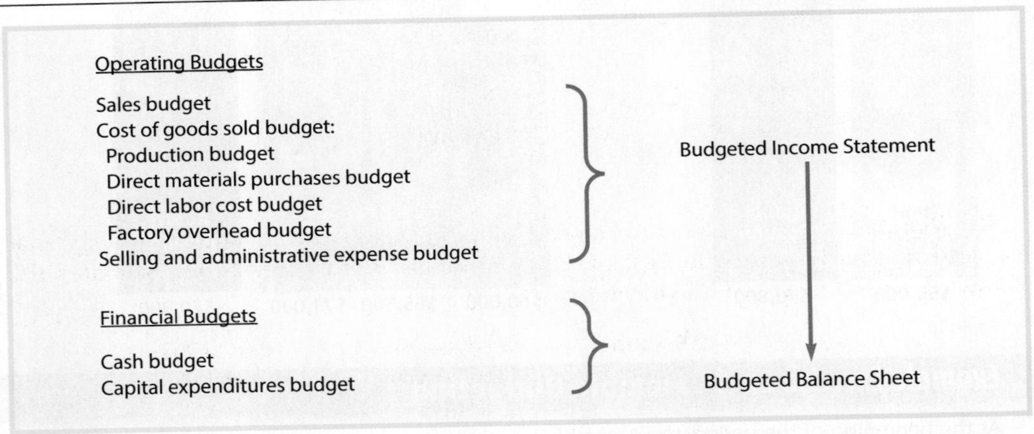

The master budget begins with preparing the operating budgets, which form the budgeted income statement. Exhibit 8 shows the relationships among the operating budgets leading to an income statement budget.

Obj. 4 Prepare the basic operating budgets for a manufacturing company.

Operating Budgets

The integrated operating budgets that support the income statement budget are illustrated for **Elite Accessories Inc.**, a small manufacturing company of personal accessories.

Sales Budget

The **sales budget** begins by estimating the quantity of sales. The prior year's sales are often used as a starting point. These sales quantities are then revised for factors such as planned advertising and promotion, projected pricing changes, and expected industry and general economic conditions.

Once sales quantities are estimated, the budgeted sales revenue can be determined as follows:

$$\text{Budgeted Revenue} = \text{Expected Sales Volume} \times \text{Expected Unit Sales Price}$$

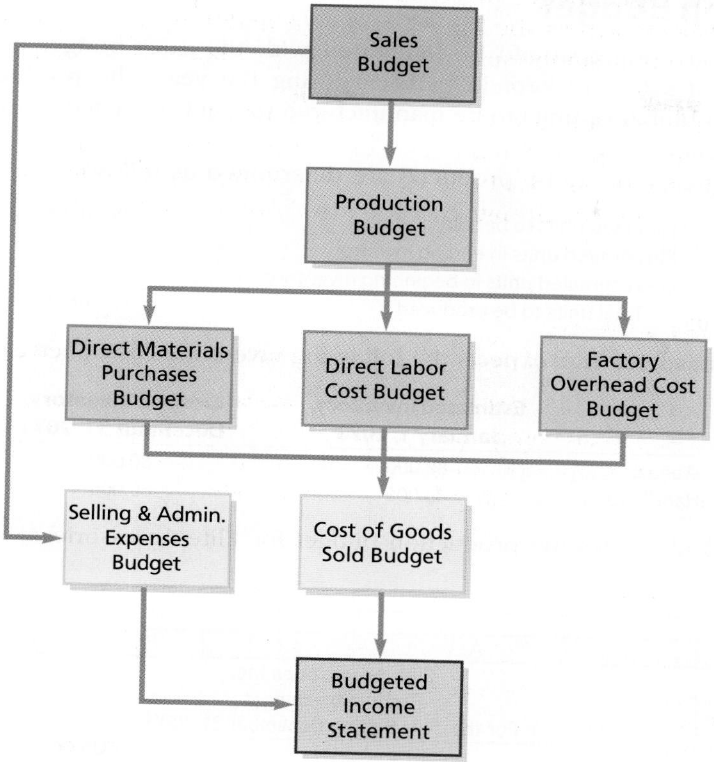

EXHIBIT 8

Operating Budgets

To illustrate, **Elite Accessories Inc.** manufactures wallets and handbags that are sold in two regions, the East and West regions. Elite Accessories estimates the following sales volumes and prices for 20Y1:

	East Region Sales Volume	West Region Sales Volume	Unit Selling Price
Wallets	287,000	241,000	$12
Handbags	156,400	123,600	25

Exhibit 9 illustrates the sales budget for Elite Accessories based on the preceding data.

EXHIBIT 9

Sales Budget

	A	B	C	D
1	**Elite Accessories Inc.**			
2	**Sales Budget**			
3	**For the Year Ending December 31, 20Y1**			
4		**Unit Sales**	**Unit Selling**	
5	**Product and Region**	**Volume**	**Price**	**Total Sales**
6	Wallet:			
7	East	287,000	$12.00	$ 3,444,000
8	West	241,000	12.00	2,892,000
9	Total	528,000		$ 6,336,000
10				
11	Handbag:			
12	East	156,400	$25.00	$ 3,910,000
13	West	123,600	25.00	3,090,000
14	Total	280,000		$ 7,000,000
15				
16	Total revenue from sales			$13,336,000
17				

Link to Hendrick Motorsports

In a recent year, Hendrick Automotive Group generated over $7 billion of revenue across 13 states.

Production Budget

The production budget should be integrated with the sales budget to ensure that production and sales are kept in balance during the year. The **production budget** estimates the number of units to be manufactured to meet budgeted sales and desired inventory levels.

The budgeted units to be produced are determined as follows:

Expected units to be sold	XXX units
Plus desired units in ending inventory	+ XXX
Less estimated units in beginning inventory	– XXX
Total units to be produced	XXX units

Elite Accessories Inc. expects the following inventories of wallets and handbags:

	Estimated Inventory, January 1, 20Y1	Desired Inventory, December 31, 20Y1
Wallets	88,000	80,000
Handbags	48,000	60,000

Exhibit 10 illustrates the production budget for Elite Accessories.

EXHIBIT 10

Production Budget

	A	B	C
1	Elite Accessories Inc.		
2	Production Budget		
3	For the Year Ending December 31, 20Y1		
4		Units	
5		Wallet	Handbag
6	Expected units to be sold (from Exhibit 9)	528,000	280,000
7	Plus desired ending inventory, December 31, 20Y1	80,000	60,000
8	Total units required	608,000	340,000
9	Less estimated beginning inventory, January 1, 20Y1	88,000	48,000
10	Total units to be produced	520,000	292,000
11			

Example Exercise 22-2 Production Budget

Obj. 4

Landon Awards Co. projected sales of 45,000 brass plaques for 20Y5. The estimated January 1, 20Y5, inventory is 3,000 units, and the desired December 31, 20Y5, inventory is 5,000 units. What is the budgeted production (in units) for 20Y5?

Follow My Example 22-2

Expected units to be sold	45,000
Plus desired ending inventory, December 31, 20Y5	5,000
Total units required	50,000
Less estimated beginning inventory, January 1, 20Y5	3,000
Total units to be produced	47,000

Practice Exercises: PE 22-2A, PE 22-2B

Direct Materials Purchases Budget

The direct materials purchases budget should be integrated with the production budget to ensure that production is not interrupted during the year. The **direct materials purchases budget** estimates the quantities of direct materials to be purchased to support budgeted production and desired inventory levels and can be developed in three steps.

Step 1 Determine the budgeted direct material required for production, which is computed as follows:

$$\text{Budgeted Direct Material Required for Production} = \text{Budgeted Production Volume (from Exhibit 10)} \times \text{Direct Material Quantity Expected per Unit}$$

To illustrate, **Elite Accessories Inc.** uses leather and lining in producing wallets and handbags. The quantity of direct materials expected to be used for each unit of product is as follows:

Wallet	Handbag
Leather: 0.30 sq. yd. per unit	Leather: 1.25 sq. yds. per unit
Lining: 0.10 sq. yd. per unit	Lining: 0.50 sq. yd. per unit

For the wallet, the direct material required for production is computed as follows:

Leather: 520,000 units × 0.30 sq. yd. per unit = 156,000 sq. yds.
Lining: 520,000 units × 0.10 sq. yd. per unit = 52,000 sq. yds.

For the handbag, the direct material required for production is computed as follows:

Leather: 292,000 units × 1.25 sq. yd. per unit = 365,000 sq. yds.
Lining: 292,000 units × 0.50 sq. yd. per unit = 146,000 sq. yds.

Step 2 The budgeted material required for production is adjusted for beginning and ending inventories to determine the direct materials to be purchased for each material, as follows:

Materials required for production (Step 1)	XXX
Plus desired ending materials inventory	+XXX
Less estimated beginning materials inventory	–XXX
Direct material quantity to be purchased	XXX

Step 3 The budgeted direct materials to be purchased is computed as follows:

$$\text{Budgeted Direct Material to be Purchased} = \text{Direct Material Quantity to be Purchased (Step 2)} \times \text{Unit Price}$$

Complete Direct Materials Purchases Budget The following inventory and unit price information for **Elite Accessories Inc.** is expected:

	Estimated Direct Materials Inventory, January 1, 20Y1	Desired Direct Materials Inventory, December 31, 20Y1
Leather	18,000 sq. yds.	20,000 sq. yds.
Lining	15,000 sq. yds.	12,000 sq. yds.

The estimated price per square yard of leather and lining during 20Y1 follows:

	Price per Square Yard
Leather	$4.50
Lining	1.20

Exhibit 11 illustrates the complete direct materials purchases budget for Elite Accessories by combining all three steps into a single schedule.

The timing of the direct materials purchases should be coordinated between the Purchasing and Production departments so that production is not interrupted.

EXHIBIT 11

Direct Materials Purchases Budget

Dynamic Exhibit

	A	B	C	D
1	Elite Accessories Inc.			
2	Direct Materials Purchases Budget			
3	For the Year Ending December 31, 20Y1			
4		Direct Materials		
5		Leather	Lining	Total
6	Square yards required for production:			
7	Wallet (Note A)	156,000	52,000	
8	Handbag (Note B)	365,000	146,000	
9	Plus desired ending inventory, December 31, 20Y1	20,000	12,000	
10	Total square yards required	541,000	210,000	
11	Less estimated beginning inventory, January 1, 20Y1	18,000	15,000	
12	Total square yards to be purchased	523,000	195,000	
13	Unit price (per square yard)	× $4.50	× $1.20	
14	Total direct materials to be purchased	$2,353,500	$234,000	$2,587,500
15				
16	Note A: Leather: 520,000 units × 0.30 sq. yd. per unit = 156,000 sq. yds.			
17	Lining: 520,000 units × 0.10 sq. yd. per unit = 52,000 sq. yds.			
18				
19	Note B: Leather: 292,000 units × 1.25 sq. yds. per unit = 365,000 sq. yds.			
20	Lining: 292,000 units × 0.50 sq. yd. per unit = 146,000 sq. yds.			
21				

Step 1 (rows 7–8); Step 2 (rows 9–12); Step 3 (rows 13–14)

Example Exercise 22-3 Direct Materials Purchases Budget

Obj. 4

Landon Awards Co. budgeted production of 47,000 brass plaques in 20Y5. Brass sheet is required to produce a brass plaque. Assume that 96 square inches of brass sheet are required for each brass plaque. The estimated January 1, 20Y5, brass sheet inventory is 240,000 square inches. The desired December 31, 20Y5, brass sheet inventory is 200,000 square inches. If brass sheet costs $0.12 per square inch, determine the direct materials purchases budget for 20Y5.

Follow My Example 22-3

Square inches required for production: Brass sheet (47,000 × 96 sq. in.)	4,512,000
Plus desired ending inventory, December 31, 20Y5	200,000
Total square inches required	4,712,000
Less estimated beginning inventory, January 1, 20Y5	240,000
Total square inches to be purchased	4,472,000
Unit price (per square inch)	× $0.12
Total direct materials to be purchased	$ 536,640

Practice Exercises: PE 22-3A, PE 22-3B

Link to Hendrick Motorsports

Hendrick Motorsports uses sheet metal in building its race cars. "Used" sections of sheet metal (from crashed cars) can be purchased from its online store.

Direct Labor Cost Budget

The **direct labor cost budget** estimates the direct labor hours and related cost needed to support budgeted production. Production managers study work methods to provide estimates used in preparing the direct labor cost budget.

The direct labor cost budget for each department is determined in two steps, as follows:

Step 1 Determine the budgeted direct labor hours required for production, which is computed as follows:

$$\text{Budgeted Direct Labor Hours Required for Production} = \text{Budgeted Production Volume (from Exhibit 10)} \times \text{Direct Labor Hours Expected per Unit}$$

To illustrate, **Elite Accessories Inc.**'s production managers estimate that the following direct labor hours are needed to produce a wallet and handbag:

Wallet	Handbag
Cutting Department: 0.10 hr. per unit	Cutting Department: 0.15 hr. per unit
Sewing Department: 0.25 hr. per unit	Sewing Department: 0.40 hr. per unit

Thus, for the wallet, the budgeted direct labor hours required for production is computed as follows:

Cutting: 520,000 units × 0.10 hr. per unit = 52,000 direct labor hours
Sewing: 520,000 units × 0.25 hr. per unit = 130,000 direct labor hours

For the handbag, the budgeted direct labor hours required for production is computed as follows:

Cutting: 292,000 units × 0.15 hr. per unit = 43,800 direct labor hours
Sewing: 292,000 units × 0.40 hr. per unit = 116,800 direct labor hours

Step 2 Determine the total direct labor cost as follows:

Direct Labor Cost = Direct Labor Required for Production (Step 1) × Hourly Rate

The estimated direct labor hourly rates for the Cutting and Sewing departments for **Elite Accessories Inc.** during 20Y1 follow:

	Hourly Rate
Cutting Department	$12
Sewing Department	15

Complete Direct Labor Cost Budget Exhibit 12 illustrates the direct labor cost budget by combining both steps for **Elite Accessories Inc.**

EXHIBIT 12

Direct Labor Cost Budget

Dynamic Exhibit

		A	B	C	D
	1	**Elite Accessories Inc.**			
	2	**Direct Labor Cost Budget**			
	3	**For the Year Ending December 31, 20Y1**			
	4		**Cutting**	**Sewing**	**Total**
	5	Hours required for production:			
Step 1	6	Wallet (Note A)	52,000	130,000	
	7	Handbag (Note B)	43,800	116,800	
Step 2	8	Total hours required	95,800	246,800	
	9	Hourly rate	× $12.00	× $15.00	
	10	Total direct labor cost	$1,149,600	$3,702,000	$4,851,600
	11				
	12	Note A: Cutting Department: 520,000 units × 0.10 hr. per unit = 52,000 hrs.			
	13	Sewing Department: 520,000 units × 0.25 hr. per unit = 130,000 hrs.			
	14				
	15	Note B: Cutting Department: 292,000 units × 0.15 hr. per unit = 43,800 hrs.			
	16	Sewing Department: 292,000 units × 0.40 hr. per unit = 116,800 hrs.			
	17				

Link to Hendrick Motorsports

Hendrick Motorsports offers an internship program for college students who want to experience and learn the operations of a NASCAR team.

The direct labor needs should be coordinated between the production and personnel departments so that there will be enough labor available for production.

Example Exercise 22-4 Direct Labor Cost Budget

Obj. 4

Landon Awards Co. budgeted production of 47,000 brass plaques in 20Y5. Each plaque requires engraving. Assume that 12 minutes are required to engrave each plaque. If engraving labor costs $11.00 per hour, determine the direct labor cost budget for 20Y5.

Follow My Example 22-4

Hours required for engraving:	
Brass plaque (47,000 × 12 min.)	564,000 min.
Convert minutes to hours	÷ 60 min.
Engraving hours	9,400 hrs.
Hourly rate	× $11.00
Total direct labor cost	$103,400

Practice Exercises: PE 22-4A, PE 22-4B

Factory Overhead Cost Budget

The **factory overhead cost budget** estimates the cost for each item of factory overhead needed to support budgeted production.

Exhibit 13 illustrates the factory overhead cost budget for **Elite Accessories Inc.**

EXHIBIT 13

Factory Overhead Cost Budget

	A	B
1	Elite Accessories Inc.	
2	Factory Overhead Cost Budget	
3	For the Year Ending December 31, 20Y1	
4	Indirect factory wages	$ 732,800
5	Supervisor salaries	360,000
6	Power and light	306,000
7	Depreciation of plant and equipment	288,000
8	Indirect materials	182,800
9	Maintenance	140,280
10	Insurance and property taxes	79,200
11	Total factory overhead cost	$2,089,080
12		

The factory overhead cost budget shown in Exhibit 13 may be supported by departmental schedules. Such schedules normally separate factory overhead costs into fixed and variable costs to better enable department managers to monitor and evaluate costs during the year.

The factory overhead cost budget should be integrated with the production budget to ensure that production is not interrupted during the year.

Cost of Goods Sold Budget

The **cost of goods sold budget** is prepared by integrating the following budgets:

- Direct materials purchases budget (Exhibit 11)
- Direct labor cost budget (Exhibit 12)
- Factory overhead cost budget (Exhibit 13)

In addition, the estimated and desired inventories for direct materials, work in process, and finished goods must be integrated into the cost of goods sold budget.

Elite Accessories Inc. expects the following direct materials, work in process, and finished goods inventories:

	Estimated Inventory, January 1, 20Y1	Desired Inventory, December 31, 20Y1
Direct materials:		
Leather	$ 81,000 (18,000 sq. yds. × $4.50)	$ 90,000 (20,000 sq. yds. × $4.50)
Lining	18,000 (15,000 sq. yds. × $1.20)	14,400 (12,000 sq. yds. × $1.20)
Total direct materials	$ 99,000	$ 104,400
Work in process	$ 214,400	$ 220,000
Finished goods	$1,095,600	$1,565,000

The cost of goods sold budget for Elite Accessories in Exhibit 14 indicates that total manufacturing costs of $9,522,780 are budgeted to be incurred in 20Y1. Of this total, $2,582,100 is budgeted for direct materials, $4,851,600 is budgeted for direct labor, and $2,089,080 is budgeted for factory overhead. After considering work in process inventories, the total budgeted cost of goods manufactured and transferred to finished goods during 20Y1 is $9,517,180. Based on expected sales, the budgeted cost of goods sold is $9,047,780.

EXHIBIT 14

Cost of Goods Sold Budget

Dynamic Exhibit

	A	B	C	D
1	Elite Accessories Inc.			
2	Cost of Goods Sold Budget			
3	For the Year Ending December 31, 20Y1			
4	Finished goods inventory, January 1, 20Y1			$ 1,095,600
5	Work in process inventory, January 1, 20Y1		$ 214,400	
6	Direct materials:			
7	Direct materials inventory,			
8	January 1, 20Y1	$ 99,000		
9	Direct materials purchases (from Exhibit 11)	2,587,500		
10	Cost of direct materials available for use	$2,686,500		
11	Less direct materials inventory,			
12	December 31, 20Y1	104,400		
13	Cost of direct materials placed in production	$2,582,100		
14	Direct labor (from Exhibit 12)	4,851,600		
15	Factory overhead (from Exhibit 13)	2,089,080		
16	Total manufacturing costs		9,522,780	
17	Total work in process during period		$9,737,180	
18	Less work in process inventory,			
19	December 31, 20Y1		220,000	
20	Cost of goods manufactured			9,517,180
21	Cost of finished goods available for sale			$10,612,780
22	Less finished goods inventory,			
23	December 31, 20Y1			1,565,000
24	Cost of goods sold			$ 9,047,780
25				

Direct materials purchases budget

Direct labor cost budget

Factory overhead cost budget

Example Exercise 22-5 Cost of Goods Sold Budget

Obj. 4

Prepare a cost of goods sold budget for Landon Awards Co. using the information in Example Exercises 22-3 and 22-4. Assume that the estimated inventories on January 1, 20Y5, for finished goods and work in process were $54,000 and $47,000, respectively. Also assume that the desired inventories on December 31, 20Y5, for finished goods and work in process were $50,000 and $49,000, respectively. Factory overhead was budgeted for $126,000.

(Continued)

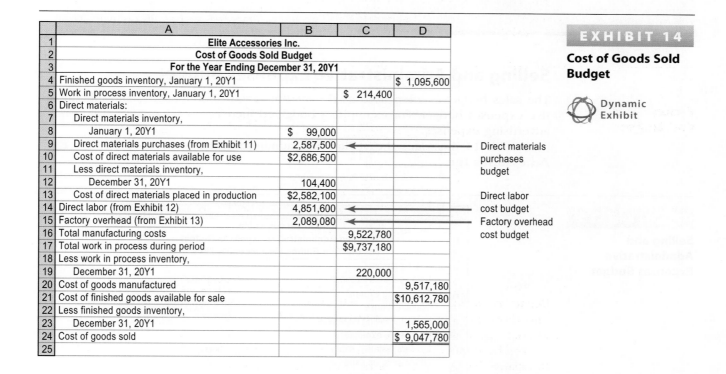

Follow My Example 22-5

Finished goods inventory, January 1, 20Y5			$ 54,000
Work in process inventory, January 1, 20Y5		$ 47,000	
Direct materials:			
Direct materials inventory, January 1, 20Y5 (240,000 × $0.12, from EE 22-3)	$ 28,800		
Direct materials purchases (from EE 22-3)	536,640		
Cost of direct materials available for use	$565,440		
Less direct materials inventory, December 31, 20Y5 (200,000 × $0.12, from EE 22-3)	24,000		
Cost of direct materials placed in production	$541,440		
Direct labor (from EE 22-4)	103,400		
Factory overhead	126,000		
Total manufacturing costs		770,840	
Total work in process during period		$817,840	
Less work in process inventory, December 31, 20Y5		49,000	
Cost of goods manufactured			768,840
Cost of finished goods available for sale			$822,840
Less finished goods inventory, December 31, 20Y5			50,000
Cost of goods sold			$772,840

Practice Exercises: PE 22-5A, PE 22-5B

Selling and Administrative Expenses Budget

The sales budget is often used as the starting point for the selling and administrative expenses budget. For example, a budgeted increase in sales may require more advertising expenses.

Exhibit 15 illustrates the selling and administrative expenses budget for **Elite Accessories Inc.**

EXHIBIT 15

Selling and Administrative Expenses Budget

	A	B	C
1	**Elite Accessories Inc.**		
2	**Selling and Administrative Expenses Budget**		
3	**For the Year Ending December 31, 20Y1**		
4	Selling expenses:		
5	Sales salaries expense	$715,000	
6	Advertising expense	360,000	
7	Travel expense	115,000	
8	Total selling expenses		$1,190,000
9	Administrative expenses:		
10	Officers' salaries expense	$360,000	
11	Office salaries expense	258,000	
12	Office rent expense	34,500	
13	Office supplies expense	17,500	
14	Miscellaneous administrative expenses	25,000	
15	Total administrative expenses		695,000
16	Total selling and administrative expenses		$1,885,000
17			

The selling and administrative expenses budget shown in Exhibit 15 is normally supported by departmental schedules. For example, an advertising expense schedule for the Marketing Department could include the advertising media to be used (newspaper, direct mail, television), quantities (column inches, number of pieces, minutes), and related costs per unit.

Business Connection

MAD MEN

The advertising budget can be one of the largest selling and administrative expenses for a business. The top 200 leading national advertisers accounted for 51% of all advertising dollars for all businesses combined. Of this amount, 68.5% went toward video broadcast advertising, 7.2% for Internet display ads, and 24.3% for print and radio. The top five spenders according to *Advertising Age* were:

Company	U.S. Advertising Spending
Procter & Gamble	$4.6 billion
AT&T	3.3 billion
General Motors	3.1 billion
Comcast	3.0 billion
Verizon	2.5 billion

The advertising budget is segmented between "measured" and "unmeasured" media. Measured media are tracked to determine the number of impressions an ad is receiving due to audience, viewership, or readership counts. Unmeasured media are not counted for impressions and include promotions, direct marketing, and coupons.

A major trend is allocating ad budget dollars toward digital strategies, such as search, social, video, and mobile. These strategies are believed to be more efficient and effective than TV or print. For Colgate-Palmolive, digital went from 2% of the advertising budget in 2006 to 13% in 2014, with expectations of growing to 25%.

Source: Bradley Johnson, "Big Spenders on a Budget: What the Top 200 U.S. Advertisers Are Doing to Spend Smarter," *Advertising Age*, July 5, 2015.

Budgeted Income Statement

The budgeted income statement for Elite Accessories Inc. in Exhibit 16 is prepared by integrating the following budgets:

- Sales budget (Exhibit 9)
- Cost of goods sold budget (Exhibit 14)
- Selling and administrative expenses budget (Exhibit 15)

EXHIBIT 16

Budgeted Income Statement

	A	B	C
1	Elite Accessories Inc.		
2	Budgeted Income Statement		
3	For the Year Ending December 31, 20Y1		
4	Revenue from sales (from Exhibit 9)		$13,336,000
5	Cost of goods sold (from Exhibit 14)		9,047,780
6	Gross profit		$ 4,288,220
7	Selling and administrative expenses:		
8	Selling expenses (from Exhibit 15)	$1,190,000	
9	Administrative expenses (from Exhibit 15)	695,000	
10	Total selling and administrative expenses		1,885,000
11	Income from operations		$ 2,403,220
12	Other revenue and expense:		
13	Interest revenue	$ 98,000	
14	Interest expense	(90,000)	8,000
15	Income before income tax		$ 2,411,220
16	Income tax		600,000
17	Net income		$ 1,811,220
18			

Sales budget (row 4); Cost of goods sold budget (row 5); Selling and administrative expenses budget (rows 8–10)

In addition, estimates of other income, other expense, and income tax are also integrated into the budgeted income statement.

This budget summarizes the budgeted operating activities of the company. In doing so, the budgeted income statement allows management to assess the effects of estimated sales, costs, and expenses on profits for the year.

Obj. 5 Prepare financial budgets for a manufacturing company.

Financial Budgets

While the operating budgets reflect the operating activities of the company, the financial budgets reflect the financing and investing activities. In this section, the following financial budgets are described and illustrated:

- Cash budget
- Capital expenditures budget

Cash Budget

Note

The cash budget presents the expected receipts and payments of cash for a period of time.

The **cash budget** estimates the expected receipts (inflows) and payments (outflows) of cash for a period of time. The cash budget is integrated with the various operating budgets. In addition, the capital expenditures budget, dividends, and equity or long-term debt financing plans of the company affect the cash budget.

To illustrate, a monthly cash budget for January, February, and March 20Y1 for Elite Accessories Inc. is prepared. The preparation of the cash budget begins by estimating cash receipts.

Estimated Cash Receipts The primary source of estimated cash receipts is from cash sales and collections on account. In addition, cash receipts may be obtained from plans to issue equity or debt financing as well as other sources such as interest revenue.

To estimate cash receipts from cash sales and collections on account, a *schedule of collections from sales* is prepared. To illustrate, the following data for Elite Accessories Inc. are used:

	January	February	March
Sales:			
Budgeted sales	$1,080,000	$1,240,000	$970,000
Accounts receivable:			
Accounts receivable January 1, 20Y1	$480,000		
Receipts from sales on account:			
From prior month's sales on account	40%		
From current month's sales on account	60		
	100%		

The budgeted cash collected for any month is the sum of the cash collected from previous month's sales and the cash collected from current month's sales. To illustrate, the cash collected in February is 40% of cash collected on sales in January ($1,080,000 × 40%) added to 60% of cash collected on sales in February ($1,240,000 × 60%), shown as follows:

	January	February
Budgeted sales	$1,080,000	$1,240,000
	× 40%	× 60%
Cash collected from prior month's sales		$432,000
Cash collected from current month's sales		744,000
Total receipts from sales on account		$1,176,000

Using the preceding data, Exhibit 17 shows the schedule of collections from sales for Elite Accessories for all three months. To simplify, it is assumed that all accounts receivable are collected and there are no cash sales.

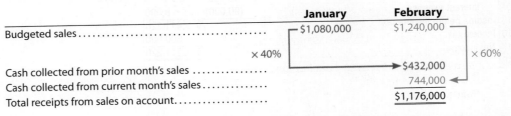

EXHIBIT 17

Schedule of Collections from Sales

	A	B	C	D
1	**Elite Accessories Inc.**			
2	**Schedule of Collections from Sales**			
3	**For the Three Months Ending March 31, 20Y1**			
4		**January**	**February**	**March**
5	Cash collected from prior month's sales—Note A	$ 480,000	$ 432,000	$ 496,000
6	Cash collected from current month's sales—Note B	648,000	744,000	582,000
7	Total receipts from sales on account	$1,128,000	$1,176,000	$1,078,000
8				
9	Note A: $480,000, given as January 1, 20Y1, Accounts Receivable balance			
10	$432,000 = $1,080,000 × 40%			
11	$496,000 = $1,240,000 × 40%			
12				
13	Note B: $648,000 = $1,080,000 × 60%			
14	$744,000 = $1,240,000 × 60%			
15	$582,000 = $970,000 × 60%			
16				

Estimated Cash Payments Estimated cash payments must be budgeted for operating costs and expenses such as manufacturing costs, selling expenses, and administrative expenses. In addition, estimated cash payments may be planned for capital expenditures, dividends, interest payments, or long-term debt payments.

To estimate cash payments for manufacturing costs, a *schedule of payments for manufacturing costs* is prepared. To illustrate, the following data for Elite Accessories Inc. are used:

	January	February	March
Manufacturing Costs:			
Budgeted manufacturing costs	$840,000	$780,000	$812,000
Depreciation on machines included in manufacturing costs	24,000	24,000	24,000
Accounts Payable:			
Accounts payable, January 1, 20Y1	$190,000		
Payments of manufacturing costs on account:			
From prior month's manufacturing costs	25%		
From current month's manufacturing costs	75		
	100%		

The budgeted cash payments for any month are the sum of the cash paid from previous month's manufacturing costs (less depreciation) and the cash paid from current month's manufacturing costs (less depreciation). To illustrate, the cash paid in February is 25% of manufacturing costs (less depreciation) in January [($840,000 – $24,000) × 25%] added to 75% of cash paid on manufacturing costs (less depreciation) in February [($780,000 – $24,000) × 75%], computed as follows:

		January	February	
Budgeted manufacturing costs		$840,000	$780,000	
Less depreciation on machines		24,000	24,000	
Manufacturing costs (less depreciation)		$816,000	$756,000	
Payments of prior month's manufacturing costs (less depreciation)	× 25%		$204,000	× 75%
Payments of current month's manufacturing costs (less depreciation)			567,000	
Total payments			$771,000	

Using the preceding data, Exhibit 18 shows the schedule of payments for manufacturing costs for Elite Accessories for all three months.

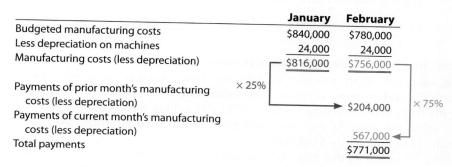

EXHIBIT 18

Schedule of Payments for Manufacturing Costs

	A	B	C	D
1	Elite Accessories Inc.			
2	Schedule of Payments for Manufacturing Costs			
3	For the Three Months Ending March 31, 20Y1			
4		January	February	March
5	Payments of prior month's manufacturing costs			
6	{[25% × previous month's manufacturing costs			
7	(less depreciation)]—Note A}	$190,000	$204,000	$189,000
8	Payments of current month's manufacturing costs			
9	{[75% × current month's manufacturing costs			
10	(less depreciation)]—Note B}	612,000	567,000	591,000
11	Total payments	$802,000	$771,000	$780,000
12				
13	Note A: $190,000, given as January 1, 20Y1, Accounts Payable balance			
14	$204,000 = ($840,000 – $24,000) × 25%			
15	$189,000 = ($780,000 – $24,000) × 25%			
16				
17	Note B: $612,000 = ($840,000 – $24,000) × 75%			
18	$567,000 = ($780,000 – $24,000) × 75%			
19	$591,000 = ($812,000 – $24,000) × 75%			
20				

Completing the Cash Budget The cash budget is structured for a budget period as follows:

Budget Period:

Estimated cash receipts	
– Estimated cash payments	
Cash increase (decrease)	
+ Cash balance at the beginning of the month	
Cash balance at the end of the month	→ Becomes the beginning balance for the next period
– Minimum cash balance	
Excess (deficiency)	

The budgeted balance at the end of the period is determined by adding the net increase (decrease) for the period to the beginning cash balance. The ending balance is compared to a minimum cash balance to support operations as determined by management. Any difference between the ending balance and the minimum cash balance represents an excess or a deficiency that may require management action.

To illustrate, assume the following additional data for **Elite Accessories Inc.**:

Cash balance on January 1, 20Y1	$225,000
Quarterly taxes paid on March 31, 20Y1	150,000
Quarterly interest expense paid on January 10, 20Y1	22,500
Quarterly interest revenue received on March 21, 20Y1	24,500
Sewing equipment purchased in February 20Y1	274,000
Selling and administrative expenses (paid in month incurred):	

January	February	March
$160,000	$165,000	$145,000

The cash budget for Elite Accessories is shown in Exhibit 19.

The estimated cash receipts include the total receipts from sales on account (Exhibit 17) and interest revenue. The estimated cash payments include the cash payments from manufacturing costs (Exhibit 18), selling and administrative expenses, capital additions, interest expense, and income taxes. In addition, assume that the minimum cash balance is $340,000.

Exhibit 19 indicates that Elite Accessories expects a cash excess at the end of January of $28,500. This excess could be invested in temporary income-producing securities such as U.S. Treasury bills or notes. In contrast, the estimated cash deficiency at the end of February of $5,500 might require Elite Accessories to borrow cash from its bank.

EXHIBIT 19

Cash Budget

	A	B	C	D
1	Elite Accessories Inc.			
2	Cash Budget			
3	For the Three Months Ending March 31, 20Y1			
4		January	February	March
5	Estimated cash receipts from:			
6	Collections of accounts receivable			
7	(from Exhibit 17)	$1,128,000	$1,176,000	$1,078,000
8	Interest revenue			24,500
9	Total cash receipts	$1,128,000	$1,176,000	$1,102,500
10	Estimated cash payments for:			
11	Manufacturing costs (from Exhibit 18)	$ 802,000	$ 771,000	$ 780,000
12	Selling and administrative expenses	160,000	165,000	145,000
13	Capital additions (sewing equipment)		274,000	
14	Interest expense	22,500		
15	Income taxes			150,000
16	Total cash payments	$ 984,500	$1,210,000	$1,075,000
17	Cash increase (decrease)	$ 143,500	$ (34,000)	$ 27,500
18	Cash balance at beginning of month	225,000	368,500	334,500
19	Cash balance at end of month	$ 368,500	$ 334,500	$ 362,000
20	Minimum cash balance	340,000	340,000	340,000
21	Excess (deficiency)	$ 28,500	$ (5,500)	$ 22,000
22				

Schedule of collections from sales

Schedule of cash payments for manufacturing costs

Example Exercise 22-6 Cash Budget

Obj. 5

Landon Awards Co. collects 25% of its sales on account in the month of the sale and 75% in the month following the sale. If sales on account are budgeted to be $100,000 for March and $126,000 for April, what are the budgeted cash receipts from sales on account for April?

Follow My Example 22-6

	April
Collections from March sales (75% × $100,000).	$ 75,000
Collections from April sales (25% × $126,000)	31,500
Total receipts from sales on account	$106,500

Practice Exercises: PE 22-6A, PE 22-6B

Capital Expenditures Budget

The **capital expenditures budget** summarizes plans for acquiring fixed assets. Such expenditures are necessary as machinery and other fixed assets wear out or become obsolete. In addition, purchasing additional fixed assets may be necessary to meet increasing demand for the company's product.

To illustrate, a five-year capital expenditures budget for **Elite Accessories Inc.** is shown in Exhibit 20.

EXHIBIT 20

Capital Expenditures Budget

	A	B	C	D	E	F
1	Elite Accessories Inc.					
2	Capital Expenditures Budget					
3	For the Five Years Ending December 31, 20Y5					
4	Item	20Y1	20Y2	20Y3	20Y4	20Y5
5	Machinery—Cutting Department	$400,000			$280,000	$360,000
6	Machinery—Sewing Department	274,000	$260,000	$560,000	200,000	
7	Office equipment		90,000			60,000
8	Total	$674,000	$350,000	$560,000	$480,000	$420,000
9						

As shown in Exhibit 20, capital expenditures budgets are often prepared for five to ten years into the future. This is necessary because fixed assets often must be ordered years in advance. Likewise, it could take years to construct new buildings or other production facilities.

The capital expenditures budget should be integrated with the operating and financing budgets. For example, depreciation of new manufacturing equipment affects the factory overhead cost budget. The plans for financing the capital expenditures also affect the cash budget.

Budgeted Balance Sheet

The budgeted balance sheet is prepared based on the operating and financial budgets of the master budget. The budgeted balance sheet is dated as of the end of the budget period and is similar to a normal balance sheet except that estimated amounts are used. For this reason, a budgeted balance sheet for Elite Accessories Inc. is not illustrated.

At a Glance 22

Obj. 1 **Describe budgeting, its objectives, and its impact on human behavior.**

Key Points Budgeting involves (1) establishing plans (planning), (2) directing operations (directing), and (3) evaluating performance (controlling). In addition, budgets should be established to avoid human behavior problems.

Learning Outcomes	*Example Exercises*	*Practice Exercises*
• Describe the planning, directing, controlling, and feedback elements of the budget process.		
• Describe the behavioral issues associated with tight goals, loose goals, and goal conflict.		

Obj. 2 Describe the basic elements of the budget process, the two major types of budgeting, and the use of computers in budgeting.

Key Points The budget estimates received by the budget committee should be carefully studied, analyzed, revised, and integrated. The static and flexible budgets are two major budgeting approaches. Computers can be used to make the budget process more efficient and organizationally integrated.

Learning Outcomes	Example Exercises	Practice Exercises
• Describe a static budget and explain when it might be used.		
• Describe and prepare a flexible budget and explain when it might be used.	EE22-1	PE22-1A, 22-1B
• Describe the role of computers in the budget process.		

Obj. 3 Describe the master budget for a manufacturing company.

Key Points The master budget consists of operating and financial budgets.

Learning Outcome	Example Exercises	Practice Exercises
• Illustrate the connection between the major operating and financial budgets.		

Obj. 4 Prepare the basic operating budgets for a manufacturing company.

Key Points The basic operating budgets are the sales budget, production budget, direct materials purchases budget, direct labor cost budget, factory overhead cost budget, cost of goods sold budget, and selling and administrative expenses budget. These can then be combined to prepare an income statement budget.

Learning Outcomes	Example Exercises	Practice Exercises
• Prepare a sales budget.		
• Prepare a production budget.	EE22-2	PE22-2A, 22-2B
• Prepare a direct materials purchases budget.	EE22-3	PE22-3A, 22-3B
• Prepare a direct labor cost budget.	EE22-4	PE22-4A, 22-4B
• Prepare a factory overhead cost budget.		
• Prepare a cost of goods sold budget.	EE22-5	PE22-5A, 22-5B
• Prepare a selling and administrative expenses budget.		
• Prepare an income statement budget.		

Obj. 5 Prepare financial budgets for a manufacturing company.

Key Points The cash budget and capital expenditures budget are financial budgets showing the investing and financing activities of the firm.

Learning Outcomes	Example Exercises	Practice Exercises
• Prepare cash receipts and cash payments schedules.	EE22-6	PE22-6A, 22-6B
• Prepare a cash budget.		
• Prepare a capital expenditures budget.		

Illustrative Problem

Selected information concerning sales and production for Cabot Co. for July are summarized as follows:

a. Estimated sales:

Product K:	40,000 units at $30 per unit
Product L:	20,000 units at $65 per unit

b. Estimated inventories, July 1:

Material A:	4,000 lb.	Product K:	3,000 units at $17 per unit	$ 51,000
Material B:	3,500 lb.	Product L:	2,700 units at $35 per unit	94,500
		Total		$145,500

There were no work in process inventories estimated for July 1.

c. Desired inventories at July 31:

Material A:	3,000 lb.	Product K:	2,500 units at $17 per unit	$ 42,500
Material B:	2,500 lb.	Product L:	2,000 units at $35 per unit	70,000
		Total		$112,500

There were no work in process inventories desired for July 31.

d. Direct materials used in production:

	Product K	Product L
Material A	0.7 lb. per unit	3.5 lb. per unit
Material B	1.2 lb. per unit	1.8 lb. per unit

e. Unit costs for direct materials:

Material A:	$4.00 per lb.
Material B:	$2.00 per lb.

f. Direct labor requirements:

	Department 1	Department 2
Product K	0.4 hr. per unit	0.15 hr. per unit
Product L	0.6 hr. per unit	0.25 hr. per unit

g.

	Department 1	Department 2
Direct labor rate	$12.00 per hr.	$16.00 per hr.

h. Estimated factory overhead costs for July:

Indirect factory wages	$200,000
Depreciation of plant and equipment	40,000
Power and light	25,000
Indirect materials	34,000
Total	$299,000

Instructions

1. Prepare a sales budget for July.
2. Prepare a production budget for July.
3. Prepare a direct materials purchases budget for July.
4. Prepare a direct labor cost budget for July.
5. Prepare a cost of goods sold budget for July.

Solution

1.

	A	B	C	D
1	**Cabot Co.**			
2	**Sales Budget**			
3	**For the Month Ending July 31**			
4	**Product**	**Unit Sales Volume**	**Unit Selling Price**	**Total Sales**
5	Product K	40,000	$30.00	$1,200,000
6	Product L	20,000	65.00	1,300,000
7	Total revenue from sales			$2,500,000
8				

2.

	A	B	C
1	**Cabot Co.**		
2	**Production Budget**		
3	**For the Month Ending July 31**		
4		**Units**	
5		**Product K**	**Product L**
6	Expected units to be sold	40,000	20,000
7	Plus desired ending inventory, July 31	2,500	2,000
8	Total units required	42,500	22,000
9	Less estimated beginning inventory, July 1	3,000	2,700
10	Total units to be produced	39,500	19,300
11			

3.

	A	B		C		D
1	**Cabot Co.**					
2	**Direct Materials Purchases Budget**					
3	**For the Month Ending July 31**					
4		**Direct Materials**				
5		**Material A**		**Material B**		**Total**
6	Pounds required for production:					
7	Product K (39,500 × lb. per unit)	27,650	lb.*	47,400	lb.*	
8	Product L (19,300 × lb. per unit)	67,550	**	34,740	**	
9	Plus desired ending inventory,					
10	July 31	3,000		2,500		
11	Total pounds required	98,200	lb.	84,640	lb.	
12	Less estimated beginning inventory,					
13	July 1	4,000		3,500		
14	Total pounds to be purchased	94,200	lb.	81,140	lb.	
15	Unit price (per pound)	× $4.00		× $2.00		
16	Total direct materials to be purchased	$376,800		$162,280		$539,080
17						
18	*27,650 = 39,500 × 0.7 47,400 = 39,500 × 1.2					
19	**67,550 = 19,300 × 3.5 34,740 = 19,300 × 1.8					
20						

(Continued)

4.

	A	B	C	D
1	**Cabot Co.**			
2	**Direct Labor Cost Budget**			
3	**For the Month Ending July 31**			
4		**Department 1**	**Department 2**	**Total**
5	Hours required for production:			
6	Product K (39,500 × hrs. per unit)	15,800 *	5,925 *	
7	Product L (19,300 × hrs. per unit)	11,580 **	4,825 **	
8	Total hours required	27,380	10,750	
9	Hourly rate	×$12.00	×$16.00	
10	Total direct labor cost	$328,560	$172,000	$500,560
11				
12	*15,800 = 39,500 × 0.4 5,925 = 39,500 × 0.15			
13	**11,580 = 19,300 × 0.6 4,825 = 19,300 × 0.25			
14				

5.

	A	B	C	D
1	**Cabot Co.**			
2	**Cost of Goods Sold Budget**			
3	**For the Month Ending July 31**			
4	Finished goods inventory, July 1			$ 145,500
5	Direct materials:			
6	Direct materials inventory, July 1 (Note A)		$ 23,000	
7	Direct materials purchases		539,080	
8	Cost of direct materials available for use		$562,080	
9	Less direct materials inventory, July 31 (Note B)		17,000	
10	Cost of direct materials placed in production		$545,080	
11	Direct labor		500,560	
12	Factory overhead		299,000	
13	Cost of goods manufactured			1,344,640
14	Cost of finished goods available for sale			$1,490,140
15	Less finished goods inventory, July 31			112,500
16	Cost of goods sold			$1,377,640
17				
18	Note A:			
19	Material A 4,000 lb. at $4.00 per lb.	$16,000		
20	Material B 3,500 lb. at $2.00 per lb.	7,000		
21	Direct materials inventory, July 1	$23,000		
22				
23	Note B:			
24	Material A 3,000 lb. at $4.00 per lb.	$12,000		
25	Material B 2,500 lb. at $2.00 per lb.	5,000		
26	Direct materials inventory, July 31	$17,000		
27				

Key Terms

budget (1076)
budgetary slack (1077)
capital expenditures budget (1095)
cash budget (1092)
continuous budgeting (1078)
cost of goods sold budget (1088)
direct labor cost budget (1086)
direct materials purchases budget (1084)
factory overhead cost budget (1088)
flexible budget (1080)
goal conflict (1077)
master budget (1082)
production budget (1084)
responsibility center (1077)
sales budget (1082)
static budget (1079)
zero-based budgeting (1079)

Discussion Questions

1. What are the three major objectives of budgeting?
2. Briefly describe the type of human behavior problems that might arise if budget goals are set too tightly.
3. What behavioral problems are associated with setting a budget too loosely?
4. What behavioral problems are associated with establishing conflicting goals within the budget?
5. Under what circumstances is a static budget appropriate?
6. How do computerized budgeting systems aid firms in the budgeting process?
7. Why should the production requirements set forth in the production budget be carefully coordinated with the sales budget?
8. Why should the timing of direct materials purchases be closely coordinated with the production budget?
9. a. Discuss the purpose of the cash budget.
   b. If the cash for the first quarter of the fiscal year indicates excess cash at the end of each of the first two months, how might the excess cash be used?
10. Give an example of how the capital expenditures budget affects other operating budgets.

Practice Exercises

Example Exercises

EE 22-1 *p. 1081*
Show Me How

PE 22-1A Flexible budgeting

OBJ. 2

At the beginning of the period, the Assembly Department budgeted direct labor of $120,000 and property tax of $16,000 for 5,000 hours of production. The department actually completed 5,600 hours of production. Determine the budget for the department, assuming that it uses flexible budgeting.

EE 22-1 *p. 1081*
Show Me How

PE 22-1B Flexible budgeting

OBJ. 2

At the beginning of the period, the Fabricating Department budgeted direct labor of $9,280 and equipment depreciation of $2,300 for 640 hours of production. The department actually completed 600 hours of production. Determine the budget for the department, assuming that it uses flexible budgeting.

EE 22-2 *p. 1084*
Show Me How

PE 22-2A Production budget

OBJ. 4

Daybook Inc. projected sales of 400,000 personal journals for 20Y6. The estimated January 1, 20Y6, inventory is 20,000 units, and the desired December 31, 20Y6, inventory is 23,500 units. What is the budgeted production (in units) for 20Y6?

EE 22-2 *p. 1084*
Show Me How

PE 22-2B Production budget

OBJ. 4

Magnolia Candle Inc. projected sales of 75,000 candles for 20Y4. The estimated January 1, 20Y4, inventory is 3,500 units, and the desired December 31, 20Y4, inventory is 2,700 units. What is the budgeted production (in units) for 20Y4?

EE 22-3 *p. 1086*
Show Me How

PE 22-3A Direct materials purchases budget

OBJ. 4

Daybook Inc. budgeted production of 403,500 personal journals in 20Y6. Paper is required to produce a journal. Assume six square yards of paper are required for each journal. The estimated January 1, 20Y6, paper inventory is 40,400 square yards. The desired December 31, 20Y6, paper inventory is 38,900 square yards. If paper costs $0.40 per square yard, determine the direct materials purchases budget for 20Y6.

Show Me How EE 22-3 p. 1086

PE 22-3B Direct materials purchases budget

OBJ. 4

Magnolia Candle Inc. budgeted production of 74,200 candles in 20Y4. Wax is required to produce a candle. Assume that eight ounces (one-half of a pound) of wax is required for each candle. The estimated January 1, 20Y4, wax inventory is 2,500 pounds. The desired December 31, 20Y4, wax inventory is 2,100 pounds. If candle wax costs $4.10 per pound, determine the direct materials purchases budget for 20Y4.

Show Me How EE 22-4 p. 1088

PE 22-4A Direct labor cost budget

OBJ. 4

Daybook Inc. budgeted production of 403,500 personal journals in 20Y6. Each journal requires assembly. Assume that eight minutes are required to assemble each journal. If assembly labor costs $13.00 per hour, determine the direct labor cost budget for 20Y6.

Show Me How EE 22-4 p. 1088

PE 22-4B Direct labor cost budget

OBJ. 4

Magnolia Candle Inc. budgeted production of 74,200 candles in 20Y4. Each candle requires molding. Assume that 12 minutes are required to mold each candle. If molding labor costs $14.00 per hour, determine the direct labor cost budget for 20Y4.

Show Me How EE 22-5 p. 1089

PE 22-5A Cost of goods sold budget

OBJ. 4

Prepare a cost of goods sold budget for Daybook Inc. using the information in Practice Exercises 22-3A and 22-4A. Assume the estimated inventories on January 1, 20Y6, for finished goods and work in process were $28,000 and $16,500, respectively. Also assume the desired inventories on December 31, 20Y6, for finished goods and work in process were $30,000 and $14,300, respectively. Factory overhead was budgeted at $214,600.

Show Me How EE 22-5 p. 1089

PE 22-5B Cost of goods sold budget

OBJ. 4

Prepare a cost of goods sold budget for Magnolia Candle Inc. using the information in Practice Exercises 22-3B and 22-4B. Assume that the estimated inventories on January 1, 20Y4, for finished goods and work in process were $9,800 and $3,600, respectively. Also assume that the desired inventories on December 31, 20Y4, for finished goods and work in process were $12,900 and $3,500, respectively. Factory overhead was budgeted at $109,600.

Show Me How EE 22-6 p. 1095

PE 22-6A Cash budget

OBJ. 5

Daybook Inc. collects 30% of its sales on account in the month of the sale and 70% in the month following the sale. If sales on account are budgeted to be $105,000 for September and $116,000 for October, what are the budgeted cash receipts from sales on account for October?

Show Me How EE 22-6 p. 1095

PE 22-6B Cash budget

OBJ. 5

Magnolia Candle Inc. pays 10% of its purchases on account in the month of the purchase and 90% in the month following the purchase. If purchases are budgeted to be $11,900 for March and $12,700 for April, what are the budgeted cash payments for purchases on account for April?

Exercises

EX 22-1 Personal budget

OBJ. 2, 5

✔ a. December 31 cash balance, $3,000

Excel

Show Me How

At the beginning of the school year, Katherine Malloy decided to prepare a cash budget for the months of September, October, November, and December. The budget must plan for enough cash on December 31 to pay the spring semester tuition, which is the same as the fall tuition. The following information relates to the budget:

Cash balance, September 1 (from a summer job)	$5,750
Purchase season football tickets in September	210
Additional entertainment for each month	275
Pay fall semester tuition in September	3,700
Pay rent at the beginning of each month	600
Pay for food each month	235
Pay apartment deposit on September 2 (to be returned December 15)	500
Part-time job earnings each month (net of taxes)	1,400

a. Prepare a cash budget for September, October, November, and December.

b. Are the four monthly budgets that are presented prepared as static budgets or flexible budgets?

c. What are the budget implications for Katherine Malloy?

EX 22-2 Flexible budget for selling and administrative expenses for a service company

OBJ. 2, 4

✔ Total selling and administrative expenses at $400,000 sales, $309,000

Excel

Show Me How

Morningside Technologies Inc. uses flexible budgets that are based on the following data:

Sales commissions	15% of sales
Advertising expense	12% of sales
Miscellaneous administrative expense	$8,000 per month plus 10% of sales
Office salaries expense	$32,000 per month
Customer support expenses	$14,000 per month plus 18% of sales
Research and development expense	$35,000 per month

Prepare a flexible selling and administrative expenses budget for April for sales volumes of $400,000, $500,000, and $600,000.

EX 22-3 Static budget versus flexible budget

OBJ. 2, 4

✔ b. Excess of actual cost over budget for March, $45,750

Excel

Show Me How

The production supervisor of the Machining Department for Niland Company agreed to the following monthly static budget for the upcoming year:

Niland Company
Machining Department
Monthly Production Budget

Wages	$1,125,000
Utilities	90,000
Depreciation	50,000
Total	$1,265,000

The actual amount spent and the actual units produced in the first three months in the Machining Department were as follows:

	Amount Spent	Units Produced
January	$1,100,000	80,000
February	1,200,000	90,000
March	1,250,000	95,000

(*Continued*)

The Machining Department supervisor has been very pleased with this performance because actual expenditures for January–March have been less than the monthly static budget of $1,265,000. However, the plant manager believes that the budget should not remain fixed for every month but should "flex" or adjust to the volume of work that is produced in the Machining Department. Additional budget information for the Machining Department is as follows:

Wages per hour	$15.00
Utility cost per direct labor hour	$1.20
Direct labor hours per unit	0.75
Planned monthly unit production	100,000

a. Prepare a flexible budget for the actual units produced for January, February, and March in the Machining Department. Assume that depreciation is a fixed cost.

b. Compare the flexible budget with the actual expenditures for the first three months. What does this comparison suggest?

EX 22-4 Flexible budget for Assembly Department

OBJ. 2

✔ Total department cost at 18,000 units, $253,700

Excel

Real World

Show Me How

Steelcase Inc. is one of the largest manufacturers of office furniture in the United States. In Grand Rapids, Michigan, it assembles filing cabinets in an Assembly Department. Assume the following information for the Assembly Department:

Direct labor per filing cabinet	12 minutes
Supervisor salaries	$150,000 per month
Depreciation	$24,500 per month
Direct labor rate	$22 per hour

Prepare a flexible budget for 18,000, 20,000, and 22,000 filing cabinets for the month of August in the Assembly Department, similar to Exhibit 5.

EX 22-5 Production budget

OBJ. 4

✔ Bath scale budgeted production, 144,500 units

Show Me How

Weightless Inc. produces a small and large version of its popular electronic scale. The anticipated unit sales for the scales by sales region are as follows:

	Bath Scale	Gym Scale
East Region unit sales	55,000	30,000
West Region unit sales	95,000	60,000
Total	150,000	90,000

The finished goods inventory estimated for October 1 for the Bath and Gym scale models is 18,000 and 10,000 units, respectively. The desired finished goods inventory for October 31 for the Bath and Gym scale models is 12,500 and 8,000 units, respectively.

Prepare a production budget for the Bath and Gym scales for the month ended October 31.

EX 22-6 Sales and production budgets

OBJ. 4

✔ b. Model Rumble total production, 25,750 units

Excel

Show Me How

Sonic Inc. manufactures two models of speakers, Rumble and Thunder. Based on the following production and sales data for June, prepare (a) a sales budget and (b) a production budget:

	Rumble	Thunder
Estimated inventory (units), June 1	750	300
Desired inventory (units), June 30	500	250
Expected sales volume (units):		
East Region	12,000	3,500
West Region	14,000	4,000
Unit sales price	$160	$200

✔ Total professional fees earned, $10,270,000

EX 22-7 Professional fees earned budget for a service company **OBJ. 4**

Rollins and Cohen, CPAs, offer three types of services to clients: auditing, tax, and small business accounting. Based on experience and projected growth, the following billable hours have been estimated for the year ending December 31, 20Y7:

	Billable Hours
Audit Department:	
Staff	22,400
Partners	7,900
Tax Department:	
Staff	13,200
Partners	5,500
Small Business Accounting Department:	
Staff	3,000
Partners	600

The average billing rate for staff is $150 per hour, and the average billing rate for partners is $320 per hour. Prepare a professional fees earned budget for Rollins and Cohen, CPAs, for the year ending December 31, 20Y7, using the following column headings and showing the estimated professional fees by type of service rendered:

Billable Hours	Hourly Rate	Total Revenue

✔ Staff total labor cost, $1,737,000

EX 22-8 Professional labor cost budget for a service company **OBJ. 4**

Based on the data in Exercise 22-7 and assuming that the average compensation per hour for staff is $45 and for partners is $140, prepare a professional labor cost budget for each department for Rollins and Cohen, CPAs, for the year ending December 31, 20Y7. Use the following column headings:

Staff	Partners

✔ Total cheese purchases, $96,603

Excel

Show Me How

EX 22-9 Direct materials purchases budget **OBJ. 4**

Lorenzo's Frozen Pizza Inc. has determined from its production budget the following estimated production volumes for 12" and 16" frozen pizzas for September:

	Units	
	12" Pizza	16" Pizza
Budgeted production volume	12,500	21,800

Three direct materials are used in producing the two types of pizza. The quantities of direct materials expected to be used for each pizza are as follows:

	12" Pizza	16" Pizza
Direct materials:		
Dough	0.80 lb. per unit	1.50 lb. per unit
Tomato	0.50	0.70
Cheese	0.70	1.30

In addition, Lorenzo's has determined the following information about each material:

	Dough	Tomato	Cheese
Estimated inventory, September 1	490 lb.	230 lb.	275 lb.
Desired inventory, September 30	580 lb.	185 lb.	340 lb.
Price per pound	$0.50	$2.20	$2.60

Prepare September's direct materials purchases budget for Lorenzo's Frozen Pizza Inc.

EX 22-10 Direct materials purchases budget

OBJ. 4

✔ Concentrate budgeted purchases, $47,400

Real World

Coca-Cola Enterprises is the largest bottler of Coca-Cola® in Western Europe. The company purchases Coke® and Sprite® concentrate from The Coca-Cola Company, dilutes and mixes the concentrate with carbonated water, and then fills the blended beverage into cans or plastic two-liter bottles. Assume that the estimated production for Coke and Sprite two-liter bottles at the Wakefield, UK, bottling plant is as follows for the month of May:

Coke	153,000 two-liter bottles
Sprite	86,500 two-liter bottles

In addition, assume that the concentrate costs $75 per pound for both Coke and Sprite and is used at a rate of 0.15 pound per 100 liters of carbonated water in blending Coke and 0.10 pound per 100 liters of carbonated water in blending Sprite. Assume that two liters of carbonated water are used for each two-liter bottle of finished product. Assume further that two-liter bottles cost $0.08 per bottle and carbonated water costs $0.06 per liter.

Prepare a direct materials purchases budget for May, assuming that inventories are ignored, because there are no changes between beginning and ending inventories for concentrate, bottles, and carbonated water.

EX 22-11 Direct materials purchases budget

OBJ. 4

✔ Total steel belt purchases, $291,200

Excel

Anticipated sales for Safety Grip Company were 42,000 passenger car tires and 19,000 truck tires. Rubber and steel belts are used in producing passenger car and truck tires as follows:

	Passenger Car	Truck
Rubber	35 lb. per unit	78 lb. per unit
Steel belts	5 lb. per unit	8 lb. per unit

The purchase prices of rubber and steel are $1.20 and $0.80 per pound, respectively. The desired ending inventories of rubber and steel belts are 40,000 and 10,000 pounds, respectively. The estimated beginning inventories for rubber and steel belts are 46,000 and 8,000 pounds, respectively.

Prepare a direct materials purchases budget for Safety Grip Company for the year ended December 31, 20Y8.

EX 22-12 Direct labor cost budget

OBJ. 4

✔ Total direct labor cost, Assembly, $30,660

MatchPoint Racket Company manufactures two types of tennis rackets, the Junior and Pro Striker models. The production budget for March for the two rackets is as follows:

	Junior	Pro Striker
Production budget	2,200 units	7,000 units

Both rackets are produced in two departments, Forming and Assembly. The direct labor hours required for each racket are estimated as follows:

	Forming Department	Assembly Department
Junior	0.10 hour per unit	0.20 hour per unit
Pro Striker	0.15 hour per unit	0.25 hour per unit

The direct labor rate for each department is as follows:

Forming Department	$15.00 per hour
Assembly Department	$14.00 per hour

Prepare the direct labor cost budget for March.

✔ Average weekday total, $2,640

EX 22-13 Direct labor budget for a service business

OBJ. 4

Ambassador Suites Inc. operates a downtown hotel property that has 300 rooms. On average, 80% of Ambassador Suites' rooms are occupied on weekdays and 40% are occupied during the weekend. The manager has asked you to develop a direct labor budget for the housekeeping and restaurant staff for weekdays and weekends. You have determined that the housekeeping staff requires 30 minutes to clean each occupied room. The housekeeping staff is paid $14 per hour. The housekeeping labor cost is fully variable to the number of occupied rooms. The restaurant has six full-time staff (eight-hour day) on duty, regardless of occupancy. However, for every 60 occupied rooms, an additional person is brought in to work in the restaurant for the eight-hour day. The restaurant staff is paid $12 per hour.

Determine the estimated housekeeping, restaurant, and total direct labor cost for an average weekday and average weekend day. Format the budget in two columns, labeled as weekday and weekend day.

✔ a. Total production of 501 Jeans, 53,300

Excel

Real World

EX 22-14 Production and direct labor cost budgets

OBJ. 4

Levi Strauss & Co. manufactures slacks and jeans under a variety of brand names, such as Dockers® and 501® Jeans. Slacks and jeans are assembled by a variety of different sewing operations. Assume that the sales budget for Dockers and 501 Jeans shows estimated sales of 23,600 and 53,100 pairs, respectively, for May. The finished goods inventory is assumed as follows:

	Dockers	501 Jeans
May 1 estimated inventory	670	1,660
May 31 desired inventory	420	1,860

Assume the following direct labor data per 10 pairs of Dockers and 501 Jeans for four different sewing operations:

	Direct Labor per 10 Pairs	
	Dockers	501 Jeans
Inseam	18 minutes	9 minutes
Outerseam	20	14
Pockets	6	9
Zipper	12	6
Total	56 minutes	38 minutes

a. Prepare a production budget for May. Prepare the budget in two columns: Dockers® and 501 Jeans®.

b. Prepare the May direct labor cost budget for the four sewing operations, assuming a $13 wage per hour for the inseam and outerseam sewing operations and a $15 wage per hour for the pocket and zipper sewing operations. Prepare the direct labor cost budget in four columns: inseam, outerseam, pockets, and zipper.

✔ Total variable factory overhead costs, $268,000

Excel

EX 22-15 Factory overhead cost budget

OBJ. 4

Sweet Tooth Candy Company budgeted the following costs for anticipated production for August:

Advertising expenses	$232,000	Production supervisor wages	$135,000
Manufacturing supplies	14,000	Production control wages	32,000
Power and light	48,000	Executive officer salaries	310,000
Sales commissions	298,000	Materials management wages	39,000
Factory insurance	30,000	Factory depreciation	22,000

Prepare a factory overhead cost budget, separating variable and fixed costs. Assume that factory insurance and depreciation are the only fixed factory costs.

EX 22-16 Cost of goods sold budget

OBJ. 4

✓ Cost of goods sold, $3,293,600

Excel

Wilmington Chemical Company uses oil to produce two types of plastic products, P1 and P2. Wilmington budgeted 50,000 barrels of oil for purchase in June for $50 per barrel. Direct labor budgeted in the chemical process was $300,000 for June. Factory overhead was budgeted $500,000 during June. The inventories on June 1 were estimated to be:

Oil	$15,500
P1	25,400
P2	22,900
Work in process	3,400

The desired inventories on June 30 were:

Oil	$16,100
P1	28,500
P2	25,000
Work in process	4,000

Use the preceding information to prepare a cost of goods sold budget for June.

EX 22-17 Cost of goods sold budget

OBJ. 4

✓ Cost of goods sold, $488,360

The controller of MingWare Ceramics Inc. wants to prepare a cost of goods sold budget for September. The controller assembled the following information for constructing the cost of goods sold budget:

Direct materials:	Enamel	Paint	Porcelain	Total
Total direct materials purchases budgeted for September	$36,780	$6,130	$145,500	$188,410
Estimated inventory, September 1	1,240	950	4,250	6,440
Desired inventory, September 30	1,890	1,070	5,870	8,830

Direct labor cost:	Kiln Department	Decorating Department	Total
Total direct labor cost budgeted for September	$47,900	$145,700	$193,600

Finished goods inventories:	Dish	Bowl	Figurine	Total
Estimated inventory, September 1	$5,780	$3,080	$2,640	$11,500
Desired inventory, September 30	3,710	2,670	3,290	9,670

Work in process inventories:	
Estimated inventory, September 1	$3,400
Desired inventory, September 30	1,990

Budgeted factory overhead costs for September:	
Indirect factory wages	$ 81,900
Depreciation of plant and equipment	14,300
Power and light	5,200
Indirect materials	4,100
Total	$105,500

Use the preceding information to prepare a cost of goods sold budget for September.

EX 22-18 Schedule of cash collections of accounts receivable

OBJ. 5

✓ Total cash collected in July, $177,550

Excel

Show Me How

Furry Friends Supplies Inc., a pet wholesale supplier, was organized on May 1. Projected sales for each of the first three months of operations are as follows:

May	$156,000
June	175,000
July	180,000

All sales are on account. Seventy percent of sales are expected to be collected in the month of the sale, 25% in the month following the sale, and the remainder in the second month following the sale.

Prepare a schedule indicating cash collections from sales for May, June, and July.

✔ Total cash collected in October, $675,000

EX 22-19 Schedule of cash collections of accounts receivable **OBJ. 5**

Office World Inc. has "cash and carry" customers and credit customers. Office World estimates that 25% of monthly sales are to cash customers, while the remaining sales are to credit customers. Of the credit customers, 40% pay their accounts in the month of sale, while the remaining 60% pay their accounts in the month following the month of sale. Projected sales for the next three months are as follows:

October	$700,000
November	650,000
December	500,000

The Accounts Receivable balance on September 30 was $290,000.

Prepare a schedule of cash collections from sales for October, November, and December.

✔ Total cash payments in May, $82,880

EX 22-20 Schedule of cash payments for a service company **OBJ. 5**

SafeMark Financial Inc. was organized on February 28. Projected selling and administrative expenses for each of the first three months of operations are as follows:

March	$78,400
April	83,500
May	96,900

Depreciation, insurance, and property taxes represent $10,000 of the estimated monthly expenses. The annual insurance premium was paid on February 28, and property taxes for the year will be paid in June. Seventy percent of the remainder of the expenses are expected to be paid in the month in which they are incurred, with the balance to be paid in the following month.

Prepare a schedule indicating cash payments for selling and administrative expenses for March, April, and May.

✔ Total cash payments in March, $113,740

Excel

EX 22-21 Schedule of cash payments for a service company **OBJ. 5**

EastGate Physical Therapy Inc. is planning its cash payments for operations for the first quarter (January–March). The Accrued Expenses Payable balance on January 1 is $15,000. The budgeted expenses for the next three months are as follows:

	January	February	March
Salaries	$56,900	$ 68,100	$ 72,200
Utilities	2,400	2,600	2,500
Other operating expenses	32,300	41,500	44,700
Total	$91,600	$112,200	$119,400

Other operating expenses include $3,000 of monthly depreciation expense and $500 of monthly insurance expense that was prepaid for the year on May 1 of the previous year. Of the remaining expenses, 70% are paid in the month in which they are incurred, with the remainder paid in the following month. The Accrued Expenses Payable balance on January 1 relates to the expenses incurred in December.

Prepare a schedule of cash payments for operations for January, February, and March.

✔ Total capital expenditures in 20Y2, $4,000,000

Excel

EX 22-22 Capital expenditures budget **OBJ. 5**

On January 1, 20Y2, the controller of Omicron Inc. is planning capital expenditures for the years 20Y2–20Y5. The following interviews helped the controller collect the necessary information for the capital expenditures budget:

Director of Facilities: A construction contract was signed in late 20Y1 for the construction of a new factory building at a contract cost of $10,000,000. The construction is scheduled to begin in 20Y2 and be completed in 20Y3.

Vice President of Manufacturing: Once the new factory building is finished, we plan to purchase $1.5 million in equipment in late 20Y3. I expect that an additional $200,000 will be needed early in the following year (20Y4) to test and install the equipment before we can begin production. If sales continue to grow, I expect we'll need to invest another $1,000,000 in equipment in 20Y5.

Chief Operating Officer: We have really been growing lately. I wouldn't be surprised if we need to expand the size of our new factory building in 20Y5 by at least 35%. Fortunately, we expect inflation to have minimal impact on construction costs over the next four years. In addition, I would expect the cost of the expansion to be proportional to the size of the expansion.

Director of Information Systems: We need to upgrade our information systems to wireless network technology. It doesn't make sense to do this until after the new factory building is completed and producing product. During 20Y4, once the factory is up and running, we should equip the whole facility with wireless technology. I think it would cost us $800,000 today to install the technology. However, prices have been dropping by 25% per year, so it should be less expensive at a later date.

Chief Financial Officer: I am excited about our long-term prospects. My only short-term concern is managing our cash flow while we expend the $4,000,000 of construction costs on the portion of the new factory building scheduled to be completed in 20Y2.

Use this interview information to prepare a capital expenditures budget for Omicron Inc. for the years 20Y2–20Y5.

Problems: Series A

✔ 3. Total revenue from sales, $878,403

Excel

PR 22-1A Forecast sales volume and sales budget **OBJ. 4**

For 20Y6, Raphael Frame Company prepared the sales budget that follows.

At the end of December 20Y6, the following unit sales data were reported for the year:

	Unit Sales	
	8" × 10" Frame	12" × 16" Frame
East	8,755	3,686
Central	6,510	3,090
West	12,348	5,616

Raphael Frame Company
Sales Budget
For the Year Ending December 31, 20Y6

Product and Area	Unit Sales Volume	Unit Selling Price	Total Sales
8" × 10" Frame:			
East	8,500	$16	$136,000
Central	6,200	16	99,200
West	12,600	16	201,600
Total	27,300		$436,800
12" × 16" Frame:			
East	3,800	$30	$114,000
Central	3,000	30	90,000
West	5,400	30	162,000
Total	12,200		$366,000
Total revenue from sales			$802,800

For the year ending December 31, 20Y7, unit sales are expected to follow the patterns established during the year ending December 31, 20Y6. The unit selling price for the 8" × 10" frame is expected to increase to $17, and the unit selling price for the 12" × 16" frame is expected to increase to $32, effective January 1, 20Y7.

Instructions

1. Compute the increase or decrease of actual unit sales for the year ended December 31, 20Y6, over budget. Place your answers in a columnar table with the following format:

	Unit Sales, Year Ended 20Y6		Increase (Decrease) Actual Over Budget	
	Budget	**Actual Sales**	**Amount**	**Percent**
8" × 10" Frame:				
East				
Central				
West				
12" × 16" Frame:				
East				
Central				
West				

2. Assuming that the increase or decrease in actual sales to budget indicated in part (1) is to continue in 20Y7, compute the unit sales volume to be used for preparing the sales budget for the year ending December 31, 20Y7. Place your answers in a columnar table similar to that in part (1) but with the following column heads. Round budgeted units to the nearest unit.

20Y6 Actual Units	Percentage Increase (Decrease)	20Y7 Budgeted Units (rounded)

3. Prepare a sales budget for the year ending December 31, 20Y7.

PR 22-2A Sales, production, direct materials purchases, and direct labor cost budgets **OBJ. 4**

✔ 3. Total direct materials purchases, $1,183,680

Excel

The budget director of Gourmet Grill Company requests estimates of sales, production, and other operating data from the various administrative units every month. Selected information concerning sales and production for March is summarized as follows:

a. Estimated sales for March by sales territory:

Maine:	
Backyard Chef	350 units at $800 per unit
Master Chef	200 units at $1,400 per unit
Vermont:	
Backyard Chef	400 units at $825 per unit
Master Chef	240 units at $1,500 per unit
New Hampshire:	
Backyard Chef	320 units at $850 per unit
Master Chef	200 units at $1,600 per unit

b. Estimated inventories at March 1:

Direct materials:		Finished products:	
Grates	320 units	Backyard Chef	30 units
Stainless steel	1,700 lb.	Master Chef	36 units
Burner subassemblies	190 units		
Shelves	350 units		

(Continued)

c. Desired inventories at March 31:

Direct materials:		Finished products:	
Grates	300 units	Backyard Chef	40 units
Stainless steel	1,500 lb.	Master Chef	26 units
Burner subassemblies	210 units		
Shelves	400 units		

d. Direct materials used in production:

In manufacture of Backyard Chef:	
Grates	3 units per unit of product
Stainless steel	24 lb. per unit of product
Burner subassemblies	2 units per unit of product
Shelves	4 units per unit of product
In manufacture of Master Chef:	
Grates	6 units per unit of product
Stainless steel	42 lb. per unit of product
Burner subassemblies	4 units per unit of product
Shelves	5 units per unit of product

e. Anticipated purchase price for direct materials:

Grates	$16 per unit	Burner subassemblies	$120 per unit
Stainless steel	$8 per lb.	Shelves	$12 per unit

f. Direct labor requirements:

Backyard Chef:	
Stamping Department	0.50 hr. at $18 per hr.
Forming Department	0.60 hr. at $16 per hr.
Assembly Department	1.00 hr. at $15 per hr.
Master Chef:	
Stamping Department	0.60 hr. at $18 per hr.
Forming Department	0.80 hr. at $16 per hr.
Assembly Department	1.50 hrs. at $15 per hr.

Instructions

1. Prepare a sales budget for March.
2. Prepare a production budget for March.
3. Prepare a direct materials purchases budget for March.
4. Prepare a direct labor cost budget for March.

PR 22-3A Budgeted income statement and supporting budgets

OBJ. 4

✔ 4. Total direct labor cost in Fabrication Dept., $44,880

Excel

The budget director of Birds of a Feather Inc., with the assistance of the controller, treasurer, production manager, and sales manager, has gathered the following data for use in developing the budgeted income statement for January:

a. Estimated sales for January:

Birdhouse	6,000 units at $55 per unit
Bird feeder	4,500 units at $75 per unit

b. Estimated inventories at January 1:

Direct materials:		Finished products:	
Wood	220 ft.	Birdhouse	300 units at $23 per unit
Plastic	250 lb.	Bird feeder	240 units at $34 per unit

c. Desired inventories at January 31:

Direct materials:		Finished products:	
Wood	180 ft.	Birdhouse	340 units at $23 per unit
Plastic	210 lb.	Bird feeder	200 units at $34 per unit

d. Direct materials used in production:

In manufacture of Birdhouse:		In manufacture of Bird Feeder:	
Wood	0.80 ft. per unit of product	Wood	1.20 ft. per unit of product
Plastic	0.50 lb. per unit of product	Plastic	0.75 lb. per unit of product

e. Anticipated cost of purchases and beginning and ending inventory of direct materials:

Wood	$8.00 per ft.	Plastic	$1.20 per lb.

f. Direct labor requirements:

Birdhouse:	
Fabrication Department	0.20 hr. at $15 per hr.
Assembly Department	0.30 hr. at $12 per hr.
Bird Feeder:	
Fabrication Department	0.40 hr. at $15 per hr.
Assembly Department	0.35 hr. at $12 per hr.

g. Estimated factory overhead costs for January:

Indirect factory wages	$80,000	Power and light	$8,000
Depreciation of plant and equipment	25,000	Insurance and property tax	2,000

h. Estimated operating expenses for January:

Sales salaries expense	$90,000
Advertising expense	20,000
Office salaries expense	18,000
Depreciation expense—office equipment	800
Telephone expense—selling	500
Telephone expense—administrative	200
Travel expense—selling	5,000
Office supplies expense	250
Miscellaneous administrative expense	450

i. Estimated other income and expense for January:

Interest revenue	$300
Interest expense	224

j. Estimated tax rate: 30%

Instructions

1. Prepare a sales budget for January.
2. Prepare a production budget for January.
3. Prepare a direct materials purchases budget for January.
4. Prepare a direct labor cost budget for January.
5. Prepare a factory overhead cost budget for January.
6. Prepare a cost of goods sold budget for January. Work in process at the beginning of January is estimated to be $29,000, and work in process at the end of January is estimated to be $35,400.
7. Prepare a selling and administrative expenses budget for January.
8. Prepare a budgeted income statement for January.

PR 22-4A Cash budget

OBJ. 5

✔ 1. July deficiency, $2,200

Excel

Show Me How

The controller of Sonoma Housewares Inc. instructs you to prepare a monthly cash budget for the next three months. You are presented with the following budget information:

	May	June	July
Sales	$86,000	$90,000	$95,000
Manufacturing costs	34,000	39,000	44,000
Selling and administrative expenses	15,000	16,000	22,000
Capital expenditures	—	—	80,000

The company expects to sell about 10% of its merchandise for cash. Of sales on account, 70% are expected to be collected in the month following the sale and the remainder the following month (second month following sale). Depreciation, insurance, and property tax expense represent $3,500 of the estimated monthly manufacturing costs. The annual insurance premium is paid in September, and the annual property taxes are paid in November. Of the remainder of the manufacturing costs, 80% are expected to be paid in the month in which they are incurred and the balance in the following month.

Current assets as of May 1 include cash of $33,000, marketable securities of $40,000, and accounts receivable of $90,000 ($72,000 from April sales and $18,000 from March sales). Sales on account for March and April were $60,000 and $72,000, respectively. Current liabilities as of May 1 include $6,000 of accounts payable incurred in April for manufacturing costs. All selling and administrative expenses are paid in cash in the period they are incurred. An estimated income tax payment of $14,000 will be made in June. Sonoma's regular quarterly dividend of $5,000 is expected to be declared in June and paid in July. Management wants to maintain a minimum cash balance of $30,000.

Instructions

1. Prepare a monthly cash budget and supporting schedules for May, June, and July.
2. On the basis of the cash budget prepared in part (1), what recommendation should be made to the controller?

PR 22-5A Budgeted income statement and balance sheet

OBJ. 4, 5

✔ 1. Budgeted net income, $96,600

Excel

As a preliminary to requesting budget estimates of sales, costs, and expenses for the fiscal year beginning January 1, 20Y4, the following tentative trial balance as of December 31, 20Y3, is prepared by the Accounting Department of Regina Soap Co.:

Cash	$ 85,000	
Accounts Receivable	125,600	
Finished Goods	69,300	
Work in Process	32,500	
Materials	48,900	
Prepaid Expenses	2,600	
Plant and Equipment	325,000	
Accumulated Depreciation—Plant and Equipment		$156,200
Accounts Payable		62,000
Common Stock, $10 par		180,000
Retained Earnings		290,700
	$688,900	$688,900

Factory output and sales for 20Y4 are expected to total 200,000 units of product, which are to be sold at $5.00 per unit. The quantities and costs of the inventories at December 31, 20Y4, are expected to remain unchanged from the balances at the beginning of the year.

Budget estimates of manufacturing costs and operating expenses for the year are summarized as follows:

	Estimated Costs and Expenses	
	Fixed (Total for Year)	**Variable (Per Unit Sold)**
Cost of goods manufactured and sold:		
Direct materials	—	$1.10
Direct labor	—	0.65
Factory overhead:		
Depreciation of plant and equipment	$40,000	—
Other factory overhead	12,000	0.40
Selling expenses:		
Sales salaries and commissions	46,000	0.45
Advertising	64,000	—
Miscellaneous selling expense	6,000	0.25
Administrative expenses:		
Office and officers salaries	72,400	0.12
Supplies	5,000	0.10
Miscellaneous administrative expense	4,000	0.05

Balances of accounts receivable, prepaid expenses, and accounts payable at the end of the year are not expected to differ significantly from the beginning balances. Federal income tax of $30,000 on 20Y4 taxable income will be paid during 20Y4. Regular quarterly cash dividends of $0.15 per share are expected to be declared and paid in March, June, September, and December on 18,000 shares of common stock outstanding. It is anticipated that fixed assets will be purchased for $75,000 cash in May.

Instructions

1. Prepare a budgeted income statement for 20Y4.
2. Prepare a budgeted balance sheet as of December 31, 20Y4, with supporting calculations.

Problems: Series B

PR 22-1B Forecast sales volume and sales budget

OBJ. 4

✔ 3. Total revenue from sales, $2,148,950

Excel

Sentinel Systems Inc. prepared the following sales budget for 20Y8:

Sentinel Systems Inc.
Sales Budget
For the Year Ending December 31, 20Y8

Product and Area	Unit Sales Volume	Unit Selling Price	Total Sales
Home Alert System:			
United States	1,700	$200	$ 340,000
Europe	580	200	116,000
Asia	450	200	90,000
Total	2,730		$ 546,000
Business Alert System:			
United States	980	$750	$ 735,000
Europe	350	750	262,500
Asia	240	750	180,000
Total	1,570		$1,177,500
Total revenue from sales			$1,723,500

(Continued)

At the end of December 20Y8, the following unit sales data were reported for the year:

	Unit Sales	
	Home Alert System	**Business Alert System**
United States	1,734	1,078
Europe	609	329
Asia	432	252

For the year ending December 31, 20Y9, unit sales are expected to follow the patterns established during the year ending December 31, 20Y8. The unit selling price for the Home Alert System is expected to increase to $250, and the unit selling price for the Business Alert System is expected to be decreased to $820, effective January 1, 20Y9.

Instructions

1. Compute the increase or decrease of actual unit sales for the year ended December 31, 20Y8, over budget. Place your answers in a columnar table with the following format:

	Unit Sales, Year Ended 20Y8		Increase (Decrease) Actual Over Budget	
	Budget	**Actual Sales**	**Amount**	**Percent**
Home Alert System:				
United States				
Europe				
Asia				
Business Alert System:				
United States				
Europe				
Asia				

2. Assuming that the increase or decrease in actual sales to budget indicated in part (1) is to continue in 20Y9, compute the unit sales volume to be used for preparing the sales budget for the year ending December 31, 20Y9. Place your answers in a columnar table similar to that in part (1) but with the following column heads. Round budgeted units to the nearest unit.

20Y8 Actual Units	Percentage Increase (Decrease)	20Y9 Budgeted Units (rounded)

3. Prepare a sales budget for the year ending December 31, 20Y9.

PR 22-2B Sales, production, direct materials purchases, and direct labor cost budgets

OBJ. 4

✔ 3. Total direct materials purchases, $987,478

Excel

The budget director of Royal Furniture Company requests estimates of sales, production, and other operating data from the various administrative units every month. Selected information concerning sales and production for February is summarized as follows:

a. Estimated sales of King and Prince chairs for February by sales territory:

Northern Domestic:	
King...	610 units at $780 per unit
Prince	750 units at $550 per unit
Southern Domestic:	
King...	340 units at $780 per unit
Prince	440 units at $550 per unit
International:	
King...	360 units at $850 per unit
Prince	290 units at $600 per unit

b. Estimated inventories at February 1:

Direct materials:		Finished products:	
Fabric	420 sq. yds.	King	90 units
Wood	580 linear ft.	Prince	25 units
Filler	250 cu. ft.		
Springs	660 units		

c. Desired inventories at February 28:

Direct materials:		Finished products:	
Fabric	390 sq. yds.	King	80 units
Wood	650 linear ft.	Prince	35 units
Filler	300 cu. ft.		
Springs	540 units		

d. Direct materials used in production:

In manufacture of King:	
Fabric	6.0 sq. yds. per unit of product
Wood	38 linear ft. per unit of product
Filler	4.2 cu. ft. per unit of product
Springs	16 units per unit of product
In manufacture of Prince:	
Fabric	4.0 sq. yds. per unit of product
Wood	26 linear ft. per unit of product
Filler	3.4 cu. ft. per unit of product
Springs	12 units per unit of product

e. Anticipated purchase price for direct materials:

Fabric	$12.00 per sq. yd.	Filler	$3.00 per cu. ft.
Wood	$7.00 per linear ft.	Springs	$4.50 per unit

f. Direct labor requirements:

King:	
Framing Department	1.2 hrs. at $12 per hr.
Cutting Department	0.5 hr. at $14 per hr.
Upholstery Department	0.8 hr. at $15 per hr.
Prince:	
Framing Department	1.0 hr. at $12 per hr.
Cutting Department	0.4 hr. at $14 per hr.
Upholstery Department	0.6 hr. at $15 per hr.

Instructions

1. Prepare a sales budget for February.
2. Prepare a production budget for February.
3. Prepare a direct materials purchases budget for February.
4. Prepare a direct labor cost budget for February.

✔ 4. Total direct labor cost in Assembly Dept., $171,766

Excel

PR 22-3B Budgeted income statement and supporting budgets — OBJ. 4

The budget director of Gold Medal Athletic Co., with the assistance of the controller, treasurer, production manager, and sales manager, has gathered the following data for use in developing the budgeted income statement for March:

a. Estimated sales for March:

Batting helmet	1,200 units at $40 per unit
Football helmet	6,500 units at $160 per unit

(Continued)

b. Estimated inventories at March 1:

Direct materials:		Finished products:	
Plastic	90 lb.	Batting helmet	40 units at $25 per unit
Foam lining	80 lb.	Football helmet	240 units at $77 per unit

c. Desired inventories at March 31:

Direct materials:		Finished products:	
Plastic	50 lb.	Batting helmet	50 units at $25 per unit
Foam lining	65 lb.	Football helmet	220 units at $78 per unit

d. Direct materials used in production:

In manufacture of batting helmet:	
Plastic	1.20 lb. per unit of product
Foam lining	0.50 lb. per unit of product
In manufacture of football helmet:	
Plastic	3.50 lb. per unit of product
Foam lining	1.50 lb. per unit of product

e. Anticipated cost of purchases and beginning and ending inventory of direct materials:

Plastic	$6.00 per lb.
Foam lining	$4.00 per lb.

f. Direct labor requirements:

Batting helmet:	
Molding Department	0.20 hr. at $20 per hr.
Assembly Department	0.50 hr. at $14 per hr.
Football helmet:	
Molding Department	0.50 hr. at $20 per hr.
Assembly Department	1.80 hrs. at $14 per hr.

g. Estimated factory overhead costs for March:

Indirect factory wages	$86,000	Power and light	$4,000
Depreciation of plant and equipment	12,000	Insurance and property tax	2,300

h. Estimated operating expenses for March:

Sales salaries expense	$184,300
Advertising expense	87,200
Office salaries expense	32,400
Depreciation expense—office equipment	3,800
Telephone expense—selling	5,800
Telephone expense—administrative	1,200
Travel expense—selling	9,000
Office supplies expense	1,100
Miscellaneous administrative expense	1,000

i. Estimated other income and expense for March:

Interest revenue	$940
Interest expense	872

j. Estimated tax rate: 30%

Instructions

1. Prepare a sales budget for March.
2. Prepare a production budget for March.
3. Prepare a direct materials purchases budget for March.
4. Prepare a direct labor cost budget for March.

5. Prepare a factory overhead cost budget for March.
6. Prepare a cost of goods sold budget for March. Work in process at the beginning of March is estimated to be $15,300, and work in process at the end of March is desired to be $14,800.
7. Prepare a selling and administrative expenses budget for March.
8. Prepare a budgeted income statement for March.

✔ 1. August deficiency, $9,000

Excel

Show Me How

PR 22-4B Cash budget

OBJ. 5

The controller of Mercury Shoes Inc. instructs you to prepare a monthly cash budget for the next three months. You are presented with the following budget information:

	June	July	August
Sales	$160,000	$185,000	$200,000
Manufacturing costs	66,000	82,000	105,000
Selling and administrative expenses	40,000	46,000	51,000
Capital expenditures	—	—	120,000

The company expects to sell about 10% of its merchandise for cash. Of sales on account, 60% are expected to be collected in the month following the sale and the remainder the following month (second month after sale). Depreciation, insurance, and property tax expense represent $12,000 of the estimated monthly manufacturing costs. The annual insurance premium is paid in February, and the annual property taxes are paid in November. Of the remainder of the manufacturing costs, 80% are expected to be paid in the month in which they are incurred and the balance in the following month.

Current assets as of June 1 include cash of $42,000, marketable securities of $25,000, and accounts receivable of $198,000 ($150,000 from May sales and $48,000 from April sales). Sales on account in April and May were $120,000 and $150,000, respectively. Current liabilities as of June 1 include $13,000 of accounts payable incurred in May for manufacturing costs. All selling and administrative expenses are paid in cash in the period they are incurred. An estimated income tax payment of $24,000 will be made in July. Mercury Shoes' regular quarterly dividend of $15,000 is expected to be declared in July and paid in August. Management wants to maintain a minimum cash balance of $40,000.

Instructions

1. Prepare a monthly cash budget and supporting schedules for June, July, and August.
2. On the basis of the cash budget prepared in part (1), what recommendation should be made to the controller?

✔ 1. Budgeted net income, $114,660

Excel

PR 22-5B Budgeted income statement and balance sheet

OBJ. 4, 5

As a preliminary to requesting budget estimates of sales, costs, and expenses for the fiscal year beginning January 1, 20Y8, the following tentative trial balance as of December 31, 20Y7, is prepared by the Accounting Department of Mesa Publishing Co.:

Cash	$ 26,000	
Accounts Receivable	23,800	
Finished Goods	16,900	
Work in Process	4,200	
Materials	6,400	
Prepaid Expenses	600	
Plant and Equipment	82,000	
Accumulated Depreciation—Plant and Equipment		$ 32,000
Accounts Payable		14,800
Common Stock, $1.50 par		30,000
Retained Earnings		83,100
	$159,900	$159,900

(Continued)

Factory output and sales for 20Y8 are expected to total 3,800 units of product, which are to be sold at $120 per unit. The quantities and costs of the inventories at December 31, 20Y8, are expected to remain unchanged from the balances at the beginning of the year.

Budget estimates of manufacturing costs and operating expenses for the year are summarized as follows:

	Estimated Costs and Expenses	
	Fixed (Total for Year)	**Variable (Per Unit Sold)**
Cost of goods manufactured and sold:		
Direct materials	—	$30.00
Direct labor	—	8.40
Factory overhead:		
Depreciation of plant and equipment	$ 4,000	—
Other factory overhead	1,400	4.80
Selling expenses:		
Sales salaries and commissions	12,800	13.50
Advertising	13,200	—
Miscellaneous selling expense	1,000	2.50
Administrative expenses:		
Office and officers salaries	7,800	7.00
Supplies	500	1.20
Miscellaneous administrative expense	400	2.40

Balances of accounts receivable, prepaid expenses, and accounts payable at the end of the year are not expected to differ significantly from the beginning balances. Federal income tax of $35,000 on 20Y8 taxable income will be paid during 20Y8. Regular quarterly cash dividends of $0.20 per share are expected to be declared and paid in March, June, September, and December on 20,000 shares of common stock outstanding. It is anticipated that fixed assets will be purchased for $22,000 cash in May.

Instructions

1. Prepare a budgeted income statement for 20Y8.
2. Prepare a budgeted balance sheet as of December 31, 20Y8, with supporting calculations.

Cases & Projects

CP 22-1 Ethics in Action

Ethics

The director of marketing for Starr Computer Co., Megan Hewitt, had the following discussion with the company controller, Cam Morley, on July 26 of the current year:

Megan: Cam, it looks like I'm going to spend much less than indicated on my July budget.

Cam: I'm glad to hear it.

Megan: Well, I'm not so sure it's good news. I'm concerned that the president will see that I'm under budget and reduce my budget in the future. The only reason I look good is because we delayed an advertising campaign. Once the campaign hits in September, I'm sure my actual expenditures will go up. You see, we are also having our sales convention in September. Having the advertising campaign and the convention at the same time is going to kill my September numbers.

Cam: I don't think that's anything to worry about. We all expect some variation in actual spending month to month. What's really important is staying within the budgeted targets for the year. Does that look as if it's going to be a problem?

Megan: I don't think so, but just the same, I'd like to be on the safe side.

Cam: What do you mean?

Megan: Well, this is what I'd like to do. I want to pay the convention-related costs in advance this month. I'll pay the hotel for room and convention space and purchase the airline tickets in advance. In this way, I can charge all these expenditures to July's budget. This would cause my actual expenses to come close to budget for July. Moreover, when the big advertising campaign hits in September, I won't have to worry about expenditures for the convention on my September budget. The convention costs will already be paid. Thus, my September expenses should be pretty close to budget.

Cam: I can't tell you when to make your convention purchases, but I'm not too sure it should be expensed on July's budget.

Megan: What's the problem? It looks like "no harm, no foul" to me. I can't see that there's anything wrong with this—it's just smart management.

How should Cam Morley respond to Megan Hewitt's request to expense the advanced payments for convention-related costs against July's budget?

Team Activity

CP 22-2 Team Activity

In a group, find the home page of a state that interests you. The home page will be of the form *www.statename.gov*. For example, the state of Tennessee would be found at www.tennessee.gov. At the home page site, search for annual budget information.

1. What are the budgeted sources of revenue and their percentage breakdown?
2. What are the major categories of budgeted expenditures (or appropriations) and their percentage breakdown?
3. Is the projected budget in balance?

Communication

CP 22-3 Communication

The city of Milton has an annual budget cycle that begins on July 1 and ends on June 30. At the beginning of each budget year, an annual budget is established for each department. The annual budget is divided by 12 months to provide a constant monthly static budget. On June 30, all unspent budgeted monies for the budget year from the various city departments must be "returned" to the General Fund. Thus, if department heads fail to use their budget by year-end, they will lose it. A budget analyst prepared a chart of the difference between the monthly actual and budgeted amounts for the recent fiscal year. The chart was as follows:

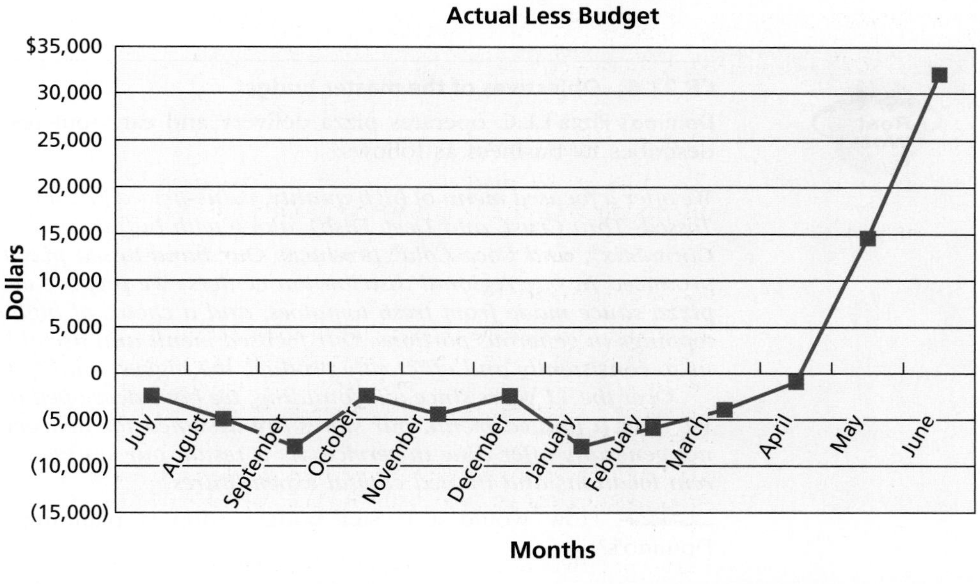

Write a memo to Stacy Collins, the city manager, interpreting the chart and suggesting improvements to the budgeting system.

CP 22-4 Evaluating budgeting systems in a service company

Real World

Children's Hospital of the King's Daughters Health System in Norfolk, Virginia, introduced a new budgeting method that allowed the hospital's annual plan to be updated for changes in operating plans. For example, if the budget was based on 400 patient-days (number of patients × number of days in the hospital) and the actual count rose to 450 patient-days, the variable costs of staffing, lab work, and medication costs could be adjusted to reflect this change. The budget manager stated, "I work with hospital directors to turn data into meaningful information and effect change before the month ends."

a. What budgeting methods are being used under the new approach?

b. Why are these methods superior to the former approaches?

CP 22-5 Static budget for a service company

A bank manager of City Savings Bank Inc. uses the managerial accounting system to track the costs of operating the various departments within the bank. The departments include Cash Management, Trust, Commercial Loans, Mortgage Loans, Operations, Credit Card, and Branch Services. The static budget and actual results for the Operations Department are as follows:

Resources	Budget	Actual
Salaries	$200,000	$200,000
Benefits	30,000	30,000
Supplies	45,000	42,000
Travel	20,000	30,000
Training	25,000	35,000
Overtime	25,000	20,000
Total	$345,000	$357,000
Excess of actual over budget		$ 12,000

a. What information is provided by the budget? Specifically, what questions can the bank manager ask of the Operations Department manager?

b. What information does the static budget fail to provide? Specifically, could the budget information be presented differently to provide even more insight for the bank manager?

CP 22-6 Objectives of the master budget

Real World

Domino's Pizza L.L.C. operates pizza delivery and carry-out restaurants. The annual report describes its business as follows:

We offer a focused menu of high-quality, value-priced pizza with three types of crust (Hand-Tossed, Thin Crust, and Deep Dish), along with buffalo wings, bread sticks, cheesy bread, CinnaStix®, and Coca-Cola® products. Our hand-tossed pizza is made from fresh dough produced in our regional distribution centers. We prepare every pizza using real cheese, pizza sauce made from fresh tomatoes, and a choice of high-quality meat and vegetable toppings in generous portions. Our focused menu and use of premium ingredients enable us to consistently and efficiently produce the highest-quality pizza.

Over the 41 years since our founding, we have developed a simple, cost-efficient model. We offer a limited menu, our stores are designed for delivery and carry-out, and we do not generally offer dine-in service. As a result, our stores require relatively small, lower-rent locations and limited capital expenditures.

How would a master budget support planning, directing, and control for Domino's?

CHAPTER 23

Evaluating Variances from Standard Costs

Concepts and Principles

Chapter 18 *Introduction to Managerial Accounting*

Developing Information

COST SYSTEMS

Chapter 19 *Job Order Costing*
Chapter 20 *Process Costing*

COST BEHAVIOR

Chapter 21 *Cost-Volume-Profit Analysis*

Decision Making

EVALUATING PERFORMANCE

Chapter 22 *Budgeting*
Chapter 23 ***Variances from Standard Costs***

COMPARING ALTERNATIVES

Chapter 24 *Decentralized Operations*
Chapter 25 *Differential Analysis, Product Pricing, and Activity-Based Costing*
Chapter 26 *Capital Investment Analysis*

PHOTOEDIT/ALAMY STOCK PHOTO

CHAPTER 23

BMW Group—Mini Cooper

When you play a sport, you are evaluated with respect to how well you perform compared to a standard or to a competitor. In bowling, for example, your score is compared to a perfect score of 300 or to the scores of your competitors. In this class, you are compared to performance standards. These standards are often described in terms of letter grades, which provide a measure of how well you achieved the class objectives. In your job, you are also evaluated according to performance standards.

Just as your class performance is evaluated, managers are evaluated according to goals and plans. For example, the **BMW Group** uses manufacturing standards at its automobile assembly plants to guide performance. The Mini Cooper, a BMW Group car, is manufactured in a modern facility in Oxford, England. A number of performance targets are used in this plant. For example, the bodyshell is welded by more than 250 robots so as to be two to three times stiffer than rival cars. In addition, the bodyshell dimensions are tested to the accuracy of the width of a human hair. Such performance standards are not surprising given the automotive racing background of John W. Cooper, the designer of the original Mini Cooper.

If you want to get a view of the BMW manufacturing process, go to the BMW website and search the phrase "How an automobile is born."

Performance is often measured as the difference between actual results and planned results. In this chapter, we will discuss and illustrate the ways in which business performance is evaluated.

Learning Objectives

After studying this chapter, you should be able to:

Example Exercises (EE) are shown in **green.**

Obj. 1 **Describe the types of standards and how they are established.**

Standards
Setting Standards
Types of Standards
Reviewing and Revising Standards
Criticisms of Standard Costs

Obj. 2 **Describe and illustrate how standards are used in budgeting.**

Budgetary Performance Evaluation
Budget Performance Report
Manufacturing Cost Variances

Obj. 3 **Compute and interpret direct materials and direct labor variances.**

Direct Materials and Direct Labor Variances
Direct Materials Variances — EE 23-1
Direct Labor Variances — EE 23-2

Obj. 4 **Compute and interpret factory overhead controllable and volume variances.**

Factory Overhead Variances
The Factory Overhead Flexible Budget
Variable Factory Overhead Controllable Variance — EE 23-3
Fixed Factory Overhead Volume Variance — EE 23-4
Reporting Factory Overhead Variances
Factory Overhead Account

Obj. 5 **Journalize the entries for recording standards in the accounts and prepare an income statement that includes variances from standard.**

Recording and Reporting Variances from Standards
Prepare Standard Cost Journal Entries — EE 23-5
Prepare Income Statement with Variances — EE 23-6

Obj. 6 **Describe and provide examples of nonfinancial performance measures.**

Nonfinancial Performance Measures
Identify Activity Inputs and Outputs — EE 23-7

At a Glance 23 Page 1148

Obj. 1 Describe the types of standards and how they are established.

Standards

Standards are performance goals. Manufacturing companies normally use **standard cost** for each of the three following product costs:

- Direct materials
- Direct labor
- Factory overhead

Accounting systems that use standards for product costs are called **standard cost systems**. Standard cost systems enable management to determine the following:

- How much a product *should* cost (standard cost)
- How much it does cost (actual cost)

When actual costs are compared with standard costs, the exceptions or cost variances are reported. This reporting by the *principle of exceptions* allows management to focus on correcting the cost variances.

Link to BMW Group

BMW began in Germany in the early 1900s as a manufacturer of airplane engines. The BMW emblem, which was first used in 1917, represents a rotating airplane propeller with the white and blue state colors of Bavaria.

Setting Standards

The standard-setting process normally requires the joint efforts of accountants, engineers, and other management personnel. The accountant converts the results of judgments and process studies into dollars and cents. Engineers with the aid of operation managers identify the materials, labor, and machine requirements needed to produce the product. For example, engineers estimate direct materials by studying the product specifications and estimating normal spoilage. Time and motion studies may be used to determine the direct labor required for each manufacturing operation. Engineering studies may also be used to determine standards for factory overhead, such as the amount of power needed to operate machinery.

Types of Standards

Standards imply an acceptable level of production efficiency. One of the major objectives in setting standards is to motivate employees to achieve efficient operations.

Ideal standards, or *theoretical standards*, are standards that can be achieved only under perfect operating conditions, such as no idle time, no machine breakdowns, and no materials spoilage. Such standards may have a negative impact on performance because they may be viewed by employees as unrealistic.

Currently attainable standards, sometimes called *normal standards*, are standards that can be attained with reasonable effort. Such standards, which are used by most companies, allow for normal production difficulties and mistakes. When reasonable standards are used, employees focus more on cost and are more likely to put forth their best efforts.

An example from the game of golf illustrates the distinction between ideal and normal standards. In golf, *par* is an ideal standard for most players. Each player's USGA (United States Golf Association) handicap is the player's normal standard. The motivation of average players is to beat their handicaps because beating par is unrealistic for most players.

Reviewing and Revising Standards

Standard costs should be reviewed periodically to ensure that they reflect current operating conditions. Standards should not be revised, however, just because they differ from actual costs. For example, the direct labor standard would not be revised just because employees are unable to meet properly set standards. On the other hand, standards should be revised when prices, product designs, labor rates, or manufacturing methods change.

INTEGRITY, OBJECTIVITY, AND ETHICS IN BUSINESS

COMPANY REPUTATION: THE BEST OF THE BEST

Harris Interactive annually ranks American corporations in terms of reputation. The ranking is based on how respondents rate corporations on 20 attributes in six major areas. The six areas are emotional appeal, products and services, financial performance, workplace environment, social responsibility, and vision and leadership. What are the five highest ranked companies in a recent survey? The five highest (best) ranked companies were Amazon.com, Apple Inc., Alphabet (Google), USAA, and The Walt Disney Company.

Source: Harris Interactive, February 2016.

Criticisms of Standard Costs

Some criticisms of using standard costs for performance evaluation include the following:

- Standards limit operating improvements by discouraging improvement beyond the standard.
- Standards are too difficult to maintain in a dynamic manufacturing environment, resulting in "stale standards."

Link to BMW Group

In addition to BMW, Mini Cooper, and Rolls-Royce automobiles, the BMW Group manufactures motorcycles.

- Standards can cause employees to lose sight of the larger objectives of the organization by focusing only on efficiency improvement.
- Standards can cause employees to focus unduly on their own operations to the possible harm of other operations that rely on them.

Regardless of these criticisms, standards are used widely. In addition, standard costs are only one part of the performance evaluation system used by most companies. As discussed in this chapter, other nonfinancial performance measures are often used to supplement standard costs, with the result that many of the preceding criticisms are overcome.

Business Connection

STANDARD COSTING IN ACTION: EXPANDING BREWING OPERATIONS

In 2011, U.S. West Coast craft brewers Sierra Nevada (CA) and New Belgium (CO) announced plans to expand their brewing operations to the Asheville, North Carolina, area. Both companies considered the standard cost of their product when making the decision to expand and in selecting Asheville as their East Coast location. The standard price of direct materials includes the cost of shipping direct materials to the manufacturers' place of business. The Asheville location was desirable when considering these costs.

In addition, New Belgium projected that its Fort Collins, Colorado, brewery would reach maximum capacity in three to five years. While consistently operating at 100% capacity creates a favorable overhead volume variance, it also can make it difficult to meet customer demand. Thus, New Belgium thought that adding a new brewery prior to reaching 100% capacity at Fort Collins was supported. In both cases, standard costing was used to support the expansion and location decisions.

Sources: H. Dornbusch, "The Case for Low Mileage Beer," www.brewersassociation.org; J. McCurry, "Hops City: Beer Culture Comes to a Head in the Asheville Region," *Site Selection*, July 2012; and J. Shikes, "New Belgium, Maker of Fat Tire, Plans a Second Brewery on the East Coast," *Denver Westword*, May 19, 2011.

Obj. 2 Describe and illustrate how standards are used in budgeting.

Budgetary Performance Evaluation

As discussed in Chapter 22, the master budget assists a company in planning, directing, and controlling performance. The control function, or budgetary performance evaluation, compares the actual performance against the budget.

To illustrate, **Western Rider Inc.**, a manufacturer of blue jeans, uses standard costs in its budgets. The standards for direct materials, direct labor, and factory overhead are separated into the following two components:

- Standard price
- Standard quantity

The standard cost per unit for direct materials, direct labor, and factory overhead is computed as follows:

$$\text{Standard Cost per Unit} = \text{Standard Price} \times \text{Standard Quantity}$$

Western Rider's standard costs per unit for its XL jeans are shown in Exhibit 1.

As shown in Exhibit 1, the standard cost per unit (pair) of XL jeans is $19.50, which consists of $7.50 for direct materials, $7.20 for direct labor, and $4.80 for factory overhead.

The standard price and standard quantity are separated for each product cost. For example, Exhibit 1 indicates that for each unit (pair) of XL jeans, the standard price for direct materials is $5.00 per square yard and the standard quantity is 1.5 square yards.

EXHIBIT 1

Standard Cost for XL Jeans

Manufacturing Costs	Standard Price	×	Standard Quantity per Unit	=	Standard Cost per Unit of XL Jeans
Direct materials	$5.00 per sq. yd.	×	1.5 sq. yds.	=	$ 7.50
Direct labor	$9.00 per hr.	×	0.80 hr. per unit	=	7.20
Factory overhead	$6.00 per hr.	×	0.80 hr. per unit	=	4.80
Total standard cost per unit					$19.50

The standard price and quantity are separated because the department responsible for their control is normally different. For example, the direct materials price per square yard is controlled by the Purchasing Department, and the direct materials quantity per unit is controlled by the Production Department.

As illustrated in Chapter 22, the master budget is prepared based on planned sales and production. The budgeted costs for materials purchases, direct labor, and factory overhead are determined by multiplying their standard costs per unit by the planned level of production. Budgeted (standard) costs are then compared to actual costs during the year for control purposes.

Budget Performance Report

The differences between actual and standard costs are called **cost variances**. A **favorable cost variance** occurs when the actual cost is less than the standard cost. An **unfavorable cost variance** occurs when the actual cost exceeds the standard cost. These cost variances are illustrated in Exhibit 2.

EXHIBIT 2

Cost Variances

Favorable Cost Variance	Unfavorable Cost Variance
Actual cost < Standard cost at actual volumes	Actual cost > Standard cost at actual volumes

The report that summarizes actual costs, standard costs, and the differences for the units produced is called a **budget performance report**. To illustrate, assume that **Western Rider Inc.** reported the following actual production data during June:

XL jeans produced and sold		5,000 units
Actual costs incurred in June:		
Direct materials	$ 40,150	
Direct labor	38,500	
Factory overhead	22,400	
Total costs incurred	$101,050	

Exhibit 3 illustrates the budget performance report for June for Western Rider.

The budget performance report shown in Exhibit 3 is based on the actual units produced in June of 5,000 XL jeans. Even though 6,000 XL jeans might have been *planned* for production, the budget performance report is based on *actual* production.

Manufacturing Cost Variances

The **total manufacturing cost variance** is the difference between total standard costs and total actual cost for the units produced. As shown in Exhibit 3, the total manufacturing cost unfavorable variance is $3,550, which consists of an unfavorable direct

EXHIBIT 3

Budget Performance Report

Western Rider Inc.
Budget Performance Report
For the Month Ended June 30

Manufacturing Costs	Actual Costs	Standard Cost at Actual Volume (5,000 units of XL Jeans)*	Cost Variance—(Favorable) Unfavorable
Direct materials	$ 40,150	$37,500	$ 2,650
Direct labor	38,500	36,000	2,500
Factory overhead	22,400	24,000	(1,600)
Total manufacturing costs	$101,050	$97,500	$ 3,550

*5,000 units × $7.50 per unit = $37,500
5,000 units × $7.20 per unit = $36,000
5,000 units × $4.80 per unit = $24,000

materials cost variance of $2,650, an unfavorable direct labor cost variance of $2,500, and a favorable factory overhead cost variance of $1,600.

For control purposes, each product cost variance is separated into two additional variances as shown in Exhibit 4.

EXHIBIT 4

Manufacturing Cost Variances

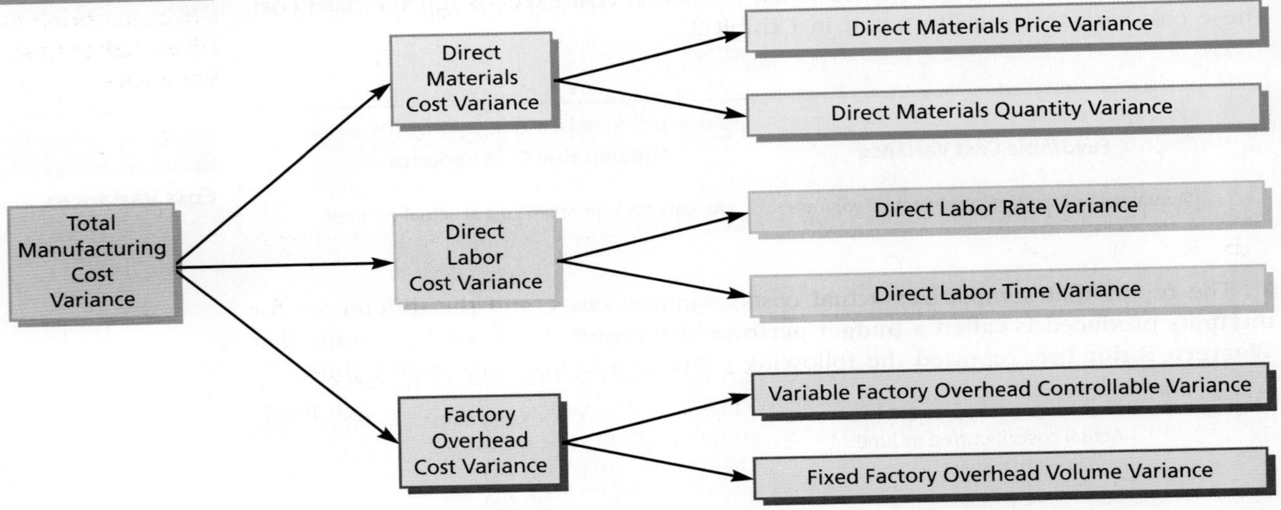

The total direct materials variance is separated into a *price* variance and a *quantity* variance. This is because standard and actual direct materials costs are computed as follows:

Actual Direct Materials Cost = Actual Price × Actual Quantity
Standard Direct Materials Cost = Standard Price × Standard Quantity

Thus, the actual and standard direct materials costs may differ because of a price difference (Actual Price − Standard Price), a quantity difference (Actual Quantity − Standard Quantity), or both.

Likewise, the total direct labor variance is separated into a *rate* variance and a *time* variance. This is because standard and actual direct labor costs are computed as follows:

Actual Direct Labor Cost = Actual Rate × Actual Time
Standard Direct Labor Cost = Standard Rate × Standard Time

Therefore, the actual and standard direct labor costs may differ because of a rate difference (Actual Rate – Standard Rate), a time difference (Actual Time – Standard Time), or both.

The total factory overhead variance is separated into a *controllable* variance and a *volume* variance. Because factory overhead has fixed and variable cost elements, it uses different variances than direct materials and direct labor, which are variable costs.

In the next sections, the price and quantity variances for direct materials, the rate and time variances for direct labor, and the controllable and volume variances for factory overhead are further described and illustrated.

Link to BMW Group

BMW's Spartanburg, South Carolina, plant employs 8,000 workers in its 6 million-square-foot facility where it manufactures X3 and X5 SUVs. Visitors may tour the manufacturing plant and company museum.

Direct Materials and Direct Labor Variances

Obj. 3 Compute and interpret direct materials and direct labor variances.

As indicated in the prior section, the total direct materials and direct labor variances are separated into the direct materials cost and direct labor cost variances for analysis and control purposes. These variances are illustrated in Exhibit 5.

EXHIBIT 5

Direct Materials and Direct Labor Cost Variances

Total Direct Materials Cost Variance	→	Direct Materials Price Variance Direct Materials Quantity Variance
Total Direct Labor Cost Variance	→	Direct Labor Rate Variance Direct Labor Time Variance

As a basis for illustration, the variances for Western Rider's June operations shown in Exhibit 3 are used.

Direct Materials Variances

During June, **Western Rider Inc.** reported an unfavorable total direct materials cost variance of $2,650 for the production of 5,000 XL style jeans, as shown in Exhibit 3. This variance was based on the following actual and standard costs:

Actual costs	$40,150
Standard costs	37,500
Total direct materials cost variance	$ 2,650

The actual costs incurred of $40,150 consist of the following:

Actual Direct Materials Cost = Actual Price × Actual Quantity
= ($5.50 per sq. yd.) × (7,300 sq. yds.)
= $40,150

The standard costs of $37,500 consist of the following:

Standard Direct Materials Cost = Standard Price × Standard Quantity
= $5.00 per sq. yd. × 7,500 sq. yds.
= $37,500

The standard price of $5.00 per square yard is established by management as shown in Exhibit 1. In addition, Exhibit 1 indicates that 1.5 square yards is the standard quantity of materials for one unit (pair) of XL jeans. Thus, 7,500 (5,000 units × 1.5 yards per unit) square yards is the standard quantity of materials for producing 5,000 units (pairs) of XL jeans.

Comparing the actual and standard cost computations indicates that the total direct materials unfavorable cost variance of $2,650 is caused by the following:

- A price per square yard of $0.50 ($5.50 – $5.00) more than standard
- A quantity usage of 200 square yards (7,300 sq. yds. – 7,500 sq. yds.) less than standard

The impact of these differences from standard is reported and analyzed as a direct materials *price* variance and direct materials *quantity* variance.

Direct Materials Price Variance The **direct materials price variance** is computed as follows:

Direct Materials Price Variance = (Actual Price – Standard Price) × Actual Quantity

If the actual price per unit exceeds the standard price per unit, the variance is unfavorable. This positive amount (unfavorable variance) can be thought of as increasing costs (a debit). If the actual price per unit is less than the standard price per unit, the variance is favorable. This negative amount (favorable variance) can be thought of as decreasing costs (a credit).

To illustrate, the direct materials price variance for **Western Rider Inc.** for June is $3,650 (unfavorable), computed as follows:[1]

Direct Materials Price Variance = (Actual Price – Standard Price) × Actual Quantity
= ($5.50 – $5.00) × 7,300 sq. yds.
= $3,650 Unfavorable Variance

Direct Materials Quantity Variance The **direct materials quantity variance** is computed as follows:

Direct Materials Quantity Variance = (Actual Quantity – Standard Quantity) × Standard Price

Link to BMW Group

Steel and aluminum are pressed into doors and side panels in BMW's stamping facility.

If the actual quantity for the units produced exceeds the standard quantity, the variance is unfavorable. This positive amount (unfavorable variance) can be thought of as increasing costs (a debit). If the actual quantity for the units produced is less than the standard quantity, the variance is favorable. This negative amount (favorable variance) can be thought of as decreasing costs (a credit).

To illustrate, the direct materials quantity variance for **Western Rider Inc.** for June is $1,000 (favorable), computed as follows:

Direct Materials Quantity Variance = (Actual Quantity – Standard Quantity) × Standard Price
= (7,300 sq. yds. – 7,500 sq. yds.) × $5.00
= $(1,000) Favorable Variance

Direct Materials Variance Relationships The relationship among the *total* direct materials cost variance, the direct materials *price* variance, and the direct materials *quantity* variance is shown in Exhibit 6.

Reporting Direct Materials Variances The direct materials quantity variances should be reported to the manager responsible for the variance. For example, an unfavorable quantity variance might be caused by either of the following:

- Equipment that has not been properly maintained
- Low-quality (inferior) direct materials

In the first case, the Operating Department responsible for maintaining the equipment should be held responsible for the variance. In the second case, the Purchasing Department should be held responsible.

1 To simplify, it is assumed that there is no change in the beginning and ending materials inventories. Thus, the amount of materials budgeted for production equals the amount purchased.

Direct Materials Variance Relationships **EXHIBIT 6**

Dynamic Exhibit

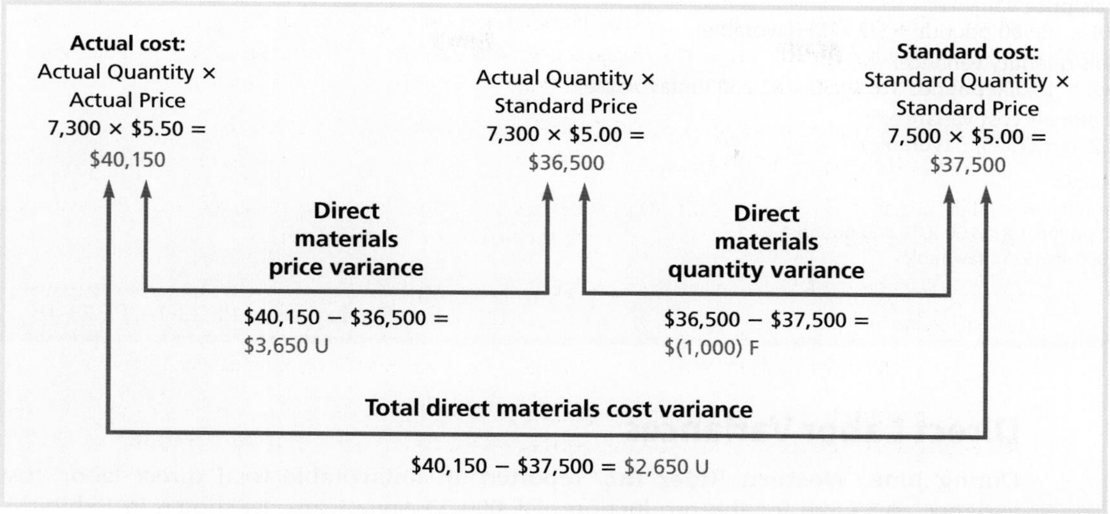

Not all variances are controllable. For example, an unfavorable materials price variance might be due to market-wide price increases. In this case, there is nothing the Purchasing Department might have done to avoid the unfavorable variance. On the other hand, if materials of the same quality could have been purchased from another supplier at the standard price, the variance was controllable.

SERVICE FOCUS

STANDARD COSTING IN THE RESTAURANT INDUSTRY

Many restaurants use standard costs to manage their business. Food costs are typically the largest expense for a restaurant. As a result, many restaurants use food quantity standards to control food costs by establishing the amount of food that is served to a customer. For example, Red Lobster restaurants, a division of **Darden Restuarants, Inc.**, establishes food quantity standards for the number of shrimp, scallops, or clams on a seafood plate.

The second largest cost to most restaurants is labor cost. Many restaurants base their labor cost standards on the labor cost percentage, which is the ratio of total labor cost to total sales. This ratio helps the restaurants of Darden Restaurants, Inc., including Olive Garden and Red Lobster, control and monitor labor costs.

Source: N. Irwin, "What Olive Garden and Red Lobster Tell Us About the Economy," *The Washington Post*, September 21, 2012.

Example Exercise 23-1 Direct Materials Variances *Obj. 3*

Tip Top Corp. produces a product that requires six standard pounds per unit. The standard price is $4.50 per pound. If 3,000 units required 18,500 pounds, which were purchased at $4.35 per pound, what is the direct materials (a) price variance, (b) quantity variance, and (c) total direct materials cost variance?

(Continued)

Follow My Example 23-1

a. Direct materials price variance:
($4.35 – $4.50) × 18,500 pounds = $(2,775) (favorable)

b. Direct materials quantity variance:
(18,500 pounds – 18,000 pounds*) × $4.50 = $2,250 (unfavorable)

c. Total direct materials cost variance:**
$(2,775) + $2,250 = $(525) (favorable)

*3,000 units × 6 pounds
**Also computed as follows:
($4.35 × 18,500 pounds) – ($4.50 × 18,000 pounds)
$80,475 – $81,000 = $(525) (favorable)

Practice Exercises: PE 23-1A, PE 23-1B

Direct Labor Variances

During June, **Western Rider Inc.** reported an unfavorable total direct labor cost variance of $2,500 for the production of 5,000 XL style jeans, as shown in Exhibit 3. This variance was based on the following actual and standard costs:

Actual costs	$38,500
Standard costs	36,000
Total direct labor cost variance	$ 2,500

The actual costs incurred of $38,500 consist of the following:

Actual Direct Labor Cost = Actual Rate per Hour × Actual Time
= $10.00 per hr. × 3,850 hrs.
= $38,500

The standard costs of $36,000 consist of the following:

Standard Direct Labor Cost = Standard Rate per Hour × Standard Time
= $9.00 per hr. × 4,000 hrs.
= $36,000

The standard rate of $9.00 per direct labor hour is set by management and provided in Exhibit 1. In addition, Exhibit 1 indicates that 0.80 hour is the standard time required for producing one unit of XL jeans. Thus, 4,000 (5,000 units × 0.80 hr.) direct labor hours is the standard for producing 5,000 units (pairs) of XL jeans.

Comparing the actual and standard cost computations indicates that the total direct labor unfavorable cost variance of $2,500 is caused by the following:

- A rate of $1.00 per hour ($10.00 – $9.00) more than standard
- A quantity of 150 hours (4,000 hrs. – 3,850 hrs.) less than standard

The impact of these differences from standard is reported and analyzed as a direct labor *rate* variance and a direct labor *time* variance.

Link to BMW Group

The camshafts of BMW's engines are manufactured using computer-controlled machine tools to a precision of one-hundredth of a human hair. Workers are used primarily to adjust the machine tools.

Direct Labor Rate Variance The **direct labor rate variance** is computed as follows:

Direct Labor Rate Variance = (Actual Rate per Hour – Standard Rate per Hour) × Actual Hours

If the actual rate per hour exceeds the standard rate per hour, the variance is unfavorable. This positive amount (unfavorable variance) can be thought of as increasing costs (a debit). If the actual rate per hour is less than the standard rate per hour, the variance is favorable. This negative amount (favorable variance) can be thought of as decreasing costs (a credit).

To illustrate, the direct labor rate variance for **Western Rider Inc.** in June is $3,850 (unfavorable), computed as follows:

Direct Labor Rate Variance = (Actual Rate per Hour – Standard Rate per Hour) × Actual Hours
= ($10.00 – $9.00) × 3,850 hours
= $3,850 Unfavorable Variance

Direct Labor Time Variance The **direct labor time variance** is computed as follows:

Direct Labor Time Variance = (Actual Direct Labor Hours – Standard Direct Labor Hours)
× Standard Rate per Hour

If the actual direct labor hours for the units produced exceeds the standard direct labor hours, the variance is unfavorable. This positive amount (unfavorable variance) can be thought of as increasing costs (a debit). If the actual direct labor hours for the units produced is less than the standard direct labor hours, the variance is favorable. This negative amount (favorable variance) can be thought of as decreasing costs (a credit).

To illustrate, the direct labor time variance for **Western Rider Inc.** for June is $1,350 (favorable) computed as follows:

Direct Labor Time Variance = (Actual Direct Labor Hours – Standard Direct Labor Hours)
× Standard Rate per Hour
= (3,850 hours – 4,000 direct labor hours) × $9.00
= $(1,350) Favorable Variance

Direct Labor Variance Relationships The relationship among the *total* direct labor cost variance, the direct labor *rate* variance, and the direct labor *time* variance is shown in Exhibit 7.

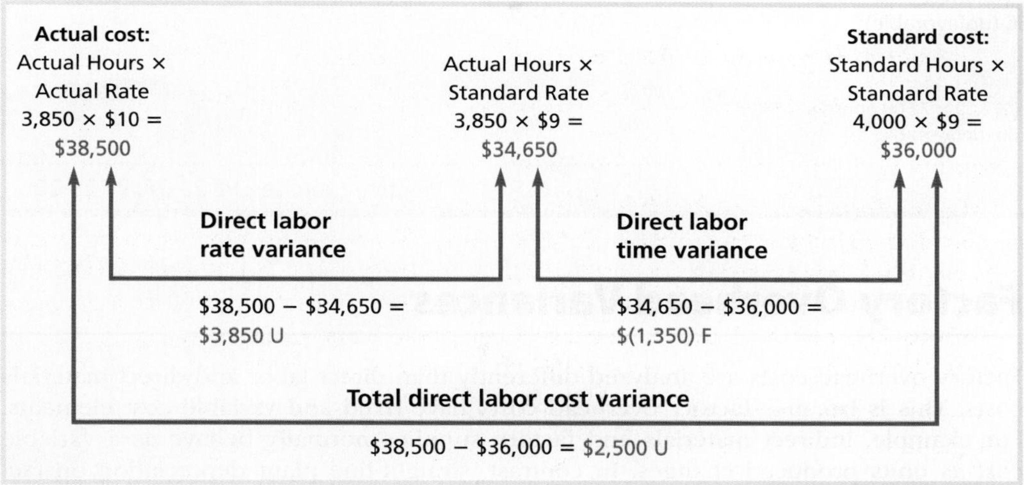

EXHIBIT 7
Direct Labor Variance Relationships

Dynamic Exhibit

Reporting Direct Labor Variances Production supervisors are normally responsible for controlling direct labor cost. For example, an investigation could reveal the following causes for unfavorable rate and time variances:

- An unfavorable rate variance may be caused by the improper scheduling and use of employees. In such cases, skilled, highly paid employees may be used in jobs that are normally performed by unskilled, lower-paid employees. In this case, the unfavorable rate variance should be reported to the managers who schedule work assignments.
- An unfavorable time variance may be caused by a shortage of skilled employees. In such cases, there may be an abnormally high turnover rate among skilled employees. In this case, production supervisors with high turnover rates should be questioned as to why their employees are quitting.

Direct Labor Standards for Nonmanufacturing Activities Direct labor time standards can also be developed for use in administrative, selling, and service activities. This is most appropriate when the activity involves a repetitive task that produces a common output. In these cases, the use of standards is similar to that for a manufactured product.

To illustrate, standards could be developed for customer service personnel who process sales orders. A standard time for processing a sales order (the output) could be developed and used to control sales order processing costs. Similar standards could be developed for computer help desk operators, nurses, and insurance application processors.

When labor-related activities are not repetitive, direct labor time standards are less commonly used. For example, the time spent by a senior executive or the work of a research and development scientist would not normally be controlled using time standards.

Example Exercise 23-2 Direct Labor Variances

Obj. 3

Tip Top Corp. produces a product that requires 2.5 standard hours per unit at a standard hourly rate of $12 per hour. If 3,000 units required 7,420 hours at an hourly rate of $12.30 per hour, what is the (a) direct labor rate variance, (b) direct labor time variance, and (c) total direct labor cost variance?

Follow My Example 23-2

a. Direct labor rate variance:
($12.30 – $12.00) × 7,420 hours = $2,226 (unfavorable)

b. Direct labor time variance:
(7,420 hours – 7,500 hours*) × $12.00 = $(960) (favorable)

c. Total direct labor cost variance:**
$2,226 – $960 = $1,266 (unfavorable)

*3,000 units × 2.5 hours
**Also computed as follows:
($12.30 × 7,420 hours) – ($12.00 × 7,500 hours)
$91,266 – $90,000 = $1,266 (unfavorable)

Practice Exercises: PE 23-2A, PE 23-2B

Obj. 4 Compute and interpret factory overhead controllable and volume variances.

Factory Overhead Variances

Factory overhead costs are analyzed differently than direct labor and direct materials costs. This is because factory overhead costs have fixed and variable cost elements. For example, indirect materials and factory supplies normally behave as a variable cost as units produced changes. In contrast, straight-line plant depreciation on factory machinery is a fixed cost.

Factory overhead costs are budgeted and controlled by separating factory overhead into fixed and variable components. Doing so allows the preparation of flexible budgets and the analysis of factory overhead controllable and volume variances.

Link to BMW Group

The **BMW Group** has significant overhead costs due to its investment in robotic and other state-of-the art technology, machinery, and facilities.

The Factory Overhead Flexible Budget

The preparation of a flexible budget was described and illustrated in Chapter 22. Exhibit 8 illustrates a flexible factory overhead budget for **Western Rider Inc.** for June.

	A	B	C	D	E
1	**Western Rider Inc.**				
2	**Factory Overhead Cost Budget**				
3	**For the Month Ending June 30**				
4	Percent of normal capacity	80%	90%	100%	110%
5	Units produced	5,000	5,625	6,250	6,875
6	Direct labor hours (0.80 hr. per unit)	4,000	4,500	5,000	5,500
7	Budgeted factory overhead:				
8	Variable costs:				
9	Indirect factory wages	$ 8,000	$ 9,000	$10,000	$11,000
10	Power and light	4,000	4,500	5,000	5,500
11	Indirect materials	2,400	2,700	3,000	3,300
12	Total variable cost	$14,400	$16,200	$18,000	$19,800
13	Fixed costs:				
14	Supervisory salaries	$ 5,500	$ 5,500	$ 5,500	$ 5,500
15	Depreciation of plant				
16	and equipment	4,500	4,500	4,500	4,500
17	Insurance and property taxes	2,000	2,000	2,000	2,000
18	Total fixed cost	$12,000	$12,000	$12,000	$12,000
19	Total factory overhead cost	$26,400	$28,200	$30,000	$31,800
20					
21	Factory overhead rate per direct labor hour, $30,000 ÷ 5,000 hours = $6.00				
22					

EXHIBIT 8

Factory Overhead Cost Budget Indicating Standard Factory Overhead Rate

Exhibit 8 indicates that the budgeted factory overhead rate for Western Rider is $6.00, computed as follows:

$$\text{Factory Overhead Rate} = \frac{\text{Budgeted Factory Overhead at Normal Productive Capacity}}{\text{Normal Productive Capacity}}$$

$$= \frac{\$30{,}000}{5{,}000 \text{ direct labor hrs.}} = \$6.00 \text{ per direct labor hr.}$$

The normal productive capacity is expressed in terms of an activity base such as direct labor hours, direct labor cost, or machine hours. For Western Rider, 100% of normal capacity is 5,000 direct labor hours. The budgeted factory overhead cost at 100% of normal capacity is $30,000, which consists of variable overhead of $18,000 and fixed overhead of $12,000.

For analysis purposes, the budgeted factory overhead rate is subdivided into a variable factory overhead rate and a fixed factory overhead rate. For Western Rider, the variable overhead rate is $3.60 per direct labor hour and the fixed overhead rate is $2.40 per direct labor hour, computed as follows:

$$\text{Variable Factory Overhead Rate} = \frac{\text{Budgeted Variable Overhead at Normal Productive Capacity}}{\text{Normal Productive Capacity}}$$

$$= \frac{\$18{,}000}{5{,}000 \text{ direct labor hrs.}} = \$3.60 \text{ per direct labor hr.}$$

$$\text{Fixed Factory Overhead Rate} = \frac{\text{Budgeted Fixed Overhead at Normal Productive Capacity}}{\text{Normal Productive Capacity}}$$

$$= \frac{\$12{,}000}{5{,}000 \text{ direct labor hrs.}} = \$2.40 \text{ per direct labor hr.}$$

To summarize, the budgeted factory overhead rates for Western Rider Inc. are as follows:

Variable factory overhead rate	$3.60
Fixed factory overhead rate	2.40
Total factory overhead rate	$6.00

As mentioned previously, factory overhead variances can be separated into a controllable variance and a volume variance as discussed in the next sections.

Variable Factory Overhead Controllable Variance

The variable factory overhead **controllable variance** is the difference between the actual variable overhead costs and the budgeted variable overhead for actual production. It is computed as follows:

$$\text{Variable Factory Overhead Controllable Variance} = \text{Actual Variable Factory Overhead} - \text{Budgeted Variable Factory Overhead}$$

If the actual variable overhead is less than the budgeted variable overhead, the variance is favorable. If the actual variable overhead exceeds the budgeted variable overhead, the variance is unfavorable.

The **budgeted variable factory overhead** is the standard variable overhead for the *actual* units produced. It is computed as follows:

$$\text{Budgeted Variable Factory Overhead} = \text{Standard Hours for Actual Units Produced} \times \text{Variable Factory Overhead Rate}$$

To illustrate, the budgeted variable overhead for **Western Rider Inc.** for June, when 5,000 units of XL jeans were produced, is $14,400, computed as follows:

$$\begin{aligned}\text{Budgeted Variable Factory Overhead} &= \text{Standard Hours for Actual Units Produced} \times \text{Variable Factory Overhead Rate}\\ &= 4{,}000 \text{ direct labor hrs.} \times \$3.60\\ &= \$14{,}400\end{aligned}$$

The preceding computation is based on the fact that Western Rider produced 5,000 XL jeans, which requires a standard of 4,000 (5,000 units × 0.8 hr.) direct labor hours. The variable factory overhead rate of $3.60 was computed earlier. Thus, the budgeted variable factory overhead is $14,400 (4,000 direct labor hrs. × $3.60).

During June, assume that Western Rider incurred the following actual factory overhead costs:

	Actual Costs in June
Variable factory overhead	$10,400
Fixed factory overhead	12,000
Total actual factory overhead	$22,400

Based on the actual variable factory overhead incurred in June, the variable factory overhead controllable variance is a $4,000 favorable variance, computed as follows:

$$\begin{aligned}\text{Variable Factory Overhead Controllable Variance} &= \text{Actual Variable Factory Overhead} - \text{Budgeted Variable Factory Overhead}\\ &= \$10{,}400 - \$14{,}400\\ &= \$(4{,}000) \text{ Favorable Variance}\end{aligned}$$

The variable factory overhead controllable variance indicates the ability to keep the factory overhead costs within the budget limits. Because variable factory overhead costs are normally controllable at the department level, responsibility for controlling this variance usually rests with department supervisors.

Example Exercise 23-3 Factory Overhead Controllable Variance **Obj. 4**

Tip Top Corp. produced 3,000 units of product that required 2.5 standard hours per unit. The standard variable overhead cost per unit is $2.20 per hour. The actual variable factory overhead was $16,850. Determine the variable factory overhead controllable variance.

Follow My Example 23-3

Variable Factory Overhead Controllable Variance = Actual Variable Factory Overhead − Budgeted Variable Factory Overhead
= $16,850 − [(3,000 units × 2.5 hrs.) × $2.20]
= $16,850 − $16,500
= $350 (unfavorable)

Practice Exercises: PE 23-3A, PE 23-3B

Fixed Factory Overhead Volume Variance

Western Rider's budgeted factory overhead is based on a 100% normal capacity of 5,000 direct labor hours, as shown in Exhibit 8. This is the expected capacity that management believes will be used under normal business conditions. Exhibit 8 indicates that the 5,000 direct labor hours is less than the total available capacity of 110%, which is 5,500 direct labor hours.

The fixed factory overhead **volume variance** is the difference between the budgeted fixed overhead at 100% of normal capacity and the standard fixed overhead for the actual units produced. It is computed as follows:

$$\text{Fixed Factory Overhead Volume Variance} = \left(\text{Standard Hours for 100\% of Normal Capacity} - \text{Standard Hours for Actual Units Produced}\right) \times \text{Fixed Factory Overhead Rate}$$

The volume variance measures the use of fixed overhead resources (plant and equipment). The interpretation of an unfavorable and a favorable fixed factory overhead volume variance is as follows:

- *Unfavorable*. The actual units produced is *less than* 100% of normal capacity; thus, the company used its fixed overhead resources (plant and equipment) less than would be expected under normal operating conditions.
- *Favorable*. The actual units produced is *more than* 100% of normal capacity; thus, the company used its fixed overhead resources (plant and equipment) more than would be expected under normal operating conditions.

To illustrate, the fixed factory overhead volume variance for **Western Rider Inc.** is a $2,400 unfavorable variance, computed as follows:

$$\text{Fixed Factory Overhead Volume Variance} = \left(\text{Standard Hours for 100\% of Normal Capacity} - \text{Standard Hours for Actual Units Produced}\right) \times \text{Fixed Factory Overhead Rate}$$

$$= \left(\text{5,000 direct labor hrs.} - \text{4,000 direct labor hrs.}\right) \times \$2.40$$

$$= \text{\$2,400 Unfavorable Variance}$$

Because Western Rider produced 5,000 units of XL jeans during June, the standard for the actual units produced is 4,000 (5,000 units × 0.80) direct labor hours. This is 1,000 hours less than the 5,000 standard hours of normal capacity. The fixed overhead rate of $2.40 was computed earlier. Thus, the unfavorable fixed factory overhead volume variance is $2,400 (1,000 direct labor hrs. × $2.40).

Exhibit 9 illustrates graphically the fixed factory overhead volume variance for **Western Rider Inc.** The budgeted fixed overhead does not change and is $12,000 at all levels of production. At 100% of normal capacity (5,000 direct labor hours), the standard fixed overhead line intersects the budgeted fixed costs line. For production levels *more than* 100% of normal capacity (5,000 direct labor hours), the volume variance is *favorable*. For production levels *less than* 100% of normal capacity (5,000 direct labor hours), the volume variance is *unfavorable*.

EXHIBIT 9

Graph of Fixed Overhead Volume Variance

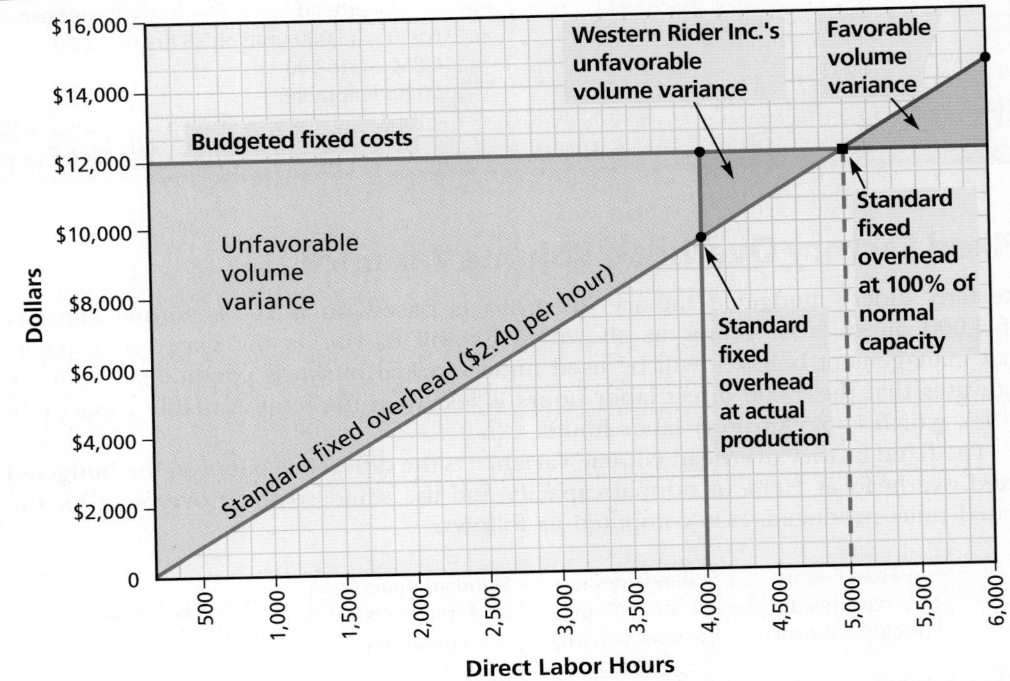

Exhibit 9 indicates that Western Rider's fixed factory overhead volume variance is unfavorable in June because the actual production is 4,000 direct labor hours, or 80% of normal volume. The unfavorable volume variance of $2,400 can be viewed as the cost of the unused capacity (1,000 direct labor hours).

An unfavorable volume variance may be due to factors such as the following:

- Failure to maintain an even flow of work
- Machine breakdowns
- Work stoppages caused by lack of materials or skilled labor
- Lack of enough sales orders to keep the factory operating at normal capacity

Management should determine the causes of the unfavorable variance and consider taking corrective action. For example, a volume variance caused by an uneven flow of work could be remedied by changing operating procedures. Lack of sales orders may be corrected through increased advertising.

Favorable volume variances may not always be desirable. For example, in an attempt to create a favorable volume variance, manufacturing managers might run the factory above the normal capacity. However, if the additional production cannot be sold, it must be stored as inventory, which would incur storage costs.

Example Exercise 23-4 Factory Overhead Volume Variance **Obj. 4**

Tip Top Corp. produced 3,000 units of product that required 2.5 standard hours per unit. The standard fixed overhead cost per unit is $0.90 per hour at 8,000 hours, which is 100% of normal capacity. Determine the fixed factory overhead volume variance.

Follow My Example 23-4

Fixed Factory Overhead Volume Variance = (Standard Hours for 100% of Normal Capacity – Standard Hours for Actual Units Produced) × Fixed Factory Overhead Rate
= [8,000 hrs. – (3,000 units × 2.5 hrs.)] × $0.90
= (8,000 hrs. – 7,500 hrs.) × $0.90
= $450 (unfavorable)

Practice Exercises: PE 23-4A, PE 23-4B

Reporting Factory Overhead Variances

The total factory overhead cost variance can also be determined as the sum of the variable factory overhead controllable and fixed factory overhead volume variances, computed as follows for **Western Rider Inc.**:

Variable factory overhead controllable variance	$(4,000)	Favorable Variance
Fixed factory overhead volume variance	2,400	Unfavorable Variance
Total factory overhead cost variance	$(1,600)	Favorable Variance

A **factory overhead cost variance report** is useful to management in controlling factory overhead costs. Budgeted and actual costs for variable and fixed factory overhead along with the related controllable and volume variances are reported by each cost element.

Exhibit 10 illustrates a factory overhead cost variance report for Western Rider Inc. for June.

EXHIBIT 10

Factory Overhead Cost Variance Report

	A	B	C	D	E
1	Western Rider Inc.				
2	Factory Overhead Cost Variance Report				
3	For the Month Ending June 30				
4	Productive capacity for the month (100% of normal)	5,000 hours			
5	Actual production for the month	4,000 hours			
6					
7			Budget		
8			(at Actual	Variances	
9		Actual	Production)	Unfavorable	Favorable
10	Variable factory overhead costs:				
11	Indirect factory wages	$ 5,100	$ 8,000		$(2,900)
12	Power and light	4,200	4,000	$ 200	
13	Indirect materials	1,100	2,400		(1,300)
14	Total variable factory				
15	overhead cost	$10,400	$14,400		
16	Fixed factory overhead costs:				
17	Supervisory salaries	$ 5,500	$ 5,500		
18	Depreciation of plant and				
19	equipment	4,500	4,500		
20	Insurance and property taxes	2,000	2,000		
21	Total fixed factory				
22	overhead cost	$12,000	$12,000		
23	Total factory overhead cost	$22,400	$26,400		
24	Total controllable variances			$ 200	$(4,200)
25					
26					
27	Net controllable variance—favorable [$(4,200) favorable + $200 unfavorable]			$(4,000)	
28	Volume variance—unfavorable:				
29	Capacity not used at the standard rate for fixed				
30	factory overhead—1,000 × $2.40			2,400	
31	Total factory overhead cost variance—favorable			$(1,600)	
32					

Factory Overhead Account

To illustrate, the applied factory overhead for **Western Rider Inc.** for the 5,000 units of XL jeans produced in June is $24,000, computed as follows:

Applied Factory Overhead = Standard Hours for Actual Units Produced × Total Factory Overhead Rate
= (5,000 jeans × 0.80 direct labor hr. per unit) × $6.00
= 4,000 direct labor hrs. × $6.00 = $24,000

The total actual factory overhead for Western Rider, as shown in Exhibit 10, was $22,400. Thus, the total factory overhead cost variance for Western Rider for June is a $1,600 favorable variance, computed as follows:

Total Factory Overhead Cost Variance = Actual Factory Overhead – Applied Factory Overhead
= $22,400 – $24,000 = $(1,600) Favorable Variance

At the end of the period, the factory overhead account typically has a debit or credit balance. A debit balance in Factory Overhead represents underapplied overhead. Underapplied overhead occurs when actual factory overhead costs exceed the applied factory overhead. A credit balance in Factory Overhead represents overapplied overhead. Overapplied overhead occurs when actual factory overhead costs are less than the applied factory overhead.

The difference between the actual factory overhead and the applied factory overhead is the total factory overhead cost variance. Thus, underapplied and overapplied factory overhead account balances represent the following total factory overhead cost variances:

- *Underapplied* Factory Overhead = *Unfavorable* Total Factory Overhead Cost Variance
- *Overapplied* Factory Overhead = *Favorable* Total Factory Overhead Cost Variance

The factory overhead account for **Western Rider Inc.** for the month ending June 30 is as follows:

Factory Overhead

Actual factory overhead ($10,400 + $12,000)	22,400		24,000 Applied factory overhead (4,000 hrs. × $6.00 per hr.)
		Bal., June 30	1,600 Overapplied factory overhead

The $1,600 overapplied factory overhead account balance and the favorable total factory overhead cost variance shown in Exhibit 10 are the same.

The variable factory overhead controllable variance and the volume variance can be computed by comparing the factory overhead account with the budgeted total overhead for the actual level produced, as shown in Exhibit 11.

The controllable and volume variances are determined as follows:

- The difference between the actual overhead incurred and the budgeted overhead is the *controllable* variance.
- The difference between the applied overhead and the budgeted overhead is the *volume* variance.

If the actual factory overhead exceeds (is less than) the budgeted factory overhead, the controllable variance is unfavorable (favorable). In contrast, if the applied factory overhead is less than (exceeds) the budgeted factory overhead, the volume variance is unfavorable (favorable).

Factory Overhead Variances EXHIBIT 11

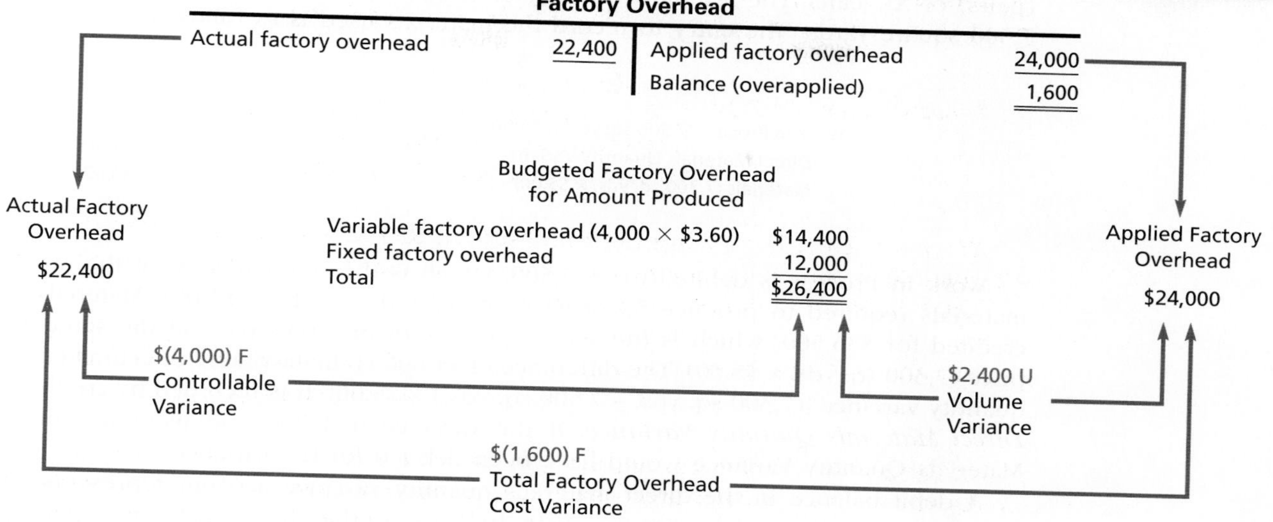

Recording and Reporting Variances from Standards

Obj. 5 Journalize the entries for recording standards in the accounts and prepare an income statement that includes variances from standard.

Standard costs may be used as a management tool to control costs separately from the accounts in the general ledger. However, many companies include standard costs in their accounts. One method for doing so records standard costs and variances at the same time the actual product costs are recorded.

To illustrate, assume that **Western Rider Inc.** purchased, on account, the 7,300 square yards of blue denim used at $5.50 per square yard. The standard price for direct materials is $5.00 per square yard. The entry to record the purchase and the unfavorable direct materials price variance is as follows:

Materials (7,300 sq. yds. × $5.00)	36,500	
Direct Materials Price Variance	3,650	
Accounts Payable (7,300 sq. yds. × $5.50)		40,150

The materials account is debited for the *actual quantity* purchased at the *standard price*, $36,500 (7,300 square yards × $5.00). Accounts Payable is credited for the $40,150 actual cost and the amount due the supplier. The difference of $3,650 is the unfavorable direct materials price variance [($5.50 – $5.00) × 7,300 sq. yds.]. It is recorded by debiting Direct Materials Price Variance. If the variance had been favorable, Direct Materials Price Variance would have been credited for the variance.

A debit balance in the direct materials price variance account represents an unfavorable variance. Likewise, a credit balance in the direct materials price variance account represents a favorable variance.

The direct materials quantity variance is recorded in a similar manner. For example, **Western Rider Inc.** used 7,300 square yards of blue denim to produce 5,000 units (pairs) of XL jeans. The standard quantity of denim for the 5,000 jeans produced is 7,500 square yards. The entry to record the materials used is as follows:

		Work in Process (7,500 sq. yds. × $5.00)		37,500	
		Direct Materials Quantity Variance			1,000
		Materials (7,300 sq. yds. × $5.00)			36,500

Work in Process is debited for $37,500, which is the standard cost of the direct materials required to produce 5,000 XL jeans (7,500 sq. yds. × $5.00). Materials is credited for $36,500, which is the actual quantity of materials used at the standard price (7,300 sq. yds. × $5.00). The difference of $1,000 is the favorable direct materials quantity variance [(7,300 sq. yds. – 7,500 sq. yds.) × $5.00]. It is recorded by crediting *Direct Materials Quantity Variance.* If the variance had been unfavorable, Direct Materials Quantity Variance would have been debited for the variance.

A debit balance in the direct materials quantity variance account represents an unfavorable variance. Likewise, a credit balance in the direct materials quantity variance account represents a favorable variance.

Example Exercise 23-5 Standard Cost Journal Entries — Obj. 5

Tip Top Corp. produced 3,000 units that require six standard pounds per unit at the $4.50 standard price per pound. The company actually used 18,500 pounds in production. Journalize the entry to record the standard direct materials used in production.

Follow My Example 23-5

Work in Process (18,000* pounds × $4.50)	81,000	
Direct Materials Quantity Variance [(18,500 pounds – 18,000 pounds) × $4.50]	2,250	
Materials (18,500 pounds × $4.50)		83,250

*3,000 units × 6 pounds per unit = 18,000 standard pounds for units produced

Practice Exercises: PE 23-5A, PE 23-5B

The journal entries to record the standard costs and variances for *direct labor* are similar to those for direct materials. These entries are summarized as follows:

- Work in Process is debited for the standard cost of direct labor.
- Wages Payable is credited for the actual direct labor cost incurred.
- Direct Labor Rate Variance is debited for an unfavorable variance and credited for a favorable variance.
- Direct Labor Time Variance is debited for an unfavorable variance and credited for a favorable variance.

As illustrated in the prior section, the factory overhead account already incorporates standard costs and variances into its journal entries. That is, Factory Overhead is debited for actual factory overhead and credited for applied (standard) factory overhead. The ending balance of factory overhead (overapplied or underapplied) is the total factory overhead cost variance. By comparing the actual factory overhead with the budgeted factory overhead, the controllable variance can be determined. By comparing the budgeted factory overhead with the applied factory overhead, the volume variance can be determined.

When goods are completed, Finished Goods is debited and Work in Process is credited for the standard cost of the product transferred.

At the end of the period, the balances of each of the variance accounts indicate the net favorable or unfavorable variance for the period. These variances may be reported in an income statement prepared for management's use.

Exhibit 12 is an example of an income statement for **Western Rider Inc.** that includes variances. In Exhibit 12, a sales price of $28 per unit (pair) of jeans, selling expenses of $14,500, and administrative expenses of $11,225 are assumed.

EXHIBIT 12

Variance from Standards in Income Statement

Western Rider Inc.
Income Statement
For the Month Ended June 30

	Unfavorable	Favorable	
Sales			$140,000[1]
Cost of goods sold—at standard			97,500[2]
Gross profit—at standard			$ 42,500
Less variance adjustments to gross profit—at standard:			
Direct materials price	$3,650		
Direct materials quantity		$ (1,000)	
Direct labor rate	3,850		
Direct labor time		(1,350)	
Factory overhead controllable		(4,000)	
Factory overhead volume	2,400		
Net variance from st.andard cost—unfavorable			3,550
Gross profit			$ 38,950
Operating expenses:			
Selling expenses		$14,500	
Administrative expenses		11,225	25,725
Income before income tax			$ 13,225

[1]5,000 × $28

[2]$37,500 + $36,000 + $24,000 (from Exhibit 3), or 5,000 × $19.50 (from Exhibit 1)

The income statement shown in Exhibit 12 is for internal use by management. That is, variances are not reported to external users. Thus, the variances shown in Exhibit 12 must be transferred to other accounts in preparing an income statement for external users.

In preparing an income statement for external users, the balances of the variance accounts are normally transferred to Cost of Goods Sold. However, if the variances are significant or if many of the products manufactured are still in inventory, the variances should be allocated to Work in Process, Finished Goods, and Cost of Goods Sold. Such an allocation, in effect, converts these account balances from standard cost to actual cost.

Example Exercise 23-6 Income Statement with Variances

Obj. 5

Prepare an income statement for the year ended December 31 through gross profit for Tip Top Corp. using the variance data in Example Exercises 23-1 through 23-4. Assume that Tip Top sold 3,000 units at $100 per unit.

(Continued)

Follow My Example 23-6

Tip Top Corp.
Income Statement Through Gross Profit
For the Year Ended December 31

Sales (3,000 units × $100)			$300,000
Cost of goods sold—at standard			194,250*
Gross profit—at standard			$105,750
	Unfavorable	**Favorable**	
Less variance adjustments to gross profit—at standard:			
Direct materials price (EE23-1)		$(2,775)	
Direct materials quantity (EE23-1)	$2,250		
Direct labor rate (EE23-2)	2,226		
Direct labor time (EE23-2)		(960)	
Factory overhead controllable (EE23-3)	350		
Factory overhead volume (EE23-4)	450		
Net variance from standard cost—unfavorable			1,541
Gross profit—actual			$104,209

*Direct materials (3,000 units × 6 lb. × $4.50)	$ 81,000
Direct labor (3,000 units × 2.5 hrs. × $12.00)	90,000
Factory overhead [3,000 units × 2.5 hrs. × ($2.20 + $0.90)]	23,250
Cost of goods sold at standard	$194,250

Practice Exercises: PE 23-6A, PE 23-6B

Obj. 6 Describe and provide examples of nonfinancial performance measures.

Nonfinancial Performance Measures

Many companies supplement standard costs and variances from standards with nonfinancial performance measures. A **nonfinancial performance measure** expresses performance in a measure other than dollars. For example, airlines use on-time performance, percent of bags lost, and number of customer complaints as nonfinancial performance measures. Such measures are often used to evaluate the time, quality, or quantity of a business activity.

Using financial and nonfinancial performance measures aids managers and employees in considering multiple performance objectives. Such measures often bring additional perspectives, such as quality of work, to evaluating performance. Some examples of nonfinancial performance measures are shown in Exhibit 13.

Link to BMW Group

The **BMW Group** uses a variety of nonfinancial performance measures for its vehicles and manufacturing operations, including energy consumption, water consumption, carbon dioxide emissions, percent of women in its workforce, average days of training per employee, and accident frequency.

EXHIBIT 13 **Nonfinancial Performance Measures**

- Inventory turnover
- Percent of on-time delivery
- Elapsed time between a customer order and product delivery
- Customer preference rankings compared to competitors
- Response time to a service call
- Time to develop new products
- Employee satisfaction
- Number of customer complaints

Nonfinancial measures are often linked to either the inputs or outputs of an activity or process. A **process** is a sequence of activities for performing a task. The relationship between an activity or a process and its inputs and outputs is shown in Exhibit 14.

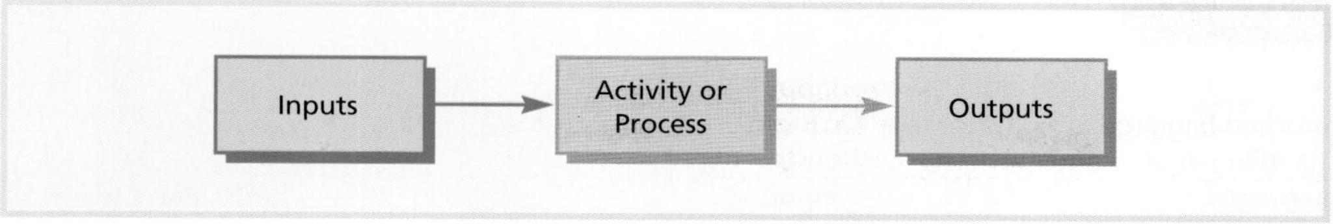

EXHIBIT 14

Relationship Between a Process and Its Inputs and Outputs

To illustrate, the counter service activity of a fast-food restaurant is used. The inputs/outputs for providing counter service at a fast-food restaurant are shown in Exhibit 15.

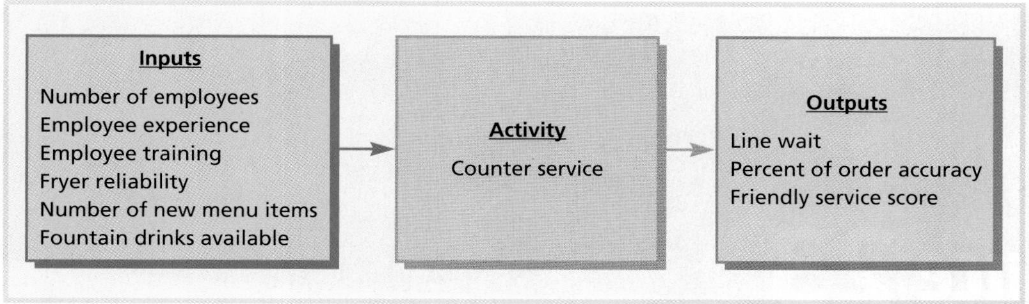

EXHIBIT 15

Inputs/Outputs for a Fast-Food Restaurant

The customer service outputs of the counter service activity include the following:

- Line wait for the customer
- Percent of order accuracy in serving the customer
- Friendly service experience for the customer

Some of the inputs that impact the customer service outputs include the following:

- Number of employees
- Employee experience
- Employee training
- Fryer (and other cooking equipment) reliability
- Number of new menu items
- Fountain drinks available

A fast-food restaurant can develop a set of linked nonfinancial performance measures across inputs and outputs. The output measures tell management how the activity is performing, such as keeping the line wait to a minimum. The input measures are used to improve the output measures. For example, if the customer line wait is too long, then improving employee training or hiring more employees could improve the output (decrease customer line wait).

Link to BMW Group

The **BMW Group** assesses its suppliers using a BMW sustainability standard that measures compliance with human rights, labor, and social issues.

Example Exercise 23-7 Activity Inputs and Outputs — Obj. 6

The following are inputs and outputs to the baggage claim process of an airline:

Baggage handler training
Time customers wait for returned baggage
Maintenance of baggage handling equipment
Number of baggage handlers
Number of damaged bags
On-time flight performance

Identify whether each is an input or output to the baggage claim process.

(Continued)

Follow My Example 23-7

Baggage handler training	Input
Time customers wait for returned baggage	Output
Maintenance of baggage handling equipment	Input
Number of baggage handlers	Input
Number of damaged bags	Output
On-time flight performance	Input

Practice Exercises: PE 23-7A, PE 23-7B

At a Glance 23

Obj. 1 Describe the types of standards and how they are established.

Key Points Standards represent performance goals that can be compared to actual results in evaluating performance. Standards are established so that they are neither too high nor too low but are attainable.

Learning Outcomes	Example Exercises	Practice Exercises
• Define *ideal* and *currently attainable standards* and explain how they are used in setting standards.		
• Describe some of the criticisms of the use of standards.		

Obj. 2 Describe and illustrate how standards are used in budgeting.

Key Points Budgets are prepared by multiplying the standard cost per unit by the planned production. To measure performance, the standard cost per unit is multiplied by the actual number of units produced, and the actual results are compared with the standard cost at actual volumes (cost variance).

Learning Outcomes	Example Exercises	Practice Exercises
• Compute the standard cost per unit of production for materials, labor, and factory overhead.		
• Compute the direct materials, direct labor, and factory overhead cost variances.		
• Prepare a budget performance report.		

Obj. 3 Compute and interpret direct materials and direct labor variances.

Key Points The direct materials cost variance can be separated into direct materials price and quantity variances. The direct labor cost variance can be separated into direct labor rate and time variances.

Learning Outcomes	Example Exercises	Practice Exercises
• Compute and interpret direct materials price and quantity variances.	EE23-1	PE23-1A, 23-1B
• Compute and interpret direct labor rate and time variances.	EE23-2	PE23-2A, 23-2B
• Describe and illustrate how time standards are used in nonmanufacturing settings.		

Obj. 4 Compute and interpret factory overhead controllable and volume variances.

Key Points The factory overhead cost variance can be separated into a variable factory overhead controllable variance and a fixed factory overhead volume variance.

Learning Outcomes	Example Exercises	Practice Exercises
• Prepare a factory overhead flexible budget.		
• Compute and interpret the variable factory overhead controllable variance.	EE23-3	PE23-3A, 23-3B
• Compute and interpret the fixed factory overhead volume variance.	EE23-4	PE23-4A, 23-4B
• Prepare a factory overhead cost variance report.		
• Evaluate factory overhead variances using a T account.		

Obj. 5 Journalize the entries for recording standards in the accounts and prepare an income statement that includes variances from standard.

Key Points Standard costs and variances can be recorded in the accounts at the same time the manufacturing costs are recorded in the accounts. Work in Process is debited at standard. Under a standard cost system, the cost of goods sold will be reported at standard cost. Manufacturing variances can be disclosed on the income statement to adjust the gross profit at standard to the actual gross profit.

Learning Outcomes	Example Exercises	Practice Exercises
• Journalize the entries to record the purchase and use of direct materials at standard, recording favorable or unfavorable variances.	EE23-5	PE23-5A, 23-5B
• Prepare an income statement, disclosing favorable and unfavorable direct materials, direct labor, and factory overhead variances.	EE23-6	PE23-6A, 23-6B

Obj. 6 **Describe and provide examples of nonfinancial performance measures.**

Key Points Many companies use a combination of financial and nonfinancial measures in order for multiple perspectives to be incorporated in evaluating performance. Nonfinancial measures are often used in conjunction with the inputs or outputs of a process or an activity.

Learning Outcomes	Example Exercises	Practice Exercises
• Define, provide the rationale for, and provide examples of nonfinancial performance measures.		
• Identify nonfinancial inputs and outputs of an activity.	EE23-7	PE23-7A, 23-7B

Illustrative Problem

Hawley Inc. manufactures designer iPod cases for national distribution. The standard costs for the manufacture of Folk Art style baskets were as follows:

	Standard Costs	Actual Costs
Direct materials	1,500 lb. at $35	1,600 lb. at $32
Direct labor	4,800 hrs. at $11	4,500 hrs. at $11.80
Factory overhead	Rates per labor hour, based on 100% of normal capacity of 5,500 labor hrs.:	
	Variable cost, $2.40	$12,300 variable cost
	Fixed cost, $3.50	$19,250 fixed cost

Instructions

1. Determine the direct materials price variance, direct materials quantity variance, and total direct materials cost variance for the designer iPod cases.
2. Determine the direct labor rate variance, direct labor time variance, and total direct labor cost variance for the designer iPod cases.
3. Determine the variable factory overhead controllable variance, fixed factory overhead volume variance, and total factory overhead cost variance for the designer iPod cases.

Solution

1. **Direct Materials Cost Variance**

Price variance:

Direct Materials Price Variance = (Actual Price – Standard Price) × Actual Quantity
= ($32 per lb. – $35 per lb.) × 1,600 lb.
= $(4,800) Favorable Variance

Quantity variance:

Direct Materials Quantity Variance = (Actual Quantity – Standard Quantity) × Standard Price
= (1,600 lb. – 1,500 lb.) × $35 per lb.
= $3,500 Unfavorable Variance

Total direct materials cost variance:

Direct Materials Cost Variance = Direct Materials Quantity Variance + Direct Materials Price Variance
= $3,500 Unfavorable + $(4,800) Favorable
= $(1,300) Favorable Variance

2.

Direct Labor Cost Variance

Rate variance:

Direct Labor Rate Variance = (Actual Rate per Hour – Standard Rate per Hour) × Actual Hours
= ($11.80 – $11.00) × 4,500 hrs.
= $3,600 Unfavorable Variance

Time variance:

Direct Labor Time Variance = (Actual Direct Labor Hours – Standard Direct Labor Hours) × Standard Rate per Hour
= (4,500 hrs. – 4,800 hrs.) × $11.00 per hour
= $(3,300) Favorable Variance

Total direct labor cost variance:

Direct Labor Cost Variance = Direct Labor Time Variance + Direct Labor Rate Variance
= $(3,300) Favorable + $3,600 Unfavorable
= $300 Unfavorable Variance

3.

Factory Overhead Cost Variance

Variable factory overhead controllable variance:

Variable Factory Overhead Controllable Variance = Actual Variable Factory Overhead – Budgeted Variable Factory Overhead
= $12,300 – (4,800 hours × $2.40 per hour)
= $780 Unfavorable Variance

Fixed factory overhead volume variance:

Fixed Factory Overhead Volume Variance = (Standard Hours for 100% of Normal Capacity – Standard Hours for Actual Units Produced) × Fixed Factory Overhead Rate
= (5,500 hrs. – 4,800 hrs.) × $3.50 per hr.
= $2,450 Unfavorable Variance

Total factory overhead cost variance:

Factory Overhead Cost Variance = Variable Factory Overhead Controllable Variance + Fixed Factory Overhead Volume Variance
= $780 Unfavorable + $2,450 Unfavorable
= $3,230 Unfavorable Variance

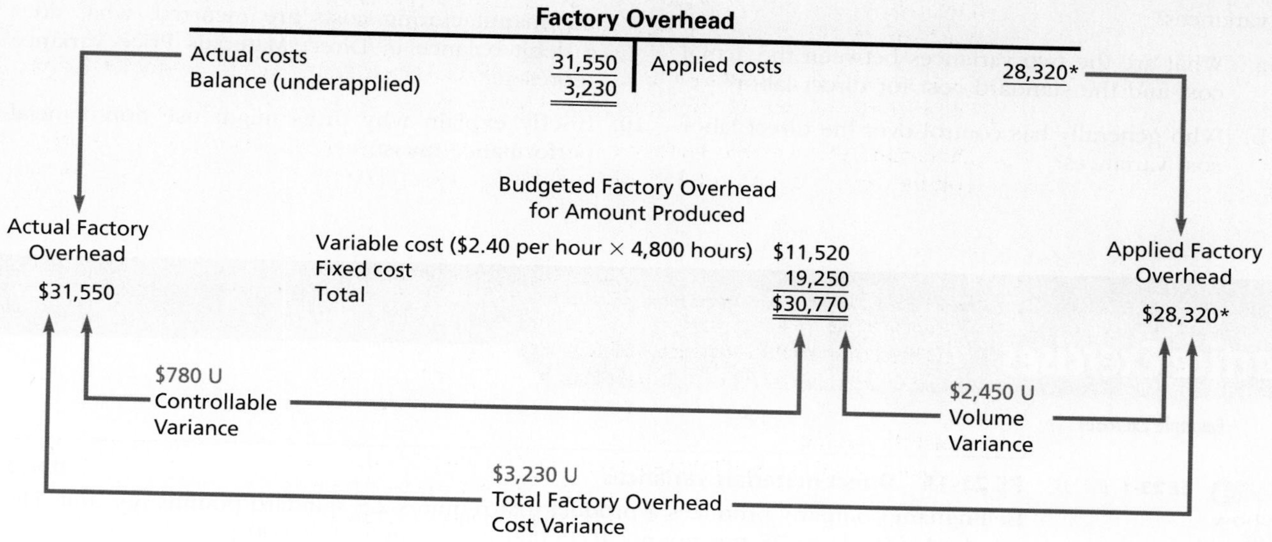

*($2.40 + $3.50) × 4,800

Key Terms

budget performance report (1129)
budgeted variable factory overhead (1138)
controllable variance (1138)
cost variance (1129)
currently attainable standards (1127)
direct labor rate variance (1134)
direct labor time variance (1135)
direct materials price variance (1132)
direct materials quantity variance (1132)
factory overhead cost variance report (1141)
favorable cost variance (1129)
ideal standards (1127)
nonfinancial performance measure (1146)
process (1146)
standard cost (1126)
standard cost systems (1126)
standards (1126)
total manufacturing cost variance (1129)
unfavorable cost variance (1129)
volume variance (1139)

Discussion Questions

1. What are the basic objectives in the use of standard costs?
2. What is meant by reporting by the "principle of exceptions" as the term is used in reference to cost control?
3. What are the two variances between the actual cost and the standard cost for direct materials?
4. The materials cost variance report for Nickols Inc. indicates a large favorable materials price variance and a significant unfavorable materials quantity variance. What might have caused these offsetting variances?
5. a. What are the two variances between the actual cost and the standard cost for direct labor?
   b. Who generally has control over the direct labor cost variances?
6. A new assistant controller recently was heard to remark: "All the assembly workers in this plant are covered by union contracts, so there should be no labor variances." Was the controller's remark correct? Discuss.
7. Would the use of standards be appropriate in a nonmanufacturing setting such as a fast-food restaurant?
8. a. Describe the two variances between the actual costs and the standard costs for factory overhead.
   b. What is a factory overhead cost variance report?
9. If variances are recorded in the accounts at the time the manufacturing costs are incurred, what does a debit balance in Direct Materials Price Variance represent?
10. Briefly explain why firms might use nonfinancial performance measures.

Practice Exercises

Example Exercises

EE 23-1 p. 1133
Show Me How

PE 23-1A Direct materials variances OBJ. 3

Bellingham Company produces a product that requires 2.5 standard pounds per unit. The standard price is $3.75 per pound. If 15,000 units required 36,000 pounds, which were purchased at $4.00 per pound, what is the direct materials (a) price variance, (b) quantity variance, and (c) total direct materials cost variance?

Show Me How **EE 23-1** *p. 1133*

PE 23-1B Direct materials variances **OBJ. 3**

Dvorak Company produces a product that requires 5 standard pounds per unit. The standard price is $2.50 per pound. If 1,000 units required 4,500 pounds, which were purchased at $3.00 per pound, what is the direct materials (a) price variance, (b) quantity variance, and (c) total direct materials cost variance?

Show Me How **EE 23-2** *p. 1136*

PE 23-2A Direct labor variances **OBJ. 3**

Bellingham Company produces a product that requires 4 standard hours per unit at a standard hourly rate of $20 per hour. If 15,000 units required 61,800 hours at an hourly rate of $19.85 per hour, what is the direct labor (a) rate variance, (b) time variance, and (c) total direct labor cost variance?

Show Me How **EE 23-2** *p. 1136*

PE 23-2B Direct labor variances **OBJ. 3**

Dvorak Company produces a product that requires 3 standard hours per unit at a standard hourly rate of $17 per hour. If 1,000 units required 2,800 hours at an hourly rate of $16.50 per hour, what is the direct labor (a) rate variance, (b) time variance, and (c) total direct labor cost variance?

Show Me How **EE 23-3** *p. 1139*

PE 23-3A Factory overhead controllable variance **OBJ. 4**

Bellingham Company produced 15,000 units of product that required 4 standard hours per unit. The standard variable overhead cost per unit is $0.90 per hour. The actual variable factory overhead was $52,770. Determine the variable factory overhead controllable variance.

Show Me How **EE 23-3** *p. 1139*

PE 23-3B Factory overhead controllable variance **OBJ. 4**

Dvorak Company produced 1,000 units of product that required 3 standard hours per unit. The standard variable overhead cost per unit is $1.40 per hour. The actual variable factory overhead was $4,000. Determine the variable factory overhead controllable variance.

Show Me How **EE 23-4** *p. 1140*

PE 23-4A Factory overhead volume variance **OBJ. 4**

Bellingham Company produced 15,000 units of product that required 4 standard hours per unit. The standard fixed overhead cost per unit is $1.15 per hour at 58,000 hours, which is 100% of normal capacity. Determine the fixed factory overhead volume variance.

Show Me How **EE 23-4** *p. 1140*

PE 23-4B Factory overhead volume variance **OBJ. 4**

Dvorak Company produced 1,000 units of product that required 3 standard hours per unit. The standard fixed overhead cost per unit is $0.60 per hour at 3,500 hours, which is 100% of normal capacity. Determine the fixed factory overhead volume variance.

Show Me How **EE 23-5** *p. 1144*

PE 23-5A Standard cost journal entries **OBJ. 5**

Bellingham Company produced 15,000 units that require 2.5 standard pounds per unit at $3.75 standard price per pound. The company actually used 36,000 pounds in production. Journalize the entry to record the standard direct materials used in production.

Show Me How **EE 23-5** *p. 1144*

PE 23-5B Standard cost journal entries **OBJ. 5**

Dvorak Company produced 1,000 units that require 5 standard pounds per unit at $2.50 standard price per pound. The company actually used 4,500 pounds in production. Journalize the entry to record the standard direct materials used in production.

Show Me How **EE 23-6** *p. 1145*

PE 23-6A Income statement with variances **OBJ. 5**

Prepare an income statement through gross profit for Bellingham Company for the month ended March 31 using the variance data in Practice Exercises 23-1A through 23-4A. Assume that Bellingham sold 15,000 units at $172 per unit.

EE 23-6 *p. 1145*

Show Me How

OBJ. 5

PE 23-6B Income statement with variances

Prepare an income statement through gross profit for Dvorak Company for the month ended July 31 using the variance data in Practice Exercises 23-1B through 23-4B. Assume that Dvorak sold 1,000 units at $90 per unit.

EE 23-7 *p. 1147*

Show Me How

OBJ. 6

PE 23-7A Activity inputs and outputs

The following are inputs and outputs to the copying process of a copy shop:

Number of employee errors
Number of times paper supply runs out
Copy machine downtime (broken)
Number of pages copied per hour
Number of customer complaints
Percent of jobs done on time

Identify whether each is an input or output to the copying process.

EE 23-7 *p. 1147*

Show Me How

OBJ. 6

PE 23-7B Activity inputs and outputs

The following are inputs and outputs to the cooking process of a restaurant:

Number of times ingredients are missing
Number of customer complaints
Number of hours kitchen equipment is down for repairs
Number of server order mistakes
Percent of meals prepared on time
Number of unexpected cook absences

Identify whether each is an input or output to the cooking process.

Exercises

Show Me How

OBJ. 2

EX 23-1 Standard direct materials cost per unit

Roanoke Company produces chocolate bars. The primary materials used in producing chocolate bars are cocoa, sugar, and milk. The standard costs for a batch of chocolate (5,200 bars) are as follows:

Ingredient	Quantity	Price
Cocoa	400 lb.	$1.25 per lb.
Sugar	80 lb.	$0.40 per lb.
Milk	120 gal.	$2.50 per gal.

Determine the standard direct materials cost per bar of chocolate.

Show Me How

OBJ. 2

EX 23-2 Standard product cost

Sana Rosa Furniture Company manufactures designer home furniture. Sana Rosa uses a standard cost system. The direct labor, direct materials, and factory overhead standards for an unfinished dining room table are as follows:

Direct labor:	standard rate	$18.00 per hr.
	standard time per unit	3.5 hrs.
Direct materials (oak):	standard price	$15.00 per bd. ft.
	standard quantity	26 bd. ft.
Variable factory overhead:	standard rate	$4.20 per direct labor hr.
Fixed factory overhead:	standard rate	$1.80 per direct labor hr.

a. Determine the standard cost per dining room table.

b. Why would Sana Rosa Furniture Company use a standard cost system?

✔ b. Direct labor cost variance, $(580) F

Excel

Show Me How

EX 23-3 Budget performance report **OBJ. 2**

Genie in a Bottle Company (GBC) manufactures plastic two-liter bottles for the beverage industry. The cost standards per 100 two-liter bottles are as follows:

Cost Category	Standard Cost per 100 Two-Liter Bottles
Direct labor	$ 2.00
Direct materials	9.10
Factory overhead	0.55
Total	$11.65

At the beginning of July, GBC management planned to produce 400,000 bottles. The actual number of bottles produced for July was 406,000 bottles. The actual costs for July of the current year were as follows:

Cost Category	Actual Cost for the Month Ended July 31
Direct labor	$ 7,540
Direct materials	35,750
Factory overhead	2,680
Total	$45,970

a. Prepare the July manufacturing standard cost budget (direct labor, direct materials, and factory overhead) for GBC, assuming planned production.

b. Prepare a budget performance report for manufacturing costs, showing the total cost variances for direct materials, direct labor, and factory overhead for July.

c. Interpret the budget performance report.

✔ a. Price variance, $7,250 U

Show Me How

EX 23-4 Direct materials variances **OBJ. 3**

The following data relate to the direct materials cost for the production of 10,000 automobile tires:

Actual:	145,000 lb. at $2.80
Standard:	150,000 lb. at $2.75

a. Determine the direct materials price variance, direct materials quantity variance, and total direct materials cost variance.

b. To whom should the variances be reported for analysis and control?

✔ Quantity variance, $300 U

Show Me How

EX 23-5 Direct materials variances **OBJ. 3**

Silicone Engine Inc. produces wrist-worn tablet computers. The company uses Thin Film Crystal (TFC) LCD displays for its products. Each tablet uses one display. The company produced 580 tablets during December. However, due to LCD defects, the company actually used 600 LCD displays during December. Each display has a standard cost of $15.00. Six hundred LCD displays were purchased for December production at a cost of $8,550.

Determine the price variance, quantity variance, and total direct materials cost variance for December.

Show Me How

EX 23-6 Standard direct materials cost per unit from variance data **OBJ. 2, 3**

The following data relating to direct materials cost for October of the current year are taken from the records of Good Clean Fun Inc., a manufacturer of organic toys:

Quantity of direct materials used	3,000 lb.
Actual unit price of direct materials	$5.50 per lb.
Units of finished product manufactured	1,400 units
Standard direct materials per unit of finished product	2 lb.
Direct materials quantity variance—unfavorable	$1,000
Direct materials price variance—unfavorable	$1,500

(Continued)

Determine the standard direct materials cost per unit of finished product, assuming that there was no inventory of work in process at either the beginning or end of the month.

EX 23-7 Standard product cost, direct materials variance **OBJ. 2, 3**

Real World

Show Me How

H.J. Heinz Company uses standards to control its materials costs. Assume that a batch of ketchup (3,128 pounds) has the following standards:

	Standard Quantity	Standard Price
Whole tomatoes	4,000 lb.	$ 0.60 per lb.
Vinegar	260 gal.	2.25 per gal.
Corn syrup	25 gal.	28.00 per gal.
Salt	100 lb.	2.25 per lb.

The actual materials in a batch may vary from the standard due to tomato characteristics. Assume that the actual quantities of materials for batch K-111 were as follows:

4,250 lb. of tomatoes
275 gal. of vinegar
22 gal. of corn syrup
90 lb. of salt

a. Determine the standard unit materials cost per pound for a standard batch.

b. Determine the direct materials quantity variance for batch K-111. Round your answer to the nearest cent.

EX 23-8 Direct labor variances **OBJ. 3**

✔ a. Rate variance, $(6,330) F

Show Me How

The following data relate to labor cost for production of 22,000 cellular telephones:

Actual:	4,220 hrs. at $44.50
Standard:	4,160 hrs. at $46.00

a. Determine the direct labor rate variance, direct labor time variance, and total direct labor cost variance.

b. Discuss what might have caused these variances.

EX 23-9 Direct labor variances **OBJ. 3, 5**

✔ a. Time variance, $(5,600) F

Show Me How

La Barte Company manufactures commuter bicycles from recycled materials. The following data for July of the current year are available:

Quantity of direct labor used	5,050 hrs.
Actual rate for direct labor	$16.80 per hr.
Bicycles completed in July	1,000 bicycles
Standard direct labor per bicycle	5.4 hrs.
Standard rate for direct labor	$16.00 per hr.

a. Determine the direct labor rate variance, time variance, and total direct labor cost variance.

b. How much direct labor should be debited to Work in Process?

EX 23-10 Direct labor variances **OBJ. 3**

✔ a. Cutting Department rate variance, $(638) F

Greeson Clothes Company produced 25,000 units during June of the current year. The Cutting Department used 6,380 direct labor hours at an actual rate of $10.90 per hour. The Sewing Department used 9,875 direct labor hours at an actual rate of $11.12 per hour. Assume that there were no work in process inventories in either department at the beginning or end of the month. The standard labor rate is $11.00. The standard labor time for the Cutting and Sewing departments is 0.25 hour and 0.40 hour per unit, respectively.

a. Determine the direct labor rate, direct labor time, and total direct labor cost variance for the (1) Cutting Department and (2) Sewing Department.

b. Interpret your results.

✔ a. $2,400

EX 23-11 Direct labor standards for nonmanufacturing expenses **OBJ. 3**

Englert Hospital began using standards to evaluate its Admissions Department. The standard was broken into two types of admissions as follows:

Type of Admission	Standard Time to Complete Admission Record
Unscheduled admission	30 min.
Scheduled admission	15 min.

The unscheduled admission took longer because name, address, and insurance information needed to be determined and verified at the time of admission. Information was collected on scheduled admissions prior to the admissions, which was less time-consuming.

The Admissions Department employs four full-time people (40 productive hours per week, with no overtime) at $15 per hour. For the most recent week, the department handled 140 unscheduled and 350 scheduled admissions.

a. How much was actually spent on labor for the week?

b. What are the standard hours for the actual volume for the week?

c. Calculate a time variance and report how well the department performed for the week.

✔ a. 28

Real World

EX 23-12 Direct labor standards for a service company **OBJ. 2, 3**

One of the operations in the United States Postal Service is a mechanical mail sorting operation. In this operation, letter mail is sorted at a rate of 1.5 letters per second. The letter is mechanically sorted from a three-digit code input by an operator sitting at a keyboard. The manager of the mechanical sorting operation wants to determine the number of temporary employees to hire for December. The manager estimates that there will be an additional 24,192,000 pieces of mail in December, due to the upcoming holiday season.

Assume that the sorting operators are temporary employees. The union contract requires that temporary employees be hired for one month at a time. Each temporary employee is hired to work 160 hours in the month.

a. How many temporary employees should the manager hire for December?

b. If each temporary employee earns a standard $16.40 per hour, what would be the labor time variance if the actual number of additional letters sorted in December was 23,895,000?

✔ a. Direct labor rate variance, $(12) F

Show Me How

EX 23-13 Direct labor variances for a service company **OBJ. 2, 3**

Hit-n-Run Food Trucks, Inc. owns and operates food trucks (mobile kitchens) throughout the West Coast. The company's employees have varying wage levels depending on their experience and length of time with the company. Employees work eight-hour shifts and are assigned to a truck each day based on labor needs to support the daily menu. One of the trucks, Jose O'Brien's Mobile Fiesta, specializes in Irish-Mexican fusion cuisine. The truck offers a single menu item that changes daily. On November 11, the truck prepared 200 of its most popular item, the Irish Breakfast Enchilada. The following data are available for that day:

Quantity of direct labor used (3 employees, working 8-hour shifts)	24 hrs.
Actual rate for direct labor	$15.00 per hr.
Standard direct labor per meal	0.1 hr.
Standard rate for direct labor	$15.50 per hr.

a. Determine the direct labor rate variance, the direct labor time variance, and the total direct labor cost variance.

b. Discuss what might have caused these variances.

✔ Direct materials quantity variance, $(1,300) F

Show Me How

EX 23-14 Direct materials and direct labor variances

OBJ. 3

At the beginning of June, Kimber Toy Company budgeted 4,800 toy action figures to be manufactured in June at standard direct materials and direct labor costs as follows:

Direct materials	$ 60,000
Direct labor	48,000
Total	$108,000

The standard materials price is $5.00 per pound. The standard direct labor rate is $20.00 per hour. At the end of June, the actual direct materials and direct labor costs were as follows:

Actual direct materials	$ 61,200
Actual direct labor	48,000
Total	$109,200

There were no direct materials price or direct labor rate variances for June. In addition, assume no changes in the direct materials inventory balances in June. Kimber Toy Company actually produced 5,000 units during June.

Determine the direct materials quantity and direct labor time variances.

✔ Total factory overhead, 22,000 hrs., $443,600

EX 23-15 Flexible overhead budget

OBJ. 4

Leno Manufacturing Company prepared the following factory overhead cost budget for the Press Department for October of the current year, during which it expected to require 20,000 hours of productive capacity in the department:

Variable overhead cost:		
Indirect factory labor	$180,000	
Power and light	12,000	
Indirect materials	64,000	
Total variable overhead cost		$256,000
Fixed overhead cost:		
Supervisory salaries	$ 80,000	
Depreciation of plant and equipment	50,000	
Insurance and property taxes	32,000	
Total fixed overhead cost		162,000
Total factory overhead cost		$418,000

Assuming that the estimated costs for November are the same as for October, prepare a flexible factory overhead cost budget for the Press Department for November for 18,000, 20,000, and 22,000 hours of production.

EX 23-16 Flexible overhead budget

OBJ. 4

Wiki Wiki Company has determined that the variable overhead rate is $4.50 per direct labor hour in the Fabrication Department. The normal production capacity for the Fabrication Department is 10,000 hours for the month. Fixed costs are budgeted at $60,000 for the month.

a. Prepare a monthly factory overhead flexible budget for 9,000, 10,000, and 11,000 hours of production.

b. How much overhead would be applied to production if 9,000 hours were used in the department during the month?

✔ Volume variance, $4,000 U

EX 23-17 Factory overhead cost variances

OBJ. 4

The following data relate to factory overhead cost for the production of 15,000 computers:

Actual:	Variable factory overhead	$240,000
	Fixed factory overhead	160,000
Standard:	19,500 hrs. at $20	390,000

If productive capacity of 100% was 20,000 hours and the total factory overhead cost budgeted at the level of 19,500 standard hours was $394,000, determine the variable factory overhead controllable variance, fixed factory overhead volume variance, and total factory overhead cost variance. The fixed factory overhead rate was $8.00 per hour.

✔ a. $(13,000) F

Excel

EX 23-18 Factory overhead cost variances **OBJ. 4**

Blumen Textiles Corporation began April with a budget for 90,000 hours of production in the Weaving Department. The department has a full capacity of 100,000 hours under normal business conditions. The budgeted overhead at the planned volumes at the beginning of April was as follows:

Variable overhead	$540,000
Fixed overhead	240,000
Total	$780,000

The actual factory overhead was $782,000 for April. The actual fixed factory overhead was as budgeted. During April, the Weaving Department had standard hours at actual production volume of 92,500 hours.

a. Determine the variable factory overhead controllable variance.

b. Determine the fixed factory overhead volume variance.

EX 23-19 Factory overhead variance corrections **OBJ. 4**

The data related to Shunda Enterprises Inc.'s factory overhead cost for the production of 100,000 units of product are as follows:

Actual:	Variable factory overhead	$458,000
	Fixed factory overhead	494,000
Standard:	132,000 hrs. at $7.30 ($3.50 for variable factory overhead)	963,600

Productive capacity at 100% of normal was 130,000 hours, and the factory overhead cost budgeted at the level of 132,000 standard hours was $956,000. Based on these data, the chief cost accountant prepared the following variance analysis:

Variable factory overhead controllable variance:		
Actual variable factory overhead cost incurred	$458,000	
Budgeted variable factory overhead for 132,000 hours	462,000	
Variance—favorable		$ (4,000)
Fixed factory overhead volume variance:		
Normal productive capacity at 100%	130,000 hrs.	
Standard for amount produced	132,000	
Productive capacity not used	2,000 hrs.	
Standard variable factory overhead rate	× $7.30	
Variance—unfavorable		14,600
Total factory overhead cost variance—unfavorable		$10,600

Identify the errors in the factory overhead cost variance analysis.

✔ Net controllable variance, $900 U

Excel

EX 23-20 Factory overhead cost variance report **OBJ. 4**

Tannin Products Inc. prepared the following factory overhead cost budget for the Trim Department for July of the current year, during which it expected to use 20,000 hours for production:

Variable overhead cost:		
Indirect factory labor	$46,000	
Power and light	12,000	
Indirect materials	20,000	
Total variable overhead cost		$ 78,000

(Continued)

Fixed overhead cost:		
Supervisory salaries	$54,500	
Depreciation of plant and equipment	40,000	
Insurance and property taxes	35,500	
Total fixed overhead cost		130,000
Total factory overhead cost		$208,000

Tannin has available 25,000 hours of monthly productive capacity in the Trim Department under normal business conditions. During July, the Trim Department actually used 22,000 hours for production. The actual fixed costs were as budgeted. The actual variable overhead for July was as follows:

Actual variable factory overhead cost:	
Indirect factory labor	$49,700
Power and light	13,000
Indirect materials	24,000
Total variable cost	$86,700

Construct a factory overhead cost variance report for the Trim Department for July.

EX 23-21 Recording standards in accounts **OBJ. 5**

Cioffi Manufacturing Company incorporates standards in its accounts and identifies variances at the time the manufacturing costs are incurred. Journalize the entries to record the following transactions:

a. Purchased 2,450 units of copper tubing on account at $52.00 per unit. The standard price is $48.50 per unit.

b. Used 1,900 units of copper tubing in the process of manufacturing 200 air conditioners. Ten units of copper tubing are required, at standard, to produce one air conditioner.

EX 23-22 Recording standards in accounts **OBJ. 5**

The Assembly Department produced 5,000 units of product during March. Each unit required 2.20 standard direct labor hours. There were 11,500 actual hours used in the Assembly Department during March at an actual rate of $17.60 per hour. The standard direct labor rate is $18.00 per hour. Assuming that direct labor for a month is paid on the fifth day of the following month, journalize the direct labor in the Assembly Department on March 31.

EX 23-23 Income statement indicating standard cost variances **OBJ. 5**

✔ Income before income tax, $85,900

The following data were taken from the records of Griggs Company for December:

Administrative expenses	$100,800
Cost of goods sold (at standard)	550,000
Direct materials price variance—unfavorable	1,680
Direct materials quantity variance—favorable	(560)
Direct labor rate variance—favorable	(1,120)
Direct labor time variance—unfavorable	490
Variable factory overhead controllable variance—favorable	(210)
Fixed factory overhead volume variance—unfavorable	3,080
Interest expense	2,940
Sales	868,000
Selling expenses	125,000

Prepare an income statement for presentation to management.

EX 23-24 Nonfinancial performance measures **OBJ. 6**

Diamond Inc. is an Internet retailer of woodworking equipment. Customers order woodworking equipment from the company, using an online catalog. The company processes these orders and delivers the requested product from its warehouse. The company wants to provide customers with an excellent purchase experience in order to expand the business through favorable word-of-mouth advertising and to drive repeat business. To help monitor performance, the company developed a set of performance measures for its order placement and delivery process:

Average computer response time to customer "clicks"
Dollar amount of returned goods
Elapsed time between customer order and product delivery
Maintenance dollars divided by hardware investment
Number of customer complaints divided by the number of orders
Number of misfilled orders divided by the number of orders
Number of orders per warehouse employee
Number of page faults or errors due to software programming errors
Number of software fixes per week
Server (computer) downtime
Training dollars per programmer

a. For each performance measure, identify it as either an input or output measure related to the "order placement and delivery" process.
b. Provide an explanation for each performance measure.

EX 23-25 Nonfinancial performance measures **OBJ. 6**

Alpha University wants to monitor the efficiency and quality of its course registration process.
a. Identify three input and three output measures for this process.
b. Why would Alpha University use nonfinancial measures for monitoring this process?

Problems: Series A

PR 23-1A Direct materials and direct labor variance analysis **OBJ. 2, 3**

✔ c. Direct labor time variance, $600 U

Show Me How

Abbeville Company manufactures faucets in a small manufacturing facility. The faucets are made from brass. Manufacturing has 90 employees. Each employee presently provides 36 hours of labor per week. Information about a production week is as follows:

Standard wage per hr.	$15.00
Standard labor time per faucet	40 min.
Standard number of lb. of brass	3 lb.
Standard price per lb. of brass	$2.40
Actual price per lb. of brass	$2.50
Actual lb. of brass used during the week	14,350 lb.
Number of faucets produced during the week	4,800
Actual wage per hr.	$14.40
Actual hrs. for the week	3,240 hrs.

Instructions

Determine (a) the standard cost per unit for direct materials and direct labor; (b) the direct materials price variance, direct materials quantity variance, and total direct materials cost variance; and (c) the direct labor rate variance, direct labor time variance, and total direct labor cost variance.

PR 23-2A Flexible budgeting and variance analysis **OBJ. 1, 2, 3**

✔ 1. a. Direct materials quantity variance, $(625) F

Excel

I Love My Chocolate Company makes dark chocolate and light chocolate. Both products require cocoa and sugar. The following planning information has been made available:

	Standard Amount per Case		
	Dark Chocolate	Light Chocolate	Standard Price per Pound
Cocoa	12 lb.	8 lb.	$7.25
Sugar	10 lb.	14 lb.	1.40
Standard labor time	0.50 hr.	0.60 hr.	

(Continued)

	Dark Chocolate	Light Chocolate
Planned production	4,700 cases	11,000 cases
Standard labor rate	$15.50 per hr.	$15.50 per hr.

I Love My Chocolate Company does not expect there to be any beginning or ending inventories of cocoa or sugar. At the end of the budget year, I Love My Chocolate Company had the following actual results:

	Dark Chocolate	Light Chocolate
Actual production (cases)	5,000	10,000
	Actual Price per Pound	**Actual Pounds Purchased and Used**
Cocoa	$7.33	140,300
Sugar	1.35	188,000
	Actual Labor Rate	**Actual Labor Hours Used**
Dark chocolate	$15.25 per hr.	2,360
Light chocolate	15.80 per hr.	6,120

Instructions

1. Prepare the following variance analyses for both chocolates and the total, based on the actual results and production levels at the end of the budget year:
   a. Direct materials price, quantity, and total variance
   b. Direct labor rate, time, and total variance
2. Why are the standard amounts in part (1) based on the actual production for the year instead of the planned production for the year?

PR 23-3A Direct materials, direct labor, and factory overhead cost variance analysis

OBJ. 3, 4

✔ c. Controllable variance, $(4,800) F

Excel

Mackinaw Inc. processes a base chemical into plastic. Standard costs and actual costs for direct materials, direct labor, and factory overhead incurred for the manufacture of 40,000 units of product were as follows:

	Standard Costs	Actual Costs
Direct materials	120,000 lb. at $3.20	118,500 lb. at $3.25
Direct labor	12,000 hrs. at $24.40	11,700 hrs. at $25.00
Factory overhead	Rates per direct labor hr., based on 100% of normal capacity of 15,000 direct labor hrs.:	
	Variable cost, $8.00	$91,200 variable cost
	Fixed cost, $10.00	$150,000 fixed cost

Each unit requires 0.3 hour of direct labor.

Instructions

Determine (a) the direct materials price variance, direct materials quantity variance, and total direct materials cost variance; (b) the direct labor rate variance, direct labor time variance, and total direct labor cost variance; and (c) the variable factory overhead controllable variance, fixed factory overhead volume variance, and total factory overhead cost variance.

PR 23-4A Factory overhead cost variance report

OBJ. 4

✔ Controllable variance, $770 U

Excel

General Ledger

Tiger Equipment Inc., a manufacturer of construction equipment, prepared the following factory overhead cost budget for the Welding Department for May of the current year. The company expected to operate the department at 100% of normal capacity of 8,400 hours.

Variable costs:		
Indirect factory wages	$30,240	
Power and light	20,160	
Indirect materials	16,800	
Total variable cost		$ 67,200
Fixed costs:		
Supervisory salaries	$20,000	
Depreciation of plant and equipment	36,200	
Insurance and property taxes	15,200	
Total fixed cost		71,400
Total factory overhead cost		$138,600

During May, the department operated at 8,860 standard hours. The factory overhead costs incurred were indirect factory wages, $32,400; power and light, $21,000; indirect materials, $18,250; supervisory salaries, $20,000; depreciation of plant and equipment, $36,200; and insurance and property taxes, $15,200.

Instructions

Prepare a factory overhead cost variance report for May. To be useful for cost control, the budgeted amounts should be based on 8,860 hours.

PR 23-5A Standards for nonmanufacturing expenses

OBJ. 3, 6

✔ 3. $1,600 U

CodeHead Software Inc. is a software development company. One important activity in software development is writing software code. The manager of the WordPro Development Team determined that the average software programmer could write 25 lines of code in an hour. The plan for the first week in May called for 4,650 lines of code to be written on the WordPro product. The WordPro Team has five programmers. Each programmer is hired from an employment firm that requires temporary employees to be hired for a minimum of a 40-hour week. Programmers are paid $32.00 per hour. The manager offered a bonus if the team could generate more lines for the week, without overtime. Due to a project emergency, the programmers wrote more code in the first week of May than planned. The actual amount of code written in the first week of May was 5,650 lines, without overtime. As a result, the bonus caused the average programmer's hourly rate to increase to $40.00 per hour during the first week in May.

Instructions

1. If the team had generated 4,650 lines of code according to the original plan, what would have been the labor time variance?
2. What was the actual labor time variance as a result of generating 5,650 lines of code?
3. What was the labor rate variance as a result of the bonus?
4. Are there any performance-related issues that the labor time and rate variances fail to consider? Explain.
5. The manager is trying to determine if a better decision would have been to hire a temporary programmer to meet the higher programming demand in the first week of May, rather than paying out the bonus. If another employee had been hired from the employment firm, what would have been the labor time variance in the first week?
6. Which decision is better, paying the bonus or hiring another programmer?

Problems: Series B

PR 23-1B Direct materials and direct labor variance analysis **OBJ. 2, 3**

✔ c. Rate variance, $(200) F

Show Me How

Lenni Clothing Co. manufactures clothing in a small manufacturing facility. Manufacturing has 25 employees. Each employee presently provides 40 hours of productive labor per week. Information about a production week is as follows:

Standard wage per hr.	$12.00
Standard labor time per unit	12 min.
Standard number of yds. of fabric per unit	5.0 yds.
Standard price per yd. of fabric	$5.00
Actual price per yd. of fabric	$5.10
Actual yds. of fabric used during the week	26,200 yds.
Number of units produced during the week	5,220
Actual wage per hr.	$11.80
Actual hrs. for the week	1,000 hrs.

Instructions

Determine (a) the standard cost per unit for direct materials and direct labor; (b) the price variance, quantity variance, and total direct materials cost variance; and (c) the rate variance, time variance, and total direct labor cost variance.

PR 23-2B Flexible budgeting and variance analysis **OBJ. 1, 2, 3**

✔ 1. a. Direct materials price variance, $12,220 U

Excel

I'm Really Cold Coat Company makes women's and men's coats. Both products require filler and lining material. The following planning information has been made available:

	Standard Amount per Unit		
	Women's Coats	**Men's Coats**	**Standard Price per Unit**
Filler	4.0 lb.	5.2 lb.	$2.00 per lb.
Liner	7.0 yds.	9.4 yds.	8.00 per yd.
Standard labor time	0.40 hr.	0.50 hr.	

	Women's Coats	Men's Coats
Planned production	5,000 units	6,200 units
Standard labor rate	$14.00 per hr.	$13.00 per hr.

I'm Really Cold Coat Company does not expect there to be any beginning or ending inventories of filler and lining material. At the end of the budget year, I'm Really Cold Coat Company experienced the following actual results:

	Women's Coats	Men's Coats
Actual production	4,400	5,800
	Actual Price per Unit	**Actual Quantity Purchased and Used**
Filler	$1.90 per lb.	48,000
Liner	8.20 per yd.	85,100
	Actual Labor Rate	**Actual Labor Hours Used**
Women's coats	$14.10 per hr.	1,825
Men's coats	13.30 per hr.	2,800

The expected beginning inventory and desired ending inventory were realized.

Instructions

1. Prepare the following variance analyses for both coats and the total, based on the actual results and production levels at the end of the budget year:
   a. Direct materials price, quantity, and total variance
   b. Direct labor rate, time, and total variance
2. Why are the standard amounts in part (1) based on the actual production at the end of the year instead of the planned production at the beginning of the year?

PR 23-3B Direct materials, direct labor, and factory overhead cost variance analysis

OBJ. 3, 4

✔ a. Direct materials price variance, $10,100 U

Excel

Road Gripper Tire Co. manufactures automobile tires. Standard costs and actual costs for direct materials, direct labor, and factory overhead incurred for the manufacture of 4,160 tires were as follows:

	Standard Costs	Actual Costs
Direct materials	100,000 lb. at $6.40	101,000 lb. at $6.50
Direct labor	2,080 hrs. at $15.75	2,000 hrs. at $15.40
Factory overhead	Rates per direct labor hr., based on 100% of normal capacity of 2,000 direct labor hrs.:	
	Variable cost, $4.00	$8,200 variable cost
	Fixed cost, $6.00	$12,000 fixed cost

Each tire requires 0.5 hour of direct labor.

Instructions

Determine (a) the direct materials price variance, direct materials quantity variance, and total direct materials cost variance; (b) the direct labor rate variance, direct labor time variance, and total direct labor cost variance; and (c) the variable factory overhead controllable variance, fixed factory overhead volume variance, and total factory overhead cost variance.

PR 23-4B Factory overhead cost variance report

OBJ. 4

✔ Controllable variance, $(1,450) F

Excel

General Ledger

Feeling Better Medical Inc., a manufacturer of disposable medical supplies, prepared the following factory overhead cost budget for the Assembly Department for October of the current year. The company expected to operate the department at 100% of normal capacity of 30,000 hours.

Variable costs:		
Indirect factory wages	$247,500	
Power and light	189,000	
Indirect materials	52,500	
Total variable cost		$489,000
Fixed costs:		
Supervisory salaries	$126,000	
Depreciation of plant and equipment	70,000	
Insurance and property taxes	44,000	
Total fixed cost		240,000
Total factory overhead cost		$729,000

During October, the department operated at 28,500 hours. The factory overhead costs incurred were indirect factory wages, $234,000; power and light, $178,500; indirect materials, $50,600; supervisory salaries, $126,000; depreciation of plant and equipment, $70,000; and insurance and property taxes, $44,000.

Instructions

Prepare a factory overhead cost variance report for October. To be useful for cost control, the budgeted amounts should be based on 28,500 hours.

PR 23-5B Standards for nonmanufacturing expenses for a service company

OBJ. 3, 6

✔ 2. $(161) F

The Radiology Department provides imaging services for Emergency Medical Center. One important activity in the Radiology Department is transcribing digitally recorded analyses of images into a written report. The manager of the Radiology Department determined that the average transcriptionist could type 700 lines of a report in an hour. The plan for the first week in May called for 81,900 typed lines to be written. The Radiology Department

(Continued)

has three transcriptionists. Each transcriptionist is hired from an employment firm that requires temporary employees to be hired for a minimum of a 40-hour week. Transcriptionists are paid $23.00 per hour. The manager offered a bonus if the department could type more lines for the week, without overtime. Due to high service demands, the transcriptionists typed more lines in the first week of May than planned. The actual amount of lines typed in the first week of May was 88,900 lines, without overtime. As a result, the bonus caused the average transcriptionist hourly rate to increase to $30.00 per hour during the first week in May.

Instructions

1. If the department had typed 81,900 lines according to the original plan, what would have been the labor time variance?
2. What was the labor time variance as a result of typing 88,900 lines?
3. What was the labor rate variance as a result of the bonus?
4. The manager is trying to determine if a better decision would have been to hire a temporary transcriptionist to meet the higher typing demands in the first week of May, rather than paying out the bonus. If another employee had been hired from the employment firm, what would have been the labor time variance in the first week?
5. Which decision is better, paying the bonus or hiring another transcriptionist?
6. Are there any performance-related issues that the labor time and rate variances fail to consider? Explain.

Comprehensive Problem 5

Genuine Spice Inc. began operations on January 1 of the current year. The company produces eight-ounce bottles of hand and body lotion called *Eternal Beauty*. The lotion is sold wholesale in 12-bottle cases for $100 per case. There is a selling commission of $20 per case. The January direct materials, direct labor, and factory overhead costs are as follows:

DIRECT MATERIALS

	Cost Behavior	Units per Case	Cost per Unit	Direct Materials Cost per Case
Cream base	Variable	100 oz.	$0.02	$ 2.00
Natural oils	Variable	30 oz.	0.30	9.00
Bottle (8-oz.)	Variable	12 bottles	0.50	6.00
				$17.00

DIRECT LABOR

Department	Cost Behavior	Time per Case	Labor Rate per Hour	Direct Labor Cost per Case
Mixing	Variable	20 min.	$18.00	$6.00
Filling	Variable	5	14.40	1.20
		25 min.		$7.20

FACTORY OVERHEAD

	Cost Behavior	Total Cost
Utilities	Mixed	$ 600
Facility lease	Fixed	14,000
Equipment depreciation	Fixed	4,300
Supplies	Fixed	660
		$19,560

Part A—Break-Even Analysis

The management of Genuine Spice Inc. wants to determine the number of cases required to break even per month. The utilities cost, which is part of factory overhead, is a mixed cost. The following information was gathered from the first six months of operation regarding this cost:

	Case Production	Utility Total Cost
January	500	$600
February	800	660
March	1,200	740
April	1,100	720
May	950	690
June	1,025	705

Instructions

✔ 2. $55.60

1. Determine the fixed and variable portion of the utility cost using the high-low method.
2. Determine the contribution margin per case.
3. Determine the fixed costs per month, including the utility fixed cost from part (1).
4. Determine the break-even number of cases per month.

Part B—August Budgets

During July of the current year, the management of Genuine Spice Inc. asked the controller to prepare August manufacturing and income statement budgets. Demand was expected to be 1,500 cases at $100 per case for August. Inventory planning information is provided as follows:

Finished Goods Inventory:

	Cases	Cost
Estimated finished goods inventory, August 1	300	$12,000
Desired finished goods inventory, August 31	175	7,000

Materials Inventory:

	Cream Base (oz.)	Oils (oz.)	Bottles (bottles)
Estimated materials inventory, August 1	250	290	600
Desired materials inventory, August 31	1,000	360	240

There was negligible work in process inventory assumed for either the beginning or end of the month; thus, none was assumed. In addition, there was no change in the cost per unit or estimated units per case operating data from January.

Instructions

✔ 6. Bottles purchased, $8,070

5. Prepare the August production budget.
6. Prepare the August direct materials purchases budget.
7. Prepare the August direct labor cost budget. Round the hours required for production to the nearest hour.
8. Prepare the August factory overhead cost budget.
9. Prepare the August budgeted income statement, including selling expenses.

Part C—August Variance Analysis

During September of the current year, the controller was asked to perform variance analyses for August. The January operating data provided the standard prices, rates, times, and quantities per case. There were 1,500 actual cases produced during August, which was 250 more cases than planned at the beginning of the month. Actual data for August were as follows:

	Actual Direct Materials Price per Unit	Actual Direct Materials Quantity per Case
Cream base	$0.016 per oz.	102 oz.
Natural oils	$0.32 per oz.	31 oz.
Bottle (8-oz.)	$0.42 per bottle	12.5 bottles

(Continued)

	Actual Direct Labor Rate	Actual Direct Labor Time per Case
Mixing	$18.20	19.50 min.
Filling	14.00	5.60 min.

Actual variable overhead	$305.00
Normal volume	1,600 cases

The prices of the materials were different from standard due to fluctuations in market prices. The standard quantity of materials used per case was an ideal standard. The Mixing Department used a higher grade labor classification during the month, thus causing the actual labor rate to exceed standard. The Filling Department used a lower grade labor classification during the month, thus causing the actual labor rate to be less than standard.

Instructions

10. Determine and interpret the direct materials price and quantity variances for the three materials.
11. Determine and interpret the direct labor rate and time variances for the two departments. Round hours to the nearest hour.
12. Determine and interpret the factory overhead controllable variance.
13. Determine and interpret the factory overhead volume variance.
14. Why are the standard direct labor and direct materials costs in the calculations for parts (10) and (11) based on the actual 1,500-case production volume rather than the planned 1,375 cases of production used in the budgets for parts (6) and (7)?

✔ 11. Mixing time variance, $(225) F

✔ 12. $5 U

Cases & Projects

CP 23-1 Ethics in Action

Ethics

Dash Riprock is a cost analyst with Safe Insurance Company. Safe is applying standards to its claims payment operation. Claims payment is a repetitive operation that could be evaluated with standards. Dash used time and motion studies to identify an ideal standard of 36 claims processed per hour. The Claims Processing Department manager, Henry Tudor, has rejected this standard and has argued that the standard should be 30 claims processed per hour. Henry and Dash were unable to agree, so they decided to discuss this matter openly at a joint meeting with the vice president of operations, who would arbitrate a final decision. Prior to the meeting, Dash wrote the following memo to the VP:

To: Anne Boleyn, Vice President of Operations
From: Dash Riprock
Re: Standards in the Claims Processing Department

As you know, Henry and I are scheduled to meet with you to discuss our disagreement with respect to the appropriate standards for the Claims Processing Department. I have conducted time and motion studies and have determined that the ideal standard is 36 claims processed per hour. Henry argues that 30 claims processed per hour would be more appropriate. I believe he is trying to "pad" the budget with some slack. I'm not sure what he is trying to get away with, but I believe a tight standard will drive up efficiency in his area. I hope you will agree when we meet with you next week.

Discuss the ethical and professional issues in this situation.

CP 23-2 Team Activity

Team Activity

Many city and county governments are discovering that you can control only what you measure. As a result, many municipal governments are introducing nonfinancial performance measures to help improve municipal services. As a team, use the Google search engine to perform a search for "municipal government performance measurement." Google will provide a list of Internet sites that outline various city efforts in using nonfinancial performance measures. As a team, report on the types of measures used by one of the cities from the search.

Communication

CP 23-3 Communication

The senior management of Tungston Company has proposed the following three performance measures for the company:

1. Net income as a percent of stockholders' equity
2. Revenue growth
3. Employee satisfaction

Management believes that these three measures combine both financial and nonfinancial measures and are thus superior to using just financial measures.

Write a brief memo to David Tungston, the company president, providing suggestions on how to improve the company's performance measurement system.

CP 23-4 Variance interpretation

You have been asked to investigate some cost problems in the Assembly Department of Ruthenium Electronics Co., a consumer electronics company. To begin your investigation, you have obtained the following budget performance report for the department for the last quarter:

Ruthenium Electronics Co.—Assembly Department
Quarterly Budget Performance Report

	Standard Quantity at Standard Rates	Actual Quantity at Standard Rates	Quantity Variances
Direct labor	$157,500	$227,500	$ 70,000 U
Direct materials	297,500	385,000	87,500 U
Total	$455,000	$612,500	$157,500 U

You also obtained the following reports:

Ruthenium Electronics Co.—Purchasing Department
Quarterly Budget Performance Report

	Actual Quantity at Standard Rates	Actual Quantity at Actual Rates	Price Variance
Direct materials	$437,500	$385,000	$(52,500) F

Ruthenium Electronics Co.—Fabrication Department
Quarterly Budget Performance Report

	Standard Quantity at Standard Rates	Actual Quantity at Standard Rates	Quantity Variances
Direct labor	$245,000	$203,000	$(42,000) F
Direct materials	140,000	140,000	0
Total	$385,000	$343,000	$(42,000) F

You also interviewed the Assembly Department supervisor. Excerpts from the interview follow:

Q: What explains the poor performance in your department?

A: Listen, you've got to understand what it's been like in this department recently. Lately, it seems no matter how hard we try, we can't seem to make the standards. I'm not sure what is going on, but we've been having a lot of problems lately.

Q: What kind of problems?

A: Well, for instance, all this quarter we've been requisitioning purchased parts from the material storeroom, and the parts just didn't fit together very well. I'm not sure what is going on, but during most of this quarter, we've had to scrap and sort purchased parts—just to get our assemblies put together. Naturally, all this takes time and material. And that's not all.

(Continued)

Q: Go on.

A: All this quarter the work we've been receiving from the Fabrication Department has been shoddy. I mean, maybe around 20% of the stuff that comes in from Fabrication just can't be assembled. The fabrication is all wrong. As a result, we've had to scrap and rework a lot of the stuff. Naturally, this has just shot our quantity variances.

Interpret the variance reports in light of the comments by the Assembly Department supervisor.

CP 23-5 Variance interpretation

Vanadium Audio Inc. is a small manufacturer of electronic musical instruments. The plant manager received the following variable factory overhead report for the period:

	Actual	Budgeted Variable Factory Overhead at Actual Production	Controllable Variance
Supplies	$ 42,000	$ 39,780	$ 2,220 U
Power and light	52,500	50,900	1,600 U
Indirect factory wages	39,100	30,600	8,500 U
Total	$133,600	$121,280	$12,320 U

Actual units produced: 15,000 (90% of practical capacity)

The plant manager is not pleased with the $12,320 unfavorable variable factory overhead controllable variance and has come to discuss the matter with the controller. The following discussion occurred:

Plant Manager: I just received this factory report for the latest month of operation. I'm not very pleased with these figures. Before these numbers go to headquarters, you and I need to reach an understanding.

Controller: Go ahead. What's the problem?

Plant Manager: What's the problem? Well, everything. Look at the variance. It's too large. If I understand the accounting approach being used here, you are assuming that my costs are variable to the units produced. Thus, as the production volume declines, so should these costs. Well, I don't believe these costs are variable at all. I think they are fixed costs. As a result, when we operate below capacity, the costs really don't go down. I'm being penalized for costs I have no control over. I need this report to be redone to reflect this fact. If anything, the difference between actual and budget is essentially a volume variance. Listen, I know that you're a team player. You really need to reconsider your assumptions on this one.

If you were in the controller's position, how would you respond to the plant manager?

CHAPTER 24

Decentralized Operations

Concepts and Principles

Chapter 18 *Introduction to Managerial Accounting*

Developing Information

COST SYSTEMS

Chapter 19 *Job Order Costing*
Chapter 20 *Process Costing*

COST BEHAVIOR

Chapter 21 *Cost-Volume-Profit Analysis*

Decision Making

EVALUATING PERFORMANCE

Chapter 22 *Budgeting*
Chapter 23 *Variances from Standard Costs*

COMPARING ALTERNATIVES

Chapter 24 ***Decentralized Operations***
Chapter 25 *Differential Analysis, Product Pricing, and Activity-Based Costing*
Chapter 26 *Capital Investment Analysis*

CHAPTER 24

©KEVIN BRINE/SHUTTERSTOCK.COM

Caterpillar, Inc.

Have you ever wondered why large retail stores like **Macy's**, **JC Penney**, and **Sears** are divided into departments? Organizing into departments allows retailers to provide products and expertise in specialized areas while offering a wide range of products. Departments also allow companies to assign responsibility for financial performance. This information can be used to make product decisions, evaluate operations, and guide company strategy. Strong departmental performance might be attributable to a good department manager, while weak departmental performance may be the result of a product mix that has low customer appeal. By tracking departmental performance, companies can identify and reward excellent performance and take corrective action in departments that are performing poorly.

Like retailers, most businesses organize into operational units such as divisions and departments. For example, **Caterpillar, Inc.**, manufactures a variety of equipment and machinery and is organized into a number of different segments, including Construction Industries, Resource Industries, Energy & Transportation, and Financial Products. The Construction Industries segment manufactures construction equipment such as tractors, dump trucks, and loaders. The Resource Industries segment makes equipment for the mining industry, such as off-highway and mining trucks. The Energy & Transportation segment manufactures equipment that is used to generate power, such as engines and turbines for power plants. The Financial Products segment provides financing for Caterpillar products to customers and dealers.

Managers at Caterpillar, Inc., are responsible for running their business segment. Each segment is evaluated on segment profit, which excludes certain expense items from the calculation of profit that are not within the control of the business segment. The company uses segment profit to determine how to allocate resources between business segments and to plan and control the company's operations.

In this chapter, the role of accounting in assisting managers in planning and controlling organizational units such as departments, divisions, and stores is described and illustrated.

Learning Objectives

After studying this chapter, you should be able to:

Example Exercises (EE) are shown in **green.**

Obj. 1 **Describe the advantages and disadvantages of decentralized operations.**

Obj. 2 **Prepare a responsibility accounting report for a cost center.**

Obj. 3 **Prepare responsibility accounting reports for a profit center.**

Obj. 4 **Compute and interpret the return on investment, the residual income, and the balanced scorecard for an investment center.**

Obj. 5 **Describe and illustrate how the market price, negotiated price, and cost price approaches to transfer pricing may be used by decentralized segments of a business.**

At a Glance 24 Page 1194

Obj. 1 Describe the advantages and disadvantages of decentralized operations.

Centralized and Decentralized Operations

In a *centralized* company, all major planning and operating decisions are made by top management. For example, a one-person, owner–manager operated company is centralized because all plans and decisions are made by one person. In a small owner–manager operated business, centralization may be desirable. This is because the owner–manager's close supervision ensures that the business will be operated the way the owner-manager chooses.

In a *decentralized* company, managers of separate divisions or units are delegated operating responsibility. The division (unit) managers are responsible for planning and controlling the operations of their divisions. Divisions are often structured around products, customers, or regions.

The proper amount of decentralization for a company depends on the company's size, organizational culture, and business strategy. For example, in some companies, division managers have authority over all operations, including fixed asset purchases. In other companies, division managers have authority over profits but not fixed asset purchases.

Advantages of Decentralization

For large companies, it is difficult for top management to:

- Maintain daily contact with all operations, and
- Maintain operating expertise in all product lines and services

In such cases, delegating authority to managers closest to the operations usually results in better decisions. These managers can typically anticipate and react to operating data more quickly than top management. Decentralization also allows managers to focus their attention on becoming "experts" in their area of operation.

Decentralized operations provide excellent training for managers. Delegating responsibility allows managers to develop managerial experience early in their careers.

This helps a company retain managers, some of whom may be later promoted to top management positions.

Managers of decentralized operations often work closely with customers. As a result, they tend to identify with customers and, thus, are often more creative in suggesting operating and product improvements. This helps create good customer relations.

Link to Caterpillar

Caterpillar uses a decentralized network of over a thousand dealers to sell its products.

Disadvantages of Decentralization

A primary disadvantage of decentralized operations is that decisions made by one manager may negatively affect the profits of the company. For example, managers of divisions whose products compete with one another might start a price war that decreases the profits of both divisions and, thus, the overall company.

Another disadvantage of decentralized operations is that assets and expenses may be duplicated across divisions. For example, each manager of a product line might have a separate sales force and office support staff.

The advantages and disadvantages of decentralization are summarized in Exhibit 1.

EXHIBIT 1

Advantages and Disadvantages of Decentralized Operations

Advantages of Decentralization

- Allows managers closest to the operations to make decisions
- Provides excellent training for managers
- Allows managers to become experts in their area of operation
- Helps retain managers
- Improves creativity and customer relations

Disadvantages of Decentralization

- Decisions made by managers may negatively affect the profits of the company
- Duplicates assets and expenses

Business Connection

DOVER CORPORATION: MANY PIECES, ONE PICTURE

Dover Corporation has grown over 45 years by acquiring more than 100 different manufacturing companies within a variety of industries. Dover uses a highly decentralized operating strategy. For example, of Dover's 30,000 employees, only about 50 employees staff the headquarters. Thus, almost all of the employees work within the 100 operating companies. The primary benefit of this approach is giving the operating companies room to respond to threats and opportunities without the bureaucratic hindrance of a centralized structure. As a result, the operating company presidents have unusual levels of autonomy. As stated by the company, "Dover company presidents set the direction of their own companies, make their own decisions, and nurture and grow their own organizations." The presidents are evaluated using metrics similar to those discussed in this chapter to keep the businesses aligned to the performance objectives of the overall organization.

Source: Dover Corporation website, Dover's Culture and Operating Philosophy.

Responsibility Accounting

In a decentralized business, accounting assists managers in evaluating and controlling their areas of responsibility, called *responsibility centers*. **Responsibility accounting** is the process of measuring and reporting operating data by responsibility center.

Link to Caterpillar
Caterpillar's corporate headquarters are located in Peoria, Illinois.

Three types of responsibility centers are as follows:

- *Cost centers*, which have responsibility over costs
- *Profit centers*, which have responsibility over revenues and costs
- *Investment centers*, which have responsibility over revenues, costs, and investment in assets

Responsibility Accounting for Cost Centers

Obj. 2 Prepare a responsibility accounting report for a cost center.

A **cost center** manager has responsibility for controlling costs. For example, the supervisor of the Power Department has responsibility for the costs of providing power. A cost center manager does not make decisions concerning sales or the amount of fixed assets invested in the center.

Cost centers may vary in size from a small department to an entire manufacturing plant. In addition, cost centers may exist within other cost centers. For example, an entire university or college could be viewed as a cost center, and each college and department within the university could also be a cost center, as shown in Exhibit 2.

EXHIBIT 2
Cost Centers in a University

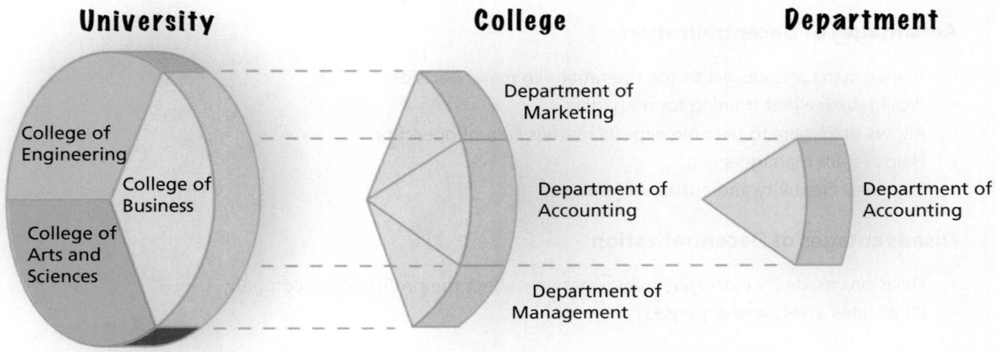

Link to Caterpillar
Caterpillar's "Corporate Services" group performs support services for its operating segments and is organized as a cost center.

Responsibility accounting for cost centers focuses on the controlling and reporting of costs. Budget performance reports that report budgeted and actual costs are normally prepared for each cost center.

Exhibit 3 illustrates budget performance reports for the following cost centers:

- Vice President, Production
- Manager, Plant A
- Supervisor, Department 1—Plant A

Exhibit 3 shows how cost centers are often linked within a company. For example, the budget performance report for Department 1—Plant A supports the report for Plant A, which supports the report for the vice president of production.

The reports in Exhibit 3 show the budgeted costs and actual costs along with the differences. Each difference is classified as either *over* budget or *under* budget. Such reports allow cost center managers to focus on areas of significant differences.

For example, the supervisor for Department 1 of Plant A can focus on why the materials cost was over budget. The supervisor might discover that excess materials were scrapped. This could be due to such factors as machine malfunctions, improperly trained employees, or low-quality materials.

As shown in Exhibit 3, responsibility accounting reports are usually more summarized for higher levels of management. For example, the budget performance report for the manager of Plant A shows only administration and departmental data. This report enables the plant manager to identify the departments responsible for major differences. Likewise, the report for the vice president of production summarizes the cost data for each plant.

EXHIBIT 3

Responsibility Accounting Reports for Cost Centers

Budget Performance Report
Vice President, Production
For the Month Ended October 31

	Actual	Budget	Over Budget	Under Budget
Administration	$ 19,700	$ 19,500	$ 200	
Plant A	470,330	467,475	2,855	
Plant B	394,300	395,225		$ (925)
	$884,330	$882,200	$3,055	$ (925)

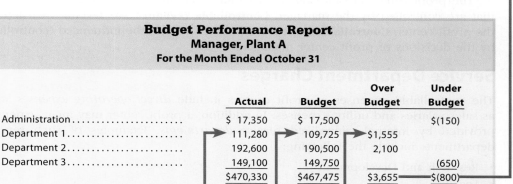

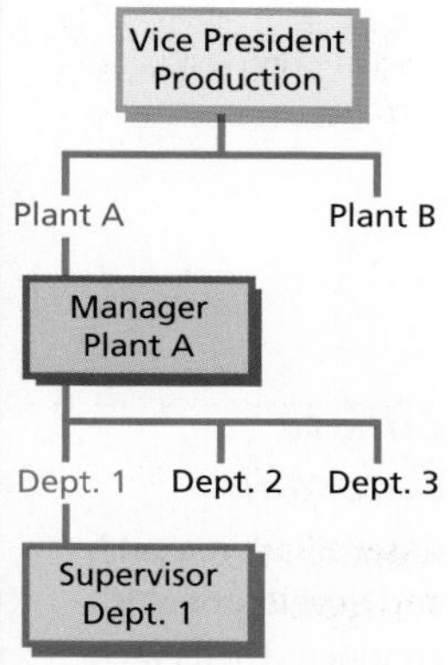

Budget Performance Report
Manager, Plant A
For the Month Ended October 31

	Actual	Budget	Over Budget	Under Budget
Administration	$ 17,350	$ 17,500		$(150)
Department 1	111,280	109,725	$1,555	
Department 2	192,600	190,500	2,100	
Department 3	149,100	149,750		(650)
	$470,330	$467,475	$3,655	$(800)

Budget Performance Report
Supervisor, Department 1—Plant A
For the Month Ended October 31

	Actual	Budget	Over Budget	Under Budget
Factory wages	$ 58,000	$ 58,100		$(100)
Materials	34,225	32,500	$1,725	
Supervisory salaries	6,400	6,400		
Power and light	5,690	5,750		(60)
Depreciation of plant and equipment	4,000	4,000		
Maintenance	1,990	2,000		(10)
Insurance and property taxes	975	975		
	$111,280	$109,725	$1,725	$(170)

Example Exercise 24-1 Budgetary Performance for Cost Center

Obj. 2

Nuclear Power Company's costs were over budget by $24,000. The company is divided into North and South regions. The North Region's costs were under budget by $2,000. Determine the amount the South Region's costs were over or under budget.

Follow My Example 24-1

$26,000 over budget [$24,000 over budget + $(2,000) under budget]

Practice Exercises: PE 24-1A, PE 24-1B

Obj. 3 Prepare responsibility accounting reports for a profit center.

Responsibility Accounting for Profit Centers

A **profit center** manager has the responsibility and authority for making decisions that affect revenues and costs and, thus, profits. Profit centers may be divisions, departments, or products.

The manager of a profit center does not make decisions concerning the fixed assets invested in the center. However, profit centers are an excellent training assignment for new managers.

Responsibility accounting for profit centers focuses on reporting revenues, expenses, and income from operations. Thus, responsibility accounting reports for profit centers take the form of income statements.

The profit center income statement should include only revenues and expenses that are controlled by the manager. **Controllable revenues** are revenues earned by the profit center. **Controllable expenses** are costs that can be influenced (controlled) by the decisions of profit center managers.

Service Department Charges

Link to Caterpillar

Caterpillar's research and development is conducted at its Tech Center in Mossville, Illinois.

The controllable expenses of profit centers include *direct operating expenses* such as sales salaries and utility expenses. In addition, a profit center may incur expenses provided by internal centralized *service departments*. Examples of such service departments include the following:

- Research and Development
- Legal
- Telecommunications
- Information and Computer Systems
- Facilities Management
- Purchasing
- Advertising
- Payroll Accounting
- Transportation
- Human Resources

Service department charges are *indirect* expenses to a profit center. They are similar to the expenses that would be incurred if the profit center purchased the services from outside the company. A profit center manager has control over service department expenses if the manager is free to choose how much service is used. In such cases, **service department charges** are allocated to profit centers based on the usage of the service by each profit center.

To illustrate, Nova Entertainment Group (NEG), a diversified entertainment company, is used. NEG has the following two operating divisions organized as profit centers:

- Theme Park Division
- Movie Production Division

The revenues and direct operating expenses for the two divisions follow. The operating expenses consist of direct expenses such as the wages and salaries of a division's employees.

	Theme Park Division	Movie Production Division
Revenues	$6,000,000	$2,500,000
Operating expenses	2,495,000	405,000

NEG's service departments and the expenses they incurred for the year ended December 31 are as follows:

Purchasing	$400,000
Payroll Accounting	255,000
Legal	250,000
Total	$905,000

An activity base for each service department is used to charge service department expenses to the Theme Park and Movie Production divisions. The activity base for each service department is a measure of the services performed. For NEG, the service department activity bases are as follows:

Department	Activity Base
Purchasing	Number of purchase requisitions
Payroll Accounting	Number of payroll checks
Legal	Number of billed hours

The use of services by the Theme Park and Movie Production divisions is as follows:

	Service Usage		
Division	**Purchasing**	**Payroll Accounting**	**Legal**
Theme Park	25,000 purchase requisitions	12,000 payroll checks	100 billed hrs.
Movie Production	15,000	3,000	900
Total	40,000 purchase requisitions	15,000 payroll checks	1,000 billed hrs.

The rates at which services are charged to each division are called *service department charge rates*. These rates are computed as follows:

$$\text{Service Department Charge Rate} = \frac{\text{Service Department Expense}}{\text{Total Service Department Usage}}$$

NEG's service department charge rates are computed as follows:

$$\text{Purchasing Charge Rate} = \frac{\$400{,}000}{40{,}000 \text{ purchase requisitions}} = \$10 \text{ per purchase requisition}$$

$$\text{Payroll Charge Rate} = \frac{\$255{,}000}{15{,}000 \text{ payroll checks}} = \$17 \text{ per payroll check}$$

$$\text{Legal Charge Rate} = \frac{\$250{,}000}{1{,}000 \text{ billed hrs.}} = \$250 \text{ per hr.}$$

The services used by each division are multiplied by the service department charge rates to determine the service charges for each division, computed as follows:

Service Department Charge = Service Usage × Service Department Charge Rate

Exhibit 4 illustrates the service department charges and related computations for NEG's Theme Park and Movie Production divisions.

EXHIBIT 4

Service Department Charges to NEG Divisions

Nova Entertainment Group
Service Department Charges to NEG Divisions
For the Year Ended December 31, 20Y8

Service Department	Theme Park Division	Movie Production Division
Purchasing (Note A)	$250,000	$150,000
Payroll Accounting (Note B)	204,000	51,000
Legal (Note C)	25,000	225,000
Total service department charges	$479,000	$426,000

Note A:
25,000 purchase requisitions × $10 per purchase requisition = $250,000
15,000 purchase requisitions × $10 per purchase requisition = $150,000

Note B:
12,000 payroll checks × $17 per check = $204,000
3,000 payroll checks × $17 per check = $51,000

Note C:
100 hours × $250 per hour = $25,000
900 hours × $250 per hour = $225,000

The differences in the service department charges between the two divisions can be explained by the nature of their operations and, thus, usage of services. For example, the Theme Park Division employs many part-time employees who are paid weekly. As a result, the Theme Park Division requires 12,000 payroll checks and incurs a $204,000 payroll service department charge (12,000 × $17). In contrast, the Movie Production Division has more permanent employees who are paid monthly. Thus, the Movie Production Division requires only 3,000 payroll checks and incurs a payroll service department charge of $51,000 (3,000 × $17).

Example Exercise 24-2 Service Department Charges

Obj. 3

The centralized legal department of Johnson Company has expenses of $600,000. The department has provided a total of 2,000 hours of service for the period. The East Division has used 500 hours of legal service during the period, and the West Division has used 1,500 hours. How much should each division be charged for legal services?

Follow My Example 24-2

East Division Service Charge for Legal Department:
$150,000 = 500 billed hours × ($600,000 ÷ 2,000 hours)

West Division Service Charge for Legal Department:
$450,000 = 1,500 billed hours × ($600,000 ÷ 2,000 hours)

Practice Exercises: PE 24-2A, PE 24-2B

Profit Center Reporting

The divisional income statements for NEG are shown in Exhibit 5.

EXHIBIT 5

Divisional Income Statements—NEG

Nova Entertainment Group
Divisional Income Statements
For the Year Ended December 31, 20Y8

	Theme Park Division	Movie Production Division
Revenues*	$6,000,000	$2,500,000
Operating expenses	2,495,000	405,000
Income from operations before service department charges	$3,505,000	$2,095,000
Less service department charges:		
Purchasing	$ 250,000	$ 150,000
Payroll Accounting	204,000	51,000
Legal	25,000	225,000
Total service department charges	$ 479,000	$ 426,000
Income from operations	$3,026,000	$1,669,000

*For a profit center that sells products, the income statement would show: Sales – Cost of goods sold = Gross profit. The operating expenses would be deducted from the gross profit to get the income from operations before service department charges.

In evaluating the profit center manager, the income from operations should be compared over time to a budget. However, it should not be compared across profit centers because the profit centers are usually different in terms of size, products, and customers.

Example Exercise 24-3 Income from Operations for Profit Center

Obj. 3

Using the data for Johnson Company from Example Exercise 24-2 along with the following data, determine the divisional income from operations for the East and West divisions:

	East Division	West Division
Sales	$3,000,000	$8,000,000
Cost of goods sold	1,650,000	4,200,000
Selling expenses	850,000	1,850,000

Follow My Example 24-3

	East Division	West Division
Sales	$3,000,000	$8,000,000
Cost of goods sold	1,650,000	4,200,000
Gross profit	$1,350,000	$3,800,000
Selling expenses	850,000	1,850,000
Income from operations before service department charges	$ 500,000	$1,950,000
Service department charges	150,000	450,000
Income from operations	$ 350,000	$1,500,000

Practice Exercises: PE 24-3A, PE 24-3B

Responsibility Accounting for Investment Centers

Obj. 4 Compute and interpret the return on investment, the residual income, and the balanced scorecard for an investment center.

An **investment center** manager has the responsibility and the authority to make decisions that affect not only costs and revenues but also the assets invested in the center. Investment centers are often used in diversified companies organized by divisions. In such cases, the divisional manager has authority similar to that of a chief operating officer or president of a company.

Because investment center managers have responsibility for revenues and expenses, *income from operations* is part of investment center reporting. In addition, because the manager has responsibility for the assets invested in the center, the following two additional measures of performance are used:

- Return on investment
- Residual income

To illustrate, DataLink Inc., a cellular phone company with three regional divisions, is used. Condensed divisional income statements for the Northern, Central, and Southern divisions of DataLink are shown in Exhibit 6.

Link to Caterpillar

Caterpillar has four group presidents who are responsible for the operations of each of its four segments: Construction Industries, Resource Industries, Energy & Transportation, and Financial Products. A fifth group president is responsible for three smaller operating segments.

Divisional Income Statements—DataLink Inc. EXHIBIT 6

DataLink Inc.
Divisional Income Statements
For the Year Ended December 31, 20Y8

	Northern Division	Central Division	Southern Division
Revenues	$560,000	$672,000	$750,000
Operating expenses	336,000	470,400	562,500
Income from operations before service department charges	$224,000	$201,600	$187,500
Service department charges	154,000	117,600	112,500
Income from operations	$ 70,000	$ 84,000	$ 75,000

Using only income from operations, the Central Division is the most profitable division. However, income from operations does not reflect the amount of assets invested in each center. For example, the Central Division could have twice as many assets as the Northern Division. For this reason, performance measures that consider the amount of invested assets, such as the return on investment and residual income, are used.

Return on Investment

Because investment center managers control the amount of assets invested in their centers, they should be evaluated based on the use of these assets. One measure that considers the amount of assets invested is the **return on investment (ROI)** or *return on assets*. It is computed as follows:

$$\text{Return on Investment (ROI)} = \frac{\text{Income from Operations}}{\text{Invested Assets}}$$

The return on investment is useful because the three factors subject to control by divisional managers (revenues, expenses, and invested assets) are considered. The higher the return on investment, the better the division is using its assets to generate income. In effect, the return on investment measures the income (return) on each dollar invested. As a result, the return on investment can be used as a common basis for comparing divisions with each other.

To illustrate, the invested assets of DataLink's three divisions are as follows:

	Invested Assets
Northern Division	$350,000
Central Division	700,000
Southern Division	500,000

Using the income from operations for each division shown in Exhibit 6, the return on investment for each division is computed as follows:

Northern Division:

$$\text{Return on Investment} = \frac{\text{Income from Operations}}{\text{Invested Assets}} = \frac{\$70{,}000}{\$350{,}000} = 20\%$$

Central Division:

$$\text{Return on Investment} = \frac{\text{Income from Operations}}{\text{Invested Assets}} = \frac{\$84{,}000}{\$700{,}000} = 12\%$$

Southern Division:

$$\text{Return on Investment} = \frac{\text{Income from Operations}}{\text{Invested Assets}} = \frac{\$75{,}000}{\$500{,}000} = 15\%$$

Link to Caterpillar

Based upon recent financial statements, the return on investment for each of Caterpillar's four segments was as follows: Construction Industries 33.8%; Resource Industries 5.2%; Energy & Transportation 48.1%; Financial Products 2.7%

Although the Central Division generated the largest income from operations, its return on investment (12%) is the lowest. Hence, relative to the assets invested, the Central Division is the least profitable division. In comparison, the return on investment of the Northern Division is 20%, and the Southern Division is 15%.

To analyze differences in the return on investment across divisions, the **DuPont formula** for the return on investment is often used.[1] The DuPont formula views the return on investment as the product of the following two factors:

- **Profit margin**, which is the ratio of income from operations to sales.
- **Investment turnover**, which is the ratio of sales to invested assets.

1 The DuPont formula was created by a financial executive of E. I. du Pont de Nemours and Company in 1919.

Using the DuPont formula, the return on investment is expressed as follows:

$$\text{Return on Investment} = \text{Profit Margin} \times \text{Investment Turnover}$$

$$\text{Return on Investment} = \frac{\text{Income from Operations}}{\text{Sales}} \times \frac{\text{Sales}}{\text{Invested Assets}}$$

The DuPont formula is useful in evaluating divisions. This is because the profit margin and the investment turnover reflect the following underlying operating relationships of each division:

- Profit margin indicates *operating profitability* by computing the rate of profit earned on each sales dollar.
- Investment turnover indicates *operating efficiency* by computing the number of sales dollars generated by each dollar of invested assets.

If a division's profit margin increases and all other factors remain the same, the division's return on investment will increase. For example, a division might add more profitable products to its sales mix and, thus, increase its operating profit, profit margin, and return on investment.

If a division's investment turnover increases and all other factors remain the same, the division's return on investment will increase. For example, a division might attempt to increase sales through special sales promotions and thus increase operating efficiency, investment turnover, and return on investment.

The return on investment, profit margin, and investment turnover operate in relationship to one another. Specifically, more income can be earned by increasing the investment turnover, increasing the profit margin, or both.

Using the DuPont formula yields the same return on investment for each of DataLink's divisions, computed as follows:

$$\text{Return on Investment} = \frac{\text{Income from Operations}}{\text{Sales}} \times \frac{\text{Sales}}{\text{Invested Assets}}$$

Northern Division:

$$\text{Return on Investment} = \frac{\$70{,}000}{\$560{,}000} \times \frac{\$560{,}000}{\$350{,}000} = 12.5\% \times 1.6 = 20\%$$

Central Division:

$$\text{Return on Investment} = \frac{\$84{,}000}{\$672{,}000} \times \frac{\$672{,}000}{\$700{,}000} = 12.5\% \times 0.96 = 12\%$$

Southern Division:

$$\text{Return on Investment} = \frac{\$75{,}000}{\$750{,}000} \times \frac{\$750{,}000}{\$500{,}000} = 10\% \times 1.5 = 15\%$$

The Northern and Central divisions have the same profit margins of 12.5%. However, the Northern Division's investment turnover of 1.6 is larger than that of the Central Division's turnover of 0.96. By using its invested assets more efficiently, the Northern Division's return on investment of 20% is 8 percentage points higher than the Central Division's return of 12%.

The Southern Division's profit margin of 10% and investment turnover of 1.5 are lower than those of the Northern Division. The product of these factors results in a return on investment of 15% for the Southern Division, compared to 20% for the Northern Division.

Even though the Southern Division's profit margin is lower than the Central Division's, its higher turnover of 1.5 results in a return of 15%, which is greater than the Central Division's return of 12%.

To increase the return on investment, the profit margin and investment turnover for a division may be analyzed. For example, assume that the Northern Division is in

Link to Caterpillar

Based upon recent financial statements, Caterpillar's Construction Industries segment had a Profit Margin of 11.3%, Investment Turnover of 3.0, resulting in a Return on Investment (ROI) of 33.9% (11.3% × 3.0).

a highly competitive industry in which the profit margin cannot be easily increased. As a result, the division manager might focus on increasing the investment turnover.

To illustrate, assume that the revenues of the Northern Division could be increased by $56,000 through increasing operating expenses, such as advertising, to $385,000. The Northern Division's income from operations will increase from $70,000 to $77,000, computed as follows:

Revenues ($560,000 + $56,000)	$616,000
Operating expenses	385,000
Income from operations before service department charges	$231,000
Service department charges	154,000
Income from operations	$ 77,000

The return on investment for the Northern Division, using the DuPont formula, is recomputed as follows:

$$\text{Return on Investment} = \frac{\$77,000}{\$616,000} \times \frac{\$616,000}{\$350,000} = 12.5\% \times 1.76 = 22\%$$

Although the Northern Division's profit margin remains the same (12.5%), the investment turnover has increased from 1.6 to 1.76, an increase of 10% (0.16 ÷ 1.6). The 10% increase in investment turnover increases the return on investment by 10% (from 20% to 22%).

The return on investment is also useful in deciding where to invest additional assets or expand operations. For example, DataLink should give priority to expanding operations in the Northern Division because it earns the highest return on investment. In other words, an investment in the Northern Division will return 20 cents (20%) on each dollar invested. In contrast, investments in the Central and Southern divisions will earn only 12 cents and 15 cents, respectively, per dollar invested.

A disadvantage of the return on investment as a performance measure is that it may lead divisional managers to reject new investments that could be profitable for the company as a whole. To illustrate, assume the following returns for the Northern Division of DataLink:

Current return on investment	20%
Minimum acceptable return on investment set by top management	10%
Expected return on investment for new project	14%

If the manager of the Northern Division invests in the new project, the Northern Division's overall return will decrease from 20% due to averaging. Thus, the division manager might decide to reject the project, even though the new project's expected return of 14% exceeds DataLink's minimum acceptable return of 10%.

Business Connection

COCA-COLA COMPANY: GO WEST YOUNG MAN

A major decision early in the history of **Coca-Cola** was to expand outside the United States to the rest of the world. As a result, Coca-Cola is known today the world over. What is revealing is how this decision has impacted the revenues and profitability of Coca-Cola across its international and North American segments. The following table shows the percent of revenues and percent of income from operations from the international and North American geographic segments.

	Revenues	Income from Operations
International segments	35.4%	94.3%
North American segment	49.2	28.5
Other (bottling companies, headquarters)	15.4	(22.8)
Total	100%	100%

The first column shows that the international segments provide over 35% of the revenues, while North America provides over 49% of the revenues, as the United States is a large market for Coca-Cola products. However, the income from operations tells a different story. More than 94% of Coca-Cola's profitability comes from international segments. Given the revenue segmentation, this suggests that the international profit margins must be much higher than the North American profit margin. Indeed this is the case, as can be seen in the following table:

	Profit Margin
International average	52.5%
North America	11.4%
Overall average	19.7%

The average profit margin for all the international segments is over four times as large as the North American segment. These results speak to the heart of the Coca-Cola marketing strategy. In the United States, Coca-Cola faces competition from many other beverage alternatives. However, outside the United States, Coca-Cola is able to earn higher profit margins because international consumers want to associate with the Coca-Cola brand identity.

Source: The Coca-Cola Company, Form 10-K for the Fiscal Year Ended December 31, 2015.

Example Exercise 24-4 Profit Margin, Investment Turnover, and ROI

Obj. 4

Campbell Company has income from operations of $35,000, invested assets of $140,000, and sales of $437,500. Use the DuPont formula to compute the return on investment and show (a) the profit margin, (b) the investment turnover, and (c) the return on investment.

Follow My Example 24-4

a. Profit Margin = $35,000 ÷ $437,500 = 8%

b. Investment Turnover = $437,500 ÷ $140,000 = 3.125

c. Return on Investment = 8% × 3.125 = 25%

Practice Exercises: PE 24-4A, PE 24-4B

Residual Income

Residual income is useful in overcoming some of the disadvantages of the return on investment. **Residual income** is the excess of income from operations over a minimum acceptable income from operations, as shown in Exhibit 7.

Income from operations	$XXX
Less minimum acceptable income from operations as a percent of invested assets	XXX
Residual income	$XXX

EXHIBIT 7

Residual Income

The minimum acceptable income from operations is computed by multiplying the company minimum return by the invested assets. The minimum return is set by top management, based on such factors as the cost of financing.

To illustrate, assume that DataLink Inc. has established 10% as the minimum acceptable return on divisional assets. The residual incomes for the three divisions are shown in Exhibit 8.

EXHIBIT 8

Residual Income—DataLink, Inc.

	Northern Division	Central Division	Southern Division
Income from operations	$70,000	$84,000	$75,000
Less minimum acceptable income from operations as a percent of invested assets:			
$350,000 × 10%	35,000		
$700,000 × 10%		70,000	
$500,000 × 10%			50,000
Residual income	$35,000	$14,000	$25,000

As shown in Exhibit 8, the Northern Division has more residual income ($35,000) than the other divisions, even though it has the least amount of income from operations ($70,000). This is because the invested assets are less for the Northern Division than for the other divisions.

The major advantage of residual income as a performance measure is that it considers the minimum acceptable return, invested assets, and the income from operations for each division. In doing so, residual income encourages division managers to maximize income from operations in excess of the minimum. This provides an incentive to accept any project that is expected to have a return in excess of the minimum.

To illustrate, assume the following return for the Northern Division of DataLink:

Current return on investment	20%
Minimum acceptable return on investment set by top management	10%
Expected return on investment for new project	14%

If the manager of the Northern Division is evaluated on new projects using only return on investment, the division manager might decide to reject the new project. This is because investing in the new project will decrease Northern's current return of 20%. While this helps the division maintain its high ROI, it hurts the company as a whole because the expected return of 14% exceeds DataLink's minimum acceptable return of 10%.

In contrast, if the manager of the Northern Division is evaluated using residual income, the new project would probably be accepted because it will increase the Northern Division's residual income. In this way, residual income supports both divisional and overall company objectives.

Example Exercise 24-5 Residual Income **Obj. 4**

The Wholesale Division of PeanutCo has income from operations of $87,000 and assets of $240,000. The minimum acceptable return on assets is 12%. What is the residual income for the division?

Follow My Example 24-5

Income from operations	$87,000
Less: minimum acceptable income from operations as a percent of assets ($240,000 × 12%)	28,800
Residual income	$58,200

Practice Exercises: PE 24-5A, PE 24-5B

The Balanced Scorecard[2]

The **balanced scorecard** is a set of multiple performance measures for a company. In addition to financial performance, a balanced scorecard normally includes performance measures for customer service, innovation and learning, and internal processes, as shown in Exhibit 9.

EXHIBIT 9

The Balanced Scorecard

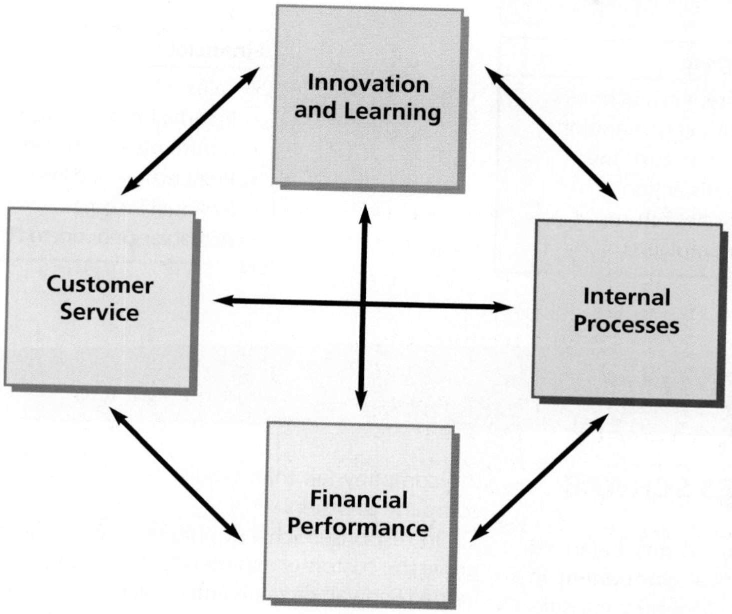

Performance measures for learning and innovation often revolve around a company's research and development efforts. For example, the number of new products developed during a year and the time it takes to bring new products to the market are performance measures for innovation. Performance measures for learning could include the number of employee training sessions and the number of employees who are cross-trained in several skills.

Performance measures for customer service include the number of customer complaints and the number of repeat customers. Customer surveys can also be used to gather measures of customer satisfaction with the company as compared to competitors.

Performance measures for internal processes include the length of time it takes to manufacture a product. The amount of scrap and waste is a measure of the efficiency of a company's manufacturing processes. The number of customer returns is a performance measure of both the manufacturing and sales ordering processes.

All companies will use financial performance measures. Some financial performance measures discussed earlier in this chapter include income from operations, return on investment, and residual income.

The balanced scorecard attempts to identify the underlying nonfinancial drivers, or causes, of financial performance related to innovation and learning, customer service, and internal processes. In this way, the financial performance may be improved. For example, customer satisfaction is often measured by the number of repeat customers. By increasing the number of repeat customers, sales and income from operations can be increased.

Some common performance measures used in the balanced scorecard approach are shown in Exhibit 10.

Link to Caterpillar

The performance of **Caterpillar's** Financial Products segment is measured by interest coverage and leverage ratios as well as its credit rating and timeliness of financial reporting.

2 The balanced scorecard was developed by R. S. Kaplan and D. P. Norton and explained in *The Balanced Scorecard: Translating Strategy into Action* (Cambridge: Harvard Business School Press, 1996).

EXHIBIT 10

Balanced Scorecard Performance Measures

Innovation and Learning

- Number of new products
- Number of new patents
- Number of cross-trained employees
- Number of training hours
- Number of ethics violations
- Employee turnover

Internal Processes

- Waste and scrap
- Time to manufacture products
- Number of defects
- Number of rejected sales orders
- Number of stockouts
- Labor utilization

Customer Service

- Number of repeat customers
- Customer brand recognition
- Delivery time to customer
- Customer satisfaction
- Number of sales returns
- Customer complaints

Financial

- Sales
- Income from operations
- Return on investment
- Profit margin and investment turnover
- Residual income
- Actual versus budgeted (standard) costs

SERVICE FOCUS

TURNING AROUND CHARLES SCHWAB

Customer service is a key component to any balanced scorecard, and it is a particularly critical component in service industries. Since 2003, **Bain & Company** consulting has helped companies improve customer service by focusing on a customer loyalty metric called the *Net Promoter Score*. This metric, when used as part of a balanced scorecard, evaluates customer service by assessing how likely a customer is to recommend the company to others.

The Charles Schwab Corporation is a full-service financial advisory firm that was founded in 1973. In 2004, the company was struggling. Although Schwab had been built on delivering exceptional customer service, the company had lost its way. When customers were surveyed, they gave Schwab a negative 35% Net Promoter Score, indicating that more customers wanted to see the company fail than would be willing to promote the company to others.

In response, Schwab enlisted Bain to help them improve the customer experience and customer loyalty. Bain helped Schwab develop and implement a Client Promoter System that focused on embedding the Client Promoter Score deep within the company's values and core strategy. As Schwab CEO Walt Bettinger describes, "If you serve clients in the way that you would like to be served, they are going to want to do more business with you." The results were significant. By 2008, the company's stock price had more than doubled, and in 2010, Schwab received a Net Promoter Score of 46%, the highest in its sector.

Sources: "Schwab Earns Highest Customer Loyalty Ranking Among Brokerage & Investment Firms in Satmetrix Net Promoter's 2010 Industry Report," *BusinessWire*, March 25, 2010 and "Seeing the World through the Client's Eyes," Bain & Co., www.netpromotersystem.com/videos/trailblazer-video/charles-schwab.aspx.

Obj. 5 Describe and illustrate how the market price, negotiated price, and cost price approaches to transfer pricing may be used by decentralized segments of a business.

Transfer Pricing

When divisions transfer products or render services to each other, a **transfer price** is used to charge for the products or services.[3] Because transfer prices will affect a division's financial performance, setting a transfer price is a sensitive matter for the managers of both the selling and buying divisions.

Three common approaches to setting transfer prices are as follows:

- Market price approach
- Negotiated price approach
- Cost approach

3 The discussion in this chapter highlights the essential concepts of transfer pricing. In-depth discussion of transfer pricing can be found in advanced texts.

Transfer prices may be used for cost, profit, or investment centers. The objective of setting a transfer price is to motivate managers to behave in a manner that will increase the overall company income. As will be illustrated, however, transfer prices may be misused in such a way that overall company income suffers.

Transfer prices can be set as low as the variable cost per unit or as high as the market price. Often, transfer prices are negotiated at some point between variable cost per unit and market price. Exhibit 11 shows the possible range of transfer prices.

EXHIBIT 11

Commonly Used Transfer Prices

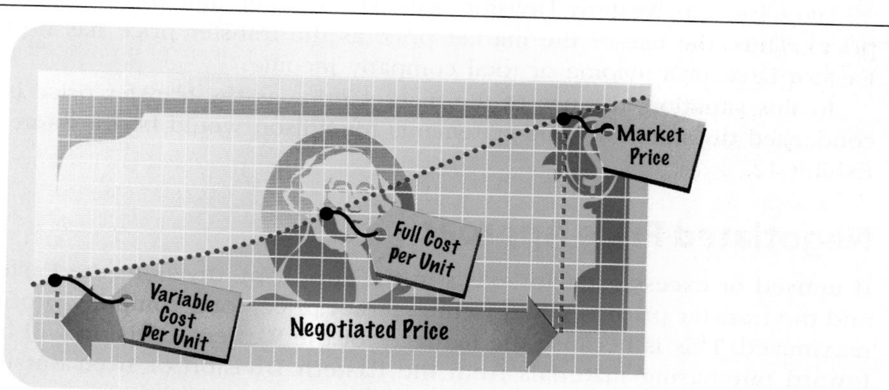

To illustrate, Wilson Company, a packaged snack food company with no service departments, is used. Wilson has two operating divisions (Eastern and Western) that are organized as investment centers. Condensed income statements for Wilson, assuming no transfers between divisions, are shown in Exhibit 12.

EXHIBIT 12

Income Statements—No Transfers Between Divisions

Wilson Company
Income Statements
For the Year Ended December 31, 20Y1

	Eastern Division	Western Division	Total Company
Sales:			
50,000 units × $20 per unit	$1,000,000		$1,000,000
20,000 units × $40 per unit		$800,000	800,000
			$1,800,000
Expenses:			
Variable:			
50,000 units × $10 per unit	$ 500,000		$ 500,000
20,000 units × $30* per unit		$600,000	600,000
Fixed	300,000	100,000	400,000
Total expenses	$ 800,000	$700,000	$1,500,000
Income from operations	$ 200,000	$100,000	$ 300,000

*$20 of the $30 per unit represents materials costs, and the remaining $10 per unit represents other variable conversion expenses incurred within the Western Division.

Market Price Approach

Using the **market price approach**, the transfer price is the price at which the product or service transferred could be sold to outside buyers. If an outside market exists for the product or service transferred, the current market price may be a proper transfer price.

Transfer Price = Market Price

To illustrate, assume that materials used by Wilson in producing snack food in the Western Division are currently purchased from an outside supplier at $20 per unit. The same materials are produced by the Eastern Division. The Eastern Division is operating at full capacity of 50,000 units and can sell all it produces to the Western Division or to outside buyers.

A transfer price of $20 per unit (the market price) has no effect on the Eastern Division's income or total company income. The Eastern Division will earn revenues of $20 per unit on all its production and sales, regardless of who buys its product.

Likewise, the Western Division will pay $20 per unit for materials (the market price). Thus, the use of the market price as the transfer price has no effect on the Eastern Division's income or total company income.

In this situation, the use of the market price as the transfer price is proper. The condensed divisional income statements for Wilson would be the same as shown in Exhibit 12.

Negotiated Price Approach

If unused or excess capacity exists in the supplying division (the Eastern Division) and the transfer price is equal to the market price, total company profit may not be maximized. This is because the manager of the Western Division will be indifferent toward purchasing materials from the Eastern Division or from outside suppliers. That is, in both cases the Western Division manager pays $20 per unit (the market price). As a result, the Western Division may purchase the materials from outside suppliers.

If, however, the Western Division purchases the materials from the Eastern Division, the difference between the market price of $20 and the variable costs of the Eastern Division of $10 per unit (from Exhibit 12) can cover fixed costs and contribute to overall company profits. Thus, the Western Division manager should be encouraged to purchase the materials from the Eastern Division.

The **negotiated price approach** allows the managers to agree (negotiate) among themselves on a transfer price. The only constraint is that the transfer price be less than the market price but greater than the supplying division's variable costs per unit, as follows:

Variable Costs per Unit < Transfer Price < Market Price

To illustrate, assume that instead of a capacity of 50,000 units, the Eastern Division's capacity is 70,000 units. In addition, assume that the Eastern Division can continue to sell only 50,000 units to outside buyers.

A transfer price less than $20 would encourage the manager of the Western Division to purchase from the Eastern Division. This is because the Western Division is currently purchasing its materials from outside suppliers at a cost of $20 per unit. Thus, its materials cost would decrease, and its income from operations would increase.

At the same time, a transfer price above the Eastern Division's variable costs per unit of $10 would encourage the manager of the Eastern Division to supply materials to the Western Division. In doing so, the Eastern Division's income from operations would also increase.

Exhibit 13 illustrates the divisional and company income statements, assuming that the Eastern and Western division managers agree to a transfer price of $15.

The Eastern Division increases its sales by $300,000 (20,000 units × $15 per unit) to $1,300,000. As a result, the Eastern Division's income from operations increases by $100,000 ($300,000 sales – $200,000 variable costs) to $300,000, as shown in Exhibit 13.

EXHIBIT 13

Income Statements—Negotiated Transfer Price

Dynamic Exhibit

Wilson Company
Income Statements
For the Year Ended December 31, 20Y1

	Eastern Division	Western Division	Total Company
Sales:			
50,000 units × $20 per unit	$1,000,000		$1,000,000
20,000 units × $15 per unit	300,000		300,000
20,000 units × $40 per unit		$800,000	800,000
	$1,300,000	$800,000	$2,100,000
Expenses:			
Variable:			
70,000 units × $10 per unit	$ 700,000		$ 700,000
20,000 units × $25* per unit		$500,000	500,000
Fixed	300,000	100,000	400,000
Total expenses	$1,000,000	$600,000	$1,600,000
Income from operations	$ 300,000	$200,000	$ 500,000

*$10 of the $25 represents variable conversion expenses incurred solely within the Western Division, and $15 per unit represents the transfer price per unit from the Eastern Division.

The increase of $100,000 in the Eastern Division's income can also be computed as follows:

Increase in Eastern (Supplying) Division's Income from Operations = (Transfer Price – Variable Cost per Unit) × Units Transferred

= ($15 – $10) × 20,000 units = $100,000

The Western Division's materials cost decreases by $5 per unit ($20 – $15) for a total of $100,000 (20,000 units × $5 per unit). Thus, the Western Division's income from operations increases by $100,000 to $200,000, as shown in Exhibit 13.

The increase of $100,000 in the Western Division's income can also be computed as follows:

Increase in Western (Purchasing) Division's Income from Operations = (Market Price – Transfer Price) × Units Transferred

= ($20 – $15) × 20,000 units = $100,000

Comparing Exhibits 12 and 13 shows that Wilson's income from operations increased by $200,000, computed as follows:

	Income from Operations		
	No Units Transferred (Exhibit 12)	20,000 Units Transferred at $15 per Unit (Exhibit 13)	Increase (Decrease)
Eastern Division	$200,000	$300,000	$100,000
Western Division	100,000	200,000	100,000
Wilson Company	$300,000	$500,000	$200,000

In the preceding illustration, any negotiated transfer price between $10 and $20 is acceptable, as shown below:

Variable Costs per Unit < Transfer Price < Market Price
$10 < Transfer Price < $20

Any transfer price within this range will increase the overall income from operations for Wilson by $200,000. However, the increases in the Eastern and Western divisions' income from operations will vary depending on the transfer price.

To illustrate, a transfer price of $16 would increase the Eastern Division's income from operations by $120,000, computed as follows:

Increase in Eastern (Supplying) Division's Income from Operations = (Transfer Price – Variable Cost per Unit) × Units Transferred

= ($16 – $10) × 20,000 units = $120,000

A transfer price of $16 would increase the Western Division's income from operations by $80,000, computed as follows:

Increase in Western (Purchasing) Division's Income from Operations = (Market Price – Transfer Price) × Units Transferred

= ($20 – $16) × 20,000 units = $80,000

With a transfer price of $16, Wilson Company's income from operations still increases by $200,000, which consists of the Eastern Division's increase of $120,000 plus the Western Division's increase of $80,000.

As shown, a negotiated price provides each division manager with an incentive to negotiate the transfer of materials. At the same time, the overall company's income from operations will also increase. However, the negotiated approach only applies when the supplying division has excess capacity. In other words, the supplying division cannot sell all its production to outside buyers at the market price.

Example Exercise 24-6 Transfer Pricing

Obj. 5

The materials used by the Winston-Salem Division of Fox Company are currently purchased from outside suppliers at $30 per unit. These same materials are produced by Fox's Flagstaff Division. The Flagstaff Division can produce the materials needed by the Winston-Salem Division at a variable cost of $15 per unit. The division is currently producing 70,000 units and has capacity of 100,000 units. The two divisions have recently negotiated a transfer price of $22 per unit for 30,000 units. By how much will each division's income increase as a result of this transfer?

Follow My Example 24-6

Increase in Flagstaff (Supplying) Division's Income from Operations = (Transfer Price – Variable Cost per Unit) × Units Transferred

= ($22 – $15) × 30,000 units = $210,000

Increase in Winston-Salem (Purchasing) Division's Income from Operations = (Market Price – Transfer Price) × Units Transferred

= ($30 – $22) × 30,000 units = $240,000

Practice Exercises: PE 24-6A, PE 24-6B

Cost Price Approach

Under the **cost price approach**, cost is used to set transfer prices. A variety of costs may be used in this approach, including the following:

- Total product cost per unit
- Variable product cost per unit

If total product cost per unit is used, direct materials, direct labor, and factory overhead are included in the transfer price. If variable product cost per unit is used, the fixed factory overhead cost is excluded from the transfer price.

Actual costs or standard (budgeted) costs may be used in applying the cost price approach. If actual costs are used, inefficiencies of the producing (supplying) division are transferred to the purchasing division. Thus, there is little incentive for the producing (supplying) division to control costs. For this reason, most companies use standard costs in the cost price approach. In this way, differences between actual and standard costs remain with the producing (supplying) division for cost control purposes.

The cost price approach is most often used when the responsibility centers are organized as cost centers. When the responsibility centers are organized as profit or investment centers, the cost price approach is normally not used.

For example, using the cost price approach when the supplying division is organized as a profit center ignores the supplying division manager's responsibility for earning profits. In this case, using the cost price approach prevents the supplying division from reporting any profit (revenues – costs) on the units transferred. As a result, the division manager has little incentive to transfer units to another division, even though it may be in the best interests of the company.

INTEGRITY, OBJECTIVITY, AND ETHICS IN BUSINESS

THE ETHICS OF TRANSFER PRICES

Transfer prices allow large multinational companies to minimize taxes by shifting taxable income from countries with high tax rates to countries with low taxes. For example, a British company will pay U.S. taxes on income from its U.S. division and British taxes on income from its British division. Because this company can set its own transfer price, it can minimize its overall tax bill by setting a high transfer price when transferring goods to the United States This increases cost of goods sold for the highly taxed U.S division and increases sales for the lesser taxed British division. The overall result is a lower tax bill for the multinational company as a whole. In recent years, government tax authorities like the Internal Revenue Service (IRS) have become concerned with tax avoidance through transfer price manipulation. In response, many countries now have guidelines for setting transfer prices that ensure that transfer prices are not subject to manipulation for tax purposes.

Source: L. Eden and L. M. Smith, "The Ethics of Transfer Pricing," unpublished working paper, Texas A&M University, 2011.

At a Glance 24

Obj. 1 Describe the advantages and disadvantages of decentralized operations.

Key Points In a centralized business, all major planning and operating decisions are made by top management. In a decentralized business, these responsibilities are delegated to unit managers. Decentralization may be more effective because operational decisions are made by the managers closest to the operations.

Learning Outcomes	Example Exercises	Practice Exercises
• Describe the advantages of decentralization.		
• Describe the disadvantages of decentralization.		
• Describe the common types of responsibility centers and the role of responsibility accounting.		

Obj. 2 Prepare a responsibility accounting report for a cost center.

Key Points Cost centers limit the responsibility and authority of managers to decisions related to the costs of their unit. The primary tools for planning and controlling are budgets and budget performance reports.

Learning Outcomes	Example Exercises	Practice Exercises
• Describe cost centers.		
• Describe the responsibility reporting for a cost center.		
• Compute the costs over (under) budget for a cost center.	EE24-1	PE24-1A, 24-1B

Obj. 3 Prepare responsibility accounting reports for a profit center.

Key Points In a profit center, managers have the responsibility and authority to make decisions that affect both revenues and costs. Responsibility reports for a profit center usually show income from operations for the unit.

Learning Outcomes	Example Exercises	Practice Exercises
• Describe profit centers.		
• Determine how service department charges are allocated to profit centers.	EE24-2	PE24-2A, 24-2B
• Describe the responsibility reporting for a profit center.		
• Compute income from operations for a profit center.	EE24-3	PE24-3A, 24-3B

Obj. 4 **Compute and interpret the return on investment, the residual income, and the balanced scorecard for an investment center.**

Key Points In an investment center, the unit manager has the responsibility and authority to make decisions that affect the unit's revenues, expenses, and assets invested in the center. Three measures are commonly used to assess investment center performance: return on investment (ROI), residual income, and the balanced scorecard. These measures are often used to compare investment center performance.

Learning Outcomes	Example Exercises	Practice Exercises
• Describe investment centers.		
• Describe the responsibility reporting for an investment center.		
• Compute the profit margin, investment turnover, and return on investment (ROI).	EE24-4	PE24-4A, 24-4B
• Compute residual income.	EE24-5	PE24-5A, 24-5B
• Describe the balanced scorecard approach.		

Obj. 5 **Describe and illustrate how the market price, negotiated price, and cost price approaches to transfer pricing may be used by decentralized segments of a business.**

Key Points When divisions within a company transfer products or provide services to each other, a transfer price is used to charge for the products or services. Transfer prices should be set so that the overall company income is increased when goods are transferred between divisions. One of three approaches is typically used to establish transfer prices: market price, negotiated price, or cost price.

Learning Outcomes	Example Exercises	Practice Exercises
• Describe how companies determine the price used to transfer products or services between divisions.		
• Determine transfer prices using the market price approach.		
• Determine transfer prices using the negotiated price approach.	EE24-6	PE24-6A, 24-6B
• Describe the cost price approach to determining transfer price.		

Illustrative Problem

Quinn Company has two divisions, Domestic and International. Invested assets and condensed income statement data for each division for the year ended December 31, 20Y8, are as follows:

	Domestic Division	International Division
Revenues	$675,000	$480,000
Operating expenses	450,000	372,400
Service department charges	90,000	50,000
Invested assets	600,000	384,000

(Continued)

Instructions

1. Prepare condensed income statements for the past year for each division.
2. Using the DuPont formula, determine the profit margin, investment turnover, and return on investment for each division.
3. If management's minimum acceptable return is 10%, determine the residual income for each division.

Solution

1.

Quinn Company
Divisional Income Statements
For the Year Ended December 31, 20Y8

	Domestic Division	International Division
Revenues	$675,000	$480,000
Operating expenses	450,000	372,400
Income from operations before service department charges	$225,000	$107,600
Service department charges	90,000	50,000
Income from operations	$135,000	$ 57,600

2. Return on Investment = Profit Margin × Investment Turnover

$$\text{Return on Investment} = \frac{\text{Income from Operations}}{\text{Sales}} \times \frac{\text{Sales}}{\text{Invested Assets}}$$

$$\text{Domestic Division: ROI} = \frac{\$135{,}000}{\$675{,}000} \times \frac{\$675{,}000}{\$600{,}000}$$

$$= 20\% \times 1.125$$

$$= 22.5\%$$

$$\text{International Division: ROI} = \frac{\$57{,}600}{\$480{,}000} \times \frac{\$480{,}000}{\$384{,}000}$$

$$= 12\% \times 1.25$$

$$= 15\%$$

3. Domestic Division: $75,000 [$135,000 – (10% × $600,000)]
International Division: $19,200 [$57,600 – (10% × $384,000)]

Key Terms

balanced scorecard (1187)
controllable expenses (1178)
controllable revenues (1178)
cost center (1176)
cost price approach (1192)
DuPont formula (1182)
investment center (1181)
investment turnover (1182)
market price approach (1189)
negotiated price approach (1190)
profit center (1178)
profit margin (1182)
residual income (1185)
responsibility accounting (1175)
return on investment (ROI) (1182)
service department charges (1178)
transfer price (1188)

Discussion Questions

1. Differentiate between centralized and decentralized operations.
2. Differentiate between a profit center and an investment center.
3. Real World **Weyerhaeuser** developed a system that assigns service department expenses to user divisions on the basis of actual services consumed by the division. Here are a number of Weyerhaeuser's activities in its central Financial Services Department:
   - Payroll
   - Accounts payable
   - Accounts receivable
   - Database administration—report preparation

   For each activity, identify an activity base that could be used to charge user divisions for service.
4. What is the major shortcoming of using income from operations as a performance measure for investment centers?
5. In a decentralized company in which the divisions are organized as investment centers, how could a division be considered the least profitable even though it earned the largest amount of income from operations?
6. How does using the return on investment facilitate comparability between divisions of decentralized companies?
7. Why would a firm use a balanced scorecard in evaluating divisional performance?
8. What is the objective of transfer pricing?
9. When is the negotiated price approach preferred over the market price approach in setting transfer prices?
10. When using the negotiated price approach to transfer pricing, within what range should the transfer price be established?

Practice Exercises

Example Exercises

Show Me How EE 24-1 *p. 1177*

PE 24-1A Budgetary performance for cost center **OBJ. 2**

Caroline Company's costs were over budget by $319,000. The company is divided into West and East regions. The East Region's costs were under budget by $47,500. Determine the amount that the West Region's costs were over or under budget.

Show Me How EE 24-1 *p. 1177*

PE 24-1B Budgetary performance for cost center **OBJ. 2**

Conley Company's costs were under budget by $198,000. The company is divided into North and South regions. The North Region's costs were over budget by $52,000. Determine the amount that the South Region's costs were over or under budget.

Show Me How EE 24-2 *p. 1180*

PE 24-2A Service department charges **OBJ. 3**

The centralized employee travel department of Croce Company has expenses of $724,000. The department has serviced a total of 5,000 travel reservations for the period. The South Division has made 2,850 reservations during the period, and the West Division has made 2,150 reservations. How much should each division be charged for travel services?

Show Me How EE 24-2 *p. 1180*

PE 24-2B Service department charges **OBJ. 3**

The centralized computer technology department of Hardy Company has expenses of $320,000. The department has provided a total of 4,000 hours of service for the period. The Retail Division has used 2,750 hours of computer technology service during the period, and the Commercial Division has used 1,250 hours of computer technology service. How much should each division be charged for computer technology department services?

OBJ. 3

Show Me How EE 24-3 *p. 1181*

PE 24-3A Income from operations for profit center

Using the data for Croce Company from Practice Exercise 24-2A along with the following data, determine the divisional income from operations for the South and West divisions:

	South Division	West Division
Sales	$2,600,000	$2,420,000
Cost of goods sold	1,352,000	1,379,400
Selling expenses	520,000	484,000

OBJ. 3

Show Me How EE 24-3 *p. 1181*

PE 24-3B Income from operations for profit center

Using the data for Hardy Company from Practice Exercise 24-2B along with the following data, determine the divisional income from operations for the Retail Division and the Commercial Division:

	Retail Division	Commercial Division
Sales	$2,150,000	$1,200,000
Cost of goods sold	1,300,000	800,000
Selling expenses	150,000	175,000

OBJ. 4

Show Me How EE 24-4 *p. 1185*

PE 24-4A Profit margin, investment turnover, and ROI

Cash Company has income from operations of $112,500, invested assets of $750,000, and sales of $1,875,000. Use the DuPont formula to compute the return on investment and show (a) the profit margin, (b) the investment turnover, and (c) the return on investment.

OBJ. 4

Show Me How EE 24-4 *p. 1185*

PE 24-4B Profit margin, investment turnover, and ROI

Briggs Company has income from operations of $36,000, invested assets of $180,000, and sales of $720,000. Use the DuPont formula to compute the return on investment and show (a) the profit margin, (b) the investment turnover, and (c) the return on investment.

OBJ. 4

Show Me How EE 24-5 *p. 1186*

PE 24-5A Residual income

The Consumer Division of Galena Company has income from operations of $12,680,000 and assets of $74,500,000. The minimum acceptable return on assets is 12%. What is the residual income for the division?

OBJ. 4

Show Me How EE 24-5 *p. 1186*

PE 24-5B Residual income

The Commercial Division of Herring Company has income from operations of $420,000 and assets of $910,000. The minimum acceptable return on assets is 8%. What is the residual income for the division?

OBJ. 5

Show Me How EE 24-6 *p. 1192*

PE 24-6A Transfer pricing

The materials used by the North Division of Horton Company are currently purchased from outside suppliers at $60 per unit. These same materials are produced by Horton's South Division. The South Division can produce the materials needed by the North Division at a variable cost of $42 per unit. The division is currently producing 200,000 units and has capacity of 250,000 units. The two divisions have recently negotiated a transfer price of $52 per unit for 30,000 units. By how much will each division's income increase as a result of this transfer?

Show Me How EE 24-6 *p. 1192*

PE 24-6B Transfer pricing

OBJ. 5

The materials used by the Multinomah Division of Isbister Company are currently purchased from outside suppliers at $90 per unit. These same materials are produced by the Pembroke Division. The Pembroke Division can produce the materials needed by the Multinomah Division at a variable cost of $75 per unit. The division is currently producing 120,000 units and has capacity of 150,000 units. The two divisions have recently negotiated a transfer price of $82 per unit for 15,000 units. By how much will each division's income increase as a result of this transfer?

Exercises

EX 24-1 Budget performance reports for cost centers

OBJ. 2

✔ a. (c) $22,950

Show Me How

Partially completed budget performance reports for Garland Company, a manufacturer of light duty motors, follow:

Garland Company
Budget Performance Report—Vice President, Production
For the Month Ended November 30

Plant	Actual	Budget	Over Budget	Under Budget
Eastern Region	$2,409,400	$2,420,000		$(10,600)
Central Region	2,998,400	3,000,000		(1,600)
Western Region	(g)	(h)	(i)	
	(j)	(k)	$ (l)	$(12,200)

Garland Company
Budget Performance Report—Manager, Western Region Plant
For the Month Ended November 30

Department	Actual	Budget	Over Budget	Under Budget
Chip Fabrication	(a)	(b)	(c)	
Electronic Assembly	$703,200	$700,000	$ 3,200	
Final Assembly	516,600	525,000		$(8,400)
	(d)	(e)	$ (f)	$(8,400)

Garland Company
Budget Performance Report—Supervisor, Chip Fabrication
For the Month Ended November 30

Cost	Actual	Budget	Over Budget	Under Budget
Factory wages	$ 95,500	$ 82,000	$13,500	
Materials	115,300	120,000		$(4,700)
Power and light	49,950	45,000	4,950	
Maintenance	37,200	28,000	9,200	
	$297,950	$275,000	$27,650	$(4,700)

a. Complete the budget performance reports by determining the correct amounts for the lettered spaces.

b. Compose a memo to Cassandra Reid, vice president of production for Garland Company, explaining the performance of the production division for November.

EX 24-2 Divisional income statements OBJ. 3

✔ Commercial Division income from operations, $179,890

The following data were summarized from the accounting records for Jersey Coast Construction Company for the year ended June 30, 20Y8:

Cost of goods sold:		Service department charges:	
Commercial Division	$912,250	Commercial Division	$112,560
Residential Division	423,675	Residential Division	67,830
Administrative expenses:		Sales:	
Commercial Division	$149,800	Commercial Division	$1,354,500
Residential Division	128,625	Residential Division	743,780

Prepare divisional income statements for Jersey Coast Construction Company.

EX 24-3 Service department charges and activity bases OBJ. 3

For each of the following service departments, identify an activity base that could be used for charging the expense to the profit center:

a. Legal
b. Duplication services
c. Information Technology Help Desk
d. Central purchasing
e. Networking
f. Accounts receivable

EX 24-4 Activity bases for service department charges OBJ. 3

✔ c. 4

For each of the following service departments, select the activity base listed that is most appropriate for charging service expenses to responsible units:

Service Department	Activity Base
a. Accounts Receivable	1. Number of employees trained
b. Central Purchasing	2. Number of payroll checks
c. Computer Support	3. Number of sales invoices
d. Conferences	4. Number of computers
e. Employee Travel	5. Number of conference attendees
f. Payroll Accounting	6. Number of travel claims
g. Telecommunications	7. Number of purchase requisitions
h. Training	8. Number of cell phone minutes used

EX 24-5 Service department charges OBJ. 3

✔ b. Residential payroll, $33,000

Show Me How

In divisional income statements prepared for LeFevre Company, the Payroll Department costs are charged back to user divisions on the basis of the number of payroll distributions, and the Purchasing Department costs are charged back on the basis of the number of purchase requisitions. The Payroll Department had expenses of $75,400 and the Purchasing Department had expenses of $42,000 for the year. The following annual data for Residential, Commercial, and Government Contract divisions were obtained from corporate records:

	Residential	Commercial	Government Contract
Sales	$1,000,000	$1,600,000	$3,200,000
Number of employees:			
Weekly payroll (52 weeks per year)	300	150	200
Monthly payroll	75	160	90
Number of purchase requisitions per year	4,000	3,500	3,000

a. Determine the total amount of payroll checks and purchase requisitions processed per year by the company and each division.

b. Using the activity base information in (a), determine the annual amount of payroll and purchasing costs charged back to the Residential, Commercial, and Government Contract divisions from payroll and purchasing services.

c. Why does the Residential Division have a larger service department charge than the other two divisions even though its sales are lower?

✔ b. Help desk, $77,200

EX 24-6 Service department charges and activity bases **OBJ. 3**

Middler Corporation, a manufacturer of electronics and communications systems, uses a service department charge system to charge profit centers with Computing and Communications Services (CCS) service department costs. The following table identifies an abbreviated list of service categories and activity bases used by the CCS department. The table also includes some assumed cost and activity base quantity information for each service for October.

CCS Service Category	Activity Base	Budgeted Cost	Budgeted Activity Base Quantity
Help desk	Number of calls	$160,000	3,200
Network center	Number of devices monitored	735,000	9,800
Electronic mail	Number of user accounts	100,000	10,000
Handheld Technology support	Number of handheld devices issued	124,600	8,900

One of the profit centers for Middler Corporation is the Communication Systems (COMM) sector. Assume the following information for the COMM sector:

- The sector has 5,200 employees, of whom 25% are office employees.
- Almost all office employees (99%) have a computer on the network.
- One hundred percent of the employees with a computer also have an e-mail account.
- The average number of help desk calls for October was 1.2 calls per individual with a computer.
- There are 600 additional printers, servers, and peripherals on the network beyond the personal computers.
- All the nonoffice employees have been issued a handheld device.

a. Determine the service charge rate for the four CCS service categories for October.

b. Determine the charges to the COMM sector for the four CCS service categories for October.

✔ Commercial income from operations, $1,071,000

Excel

Show Me How

EX 24-7 Divisional income statements with service department charges **OBJ. 3**

Grael Technology has two divisions, Consumer and Commercial, and two corporate service departments, Tech Support and Purchasing. The corporate expenses for the year ended December 31, 20Y7, are as follows:

Tech Support Department	$336,000
Purchasing Department	67,500
Other corporate administrative expenses	448,000
Total corporate expense	$851,500

The other corporate administrative expenses include officers' salaries and other expenses required by the corporation. The Tech Support Department charges the divisions for services rendered, based on the number of computers in the department, and the Purchasing Department charges divisions for services, based on the number of purchase orders for each department. The usage of service by the two divisions is as follows:

	Tech Support	Purchasing
Consumer Division	300 computers	1,800 purchase orders
Commercial Division	180	2,700
Total	480 computers	4,500 purchase orders

(Continued)

The service department charges of the Tech Support Department and the Purchasing Department are considered controllable by the divisions. Corporate administrative expenses are not considered controllable by the divisions. The revenues, cost of goods sold, and operating expenses for the two divisions are as follows:

	Consumer	Commercial
Revenues	$5,900,000	$4,950,000
Cost of goods sold	3,304,000	2,475,000
Operating expenses	1,180,000	1,237,500

Prepare the divisional income statements for the two divisions.

EX 24-8 Corrections to service department charges for a service company — OBJ. 3

✔ b. Income from operations, Cargo Division, $84,400

Wild Sun Airlines Inc. has two divisions organized as profit centers, the Passenger Division and the Cargo Division. The following divisional income statements were prepared:

Wild Sun Airlines Inc.
Divisional Income Statements
For the Year Ended December 31, 20Y9

	Passenger Division		Cargo Division	
Revenues		$3,025,000		$3,025,000
Operating expenses		2,450,000		2,736,000
Income from operations before service department charges		$ 575,000		$ 289,000
Less service department charges:				
Training	$125,000		$125,000	
Flight scheduling	108,000		108,000	
Reservations	151,200	384,200	151,200	384,200
Income from operations		$ 190,800		$ (95,200)

The service department charge rate for the service department costs was based on revenues. Because the revenues of the two divisions were the same, the service department charges to each division were also the same.

The following additional information is available:

	Passenger Division	Cargo Division	Total
Number of personnel trained	350	150	500
Number of flights	800	1,200	2,000
Number of reservations requested	20,000	0	20,000

a. Does the income from operations for the two divisions accurately measure performance? Explain.

b. Correct the divisional income statements, using the activity bases provided in revising the service department charges.

EX 24-9 Profit center responsibility reporting — OBJ. 3

✔ Income from operations, Summer Sports Division, $1,717,920

Excel

Show Me How

Glades Sporting Goods Co. operates two divisions—the Winter Sports Division and the Summer Sports Division. The following income and expense accounts were provided from the trial balance as of December 31, 20Y8, the end of the fiscal year, after all adjustments, including those for inventories, were recorded and posted:

Sales—Winter Sports Division	$12,600,000
Sales—Summer Sports Division	16,300,000
Cost of Goods Sold—Winter Sports Division	7,560,000
Cost of Goods Sold—Summer Sports Division	9,454,000
Sales Expense—Winter Sports Division	2,016,000
Sales Expense—Summer Sports Division	2,282,000
Administrative Expense—Winter Sports Division	1,260,000
Administrative Expense—Summer Sports Division	1,450,700
Advertising Expense	578,000
Transportation Expense	265,660
Accounts Receivable Collection Expense	174,000
Warehouse Expense	1,540,000

The bases to be used in allocating expenses, together with other essential information, are as follows:

a. Advertising expense—incurred at headquarters, charged back to divisions on the basis of usage: Winter Sports Division, $252,000; Summer Sports Division, $326,000.

b. Transportation expense—charged back to divisions at a charge rate of $7.40 per bill of lading: Winter Sports Division, 17,200 bills of lading; Summer Sports Division, 18,700 bills of lading.

c. Accounts receivable collection expense—incurred at headquarters, charged back to divisions at a charge rate of $6.00 per invoice: Winter Sports Division, 11,500 sales invoices; Summer Sports Division, 17,500 sales invoices.

d. Warehouse expense—charged back to divisions on the basis of floor space used in storing division products: Winter Sports Division, 102,000 square feet; Summer Sports Division, 118,000 square feet.

Prepare a divisional income statement with two column headings: Winter Sports Division and Summer Sports Division. Provide supporting calculations for service department charges.

✔ a. Retail, 18%

Show Me How

EX 24-10 Return on investment

OBJ. 4

The income from operations and the amount of invested assets in each division of Beck Industries are as follows:

	Income from Operations	Invested Assets
Retail Division	$5,400,000	$30,000,000
Commercial Division	6,250,000	25,000,000
Internet Division	1,800,000	12,000,000

a. Compute the return on investment for each division.

b. Which division is the most profitable per dollar invested?

✔ a. Retail Division, $2,700,000

Show Me How

EX 24-11 Residual income

OBJ. 4

Based on the data in Exercise 24-10, assume that management has established a 9% minimum acceptable return for invested assets.

a. Determine the residual income for each division.

b. Which division has the most residual income?

EX 24-12 Determining missing items in return computation **OBJ. 4**

✔ d. 3.00

One item is omitted from each of the following computations of the return on investment:

Return on Investment	=	Profit Margin	×	Investment Turnover
13.2%	=	6%	×	(a)
(b)	=	10%	×	1.80
10.5%	=	(c)	×	1.50
15.0%	=	5%	×	(d)
(e)	=	12%	×	1.10

Determine the missing items, identifying each by the appropriate letter.

EX 24-13 Profit margin, investment turnover, and return on investment **OBJ. 4**

✔ a. ROI, 24%

Show Me How

The condensed income statement for the Consumer Products Division of Fargo Industries Inc. is as follows (assuming no service department charges):

Sales	$82,500,000
Cost of goods sold	53,625,000
Gross profit	$28,875,000
Administrative expenses	15,675,000
Income from operations	$13,200,000

The manager of the Consumer Products Division is considering ways to increase the return on investment.

a. Using the DuPont formula for return on investment, determine the profit margin, investment turnover, and return on investment of the Consumer Products Division, assuming that $55,000,000 of assets have been invested in the Consumer Products Division.

b. If expenses could be reduced by $1,650,000 without decreasing sales, what would be the impact on the profit margin, investment turnover, and return on investment for the Consumer Products Division?

EX 24-14 Return on investment **OBJ. 4**

✔ a. Media Networks ROI, 24.5%

Real World

The Walt Disney Company has four profitable business segments, described as follows:

- **Media Networks:** The ABC television and radio network, Disney channel, ESPN, A&E, E!, and Disney.com
- **Parks and Resorts:** Walt Disney World Resort, Disneyland, Disney Cruise Line, and other resort properties
- **Studio Entertainment:** Walt Disney Studios, which releases films by Pixar Animation Studios, Marvel Studios, Disney/Lucasfilm, and Touchstone Pictures
- **Consumer Products:** Character merchandising, Disney stores, books, and magazines

Disney recently reported sector income from operations, revenue, and invested assets (in millions) as follows:

	Income from Operations	Revenue	Invested Assets
Media Networks	$7,321	$21,152	$29,887
Parks and Resorts	2,663	15,099	23,335
Studio Entertainment	1,549	6,988	15,155
Consumer Products	1,356	4,274	7,526

a. Use the DuPont formula to determine the return on investment for the four Disney sectors. Round whole percents to one decimal place and investment turnover to two decimal places.

b. How do the four sectors differ in their profit margin, investment turnover, and return on investment?

✔ c. $46,250

EX 24-15 Determining missing items in return and residual income computations **OBJ. 4**

Data for Uberto Company are presented in the following table of returns on investment and residual incomes:

Invested Assets	Income from Operations	Return on Investment	Minimum Return	Minimum Acceptable Income from Operations	Residual Income
$925,000	$185,000	(a)	15%	(b)	(c)
$775,000	(d)	(e)	(f)	$93,000	$23,250
$450,000	(g)	18%	(h)	$58,500	(i)
$610,000	$97,600	(j)	12%	(k)	(l)

Determine the missing items, identifying each item by the appropriate letter.

✔ a. (e) $300,000

EX 24-16 Determining missing items from computations **OBJ. 4**

Data for the North, South, East, and West divisions of Free Bird Company are as follows:

	Sales	Income from Operations	Invested Assets	Return on Investment	Profit Margin	Investment Turnover
North	$860,000	(a)	(b)	17.5%	7.0%	(c)
South	(d)	$51,300	(e)	(f)	4.5%	3.8
East	$1,020,000	(g)	$680,000	15.0%	(h)	(i)
West	$1,120,000	$89,600	$560,000	(j)	(k)	(l)

a. Determine the missing items, identifying each by the letters (a) through (l). Round percents and investment turnover to one decimal place.

b. Determine the residual income for each division, assuming that the minimum acceptable return established by management is 12%.

c. Which division is the most profitable in terms of (1) return on investment and (2) residual income?

Real World

EX 24-17 Return on investment, residual income for a service company **OBJ. 4**

H&R Block Inc. provides tax preparation services throughout the United States and other parts of the world. These services are provided through two segments: company-owned offices and franchised operations.

Recent financial information provided by H&R Block for its company-owned and franchised operations is as follows (in millions):

	Company-Owned	Franchised Operations
Revenues	$2,651	$335
Income from operations	617	86
Total assets	3,930	586

a. Use the DuPont formula to determine the return on investment for each business divisions. Round whole percents to one decimal place and investment turnover to two decimal places.

b. Determine the residual income for each division, assuming a minimum acceptable income of 15% of total assets. Round minimal acceptable return to the nearest million dollars.

c. Interpret your results.

EX 24-18 Balanced scorecard for a service company **OBJ. 4**

Real World

American Express Company is a major financial services company, noted for its American Express® card. Some of the performance measures used by the company in its balanced scorecard follow:

- Average card member spending
- Cards in force
- Earnings growth
- Hours of credit consultant training
- Investment in information technology
- Number of card choices
- Number of Internet features
- Number of merchant signings
- Number of new card launches
- Return on equity
- Revenue growth

For each measure, identify whether the measure best fits the innovation, customer, internal process, or financial dimension of the balanced scorecard.

EX 24-19 Building a balanced scorecard **OBJ. 4**

Hit-n-Run Inc. owns and operates 10 food trucks (mobile kitchens) throughout metropolitan Los Angeles. Each food truck has a different food theme, such as Irish-Mexican fusion, traditional Mexican street food, Ethiopian cuisine, and Lebanese-Italian fusion. The company was founded three years ago by Juanita O'Brien when she opened a single food truck with a unique menu. As her business has grown, she has become concerned about her ability to manage and control the business. O'Brien describes how the company was built, its key success factors, and its recent growth.

"I built the company from the ground up. In the beginning it was just me. I drove the truck, set the menu, bought the ingredients, prepared the meals, served the meals, cleaned the kitchen, and maintained the equipment. I made unique meals from quality ingredients and didn't serve anything that wasn't perfect. I changed my location daily and notified customers of my location via Twitter.

As my customer base grew, I hired employees to help me in the truck. Then one day I realized that I had a formula that could be expanded to multiple trucks. Before I knew it, I had 10 trucks and was hiring people to do everything that I used to do by myself. Now I work with my team to build the menu, set daily locations for the trucks, and manage the operations of the business.

My business model is based on providing the highest quality street food and charging more for it than other trucks do. You won't get the cheapest meal at one of my trucks, but you will get the best. The superior quality allows me to price my meals a little bit higher than the other trucks do. My employees are critical to my success. I pay them a better wage than they could make on other food trucks, and I expect more from them. I rely on them to maintain the quality that I established when I opened my first truck.

Things are going great, but I'm feeling overwhelmed. So far, the growth in sales has led to a growth in profitability—but I'm getting nervous. If quality starts to fall off, my brand value erodes, and that could affect the prices that I charge for my meals and the success of my business."

Create balanced scorecard measures for Hit-n-Run Food Trucks. Identify whether these measures best fit the innovation, customer, internal process, or financial dimension of the balanced scorecard.

EX 24-20 Decision on transfer pricing **OBJ. 5**

✔ a. $2,650,000

Materials used by the Instrument Division of T_Kong Industries are currently purchased from outside suppliers at a cost of $175 per unit. However, the same materials are available from the Components Division. The Components Division has unused capacity and can produce the materials needed by the Instrument Division at a variable cost of $122 per unit.

a. If a transfer price of $148 per unit is established and 50,000 units of materials are transferred, with no reduction in the Components Division's current sales, how much would T_Kong Industries' total income from operations increase?

b. How much would the Instrument Division's income from operations increase?

c. How much would the Components Division's income from operations increase?

EX 24-21 Decision on transfer pricing **OBJ. 5**

✔ b. $750,000

Based on T_Kong Industries' data in Exercise 24-20, assume that a transfer price of $160 has been established and that 50,000 units of materials are transferred, with no reduction in the Components Division's current sales.

a. How much would T_Kong Industries' total income from operations increase?
b. How much would the Instrument Division's income from operations increase?
c. How much would the Components Division's income from operations increase?
d. If the negotiated price approach is used, what would be the range of acceptable transfer prices and why?

Problems: Series A

Excel

PR 24-1A Budget performance report for a cost center

OBJ. 2

Valotic Tech Inc. sells electronics over the Internet. The Consumer Products Division is organized as a cost center. The budget for the Consumer Products Division for the month ended January 31 is as follows (in thousands):

Customer service salaries	$ 546,840
Insurance and property taxes	114,660
Distribution salaries	872,340
Marketing salaries	1,028,370
Engineer salaries	836,850
Warehouse wages	586,110
Equipment depreciation	183,792
Total	$4,168,962

During January, the costs incurred in the Consumer Products Division were as follows:

Customer service salaries	$ 602,350
Insurance and property taxes	110,240
Distribution salaries	861,200
Marketing salaries	1,085,230
Engineer salaries	820,008
Warehouse wages	562,632
Equipment depreciation	183,610
Total	$4,225,270

Instructions

1. Prepare a budget performance report for the director of the Consumer Products Division for the month of January.
2. For which costs might the director be expected to request supplemental reports?

✔ 1. Income from operations, Central Division, $930,100

Excel

Show Me How

PR 24-2A Profit center responsibility reporting for a service company

OBJ. 3

Red Line Railroad Inc. has three regional divisions organized as profit centers. The chief executive officer (CEO) evaluates divisional performance, using income from operations as a percent of revenues. The following quarterly income and expense accounts were provided from the trial balance as of December 31:

Revenues—East	$1,400,000
Revenues—West	2,000,000
Revenues—Central	3,200,000
Operating Expenses—East	800,000
Operating Expenses—West	1,350,000
Operating Expenses—Central	1,900,000
Corporate Expenses—Shareholder Relations	300,000
Corporate Expenses—Customer Support	320,000
Corporate Expenses—Legal	500,000
General Corporate Officers' Salaries	1,200,000

(Continued)

The company operates three service departments: Shareholder Relations, Customer Support, and Legal. The Shareholder Relations Department conducts a variety of services for shareholders of the company. The shareholder Relations Department and general corporate officers' salaries are not controllable by division management. The Customer Support Department is the company's point of contact for new service, complaints, and requests for repair. The department believes that the number of customer contacts is an activity base for this work. The Legal Department provides legal services for division management. The department believes that the number of hours billed is an activity base for this work. The following additional information has been gathered:

	East	West	Central
Number of customer contacts	1,500	2,800	5,700
Number of hours billed	750	1,750	1,500

Instructions

1. Prepare quarterly income statements showing income from operations for the three divisions. Use three column headings: East, West, and Central.
2. Identify the most successful division according to the profit margin.
3. Provide a recommendation to the CEO for a better method for evaluating the performance of the divisions. In your recommendation, identify the major weakness of the present method.

PR 24-3A Divisional income statements and return on investment analysis

OBJ. 4

✔ 2. Cereal Division ROI, 11.0%

Excel

The Whole Life Baked Goods Company is a diversified food company that specializes in all natural foods. The company has three operating divisions organized as investment centers. Condensed data taken from the records of the three divisions for the year ended June 30, 20Y7, are as follows:

	Cereal Division	Snack Cake Division	Retail Bakeries Division
Sales	$17,600,000	$18,000,000	$9,520,000
Cost of goods sold	10,600,000	12,550,000	6,630,000
Operating expenses	6,120,000	4,730,000	2,318,800
Invested assets	8,000,000	6,000,000	6,800,000

The management of The Whole Life Baked Goods Company is evaluating each division as a basis for planning a future expansion of operations.

Instructions

1. Prepare condensed divisional income statements for the three divisions, assuming that there were no service department charges.
2. Using the DuPont formula for return on investment, compute the profit margin, investment turnover, and return on investment for each division. Round percentages and the investment turnover to one decimal place.
3. If available funds permit the expansion of operations of only one division, which of the divisions would you recommend for expansion, based on parts (1) and (2)? Explain.

PR 24-4A Effect of proposals on divisional performance

OBJ. 4

✔ 1. ROI, 16.8%

Excel

A condensed income statement for the Commercial Division of Maxell Manufacturing Inc. for the year ended December 31 is as follows:

Sales	$3,500,000
Cost of goods sold	2,480,000
Gross profit	$1,020,000
Operating expenses	600,000
Income from operations	$ 420,000
Invested assets	$2,500,000

Assume that the Commercial Division received no charges from service departments. The president of Maxell Manufacturing has indicated that the division's return on a $2,500,000 investment must be increased to at least 21% by the end of the next year if operations are to continue. The division manager is considering the following three proposals:

Proposal 1: Transfer equipment with a book value of $312,500 to other divisions at no gain or loss and lease similar equipment. The annual lease payments would exceed the amount of depreciation expense on the old equipment by $105,000. This increase in expense would be included as part of the cost of goods sold. Sales would remain unchanged.

Proposal 2: Purchase new and more efficient machining equipment and thereby reduce the cost of goods sold by $560,000 after considering the effects of depreciation expense on the new equipment. Sales would remain unchanged, and the old equipment, which has no remaining book value, would be scrapped at no gain or loss. The new equipment would increase invested assets by an additional $1,875,000 for the year.

Proposal 3: Reduce invested assets by discontinuing a product line. This action would eliminate sales of $595,000, reduce cost of goods sold by $406,700, and reduce operating expenses by $175,000. Assets of $1,338,000 would be transferred to other divisions at no gain or loss.

Instructions

1. Using the DuPont formula for return on investment, determine the profit margin, investment turnover, and return on investment for the Commercial Division for the past year.
2. Prepare condensed estimated income statements and compute the invested assets for each proposal.
3. Using the DuPont formula for return on investment, determine the profit margin, investment turnover, and return on investment for each proposal. Round percentages and the investment turnover to one decimal place.
4. Which of the three proposals would meet the required 21% return on investment?
5. If the Commercial Division were in an industry where the profit margin could not be increased, how much would the investment turnover have to increase to meet the president's required 21% return on investment? Round to one decimal place.

✔ 2. Business Division ROI, 20.0%

Excel

Show Me How

PR 24-5A Divisional performance analysis and evaluation

OBJ. 4

The vice president of operations of Pavone Company is evaluating the performance of two divisions organized as investment centers. Invested assets and condensed income statement data for the past year for each division are as follows:

	Business Division	Consumer Division
Sales	$2,500,000	$2,550,000
Cost of goods sold	1,320,000	1,350,000
Operating expenses	930,000	843,000
Invested assets	1,250,000	2,125,000

Instructions

1. Prepare condensed divisional income statements for the year ended December 31, assuming that there were no service department charges.
2. Using the DuPont formula for return on investment, determine the profit margin, investment turnover, and return on investment for each division. Round percentages and the investment turnover to one decimal place.
3. If management wants a minimum acceptable return of 17%, determine the residual income for each division.
4. Discuss the evaluation of the two divisions, using the performance measures determined in parts (1), (2), and (3).

PR 24-6A Transfer pricing

OBJ. 5

✓ 3. Total income from operations, $1,759,680

Excel

Garcon Inc. manufactures electronic products, with two operating divisions, the Consumer and Commercial divisions. Condensed divisional income statements, which involve no intracompany transfers and include a breakdown of expenses into variable and fixed components, are as follows:

Garcon Inc.
Divisional Income Statements
For the Year Ended December 31, 20Y8

	Consumer Division	Commercial Division	Total
Sales:			
14,400 units @ $144 per unit	$2,073,600		$2,073,600
21,600 units @ $275 per unit		$5,940,000	5,940,000
	$2,073,600	$5,940,000	$8,013,600
Expenses:			
Variable:			
14,400 units @ $104 per unit	$1,497,600		$1,497,600
21,600 units @ $193* per unit		$4,168,800	4,168,800
Fixed	200,000	520,000	720,000
Total expenses	$1,697,600	$4,688,800	$6,386,400
Income from operations	$ 376,000	$1,251,200	$1,627,200

*$150 of the $193 per unit represents materials costs, and the remaining $43 per unit represents other variable conversion expenses incurred within the Commercial Division.

The Consumer Division is presently producing 14,400 units out of a total capacity of 17,280 units. Materials used in producing the Commercial Division's product are currently purchased from outside suppliers at a price of $150 per unit. The Consumer Division is able to produce the materials used by the Commercial Division. Except for the possible transfer of materials between divisions, no changes are expected in sales and expenses.

Instructions

1. Would the market price of $150 per unit be an appropriate transfer price for Garcon Inc.? Explain.
2. If the Commercial Division purchased 2,880 units from the Consumer Division, rather than externally, at a negotiated transfer price of $115 per unit, how much would the income from operations of each division and the total company income from operations increase?
3. Prepare condensed divisional income statements for Garcon Inc. based on the data in part (2).
4. If a transfer price of $126 per unit was negotiated, how much would the income from operations of each division and the total company income from operations increase?
5. a. What is the range of possible negotiated transfer prices that would be acceptable for Garcon Inc.?
   b. Assuming that the managers of the two divisions cannot agree on a transfer price, what price would you suggest as the transfer price?

Problems: Series B

PR 24-1B Budget performance report for a cost center

OBJ. 2

Excel

The Eastern District of Adelson Inc. is organized as a cost center. The budget for the Eastern District of Adelson Inc. for the month ended December 31 is as follows (in thousands):

Sales salaries	$ 819,840
System administration salaries	448,152
Customer service salaries	152,600
Billing salaries	98,760
Maintenance	271,104
Depreciation of plant and equipment	92,232
Insurance and property taxes	41,280
Total	$1,923,968

During December, the costs incurred in the Eastern District were as follows:

Sales salaries	$ 818,880
System administration salaries	447,720
Customer service salaries	183,120
Billing salaries	98,100
Maintenance	273,000
Depreciation of plant and equipment	92,232
Insurance and property taxes	41,400
Total	$1,954,452

Instructions

1. Prepare a budget performance report for the manager of the Eastern District of Adelson for the month of December.
2. For which costs might the supervisor be expected to request supplemental reports?

✔ 1. Income from operations, West Region, $820,800

Excel

Show Me How

PR 24-2B Profit center responsibility reporting for a service company **OBJ. 3**

Thomas Railroad Company organizes its three divisions, the North (N), South (S), and West (W) regions, as profit centers. The chief executive officer (CEO) evaluates divisional performance using income from operations as a percent of revenues. The following quarterly income and expense accounts were provided from the trial balance as of December 31:

Revenues—N Region	$3,780,000
Revenues—S Region	5,673,000
Revenues—W Region	5,130,000
Operating Expenses—N Region	2,678,500
Operating Expenses—S Region	4,494,890
Operating Expenses—W Region	3,770,050
Corporate Expenses—Dispatching	182,000
Corporate Expenses—Equipment Management	1,200,000
Corporate Expenses—Treasurer's	734,000
General Corporate Officers' Salaries	1,380,000

The company operates three service departments: the Dispatching Department, the Equipment Management Department, and the Treasurer's Department. The Treasurer's Department and general corporate officers' salaries are not controllable by division management. The Dispatching Department manages the scheduling and releasing of completed trains. The Equipment Management Department manages the inventories of railroad cars. It makes sure the right freight cars are at the right place at the right time. The Treasurer's Department conducts a variety of services for the company as a whole. The following additional information has been gathered:

	North	South	West
Number of scheduled trains	650	1,105	845
Number of railroad cars in inventory	6,000	8,400	9,600

(Continued)

Instructions

1. Prepare quarterly income statements showing income from operations for the three regions. Use three column headings: North, South, and West.
2. Identify the most successful region according to the profit margin.
3. Provide a recommendation to the CEO for a better method for evaluating the performance of the regions. In your recommendation, identify the major weakness of the present method.

PR 24-3B Divisional income statements and return on investment analysis **OBJ. 4**

✔ 2. Mutual Fund Division, ROI, 22.4%

Excel

E.F. Lynch Company is a diversified investment company with three operating divisions organized as investment centers. Condensed data taken from the records of the three divisions for the year ended June 30, 20Y8, are as follows:

	Mutual Fund Division	Electronic Brokerage Division	Investment Banking Division
Fee revenue	$4,140,000	$3,360,000	$4,560,000
Operating expenses	2,980,800	3,091,200	3,739,200
Invested assets	5,175,000	1,120,000	3,800,000

The management of E.F. Lynch Company is evaluating each division as a basis for planning a future expansion of operations.

Instructions

1. Prepare condensed divisional income statements for the three divisions, assuming that there were no service department charges.
2. Using the DuPont formula for return on investment, compute the profit margin, investment turnover, and return on investment for each division. Round percentages and the investment turnover to one decimal place.
3. If available funds permit the expansion of operations of only one division, which of the divisions would you recommend for expansion, based on parts (1) and (2)? Explain.

PR 24-4B Effect of proposals on divisional performance **OBJ. 4**

✔ 3. Proposal 3 ROI, 16.0%

Excel

A condensed income statement for the Electronics Division of Gihbli Industries Inc. for the year ended December 31 is as follows:

Sales	$1,575,000
Cost of goods sold	891,000
Gross profit	$ 684,000
Operating expenses	558,000
Income from operations	$ 126,000
Invested assets	$1,050,000

Assume that the Electronics Division received no charges from service departments. The president of Gihbli Industries Inc. has indicated that the division's return on a $1,050,000 investment must be increased to at least 20% by the end of the next year if operations are to continue. The division manager is considering the following three proposals:

Proposal 1: Transfer equipment with a book value of $300,000 to other divisions at no gain or loss and lease similar equipment. The annual lease payments would be less than the amount of depreciation expense on the old equipment by $31,400. This decrease in expense would be included as part of the cost of goods sold. Sales would remain unchanged.

Proposal 2: Reduce invested assets by discontinuing a product line. This action would eliminate sales of $180,000, reduce cost of goods sold by $119,550, and reduce operating expenses by $60,000. Assets of $112,500 would be transferred to other divisions at no gain or loss.

Proposal 3: Purchase new and more efficient machinery and thereby reduce the cost of goods sold by $189,000 after considering the effects of depreciation expense on the new equipment. Sales would remain unchanged, and the old machinery, which has no remaining book value, would be scrapped at no gain or loss. The new machinery would increase invested assets by $918,750 for the year.

Instructions

1. Using the DuPont formula for return on investment, determine the profit margin, investment turnover, and return on investment for the Electronics Division for the past year. Round percentages and the investment turnover to one decimal place.
2. Prepare condensed estimated income statements and compute the invested assets for each proposal.
3. Using the DuPont formula for return on investment, determine the profit margin, investment turnover, and return on investment for each proposal. Round percentages and the investment turnover to one decimal place.
4. Which of the three proposals would meet the required 20% return on investment?
5. If the Electronics Division were in an industry where the profit margin could not be increased, how much would the investment turnover have to increase to meet the president's required 20% return on investment? Round to one decimal place.

✔ 2. Road Bike Division ROI, 12.0%

Excel

Show Me How

PR 24-5B Divisional performance analysis and evaluation

OBJ. 4

The vice president of operations of Free Ride Bike Company is evaluating the performance of two divisions organized as investment centers. Invested assets and condensed income statement data for the past year for each division are as follows:

	Road Bike Division	Mountain Bike Division
Sales	$1,728,000	$1,760,000
Cost of goods sold	1,380,000	1,400,000
Operating expenses	175,200	236,800
Invested assets	1,440,000	800,000

Instructions

1. Prepare condensed divisional income statements for the year ended December 31, 20Y7, assuming that there were no service department charges.
2. Using the DuPont formula for return on investment, determine the profit margin, investment turnover, and return on investment for each division. Round percentages and the investment turnover to one decimal place.
3. If management's minimum acceptable return is 10%, determine the residual income for each division.
4. Discuss the evaluation of the two divisions, using the performance measures determined in parts (1), (2), and (3).

OBJ. 5

PR 24-6B Transfer pricing

✓ 3. Navigational Systems Division, $179,410

Excel

Exoplex Industries Inc. is a diversified aerospace company, including two operating divisions, Semiconductors and Navigational Systems divisions. Condensed divisional income statements, which involve no intracompany transfers and include a breakdown of expenses into variable and fixed components, are as follows:

Exoplex Industries Inc.
Divisional Income Statements
For the Year Ended December 31, 20Y8

	Semiconductors Division	Navigational Systems Division	Total
Sales:			
2,240 units @ $396 per unit	$887,040		$ 887,040
3,675 units @ $590 per unit		$2,168,250	2,168,250
	$887,040	$2,168,250	$3,055,290
Expenses:			
Variable:			
2,240 units @ $232 per unit	$519,680		$ 519,680
3,675 units @ $472* per unit		$1,734,600	1,734,600
Fixed	220,000	325,000	545,000
Total expenses	$739,680	$2,059,600	$2,799,280
Income from operations	$147,360	$ 108,650	$ 256,010

*$432 of the $472 per unit represents materials costs, and the remaining $40 per unit represents other variable conversion expenses incurred within the Navigational Systems Division.

The Semiconductors Division is presently producing 2,240 units out of a total capacity of 2,820 units. Materials used in producing the Navigational Systems Division's product are currently purchased from outside suppliers at a price of $432 per unit. The Semiconductors Division is able to produce the components used by the Navigational Systems Division. Except for the possible transfer of materials between divisions, no changes are expected in sales and expenses.

Instructions

1. Would the market price of $432 per unit be an appropriate transfer price for Exoplex Industries Inc.? Explain.
2. If the Navigational Systems Division purchased 580 units from the Semiconductors Division, rather than externally, at a negotiated transfer price of $310 per unit, how much would the income from operations of each division and total company income from operations increase?
3. Prepare condensed divisional income statements for Exoplex Industries Inc. based on the data in part (2).
4. If a transfer price of $340 per unit was negotiated, how much would the income from operations of each division and total company income from operations increase?
5. a. What is the range of possible negotiated transfer prices that would be acceptable for Exoplex Industries Inc.?
   b. Assuming that the managers of the two divisions cannot agree on a transfer price, what price would you suggest as the transfer price?

Cases & Projects

CP 24-1 Ethics in Action

Ethics

Sembotix Company has several divisions including a Semiconductor Division that sells semiconductors to both internal and external customers. The company's X-ray Division uses semiconductors as a component in its final product and is evaluating whether to purchase them from the Semiconductor Division or from an external supplier. The market price for semiconductors is $100 per 100 semiconductors. Dave Bryant is the controller of the X-ray Division, and Howard Hillman is the controller of the Semiconductor Division. The following conversation took place between Dave and Howard:

Dave: I hear you are having problems selling semiconductors out of your division. Maybe I can help.

Howard: You've got that right. We're producing and selling at about 90% of our capacity to outsiders. Last year we were selling 100% of capacity. Would it be possible for your division to pick up some of our excess capacity? After all, we are part of the same company.

Dave: What kind of price could you give me?

Howard: Well, you know as well as I that we are under strict profit responsibility in our divisions, so I would expect to get market price, $100 for 100 semiconductors.

Dave: I'm not so sure we can swing that. I was expecting a price break from a "sister" division.

Howard: Hey, I can only take this "sister" stuff so far. If I give you a price break, our profits will fall from last year's levels. I don't think I could explain that. I'm sorry, but I must remain firm—market price. After all, it's only fair—that's what you would have to pay from an external supplier.

Dave: Fair or not, I think we'll pass. Sorry we couldn't have helped.

Is Dave behaving ethically by trying to force the Semiconductor Division into a price break? Comment on Howard's reactions.

Team Activity

CP 24-2 Team Activity

In teams, visit the website of a company that uses the balanced scorecard to evaluate its performance. Identify the performance measures used by the company on its balanced scorecard. For each measure, identify whether the measure best fits the innovation, customer, internal process, or financial dimension of the balanced scorecard.

Communication

CP 24-3 Communication

The Norsk Division of Gridiron Concepts Inc. has been experiencing revenue and profit growth during the years 20Y6–20Y8. The divisional income statements follow:

Gridiron Concepts Inc.
Divisional Income Statements, Norsk Division
For the Years Ended December 31, 20Y6–20Y8

	20Y6	20Y7	20Y8
Sales	$1,470,000	$2,100,000	$2,450,000
Cost of goods sold	1,064,000	1,498,000	1,680,000
Gross profit	$ 406,000	$ 602,000	$ 770,000
Operating expenses	185,500	224,000	231,000
Income from operations	$ 220,500	$ 378,000	$ 539,000
Invested assets	$ 735,000	$1,500,000	$3,500,000

There are no service department charges, and the division operates as an investment center that must maintain a 15% return on invested assets.

Determine the profit margins, investment turnover, and return on investment for the Norse Division for 20Y6–20Y8. Based on your calculations, write a brief memo to the president of Gridiron Concepts Inc., Tom Yang, evaluating the division's performance.

CP 24-4 Service department charges

The Customer Service Department of Door Industries Inc. asked the Publications Department to prepare a brochure for its training program. The Publications Department delivered the brochures and charged the Customer Service Department a rate that was 25% higher than could be obtained from an outside printing company. The policy of the company required the Customer Service Department to use the internal publications group for brochures. The Publications Department claimed that it had a drop in demand for its services during the fiscal year, so it had to charge higher prices in order to recover its payroll and fixed costs.

(Continued)

Should the cost of the brochure be transferred to the Customer Service Department in order to hold the Customer Service Department head accountable for the cost of the brochure? What changes in policy would you recommend?

CP 24-5 Evaluating divisional performance

The three divisions of Yummy Foods are Snack Goods, Cereal, and Frozen Foods. The divisions are structured as investment centers. The following responsibility reports were prepared for the three divisions for the prior year:

	Snack Goods	Cereal	Frozen Foods
Revenues	$2,200,000	$2,520,000	$2,100,000
Operating expenses	1,366,600	1,122,000	976,800
Income from operations before service department charges	$ 833,400	$1,398,000	$1,123,200
Service department charges:			
Promotion	$ 300,000	$ 600,000	$ 468,000
Legal	137,400	243,600	235,200
Total service department charges	$ 437,400	$ 843,600	$ 703,200
Income from operations	$ 396,000	$ 554,400	$ 420,000
Invested assets	$2,000,000	$1,680,000	$1,750,000

1. Which division is making the best use of invested assets and should be given priority for future capital investments?
2. Assuming that the minimum acceptable return on new projects is 19%, would all investments that produce a return in excess of 19% be accepted by the divisions? Explain.
3. Identify opportunities for improving the company's financial performance.

CP 24-6 Evaluating division performance

Last Resort Industries Inc. is a privately held diversified company with five separate divisions organized as investment centers. A condensed income statement for the Specialty Products Division for the past year, assuming no service department charges, is as follows:

Last Resort Industries Inc.—Specialty Products Division
Income Statement
For the Year Ended December 31, 20Y5

Sales	$32,400,000
Cost of goods sold	24,300,000
Gross profit	$ 8,100,000
Operating expenses	3,240,000
Income from operations	$ 4,860,000
Invested assets	$27,000,000

The manager of the Specialty Products Division was recently presented with the opportunity to add an additional product line, which would require invested assets of $14,400,000. A projected income statement for the new product line is as follows:

New Product Line
Projected Income Statement
For the Year Ended December 31, 20Y6

Sales	$12,960,000
Cost of goods sold	7,500,000
Gross profit	$ 5,460,000
Operating expenses	3,127,200
Income from operations	$ 2,332,800

The Specialty Products Division currently has $27,000,000 in invested assets, and Last Resort Industries Inc.'s overall return on investment, including all divisions, is 10%. Each division manager is evaluated on the basis of divisional return on investment. A bonus is paid, in $8,000 increments, for each whole percentage point that the division's return on investment exceeds the company average.

The president is concerned that the manager of the Specialty Products Division rejected the addition of the new product line, even though all estimates indicated that the product line would be profitable and would increase overall company income. You have been asked to analyze the possible reasons the Specialty Products Division manager rejected the new product line.

1. Determine the return on investment for the Specialty Products Division for the past year.
2. Determine the Specialty Products Division manager's bonus for the past year.
3. Determine the estimated return on investment for the new product line. Round whole percents to one decimal place and investment turnover to two decimal places.
4. Why might the manager of the Specialty Products Division decide to reject the new product line? Support your answer by determining the projected return on investment for 20Y6, assuming that the new product line was launched in the Specialty Products Division, and 20Y6 actual operating results were similar to those of 20Y5.
5. Suggest an alternative performance measure for motivating division managers to accept new investment opportunities that would increase the overall company income and return on investment.

CHAPTER 25

Differential Analysis, Product Pricing, and Activity-Based Costing

Concepts and Principles

Chapter 18 *Introduction to Managerial Accounting*

Developing Information

COST SYSTEMS

Chapter 19 *Job Order Costing*
Chapter 20 *Process Costing*

COST BEHAVIOR

Chapter 21 *Cost-Volume-Profit Analysis*

Decision Making

EVALUATING PERFORMANCE

Chapter 22 *Budgeting*
Chapter 23 *Variances from Standard Costs*

COMPARING ALTERNATIVES

Chapter 24 *Decentralized Operations*
Chapter 25 ***Differential Analysis, Product Pricing, and Activity-Based Costing***
Chapter 26 *Capital Investment Analysis*

CHAPTER 25

BLOOMBERG/GETTY IMAGES

Facebook

Managers must evaluate the costs and benefits of alternative actions. **Facebook**, the largest social networking site in the world, was cofounded by Mark Zuckerberg in 2004. Since then, it has grown to nearly 1 billion users and made Zuckerberg a multibillionaire.

Facebook has plans to grow to well over 1 billion users worldwide. Such growth involves decisions about where to expand. For example, expanding the site to new languages and countries involves software programming, marketing, and computer hardware costs. The benefits include adding new users to Facebook.

Analysis of the benefits and costs might lead Facebook to expand in some languages before others. For example, such an analysis might lead Facebook to expand in Swedish before it expands in Tok Pisin (the language of Papua New Guinea).

In this chapter, differential analysis, which reports the effects of decisions on total revenues and costs, is discussed. Practical approaches to setting product prices are also described and illustrated. Finally, how production bottlenecks and activity-based costing influence pricing and other decisions is also discussed.

Learning Objectives

After studying this chapter, you should be able to:

Example Exercises (EE) are shown in **green**.

Obj. 1 **Prepare differential analysis reports for a variety of managerial decisions.**

Differential Analysis

Lease or Sell	EE 25-1
Discontinue a Segment or Product	EE 25-2
Make or Buy	EE 25-3
Replace Equipment	EE 25-4
Process or Sell	EE 25-5
Accept Business at a Special Price	EE 25-6

Obj. 2 **Determine the selling price of a product, using the product cost concept.**

Setting Normal Product Selling Prices

Product Cost Concept	EE 25-7
Target Costing	

Obj. 3 **Compute the relative profitability of products in bottleneck production processes.**

Production Bottlenecks

Bottleneck profit	EE 25-8

Obj. 4 **Allocate product costs using activity-based costing.**

Activity-Based Costing

Estimated Activity Costs	
Activity Rates	EE 25-9
Overhead Allocation	EE 25-9
Dangers of Product Cost Distortion	

At a Glance 25 Page 1246

Obj. 1 Prepare differential analysis reports for a variety of managerial decisions.

Link to Facebook

Facebook's purchase of **WhatsApp** in 2014 was estimated to yield differential income.

Differential Analysis

Managerial decision making involves choosing between alternative courses of action. **Differential analysis**, sometimes called *incremental analysis*, analyzes differential revenues and costs in order to determine the differential impact on income of two alternative courses of action.

Differential revenue is the amount of increase or decrease in revenue that is expected from a course of action compared to an alternative. **Differential cost** is the amount of increase or decrease in cost that is expected from a course of action as compared to an alternative. **Differential income (loss)** is the difference between the differential revenue and differential costs. Differential income indicates that a decision is expected to increase income, while a differential loss indicates that the decision is expected to decrease income.

To illustrate, assume Bryant Restaurants is deciding between using selected floor space for existing tables (Alternative 1) or replacing the tables with a salad bar (Alternative 2). Each alternative will produce revenues, costs, and income as shown below:

	Tables (Alternative 1)	Salad Bar (Alternative 2)
Revenues	$100,000	$120,000
Costs	60,000	65,000
Income (loss)	$ 40,000	$ 55,000

The differential analysis as of July 11 for Bryant Restaurants is shown in Exhibit 1. The differential analysis is prepared in three columns, where positive amounts indicate that the effect is to increase income and negative amounts indicate that the effect is to decrease income. The first column is the revenues, costs, and income for maintaining floor space for tables (Alternative 1). The second column is the revenues, costs, and income for using that floor space for a salad bar (Alternative 2).

Exhibit 1 compares the income from keeping the existing tables (Alternative 1 in column 1) to the income from a salad bar (Alternative 2 in column 2). The difference (column 3), is the differential income from selecting Alternative 2 over Alternative 1.

EXHIBIT 1

Differential Analysis—Bryant Restaurants

Differential Analysis
Tables (Alternative 1) or Salad Bar (Alternative 2)
July 11

	Tables (Alternative 1)	Salad Bar (Alternative 2)	Differential Effect on Income (Alternative 2)
Revenues	$100,000	$120,000	$20,000
Costs	–60,000	–65,000	–5,000
Income (loss)	$ 40,000	$ 55,000	$15,000

In Exhibit 1, the differential revenue of a salad bar over tables is $20,000 ($120,000 – $100,000). Because the increased revenue would increase income, it is entered as a positive $20,000 in the Differential Effect on Income column. The differential cost of a salad bar over tables is $5,000 ($65,000 – $60,000). Because the increased costs will decrease income, it is entered as a negative $5,000 in the Differential Effect on Income column.

The differential income (loss) of a salad bar over tables of $15,000 is determined by subtracting the differential costs from the differential revenues in the Differential Effect on Income column. Thus, installing a salad bar increases income by $15,000.

The preceding differential revenue, costs, and income can also be determined using the following formulas:

Differential Revenue = Revenue (Alt. 2) – Revenue (Alt. 1)
= $120,000 – $100,000 = $20,000

Differential Costs = Costs (Alt. 2) – Costs (Alt. 1)
= –$65,000 – (–$60,000) = –$5,000

Differential Income (Loss) = Income (Alt. 2) – Income (Alt. 1)
= $55,000 – $40,000 = $15,000

Based upon the differential analysis report shown in Exhibit 1, Bryant Restaurants should replace some of its tables with a salad bar. Doing so will increase its income by $15,000. Over time, this decision should be reviewed based upon actual revenues and costs. If the actual revenues and costs differ significantly from those gathered in the analysis, another differential analysis may be needed to verify the decision.

In this chapter, differential analysis is illustrated for the following common decisions:

- Leasing or selling equipment
- Discontinuing an unprofitable segment
- Manufacturing or purchasing a needed part
- Replacing fixed assets
- Selling a product or processing further
- Accepting additional business at a special price

Lease or Sell

Link to Facebook

Facebook used differential analyses in deciding to own data centers in Iowa, North Carolina, Oregon, and Lulea, Sweden, but to lease (rent) data centers in California and Virginia.

Management may lease or sell a piece of equipment that is no longer needed. This may occur when a company changes its manufacturing process and can no longer use the equipment in the manufacturing process. In making a decision, differential analysis can be used.

To illustrate, assume that on June 22 of the current year, Marcus Company is considering leasing or disposing of the following equipment:

Cost of equipment	$200,000
Less accumulated depreciation	120,000
Book value	$ 80,000
Lease (Alternative 1):	
Total revenue for five-year lease	$160,000
Total estimated repair, insurance, and property tax expenses during life of lease	35,000
Residual value at end of fifth year of lease	0
Sell (Alternative 2):	
Sales price	$100,000
Commission on sales	6%

Exhibit 2 shows the differential analysis of whether to lease (Alternative 1) or sell (Alternative 2) the equipment.

EXHIBIT 2

Differential Analysis—Lease or Sell Equipment

Differential Analysis
Lease Equipment (Alternative 1) or Sell Equipment (Alternative 2)
June 22

	Lease Equipment (Alternative 1)	Sell Equipment (Alternative 2)	Differential Effect on Income (Alternative 2)
Revenues	$160,000	$100,000	−$60,000
Costs	−35,000	−6,000*	29,000
Income (loss)	$125,000	$ 94,000	−$31,000

* $100,000 × 6%

If the equipment is sold, differential revenues will decrease by $60,000, differential costs will decrease by $29,000, and the differential effect on income is a decrease of $31,000. Thus, the decision should be to lease the equipment.

Exhibit 2 includes only the differential revenues and differential costs associated with the lease-or-sell decision. The $80,000 book value ($200,000 – $120,000) of the equipment is a *sunk* cost and is not considered in the differential analysis. **Sunk costs** are costs that have been incurred in the past, cannot be recouped, and are not relevant to future decisions. That is, the $80,000 is not affected regardless of which decision is made. For example, if the $80,000 were included in Exhibit 2, the costs for each alternative would both increase by $80,000, but the differential effect on income of −$31,000 would remain unchanged.

To simplify, the following factors were not considered in Exhibit 2:

- Differential revenue from investing funds
- Differential income tax

Differential revenue, such as interest revenue, could arise from investing the cash created by the two alternatives. Differential income tax could also arise from differences in income. These factors are discussed in Chapter 26.

Example Exercise 25-1 Lease or Sell

Obj. 1

Casper Company owns office space with a cost of $100,000 and accumulated depreciation of $30,000 that can be sold for $150,000, less a 6% broker commission. Alternatively, the office space can be leased by Casper Company for 10 years for a total of $170,000, at the end of which there is no residual value. In addition, repair, insurance, and property tax that would be incurred by Casper Company on the rented office space would total $24,000 over the 10 years. Prepare a differential analysis on May 30 as to whether Casper Company should lease (Alternative 1) or sell (Alternative 2) the office space.

Follow My Example 25-1

Differential Analysis
Lease Office Space (Alternative 1) or Sell Office Space (Alternative 2)
May 30

	Lease Office Space (Alternative 1)	Sell Office Space (Alternative 2)	Differential Effect on Income (Alternative 2)
Revenues	$170,000	$150,000	–$20,000
Costs	–24,000	–9,000*	15,000
Income (loss)	$146,000	$141,000	–$ 5,000

*$150,000 × 6%

Casper Company should lease the office space.

Practice Exercises: PE 25-1A, PE 25-1B

Discontinue a Segment or Product

A product, department, branch, territory, or other segment of a business may be generating losses. As a result, management may consider discontinuing (eliminating) the product or segment. In such cases, it may be erroneously assumed that the total company income will increase by eliminating the operating loss.

Discontinuing the product or segment usually eliminates all of the product's or segment's variable costs. Such costs include direct materials, direct labor, variable factory overhead, and sales commissions. However, fixed costs such as depreciation, insurance, and property taxes may not be eliminated. Thus, it is possible for total company income to decrease rather than increase if the unprofitable product or segment is discontinued.

To illustrate, the income statement for Battle Creek Cereal Co. is shown in Exhibit 3. As shown in Exhibit 3, Bran Flakes incurred an operating loss of $11,000. Because Bran Flakes has incurred annual losses for several years, management is considering discontinuing it.

EXHIBIT 3

Income (Loss) by Product

Battle Creek Cereal Co.
Condensed Income Statement
For the Year Ended August 31, 20Y7

	Corn Flakes	Toasted Oats	Bran Flakes	Total Company
Sales	$500,000	$400,000	$100,000	$1,000,000
Cost of goods sold:				
Variable costs	$220,000	$200,000	$ 60,000	$ 480,000
Fixed costs	120,000	80,000	20,000	220,000
Total cost of goods sold	$340,000	$280,000	$ 80,000	$ 700,000
Gross profit	$160,000	$120,000	$ 20,000	$ 300,000
Operating expenses:				
Variable expenses	$ 95,000	$ 60,000	$ 25,000	$ 180,000
Fixed expenses	25,000	20,000	6,000	51,000
Total operating expenses	$120,000	$ 80,000	$ 31,000	$ 231,000
Income (loss) from operations	$ 40,000	$ 40,000	$ (11,000)	$ 69,000

However, the differential analysis dated September 29, 20Y7, in Exhibit 4 indicates that discontinuing Bran Flakes (Alternative 2) actually decreases operating income by $15,000, even though it incurs a net loss of $11,000. This is because discontinuing Bran Flakes has no effect on fixed costs and expenses.

Exhibit 4 only considers the short-term (one-year) effects of discontinuing Bran Flakes. When discontinuing a product or segment, long-term effects should also be considered. For example, employee morale and productivity might suffer if employees are laid off or relocated.

EXHIBIT 4

Differential Analysis—Continue or Discontinue Bran Flakes

Differential Analysis
Continue Bran Flakes (Alternative 1) or Discontinue Bran Flakes (Alternative 2)
September 29, 20Y7

	Continue Bran Flakes (Alternative 1)	Discontinue Bran Flakes (Alternative 2)	Differential Effect on Income (Alternative 2)
Revenues	$100,000	$ 0	–$100,000
Costs:			
Variable	–$ 85,000	$ 0	$ 85,000
Fixed	–26,000	–26,000	0
Total costs	–$111,000	–$26,000	$ 85,000
Income (loss)	–$ 11,000	–$26,000	–$ 15,000

Example Exercise 25-2 Discontinue a Segment **Obj. 1**

Product K has revenue of $65,000, variable cost of goods sold of $50,000, variable selling expenses of $12,000, and fixed costs of $25,000, creating a loss from operations of $22,000. Prepare a differential analysis dated February 22 to determine whether Product K should be continued (Alternative 1) or discontinued (Alternative 2), assuming that fixed costs are unaffected by the decision.

Follow My Example 25-2

Differential Analysis
Continue K (Alternative 1) or Discontinue K (Alternative 2)
February 22

	Continue Product K (Alternative 1)	Discontinue Product K (Alternative 2)	Differential Effect on Income (Alternative 2)
Revenues	$65,000	$ 0	–$65,000
Costs:			
Variable	–$62,000*	$ 0	$62,000
Fixed	–25,000	–25,000	0
Total costs	–$87,000	–$25,000	$62,000
Income (loss)	–$22,000	–$25,000	–$ 3,000

*$50,000 + $12,000

Product K should be continued.

Practice Exercises: PE 25-2A, PE 25-2B

Make or Buy

Companies often manufacture products made up of components that are assembled into a final product. For example, an automobile manufacturer assembles tires, radios, motors, interior seats, transmissions, and other parts into a finished automobile. In such cases, the manufacturer must decide whether to make a part or purchase it from a supplier.

Differential analysis can be used to decide whether to make or buy a part. The analysis is similar whether management is considering making a part that is currently being purchased or purchasing a part that is currently being made.

To illustrate, assume that an automobile manufacturer has been purchasing instrument panels for $240 a unit. The factory is currently operating at 80% of capacity, and no major increase in production is expected in the near future. The cost per unit of manufacturing an instrument panel internally is estimated on February 15 as follows:

Direct materials	$ 80
Direct labor	80
Variable factory overhead	52
Fixed factory overhead	68
Total cost per unit	$280

If the make price of $280 is simply compared with the buy price of $240, the decision is to buy the instrument panel. However, if unused capacity could be used in manufacturing the part, only the variable factory overhead costs would increase.

The differential analysis for this make (Alternative 1) or buy (Alternative 2) decision is shown in Exhibit 5. The first line shows that no revenue is earned in this decision, since the component is not sold, but is used in production. The remaining lines show the cost per unit under each alternative. The fixed factory overhead cannot be eliminated by purchasing the panels. Thus, both alternatives include the fixed factory overhead. The differential analysis indicates that there is a loss of $28 per unit from buying the instrument panels. Thus, the instrument panels should be manufactured.

EXHIBIT 5

Differential Analysis—Make or Buy Instrument Panels

Differential Analysis
Make Panels (Alternative 1) or Buy Panels (Alternative 2)
February 15

	Make Panels (Alternative 1)	Buy Panels (Alternative 2)	Differential Effect on Income (Alternative 2)
Sales price	$ 0	$ 0	$ 0
Unit costs:			
Purchase price	$ 0	−$240	−$240
Direct materials	−80	0	80
Direct labor	−80	0	80
Variable factory overhead	−52	0	52
Fixed factory overhead	−68	−68	0
Income (loss)	−$280	−$308	−$ 28

Link to Facebook

Rather than develop its own virtual reality technology, **Facebook** purchased **Oculus VR, LLC**, a privately held company, in 2014.

Other factors should also be considered in the analysis. For example, productive capacity used to make the instrument panel would not be available for other production. The decision may also affect the future business relationship with the instrument panel supplier. For example, if the supplier provides other parts, the company's decision to make instrument panels might jeopardize the timely delivery of other parts.

Example Exercise 25-3 Make or Buy

Obj. 1

A company manufactures a subcomponent of an assembly for $80 per unit, including fixed costs of $25 per unit. A proposal is offered to purchase the subcomponent from an outside source for $60 per unit plus $5 per unit freight. Prepare a differential analysis dated November 2 to determine whether the company should make (Alternative 1) or buy (Alternative 2) the subcomponent, assuming that fixed costs are unaffected by the decision.

Follow My Example 25-3

Differential Analysis
Make Subcomponent (Alternative 1) or Buy Subcomponent (Alternative 2)
November 2

	Make Subcomponent (Alternative 1)	Buy Subcomponent (Alternative 2)	Differential Effect on Income (Alternative 2)
Sales price	$ 0	$ 0	$ 0
Unit costs:			
Purchase price	$ 0	−$60	−$60
Freight	0	−5	−5
Variable costs ($80 − $25)	−55	0	55
Fixed factory overhead	−25	−25	0
Income (loss)	−$80	−$90	−$10

The company should make the subcomponent.

Practice Exercises: PE 25-3A, PE 25-3B

Replace Equipment

The usefulness of a fixed asset may decrease before it is worn out. For example, old equipment may no longer be as efficient as new equipment.

Differential analysis can be used for decisions to replace fixed assets such as equipment and machinery. The analysis normally focuses on the costs of continuing to use the old equipment versus replacing the equipment. The book value of the old equipment is a sunk cost and, thus, is irrelevant.

To illustrate, assume that on November 28 of the current year, a business is considering replacing an old machine with a new machine:

Old Machine	
Book value	$100,000
Estimated annual variable manufacturing costs	225,000
Estimated selling price	25,000
Estimated remaining useful life	5 years
New Machine	
Purchase price of new machine	$250,000
Estimated annual variable manufacturing costs	150,000
Estimated residual value	0
Estimated useful life	5 years

The differential analysis for whether to continue with the old machine (Alternative 1) or replace the old machine with a new machine (Alternative 2) is shown in Exhibit 6.

EXHIBIT 6

Differential Analysis—Continue with or Replace Old Equipment

Differential Analysis
Continue with Old Machine (Alternative 1) or Replace Old Machine (Alternative 2)
November 28

	Continue with Old Machine (Alternative 1)	Replace Old Machine (Alternative 2)	Differential Effect on Income (Alternative 2)
Revenues:			
Proceeds from sale of old machine	$ 0	$ 25,000	$ 25,000
Costs:			
Purchase price	$ 0	–$ 250,000	–$250,000
Variable manufacturing costs (5 years)	–1,125,000*	–750,000**	375,000
Total costs	–$1,125,000	–$1,000,000	$125,000
Income (loss)	–$1,125,000	–$ 975,000	$150,000

*$225,000 × 5 years
**$150,000 × 5 years

As shown in Exhibit 6, there is five-year differential effect on income of $150,000 (or $30,000 per year) from replacing the machine. Thus, the decision should be to purchase the new machine and sell the old machine.

Other factors are often important in equipment replacement decisions. For example, differences between the remaining useful life of the old equipment and the estimated life of the new equipment could exist. In addition, the new equipment might improve the overall quality of the product and, thus, increase sales.

The time value of money and other uses for the cash needed to purchase the new equipment could also affect the decision to replace equipment.[1] The revenue that is forgone from an alternative use of an asset, such as cash, is called an **opportunity cost**. Although the opportunity cost is not recorded in the accounting records, it is useful in analyzing alternative courses of action.

Link to Facebook

Facebook used cash to purchase $1,812 million of property and equipment in 2014.

1 The time value of money in purchasing equipment (capital assets) is discussed in Chapter 26.

Example Exercise 25-4 Replace Equipment

Obj. 1

A machine with a book value of $32,000 has an estimated four-year life. A proposal is offered to sell the old machine for $10,000 and replace it with a new machine at a cost of $45,000. The new machine has a four-year life with no residual value. The new machine would reduce annual direct labor costs from $33,000 to $22,000. Prepare a differential analysis dated October 7 on whether to continue with the old machine (Alternative 1) or replace the old machine (Alternative 2).

Follow My Example 25-4

Differential Analysis
Continue with Old Machine (Alternative 1) or Replace Old Machine (Alternative 2)
October 7

	Continue with Old Machine (Alternative 1)	Replace Old Machine (Alternative 2)	Differential Effect on Income (Alternative 2)
Revenues:			
Proceeds from sale of old machine	$ 0	$ 10,000	$10,000
Costs:			
Purchase price	$ 0	–$ 45,000	–$45,000
Direct labor (4 years)	–132,000*	–88,000**	44,000
Total costs	–$132,000	–$133,000	–$ 1,000
Total income (loss)	–$132,000	–$123,000	$ 9,000

*$33,000 × 4 years
**$22,000 × 4 years

The old machine should be sold and replaced with the new machine.

Practice Exercises: PE 25-4A, PE 25-4B

Process or Sell

During manufacturing, a product normally progresses through various stages or processes. In some cases, a product can be sold at an intermediate stage of production, or it can be processed further and then sold.

Differential analysis can be used to decide whether to sell a product at an intermediate stage or to process it further. In doing so, the differential revenues and costs from further processing are compared. The costs of producing the intermediate product do not change, regardless of whether the intermediate product is sold or processed further.

To illustrate, assume that a business produces kerosene as an intermediate product as follows:

Kerosene:	
Batch size	4,000 gallons
Cost of producing kerosene	$2,400 per batch
Selling price	$2.50 per gallon

The kerosene can be processed further to yield gasoline. When processing kerosene into gasoline, the process will incur additional costs and some evaporation, shown as follows:

Gasoline:	
Input batch size	4,000 gallons
Less evaporation (20%)	800 (4,000 × 20%)
Output batch size	3,200 gallons
Cost of producing gasoline	$3,050 per batch
Selling price	$3.50 per gallon

Exhibit 7 shows the differential analysis dated October 1 for whether to sell kerosene (Alternative 1) or process it further into gasoline (Alternative 2).

As shown in Exhibit 7, there is additional income of $550 per batch from further processing the kerosene into gasoline. Therefore, the decision should be to process the kerosene further into gasoline.

EXHIBIT 7

Differential Analysis—Sell Kerosene or Process Further into Gasoline

Differential Analysis
Sell Kerosene (Alternative 1) or Process Further into Gasoline (Alternative 2)
October 1

	Sell Kerosene (Alternative 1)	Process Further into Gasoline (Alternative 2)	Differential Effect on Income (Alternative 2)
Revenues	$10,000*	$11,200**	$1,200
Costs	−2,400	−3,050	−650
Income (loss)	$ 7,600	$ 8,150	$ 550

*4,000 gallons × $2.50
**(4,000 gallons − 800 gallons) × $3.50

Example Exercise 25-5 Process or Sell

Obj. 1

Product T is produced for $2.50 per gallon. Product T can be sold without additional processing for $3.50 per gallon or processed further into Product V at an additional total cost of $0.70 per gallon. Product V can be sold for $4.00 per gallon. Prepare a differential analysis dated April 8 on whether to sell Product T (Alternative 1) or process it further into Product V (Alternative 2).

Follow My Example 25-5

Differential Analysis
Sell Product T (Alternative 1) or Process Further into Product V (Alternative 2)
April 8

	Sell Product T (Alternative 1)	Process Further into Product V (Alternative 2)	Differential Effect on Income (Alternative 2)
Revenues, per unit	$3.50	$4.00	$0.50
Costs, per unit	−2.50	−3.20*	−0.70
Income (loss), per unit	$1.00	$0.80	−$0.20

*$2.50 + $0.70

This analysis is conducted on a per-unit basis, as opposed to a per-batch basis as illustrated in the text. Without evaporation, the per-unit approach is acceptable; thus the decision should be to sell Product T.

Practice Exercises: PE 25-5A, PE 25-5B

Accept Business at a Special Price

A company may be offered the opportunity to sell its products at prices other than normal prices. For example, an exporter may offer to sell a company's products overseas at special discount prices.

Differential analysis can be used to decide whether to accept additional business at a special price. The differential revenue from accepting the additional business is compared to the differential costs of producing and delivering the product to the customer.

The differential costs of accepting additional business depend on whether the company is operating at less than capacity. If the company is operating at less than full capacity, then the additional production does not increase fixed manufacturing costs. However, selling and administrative expenses may change because of the additional business.

To illustrate, assume that B-Ball Inc. manufactures basketballs as follows:

Monthly productive capacity	12,500 basketballs
Current monthly sales	10,000 basketballs
Normal (domestic) selling price	$30.00 per basketball
Manufacturing costs:	
Variable costs	$12.50 per basketball
Fixed costs	7.50
Total	$20.00 per basketball

On March 10 of the current year, B-Ball Inc. received an offer from an exporter for 5,000 basketballs at $18 each. Production can be spread over three months without interfering with normal production or incurring overtime costs. Pricing policies in the domestic market will not be affected.

As shown in Exhibit 8, a differential analysis on whether to reject the order (Alternative 1) or accept the order (Alternative 2) shows that the special order should be accepted. The special business is accepted even though the sales price of $18 per unit is less than the manufacturing cost of $20 per unit because the fixed costs are not affected by the decision and are, thus, omitted from the analysis.

EXHIBIT 8

Differential Analysis—Accept Business at a Special Price

Differential Analysis
Reject Order (Alternative 1) or Accept Order (Alternative 2)
March 10

	Reject Order (Alternative 1)	Accept Order (Alternative 2)	Differential Effect on Income (Alternative 2)
Revenues	$0	$90,000*	$90,000
Costs:			
Variable manufacturing costs	0	−62,500**	−62,500
Income (loss)	$0	$27,500	$27,500

*5,000 units × $18
**5,000 units × $12.50 variable cost per unit

Proposals to sell products at special prices often require additional considerations. For example, special prices in one geographic area may result in price reductions in other areas, with the result that total company sales revenues decrease. Manufacturers must also conform to the Robinson-Patman Act, which prohibits price discrimination within the United States unless price differences can be justified by different costs.

Business Connection

60% OFF!

Priceline.com Inc. was founded in the late 1990s and has become a successful online retailer. Priceline offers deep discounts of up to 60% for travel services, such as hotels and travel. How does it work? For hotel services, Priceline has arrangements with hotels to provide deeply discounted rooms. These rooms are resold to customers on Priceline's website. Why do hotels provide rooms at such a large discount? If the hotel has unused rooms, the variable cost of an incremental guest is low relative to the fixed cost of the room. Thus, during low occupancy times, any price greater than the variable cost of providing the room can add to the profitability of the hotel. Thus, hotels view Priceline as an additional source of profit from filling unused rooms during low demand periods.

Example Exercise 25-6 Accept Business at Special Price *Obj. 1*

Product D is normally sold for $4.40 per unit. A special price of $3.60 is offered for the export market. The variable production cost is $3.00 per unit. An additional export tariff of 10% of revenue must be paid for all export products. Assume that there is sufficient capacity for the special order. Prepare a differential analysis dated January 14 on whether to reject (Alternative 1) or accept (Alternative 2) the special order.

Follow My Example 25-6

Differential Analysis
Reject Order (Alternative 1) or Accept Order (Alternative 2)
January 14

	Reject Order (Alternative 1)	Accept Order (Alternative 2)	Differential Effect on Income (Alternative 2)
Per unit:			
Revenues	$0	$3.60	$3.60
Costs:			
Variable manufacturing costs	$0	–$3.00	–$3.00
Export tariff	0	–0.36*	–0.36
Total costs	$0	–$3.36	–$3.36
Income (loss)	$0	$0.24	$0.24

*$3.60 × 10%

The special order should be accepted.

Practice Exercises: PE 25-6A, PE 25-6B

Setting Normal Product Selling Prices

Obj. 2 Determine the selling price of a product, using the product cost concept.

The *normal* selling price is the target selling price to be achieved in the long term. The normal selling price must be set high enough to cover all costs and expenses (fixed and variable) and provide a reasonable profit. Otherwise, the business will not survive.

In contrast, in deciding whether to accept additional business at a special price, only differential costs are considered. Any price greater than the differential costs will increase profits in the short term. However, in the long term, products are sold at normal prices rather than special prices.

Managers can use one of two market methods to determine selling price:

- Demand-based concept
- Competition-based concept

The demand-based concept sets the price according to the demand for the product. If there is high demand for the product, then the price is set high. Likewise, if there is a low demand for the product, then the price is set low.

The competition-based concept sets the price according to the price offered by competitors. For example, if a competitor reduces the price, then management adjusts the price to meet the competition. The market-based pricing approaches are discussed in greater detail in marketing courses.

Managers can also use one of three cost-plus methods to determine the selling price:

- Product cost concept
- Total cost concept
- Variable cost concept

The product cost concept is illustrated in this section. The total cost and variable cost concepts are illustrated in the appendix to this chapter.

Link to Facebook

Facebook's prices are affected by its competitors, such as **Google**.

SERVICE FOCUS

REVENUE MANAGEMENT

Did you know that it is common to sit next to a person on a flight who paid much more for that seat than you did for yours (or vice versa)? While this may not seem fair, this practice is consistent with a type of differential analysis called revenue management. Revenue management strives to yield the maximum amount of profit from a perishable good. Examples of perishable goods in service include a seat on a flight, a hotel room for a given night, a ticket for a given event, or a cruise ship berth for a given voyage. The service is perishable because once the date passes, the "product" expires.

Consider Delta Air Lines. Delta maximizes the profitability on a given flight by taking into account different customer behaviors and preferences. For example, a businessperson may pay a very high price for an airline ticket booked one day in advance to attend an emergency meeting. Next to her may be a college student on the same flight who booked two months in advance at a very low price. The difference in behavior yields a different price. The airline sells early bookings at very favorable prices to fill out the flight. However, late emergency business bookings are priced high because the inventory of seats has diminished and, thus, seats have become valuable. However, if too many seats remain unoccupied very close to the flight time, the airline may release them at deep discounts to standby passengers to fill the flight. Thus, the flight is filled with different priced seats for different customers, all in attempt to fill the flight as profitably as possible.

Product Cost Concept

Cost-plus methods determine the normal selling price by estimating a cost amount per unit and adding a markup, computed as follows:

Normal Selling Price = Cost Amount per Unit + Markup

Management determines the markup based on the desired profit for the product. The markup should be sufficient to earn the desired profit and cover any costs and expenses that are not included in the cost amount.

As shown in Exhibit 9, under the **product cost concept**, only the costs of manufacturing the product, termed the *product costs,* are included in the cost amount per unit to which the markup is added. Estimated selling expenses, administrative expenses, and desired profit are included in the markup. The markup per unit is then computed and added to the product cost per unit to determine the normal selling price.

EXHIBIT 9

Product Cost Concept

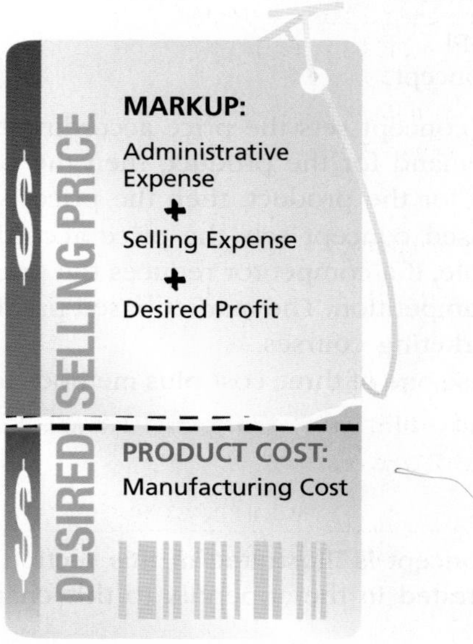

The product cost concept is applied using the following steps:

Step 1. Estimate the total product costs as follows:

Product costs:	
Direct materials	$XXX
Direct labor	XXX
Factory overhead	XXX
Total product cost	$XXX

Step 2. Estimate the total selling and administrative expenses.

Step 3. Divide the total product cost by the number of units expected to be produced and sold to determine the total product cost per unit, computed as follows:

$$\text{Product Cost per Unit} = \frac{\text{Total Product Cost}}{\text{Estimated Units Produced and Sold}}$$

Step 4. Compute the markup percentage as follows:

$$\text{Markup Percentage} = \frac{\text{Desired Profit} + \text{Total Selling and Administrative Expenses}}{\text{Total Product Cost}}$$

The numerator of the markup percentage is the desired profit plus the total selling and administrative expenses. These expenses must be included in the markup percentage because they are not included in the cost amount to which the markup is added.

The desired profit is normally computed based on a rate of return on assets as follows:

$$\text{Desired Profit} = \text{Desired Rate of Return} \times \text{Total Assets}$$

Step 5. Determine the markup per unit by multiplying the markup percentage times the product cost per unit as follows:

$$\text{Markup per Unit} = \text{Markup Percentage} \times \text{Product Cost per Unit}$$

Step 6. Determine the normal selling price by adding the markup per unit to the product cost per unit as follows:

Product cost per unit	$XXX
Markup per unit	XXX
Normal selling price per unit	$XXX

To illustrate, assume the following data for 100,000 calculators that Digital Solutions Inc. expects to produce and sell during the current year:

Manufacturing costs:	
Direct materials ($3.00 × 100,000)	$ 300,000
Direct labor ($10.00 × 100,000)	1,000,000
Factory overhead	200,000
Total manufacturing costs	$1,500,000
Selling and administrative expenses	170,000
Total cost	$1,670,000
Total assets	$ 800,000
Desired rate of return	20%

The normal selling price of $18.30 is determined under the product cost concept as follows:

Step 1. Total product cost: $1,500,000

Step 2. Total selling and administrative expenses: $170,000

Step 3. Total product cost per unit: $15.00

$$\text{Total Cost per Unit} = \frac{\text{Total Product Cost}}{\text{Estimated Units Produced and Sold}} = \frac{\$1{,}500{,}000}{100{,}000 \text{ units}} = \$15.00 \text{ per unit}$$

Step 4. Markup percentage: 22%

Desired Profit = Desired Rate of Return × Total Assets = 20% × $800,000 = $160,000

$$\text{Markup Percentage} = \frac{\text{Desired Profit} + \text{Total Selling and Administrative Expenses}}{\text{Total Product Cost}}$$

$$= \frac{\$160,000 + \$170,000}{\$1,500,000} = \frac{\$330,000}{\$1,500,000} = 22\%$$

Step 5. Markup per unit: $3.30

Markup per Unit = Markup Percentage × Product Cost per Unit
= 22% × $15.00 = $3.30 per unit

Step 6. Normal selling price: $18.30

Total product cost per unit	$15.00
Markup per unit	3.30
Normal selling price per unit	$18.30

Product cost estimates, rather than actual costs, may be used in computing the markup. Management should be careful, however, when using estimated or standard costs in applying the cost-plus approach. Specifically, estimates should be based on normal (attainable) operating levels and not theoretical (ideal) levels of performance. In product pricing, the use of estimates based on ideal operating performance could lead to setting product prices too low.

Example Exercise 25-7 Product Cost Markup Percentage **Obj. 2**

Apex Corporation produces and sells Product Z at a total cost of $30 per unit, of which $20 is product cost and $10 is selling and administrative expenses. In addition, the total cost of $30 is made up of $18 variable cost and $12 fixed cost. The desired profit is $3 per unit. Determine the markup percentage on product cost.

Follow My Example 25-7

Markup percentage on product cost: $\frac{\$3 + \$10}{\$20} = 65\%$

Practice Exercises: PE 25-7A, PE 25-7B

INTEGRITY, OBJECTIVITY, AND ETHICS IN BUSINESS

PRICE FIXING

Federal law prevents companies competing in similar markets from sharing cost and price information, or what is commonly termed "price fixing." For example, the Federal Trade Commission (FTC) brought a suit against U-Haul for releasing company-wide memorandums to its managers telling them to encourage competitors to match U-Haul price increases. Commenting on the case, the chairman of the FTC stated, "It's a bedrock principle that you can't conspire with your competitors to fix prices, and shouldn't even try."

Source: Edward Wyatt, "U-Haul to Settle with Trade Agency in Case on Truck Rental Price-Fixing," *New York Times*, June 10, 2010, p. B3.

Target Costing

Target costing is a method of setting prices that combines market-based pricing with a cost-reduction emphasis. Under target costing, a future selling price is anticipated, using the demand or competition-based concepts. The target cost is then determined by subtracting a desired profit from the expected selling price, computed as follows:

Target Cost = Expected Selling Price – Desired Profit

Target costing tries to reduce costs as shown in Exhibit 10. The bar at the left in Exhibit 10 shows the actual cost and profit that can be earned during the current period. The bar at the right shows that the market price is expected to decline in the future. The target cost is estimated as the difference between the expected market price and the desired profit.

The target cost is normally less than the current cost. Thus, managers must try to reduce costs from the design and manufacture of the product. The planned cost reduction is sometimes referred to as the cost drift. Costs can be reduced in a variety of ways such as the following:

- Simplifying the design
- Reducing the cost of direct materials
- Reducing the direct labor costs
- Eliminating waste

Target costing is especially useful in highly competitive markets such as the market for personal computers. Such markets require continual product cost reductions to remain competitive.

EXHIBIT 10

Target Cost Concept

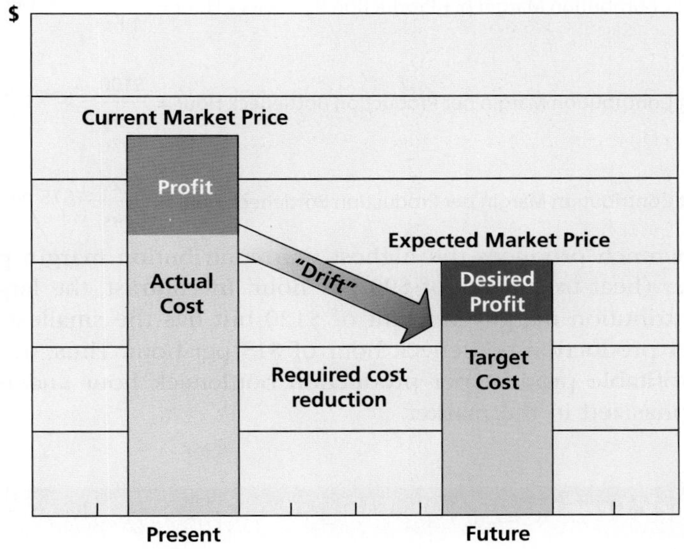

Production Bottlenecks

Obj. 3 Compute the relative profitability of products in bottleneck production processes.

A **production bottleneck** (or *constraint*) is a point in the manufacturing process where the demand for the company's product exceeds the ability to produce the product. The **theory of constraints (TOC)** is a manufacturing strategy that focuses on reducing the influence of bottlenecks on production processes.

When a company has a production bottleneck in its production process, it should attempt to maximize its profits, subject to the production bottleneck. In doing so, the unit contribution margin of each product per production bottleneck constraint is used.

To illustrate, assume that PrideCraft Tool Company makes three types of wrenches: small, medium, and large. All three products are processed through a heat treatment operation, which hardens the steel tools. PrideCraft Tool's heat treatment process is operating at full capacity and is a production bottleneck. The product unit contribution margin and the number of hours of heat treatment used by each type of wrench are as follows:

	Small Wrench	Medium Wrench	Large Wrench
Unit selling price	$130	$140	$160
Unit variable cost	40	40	40
Unit contribution margin	$ 90	$100	$120
Heat treatment hours per unit	1 hr.	4 hrs.	8 hrs.

The large wrench appears to be the most profitable product because its unit contribution margin of $120 is the greatest. However, the unit contribution margin can be misleading in a production bottleneck operation.

In a production bottleneck operation, the best measure of profitability is the unit contribution margin per production bottleneck constraint. For PrideCraft Tool, the production bottleneck constraint is heat treatment process hours. Therefore, the unit contribution margin per bottleneck constraint is expressed as follows:

$$\text{Unit Contribution Margin per Production Bottleneck Hour} = \frac{\text{Unit Contribution Margin}}{\text{Heat Treatment Hours per Unit}}$$

The unit contribution per production bottleneck hour for each of the wrenches produced by PrideCraft Tool is computed as follows:

Small Wrenches

$$\text{Unit Contribution Margin per Production Bottleneck Hour} = \frac{\$90}{1\text{ hr.}} = \$90\text{ per hr.}$$

Medium Wrenches

$$\text{Unit Contribution Margin per Production Bottleneck Hour} = \frac{\$100}{4\text{ hrs.}} = \$25\text{ per hr.}$$

Large Wrenches

$$\text{Unit Contribution Margin per Production Bottleneck Hour} = \frac{\$120}{8\text{ hrs.}} = \$15\text{ per hr.}$$

The small wrench produces the highest unit contribution margin per production bottleneck hour (heat treatment) of $90 per hour. In contrast, the large wrench has the largest contribution margin per unit of $120 but has the smallest unit contribution margin per production bottleneck hour of $15 per hour. Thus, the small wrench is the most profitable product per production bottleneck hour and is the one that should be emphasized in the market.

Example Exercise 25-8 Bottleneck Profit **Obj. 3**

Product A has a unit contribution margin of $15. Product B has a unit contribution margin of $20. Product A requires three furnace hours, while Product B requires five furnace hours. Determine the most profitable product, assuming that the furnace is a production bottleneck.

Follow My Example 25-8

	Product A	Product B
Unit contribution margin	$15	$20
Furnace hours per unit	÷ 3	÷ 5
Unit contribution margin per production bottleneck hour	$ 5	$ 4

Product A is the most profitable in using bottleneck resources.

Practice Exercises: PE 25-8A, PE 25-8B

Activity-Based Costing

Obj. 4 Allocate product costs using activity-based costing.

Normal product prices can be computed from a markup on product cost, as illustrated earlier in this chapter. Product cost is the sum of direct material, direct labor, and factory overhead. In Chapter 19, factory overhead was allocated to products (jobs) using a predetermined factory overhead rate. This rate was computed as follows:

$$\text{Predetermined Factory Overhead Rate} = \frac{\text{Estimated Total Factory Overhead Costs}}{\text{Estimated Activity Base}}$$

The use of a single, predetermined factory overhead rate may, however, allocate factory overhead inaccurately. In such cases, normal product prices based on product cost markup may also be inaccurate. This may occur in manufacturing operations involving more than one product. In such cases, each product may use different types of factory overhead in different ways. Under such conditions, a single factory overhead rate will distort factory overhead allocation.

Activity-based costing (ABC) identifies and traces costs and expenses to activities and then to specific products. The ABC method is an alternative approach for allocating factory overhead when there are diverse products and processes. ABC uses multiple factory overhead rates based on activities. **Activities** are the types of work, or actions, involved in a manufacturing process or service activity. For example, assembly, inspection, and engineering design are activities.

Link to Facebook

One of **Facebook's** significant activities is research and development, with a cost of $4.8 billion in a recent year.

Estimated Activity Costs

ABC initially assigns estimated factory overhead costs to activities, resulting in estimated activity costs. To illustrate, assume that Ruiz Company produces snowmobiles and riding mowers. The overhead activities used in producing each product are as follows:

- *Fabrication*, which consists of cutting metal to shape the product. This activity is machine-intensive.
- *Assembly*, which consists of manually assembling machined pieces into a final product. This activity is labor-intensive.
- *Setup*, which consists of changing the characteristics of a machine to produce a different product. Each production run requires a **setup**.
- *Quality-control inspections*, which consist of inspecting the product for conformance to specifications. Inspection requires product teardown and reassembly.
- *Engineering changes*, which consist of processing changes in design or process specifications for a product. The document that initiates changing a product or process is called an **engineering change order (ECO)**.

Ruiz Company's total estimated factory overhead of $1,600,000 is assigned to each activity as shown in Exhibit 11.

EXHIBIT 11

Estimated Activity Costs

Activity	Estimated Activity Cost
Fabrication	$ 530,000
Assembly	70,000
Setup	480,000
Quality-control inspection	312,000
Engineering changes	208,000
Total estimated activity costs	$1,600,000

Activity Rates

The estimated activity costs are allocated to products using an **activity rate**. Activity rates are determined as follows:

$$\text{Activity Rate} = \frac{\text{Estimated Activity Cost}}{\text{Estimated Activity-Base Usage}}$$

The **activity base** is a measure of physical activity for each activity. For example, the activity base for the setup activity is the number of setups. The activity-base *usage* is the number of setups estimated to be used by the operations.

As shown in Exhibit 11, the estimated activity cost for setups is $480,000. Assume that the activity-base usage for the setup activity is estimated to be 120 setups. The setup activity rate is $4,000 per setup, computed as follows:

$$\text{Setup Activity Rate} = \frac{\$480{,}000}{120 \text{ setups}} = \$4{,}000 \text{ per setup}$$

The estimated activity-base usage for each activity is shown in Exhibit 12.

EXHIBIT 12

Ruiz Company Activity-Base Usage

Activity Base	Estimated Activity-Base Usage by Product: Snowmobile	Estimated Activity-Base Usage by Product: Riding Mower	Total Estimated Activity-Base Usage
Number of fabrication direct labor hours	8,000 dlh	2,000 dlh	10,000 dlh
Number of assembly direct labor hours	2,000 dlh	8,000 dlh	10,000 dlh
Number of setups	100 setups	20 setups	120 setups
Number of quality-control inspections	100 insp.	4 insp.	104 insp.
Number of engineering change orders	12 ECOs	4 ECOs	16 ECOs

The activity rates for each activity are determined by dividing the estimated activity cost in Exhibit 11 by the total estimated activity-base usage for each activity in Exhibit 12. The activity rates for Ruiz Company are computed in Exhibit 13.

EXHIBIT 13

Activity Rates—Ruiz Company

Activity	Estimated Activity Cost	÷	Estimated Activity-Base Usage	=	Activity Rate
Fabrication	$530,000	÷	10,000 direct labor hours	=	$53 per direct labor hour
Assembly	$ 70,000	÷	10,000 direct labor hours	=	$7 per direct labor hour
Setup	$480,000	÷	120 setups	=	$4,000 per setup
Quality-control inspection	$312,000	÷	104 inspections	=	$3,000 per inspection
Engineering changes	$208,000	÷	16 engineering changes	=	$13,000 per engineering change order

Overhead Allocation

The estimated activity costs are allocated to the snowmobiles and riding mowers by using the following equation for each product:

$$\text{Activity-Base Usage} \times \text{Activity Rate} = \text{Activity Cost}$$

The sum of these activity costs for each product is the total factory overhead cost for the product. This amount is divided by the total number of units produced to determine the factory overhead cost per unit. These computations are shown in Exhibit 14 for Ruiz Company.

Activity-Based Product Cost Calculations **EXHIBIT 14**

	A	B	C	D	E	F	G	H	I	J	K	L
1		Snowmobile						Riding Mower				
2		Activity-		Activity		Activity		Activity-		Activity		Activity
3	Activity	Base Usage	×	Rate	=	Cost		Base Usage	×	Rate	=	Cost
4												
5	Fabrication	8,000 dlh		$53/dlh		$ 424,000		2,000 dlh		$53/dlh		$106,000
6	Assembly	2,000 dlh		$7/dlh		14,000		8,000 dlh		$7/dlh		56,000
7	Setup	100 setups		$4,000/setup		400,000		20 setups		$4,000/setup		80,000
8	Quality-control											
9	inspections	100 insp.		$3,000/insp.		300,000		4 insp.		$3,000/insp.		12,000
10	Engineering											
11	changes	12 ECOs		$13,000/ECO		156,000		4 ECOs		$13,000/ECO		52,000
12	Total factory											
13	overhead cost					$1,294,000						$306,000
14	Budgeted units											
15	of production					÷ 1,000						÷ 1,000
16	Factory overhead											
17	cost per unit					$ 1,294						$ 306
18												

The allocation of factory overhead using the ABC method for Ruiz Company is illustrated in Exhibit 15.

Activity-Based Costing Method—Ruiz Company **EXHIBIT 15**

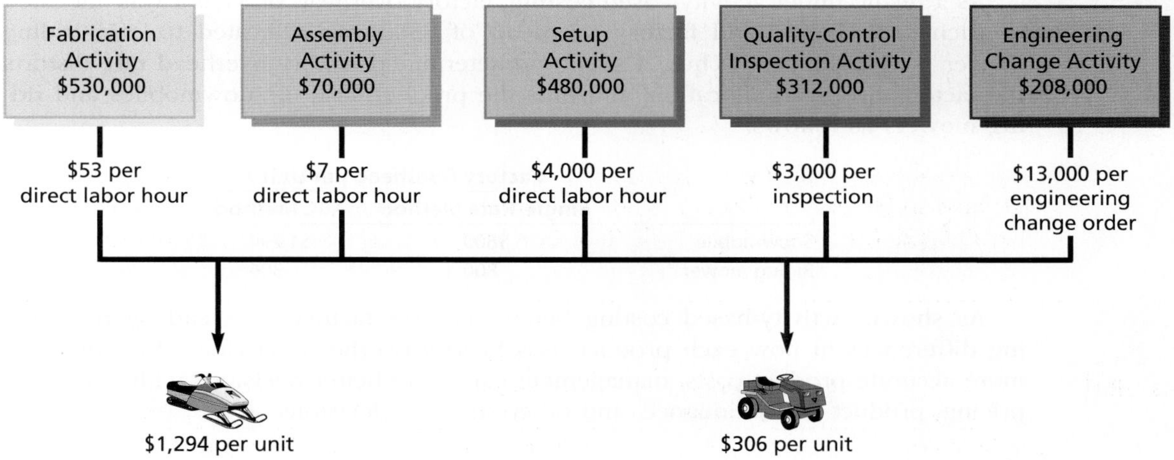

Business Connection

THE ABC'S OF SCHWAB

The Charles Schwab Corporation provides financial and brokerage services to individuals and businesses. The company operates two segments: Investor Services and Advisor Services. The Investor Services segment provides retail brokerage services, while the Advisor Services business provides services to independent investment advisors. Independent investment advisors use Schwab software, support, and products to serve their clients. Schwab uses activity-based costing to allocate salaries and depreciation expenses to these two segments, using activities such as client service, new accounts, and business development.

Source: The Charles Schwab Corporation 2015 10-K Annual Report, Note 24.

Dangers of Product Cost Distortion

The allocation of factory overhead affects the accuracy of product costs. In turn, product costs are used for decisions such as establishing product price and determining whether to discontinue a product line.

Using an inappropriate factory overhead allocation method can lead to distorted product costs. To illustrate, assume that Ruiz Company used a single predetermined factory overhead rate to allocate factory overhead to the riding mower and snowmobile. Assume that total estimated factory overhead was allocated using direct labor hours. The single predetermined factory overhead rate for Ruiz is computed as follows:

$$\text{Predetermined Factory Overhead Rate} = \frac{\text{Estimated Total Factory Overhead Costs}}{\text{Estimated Activity Base}}$$

$$= \frac{\$1{,}600{,}000}{20{,}000 \text{ direct labor hours}}$$

$$= \$80 \text{ per direct labor hour}$$

Using this rate, riding mowers and snowmobiles are each allocated $800,000 of factory overhead ($80 per direct labor hour × 10,000 direct labor hours), or $800 per unit ($800,000 ÷ 1,000 units). Under the single predetermined factory overhead rate method, each product is allocated the same factory overhead. This is because riding mowers and snowmobiles consume the same amount of direct labor hours.

However, the snowmobiles and riding mowers do not consume setup, quality-control inspection, and engineering change activities in proportion to direct labor hours. For example, each snowmobile consumes more of these activities than does the riding mower even though each product is budgeted for 10,000 direct labor hours.

As a result, under activity-based costing, factory overhead of $1,294 was allocated to each snowmobile and factory overhead of $306 was allocated to each riding mower (see Exhibit 14). Thus, a single predetermined factory overhead rate distorts the factory overhead allocation, and thus the product cost, of snowmobiles and riding mowers as follows:

	Factory Overhead per Unit	
	Single-Rate Method	**ABC Method**
Snowmobile	$800	$1,294
Riding mower	800	306

As shown, activity-based costing better allocates factory overhead by recognizing differences in how each product uses factory overhead activities. As a result of more accurate product costs, management can make better decisions with respect to pricing, product discontinuance, and other strategic decisions.

Example Exercise 25-9 Activity-Based Costing — Obj. 4

Thor Company has total estimated factory overhead for the year of $600,000, divided into four activities: fabrication, $300,000; assembly, $120,000; setup, $100,000; and materials handling, $80,000. Thor manufactures two products: snowboards and skis. The activity-base usage quantities for each product by each activity are as follows:

	Fabrication	**Assembly**	**Setup**	**Materials Handling**
Snowboards	5,000 dlh	15,000 dlh	30 setups	50 moves
Skis	15,000	5,000	220	350
	20,000 dlh	20,000 dlh	250 setups	400 moves

Each product is budgeted for 5,000 units of production for the year. Determine (a) the activity rates for each activity and (b) the factory overhead cost per unit for each product, using activity-based costing.

Follow My Example 25-9

a. Fabrication: $300,000 ÷ 20,000 direct labor hours = $15 per dlh
Assembly: $120,000 ÷ 20,000 direct labor hours = $6 per dlh
Setup: $100,000 ÷ 250 setups = $400 per setup
Materials handling: $80,000 ÷ 400 moves = $200 per move

b.

	A	B	C	D	E	F	G	H	I	J	K	L
1				Snowboards						Skis		
2		Activity-Base		Activity		Activity		Activity-Base		Activity		Activity
3	Activity	Usage	×	Rate	=	Cost		Usage	×	Rate	=	Cost
4												
5	Fabrication	5,000 dlh		$15/dlh		$ 75,000		15,000 dlh		$15/dlh		$225,000
6	Assembly	15,000 dlh		$6/dlh		90,000		5,000 dlh		$6/dlh		30,000
7	Setup	30 setups		$400/setup		12,000		220 setups		$400/setup		88,000
8	Materials handling	50 moves		$200/move		10,000		350 moves		$200/move		70,000
9	Total					$187,000						$413,000
10	Budgeted units					÷ 5,000						÷ 5,000
11	Factory overhead											
12	per unit					$ 37.40						$ 82.60
13												

Practice Exercises: PE 25-9A, PE 25-9B

APPENDIX

Total and Variable Cost Concepts to Setting Normal Price

Recall from the chapter that cost-plus methods determine the normal selling price by estimating a cost amount per unit and adding a markup, as follows:

Normal Selling Price = Cost Amount per Unit + Markup

Management determines the markup based on the desired profit for the product. The markup should be sufficient to earn the desired profit and cover any cost and expenses that are not included in the cost amount. The product cost concept was discussed in the chapter, and the total and variable cost concepts are discussed in this appendix.

Total Cost Concept

As shown in Exhibit 16, under the **total cost concept**, manufacturing cost plus the selling and administrative expenses are included in the total cost per unit. The markup per unit is then computed and added to the total cost per unit to determine the normal selling price.

The total cost concept is applied using the following steps:

Step 1. Estimate the total manufacturing cost as follows:

Manufacturing costs:	
Direct materials	$XXX
Direct labor	XXX
Factory overhead	XXX
Total manufacturing cost	$XXX

EXHIBIT 16

Total Cost Concept

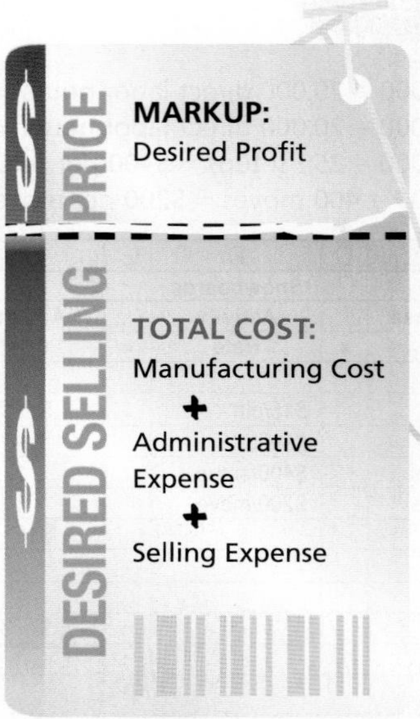

Step 2. Estimate the total selling and administrative expenses.

Step 3. Estimate the total cost as follows:

Total manufacturing costs	$XXX
Selling and administrative expenses	XXX
Total cost	$XXX

Step 4. Divide the total cost by the number of units expected to be produced and sold to determine the total cost per unit, as follows:

$$\text{Total Cost per Unit} = \frac{\text{Total Cost}}{\text{Estimated Units Produced and Sold}}$$

Step 5. Compute the markup percentage as follows:

$$\text{Markup Percentage} = \frac{\text{Desired Profit}}{\text{Total Cost}}$$

The desired profit is normally computed based on a rate of return on assets as follows:

$$\text{Desired Profit} = \text{Desired Rate of Return} \times \text{Total Assets}$$

Step 6. Determine the markup per unit by multiplying the markup percentage times the total cost per unit as follows:

$$\text{Markup per Unit} = \text{Markup Percentage} \times \text{Total Cost per Unit}$$

Step 7. Determine the normal selling price by adding the markup per unit to the total cost per unit as follows:

Total cost per unit	$XXX
Markup per unit	XXX
Normal selling price per unit	$XXX

To illustrate, assume the following data for 100,000 calculators that Digital Solutions Inc. expects to produce and sell during 20Y4:

Manufacturing costs:		
Direct materials ($3.00 × 100,000)		$ 300,000
Direct labor ($10.00 × 100,000)		1,000,000
Factory overhead:		
Variable costs ($1.50 × 100,000)	$150,000	
Fixed costs	50,000	200,000
Total manufacturing cost		$1,500,000
Selling and administrative expenses:		
Variable expenses ($1.50 × 100,000)	$150,000	
Fixed costs	20,000	
Total selling and administrative expenses		170,000
Total cost		$1,670,000
Desired rate of return		20%
Total assets		$ 800,000

Using the total cost concept, the normal selling price of $18.30 is determined as follows:

Step 1. Total manufacturing cost: $1,500,000
Step 2. Total selling and administrative expenses: $170,000
Step 3. Total cost: $1,670,000
Step 4. Total cost per unit: $16.70

$$\text{Total Cost per Unit} = \frac{\text{Total Cost}}{\text{Estimated Units Produced and Sold}} = \frac{\$1{,}670{,}000}{100{,}000 \text{ units}} = \$16.70 \text{ per unit}$$

Step 5. Markup percentage: 9.6% (rounded)

$$\text{Desired Profit} = \text{Desired Rate of Return} \times \text{Total Assets} = 20\% \times \$800{,}000 = \$160{,}000$$

$$\text{Markup Percentage} = \frac{\text{Desired Profit}}{\text{Total Cost}} = \frac{\$160{,}000}{\$1{,}670{,}000} = 9.6\% \text{ (rounded)}$$

Step 6. Markup per unit: $1.60

$$\text{Markup per Unit} = \text{Markup Percentage} \times \text{Total Cost per Unit}$$
$$= 9.6\% \times \$16.70 = \$1.60 \text{ per unit}$$

Step 7. Normal selling price: $18.30

Total cost per unit	$16.70
Markup per unit	1.60
Normal selling price per unit	$18.30

The ability of the selling price of $18.30 to generate the desired profit of $160,000 is illustrated by the income statement that follows:

Digital Solutions Inc.
Income Statement
For the Year Ended December 31, 20Y4

Sales (100,000 units × $18.30)		$1,830,000
Expenses:		
Variable (100,000 units × $16.00)	$1,600,000	
Fixed ($50,000 + $20,000)	70,000	1,670,000
Income from operations		$ 160,000

The total cost concept is often used by contractors who sell products to government agencies. This is because in many cases, government contractors are required by law to be reimbursed for their products on a total-cost-plus-profit basis.

Variable Cost Concept

As shown in Exhibit 17, under the **variable cost concept**, only variable costs are included in the cost amount per unit to which the markup is added. All variable manufacturing costs, as well as variable selling and administrative expenses, are included in the cost amount. Fixed manufacturing costs, fixed selling and administrative expenses, and desired profit are included in the markup. The markup per unit is then added to the variable cost per unit to determine the normal selling price.

EXHIBIT 17

Variable Cost Concept

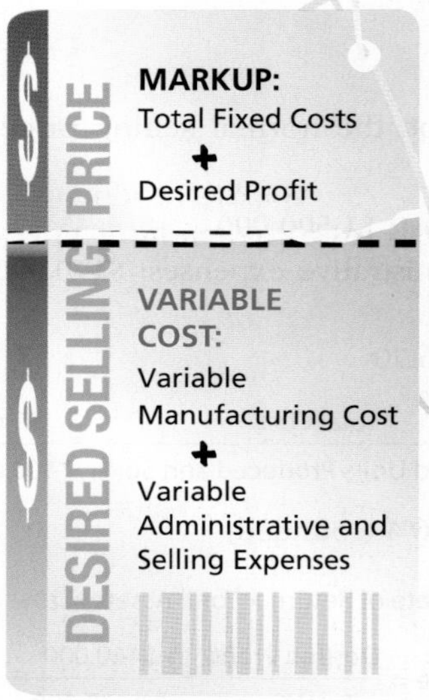

The variable cost concept is applied using the following steps:

Step 1. Estimate the total variable product cost as follows:

Variable product costs:	
Direct materials	$XXX
Direct labor	XXX
Variable factory overhead	XXX
Total variable product cost	$XXX

Step 2. Estimate the total variable selling and administrative expenses.

Step 3. Determine the total variable cost as follows:

Total variable product cost	$XXX
Total variable selling and administrative expenses	XXX
Total variable cost	$XXX

Step 4. Compute the variable cost per unit as follows:

$$\text{Variable Cost per Unit} = \frac{\text{Total Variable Cost}}{\text{Estimated Units Produced and Sold}}$$

Step 5. Compute the markup percentage as follows:

$$\text{Markup Percentage} = \frac{\text{Desired Profit} + \text{Total Fixed Costs and Expenses}}{\text{Total Variable Cost}}$$

The numerator of the markup percentage is the desired profit plus the total fixed costs (fixed factory overhead) and expenses (selling and administrative). These fixed costs and expenses must be included in the markup percentage because they are not included in the cost amount to which the markup is added.

As illustrated for the total and product cost concepts, the desired profit is normally computed based on a rate of return on assets as follows:

$$\text{Desired Profit} = \text{Desired Rate of Return} \times \text{Total Assets}$$

Step 6. Determine the markup per unit by multiplying the markup percentage times the variable cost per unit as follows:

$$\text{Markup per Unit} = \text{Markup Percentage} \times \text{Variable Cost per Unit}$$

Step 7. Determine the normal selling price by adding the markup per unit to the variable cost per unit as follows:

Variable cost per unit	$XXX
Markup per unit	XXX
Normal selling price per unit	$XXX

To illustrate, assume the same data for the production and sale of 100,000 calculators by Digital Solutions Inc. as in the preceding example. The normal selling price of $18.30 is determined under the variable cost concept as follows:

Step 1. Total variable product cost: $1,450,000

Variable product costs:	
Direct materials ($3 × 100,000)	$ 300,000
Direct labor ($10 × 100,000)	1,000,000
Variable factory overhead ($1.50 × 100,000)	150,000
Total variable product cost	$1,450,000

Step 2. Total variable selling and administrative expenses: $150,000 ($1.50 × 100,000)

Step 3. Total variable cost: $1,600,000 ($1,450,000 + $150,000)

Step 4. Variable cost per unit: $16.00

$$\text{Variable Cost per Unit} = \frac{\text{Total Variable Cost}}{\text{Estimated Units Produced and Sold}} = \frac{\$1{,}600{,}000}{100{,}000 \text{ units}} = \$16 \text{ per unit}$$

Step 5. Markup percentage: 14.4% (rounded)

$$\text{Desired Profit} = \text{Desired Rate of Return} \times \text{Total Assets} = 20\% \times \$800{,}000 = \$160{,}000$$

$$\text{Markup Percentage} = \frac{\text{Desired Profit} + \text{Total Fixed Costs and Expenses}}{\text{Total Variable Cost}}$$

$$= \frac{\$160{,}000 + \$50{,}000 + \$20{,}000}{\$1{,}600{,}000} = \frac{\$230{,}000}{\$1{,}600{,}000}$$

$$= 14.4\% \text{ (rounded)}$$

Step 6. Markup per unit: $2.30

$$\text{Markup per Unit} = \text{Markup Percentage} \times \text{Variable Cost per Unit}$$
$$= 14.4\% \times \$16.00 = \$2.30 \text{ per unit}$$

Step 7. Normal selling price: $18.30

Total variable cost per unit	$16.00
Markup per unit	2.30
Normal selling price per unit	$18.30

At a Glance 25

Obj. 1 Prepare differential analysis reports for a variety of managerial decisions.

Key Points Differential analysis reports for various decisions are illustrated in the text. Each analysis focuses on the differential effects on income (loss) for alternative courses of action.

Learning Outcomes	Example Exercises	Practice Exercises
• Prepare a lease-or-sell differential analysis.	EE25-1	PE25-1A, 25-1B
• Prepare a discontinued segment differential analysis.	EE25-2	PE25-2A, 25-2B
• Prepare a make-or-buy differential analysis.	EE25-3	PE25-3A, 25-3B
• Prepare an equipment replacement differential analysis.	EE25-4	PE25-4A, 25-4B
• Prepare a process-or-sell differential analysis.	EE25-5	PE25-5A, 25-5B
• Prepare an accept business at a special price differential analysis.	EE25-6	PE25-6A, 25-6B

Obj. 2 Determine the selling price of a product, using the product cost concept.

Key Points The three cost concepts commonly used in applying the cost-plus approach to product pricing are the product cost, total cost (appendix), and variable cost (appendix) concepts.

Target costing combines market-based methods with a cost-reduction emphasis.

Learning Outcomes	Example Exercises	Practice Exercises
• Compute the markup percentage, using the product cost concept.	EE25-7	PE25-7A, 25-7B
• Define and describe target costing.		

Obj. 3 Compute the relative profitability of products in bottleneck production processes.

Key Points The relative profitability of a product in a bottleneck production environment is determined by dividing the unit contribution margin by the bottleneck hours per unit.

Learning Outcome	Example Exercises	Practice Exercises
• Compute the unit contribution margin per bottleneck hour.	EE25-8	PE25-8A, 25-8B

Obj. 4 Allocate product costs using activity-based costing.

Key Points Activity-based costing requires factory overhead to be assigned to activities. The estimated activity costs are allocated to products by multiplying activity rates by the activity-base usage quantity consumed for each product. Activity-based costing may provide more accurate allocation of factory overhead in complex product and manufacturing environments.

Learning Outcomes	Example Exercises	Practice Exercises
• Compute activity rates.		
• Allocate factory overhead costs to products using ABC.	EE25-9	PE25-9A, 25-9B

Illustrative Problem

Inez Company recently began production of a new product, a digital clock, which required the investment of $1,600,000 in assets. The costs of producing and selling 80,000 units of the digital clock are estimated as follows:

Variable costs:		
Direct materials		$10.00 per unit
Direct labor		6.00
Factory overhead		4.00
Selling and administrative expenses		5.00
Total		$25.00 per unit
Fixed costs:		
Factory overhead	$800,000	
Selling and administrative expenses	400,000	

Inez Company is currently considering establishing a selling price for the digital clock. The president of Inez Company has decided to use the cost-plus approach to product pricing and has indicated that the digital clock must earn a 10% rate of return on invested assets.

Instructions

1. Determine the amount of desired profit from the production and sale of the digital clock.
2. Assuming that the product cost concept is used, determine (a) the cost amount per unit, (b) the markup percentage, and (c) the selling price of the digital clock.
3. Under what conditions should Inez Company consider using activity-based costing rather than a single factory overhead allocation rate in allocating factory overhead to the digital clock?
4. Assume that the market price for similar digital clocks was estimated at $38. Compute the reduction in manufacturing cost per unit needed to maintain the desired profit and existing selling and administrative expenses under target costing.
5. Assume that for the current year, the selling price of the digital clock was $42 per unit. To date, 60,000 units have been produced and sold, and analysis of the domestic market indicates that 15,000 additional units are expected to be sold during the remainder of the year. On August 7, Inez Company received an offer from Wong Inc. for 4,000 units of the digital clock at $28 each. Wong Inc. will market the units in Korea under its own brand name, and no selling and administrative expenses associated with the sale will be incurred by Inez Company. The additional business is not expected to affect the domestic sales of the digital clock, and the additional units could be produced during the current year, using existing capacity. Prepare a differential analysis dated August 7 to determine whether to reject (Alternative 1) or accept (Alternative 2) the special order from Wong.

Solution

1. $160,000 ($1,600,000 × 10%)
2. a. Total manufacturing costs:

Variable ($20 × 80,000 units)	$1,600,000
Fixed factory overhead	800,000
Total	$2,400,000

Cost amount per unit: $2,400,000 ÷ 80,000 units = $30.00

(Continued)

b. $$\text{Markup Percentage} = \frac{\text{Desired Profit} + \text{Total Selling and Administrative Expenses}}{\text{Total Product Cost}}$$

$$= \frac{\$160{,}000 + \$400{,}000 + (\$5 \times 80{,}000 \text{ units})}{\$2{,}400{,}000}$$

$$= \frac{\$160{,}000 + \$400{,}000 + \$400{,}000}{\$2{,}400{,}000}$$

$$= \frac{\$960{,}000}{\$2{,}400{,}000} = 40\%$$

c.

Cost amount per unit	$30.00
Markup ($30 × 40%)	12.00
Selling price	$42.00

3. Inez should consider using activity-based costing for factory overhead allocation when the product and manufacturing operations are complex. For example, if the digital clock was introduced as one among many different consumer digital products, these products will likely consume factory activities in different ways. If this is combined with complex manufacturing and manufacturing support processes, a single overhead allocation rate will likely lead to distorted factory overhead allocation. Specifically, the digital clock is a new product. Thus, it will likely consume more factory overhead than existing stable and mature products. In this case, a single rate would result in the digital clock being undercosted compared to results using activity-based rates for factory overhead allocation.

4.

Current selling price	$42
Expected selling price	−38
Required reduction in manufacturing cost to maintain same profit	$ 4

Revised revenue and cost figures:

	Current	Desired
Selling price	$42	$38
Costs:		
Variable selling and administrative expenses per unit	$ 5	$ 5
Fixed selling and administrative expenses per unit ($400,000 ÷ 80,000 units)	5	5
Existing manufacturing cost per unit [part (2)]	30	
Target manufacturing cost per unit ($30 − $4)		26
Total costs	$40	$36
Profit	$ 2	$ 2

5.

Differential Analysis—Wong Inc. Special Order
Reject Order (Alternative 1) or Accept Order (Alternative 2)
August 7

	Reject Order (Alternative 1)	Accept Order (Alternative 2)	Differential Effect on Income (Alternative 2)
Revenues	$0	$112,000*	$112,000
Costs:			
Variable manufacturing costs	0	−80,000**	−80,000
Income (loss)	$0	$ 32,000	$ 32,000

*4,000 units × $28 per unit
**4,000 units × $20 per unit

The proposal should be accepted.

Key Terms

activities (1237)
activity base (1238)
activity-based costing (ABC) (1237)
activity rate (1238)
differential analysis (1220)
differential cost (1220)
differential income (loss) (1220)
differential revenue (1220)
engineering change order (ECO) (1237)
opportunity cost (1227)
product cost concept (1232)
production bottleneck (1235)
setup (1237)
sunk cost (1222)
target costing (1234)
theory of constraints (TOC) (1235)
total cost concept (1241)
variable cost concept (1244)

Discussion Questions

1. Explain the meaning of (a) differential revenue, (b) differential cost, and (c) differential income.
2. A company could sell a building for $250,000 or lease it for $2,500 per month. What would need to be considered in determining if the lease option would be preferred?
3. A chemical company has commodity-grade and premium-grade products. Why might the company elect to process the commodity-grade product further to the premium-grade product?
4. A company accepts incremental business at a special price that exceeds the variable cost. What other issues must the company consider in deciding whether to accept the business?
5. A company fabricates a component at a cost of $6.00. A supplier offers to supply the same component for $5.50. Under what circumstances is it reasonable to purchase from the supplier?
6. Real World Many fast-food restaurant chains such as **McDonald's** occasionally discontinue restaurants in their system. What are some financial considerations in deciding to eliminate a store?
7. In the long run, the normal selling price must be set high enough to cover what factors?
8. Although the cost-plus approach to product pricing may be used by management as a general guideline, what are examples of other factors that managers should consider in setting product prices?
9. How does the target cost concept differ from cost-plus approaches?
10. What is the appropriate measure of a product's value when a firm is operating under production bottlenecks?
11. Under what conditions might a company use activity-based costing to allocate factory overhead to products?

Practice Exercises

Example Exercises

Show Me How **EE 25-1** *p. 1223*

PE 25-1A Lease or sell **OBJ. 1**

Duncan Company owns a machine with a cost of $75,000 and accumulated depreciation of $15,000 that can be sold for $54,000 less a 5% sales commission. Alternatively, Duncan Company can lease the machine to another company for three years for a total of $60,000, at the end of which there is no residual value. In addition, the repair, insurance, and property tax expense that would be incurred by Duncan Company on the machine would total $8,500 over the three years. Prepare a differential analysis on February 21 as to whether Duncan Company should lease (Alternative 1) or sell (Alternative 2) the machine.

EE 25-1 p. 1223 Show Me How

PE 25-1B Lease or sell **OBJ. 1**

Timberlake Company owns equipment with a cost of $165,000 and accumulated depreciation of $60,000 that can be sold for $82,000 less a 6% sales commission. Alternatively, Timberlake Company can lease the equipment to another company for five years for a total of $84,600, at the end of which there is no residual value. In addition, the repair, insurance, and property tax expense that would be incurred by Timberlake Company on the equipment would total $7,950 over the five years. Prepare a differential analysis on March 23 as to whether Timberlake Company should lease (Alternative 1) or sell (Alternative 2) the equipment.

EE 25-2 p. 1224 Show Me How

PE 25-2A Discontinue a segment **OBJ. 1**

Product Alpha has revenue of $545,000, variable cost of goods sold of $400,000, variable selling expenses of $65,000, and fixed costs of $90,000, creating a loss from operations of $10,000. Prepare a differential analysis as of December 10 to determine whether Product Alpha should be continued (Alternative 1) or discontinued (Alternative 2), assuming that fixed costs are unaffected by the decision.

EE 25-2 p. 1224 Show Me How

PE 25-2B Discontinue a segment **OBJ. 1**

Product B has revenue of $39,500, variable cost of goods sold of $25,500, variable selling expenses of $16,500, and fixed costs of $15,000, creating a loss from operations of $17,500. Prepare a differential analysis as of May 9 to determine whether Product B should be continued (Alternative 1) or discontinued (Alternative 2), assuming fixed costs are unaffected by the decision.

EE 25-3 p. 1226 Show Me How

PE 25-3A Make or buy **OBJ. 1**

A restaurant bakes its own bread for a cost of $230 per unit (100 loaves), including fixed costs of $47 per unit. A proposal is offered to purchase bread from an outside source for $180 per unit, plus $18 per unit for delivery. Prepare a differential analysis dated July 7 to determine whether the company should make (Alternative 1) or buy (Alternative 2) the bread, assuming that fixed costs are unaffected by the decision.

EE 25-3 p. 1226 Show Me How

PE 25-3B Make or buy **OBJ. 1**

A company manufactures various sized plastic bottles for its medicinal product. The manufacturing cost for small bottles is $67 per unit (100 bottles), including fixed costs of $22 per unit. A proposal is offered to purchase small bottles from an outside source for $35 per unit, plus $5 per unit for freight. Prepare a differential analysis dated March 30 to determine whether the company should make (Alternative 1) or buy (Alternative 2) the bottles, assuming that fixed costs are unaffected by the decision.

EE 25-4 p. 1228 Show Me How

PE 25-4A Replace equipment **OBJ. 1**

A machine with a book value of $250,000 has an estimated six-year life. A proposal is offered to sell the old machine for $320,000 and replace it with a new machine at a cost of $390,000. The new machine has a six-year life with no residual value. The new machine would reduce annual direct labor costs from $75,000 to $61,000. Prepare a differential analysis dated October 3 on whether to continue with the old machine (Alternative 1) or replace the old machine (Alternative 2).

EE 25-4 p. 1228 Show Me How

PE 25-4B Replace equipment **OBJ. 1**

A machine with a book value of $80,000 has an estimated five-year life. A proposal is offered to sell the old machine for $50,500 and replace it with a new machine at a cost of $75,000. The new machine has a five-year life with no residual value. The new machine would reduce annual direct labor costs from $11,200 to $7,400. Prepare a differential analysis dated April 11 on whether to continue with the old machine (Alternative 1) or replace the old machine (Alternative 2).

Show Me How EE 25-5 p. 1229

PE 25-5A Process or sell **OBJ. 1**

Product K is produced for $155 per pound. Product K can be sold without additional processing for $220 per pound or processed further into Product L at an additional cost of $28 per pound. Product L can be sold for $250 per pound. Prepare a differential analysis dated November 15 on whether to sell Product K (Alternative 1) or process further into Product L (Alternative 2).

Show Me How EE 25-5 p. 1229

PE 25-5B Process or sell **OBJ. 1**

Product D is produced for $24 per gallon. Product D can be sold without additional processing for $36 per gallon or processed further into Product E at an additional cost of $9 per gallon. Product E can be sold for $43 per gallon. Prepare a differential analysis dated February 26 on whether to sell Product D (Alternative 1) or process further into Product E (Alternative 2).

Show Me How EE 25-6 p. 1231

PE 25-6A Accept business at special price **OBJ. 1**

Product AA is normally sold for $120 per unit. A special price of $112 is offered for the export market. The variable production cost is $80 per unit. An additional export tariff of 30% of revenue must be paid for all export products. Assume that there is sufficient capacity for the special order. Prepare a differential analysis dated March 5 on whether to reject (Alternative 1) or accept (Alternative 2) the special order.

Show Me How EE 25-6 p. 1231

PE 25-6B Accept business at special price **OBJ. 1**

Product A is normally sold for $9.60 per unit. A special price of $7.20 is offered for the export market. The variable production cost is $5.00 per unit. An additional export tariff of 15% of revenue must be paid for all export products. Assume that there is sufficient capacity for the special order. Prepare a differential analysis dated March 16 on whether to reject (Alternative 1) or accept (Alternative 2) the special order.

Show Me How EE 25-7 p. 1234

PE 25-7A Product cost markup percentage **OBJ. 2**

Light Force Inc. produces and sells lighting fixtures. An entry light has a total cost of $180 per unit, of which $100 is product cost and $80 is selling and administrative expenses. In addition, the total cost of $180 is made up of $110 variable cost and $70 fixed cost. The desired profit is $45 per unit. Determine the markup percentage on product cost.

Show Me How EE 25-7 p. 1234

PE 25-7B Product cost markup percentage **OBJ. 2**

Green Thumb Garden Tools Inc. produces and sells home and garden tools and equipment. A lawn mower has a total cost of $230 per unit, of which $160 is product cost and $70 is selling and administrative expenses. In addition, the total cost of $230 is made up of $120 variable cost and $110 fixed cost. The desired profit is $58 per unit. Determine the markup percentage on product cost.

Show Me How EE 25-8 p. 1236

PE 25-8A Bottleneck profit **OBJ. 3**

Product A has a unit contribution margin of $24. Product B has a unit contribution margin of $30. Product A requires four testing hours, while Product B requires six testing hours. Determine the most profitable product, assuming that the testing is a production bottleneck.

Show Me How — EE 25-8 p. 1236

PE 25-8B Bottleneck profit OBJ. 3

Product K has a unit contribution margin of $120. Product L has a unit contribution margin of $100. Product K requires five furnace hours, while Product L requires four furnace hours. Determine the most profitable product, assuming that the furnace is a production bottleneck.

Show Me How — EE 25-9 p. 1240

PE 25-9A Activity-based costing OBJ. 4

Mainline Marine Company has total estimated factory overhead for the year of $2,090,000, divided into four activities: fabrication, $750,000; assembly, $240,000; setup, $600,000; and inspection, $500,000. Mainline manufactures two types of boats: a speedboat and a bass boat. The activity-base usage quantities for each product by each activity are as follows:

	Fabrication	Assembly	Setup	Inspection
Speedboat	1,200 dlh	1,800 dlh	60 setups	600 inspections
Bass boat	1,800	1,200	100	200
	3,000 dlh	3,000 dlh	160 setups	800 inspections

Each product is budgeted for 200 units of production for the year. Determine (a) the activity rates for each activity and (b) the factory overhead cost per unit for each product, using activity-based costing.

Show Me How — EE 25-9 p. 1240

PE 25-9B Activity-based costing OBJ. 4

Casual Cuts Inc. has total estimated factory overhead for the year of $225,000, divided into four activities: cutting, $90,000; sewing, $22,500; setup, $80,000; and inspection, $32,500. Casual Cuts manufactures two types of men's pants: jeans and khakis. The activity-base usage quantities for each product by each activity are as follows:

	Cutting	Sewing	Setup	Inspection
Jeans	500 dlh	1,000 dlh	250 setups	100 inspections
Khakis	1,000	500	750	400
	1,500 dlh	1,500 dlh	1,000 setups	500 inspections

Each product is budgeted for 10,000 units of production for the year. Determine (a) the activity rates for each activity and (b) the factory overhead cost per unit for each product, using activity-based costing.

Exercises

EX 25-1 Differential analysis for a lease-or-sell decision OBJ. 1

✔ a. Differential revenue from selling, $3,500

Show Me How

Matrix Construction Company is considering selling excess machinery with a book value of $75,000 (original cost of $200,000 less accumulated depreciation of $125,000) for $60,000 less a 5% brokerage commission. Alternatively, the machinery can be leased to another company for a total of $75,000 for five years, after which it is expected to have no residual value. During the period of the lease, Matrix Construction Company's costs of repairs, insurance, and property tax expenses are expected to be $21,500.

a. Prepare a differential analysis dated May 25 to determine whether Matrix should lease (Alternative 1) or sell (Alternative 2) the machinery.

b. On the basis of the data presented, would it be advisable to lease or sell the machinery? Explain.

EX 25-2 Differential analysis for a lease-or-buy decision OBJ. 1

✔ Loss from buying equipment, –$378,000

D'Amato Corporation is considering new equipment. The equipment can be purchased from an overseas supplier for $315,000. The freight and installation costs for the equip-

Show Me How

ment are $15,000. If purchased, annual repairs and maintenance are estimated to be $12,000 per year over the four-year useful life of the equipment. Alternatively, D'Amato can lease the equipment from a domestic supplier for $95,000 per year for four years, with no additional costs. Prepare a differential analysis dated December 11 to determine whether D'Amato should lease (Alternative 1) or purchase (Alternative 2) the equipment. *Hint:* This is a lease-or-buy decision, which must be analyzed from the perspective of the equipment user, as opposed to the equipment owner.

✔ a. Loss to discontinue Star Cola, –$113,300

Show Me How

EX 25-3 Differential analysis for a discontinued product

OBJ. 1

A condensed income statement by product line for Celestial Beverage Inc. indicated the following for Star Cola for the past year:

Sales	$390,000
Cost of goods sold	184,000
Gross profit	$206,000
Operating expenses	255,000
Loss from operations	$ (49,000)

It is estimated that 20% of the cost of goods sold represents fixed factory overhead costs and that 30% of the operating expenses are fixed. Because Star Cola is only one of many products, the fixed costs will not be materially affected if the product is discontinued.

a. Prepare a differential analysis dated January 21 to determine whether Star Cola should be continued (Alternative 1) or discontinued (Alternative 2).

b. Should Star Cola be retained? Explain.

✔ a. Alternative 1 loss, $4,300

Excel

EX 25-4 Differential analysis for a discontinued product

OBJ. 1

The condensed product-line income statement for Dish N' Dat Company for the month of May is as follows:

Dish N' Dat Company
Product-Line Income Statement
For the Month Ended May 31

	Bowls	Plates	Cups
Sales	$71,000	$105,700	$33,500
Cost of goods sold	32,600	42,300	20,600
Gross profit	$38,400	$ 63,400	$12,900
Selling and administrative expenses	27,400	42,800	17,200
Income from operations	$11,000	$ 20,600	$ (4,300)

Fixed costs are 15% of the cost of goods sold and 30% of the selling and administrative expenses. Dish N' Dat assumes that fixed costs would not be materially affected if the Cups line were discontinued.

a. Prepare a differential analysis dated May 31 to determine if Cups should be continued (Alternative 1) or discontinued (Alternative 2).

b. Should the Cups line be retained? Explain.

Real World

EX 25-5 Segment analysis for a service company

OBJ. 1

Charles Schwab Corporation is one of the more innovative brokerage and financial service companies in the United States. The company recently provided information about its major business segments as follows (in millions):

	Investor Services	Advisor Services
Revenues	$4,771	$4,597
Income from operations	1,681	1,660
Depreciation	171	154

(Continued)

a. How does a brokerage company like Schwab define the Investor Services and Advisor Services segments? Use the Internet and the Business Connection box in this chapter to develop your answer.

b. Provide a specific example of a variable and fixed cost in the Investor Services segment.

c. Estimate the contribution margin for each segment, assuming that depreciation represents the majority of fixed costs.

d. If Schwab decided to sell its Advisor Services business to another company, estimate how much operating income would decline.

EX 25-6 Decision to discontinue a product

OBJ. 1

On the basis of the following data, the general manager of Foremost Footwear Inc. decided to discontinue Children's Shoes because it reduced income from operations by $10,000. What is the flaw in this decision if it is assumed that fixed costs would not be materially affected by the discontinuance?

Foremost Footwear Inc.
Product-Line Income Statement
For the Year Ended April 30, 20Y7

	Children's Shoes	Men's Shoes	Women's Shoes	Total
Sales	$165,000	$300,000	$500,000	$965,000
Costs of goods sold:				
Variable costs	$105,000	$150,000	$220,000	$475,000
Fixed costs	32,000	60,000	120,000	212,000
Total cost of goods sold	$137,000	$210,000	$340,000	$687,000
Gross profit	$ 28,000	$ 90,000	$160,000	$278,000
Selling and adminstrative expenses:				
Variable selling and admin. expenses	$ 21,000	$ 45,000	$ 95,000	$161,000
Fixed selling and admin. expenses	17,000	20,000	25,000	62,000
Total selling and admin. expenses	$ 38,000	$ 65,000	$120,000	$223,000
Income (loss) from operations	$ (10,000)	$ 25,000	$ 40,000	$ 55,000

EX 25-7 Make-or-buy decision

OBJ. 1

✔ a. Differential loss from buying, $3.30 per case

Excel

Show Me How

Diamond Computer Company has been purchasing carrying cases for its portable computers at a purchase price of $59 per unit. The company, which is currently operating below full capacity, charges factory overhead to production at the rate of 40% of direct labor cost. The fully absorbed unit costs to produce comparable carrying cases are expected to be as follows:

Direct materials	$35.00
Direct labor	18.00
Factory overhead (40% of direct labor)	7.20
Total cost per unit	$60.20

If Diamond Computer Company manufactures the carrying cases, fixed factory overhead costs will not increase and variable factory overhead costs associated with the cases are expected to be 15% of the direct labor costs.

a. Prepare a differential analysis dated February 24 to determine whether the company should make (Alternative 1) or buy (Alternative 2) the carrying case.

b. On the basis of the data presented, would it be advisable to make the carrying cases or to continue buying them? Explain.

✔ a. Loss from purchasing layout services, –$364,000

Excel

EX 25-8 Make-or-buy decision for a service company **OBJ. 1**

The Theater Arts Guild of Dallas (TAG-D) employs five people in its Publication Department. These people lay out pages for pamphlets, brochures, magazines, and other publications for the TAG-D productions. The pages are delivered to an outside company for printing. The company is considering an outside publication service for the layout work. The outside service is quoting a price of $13 per layout page. The budget for the Publication Department for the current year is as follows:

Salaries	$224,000
Benefits	36,000
Supplies	21,000
Office expenses	39,000
Office depreciation	28,000
Computer depreciation	24,000
Total	$372,000

The department expects to lay out 24,000 pages for the current year. The Publication Department office space and equipment would be used for future administrative needs if the department's function were purchased from the outside.

a. Prepare a differential analysis dated February 22 to determine whether TAG-D should lay out pages internally (Alternative 1) or purchase layout services from the outside (Alternative 2).

b. On the basis of your analysis in part (a), should the page layout work be purchased from an outside company? Explain.

c. What additional considerations might factor into the decision making?

✔ a. Loss from replacing old machine, –$66,700

Show Me How

EX 25-9 Machine replacement decision **OBJ. 1**

A company is considering replacing an old piece of machinery, which cost $105,000 and has $55,000 of accumulated depreciation to date, with a new machine that has a purchase price of $83,000. The old machine could be sold for $56,300. The annual variable production costs associated with the old machine are estimated to be $8,500 per year for eight years. The annual variable production costs for the new machine are estimated to be $5,000 per year for eight years.

a. Prepare a differential analysis dated April 29 to determine whether to continue with (Alternative 1) or replace (Alternative 2) the old machine.

b. What is the sunk cost in this situation?

✔ a. Differential loss, $2,500

Excel

EX 25-10 Differential analysis for machine replacement **OBJ. 1**

Kim Kwon Digital Components Company assembles circuit boards by using a manually operated machine to insert electronic components. The original cost of the machine is $60,000, the accumulated depreciation is $24,000, its remaining useful life is five years, and its residual value is negligible. On May 4 of the current year, a proposal was made to replace the present manufacturing procedure with a fully automatic machine that has a purchase price of $180,000. The automatic machine has an estimated useful life of five years and no significant residual value. For use in evaluating the proposal, the accountant accumulated the following annual data on present and proposed operations:

	Present Operations	Proposed Operations
Sales	$205,000	$205,000
Direct materials	$ 72,000	$ 72,000
Direct labor	51,000	—
Power and maintenance	5,000	18,000
Taxes, insurance, etc.	1,500	4,000
Selling and administrative expenses	45,000	45,000
Total expenses	$174,500	$139,000

(Continued)

a. Prepare a differential analysis dated May 4 to determine whether to continue with the old machine (Alternative 1) or replace the old machine (Alternative 2). Prepare the analysis over the useful life of the new machine.

b. Based only on the data presented, should the proposal be accepted?

c. What other factors should be considered before a final decision is made?

EX 25-11 Sell or process further **OBJ. 1**

✔ Income from processing further, $145

Show Me How

Big Fork Lumber Company incurs a cost of $402 per hundred board feet (hbf) in processing certain "rough-cut" lumber, which it sells for $540 per hbf. An alternative is to produce a "finished cut" at a total processing cost of $523 per hbf, which can be sold for $668 per hbf. Prepare a differential analysis dated August 9 on whether to sell rough-cut lumber (Alternative 1) or process further into finished-cut lumber (Alternative 2).

EX 25-12 Sell or process further **OBJ. 1**

✔ a. Income from processing further, $24,486

Excel

Rise N' Shine Coffee Company produces Columbian coffee in batches of 6,000 pounds. The standard quantity of materials required in the process is 6,000 pounds, which cost $5.50 per pound. Columbian coffee can be sold without further processing for $9.22 per pound. Columbian coffee can also be processed further to yield Decaf Columbian, which can be sold for $11.88 per pound. The processing into Decaf Columbian requires additional processing costs of $10,230 per batch. The additional processing also causes a 5% loss of product due to evaporation.

a. Prepare a differential analysis dated October 6 on whether to sell regular Columbian (Alternative 1) or process further into Decaf Columbian (Alternative 2).

b. Should Rise N' Shine sell Columbian coffee or process further and sell Decaf Columbian?

c. Determine the price of Decaf Columbian that would cause neither an advantage nor a disadvantage for processing further and selling Decaf Columbian.

EX 25-13 Decision on accepting additional business **OBJ. 1**

✔ a. Differential income, $54,000

Homestead Jeans Co. has an annual plant capacity of 65,000 units, and current production is 45,000 units. Monthly fixed costs are $54,000, and variable costs are $29 per unit. The present selling price is $42 per unit. On November 12 of the current year, the company received an offer from Dawkins Company for 18,000 units of the product at $32 each. Dawkins Company will market the units in a foreign country under its own brand name. The additional business is not expected to affect the domestic selling price or quantity of sales of Homestead Jeans Co.

a. Prepare a differential analysis dated November 12 on whether to reject (Alternative 1) or accept (Alternative 2) the Dawkins order.

b. Briefly explain why accepting this additional business will increase operating income.

c. What is the minimum price per unit that would produce a positive contribution margin?

EX 25-14 Accepting business at a special price **OBJ. 1**

Portable Power Company expects to operate at 80% of productive capacity during July. The total manufacturing costs for July for the production of 25,000 batteries are budgeted as follows:

Direct materials	$162,500
Direct labor	70,000
Variable factory overhead	30,000
Fixed factory overhead	112,500
Total manufacturing costs	$375,000

The company has an opportunity to submit a bid for 2,500 batteries to be delivered by July 31 to a government agency. If the contract is obtained, it is anticipated that the additional activity will not interfere with normal production during July or increase the selling or administrative expenses. What is the unit cost below which Portable Power Company should not go in bidding on the government contract?

✔ a. Differential revenue, $2,320,000

Excel

Show Me How

EX 25-15 Decision on accepting additional business **OBJ. 1**

Brightstone Tire and Rubber Company has capacity to produce 170,000 tires. Brightstone presently produces and sells 130,000 tires for the North American market at a price of $175 per tire. Brightstone is evaluating a special order from a European automobile company, Euro Motors. Euro is offering to buy 20,000 tires for $116 per tire. Brightstone's accounting system indicates that the total cost per tire is as follows:

Direct materials	$ 56
Direct labor	22
Factory overhead (60% variable)	25
Selling and administrative expenses (45% variable)	26
Total	$129

Brightstone pays a selling commission equal to 5% of the selling price on North American orders, which is included in the variable portion of the selling and administrative expenses. However, this special order would not have a sales commission. If the order was accepted, the tires would be shipped overseas for an additional shipping cost of $7.50 per tire. In addition, Euro has made the order conditional on receiving European safety certification. Brightstone estimates that this certification would cost $165,000.

a. Prepare a differential analysis dated January 21 on whether to reject (Alternative 1) or accept (Alternative 2) the special order from Euro Motors.

b. What is the minimum price per unit that would be financially acceptable to Brightstone?

EX 25-16 Accepting business at a special price for a service company

Cityscape Hotels has 200 rooms available in a major metropolitan city. The hotel is able to attract business customers during the weekdays and leisure customers during the weekend. However, the leisure customers on weekends occupy fewer rooms than do business customers on weekdays. Thus, Cityscape plans to provide special weekend pricing to attract additional leisure customers. A hotel room is priced at $180 per room night. The cost of a hotel room night includes the following:

	Cost per Room Night (at normal occupancy)
Housekeeping service	$ 23
Utilities	7
Amenities	3
Hotel depreciation	55
Hotel staff (excluding housekeeping)	42
Total	$130

a. What is the contribution margin for a room night if only the hotel depreciation and hotel staff are assumed fixed for all occupancy levels?

b. What should be considered in setting a discount price for the weekends?

✔ b. $40

Show Me How

EX 25-17 Product cost concept of product pricing **OBJ. 2**

La Femme Accessories Inc. produces women's handbags. The cost of producing 800 handbags is as follows:

Direct materials	$18,000
Direct labor	8,500
Factory overhead	5,500
Total manufacturing cost	$32,000

(Continued)

The selling and administrative expenses are $17,000. The management wants a profit equal to 22% of invested assets of $250,000.

a. Determine the amount of desired profit from the production and sale of 800 handbags.
b. Determine the product cost per unit for the production of 800 handbags.
c. Determine the product cost markup percentage for handbags.
d. Determine the selling price of handbags.

EX 25-18 Product cost concept of product costing OBJ. 2

✔ d. $325

Show Me How

Smart Stream Inc. uses the product cost concept of applying the cost-plus approach to product pricing. The costs of producing and selling 10,000 cellular phones are as follows:

Variable costs per unit:	
Direct materials	$150
Direct labor	25
Factory overhead	40
Selling and administrative expenses	25
Total	$240

Fixed costs:	
Factory overhead	$350,000
Selling and administrative expenses	140,000

Smart Stream wants a profit equal to a 30% rate of return on invested assets of $1,200,000.

a. Determine the amount of desired profit from the production and sale of 10,000 cellular phones.
b. Determine the product cost and the cost amount per unit for the production of 10,000 cellular phones.
c. Determine the product cost markup percentage for cellular phones.
d. Determine the selling price of cellular phones.

EX 25-19 Target costing OBJ. 2

Real World

Toyota Motor Corporation uses target costing. Assume that Toyota marketing personnel estimate that the competitive selling price for the Camry in the upcoming model year will need to be $27,000. Assume further that the Camry's total unit cost for the upcoming model year is estimated to be $22,500 and that Toyota requires a 20% profit margin on selling price (which is equivalent to a 25% markup on total cost).

a. What price will Toyota establish for the Camry for the upcoming model year?
b. What impact will target costing have on Toyota, given the assumed information?

EX 25-20 Target costing OBJ. 2

✔ b. $30

Instant Image Inc. manufactures color laser printers. Model J20 presently sells for $460 and has a product cost of $230, as follows:

Direct materials	$175
Direct labor	40
Factory overhead	15
Total	$230

It is estimated that the competitive selling price for color laser printers of this type will drop to $400 next year. Instant Image has established a target cost to maintain its historical markup percentage on product cost. Engineers have provided the following cost-reduction ideas:

1. Purchase a plastic printer cover with snap-on assembly rather than with screws. This will reduce the amount of direct labor by 15 minutes per unit.
2. Add an inspection step that will add six minutes per unit of direct labor but reduce the materials cost by $20 per unit.

3. Decrease the cycle time of the injection molding machine from four minutes to three minutes per part. Forty percent of the direct labor and 48% of the factory overhead are related to running injection molding machines.

The direct labor rate is $30 per hour.

a. Determine the target cost for Model J20, assuming that the historical markup on product cost and selling price is maintained.

b. Determine the required cost reduction.

c. Evaluate the three engineering improvements together to determine whether the required cost reduction (drift) can be achieved.

✔ Unit contribution per furnace hour Type 5, $0.30

EX 25-21 Product decisions under bottlenecked operations **OBJ. 3**

Mill Metals Inc. has three grades of metal product, Type 5, Type 10, and Type 20. Financial data for the three grades are as follows:

	Type 5	Type 10	Type 20
Revenues	$43,000	$49,000	$56,500
Variable cost	$34,000	$28,000	$26,500
Fixed cost	8,000	8,000	8,000
Total cost	$42,000	$36,000	$34,500
Income from operations	$ 1,000	$13,000	$22,000
Number of units	÷ 5,000	÷ 5,000	÷ 5,000
Income from operations per unit	$ 0.20	$ 2.60	$ 4.40

Mill's operations require all three grades to be melted in a furnace before being formed. The furnace runs 24 hours a day, 7 days a week, and is a production bottleneck. The furnace hours required per unit of each product are as follows:

Type 5:	6 hours
Type 10:	6 hours
Type 20:	12 hours

The Marketing Department is considering a new marketing and sales campaign.

Which product should be emphasized in the marketing and sales campaign in order to maximize profitability?

✔ a. Total income from operations, $269,000

EX 25-22 Product decisions under bottlenecked operations **OBJ. 3**

Youngstown Glass Company manufactures three types of safety plate glass: large, medium, and small. All three products have high demand. Thus, Youngstown Glass is able to sell all the safety glass it can make. The production process includes an autoclave operation, which is a pressurized heat treatment. The autoclave is a production bottleneck. Total fixed costs are $85,000 for the company as a whole. In addition, the following information is available about the three products:

	Large	Medium	Small
Unit selling price	$184	$160	$100
Unit variable cost	130	120	76
Unit contribution margin	$ 54	$ 40	$ 24
Autoclave hours per unit	3	2	1
Total process hours per unit	5	4	2
Budgeted units of production	3,000	3,000	3,000

a. Determine the contribution margin by glass type and the total company income from operations for the budgeted units of production.

b. Prepare an analysis showing which product is the most profitable per bottleneck hour.

OBJ. 4

✔ Activity cost per stationary bicycle, $92.40

Excel

EX 25-23 Activity-based costing

CardioTrainer Equipment Company manufactures stationary bicycles and treadmills. The products are produced in the Fabrication and Assembly production departments. In addition to production activities, several other activities are required to produce the two products. These activities and their associated activity rates are as follows:

Activity	Activity Rate
Fabrication	$22 per machine hour (mh)
Assembly	$12 per direct labor hour (dlh)
Setup	$40 per setup
Inspecting	$18 per inspection
Production scheduling	$8 per production order
Purchasing	$5 per purchase order

The activity-base usage quantities and units produced for each product were as follows:

	Stationary Bicycle	Treadmill
Machine hours	1,680	1,070
Direct labor hours	243	131
Setups	45	20
Inspections	158	94
Production orders	60	32
Purchase orders	240	98
Units produced	500	350

Use the activity rate and usage information to compute the total activity costs and the activity costs per unit for each product.

OBJ. 4

✔ b. Custom, $90.65 per unit

EX 25-24 Activity-based costing

Zeus Industries manufactures two types of electrical power units, custom and standard, which involve four factory overhead activities—production setup, procurement, quality control, and materials management. An activity analysis of the overhead revealed the following estimated activity costs and activity bases for these activities:

Activity	Activity Cost	Activity Base
Production setup	$ 44,000	Number of setups
Procurement	13,500	Number of purchase orders (PO)
Quality control	97,500	Number of inspections
Materials management	84,000	Number of components
Total	$239,000	

The activity-base usage quantities for each product are as follows:

	Setups	Purchase Orders	Inspections	Components	Unit Volume
Custom	290	760	1,200	500	2,000
Standard	110	140	300	200	2,000
Total	400	900	1,500	700	4,000

a. Determine an activity rate for each activity.

b. Assign activity costs to each product and determine the unit activity cost, using the activity rates from part (a).

c. Assume that each product required one direct labor hour per unit. Determine the per-unit cost if factory overhead is allocated on the basis of direct labor hours.

d. Explain why the answers in parts (b) and (c) are different.

EX 25-25 Activity rates and product costs using activity-based costing

OBJ. 4

✔ b. Dining room lighting fixtures, $71.60 per unit

BriteLite Inc. manufactures entry and dining room lighting fixtures. Five activities are used in manufacturing the fixtures. These activities and their associated activity costs and activity bases are as follows:

Activity	Activity Costs (Budgeted)	Activity Base
Casting	$42,000	Machine hours
Assembly	13,500	Direct labor hours
Inspecting	5,800	Number of inspections
Setup	16,800	Number of setups
Materials handling	3,600	Number of loads

Corporate records were obtained to estimate the amount of activity to be used by the two products. The estimated activity-base usage quantities and units produced for each product and in total are provided in the following table:

Activity Base	Entry	Dining	Total
Machine hours	800	600	1,400
Direct labor hours	500	400	900
Number of inspections	140	150	290
Number of setups	80	60	140
Number of loads	50	40	90
Units produced	1,200	500	1,700

a. Determine the activity rate for each activity.

b. Use the activity rates in (a) to determine the total and per-unit activity costs associated with each product.

Appendix

EX 25-26 Total cost concept of product pricing

✔ b. 12.46%

Based on the data presented in Exercise 25-18, assume that Smart Stream Inc. uses the total cost concept of applying the cost-plus approach to product pricing.

a. Determine the total costs and the total cost amount per unit for the production and sale of 10,000 cellular phones.

b. Determine the total cost markup percentage (rounded to two decimal places) for cellular phones.

c. Determine the selling price of cellular phones. Round to the nearest dollar.

Appendix

EX 25-27 Variable cost concept of product pricing

✔ b. 35.42%

Based on the data presented in Exercise 25-18, assume that Smart Stream Inc. uses the variable cost concept of applying the cost-plus approach to product pricing.

a. Determine the variable costs and the variable cost amount per unit for the production and sale of 10,000 cellular phones.

b. Determine the variable cost markup percentage (rounded to two decimal places) for cellular phones.

c. Determine the selling price of cellular phones. Round to the nearest dollar.

Problems: Series A

PR 25-1A Differential analysis involving opportunity costs

OBJ. 1

✔ 1. Income from investing in bonds, $172,800

Excel

On October 1, White Way Stores Inc. is considering leasing a building and purchasing the necessary equipment to operate a retail store. Alternatively, the company could use the funds to invest in $180,000 of 6% U.S. Treasury bonds that mature in 16 years. The bonds could be purchased at face value. The following data have been assembled:

Cost of store equipment	$180,000
Life of store equipment	16 years
Estimated residual value of store equipment	$15,000
Yearly costs to operate the store, excluding depreciation of store equipment	$58,000
Yearly expected revenues—years 1–8	$85,000
Yearly expected revenues—years 9–16	$73,000

Instructions

1. Prepare a differential analysis as of October 1 presenting the proposed operation of the store for the 16 years (Alternative 1) as compared with investing in U.S. Treasury bonds (Alternative 2).
2. Based on the results disclosed by the differential analysis, should the proposal be accepted?
3. If the proposal is accepted, what would be the total estimated income from operations of the store for the 16 years?

PR 25-2A Differential analysis for machine replacement proposal

OBJ. 1

✔ 1. Loss to replace the old machine, –$131,400

Excel

Lexigraphic Printing Company is considering replacing a machine that has been used in its factory for four years. Relevant data associated with the operations of the old machine and the new machine, neither of which has any estimated residual value, are as follows:

Old Machine	
Cost of machine, 10-year life	$89,000
Annual depreciation (straight-line)	8,900
Annual manufacturing costs, excluding depreciation	23,600
Annual nonmanufacturing operating expenses	6,100
Annual revenue	74,200
Current estimated selling price of machine	29,700

New Machine	
Purchase price of machine, six-year life	$119,700
Annual depreciation (straight-line)	19,950
Estimated annual manufacturing costs, excluding depreciation	6,900

Annual nonmanufacturing operating expenses and revenue are not expected to be affected by purchase of the new machine.

Instructions

1. Prepare a differential analysis as of April 30 comparing operations using the present machine (Alternative 1) with operations using the new machine (Alternative 2). The analysis should indicate the total differential income that would result over the six-year period if the new machine is acquired.
2. List other factors that should be considered before a final decision is reached.

✔ 1. Differential revenue, −$10,000

Excel

Show Me How

PR 25-3A Differential analysis for sales promotion proposal

OBJ. 1

Parisian Cosmetics Company is planning a one-month campaign for September to promote sales of one of its two cosmetics products. A total of $140,000 has been budgeted for advertising, contests, redeemable coupons, and other promotional activities. The following data have been assembled for their possible usefulness in deciding which of the products to select for the campaign:

	Moisturizer	Perfume
Unit selling price	$55	$60
Unit production costs:		
Direct materials	$ 9	$14
Direct labor	3	5
Variable factory overhead	3	5
Fixed factory overhead	6	4
Total unit production costs	$21	$28
Unit variable selling expenses	16	15
Unit fixed selling expenses	12	6
Total unit costs	$49	$49
Operating income per unit	$ 6	$11

No increase in facilities would be necessary to produce and sell the increased output. It is anticipated that 22,000 additional units of moisturizer or 20,000 additional units of perfume could be sold from the campaign without changing the unit selling price of either product.

Instructions

1. Prepare a differential analysis as of August 21 to determine whether to promote moisturizer (Alternative 1) or perfume (Alternative 2).
2. The sales manager had tentatively decided to promote perfume, estimating that operating income would be increased by $80,000 ($11 operating income per unit for 20,000 units less promotion expenses of $140,000). The manager also believed that the selection of moisturizer would reduce operating income by $8,000 ($6 operating income per unit for 22,000 units less promotion expenses of $140,000). State briefly your reasons for supporting or opposing the tentative decision.

✔ 1. Raw sugar income, $23,800

PR 25-4A Differential analysis for further processing

OBJ. 1

The management of Dominican Sugar Company is considering whether to process further raw sugar into refined sugar. Refined sugar can be sold for $2.20 per pound, and raw sugar can be sold without further processing for $1.40 per pound. Raw sugar is produced in batches of 42,000 pounds by processing 100,000 pounds of sugar cane, which costs $0.35 per pound of cane. Refined sugar will require additional processing costs of $0.50 per pound of raw sugar, and 1.25 pounds of raw sugar will produce 1 pound of refined sugar.

Instructions

1. Prepare a differential analysis as of March 24 to determine whether to sell raw sugar (Alternative 1) or process further into refined sugar (Alternative 2).
2. Briefly report your recommendations.

PR 25-5A Product pricing using the cost-plus approach concepts; differential analysis for accepting additional business

OBJ. 1, 2

✔ 2. b. Markup percentage, 44%

Crystal Displays Inc. recently began production of a new product, flat panel displays, which required the investment of $1,500,000 in assets. The costs of producing and selling 5,000 units of flat panel displays are estimated as follows:

Variable costs per unit:		Fixed costs:	
Direct materials	$120	Factory overhead	$250,000
Direct labor	30	Selling and administrative expenses	150,000
Factory overhead	50		
Selling and administrative expenses	35		
Total	$235		

Crystal Displays Inc. is currently considering establishing a selling price for flat panel displays. The president of Crystal Displays has decided to use the cost-plus approach to product pricing and has indicated that the displays must earn a 15% rate of return on invested assets.

Instructions

1. Determine the amount of desired profit from the production and sale of flat panel displays.
2. Assuming that the product cost concept is used, determine (a) the cost amount per unit, (b) the markup percentage, and (c) the selling price of flat panel displays.
3. (*Appendix*) Assuming that the total cost concept is used, determine (a) the cost amount per unit, (b) the markup percentage (rounded to two decimal places), and (c) the selling price of flat panel displays (rounded to nearest whole dollar).
4. (*Appendix*) Assuming that the variable cost concept is used, determine (a) the cost amount per unit, (b) the markup percentage (rounded to two decimal places), and (c) the selling price of flat panel displays (rounded to nearest whole dollar).
5. Comment on any additional considerations that could influence establishing the selling price for flat panel displays.
6. Assume that as of August 1, 3,000 units of flat panel displays have been produced and sold during the current year. Analysis of the domestic market indicates that 2,000 additional units are expected to be sold during the remainder of the year at the normal product price determined under the product cost concept. On August 3, Crystal Displays Inc. received an offer from Maple Leaf Visual Inc. for 800 units of flat panel displays at $225 each. Maple Leaf Visual Inc. will market the units in Canada under its own brand name, and no variable selling and administrative expenses associated with the sale will be incurred by Crystal Displays Inc. The additional business is not expected to affect the domestic sales of flat panel displays, and the additional units could be produced using existing factory, selling, and administrative capacity.
   a. Prepare a differential analysis of the proposed sale to Maple Leaf Visual Inc.
   b. Based on the differential analysis in part (a), should the proposal be accepted?

PR 25-6A Product pricing and profit analysis with bottleneck operations

OBJ. 3

✔ 1. High Grade, $10

Excel

Hercules Steel Company produces three grades of steel: high, good, and regular grade. Each of these products (grades) has high demand in the market, and Hercules is able to sell as much as it can produce of all three. The furnace operation is a bottleneck in the process and is running at 100% of capacity. Hercules wants to improve steel operation profitability. The variable conversion cost is $15 per process hour. The fixed cost is $200,000. In addition, the cost analyst was able to determine the following information about the three products:

	High Grade	Good Grade	Regular Grade
Budgeted units produced	5,000	5,000	5,000
Total process hours per unit	12	11	10
Furnace hours per unit	4	3	2.5
Unit selling price	$280	$270	$250
Direct materials cost per unit	$90	$84	$80

The furnace operation is part of the total process for each of these three products. Thus, for example, 4.0 of the 12.0 hours required to process High Grade steel are associated with the furnace.

Instructions

1. Determine the unit contribution margin for each product.
2. Provide an analysis to determine the relative product profitability, assuming that the furnace is a bottleneck.

PR 25-7A Activity-based costing

OBJ. 4

✔ 2. Brown sugar total activity cost, $138,550

Excel

Pure Cane Sugar Company manufactures three products (white sugar, brown sugar, and powdered sugar) in a continuous production process. Senior management has asked the controller to conduct an activity-based costing study. The controller identified the amount of factory overhead required by the critical activities of the organization as follows:

Activity	Activity Costs
Production	$247,500
Setup	48,000
Inspection	12,500
Shipping	69,300
Customer service	27,600
Total	$404,900

The activity bases identified for each activity are as follows:

Activity	Activity Base
Production	Machine hours
Setup	Number of setups
Inspection	Number of inspections
Shipping	Number of customer orders
Customer service	Number of customer service requests

The activity-base usage quantities and units produced for the three products were determined from corporate records as follows:

	Machine Hours	Number of Setups	Number of Inspections	Number of Customer Orders	Number of Customer Service Requests	Units
White sugar	2,000	50	100	410	25	8,000
Brown sugar	1,250	70	160	1,100	200	5,000
Powdered sugar	1,250	80	240	800	120	5,000
Total	4,500	200	500	2,310	345	18,000

Each product requires 0.25 machine hour per unit.

Instructions

1. Determine the activity rate for each activity.
2. Determine the total and per-unit activity costs for all three products.
3. Why aren't the activity unit costs equal across all three products since they require the same machine time per unit?

Problems: Series B

PR 25-1B Differential analysis involving opportunity costs

OBJ. 1

✔ 1. Income from investing in bonds, $518,000

Excel

On July 1, Coastal Distribution Company is considering leasing a building and buying the necessary equipment to operate a public warehouse. Alternatively, the company could use the funds to invest in $740,000 of 5% U.S. Treasury bonds that mature in 14 years. The bonds could be purchased at face value. The following data have been assembled:

Cost of equipment	$740,000
Life of equipment	14 years
Estimated residual value of equipment	$75,000
Yearly costs to operate the warehouse, excluding depreciation of equipment	$175,000
Yearly expected revenues—years 1–7	$280,000
Yearly expected revenues—years 8–14	$240,000

Instructions

1. Prepare a differential analysis as of July 1 presenting the proposed operation of the warehouse for the 14 years (Alternative 1) as compared with investing in U.S. Treasury bonds (Alternative 2).
2. Based on the results disclosed by the differential analysis, should the proposal be accepted?
3. If the proposal is accepted, what is the total estimated income from operations of the warehouse for the 14 years?

PR 25-2B Differential analysis for machine replacement proposal

OBJ. 1

✔ 1. Loss to replace the old machine, –$64,500

Excel

Flint Tooling Company is considering replacing a machine that has been used in its factory for two years. Relevant data associated with the operations of the old machine and the new machine, neither of which has any estimated residual value, are as follows:

Old Machine	
Cost of machine, eight-year life	$38,000
Annual depreciation (straight-line)	4,750
Annual manufacturing costs, excluding depreciation	12,400
Annual nonmanufacturing operating expenses	2,700
Annual revenue	32,400
Current estimated selling price of the machine	12,900

New Machine	
Cost of machine, six-year life	$57,000
Annual depreciation (straight-line)	9,500
Estimated annual manufacturing costs, exclusive of depreciation	3,400

Annual nonmanufacturing operating expenses and revenue are not expected to be affected by purchase of the new machine.

Instructions

1. Prepare a differential analysis as of November 8 comparing operations using the present machine (Alternative 1) with operations using the new machine (Alternative 2). The analysis should indicate the differential income that would result over the six-year period if the new machine is acquired.
2. List other factors that should be considered before a final decision is reached.

PR 25-3B Differential analysis for sales promotion proposal

OBJ. 1

✔ 1. Differential revenue, $105,000

Excel

Show Me How

Sole Mates Inc. is planning a one-month campaign for July to promote sales of one of its two shoe products. A total of $100,000 has been budgeted for advertising, contests, redeemable coupons, and other promotional activities. The following data have been assembled for their possible usefulness in deciding which of the products to select for the campaign:

	Tennis Shoe	Walking Shoe
Unit selling price	$85	$100
Unit production costs:		
Direct materials	$19	$ 32
Direct labor	8	12
Variable factory overhead	7	5
Fixed factory overhead	16	11
Total unit production costs	$50	$ 60
Unit variable selling expenses	6	10
Unit fixed selling expenses	20	15
Total unit costs	$76	$ 85
Operating income per unit	$ 9	$ 15

No increase in facilities would be necessary to produce and sell the increased output. It is anticipated that 7,000 additional units of tennis shoes or 7,000 additional units of walking shoes could be sold without changing the unit selling price of either product.

Instructions

1. Prepare a differential analysis as of June 19 to determine whether to promote tennis shoes (Alternative 1) or walking shoes (Alternative 2).
2. The sales manager had tentatively decided to promote walking shoes, estimating that operating income would be increased by $5,000 ($15 operating income per unit for 7,000 units less promotion expenses of $100,000). The manager also believed that the selection of tennis shoes would reduce operating income by $37,000 ($9 operating income per unit for 7,000 units less promotion expenses of $100,000). State briefly your reasons for supporting or opposing the tentative decision.

PR 25-4B Differential analysis for further processing

OBJ. 1

✔ 1. Ingot income, $35,500

The management of International Aluminum Co. is considering whether to process aluminum ingot further into rolled aluminum. Rolled aluminum can be sold for $2,200 per ton, and ingot can be sold without further processing for $1,100 per ton. Ingot is produced in batches of 80 tons by smelting 500 tons of bauxite, which costs $105 per ton of bauxite. Rolled aluminum will require additional processing costs of $620 per ton of ingot, and 1.25 tons of ingot will produce 1 ton of rolled aluminum (due to trim losses).

Instructions

1. Prepare a differential analysis as of February 5 to determine whether to sell aluminum ingot (Alternative 1) or process further into rolled aluminum (Alternative 2).
2. Briefly report your recommendations.

PR 25-5B Product pricing using the cost-plus approach concepts; differential analysis for accepting additional business

OBJ. 1, 2

✔ 2. b. Markup percentage, 30%

Night Glow Inc. recently began production of a new product, the halogen light, which required the investment of $600,000 in assets. The costs of producing and selling 10,000 halogen lights are estimated as follows:

Variable costs per unit:		Fixed costs:	
Direct materials	$32	Factory overhead	$180,000
Direct labor	12	Selling and administrative expenses	80,000
Factory overhead	8		
Selling and administrative expenses	7		
Total	$59		

Night Glow Inc. is currently considering establishing a selling price for the halogen light. The president of Night Glow Inc. has decided to use the cost-plus approach to product pricing and has indicated that the halogen light must earn a 10% rate of return on invested assets.

Instructions

1. Determine the amount of desired profit from the production and sale of the halogen light.
2. Assuming that the product cost concept is used, determine (a) the cost amount per unit, (b) the markup percentage, and (c) the selling price of the halogen light.
3. (*Appendix*) Assuming that the total cost concept is used, determine (a) the cost amount per unit, (b) the markup percentage (rounded to two decimal places), and (c) the selling price of the halogen light (rounded to the nearest whole dollar).
4. (*Appendix*) Assuming that the variable cost concept is used, determine (a) the cost amount per unit, (b) the markup percentage (rounded to two decimal places), and (c) the selling price of the halogen light (rounded to nearest whole dollar).
5. Comment on any additional considerations that could influence establishing the selling price for the halogen light.
6. Assume that as of September 1, 7,000 units of halogen light have been produced and sold during the current year. Analysis of the domestic market indicates that 3,000 additional units of the halogen light are expected to be sold during the remainder of the year at the normal product price determined under the product cost concept. On September 5, Night Glow Inc. received an offer from Tokyo Lighting Inc. for 1,600 units of the halogen light at $57 each. Tokyo Lighting Inc. will market the units in Japan under its own brand name, and no variable selling and administrative expenses associated with the sale will be incurred by Night Glow Inc. The additional business is not expected to affect the domestic sales of the halogen light, and the additional units could be produced using existing productive, selling, and administrative capacity.
   a. Prepare a differential analysis of the proposed sale to Tokyo Lighting Inc.
   b. Based on the differential analysis in part (a), should the proposal be accepted?

PR 25-6B Product pricing and profit analysis with bottleneck operations

OBJ. 3

✔ 1. Ethylene, $15

Excel

Wilmington Chemical Company produces three products: ethylene, butane, and ester. Each of these products has high demand in the market, and Wilmington Chemical is able to sell as much as it can produce of all three. The reaction operation is a bottleneck in the process and is running at 100% of capacity. Wilmington wants to improve chemical operation profitability. The variable conversion cost is $10 per process hour. The fixed cost is $400,000. In addition, the cost analyst was able to determine the following information about the three products:

	Ethylene	Butane	Ester
Budgeted units produced	9,000	9,000	9,000
Total process hours per unit	4.0	4.0	3.0
Reactor hours per unit	1.5	1.0	0.5
Unit selling price	$170	$155	$130
Direct materials cost per unit	$115	$88	$85

The reaction operation is part of the total process for each of these three products. Thus, for example, 1.5 of the 4.0 hours required to process ethylene is associated with the reactor.

Instructions

1. Determine the unit contribution margin for each product.
2. Provide an analysis to determine the relative product profitabilities, assuming that the reactor is a bottleneck.

PR 25-7B Activity-based costing

OBJ. 4

✔ 2. Newsprint total activity cost, $139,650

Excel

Southeastern Paper Company manufactures three products (computer paper, newsprint, and specialty paper) in a continuous production process. Senior management has asked the controller to conduct an activity-based costing study. The controller identified the amount of factory overhead required by the critical activities of the organization as follows:

Activity	Activity Costs
Production	$220,000
Setup	117,000
Moving	21,000
Shipping	105,000
Product engineering	102,000
Total	$565,000

The activity bases identified for each activity are as follows:

Activity	Activity Base
Production	Machine hours
Setup	Number of setups
Moving	Number of moves
Shipping	Number of customer orders
Product engineering	Number of test runs

The activity-base usage quantities and units produced for the three products were determined from corporate records and are as follows:

	Machine Hours	Number of Setups	Number of Moves	Number of Customer Orders	Number of Test Runs	Units
Computer paper	400	80	230	310	50	1,000
Newsprint	500	30	70	140	15	1,250
Specialty paper	200	150	300	550	105	500
Total	1,100	260	600	1,000	170	2,750

Each product requires 0.4 machine hour per unit.

Instructions

1. Determine the activity rate for each activity.
2. Determine the total and per-unit activity cost for all three products.
3. Why aren't the activity unit costs equal across all three products, since they require the same machine time per unit?

Cases & Projects

Ethics

CP 25-1 Ethics in Action

Aaron McKinney is a cost accountant for Majik Systems Inc. Martin Dodd, vice president of marketing, has asked Aaron to meet with representatives of Majik Systems' major competitor to discuss product cost data. Martin indicates that the sharing of these data will enable Majik Systems to determine a fair and equitable price for its products.

Would it be ethical for Aaron to attend the meeting and share the relevant cost data? Why or why not?

Team Activity

Real World

CP 25-2 Team Activity

Many businesses are offering their products and services over the Internet. Some of these companies and their Internet addresses follow:

Company Name	Internet Address (URL)	Product
Delta Air Lines	www.delta.com	Airline tickets
Amazon.com	www.amazon.com	Merchandise
Dell Inc.	www.dell.com	Personal computers

In groups of three, assign each person in your group to one of the Internet sites listed. For each site, determine the following:

1. A product (or service) description
2. A product price
3. Based on your responses to parts (1) and (2), along with the description of the company's business, identify the potential costs that are required to provide the product selected in part (1) and categorize them as fixed or variable.
4. Which product do you believe has the largest contribution margin per incremental unit sold?

Communication

CP 25-3 Communication

The following conversation took place between Juanita Jackson, vice president of marketing, and Les Miles, controller of Diamond Computer Company:

Juanita: I am really excited about our new computer coming out. I think it will be a real market success.

Les: I'm really glad you think so. I know that our success will be determined by our price. If our price is too high, our competitors will be the ones with the market success.

Juanita: Don't worry about it. We'll just mark our product cost up by 25%, and it will all work out. I know we'll make money at those markups. By the way, what does the estimated product cost look like?

Les: Well, there's the rub. The product cost looks as if it's going to come in at around $1,200. With a 25% markup, that will give us a selling price of $1,500.

Juanita: I see your concern. That's a little high. Our research indicates that computer prices are dropping and that this type of computer should be selling for around $1,250 when we release it to the market.

Les: I'm not sure what to do.

Juanita: Let me see if I can help. How much of the $1,200 is fixed cost?

Les: About $200.

Juanita: There you go. The fixed cost is sunk. We don't need to consider it in our pricing decision. If we reduce the product cost by $200, the new price with a 25% markup would be right at $1,250. Boy, I was really worried for a minute there. I knew something wasn't right.

Write a brief memo from Les Miles to Juanita Jackson (1) responding to her solution to the pricing problem and (2) explaining how target costing could be used to solve the problem.

CP 25-4 Decision on accepting additional business

A manager of Varden Sporting Goods Company is considering accepting an order from an overseas customer. This customer has requested an order for 20,000 dozen golf balls at a price of $22 per dozen. The variable cost to manufacture a dozen golf balls is $18 per dozen. The full cost is $25 per dozen. Varden has a normal selling price of $35 per dozen. Varden's plant has just enough excess capacity on the second shift to make the overseas order.

What are some considerations in accepting or rejecting this order?

CP 25-5 Accept business at a special price for a service company

Real World

If you are not familiar with Priceline.com Inc., go to its website. Assume that an individual "names a price" of $85 on Priceline.com for a room in Nashville, Tennessee, on August 22. Assume that August 22 is a Saturday, with low expected room demand in Nashville at a Marriott International, Inc., hotel, so there is excess room capacity. The fully allocated cost per room per day is assumed from hotel records as follows:

Housekeeping labor cost*	$ 38
Hotel depreciation expense	43
Cost of room supplies (soap, paper, etc.)	8
Laundry labor and material cost*	10
Cost of desk staff	6
Utility cost (mostly air conditioning)	5
Total cost per room per day	$110

*Both housekeeping and laundry staff include many part-time workers so that the workload is variable to demand.

Should Marriott accept the customer bid for a night in Nashville on August 22 at a price of $85? Why or why not?

CP 25-6 Identifying product cost distortion

Peachtree Beverage Company manufactures soft drinks. Information about two products is as follows:

	Volume	Sales Price per Case	Gross Profit per Case
Jamaican Punch	10,000 cases	$30	$12
King Kola	800,000 cases	30	12

It is known that both products have the same direct materials and direct labor costs per case. Peachtree Beverage allocates factory overhead to products by using a single plant-wide factory overhead rate, based on direct labor cost. Additional information about the two products is as follows:

Jamaican Punch: Requires extensive process preparation and sterilization prior to processing. The ingredients are from Jamaica, requiring complex import controls. The formulation is complex, and it is thus difficult to maintain quality. Finally, the product is produced in small production run sizes.

King Kola: Requires minor process preparation and sterilization prior to processing. The ingredients are acquired locally. The formulation is simple, and it is easy to maintain quality. Finally, the product is produced in large production run sizes.

Explain the weakness in the per-case product profitability report in light of the additional data.

CHAPTER

26

Capital Investment Analysis

Concepts and Principles

Chapter 18 *Introduction to Managerial Accounting*

Developing Information

COST SYSTEMS

Chapter 19 *Job Order Costing*
Chapter 20 *Process Costing*

COST BEHAVIOR

Chapter 21 *Cost-Volume-Profit Analysis*

Decision Making

EVALUATING PERFORMANCE

Chapter 22 *Budgeting*
Chapter 23 *Variances from Standard Costs*

COMPARING ALTERNATIVES

Chapter 24 *Decentralized Operations*
Chapter 25 *Differential Analysis, Product Pricing, and Activity-Based Costing*
Chapter 26 ***Capital Investment Analysis***

J STOCK/STOCKSHOT/ALAMY STOCK PHOTO

CHAPTER 26

Vail Resorts, Inc.

Why are you paying tuition, studying this text, and spending time and money on a higher education? Most people believe that the money and time spent now will return them more earnings in the future. That is, the cost of higher education is an investment in your future earning ability. How would you know if this investment is worth it?

One method would be for you to compare the cost of a higher education with the estimated increase in your future earning power. The bigger the difference between your expected future earnings and the cost of your education, the better the investment. A business also evaluates its investments in fixed assets by comparing the initial cost of the investment to its future earnings and cash flows.

For example, **Vail Resorts, Inc.**, is one of the largest ski resort owner-operators in the world. It is known for its Vail, Breckenridge, and Keystone ski resorts, among others. A ski resort requires significant investments in property and equipment. Thus, Vail routinely makes major investments in new or improved amenities, lodging, retail, lifts, snowmaking and grooming equipment, and technology infrastructure. These investments are evaluated by their ability to enhance cash flows.

In this chapter, the methods used to make investment decisions, which may involve thousands, millions, or even billions of dollars, are described and illustrated. The similarities and differences among the most commonly used methods of evaluating investment proposals, as well as the benefits of each method, are emphasized. Factors that can complicate the analysis are also discussed.

Learning Objectives

After studying this chapter, you should be able to:

Example Exercises (EE) are shown in **green.**

At a Glance 26 Page 1292

Obj. 1 Explain the nature and importance of capital investment analysis.

Nature of Capital Investment Analysis

Companies use capital investment analysis to evaluate long-term investments. **Capital investment analysis** (or *capital budgeting*) is the process by which management plans, evaluates, and controls investments in fixed assets. Capital investments use funds and affect operations for many years and must earn a reasonable rate of return. Thus, capital investment decisions are some of the most important decisions that management makes.

Capital investment evaluation methods can be grouped into the following categories:

Methods That Do Not Use Present Values

- Average rate of return method
- Cash payback method

Methods That Use Present Values

- Net present value method
- Internal rate of return method

The two methods that use present values consider the time value of money. The **time value of money concept** recognizes that a dollar today is worth more than a dollar tomorrow because today's dollar can earn interest.

Link to Vail Resorts, Inc.

In 2014, **Vail Resorts, Inc.**, purchased the Park City Mountain Resort and ski area in Park City, Utah, for $182.5 million.

Business Connection

BUSINESS USE OF INVESTMENT ANALYSIS METHODS

A survey of chief financial officers of large U.S. companies reported their use of the four investment methods as follows:

Percentage of Respondents Reporting the Use of the Method as "Always" or "Often"

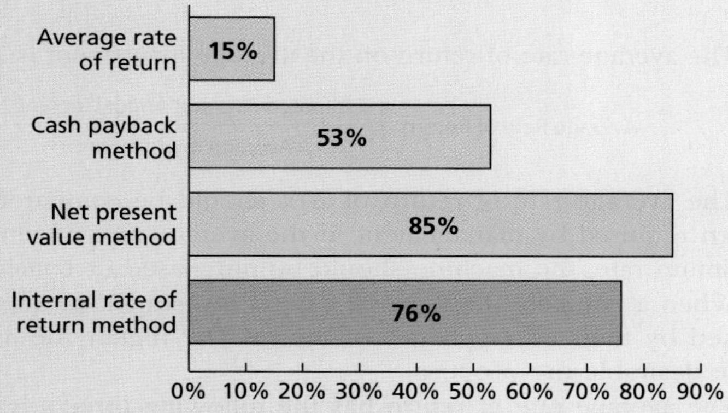

Source: Patricia A. Ryan and Glenn P. Ryan, "Capital Budgeting Practice of the Fortune 1000: How Have Things Changed?" *Journal of Business and Management* (Winter 2002).

Methods Not Using Present Values

Obj. 2 Evaluate capital investment proposals, using the average rate of return and cash payback methods.

The methods not using present values are often useful in evaluating capital investment proposals that have relatively short useful lives. In such cases, the timing of the cash flows (the time value of money) is less important.

Because the methods not using present values are easy to use, they are often used to screen proposals. Minimum standards for accepting proposals are set, and proposals not meeting these standards are dropped. If a proposal meets the minimum standards, it may be subject to further analysis using the present value methods.

Average Rate of Return Method

The **average rate of return**, sometimes called the *accounting rate of return*, measures the average income as a percent of the average investment. The average rate of return is computed as follows:

$$\text{Average Rate of Return} = \frac{\text{Estimated Average Annual Income}}{\text{Average Investment}}$$

In the preceding equation, the numerator is the average of the annual income expected to be earned from the investment over its life, after deducting depreciation. The denominator is the average investment (book value) over the life of the investment. Assuming straight-line depreciation, the average investment is computed as follows:

$$\text{Average Investment} = \frac{\text{Initial Cost} + \text{Residual Value}}{2}$$

To illustrate, assume that management is evaluating the purchase of a new machine as follows:

Cost of new machine	$500,000
Residual value	$0
Estimated total income from machine	$200,000
Expected useful life	4 years

The average estimated annual income from the machine is $50,000 ($200,000 ÷ 4 years). The average investment is $250,000, computed as follows:

$$\text{Average Investment} = \frac{\text{Initial Cost} + \text{Residual Value}}{2} = \frac{\$500{,}000 + \$0}{2} = \$250{,}000$$

The average rate of return on the average investment is 20%, computed as follows:

$$\text{Average Rate of Return} = \frac{\text{Estimated Average Annual Income}}{\text{Average Investment}} = \frac{\$50{,}000}{\$250{,}000} = 20\%$$

The average rate of return of 20% should be compared to the minimum rate of return required by management. If the average rate of return equals or exceeds the minimum rate, the machine should be purchased or considered for further analysis.

When a company has several capital investment proposals, the proposals can be ranked by their average rates of return. The higher the average rate of return, the more desirable the proposal.

Note

The average rate of return method considers the amount of income earned over the life of a proposal.

The average rate of return has the following three advantages:

- It is easy to compute.
- It includes the entire amount of income earned over the life of the proposal.
- It emphasizes accounting income, which is often used by investors and creditors in evaluating management performance.

The average rate of return has the following two disadvantages:

- It does not directly consider the expected cash flows from the proposal.
- It does not directly consider the timing of the expected cash flows.

Example Exercise 26-1 Average Rate of Return **Obj. 2**

Determine the average rate of return for a project that is estimated to yield total income of $273,600 over three years, has a cost of $690,000, and has a $70,000 residual value.

Follow My Example 26-1

Estimated average annual income	$91,200 ($273,600 ÷ 3 years)
Average investment	$380,000 ($690,000 + $70,000) ÷ 2
Average rate of return	24% ($91,200 ÷ $380,000)

Practice Exercises: PE 26-1A, PE 26-1B

Link to Vail Resorts, Inc.

Vail Resorts' average rate of return on its property, plant, and equipment is slightly more than 10%.

Cash Payback Method

A capital investment uses cash and must return cash in the future to be successful. The expected period of time between the date of an investment and the recovery in cash of the amount invested is the **cash payback period**.

When annual net cash inflows are equal, the cash payback period is computed as follows:

$$\text{Cash Payback Period} = \frac{\text{Initial Cost}}{\text{Annual Net Cash Inflow}}$$

To illustrate, assume that management is evaluating the purchase of the following new machine:

Cost of new machine	$200,000
Cash revenues from machine per year	50,000
Expenses of machine per year (incl. depreciation)	30,000
Depreciation per year	20,000

To simplify, the revenues and expenses other than depreciation are assumed to be in cash. Hence, the expected net cash inflow per year from use of the machine is as follows:

Net cash inflow per year:		
Cash revenues from machine		$50,000
Less cash expenses of machine:		
Expenses of machine (incl. depreciation)	$30,000	
Less depreciation	20,000	10,000
Net cash inflow per year		$40,000

The time required for the net cash flow to equal the cost of the new machine is the payback period. Thus, the estimated cash payback period for the investment is five years, computed as follows:

$$\text{Cash Payback Period} = \frac{\text{Initial Cost}}{\text{Annual Net Cash Inflow}} = \frac{\$200{,}000}{\$40{,}000} = 5 \text{ years}$$

In the preceding illustration, the annual net cash inflows are equal ($40,000 per year). When the annual net cash inflows are not equal, the cash payback period is determined by adding the annual net cash inflows until the cumulative total equals the initial cost of the proposed investment.

To illustrate, assume that a proposed investment has an initial cost of $400,000. The annual and cumulative net cash inflows over the proposal's six-year life are as follows:

Year	Net Cash Flow	Cumulative Net Cash Flow
1	$ 60,000	$ 60,000
2	80,000	140,000
3	105,000	245,000
4	155,000	400,000
5	100,000	500,000
6	90,000	590,000

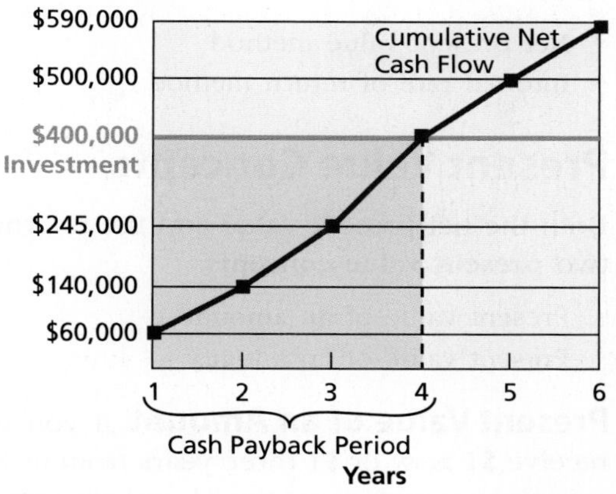

The cumulative net cash flow at the end of Year 4 equals the initial cost of the investment, $400,000. Thus, the payback period is four years.

If the initial cost of the proposed investment had been $450,000, the cash payback period would occur during Year 5. Because $100,000 of net cash flow is expected during Year 5, the additional $50,000 to increase the cumulative total to $450,000 occurs halfway through the year ($50,000 ÷ $100,000). Thus, the cash payback period would be 4½ years.[1]

A short cash payback period is desirable. This is because the sooner cash is recovered, the sooner it can be reinvested in other projects. In addition, there is less chance of losses from changing economic or business conditions. A short cash payback period is also desirable for quickly repaying any debt used to purchase the investment.

Link to Vail Resorts, Inc.

The ski operations are seasonal in nature and typically run from mid-November to mid-April. To increase cash flows, **Vail Resorts** promotes nonski activities in the summer months, including sightseeing, mountain biking, and zip tours.

1 Unless otherwise stated, net cash inflows are received uniformly throughout the year.

The cash payback method has the following two advantages:

- It is simple to use and understand.
- It analyzes cash flows, which provides insight into how long it takes to return cash equal to the original investment.

The cash payback method has the following two disadvantages:

- It ignores cash flows occurring after the payback period.
- It does not use present value concepts in valuing cash flows occurring in different periods.

Example Exercise 26-2 Cash Payback Period — Obj. 2

A project has estimated annual net cash flows of $30,000. It is estimated to cost $105,000. Determine the cash payback period.

Follow My Example 26-2

3.5 years ($105,000 ÷ $30,000)

Practice Exercises: PE 26-2A, PE 26-2B

Obj. 3 Evaluate capital investment proposals, using the net present value and internal rate of return methods.

Methods Using Present Values

An investment in fixed assets may be viewed as purchasing a series of net cash flows over a period of time. The timing of when the net cash flows will be received is important in determining the value of a proposed investment.

Present value methods use the amount and timing of the net cash flows in evaluating an investment. The two methods of evaluating capital investments using present values are as follows:

- Net present value method
- Internal rate of return method

Present Value Concepts

Both the net present value and the internal rate of return methods use the following two **present value concepts**:

- Present value of an amount
- Present value of an annuity

Present Value of an Amount If you were given the choice, would you prefer to receive $1 now or $1 three years from now? You should prefer to receive $1 now, because you could invest the $1 and earn interest for three years. As a result, the amount you would have after three years would be greater than $1.

To illustrate, assume that you have $1 to invest as follows:

Amount to be invested	$1
Period to be invested	3 years
Interest rate	12%

After one year, the $1 earns interest of $0.12 ($1 × 12%) and, thus, will grow to $1.12 ($1 × 1.12). In the second year, the $1.12 earns 12% interest of $0.134 ($1.12 × 12%) and, thus, will grow to $1.254 ($1.12 × 1.12) by the end of the second year. This process of interest earning interest is called *compounding*. By the end of the third year, your $1 investment will grow to $1.404 as shown in Exhibit 1.

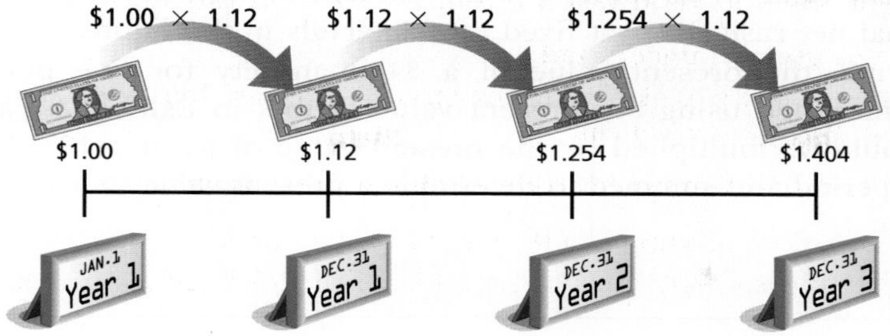

EXHIBIT 1

Compound Amount of $1 for Three Periods at 12%

On January 1, Year 1, what is the present value of $1.404 to be received on December 31, Year 3? This is a present value question. The answer can be determined with the aid of a present value of $1 table. For example, the partial table in Exhibit 2 indicates that the present value of $1 to be received in three years with earnings compounded at the rate of 12% per year is 0.712.[2]

EXHIBIT 2

Partial Present Value of $1 Table

Present Value of $1 at Compound Interest

Year	6%	10%	12%	15%	20%
1	0.943	0.909	0.893	0.870	0.833
2	0.890	0.826	0.797	0.756	0.694
3	0.840	0.751	0.712	0.658	0.579
4	0.792	0.683	0.636	0.572	0.482
5	0.747	0.621	0.567	0.497	0.402
6	0.705	0.564	0.507	0.432	0.335
7	0.665	0.513	0.452	0.376	0.279
8	0.627	0.467	0.404	0.327	0.233
9	0.592	0.424	0.361	0.284	0.194
10	0.558	0.386	0.322	0.247	0.162

Multiplying 0.712 by $1.404 yields $1 as follows:

Present Value		Amount to Be Received in 3 Years		Present Value of $1 to Be Received in 3 Years (from Exhibit 2)
$1	=	$1.404	×	0.712

That is, the present value of $1.404 to be received in three years using a compound interest rate of 12% is $1, as shown in Exhibit 3.

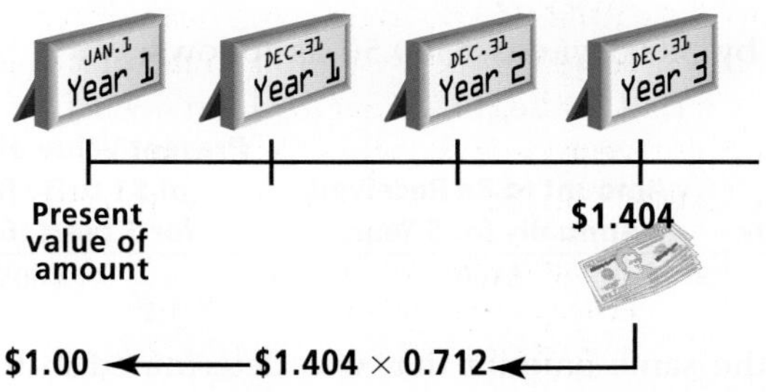

EXHIBIT 3

Present Value of an Amount of $1.404

Present Value of an Annuity An **annuity** is a series of equal net cash flows at fixed time intervals. Annuities are very common in business. Cash payments for monthly rent, salaries, and bond interest are all examples of annuities.

2 The present value factors in the table are rounded to three decimal places. More complete tables of present values are in Appendix A.

The **present value of an annuity** is the amount of cash needed today to yield a series of equal net cash flows at fixed time intervals in the future.

To illustrate, the present value of a $100 annuity for five periods at 12% could be determined using the present value factors in Exhibit 2. Each $100 net cash flow could be multiplied by the present value of $1 at a 12% factor for the appropriate period and summed to determine a present value of $360.50, as shown in Exhibit 4.

EXHIBIT 4

Present Value of a $100 Amount for Five Consecutive Periods

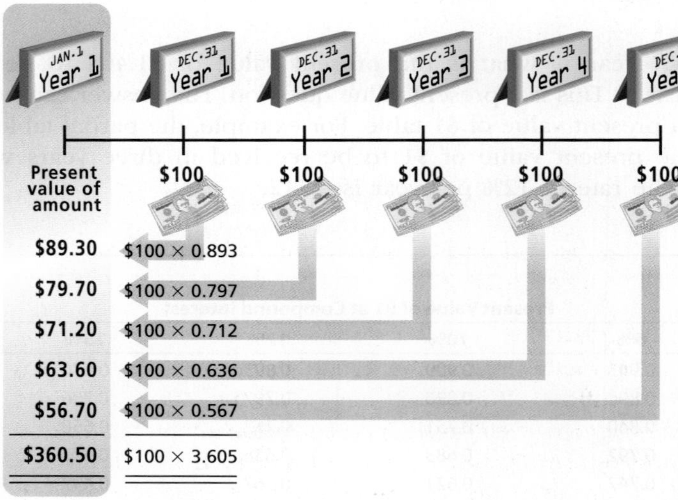

Using a present value of an annuity table is a simpler approach. Exhibit 5 is a partial table of present value annuity factors.[3]

The present value factors in the table shown in Exhibit 5 are the sum of the present value of $1 factors in Exhibit 2 for the number of annuity periods. Thus, 3.605 in the annuity table (Exhibit 5) is the sum of the five present value of $1 factors at 12% from Exhibit 2, computed as follows:

	Present Value of $1 (Exhibit 2)
Present value of $1 for 1 year @12%	0.893
Present value of $1 for 2 years @12%	0.797
Present value of $1 for 3 years @12%	0.712
Present value of $1 for 4 years @12%	0.636
Present value of $1 for 5 years @12%	0.567
Present value of an annuity of $1 for 5 years (from Exhibit 5)	3.605

Multiplying $100 by 3.605 yields $360.50 as follows:

Present Value		**Amount to Be Received Annually for 5 Years**		**Present Value of an Annuity of $1 to Be Received for 5 Years (Exhibit 5)**
$360.50	=	$100	×	3.605

Thus, $360.50 is the same amount that was determined in the preceding illustration by five successive multiplications.

3 The present value factors in the table are rounded to three decimal places. More complete tables of present values are in Appendix A.

EXHIBIT 5

Partial Present Value of an Annuity Table

Present Value of an Annuity of $1 at Compound Interest

Year	6%	10%	12%	15%	20%
1	0.943	0.909	0.893	0.870	0.833
2	1.833	1.736	1.690	1.626	1.528
3	2.673	2.487	2.402	2.283	2.106
4	3.465	3.170	3.037	2.855	2.589
5	4.212	3.791	3.605	3.353	2.991
6	4.917	4.355	4.111	3.785	3.326
7	5.582	4.868	4.564	4.160	3.605
8	6.210	5.335	4.968	4.487	3.837
9	6.802	5.759	5.328	4.772	4.031
10	7.360	6.145	5.650	5.019	4.192

Net Present Value Method and Index

The net present value method and present value index are often used in combination, as illustrated in this section.

Net Present Value Method

The **net present value method** compares the amount to be invested with the present value of the net cash inflows. It is sometimes called the *discounted cash flow method.*

The interest rate (return) used in net present value analysis is the company's minimum desired rate of return. This rate, sometimes termed the *hurdle rate*, is based on such factors as the purpose of the investment and the cost of obtaining funds for the investment. If the present value of the cash inflows equals or exceeds the amount to be invested, the proposal is desirable.

To illustrate, assume the following data for a proposed investment in new equipment:

Note

The net present value method compares an investment's initial cash outflow with the present value of its cash inflows.

Cost of new equipment	$200,000
Expected useful life	5 years
Minimum desired rate of return	10%
Expected cash flows to be received each year:	
Year 1	$ 70,000
Year 2	60,000
Year 3	50,000
Year 4	40,000
Year 5	40,000
Total expected cash flows	$260,000

The present value of the net cash flow for each year is computed by multiplying the net cash flow for the year by the present value factor of $1 for that year, as follows:

Year	Present Value of $1 at 10%	×	Net Cash Flow	=	Present Value of Net Cash Flow
1	0.909		$ 70,000		$ 63,630
2	0.826		60,000		49,560
3	0.751		50,000		37,550
4	0.683		40,000		27,320
5	0.621		40,000		24,840
Total			$260,000		$202,900
Less amount to be invested					200,000
Net present value					$ 2,900

The preceding computations are also graphically illustrated in Exhibit 6.

EXHIBIT 6

Present Value of Equipment Cash Flows

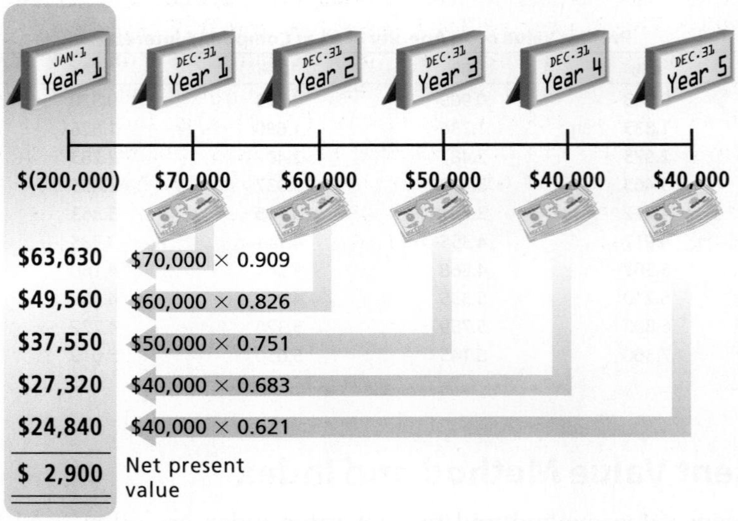

The net present value of $2,900 indicates that the purchase of the new equipment is expected to recover the investment and provide more than the minimum rate of return of 10%. Thus, the purchase of the new equipment is desirable.

The net present value method has the following three advantages:

- It considers the cash flows of the investment.
- It considers the time value of money.
- It can rank projects with equal lives using the present value index, as shown in the next section.

The net present value method has the following two disadvantages:

- It has more complex computations than methods that don't use present value.
- It assumes that the cash flows can be reinvested at the minimum desired rate of return, which may not be valid.

Present Value Index

When capital investment funds are limited and the proposals involve different investments, a ranking of the proposals can be prepared using a present value index. The **present value index** is computed as follows:

$$\text{Present Value Index} = \frac{\text{Total Present Value of Net Cash Flow}}{\text{Amount to Be Invested}}$$

Link to Vail Resorts, Inc.

Vail Resorts uses present values in determining the value of assets and liabilities acquired in business acquisitions.

Source: Vail Resorts, Inc., *Form 10-K for the Fiscal Year Ended July 31, 2015.*

The present value index for the investment in the preceding illustration is 1.0145, computed as follows:

$$\text{Present Value Index} = \frac{\$202{,}900}{\$200{,}000} = 1.0145$$

Assume that a company is considering three proposals. The net present value and the present value index for each proposal are as follows:

	Proposal A	Proposal B	Proposal C
Total present value of net cash flow	$107,000	$86,400	$86,400
Less amount to be invested	100,000	80,000	90,000
Net present value	$ 7,000	$ 6,400	$ (3,600)
Present value index:			
Proposal A ($107,000 ÷ $100,000)	1.07		
Proposal B ($86,400 ÷ $80,000)		1.08	
Proposal C ($86,400 ÷ $90,000)			0.96

A project will have a present value index greater than 1 when the net present value is positive. This is the case for Proposals A and B. When the net present value is negative, the present value index will be less than 1, as is the case for Proposal C.

Although Proposal A has the largest net present value, the present value indices indicate that it is not as desirable as Proposal B. That is, Proposal B returns $1.08 present value per dollar invested, whereas Proposal A returns only $1.07. Proposal B requires an investment of $80,000, compared to an investment of $100,000 for Proposal A. The possible use of the $20,000 difference between Proposals A and B investments should also be considered before making a final decision.

Example Exercise 26-3 Net Present Value **Obj. 3**

A project has estimated annual net cash flows of $50,000 for seven years and is estimated to cost $240,000. Assume a minimum acceptable rate of return of 12%. Using Exhibit 5, determine (a) the net present value of the project and (b) the present value index, rounded to two decimal places.

Follow My Example 26-3

a. ($11,800) [($50,000 × 4.564) – $240,000]

b. 0.95 ($228,200 ÷ $240,000)

Practice Exercises: PE 26-3A, PE 26-3B

Internal Rate of Return Method

The **internal rate of return (IRR) method** determines the rate of return wherein the net present value of a project is zero. This method, sometimes called the *time-adjusted rate of return method*, starts with the proposal's net cash flows and works backward to estimate the proposal's expected rate of return.

To illustrate, assume that management is evaluating the following proposal to purchase new equipment:

Cost of new equipment	$33,530
Yearly expected cash flows to be received	$10,000
Expected life	5 years
Minimum desired rate of return	12%

The present value of the net cash flows, using the present value of an annuity table in Exhibit 5, is $2,520, as shown in Exhibit 7.

Annual net cash flow (at the end of each of five years)	$10,000
Present value of an annuity of $1 at 12% for five years (Exhibit 5)	× 3.605
Present value of annual net cash flows	$36,050
Less amount to be invested	33,530
Net present value	$ 2,520

EXHIBIT 7

Net Present Value Analysis at 12%

Dynamic Exhibit

In Exhibit 7, the $36,050 present value of the cash inflows, based on a 12% rate of return, is greater than the $33,530 to be invested. Thus, the internal rate of return must be greater than 12%. Through trial and error, the rate of return equating the $33,530 cost of the investment with the present value of the net cash flows can be determined to be 15%, as shown in Exhibit 8.

EXHIBIT 8

Present Value of an Annuity at the Internal Rate of Return

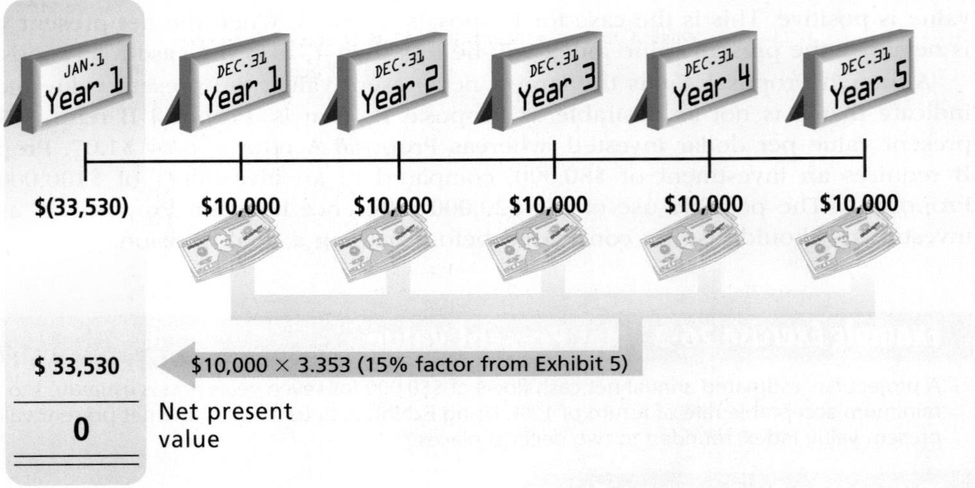

When equal annual net cash flows are expected from a proposal, as in the preceding example, the internal rate of return can be determined as follows:[4]

Step 1. Determine a present value factor for an annuity of $1 as follows:

$$\text{Present Value Factor for an Annuity of \$1} = \frac{\text{Amount to Be Invested}}{\text{Equal Annual Net Cash Flows}}$$

Step 2. Locate the present value factor determined in Step 1 in the present value of an annuity of $1 table (Exhibit 5) as follows:

a. Locate the number of years of expected useful life of the investment in the Year column.

b. Proceed horizontally across the table until you find the present value factor computed in Step 1.

Step 3. Identify the internal rate of return by the heading of the column in which the present value factor in Step 2 is located.

To illustrate, assume that management is evaluating the following proposal to purchase new equipment:

Cost of new equipment	$97,360
Yearly expected cash flows to be received	$20,000
Expected useful life	7 years

The present value factor for an annuity of $1 is 4.868, computed as follows:

$$\text{Present Value Factor for an Annuity of \$1} = \frac{\text{Amount to Be Invested}}{\text{Equal Annual Net Cash Flows}}$$

$$= \frac{\$97,360}{\$20,000} = 4.868$$

Using the partial present value of an annuity of $1 table shown in Exhibit 9 and a period of seven years, the factor 4.868 is related to 10%. Thus, the internal rate of return for this proposal is 10%.

4 To simplify, equal annual net cash flows are assumed. If the net cash flows are not equal, spreadsheet software can be used to determine the rate of return.

EXHIBIT 9

Steps to Determine the Internal Rate of Return

Present Value of an Annuity of $1 at Compound Interest

	Year	6%		Step 3 10%	12%
	1	0.943		0.909	0.893
	2	1.833		1.736	1.690
	3	2.673		2.487	2.402
	4	3.465		3.170	3.037
	5	4.212		3.791	3.605
	6	4.917	**Step 2(b)**	4.355	4.111
Step 2(a)	7	5.582	→	4.868	4.564
	8	6.210		5.335	4.968
	9	6.802		5.759	5.328
	10	7.360		6.145	5.650

Step 1: Determine present value factor for an annuity of $1 $= \frac{\$97,360}{\$20,000} = 4.868$

If the minimum acceptable rate of return is 10%, then the proposal is considered acceptable. Several proposals can be ranked by their internal rates of return. The proposal with the highest rate is the most desirable.

The internal rate of return method has the following three advantages:

- It considers the cash flows of the investment.
- It considers the time value of money.
- It ranks proposals based upon the cash flows over their complete useful life, even if the project lives are not the same.

The internal rate of return method has the following two disadvantages:

- It has complex computations, requiring a computer if the periodic cash flows are not equal.
- It assumes that the cash received from a proposal can be reinvested at the internal rate of return, which may not be valid.

Example Exercise 26-4 Internal Rate of Return *Obj. 3*

A project is estimated to cost $208,175 and provide annual net cash flows of $55,000 for six years. Determine the internal rate of return for this project, using Exhibit 5.

Follow My Example 26-4

15% [($208,175 ÷ $55,000) = 3.785, the present value of an annuity factor for six periods at 15%, from Exhibit 5]

Practice Exercises: PE 26-4A, PE 26-4B

Business Connection

PANERA BREAD RATE OF RETURN

Panera Bread owns, operates, and franchises bakery-cafés throughout the United States. A recent annual report to the Securities and Exchange Commission (SEC Form 10-K) allowed the following information to be determined about an average company-owned store:

Operating profit	$ 405,000
Depreciation	115,000
Investment book value	1,500,000

Assume that the operating profit and depreciation will remain unchanged for the next 15 years. Assume that operating profit plus depreciation approximates annual net cash

(Continued)

flows and that the investment residual value will be zero. The average rate of return on a company-owned store is:

$$\frac{\$405{,}000}{\$1{,}500{,}000 \div 2} = 54\%$$

The internal rate of return is calculated by first determining the present value of an annuity of $1:

$$\text{Present Value of an Annuity of \$1} = \frac{\$1{,}500{,}000}{\$405{,}000 + \$115{,}000} = 2.88$$

For a period of five years, this factor implies an internal rate of return of more than 20% (from Exhibit 5). However, if we more realistically assumed these cash flows for 15 years, Panera's company-owned stores generate an estimated internal rate of return of approximately 34% (from a spreadsheet calculation). Clearly, both investment evaluation methods indicate a highly successful business.

Source: Panera Bread, *Form 10-K for the Fiscal Year Ended December 25, 2015.*

Obj. 4 List and describe additional factors in capital investment analysis.

Additional Factors in Capital Investment Analysis

Four widely used methods of evaluating capital investment proposals have been described and illustrated in this chapter. In practice, additional factors such as the following may impact capital investment decisions:

- Income tax
- Proposals with unequal lives
- Lease versus purchase
- Uncertainty
- Changes in price levels
- Qualitative factors
- Capital investment for sustainability

Income Tax

The impact of income taxes on capital investment decisions can be material. For example, in determining depreciation for federal income tax purposes, useful lives that are much shorter than the actual useful lives are often used. Also, depreciation for tax purposes often differs from depreciation for financial statement purposes. As a result, the timing of the cash flows for income taxes can have a significant impact on capital investment analysis.[5]

Unequal Proposal Lives

The prior capital investment illustrations assumed that the alternative proposals had the same useful lives. In practice, however, proposals often have different lives.

To illustrate, assume that a company is considering purchasing a new truck or a new computer network. The data for each proposal follow:

	Truck	Computer Network
Cost	$100,000	$100,000
Minimum desired rate of return	10%	10%
Expected useful life	8 years	5 years
Yearly expected cash flows to be received:		
Year 1	$ 30,000	$ 30,000
Year 2	30,000	30,000
Year 3	25,000	30,000
Year 4	20,000	30,000
Year 5	15,000	35,000
Year 6	15,000	0
Year 7	10,000	0
Year 8	10,000	0
Total	$155,000	$155,000

5 The impact of taxes on capital investment analysis is covered in advanced accounting textbooks.

The expected cash flows and net present value for each proposal are shown in Exhibit 10. Because of the unequal useful lives, however, the net present values in Exhibit 10 are not comparable.

Net Present Value Analysis—Unequal Lives of Proposals EXHIBIT 10

	A	B	C	D
1			Truck	
2		Present	Net	Present
3		Value of	Cash	Value of
4	Year	$1 at 10%	Flow	Net Cash Flow
5	1	0.909	$ 30,000	$ 27,270
6	2	0.826	30,000	24,780
7	3	0.751	25,000	18,775
8	4	0.683	20,000	13,660
9	5	0.621	15,000	9,315
10	6	0.564	15,000	8,460
11	7	0.513	10,000	5,130
12	8	0.467	10,000	4,670
13	Total		$155,000	$112,060
14				
15	Less amount to be invested			100,000
16	Net present value			$ 12,060
17				

	A	B	C	D
1			Computer Network	
2		Present	Net	Present
3		Value of	Cash	Value of
4	Year	$1 at 10%	Flow	Net Cash Flow
5	1	0.909	$ 30,000	$ 27,270
6	2	0.826	30,000	24,780
7	3	0.751	30,000	22,530
8	4	0.683	30,000	20,490
9	5	0.621	35,000	21,735
10	Total		$155,000	$116,805
11				
12	Less amount to be invested			100,000
13	Net present value			$ 16,805
14				

Cannot be compared (unequal lives)

EXHIBIT 11

Net Present Value Analysis—Equalized Lives of Proposals

	A	B	C	D
1			Truck—Revised to 5-Year Life	
2		Present	Net	Present
3		Value of	Cash	Value of
4	Year	$1 at 10%	Flow	Net Cash Flow
5	1	0.909	$ 30,000	$ 27,270
6	2	0.826	30,000	24,780
7	3	0.751	25,000	18,775
8	4	0.683	20,000	13,660
9	5	0.621	15,000	9,315
10	5 (Residual			
11	value)	0.621	40,000	24,840
12	Total		$160,000	$118,640
13				
14	Less amount to be invested			100,000
15	Net present value			$ 18,640
16				

Truck Net Present Value Greater Than Computer Network Net Present Value by $1,835

Compared (equal lives)

To make the proposals comparable, the useful lives are adjusted to end at the same time. In this illustration, this is done by assuming that the truck will be sold at the end of five years. The selling price (residual value) of the truck at the end of five years is estimated and included in the cash inflows. Both proposals will then cover five years; thus, the net present value analyses will be comparable.

To illustrate, assume that the truck's estimated selling price (residual value) at the end of Year 5 is $40,000. Exhibit 11 shows the truck's revised present value analysis assuming a five-year life.

As shown in Exhibit 11, the net present value for the truck exceeds the net present value for the computer network by $1,835 ($18,640 – $16,805). Thus, the truck is the more attractive of the two proposals.

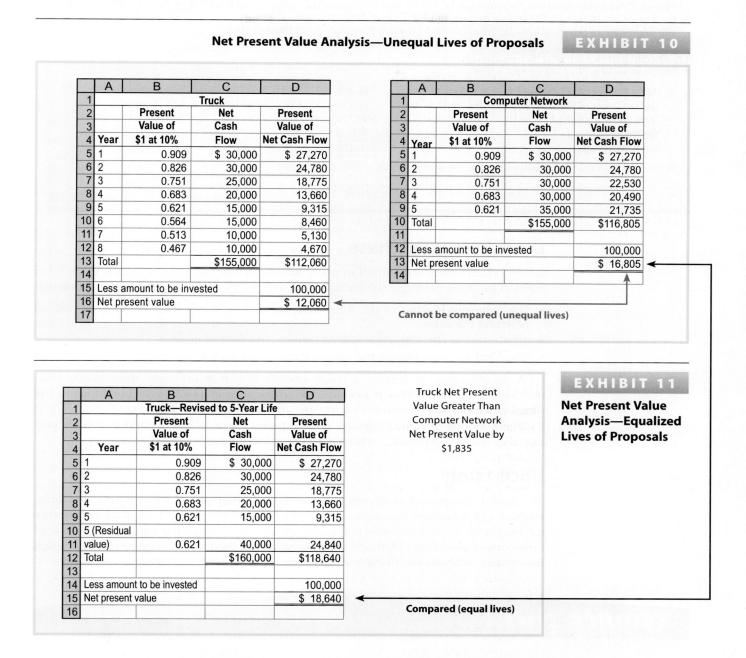

Example Exercise 26-5 Net Present Value—Unequal Lives

Obj. 4

Project 1 requires an original investment of $50,000. The project will yield cash flows of $12,000 per year for seven years. Project 2 has a calculated net present value of $8,900 over a five-year life. Project 1 could be sold at the end of five years for a price of $30,000. (a) Determine the net present value of Project 1 over a five-year life, with residual value, assuming a minimum rate of return of 12%. (b) Which project provides the greatest net present value?

Follow My Example 26-5

a. Present value of $12,000 per year at 12% for 5 years	$43,260	[$12,000 × 3.605 (Exhibit 5, 12%, 5 years)]
Present value of $30,000 at 12% at the end of 5 years	17,010	[$30,000 × 0.567 (Exhibit 2, 12%, 5 years)]
Total present value of Project 1	$60,270	
Total cost of Project 1	50,000	
Net present value of Project 1	$10,270	

b. Project 1—$10,270 is greater than the net present value of Project 2, $8,900.

Practice Exercises: PE 26-5A, PE 26-5B

Lease Versus Purchase

Leasing fixed assets is common in many industries. For example, hospitals often lease medical equipment. Some advantages of leasing a fixed asset include the following:

- The company has use of the fixed asset without spending large amounts of cash to purchase the asset.
- The company eliminates the risk of owning an obsolete asset.
- The company may deduct the annual lease payments for income tax purposes.

A disadvantage of leasing a fixed asset is that it is normally more costly than purchasing the asset. This is because the lessor (owner of the asset) includes in the rental price not only the costs of owning the asset but also a profit.

The methods of evaluating capital investment proposals illustrated in this chapter can also be used to decide whether to lease or purchase a fixed asset.

Uncertainty

All capital investment analyses rely on factors that are uncertain. For example, estimates of revenues, expenses, and cash flows are uncertain. This is especially true for long-term capital investments. Errors in one or more of the estimates could lead to incorrect decisions. Methods that consider the impact of uncertainty on capital investment analysis are discussed in advanced accounting and finance textbooks.

SERVICE FOCUS

IF YOU BUILD IT, THEY WILL COME

A business model describes how an organization delivers products or services to make a profit. Many service companies use what is termed a *network business model*. A network business model connects people and businesses with each other or to a centralized service. Examples of network service businesses include telecommunication, transportation, power and natural gas distribution, cable, satellite, and Internet companies. Network businesses often require significant investment in physical assets in order to create the network. Often, this is described as a *Field of Dreams strategy* (from the movie of that name) because the network can only generate revenue once it is largely built. For example, a cell phone company draws value from having many cell towers linking many callers. A critical mass of cell towers must be pre-built in order to establish the business. This is risky. As a result, network businesses carefully evaluate capital investments prior to building networks.

Changes in Price Levels

Price levels normally change as the economy improves or deteriorates. General price levels often increase in a rapidly growing economy, which is called **inflation**. During such periods, the rate of return on an investment should exceed the rising price level. If this is not the case, the cash returned on the investment will be less than expected.

Price levels may also change for foreign investments. This occurs as currency exchange rates change. **Currency exchange rates** are the rates at which currency in another country can be exchanged for U.S. dollars.

If the amount of local dollars that can be exchanged for one U.S. dollar increases, then the local currency is said to be weakening to the dollar. When a company has an investment in another country where the local currency is weakening, the return on the investment, as expressed in U.S. dollars, is adversely impacted. This is because the expected amount of local currency returned on the investment would purchase fewer U.S. dollars.

Link to Vail Resorts, Inc.

Some of Vail Resorts' rental (lease) agreements include increases for inflation that are linked to the Consumer Price Index (CPI).

Qualitative Considerations

Some benefits of capital investments are qualitative in nature and cannot be estimated in dollar terms. However, if a company does not consider qualitative considerations, an acceptable investment proposal could be rejected.

Some examples of qualitative considerations that may influence capital investment analysis include the investment proposal's impact on the following:

- Product quality
- Manufacturing flexibility
- Employee morale
- Manufacturing productivity
- Market (strategic) opportunities

Many qualitative factors may be as important as, if not more important than, quantitative factors.

Link to Vail Resorts, Inc.

Vail recycles 300 tons of material from the resort mountain each year. An example includes vegetable oil from the mountain restaurants being recycled into biodiesel.

Source: www.vail.com sustainability page

Capital Investment for Sustainability

Chapter 18 defined sustainability as "the practice of operating a business to maximize profits while attempting to preserve the environment, economy, and needs of future generations." Sustainability practices often require capital investments in order to establish these priorities. Some examples are listed in Exhibit 12.

EXHIBIT 12

Examples of Capital Investments in Sustainability

Sustainability Objective	Capital Investment Example
Minimize resource waste and environmental degradation	Invest in land, soil, and water reclamation projects for a mining company.
Develop new sustainable markets	Invest in equipment to produce an environmentally safe cleaning product for a consumer product company.
Reduce litigation risks	Invest in wastewater recycling to avoid river contamination and potential legal liability for a papermaking company.
Maintain an attractive and safe working environment	Invest in an employee wellness and fitness center to attract and retain high-performance employees for a software company.

Often, sustainability investments can be analyzed using methods described in this chapter. An example is manufacturing equipment for the new environmentally safe cleaning product listed in Exhibit 12. In contrast, the benefits of some sustainability investments may be difficult to measure and, thus, must be evaluated qualitatively.

An example is the wellness and fitness center for employees listed in Exhibit 12. In addition, sustainability investments may be legally mandated and, thus, are justified more by the requirements of law than by their immediate economic benefits. Examples are the land, soil, and water reclamation project and wastewater recycling projects listed in Exhibit 12.

To illustrate a capital investment analysis, Carpenter Company proposes to install solar panels to satisfy a portion of the power requirements for its manufacturing plant. The cost of the solar panel investment is $150,000. The solar panel operating and maintenance cost is expected to be $20,000 per year. The plant uses an average of 3,000 kilowatt-hours (kwh) per day for 250 sunny days per year. A kilowatt-hour is the use of 1,000 watts per hour and is a standard measure of electricity consumption. The solar panels replace metered electricity from the power company that costs Carpenter $0.12 per kwh. The solar panels are expected to last 10 years with no salvage value.

The annual cost savings can be computed as follows:

Kilowatt-hours per day	3,000	kwh
× Number of sunny operating days	250	days
Kilowatt-hours per year	750,000	kwh
× Metered electricity cost per kwh	$0.12	per kwh
Total metered cost savings	$ 90,000	
Less annual solar panel maintenance cost	20,000	
Net annual savings	$ 70,000	

The net present value of the project assuming a minimum rate of return of 10% is as follows:

Annual net cash flow savings from installing solar panels	$ 70,000
× Present value of a $1 annuity at 10% for 10 periods (Exhibit 5)	× 6.145
Present value of annual savings	$ 430,150
Less amount to be invested	150,000
Net present value	$ 280,150

The net present value is positive; thus, the solar panel proposal is supported by the analysis.

INTEGRITY, OBJECTIVITY, AND ETHICS IN BUSINESS

ASSUMPTION FUDGING

The results of any capital budgeting analysis depend on many subjective estimates, such as the cash flows, discount rate, time period, and total investment amount. The results of the analysis should be used to either support or reject a project. Capital budgeting should not be used to justify an assumed net present value. That is, the analyst should not work backwards, filling in assumed numbers that will produce the desired net present value. Such a reverse approach reduces the credibility of the entire process.

Obj. 5 Diagram the capital rationing process.

Capital Rationing

Capital rationing is the process by which management allocates funds among competing capital investment proposals. In this process, management often uses a combination of the methods described in this chapter.

Exhibit 13 illustrates the capital rationing decision process. Alternative proposals are initially screened by establishing minimum standards, using the cash payback and the average rate of return methods. The proposals that survive this screening are further analyzed, using the net present value and internal rate of return methods.

Capital Rationing Decision Process EXHIBIT 13

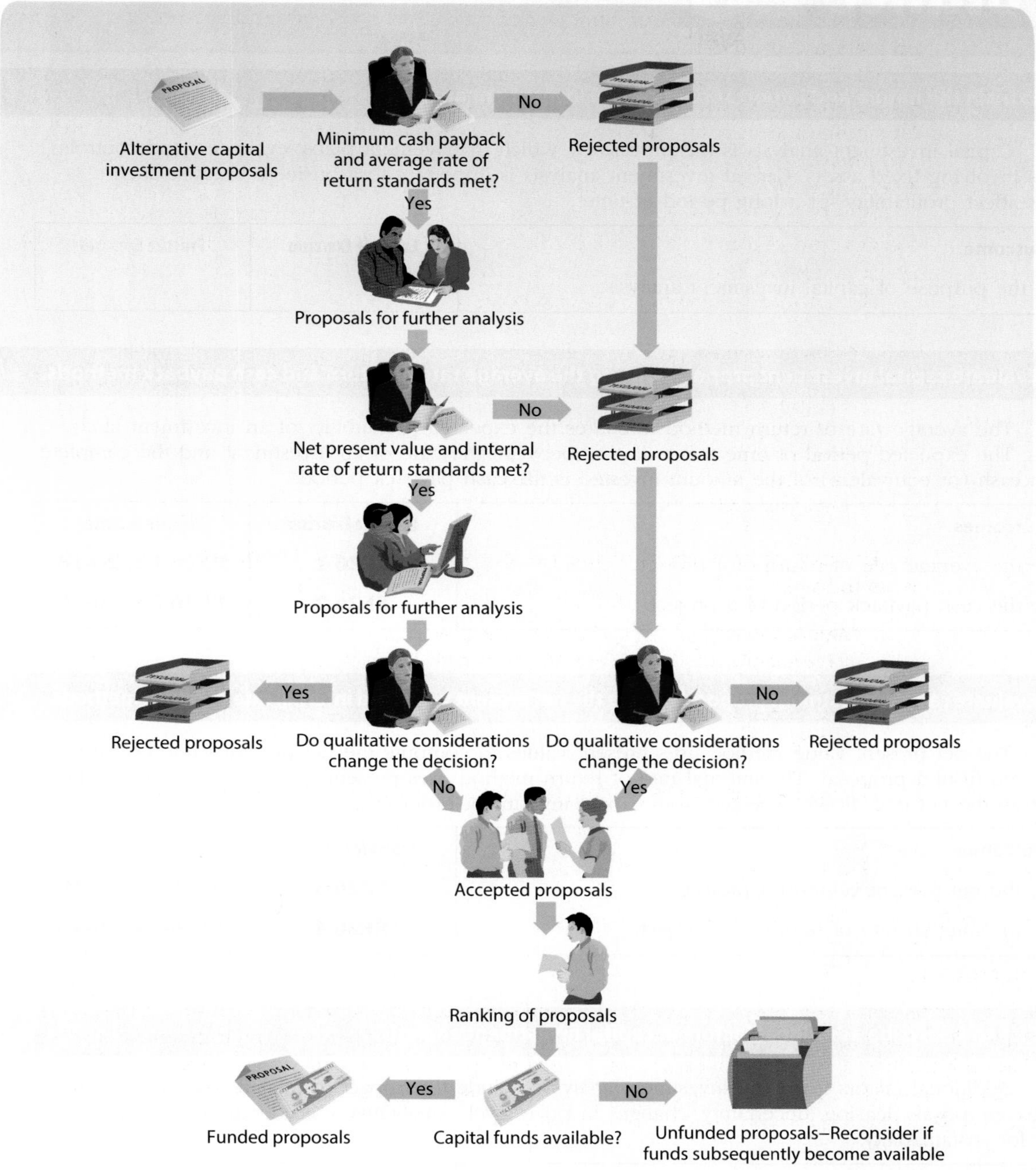

Qualitative factors related to each proposal should also be considered throughout the capital rationing process. For example, new equipment might improve the quality of the product and, thus, increase consumer satisfaction and sales.

At the end of the capital rationing process, accepted proposals are ranked and compared with the funds available. Proposals that are selected for funding are included in the capital expenditures budget. Unfunded proposals may be reconsidered if funds later become available.

At a Glance 26

Obj. 1 Explain the nature and importance of capital investment analysis.

Key Points Capital investment analysis is the process by which management plans, evaluates, and controls investments involving fixed assets. Capital investment analysis is important to a business because such investments affect profitability for a long period of time.

Learning Outcome	Example Exercises	Practice Exercises
• Describe the purpose of capital investment analysis.		

Obj. 2 Evaluate capital investment proposals, using the average rate of return and cash payback methods.

Key Points The average rate of return method measures the expected profitability of an investment in fixed assets. The expected period of time that will pass between the date of an investment and the complete recovery in cash (or equivalent) of the amount invested is the cash payback period.

Learning Outcomes	Example Exercises	Practice Exercises
• Compute the average rate of return of a project.	EE26-1	PE26-1A, 26-1B
• Compute the cash payback period of a project.	EE26-2	PE26-2A, 26-2B

Obj. 3 Evaluate capital investment proposals, using the net present value and internal rate of return methods.

Key Points The net present value method uses present values to compute the net present value of the cash flows expected from a proposal. The internal rate of return method uses present values to compute the rate of return from the net cash flows expected from capital investment proposals.

Learning Outcomes	Example Exercises	Practice Exercises
• Compute the net present value of a project.	EE26-3	PE26-3A, 26-3B
• Compute the internal rate of return of a project.	EE26-4	PE26-4A, 26-4B

Obj. 4 List and describe additional factors in capital investment analysis.

Key Points Additional factors in capital investment analysis include the impact of income tax, unequal lives of alternative proposals, leasing, uncertainty, changes in price levels, qualitative considerations, and capital investment for sustainability.

Learning Outcomes	Example Exercises	Practice Exercises
• Describe the impact of income taxes in capital investment analysis.		
• Evaluate projects with unequal lives.	EE26-5	PE26-5A, 26-5B
• Describe leasing versus capital investment.		
• Describe uncertainty, changes in price levels, and qualitative considerations in capital investment analysis.		
• Describe and illustrate capital investment analysis for sustainability.		

Obj. 5 **Diagram the capital rationing process.**

Key Points Capital rationing refers to the process by which management allocates available investment funds among competing capital investment proposals. A diagram of the capital rationing process appears in Exhibit 13.

Learning Outcomes	*Example Exercises*	*Practice Exercises*
• Define *capital rationing.* • Diagram the capital rationing process.		

Illustrative Problem

The capital investment committee of Hopewell Company is currently considering two investments. The estimated income from operations and net cash flows expected from each investment are as follows:

	Truck		Equipment	
Year	**Income from Operations**	**Net Cash Flow**	**Income from Operations**	**Net Cash Flow**
1	$ 6,000	$ 22,000	$13,000	$ 29,000
2	9,000	25,000	10,000	26,000
3	10,000	26,000	8,000	24,000
4	8,000	24,000	8,000	24,000
5	11,000	27,000	3,000	19,000
	$44,000	$124,000	$42,000	$122,000

Each investment requires $80,000. Straight-line depreciation will be used, and no residual value is expected. The committee has selected a rate of 15% for purposes of the net present value analysis.

Instructions

1. Compute the following:
   a. The average rate of return for each investment.
   b. The net present value for each investment. Use the present value of $1 table appearing in this chapter (Exhibit 2).
2. Why is the net present value of the equipment greater than the truck even though its average rate of return is less?
3. Prepare a summary for the capital investment committee, advising it on the relative merits of the two investments.

Solution

1. a. Average rate of return for the truck:

$$\frac{\$44{,}000 \div 5}{(\$80{,}000 + \$0) \div 2} = 22\%$$

Average rate of return for the equipment:

$$\frac{\$42{,}000 \div 5}{(\$80{,}000 + \$0) \div 2} = 21\%$$

(*Continued*)

b. Net present value analysis:

Year	Present Value of $1 at 15%	Net Cash Flow		Present Value of Net Cash Flow	
		Truck	Equipment	Truck	Equipment
1	0.870	$ 22,000	$ 29,000	$19,140	$25,230
2	0.756	25,000	26,000	18,900	19,656
3	0.658	26,000	24,000	17,108	15,792
4	0.572	24,000	24,000	13,728	13,728
5	0.497	27,000	19,000	13,419	9,443
Total		$124,000	$122,000	$82,295	$83,849
Less amount to be invested				80,000	80,000
Net present value				$ 2,295	$ 3,849

2. The equipment has a lower average rate of return than the truck because the equipment's total income from operations for the five years is $42,000, which is $2,000 less than the truck's. Even so, the net present value of the equipment is greater than that of the truck because the equipment has higher cash flows in the early years.

3. Both investments exceed the selected rate established for the net present value analysis. The truck has a higher average rate of return, but the equipment offers a larger net present value. Thus, if only one of the two investments can be accepted, the equipment would be the more attractive.

Key Terms

annuity (1279)
average rate of return (1275)
capital investment analysis (1274)
capital rationing (1290)
cash payback period (1276)
currency exchange rate (1289)
inflation (1289)
internal rate of return (IRR) method (1283)
net present value method (1281)
present value concept (1278)
present value index (1282)
present value of an annuity (1280)
time value of money concept (1274)

Discussion Questions

1. What are the principal objections to the use of the average rate of return method in evaluating capital investment proposals?
2. Discuss the principal limitations of the cash payback method for evaluating capital investment proposals.
3. Why would the average rate of return differ from the internal rate of return on the same project?
4. Your boss has suggested that a one-year payback period is the same as a 100% average rate of return. Do you agree? Explain.
5. Why would the cash payback method understate the attractiveness of a project with a large residual value?
6. Why would the use of the cash payback period for analyzing the financial performance of theatrical releases from a motion picture production studio be supported over the net present value method?
7. A net present value analysis used to evaluate a proposed equipment acquisition indicated a $7,900 net present value. What is the meaning of the $7,900 as it relates to the desirability of the proposal?
8. Two projects have an identical net present value of $9,000. Are both projects equal in desirability? Explain.
9. What are the major disadvantages of the use of the net present value method of analyzing capital investment proposals?

10. What are the major disadvantages of the use of the internal rate of return method of analyzing capital investment proposals?
11. What are the major advantages of leasing a fixed asset rather than purchasing it?
12. Give an example of a qualitative factor that should be considered in a capital investment analysis related to acquiring automated factory equipment.
13. How are investments in sustainability justified?

Practice Exercises

Example Exercises

EE 26-1 *p. 1276*

PE 26-1A Average rate of return **OBJ. 2**

Determine the average rate of return for a project that is estimated to yield total income of \$180,000 over five years, has a cost of \$400,000, and has a \$50,000 residual value.

EE 26-1 *p. 1276*

PE 26-1B Average rate of return **OBJ. 2**

Determine the average rate of return for a project that is estimated to yield total income of \$36,000 over three years, has a cost of \$70,000, and has a \$10,000 residual value.

EE 26-2 *p. 1278*

PE 26-2A Cash payback period **OBJ. 2**

A project has estimated annual net cash flows of \$95,200. It is estimated to cost \$580,720. Determine the cash payback period. Round to one decimal place.

EE 26-2 *p. 1278*

PE 26-2B Cash payback period **OBJ. 2**

A project has estimated annual net cash flows of \$9,300. It is estimated to cost \$41,850. Determine the cash payback period. Round to one decimal place.

EE 26-3 *p. 1283*

PE 26-3A Net present value **OBJ. 3**

A project has estimated annual net cash flows of \$8,000 for five years and is estimated to cost \$28,000. Assume a minimum acceptable rate of return of 12%. Using Exhibit 5, determine (1) the net present value of the project and (2) the present value index, rounded to two decimal places.

EE 26-3 *p. 1283*

PE 26-3B Net present value **OBJ. 3**

A project has estimated annual net cash flows of \$96,200 for four years and is estimated to cost \$315,500. Assume a minimum acceptable rate of return of 10%. Using Exhibit 5, determine (1) the net present value of the project and (2) the present value index, rounded to two decimal places.

EE 26-4 *p. 1285*

PE 26-4A Internal rate of return **OBJ. 3**

A project is estimated to cost \$90,045 and provide annual net cash flows of \$14,500 for eight years. Determine the internal rate of return for this project, using Exhibit 5.

EE 26-4 *p. 1285*

PE 26-4B Internal rate of return **OBJ. 3**

A project is estimated to cost \$362,672 and provide annual net cash flows of \$76,000 for nine years. Determine the internal rate of return for this project, using Exhibit 5.

EE 26-5 *p. 1288*

PE 26-5A Net present value—unequal lives **OBJ. 4**

Project A requires an original investment of $32,600. The project will yield cash flows of $7,000 per year for nine years. Project B has a calculated net present value of $3,500 over a six-year life. Project A could be sold at the end of six years for a price of $15,000. (a) Determine the net present value of Project A over a six-year life, with residual value, assuming a minimum rate of return of 12%. (b) Which project provides the greatest net present value?

EE 26-5 *p. 1288*

PE 26-5B Net present value—unequal lives **OBJ. 4**

Project 1 requires an original investment of $55,000. The project will yield cash flows of $15,000 per year for seven years. Project 2 has a calculated net present value of $5,000 over a four-year life. Project 1 could be sold at the end of four years for a price of $38,000. (a) Determine the net present value of Project 1 over a four-year life, with residual value, assuming a minimum rate of return of 20%. (b) Which project provides the greatest net present value?

Exercises

EX 26-1 Average rate of return **OBJ. 2**

✔ 3D Printer, 16%

Show Me How

The following data are accumulated by Lone Peak Inc. in evaluating two competing capital investment proposals:

	3D Printer	Truck
Amount of investment	$40,000	$50,000
Useful life	7 years	10 years
Estimated residual value	$3,000	$6,000
Estimated total income over the useful life	$24,080	$36,400

Determine the expected average rate of return for each proposal.

EX 26-2 Average rate of return—cost savings **OBJ. 2**

Midwest Fabricators Inc. is considering an investment in equipment that will replace direct labor. The equipment has a cost of $132,000 with a $16,000 residual value and a 10-year life. The equipment will replace one employee who has an average wage of $34,000 per year. In addition, the equipment will have operating and energy costs of $5,380 per year.

Determine the average rate of return on the equipment, giving effect to straight-line depreciation on the investment.

EX 26-3 Average rate of return—new product **OBJ. 2**

✔ Average annual income, $744,000

Show Me How

Micro Tek Inc. is considering an investment in new equipment that will be used to manufacture a smartphone. The phone is expected to generate additional annual sales of 4,000 units at $450 per unit. The equipment has a cost of $940,000, residual value of $20,000, and an eight-year life. The equipment can only be used to manufacture the phone. The cost to manufacture the phone follows:

Cost per unit:	
Direct labor	$ 20
Direct materials	205
Factory overhead (including depreciation)	39
Total cost per unit	$264

Determine the average rate of return on the equipment.

EX 26-4 Calculate cash flows

OBJ. 2

Year 1: $(217,400)

Show Me How

Nature's Way Inc. is planning to invest in new manufacturing equipment to make a new garden tool. The garden tool is expected to generate additional annual sales of 1,600 units at $75 each. The new manufacturing equipment will cost $257,000 and is expected to have a 10-year life and $17,000 residual value. Selling expenses related to the new product are expected to be 5% of sales revenue. The cost to manufacture the product includes the following on a per-unit basis:

Direct labor	$12.00
Direct materials	30.00
Fixed factory overhead—depreciation	15.00
Variable factory overhead	4.50
Total	$61.50

Determine the net cash flows for the first year of the project, Years 2–9, and for the last year of the project.

EX 26-5 Cash payback period for a service company

OBJ. 2

✔ Location 1: 5 years

Show Me How

Prime Financial Inc. is evaluating two capital investment proposals for a drive-up ATM kiosk, each requiring an investment of $200,000 and each with an eight-year life and expected total net cash flows of $320,000. Location 1 is expected to provide equal annual net cash flows of $40,000, and Location 2 is expected to have the following unequal annual net cash flows:

Year 1	$60,000	Year 5	$30,000
Year 2	50,000	Year 6	30,000
Year 3	50,000	Year 7	30,000
Year 4	40,000	Year 8	30,000

Determine the cash payback period for both location proposals.

EX 26-6 Cash payback method

OBJ. 2

Excel

Lily Products Company is considering an investment in one of two new product lines. The investment required for either product line is $540,000. The net cash flows associated with each product are as follows:

Year	Liquid Soap	Body Lotion
1	$170,000	$ 90,000
2	150,000	90,000
3	120,000	90,000
4	100,000	90,000
5	70,000	90,000
6	40,000	90,000
7	40,000	90,000
8	30,000	90,000
Total	$720,000	$720,000

a. Recommend a product offering to Lily Products Company, based on the cash payback period for each product line.

b. Why is one product line preferred over the other even though they both have the same total net cash flows through eight periods?

EX 26-7 Net present value method — OBJ. 3

✔ a. NPV, $24,520

Show Me How

The following data are accumulated by Paxton Company in evaluating the purchase of $150,000 of equipment having a four-year useful life:

	Net Income	Net Cash Flow
Year 1	$42,500	$80,000
Year 2	27,500	65,000
Year 3	12,500	50,000
Year 4	2,500	40,000

a. Assuming that the desired rate of return is 15%, determine the net present value for the proposal. Use the table of the present value of $1 appearing in Exhibit 2 of this chapter.

b. Would management be likely to look with favor on the proposal? Explain.

EX 26-8 Net present value method for a service company — OBJ. 3

✔ a. 20Y1, $13,000

AM Express Inc. is considering the purchase of an additional delivery vehicle for $55,000 on January 1, 20Y1. The truck is expected to have a five-year life with an expected residual value of $15,000 at the end of five years. The expected additional revenues from the added delivery capacity are anticipated to be $58,000 per year for each of the next five years. A driver will cost $42,000 in 20Y1, with an expected annual salary increase of $1,000 for each year thereafter. The annual operating costs for the truck are estimated to be $3,000 per year.

a. Determine the expected annual net cash flows from the delivery truck investment for 20Y1–20Y5.

b. Calculate the net present value of the investment, assuming that the minimum desired rate of return is 12%. Use the present value of $1 table appearing in Exhibit 2 of this chapter.

c. Is the additional truck a good investment based on your analysis? Explain.

EX 26-9 Net present value method—annuity for a service company — OBJ. 3

✔ a. $14 million

Show Me How

Welcome Inn Hotels is considering the construction of a new hotel for $90 million. The expected life of the hotel is 30 years, with no residual value. The hotel is expected to earn revenues of $26 million per year. Total expenses, including depreciation, are expected to be $15 million per year. Welcome Inn management has set a minimum acceptable rate of return of 14%.

a. Determine the equal annual net cash flows from operating the hotel.

b. Calculate the net present value of the new hotel, using the present value of an annuity of $1 table found in Appendix A. Round to the nearest million dollars.

c. Does your analysis support construction of the new hotel? Explain.

EX 26-10 Net present value method—annuity — OBJ. 3

✔ a. $46,000

Briggs Excavation Company is planning an investment of $132,000 for a bulldozer. The bulldozer is expected to operate for 1,500 hours per year for five years. Customers will be charged $110 per hour for bulldozer work. The bulldozer operator costs $28 per hour in wages and benefits. The bulldozer is expected to require annual maintenance costing $8,000. The bulldozer uses fuel that is expected to cost $46 per hour of bulldozer operation.

a. Determine the equal annual net cash flows from operating the bulldozer.

b. Determine the net present value of the investment, assuming that the desired rate of return is 10%. Use the present value of an annuity of $1 table in the chapter (Exhibit 5). Round to the nearest dollar.

c. Should Briggs invest in the bulldozer, based on this analysis? Explain.

d. Determine the number of operating hours such that the present value of cash flows equals the amount to be invested.

✔ a. $146,320,000

Real World

EX 26-11 Net present value method for a service company **OBJ. 3**

Carnival Corporation has recently placed into service some of the largest cruise ships in the world. One of these ships, the *Carnival Breeze*, can hold up to 3,600 passengers, and it can cost $800 million to build. Assume the following additional information:

- There will be 330 cruise days per year operated at a full capacity of 3,600 passengers.
- The variable expenses per passenger are estimated to be $110 per cruise day.
- The revenue per passenger is expected to be $250 per cruise day.
- The fixed expenses for running the ship, other than depreciation, are estimated to be $20,000,000 per year.
- The ship has a service life of 10 years, with a residual value of $200,000,000 at the end of 10 years.

a. Determine the annual net cash flow from operating the cruise ship.

b. Determine the net present value of this investment, assuming a 12% minimum rate of return. Use the present value tables (Exhibits 2 and 5) provided in the chapter in determining your answer.

✔ Fort Collins, 0.98

EX 26-12 Present value index **OBJ. 3**

Dip N' Dunk Doughnuts has computed the net present value for capital expenditure at two locations. Relevant data related to the computation are as follows:

	Fort Collins	Boulder
Total present value of net cash flow	$607,600	$624,000
Less amount to be invested	620,000	600,000
Net present value	$(12,400)	$ 24,000

a. Determine the present value index for each proposal.

b. Which location does your analysis support? Explain.

✔ b. Packing machine, 1.55

EX 26-13 Net present value method and present value index **OBJ. 3**

Diamond & Turf Inc. is considering an investment in one of two machines. The sewing machine will increase productivity from sewing 150 baseballs per hour to sewing 290 per hour. The contribution margin per unit is $0.32 per baseball. Assume that any increased production of baseballs can be sold. The second machine is an automatic packing machine for the golf ball line. The packing machine will reduce packing labor cost. The labor cost saved is equivalent to $21 per hour. The sewing machine will cost $260,000, will have an eight-year life, and will operate for 1,800 hours per year. The packing machine will cost $85,000, will have an eight-year life, and will operate for 1,400 hours per year. Diamond & Turf seeks a minimum rate of return of 15% on its investments.

a. Determine the net present value for the two machines. Use the present value of an annuity of $1 table in the chapter (Exhibit 5). Round to the nearest dollar.

b. Determine the present value index for the two machines. Round to two decimal places.

c. If Diamond & Turf has sufficient funds for only one of the machines and qualitative factors are equal between the two machines, in which machine should it invest? Explain.

✔ b. 5 years

Show Me How

EX 26-14 Average rate of return, cash payback period, net present value method for a service company **OBJ. 2, 3**

Bi-Coastal Railroad Inc. is considering acquiring equipment at a cost of $520,000. The equipment has an estimated life of eight years and no residual value. It is expected to provide yearly net cash flows of $104,000. The company's minimum desired rate of return for net present value analysis is 10%.

(Continued)

Compute the following:

a. The average rate of return, assuming the annual earnings are equal to the net cash flows less the annual depreciation expense on the equipment.

b. The cash payback period.

c. The net present value. Use the present value of an annuity of $1 table appearing in this chapter (Exhibit 5). Round to the nearest dollar.

EX 26-15 Cash payback period, net present value analysis, and qualitative considerations

OBJ. 2, 3, 4

✔ a. 4 years

The plant manager of Shenzhen Electronics Company is considering the purchase of new automated assembly equipment. The new equipment will cost $1,400,000. The manager believes that the new investment will result in direct labor savings of $350,000 per year for 10 years.

a. What is the payback period on this project?

b. What is the net present value, assuming a 10% rate of return? Use the present value of an annuity of $1 table in Exhibit 5.

c. What else should the manager consider in the analysis?

EX 26-16 Internal rate of return method

OBJ. 3

✔ a. 4.111

Show Me How

The internal rate of return method is used by King Bros. Construction Co. in analyzing a capital expenditure proposal that involves an investment of $156,218 and annual net cash flows of $38,000 for each of the six years of its useful life.

a. Determine a present value factor for an annuity of $1, which can be used in determining the internal rate of return. Round to three decimal places.

b. Using the factor determined in part (a) and the present value of an annuity of $1 table appearing in this chapter (Exhibit 5), determine the internal rate of return for the proposal.

EX 26-17 Internal rate of return method for a service company

OBJ. 3, 4

Real World

Park City Mountain Resort, a Utah ski resort, recently announced a $415 million expansion of lodging properties, lifts, and terrain. Assume that this investment is estimated to produce $99 million in equal annual cash flows for each of the first 10 years of the project life.

a. Determine the expected internal rate of return of this project for 10 years, using the present value of an annuity of $1 table found in Exhibit 5.

b. What are some uncertainties that could reduce the internal rate of return of this project?

EX 26-18 Internal rate of return method—two projects

OBJ. 3

✔ a. Delivery truck, 15%

Munch N' Crunch Snack Company is considering two possible investments: a delivery truck or a bagging machine. The delivery truck would cost $43,056 and could be used to deliver an additional 95,000 bags of pretzels per year. Each bag of pretzels can be sold for a contribution margin of $0.45. The delivery truck operating expenses, excluding depreciation, are $1.35 per mile for 24,000 miles per year. The bagging machine would replace an old bagging machine, and its net investment cost would be $61,614. The new machine would require three fewer hours of direct labor per day. Direct labor is $18 per hour. There are 250 operating days in the year. Both the truck and the bagging machine are estimated to have seven-year lives. The minimum rate of return is 13%. However, Munch N' Crunch has funds to invest in only one of the projects.

a. Compute the internal rate of return for each investment. Use the present value of an annuity of $1 table appearing in this chapter (Exhibit 5).

b. Provide a recommendation to management in a memo.

EX 26-19 Net present value method and internal rate of return method for a service company

OBJ. 3

✔ a. $(36,750)

Keystone Healthcare Corp. is proposing to spend $260,820 on an eight-year project that has estimated net cash flows of $42,000 for each of the eight years.

a. Compute the net present value, using a rate of return of 10%. Use the present value of an annuity of $1 table in the chapter (Exhibit 5).

b. Based on the analysis prepared in part (a), is the rate of return (1) more than 10%, (2) 10%, or (3) less than 10%? Explain.

c. Determine the internal rate of return by computing a present value factor for an annuity of $1 and using the present value of an annuity of $1 table presented in the text (Exhibit 5).

EX 26-20 Identify error in capital investment analysis calculations

OBJ. 3

Artscape Inc. is considering the purchase of automated machinery that is expected to have a useful life of five years and no residual value. The average rate of return on the average investment has been computed to be 20%, and the cash payback period was computed to be 5.5 years.

Do you see any reason to question the validity of the data presented? Explain.

EX 26-21 Net present value—unequal lives

OBJ. 3, 4

✔ Net present value, Processing mill, $196,220

Excel

Bunker Hill Mining Company has two competing proposals: a processing mill and an electric shovel. Both pieces of equipment have an initial investment of $750,000. The net cash flows estimated for the two proposals are as follows:

	Net Cash Flow	
Year	**Processing Mill**	**Electric Shovel**
1	$310,000	$330,000
2	260,000	325,000
3	260,000	325,000
4	260,000	320,000
5	180,000	
6	130,000	
7	120,000	
8	120,000	

The estimated residual value of the processing mill at the end of Year 4 is $280,000.

Determine which equipment should be favored, comparing the net present values of the two proposals and assuming a minimum rate of return of 15%. Use the present value table presented in this chapter (Exhibit 2).

EX 26-22 Net present value—unequal lives

OBJ. 3, 4

Daisy's Creamery Inc. is considering one of two investment options. Option 1 is a $75,000 investment in new blending equipment that is expected to produce equal annual cash flows of $19,000 for each of seven years. Option 2 is a $90,000 investment in a new computer system that is expected to produce equal annual cash flows of $27,000 for each of five years. The residual value of the blending equipment at the end of the fifth year is estimated to be $15,000. The computer system has no expected residual value at the end of the fifth year.

Assume that there is sufficient capital to fund only one of the projects. Determine which project should be selected, comparing the (a) net present values and (b) present value indices of the two projects. Assume a minimum rate of return of 10%. Round the present value index to two decimal places. Use the present value tables presented in this chapter (Exhibits 2 and 5).

EX 26-23 Sustainable energy capital investment analysis OBJ. 3, 4

Central Plains Power Company is considering an investment in wind farm technology to replace natural gas-generating capacity. Initial installation cost of a wind turbine is expected to be $1,200 per kilowatt-hour of capacity. The wind turbine has a capacity of generating 2 megawatts per hour. A kilowatt-hour is 1,000 watts generated per hour, and a megawatt hour is 1,000 kilowatts generated per hour.

Annual operating information related to the wind turbine project was developed as follows:

Operating cost per wind turbine megawatt hour	$10
Variable operating, fuel, and maintenance costs of natural gas per megawatt hour	$95
Wind turbine operating days per year	90

a. Determine the initial investment cost of the wind turbine.

b. Determine the annual cost savings from the wind turbine in replacing natural gas generation. Round to the nearest dollar.

c. Determine the net present value of the project assuming a 15-year life and 12% minimum rate of return (use the present value tables in Appendix A). Round to the nearest dollar.

EX 26-24 Sustainable product capital investment analysis OBJ. 3, 4

AutoSource Inc. designs and manufactures tires for automobiles. The company's strategy is to design products that incorporate the full environmental impact of the product over its life cycle. This includes designing tires for fuel efficiency.

The technical team has determined that the tires manufactured with a silica blend will reduce road resistance. Thus, silica-blended tires will be significantly more fuel-efficient for the consumer, without compromising tire life. To produce the silica-blended tires, AutoSource will need to invest $5,000,000 in new equipment. It is expected that the new tire will be attractive to consumers and will result in increased tire sales. However, sales of conventional tires will be reduced as a result of the new silica-based tires. To evaluate the project, the cost and prices of silica and conventional tires are estimated as follows:

	Silica Tires	Conventional Tires
Sales price per tire	$160	$140
Material cost per tire	80	70
Variable manufacturing cost per tire	15	12

It is anticipated that 80,000 silica tires will be sold annually, while the sales of conventional tires will be reduced by 70,000 tires annually.

a. Determine the annual contribution margin for manufacturing and selling the silica-blended tires.

b. Determine the annual cash flows of manufacturing and selling silica-blended tires, incorporating the impact of lost sales from conventional tires.

c. Prepare a net present value analysis of the silica equipment investment, assuming an eight-year life and 12% minimum rate of return (use the Present Value tables in Appendix A). Round to the nearest dollar.

Problems: Series A

PR 26-1A Average rate of return method, net present value method, and analysis

OBJ. 2, 3

✔ 1. a. 30.0%

Excel

Show Me How

The capital investment committee of Nature's Portrait Landscaping Company is considering two capital investments. The estimated income from operations and net cash flows from each investment are as follows:

	Front-End Loader		Greenhouse Fixtures	
Year	Income from Operations	Net Cash Flow	Income from Operations	Net Cash Flow
1	$25,000	$ 40,000	$11,250	$ 26,250
2	20,000	35,000	11,250	26,250
3	7,000	22,000	11,250	26,250
4	3,000	18,000	11,250	26,250
5	1,250	16,250	11,250	26,250
Total	$56,250	$131,250	$56,250	$131,250

Each project requires an investment of $75,000. Straight-line depreciation will be used, and no residual value is expected. The committee has selected a rate of 12% for purposes of the net present value analysis.

Instructions

1. Compute the following:
   a. The average rate of return for each investment. Round to one decimal place.
   b. The net present value for each investment. Use the present value of $1 table appearing in this chapter (Exhibit 2). Round present values to the nearest dollar.
2. Prepare a brief report for the capital investment committee, advising it on the relative merits of the two investments.

PR 26-2A Cash payback period, net present value method, and analysis

OBJ. 2, 3

✔ 1. b. Plant expansion, $305,040

Excel

Elite Apparel Inc. is considering two investment projects. The estimated net cash flows from each project are as follows:

Year	Plant Expansion	Retail Store Expansion
1	$ 450,000	$ 500,000
2	450,000	400,000
3	340,000	350,000
4	280,000	250,000
5	180,000	200,000
Total	$1,700,000	$1,700,000

Each project requires an investment of $900,000. A rate of 15% has been selected for the net present value analysis.

Instructions

1. Compute the following for each product:
   a. Cash payback period.
   b. The net present value. Use the present value of $1 table appearing in this chapter (Exhibit 2).
2. Prepare a brief report advising management on the relative merits of each project.

PR 26-3A Net present value method, present value index, and analysis — OBJ. 3

✔ 2. Computer network, 1.20

Excel

Continental Railroad Company is evaluating three capital investment proposals using the net present value method. Relevant data related to the proposals are summarized as follows:

	Maintenance Equipment	Ramp Facilities	Computer Network
Amount to be invested	$8,000,000	$20,000,000	$9,000,000
Annual net cash flows:			
Year 1	4,000,000	12,000,000	6,000,000
Year 2	3,500,000	10,000,000	5,000,000
Year 3	2,500,000	9,000,000	4,000,000

Instructions

1. Assuming that the desired rate of return is 20%, prepare a net present value analysis for each proposal. Use the present value of $1 table appearing in this chapter (Exhibit 2).
2. Determine a present value index for each proposal. Round to two decimal places.
3. Which proposal offers the largest amount of present value per dollar of investment? Explain.

PR 26-4A Net present value method, internal rate of return method, and analysis — OBJ. 3, 4

✔ 1. a. Wind turbines, $82,600

The management of Advanced Alternative Power Inc. is considering two capital investment projects. The estimated net cash flows from each project are as follows:

Year	Wind Turbines	Biofuel Equipment
1	$280,000	$300,000
2	280,000	300,000
3	280,000	300,000
4	280,000	300,000

The wind turbines require an investment of $887,600, while the biofuel equipment requires an investment of $911,100. No residual value is expected from either project.

Instructions

1. Compute the following for each project:
   a. The net present value. Use a rate of 6% and the present value of an annuity of $1 table appearing in this chapter (Exhibit 5).
   b. A present value index. Round to two decimal places.
2. Determine the internal rate of return for each project by (a) computing a present value factor for an annuity of $1 and (b) using the present value of an annuity of $1 table appearing in this chapter (Exhibit 5).
3. What advantage does the internal rate of return method have over the net present value method in comparing projects?

PR 26-5A Alternative capital investments — OBJ. 3, 4

✔ 1. Server upgrade, $11,105

Excel

The investment committee of Sentry Insurance Co. is evaluating two projects, office expansion and upgrade to computer servers. The projects have different useful lives, but each requires an investment of $490,000. The estimated net cash flows from each project are as follows:

	Net Cash Flows	
Year	**Office Expansion**	**Servers**
1	$125,000	$165,000
2	125,000	165,000
3	125,000	165,000
4	125,000	165,000
5	125,000	
6	125,000	

The committee has selected a rate of 12% for purposes of net present value analysis. It also estimates that the residual value at the end of each project's useful life is $0, but at the end of the fourth year, the office expansion's residual value would be $180,000.

Instructions

1. For each project, compute the net present value. Use the present value of an annuity of $1 table appearing in this chapter (Exhibit 5). (Ignore the unequal lives of the projects.)
2. For each project, compute the net present value, assuming that the office expansion is adjusted to a four-year life for purposes of analysis. Use the present value of $1 table appearing in this chapter (Exhibit 2).
3. Prepare a report to the investment committee, giving your advice on the relative merits of the two projects.

PR 26-6A Capital rationing decision for a service company involving four proposals

OBJ. 2, 3, 5

✔ 5. Proposal B, 1.13

Excel

Clearcast Communications Inc. is considering allocating a limited amount of capital investment funds among four proposals. The amount of proposed investment, estimated income from operations, and net cash flow for each proposal are as follows:

	Investment	Year	Income from Operations	Net Cash Flow
Proposal A:	$450,000	1	$ 30,000	$120,000
		2	30,000	120,000
		3	20,000	110,000
		4	10,000	100,000
		5	(30,000)	60,000
			$ 60,000	$510,000
Proposal B:	$200,000	1	$ 60,000	$100,000
		2	40,000	80,000
		3	20,000	60,000
		4	(10,000)	30,000
		5	(20,000)	20,000
			$ 90,000	$290,000
Proposal C:	$320,000	1	$ 36,000	$100,000
		2	26,000	90,000
		3	26,000	90,000
		4	16,000	80,000
		5	16,000	80,000
			$120,000	$440,000
Proposal D:	$540,000	1	$ 92,000	$200,000
		2	72,000	180,000
		3	52,000	160,000
		4	12,000	120,000
		5	(8,000)	100,000
			$220,000	$760,000

(Continued)

The company's capital rationing policy requires a maximum cash payback period of three years. In addition, a minimum average rate of return of 12% is required on all projects. If the preceding standards are met, the net present value method and present value indexes are used to rank the remaining proposals.

Instructions

1. Compute the cash payback period for each of the four proposals.
2. Giving effect to straight-line depreciation on the investments and assuming no estimated residual value, compute the average rate of return for each of the four proposals. Round to one decimal place.
3. Using the following format, summarize the results of your computations in parts (1) and (2). By placing the calculated amounts in the first two columns on the left and by placing a check mark in the appropriate column to the right, indicate which proposals should be accepted for further analysis and which should be rejected.

Proposal	Cash Payback Period	Average Rate of Return	Accept for Further Analysis	Reject
A				
B				
C				
D				

4. For the proposals accepted for further analysis in part (3), compute the net present value. Use a rate of 12% and the present value of $1 table appearing in this chapter (Exhibit 2).
5. Compute the present value index for each of the proposals in part (4). Round to two decimal places.
6. Rank the proposals from most attractive to least attractive, based on the present values of net cash flows computed in part (4).
7. Rank the proposals from most attractive to least attractive, based on the present value indexes computed in part (5).
8. Based on the analyses, comment on the relative attractiveness of the proposals ranked in parts (6) and (7).

Problems: Series B

PR 26-1B Average rate of return method, net present value method, and analysis

OBJ. 2, 3

✔ 1. a. 18.7%

Excel

Show Me How

The capital investment committee of Ellis Transport and Storage Inc. is considering two investment projects. The estimated income from operations and net cash flows from each investment are as follows:

	Warehouse		Tracking Technology	
Year	Income from Operations	Net Cash Flow	Income from Operations	Net Cash Flow
1	$ 61,400	$135,000	$ 34,400	$108,000
2	51,400	125,000	34,400	108,000
3	36,400	110,000	34,400	108,000
4	26,400	100,000	34,400	108,000
5	(3,600)	70,000	34,400	108,000
Total	$172,000	$540,000	$172,000	$540,000

Each project requires an investment of $368,000. Straight-line depreciation will be used, and no residual value is expected. The committee has selected a rate of 15% for purposes of the net present value analysis.

Instructions

1. Compute the following:
   a. The average rate of return for each investment. Round to one decimal place.
   b. The net present value for each investment. Use the present value of $1 table appearing in this chapter (Exhibit 2). Round present values to the nearest dollar.
2. Prepare a brief report for the capital investment committee, advising it on the relative merits of the two projects.

PR 26-2B Cash payback period, net present value method, and analysis OBJ. 2, 3

✔ 1. b. *Pro Gamer,* $49,465

Excel

Social Circle Publications Inc. is considering two new magazine products. The estimated net cash flows from each product are as follows:

Year	*Sound Cellar*	*Pro Gamer*
1	$ 65,000	$ 70,000
2	60,000	55,000
3	25,000	35,000
4	25,000	30,000
5	45,000	30,000
Total	$220,000	$220,000

Each product requires an investment of $125,000. A rate of 10% has been selected for the net present value analysis.

Instructions

1. Compute the following for each product:
   a. Cash payback period.
   b. The net present value. Use the present value of $1 table appearing in this chapter (Exhibit 2).
2. Prepare a brief report advising management on the relative merits of each of the two products.

PR 26-3B Net present value method, present value index, and analysis OBJ. 3

✔ 2. Branch office expansion, 0.95

Excel

First United Bank Inc. is evaluating three capital investment projects using the net present value method. Relevant data related to the projects are summarized as follows:

	Branch Office Expansion	Computer System Upgrade	ATM Kiosk Expansion
Amount to be invested	$420,000	$350,000	$520,000
Annual net cash flows:			
Year 1	200,000	190,000	275,000
Year 2	160,000	180,000	250,000
Year 3	160,000	170,000	250,000

Instructions

1. Assuming that the desired rate of return is 15%, prepare a net present value analysis for each project. Use the present value of $1 table appearing in this chapter (Exhibit 2).
2. Determine a present value index for each project. Round to two decimal places.
3. Which project offers the largest amount of present value per dollar of investment? Explain.

✓ 1. a. *After Hours,* $100,800

PR 26-4B Net present value method, internal rate of return method, and analysis **OBJ. 3**

The management of Style Networks Inc. is considering two TV show projects. The estimated net cash flows from each project are as follows:

Year	*After Hours*	*Sun Fun*
1	$320,000	$290,000
2	320,000	290,000
3	320,000	290,000
4	320,000	290,000

After Hours requires an investment of $913,600, while *Sun Fun* requires an investment of $880,730. No residual value is expected from either project.

Instructions

1. Compute the following for each project:
   a. The net present value. Use a rate of 10% and the present value of an annuity of $1 table appearing in this chapter (Exhibit 5).
   b. A present value index. Round to two decimal places.
2. Determine the internal rate of return for each project by (a) computing a present value factor for an annuity of $1 and (b) using the present value of an annuity of $1 table appearing in this chapter (Exhibit 5).
3. What advantage does the internal rate of return method have over the net present value method in comparing projects?

✓ 1. Topeka, $135,600

Excel

PR 26-5B Alternative capital investments **OBJ. 3, 4**

The investment committee of Auntie M's Restaurants Inc. is evaluating two restaurant sites. The sites have different useful lives, but each requires an investment of $900,000. The estimated net cash flows from each site are as follows:

	Net Cash Flows	
Year	**Wichita**	**Topeka**
1	$310,000	$400,000
2	310,000	400,000
3	310,000	400,000
4	310,000	400,000
5	310,000	
6	310,000	

The committee has selected a rate of 20% for purposes of net present value analysis. It also estimates that the residual value at the end of each restaurant's useful life is $0, but at the end of the fourth year, Wichita's residual value would be $500,000.

Instructions

1. For each site, compute the net present value. Use the present value of an annuity of $1 table appearing in this chapter (Exhibit 5). (Ignore the unequal lives of the projects.)
2. For each site, compute the net present value, assuming that Wichita is adjusted to a four-year life for purposes of analysis. Use the present value of $1 table appearing in this chapter (Exhibit 2).
3. Prepare a report to the investment committee, giving your advice on the relative merits of the two sites.

PR 26-6B Capital rationing decision for a service company involving four proposals

OBJ. 2, 3, 5

✔ 5. Proposal C, 1.57

Excel

Renaissance Capital Group is considering allocating a limited amount of capital investment funds among four proposals. The amount of proposed investment, estimated income from operations, and net cash flow for each proposal are as follows:

	Investment	Year	Income from Operations	Net Cash Flow
Proposal A:	$680,000	1	$ 64,000	$ 200,000
		2	64,000	200,000
		3	64,000	200,000
		4	24,000	160,000
		5	24,000	160,000
			$240,000	$ 920,000
Proposal B:	$320,000	1	$ 26,000	$ 90,000
		2	26,000	90,000
		3	6,000	70,000
		4	6,000	70,000
		5	(44,000)	20,000
			$ 20,000	$ 340,000
Proposal C:	$108,000	1	$ 33,400	$ 55,000
		2	31,400	53,000
		3	28,400	50,000
		4	25,400	47,000
		5	23,400	45,000
			$142,000	$ 250,000
Proposal D:	$400,000	1	$100,000	$ 180,000
		2	100,000	180,000
		3	80,000	160,000
		4	20,000	100,000
		5	0	80,000
			$300,000	$700,000

The company's capital rationing policy requires a maximum cash payback period of three years. In addition, a minimum average rate of return of 12% is required on all projects. If the preceding standards are met, the net present value method and present value indexes are used to rank the remaining proposals.

Instructions

1. Compute the cash payback period for each of the four proposals.
2. Giving effect to straight-line depreciation on the investments and assuming no estimated residual value, compute the average rate of return for each of the four proposals. Round to one decimal place.
3. Using the following format, summarize the results of your computations in parts (1) and (2). By placing the calculated amounts in the first two columns on the left and by placing a check mark in the appropriate column to the right, indicate which proposals should be accepted for further analysis and which should be rejected.

Proposal	Cash Payback Period	Average Rate of Return	Accept for Further Analysis	Reject
A				
B				
C				
D				

4. For the proposals accepted for further analysis in part (3), compute the net present value. Use a rate of 15% and the present value of $1 table appearing in this chapter (Exhibit 2).

(Continued)

5. Compute the present value index for each of the proposals in part (4). Round to two decimal places.
6. Rank the proposals from most attractive to least attractive, based on the present values of net cash flows computed in part (4).
7. Rank the proposals from most attractive to least attractive, based on the present value indexes computed in part (5).
8. Based on the analyses, comment on the relative attractiveness of the proposals ranked in parts (6) and (7).

Cases & Projects

Ethics

CP 26-1 Ethics in Action

Danielle Hastings was recently hired as a cost analyst by CareNet Medical Supplies Inc. One of Danielle's first assignments was to perform a net present value analysis for a new warehouse. Danielle performed the analysis and calculated a present value index of 0.75. The plant manager, Jerrod Moore, is intent on purchasing the warehouse because he believes that more storage space is needed. Jerrod asks Danielle to come to his office, where the following conversation takes place:

Jerrod: Danielle, you're new here, aren't you?

Danielle: Yes, I am.

Jerrod: Well, Danielle, I'm not at all pleased with the capital investment analysis that you performed on this new warehouse. I need that warehouse for my production. If I don't get it, where am I going to place our output?

Danielle: Well, we need to get product into our customers' hands.

Jerrod: I agree, and we need a warehouse to do that.

Danielle: My analysis does not support constructing a new warehouse. The numbers don't lie; the warehouse does not meet our investment return targets. In fact, it seems to me that purchasing a warehouse does not add much value to the business. We need to be producing product to satisfy customer orders, not to fill a warehouse.

Jerrod: The headquarters people will not allow me to build the warehouse if the numbers don't add up. You know as well as I that many assumptions go into your net present value analysis. Why don't you relax some of your assumptions so that the financial savings will offset the cost?

Danielle: I'm willing to discuss my assumptions with you. Maybe I overlooked something.

Jerrod: Good. Here's what I want you to do. I see in your analysis that you don't project greater sales as a result of the warehouse. It seems to me that if we can store more goods, we will have more to sell. Thus, logically, a larger warehouse translates into more sales. If you incorporate this into your analysis, I think you'll see that the numbers will work out. Why don't you work it through and come back with a new analysis. I'm really counting on you on this one. Let's get off to a good start together and see if we can get this project accepted.

What is your advice to Danielle?

Team Activity

CP 26-2 Team Activity

Divide your team into two groups. In one group, find a local business, such as a copy shop, that rents time on desktop computers for an hourly rate. Determine the hourly rate. In the other group, determine the price of a mid-range desktop computer at www.dell.com. Combine this information from the two groups and perform a capital investment analysis. Assume that one student will use the computer for 40 hours per semester for the next three years. Also assume that the minimum rate of return is 10%. Use the interest tables in Appendix A in performing your analysis. [*Hint:* Use the appropriate present value of an annuity of $1 factor for 5% compounded for six semiannual periods (periods = 6).]

Does your analysis support the student purchasing the computer? Why or why not?

Communication

CP 26-3 Communication

Global Electronics Inc. invested $1,000,000 to build a plant in a foreign country. The labor and materials used in production are purchased locally. The plant expansion was estimated to produce an internal rate of return of 20% in U.S. dollar terms. Due to a currency crisis, the currency exchange rate between the local currency and the U.S. dollar doubled from two local units per U.S. dollar to four local units per U.S. dollar.

Write a brief memo to the chief financial officer, Tom Greene, explaining the impact the currency exchange rate change would have on the project's internal rate of return if (1) the plant produced and sold all product in the local economy only and (2) the plant produced all product locally and exported all product to the United States for sale.

CP 26-4 Personal investment analysis for a service company

A Masters of Accountancy degree at Central University costs $12,000 for an additional fifth year of education beyond the bachelor's degree. Assume that all tuition is paid at the beginning of the year. A student considering this investment must evaluate the present value of cash flows from possessing a graduate degree versus holding only the undergraduate degree. Assume that the average student with an undergraduate degree is expected to earn an annual salary of $50,000 per year (assumed to be paid at the end of the year) for 10 years. Assume that the average student with a graduate Masters of Accountancy degree is expected to earn an annual salary of $66,000 per year (assumed to be paid at the end of the year) for nine years after graduation. Assume a minimum rate of return of 10%.

1. Determine the net present value of cash flows from an undergraduate degree. Use the present value table provided in this chapter in Exhibit 5.
2. Determine the net present value of cash flows from a Masters of Accountancy degree, assuming that no salary is earned during the graduate year of schooling.
3. What is the net advantage or disadvantage of pursuing a graduate degree under these assumptions?

Real World

CP 26-5 Qualitative issues in investment analysis

The following are some selected quotes from senior executives:

CEO, Worthington Industries (a high-technology steel company): "We try to find the best technology, stay ahead of the competition, and serve the customer. . . . We'll make any investment that will pay back quickly . . . but if it is something that we really see as a must down the road, payback is not going to be that important."

Chairman of Amgen Inc. (a biotech company): "You cannot really run the numbers, do net present value calculations, because the uncertainties are really gigantic. . . . You decide on a project you want to run, and then you run the numbers [as a reality check on your assumptions]. Success in a business like this is much more dependent on tracking rather than on predicting, much more dependent on seeing results over time, tracking and adjusting and readjusting, much more dynamic, much more flexible."

Chief financial officer of Merck & Co., Inc. (a pharmaceutical company): ". . . at the individual product level—the development of a successful new product requires on the order of $230 million in R&D, spread over more than a decade—discounted cash flow style analysis does not become a factor until development is near the point of manufacturing scale-up effort. Prior to that point, given the uncertainties associated with new product development, it would be lunacy in our business to decide that we know exactly what's going to happen to a product once it gets out."

Explain the role of capital investment analysis for these companies.

Excel

Real World

CP 26-6 Net present value method for a service company

Metro-Goldwyn-Mayer Studios Inc. (MGM) is a major producer and distributor of theatrical and television filmed entertainment. Regarding theatrical films, MGM states, "Our feature films are exploited through a series of sequential domestic and international distribution channels, typically beginning with theatrical exhibition. Thereafter, feature films are first made available for home video (online downloads) generally six months after theatrical release; for pay television, one year after theatrical release; and for syndication, approximately three to five years after theatrical release."

(Continued)

Assume that MGM produces a film during early 2018 at a cost of $340 million and releases it halfway through the year. During the last half of 2018, the film earns revenues of $420 million at the box office. The film requires $90 million of advertising during the release. One year later, by the end of 2019, the film is expected to earn MGM net cash flows from online downloads of $60 million. By the end of 2020, the film is expected to earn MGM $20 million from pay TV, and by the end of 2021, the film is expected to earn $10 million from syndication.

a. Determine the net present value of the film as of the beginning of 2018 if the desired rate of return is 20%. To simplify present value calculations, assume that all annual net cash flows occur at the end of each year. Use the table of the present value of $1 appearing in Exhibit 2 of this chapter. Round to the nearest whole million dollars.

b. Under the assumptions provided here, is the film expected to be financially successful? Explain.

Mornin' Joe

Financial Statements for Mornin' Joe

Financial Statements for Mornin' Joe International

Financial Statements for Mornin' Joe

The financial statements for **Mornin' Joe** follow. Mornin' Joe is a fictitious coffeehouse chain featuring drip and espresso coffee in cafés. The financial statements for Mornin' Joe are provided to illustrate the complete financial statements of a corporation, using the terms, formats, and reporting illustrated throughout this text. In addition, excerpts of the Mornin' Joe financial statements are used to illustrate the financial reporting for the topics discussed in Chapters 7–15. The complete financial statements are shown in Exhibits 1, 2, 3, and 4.

EXHIBIT 1

Income Statement for Mornin' Joe

Mornin' Joe
Income Statement
For the Year Ended December 31, 20Y6

Sales			$5,402,100
Cost of merchandise sold			2,160,000
Gross profit			$3,242,100
Operating expenses			
Selling expenses:			
Wages expense	$825,000		
Advertising expense	678,900		
Depreciation expense—buildings	124,300		
Miscellaneous selling expense	26,500		
Total selling expenses		$ 1,654,700	
Administrative expenses:			
Office salaries expense	$325,000		
Rent expense	425,600		
Payroll tax expense	110,000		
Depreciation expense—office equipment	68,900		
Bad debt expense	14,000		
Amortization expense	10,500		
Total administrative expenses		954,000	
Total operating expenses			2,608,700
Income from operations			$ 633,400
Other income and expense:			
Interest revenue		$ 18,000	
Interest expense		(136,000)	
Loss on disposal of fixed asset		(23,000)	
Unrealized gain on trading investments		5,000	
Equity income in AM Coffee		57,000	(79,000)
Income before income taxes			$ 554,400
Income tax expense			132,800
Net income			$ 421,600
Basic earnings per share [($421,600 – $30,000) ÷ 44,000 shares issued and outstanding]			$ 8.90

EXHIBIT 2

Balance Sheet for Mornin' Joe

Mornin' Joe
Balance Sheet
December 31, 20Y6

Assets			
Current assets:			
Cash and cash equivalents		$ 235,000	
Trading investments (at cost)	$ 420,000		
Plus valuation allowance for trading investments	45,000	465,000	
Accounts receivable	$ 305,000		
Less allowance for doubtful accounts	12,300	292,700	
Merchandise inventory—at lower of cost (first-in, first-out method) or market		120,000	
Prepaid insurance		24,000	
Total current assets			$1,136,700
Investments:			
Investment in AM Coffee (equity method)			565,000
Property, plant, and equipment:			
Land		$1,850,000	
Buildings	$2,650,000		
Less accumulated depreciation	420,000	2,230,000	
Office equipment	$ 350,000		
Less accumulated depreciation	102,000	248,000	
Total property, plant, and equipment			4,328,000
Intangible assets:			
Patents			140,000
Total assets			$6,169,700
Liabilities			
Current liabilities:			
Accounts payable		$ 133,000	
Notes payable (current portion)		200,000	
Salaries and wages payable		42,000	
Payroll taxes payable		16,400	
Interest payable		40,000	
Total current liabilities			$ 431,400
Long-term liabilities:			
Bonds payable, 8%, due in 25 years		$ 500,000	
Unamortized discount		(16,000)	$ 484,000
Notes payable			1,400,000
Total long-term liabilities			$1,884,000
Total liabilities			$2,315,400
Stockholders' Equity			
Paid-in capital:			
Preferred 10% stock, $50 par (6,000 shares authorized and issued)		$ 300,000	
Excess of issue price over par		50,000	$ 350,000
Common stock, $20 par (50,000 shares authorized, 45,000 shares issued)		$ 900,000	
Excess of issue price over par		1,450,000	2,350,000
Total paid-in capital			$2,700,000
Retained earnings			1,200,300
Total			$3,900,300
Treasury stock (1,000 shares at cost)			(46,000)
Total stockholders' equity			$3,854,300
Total liabilities and stockholders' equity			$6,169,700

EXHIBIT 3

Retained Earnings Statement for Mornin' Joe

Mornin' Joe
Retained Earnings Statement
For the Year Ended December 31, 20Y6

Retained earnings, January 1, 20Y6		$ 852,700
Net income	$421,600	
Dividends:		
Preferred stock	(30,000)	
Common stock	(44,000)	
Increase in retained earnings		347,600
Retained earnings, December 31, 20Y6		$1,200,300

EXHIBIT 4

Statement of Stockholders' Equity for Mornin' Joe

Mornin' Joe
Statement of Stockholders' Equity
For the Year Ended December 31, 20Y6

	Preferred Stock	Common Stock	Additional Paid-In Capital	Retained Earnings	Treasury Stock	Total
Balance, January 1, 20Y6	$300,000	$800,000	$1,325,000	$ 852,700	$(36,000)	$3,241,700
Issuance of additional common stock		100,000	175,000			275,000
Purchase of treasury stock					(10,000)	(10,000)
Net income				421,600		421,600
Dividends on preferred stock				(30,000)		(30,000)
Dividends on common stock				(44,000)		(44,000)
Balance, December 31, 20Y6	$300,000	$900,000	$1,500,000	$1,200,300	$(46,000)	$3,854,300

Financial Statements for Mornin' Joe International

Mornin' Joe is planning to expand operations to various places around the world. Financing for this expansion will come from foreign banks. While financial statements prepared under U.S. GAAP may be appropriate for U.S. operations, financial statements prepared for foreign bankers should be prepared using international accounting standards.

IFRS

Mornin' Joe

The European Union (EU) has developed accounting standards similar in structure to U.S. standards. Its accounting standards board is called the International Accounting Standards Board (IASB). The IASB issues accounting standards that are termed *International Financial Reporting Standards (IFRS)*. The intent of the IASB is to create a set of financial standards that can be used by public companies worldwide, not just in the EU.

Currently, the EU countries and more than 100 other countries around the world have adopted or are planning to adopt IFRS.

Key Reporting Differences Between IFRS and U.S. GAAP

The financial statements of **Mornin' Joe International** using IFRS are presented in Exhibits 1, 2, and 3. This illustration highlights reporting and terminology differences between IFRS and U.S. GAAP. Differences in recording transactions under IFRS and U.S. GAAP are discussed in Appendix B and in various International Connection boxes throughout the text.

The Mornin' Joe International financial statements in Exhibits 5, 6, and 7 are simplified and illustrate only portions of IFRS that are appropriate for introductory accounting. The financial statements are presented in euros (€), which is the standard currency of the European Union. The euro is translated at a 1:1 ratio from the dollar to simplify comparisons. Throughout the illustration, call-outs and end notes to each statement are used to highlight the differences between financial statements prepared under IFRS and under U.S. GAAP.

Statements of Comprehensive Income Versus Income Statements

Exhibit 5 illustrates the statement of comprehensive income for **Mornin' Joe International** and shows key differences from the income statements prepared under U.S. GAAP.

EXHIBIT 5 **Statement of Comprehensive Income for Mornin' Joe International**

Mornin' Joe International
Statement of Comprehensive Income
For the Year Ended December 31, 20Y6

Sales (net)*	€ 5,402,100
Cost of merchandise sold	(2,160,000)
Gross profit	€ 3,242,100
Selling expenses	(1,654,700)
Administrative expenses	(954,000)
Loss on disposal of fixed asset	(23,000)
Other income (expenses)	23,000
Share in profit (loss) of associates*	57,000
Operating profit	€ 690,400
Finance costs*	(136,000)
Profit before income tax	€ 554,400
Tax expense*	(132,800)
Profit for the year*	€ 421,600
Other comprehensive income	
Gain on revaluation of properties*	44,800
Total comprehensive income for the year, net of tax*	€ 466,400
Earnings per share basic* (€421,600 ÷ 44,000 shares)	€ 9.58

*A required disclosure on the face of the statement of comprehensive income

Title includes the word *Comprehensive*.

This is a common term for an equity method investment.

The term *Finance costs* is used rather than *Interest expense*.

The term *Profit for the year* is used rather than *Net income*.

Expenses are organized by their nature. See Note 2.

Diversity allowed with regard to subtotal definitions. See Note 3.

Other comprehensive income is a required disclosure. See Note 4.

IFRS allow latitude on how statements are organized but do list minimum disclosure requirements that are less restrictive than required by the SEC. See Note 1.

1. IFRS statements are often more summarized than U.S. GAAP statements. To compensate, IFRS require specific disclosures on the face of the financial statements (denoted*) and additional disclosures in the footnotes to the financial statements. Because additions and subtractions are grouped together in sections of IFRS statements, parentheses are used to indicate subtractions.
2. Expenses in an IFRS income statement are classified by either their nature or function. The nature of an expense is how the expense would naturally be recorded in a journal entry reflecting the economic benefit received for that expense. Examples include salaries, depreciation, advertising, and utilities. The function of an expense identifies the purpose of the expense, such as a selling expense or an administrative expense.

   IFRS do not permit the natural and functional classifications to be mixed together on the same statement. That is, all expenses must be classified by either nature or function. However, if a functional classification of expenses is used, a footnote to the income statement must show the natural classification of expenses. To illustrate, because **Mornin' Joe International** uses the functional classification of expenses in its income statement, it must also show the following natural classification of expenses in a footnote:

Cost of product	€2,100,000	The cost of product purchased for resale
Employee benefits expense	1,260,000	Required natural disclosure
Depreciation and amortization expense	203,700	Required natural disclosure
Rent expense	425,600	
Advertising expense	678,900	
Other expenses	58,500	
Total natural expenses	€4,726,700	

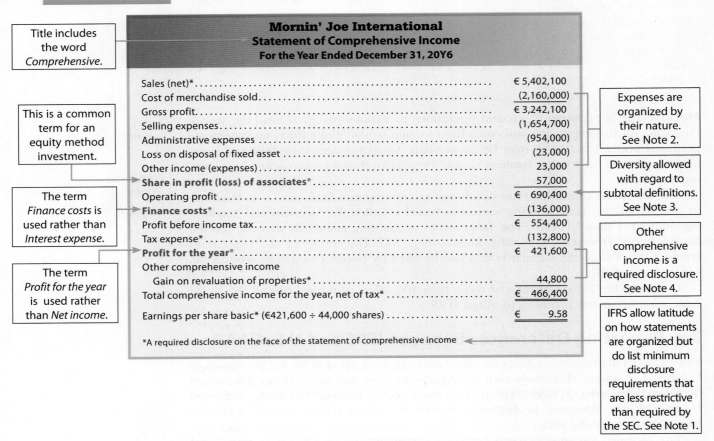

3. IFRS provide flexibility with regard to line items, headings, and subtotals on the income statement. There is less flexibility under U.S. GAAP for public companies.
4. IFRS require the reporting of other comprehensive income (see appendix to Chapter 15) either on the income statement (see Exhibit 5) or in a separate statement. U.S. GAAP has a similar disclosure treatment. For **Mornin' Joe International**, other comprehensive income consists of the restatement of café locations to fair value (see Note 6 for more details).
5. Under IFRS, there is no standard format for the balance sheet (statement of financial position, see Exhibit 6). A typical format for European Union companies is to begin the Asset section of the balance sheet with noncurrent assets. This is followed by current assets listed in reverse order of liquidity. That is, the asset side of the balance sheet is reported in reverse order of liquidity from least liquid to most liquid. Listing noncurrent assets first emphasizes the going concern nature of the entity.

   The liability and owners' equity side of the balance sheet is also reported differently than under U.S. GAAP. Specifically, owners' equity is reported first followed by noncurrent liabilities and current liabilities. Listing equity first emphasizes the going concern nature of the entity and the long-term financial interest of the owners in the business.
6. Under IFRS, property, plant, and equipment (PP&E) may be measured at historical cost or fair value. If fair value is used, the revaluation must be for similar classifications of PP&E but need not be for all PP&E. This departs from U.S. GAAP, which requires PP&E to be measured at historical cost. **Mornin' Joe International** restated its Land and Buildings to fair value because the café sites have readily available real estate market prices. Land and buildings are included together because their fair values are not separable. The office equipment remains at historical cost because it does not have a readily available market price. The increase in fair value is recorded by reducing accumulated depreciation and recognizing the gain as other comprehensive income. This element of other comprehensive income is accumulated in stockholders' equity under the heading Property revaluation reserve.* This treatment is similar (with different titles) to the U.S. GAAP treatment of unrealized gains (losses) from available-for-sale securities. For Mornin' Joe International, there is an increase in the property revaluation reserve of €44,800. This amount is the only difference between Mornin' Joe's U.S. GAAP net income, total assets, and total stockholders' equity and Mornin' Joe International's IFRS total comprehensive income, total assets, and total stockholders' equity.
7. **Mornin' Joe International** recently acquired a coffee plantation. This is an example of a biological asset. IFRS require separate reporting of biological assets (principally agricultural assets) at fair value.
8. Inventories are valued at lower of cost or market; however, "market" is defined as net realizable value under IFRS. U.S. GAAP defines "market" as replacement cost under most conditions. In addition, IFRS prohibit LIFO cost valuation.
9. Under IFRS, some elements of other comprehensive income and owner's equity are often aggregated under the term *reserves*. In contrast, under U.S. GAAP, *reserve* is used to identify a liability. IFRS also do not require separate disclosure of treasury stock as does U.S. GAAP. Specifically, treasury stock may be reported as a reduction of a reserve, as a reduction of a stock premium, or as a separate item.
10. The term *provision* is used to denote a liability under IFRS, whereas this term often indicates an expense under U.S. GAAP. For example, *Provision for income taxes* means "Income tax expense" under U.S. GAAP, whereas it would mean "Income taxes payable" under IFRS.
11. Under U.S. GAAP, other comprehensive income items must be included as changes in accumulated other comprehensive income in the statement of changes in stockholders' equity (see Exhibit 7). IFRS allow for similar treatment, with wider latitude for terminology, such as *Property Revaluation Reserve* illustrated by the column title here. In this illustration, treasury stock is included as part of a reserve (Reserve for Own Shares). As discussed in Note 9, under U.S. GAAP, the term *reserve* denotes a liability.

Statements of Financial Position Versus Balance Sheets Exhibit 6 illustrates the statement of financial position for **Mornin' Joe International** and shows key differences from the balance sheets prepared under U.S. GAAP.

EXHIBIT 6 **Statement of Financial Position for Mornin' Joe International**

Mornin' Joe International
Statement of Financial Position
December 31, 20Y6

Assets			
Noncurrent assets			
Property, plant, and equipment*			
Land and buildings at fair value	€4,180,000		
Less: Accumulated depreciation	375,200	€3,804,800	
Office equipment at cost	€ 350,000		
Less: Accumulated depreciation	102,000	248,000	
Biological assets at fair value*		320,000	
Patents at amortized cost*		140,000	
Investment in AM Coffee (equity method)*		565,000	
Total noncurrent assets			€5,077,800
Current assets			
Prepaid insurance		€ 24,000	
Merchandise inventory—**at lower of cost (first-in, first-out) or realizable value***		120,000	
Accounts receivable (net of allowance for doubtful accounts)*		292,700	
Financial assets at fair value through profit or loss*		465,000	
Cash and cash equivalents*		235,000	
Total current assets			1,136,700
Total assets*			€6,214,500
Equity attributable to owners			
Preferred 10% stock, €50 par (6,000 shares authorized and issued)*		€ 300,000	
Common stock, €20 par (50,000 shares authorized, 45,000 shares issued)*		900,000	
Share premium*		1,500,000	
Reserves*		(1,200)	
Retained earnings*		1,200,300	
Total equity attributable to owners*			€3,899,100
Liabilities			
Noncurrent liabilities*			
Bonds payable, 8%, due December 31, 2036 (net of discount)		€ 484,000	
Notes payable		1,400,000	
Total noncurrent liabilities			€1,884,000
Current liabilities			
Accounts payable*		€ 133,000	
Loans*		200,000	
Employee provisions*		58,400	
Interest payable		40,000	
Total current liabilities			431,400
Total liabilities*			€2,315,400
Total equity and liabilities*			€6,214,500

*Required disclosures. Footnotes provide additional subclassification detail.

- Preferred title for the balance sheet.
- Biological assets are a required disclosure at fair value. See Note 7.
- Inventory valuation. See Note 8.
- International terminology for "Trading investments." Same accounting treatment.
- International terminology for "Excess of issue price over par."
- Other comprehensive items and treasury stock. See Note 9.
- Employee provisions are wages, salaries, and payroll taxes payable. See Note 10.
- Sub-classifications of PP&E may be valued at fair value. See Note 6.
- Reverse liquidity account order. See Note 5.
- Equities listed first, then liabilities. See Note 5.
- Noncurrent liabilities listed prior to current liabilities.

Statements of Changes in Equity Versus Statements of Stockholders' Equity Exhibit 7 illustrates the statement of changes in equity for **Mornin' Joe International** and shows key differences from the statements of stockholders' equity prepared under U.S. GAAP.

Statement of Changes in Equity for Mornin' Joe International EXHIBIT 7

Mornin' Joe International
Statement of Changes in Equity
For the Year Ended December 31, 20Y6

	Preferred Stock	Common Stock	Share Premium	Reserves: Property Revaluation Reserve	Reserves: Reserve for Own Shares	Retained Earnings	Total Equity Attributable to Owners
Balance, January 1, 20Y6	€300,000	€800,000	€1,325,000	€ 0	€(36,000)	€ 852,700	€3,241,700
Profit for the year						421,600	421,600
Other comprehensive income							
Property revaluation (gain)				44,800			44,800
Total comprehensive income				€44,800		€ 421,600	€ 466,400
Contributions by and distributions to owners							
Dividends on preferred stock						(30,000)	(30,000)
Dividends on common stock						(44,000)	(44,000)
Issuance of additional common stock		100,000	175,000				275,000
Purchase of own shares					(10,000)		(10,000)
Total contributions and distributions to owners	€ 0	€100,000	€ 175,000	€ 0	€(10,000)	€ (74,000)	€ 191,000
Balance, December 31, 20Y6	€300,000	€900,000	€1,500,000	€44,800	€(46,000)	€1,200,300	€3,899,100

"Reserves," see Notes 9 and 11.

Discussion Questions

1. Contrast U.S. GAAP financial statement terms with their different IFRS terms.
2. What is the difference between classifying an expense by nature or function?
3. If a functional expense classification is used for the statement of comprehensive income, what must also be disclosed?
4. How is the term *provision* used differently under IFRS than under U.S. GAAP?
5. What are two main differences in inventory valuation under IFRS compared to U.S. GAAP?
6. What is a "biological asset"?
7. What is the most significant IFRS departure from U.S. GAAP for valuing property, plant, and equipment?
8. What is a "share premium"?
9. How is the term *reserve* used under IFRS, and how does it differ from its meaning under U.S. GAAP?

IFRS IFRS Activity 1

Unilever Group is a global company that markets a wide variety of products, including Lever® soap, Breyer's® ice cream, and Hellman's® mayonnaise. A recent income statement and statement of comprehensive income for the Dutch company, Unilever Group, follow:

Unilever Group
Consolidated Income Statement
For the Year Ended December 31
(in millions of euros)

Turnover		€51,324
Operating profit		6,989
After (charging)/crediting:		
Non-core items	(73)	
Net finance costs	(397)	
Finance income	136	
Finance costs	(526)	
Pensions and similar obligations	(7)	
Share of net profit/(loss) of joint ventures and associations		105
Other income from non-current investments		(14)
Profit before taxation		€ 6,683
Taxation		(1,735)
Net profit		€ 4,948
Earnings per share—basic		€ 1.58
Earnings per share—diluted		€ 1.54

Consolidated Statement of Comprehensive Income
For the Year Ended December 31

Fair value gains (losses), net of tax	€ (125)
Actuarial gains (losses) on pensions, net of tax	(644)
Currency retranslation gains (losses), net of tax	(316)
Net income (expense) recognized directly into equity	€(1,085)
Net profit	4,948
Total comprehensive income	€3,863

a. What do you think is meant by "turnover"?

b. How does Unilever's income statement presentation differ significantly from that of Mornin' Joe?

c. How is the total for net finance costs presented differently from what typically would be found under U.S. GAAP?

IFRS IFRS Activity 2

The following is a recent consolidated statement of financial position on December 31 of a recent year for LVMH, a French company that markets the Louis Vuitton® and Moët Hennessy® brands:

LVMH Statement of Financial Position December 31 (in millions of euros)	
Assets	
Brands and other intangible assets—net	€11,510
Goodwill—net	7,806
Property, plant, and equipment—net	8,769
Investment in associates	163
Non-current available for sale financial assets	6,004
Other non-current assets	524
Deferred tax	881
Non-current assets	€35,657
Inventories	€ 8,080
Trade accounts receivable	1,985
Income taxes	201
Other current assets	1,811
Cash and cash equivalents	2,196
Current assets	€14,273
TOTAL ASSETS	€49,930
Liabilities and Equity	
Share capital	€ 152
Share premium	3,848
Treasury shares	(414)
Revaluation reserves	2,819
Other reserves	14,393
Cumulative translation adjustment	342
Net profit, group share	3,424
Equity, group share	€24,564
Minority interests	1,102
Total equity	€25,666
Long-term borrowings	€ 3,836
Provisions	1,530
Deferred tax	3,960
Other non-current liabilities	5,456
Total non-current liabilities	€14,782
Short-term borrowings	€ 2,976
Trade accounts payable	3,134
Income taxes payable	442
Provisions	335
Other current liabilities	2,595
Total current liabilities	€ 9,482
TOTAL LIABILITIES AND EQUITY	€49,930

a. Identify presentation differences between the balance sheet of LVMH and a balance sheet prepared under U.S. GAAP. Use the Mornin' Joe balance sheet (Exhibit 2) as an example of a U.S. GAAP balance sheet. (Ignore minority interests and cumulative translation adjustment.)

b. Compare the terms used in this balance sheet with the terms used by Mornin' Joe (Exhibit 2), using the table that follows:

LVMH Term	Mornin' Joe U.S. GAAP Term
Statement of financial position	
Share capital	
Share premium	
Other reserves	
Provisions	

c. What does the "Revaluation reserves" in the Equity section of the balance sheet represent?

IFRS IFRS Activity 3

Under U.S. GAAP, LIFO is an acceptable inventory method. Financial statement information for three companies that use LIFO follows. All table numbers are in millions of dollars.

	LIFO Inventory	FIFO Inventory (from notes)	Impact on Net Income from Using LIFO Rather Than FIFO (from notes)	Total Current Assets	Net Income as Reported
ExxonMobil	$9,852	$31,200	$317	$58,984	$30,460
Kroger	4,966	5,793	(57)	7,621	1,116
Ford Motor*	5,917	6,782	4	34,368	4,690

*Autos and trucks only

Assume that these companies adopted IFRS and thus were required to use FIFO rather than LIFO.

a. Prepare a table with the following columns:

(1)	(2)	(3)	(4)
FIFO less LIFO	IFRS Net Income	(FIFO less LIFO) / Total Current Assets	IFRS Net Income (Col. 2) / Reported Net Income

(1) Difference between FIFO and LIFO inventory valuation

(2) Revised IFRS net income using FIFO

(3) Difference between FIFO and LIFO inventory valuation as a percent of total current assets (rounded to the nearest whole percent)

(4) Revised IFRS net income as a percent of the reported net income (rounded to the nearest whole percent)

b. Complete the table for the three companies.

c. For which company would a change to IFRS for inventory valuation have the largest percentage impact on total current assets (Col. 3)?

d. For which company would a change to IFRS for inventory valuation have the largest percentage impact on net income (Col. 4)?

e. Why might Kroger have a negative impact on net income from using LIFO, while the other two companies have a positive impact on net income from using LIFO?

Appendices

Appendix A

Interest Tables

Present Value of $1 at Compound Interest Due in *n* Periods

Periods	4.0%	4.5%	5%	5.5%	6%	6.5%	7%
1	0.96154	0.95694	0.95238	0.94787	0.94340	0.93897	0.93458
2	0.92456	0.91573	0.90703	0.89845	0.89000	0.88166	0.87344
3	0.88900	0.87630	0.86384	0.85161	0.83962	0.82785	0.81630
4	0.85480	0.83856	0.82270	0.80722	0.79209	0.77732	0.76290
5	0.82193	0.80245	0.78353	0.76513	0.74726	0.72988	0.71299
6	0.79031	0.76790	0.74622	0.72525	0.70496	0.68533	0.66634
7	0.75992	0.73483	0.71068	0.68744	0.66506	0.64351	0.62275
8	0.73069	0.70319	0.67684	0.65160	0.62741	0.60423	0.58201
9	0.70259	0.67290	0.64461	0.61763	0.59190	0.56735	0.54393
10	0.67556	0.64393	0.61391	0.58543	0.55839	0.53273	0.50835
11	0.64958	0.61620	0.58468	0.55491	0.52679	0.50021	0.47509
12	0.62460	0.58966	0.55684	0.52598	0.49697	0.46968	0.44401
13	0.60057	0.56427	0.53032	0.49856	0.46884	0.44102	0.41496
14	0.57748	0.53997	0.50507	0.47257	0.44230	0.41410	0.38782
15	0.55526	0.51672	0.48102	0.44793	0.41727	0.38883	0.36245
16	0.53391	0.49447	0.45811	0.42458	0.39365	0.36510	0.33873
17	0.51337	0.47318	0.43630	0.40245	0.37136	0.34281	0.31657
18	0.49363	0.45280	0.41552	0.38147	0.35034	0.32189	0.29586
19	0.47464	0.43330	0.39573	0.36158	0.33051	0.30224	0.27651
20	0.45639	0.41464	0.37689	0.34273	0.31180	0.28380	0.25842
21	0.43883	0.39679	0.35894	0.32486	0.29416	0.26648	0.24151
22	0.42196	0.37970	0.34185	0.30793	0.27751	0.25021	0.22571
23	0.40573	0.36335	0.32557	0.29187	0.26180	0.23494	0.21095
24	0.39012	0.34770	0.31007	0.27666	0.24698	0.22060	0.19715
25	0.37512	0.33273	0.29530	0.26223	0.23300	0.20714	0.18425
26	0.36069	0.31840	0.28124	0.24856	0.21981	0.19450	0.17220
27	0.34682	0.30469	0.26785	0.23560	0.20737	0.18263	0.16093
28	0.33348	0.29157	0.25509	0.22332	0.19563	0.17148	0.15040
29	0.32065	0.27902	0.24295	0.21168	0.18456	0.16101	0.14056
30	0.30832	0.26700	0.23138	0.20064	0.17411	0.15119	0.13137
31	0.29646	0.25550	0.22036	0.19018	0.16425	0.14196	0.12277
32	0.28506	0.24450	0.20987	0.18027	0.15496	0.13329	0.11474
33	0.27409	0.23397	0.19987	0.17087	0.14619	0.12516	0.10723
34	0.26355	0.22390	0.19035	0.16196	0.13791	0.11752	0.10022
35	0.25342	0.21425	0.18129	0.15352	0.13011	0.11035	0.09366
40	0.20829	0.17193	0.14205	0.11746	0.09722	0.08054	0.06678
45	0.17120	0.13796	0.11130	0.08988	0.07265	0.05879	0.04761
50	0.14071	0.11071	0.08720	0.06877	0.05429	0.04291	0.03395

Present Value of $1 at Compound Interest Due in *n* Periods

Periods	8%	9%	10%	11%	12%	13%	14%
1	0.92593	0.91743	0.90909	0.90090	0.89286	0.88496	0.87719
2	0.85734	0.84168	0.82645	0.81162	0.79719	0.78315	0.76947
3	0.79383	0.77218	0.75131	0.73119	0.71178	0.69305	0.67497
4	0.73503	0.70843	0.68301	0.65873	0.63552	0.61332	0.59208
5	0.68058	0.64993	0.62092	0.59345	0.56743	0.54276	0.51937
6	0.63017	0.59627	0.56447	0.53464	0.50663	0.48032	0.45559
7	0.58349	0.54703	0.51316	0.48166	0.45235	0.42506	0.39964
8	0.54027	0.50187	0.46651	0.43393	0.40388	0.37616	0.35056
9	0.50025	0.46043	0.42410	0.39092	0.36061	0.33288	0.30751
10	0.46319	0.42241	0.38554	0.35218	0.32197	0.29459	0.26974
11	0.42888	0.38753	0.35049	0.31728	0.28748	0.26070	0.23662
12	0.39711	0.35553	0.31863	0.28584	0.25668	0.23071	0.20756
13	0.36770	0.32618	0.28966	0.25751	0.22917	0.20416	0.18207
14	0.34046	0.29925	0.26333	0.23199	0.20462	0.18068	0.15971
15	0.31524	0.27454	0.23939	0.20900	0.18270	0.15989	0.14010
16	0.29189	0.25187	0.21763	0.18829	0.16312	0.14150	0.12289
17	0.27027	0.23107	0.19784	0.16963	0.14564	0.12522	0.10780
18	0.25025	0.21199	0.17986	0.15282	0.13004	0.11081	0.09456
19	0.23171	0.19449	0.16351	0.13768	0.11611	0.09806	0.08295
20	0.21455	0.17843	0.14864	0.12403	0.10367	0.08678	0.07276
21	0.19866	0.16370	0.13513	0.11174	0.09256	0.07680	0.06383
22	0.18394	0.15018	0.12285	0.10067	0.08264	0.06796	0.05599
23	0.17032	0.13778	0.11168	0.09069	0.07379	0.06014	0.04911
24	0.15770	0.12640	0.10153	0.08170	0.06588	0.05323	0.04308
25	0.14602	0.11597	0.09230	0.07361	0.05882	0.04710	0.03779
26	0.13520	0.10639	0.08391	0.06631	0.05252	0.04168	0.03315
27	0.12519	0.09761	0.07628	0.05974	0.04689	0.03689	0.02908
28	0.11591	0.08955	0.06934	0.05382	0.04187	0.03264	0.02551
29	0.10733	0.08215	0.06304	0.04849	0.03738	0.02889	0.02237
30	0.09938	0.07537	0.05731	0.04368	0.03338	0.02557	0.01963
31	0.09202	0.06915	0.05210	0.03935	0.02980	0.02262	0.01722
32	0.08520	0.06344	0.04736	0.03545	0.02661	0.02002	0.01510
33	0.07889	0.05820	0.04306	0.03194	0.02376	0.01772	0.01325
34	0.07305	0.05339	0.03914	0.02878	0.02121	0.01568	0.01162
35	0.06763	0.04899	0.03558	0.02592	0.01894	0.01388	0.01019
40	0.04603	0.03184	0.02209	0.01538	0.01075	0.00753	0.00529
45	0.03133	0.02069	0.01372	0.00913	0.00610	0.00409	0.00275
50	0.02132	0.01345	0.00852	0.00542	0.00346	0.00222	0.00143

Present Value of Ordinary Annuity of $1 per Period

Periods	4.0%	4.5%	5%	5.5%	6%	6.5%	7%
1	0.96154	0.95694	0.95238	0.94787	0.94340	0.93897	0.93458
2	1.88609	1.87267	1.85941	1.84632	1.83339	1.82063	1.80802
3	2.77509	2.74896	2.72325	2.69793	2.67301	2.64848	2.62432
4	3.62990	3.58753	3.54595	3.50515	3.46511	3.42580	3.38721
5	4.45182	4.38998	4.32948	4.27028	4.21236	4.15568	4.10020
6	5.24214	5.15787	5.07569	4.99553	4.91732	4.84101	4.76654
7	6.00205	5.89270	5.78637	5.68297	5.58238	5.48452	5.38929
8	6.73274	6.59589	6.46321	6.33457	6.20979	6.08875	5.97130
9	7.43533	7.26879	7.10782	6.95220	6.80169	6.65610	6.51523
10	8.11090	7.91272	7.72173	7.53763	7.36009	7.18883	7.02358
11	8.76048	8.52892	8.30641	8.09254	7.88687	7.68904	7.49867
12	9.38507	9.11858	8.86325	8.61852	8.38384	8.15873	7.94269
13	9.98565	9.68285	9.39357	9.11708	8.85268	8.59974	8.35765
14	10.56312	10.22283	9.89864	9.58965	9.29498	9.01384	8.74547
15	11.11839	10.73955	10.37966	10.03758	9.71225	9.40267	9.10791
16	11.65230	11.23402	10.83777	10.46216	10.10590	9.76776	9.44665
17	12.16567	11.70719	11.27407	10.86461	10.47726	10.11058	9.76322
18	12.65930	12.15999	11.68959	11.24607	10.82760	10.43247	10.05909
19	13.13394	12.59329	12.08532	11.60765	11.15812	10.73471	10.33560
20	13.59033	13.00794	12.46221	11.95038	11.46992	11.01851	10.59401
21	14.02916	13.40472	12.82115	12.27524	11.76408	11.28498	10.83553
22	14.45112	13.78442	13.16300	12.58317	12.04158	11.53520	11.06124
23	14.85684	14.14777	13.48857	12.87504	12.30338	11.77014	11.27219
24	15.24696	14.49548	13.79864	13.15170	12.55036	11.99074	11.46933
25	15.62208	14.82821	14.09394	13.41393	12.78336	12.19788	11.65358
26	15.98277	15.14661	14.37519	13.66250	13.00317	12.39237	11.82578
27	16.32959	15.45130	14.64303	13.89810	13.21053	12.57500	11.98671
28	16.66306	15.74287	14.89813	14.12142	13.40616	12.74648	12.13711
29	16.98371	16.02189	15.14107	14.33310	13.59072	12.90749	12.27767
30	17.29203	16.28889	15.37245	14.53375	13.76483	13.05868	12.40904
31	17.58849	16.54439	15.59281	14.72393	13.92909	13.20063	12.53181
32	17.87355	16.78889	15.80268	14.90420	14.08404	13.33393	12.64656
33	18.14765	17.02286	16.00255	15.07507	14.23023	13.45909	12.75379
34	18.41120	17.24676	16.19290	15.23703	14.36814	13.57661	12.85401
35	18.66461	17.46101	16.37419	15.39055	14.49825	13.68696	12.94767
40	19.79277	18.40158	17.15909	16.04612	15.04630	14.14553	13.33171
45	20.72004	19.15635	17.77407	16.54773	15.45583	14.48023	13.60552
50	21.48218	19.76201	18.25593	16.93152	15.76186	14.72452	13.80075

Present Value of Ordinary Annuity of $1 per Period

Periods	8%	9%	10%	11%	12%	13%	14%
1	0.92593	0.91743	0.90909	0.90090	0.89286	0.88496	0.87719
2	1.78326	1.75911	1.73554	1.71252	1.69005	1.66810	1.64666
3	2.57710	2.53129	2.48685	2.44371	2.40183	2.36115	2.32163
4	3.31213	3.23972	3.16987	3.10245	3.03735	2.97447	2.91371
5	3.99271	3.88965	3.79079	3.69590	3.60478	3.51723	3.43308
6	4.62288	4.48592	4.35526	4.23054	4.11141	3.99755	3.88867
7	5.20637	5.03295	4.86842	4.71220	4.56376	4.42261	4.28830
8	5.74664	5.53482	5.33493	5.14612	4.96764	4.79677	4.63886
9	6.24689	5.99525	5.75902	5.53705	5.32825	5.13166	4.94637
10	6.71008	6.41766	6.14457	5.88923	5.65022	5.42624	5.21612
11	7.13896	6.80519	6.49506	6.20652	5.93770	5.68694	5.45273
12	7.53608	7.16073	6.81369	6.49236	6.19437	5.91765	5.66029
13	7.90378	7.48690	7.10336	6.74987	6.42355	6.12181	5.84236
14	8.22424	7.78615	7.36669	6.96187	6.62817	6.30249	6.00207
15	8.55948	8.06069	7.60608	7.19087	6.81086	6.46238	6.14217
16	8.85137	8.31256	7.82371	7.37916	6.97399	6.60388	6.26506
17	9.12164	8.54363	8.02155	7.54879	7.11963	6.72909	6.37286
18	9.37189	8.75563	8.20141	7.70162	7.24967	6.83991	6.46742
19	9.60360	8.95011	8.36492	7.83929	7.36578	6.93797	6.55037
20	9.81815	9.12855	8.51356	7.96333	7.46944	7.02475	6.62313
21	10.01680	9.29224	8.64869	8.07507	7.56200	7.10155	6.68696
22	10.20074	9.44243	8.77154	8.17574	7.64465	7.16951	6.74294
23	10.37106	9.58021	8.88322	8.26643	7.71843	7.22966	6.79206
24	10.52876	9.70661	8.98474	8.34814	7.78432	7.28288	6.83514
25	10.67478	9.82258	9.07704	8.42174	7.84314	7.32998	6.87293
26	10.80998	9.92897	9.16095	8.48806	7.89566	7.37167	6.90608
27	10.93516	10.02658	9.23722	8.54780	7.94255	7.40856	6.93515
28	11.05108	10.11613	9.30657	8.60162	7.98442	7.44120	6.96066
29	11.15841	10.19828	9.36961	8.65011	8.02181	7.47009	6.98304
30	11.25778	10.27365	9.42691	8.69379	8.05518	7.49565	7.00266
31	11.34980	10.34280	9.47901	8.73315	8.08499	7.51828	7.01988
32	11.43500	10.40624	9.52638	8.76860	8.11159	7.53830	7.03498
33	11.51389	10.46444	9.56943	8.80054	8.13535	7.55602	7.04823
34	11.58693	10.51784	9.60857	8.82932	8.15656	7.57170	7.05985
35	11.65457	10.56682	9.64416	8.85524	8.17550	7.58557	7.07005
40	11.92461	10.75736	9.77905	8.95105	8.24378	7.63438	7.10504
45	12.10840	10.88120	9.86281	9.00791	8.28252	7.66086	7.12322
50	12.23348	10.96168	9.91481	9.04165	8.30450	7.67524	7.13266

Appendix B

IFRS

International Financial Reporting Standards (IFRS)

The Need for Global Accounting Standards

As discussed in Chapter 1, the Financial Accounting Standards Board (FASB) establishes generally accepted accounting principles (GAAP) for public companies in the United States. Of course, there is a world beyond the borders of the United States. In recent years, the removal of trade barriers and the growth in cross-border equity and debt issuances have led to a dramatic increase in international commerce. As a result, often companies are reporting financial results to users outside of the United States.

Historically, accounting standards have varied considerably across countries. These variances have been driven by cultural, legal, and political differences and resulted in financial statements that were not easily comparable and difficult to interpret. These differences caused problems for companies in Europe and Asia, where local economies have become increasingly tied to international commerce.

A common set of International Financial Reporting Standards (IFRS) has begun to emerge to reduce cross-country differences in accounting standards. While much of the world has migrated to IFRS, the United States has not. Because of the size of the United States and its significant role in world commerce, U.S. GAAP still has a global impact. As a result, there are currently two major accounting standard-setting efforts in the world, U.S. GAAP and IFRS. These two sets of accounting standards add cost and complexity for companies operating internationally.

Overview of IFRS

International Financial Reporting Standards are designed to meet the financial reporting needs of an increasingly global business environment.

What Is IFRS? International Financial Reporting Standards are a set of global accounting standards developed by an international standard-setting body called the International Accounting Standards Board (IASB). Like the Financial Accounting Standards Board, the IASB is an independent entity that establishes accounting rules. Unlike the FASB, the IASB does not establish accounting rules for any specific country. Rather, it develops accounting rules that can be used by a variety of countries, with the goal of developing a single set of global accounting standards.

Who Uses IFRS? IFRS applies to companies that issue publicly traded debt or equity securities, called **public companies**, in countries that have adopted IFRS as their accounting standards. For example, public companies in the European Union (EU) are required to prepare financial statements using IFRS. The 140 countries and jurisdictions that have adopted or permit the use of IFRS for financial reporting are shown in Exhibit 1.

EXHIBIT 1 **IFRS Adopters**

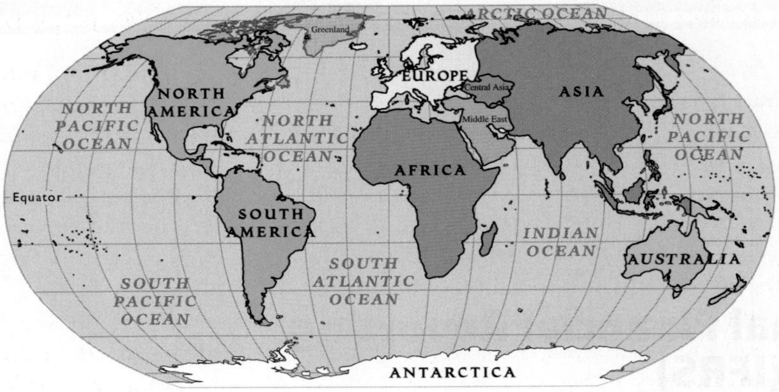

Afghanistan
Albania
Angola
Anguilla
Antigua and Barbuda
Argentina
Armenia
Australia
Austria
Azerbaijan
Bahamas
Bahrain
Bangladesh
Barbados
Belarus
Belgium
Belize
Bermuda
Bhutan
Bolivia
Bosnia and Herzegovina
Botswana
Brazil
Brunei
Bulgaria
Cambodia
Canada
Cayman Islands
Chile
China
Colombia
Costa Rica
Croatia
Cyprus
Czech Republic
Denmark
Dominica
Dominican Republic
Ecuador
Egypt
El Salvador
Estonia
European Union
Fiji
Finland
France
Georgia
Germany
Ghana
Greece
Grenada
Guatemala
Guinea-Bissau
Guyana
Honduras
Hong Kong
Hungary
Iceland
India
Indonesia
Iraq
Ireland
Israel
Italy
Jamaica
Japan
Jordan
Kenya
Korea (South)
Kosovo
Latvia
Lesotho
Liechtenstein
Lithuania
Luxembourg
Macao
Macedonia
Madagascar
Malaysia
Maldives
Malta
Mauritius
Mexico
Moldova
Mongolia
Montserrat
Myanmar
Nepal
Netherlands
New Zealand
Nicaragua
Niger
Nigeria
Norway
Oman
Pakistan
Palestine
Panama
Paraguay
Peru
Philippines
Poland
Portugal
Romania
Russia
Rwanda
Saint Lucia
Saudi Arabia
Serbia
Sierra Leone
Singapore
Slovakia
Slovenia
South Africa
Spain
Sri Lanka
St Kitts and Nevis
St Vincent and the Grenadines
Suriname
Swaziland
Sweden
Switzerland
Syria
Taiwan
Tanzania
Thailand
Trinidad and Tobago
Turkey
Uganda
Ukraine
United Arab Emirates
United Kingdom
United States
Uruguay
Uzbekistan
Venezuela
Vietnam
Yemen
Zambia
Zimbabwe

Source: *Financial Reporting Standards for the World Economy*, IFRS, June 2015.

U.S. GAAP and IFRS: The Road Forward

The United States has not formally adopted IFRS for U.S. companies. The wide acceptance being gained by IFRS around the world, however, has placed considerable pressure on the United States to align U.S. GAAP with IFRS. There are two possible paths that the United States could take to achieve this: (1) adoption of IFRS by the U.S. Securities and Exchange Commission or (2) convergence of U.S. GAAP and IFRS. These two options are briefly discussed in this section.

Adoption of IFRS by the SEC The U.S. Securities and Exchange Commission (SEC) is the U.S. governmental agency that has authority over the accounting and financial disclosures for U.S. public companies. Only the SEC has the authority to adopt IFRS for U.S. public companies. After considerable deliberation over a period of nearly five years, the SEC published a Final

Report on the issues surrounding IFRS adoption.[1] Notably, this report did not include a final policy decision or recommendation in favor of U.S. public companies adopting IFRS. Indeed, since this report, the SEC has distanced itself from the adoption position, and it is now acknowledged as unsupported. This leaves what remains of the convergence pathway.

Convergence of U.S. GAAP and IFRS Convergence involves aligning IFRS and U.S. GAAP one topic at a time, by slowly merging IFRS and U.S. GAAP into two broadly uniform sets of accounting standards. To this end, the FASB and IASB have agreed to work together on a select number of difficult and high-profile accounting issues. These issues frame a large portion of the disagreement between the two sets of standards and, if accomplished, will significantly reduce the differences between U.S. GAAP and IFRS. The projects selected for the convergence effort represent some of the more technical topics in accounting and are covered in intermediate and advanced accounting courses.

One of the major limitations of convergence is that both the FASB and IASB continue to operate as the accounting standard-setting bodies for their respective jurisdictions. As such, convergence would not result in a single set of global accounting standards. Only those standards that go through the joint FASB–IASB standard-setting process would be released as uniform. Standards that do not go through a joint standard-setting process may create inconsistencies between U.S. GAAP and IFRS.

Differences Between U.S. GAAP and IFRS

U.S. GAAP and IFRS differ both in their approach to standard setting, as well as their financial statement presentation and recording of transactions.

Rules-Based Versus Principles Approach to Standard Setting U.S. GAAP is considered to be a "rules-based" approach to accounting standard setting. The accounting standards provide detailed and specific rules on the accounting for business transactions. There are few exceptions or varying interpretations of the accounting for a business event. This structure is consistent with the U.S. legal and regulatory system, reflecting the social and economic values of the United States.

In contrast, IFRS is designed to meet the needs of many countries. Differences in legal, political, and economic systems create different needs for and uses of financial information in different countries. For example, Germany needs a financial reporting system that reflects the central role of banks in its financial system, while the Netherlands needs a financial reporting system that reflects the significant role of outside equity in its financial system.

To accommodate economic, legal, and social diversity, IFRS must be broad enough to capture these differences while still presenting comparable financial statements. Under IFRS, there is greater opportunity for different interpretations of the accounting treatment of a business event across different business entities. To support this, IFRS often has more extensive disclosures that support alternative assumptions. Thus, IFRS provides more latitude for professional judgment than typically found in comparable U.S. GAAP. Many countries find this feature attractive in reducing regulatory costs associated with using and auditing financial reports. This "principles-based" approach presents one of the most significant challenges to adopting IFRS in the United States.

Technical Differences Between IFRS and U.S. GAAP Although U.S. GAAP is similar to IFRS, differences arise in the presentation format, balance sheet valuations, and technical accounting procedures. The Mornin' Joe International financial statements presented at the end of the last chapter highlight the financial statement format, presentation, and recording differences between U.S. GAAP and IFRS. A more comprehensive summary of the key differences between U.S. GAAP and IFRS that are relevant to an introductory accounting course is provided in Exhibit 2.

1 Work Plan for the Consideration of Incorporating International Financial Accounting Standards into the Financial Reporting System for U.S. Issuers: Final Staff Report, U.S. Securities Exchange Commission, July 13, 2012.

EXHIBIT 2 **Comparison of Accounting for Selected Items Under U.S. GAAP and IFRS**

	U.S. GAAP	IFRS	Text Reference
General:			
Financial statement titles	Balance Sheet Statement of Stockholders' Equity Statement of Cash Flows	Statement of Financial Position Statement of Changes in Equity Statement of Cash Flows	General
Financial periods presented	Public companies must present two years of comparative information for income statement, statement of stockholders' equity, and statement of cash flows	One year of comparative information must be presented	General
Conceptual basis for standard setting	"Rules-based" approach	"Principles-based" approach	General
Internal control requirements	Sarbanes-Oxley Act (SOX) Section 404		Ch 7
Balance Sheet:	***Balance Sheet***	***Statement of Financial Position***	
Terminology differences	"Payable" "Stockholders' Equity" "Net Income (Loss)"	"Provision" "Capital and Reserves" "Profit or (Loss)"	Ch 10 Ch 12 General
Inventory—LIFO	LIFO allowed	LIFO prohibited	Ch 6
Inventory—valuation	Reversal of lower-of-cost-or-market write-downs not allowed	Reversal of write-downs allowed	Ch 6 Ch 6
Long-lived assets	May NOT be revalued to fair value	May be revalued to fair value on a regular basis	Ch 9

(Continued)

EXHIBIT 2 **Comparison of Accounting for Selected Items Under U.S. GAAP and IFRS (Continued)**

	U.S. GAAP	IFRS	Text Reference
Land held for investment	Treated as held for use or sale, and recorded at historical cost	May be accounted for on a historical cost basis or on a fair value basis with changes in fair value recognized through profit and loss	Ch 9
Property, plant, and equipment—valuation	Historical cost If impaired, impairment loss may NOT be reversed in future periods	May select between historical cost or revalued amount (a form of fair value) If impaired, impairment loss may be reversed in future periods	Ch 9
Cost of major overhaul (Capital and revenue expenditures)	Different treatment for ordinary repairs and maintenance, asset improvement, extraordinary repairs	Typically included as part of the cost of the asset or asset component if future economic benefit is probable and can be reliably measured	Ch 9
Intangible assets—valuation	Acquisition cost, unless impaired	Fair value permitted if the intangible asset trades in an active market	Ch 9
Intangible assets—impairment loss reversal	Prohibited	Prohibited for goodwill but allowed for other intangible assets	Ch 9
Income Statement:	***Income Statement***	***Statement of Comprehensive Income***	
Classification of expenses on income statement	Public companies must present expenses on the income statement by function (e.g., cost of goods sold, selling, administrative)	Expenses may be presented based either by function (e.g., cost of goods sold, selling) or by the nature of expense (e.g., wages expense, interest expense)	Chs 3, 4, 5
Statement of Cash Flows:	***Statement of Cash Flows***	***Statement of Cash Flows***	
Classification of interest paid or received	Treated as an operating activity	Interest paid may be treated as either an operating or a financing activity; interest received may be treated as an operating or investing activity	Ch. 13
Classification of dividend paid or received	Dividend paid treated as a financing activity, dividend received treated as an operating activity	Dividend paid may be treated as either an operating or a financing activity; dividend received may be treated as an operating or investing activity	Ch. 13

Discussion Questions

1. Briefly discuss why global accounting standards are needed in today's business environment.
2. What are International Financial Reporting Standards? Who uses these accounting standards?
3. What body is responsible for setting International Financial Reporting Standards?
4. Briefly discuss the differences between (A) adoption of IFRS by the U.S. Securities and Exchange Commission and (B) convergence of U.S. GAAP with IFRS.
5. Briefly discuss the difference between (A) a "rules-based" approach to accounting standard setting and (B) a "principles-based" approach to accounting standard setting.
6. How is property, plant, and equipment measured on the balance sheet under IFRS? How does this differ from the way property, plant, and equipment is measured on the balance sheet under U.S. GAAP?
7. What inventory costing methods are allowed under IFRS? How does this differ from the treatment under U.S. GAAP?

Appendix C

Revenue Recognition

Companies recognize revenue when services have been performed or products have been delivered to customers. For example, when **McDonald's** sells a hamburger, the revenue is earned when the hamburger is delivered to the customer. In this example, revenue recognition is simple because the hamburger is delivered and cash is received at a single point in time.

Revenue recognition is more complex, however, when a transaction includes several items that are sold together, items that are delivered over time, or items whose prices depend upon future events. To address these more complex transactions, the Financial Accounting Standards Board (FASB) issued a new accounting standard in May 2014.[1] The new Standard uses a five-step method for determining when revenue should be recognized. The five steps are as follows:

Step 1. *Identify the contract with the customer.* The new Standard treats every revenue transaction as a contract. A contract is an agreement by the seller to provide a good or service in exchange for payment from the buyer. A contract may be verbal and implicit, such as the purchase of a **McDonald's** hamburger, or written and explicit, such as a cell phone contract.

Step 2. *Identify the separate performance obligations in the contract.* Every contract requires the seller and buyer to perform. For example, when you purchase a **McDonald's** hamburger, you (the buyer) perform by paying and McDonald's (the seller) performs by delivering a hamburger. When you purchase a cell phone from **Verizon**, the transaction is more complex. You perform by paying cash or charging your credit card and signing a written contract. Verizon performs by delivering you the phone and promising to provide you cellular service in the future. In this case, Verizon has two performance obligations: (1) to provide the phone and (2) to provide cellular service in the future.

Step 3. *Determine the transaction price.* The transaction price is the amount the seller is entitled to receive in exchange for the goods and services they have provided. In the case of the **McDonald's** hamburger, the transaction price is the amount paid for the hamburger. In the case of **Verizon**, the transaction price must be estimated for the phone (the first performance obligation) and cellular service (the second performance obligation).

Step 4. *Allocate the transaction price to the separate performance obligations.* Since the sale of a **McDonald's** hamburger involves the sale of a single item that is immediately delivered, the entire transaction price is allocated to the hamburger. In more complex transactions, such as a **Verizon** cellular service contract, the revenue received from the customer must be allocated among the performance obligations. This allocation is often based on the stand-alone (separate) price of each good or service. For example, Verizon should allocate the revenue from the

1 Accounting Standards Update, *Revenue from Contracts with Customers (Topic 606),* Financial Accounting Standards Board, May 2014, Norwalk, CT.

customer between the phone (first performance obligation) and the commitment to provide cellular service (second performance obligation).

Step 5. *Recognize revenue when each separate performance obligation is satisfied.* The seller should recognize (record) revenue as each performance obligation is satisfied. In the case of **McDonald's**, the performance obligation is satisfied when the clerk delivers the hamburger to the customer. At this point, the control of the hamburger has passed to the customer. In the case of **Verizon**, it satisfies its first performance obligation when it delivers you the phone. Verizon satisfies its second performance obligation over time by providing you cellular service. Thus, Verizon should record a portion of the total revenue at the time you sign the contract and receive your phone and the remaining revenue over the period cellular service is provided.

To illustrate, assume that on March 1, Chandler Evans upgrades (replaces) his cell phone with Star Cellular at no cost by signing a two-year agreement. The new agreement cannot be cancelled and requires a payment of $90 per month. The cell phone selected by Evans cost Star Cellular $250.

The five-step method for recognizing revenue from this transaction would be applied as follows:

Step 1. *Identify the contract with the customer.* The contract with Chandler Evans is the two-year cellular service agreement that includes delivery of a new cell phone.

Step 2. *Identify the separate performance obligations in the contract.* Star Cellular has two separate performance obligations under this contract. First, Star Cellular must deliver a new cell phone at the time that Evans signs the service agreement. Second, Star Cellular must provide Evans with cell service for two years.

Step 3. *Determine the transaction price.* The transaction price is the total amount Star Cellular will receive over the contract period. In this case, Star Cellular will receive $2,160 ($90 × 24 months) over the contract period.[2]

Step 4. *Allocate the transaction price to the separate performance obligations.* If Star Cellular sold the cell phone and cell service separately, the individual prices would be as follows:

Cell phone (sold separately)	$ 600
Cell service for two years	3,000
Total price if sold separately	$3,600

The transaction price is allocated to each performance obligation based upon what each obligation would sell for separately as a stand-alone product. To illustrate, the cell phone is allocated $360 of the transaction price of $2,160, computed as follows:

$$\text{Cell Phone} = \text{Transaction Price} \times \frac{\text{Price of Cell Phone Sold Separately}}{\text{Total Price of Cell Phone and Cell Service Sold Separately}}$$

$$= \$2{,}160 \times \frac{\$600}{\$3{,}600} = \$360$$

The cell service is allocated $1,800 of the transaction price of $2,160, computed as follows:

$$\text{Cell Service} = \text{Transaction Price} \times \frac{\text{Price of Cell Service Sold Separately}}{\text{Total Price of Cell Phone and Cell Service Sold Separately}}$$

$$= \$2{,}160 \times \frac{\$3{,}000}{\$3{,}600} = \$1{,}800$$

Step 5. *Recognize revenue when each separate performance obligation is satisfied.* The $360 of revenue assigned to the cell phone is recognized when the customer signs the service agreement and receives the phone. At this point, the first performance obligation has been satisfied by Star Cellular and the control of the phone has passed to the customer. The journal entry to record revenue on March 1 is as follows:

2 An interest component may need to be considered in long-term contracts. To simplify, we ignore interest.

Mar.	1	Accounts Receivable—Chandler Evans	360	
		Sales		360
	1	Cost of Goods Sold	250	
		Inventory		250

The $1,800 of cell service revenue is recognized as the performance obligation is satisfied over the two-year term of the contract. For example, $75 ($1,800 ÷ 24 months) of service revenue would be recorded each month. The journal entry to record the service revenue for March is as follows:

Mar.	31	Cash	90	
		Accounts Receivable ($360 ÷ 24 months)		15
		Cell Service Revenue ($1,800 ÷ 24 months)		75

The preceding journal entries illustrate how over the life of the two-year contract the total revenue from the contract of $2,160 is divided between the sale of the cell phone ($360 of revenue) and providing of cell service ($1,800 of revenue). In addition, the journal entries illustrate when revenue from the phone and service is recorded.

Exhibit 1 summarizes the division of revenue and its recording over the two-year contract.

Recording Revenue over Two-Year Contract EXHIBIT 1

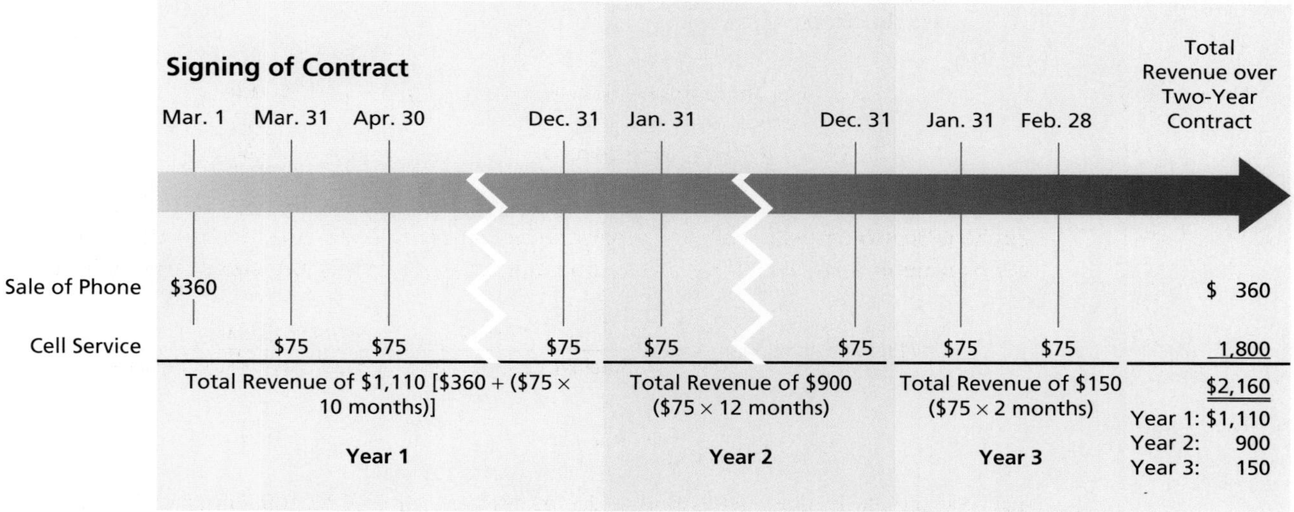

Appendix D

Selected Excerpts from Nike Inc., Form 10-K for the Fiscal Year Ended May 31, 2016

NIKE, Inc .

(Exact name of Registrant as specified in its charter)

Management's Annual Report on Internal Control Over Financial Reporting

Management is responsible for establishing and maintaining adequate internal control over financial reporting, as such term is defined in Rule 13(a) - 15(f) and Rule 15(d) - 15(f) of the Securities Exchange Act of 1934, as amended. Internal control over financial reporting is a process designed to provide reasonable assurance regarding the reliability of financial reporting and the preparation of the financial statements for external purposes in accordance with generally accepted accounting principles in the United States of America. Internal control over financial reporting includes those policies and procedures that: (i) pertain to the maintenance of records that, in reasonable detail, accurately and fairly reflect the transactions and dispositions of assets of the Company; (ii) provide reasonable assurance that transactions are recorded as necessary to permit preparation of financial statements in accordance with generally accepted accounting principles, and that receipts and expenditures of the Company are being made only in accordance with authorizations of our management and directors; and (iii) provide reasonable assurance regarding prevention or timely detection of unauthorized acquisition, use or disposition of assets of the Company that could have a material effect on the financial statements.

While "reasonable assurance" is a high level of assurance, it does not mean absolute assurance. Because of its inherent limitations, internal control over financial reporting may not prevent or detect every misstatement and instance of fraud. Controls are susceptible to manipulation, especially in instances of fraud caused by the collusion of two or more people, including our senior management. Also, projections of any evaluation of effectiveness to future periods are subject to the risk that controls may become inadequate because of changes in conditions, or that the degree of compliance with the policies or procedures may deteriorate.

Under the supervision and with the participation of our Chief Executive Officer and Chief Financial Officer, our management conducted an evaluation of the effectiveness of our internal control over financial reporting based upon the framework in *Internal Control — Integrated Framework (2013)* issued by the Committee of Sponsoring Organizations of the Treadway Commission (COSO). Based on the results of our evaluation, our management concluded that our internal control over financial reporting was effective as of May 31, 2016.

PricewaterhouseCoopers LLP, an independent registered public accounting firm, has audited (1) the Consolidated Financial Statements and (2) the effectiveness of our internal control over financial reporting as of May 31, 2016, as stated in their report herein.

Mark G. Parker
Chairman, President and Chief Executive Officer

Andrew Campion
Chief Financial Officer

Report of Independent Registered Public Accounting Firm

To the Board of Directors and Shareholders of NIKE, Inc.:

In our opinion, the consolidated financial statements listed in the index appearing under Item 15(a)(1) present fairly, in all material respects, the financial position of NIKE, Inc. and its subsidiaries at May 31, 2016 and 2015 , and the results of their operations and their cash flows for each of the three years in the period ended May 31, 2016 in conformity with accounting principles generally accepted in the United States of America. In addition, in our opinion, the financial statement schedule listed in the index appearing under Item 15(a)(2) presents fairly, in all material respects, the information set forth therein when read in conjunction with the related consolidated financial statements. Also in our opinion, the Company maintained, in all material respects, effective internal control over financial reporting as of May 31, 2016 , based on criteria established in *Internal Control — Integrated Framework (2013)* issued by the Committee of Sponsoring Organizations of the Treadway Commission (COSO). The Company's management is responsible for these financial statements and financial statement schedule, for maintaining effective internal control over financial reporting and for its assessment of the effectiveness of internal control over financial reporting, included in Management's Annual Report on Internal Control over Financial Reporting appearing under Item 8. Our responsibility is to express opinions on these financial statements, on the financial statement schedule and on the Company's internal control over financial reporting based on our integrated audits. We conducted our audits in accordance with the standards of the Public Company Accounting Oversight Board (United States). Those standards require that we plan and perform the audits to obtain reasonable assurance about whether the financial statements are free of material misstatement and whether effective internal control over financial reporting was maintained in all material respects. Our audits of the financial statements included examining, on a test basis, evidence supporting the amounts and disclosures in the financial statements, assessing the accounting principles used and significant estimates made by management and evaluating the overall financial statement presentation. Our audit of internal control over financial reporting included obtaining an understanding of internal control over financial reporting, assessing the risk that a material weakness exists and testing and evaluating the design and operating effectiveness of internal control based on the assessed risk. Our audits also included performing such other procedures as we considered necessary in the circumstances. We believe that our audits provide a reasonable basis for our opinions.

A company's internal control over financial reporting is a process designed to provide reasonable assurance regarding the reliability of financial reporting and the preparation of financial statements for external purposes in accordance with generally accepted accounting principles. A company's internal control over financial reporting includes those policies and procedures that (i) pertain to the maintenance of records that, in reasonable detail, accurately and fairly reflect the transactions and dispositions of the assets of the company; (ii) provide reasonable assurance that transactions are recorded as necessary to permit preparation of financial statements in accordance with generally accepted accounting principles, and that receipts and expenditures of the company are being made only in accordance with authorizations of management and directors of the company; and (iii) provide reasonable assurance regarding prevention or timely detection of unauthorized acquisition, use, or disposition of the company's assets that could have a material effect on the financial statements.

Because of its inherent limitations, internal control over financial reporting may not prevent or detect misstatements. Also, projections of any evaluation of effectiveness to future periods are subject to the risk that controls may become inadequate because of changes in conditions, or that the degree of compliance with the policies or procedures may deteriorate.

/S/ PRICEWATERHOUSECOOPERS LLP

Portland, Oregon

July 21, 2016

NIKE, Inc. Consolidated Statements of Income

(In millions, except per share data)	Year Ended May 31, 2016	2015	2014
Revenues	$ 32,376	$ 30,601	$ 27,799
Cost of sales	17,405	16,534	15,353
Gross profit	14,971	14,067	12,446
Demand creation expense	3,278	3,213	3,031
Operating overhead expense	7,191	6,679	5,735
Total selling and administrative expense	10,469	9,892	8,766
Interest expense (income), net	19	28	33
Other (income) expense, net	(140)	(58)	103
Income before income taxes	4,623	4,205	3,544
Income tax expense	863	932	851
NET INCOME	**$ 3,760**	**$ 3,273**	**$ 2,693**
Earnings per common share:			
Basic	$ 2.21	$ 1.90	$ 1.52
Diluted	$ 2.16	$ 1.85	$ 1.49
Dividends declared per common share	$ 0.62	$ 0.54	$ 0.47

The accompanying Notes to the Consolidated Financial Statements are an integral part of this statement.

The Notes may be found on the companion website at CengageBrain.com

NIKE, Inc. Consolidated Statements of Comprehensive Income

(In millions)	Year Ended May 31, 2016	2015	2014
Net income	$ 3,760	$ 3,273	$ 2,693
Other comprehensive income (loss), net of tax:			
Change in net foreign currency translation adjustment[(1)]	(176)	(20)	(32)
Change in net gains (losses) on cash flow hedges[(2)]	(757)	1,188	(161)
Change in net gains (losses) on other[(3)]	5	(7)	4
Total other comprehensive income (loss), net of tax	(928)	1,161	(189)
TOTAL COMPREHENSIVE INCOME	**$ 2,832**	**$ 4,434**	**$ 2,504**

(1) Net of tax benefit (expense) of $0 million , $0 million and $0 million , respectively.

(2) Net of tax benefit (expense) of $35 million , $(31) million and $18 million , respectively.

(3) Net of tax benefit (expense) of $0 million , $0 million and $0 million , respectively.

The accompanying Notes to the Consolidated Financial Statements are an integral part of this statement.

The Notes may be found on the companion website at CengageBrain.com

NIKE, Inc. Consolidated Balance Sheets

	May 31,	
(In millions)	**2016**	**2015**
ASSETS		
Current assets:		
Cash and equivalents	$ 3,138	$ 3,852
Short-term investments	2,319	2,072
Accounts receivable, net	3,241	3,358
Inventories	4,838	4,337
Prepaid expenses and other current assets	1,489	1,968
Total current assets	15,025	15,587
Property, plant and equipment, net	3,520	3,011
Identifiable intangible assets, net	281	281
Goodwill	131	131
Deferred income taxes and other assets	2,439	2,587
TOTAL ASSETS	**$ 21,396**	**$ 21,597**
LIABILITIES AND SHAREHOLDERS' EQUITY		
Current liabilities:		
Current portion of long-term debt	$ 44	$ 107
Notes payable	1	74
Accounts payable	2,191	2,131
Accrued liabilities	3,037	3,949
Income taxes payable	85	71
Total current liabilities	5,358	6,332
Long-term debt	2,010	1,079
Deferred income taxes and other liabilities	1,770	1,479
Commitments and contingencies		
Redeemable preferred stock	—	—
Shareholders' equity:		
Common stock at stated value:		
Class A convertible — 353 and 355 shares outstanding	—	—
Class B — 1,329 and 1,357 shares outstanding	3	3
Capital in excess of stated value	7,786	6,773
Accumulated other comprehensive income	318	1,246
Retained earnings	4,151	4,685
Total shareholders' equity	12,258	12,707
TOTAL LIABILITIES AND SHAREHOLDERS' EQUITY	**$ 21,396**	**$ 21,597**

The accompanying Notes to the Consolidated Financial Statements are an integral part of this statement.

The Notes may be found on the companion website at CengageBrain.com

NIKE, Inc. Consolidated Statements of Cash Flows

(In millions)	Year Ended May 31, 2016	2015	2014
Cash provided by operations:			
Net income	$ 3,760	$ 3,273	$ 2,693
Income charges (credits) not affecting cash:			
Depreciation	649	606	518
Deferred income taxes	(80)	(113)	(11)
Stock-based compensation	236	191	177
Amortization and other	13	43	68
Net foreign currency adjustments	98	424	56
Changes in certain working capital components and other assets and liabilities:			
Decrease (increase) in accounts receivable	60	(216)	(298)
(Increase) in inventories	(590)	(621)	(505)
(Increase) in prepaid expenses and other current assets	(161)	(144)	(210)
(Decrease) increase in accounts payable, accrued liabilities and income taxes payable	(889)	1,237	525
Cash provided by operations	3,096	4,680	3,013
Cash used by investing activities:			
Purchases of short-term investments	(5,367)	(4,936)	(5,386)
Maturities of short-term investments	2,924	3,655	3,932
Sales of short-term investments	2,386	2,216	1,126
Investments in reverse repurchase agreements	150	(150)	—
Additions to property, plant and equipment	(1,143)	(963)	(880)
Disposals of property, plant and equipment	10	3	3
Decrease (increase) in other assets, net of other liabilities	6	—	(2)
Cash used by investing activities	(1,034)	(175)	(1,207)
Cash used by financing activities:			
Net proceeds from long-term debt issuance	981	—	—
Long-term debt payments, including current portion	(106)	(7)	(60)
(Decrease) increase in notes payable	(67)	(63)	75
Payments on capital lease obligations	(7)	(19)	(17)
Proceeds from exercise of stock options and other stock issuances	507	514	383
Excess tax benefits from share-based payment arrangements	281	218	132
Repurchase of common stock	(3,238)	(2,534)	(2,628)
Dividends — common and preferred	(1,022)	(899)	(799)
Cash used by financing activities	(2,671)	(2,790)	(2,914)
Effect of exchange rate changes on cash and equivalents	(105)	(83)	(9)
Net (decrease) increase in cash and equivalents	(714)	1,632	(1,117)
Cash and equivalents, beginning of year	3,852	2,220	3,337
CASH AND EQUIVALENTS, END OF YEAR	**$ 3,138**	**$ 3,852**	**$ 2,220**
Supplemental disclosure of cash flow information:			
Cash paid during the year for:			
Interest, net of capitalized interest	$ 70	$ 53	$ 53
Income taxes	748	1,262	856
Non-cash additions to property, plant and equipment	252	206	167
Dividends declared and not paid	271	240	209

The accompanying Notes to the Consolidated Financial Statements are an integral part of this statement.

The Notes may be found on the companion website at CengageBrain.com

NIKE, Inc. Consolidated Statements of Shareholders' Equity

(In millions, except per share data)	Common Stock Class A Shares	Common Stock Class A Amount	Common Stock Class B Shares	Common Stock Class B Amount	Capital in Excess of Stated Value	Accumulated Other Comprehensive Income	Retained Earnings	Total
Balance at May 31, 2013	**356**	**$ —**	**1,433**	**$ 3**	**$ 5,184**	**$ 274**	**$ 5,620**	**$ 11,081**
Stock options exercised	(1)		22		445			445
Conversion to Class B Common Stock		—	1	—				—
Repurchase of Class B Common Stock			(73)		(11)		(2,617)	(2,628)
Dividends on common stock ($0.47 per share)							(821)	(821)
Issuance of shares to employees			3		78			78
Stock-based compensation					177			177
Forfeiture of shares from employees			(1)		(8)		(4)	(12)
Net income							2,693	2,693
Other comprehensive income (loss)						(189)		(189)
Balance at May 31, 2014	**355**	**$ —**	**1,385**	**$ 3**	**$ 5,865**	**$ 85**	**$ 4,871**	**$ 10,824**
Stock options exercised			27		639			639
Repurchase of Class B Common Stock			(58)		(9)		(2,525)	(2,534)
Dividends on common stock ($0.54 per share)							(931)	(931)
Issuance of shares to employees			3		92			92
Stock-based compensation					191			191
Forfeiture of shares from employees			—		(5)		(3)	(8)
Net income							3,273	3,273
Other comprehensive income (loss)						1,161		1,161
Balance at May 31, 2015	**355**	**$ —**	**1,357**	**$ 3**	**$ 6,773**	**$ 1,246**	**$ 4,685**	**$ 12,707**
Stock options exercised			22		680			680
Conversion to Class B Common Stock	(2)	—	2	—				—
Repurchase of Class B Common Stock			(55)		(8)		(3,230)	(3,238)
Dividends on common stock ($0.62 per share)							(1,053)	(1,053)
Issuance of shares to employees			3		115			115
Stock-based compensation					236			236
Forfeiture of shares from employees			—		(10)		(11)	(21)
Net income							3,760	3,760
Other comprehensive income (loss)						(928)		(928)
Balance at May 31, 2016	**353**	**$ —**	**1,329**	**$ 3**	**7,786**	**$ 318**	**$ 4,151**	**$ 12,258**

The accompanying Notes to the Consolidated Financial Statements are an integral part of this statement.

The Notes may be found on the companion website at CengageBrain.com

Glossary

A

absorption costing The reporting of the costs of manufactured products, normally direct materials, direct labor, and factory overhead, as product costs. (Ch. 21)

accounts receivable analysis A company's ability to collect its accounts receivable. (Ch. 17)

accounts receivable turnover The relationship between net sales and accounts receivable, computed by dividing the net sales by the average net accounts receivable; measures how frequently during the year the accounts receivable are being converted to cash. (Ch. 17)

accumulated other comprehensive income The cumulative effects of other comprehensive income items reported separately in the Stockholders' Equity section of the balance sheet. (Ch. 15)

activities The types of work, or actions, involved in a manufacturing process or service activity. (Ch. 25)

activity base (driver) A measure of activity that is related to changes in cost. Used in analyzing and classifying cost behavior. Activity bases are also used in the denominator in calculating the predetermined factory overhead rate to assign overhead costs to cost objects. (Chs. 19, 21, 25)

activity rate The estimated activity cost divided by estimated activity-base usage. (Ch. 25)

activity-based costing (ABC) A cost allocation method that identifies activities causing the incurrence of costs and allocates these costs to products (or other cost objects), based on activity drivers (bases). (Chs. 19, 25)

amortization The periodic transfer of the cost of an intangible asset to expense. (Ch. 14)

analytical methods Methods that examine changes in the amount and percentage of financial statement items within and across periods. (Ch. 17)

annuity A series of equal cash flows at fixed intervals. (Chs. 14, 26)

asset turnover A measure of how effectively a business is using its assets to generate sales. (Ch. 17)

available-for-sale securities Securities that management expects to sell in the future but which are not actively traded for profit. (Ch. 15)

average rate of return A method of evaluating capital investment proposals that focuses on the expected profitability of the investment. (Ch. 26)

B

balanced scorecard A performance evaluation approach that incorporates multiple performance dimensions by combining financial and nonfinancial measures. (Ch. 24)

bond A form of an interest-bearing note used by corporations to borrow on a long-term basis. (Ch. 14)

bond indenture The contract between a corporation issuing bonds and the bondholders. (Ch. 14)

break-even point The level of business operations at which revenues and expired costs are equal. (Ch. 21)

budget An accounting device used to plan and control resources of operational departments and divisions. (Ch. 22)

budget performance report A report comparing actual results with budget figures. (Ch. 23)

budgetary slack Excess resources set within a budget to provide for uncertain events. (Ch. 22)

budgeted variable factory overhead The standard variable overhead for the actual units produced. (Ch. 23)

business combination A business making an investment in another business by acquiring a controlling share, often greater than 50%, of the outstanding voting stock of another corporation by paying cash or exchanging stock. (Ch. 15)

C

capital expenditures budget The budget summarizing future plans for acquiring plant facilities and equipment. (Ch. 22)

capital investment analysis The process by which management plans, evaluates, and controls long-term capital investments involving property, plant, and equipment. (Ch. 26)

capital rationing The process by which management plans, evaluates, and controls long-term capital investments involving fixed assets. (Ch. 26)

carrying amount The balance of the bonds payable account (face amount of the bonds) less any unamortized discount or plus any unamortized premium. (Ch. 14)

cash budget A budget of estimated cash receipts and payments. (Ch. 22)

cash flow per share Normally computed as cash flow from operations per share. (Ch. 16)

cash flows from (used for) financing activities The section of the statement of cash flows that reports cash flows from transactions affecting the equity and debt of the business. (Ch. 16)

cash flows from (used for) investing activities The section of the statement of cash flows that reports cash flows from transactions affecting investments in noncurrent assets. (Ch. 16)

cash flows from operating activities The section of the statement of cash flows that reports the cash transactions affecting the determination of net income. (Ch. 16)

cash payback period The expected period of time that will elapse between the date of a capital expenditure and the complete recovery in cash (or equivalent) of the amount invested. (Ch. 26)

common-sized statement A financial statement in which all items are expressed only in relative terms. (Ch. 17)

comprehensive income All changes in stockholders' equity during a period, except those resulting from dividends and stockholders' investments. (Ch. 15)

consolidated financial statements Financial statements resulting from combining parent and subsidiary statements. (Ch. 15)

continuous budgeting A method of budgeting that provides for maintaining a 12-month projection into the future. (Ch. 22)

continuous process improvement A management approach that is part of the overall total quality management philosophy. The approach requires all employees to constantly improve processes of which they are a part or for which they have managerial responsibility. (Ch. 18)

contract rate The periodic interest to be paid on the bonds that is identified in the bond indenture; expressed as a percentage of the face amount of the bond. (Ch. 14)

contribution margin The excess of sales over variable costs. (Ch. 21)

contribution margin ratio The percentage of each sales dollar that is available to cover the fixed costs and provide an operating income. (Ch. 21)

controllable expenses Costs that can be influenced by the decisions of a manager. (Ch. 24)

controllable revenues Revenues earned by the profit center. (Ch. 24)

controllable variance The difference between the actual amount of variable factory overhead cost incurred and the amount of variable factory overhead budgeted for the standard product. (Ch. 23)

controller The chief management accountant of a division or other segment of a business. (Ch. 18)

controlling A phase in the management process that consists of monitoring the operating results of implemented plans and comparing the actual results with the expected results. (Ch. 18)

conversion costs The combination of direct labor and factory overhead costs. (Ch. 18)

cost A payment of cash (or a commitment to pay cash in the future) for the purpose of generating revenues. (Ch. 18)

cost accounting systems Systems that measure, record, and report product costs. (Ch. 19)

cost allocation The process of assigning indirect cost to a cost object, such as a job. (Ch. 19)

cost behavior The manner in which a cost changes in relation to its activity base (driver). (Ch. 21)

cost center A decentralized unit in which the department or division manager has responsibility for the control of costs incurred and the authority to make decisions that affect these costs. (Ch. 24)

cost method A method of accounting for equity investments representing less than 20% of the outstanding shares of the investee. The purchase is at original cost, and any gains or losses upon sale are recognized by the difference between the sale proceeds and the original cost. (Ch. 15)

cost object The object or segment of operations to which costs are related for management's use, such as a product or department. (Ch. 18)

cost of finished goods available for sale The beginning finished goods inventory added to the cost of goods manufactured during the period. (Ch. 18)

cost of goods manufactured The total cost of making and finishing a product. (Ch. 18)

cost of goods sold The cost of finished goods available for sale minus the ending finished goods inventory. (Ch. 18)

cost of goods sold budget A budget of the estimated direct materials, direct labor, and factory overhead consumed by sold products. (Ch. 22)

cost of merchandise sold The cost that is reported as an expense when merchandise is sold. (Ch. 18)

cost of production report A report prepared periodically by a processing department, summarizing (1) the units for which the department is accountable and the disposition of those units and (2) the costs incurred by the department and the allocation of those costs between completed and incomplete production. (Ch. 20)

cost per equivalent unit The rate used to allocate costs between completed and partially completed production. (Ch. 20)

cost price approach An approach to transfer pricing that uses cost as the basis for setting the transfer price. (Ch. 24)

cost variance The difference between actual cost and the flexible budget at actual volumes. (Ch. 23)

cost-volume-profit analysis The systematic examination of the relationships among selling prices, volume of sales and production, costs, expenses, and profits. (Ch. 21)

cost-volume-profit chart A chart that graphically shows sales, costs, and the related profit or loss for various levels of units sold. (Ch. 21)

currency exchange rate The rate at which currency in another country can be exchanged for local currency. (Ch. 26)

current position analysis A company's ability to pay its current liabilities. (Ch. 17)

current ratio A financial ratio that is computed by dividing current assets by current liabilities. (Ch. 17)

currently attainable standards Standards that represent levels of operation that can be attained with reasonable effort. (Ch. 23)

D

debt securities Notes and bond investments that provide interest revenue over a fixed maturity. (Ch. 15)

decision making A component inherent in the other management processes of planning, directing, controlling, and improving. (Ch. 18)

differential analysis The area of accounting concerned with the effect of alternative courses of action on revenues and costs. (Ch. 25)

differential cost The amount of increase or decrease in cost expected from a particular course of action compared with an alternative. (Ch. 25)

differential income (loss) The difference between the differential revenue and the differential costs. (Ch. 25)

differential revenue The amount of increase or decrease in revenue expected from a particular course of action as compared with an alternative. (Ch. 25)

direct costs Costs that can be traced directly to a cost object. (Ch. 18)

direct labor cost The wages of factory workers who are directly involved in converting materials into a finished product. (Ch. 18)

direct labor cost budget Budget that estimates direct labor hours and related costs needed to support budgeted production. (Ch. 22)

direct labor rate variance The cost associated with the difference between the actual rate and the standard rate paid for direct labor multiplied by the actual direct labor hours used in producing a commodity. (Ch. 23)

direct labor time variance The cost associated with the difference between the actual hours and the standard hours of direct labor spent producing a commodity multiplied by the standard direct labor rate per hour. (Ch. 23)

direct materials cost The cost of materials that are an integral part of the finished product. (Ch. 18)

direct materials price variance The cost associated with the difference between the actual price and the standard price of direct materials multiplied by the actual quantity of direct materials used in producing a commodity. (Ch. 23)

direct materials purchases budget A budget that uses the production budget as a starting point to budget materials purchases. (Ch. 22)

direct materials quantity variance The cost associated with the difference between the actual quantity and the standard quantity of direct materials used in producing a commodity multiplied by the standard direct materials price. (Ch. 23)

direct method A method of reporting the cash flows from operating activities as the difference between the operating cash receipts and the operating cash payments. (Ch. 16)

directing The process by which managers, given their assigned level of responsibilities, run day-to-day operations. (Ch. 18)

discount The interest deducted from the maturity value of a note or the excess of the face amount of bonds over their issue price. (Ch. 14)

dividend yield A ratio, computed by dividing the annual dividends paid per share of common stock by the market price per share at a specific date, that indicates the rate of return to stockholders in terms of cash dividend distributions. (Chs. 15, 17)

dividends per share Measures the extent to which earnings are being distributed to common shareholders. (Ch. 17)

DuPont formula An expanded expression of return on investment determined by multiplying the profit margin by the investment turnover. (Ch. 24)

E

earnings per common share (EPS) Net income per share of common stock outstanding during a period. (Ch. 14)

earnings per share (EPS) on common stock The profitability ratio of net income available to common shareholders to the number of common shares outstanding. (Ch. 17)

eco-efficiency measures Measures that help managers evaluate the savings generated by using fewer natural resources in a company's operations. (Ch. 18)

effective interest rate method The method of amortizing discounts and premiums that provides for a constant rate of interest on the carrying amount of the bonds at the beginning of each period; often called simply the "interest method." (Ch. 14)

effective rate of interest The market rate of interest at the time bonds are issued. (Ch. 14)

engineering change order (ECO) The document that initiates changing a product or process. (Ch. 25)

equity method A method of accounting for an investment in common stock by which the investment account is adjusted for the investor's share of periodic net income and cash dividends of the investee. (Ch. 15)

equity securities The common and preferred stock of a firm. (Ch. 15)

equivalent units of production The number of production units that could have been completed within a given accounting period, given the resources consumed. (Ch. 20)

F

face amount An amount at which bonds sell if the market rate equals the contract rate. (Ch. 14)

factory burden Another term for manufacturing overhead or factory overhead. (Ch. 18)

factory overhead cost All of the costs of producing a product except for direct materials and direct labor. (Ch. 18)

factory overhead cost budget Budget that estimates the cost for each item of factory overhead needed to support budgeted production. (Ch. 22)

factory overhead cost variance report Reports budgeted and actual costs for variable and fixed factory overhead along with the related controllable and volume variances. (Ch. 23)

fair value The price that would be received for selling an asset or paying off a liability, often the market price for an equity or debt security. (Ch. 15)

favorable cost variance A variance that occurs when the actual cost is less than standard cost. (Ch. 23)

feedback Measures provided to operational employees or managers on the performance of subunits of the organization. These measures are used by employees to adjust a process or a behavior to achieve goals. See management by exception. (Ch. 18)

financial accounting The branch of accounting that is concerned with recording transactions using generally accepted accounting principles (GAAP) for a business or other economic unit and with a periodic preparation of various statements from such records. (Ch. 18)

finished goods inventory The direct materials costs, direct labor costs, and factory overhead costs of finished products that have not been sold. (Ch. 18)

finished goods ledger The subsidiary ledger that contains the individual accounts for each kind of commodity or product produced. (Ch. 19)

first-in, first-out (FIFO) inventory cost flow method The method of inventory costing based on the assumption that the costs of merchandise sold should be charged against revenue in the order in which the costs were incurred. (Ch. 20)

fixed costs Costs that tend to remain the same in amount, regardless of variations in the level of activity. (Ch. 21)

flexible budget A budget that adjusts for varying rates of activity. (Ch. 22)

free cash flow The amount of operating cash flow remaining after replacing current productive capacity. (Ch. 16)

future value The value of an asset or cash at a specified date in the future that is equivalent in value to a specified sum today. (Ch. 14)

G

goal conflict A condition that occurs when individual objectives conflict with organizational objectives. (Ch. 22)

H

held-to-maturity securities Investments in bonds or other debt securities that management intends to hold to their maturity. (Ch. 15)

high-low method A technique that uses the highest and lowest total costs as a basis for estimating the variable cost per unit and the fixed cost component of a mixed cost. (Ch. 21)

horizontal analysis Financial analysis that compares an item in a current statement with the same item in prior statements. (Ch. 17)

I

ideal standards Standards that can be achieved only under perfect operating conditions, such as no idle time, no machine breakdowns, and no materials spoilage; also called theoretical standards. (Ch. 23)

indirect costs Costs that cannot be traced directly to a cost object. (Ch. 18)

indirect method A method of reporting the cash flows from operating activities as the net income from operations adjusted for all deferrals of past cash receipts and payments and all accruals of expected future cash receipts and payments. (Ch. 16)

inflation A period when prices in general are rising and the purchasing power of money is declining. (Ch. 26)

installment note A debt that requires the borrower to make equal periodic payments to the lender for the term of the note. (Ch. 14)

internal rate of return (IRR) method A method that determines the rate of return wherein the net present value of a project is zero. (Ch. 26)

inventory analysis A company's ability to manage its inventory effectively. (Ch. 17)

inventory turnover The relationship between the volume of goods sold and inventory, computed by dividing the cost of goods sold by the average inventory. (Ch. 17)

investee The company whose stock is purchased by the investor. (Ch. 15)

investment center A decentralized unit in which the manager has the responsibility and authority to make decisions that affect not only costs and revenues but also the fixed assets available to the center. (Ch. 24)

investment turnover A component of the rate of return on investment, computed as the ratio of sales to invested assets. (Ch. 24)

investments The balance sheet caption used to report long-term investments in stocks not intended as a source of cash in the normal operations of the business. (Ch. 15)

investor The company investing in another company's stock. (Ch. 15)

J

job cost sheet An account in the work in process subsidiary ledger in which the costs charged to a particular job order are recorded. (Ch. 19)

job order cost system A type of cost accounting system that provides for a separate record of the cost of each particular quantity of product that passes through the factory. (Ch. 19)

L

lean manufacturing A manufacturing enterprise that uses lean principles. (Ch. 20)

leverage Using debt to increase the return on an investment. (Ch. 17)

line department A unit that is directly involved in the basic objectives of an organization. (Ch. 18)

liquidity The ability to convert assets into cash. (Ch. 17)

M

management (or managerial) accounting The branch of accounting that uses both historical and estimated data in providing information that management uses in conducting daily operations, in planning future operations, and in developing overall business strategies. (Ch. 18)

management by exception The philosophy of managing that involves monitoring the operating results of implemented plans and comparing the expected results with the actual results. This feedback allows management to isolate significant variations for further investigation and possible remedial action. (Ch. 18)

management process The five basic management functions of (1) planning, (2) directing, (3) controlling, (4) improving, and (5) decision making. (Ch. 18)

Management's Discussion and Analysis (MD&A) An annual report disclosure that provides management's analysis of the results of operations and financial condition. (Ch. 17)

manufacturing cells A grouping of processes where employees are cross-trained to perform more than one function. (Ch. 20)

manufacturing overhead Costs, other than direct materials and direct labor costs, that are incurred in the manufacturing process. (Ch. 18)

margin of safety Indicates the possible decrease in sales that may occur before an operating loss results. (Ch. 21)

market price approach An approach to transfer pricing that uses the price at which the product or service transferred could be sold to outside buyers as the transfer price. (Ch. 24)

market rate of interest The rate determined from sales and purchases of similar bonds. (Ch. 14)

master budget The comprehensive budget plan linking all the individual budgets related to sales, cost of goods sold, operating expenses, projects, capital expenditures, and cash. (Ch. 22)

materials inventory The cost of materials that have not yet entered into the manufacturing process. (Ch. 18)

materials ledger The subsidiary ledger containing the individual accounts for each type of material. (Ch. 19)

materials requisition The form or electronic transmission used by a manufacturing department to authorize materials issuances from the storeroom. (Ch. 19)

merchandise available for sale The cost of merchandise available for sale to customers calculated by adding the beginning merchandise inventory to net purchases. (Ch. 18)

mixed costs Costs with both variable and fixed characteristics, sometimes called semivariable or semifixed costs. (Ch. 21)

mortgage notes An installment note that may be secured by a pledge of the borrower's assets. (Ch. 14)

N

negotiated price approach An approach to transfer pricing that allows managers of decentralized units to agree (negotiate) among themselves as to the transfer price. (Ch. 24)

net present value method A method of analysis of proposed capital investments that subtracts the amount to be invested from the present value of the cash flows expected from the investments. (Ch. 26)

nonfinancial performance measure A performance measure expressed in units rather than dollars. (Ch. 23)

number of days' sales in inventory The relationship between the volume of sales and inventory, computed by dividing the inventory at the end of the year by the average daily cost of goods sold. (Ch. 17)

number of days' sales in receivables The relationship between sales and accounts receivable, computed by dividing the net accounts receivable at the end of the year by the average daily sales. (Ch. 17)

O

objectives (goals) Developed in the planning stage, these reflect the direction and desired outcomes of certain courses of action. (Ch. 18)

operating leverage A measure of the relative mix of a business's variable costs and fixed costs, computed as contribution margin divided by operating income. (Ch. 21)

operational planning The development of short-term plans to achieve goals identified in a business's strategic plan. Sometimes called tactical planning. (Ch. 18)

opportunity cost The amount of income forgone from an alternative to a proposed use of cash or its equivalent. (Ch. 25)

other comprehensive income Specified items that are reported separately from net income, including foreign currency items, pension liability adjustments, and unrealized gains and losses on investments. (Ch. 15)

overapplied factory overhead The amount of factory overhead applied in excess of the actual factory overhead costs incurred for production during a period. (Ch. 19)

P

parent company The corporation owning all or a majority of the voting stock of the other corporation. (Ch. 15)

period costs Those costs that are used up in generating revenue during the current period and that are not involved in manufacturing a product, such as selling, general, and administrative expenses. (Ch. 18)

planning A phase of the management process whereby objectives are outlined and courses of action determined. (Ch. 18)

predetermined factory overhead rate The rate used to apply factory overhead costs to the goods manufactured. The rate is determined by dividing the budgeted overhead cost by the estimated activity usage at the beginning of the fiscal period. (Ch. 19)

premium The excess of the issue price of a stock over its par value or the excess of the issue price of bonds over their face amount. (Ch. 14)

present value concept Cash to be received (or paid) in the future is not the equivalent of the same amount of money received at an earlier date. (Chs. 14, 26)

present value index An index computed by dividing the total present value of the net cash flow to be received from a proposed capital investment by the amount to be invested. (Ch. 26)

present value of an annuity The sum of the present values of a series of equal cash flows to be received at fixed intervals. (Chs. 14, 26)

price-earnings (P/E) ratio The ratio of the market price per share of common stock, at a specific date, to the annual earnings per share. (Ch. 17)

prime costs The combination of direct materials and direct labor costs. (Ch. 18)

process A sequence of activities linked together for performing a particular task. (Ch. 23)

process cost system A type of cost system that accumulates costs for each of the various departments within a manufacturing facility. (Chs. 19, 20)

process manufacturer A manufacturer that uses large machines to process a continuous flow of raw materials through various stages of completion into a finished state. (Ch. 20)

product cost concept A concept used in applying the cost-plus approach to product pricing in which only the costs of manufacturing the product, termed the product cost, are included in the cost amount to which the markup is added. (Ch. 25)

product costs The three components of manufacturing cost: direct materials, direct labor, and factory overhead costs. (Ch. 18)

production bottleneck A condition that occurs when product demand exceeds production capacity. (Ch. 25)

production budget A budget of estimated unit production. (Ch. 22)

profit center A decentralized unit in which the manager has the responsibility and the authority to make decisions that affect both costs and revenues (and thus profits). (Ch. 24)

profit margin A component of the rate of return on investment, computed as the ratio of income from operations to sales. (Ch. 24)

profit-volume chart A chart used to assist management in understanding the relationship between profit and volume. (Ch. 21)

profitability The ability of a firm to earn income. (Ch. 17)

public companies Companies that issue publicly traded debt or equity securities. (App. B)

Q

quick assets Cash and other current assets that can be quickly converted to cash, such as marketable securities and receivables. (Ch. 17)

quick ratio A financial ratio that measures the ability to pay current liabilities with quick assets (cash, marketable securities, accounts receivable). (Ch. 17)

R

ratio of fixed assets to long-term liabilities A leverage ratio that measures the margin of safety of long-term creditors, calculated as the net fixed assets divided by the long-term liabilities. (Ch. 17)

ratio of liabilities to owner's (stockholders') equity A comprehensive leverage ratio that measures the relationship of the claims of creditors to stockholders' equity. (Ch. 17)

ratios A number that expresses a financial statement item or set of financial statement items as a percentage of another financial item, in order to measure an important economic relationship as a single number. (Ch. 17)

receiving report The form or electronic transmission used by the receiving personnel to indicate that materials have been received and inspected. (Ch. 19)

relevant range The range of activity over which changes in cost are of interest to management. (Ch. 21)

residual income The excess of divisional income from operations over a "minimum" acceptable income from operations. (Ch. 24)

responsibility accounting The process of measuring and reporting operating data by areas of responsibility. (Ch. 24)

responsibility center An organizational unit for which a manager is assigned responsibility over costs, revenues, or assets. (Ch. 22)

return on common stockholders' equity A measure of profitability computed by dividing net income, reduced by preferred dividend requirements, by common stockholders' equity. (Ch. 17)

return on investment (ROI) A measure of managerial efficiency in the use of investments in assets, computed as income from operations divided by invested assets. (Ch. 24)

return on stockholders' equity A measure of profitability computed by dividing net income by total stockholders' equity. (Ch. 17)

return on total assets A measure of the profitability of assets, without regard to the equity of creditors and stockholders in the assets. (Ch. 17)

S

sales budget One of the major elements of the income statement budget that indicates the quantity of estimated sales and the expected unit selling price. (Ch. 22)

sales mix The relative distribution of sales among the various products available for sale. (Ch. 21)

service department charges The costs of services provided by an internal service department and transferred to a responsibility center. (Ch. 24)

setup An overhead activity that consists of changing tooling in machines in preparation for making a new product. (Ch. 25)

solvency The ability of a firm to pay its debts as they come due. (Ch. 17)

staff department A unit that provides services, assistance, and advice to the departments with line or other staff responsibilities. (Ch. 18)

standard cost A detailed estimate of what a product should cost. (Ch. 23)

standard cost systems Accounting systems that use standards for each element of manufacturing cost entering into the finished product. (Ch. 23)

standards Performance goals, often relating to how much a product should cost. (Ch. 23)

statement of cash flows A summary of the cash receipts and cash payments for a specific period of time, such as a month or a year. (Ch. 16)

statement of cost of goods manufactured The income statement of manufacturing companies. (Ch. 18)

static budget A budget that does not adjust to changes in activity levels. (Ch. 22)

strategic planning The development of a long-range course of action to achieve business goals. (Ch. 18)

strategies The means by which business goals and objectives will be achieved. (Ch. 18)

subsidiary company The corporation that is controlled by a parent company. (Ch. 15)

sunk cost A cost that is not affected by subsequent decisions. (Ch. 25)

sustainability The practice of operating a business to maximize profits while attempting to preserve the environment, economy, and needs of future generations. (Ch. 18)

Sustainability Accounting Standards Board (SASB) A board that was organized in 2011 to develop accounting standards that help companies report decision-useful sustainability information to external financial statement users. (Ch. 18)

T

target costing The target cost is determined by subtracting a desired profit from a market method determined price. The resulting target cost is used to motivate cost improvements in design and manufacture. (Ch. 25)

theory of constraints (TOC) A manufacturing strategy that attempts to remove the influence of bottlenecks (constraints) on a process. (Ch. 25)

time tickets The form on which the amount of time spent by each employee and the labor cost incurred for each individual job, or for factory overhead, are recorded. (Ch. 19)

time value of money concept The concept that an amount of money invested today will earn income. (Ch. 26)

times interest earned A ratio that measures creditor margin of safety for interest payments, calculated as income before interest and taxes divided by interest expense. (Chs. 14, 17)

total cost concept A concept used in applying the cost-plus approach to product pricing in which all the costs of manufacturing the product plus the selling and administrative expenses are included in the cost amount to which the markup is added. (Ch. 25)

total manufacturing cost variance The difference between total standard costs and total actual costs for units produced. (Ch. 23)

trading securities Securities that management intends to actively trade for profit. (Ch. 15)

transfer price The price charged one decentralized unit by another for the goods or services provided. (Ch. 24)

U

underapplied factory overhead The amount of actual factory overhead in excess of the factory overhead applied to production during a period. (Ch. 19)

unfavorable cost variance A variance that occurs when the actual cost exceeds the standard cost. (Ch. 23)

unit contribution margin The dollars available from each unit of sales to cover fixed costs and provide operating profits. (Ch. 21)

unrealized gain or loss Changes in the fair value of equity or debt securities for a period. (Ch. 15)

V

variable cost concept A concept used in applying the cost-plus approach to product pricing in which only the variable costs are included in the cost amount to which the markup is added. (Ch. 25)

variable costing The concept that considers the cost of products manufactured to be composed only of those manufacturing costs that increase or decrease as the volume of production rises or falls (direct materials, direct labor, and variable factory overhead). (Ch. 21)

variable costs Costs that vary in total dollar amount as the level of activity changes. (Ch. 21)

vertical analysis An analysis that compares each item in a current statement with a total amount within the same statement. (Ch. 17)

volume variance The difference between the budgeted fixed overhead at 100% of normal capacity and the standard fixed overhead for the actual production achieved during the period. (Ch. 23)

W

whole units The number of units in production during a period, whether completed or not. (Ch. 20)

work in process inventory The direct materials costs, the direct labor costs, and the applied factory overhead costs that have entered into the manufacturing process but are associated with products that have not been finished. (Ch. 18)

working capital The excess of the current assets of a business over its current liabilities. (Ch. 17)

Y

yield A measure of materials usage efficiency. (Ch. 20)

Z

zero-based budgeting A concept of budgeting that requires all levels of management to start from zero and estimate budget data as if there had been no previous activities in their units. (Ch. 22)

Index

A

B

C

J

K

L

M

Q

R

S

T

The Basics

Accounting Equation:

Assets = Liabilities + Owner's Equity

T Account:

Account Title	
Left side	Right side
debit	credit

Rules of Debit and Credit:

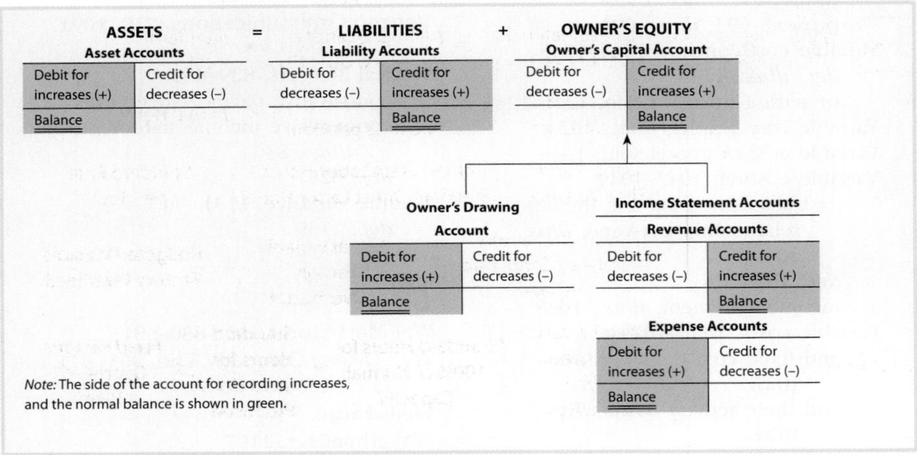

Analyzing and Journalizing Transactions

1. Carefully read the description of the transaction to determine whether an asset, a liability, an owner's equity, a revenue, an expense, or a drawing account is affected.
2. For each account affected by the transaction, determine whether the account increases or decreases.
3. Determine whether each increase or decrease should be recorded as a debit or a credit, following the rules of debit and credit.
4. Record the transaction using a journal entry.
5. Periodically post journal entries to the accounts in the ledger.
6. Prepare an unadjusted trial balance at the end of the period.

Financial Statements:

- **Income statement:** A summary of the revenue and expenses of a business entity for a specific period of time, such as a month or a year.
- **Statement of owner's equity:** A summary of the changes in the owner's equity of a business entity that have occurred during a specific period of time, such as a month or a year.
- **Balance sheet:** A list of the assets, liabilities, and owner's equity of a business entity as of a specific date, usually at the close of the last day of a month or a year.
- **Statement of Cash Flows:** A summary of the cash receipts and cash payments of a business entity for a specific period of time, such as a month or a year.

Accounting Cycle:

1. Transactions are analyzed and recorded in the journal.
2. Transactions are posted to the ledger.
3. An unadjusted trial balance is prepared.
4. Adjustment data are assembled and analyzed.
5. An optional end-of-period spreadsheet is prepared.
6. Adjusting entries are journalized and posted to the ledger.
7. An adjusted trial balance is prepared.
8. Financial statements are prepared.
9. Closing entries are journalized and posted to the ledger.
10. A post-closing trial balance is prepared.

Types of Adjusting Entries:

- Accrued revenue (accrued asset)
- Accrued expense (accrued liability)
- Unearned revenue (deferred revenue)
- Prepaid expense (deferred expense)
- Depreciation expense

Each entry will always affect both a balance sheet account and an income statement account.

Closing Entries:

1. Debit each revenue account for its balance, credit each expense account for its balance, and credit (net income) or debit (net loss) the owner's capital account.
2. Debit the owner's capital account for the balance of the drawing account and credit the drawing account.

Special Journals:

Providing services on account ⟶ recorded in ⟶ Revenue journal

Receipt of cash from any source ⟶ recorded in ⟶ Cash receipts journal

Purchase of items on account ⟶ recorded in ⟶ Purchases journal

Payments of cash for any purpose ⟶ recorded in ⟶ Cash payments journal

Shipping Terms:

	FOB Shipping Point	FOB Destination
Ownership (title) passes to buyer when merchandise is..................	delivered to freight carrier	delivered to buyer
Freight costs are paid by.........................	buyer	seller

Format for Bank Reconciliation:

Cash balance according to bank statement		$XXX
Add: Additions by company not on bank statement	$XXX	
Bank errors	XXX	XXX
		$XXX
Deduct: Deductions by company not on bank statement	$XXX	
Bank errors	XXX	XXX
Adjusted balance		$XXX
Cash balance according to company's records		$XXX
Add: Additions by bank not recorded by company	$XXX	
Company errors	XXX	XXX
		$XXX
Deduct: Deductions by bank not recorded by company	$XXX	
Company errors	XXX	XXX
Adjusted balance		$XXX

Inventory Costing Methods:

- First-in, First-out (FIFO)
- Last-in, First-out (LIFO)
- Weighted-Average

Interest Computations:

Interest = Face Amount (or Principal) × Rate × Time

Methods of Determining Annual Depreciation:

Straight-Line: $\frac{\text{Cost} - \text{Estimated Residual Value}}{\text{Estimated Life}}$

Double-Declining-Balance: Rate* × Book Value at Beginning of Period

*Rate is commonly twice the straight-line rate (1 ÷ Estimated Life).

Adjustments to Net Income (Loss) Using the Indirect Method:

	Increase (Decrease)
Net income (loss)	$ XXX
Adjustments to reconcile net income to net cash flow from operating activities:	
Depreciation of fixed assets	XXX
Amortization of intangible assets	XXX
Losses on disposal of assets	XXX
Gains on disposal of assets	(XXX)
Changes in current operating assets and liabilities:	
Increases in noncash current operating assets	(XXX)
Decreases in noncash current operating assets	XXX
Increases in current operating liabilities	XXX
Decreases in current operating liabilities	(XXX)
Net cash flow from operating activities	$ XXX or $(XXX)

Contribution Margin Ratio = $\frac{\text{Sales} - \text{Variable Costs}}{\text{Sales}}$

Break-Even Sales (Units) = $\frac{\text{Fixed Costs}}{\text{Unit Contribution Margin}}$

Sales (Units) = $\frac{\text{Fixed Costs} + \text{Target Profit}}{\text{Unit Contribution Margin}}$

Margin of Safety = $\frac{\text{Sales} - \text{Sales at Break-Even Point}}{\text{Sales}}$

Operating Leverage = $\frac{\text{Contribution Margin}}{\text{Income from Operations}}$

Variances:

Direct Materials Price Variance = (Actual Price − Standard Price) × Actual Quantity

Direct Materials Quantity Variance = (Actual Quantity − Standard Quantity) × Standard Price

Direct Labor Rate Variance = (Actual Rate per Hour − Standard Rate per Hour) × Actual Hours

Direct Labor Time Variance = (Actual Direct Labor Hours − Standard Direct Labor Hours) × Standard Rate per Hour

Variable Factory Overhead Controllable Variance = Actual Variable Factory Overhead − Budgeted Variable Factory Overhead

Fixed Factory Overhead Volume Variance = (Standard Hours for 100% of Normal Capacity − Standard Hours for Actual Units Produced) × Fixed Factory Overhead Rate

Rate of Return on Investment (ROI) = $\frac{\text{Income from Operations}}{\text{Invested Assets}}$

Alternative ROI Computation:

$$\text{ROI} = \frac{\text{Income from Operations}}{\text{Sales}} \times \frac{\text{Sales}}{\text{Invested Assets}}$$

Capital Investment Analysis Methods:

Methods That Ignore Present Values:

- Average Rate of Return Method
- Cash Payback Method

Methods That Use Present Values:

- Net Present Value Method
- Internal Rate of Return Method

Average Rate of Return = $\frac{\text{Estimated Average Annual Income}}{\text{Average Investment}}$

Present Value Index = $\frac{\text{Total Present Value of Net Cash Flow}}{\text{Amount to Be Invested}}$

Present Value Factor for an Annuity of $1 = $\frac{\text{Amount to Be Invested}}{\text{Equal Annual Net Cash Flows}}$

Abbreviations and Acronyms Commonly Used in Business and Accounting

AAA	American Accounting Association
ABC	Activity-based costing
AICPA	American Institute of Certified Public Accountants
B2B	Business-to-business
B2C	Business-to-consumer
CFO	Chief Financial Officer
CMA	Certified Management Accountant
COGM	Cost of goods manufactured
COGS	Cost of goods sold
CPA	Certified Public Accountant
Cr.	Credit
CVP	Cost-volume-profit
Dr.	Debit
EFT	Electronic funds transfer
EPS	Earnings per share
ERP	Enterprise resource planning
FASB	Financial Accounting Standards Board
FICA tax	Federal Insurance Contributions Act tax
FIFO	First-in, first-out
FOB	Free on board
FUTA	Federal unemployment compensation tax
GAAP	Generally accepted accounting principles
IASB	International Accounting Standards Board
IFRS	International Financial Reporting Standards
IMA	Institute of Management Accountants
IRC	Internal Revenue Code
IRR	Internal rate of return
IRS	Internal Revenue Service
JIT	Just-in-time
LIFO	Last-in, first-out
LCM	Lower of cost or market
MACRS	Modified Accelerated Cost Recovery System
MD&A	Management's Discussion and Analysis
n/30	Net 30
n/eom	Net, end-of-month
NPV	Net present value
NSF	Not sufficient funds
P/E Ratio	Price-earnings ratio
POS	Point of sale
ROI	Return on investment
R&D	Research and development
SCM	Supply chain management
SEC	Securities and Exchange Commission
SOX	Sarbanes-Oxley Act
TQC	Total quality control
W-4	Employee's Withholding Allowance Certificate
WIP	Work in process

Classification of Accounts

Account Title	*Account Classification*	*Normal Balance*	*Financial Statement*
Accounts Payable	Current liability	Credit	Balance sheet
Accounts Receivable	Current asset	Debit	Balance sheet
Accumulated Depletion	Contra fixed asset	Credit	Balance sheet
Accumulated Depreciation	Contra fixed asset	Credit	Balance sheet
Advertising Expense	Operating expense	Debit	Income statement
Allowance for Doubtful Accounts	Contra current asset	Credit	Balance sheet
Amortization Expense	Operating expense	Debit	Income statement
Bonds Payable	Long-term liability	Credit	Balance sheet
Building	Fixed asset	Debit	Balance sheet
__________ Capital	Owner's equity	Credit	Statement of owner's equity/ Balance sheet
Cash	Current asset	Debit	Balance sheet
Cash Dividends	Stockholders' equity	Debit	Retained earnings statement
Cash Dividends Payable	Current liability	Credit	Balance sheet
Common Stock	Stockholders' equity	Credit	Balance sheet
Cost of Merchandise (Goods) Sold	Cost of merchandise (goods) sold	Debit	Income statement
Customer Refunds Payable	Current liability	Credit	Balance sheet
Delivery Expense	Operating expense	Debit	Income statement
Depletion Expense	Operating expense	Debit	Income statement
Discount on Bonds Payable	Long-term liability	Debit	Balance sheet
Dividend Revenue	Other income	Credit	Income statement
Dividends	Stockholders' equity	Debit	Retained earnings statement
__________ Drawing	Owner's equity	Debit	Statement of owner's equity
Employees Federal Income Tax Payable	Current liability	Credit	Balance sheet
Equipment	Fixed asset	Debit	Balance sheet
Estimated Returns Inventory	Current asset	Debit	Balance sheet
Factory Overhead (Overapplied)	Deferred credit	Credit	Balance sheet (interim)
Factory Overhead (Underapplied)	Deferred debit	Debit	Balance sheet (interim)
Federal Income Tax Payable	Current liability	Credit	Balance sheet
Federal Unemployment Tax Payable	Current liability	Credit	Balance sheet
Finished Goods	Current asset	Debit	Balance sheet
Freight In	Cost of merchandise sold	Debit	Income statement
Freight Out	Operating expense	Debit	Income statement
Gain on Disposal of Fixed Assets	Other income	Credit	Income statement
Gain on Redemption of Bonds	Other income	Credit	Income statement
Gain on Sale of Investments	Other income	Credit	Income statement
Goodwill	Intangible asset	Debit	Balance sheet
Income Tax Expense	Income tax	Debit	Income statement
Income Tax Payable	Current liability	Credit	Balance sheet
Insurance Expense	Operating expense	Debit	Income statement
Interest Expense	Other expense	Debit	Income statement
Interest Receivable	Current asset	Debit	Balance sheet
Interest Revenue	Other income	Credit	Income statement
Investment in Bonds	Investment	Debit	Balance sheet
Investment in Stocks	Investment	Debit	Balance sheet
Investment in Subsidiary	Investment	Debit	Balance sheet
Land	Fixed asset	Debit	Balance sheet
Loss on Disposal of Fixed Assets	Other expense	Debit	Income statement
Loss on Redemption of Bonds	Other expense	Debit	Income statement

Account Title	*Account Classification*	*Normal Balance*	*Financial Statement*
Loss on Sale of Investments	Other expense	Debit	Income statement
Marketable Securities	Current asset	Debit	Balance sheet
Materials	Current asset	Debit	Balance sheet
Medicare Tax Payable	Current liability	Credit	Balance sheet
Merchandise Inventory	Current asset/Cost of merchandise sold	Debit	Balance sheet/Income statement
Net Sales	Revenue from sales	Credit	Income statement
Notes Payable	Current liability/Long-term liability	Credit	Balance sheet
Notes Receivable	Current asset/Investment	Debit	Balance sheet
Patents	Intangible asset	Debit	Balance sheet
Paid-In Capital from Sale of Treasury Stock	Stockholders' equity	Credit	Balance sheet
Paid-In Capital in Excess of Par (Stated Value)	Stockholders' equity	Credit	Balance sheet
Payroll Tax Expense	Operating expense	Debit	Income statement
Pension Expense	Operating expense	Debit	Income statement
Petty Cash	Current asset	Debit	Balance sheet
Preferred Stock	Stockholders' equity	Credit	Balance sheet
Premium on Bonds Payable	Long-term liability	Credit	Balance sheet
Prepaid Insurance	Current asset	Debit	Balance sheet
Prepaid Rent	Current asset	Debit	Balance sheet
Purchases	Cost of merchandise sold	Debit	Income statement
Purchases Discounts	Cost of merchandise sold	Credit	Income statement
Purchases Returns and Allowances	Cost of merchandise sold	Credit	Income statement
Rent Expense	Operating expense	Debit	Income statement
Rent Revenue	Other income	Credit	Income statement
Retained Earnings	Stockholders' equity	Credit	Balance sheet/Retained earnings statement
Salaries Expense	Operating expense	Debit	Income statement
Salaries Payable	Current liability	Credit	Balance sheet
Sales Tax Payable	Current liability	Credit	Balance sheet
Social Security Tax Payable	Current liability	Credit	Balance sheet
State Unemployment Tax Payable	Current liability	Credit	Balance sheet
Stock Dividends	Stockholders' equity	Debit	Retained earnings statement
Stock Dividends Distributable	Stockholders' equity	Credit	Balance sheet
Supplies	Current asset	Debit	Balance sheet
Supplies Expense	Operating expense	Debit	Income statement
Treasury Stock	Stockholders' equity	Debit	Balance sheet
Uncollectible Accounts Expense	Operating expense	Debit	Income statement
Unearned Rent	Current liability	Credit	Balance sheet
Utilities Expense	Operating expense	Debit	Income statement
Vacation Pay Expense	Operating expense	Debit	Income statement
Vacation Pay Payable	Current liability/Long-term liability	Credit	Balance sheet
Work in Process	Current asset	Debit	Balance sheet